Critics across America acclaim "A People's History"

"This People's History is a celebration."   —*The New York Times Book Review*

"Readers are sure to be rewarded. . . . Smith's multi-volume story of who we Americans are and how we came to be is an admirable project."
—*The Washington Post Book World*

"Engrossing narrative history . . . bound to invigorate and instruct . . . Amazing in its sweep and scope"   —*Chicago Sun-Times*

"Popular history set down with the candor of a maturing New Journalism"
—*Publishers Weekly*

"Smith's achievement is truly remarkable. No American historian since Charles Beard has produced anything comparable in length, scope, or readability. To find standards with which to judge this work we must go back to 19th-century masters like George Bancroft, Francis Parkman, and Henry Adams."   —*San Francisco Chronicle Book Review*

"A remarkable achievement in the writing of popular history"
—*Dallas Times Herald*

"The individual characters' lives Smith dramatizes truly live."   —*Miami Herald*

"Distinguished . . . Belongs on the shelves of anyone who wants to understand where we've been, so he can form a more educated opinion on where we're going."   —*Milwaukee Journal*

"Smith brings to his work not only a clear and thorough knowledge of his subject, but a literary elegance rarely found among today's scholars."
—*The Boston Sunday Globe*

"The author's great gift lies in his unerring eye for the evocative or perceptive quotation that opens for the reader a view of the times as seen by the women and men living in them."   —*The Philadelphia Inquirer*

"Smith writes as a lover loves—from the heart. . . . Not since the 19th century has an American historian written so extensively and passionately about his country."   —*Los Angeles Times Book Review*

PENGUIN BOOKS

THE RISE OF INDUSTRIAL AMERICA

Page Smith was educated at the Gilman School in Baltimore, Dartmouth College, and Harvard University. He has served as research associate at the Institute of Early American History and Culture and has taught at the University of California at Los Angeles and at Santa Cruz, where he makes his home. Dr. Smith is author of *The Historian and History*; *The Constitution: A Documentary and Narrative History*; *Daughters of the Promised Land: Women in American History*; the highly acclaimed two-volume biography *John Adams*, winner of the Bancroft Prize; *Jefferson: A Revealing Biography*; *The Chicken Book*, with Charles Daniel; and *Killing the Spirit: Higher Education in America*. *The Rise of Industrial America* is the sixth volume in the first extensive history of the United States written by a professional historian since the beginning of this century. The previous volumes are *A New Age Now Begins: A People's History of the American Revolution* (two volumes); *The Shaping of America: A People's History of the Young Republic* (an American Book Award Nominee); *The Nation Comes of Age: A People's History of the Ante-Bellum Years*; and *Trial by Fire: A People's History of the Civil War and Reconstruction*, all Main Selections of the Book-of-the-Month Club.

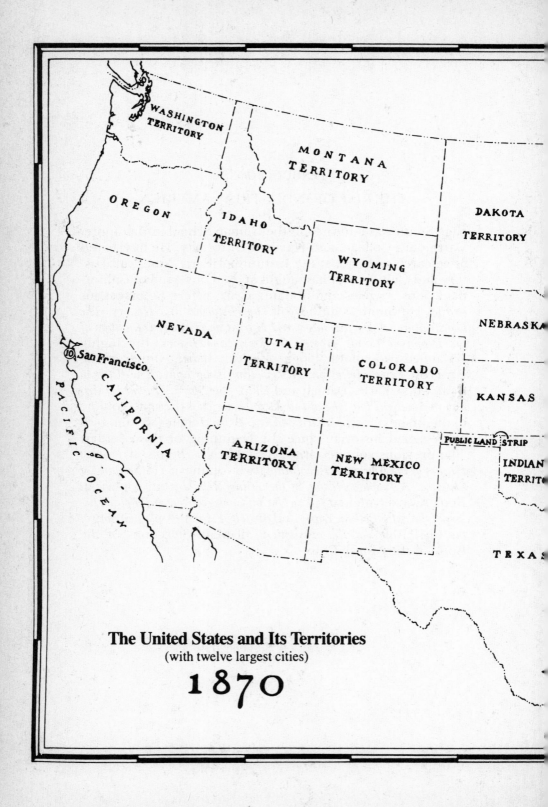

The United States and Its Territories

(with twelve largest cities)

1870

MINNESOTA

WISCONSIN

MICHIGAN

IOWA

⑤Chicago

ILLINOIS   INDIANA   OHIO

⑧Cincinnati

St.Louis④

MISSOURI

KENTUCKY

ARKANSAS

TENNESSEE

WEST VIRGINIA

VIRGINIA

NORTH CAROLINA

SOUTH CAROLINA

ALABAMA   GEORGIA

MISSISSIPPI

LOUISIANA

⑨New Orleans

FLORIDA

GULF OF MEXICO

PENNSYLVANIA

⑪Buffalo

NEW YORK

MAINE

VT.   N.H.

MASS. ⑦Boston

CONN.

R.I.

New York ①③Brooklyn

Philadelphia
Baltimore ②
MD. ⑥   N.J.
⑫
Washington

DEL.

ATLANTIC OCEAN

MILES
0   100   200   300   400

A PEOPLE'S HISTORY OF THE POST-RECONSTRUCTION ERA

THE
RISE OF
INDUSTRIAL
AMERICA

Page Smith

VOLUME SIX

PENGUIN BOOKS

PENGUIN BOOKS
Published by the Penguin Group
Viking Penguin, a division of Penguin Books USA Inc.,
375 Hudson Street, New York, New York 10014, U.S.A.
Penguin Books Ltd, 27 Wrights Lane, London W8 5TZ, England
Penguin Books Australia Ltd, Ringwood, Victoria, Australia
Penguin Books Canada Ltd, 2801 John Street, Markham, Ontario, Canada L3R 1B4
Penguin Books (N.Z.) Ltd, 182–190 Wairau Road, Auckland 10, New Zealand

Penguin Books Ltd, Registered Offices:
Harmondsworth, Middlesex, England

First published in the United States of America by
McGraw-Hill Book Company, 1984
Reprinted by arrangement with McGraw-Hill, Inc.
Published in Penguin Books 1990

10 9 8 7 6 5 4 3 2 1

LIBRARY OF CONGRESS CATALOGING IN PUBLICATION DATA
Smith, Page.
The rise of industrial America: a people's history of the post-
reconstruction era/Page Smith.
p.   cm.
Reprint. Originally published: New York: McGraw-Hill, c1984.
"Volume six."
ISBN 0 14 01.2262 1
1. United States—History—1865–1898.   I. Title.
E661.S58   1990
973.8—dc20   90–7002

Printed in the United States of America

Contents

VOLUME SIX

Introduction	*ix*
1. *Indian Affairs: The Sand Creek Massacre*	*1*
2. *An Indian Policy*	*15*
3. *War in the Southwest*	*34*
4. *Scattered Campaigns*	*50*
5. *The End of the Indian Wars*	*61*
6. *The Railroads*	*89*
7. *The New Technology*	*113*
8. *The Rise of the Trusts*	*128*
9. *The Darwinians*	*140*
10. *The Great Strikes*	*164*
11. *Progress and Poverty*	*193*
12. *The Conditions of Labor*	*213*
13. *Unions*	*227*
14. *Haymarket*	*241*
15. *Free Love*	*258*
16. *From Free Thought to Anarchism*	*284*
17. *The James Family*	*295*
18. *The Adamses*	*317*
19. *Immigration*	*332*
20. *The Promised Land*	*344*
21. *The City*	*364*
22. *The New Journalists*	*376*
23. *Jane Addams and Hull House*	*404*

24. *The Farmers' Revolt*   422
25. *Politics*   452
26. *Homestead*   469
27. *1893*   482
28. *Coxey's Army*   508
29. *Pullman*   517
30. *The Election of 1896*   536
31. *Religion*   554
32. *Education*   587
33. *Blacks*   614
34. *The Women*   661
35. *The Empire of Reform*   696
36. *The Literary Scene*   716
37. *American Literature: Women's Division*   757
38. *The Arts*   772
39. *The West*   798
40. *North and South*   826
41. *Sports*   841
42. *The Upper Classes*   853
43. *The New Empire*   864
44. *The End of the Century*   887
45. *Retrospections*   907
    Index   931

Introduction

When Charles Francis Adams returned to the United States in 1868 from his post as ambassador to the Court of St. James's, he had been away from the United States for seven years. What he saw around him was as novel and surprising as the outside world might be to a long-incarcerated prisoner or a modern-day Rip Van Winkle. The most noticeable change of all, he wrote, "is perhaps to be found in a greatly enlarged grasp of enterprise and increased facility of combination. The great operations of war, the handling of large masses of men, the influence of discipline, the lavish expenditures of unprecedented sums of money, the immense financial operations, the possibilities of effective cooperation were lessons not likely to be lost on men quick to receive and apply new ideas." The Civil War not only had been a long and bloody tragedy but had changed the temper and quality of American life in profound ways. Above all, it had vastly enlarged the practical scope of the American imagination. One could hardly improve on Adams's inventory of new techniques or processes that the war had brought in its wake.

Adams, a man who believed that moral laws must govern human

affairs, had no illusions about the consequences of the war. The years following the war, he wrote, "have witnessed some of the most remarkable examples of organized lawlessness, under the forms of law, which mankind has yet had an opportunity to study. If individuals have, as a rule, quietly pursued their peaceful vocations, the same cannot be said of certain single men at the head of vast combinations of private wealth. This has been particularly the case as regards those controlling the rapidly developed railroad interests. These modern potentates have declared war, negotiated peace, reduced courts, legislatures, and sovereign States to an unqualified obedience to their will, disturbed trade, agitated the currency, imposed taxes, and, boldly setting both law and public opinion at defiance, have freely exercised many other attributes of sovereignty. . . . Single men have controlled hundreds of miles of railway, thousands of men, tens of millions of revenue, and hundreds of millions of capital. The strength implied in all this they wielded in practical independence of the control both of governments and of individuals; much as petty German despots might have governed their little principalities a century or two ago."

The Civil War and the period that followed it—so-called Reconstruction—were without question the most traumatic events of our history. At the end of the war the nation had experienced a wave of euphoria perhaps best expressed in James Russell Lowell's ecstatic letter to an English friend, telling him that now that the stain of slavery had been eradicated, he was at last able to love his country.

For that substantial number of Americans of an apocalyptic turn of mind who, in every generation, longed for the millennium, hope for the Second Coming was more abundant than it had been since the earliest days of the Republic. Secular-minded reformers such as young Lester Ward anticipated a kind of heaven on earth, a new era of freedom, justice, and economic equality, a revival, in effect, of the Jeffersonian dream of a progressive and ultimately perfectible world. But Reconstruction turned into a nightmare. The very word abounded in irony. "Destruction" would have been a more accurate word. Only the war had divided Americans more bitterly. In addition, a fever of avariciousness seized the country, a pathology of uncontrolled expansion and acquisitiveness. In a nation that honored self-control above all else, everything seemed as out of control as it had in the decades preceding the war itself. This time the enemy was harder to identify. To many Americans the successful outcome of the war had been, above all, a vindication of democracy—an appraisal that had been declaimed from pulpits and proclaimed by politicians, Lincoln most prominent among them. Now the suspicion grew that "the democracy," the people— whoever they were, however defined—were not perhaps, after all, up to self-government. Among the skeptics was at least one future pres- ident of the United States. In 1876, on the occasion of the nation's centennial, young Woodrow Wilson, an undergraduate at Princeton, had expressed his doubts that the country would survive another hundred years, so grave were the shortcomings of democracy.

For one thing, the entrepreneurial spirit (or, more simply, the desire to make as much money as possible by any means possible), a spirit which existed from the beginning of the Republic (and caused so much concern among upper-class Americans of inherited wealth and position), appeared to be a passion without limits. It was evident in retrospect that, prior to the Civil War, the conservative, agrarian, slaveholding South in alliance with Northern Democrats, Irish and Germans prominent among them—an alliance established by Thomas Jefferson as the basis of the political power of the Jeffersonian Re- publicans and later the Jacksonian Democrats—had, by laying a per- sistent claim to power, inhibited the entrepreneurial temper. Indeed, some historians were soon to argue that it was this inhibition, far more than moral outrage over slavery, that induced Northern capitalists to support the Union cause. While such a proposition not only is un- provable but runs counter to the great mass of evidence, there is no question that once the war was over and the Union restored, entre- preneurs, free of the restraining influence of the South, took matters into their own hands. They strengthened their grip on the Republican Party, conceived as the party of reform and resistance to slavery, and made it their instrument.

In the debates at the Federal Convention in 1787, Gouverneur Morris had urged the delegates to build into the Constitution provisions that would, so far as possible, prevent classes from exploiting each other. "The Rich," he declared, "will strive to establish their dominion & enslave the rest. They always did. They always will. . . . Let the rich mix with the poor and in Commercial Country, they will establish an oligarchy." If the check of the commercial class was removed, "the democracy will triumph." He added: "Thus it has been the world over. So will it be among us. Reason tells us we are but men." Morris persisted in his theme. The mass of people never acted from reason alone. The rich would take advantage of their passions and "make these the in- struments for oppressing them." The ordinary people could not "communicate and act in concert"; they would thus be the "dupes of those who have more knowledge & intercourse."

William Manning in his *Key to Libberty*, written a few years later on the occasion of Jay's Treaty settling disputes with England, expressed similar sentiments. He also argued, in almost the same, if much less literate, words, that workingmen would be exploited by those who lived without working—businessmen, doctors, lawyers, professors, the educated elite. It was in the nature of man to pursue selfish ends— "self-aggrandisement," as Manning put it. Forty-some years later Alexis de Tocqueville expressed the same anxiety. "In commercial country," he wrote, "the rich might come to fasten a particularly onerous yoke on the backs of the less powerful, primarily the working men and women of the nation."

Now, it might be said, the day was at hand. But it is important to emphasize that this end could not have been achieved without, in a very real sense, the active complicity of the mass of Americans. In the third volume of this work we emphasized that Americans, in the absence of any of the traditional ways of authenticating themselves and finding their places in the system—caste, clan, or "order"—had to depend primarily upon money; making money became the validation of personal worth very early in our history. Moreover, it seems safe to say that in a nation with a strong tradition of centralized government individual capitalists simply could not have assumed control over the principal agencies of the nation's economic life; above all, over what Brooks Adams called "the public highways," the railroads. That this could happen was, in a curious way, the consequence, once again, of slavery, of the war, and of the political principle which underlay them both—the ubiquitous doctrine of states' rights, an anachronism unwilling to die. John Roy Lynch, the black Congressman, reported that Ulysses S. Grant had told him in the Reconstruction Era that he believed that the Civil War had been fought to free the slaves and bury, once and for all, the notion of states' rights but that he had come reluctantly to recognize that only half the task had been accomplished; states' rights was not only still alive but reasserting itself with astonishing tenacity. The South, by its stubborn resistance to the Federal government's efforts to protect the civil and political rights of the freedmen and women, had worn down and ultimately defeated the North and retrieved the greater part of what it at first appeared to have lost in the war in social and political, if not in economic, terms. Indeed, it could be argued that it was not the Southern blacks who were freed by the war (they remained slaves or became once again slaves in all but name after a brief interlude of freedom guarded by Northern guns) but the white population of the South, which was freed of the terrible onus of slavery while continuing to enjoy the essentially servile labor of "free" blacks. The tacit agreement which gave the presidency to Rutherford Hayes in 1876 also re-established states' rights as the dominant fact of American political life. The same doctrine that allowed Southern whites to thrust Southern blacks back into a slavery in all but name gave free rein to the most rapacious instincts of the new class of capitalists. All efforts by the Federal government to check the depredations of the "robber barons"—and these efforts were relatively few in any event—were denounced as infringements of the once more sacred doctrine of states' rights.

In the period with which we are here concerned—roughly 1876 to 1901—two themes dominate: "the rise of science" (primarily Darwinism) and "the war between capital and labor." Darwinism, or what we might call more accurately the notion of the evolutionary development of the universe, pervades every aspect of American thought and life. It demands a response from the churches and from the theologians, from the schools and academies, from individuals and from social groups. It is argued about, debated, attacked, and defended with a passion that recalls the religious wars of the sixteenth century—the Reformation and the Counterreformation. It colors the way social classes view themselves and, more important, the way they view other classes. It affects attitudes toward other races—aborigines, especially American Indians, blacks, Orientals, all of whom are generally viewed as representing lower stages of evolutionary development. It is taken by some Americans, generally wealthy and "successful," as confirming the model of competitive individualism and thereby justifying capitalism, and it is taken by many others as anticipating socialism as a higher and more humane form of political and economic organization. It divides clerics and professors of philosophy, natural scientists and "social scientists," husbands and wives, parents and children. Taken all in all, it represents the most startling and dramatic change in human beings' perception of the origin, nature, and goals of human existence since the beginning of the Christian Era.

The war between capital and labor was, in essence, a struggle to regain what had been lost in the tumultuous years since the Declaration of Independence: the conviction that in some odd metaphysical sense that defied the lessons of history and the observable facts of man's social life, all human beings had been born equal and were entitled to equal rights and opportunities, foremost among which were "life, liberty, and the pursuit of happiness." While it was certainly true that the injunctions of the Founders were always fitfully and inadequately attended to, more honored in the breach and in patriotic oratory than in fact, they provided the leitmotiv of our existence as a people. As a nation, as the United States, odd congeries of wildly disparate social and political units called states, we were often the despair of decent and humane persons, within and without, but as "a people" we clung to the visions evoked by the original contract, knowing that our lives, in a profound sense, depended on it. As with the war against slavery there could be no peace in Zion until the war between capital and labor had been at least provisionally settled. So the central intellectual and moral issue of this volume is the rise of science, most strikingly in the form of Darwinism, and the central problem is the war between capital and labor.

A subsidiary, but extremely important, theme is the emergence of the West or Wests: the so-called Midwest (what I called in an earlier volume the Near West, the region of the Mississippi Valley); the Fur West, or the Rocky Mountain West; and the Far West—the Pacific Coast West. While, as I have earlier argued at length, these three Wests, not to mention the Southwest, were clearly distinguishable in their own respective styles, economies, and values, they were united in the consideration of one overriding fact, a bond that often united them when nothing else could—they all were "not the East." They all were, in varying degrees, colonies of the East, held in social and, above all, economic bondage. They all looked toward the East with envy, hostility, resentment, awe, anger, longing—with one or another or all of those emotions and doubtless others beside. The East was the mother, the exploiter, the ideal, the enemy. The West was obsessed with the East. The East was, for the most part, only vaguely aware of the West. The West, when it was thought of at all by the East, was primarily landscape—breathtaking vistas; geysers of steam, as in Yellowstone Park; dazzling canyons; cattle and cowboys; and large dividends from mines and forests and the incremental growth of Western cities. The ruined and improvident went West: the young and ambitious to make their fortunes; the old and ailing to enjoy its salubrious climates and invigorating airs. More enterprising tourists visited such exotic spots as Omaha, Denver, Salt Lake City (the Mormons were an endless source of wonder and astonishment), Los Angeles, and San Francisco (the latter was given the highest accolade, that of being an "Eastern" city still imbued with the romantic aura of the gold rush days) and returned to report that there were encouraging signs of cultivation in such unlikely places as Portland and Seattle.

The Civil War had, of course, done a vast deal to give the East and Middle West a sense of unity and commonality, especially through the agency of the Republican Party. Midwesterners had, if anything, borne a disproportionate share of the burden of the war, both materially and in lives lost. They had acquitted themselves well and sometimes brilliantly as soldiers. It could even be argued (and I, for one, am disposed to argue it) that the war was actually won, not in Virginia at Appomattox but in the West and, particularly, along the line of the Mississippi River. Finally, the savior of the Union and the conflict's greatest general both had come from the same archetypically Midwestern state of Illinois. Those are all facts familiar enough, so familiar that we often fail to take account of their significance. With the war as a kind of economic and even social starting point, relations between the East and the West developed with astonishing rapidity. The railroads, of course, helped enormously as did simple greed—the desire of the East to exploit the extraordinary material resources of the West. The conflicts, it must be emphasized, remained real and deep, and in many respects—the political and economic most notably—they grew deeper and wider as the decades passed. But on the intellectual level and on the social level a new kind of national consciousness took form. It was essentially conservative, reformist (temperance was, of course, its favorite reform), predominantly middle-class, Anglo-Saxon or Teutonic, and overwhelmingly Protestant.

The period between the Centennial Exposition of 1876 and the end of the nineteenth century is a singularly complex and inchoate era. An age of unparalleled growth and expansion, of imperialist ventures and American involvement in the world, it was also a time of crisis for the American consciousness bound to an older and simpler tradition and challenged to adjust to a bewilderingly new world in which all the old verities were called into question. A modern writer has spoken of the accelerating pace of technological innovation as producing "future shock." Future shock has been part of the experience of Americans ever since the Pilgrims landed on the New England coast in 1620, but, in the period following the Civil War, future shock imposed an increasing strain on the collective American psyche. Before the war the dramatic advances in technology—railroads, steamboats, the telegraph, the camera, electricity—awesome and wonder-inducing as they were, did little to disturb Americans' basic conception of the nature of the universe and their place in it. The postwar world made a direct and concerted assault on that basic conception, worrying it as a dog worries a bone and all but demolishing it.

Underlying all other themes of the period is that of the adjustment of Americans to a new order of things: the formation of a new consciousness. Jane Addams, the founder of Hull House, wrote: "Perhaps no presentation of history is so difficult as that which treats of the growth of a new consciousness." That, nonetheless, is our most essential task.

But first there is unfinished business to attend to. Indians.

Indian Affairs:
The Sand Creek Massacre

Word of the destruction of General George Custer's cavalry by the Sioux at Little Big Horn reached Philadelphia shortly after the opening of the Centennial Exposition in 1876. But that lurid event was only the climax in a series of wars and lesser engagements. In the years following the Black Hawk War in the upper Mississippi Valley in 1832, the pressure of white settlers on Indian lands had remained constant. The Indians, of course, had continued to raid white settlements that in their view encroached on their lands.

The Mexican War, the annexation of Texas, and the acquisition, under the terms of the Treaty of Guadalupe Hidalgo in 1848, of present-day Arizona and New Mexico had presented the Federal government with vastly enlarged Indian problems by adding to its jurisdiction the tribes of the Southwest, the Apache and Comanche among them. While the Federal government had from the first accepted the principle that the Indians had rights in the lands that they occupied, the states had been equally insistent that the Indians within their borders were subject to *their* jurisdiction. It was this controversy which had led to the Indian Removal. The Southern states had rejected the argument of John Quincy Adams and the Supreme Court that Indians were wards of the national government. Texans likewise rejected the

1

argument. The first Texas legislature had declared in 1846: "We recognize no title in the Indian tribes resident within the limits of the state to any portion of the soil thereof; and . . . we recognize no right of the Government of the United States to make any treaty with the said Indian tribes without the consent of the Government of this state."

A number of the tribes, the Apache most prominently, had long been accustomed to raiding Mexican villages with impunity and saw no reason to desist simply because Americans had replaced Mexicans as intruders. But when Federal commissioners concluded a treaty with the eleven principal tribes in Texas, promising trading posts, presents, and protection, Texans in Congress were furious. Congress backed away from the issue, and the tribes found themselves, as so many others had, caught between the claims of the Federal government and those of the state. In the words of one Comanche chief: "For a long time a great many people have been passing through my country; they kill all the game, and burn the country, and trouble me very much. The commissioners of our Great Father promised to keep these people out of our country. I believe our white brothers do not wish to run a line between us, because they wish to settle in this country. I object to any more settlements."

State authorities were indifferent to pleas or warnings. Indian lands were freely granted to speculators. Four surveyors were killed on land claimed by the Comanche, and a familiar pattern of white intrusion and Indian response emerged. As the danger of open warfare increased, the Texas governor at last drew a line beyond which he forbade white settlers to encroach. The order was largely ignored. The Texas Emigration and Land Company, made up of some of the most powerful men in the state, began to recruit its own army to fight the Indians. When Texas Rangers, seeking retribution for the murder of a white settler, massacred twenty-five Wichita who apparently had nothing to do with the murder, war was inevitable. Wichita, Waco, and Comanche went on the warpath, destroying crops, burning buildings, and driving off horses. The Texas legislature, under strong pressure from the Federal government, agreed to sell land to the United States to be used for Indian reservations. Needless to say, the Indians were not consulted. But even on reservations the Indians were not safe from the hostility of the whites. Texans invaded the reservations and hunted Indians down like deer or bear for the sport. Finally the Federal government undertook to move the tribes out of Texas entirely.

With the acquisition of New Mexico, General Stephen Kearny

assured the Mexicans who had been preyed on for years by bands of Apache, Comanche, and Navaho that the United States would protect them. As soon as Kearny left for California, however, the Indian raids resumed. When the news reached Kearny, he directed Colonel Alexander Doniphan to organize the Mexicans and the Pueblo Indians, also the victims of frequent raids, into "war parties, to march into the country of their enemies, the Navajos, to recover their property, to make reprisals." A series of forts was built to check Indian raids and confine the more warlike tribes to vaguely defined reservations, where Indian agents were assigned to help them adapt to settled agricultural life.

If some tribes, especially those whose original habitat was in the Old Northwest, in the Ohio country and the region of the Great Lakes, were prevailed upon by various blandishments, typically in the form of presents and subsidies, to try the novel experiment of a settled, primarily agricultural life, they were almost invariably the victims of raids by nomadic tribes that scorned them for adapting the white man's ways. The Missouri, Potawatomi, Ottawa, Winnebago, Delaware, and some remnants of Black Hawk's Sac and Fox were among the tribes that turned to the Federal government for protection. Certainly their condition did little to encourage the less tractable Indians to accept domestication. Filthy and squalid, they suffered from a variety of white man's diseases and vices. The plight of the Pawnee was particularly awkward. North of the Platte they were subject to constant harassment from the Sioux, who viewed them as encroaching on their own territory. When they withdrew south of the Platte, their young braves could not be restrained from preying on the emigrant wagon trains moving West and being, in turn, hunted down by U.S. cavalry.

By 1850 the notion had emerged of clearly defined reservations, where Indians could be both protected from white incursions and restrained from harassing emigrants or raiding the "civilized" tribes. Related to the reservation plan was the agitation for a transcontinental railroad, which must, of necessity, run through land claimed by various Indian tribes. If these Indians could be persuaded to take up residence on clearly defined reservations, conflict might be avoided. The commissioner of Indian affairs, Orlando Brown, urged that reservations be established for each tribe in areas "adapted to agriculture, of limited extent and well-defined boundaries; within which all with occasional exceptions should be compelled constantly to remain until such time as their general improvement and good conduct may supersede the necessity of such restrictions." The government should give the tribes "agricultural implements, and useful materials for clothing; encourage and assist them in the erection of comfortable dwellings and secure to them the means and facilities of education, intellectual, moral and religious."

Brown's proposals indicated that there had been no essential change in American attitudes toward the "Indian problem" since the days of Thomas Jefferson. Men were rational creatures; Indians were men—therefore, Indians were rational beings. It thus followed that when given education, "intellectual, moral and religious," they must become indistinguishable from white Americans and soon assimilated into the general population. But generation after generation the American aborigines showed a stubborn determination to remain irredeemably Indian.

The Plains Indians presented a special problem. One writer has divided the tribes in the decade of the 1850s into "wild, undecided, and subdued" Indians. The wild Indians resisted every effort to prevail on them to limit their depredations or confine their hunting ranges. The "undecideds" sometimes remained aloof and sometimes, if sufficiently angered by the actions of whites, whether of the army, the Indian Bureau, or aggressive civilians, threw in their lot with the unregenerate. The "subdued," having decided that caution was the better part of valor or having had their spirits broken by a series of disastrous encounters with whites, did what they were instructed to do and avoided any actions that might bring further suffering and destruction upon them. Part of the difficulty was that there was no surefire way to distinguish between "wild" and "undecided." They dressed the same, looked the same, and often belonged to the same tribe.

The first great council called by the government to try to stabilize the situation of the Plains Indians was charged with responsibility for negotiating a treaty or series of treaties with the tribes through whose territory emigrant trains headed for the Pacific coast. The direction of the council was in the hands of the famous trapper and mountain man Thomas Fitzpatrick, onetime partner of Jedediah Smith. Known as Broken Hand to the Indians because of a crippled hand, Fitzpatrick had written one of the best-known guides for the wagon trains that wound their way across the prairie and through mountain passes he knew so well. Since 1846 he had been Indian agent for the tribes in the region of the Platte and Arkansas. He called on all the major Plains tribes to meet on September 1, 1851, at Fort Laramie, in the Wyoming

Territory. Weeks before the meeting the tribes began to assemble—the Oglala, Teton, and Brulé bands of the Sioux; the Arapaho and the Cheyenne. When the Shoshone, traditional enemies of the Sioux, arrived, a fight almost broke out between the two tribes. Day after day tribes or portions of tribes arrived—Assiniboine, Crow, Arikara, Pawnee—until a city of tepees covered the plain around the fort. It was the greatest gathering of tribes in the history of the West, numbering, by various estimates, between 8,000 and 12,000 with as many ponies. While they waited for gifts to arrive from the Federal government, the tribes entertained themselves with games and contests. Finally the parley began in a large tent where the brilliantly caparisoned chiefs gathered each day for twenty days. In the parley the superintendent of Indian affairs, David Mitchell, insisted that the tribes must not attack or harass travelers on the Oregon Trail. To do so would mean war with the United States. Moreover, they must give the government the right to establish forts for the maintenance of the trail and as places where emigrants could get supplies and assistance in case of need. Most important of all, the tribes must cease their constant warfare among themselves; as long as the repeated raids and counterraids continued the whites had great difficulty avoiding involvement. Finally, to ensure peace, the tribes must accept boundaries that would define their hunting ranges. In return the government would provide each of the tribes with the equivalent of $50,000 a year in supplies, much-needed food for the winter months, farm animals, and tools, the latter items representing the perpetually renewed hope that the Indians could, in time, be prevailed upon to take up a more settled agricultural life. When the great council broke up at the end of September and the bands of Indians drifted away—it was hoped to their assigned ranges—the feeling that the stormy relations between whites and Indians in the Great Plains had been fairly resolved and an era of peace lay ahead lingered in the air like the smoke of their campfires.

Fitzpatrick moved on to Fort Atkinson on the Arkansas River to meet with the Comanche and Kiowa and conclude a treaty with them. The message was substantially the same. Forts, they were told, would be built to protect them from incursions by marauding whites. In turn, they must allow passage over the Santa Fe Trail and, most difficult of all, refrain from raids into Mexico. One of the purposes of the Fort Atkinson council failed. The Kiowa and Comanche had captured a number of children, the majority of them Mexican, in raids on isolated farms and ranches, raids in which, generally, the children's parents had been killed. Fitzpatrick had been instructed to secure the return of such captives, but on this point the Indians were adamant. More important, the captives themselves refused to leave the families that had adopted them. Many of the males had become warriors, and the females had grown up to become the wives of Comanche or Kiowa braves.

In 1853 at a conference at Fort Benton, Isaac Stevens, the governor of Washington Territory, met the Blackfoot and their allied tribes and declared: "Your Great Father . . . wishes you to live at peace with each other and the whites. He desires that you should be under his protection, and partake equally with the Crows and the Assiniboines of his bounty. Live in peace with all the neighboring Indians, protect all the whites passing through your country, and the Great Father will be your best friend."

Chief Low Horn of the Piegan replied that the problem was restraining their young men, who "were wild and ambitious in their turn to be braves and chiefs. They wanted by some brave act to win the favor of their young women and bring scalps and horses to show their prowess." The governor professed to believe that the Blackfoot Indians could be prevailed upon to abandon their nomadic ways and adopt the life of peaceful farmers. To ask them (or any other of the hunting tribes for that matter) to do so was to ask them to abandon the very essence of their existence. The whites, of course, saw nothing degrading in being a farmer; most of them were farmers themselves. It was a matter, once again, of an inadequate anthropology. In return for giving up their way of life, the "vital root" of their existence, the Indians were to receive the classic benefits—presents—at the conclusion of the treaty, yearly subsidies to the extent of $20,000 a year among the four tribes, and $15,000 to carry on the work of Christianization.

With the conclusion of the Blackfoot treaty, the Indian problem appeared "solved." All the tribes had been assigned, if not precisely to reservations, at least to areas marked by definite features of the terrain—most commonly rivers and mountain ranges.

In 1854 the Eastern Indians who had been removed to the Indian Territory about twenty-five years earlier with the assurance that they could remain there until the end of time were told that they must move again; their lands were wanted by the white man. By that time it was already clear that the treaties so hopefully concluded three years earlier had begun to break down. When Thomas Fitzpatrick traveled through the region under his superintendency, he found the condition of the Indians had deteriorated. "They are in abject want of food half the year," he wrote. "The travel upon the road [the Oregon Trail] drives the buffalo off or else confines them to a narrow path during the period of migration, and the different tribes are forced to contend with hostile nations in seeking support for their villages. The women are pinched with want and their children are constantly crying with hunger. . . . Already, under the pressure of such hardships, they are beginning to gather around a few licensed hunters . . . acting as herdsmen, runners, and interpreters, living on their bounty; while others accept most immoral methods with their families to eke out an existence." Within the year Fitzpatrick, a great figure in the early history of the West, was dead, and the Indians were deprived of the services of one of their most sympathetic advocates.

A few months later a hungry Brulé Sioux, coming on a lame cow near Fort Laramie, killed and ate it with some fellow braves. The owner, an indignant Mormon, demanded that the Sioux brave be punished. A Sioux chief, Conquering Bear, offered to pay $10 for the cow and, when the emigrant demanded more, angrily broke off the discussion and returned to his lodge. When the lieutenant in charge of the fort was appealed to by the Mormon, he mustered up a party of thirty soldiers and two cannon, made his way to the Sioux camp, emplaced his artillery, and threatened to blow up the camp unless the cow was paid for or the brave who had killed her was surrendered to him. When Conquering Bear expostulated, the lieutenant ordered his men to open fire. Three Indians were killed, and Conquering Bear was fatally wounded. The Sioux then annihilated the soldiers.

The matter did not end there. The generally accepted principle of the army in dealing with Indians of whatever tribe was that the killing of United States soldiers could not go unpunished whatever the provocation. Colonel William Harney, therefore, set out as soon as the weather permitted with 1,300 troopers to chastise the Sioux. He soon came on a camp of Sioux who had had nothing to do with the Fort Laramie episode. Harney opened fire with his artillery, and before the fighting was over, eighty-six Sioux, many of them women and children, had been killed.

It would have been odd indeed if, in an age dedicated to reform, the American aborigine had not had many devoted advocates. The Black Hawk War had called forth a substantial body of pro-Indian sentiment, as, indeed, had the infamous Indian Removal. One of the earliest and most effective advocates of the Indian cause was John Beeson, whose indignation at the treatment of the Nez Percé in Oregon aroused the ire of his neighbors to such a degree that he was shot at and his house burned down. Beeson toured the Eastern cities in the late 1850s, speaking in Faneuil Hall in Boston, among other places, and helping found the National Indian Aid Association.

Henry Benjamin Whipple, the Episcopal bishop of the diocese of Minnesota, was a coadjutor of Beeson's. He made the condition of the Chippewa and Minnesota Sioux his special concern. Two years before the bloody Sioux uprising in Minnesota he had warned President James Buchanan that, unless there was a reform of the Indian Bureau and its agency, there would be an explosion of Indian wrath; "a nation which sowed robbery would reap a harvest of blood." When, in the aftermath of the uprising in which more than 100 white settlers were killed, Whipple, whose Indian name was Straight Tongue, drew up a proposal to reform Indian policy, he collected the signatures of thirty-eight Episcopal bishops (pretty much the whole lot) and a number of prominent citizens and went to Washington to plead with Lincoln to commute the sentences of those Indians who had been captured and sentenced to be hanged. Lincoln was horrified at Whipple's account of "the rascality of this Indian business. . . . If we get through this war, and I live," he told an aide, "this Indian system shall be reformed."

Beeson also secured an audience with Lincoln to press the cause of the Sioux, and the President told him to "rest assured that as soon as the pressing matters of this war are settled the Indians shall have my first care and I will not rest until Justice is done to their and to your Satisfaction."

Beeson, a farmer of only modest literacy, made a striking contrast with the articulate, college-educated Whipple. The bishop's office gave him financial independence and enabled him to tap philanthropic funds to carry on his mission, while Beeson lived a hand-to-mouth existence, retiring to his Oregon farm when he had exhausted his funds.

With the outbreak of the Civil War the Confederacy asserted its authority over the Indian Territory, the region, including much of present-day Oklahoma, to which the Five Civilized Nations had, not many years before, been driven. The Seneca and the Shawnee were recruited for the Confederate army along with many warriors from the Civilized Nations. The North Carolina Volunteers counted in their ranks 850 Cherokee Indians, and Georgia enlisted 1,000 more. Many more Indians could be recruited, Emma Holmes, the Charleston diarist, noted, if the Confederate generals would consent to a policy of no quarter asked or given. The principal obstacle to the use of Indians was that they could not be restrained from killing Union soldiers taken prisoner or wounded.

The forays by Federal and Confederate forces into the Indian Territory, the confused fighting, and the acts of retribution directed against Indians who had cast their lot with the Union or the Confederacy make too involved a story to retrace here. It is enough to say that, whichever side they adhered to (and some changed their allegiance with changes in the fortunes of the war), events worked as always to the eventual disadvantage of the Indians.

When the Minnesota Sioux, incited by Confederate agents and angry at the violation of treaty agreements, broke out in a rampage of killing, Lincoln was subjected to strong pressure to remove the inoffensive Winnebago and Chippewa as well as the Sioux. Gideon Welles, secretary of the navy, noted in his diary: "The members of Congress from Minnesota are urging the President vehemently to give his assent to the execution of three hundred Indians captured, but they will not succeed . . . it would seem the sentiments of the Representatives were but slightly removed from the barbarians whom they would execute. The Minnesotians are greatly exasperated and threaten the administration if it shows clemency." When the report on the Minnesota "Indian Wars" was received by the Cabinet, Welles wrote: "It shows that the Indian War was not war at all; that our people, not the Indians, were in fault. . . . After aggressions on the part of the whites, the Indians killed a number, and our army succeeded in killing six Indians. This war will cost the country scarcely less than fifty millions."

Conflict with the Cheyenne in the Colorado Territory increased as miners encroached on Indian hunting ranges. John Chivington, a circuit-riding Methodist minister of mammoth proportions, who had dedicated his life to the Free Soil cause and had defied the efforts of the proslavery men in Missouri to drive him from the pulpit, had moved on to Denver. At the outbreak of hostilities Chivington had volunteered to serve in a Union force being organized by the governor of the territory. The governor offered to make him a chaplain, but Chivington reportedly replied, "I feel compelled to strike a blow in person for the destruction of human slavery and to help in some measure to make this a truly free country." He was commissioned a major and began whipping the raw recruits of the 1st Colorado Regiment of Volunteers into some semblance of military order. When outnumbered Union forces in New Mexico appealed to the governor of Colorado for help, he dispatched Chivington. Joining forces with Colonel John Slough, a lawyer from Denver, after a 300-mile forced march, Chivington came upon a Confederate supply train of eighty-five wagons loaded with ammunition and supplies intended to support an invasion of California. In a battle at Apache Canyon near Santa Fe, his men destroyed the train, killing 500 horses and mules in the process. It was undoubtedly the most decisive single engagement of the war in the Rocky Mountain region and may well have saved both Colorado and California for the Union. With the Southern invaders forced to retreat to Texas, Chivington's main responsibility became the protection of the settlers of the area from the raids of the Cheyenne and the Arapaho, who operated between the Platte and the Arkansas, and to preserve peace between those tribes and the Ute and Pawnee. Disturbed by the influx of settlers, the Arapaho chief Little Raven went to Denver with some of his principal braves to urge the authorities there to impose restrictions on the settlement of whites on Arapaho land. In a spirit of mutual forbearance promises were made on both sides to practice restraint.

Despite the efforts of the famous trapper and "squawman," Jim Beckwourth, and whites friendly to the Indians, the Arapahos and Cheyenne had been prevailed upon to sign a treaty—the Fort Wise Treaty—much like those signed earlier by the Sioux and their associated tribes, a treaty which in effect surrendered their rights to large portions of their hunting lands in return for subsidies and assistance in adopting a farming rather than a nomadic life. But the Cheyenne had continued to raid the Ute and threaten the settlers. Returning from a war party against the Ute, they flourished fresh scalps in a white settlement and frightened the whites half out of their wits with their war whoops and wild yells.

Arapaho, debauched by the white man's whiskey, stole horses and supplies and raided white ranches. An officer sent to try to find and arrest the culprits reported: "The Indians talk very bitterly about the whites—say they have stolen their ponies and abused their women, taken their hunting grounds, and they expected that they would have to fight for their rights." More cattle stealing followed; a party of soldiers, sent to retrieve the cattle, killed three Indians. Public feeling in Denver was further exacerbated when the mutilated bodies of a rancher, his wife, and their children were brought into the town. Supply trains, hearing rumors of an Indian war, refused to venture on the trail, and Denver and nearby mining towns found themselves short of supplies. The governor of the territory, hoping to avert open hostilities, ordered the various tribes to go to the nearest fort to receive food and protection from soldiers on the hunt for hostiles, but when the Kiowa chief Satanta rode up to Fort Larned, he was refused admission. The enraged chief wounded a soldier, and he and his warriors drove off all the fort's horses. A number of Cheyenne and Arapaho were treated in a similarly cavalier fashion by the army. The infuriated Indians were soon on the warpath. Remote ranches were burned, their occupants tortured and killed. In a period of a few weeks more than 200 settlers and emigrants lost their lives. One woman who was later rescued declared, "An old chief . . . forced me, by the most terrible threats and menaces, to yield my person to him." Other chiefs then raped her in turn. Some whites, like William Bent, who understood the provocations suffered by the Indians, tried to arrange a peace council, but Chivington's superior had telegraphed him: "I shall require the bad Indians delivered up; restoration of stock; also hostages to secure. I want no peace until the Indians suffer more. . . . I fear the Agent of the Indian Department will be ready to make presents too soon. . . . No peace must be made without my direction."

Governor John Evans of Colorado was more conciliatory. Black Kettle, the Cheyenne chief, took his grievances to Evans at a council. The governor reminded him that he had earlier refused to parley and had sent word that he wanted nothing to do with Evans or the Great White Father in Washington, the United States government. A state of war existed, Evans declared, and matters were out of the hands of the military. General Patrick Connor, who had won his laurels as an Indian fighter against the Bannock and Shoshone, was dispatched in pursuit of the Sioux and Cheyenne. His orders to his troops declared: "You will not receive overtures of peace or submission from Indians, but will attack and kill every male Indian over twelve years of age."

Under the threat of punishment, one of the Arapaho bands returned some of the plunder from its raids. Meanwhile, a Major Wynkoop at Fort Lyon had negotiated an exchange of prisoners with the Cheyenne chief Black Kettle. Chivington immediately replaced Wynkoop with Scott Anthony, who soon was confronted with the problem of 650 Arapaho under Left Hand, who had come to Fort Lyon for gifts and protection. Unable to feed them and uneasy over rumors that they intended to attack the fort, Anthony sent them off. To a request for peace from Black Kettle and his Cheyenne, Anthony replied that he had no authority to negotiate peace but that they could camp at Sand Creek, forty miles away. The Cheyenne, to the number of some 700 men, women, and children, established a village at Sand Creek.

Meanwhile, Chivington received a message from the army commander in the state, General Martin Curtis, ordering him "to pursue everywhere and chastise the Cheyennes and Arapahos."

In the late fall of 1864 Chivington, at the head of the 3d Colorado and six companies of the 1st plus four twelve-pound howitzers, began a forced march through snow and bitter cold to Fort Lyon. There Anthony told him that the Cheyenne were camped at Sand Creek, and Chivington and his troopers pushed on, traveling all night and guided unwillingly by Robert Bent, son of William Bent—the first white settler in Colorado—and a Cheyenne woman. Robert Bent believed that the planned attack on the Cheyenne village where the chiefs were awaiting word of further negotiation was a classic example of white treachery. Chivington suspected that Bent was deliberately leading the cavalry astray; he tapped his revolver suggestively and told Bent, "I haven't had an Indian to eat for a long time. If you fool with me and don't lead me to that camp, I'll have you for breakfast."

At daybreak the soldiers found themselves within a mile of the Cheyenne camp. When it was evident that Chivington planned to attack the sleeping Indians, Lieutenant Joseph Cramer, who had served under Wynkoop, protested that the Indians were peaceful, that they felt confident that Wynkoop's word protected them, and that an attack would be an unjustifiable breach of faith. Chivington reportedly replied: "The Cheyenne nation has been waging bloody war against the whites all spring, summer, and fall, and Black Kettle is their principal chief. They have been guilty of robbery, arson, murder, rape, and fiendish torture, not even sparing women and little children. I believe it right and honorable to use any means under God's heaven to kill Indians who kill and torture women and children. Damn any man who is in sympathy with them." Chivington was later accused of having declared: "Kill and scalp all, big and little; nits make lice." He denied having made such a statement, but two of his officers testified that he did say, "No, boys, I shan't say who you shall kill, but remember who murdered our women and children."

Thereupon Chivington's men fell upon the unsuspecting Cheyenne. A hastily formed line of Cheyenne warriors met the attack and turned it back. White Antelope, an old chief, refused to take refuge along the riverbanks. He folded his arms and began the Cheyenne death song: "Nothing lives long except the earth and the mountains." Soon he was dead by a soldier's bullet. Major Scott Anthony wrote later: "I never saw more bravery displayed by any set of people on the face of the earth than by these Indians. They would charge on the whole company singly, determined to kill someone before being killed themselves." The fighting continued throughout the day. Some women and children escaped, but the warriors suffered heavy casualties. By four in the afternoon the Colorado volunteers were in complete command. The Indians who had not escaped had been killed, among them a number of women and children. Twenty-five soldiers had been killed or wounded.

Back in Denver, Chivington and his men were acclaimed as heroes. The *Denver News* declared: "Colorado soldiers have again covered themselves with glory." Some of the volunteers were introduced between the acts of a play at a Denver theater and exhibited Indian scalps to loud applause.

Soon ugly stories began to leak out of Indians killed in cold blood. Equally troubling was the circulated story that the Cheyenne and Arapaho had been attacked when they were confident that they were at peace with the whites and indeed under the nominal protection of Fort Lyon. In rebuttal to the argument that the Indians were entirely peaceful, some weight should be given to testimony that fresh scalps of whites were found in some of the Indian lodges by Chivington's soldiers.

Two congressional investigations produced a mass of conflicting testimony. There was no agreement even on the number of Indians killed. Estimates ranged from sixty-nine to "five and six hundred Indians left dead upon the field." Since the Cheyenne carried off all the wounded and many of the dead, the true number could not be determined. The most controversial issue of all was the number of women and children who had been killed. Some said two-thirds of the dead were women and children. A corporal testified that only "twenty-five of the dead were full-grown men." Robert Bent reported seeing a dead woman "cut open with an unborn child lying by her side. I saw the body of White Antelope, with the privates cut off." An Indian agent testified, "I saw the bodies of those lying there cut all to pieces, worse mutilated than any I ever saw before, the women cut all to pieces . . . children two or three months old . . . from sucking infants up to warriors."

The congressional committee that came to Denver to investigate the Sand Creek episode called Kit Carson as a witness and asked him what he thought of Chivington's actions, and Carson replied with a bitter denunciation. The Commission on Indian Affairs concluded in its report that the war which ensued "cost the government $30,000,000 and carried conflagration and death to the border settlements." During the summer of 1865 no fewer than 8,000 troops were withdrawn from the effective force engaged in suppressing the rebellion to meet this Indian war. "The result of the year's campaign . . . was useless and expensive. Fifteen or twenty Indians were killed at an expense of more than a million dollars apiece while hundreds of our soldiers had lost their lives."

By 1866 the "war" had dwindled down to sporadic raids. William Bent and Kit Carson, strong advocates of the Indian cause, could offer no better solution than the often-tried notion of persuading the tribes to take up an agricultural way of life. Charles Bent, a Cheyenne warrior and half brother of Robert, survived the Sand Creek battle. He devoted himself to hunting down white men and women and torturing them to death. Having lured two settlers out of a station on the Smoky Hill Trail, he staked one to the ground, cut out his tongue, built a fire on his stomach, and castrated and disemboweled him. William Bent disowned him for his cruelties, and Charles set out to kill his father.

Chivington's reputation never recovered. He remained under a cloud as the instigator of the "Sand Creek Massacre."

2

An Indian Policy

B y the end of the Civil War, with the national government firmly
in the hands of the Radical Republicans, there was a strong disposition on the part of Congress to do justice to the Indians as well as
to the ex-slaves. There were three major proposals for dealing with
the aborigines. One, generally espoused by the military, was a policy
of armed force combined with fairness. Its proponents argued that the
Indians, in the last analysis, respected only force. To impose order on
the constantly warring tribes, it was essential to demonstrate the determination of the United States government, through the agency of
the army, to suppress warfare between tribes as well as raids against
white settlements.

The most conspicuous alternate proposal, backed by a majority
of abolitionists, who enjoyed a considerable, if fleeting, prestige as the
agents of emancipation, as well as by the pacifists (in many cases one
and the same), was called the peace policy and eschewed all use of
force in dealing with the tribes. Force bred force, the argument ran.
If the Indians' better natures were appealed to, if they were provided
with schools and teachers and missionaries, they would welcome civilization. The army was not the solution but the problem. All matters

having to do with the Plains tribes should be placed in the hands of civilians committed to civilizing the aborigines.

The third proposal, held by a considerable majority of Americans living west of the Mississippi and north of the Ohio, was to exterminate the "uncivilized" Indians on the ground that they were beyond hope of reform.

The government policy in the period from the end of the Civil War to the end of the century was a combination of the first two proposals or an alternation between them. As early as 1865 the proponents of the peace policy had mustered their forces for an all-out campaign to win over the Johnson administration. Included in their ranks were such veterans of the abolitionist movement as Wendell Phillips, Frederick Douglass, Harriet Beecher Stowe and her brother Henry Ward Beecher, Lydia Maria Child, Julia Ward Howe, and Lucretia Mott and her faithful husband, James, now in their seventies but still on fire with righteous wrath wherever injustice might reveal itself.

Wendell Phillips, always outspoken, described the treatment of the Indians as "one of the foulest blots in our history." It was the task of the coming generation, he said, to give effect to the Fifteenth Amendment. "With infinite toil, at vast expense, sealing with 500,000 graves, we have made it true of the negro. With what toil, at what cost, with what devotion, you will make it true of the Indian and the Chinese, the coming Years will tell." When peace agreements with the Sioux began to unravel a few months after they were achieved, Phillips wrote in *The New York Times* that "the Indians have begun to tear up the rails, [and] to shoot passengers and conductors on the Pacific Road. . . . We see great good in this." The work started by the Indians should be completed, Phillips declared, and the Great Plains returned to them. While few reformers were willing to go as far as Phillips, it was certainly true that many cheered on the Indians in their clashes with army troops.

In the view of the reformers, justice for the aborigines meant observing the terms of existing treaties when possible or practical and, when either not possible or not practical, negotiating in good faith with *all* the members of particular tribes, not merely with some splinter group of more compliant Indians; it meant paying the tribes a fair price for their lands and, finally, undertaking to "civilize" the aborigines through training in agriculture and, through Christian education (there was, in their view, no other), the inculcation of the virtues of thrift, hard work, piety—the so-called Protestant ethic—and perhaps, above all, individualism. This was the task in which all friends of the Indians combined their very considerable talents and resources, social and political. They commanded, in their crusade, a network of liberal publications, journals and newspapers, from the sometimes wavering support of Godkin's *Nation* to *Harper's Weekly*, the *Boston Advertiser*, the *Boston Evening Transcript*, *The New York Times*, and, usually, the *New York Tribune*. All the antislavery and reform journals that survived were eager to contribute their bit, and soon there were a number of ephemeral journals concerned only with the reform of Indian affairs.

The policy of prevailing on Indians to settle on reservations was at least as old as the Indian Removal. The argument for reservations on the part of those friendly to the Indians was that it was only on reservations that Indians could be protected from predatory whites. The "assimilationists," on the other hand, attacked the reservations on the ground that they postponed assimilation.

Lyman Abbott, a Congregational clergyman, editor of the *Christian Union*, coadjutor to Henry Ward Beecher, and a champion of the Indian cause, was convinced that the long record of "dishonor which justly attaches to the history of our dealing with the North American Indians is due to a lack of prophetic vision . . . and an ignorance and indifference, not pardonable, in the nation at large, rather than to any deliberate policy of injustice adopted by the nation." To Abbott, the reservation system was the villain of the piece. "From the reservation," he wrote, "all the currents of civilization were excluded by federal law. The railroad, the telegraph, the newspaper, the open market, free competition—all halted at its walls." The reservation system had "made a prisoner [of the Indian] that it might civilize him, under the illusion that it is possible to civilize a race without subjecting it to the perils of civilization. . . . The reservation system is absolutely, hopelessly, incurably bad, 'evil and wholly evil' and that continually."

Abbott's remedy was to treat the Indians "as we have treated the Poles, Hungarians, Italians, Scandinavians. Many of them are no better able to take care of themselves than the Indians; but we have thrown on them the responsibility of their own custody, and they have learned to live by living. Treat them as we have treated the negro. As a race the African is less competent than the Indian; but we do not shut the negroes up in reservations and put them in charge of politically appointed parents called agents. The lazy grow hungry; the criminal are punished; the industrious get on. . . . Let the Indian administer his own affairs and take his chances. . . . Turn the Indian loose on the continent and the race will disappear! Certainly. The sooner the better. There is no more reason why we should endeavor to preserve intact the Indian race than the Hungarians, the Poles, or the Italians. Americans all, from ocean to ocean, should be the aim of American statesmanship. Let us understand once for all that an inferior race must either adapt and conform itself to the higher civilization, wherever the two come in conflict, or else die. This is the law of God, from which there is no appeal."

Richard Henry Pratt, perhaps the most notable "educator" of Indians in the post-Civil War period, also supported assimilation. Pratt estimated that there were some 250,000 Indians in the United States. Since there were approximately 3,000 counties in the various states, Pratt recommended dividing up the Indians "in the proportion of about ninety Indians to a county, and [finding] them homes and work among our people; that would solve the knotty problem in three years' time, and there would be no more an 'Indian Question.' It is folly to handle them at arms-length; we should absorb them into our national life for their own good and ours," he wrote. "It is wicked to stand them up as targets for sharp-shooters. The Indians are just like other men, only minus their environment. . . . We can, by planting the Indians among us, make educated and industrious citizens of them." Indians were "naturally religious." All that was necessary was "to familiarize their reverent minds with the truths of the New Testament." Captain Pratt told Frances Willard that "the history of the Indians as set forth in books is a bundle of falsehoods. They are like other people, and, unprovoked by outrage and injustice, behave far more peaceably than they get credit for."

It is important to emphasize here that, Lyman Abbott and Richard Pratt aside, among the great majority of Americans who considered themselves the friends of the Indian there was no substantial difference on the reservation issue. From reformers like Beeson and Whipple to President Grant himself, there was virtual unanimity on the reservation plan as the only fair solution to the Indian problem; the Indians must consent to go onto reservations and must be fairly compensated for the lands they surrendered. What if they refused all arguments and inducements? That, clearly, was the sticking point. No one could think of any better solution than sweetening the pie with more money and more gifts and larger annuities—bigger bribes. And then what? If all those inducements failed? Here force must obviously be used, however reluctantly. And what if, once on reservations, the Indians refused to remain, slipped away to prey on other tribes or on white settlers or emigrants within their range? Again, they must be punished by the army. But everyone was confident it would not come to that. The key was fair dealing, fair compensation, kindness, and good will.

In addition to the Eastern philanthropists there were men like Jim Bridger, Jim Meeker, and Thomas Fitzpatrick who knew the Indians as intimately as any white man could know them, who married or lived with Indian women and played and fought with the warriors. For them Indian life, compared with the life of the average white American, was irresistibly alluring. Some of them simply became "squaw men," white men who "went native"; others served in a variety of capacities: as guides for emigrant wagon trains; as scouts for the army; as Indian agents; even as Indian traders distinguished by their honesty and fair dealing with the aborigines. Their efforts were devoted to trying to protect those tribes with which they were most closely associated from the vagaries of state and federal policy and from particular acts of cruelty and violence. The connecting links between the Eastern reformers and the Western advocates of the Indian cause were the Christian missionaries, who carried on their hazardous and often fruitless labors wherever they could find Indians "settled" enough to listen to the Gospel or to send their children to mission schools.

Westerners were furious at what they considered the foolishly sentimental attitude of Eastern reformers toward the Indians. The *Kearney* (Nebraska) *Herald* in July, 1866, declared: "The earnest defenders of this barbarian monster would turn away in disgust could they see him in all of his original desperation. The best and only way to reconcile the blood-washed animal will be to impose upon him a worse schooling than has ever befallen the inferior races." The editor of a Boise, Idaho, newspaper suggested that the Nez Percé, who were protesting the invasion of their reservation by whites, be sent a shipment of blankets infected by smallpox. In Montana, when several Indians were killed in a fight with miners, the whites cut off their ears and pickled them in whiskey, stripped and bleached their skulls and wrote on them: "I am on the Reservation at Last" and "Let Harper's Tell of My Virtues." The *Kansas Daily Tribune* stated in July, 1866: "There can be no permanent, lasting peace on our frontiers till these devils are exterminated. Our eastern friends may be slightly shocked at such a sentiment, but a few years' residence in the West, and acquaintance with the continued history of their outrages upon settlers and travelers in the West, has dispersed the romance with which these people are regarded in the East." That, indeed, proved to be the case with a number of reformers who went West and encountered real Indians. They promptly, and sometimes publicly, recanted and came to sound disconcertingly like the most unreconstructed pioneers. Mark Twain, an avowed "Indian worshipper," was dismayed at the Goshute Indians of Nevada and confessed that he had been viewing the Indian "through the mellow moonshine of romance." A. J. Grover wrote to the *National Anti-Slavery Standard* that he was convinced the editor of that journal and Wendell Phillips himself would experience a change of heart if they were to travel through the West. "My sympathies have changed sides," he wrote, "and are now decidedly with the settlers and against the Indians who are prowling, stealing and murdering continually. . . . How would you and Wendell Phillips denounce such a policy as against the Ku-Klux of the South? And yet the Indians are ten times as savage and blood thirsty." An even more serious defection was that of Samuel Bowles, the liberal editor of the *Springfield* (Massachusetts) *Republican*, one of the founders and leaders of the Republican Party in Massachusetts, and a staunch antislavery man. Bowles traveled through the West and reported to his readers that "the wild clamor of the border population for the indiscriminate extermination of the savages . . . is as unintelligent and barbarous, as the long dominant thought of the East against the use of force, and its incident policy of treating the Indians as of equal responsibility and intelligence with the whites, are unphilosophical and impracticable." Bowles was convinced that the best that could be done for the Indian would be to "make decent the pathway to his grave." He could not survive as a "wild" Indian, and he could not be tamed.

In fairness to the Westerners, it must be kept in mind that customs and manners of the Indians were, for the most part, antithetical to everything that the white American valued and esteemed. Indian revenge, as we have noted, fell most commonly on the innocent. (The reverse, of course, was often true of white revenge for Indian depredations.) The practice of most tribes of mutilating the dead (so that they would enter the afterlife bereft of vital organs), of subjecting captives or the wounded to terrible tortures, and, above all, of raping captured white women placed the aborigines, in the minds of many of those whites most often in contact with them, beyond the pale of humanity. John Holmes grew up in one of the most enlightened towns of western Ohio—Mastersville. It was solidly Republican and antislavery in the era before the war. Many of the citizens subscribed to or shared William Lloyd Garrison's *Liberator* and the *Boston Evening Transcript*, a tireless organ of reform. There was an Indian reservation not far away, and small parties of Sac passed near the town occasionally, often on the prowl for stray Indians of rival tribes. On one occasion a resident of the town discovered the body of a young brave who had been skinned alive, the flesh torn from his body in great strips. If there had been any residual sympathy for Indians in Mastersville, that one episode dissipated it. A few years later an Indian woman, married to a white man, was shot by an Indian of a rival tribe as she sat on the porch of her house. It is not surprising that one of the topics of the Mastersville Literary and Debating Society was "Should the uncivilized Indians be exterminated?" What was surprising was not the topic but that it was considered debatable. Included in the topics listed in the society's minutes as having been debated in the same era were: "Should capital punishment be abolished?" and "Is a liberal education essential to a happy life?" In a town hospitable to blacks and even willing to tolerate Democrats, there was no sympathy for Indians. Seventy years later, reading the minutes of the Literary and Debating Society that he had recorded as a boy, John Holmes shook his head in bewilderment that such a topic as the extermination of the Indians could have been seriously debated by decent and liberally disposed men, many of them his relatives.

We might try the exercise of simply listing those qualities which white Americans most commonly attributed to red Americans. To the Eastern reformers, Indians were noble, free, wild, courageous, stoic, daring, nature-loving, worshipers of the Great Spirit, loyal, faithful, honorable (the white man, on the other hand, spoke with "forked tongue"). By contrast, the settlers and soldiers who were in most direct contact with the aborigines were inclined to describe them with such words as vile, savage, inhuman, barbarous, cunning, deceitful, treacherous, cruel, dirty, foul-smelling, insolent, adjectives often followed by a lurid list of particulars. I think we must concede that the Indians were, in varying degrees, all these things—characteristics, of course, varied widely from tribe to tribe—in different degrees and at different times and among different people. But taken together the words were, in essence, meaningless. They were white perceptions of the Indian. They did not begin to exhaust or even to describe sufficiently the reality that was the aborigine. In the most fundamental sense the Indian was the victim of the inadequacy of the white man's categories. The categories were both real and not real. They delineated a line or a feature, described an episode or evoked an aroma, but they failed to touch the indescribable heart of the reality. The issue was much larger and more complex than Indian cruelty or white prejudice.

The reformers had another irony to contend with. At the end of the war some 15,000 to 20,000 blacks were held by the Choctaw, Cherokee, and Chickasaw Indians as slaves. Forced by the terms of the peace treaty to free their slaves, the Indians kept them in a state of subordination very similar to that imposed on Southern blacks by white Southerners, the difference being that there was no Reconstruction army in the Indian Territory to protect the rights of the ex-slaves, who complained of "many ills and outrages" at the hand of their former owners, "even to the loss of many a life." Congress did its best to prevail upon the Indians to incorporate some 3,000 freed slaves into their tribes and give them each forty acres of land, offering $300,000 to facilitate matters. The Choctaw and Cherokee reluctantly complied, but the Chickasaw declared, tellingly, that they could not "see any reason or just cause why they should be required to do more for their freed slaves than the white people have done in the slave-holding states for theirs."

After the Civil War, William Tecumseh Sherman was given command of the Division of the Missouri, which extended as far south as Texas and as far west as the Rockies. Sherman's sympathies seemed, at least initially, with the Indians. He had a soldier's admiration of their bravery and skill in battle, and he looked on the white settlers, miners, and traders who crowded westward as greedy and unscrupulous civilians. At Colorado Springs, when the residents asked the general to build a fort to protect them from the Indians, Sherman suggested that they were more interested in the business that a military installation would bring than in warding off the Indians, whom they seemed eager to exploit. When Sherman was appealed to by importunate miners and prospective settlers for protection, he wrote to General Alfred Terry: "I agree with you perfectly that we are not in a position to permit an invasion of that region, for no sooner would a settlement be inaugurated, than an appeal would come for protection. . . . You may, therefore, forbid all white people going there at present, and warn all those who go in spite of your prohibition, that the United States will not protect them now, or until public notice is given that the Indian title is extinguished." When a party of 300 men was recruited in Yankton by an ex-army officer for an incursion into the Black Hills reservation under the name of the Black Hills Exploring and Mining Association, the military commander of the Dakota district was ordered to stop the party by force if persuasion failed.

Many whites in the region were calling for a war of extermination against the tribes and proposing a bounty of $100 per scalp. Sherman had no patience with such talk and made it clear wherever he went that he was as concerned with protecting the rights of the Indians under existing treaty arrangements as he was with protecting the lives of the whites. He discerned readily the difficulty of using locally recruited soldiers, poorly disciplined and filled with hatred of the Indians, to preserve order on the frontier and set about to replace such volunteers with regular army officers and enlisted men.

Sherman took it as his principal responsibility to keep open the Oregon, Smoky Hill, and Santa Fe trails. He was convinced that only by ensuring access on those now well-traveled roads to the Southwest and to the Pacific coast could the clamor for intervention by the military be stopped. If emigrants could pass over those roads with safety, time might be bought to "solve" the Indian problem on a permanent basis. There was one other potentially dangerous issue on the horizon: the building of a transcontinental railroad. Ever since the end of the Mexican War there had been talk of such a line, tying together the east and west coasts of the continent. It had grown insistent by the time of Fort Sumter, and only the coming of the war had delayed it. Now half a dozen "corporations" were vying for the right to run the line across the Great Plains through the Rockies, over the deserts of the Great Basin and on to San Francisco, Los Angeles, and the Northwest. It was clear that nothing could prevent or deflect the building of such a line or, eventually, lines. They must go through Indian hunting grounds, and there was ample reason to believe that the Plains tribes would resist that final intrusion. Indeed, the Union Pacific was moving west from Omaha at the rate of ten miles or so a day when Sherman assumed his responsibilities as military commander of the region through which the line was destined to run. The Kansas Pacific was also running a roughly parallel line from Kansas City to Denver.

To complicate matters further, the so-called Bozeman Trail had been discovered by John Bozeman and a companion who had been seeking gold in Montana. The two men found their way through a pass from Virginia City into the valley of the Yellowstone and thence to the Oregon Trail near Fort Laramie. For their pains, the Sioux stripped them of their horses, rifles, and clothes. They were back, nonetheless, the next spring with a large party of miners, determined to run the risks of Indian attack. Sherman was ordered to establish army posts along the established trail to protect those using it. He dispatched Colonel Henry Carrington with a battalion of 700 men, 226 wagons, a 26-piece band, a number of ambulances carrying the wives and children of some of the officers who were to garrison the forts along the trail, and 1,000 cattle to provide food for the expedition. Jim Bridger, a relic of the great fur trapping days in the Yellowstone, was the guide.

Just as Carrington departed, the Sioux chiefs were summoned to Fort Laramie for a parley. Chief Red Cloud of the Oglala Sioux protested: "Great Father sends us presents and wants new road but White Chief goes with soldiers to steal road before Indian says yes or no." When Red Cloud and Young-Man-Afraid-of-His-Horses refused further discussions, Carrington repaired to Fort Reno (formerly Fort Connor) on the Powder River and then pushed on and established Fort Phil Kearny at Big Piney Creek—a substantial settlement of twenty or so buildings in a space 400 by 400 feet surrounded by palisades. Before the fort was completed, a party of Sioux drove off 175 horses and mules. Pursued, they killed two soldiers and wounded three. Fifty-one such attacks were made in the space of five months. A favorite tactic of the Sioux was to raid the parties bringing lumber for the construction of Fort Kearny from the nearby foothills, the slopes of which were covered with pine trees.

Emigrant trains were shadowed and attacked whenever vigilance was relaxed. Bozeman himself was killed in 1867 on the trail that bore his name by a party of Blackfoot. Despite the attacks, Carrington pushed the construction of a third fort, Fort C. F. Smith, ninety miles beyond Kearny.

The Sioux attacks continued, gradually wearing away the morale of the expedition and driving off horses and cattle. In November, Carrington was reinforced by a company of cavalry and two officers, Captains James Powell and William Fetterman. Fetterman was a fire-eater with an outstanding record as a regimental officer in the Civil War. He ridiculed Carrington for his caution in not pursuing the Sioux raiders more aggressively and volunteered to be a scourge to the savages. When a party of Sioux were spotted headed for the "wood train," Carrington sent Fetterman with the cavalry company to reinforce the guards that accompanied the train. Fetterman and his junior officers, having driven off the Sioux, could not refrain from headlong pursuit.

They promptly ran into an ambush; one of the lieutenants was found later with more than fifty arrows in his body. Encouraged by the success of the skirmish, Red Cloud and his fellow chiefs decided to employ similar tactics to try to draw a larger force out of the fort and into an ambush.

Everything went according to Red Cloud's plan. The wood train was attacked; the soldiers at the fort prepared to go to its relief. Captain Fetterman, as the next in line to Carrington, demanded to be given command of the relief party of eighty men, including a number of volunteers anxious to get in on the action. Carrington's orders to Fetterman were: "Support the wood train. Relieve it and report to me. Do not engage or pursue Indians at its expense. Under no circumstances pursue over Lodge Trail Ridge." Carrington took special pains to be sure Fetterman understood his orders. The cavalry followed Fetterman's infantry detachment, and Carrington again repeated his instructions: no pursuit of the Indians over Lodge Trail Ridge.

When the detachment from the fort appeared, the Indian raiders withdrew, as they commonly did, to avoid being cut off or outflanked. Fetterman, in open defiance of his orders, took up the pursuit. Soon he and his men found themselves surrounded by Indians and vastly outnumbered. The fighting was fierce, and Carrington, hearing the shots and suspecting what had happened, dispatched a relief force of fifty-four men with an ambulance and wagons to reinforce Fetterman. The relief party arrived just as the Indians withdrew, leaving the ground strewn with the dead and mutilated bodies of the soldiers. Fetterman and a fellow officer had apparently shot each other to prevent capture and torture. The scene which confronted the rescue party was a grim one. Two civilian employees of the army, experienced Indian fighters armed with the sixteen-shot repeating Henry rifles, had held off the Indians for some time before their ammunition ran out. Sixty-five pools of frozen blood were counted in front of the rocks where they had taken refuge. Indian fury was indicated by the fact that one body had 105 arrows in it when it was retrieved by a burial detail from the fort.

Fire Thunder, a young Sioux brave, later recalled the battle: "[T]here were many bullets, but there were more arrows—so many that it was like a cloud of grasshoppers, all above and around the soldiers; and our people shooting across, hit each other. The soldiers were falling all the while they were fighting back up the hill, and their horses got loose. . . . When the soldiers got on top, there were not many of them left and they had no place to hide. . . . We were told to crawl up on them, and we did. When we were close, someone yelled: 'Let us go! This is a good day to die. Think of the helpless ones at home!' . . . I was . . . quick on my feet, and I was one of the first to get in among the soldiers. They got up and fought until not one of them was alive." Only a dog was left and it ran away howling. "Dead men and horses and wounded Indians were scattered all the way up the hill, and their blood was frozen. . . ."

Carrington reported on the condition of the corpses: "Eyes torn out and laid on rocks; noses cut off, ears cut off; chins hewn off; teeth chopped out; joints of fingers, brains taken out and placed on rocks with other members of the body; entrails taken out and exposed; hands cut off; feet cut off, arms taken out from sockets. . . ." The engagement into which the rash Fetterman had led his command to death was one of only two battles in our history in which there were no survivors; the other would be also at the hands of the Sioux.

When word of the debacle, along with the news that the hills around the fort were swarming with several thousand hostile Indians, reached Carrington, he made hasty preparations for defense, doubtless having in mind the fate of the 10 women (among them his own wife) and 11 children under his protection. Only some 120 men remained in the fort to defend it. With the wood train were 50 soldiers and 30 civilians, and 94 were in the relief party, which had not yet returned and the fate of which was still uncertain. Under the cover of darkness the wood train reached the fort and was soon followed by the relief party. Everything was done to prepare for an all-out assault, but it failed to materialize. The Sioux, who themselves had suffered heavy casualties, withdrew to bury their dead, treat the wounded, and savor their victory.

General Philip St. George Cooke, in command of the Department of the Platte, relieved Carrington of his command when word reached him of Fetterman's disaster. But Cooke, who had fought in the Black Hawk War thirty-four years earlier, was in turn relieved by Sherman. Although he had taken up his duties with a determination to deal justly with the Indians, Sherman experienced a change of heart on hearing the news of the annihilation of Fetterman's party. "I do not understand how the massacre of Colonel Fetterman's party could have been so complete . . ." he wrote. "We must act with vindictive earnestness against the Sioux, even to their extermination, men, women and children. Nothing else will do." Sherman soon had second thoughts about such a draconian policy, but his words, written in the heat of his anger and dismay over the gory news, were to haunt him. They would be cited by innumerable historians of the Indian wars as evidence that the hero of Atlanta and the March to the Sea was bent on the destruction of the Indians.

It was apparent that maintaining the three forts along the Bozeman Trail—Reno, Kearny, and Smith—was going to be a major drain on the resources of the army. Red Cloud and his Sioux warriors kept up a constant pressure, attacking any party that ventured out of the forts. The parties dispatched to cut wood were especially vulnerable, and they were the frequent objects of classic attacks by yelping warriors, who circled the woodcutters' camps on their ponies, hanging over the offsides of their mounts and firing underneath their necks at the beleaguered whites. The forts and their occupants, surrounded by thousands of hostile Indians, were actually little more than hostages to the tribes.

In the aftermath of the Fetterman episode a good deal of soul-searching was done on the subject of Indian policy. The Indian Bureau of the Department of the Interior and the War Department accused each other of various sins of omission and commission. The War Department charged the bureau with a weak and inconsistent policy toward the tribes, with corruption among its agents, and with condoning the exploitation of the Indians by rapacious traders. The bureau replied that it was expending millions of dollars each year in subsidies to the tribes and to assist in missionary work among those settled on reservations, especially in the establishment and maintenance of schools. The army, on the other hand, had no policy other than beating the Indians into submission in campaigns that were extremely costly in money and lives and often unsuccessful to boot. The army held to the line that the Indians were warriors who understood only force. Compromise and concession were to them evidence of weakness. They respected soldiers (warriors), and the soldiers should be left to deal with them. The Fetterman fiasco undercut the military, and for at least the moment the balance shifted to the Department of the Interior and its Indian Bureau. Congress, firmly in the hands of the Radical Republicans, intervened with a bill, passed in March, 1867, that established a peace commission to work out a blueprint for achieving peace with the Plains tribes.

A wave of optimism was created by the appointment of the Peace Commission, chaired by the commissioner of Indian affairs and including among its members such Radical Republicans and friends of the Indian as Senator John B. Henderson of Missouri, George Julian of Indiana, William Windom of Minnesota, and Samuel Tappan, a member of the great family of reformers and an early recruit to the Indian cause. Alfred Terry and William Harney, both strong antislavery men with outstanding war records, were also members of the commission, as was General Sherman. While the military was thus strongly represented, it was the best and most liberal element of the army. The charge to the commissioners was to make a thorough investigation of the general state of affairs regarding the Plains Indians, to negotiate treaties with the tribes in question, and to propose a long-range plan for civilizing the aborigines.

When the commissioners' report was delivered in 1868, it was overflowing with enlightened sentiments. "We have spent 200 years in creating the present state of things," it declared. "If we can civilize [the Indians] in twenty-five years, it will be a vast improvement on the operations of the past." They recommended a "hitherto untried policy of endeavoring to conquer by kindness." At the same time the commissioners rejected the notion that a "handful of savages" could seriously impede the age of progress and enlightenment that clearly lay ahead for the American people and in which the orderly settlement of the West and the exploitation of its natural resources were clearly essential elements.

The military members of the Peace Commission who knew the Indians best, Sherman most prominent among them, suppressed their doubts and acquiesced in the report, primarily on the ground that time would demonstrate whether the hopes expressed were extravagant. Sherman took the view that even if the report were excessively optimistic, its goals might be realized in the long run after the more recalcitrant tribes had been so chastened that they would accept life on their reservations. Enlightened as the report was, in many ways, it bore unmistakable evidence of white prejudices and predilections, most notably perhaps in its ban on polygamy. It was to that aspect that Lydia Maria Child objected strongly. "Let it be discountenanced, and reasoned against, and privileges conferred on those who live with one wife . . ." she wrote. "Indians, like other human beings are more easily led by the Angel Attraction, than driven by the Demon Penalty." The aborigines should be treated "simply as younger members of the great human family, who need to be protected, instructed and encouraged, till they are capable of appreciating and sharing all our advantages."

On the other side, Samuel Crawford of Kansas was unequivocal in his condemnation of the commissioners' report. "It was largely through their recommendations and misrepresentations," he declared, "that the wicked policy . . . was adopted by the government and persisted in by the Interior Department." Behind the Interior Department "was a gang of thieving Indian agents in the West, and a maudlin sentimentality in the East."

In the spring of 1868 at Fort Laramie, the commissioners signed a treaty with the Sioux and the Cheyenne that abandoned the forts on the Bozeman Trail (and, of course, the trail itself) in return for a promise on the part of the Indians to remain on their reservations, not to wage war against each other, and, most important, to permit the passage of the Union Pacific roadbed through their lands. William Dodge, chairman of the commissioners, explained to the Indians: "There are a great many people east who love the Indians and want to do them good. They wish to save the Indian from ruin. They remember that many moons ago the red man lived where the white man now lives but they are gone." Now the Indians must "begin to live like the white man. Cultivate your land, and we will send good men to teach your children to work, to read and write, and then they will grow up able to support themselves after the buffalo has gone."

The abandoned forts on the Bozeman Trail were burned by the triumphant Sioux. The last dramatic touch was added when Red Cloud, who had remained aloof from all the treaty negotiations, rode up to Fort Laramie in November after the forts on the Bozeman Trail had been abandoned and added his signature to the treaty. He must have done so with the conscious air of the victor.

Having concluded the treaty with the Sioux and Cheyenne at Laramie, the peace commissioners proceeded to Medicine Lodge Creek in Kansas to negotiate a similar treaty with the Comanche, Kiowa, Arapaho, and Southern Cheyenne. Three thousand Indians gathered in a wildly romantic scene. The purpose was similar, and the technique the same: the classic combination of gifts and threats. The Indians must accept limitations to their hunting ranges. It was clear that many were resistant. The Kiowa chief Satanta declared: "I love the land and the buffalo and will not part with it. I want the children raised as I was. I don't want to settle. I love to roam over the prairies. A long time ago this land belonged to our fathers, but when I go to the river I see camps of the soldiers on its banks. These soldiers cut down my timber; they kill my buffalo; and when I see that it feels as if my heart would burst with sorrow."

Albert Barnitz, a young lieutenant in Custer's 7th Cavalry, described how the Indians pressed into the regimental camps of the cavalry. "We are drilling daily," he wrote, "and the camp is daily thronged with Indian spectators of all ages, sexes and tribes. Last night 'White Man' an Arapaho Indian brought me a young squaw which he assured me was 'heap good' and which he desired to present to me for the evening." The officers in turn visited the camps of various tribes, among them the band of the Comanche leader Ten Bears. The Comanche, Ten Bears told his visitors, called themselves "nim" or "a people," and his band was called "nim-nim" or "a people of people." The Indians crowded in, observing every detail of army life with fascinated curiosity, the chiefs often "inviting themselves for dinner," Lieutenant Barnitz wrote his fiancée.

Reluctantly but inevitably, as they had done many times before, the tribes assented to the treaty. The Cheyenne and Arapaho were assigned some 3,000,000 acres north of the Washita River. There were the now standard promises of yearly subsidies—food, clothing, farm implements, and teachers—and then the distribution of the presents, bribes in truth.

From Medicine Lodge Creek the commissioners proceeded farther west to conclude treaties with the friendly Crow, the Ute of Colorado and Utah, the Bannock and the Shoshone, who, like the Crow, had kept peace with the whites. The Navaho and Snake, beguiled by mounds of presents, likewise fell in line, and now the system seemed complete. Under the terms of the treaties no white might "ever" enter the reserved areas "except those . . . designated and authorized to do so, and . . . such officers, agents, and employees of the government may be authorized to enter upon Indian reservations in discharge of duties enjoined by law. . . ."

The response of the frontier was what might have been expected. The *Yankton Press and Dakotan* declared indignantly: "This abominable compact with the marauding bands that regularly make war on the white in the summer and live on government bounty all winter, is now pleaded as a barrier to the improvement and development of one of the richest and most fertile sections in America. What shall be done with these Indian dogs in our manger? They will not dig the gold or let others do it. . . . They are too lazy and too much like mere animals to cultivate the fertile soil, mine the coal, develop the salt mines, bore the petroleum wells, or wash the gold. Having all these things in their hands, they prefer to live as paupers, thieves and beggars, fighting, torturing, hunting, gorging, yelling and dancing all night to the beating of old tin kettles. . . . Anyone who knows how utterly they depend on the government for subsistence will see that if they have to be supported at all, they might far better occupy small reservations and be within military reach, than to have the exclusive control of a tract of country as large as the whole State of Pennsylvania or New York, which they can neither improve or utilize."

Grant's election in 1868 spurred the friends of the Indians to renewed efforts on their behalf. The most enlightened viewpoint was expressed by valiant old Lydia Maria Child. She cautioned against the heavy-handed approach to "civilizing" the aborigines. The teachers of the Indian must respect the Indian's own culture, scrupulously avoid "our haughty Anglo-Saxon ideas of force." In her eloquent *An Appeal for the Indians* (1868), she urged: "Let their books, at first, be printed in Indian, with English translations, and let them contain selections from the best of their own traditionary stories."

Peter Cooper, the indefatigable philanthropist, the bankroller of a hundred good causes, inspired by Lydia Maria Child's *Appeal*, assembled a company of kindred spirits at the Cooper Union to form an association—the United States Indian Commissioners—"for the protection and elevation of the Indians, and to co-operate with the United States government in its efforts to prevent desolation and wars on the frontiers of our country." Like the Peace Commission, the report of which it endorsed, the new association emphasized that peace, not the sword, and justice, not expropriation, were the proper path to follow in all dealings with the aborigines. The Indian Commission, somewhat a misnomer since it suggested an official governmental tie, called for Indian representation in Congress and a separate department of Indian affairs not under the jurisdiction of the army *or* the Department of the Interior. John Beeson and Bishop Whipple were active in the new organization as were a number of clergymen and prosperous merchants along with the usual company of reformers.

Vincent Colyer, sent by the commission to report on the state of mind of the Indians, returned with the assurance that "in less than two years we shall have heard the last of 'Indian outrages.'"

The principal task undertaken by the Indian Commission was to arouse the public to the wrongs suffered by the Indians and to advance the peace policy in dealing with the Indians. All the wars with the Indians, they insisted in a spirit that ensured the angry opposition of the West, had been the result of injustices perpetrated by white men.

In a memorandum to Congress, drafted by Beeson, the commission declared that "when the true history of the Indian wrongs is laid before our countrymen, their united voice will demand that the honor and interests of the nation shall no longer be sacrificed to the insatiable lust and avarice of unscrupulous men."

The formation of the United States Indian Commission was followed by the founding of numerous associations dedicated to advancing, in one way or another, the welfare of the aborigines. Other reform and philanthropic organizations extended their interests to include the Indians—the Radical Club of Boston, the Union League, the Friends Social Union, and the Equal Rights Association prominent among them. Foremost in its eleemosynary activities was the American Peace Society under the leadership of Alfred Love. In addition to pushing for Indian representation in Congress and for vastly extended Federal assistance to the tribes to establish schools, build houses, buy agricultural implements and train the Indians in their proper use, the reformers proposed that Congress, after ridding itself of the horde of corrupt Indian agents, dispatch "true friends" of the aborigines to "mingle among the Indians, and in a few months settle the existing troubles." One rather wishes this bizarre proposal had been put to the test. Certainly a meeting of Alfred Love, Lucretia Mott, Gerrit Smith, and Lydia Maria Child with Red Cloud, Two Bears, Spotted Calf, and Crazy Horse would have provided inexhaustible material for parodists.

On the eve of the worst period of Indian troubles in our history, the optimum conditions prevailed in the government for fair and just treatment for the aborigines. Never before and never again would a national administration be as deeply committed to what it conceived of as a humane and liberal policy.

Moreover, no one could doubt the sincerity of President Grant himself. He endorsed the plan to bring delegations of Indians to Washington to present and dramatize their grievances, and Congress authorized him to "organize a board of Commissioners, to consist of not more than ten persons . . . eminent for their intelligence and philanthropy," to play an active role not only in advising on Indian policy but in supervising, jointly with the Department of the Interior, the proper observation of treaties and the best use of a so-called civilization fund of $2,000,000.

Determined to protect the emigrants while dealing justly with the tribes, Grant wished to remove, so far as possible, any grounds for Indian recalcitrance. Clearly one of the reasons most tribes were reluctant to remain on reservations was that they had no confidence that they would be treated fairly by the Indian agents. Grant's solution to this classic grievance was ingenious. The various Christian churches, which, since the turn of the century and in many instances well before, had been dispatching missionaries to the various settled tribes to try to convert them to Christianity and to establish mission schools (often subsidized by the government), had performed a thankless task, but they had also shown, with the inevitable exceptions, a genuine concern for the aborigines and a degree of honesty considerably above that of the average government agent. Grant therefore decided to seek his Indian agents among the Christian denominations. Because many of those chosen were Quakers, Grant's innovation came to be called the Quaker policy, and it did indeed substantially improve the quality of Indian agents and, in consequence, life on the reservations.

3

War in the Southwest

In the winter of 1866, while Sherman was attempting to keep the Bozeman Trail open by dispatching Colonel Carrington to establish a line of forts, a bloody conflict was taking place in the Arizona Territory between the military forces of the United States and the Chiricahua Apache. The trouble began when Colonel Pitcairn Morrison dispatched a young lieutenant to recapture a white boy kidnapped by an Apache band. The chief of the Apache was Cochise, one of the greatest Indian leaders in the country's history. Over six feet tall and famous for his strength and agility, he had carried on a long and bitter warfare with Mexico. When the Arizona region passed into American hands at the end of the Mexican War, Cochise decided that the Americans were too numerous and too warlike to attack. His policy, therefore, became one of caution and restraint. He believed that in the long run the only hope for his tribe was to adopt some of the ways of the white settlers, specifically to abandon a nomadic life for the more settled one of ranchers. The role that Cochise envisioned for the Apache was one that they had already undertaken—that of providing beef for emigrant trains moving West, for miners, and for new settlers. The beef initially had been stolen from Mexican rancheros, but Cochise was determined to establish the raising of cattle as a legitimate business whereby his tribe could preserve much of its culture. As the country filled up with white settlers, the relations between them and the Apache, guided by Cochise, were exemplary.

Such was the general state of things when a Lieutenant Bascom, unfamiliar with Indian ways and innocent of any knowledge of Cochise, summoned the Apache chief to his camp to answer for the kidnapping. Cochise came with his wife and son, two nephews, and a brother. Bascom charged him with responsibility for the kidnapping and threatened retribution unless the boy was returned. Cochise replied mildly enough that he had no knowledge of the kidnapping and would be glad to do what he could to ensure the boy's return. Thereupon Bascom is said to have declared, "Cochise, you are a liar! You and your people are my prisoners until the child is returned." At that Cochise slashed his way out of Bascom's tent and although wounded, made his escape, calling to the members of his family to follow him. They failed to escape, however, and the enraged Cochise attacked the Butterfield stage, intent on capturing whites to exchange for the members of his family. The braves captured three whites and killed eight others in the attack. Cochise then surrounded the stage station and kept the soldiers and civilians pinned down by musket fire until they began to suffer acutely from thirst. When the manager of the station, who knew Cochise well, went with two employees to parley with the chief, the three men were added to the group of whites offered by Cochise in exchange for his family. Bascom refused to make the exchange, although the manager called out to him that the result would be the death of the six white prisoners and the beginning of a fearful war. When one of Bascom's sergeants, who knew the ways of the Apache well, expostulated with Bascom, he was placed under arrest for insubordination.

At this point Bascom either hanged Cochise's wife, son, brother, and nephews and Cochise retaliated by killing his white prisoners, or vice versa. Another version has it that reinforcements arrived and took Cochise's wife and son back to Tucson, where they were set free. In any event the consequences are not in doubt: bitter and merciless warfare between the whites and the Chiricahua Apache, led by Cochise. Cochise's policy was now extirpation of the whites. His warriors spread out in deadly raids on ranches, stagecoach stations, and unwary travelers throughout the territory. Reuben Bernard, the sergeant who had tried to prevail on Bascom to accept Cochise's terms, wrote that he "personally knew of thirteen white men whom Cochise had burned alive, five of whom he tortured to death by cutting small pieces out of their feet, and fifteen whom he dragged to death after tying their hands and putting lariats around their necks. . . . This Indian was at peace," he noted, "until betrayed and wounded by white men. He now, when spoken to about peace, points to his scars and says, 'I was at peace with the whites until they tried to kill me for what other Indians did. I now live and die at war with them.' "

In 1865 an army colonel sent out to command the U.S. troops in the territory reported: "When I arrived, every ranch had been deserted south of Gila. The town of Tucson had but two hundred souls. North of Gila, roads were completely blocked, ranches abandoned and most of the settlements threatened with annihilation."

Cochise found a ready ally in Mangas Coloradas ("Red Sleeves"), the Mimbreño Apache chief, but the two of them together could seldom muster more than a 100 or so warriors. With these slim numbers they held the United States Army at bay. Moreover, Cochise prevented the mail from moving freely from the East to Tucson. Time and again couriers riding from Fort Bowie to Tucson were intercepted—fourteen in the first sixteen months of the line. In charge of getting the mail through was a remarkable Indian scout named Tom Jeffords. Jeffords finally decided to seek Cochise out and try to prevail upon him to let the mail go through. It was a bold and extremely dangerous enterprise that would, in a later day, provide dramatic scenes for a dozen or more movie westerns: the intrepid scout confronting one of the most feared Indian chieftains of the age. Jeffords reached Cochise's village, gave his gun and revolver to a woman, and walked to Cochise's lodge. For seven years no white man had come near Cochise; but Indians honored courage, and Cochise was fascinated by the resolution of "Sandy Whiskers," as he called Jeffords. He promised to protect the mail and told Jeffords he was free to visit the band whenever he wished. Jeffords took advantage of Cochise's offer and in time became a blood brother and Cochise's biographer.

When peace seemed a possibility in the winter of 1870, a band of renegade whites with ninety-two Papago Indians, longtime enemies of the Apache, and forty-eight Tucson Mexicans fell on a band of un-suspecting Aravaipa Apache, most of them women and children, and slaughtered them all. The episode roused a storm of indignation in the East. President Grant initiated an investigation and ordered that the culprits be tried. All of them were acquitted. In the summer of 1871 Grant reached the conclusion that the only hope for protecting the Indians against whites as well as against other Indians was by locating them "upon suitable territories . . . under control of the proper officers of the Indian Department." A central aim was making peace with Cochise and his Chiricahua Apache. For this assignment, the President chose the secretary of the Board of Indian Commissioners, Vincent Colyer, a man known to be sympathetic to the Indians.

Cochise agreed to meet with Colyer and the army officer in charge of the military forces of the territory. The suggestion was made by Colyer that Cochise and the Chiricahua Apache live on the Tularosa Reservation, almost 200 miles from the country where they had lived and fought the intrusion of the white man so successfully. Cochise replied: "I have come with my hands open to you to live in peace with you. I speak straight and do not wish to deceive or be deceived. I want a strong, lasting peace.

"When I was young I walked all over this country, east and west, and saw no other people than the Apaches. After many summers I walked again and found another race of people had come to take it. How is that? Why is it that the Apache want to die . . . ? They roam over the hills and plains and want the heavens to fall on them. The Apache were once a great nation; they are now but a few, and because of this they want to die. . . . Many have been killed in battle. You must speak straight so that your words may go as sunlight into our hearts. Tell me, if the Virgin Mary has walked throughout all the land why has she never entered the wigwam of the Apache? Why have we never seen or heard her? . . . When I was going around the world, all were asking for Cochise. Now he is here—you see him and hear him—are you glad? If so, say so. Speak, Americans and Mexicans. I do not wish to hide anything from you nor have you hide anything from me. I will not lie to you; do not lie to me." As for the Tularosa, that was far away. "The flies on those mountains eat out the eyes of the horses. The bad spirits live there. I want to live in these mountains. I have drunk of these waters and they have cooled me; I do not want to leave here."

General Gordon Granger, the military commander, gave Cochise his word that he and his people could remain in their mountains. Cochise thereupon declared the war at an end and prepared to adapt the life of his tribe to the limitations of a reservation, broad though it might be. But Washington rejected the part of the treaty that allowed Cochise and his people to remain on their tribal land. They must go, with the other Apache, to Tularosa. Cochise took to the warpath once more with almost 1,000 Apache, many from other tribes. Again settlers lived in fear of their lives. Horses and cattle by the hundreds were driven off, and fifty settlers killed or wounded in raids. No isolated settlement or ranch in the Southwest was safe from Apache revenge. This time Grant sent two of his favorite generals to subdue the Apaches and bring peace to the region: George Crook and Oliver Otis Howard. Crook, who had graduated from West Point, class of '52, had served for almost eight years in the West, in California, on the Rogue River expedition against the tribes of the Northwest and in command of the Pitt River expedition, during which he was wounded by an arrow. With the outbreak of the Civil War he had advanced to the rank of brigadier, distinguished himself at the Battle of Chickamauga, and subsequently served as Sheridan's right-hand man in his famous raid on the Shenandoah Valley. By the end of the war he had attained the rank of major general. After the war Crook was sent to Boise, in the Idaho Territory, where he proved himself adept at Indian warfare and forced peace on the tribes in the region around Boise. Oliver Otis Howard, a year younger than Crook, was one of the genuine heroes of the Civil War. He was the pious officer whom Sherman teased by saying "damn" in his presence. He had lost an arm at Fair Oaks, won the Congressional Medal of Honor for his heroism, and distinguished himself at Gettysburg. An ardent abolitionist, Howard had served as commissioner of the Freedmen's Bureau, founded Howard University, and been its first president. Now he was given the assignment of pacifying Cochise while Crook was given the task of rounding up the rest of the Apache and forcing them to return to the reservation at Tularosa. Crook was of the threat-and-intimidation school of Indian fighters, as, it must be said, most military men were. He ordered the rebellious chiefs to return to their reservations or "be wiped from the face of the earth."

Howard, by contrast, was determined to try to put his Christian precepts to use, and Grant promised that he would support any peace plan that Howard might negotiate with Cochise. Howard knew of Tom Jeffords's friendship with Cochise, and he asked Jeffords to take him to the Apache chief without any accompanying soldiers, other than the general's aide, Captain John Sladen. After a long, trying trip the little party reached Cochise's mountain stronghold. Howard was introduced to Cochise. "He gave me a grasp of the hand," Howard wrote later, "and said very pleasantly, 'Buenas dias.' His face was really pleasant to look upon, making me say to myself, 'How strange it is that such a man can be the robber and murderer so much complained of. . . . We walked together, and sat down side by side on the blanket seat beneath a fine spreading oak." With Jeffords acting as interpreter, Howard told Cochise, "I came with the hope of making peace between you and the citizens, and thus saving life and property." Cochise replied, "I am as much in favor of peace as anyone. I have not been out to do mischief for the past year. But I am poor; my horses are poor and few in number. I could have taken more horses on the Tucson road but have not done it. I have twelve captains out in different directions who have been instructed to go and get their living." Cochise's reply suggested the real nature of the problem. Ever since the whites had come to the land of the Apache, that warlike people had lived off the horses and cattle of the invaders. It was an essential part of the Indian economy. Under the Mexican government the efforts to force the Apache, the Waco, and the Comanche especially to stop their depredations had been intermittent and, for the most part, unsuccessful. With the Americans it was different. They were determined to make good their claims to inhabit the region. The Indians must become farmers. But that was, in essence, asking them to cease being Indians and to become some indeterminate, undefined creature that was neither an Indian nor a white man. The fact was that the Apache could not live as *Apache* without taking from white Americans, as they had taken from Mexicans for generations, an essential increment of food and other white artifacts. Denied the right to raid, they faced starvation. The white answer was "Stay on the reservations, and we will take care of you. Leave the reservation, raid white ranches and white settlements, and we will destroy you."

But Cochise and Howard could not say precisely this to each other. Howard instead urged Cochise to accept life-death on a reservation. "I would like to have a common reservation on the Rio Grande," he told Cochise, "for the Mimbreño Apache and Chiricahua Apache."

"I have been there and like the country," Cochise replied. Rather than not have peace, he would go there, but he could not guarantee that all his people would follow him. He believed, rather, that the move would "break my band." If Howard would give him a reservation at Apache Pass, then he might indeed be able to control his young braves and assure the safety of emigrants and settlers.

How long could Howard stay? Cochise asked. He must consult with his twelve subchiefs before he could agree to any move. "I came from Washington for the purpose of making peace," Howard replied, "and I will stay as long as necessary." Cochise seemed pleased with the general's response, but suddenly he broke out with a bitter recitation of the wrongs his people had suffered at the hands of the whites. "My best friends were taken by treachery and murdered," he reminded Howard. The infamous Bascom had left their bodies hanging until the elements and the predators had stripped their bones. "The Mexicans and Americans kill an Apache whenever they see him. I have fought back with all my might. My people have killed many Mexicans and Americans and have captured much property. Their losses are greater than ours; yet I know we are all the time diminishing in numbers. Why do you shut us upon a reservation? We want to make peace, and we will faithfully keep it; but let us go wherever we please, as the Americans do." To this Howard had no answer except to repeat that the Apache must accept settlement on a reservation. That was now the government's policy. Otherwise they could not be protected from the rapacity of the white settlers who were determined to occupy their lands. The land belonged to God, Howard decided. It did not belong to the white man or to the Indian. So there must be boundaries. The second point did not seem to Cochise to follow from the first. If the land belonged to God, why was it not open to all His children without distinction and without boundaries? Cochise did not, of course, allude to the fact that the Apache had, at the height of their power, appropriated the lands claimed by weaker tribes. It was, in any event, beside the point.

When the subchiefs arrived, the council began, and now Cochise, speaking for the others, insisted that the land of the Chiricahua must be their reservation. Howard at last reluctantly agreed. Jeffords must be the Indian agent for the reservation, Cochise declared, but Jeffords, knowing only too well the kinds of political pressures to which Indian agents were subject, refused. No Jeffords, Cochise declared, no treaty. Jeffords gave in. He would be agent if he were given complete authority so that no person could come onto the reservation without his permission. Confident that Grant would back him up, Howard agreed to Cochise's and Jeffords's conditions. The treaty, perhaps the most remarkable negotiated with any tribe in the post-Civil War period, was concluded, dispatched to Washington, and there twelve days later accepted by the President. "Hereafter," Cochise declared upon hearing the news, "the white man and the Indian are to drink of the same water, eat of the same bread, and be at peace."

Cochise observed the terms of the treaty. The Apache, unwilling to farm, cut hay and wood for the military units in the area, but the work was uncongenial to the warriors, and the promised supplies of government food were delayed in arriving. Cochise led a raiding party into Mexico on the ground that he had no treaty agreement with the Mexicans. He was wounded in the raid. The wound became infected, and soon it was evident that Cochise was dying. Jeffords remained with him much of the time. According to Jeffords's account, one day when he was about to leave, Cochise said, "Chickasaw [brother], do you think you will ever see me alive again?"

"No, I do not think I will. I think that by tomorrow night you will be dead."

"Yes, I think so too—about ten o'clock tomorrow morning. Do you think we will ever meet again?"

"I don't know," Jeffords replied. "What is your opinion about it?"

"I have been thinking a good deal about it while I have been sick here, and I believe we will; good friends will meet again—up there."

"Where?"

"That I do not know—somewhere; up yonder, I think," Cochise said, pointing to the sky.

Early the next morning he asked his warriors to bear him up the mountain to watch the sun rise over the mountain peaks. After Cochise's death Jeffords, knowing the white man's passion for exhuming the bones of Indians, told several conflicting stories of where the great chief's remains were placed. Twenty years later he took Nino Cochise, the chief's grandson, to the country of the Chiricahua Apache. It was dotted with ramshackle settlements and marginal ranches. Jeffords and young Cochise stopped at a ranch run by an old friend of the former scout, Billy Fourr, and Fourr declared bluntly, "If old Cochise were alive and could see what happened to his land he'd blow a gasket."

Two years after his death the treaty he and Howard had negotiated was broken. Without Cochise's restraining influence incidents occurred. Ranchers complained of losing horses and cattle. The Chiricahua Apache were ordered to move to a reservation in New Mexico. Many of the young braves refused, and once more there was warfare in the territory.

It has been estimated that in the efforts to bring Cochise and the Chiricahua Apache to account, more than 1,000 soldiers were killed or died of disease with a loss of barely 100 Apache. Nowhere else was there such an imbalance in white-Indian casualties. Cochise and his warriors ranged over a land they knew like the palms of their hands, a land so bleak and barren that soldiers followed at their peril.

If the Chiricahua Apache were the terror of the Southwest, other Apache tribes and their allies ranged over the area from south of the Platte to the Missouri. This territory was assigned to George Crook for pacification. Crook, as we have noted, was an experienced Indian fighter. He had won the admiration of many of the Indians he had defeated in battle, particularly the Shoshone. He accepted as inevitable the reservation system. Within its narrow limits, he was determined to deal fairly with the various tribes, knowing that they respected the military virtues and felt a kind of rapport with soldiers that did not extend to the civilians who pushed their way onto their lands. Crook clearly had a flair. Tall and thin, he wore a stained canvas hunting jacket and a pith helmet, both items strictly nonissue, and rode a handsome mule named Apache. With patient attention to the smallest detail, especially to the condition of his prized mules, he created excellent morale in the officers and men under his command. Not content to remain at the headquarters of his command, Crook undertook an expedition through Indian country, seeking out the various Apache chiefs and assuring them that they must cease their warlike ways or be utterly defeated. His story was always the same. If they would consent to adapt to a settled, agricultural life, he would protect them from any whites who tried to disturb them. He also stated that he would find work for all Indians who wished work and would pay them the same wages as those given to white men. Well aware of their resistance to reservation life, Crook assured them that they would be confined to reservations only until, with the help of Indian agents and teachers, they had learned white ways well enough to hold their own in white society. Then they would be free to mix in white society, attend white schools and churches, and become full citizens of the United States rather than wards of the Federal government. It was an enlightened, if perhaps excessively optimistic, picture that Crook, in good conscience, painted for the suspicious chiefs. To modern critics it smacks of ethnocentricity. The white man's ways were better; therefore, the Indians must abandon their traditional ways and become, for all practical purposes, nineteenth-century whites. But, it must be said, with the benefit of more than 100 years of hindsight, no one has proposed a better solution to the "Indian problem." Considering that virtually all frontier settlers and many Americans who were in all other respects kindly and charitable wished to exterminate all Indians, Crook's policies and, even more, his attitude appear exemplary.

With his headquarters temporarily at Prescott, Crook displayed an insatiable curiosity about the surrounding countryside. Not only was he an eager anthropologist, anxious to learn everything he could about the cultural life of the tribes, but he was equally curious about the flora and fauna of the region. In addition, the general formed an alliance with the Paiute and Hualpais tribes, planning to enlist them if the efforts to persuade the Apache to accept reservation life failed and it was necessary to resort to force.

Believing that there was no hope of an enduring peace until the Apache bands felt the weight of military force, Crook prepared for that type of fighting for which the Indians were least prepared—winter campaigning. Winter was at best a precarious time for the Plains Indians. Like the deer and buffalo they depended upon, they grew lean and hungry, scratching up food where they could find it, often suffering acutely in hard winters. Their mobility was severely limited. Often they were reduced to eating their ponies or raiding neighboring tribes. The women and children were a heavy responsibility as well. Hence the disposition of all tribes was to sue for peace at the approach of winter. As important as his winter strategy was Crook's systematic enlistment of Apache who were disposed to peace or simply willing to work for a white man's wages. It was a policy that aroused the resentment of soldiers and settlers alike. The notion of paying an Indian a white man's wages offended them profoundly, but it drained away Apache strength, and when fighting came it provided Crook with a substantial body of Indian scouts familiar with the locations of the various Indian refuges.

Crook's practice was to place well-equipped and well-disciplined troops under the independent leadership of officers whose resourcefulness he trusted, with instructions to give the Indians no respite, to pursue them until they were defeated or until they could flee no longer. Women and children were not to be harmed, or prisoners mistreated. The strategy soon proved its effectiveness. Some Indians surrendered, others were killed. A troop commanded by Major William Brown surprised a large band of Apache in the Salt River Canyon and killed seventy-four braves. Those who escaped intercepted a party of Englishmen, killed a number, and tortured two to death. Crook caught up with the war party at Turret Butte a week later, and soon the survivors of the winter campaign were suing for peace in behalf of some 2,300 Apaches. Crook's terms were that those who surrendered must start work at once on an irrigation project designed to bring water to the farms they would be required to till. Crook would see that the Indians were fairly paid for the crops they grew and that order was preserved on the reservation by Apache police. Those Indians who committed crimes would be tried by Apache juries. The Apache turned to and dug a canal five miles long, three feet deep, and four feet wide, the first such physical labor most of them had ever performed. Crook had also promised schools, but the Federal government proved delinquent in providing them, and the general turned to missionaries for assistance.

Crook's principal obstacle proved to be the so-called Indian Ring, made up of private traders who fattened on exploiting the Indians and providing supplies for the army units sent out to fight them. They had a vested interest in perpetuating a state of warfare and did their best to discredit Crook with those authorities in Washington to whom he was accountable. Grant, however, gave the general his full support, and Crook in turn showed remarkable tact and skill in keeping the restless Apache appeased.

It might be well at this point to consider the life of the army officers and enlisted men charged with keeping peace in Indian country and with fighting the Indians when treaty agreements broke down.

There was a strange, symbiotic relationship between the "wild" Indians and the military men sent out to "tame" them. Men like Terry, Crook, and Howard were the best representatives of the army, decent and humane men who suffered pangs of remorse and bitter frustration when the government failed to make good on the promises it had authorized them to make to persuade hostiles to stop their predatory ways and remain on or return to their reservations. Better than bureaucrats of the Department of the Interior and the higher echelons of the War Department, better even than the pro-Indian lobby, they understood and respected the savage ethos of the tribes they were directed to bring to account. When the Bannock or Snake Indians, who had accepted reservation life in good faith and cooperated with the army in a number of its campaigns against other tribes, failed to receive their promised supplies from the government and were, in consequence, faced with starvation, Crook wrote a bitterly critical article for the *Army and Navy Journal*, describing the situation in the bluntest terms. When there were not enough jackrabbits or buffalo to sustain them, "What," he asked, "were they to do? Starvation is staring them in the face, and if they wait much longer, they will not be able to fight. . . . I do not wonder, and you will not either that when these Indians see their wives and children starving, and their last resources of supplies cut off, they go to war. And then we are sent out to kill. It is an outrage."

The life in the frontier posts was not without its pleasures and comforts, at least for the officers. Frances Roe, the wife of Lieutenant Faye Roe, described Fort Lyon, in the Colorado Territory, as resembling "a prim little village built around a square, in the center of which is a high flagstaff and a big cannon. The buildings are very low and broad and are made of adobe—a kind of clay and mud mixed together—and the walls are very thick. At every window are heavy wooden shutters that can be closed during severe sand and wind storms." Where timber was available, forts generally were surrounded by wooden palisades, so often depicted in western films.

Christmas at Fort Lyon was celebrated with some style. Frances Roe described "three long tables, fairly groaning with things upon them: buffalo, antelope, boiled ham, several kinds of vegetables, pies, cakes, quantities of pickles, dried 'apple-duff,' and coffee." It was the custom for the officers' wives to send the enlisted men of their husbands' companies "large plum cakes rich with fruit and sugar. Turkeys, celery, canned oysters and other delicacies had been imported from St. Louis." After the sumptuous meal there was a dance with the officers in full-dress uniforms and the wives in their finest gowns.

When the men were not fighting Indians, the forts offered a variety of diversions for the officers and their spouses, from riding with greyhounds in pursuit of elusive jackrabbits or antelope to costume balls. At Camp Supply in the Indian Territory, Indians were all about—Arapaho, Comanche, Southern Cheyenne, Apache, and Kiowa—and one was never quite sure of their disposition. They were bolder than the Ute and Frances Roe was often disconcerted to find them staring through the windows of her quarters, their painted faces pressed against the glass. "It is enough to drive one mad," she wrote a friend. "You never know when they are about, their tread is so stealthy with their moccasined feet."

For the enlisted men, many of them Irish immigrants, with an admixture of Germans and Italians (Custer's messenger at the Little Bighorn was Giovanni Martini, known as John Martin, whose difficulties with English caused confusion in the initial stages of the battle), life was much like that of the private soldiers of the Civil War. Indeed, most of the U.S. regulars fighting in the frontier were veterans of the war. For them the life of a frontier military post was a monotonous routine of camp duties, of army food—prepared often by Chinese cooks ("Chinks" or "Chinee")—and of foraging parties, scouting missions, and brief interludes of active campaigning, often under the desperately hard conditions of a Rocky Mountain winter. The toll from illness and disease as well as Indian arrows and bullets was heavy, and the job, in a large measure, thankless. What glory there was went to the officers. For many white Americans it was, after all, the Indians, not the U.S. Army, who were the heroes. On the more positive side, the wild beauty of the landscape itself, combined with the aura of romance that hung over everything that had to do with the Indians, gave the life a strong appeal to the young and venturesome. Even the private soldier was caught up in the glamour associated with being an "Indian fighter." Custer, trying to persuade a civilian friend to accompany the Black Hills expedition of 1874, wrote: "You shall taste of greater varieties of game than a New Yorker ever dreamed of and it will not be such as you obtain in the market houses . . . but it will be of such delicious flavor and condition as will make you wonder if you ever tasted game before. . . . The appetite you will have for food and the soundness of your sleep will be so different from those usually enjoyed by professional gentlemen in all kinds of life, that you will think you have fallen into fairyland and when you return to the states you will feel like a man who has been granted a renewed lease of life."

Among the most experienced troopers were the black cavalrymen of the 9th and 10th regiments—buffalo soldiers the Indians called them because of kinky black hair like a buffalo's mane. They made excellent soldiers. "They fight like fiends," Frances Roe reported. "They certainly manage to stick on their horses like monkeys."

If Indian chiefs and U.S. Army officers respected each other as warriors, relations between the aborigines and the soldiers assigned to "protect" or to fight them were often tense. Those aborigines who were "at peace," or, as they were referred to, "treaty Indians," often got their kicks by scaring and harassing the soldiers and civilians at the forts and Indian agencies where they came for supplies, to trade, or simply to cause mischief. Well aware that soldiers were forbidden to fire at "friendly" Indians, they did not hesitate to take advantage of that fact by assuming arrogant or threatening manners. The wives of officers and new recruits were often the special targets of the devilry. Frances Roe was horrified by her first contact with the "savages" at her husband's post at Fort Lyon. "Well, I have seen an Indian—number of Indians—but they were not Red Jackets," she wrote a friend; "neither were they noble red men. They were simply, and only, painted, dirty, and nauseous-smelling savages!" Shopping with a friend in a store at Las Animas, a small Mexican town near the fort, Frances Roe was alarmed when ten or twelve Indians dashed up on ponies, crowded into the little store "in their imperious way," and pushed the two white women aside "with such an impatient force that we both fell over the counter." They demanded from the intimidated shopkeeper powder, balls, and percussion caps, and one of those who had remained outside rode his piebald pony into the doorway of the store, preventing the frightened women from escaping. When the Indians departed, the storekeeper told the women that the visitors were Ute, much excited at the news that their traditional enemies, the Cheyenne, were in the vicinity. "Not one penny did they pay for the things they carried off," Frances Roe reported indignantly. "They were all hideous—with streaks of red or green paint on their faces that made them look like fiends. Their hair was roped with strips of bright-colored stuff, and hung down on each side of their shoulders in front, and on the crown of each black head was a small, tightly plaited lock, ornamented at the top with a feather, a piece of tin, or something fantastic. These were their scalp locks. They wore blankets over dirty old shirts, and of course had on long, trouserlike leggings of skin and moccasins. . . . The odor of those skins, and of the Indians themselves, in that stuffy little shop, I expect to smell the rest of my life!"

At Camp Supply, Frances Roe reported, a party of forty or fifty Comanche "came rushing down the drive in front of the officers' quarters, frightening some of us almost out of our senses. . . . They rode past the houses like mad creatures, and out on the company gardens, where they made their ponies trample and destroy every growing thing." The Indians were "young bucks out on a frolic, but quite ready, officers say, for any kind of devilment. They rode around the post three or four times at breakneck speed, each circle being larger, and taking them further away. . . . I presume there were dozens of Indians on the sand hills around the post peeking to see how the fun went on." A few nights later Frances Roe and her husband were awakened by rifle shots and cries of "Indians! Indians!" Pandemonium followed. Drums beat the long roll call to arms, and the cavalry bugles sounded boots and saddles, sounds that "strike terror," Frances Roe wrote, "to the heart of every army woman." With the fort thoroughly aroused, the Indians rode off with triumphant shouts. It was all a game.

The sense that they were always under surveillance by Indian lookouts was strengthened by the not uncommon experience of being out hunting or simply riding for pleasure only to discover that one was being watched by some motionless brave. Frances Roe, through her husband's binoculars, watched an Indian sentinel on a distant ridge. "He sat there on his pony for hours," she noted, "both Indian and horse apparently perfectly motionless, but his face always turned toward the post, ready to signal to his people the slightest movement of the troops."

White men continued, as they had since the days of the Yellowstone rendezvous, to live with various Indian tribes. Often the reasons were more "anthropological" than commercial, a fascination with Indian culture and Indian ways.

Thomas Henry Tibbles, a journalist, Populist, and ardent friend of the Indians, spent a winter with the Omaha and eventually married an Indian woman. Tibbles gave a delightful account of tribes at play, of the endless dancing and storytelling, the garrulousness of the older braves and the bravado of the young. The lodges of the tribe were divided into groups Tibbles called clubs, the primary purpose of which was entertainment. The clubs vied among themselves for Tibbles's company. At Prairie Chicken's club, the young men danced first, "gaily painted and covered with bells. Then came a masked dance in which the men covered their faces with the heads of animals, then the young women danced and partners were chosen by means of a guessing game." Tibbles was pressed to teach his Indian friends some white dance steps. A drum was brought, he whistled a waltz, and after a time an Indian girl came forward to join. She had learned the "Rocky Mountain Waltz" from another tribe, and as she and Tibbles sang and danced the others joined in. "The whole group," Tibbles wrote, "was wild with excitement . . . and soon the tent was filled with pairs of Indians whirling around in a half-civilized, half-barbaric style that seemed to take all our senses away." Half the tribe, attracted by the noise, joined in; "everywhere there were shouts of laughter, screams of delight, the racket of drums." Finally the older women and men of the tribe, aroused by the revels, appeared and angrily put a halt to the festivities. White men's dances were forbidden to Indians; they were a corruption, "dangerous and indecent," prohibited by the tribal council "as long as the grass grows and the waters run."

When Tibbles next visited the Omaha, they had been forced to accept life on a reservation, and they were dramatically changed in health and appearance from the Indians he had visited a few years earlier. "The reserve was the poorest soil in the state and the Indian agency was made up of a few rough structures housing a blacksmith shop, a sawmill and a government storehouse." Seeing his friends reduced to hunger and misery and jeered at by the white loafers around the agency, Tibbles "felt a wave of fury toward our government's whole Indian policy. . . . Could it be God's will," he asked himself, "that men [like those he had known] brave, generous to a fault, dignified, intelligent, faithful to every trust, loving their families and children and every inch of their native plains, should become beggars and gradually be swept off the face of the earth? Must they make room for a race of sordid people who were subordinating every noble instinct to a ruling passion for accumulating property?" The Indian's greatest failing, Tibbles reflected, was giving; the white man's custom was taking. He took everything the Indian gave and demanded more.

4

Scattered Campaigns

When Grant had been elected President in 1868, he had summoned Sherman back to Washington to take overall command of the army. Philip Sheridan had replaced him as commander of the Division of the Missouri, with responsibility to preserve peace with the Indians by making every effort to meet their most serious grievances.

Sheridan found his hands full. Among the Southern tribes the Comanche and Kiowa kept New Mexico and Texas in a state of continual agitation by their daring raids. While they were nominally confined to their reservations, they used them primarily as a base of operations for their raids. A chorus of outraged cries from settlers and traders penetrated the halls of Congress, and a proposal was made to shut off the Texas border by constructing a string of military reservations along the Texas boundary with New Mexico. In May, 1869, a Kiowa chief named Satanta led an attack on a wagon train and killed six teamsters. Satanta freely admitted that he was responsible. He was arrested, tried in a civil court, convicted of the murders, and sentenced to be hanged. Such a storm of protest was raised by champions of the Indians that Grant brought pressure on the governor of Texas to commute Satanta's sentence to life imprisonment. When the public clamor continued, the governor pardoned the chief and another Indian, to the rage of his Texas constituents. The episode is significant for what it reveals of the strength and numbers of what today we would call the Indian lobby. Upon the news of the chief's release, Sherman wrote to the offending governor that he hoped the first scalp that Satanta took would be his.

Raids and murders increased in number in the Southwest, motivated in large part by the frustration of the tribes over the systematic slaughter of their principal source of food, clothing, and many other essential items: the buffalo. The Kansas Pacific Railroad, for example, ran excursions from Leavenworth to the areas along its line where the buffalo abounded, and hunters, armed to the teeth, shot the great beasts, often from the train windows. Many were shot only for the tongue, others for their hides; in most cases their carcasses were left to rot. The situation was exacerbated by the fact that a new method of tanning buffalo hides greatly increased their value and started a kind of "buffalo rush" of professional hunters, who often killed more than 100 buffalo at a single stand, or shooting station. Buffalo Bill Cody was famous for shooting hundreds of the animals at a time.

Raiding and fighting began anew. This time Nelson Miles was given command of five columns of regulars, infantry and cavalry, and the assignment of tracking down the Cheyenne, Comanche, and Kiowa who had strayed off their reservations. Nelson A. Miles's 4th Cavalry found the tribes in winter camp in the Palo Duro Canyon on a fork of the Red River, surprised them, drove them out of their villages, and then systematically destroyed tepees, food supplies, cooking utensils, and more than 1,400 horses and mules. Soon hungry and demoralized Indians began trickling into the reservations, asking for food and shelter. They were disarmed and fed. Miles's troopers continued their pursuit relentlessly, fighting fourteen battles or skirmishes and destroying seven or eight Indian villages. Finally, the word came from Sherman to "ease down on the parties hostile at present." By March the last of the Southern Cheyenne had come into the agency at Darlington near Fort Reno, but when they considered themselves abused, a party broke free and took to the hills once again. The Comanche and Kiowa came into their reservations in June. Chiefs identified as leaders in the "revolts" from the reservations were sent into exile in Florida. Some went to Hampton Institute in Virginia for a white man's education and a school, headed by Richard Pratt, was started at Carlisle, Pennsylvania, for others.

By the late summer of 1869 the Cheyenne and Arapaho were also on the warpath once more, raiding settlements, killing 117 men, women, and children, and taking women captive, most of them to suffer the proverbial "fate worse than death," not once but numerous times. Short of regulars, Miles rounded up an odd lot of some fifty available males with a taste for Indian fighting and sent them off as scouts under Major George Forsyth with instructions to maintain contact with the Indians. When the Indians, several thousand in number, discovered they were being pursued by only a handful of soldiers, they launched an all-out attack on Forsyth's camp. The recruits were armed with seven-shot Spencer carbines. Classic Indian tactics were to ride close enough to the soldiers to draw fire from their laboriously loaded guns and then attack before they could reload. Now the Indians found that the new repeating rifles denied them that precious interval to close with the troopers. Nonetheless, they so far outnumbered the soldiers that it seemed as though the latter must suffer the fate of Fetterman's force. Forsyth's legs were broken by bullets, and another bullet fractured his skull, at which point he cried out, "We are beyond all human aid, and if God does not help us, there is none for us." Lieutenant Frederick Henry Beecher was fatally wounded, and Roman Nose, one of the most famous of the Cheyenne warriors, was killed. At dusk the attackers drew back, disheartened at the tenacity of the scouts' defense but confident that they could finish off the survivors the next day. Three scouts were dead, and seventeen wounded. After dark two men volunteered to go for help, and the rest dug foxholes in the sand. After a siege that lasted five days, the Cheyenne withdrew in frustration. Without horses and encumbered with wounded, Forsyth, suffering acutely from his wounds, had no choice but to wait for help to arrive. Nine days after the engagement had begun, a black cavalry regiment, the 10th, arrived. Forsyth's experience convinced Sherman that there was no alternative to forcing the Indians to remain, as the treaty provided, on the reservations assigned to them. "All who cling to their old hunting grounds are hostile," he wrote, "and will remain so until they are killed off." And to his brother, John, the Senator, he wrote: "The more we can kill this year, the less will have to be killed in the next war, for the more I see of these Indians the more convinced I am that all have to be killed or maintained as a species of pauper. Their attempts at civilization are simply ridiculous."

Meantime, the spectacular career of Colonel George Custer suffered a severe setback. Custer had graduated from West Point in the class of 1861. He promptly displayed qualities of leadership, along with a flamboyant style, that won him a series of promotions until at the end of the Civil War he was one of the youngest brevet major generals in the Union army. At the close of the war he reverted to his regular army rank of lieutenant colonel and was given command of the 7th Cavalry.

Annoyed by the evasiveness of the Cheyenne and bored by the monotonous routine of campaigning against such an elusive adversary, Custer abandoned his men and headed back to Fort Riley for a conjugal visit to his adoring wife, Elizabeth. He covered the 150 miles to Fort Riley in fifty-five hours, but twenty soldiers of his troop, exhausted by their commander's relentless pace, deserted, and he ordered twelve of the deserters shot. Custer was subsequently court-martialed for leaving his command in the field, for ordering the shooting of the deserters, and on five lesser charges. Convicted, he was sentenced to be suspended from his command for a year.

In the aftermath of the breakdown of the treaties of 1868–69, on which so much time and money had been expended, even Grant's patience began to run short. Doubtless influenced by Sherman, he expressed his determination to ensure the peaceful passage of emigrants across the Plains "even if the extermination of every Indian tribe was necessary to secure such a result." Despite such privately expressed opinions, no war of extermination took place. Efforts, fumbling and ineffective as they were, continued to be made to cajole or force the tribes to observe the terms of the treaties. It was as certain as the tides that Americans were going to pour westward. That issue had been settled by the gold rush of '49, by the subsequent discovery of gold and silver in the Rockies, by the settlement of the Northwest, and by every emigrant train that ventured out of Independence or Omaha, as well as by the laborious but irresistible movement of the railroads west (and eastward from the Pacific). It was just as inevitable that the tribes would do the only thing they knew how to do: hunt and fight for their way of life. Even if the United States government had faithfully observed every provision of every treaty, the westward progress of the nation could not have been arrested. The destruction of the tribes would have continued by one means or another. So the tragedy was played out, the relentless pressure continued, and the doomed tribes fought back, ferociously, cunningly, unavailingly.

Sherman decided to use a variation of the tactics he had employed successfully, on a smaller scale, in Georgia: a winter campaign of attrition that would give the Indians no rest and no opportunity to hunt or to protect their women and children in winter camps. Accordingly, Sheridan planned a three-pronged attack on the winter camp of the Cheyenne and Arapaho. He himself would lead the campaign. "I deemed it best to go in person," he wrote, "as the campaign was an experimental one—campaigns at such a season having been deemed impractical and reckless by old and experienced frontiersmen, and I did not like to expose the troops to great hazards without being present myself to judge of their hardships and privations." The words were those of a seasoned soldier. Under him was Custer, who, having served his year of exile, now was restored to command of the 7th Cavalry, the horses and men of which he had so cruelly abused. Custer made amends by reorganizing and drilling the regiment until it was the best disciplined in Sheridan's expeditionary force. Sheridan knew that good soldiering began with discipline, though it did not end there. He instructed Custer, who was to lead one of the columns, to hang all Indians found off the reservation and to take women and children prisoners. No distinction was to be made, and probably none could have been made, between Indians off the reservations who had been engaged in raids on white settlers and wagon trains and those who were simply roaming about, hunting.

A band of Cheyenne under Black Kettle, who had been present at Sand Creek, was surprised in its village on the Washita River. Although the Cheyenne fought back courageously, Black Kettle and many of his warriors were killed, the village itself was destroyed, and 875 ponies were killed; but there was none of the wanton killing that had disgraced the attack of Chivington's undisciplined soldiers. Although some women and boys were killed, it was alleged that they had been engaged in the fighting and were killed in self-defense. Meanwhile, word reached Custer that another column under the command of Joel Elliott was heavily engaged by a large war party. Custer, inexplicably, made no move to go to Elliott's support, and the glory, such as it was, of Custer's victory was severely compromised by the fact that the column was destroyed, and more than 1,000 horses captured. Elliott and his staff were killed and mutilated. The uncharitable conjectured that Custer's failure to go to Elliott's support may have been related to the fact that Elliott had commanded the 7th Cavalry during Custer's period of punishment.

Sherman wrote to Sheridan: "I am well satisfied with Custer's attack and would not have wept if he had served Satanta [the Kiowa chief] and Bull Bear's band in the same style. I want you to go ahead;

kill and punish the hostile, rescue the captive white women and children, capture and destroy the ponies, lances, carbines, etc, etc, of the Cheyennes, Arapahos and Kiowas; mark out the spots where they must stay, and then systemize the whole (friendly and hostile) into camps with a view to economical support until we can get them to be self-supporting like the Cherokees and Choctaws."

Custer and Sheridan, perhaps sobered by the destruction of Elliott's column, decided on a more conciliatory line. Custer followed a Cheyenne band, caught up with it, rode into the camp with two aides, and persuaded Dull Knife, Fat Bear, and Big Head to go to their reservation without further resistance. The incident suggested that there were better ways to prevail on the tribes to observe the terms of the treaty than killing them. Sheridan's Washita campaign against the Southern Cheyenne brought a storm of protest from the Indian advocates. Grant was implored to withdraw the army and confer citizenship upon the Cheyenne, thereby ending the conflict.

On January 23, 1870, another Sand Creek "massacre" was enacted when Colonel E. M. Baker made a surprise attack on a band of Piegan in Wyoming Territory and killed 173 Indians, the great majority women and children. Piegan had been raiding white settlements, stealing cattle and horses and whatever else was not nailed down. When news of the attack reached the East, there was once again a storm of angry protest. In Congress Daniel Voorhees, an Indiana Democrat, declared that such attacks "cannot be justified before God or man," and *The New York Times* denounced the "sickening slaughter." Correspondingly, the response in the territory was to praise Baker and call for more such actions until all the Plains tribes were disarmed and placed on reservations. Lydia Maria Child placed the blame squarely on the military. The army's "approved method of teaching red men not to commit murder is to slaughter their wives and children . . . indiscriminate slaughter of helpless women and innocent babies is not war—it is butchery; it is murder. . . ." Wendell Phillips, in his characteristic vein, declared at a meeting of the Reform League: "I only know the names of three savages upon the Plains—Colonel Baker, General Custer, and at the head of all, General Sheridan (applause). . . . Thank God for a President in the White House whose first word was for the negro, and the second for the Indian; (applause). Who saw protection for the Indian, not in the rude and blood-thirsty policy of Sheridan and Sherman, but in the ballot, in citizenship, the great panacea that has always protected the rights of Saxon individuals." Frederick Douglass sounded the same theme, declaring that, slavery aside, the condition of the Indian was "the saddest chapter of our history. The most terrible reproach that can be hurled at the moment at the head of American Christianity and civilization is the fact that there is a general consent all over this country that the aboriginal inhabitants . . . should die out in the presence of that Christianity and civilization." Both houses of Congress joined in with a resolution declaring that the "present military policy is unwise, unjust, oppressive, extravagant, and incompatible with Christian civilization."

Lydia Maria Child, always firm in her convictions, was determined to see the matter from the settlers' side as well as that of the Indians. In the aftermath of the Piegan Massacre, which she roundly condemned, she declared that the settlers "must be protected! . . . It is more than can be expected of human nature that the white frontier settlers, living as they do in the midst of deadly peril, should think dispassionately of the Indians, or treat them fairly." It was the responsibility of the government, she said, to protect both the lives of the settlers and the rights of the Indians.

The Piegan Massacre gave fresh impetus to the move to bring certain Indian chiefs to Washington. Red Cloud, who had wiped out Captain Fetterman's company in 1866, sent word to the army office in charge of Fort Fetterman that he and some of his chiefs were ready to go to Washington to inform the Great White Father at first hand of their grievances. They were received in Washington by Peter Cooper and other members of the United States Indian Commission like visiting royalty with parties and receptions that were concluded with a reception and splendid feast at the White House. Red Cloud, unimpressed by all the pageantry, addressed the members of the Board of Indian Commissioners in direct language: "The Great Father may be good and kind but I can't see it. . . . [He] has sent his people out there and left me nothing but an island. Our nation is melting away like the snow on the sides of the hills where the sun is warm; while your people are like the blades of grass in the spring when summer is coming."

Convinced that nothing was to be gained by further parleying in Washington, Red Cloud and his fellows demanded to be sent back to the Black Hills, but numbers of enthusiastic friends of the Indians were waiting to greet them in New York City. The chiefs professed indifference; they wanted to return to their tribe. They were put on the train, presumably headed for Omaha, but they found themselves a few hours later in New York—another instance of white deceitfulness. Peter Cooper did his best to smooth their ruffled feathers. When Red Cloud mentioned that Grant had refused him a gift of seventeen horses, Cooper promised to provide them. But before the chieftains could be presented to their sponsors, wicked Jim Fisk, the Wall Street speculator, spirited them away to his Grand Opera House, where, reporters noted, "they appeared to take especial delight in the fantastic gambols of the semi-nude coryphees and the gorgeous display of parti-colored fustian, glittering tinsel and red fire." It seems safe to assume that the chiefs felt far more at home with Jim Fisk than with serious, sober old Peter Cooper.

The next night Red Cloud and his chiefs were introduced to a packed house by Peter Cooper himself. Red Cloud, wearing a high beaver hat, spoke through an interpreter. The Sioux were being punished, he declared, for the actions of a few maverick warriors who had been debauched by the whiskey given them by whites. "You have children," he said. "So have we. We want to rear our children well and ask you to help us in doing so. . . . We do not want riches, we want peace and love."

Red Dog, now an ancient chief but a famous orator, followed Red Cloud. "I have but a few words to say to you, my friends. When the Great Spirit raised us, he raised us with good men for counselors and he raised you with good men for counselors. But yours are all the time getting bad while ours remain good. . . . I know all of you are men of sense and men of respect, and I therefore ask you confidently that when men are sent out to our country, they shall be righteous men and just men, and will not do us harm.

"I don't want any more men sent out there who are so poor that they think only of filling their pockets. We want those who will help to protect us on our reservations, and save us from those who are viciously disposed toward us."

The success of the visit by Red Cloud, Spotted Tail, and the other Sioux chiefs, which led to the formation of a whole new group of organizations dedicated to helping the Indians, was followed by another such excursion the next year, also sponsored by the United States Indian Commission. This time there were Cheyenne, Arapaho, and Wichita chiefs. The crucial issue, the chiefs made clear, as their predecessors had done, was the intrusion of the railroads on Indian land. All else might be compromised or resolved, but they would not tolerate the "iron horses" snorting their fiery way across their hunting grounds, frightening the buffalo, and periodically setting fire to the dry grass.

Columbus Delano, the new secretary of the interior, told the delegation, "We cannot stop this clearing of land and building of cities and railroads all over the country. The Great Spirit has decreed it and it must go on." When the chiefs addressed another overflow crowd at Cooper Union, they begged their white friends to stop the building of railroads. Buffalo Good, a Wichita, declared, "The white people have done a great deal of wrong to our people and we want to have it stopped. If you are going to do anything for us we want you to do it quick."

In reply William Dodge promised that the commissioners would continue to do their best to "manufacture public opinion" favorable to the Indians and reiterated the commission's commitment to "educate, elevate and Christianize them." A vast gap, which the enthusiastic audience perforce ignored, lay between the Indian plea to be left alone in the enjoyment of their lands and the white assurances that they would help in every way to "civilize" them. It was plain beyond doubt or equivocation that the Indians had not the slightest disposition to be "civilized." That was the whole point; that was why they were there, pleading to be spared further infringements of their hunting ranges. Dramatic, absurd, and, above all, heartbreaking as these ritual meetings were, doomed as they were to fail in the overall hopes and expectations invested in them by Indians and reformers alike, they nonetheless served to emphasize the determination of the reformers to see justice done for the aborigines.

In Boston at the Tremont Temple, before another vast crowd, the theme was the same. This time Stone Calf was even more explicit: "Stop at once the progress of any railroads through our country, so that we may live in peace for a long time with the American people." It was like asking that the sun be arrested in its course or that the earth cease to turn. Wendell Phillips's plea that the sense of justice of the American people would ordain protection "to every atom of property and the most trifling right of the smallest Indian tribe" rang hollowly.

Now chiefs of the most militant tribes came thick and fast. Red Cloud and twenty-nine members of his tribe were back again in 1872, this time under pressure to make way for the Northern Pacific Railroad, which was nearing the Powder River. Before the summer of 1872 was over, six more delegations of chiefs had visited the Eastern cities and the capital, presented their grievances to various official and unofficial bodies, drawn huge crowds at public meetings, and returned home to tell their fellow tribesmen of the great wealth and power of the United States as well as of support of many white friends. In the end the ardent assurances of those same friends may have encouraged the more militant tribes to resist and thereby, inadvertently, made more fighting and more bloodshed inevitable. That was certainly what the furious Westerners believed with all their hearts and souls.

The year of 1872 was also the year of the presidential election, the year of the defection of the Liberal Republicans, under the leadership of Carl Schurz, Charles Francis Adams, and other dissenters, from the policies and scandals of Grant's administration. At this juncture Grant's strong support of the Indian peace policy, the so-called Quaker policy, stood him in good stead with the reformers. Many, like Wendell Phillips, who stood by him and refused to defect to Horace Greeley, cited, as their principal reason, Grant's firm and just treatment of the freedmen and the Indians. William Dodge praised the President's Indian policy, which, he declared, has "attracted the attention and sympathy of the whole Christian and philanthropic world."

Grant's victory in the election was not long past when the so-called Modoc War in California reactivated the friends of the Indians. The Modoc tribe, led by a skillful and rather devious chief named Captain Jack, had been rudely shuttled about from reservation to reservation (starting out in unhappy conjunction with their traditional enemies, the Klamath Indians). They rebelled against further shifts, and a force moved into their camp to round them up at gunpoint. They resisted, and a fight began. The Modoc withdrew to nearby lava beds, where they held the soldiers at bay. Finally, Captain Jack agreed to a meeting with General E. R. S. Canby and two peace commissioners to discuss terms for peace. Canby and one of the commissioners were thereupon killed by Captain Jack and his chiefs, and the other commissioner, Alfred B. Meacham, was so severely wounded that he was left for dead. Californians immediately demanded severe punishment for the treacherous attack, and seventeen Modoc, Captain Jack among them, were rounded up by the army. The Eastern reformers were shaken by the episode, and the President's peace policy suffered a severe setback; but the philanthropists rallied vigorously, declaring that the murders, reprehensible as they were, were simply the inevitable fruit of decades of abuse and exploitation of the Western tribes. In the midst of a loud and bitter controversy over the murder of Canby and the peace commission, a group of whites waylaid the Modoc captives and captors and killed three of the Indians before they were driven off. Now the cry was raised in the East for equal justice under the law. The killers of the Indians must be apprehended and brought to trial. Alfred Meacham, the surviving commissioner, added his voice to those who called for restraint and moderation in meting out punishment to the Modoc, declaring that there were "white men in California and Oregon more responsible for the blood of General Canby than Captain Jack himself." Meacham's emergence as an advocate of peace with the Indians caused joy in the ranks of the reformers. When he spoke at the Park Street Church in Boston, defending the Modoc Indians, Wendell Phillips declared, "Never before have we had such a witness upon the stand. Covered all over with wounds received at the hands of the Indians; having suffered all that man can suffer and still live—that he should yet lift up his voice in their behalf, affords a marvelous instance of fidelity to principle, against every temptation and injury." Recovered from his wounds, Meacham gave as many as five lectures a week in churches of the Northeast.

When Jack and five other Modoc were sentenced by an army court-martial to be hanged, the peace forces, led by the Universal Peace Union, turned their attention to trying to win executive clemency from the President. A party that included Lydia Maria Child was given an audience with Grant, who assured its members that "all the condemned Modocs should not be hung." After months under siege by delegations, memorials, and petitions the President commuted the sentences of two of the convicted Modoc to life imprisonment. Under the circumstances it represented at least a partial victory for the reformers and was taken as a reaffirmation of Grant's commitment to a policy of peace and reconciliation.

The reformers now began to place their principal emphasis on persuading the aborigines to accept land in severalty—i.e., individual landholdings. This campaign, undertaken with the best of intentions, had little support from the tribes themselves. The charge that it was simply another ruse to deprive them of what little was left of their reservations was answered by the provision that once each male Indian had received 160 acres, the remaining lands on the reservation would be held in trust for the tribe, with any income that might accrue from their rental to be allocated for the use of the tribe.

5

The End of the
Indian Wars

The so-called Red River War of the winter of 1874–75 was, in fact, far less a war than a campaign of attrition waged to force the destitute Indians to accept life on the reservations. It did mark the end, however, of the free hunting life of the Southern Plains Indians, specifically the Southern Cheyenne, the Kiowa, and most tribes of the Comanche.

In the region set aside for the Sioux and the Northern Cheyenne, a vast area the centerpiece of which was the Black Hills, Sherman and his lieutenants had demonstrated their determination to keep whiteskins out as well as redskins in. But pressure from prospectors and lumbermen to open the area built up constantly. Rumors persisted that the Black Hills were full of gold and silver. The Panic and Depression of 1873, it was argued, might be relieved by the economic stimulus provided by the discovery of great new gold mines. For the Sioux and the Cheyenne the Black Hills were objects of religious veneration, filled, the aborigines believed, by spirits; their concern was also that the deer and buffalo of the Yellowstone Basin not be endangered.

The Cheyenne and Sioux were suspected of raiding south of their southern boundary line into the Department of the Platte, where General E. O. C. Ord was charged with protecting the Pawnee and the

Osage. General Alfred H. Terry, in command of the Department of the Dakota, which included the Black Hills region, argued that the only way he could control the activities of the Sioux and Cheyenne was by establishing a strong military post on the reservation. He put his case to Sheridan, who recommended to Sherman that "In order to better control the Indians making these raids toward the south," a large post be established "so that by holding an interior point in the heart of Indian country we could threaten the villages and stock of the Indians, if they made raids on our settlements." With this in mind it was necessary to make a reconnaissance into the Indian Territory. Custer was chosen to make a detailed report on the country with special attention to the Black Hills themselves.

In addition to ten companies of cavalry and a vast wagon train of supplies, the Custer expedition included five newspaper reporters, among them twenty-three-year-old William Eleroy Curtis, reporting for the *New York World*. Curtis fell immediately under Custer's spell and soon became a kind of personal flack man for the colonel. "He is a great man—a noble man," Curtis wrote, " . . . a slender, quiet gentleman, with a face as fair as a girl's, and manners as gentle and courtly as the traditional prince." The reporter found the great Indian fighter teaching two small girls to read—one was white and one black.

Prominent in the expeditionary force was Bloody Knife, an Arikara warrior, a number of whose relatives had been killed by the Sioux and who served as chief Indian scout and personal aide to Custer. Even before the expedition was under way, a national debate began over whether it should have been authorized. The friends of the redskins denounced Grant for allowing it. William Hare, Episcopal bishop and special commissioner to the Sioux, declared it a "high-handed outrage," but General Terry insisted it was merely a necessary reconnaissance, consistent with the government's policy—going back more than fifty years to the days of Stephen Long—of "sending exploring parties of a military character into unceded territory. . . . Can it be supposed," Terry wrote, "that it was the intent of the treaty [of 1868] to set apart, in the heart of the national territory, a district nearly as great as the largest State east of the Mississippi River—two-thirds as large as the combined area of the six New England States—within which the government would be forbidden to exercise the power which it everywhere else possesses, of sending its military forces where they may be required?"

When the expedition set out in early July, 1874, it was a classic

Custer performance. Sixteen musicians on white horses played "The Girl I Left Behind." Custer rode at the head of the column, gay with flags and company guidons, in his buckskins with his famous broad-brimmed hat and red neckerchief; his greyhounds ranged ahead, and Frederick Grant, the President's son, rode alongside. Fred had earlier been sent on a sea voyage by his father in hopes of drying him out. Now he would try a land expedition, with, as it turned out, no more success.

At least one member of the expedition, Private Theodore Ewert, had no illusions about the expedition or its commander. One of the burdens of American officers has always been that they have had in the ranks of enlisted men well-educated and literate individuals eager to record their superiors' foibles and shortcomings. Ewert was a German immigrant who had served as a lieutenant in the Civil War. In his view, Custer was more interested in winning military acclaim than in collecting scientific data. "The unknown and unexplored Black Hills offered all the inducements for more fresh laurels, and to enable him to gather these, no matter at what cost of labor, trouble, or life, became his study by night and by day," Ewert wrote. "The honor of himself and his country weighed lightly in the scale against the 'glorious!' name of Geo. A. Custer. . . . The United States Government forgot its honor, forgot the sacred treaty in force between itself and the Dakota Sioux, forgot its integrity, and ordered the organization of an Expedition for the invasion of the Black Hills."

Ewert was by no means an uncritical champion of the Indians. He expressed indignation that chiefs like Red Cloud ("the cause, author and instigator of the Fort Phil Kearny massacre"), who were guilty of murdering settlers and killing numerous Indians of other tribes, were allowed to go about unmolested. "Indian agents," he wrote, "would lose their profitable situations, were every red scamp punished according to their deeds. . . . " The victims, in Ewert's view, were the common soldiers sent off on a perilous mission the ultimate aim of which was to provide profits for avaricious speculators.

The expedition seldom saw Indians, but it was kept under constant surveillance by lookouts, and word of its progress was sent ahead by smoke signals. "So far," Curtis wrote at the end of July, "we have seen nothing remarkable; the miners have discovered no gold; the geologists have wacked in vain for the fossil of the 'missing link'; the naturalists have emptied their saddle pockets day after day without revealing the existences of any new wonders in life; the soldiers have fought no

Indians, and so far, the expedition in a positive sense, has been un-successful." In the Black Hills the expedition came on an Edenic valley, filled with wild flowers. The band played "How So Fair," and the troopers stuck flowers in their caps. The soldiers got up a baseball game between the Actives and the Athletes; a glee club performed, and the expedition became rather like an extended camping trip. Fi-nally, the miners in the party began to find indications of gold-bearing quartz, and soon most of the members of the expedition were panning for gold. It was far from a gold strike or the "new El Dorado" that many advocates of the expedition had predicted, but it was enough to feed the rumors. Although Custer in his report to Sheridan warned that on such a slim basis "no opinion should be formed . . . regarding the richness of the gold," opinions *were* formed. When word of the modest finds reached Fort Laramie, the *Yankton Press and Dakotan* an-nounced: "STRUCK IT AT LAST! Rich Mines of Gold and Silver Reported Found by Custer. PREPARE FOR LIVELY TIMES! . . . National Debt to Be Paid When Custer Returns."

A correspondent's dispatch to the *New York Tribune* was far less fervent. "Those who seek the Hills only for gold must be prepared to take their chances," he wrote. "Let the over-confident study the history of Pike's Peak. The Black Hills, too, are not without ready-made mon-uments for the martyrs who may perish in their parks." After eight weeks the expedition was back at Fort Lincoln. It had covered more than 800 miles and seen only a handful of Indians. Elizabeth Custer added a final dramatic touch by fainting in her husband's arms on his return.

A prolonged and acrimonious debate on the gold question now followed. The Eastern, generally pro-Indian, press took the line that the talk of gold was all fantasy intended to draw miners to the region and nullify the Treaty of 1868. Fred Grant was widely quoted as de-claring that he had seen no gold, news which enraged the citizens of such towns as Bismarck and Yankton. Army or no army, there was no stopping the gold-hungry whites. Within six months it was estimated that at least 800 miners were prowling about the hills, many of them anticipating a new treaty with the Sioux that would open the hills to mining for gold and silver. The treaty meeting took place in the sum-mer of 1875. Twenty thousand Sioux gathered along the banks of the White River. They and their chiefs, now convinced that vast wealth was hidden in the Black Hills, were divided between those who were opposed to ceding the land under any terms and those determined to strike a hard bargain with the government negotiators.

When the parleying began, Red Dog announced that he and his tribe, in return for abandoning their claim to the Black Hills, wished to be taken care of by the government for "seven generations ahead." Red Cloud echoed the demand. Little Bear added: "Our Great Father has a house full of money. . . . The Black Hills are the house of gold for the Indians. We watch it to get rich. . . ." Spotted Tail, who had carefully abstained from making war against the whites, added his own note: "As long as we live on this earth we will expect pay. We want to leave the amount with the President at interest forever. . . . I want to live on the interest of my money. . . ." What would the government pay? It offered $400,000 a year for the mining rights or $6,000,000 for purchase. That was not enough, the chiefs declared, and the negotiations were broken off.

The government had a final weapon to use. Under the terms of the Treaty of 1868 the government was obliged to provide "annuities" for the tribes for four years. After the four years had expired, the government had continued the subsidies. Unless the tribes now agreed to sell or lease the Black Hills, the government would withdraw the subsidies. In a real sense the independence of the Plains Indians (and, indeed, all the rest of the tribes) had ended the day they first agreed to accept a yearly issue of food and goods. Thereafter the life of each tribe revolved, to a greater or lesser degree, around the yearly distribution of highly desired items. In addition to making the Indians hopelessly dependent, the purchase and distribution of the supplies provided, as we have noted, endless temptations for cheating and corruption on the part of those whites (and, in some instances, Indians) charged with making the distributions. Often the annuity goods arrived late while the aborigines grew increasingly impatient and hostile. Indeed, the terrible Minnesota uprising that resulted in the deaths of so many unsuspecting settlers had derived some of its impetus from the delay of the government's yearly quota and dissatisfaction over its distribution. The Indians both longed for, and often desperately needed, the foodstuffs and resented that longing, knowing that it was the mark of their dependence.

The more militant Indians from every tribe began to repair to the standards of the more intractable chiefs, Crazy Horse and Sitting Bull most prominent among them. The tales of Indian outrages mounted, along with rumors that the Sioux and Northern Cheyenne were joining forces for a campaign of extermination against all whites. Many of the chiefs were convinced that they must make a stand at all costs or lose whatever remained of the game. Others warned against provoking a showdown with the army. There were far too many white men to conquer. These chiefs argued that the best that could be hoped for was an agreement that would protect the tribes from starvation—through yearly allotments of food—and guarantee them sufficient land on which to establish themselves as farmers or ranchers. The more warlike argued, much as the United States military men did, that the only thing the whites understood was force. Recent experience had proved that killing substantial numbers of white soldiers was the only way to make the United States government more tractable. Hadn't the destruction of Fetterman's force led directly to the Treaty of 1868, the abandonment of the forts on the Bozeman Trail, and eight years of relative peace? It was a hard argument to answer. Red Cloud's reputation was tarnished by the fact that he had settled down in good faith to try to prevail on his people to learn the white man's agricultural techniques. The more militant Indians, while rejecting Red Cloud's leadership, pointed to his victories in 1868 as evidence that the United States Army could be decisively defeated in battle. Gall, leader of the Hunkpapa Sioux, threw his weight and that of his tribe behind Sitting Bull and Crazy Horse. The so-called nontreaty Indians withdrew to the Yellowstone Basin and, in effect, dared the U.S. Army to try to root them out. Things were brought to a head by the advance of the railroad line into territory reserved to the Sioux and Cheyenne under the Treaty of 1868. One of the purposes of that treaty had been to ensure the peaceful construction of the railroad; but the commissioners had failed to define the route carefully, and now it was evident that it would pass south of the Yellowstone, in Sioux country. Two commissioners were sent to try to negotiate a passage for the railroad, but the Indians were adamant. No railroad.

After the failure of the White River parley, the Indian Bureau ordered all the tribes in the Black Hills Reservation to report to Fort Laramie. It was the dead of winter, a time of year when traveling in the Montana-Wyoming region was exhausting and hazardous. It is not even clear that all the tribes were notified of the order. In any event only one tribe responded to the call. Those that did not were assumed to be hostiles, and Sheridan made plans to launch a campaign against them. Again he decided on the three converging columns strategy. Terry was to command one column of some 1,000 soldiers. General George Crook was to advance from the region of the North Platte River toward the Yellowstone Valley. Colonel John Gibbon would proceed along the Yellowstone from Fort Ellis. The three columns would meet near the junction of the Bighorn and the Yellowstone.

The campaign of 1875–76 began in the dead of winter, and the soldiers, in consequence, suffered severely from the weather. Pushing on to the Powder River, Crook encountered the tracks of Indian ponies in the snow, followed them, and fell on a camp of sleeping Cheyenne, who were, in fact, preparing to return to their agency. The Indians fought back doggedly and finally routed the soldiers, who fled, leaving their dead and, it was said, a wounded soldier. The Cheyenne chief, Two Cloud, swore revenge on the whites for what he believed to have been a treacherous attack. It was not a promising beginning. The tribes took heart, and the numbers of hostile Indians increased dramatically. Meanwhile, Sheridan called off further campaigning until early spring.

A renewal of the campaigning was delayed by the prolonged absence of Custer from his command. When Secretary of War William Belknap's bribe-taking had begun to come to light, Custer had offered to testify about the secretary's misuse of his powers in various army posts on the frontier. He was called to Washington, where his testimony turned out to be primarily hearsay and conjecture. Indeed, Custer went so far as to implicate Grant's brother and hint that the President himself had been involved in dubious practices in regard to the boundaries of Indian reservations. All this delayed the beginning of the campaign against the Indians since Custer was still in command of the 7th Cavalry and was to have led the column under Terry's overall command. Finally, orders came from Sherman that Custer was to be relieved of his command and that Terry himself was to take personal charge of the column. Custer was to remain at St. Paul. Custer's numerous friends and admirers hastened to intercede with Grant, to whom Custer wrote a pleading letter which contained the sentence, "I appeal to you as a soldier to spare me the humiliation of seeing my regiment march to meet the enemy and I not to share its dangers." Doubtless aware of the public clamor that would be aroused by grounding Custer and conscious that his enemies would charge him with vindictiveness, Grant reluctantly gave his consent. In forwarding the President's permission, Sherman added a cautionary note to Terry:

"Advise Custer to be prudent, not to take along any newspaper men, who always make mischief, and to abstain from personalities in the future." But Custer was beyond redemption or reform. He took a newspaper reporter with him, and he told a fellow officer that he intended to "cut loose from General Terry during the summer," even though it was to Terry's support that he largely owed his restoration.

With Terry in command, the column of 1,200 men left Fort Lincoln at dawn on May 17, 1876; Custer's 7th Cavalry was the largest and most experienced unit. The column contained 45 Indian scouts, most of them Arikara, and 190 civilians. Custer's brother Thomas commanded C Company, and his brother-in-law James Calhoun was in command of L Company. A nephew, Armstrong Reed, was also a member of the expedition, as was another of Custer's brothers, Boston. Terry's column made contact with that of Colonel Gibbon near Rosebud Creek, and the two forces awaited the arrival of Crook, coming up from the Platte. Crook, with 180 Crow scouts and a force generally comparable to that of Terry, advanced along the Bozeman Trail past the sites of the three forts once intended to guard it. As Crook approached Rosebud Creek, having forded the Powder, his scouts informed him that a large party of Sioux lay ahead. On June 16 Crook prepared to do battle.

The Sioux were spoiling for a fight. Sitting Bull, after undergoing ritual torture involving the cutting of some fifty pieces of flesh from his arms and chest, had had a vision of the soldiers being defeated. The next day the Cheyenne and the Sioux, some 1,000 strong, led by Crazy Horse, swept down on Crook's column. Crazy Horse, the Oglala chieftain, gave his cry, "Come on, Dakotas, it is a good day to die." The fighting soon broke down into small groups of whites and Indians engaged in desperate combat, often hand to hand. Crook's efforts to form conventional lines failed, and throughout the day the battle was a standoff, with neither side able to gain a decisive advantage. What was unsettling to Crook was the fact that the Indians fought with much more than ordinary tenacity. Generally, if an attack failed, the Indians, easily discouraged and seldom under any overall discipline, would withdraw after an hour or so. Now they fought all day long, not abandoning the field until dusk. Crook claimed victory—"My troops beat these Indians on a field of their own choosing and drove them in utter rout from it . . ."—but it was soon apparent that he had accomplished nothing in terms of routing the tribes or seriously diminishing either their capacity or their resolution to resist the intrusion of the white soldiers.

Meanwhile, finding no Indians on the Yellowstone or the lower reaches of the Rosebud, Major Marcus Reno, second-in-command of the 7th Cavalry, had been sent with six companies on a reconnaissance toward the Powder River. Disobeying orders, Reno headed for the Tongue, crossed the valley of that river, and turned toward the Rosebud, where Crook was already engaged with Crazy Horse's warriors. When Reno returned without encountering any Indians, Terry concluded that the main body of aborigines must be in the vicinity of the Little Bighorn. His strategy was to send Gibbon up the Bighorn while Custer and the 7th circled around by way of the Little Bighorn to take the enemy in the flank or rear. Custer resisted all suggestions for augmenting the 7th with howitzers or additional companies of cavalry. The 7th could take care of itself, he assured Terry. Before it departed on its mission, Custer presented a dashing review with the regimental band playing and the men smartly turned out. Terry's parting words were "God bless you." Colonel Gibbon, often a rival, called out, "Now, Custer, don't be greedy. Wait for us."

It was, of course, just the moment Custer had been waiting and hoping for: to be off on his own beyond Terry's immediate control with a golden opportunity to whip Indians and acquire more fame and glory. At the point where the trail, followed a few days earlier by Reno, dropped into the valley of the Rosebud, another trail diverged toward the Little Bighorn. This trail Terry had specifically told Custer to avoid. He was to push farther along toward the waters of the Tongue before he turned west toward the Little Bighorn, but Custer, greedy to engage the hostiles before the rest of the expedition could arrive to share the glory, devised a very different plan. He would cross over to the Little Bighorn, thereby stealing a march on Terry's main force (actually the troops were almost evenly divided between Terry and Custer), and spend the next day concealed, while his scouts located the lodges of the Sioux and Cheyenne. Custer's men moved by night. At dawn the scouts, climbing the divide between the valley of the Rosebud and that of the Little Bighorn, observed a large Indian camp along the banks of that river. The campfires of the 7th, meanwhile, were visible for miles, and any hope of a surprise attack was lost. Custer, without waiting for support from Gibbon, decided to attack at once. Rousing his weary men, he hurried them along into the valley of the Little Bighorn, where he divided his force into combat units. One, under the command of Captain Frederick Benteen, consisting of approximately 125 troopers, was sent off in pursuit of any Indians that could be discovered. (Benteen, it should be noted, despised Custer as a self-promoter, who had callously abandoned Joel Elliott at the Washita battle, and he referred to Custer's account of his accomplishments—*My Life on the Plains*—as "My Lie on the Plains.")

Custer, meanwhile, advanced with the remaining companies toward the river. The objective he was approaching in such cavalier fashion was, it turned out, a vast encampment, as large as any recorded (except for treaty meetings) in the history of the Plains Indians. It has been estimated that there were more than 2,000 lodges and, with the rough rule of thumb being at least two warriors to a lodge, some 4,000 warriors and perhaps 12,000 Indians, counting women, children, and old men. There were Gall of the Hunkpapa, Crow King, Sitting Bull, Hump, Spotted Eagle, Low Dog, Big Road, and, most important of all, Crazy Horse, elated by his victory over Crook a week earlier, a victory of which, incidentally, Custer knew nothing.

When Custer saw a small party of Indians fleeing, he concluded that the hostiles were already on the run. Anxious to prevent their escape, he ordered Major Reno to pursue them, promising that he would be "supported by the whole outfit." Reno took off with some 112 soldiers and 25 Indian scouts. As soon as he had crossed the river, he was disabused of the notion that the Sioux and Cheyenne were in flight. A large party of warriors—it was later estimated at 1,000 or so—rode out of the encampment to meet him. Reno sent word at once to Custer, undoubtedly assuming that he would, as he had promised, come to his support. But Custer had other plans, and Reno was left to fight his way out of the mass of attacking Indians as best he could, taking heavy casualties in the process and abandoning the wounded to slow deaths by torture. By the time Reno had recrossed the river half his men were dead or wounded, and he deployed the survivors among the rocks to hold off the assailants as best they could. Meanwhile, Benteen, on the way back from his fruitless expedition in search of Indians, was met by a messenger, Giovanni Martini, ordering him to hurry on to support an attack on a "big village." In a few miles Benteen came on the remnants of Reno's battalion, making a desperate, last-ditch defense. Benteen took command of the combined units from the demoralized Reno.

As the warriors opposing the Reno-Benteen force drifted away, Benteen moved his command, trying to make contact with Custer. Before he could, he found himself surrounded by hundreds of mounted warriors, who forced him to take up defensive positions once again.

When nightfall came, Benteen's men were still beleaguered, and they began to work with any implement at hand to strengthen their defenses. The position that Benteen had chosen on a hilltop was a natural fortification, and the following day the soldiers kept the enemy at bay, even making several charges to drive back Indians who ventured too close for comfort.

Custer had followed Reno until he received word that the latter was under attack; he then turned along the east bank of the river, apparently with the intention of attacking the Indians on their flank. The Sioux had seen Custer and anticipated this attack. To Custer it appeared that the Sioux and Cheyenne had abandoned their villages, and he prepared to gallop gloriously into the encampment and rout out whatever Indians might remain. Before he could carry out his plan, more Indians than the colonel had ever seen before in a single engagement poured over a nearby ridge, screaming their war cries. Custer hardly had time to dispose his troops in defensive positions before they were inundated by Gall's Hunkpapa, followed by successive waves of warriors, Crazy Horse's Oglala Sioux and Two Moon's Cheyenne. In almost less time than it takes to tell, the outnumbered soldiers were beaten down. Fifty-one of the survivors, many wounded, gathered around their colonel for a last desperate stand and were cut down one after another. Custer had had his famous shoulder-length golden hair, now streaked with gray, cut before the campaign began, and the Indians left his hair and his naked body intact. It was a gesture of respect for the most famous of the Indian fighters.

Meanwhile, the combined companies of Reno and Benteen held off their attackers. The Indian fire became desultory, and after noon on June 26 Benteen's scouts brought word that the Indians, having learned of the approach of Terry and Gibbon, were breaking camp and preparing to move. The next day Gibbon's column arrived to lift the siege. Reno and Benteen between them had lost some 50 killed and as many wounded out of a combined force of fewer than 250 men.

No one knew where Custer and his troopers were. Finally, they were discovered by scouts—the stripped, scalped, and mutilated bodies of 197 men, scouts, soldiers, Custer's brothers and brother-in-law, Custer himself, and the unfortunate newspaper reporter who had accompanied him to record his brilliant deeds. Not one man was left to tell the tale of the worst military disaster in the long series of Indian wars that stretched back to the beginning of the century.

Undoubtedly Benteen and Reno and the men under their command who survived did so, in large part, because the Indians were drawn off by the threat that Custer posed to the village. There has been much controversy over the question of mutilation—how many bodies were mutilated, how many scalped, etc. The matter is, to a large degree, irrelevant. The Indians commonly mutilated the bodies of their enemies—white or red. Indian representations of the battle, of which there are a number, indicated mutilations. If the bodies of some of the slain soldiers were not scalped or mutilated, it was due to the fact that the victors had more pressing matters on their minds rather than to any change in traditional practices.

Grant, remorseful that he had weakened in his resolution not to allow Custer to accompany the expedition, did not hesitate to place the blame on that officer, but in all the charges and countercharges that followed the Battle of the Little Bighorn, the popular disposition to see Custer as hero proved insurmountable. Truth was powerless before the myth. Although the soldiers themselves were well aware of the series of horrendous blunders that had led to the disaster, it would be years before the full story was unraveled. Custer's image as heroic Indian fighter was so firmly established in the public mind—primarily, of course, by Custer himself—that it would prove impervious to anything as simple as the truth. Moreover, all efforts to reveal the facts were relentlessly opposed by the bereaved widow, who spent the balance of her long life protecting the reputation of her hero, going so far as to threaten lawsuits against anyone bold enough to step forward with the truth.

The fact that the news of the "massacre," as it was called, or, more commonly, "Custer's Last Stand," reached the nation just at the moment of national apotheosis, when Americans were engaged in an orgy of self-congratulation over the first glorious hundred years of the Republic, made it perhaps inevitable that the episode would be taken as proof that the remaining aborigines must be punished in such a conclusive way that they would never again pose a serious threat to the lives of American citizens. Viewed in the light of the widespread public reaction of horror and anger, Little Bighorn may have been the costliest victory ever suffered by a people fighting for survival against enormous odds. The voices of that not inconsiderable company that espoused the cause of the Indians were drowned out by those who pressed for a "final solution" to the Indian problem.

General Terry was supplied with new recruits, and he and Crook, who had come off comparatively lightly at Rosebud, were heavily reinforced by Sheridan and given the assignment of bringing the culprits to account. They set off in early August with 2,100 soldiers and 225 scouts, primarily Shoshone and Ute, after the elusive Cheyenne and Sioux. In Terry's command was a white scout named Bill Cody. Their efforts proved abortive. Combing the vast area of the Black Hills Reservation, they found no Indians and engaged in no battles. At last, Crook, largely through the efforts of his Indian scouts, some of them Sioux and Cheyenne, found the village of Dull Knife and his band of Cheyenne, killed a number of Indians in a pitched battle, and destroyed their village. Colonel Miles, meanwhile, drove Gall and Sitting Bull into Canada and persuaded many of their followers to return to their Indian agency. With Gall and Sitting Bull in Canada, the military forces under Miles and Crook concentrated on hunting down Crazy Horse, the last of the great Sioux leaders still at large. Crook finally persuaded Crazy Horse and some 800 of his followers to come to the Red Cloud agency and give up their arms.

In the course of the peace conference the now powerless Sioux, Cheyenne, and Arapaho were deprived of a third of the region reserved to them in the Treaty of 1868, including the Black Hills. Crook, who had prevailed on Crazy Horse to abandon his intransigence with the promise of a reservation on the Tongue River, an area that the chief prized, found that he was unable to deliver on his promise, though to his credit, it must be said, he left no politician or bureaucrat unturned in his efforts to make good on his word. There was to be a tragic denouement. Crook was determined to try to enlist Crazy Horse in a campaign against the Nez Percé who had left their reservation and were raiding in the area of eastern Montana. A sequence of misunderstandings led Crook to order the arrest of Crazy Horse. When Crazy Horse saw that he was being taken to the guardhouse at the agency, he began to resist and was stabbed and fatally wounded by a soldier's bayonet. It seems apparent that part of the confusion that led to the death of the famous chief was caused by Indians at the agency hostile to Crazy Horse. The incident might thus serve to remind us of one of the major disadvantages that the tribes labored under in their effort to preserve their land and their way of life against white encroachments. The hostility among the various tribes was almost invariably greater than the hostility of the respective tribes for the whites. Black Elk, one of the Sioux warriors, was convinced that Crazy Horse was deliberately assassinated. "Afterwards," he declared, "the Hang-Around-the-Fort people said that he was getting ready to tie up his horse's tail again and make war on the Wasichus [the whites]. How could he do that when he had no guns and could not get any? It was a story the Wasichus told, and their tongues were forked when they told it. Our people believe they did what they did because he was a great man and they could not kill him in battle and he would not make himself over into a Wasichu, as Spotted Tail and the others did."

As the most powerful and warlike tribe in the Great Plains the Sioux had, over decades, driven other tribes—the Pawnee, Crow, and Shoshone prominent among them—from their ancient hunting grounds. Thus, when they came at last to stand as the principal barrier to the white man's westward advance, their only substantial allies were the Northern Cheyenne and a handful of Arapaho. The hands of most other tribes were turned against them. Nonetheless, the various tribes of Sioux, along with the Cheyenne and Arapaho in the north, for forty years impeded, if they could not stop, the westward movement of emigrating white Americans, while the Apache, Comanche, and Southern Cheyenne did the same in the region of the Red River, in New Mexico, and along the borders of Texas. They exacted a heavy toll in lives and money. Subsidies, annuities, and treaty payments aside, the campaigns to suppress them cost the United States government millions upon millions of dollars (it was estimated that it cost the United States Army $1,000,000 to kill a single Indian). Any people less hardy, less courageous, and perhaps, above all, less greedy would have flinched in the face of such determined resistance, but not the settlers, miners, or emigrants who year after year poured into Indian country at the risk of their possessions and, not infrequently, their lives. They literally bet their lives on the fact that the United States government, however it might warn, discourage, or outright forbid them to venture onto Indian land, must in the end extend its protection over them and undertake to punish those tribes that, whatever their justification, murdered the intruders.

The killing of Crazy Horse was not, of course, the end of the tragedy of the Plains Indians. A few months after his death one of the most unhappy episodes involving Indians and whites took place with the Nez Percé, a northwestern tribe that was proud of never having killed a white man or having had any but peaceful relations with the settlers who pressed constantly on its lands. With an ancient and sophisticated culture of their own, the Nez Percé, like so many other tribes, had been seduced by the opportunities presented by the horse culture and had ventured over the Cascades and the Bitteroot Range into what is today Idaho and western Montana to hunt buffalo. Their most famous chief had been Chief Joseph, a convert to Christianity, who had guided his people with extraordinary tact and diplomacy through their initial contacts with the whites. On his death his mantle had fallen on his son, Hinmaton-Yalatkit, or Rolling-Thunder-in-Mountains, also called Young Joseph. Under the reservation policy, the Wallowa Valley in northeastern Oregon was designated as Nez Percé country, but the pressure of settlers who coveted the beautiful valley caused the government to declare the area open to homesteaders. Joseph's father had told him in his dying hours: "This country holds your father's body. Never sell the bones of your father and mother."

An army commission that included General Oliver Otis Howard had met with Joseph to try to persuade him to sell the land. The commissioners were clearly impressed by Joseph's presence and by the quiet but determined skill with which he defended the right of the Nez Percé to their homeland. "If we ever owned the land we own it still, for we have never sold it. . . . In the treaty councils the commissioners have claimed that our country has been sold to the government. Suppose a white man should come to me and say, 'Joseph, I like your horses, and I want to buy them but he refuses to sell.' My neighbor answers, 'Pay me the money and I will sell you Joseph's horses.' The white man returns to me and says, 'Joseph, I have bought your horses and you must let me have them.' If we sold our lands to the government, that is the way they were bought."

The decision of the commissioners was that Joseph's Nez Percé should be required to join the other Nez Percé on the Lapwai Reservation by persuasion or force. Howard, who was in charge of the territory that included the Lapwai Reservation, gave Joseph a month to bring his tribe, which numbered fewer than 100 warriors, into the reservation. Joseph protested that the Snake was too high for his band to cross safely, but Howard refused to allow him more time. After the Nez Percé band had crossed the river a group of young braves, who were not members of Joseph's band and were furious at being forced onto the reservation, broke out in an orgy of killing. It was a classic Indian uprising, triggered by a profound sense of grievance and frustration and fueled by traders' whiskey. Before they were through, some 20 whites had been killed, with farms burned and women raped.

Howard started out from the Lapwai Reservation immediately with some 110 soldiers and volunteers. The soldiers came up to Joseph's small band and, rejecting the offer of a truce, attacked its camp in White Bird Canyon. Although outnumbered, the Nez Percé, led by Joseph, killed 34 soldiers and wounded 4, administering a severe defeat to Howard's small force. Howard began to round up a larger contingent of troops, and, since nothing succeeds like success, Joseph found his own band augmented by other discontented groups of Indians spoiling for a fight. Howard, now with 400 soldiers and 180 Indian scouts, surprised Joseph's party, which now included five other bands of Nez Percé, on the Clearwater River, in early July. The first warning the Indians had was the fire from Howard's howitzer and Gatling guns from a bluff above their camp. The Indians rallied, and once more Howard suffered a humiliating setback. The Nez Percé chiefs believed that if they could get over the Bitterroot Mountains into Idaho, they would be safe from pursuit. In a remarkable hegira, herding along several thousand horses as well as children, the sick, and those wounded at the Clearwater River, they reached western Montana, where they found their path blocked by some 35 army infantrymen. The Nez Percé made their way around the soldiers and stopped at Stevensville, where they bought much needed supplies from the townspeople. After crossing the Continental Divide, they made camp in the Big Hole Valley, near the present-day town of Dillon, Montana. There Colonel John Gibbon, veteran of the fighting against Crazy Horse and the Sioux, came on the camp and caught the sleeping Nez Percé by surprise in a dawn attack. Men, women, and children were killed indiscriminately. Once more the warriors rallied and gave such a good account of themselves that Gibbon's larger force soon found itself on the defensive (the Nez Percé were noted for being the finest marksmen of all the Indian tribes). Gibbon lost 33 dead and as many wounded, and his command may well have been saved from Custer's fate only by the arrival of Howard. The Nez Percé lost 89, most of them apparently women and children and old men. Among the Nez Percé dead were two of their most noted warriors, Rainbow and Five Wounds. The Nez Percé buried their dead before abandoning their camp, but the Bannock scouts dug up the bodies and scalped them.

What was most notable about all the engagements involving the Nez Percé was that the outnumbered Indians inflicted a series of defeats on superior forces of, in the main, army regulars. There was no parallel in all the years of fighting to the "victories" (victories in the rather modest sense of avoiding annihilation and inflicting heavier casualties than they suffered) of the Nez Percé over their pursuers, led by two of the ablest and most experienced Indian fighters in the

West. By the time of the Big Hole Battle, the attention of the nation had become fixed on the dramatic odyssey of the Nez Percé. Chief Joseph, although only one among equals and not, in fact, the most accomplished of the Nez Percé leaders, was credited with the victories and became an instant hero. Indeed, it is safe to say that, Montana and Idaho settlers aside, there were more Americans rooting for Joseph and "his" Nez Percé than for Howard and the United States Army. Never able to resist a military hero, whatever the color of his skin, Americans elevated Joseph to that pantheon of Indian heroes that included Tecumseh (the middle name of the commanding general of the United States Army was Tecumseh), Black Hawk, Osceola, and, more recently, Crazy Horse and Sitting Bull.

Fleeing from Howard's implacable pursuit, the Nez Percé passed through Yellowstone Park, which was already attracting tourists. They had hoped to find refuge among the Crow, allies from other days against the Sioux and Cheyenne, but they found that the Crow were not only at peace with the whites but acting as army scouts. It was decided to press on to Canada, as the remnants of the Sioux under Sitting Bull had recently done, but in camp not far from the border they were overtaken by Nelson Miles, who had been called up from Fort Keogh with 600 soldiers, including part of the 7th Cavalry. Miles ordered a charge which was stopped with heavy casualties; 24 officers and men were killed, and another 42 wounded. The Nez Percé, after four months of fighting against three different expeditions dispatched against them in a journey that had covered more than 1,300 miles, were still dangerous. Some of the Nez Percé women and children, among them Joseph's twelve-year-old daughter, escaped but the remaining warriors—some 120—found themselves besieged by Miles's much larger force. A few days later Howard arrived with more troops, ending all hope of escape. Joseph persuaded the remaining warriors, cold and hungry, to surrender. He sent his message of surrender to Howard by way of Captain John, a Nez Percé interpreter, who wept as he delivered it: "Tell General Howard I know his heart. What he told me before I have in my heart. I am tired of fighting. Our chiefs are killed. Looking Glass is dead. . . . The old men are all dead. It is the young men who say yes and no. He who led the young men is dead. It is cold and we have no blankets. The little children are freezing to death. My people, some of them, have run away to the hills, and have no blankets, no food; no one knows where they are—perhaps freezing to death. I want to have time to look for my children and see how many I can find. Maybe I shall find them among the dead. Hear me, my chiefs, I am tired; my heart is sick and sad. From where the sun now stands, I will fight no more forever." From Chief Logan, mourning the murder of his wife and children by renegade whites almost 100 years earlier, to the words of Chief Joseph, there had been the same refrain of unfathomable sadness by Indian chieftains caught in the web of an inexorable fate.

Joseph rode into the lines of the soldiers and handed his gun to Miles. Of the handful of Nez Percé who escaped to Canada, some were killed by the Assiniboine and Hidatsa. Joseph's six children survived. Miles did what he could to assist those who surrendered, some 400 in all. They were taken by train to Bismarck on the way to Fort Abraham Lincoln, and there they were greeted by the citizens of that frontier Indian-hating town as heroes, showered with gifts of food and clothing. Joseph and other chiefs were given a dinner by the women of the town. But the reservation they were placed on was hundreds of miles from the land where their ancestors were buried; they were moved from the luxuriant forests and clean winds to an area of malarial dampness. Within a few months a fourth of their number was dead from disease (among them all of Joseph's children), some doubtless from heartbreak. "I will fight no more forever," became a kind of epitaph for the American aborigines.

The heroic story of Chief Joseph and the Nez Percé put the Indians once more on the front pages of the nation's newspapers, with public sentiment overwhelmingly in favor of the aborigines. Chief Joseph was brought to Washington to experience another of those strange orgies of public adulation by now so familiar a part of the relationship between the aborigines and their white supporters.

Although few historians have taken notice of Grant's efforts in behalf of the Indians, for his reform-minded contemporaries it was the most notable achievement of his administration. A grateful Bishop Whipple wrote the President in 1875: "No act of any President will stand out in brighter relief on the pages of history than your kindness to a perishing race. When this change was made an honest agent was a rare exception. . . . For all this you are held in esteem by thousands of the best men in America. I cannot find words to express my own deep sense of obligation for your perseverance when a less brave man would have faltered." But within a year the Sioux were once more on the warpath, Custer and his men were dead, and the peace policy on which so much hope had been placed was in jeopardy. It was increasingly difficult to answer the charges of the Westerners that its principal effect had been to encourage and indeed to reward Indian recalcitrance. E. L. Godkin announced the failure of the policy in the *Nation*: "Our philanthropy and our hostility tend to about the same end, and this is the destruction of the Indian race . . . the missionary expedient may be said to have failed." But the reformers were far from ready to concede defeat. They reiterated all the familiar arguments. The bad behavior of the Indians had been provoked by the whites. Now, above all, was the time for forbearance. Others took the line that while it was evident that the Sioux must be brought to account, public indignation should not be allowed to prejudice the cases of those tribes that had remained peaceable. Still others took the occasion to reiterate that the army, not the Indians, was the problem.

The election of Rutherford Hayes to the presidency in 1876 brought with it a new secretary of the interior, Carl Schurz. Schurz, while sympathetic to the calls for fair dealing with the Indians, was determined to replace Grant's Quaker policy—a heavy dependence on the denominational churches for the actual management of the Indian agencies—with a more orthodox bureaucratic arrangement. Meanwhile, the debate over the Indian policy grew, if possible, more intense. The country seemed filled with self-appointed experts recommending one or another solution, ranging, at the most extreme, from turning the Great Plains and Rocky Mountain West into a vast Indian reservation to blueprints for turning Indians into white men. In his first annual message to Congress, Hayes came out strongly in support of a "just and humane policy" which would lead to citizenship for all Indians who could be prevailed upon to abandon their tribal alliances. The issue of transference, of placing the responsibility for Indian welfare under the War Department rather than the Department of the Interior, was perhaps the most bitterly debated issue of all. A move in that direction by Congress brought out the full force of the embattled reformers, and after a struggle that lasted for several years it was beaten back.

There was at least one more excruciating chapter to be written. At the end of the Sioux war, the band of Cheyenne under the leadership of Dull Knife had been placed on the reservation of the Southern Cheyenne and Arapaho in the Indian Territory. There they grew increasingly restless and dissatisfied, both with their surroundings and with the failure of the government to deliver the food and supplies it had promised. In 1878 they announced that they were determined to go home. Troops were summoned from Fort Reno, and their camp was surrounded, but during the night some seventy warriors and their wives and children slipped away and headed northwest to their home range, pursued by U.S. cavalry and fighting a number of skirmishes as they went, replenishing their herds from ranches along the way. With hundreds of soldiers spread out to intercept them, they crossed three railroad lines and continued their flight toward the sand hills in northern Nebraska. In a snowstorm Dull Knife ran into two companies of cavalry. As the two parties parleyed, more and more soldiers arrived until finally Dull Knife felt he had no recourse except to surrender and agree to go to Camp Robinson on the White River near the Dakota-Nebraska boundary. Pressed to return to the reservation in the south, Dull Knife declared, "We will not go there to live. That is not a healthful country, and if we should stay there we will all die. We do not wish to go back there and we will not go. You may kill me here, but you cannot make me go back."

The sympathy that had been roused by the dramatic journey of the Nez Percé was again manifest for the plight of the Cheyenne. Even the editor of the *Omaha Herald* urged that they be allowed to remain in the country that they knew and loved. To take them back would mean starvation. "I implore you," he addressed the Indian Bureau, "for justice and humanity to those wronged red men, let them stay in their own country." The authorities in Washington were adamant, however. Amid a storm of public protest the order came to return the Cheyenne to the southern reservation lest their example encourage other tribes to leave the reservations assigned to them. The Indians repeated that they would rather die where they were than return. The officer in charge tried to force compliance by withholding food and then water. They refused to budge. Finally, when the officer in charge had tricked two of their principal warriors into a parley and put them in chains, the remaining warriors retrieved rifles that they had hidden under the barracks where they were quartered and prepared to fight to the last. At nightfall they broke out of their quarters and fled for the hills, with soldiers close on their trail. A number were killed or wounded in the escape. Others, fighting off their pursuers, pushed on for ten days until, surrounded and vastly outnumbered, they were driven to earth and killed or wounded. Dull Knife and his family made their way to the Pine Ridge Reservation, where friendly Indians concealed them. Of those who had broken out of the barracks, all who survived, some fifty-eight, were allowed to go to the Pine Ridge agency. Seven leaders were tried for killing white settlers in the course of their flight; but the cases were dismissed, and they, too, joined the remnant of the band at Pine Ridge. Public feeling rallied so strongly now to the Cheyenne cause that soon all the Northern Cheyenne who survived were gathered on the Tongue River Reservation in the heart of the country they knew and loved.

The Ponca, related to the Omaha, had been living peacefully, if sordidly, on the southeast corner of an area claimed by the Sioux. The Sioux raided and pillaged the Ponca while complaining of their presence, and the Department of the Interior, anxious to placate the more active and dangerous tribe, undertook to move the Ponca to another reservation. The Ponca, rather to everyone's surprise, refused, but, faced with the threat of forceable removal, a portion of the tribe began what proved to be a terribly arduous trek to the new reservation. Many fell ill along the way, and a number died. The man who took up their cause and focused national attention on it was Thomas Tibbles, a skillful journalist and propagandist. Tibbles soon had the attention of the Eastern press focused on the desperate situation of the Ponca. A delegation of Ponca was given an audience with President Hayes and it asked, reasonably enough, that the tribe be sent back to its old reservation or to Nebraska, where the main body of Omaha lived. Once again the legions of reform rallied to an Indian cause. President Hayes admitted publicly that an injustice had been done to the Ponca, and Congress passed a bill for their relief. Meanwhile, their chief, Standing Bear, seeing the members of his band dying off from disease, primarily malaria, gathered the survivors together and headed for the Omaha reservation. Now the Eastern reformers, joined by a number of white residents of the Dakotas and Nebraska, drafted petitions, asking that they be allowed to remain. Encouraged by white supporters, Standing Bear went so far as to bring suit for habeas corpus in a U.S. circuit court to prevent the return of the tribe to the malarial reservation from which it had fled. In May, 1879, Judge Dundy ruled that "in time of peace no authority, civil or military, exists for transporting Indians from one section of the country to another, without the consent of the Indians. . . ." Any Indians confined for the purpose of removal would be released on habeas corpus. Encouraged by the court victory, the friends of the Ponca renewed the fight. Tibbles organized an extensive lecture tour featuring Chief Standing Bear and an attractive, missionary-school-educated young Omaha woman, Susette La Flesche, whose Indian name was Bright Eyes. The tour "opened in Boston" to enthusiastic audiences. Tibbles raised some $7,000 to carry on a legal battle for the Ponca. Carl Schurz, to his indignation, found himself squarely in the center of the battle. A Boston woman, Martha Goddard, was typical of those who took him to task for not responding generously enough to the plight of the Ponca. The condition of the Indians, she wrote him, was "the great question now, and you would be surprised if you knew how much people here think about it & care for it, not passionately, or with any political afterthought, but earnestly, and as a matter of humanity & justice & national honor, as they cared for the emancipation of the slaves."

The most formidable recruit to the Ponca cause was a Colorado woman, Helen Hunt Jackson, who, visiting Boston, heard Tibbles, Standing Bear, and Susette La Flesche and discovered the cause that was to obsess her for the remaining years of her life. While Wendell Phillips, under a pseudonym, produced a tract called *The Ponca Chiefs*, which charged the government with being "incompetent, cruel and faithless," thereby earning "the contempt and detestation of all honest men and the distrust and hate of the Indian tribes," Mrs. Jackson began work on what was to be the most devastating indictment of the treatment of the Indians yet written—*A Century of Dishonor*. The marriage of Thomas Tibbles and Susette La Flesche added a decidedly romantic note to the three-year-long campaign on behalf of the Ponca.

Justice, so far as that was possible—legal justice at least—was finally done for the Ponca or what remained of them—somewhat more than 600 members of the tribe. Congress voted $165,000 to compensate them for their losses, and they were given the choice of living either on their old reservation or with the Omaha. All in all, the Ponca controversy was one of the more remarkable episodes in American history. With the Indian wars finally at an end and the Indian "problem" to all intents and purposes "solved," with the vast majority of the Indians settled on reservations and presumably involved in the process of being "civilized," the nation indulged itself in a final orgy of guilt over the Indian question. Seen in this light, the Ponca affair, involving a small, obscure tribe that most Americans had never even heard of, set off rites of expiation designed, quite unconsciously, to ease a bad collective conscience. If the Ponca in the end could be treated justly and humanely, the books might be closed on the extended tragedy of the aboriginal Americans. During the Ponca controversy a number of the antislavery old guard, among them the greatest spirits of the age, died—William Lloyd Garrison in the spring of 1879, Lydia Maria Child and Lucretia Mott the following year.

The Apache under Geronimo continued to disturb the Southwest, and the Ghost Dance uprising would flair up into a bloody finale in the 1880s; but with the surrender of the Sioux and the Cheyenne for all intents and purposes the Indian wars were over. They had entered the realm of mythology and become as much a part of the nation's collective memory as the Trojan War for the Greeks, the material of countless romances and innumerable "westerns," told and retold, interpreted and reinterpreted. But somehow the truth remained as elusive as ever. The issue became polemical rather than tragical. The government erected historical markers along busy, traveled roads, which told the brief and unrevealing facts. "Near here Crazy Horse and his Sioux warriors were defeated by. . . ." "At this spot, Chief Joseph surrendered to Colonel Nelson Miles." But sadness haunted the land.

By 1881 the Indians had had 155,632,000 acres of land allocated to them. Indians on reservations and in the Indian Territory numbered 189,447. In addition, 117,368 white men and women lived in the Indian Territory and on reservations, as did more than 18,000 blacks, most of them former slaves of the Civilized Tribes.

In 1885 Grover Cleveland returned some of the Indian lands which his predecessor, Chester Arthur, had taken from the Indians, and three years later he reported to Congress that "over 80,000,000 acres have been arrested from illegal usurpation, improvident grants, and fraudulent entries and claims to be taken for the homesteads of honest industry. . . ." Nonetheless, Indian lands were whittled away until by 1900 only 84,000,000 acres were still reserved. But all such statistics are, in a sense, beside the point. Whether the approximately 200,000 Indians scattered on some 300 reservations from Maine to Florida and from New York to Oregon had been on 20,000,000 acres (with an allocation of 100 acres for each Indian, man, woman, and child) or on 200,000,000 (with 1,000 acres for each member of every tribe) would in the long run have made no difference. As tribal people they lived in a world without any conception of "work," and they lived in the midst of a society in which "work" was only slightly less venerated than "property."

The organizations dedicated to the welfare of the Indian did not diminish in numbers or ardor. Rather the reverse. The last decades of the century saw the establishment of a journal devoted to progressive improvement in the condition of the Indian called *The Council Fire*, edited by Alfred Meacham until his premature death, caused by the wounds he had received at the hands of Captain Jack and his Modoc chiefs. The Boston Indian Citizenship Association, as its name indicated, was devoted to the cause of winning citizenship for the Indians. The Women's National Indian Association of Philadelphia was organized in 1879 and counted among its more prominent members Mrs. John Jacob Astor. In a few years it had sixty chapters, the most active being the Connecticut Indian Association, of which Harriet Beecher Stowe was vice-president. Inspired by Helen Hunt Jackson's *A Century of Dishonor*, Herbert Welsh founded the Indian Rights Association in 1882. Together the various organizations contributed sums in excess of $100,000 a year to support educational programs on the various reservations. Perhaps most important was their watchdog role. They kept, through their agents and through the numerous missionaries to the Indians, a close eye on the government's dealings with the tribes and were ready at any moment to step forth to try to right a wrong or repair an injustice.

The passage of the Dawes Act in 1887 was the culmination of almost eighteen years of agitation in behalf of the Indian, and it might be taken also as the last nail driven into the coffin of the tribal culture of the North American Indian. The committee which proposed the bill had it in mind that "the sun dance shall be stricken down, and that in its stead we shall have industrial schools; that the commune shall give way to the dignity and rights of American citizens; that the heathen idols shall give place to the Christian altars, and that the tribal organization shall be broken up and the individuality of the Indian encouraged and developed, and the lands unnecessarily reserved for them opened to the pioneer, that intelligence and thrift may find lodging there." At last, we might say, Thomas Jefferson's program for civilizing the Indians was to be given practical effect. Such sentiments are, of course, uncongenial to the more anthropologically enlightened consciousness of today, but they were the best that the age could come up with; they were, in any event, the very opposite of "extermination," although it could well be argued that they killed the spirit if they left the body intact.

What the most enlightened and humane reformers and friends of the Indian could not, of course, understand was the power of "culture" over "civilization." In any serious contest between culture and so-called civilization for the soul of a people, culture must win even if winning means dying. As we have tediously reiterated, there were no "Indians" in the Americas; there were tribes of aborigines, hundreds of tribes that ranged from the "civilized" Cherokee, with their sophisticated agricultural-hunting mode of life, to the Ute of the Great Desert Basin, whose existence was as marginally human as any on this planet. Between the more highly developed tribes and the more primitive there was a vaster difference than between a British lord and a Cherokee chief (who, it might be argued, were, in fact, quite similar). What all those several hundred astonishingly diverse peoples shared was a common tribal consciousness, and to that tribal consciousness or culture they clung with a tenacity that confused, bewildered, and demoralized the exponents of civilizing the Indian, from Thomas Jefferson to the most recent twentieth-century authority on the subject. Tribal culture could not survive intact, and the aborigines could not wholly abandon it. They must, perforce, live in a limbo.

If money and good intentions could have solved the "Indian problem," it would certainly have been solved early in the history of the Republic. By 1823 the Federal government had spent more than $85,000,000 on Indian affairs—treaties, subsidies, gifts (not, of course, to mention the uncounted millions spent killing recalcitrant Indians). The total sum appropriated to pay for Indian lands and to pay the Indians subsequently to live on them would mount into the billions of dollars. But buying off the Indians was simply another way of killing them. They were made dependent wards of the government, living, for the most part, in idleness and squalor.

It is a truism to say that the Indians were robbed of their lands, but even if a fair market value had been put on every acre of land purchased from the Indians, it would, in the long run, have done them little good. They had no use for or understanding of money. Their land had no value that could be equated with money for them. It was their life.

In addition to money (uncounted millions more were contributed through private philanthropy), thousands of white Americans devoted some or all of their lives to trying to "raise up" the Indians, to educate, Christianize, "civilize" them. But no one found a way to "empower" the Indians. The powerless are always, with the best of intentions, exploited by the powerful because those with power must treat them as wards, as dependents with no real control over their own destinies. So, as it turned out, everything done *for* the American aborigines made their situation worse. The reservations, which began, in part at least, as a way of protecting tribes from avaricious whites and, equally important, from each other, became a prison of the spirit. Better, by far, Richard Pratt's notion, eccentric as it was, of parceling out the aborigines all over the United States, ninety to a county, to be taken in by good Christian families. But it may be doubted that the Indians themselves would have taken kindly to such a solution.

We have had more than one occasion to speak of America as full of heartbreak—violent deaths in lonely places, wasting disease in malarial lowlands, the desperate life of the city poor, defeated hopes and frustrated expectations, truncated youth and barren old age, a kind of cosmic homesickness when home was so often so far away, all part of the price of being an American, a price that, generation after generation, millions of people seemed willing, indeed eager to pay to be American. But the aborigine had no choice. The limitless and incommensurable sadness was that he was dispossessed from the earth he loved by forces he could not comprehend. He had no choice in the matter. Civilization swallowed up culture, and, turn one way and another as we may, it is hard indeed to see how it could have been otherwise. A far more exact justice might, indeed, have been done, but considering the ways of conquering peoples with the conquered in the long record of history, there turns out to have been much, after all, that was done or that at least was tried in the best spirit. But, as E. L. Godkin pointed out, the good and the bad seemed to have much the same result. If we could have repaired all the instances of bad faith and broken treaties, would not the outcome have been the same—the remnants of once proud tribes living hopeless lives on reservations?

Beyond the endless drama, the scenes so vividly painted in words and on canvas, beginning with James Fenimore Cooper and extending to the most recent novels and historical and anthropological studies, there was above everything else the ineffable sadness of the destruction of tribal societies that, with all their cruelty and violence, contained much of beauty. In every generation and in perhaps none more than the present, the American aborigines have found their champions and admirers, men and women who, if they often shamelessly romanticize Indian life, nonetheless adore an essence of tribal experience beside which the corruptions and falsities of civilization have been constantly contrasted.

Finally, we are prone to overlook the fact that tens of thousands of Indians did indeed become "civilized." The greater number of those who did entered into the white man's culture by the only sure door open to them—through his religion. They thus adopted a new and larger cosmology and simply disappeared, were assimilated, so that their descendants were proud to say, "My grandmother [it was grand-mother generally rather than grandfather since women assimilated more readily than men] was a Cherokee" or Sioux or Cheyenne or Navaho. Certainly those Indians who "passed" or amalgamated gave ample evidence that there was no "racial" or genetic inferiority in the American aborigines. They proved what the abolitionists claimed: that men, "primitive" as they might be, were in an astonishing (and, in Darwinian terms, inexplicable) degree "equal" for all practical purposes.

One thing is clear: However the great majority of Americans may have been caught in the terrible and unremitting sin of racism in regard to black Americans, it was not racism per se that cast such a dark cloud over the red-white clash. John Rolfe's marriage to Pocahontas was the unshakable symbol of that fact. In the first place, the American aborigines were not "Indians," were not a *race* in any rational meaning of that dangerously elusive word. They were innumerable tribes, some "noble," some "degraded," all "aboriginal" for want of a better word. Thousands of "white" men or, more accurately, men ranging in complexion from pink to swarthy married thousands of aboriginal women without experiencing more than a modicum of hostility from their fellow whites. Often the reverse. A handsome Indian woman was an object, certainly in the higher social circles, of fascinated attention, just as the appearance of a famous Indian chief would turn out the citizenry by the thousands wherever he appeared in the "civilized" world. To mix "racism" in with the jumble of catchwords and clichés through which we must hack our way in order even to approach the truth is, in my opinion, hopelessly to compromise the whole issue. We have enough to answer for in the bona fide area of racism. Certainly settlers and other Americans unsympathetic to the Indians did not hesitate to speak of them as a "savage and degraded race," but worse things were said of the Irish, the Italians, and the Poles.

Wendell Phillips liked to pair the problems of the treatment of the Indians and that of the Chinese immigrants. But few took up the analogy; it was far too eccentric. Phillips's point, of course, was that both Indians and Chinese, each so different, were part of a common human brotherhood and must be so perceived and so treated. The pairing of the two "races," one a genuine race, the other a category, had the actual effect of highlighting the difference between the two issues. The Chinese were, from the moment they arrived on the American shores, the victims of flagrantly racist attitudes. That was never the Indian problem. We could do worse than leave the last word to the Reverend David Macrae, the touring Scottish minister. Many Americans expressed a sincere desire, he noted in 1854, to "improve" the Indian—i.e., make him more like a white man. "Before there is time to civilize him, he is likely to be 'improved' from the face of the earth," Macrae wrote. "American civilization is impatient, and cannot wait for him. People who eat their meals in four minutes and a half, and push railway lines across the prairie at the rate of two miles a day, cannot wait a hundred years to give the Indian time to bury his tomahawk, wash his face, and put on a pair of trousers." Especially if the Indian had no interest in such a transformation.

6

The Railroads

While many other issues concerning the Indian problem were debated by friends and enemies of the Indians—civilizers and exterminators—it was clear that at least for the Sioux, Cheyenne, Arapaho, and Kiowa, the principal obstacle to peace on the Great Plains was the issue of the railroads bi- and trisecting their hunting grounds. On this, as we have seen, there could be in the long run no compromise. The rails must run their irresistible way through the heart of Indian country.

There was clearly no artifact of the new industrial culture as powerfully symbolic as the steam locomotive. It aroused the deepest emotions of which Americans were capable—awe at its power, at the thrust of its great wheels, the clouds of trailing smoke, the tolling bell, the eerie whistle borne mournfully on the wind (the most haunting music of the new age); greed at the wealth it promised; rage at its dictatorial and unpredictable ways and at the corruption that followed it everywhere like a dark cloud. All that was best and worst in America seemed caught up in the railroad mania.

The growth of the railroads was undoubtedly the most impressive fact about them. In the fifteen years between the end of the Civil War and 1880 the ton-miles of freight carried by the thirteen principal lines in the country rose from 2.16 billion to 14.48 billion, an increase of 600 percent. In the fifteen-year period track mileage more than tripled—from 35,000 miles to 115,647—and 18,000 locomotives were in service. In the next decade the number of passengers carried on all roads increased from 289,000,000 to 520,000,000, and passenger-miles from 7 billion to 12 billion. Ton-miles of freight climbed from 39 to 79 billion. Between 1880 and 1890 the average railroad mileage constructed per year totaled more than 6,000 miles; the peak year was 1887, when 12,000 miles of track were laid.

Henry Adams put the matter in a larger context. "On the scale of power," he wrote, "merely to make the continent habitable for civilized people would require an immediate outlay that would have bankrupted the world. . . . The new Americans . . . must, whether they were fit or unfit, create a world of their own, a science, a society, a philosophy, a universe, where they had not created a road or even learned to dig their own iron. They had no time for thought; they saw, and could see, nothing beyond their own day's work." Faced with the staggering task of inhabiting and organizing a continent, "the society dropped every thought of dealing with anything more than the single fraction called a railway system. This relatively small part of its task was still so big as to need the energies of a generation, for it required all the new machinery to be created—capital, banks, mines, furnaces, shops, powerhouses, technical knowledge, mechanical population, together with a steady remodeling of social and political habits, ideas, and institutions to fit the new scale and the new conditions. The generation between 1865 and 1895 was already mortgaged to the railways, and no one knew it better than the generation itself. . . ."

In the congressional legislation that paved the way for the transcontinental railroads, it was provided that the line should move west from Council Bluffs under the direction of the Union Pacific and east from Sacramento under the auspices of the Central Pacific. Each company was to receive ten alternating sections along its right-of-way to help defray the cost of construction. Fraud and corruption, culminating in the Crédit Mobilier scandal involving bribes to Congressmen, marked the venture from its inception.

The Central Pacific was a partnership of five men, all newcomers to railroad building. Collis Potter Huntington was a coarse, rough man who, like Jay Gould, began his career as a peddler. Born in Connecticut in 1821, Huntington was graduated to storekeeping and then moved to California at the time of the gold rush, establishing a successful hardware store at Sacramento. Along with three other small merchants—Mark Hopkins, his partner in the hardware store; Leland Stanford, a grocer; and Charles Crocker, a former gold miner—and a brilliant engineer, Theodore Dehone Judah, the ambitious Huntington formed a partnership to build a railroad across the Sierra Nevada.

Determined to win the contract to build the western portion of the line, the partners dispatched Judah to Washington, where he persuaded Congress that only he and his backers were competent to build the line eastward from Sacramento. After the legislation had passed through Congress, Judah wired a cryptic message to his partners: "We have drawn the elephant. Now let us see if we can harness him up."

Soon after his return from the East Judah died of yellow fever, and the "Big Four" pushed on without him. After a good deal of feverish lobbying, Congress set Promontory Point in Utah as the meeting place of the two lines.

The Casement Brothers, Daniel and Jack, were the contractors for much of the Union Pacific track, gathering up more than 1,000 men: ex-soldiers from both North and South, Irishmen from Chicago and New York, and a mixed bag of drifters, ex-mountain men, and fugitives from the law. General Sherman was convinced that such a formidable collection of hard-rock types had nothing to fear from the Indians. "So large a number of workmen distributed along the line will introduce enough whisky to kill all the Indians within 300 miles of the road," he wrote.

On the other end of the line, advancing from California, huge, profane Charles Crocker had trouble rounding up workers who could endure the blistering heat of the Great Desert Basin. He tried to import Mexicans, but the Mexican government was unsympathetic. Next, he turned to Chinese laborers, who had been imported to work the placer mines in California. Most construction men considered them too small and frail to sustain heavy construction; but Crocker tried out fifty, and they proved as hardy as their Caucasian counterparts and far more tidy and efficient. Two thousand were rounded up in San Francisco, Stockton, Sacramento, and scattered mining towns, and several thousand more imported from Canton. With their wide-brimmed straw hats and blue work clothes they doubtlessly looked much as their ancestors had centuries earlier, working on the Great Wall of China.

The rails were pushed forward relentlessly in the face of heavy snowfalls, avalanches, and, in the summer, blistering heat. On several occasions whole construction camps were buried under a hundred feet of rock and earth by avalanches.

As the track moved west and east, laying the rails developed into a race between the construction crews of the Central Pacific and those of the Union Pacific; the line that built the longest stretch of railroad bed could claim the largest number of sections and, it was hoped, the largest profits for its stockholders. As many as 10,000 men—a vast polyglot army of laborers, plagued by disease, Indians, whiskey, and the elements—pushed the lines as much as eight miles a day. (Progress was much slower, of course, through the Sierra Nevada and the Rocky Mountains.) Four hundred and fifty miles of track were laid in 1867–68, many stretches improperly graded, many bridges flimsily constructed.

Prostitutes, gamblers, sutlers—a whole additional army of leeches that preyed on the laborers—followed in their rear. Some camps turned into rough, rowdy cities—Julesburg, Cheyenne, and Laramie among them. Robert Louis Stevenson called them "roaring, impromptu cities full of gold and lust and death." Collis Huntington handled the Indian problem by issuing free passes to all the chiefs and letting "the common Indians ride on the freight cars whenever they saw fit."

On May 10, 1869, trains arrived from California with Leland Stanford and his party (the Central Pacific had constructed 742 miles; the Union Pacific 1,038), and a few hours later Sidney Dillon, a director of the Union Pacific and the Crédit Mobilier, arrived in his private car. In front of a motley crowd of Chinese and Irish workers, public officials, and the soldiers of the 21st U.S. Infantry Regiment, a golden spike was driven by a silver sledge to complete the first transcontinental railroad line. When word of the historic event, which ranked with the first telegraph message sent by Samuel F. B. Morse to Baltimore from Washington and the initial message on the Atlantic cable, was flashed over the wires, many towns and cities gave themselves over to enthusiastic celebrations. In Chicago a parade four miles long honored the linking of the two coasts. In San Francisco the air rang with the sounds of fire bells, and in small towns along the right of way there were fireworks and bars stayed open far into the night. The California poet Joaquin Miller wrote: "There is more poetry in the rush of a single railroad train across the continent than in all the gory story of the burning of Troy."

Soon the great event was clouded with the revelations of corruption which made all previous defalcations seem modest by comparison. Although Stanford, Hopkins, Huntington, and Crocker were hardly equal in their thievery to the more experienced financiers of the Union Pacific, they laid the foundations of vast fortunes (estimated at a total in excess of $23,000,000).

At this point a startlingly different type of tycoon entered the picture. Henry Villard was a German immigrant who had been a newspaper correspondent during the Civil War. His wife was Frances Garrison, the daughter of William Lloyd Garrison. His son, Oswald Garrison Villard, revered his grandfather, and his earliest memories were of that rather awesome figure at his home in Massachusetts. Villard recalled that the mild eyes behind the gold-rimmed spectacles could grow quite fierce at any infraction of the household rules or news of any injustice in the world. Henry Villard was one of that company of German "liberationists" that included such figures as Carl Schurz. He had landed in the United States in 1853, found a job as a reporter for the German-language paper *Staats-Zeitung*, and became a friend of Lincoln. From there he advanced to the *Cincinnati Commercial*, under the famous editor Murat Halstead. As a correspondent for the *Commercial* Henry Villard was on the first stagecoach run from Leavenworth to Denver, a trip of seven and a half days. After reporting the presidential campaign of 1860, Villard covered many of the most important battles of the war from Bull Run to the Wilderness.

Villard's wife, Frances Garrison, had lived at the center of the abolitionist movement since her birth. She had known John Brown and been present at the meeting in the Tremont Temple in Boston on January 1, 1863, to celebrate the Emancipation Proclamation. She had been a member of Dr. Dio Lewis's famous gymnastic class, the first ever organized in Boston. It was there she met the young war correspondent Henry Villard. They were married a year later.

When Villard's health broke down, he returned to his native Heidelberg to recuperate. There he was approached by a group of German bondholders of the Oregon and California Railroad, then in bankruptcy, with the proposal that he represent them in the United States in an effort to retrieve something from the collapse of the railroad. Back in the United States Villard discovered that one of the railroad lines, for which $3,000,000 in bonds had been sold to the German investors, had never been built. As he began to unravel the tangled affairs of the Oregon and California Railroad Company, Villard found himself in effect running the enterprise, which was reorganized as the Kansas Pacific Railway Company. Soon, in one of the most spectacular ascents in the frantic railroad building era, Villard was president of a half dozen companies formed to develop "the material and natural resources of Oregon." Prominent among them was the Oregon Steamship Company. He next used an invention of his own, the so-called blind pool, to purchase a controlling interest in the Northern Pacific, and as president of that line he acquired the right to complete another transcontinental railroad line.

Villard set a new standard for mass construction by employing 25,000 men, half of them Chinese, working from both East and West; on September 8, 1883, the rails met west of Helena, in the Montana Territory, as they had fourteen years earlier at Promontory Point. Villard, with his newspaper background, had a flair for publicity. Determined to make the meeting of the two roadbeds one of the most spectacular events of the century, he arranged for a special train or, more accurately, a series of special trains to carry distinguished guests to Gold Creek, fifty-five miles west of Helena, where the rails were to meet. The trip was a kind of protracted celebration of American technological accomplishment.

The British section included James Bryce, a Member of Parliament and expert on American government, two earls, and several other lords. There were some 500 in all in the official party, including the Villard and Garrison families. Among the dozens of American journalists the most distinguished were E. L. Godkin, Carl Schurz, Joseph Medill, editor of the *Chicago Tribune*, Joseph Pulitzer, and Henry Loomis Nelson. An assortment of American dignitaries completed the roster. The generals were led by former President Ulysses S. Grant, accompanied by Generals Sheridan, Terry, and Miles. President Chester Arthur, on his way back from a vacation in the Yellowstone, met the expedition at Minneapolis for a celebration. Similar events occurred at various stops along the line. Occasionally, angry protesters, gathered to denounce the railroads, had to be hustled away by embarrassed officials. At Bismarck, North Dakota, Sitting Bull joined Carl Schurz to lay the cornerstone of the state Capitol. The trains stopped at the Crow village near Gold Creek, and the passengers were given an opportunity to visit a real Indian encampment.

The Crow—3,000 strong—were present as a reward, presumably, for their long history of friendly relations with the whites. They were a dismal remnant of a once great tribe. They crowded around begging for money, while a dozen or so of their chiefs joined the expedition to participate in the ceremonies.

At Gold Creek, 1,025 miles from St. Paul and 706 from Portland, Oregon, the official last spike was to be driven. A pavilion and bandstand large enough to shade 5,000 spectators from sun or rain had been constructed. The four long trains from the East, colorfully festooned with flags and ribbons, drew up to meet a train from the Pacific coast. The grandstand was well filled, and the ceremony was protracted. Henry Villard's young son, Oswald Garrison Villard, recalled: "Around it swirled a motley crowd, cowboys, tracklayers, railroad men, settlers who had driven many miles . . . soldiers from General Nelson Miles's Fifth Infantry . . ." and the seven Crow chiefs, headed by Iron Bull. Henry Villard delivered the opening remarks, making special mention of the men who had laid the ties and rails, among them 15,000 Chinese. Their achievements "formed a great sum of human patience and perseverance, energy and bravery, hardship and privation . . . a mighty struggle of mechanical and manual force against the direct obstacles of primitive nature." Turning to the foreign guests, Villard declared, "You have the testimony of your own eyes that this highway had to be carved out of a very wilderness where we found nothing to help us—no labor, no food, no habitations, no material, no means of transportation."

William Evarts, former secretary of state, spoke, characteristically at length, without saying anything memorable and was followed by representatives of Great Britain and Germany, five state and territorial governors, and, at the demand of the crowd, General Grant, who recalled that when Jefferson Davis was secretary of war in Pierce's Cabinet and Grant a lieutenant at an army post on the Columbia River, he had issued supplies for the first survey expedition of the railroad's route. (It was at the same post that Grant, overcome by loneliness and faced with the threat of a court-martial for drunkenness, decided to resign his commission and go back to Galena to work as a clerk in his father's store.)

Iron Bull, the Crow chief, gave the last speech in sign language as the sun was setting and the weary crowd was drifting away. "There is a meaning in my part of the ceremony and I understand it," Iron Bull declared. "We have reached the end of our rule and a new one has come. The end of our lives, too, is near at hand. . . . Of our once powerful nation there are now but a few left—just a handful—and we, too, will soon be gone. After the Indian has given way to civilization the whites will come."

At last the time had come for the driving of the spike. At a signal crews from West and East rushed to the missing rails, cheering and yelling, urged on by their partisans. The rails of the Eastern gang were drawn by a horse carrying the sign, "My name is Nig. I have drawn rails 750 miles." When the rails were down and Henry Villard started forward to drive the last spike, the crowd broke ranks and rushed to the spot. The mass of bodies was so dense that it was difficult for those assigned to swing the maul to find sufficient space. H. C. Davis, an official of the Manitoba Railroad, struck the first blow, followed by Villard, Mayor Carter Harrison of Chicago, Evarts, Carl Schurz, Grant, Fanny Villard, and last of all Iron Bull. Plans to record the historic moment on film were aborted by the throng that pressed around the principals, barring the photographers' view.

The New York Times wrote on September 9, 1883: "A wilderness is now open to civilization, and one which is adequate to support in comfort the surplus population of all Europe . . . which will within a few years work economic and social changes of which what has already happened in Great Britain affords but a faint far-off hint."

As the entourage proceeded West through numerous small towns, "the popular demonstrations . . . were amazing," according to the editor of the *Columbus* (Ohio) *Sunday Herald.* "We saw literally during our journey, more than 2,000 miles of decorations and flags; and the merchant millionaires of the city, the lonely squatter on the prairie, the Chinese woodcutter in the forest, all had 'welcome,' written over their doors, as well as on their faces and in their hearts."

But there was a final and crowning irony. The Great Scriptwriter in the Sky seldom has composed a stranger scenario. As the last spike expedition made its way across the country, the reverse of what Henry Villard had anticipated happened: The stock of the Northern Pacific fell precipitously. The whole line appeared in the gravest danger of bankruptcy. Some of the foreign investors, appalled at the desolate and uninhabited character of the country over which the railroad passed, wired their associates to sell their bonds. The enormous cost of the expedition itself aroused apprehension among investors. Crowds gathered in front of the recently completed Villard mansion on Fifth Avenue, which appeared to occupy a whole block (it was actually six separate houses), jeering and displaying hostile signs. Suddenly the Villard financial empire was in jeopardy. The Oregon and Transcontinental Company, a holding company created by Villard primarily to funnel money to the Northern Pacific, went under. He was forced out of the presidency of his various companies and, once again on the verge of a nervous breakdown, fled "home" to Germany for his health and to escape both his creditors and the humiliation of his fall from the pinnacle of capitalist glory.

After two years in self-imposed exile Villard and his family returned to New York. There, acting as a representative of German financial interests once more, he began to reassemble his once vast holdings, starting with the Oregon Railway and Navigation Company, which he rescued from bankruptcy by getting a $5,000,000 loan from his German backers.

Henry Villard was cut from a different cloth from the run-of-the-mill tycoons of the day. His own interests in art and music were supplemented by the cultural and philanthropic concerns of his wife. "He was far more interested in his great gifts to education and to philanthropies," his admiring son wrote, "than in augmenting the family fortune. He never urged that we should learn to make money; on the contrary he wished us to be professional men. . . ." Yet he built what was the greatest mansion of its day in New York on Fifth Avenue, designed by McKim, Mead and White, and a lavish home on the Hudson, Thorwood, which was a gathering place for German visitors to the United States as well as for prominent members of the Revolutionary Class of '48, the most famous of whom was, of course, Carl Schurz. Schurz told thrilling stories of his adventures in the upheavals in Germany that forced him to flee to the United States and of his experiences as a Civil War general. The Americans who came were "always a liberal group and never conservative or Big Business," Oswald Garrison Villard recalled. Indeed, Villard's fellow tycoons shied away from him. He did not go to church on Sunday, he did not engage in sports, and he belonged to no clubs. Worst of all, he was a free-trader and a Democrat. After Villard had bought the *Nation* and the *Evening Post* and installed E. L. Godkin as editor in chief of both, he was more persona non grata than ever.

Stanford, Hopkins, Crocker, and Villard were only the most prominent of the railroad tycoons. Cyrus Holliday, founder of Topeka, Kansas, pushed his Atchison, Topeka & Santa Fe line west to Dodge City. Holliday was determined to tap the growing cattle market by running his railroad nearer to the cattle country of Texas, Colorado, and New Mexico. Denver business interests extended the Denver and

Rio Grande south and west. The Denver and Rio Grande and the Santa Fe then engaged in a race for the mountain passes. The Santa Fe made it to Raton Pass ahead of the Denver and Rio Grande, but the latter found its way through the Royal Gorge along the Arkansas River.

William Strong, president of the Santa Fe, proved one of the great railroad innovators of his day, extending his line to cover some 7,000 miles by 1889 and introducing the first great chain of railroad restaurants in the Santa Fe stations. Good food, served by handsome waitresses—"young women of good character, attractive and intelligent, 18 to 30," the help wanted ads read—made the Harvey restaurants and the Harvey Girls famous.

One of the most successful of all the railroad barons was Jim Hill—James Jerome Hill, who had arrived in St. Paul at the age of eighteen and become a power in the city's financial circles ten years later. Born in Canada, Hill had connections with the Hudson's Bay Company. He persuaded the company to help him take over a bankrupt line and extend it first to Great Falls, in the Montana Territory, and then through to Seattle. Hill named it the Great Northern Railway. While the other transcontinental lines faced bankruptcy and receivership, Hill's Great Northern showed the results of better management, superior construction, and Hill's genius for promotion. In Hill's words, "Make it desirable for people to come here [Oregon and Washington], make it easy for them to carry on their business and we will get the freight. We consider ourselves and the people along our line as co-partners in the prosperity of the country we both occupy; and the prosperity of the one should mean the prosperity of both, and their adversity will be quickly followed by ours." In this spirit Hill took an active role as a community builder, encouraging the building of schools and churches and providing instruction for emigrants on the best methods of farming and cattle raising.

By the mid-1880s the major trans-Mississippi railroad systems were complete. Only the Santa Fe and its affiliated lines remained to be finished. The four so-called Granger lines were made up of the Chicago, Burlington & Quincy; the Chicago, Milwaukee & St. Paul; the Chicago & North Western; and the Chicago, Rock Island & Pacific. These roads covered the great hog-raising, grain-producing region of the Midwest that found its focus in Chicago.

Andrew Carnegie, rhapsodizing in *Triumphant Democracy* over the growth of the railroads in the United States, pointed out that the railroad mileage in America exceeded that of the whole rest of the world. "Monster, you were called into existence only to redress the balance of the Old World, and within one short century we find you threatening to weight it down! The Republic against 'the field' and no takers!"

Basic, of course, to the rapid expansion of the railroads was the policy of the Federal government, and in some instances the states, of subsidizing the railroads by vast land grants. Such grants worked, presumably, for the good of the nation in that they provided a highly practical incentive for the railroads to populate the Western states in order to make a profit by selling off their grants to settlers. By March 3, 1871, more than 170,000,000 acres had been allocated to eighty railroads by the Federal government, but since only half the roads planned were ever built, approximately 35,000,000 acres eventually returned to the government. If the grants given by the states, particularly Texas, are included, the number of acres given the railroads totals some 164,000,000—an area larger than all the lands granted individuals under the terms of the Homestead Act, four-fifths as large as the five states of the Old Northwest, or almost as large as the combined acreages of California and Nevada.

One of the most important functions of the railroads was to fill out, so to speak, the remaining states or the territories that would become states. In almost every instance, railroads preceded and were essential to statehood. When Wyoming, Utah, Oklahoma, New Mexico, and Arizona became states, they each had more than 1,000 miles of railroad running through them and a total of 23,000 miles.

The problem was to get settlers on those interminable Western acres. By 1876 the Northern Pacific ran from St. Paul north to Brainerd, Minnesota, turned directly west through the Dakota Territory to Bismarck and thence into Montana to Livingston, Helena, Missoula, across the Idaho panhandle to Washington, and then southwest to Portland, Oregon. The Northern Pacific advertised proudly that the Pacific Express "with Pullman and Dining Cars attached" ran from St. Paul to Portland in four days without change of train. Its passengers could be dropped off at innumerable spots en route to hunt for deer and bear, for antelope, buffalo, and, even, spare the mark, prairie dogs. Ducks, prairie chicken, grouse, and plover were plentiful in the lake regions of Minnesota and numerous stations throughout Montana, and the Northwest offered a variety of splendid fishing. The railroad advertised: "Millions and millions of acres of Northern Pacific LANDS FOR SALE at the lowest prices ever offered by any railroad company ranging chiefly from $2.60 to $4.00 per acre. Best Wheat Lands Best Farming Lands Best Grazing Lands in the World." In alternating quarter sections there was government land to be had for the homesteading. "Large and sure crops every year" were promised by the railroad's promotional literature.

The Best Homes
For 10,000,000 People Now Await Occupancy in
Minnesota, Dakota, Montana, Idaho, Washington
and Oregon
The great new
Northern Pacific Country

Those bold spirits who venture into the region "will soon become the first families, and leaders, socially and politically, in this newly opened section of the United States." One-sixth down was the basic requirement, the balance in five equal annual installments.

Dakota boasted six lines—Chicago & North Western, Dakota Southern (running from Yankton to Sioux City), Dakota & North Western, Northern Pacific, Sioux City & Pembina, and Winona & St. Peter. Of the approximately 300 "towns"—some were with excessive optimism called cities, such as Brulé City, Custer City, and Dell City— many had no more than half a dozen inhabitants, and most have long since disappeared entirely. The great majority, of course, were strung along the railroad lines like beads on a string. Thus between Jamestown, Dakota, and Bismarck, a distance of perhaps 100 miles, the traveler was whirled past Eldridge, Cleveland, Medina, Crystal Springs, Tappen, Dawson, Steele, Sterling, and Clark.

Nebraska, older and more civilized, had nine lines: Atchison & Nebraska, Burlington & Missouri, Frémont, Elkhorn & Missouri Valley, Midland Pacific, Nebraska Railway, Omaha & Northwestern, Sioux City & Pacific, St. Joseph & Denver City, and, most important, the Union Pacific. Kansas had fourteen, the most famous being the Atchison, Topeka & Santa Fe, which ran along the Arkansas River from Wichita through Dodge City to Fort Lyon in Colorado. It had, in addition, the Missouri, Kansas & Texas, and the Kansas Central. The Atchison, Topeka & Santa Fe staked out the mining regions of Colorado, New Mexico, and Arizona as its special preserve. From La Junta in eastern Colorado, it joined with the Southern Pacific, turning southwest to Santa Fe and Albuquerque, Mesilla, and Tucson. From Albuquerque the Atlantic & Pacific ran due west to Los Angeles and San Diego. Its special appeal was to "tourists bound for the Mines and Health Resorts of Colorado, $38 dollars from Denver round-trip."

The Great Rock Island Route offered to carry its patrons 10,840 miles from Australia, including 3,310 miles to England and straight across the continent of North America from New York to San Francisco. The Union Pacific ran from Omaha, or, more precisely, Council Bluffs, along the Platte to Julesburg, where a line branched off to Denver. From Julesburg it followed the now familiar route to Ogden, Utah (with a spur to Salt Lake City), and across the Great American Desert, through Elko, Nevada, to Reno, and then a final push through the Sierra Nevada to Sacramento and San Francisco.

Towns not on railroad lines, struggling to survive, not uncommonly concluded that their only hope for prosperity was to prevail on a railroad to run a spur to the town, thereby connecting it to the great national network of rails. Railroads often "auctioned off" a lifesaving spur line to the town that made the highest bid; towns not infrequently bankrupted themselves to win a railroad line that, it was hoped, would make them flourishing cities, only to find their hopes defeated and their future bleaker than ever.

Railroad lines not only exploited the public—farmers, mine owners, and ranchers—who shipped their products on railroads and the stockholders (by means of "watered"—i.e., wildly inflated stocks) but also engaged in ruthless competition with each other and failed more often than not. Bankruptcy was also manipulated, and the principal losers were generally the smaller stockholders.

Rate wars with rival lines competing for a limited number of passengers reached such a point that a traveler in the 1880s could go from New York to San Francisco for $21.50. The same was true, of course, of freight rates. Where two rival lines competed for freight in the same region or along parallel lines, one line often reduced its rates to the point where its rival was driven into bankruptcy, whereupon the victor would raise rates excessively to recoup its losses. When Cornelius Vanderbilt, in his war with Jim Fisk, lowered the shipping rates to less than $1 a head, Fisk shrewdly bought a large number of cattle and shipped them on Vanderbilt's line.

In 1886 (not a depression year) 108 railroads, with 11,000 miles of track, were in receivership. By 1895 the Federal courts were operating nearly one-fourth of all the railroads in the nation through court-appointed receivers, many of whom were the men who had run the lines into bankruptcy by stock manipulations. The author of a book entitled *American Railroads as Investments*, published in the late 1880s, estimated that for shares at a market value of more than 4 billion, the investors had originally paid not more than a tenth of that sum. To George Herron, the evangelist and Christian Socialist, the railway system was "a greater menace to the integrity and perpetuity of the nation than was ever the institution of slavery; it is the strongest enemy of society and the chief danger of anarchy . . ." he wrote in 1894. At the end of the century it was estimated that $3 billion had been lost in railroad bankruptcies.

The railroads nevertheless gave an enormous stimulus to industrial growth. Besides the great factories where the locomotives and the freight cars and passenger trains were built, and the steel mills that rolled out the rails as well as the steel that made up the wheels and the frames of the cars, the railroads gave impetus to the inclination toward large-scale single-crop agriculture. Traditional small-scale multicrop farming gave way to farming that in its need for capital, expensive machinery, and large acreages, imitated more and more the specialized capital-intensive world of the factory.

In the wake of the railroad barons came the coal barons, the timber barons—whole forests could be cut down wherever a railroad line ran and shipped off to burgeoning cities—and the steel barons, constituting, in Matthew Josephson's memorable phrase, the "robber barons." The railroads, carrying goods 100 or 1,000 times farther and faster than they had ever been carried before, made possible all the satellite baronies. Hundreds of thousands of acres of grazing lands—once the support of millions of buffalo—could support thousands of head of cattle that could, it was soon demonstrated, be driven to railheads to be carried in cattle cars to Omaha or Kansas City, fattened in the stockyards, and butchered, with substantial profits at every step of the way.

Joseph McCoy, a pioneer cattleman who helped open the Chisholm Trail, founded a railhead for Texas cattle in Abilene, Kansas. He contracted with the Kansas Pacific to ship cattle out of Abilene and dispatched twenty carloads of longhorn on September 5, 1867. A year later 1,000 carloads of steers had been shipped from Abilene, and by 1871 the number had passed 700,000 for the year. By 1880, when the great cattle drives were already being impeded by farmers and fences and hastily passed laws, more than 4,000,000 cattle had come up the Chisholm and other famous trails to Ellis and Dodge City, which rivaled Abilene as shipping points. That decade, 1870 to 1880, bred the legends of the famous cattle drives and the endlessly reiterated saga of the cowboy West.

In retrospect it appeared it had been the lack of adequate transportation, above all else, that had kept civilization moving at a mere camel's pace, or a mule's or ox's pace, prior to the railroad era. The steamboats and canals had, to be sure, broken through the many-thousand-years-old pace of overland caravans, but the railroads accelerated the process to a degree that the mind could hardly comprehend. The difficulties of getting to gold-bearing streams and the laborious task of getting gold out, usually in the form of a few ounces of dust carried in a miner's poke, had limited the extent and duration of the California gold rush, fabulous as it had been. With the coming of the steam locomotive, tons of ore could be hauled off to be crushed and smelted, and low-grade ore became more profitable than the richest strike of an individual miner. Iron ore, copper, silver, even gold yielded to mass-production techniques. All this required labor of a kind that few native-born Americans were willing to perform. The cry for cheap labor willing to do backbreaking work under conditions of appalling hardship and danger, where disease and industrial accidents decimated the work forces, seemed insatiable.

As the railroads grew, they became the nation's principal employer—749,000 workers by 1890—and the principal killer and maimer of Americans. In 1890, 6,335 died in railroad accidents and 29,000 were injured. The toll of railroad disasters seemed endless. Many occurred when bridge spans gave under the ever greater weight of locomotives and trains. In 1867 at Angola, New York, the last two cars of a train of the New York Central broke through a truss bridge above Big Sisters Creek and fell forty feet to the frozen water below; 49 people were killed, and 40 injured. Four years later the Portland Express, running from Boston to Portland, Maine, ran into the rear end of a local train, killing 29 persons and injuring 57. Eleven cars of the Pacific Express of the Lake Shore & Michigan Southern, drawn by two locomotives, fell into the creek at Ashtabula, Ohio, as a bridge collapsed. Again there was a long toll of passengers and crew killed or badly injured. But these famous wrecks were only the most spectacular. While the casualties were never as heavy as they had been during the height of the steamboating days, thousands perished every year, tens of thousands in the aggregate.

As the locomotives evolved through a multitude of progressively more powerful forms, the passenger cars grew more comfortable and indeed ornate. Undoubtedly the most striking development here was the Pullman sleeper. Andrew Carnegie told the story of a clerk, "a tall,

spare, farmer-looking kind of man" named T. T. Woodruff, who came
to him when he was riding on the rear car of a Pennsylvania Railroad
train and drew from a green bag a model of a sleeping berth for
railroad cars. "He had not spoken a moment," according to Carnegie's
recollection, "before, like a flash, the whole range of discovery burst
upon me. 'Yes,' I said, 'that is something which this continent must
have.' " Carnegie persuaded Thomas Scott, president of the Pennsylvania Railroad, to build two trial cars. Carnegie borrowed money to
pay for his share of the enterprise, and before long he had his first
fortune. George Pullman soon made himself the tycoon of the sleeping
car world, and in 1885 he seemed to Andrew Carnegie the very model
of the enlightened self-made man (like Carnegie himself), one of those
who, "springing from honest poverty, have made fortunes through
honest toil, and then, . . . turning back to look upon the poor workers
where they started, have thereafter devoted their fortune and abilities
so to improve the industrial system as to give to that class a better
chance in life than it was possible for themselves to obtain."

In addition to the elegant Pullman car, designed and built by
George Pullman's company, every transcontinental express had a luxurious dining car, where on dazzling white tablecloths with gleaming
railroad silver, bearing the railroad's logo or "coat of arms," gourmet
food was served by black waiters resplendent in white jackets and smart
blue trousers. The Pullman cars were a marvel in themselves—"palaces" rich in gilt and plush, elaborately decorated, where an attentive
black porter could be summoned by the touch of a bell and where at
night the overstuffed couchlike seats were converted magically by the
same attentive black porters into upper and lower berths. Passengers
mounted to the upper berth by a ladder and disrobed and donned
sleeping clothes in the berth. There, cradled above the rhythmical
clackety-clack of the wheels on the endless rails, the more prosperous
passengers were wafted into the tenderest of slumbers. For $21.50
extra a passenger could ride from New York to San Francisco, sleeping
each night in a double berth.

The railroad barons vied with each other in the magnificence of
their private cars. They rode like Renaissance princes through the
unnumbered acres of their vast domains, some as big as countries.
From these minipalaces they disposed of the fate of tens of thousands
of their fellow citizens.

Finally, there were the train robbers, not the robber barons who
owned the railroads and robbed the citizenry in general, but robbers

on a more modest scale. On October 6, 1866, the first train robbery took place as two enterprising robbers held up a train on the Ohio & Mississippi Railroad in Jackson County, Indiana. Wearing masks, they took keys to the safe from the conductor and extracted $13,000, a substantial sum for those days. They then yanked on the bell cord to stop the train and jumped off. A year later the crime was repeated on the same line near the same spot. The robberies were reputed to be the work of the Reno Gang, the leaders of which were four brothers by that name. Their next haul was on the Jefferson, Madison & Indianapolis, and the take was $96,000. Suddenly train robbery was all the rage. After several more holdups, in the course of which· an employee of the line was killed, vigilantes broke into the jail where three of the Renos had been incarcerated and hanged them without ceremony. In the face of such discouragement it was two years before another train was robbed; then there were three in succession in Nevada, Tennessee, and Kentucky. After the Tennessee holdup Pinkerton detectives were dispatched on the trail of the Farrington brothers (train robbery was, initially, a family enterprise) and ran them to earth in a hideout near Gilman, Tennessee. One of the suspected bandits was shot to death, and two surrendered to the agents.

Another Nevada holdup took place in Truckee, just over the California line, and the bandits escaped with $40,000. The next night the same train was held up with an equivalent haul. The way was thus paved for two more sets of brothers, Frank and Jesse James, ambitious young Missourians, and the Younger brothers, Coleman, Bob, Jim, and John. They improved on the existing technique by wrecking the trains prior to looting them and by giving equal attention to the passengers and their possessions. In July, 1873, the James and Younger gangs pulled a tie and wrecked a train of the Chicago, Rock Island & Pacific not far from Adair, Iowa. The engineer was killed, and the passengers were bruised and shaken. After another robbery six months later in Missouri the Pinkertons closed in. In a gunfight between the railroad agents and the Youngers, two of the agents were killed, as was one of the brothers, Jack. The Pinkertons then threw a bomb into the Jameses' home in Missouri. Frank and James were away, and the bomb blew off their mother's arm and killed their half brother. The affair had the effect of turning the Jameses into folk heroes and giving a fresh impetus to their career. A year later a train of the Kansas Pacific was stopped by a pile of ties on the track. This time the loot was $30,000 from the train's safe and whatever valuables the passengers carried.

For two more years the James and Younger gang or gangs robbed banks, stagecoaches, and trains from Texas to West Virginia. Since hostility to banks and railroads was everywhere on the increase, the public followed the fortunes of the train robbers with interest mixed with growing sympathy. Finally, emboldened by success, the gang rode into Northfield, Minnesota, to rob the town's principal bank. Rumors of the intended heist preceded the bandits, and they found themselves in a hornet's nest of embattled citizen-sharpshooters who killed three of the gang and wounded the three Youngers, who were pursued, overtaken, and shipped off to the state penitentiary. Bob died, Jim committed suicide, and Coleman survived to be paroled in 1901 and become a star attraction in the Frank James Wild West Show.

Frank and Jesse James escaped unscathed and three years later resumed their careers by robbing a train near Glendale, Missouri. Two years later, in the course of holding up a train on the Rock Island line, they killed two crew members. Another train robbery at Blue Art, Missouri, followed, but the next spring "a dirty little coward," Bob Ford, along with his brother Charlie, shot Jesse James in the back for the $10,000 reward money with a gun that James was said to have given him. (A friend of James called the Ford brothers, uncharitably, "two weasel-eyed degenerates with pimpled faces and bad teeth.") The manner of his murder sealed Jesse James's fame. Charlie Ford committed suicide in an agony of remorse, and Red Kenney cut down Bob Ford in the saloon in Creede, Colorado, a few years later with a blast of buckshot.

The Jameses and the Youngers were the most famous of the train robbers but they had many counterparts, most of them gangs, although there were a few partnerships and single bandits. Despite the best efforts of the Pinkertons and squads of railroad detectives and guards, train robbery was a popular and lucrative, if often terminal, career down to the end of the century. With the railroads in bad odor, a Robin Hood-like glamour clung to the profession. The most famous fugitives on the West Coast (it was never proved beyond doubt that they were train robbers) were Chris Evans and John Sontag, men who felt they had been defrauded by the Southern Pacific and who held off, in numerous shoot-outs, a small army of law officers and agents of the Southern Pacific, killing or wounding some twenty of their pursuers over the course of three years. Eventually Evans was captured, and Sontag shot.

If many of the railroad entrepreneurs were simply more ambitious versions of the Jameses or Youngers, the system of transportation that they produced was at best a marvel. The Reverend David Macrae, the touring Scotsman, was ecstatic about the American railroads. On a Western line, a few dollars extra secured for him "a beautiful little parlour and bedroom. . . . The parlour is furnished with richly cushioned sofa and chairs, a stove, gilded racks for parcels and books, and a table at which you can sit and write, or have your meals. . . . the conductor, who awakes you in the morning, brings in your breakfast and the morning papers of the district through which you are passing at the time. It is like a little travelling hotel." Every train had an enterprising boy aboard who first came through, selling newspapers. Then, having disposed of his papers, he "by-and-by makes his appearance with a basket of apples, or nuts, or grapes, or whatever happens to be in season. Should he fail to tempt you with these, he returns with maple sugar, or figs, or candy." Having displayed these temptations to every passenger and "come to the conclusion that by this time (your appetite for confections and the latest news being satisfied) the desire for general information may be successfully appealed to," the indefatigable boy "re-appears with an armful of books, magazines, or illustrated papers," offering each one to the passenger most fitted to appreciate it, thus "to the curly-headed youth with his hat cocked over his eye he throws an illustrated police paper; to the gentleman with the cheesy hat he administers an agricultural journal. . . ."

To Macrae the railway train was a splendid parable on American equality where the Irish serving girl might take her seat beside the vice-president of the United States and a hod carrier sit beside a bishop's daughter. "It is one of the ways," Macrae added, "in which the people, high and low, are being educated for the new form of society to which the world is moving. The high must stoop to help the low. All down the scale, the work of God incarnating Himself to redeem mankind has to be reproduced. The result in many respects is beneficial to all classes." Even the millionaire in such circumstances "learns to be accommodating and to take his seat not as a millionaire but as a man. . . . Of course men and masses of men are not refined in a day, but the process of education is going on."

The train stations had perforce to convey the same sense of splendor as the parlor car; they had to evoke images of power and religious awe—of crenellated castles, inflated Roman temples, Renaissance palaces, Gothic cathedrals. One rose up in every town with pretensions to be taken seriously as a city, the largest and most ornate structure in sight. Money, multiplied by steam, raised temples to progress and power, many of which, converted to more mundane purposes, remain to remind us of the extraordinary material accomplishments of the age of steam with all its sacred symbols and insistent iconography.

In the stations, battalions of black redcaps were ready to convey to coach or carriage the very considerable array of suitcases and trunks considered essential for any well-equipped traveler. It was an odd mating—the railroad train, bespeaking power, served by the race most lacking in power. The trains, it might be argued, offered American blacks their first substantial vocation. Black porters and waiters became in many instances the leaders of their race. After bitter struggles they formed the first black unions.

One of the most astute scholars of the burgeoning railroads was Charles Francis Adams, Jr. After the Civil War Adams, like so many of the young men of his generation, had somewhat belatedly to find a career. His "war education," far more important, in his view, than his Harvard education, had left him determined to abandon the law. Like every ambitious, independent minded young American, he wished above all else to be a writer, but since that was a notoriously risky and poorly paid calling, Adams, as he tells it, "fixed on the railroad system as the most developing force and the largest field of the day, and determined to attach myself to it." His method was ingenious. He wrote an article on "Railroads" for the *North American Review*, then edited by James Russell Lowell and Charles Eliot Norton. The burden of the article was that the country had hardly yet awakened to the enormous importance of railroads both presently and upon the future development of the country. Moreover, the railroads were too important to the nation's economy to be allowed to proceed on their own, unsupervised and unchecked. Ruthless capitalists and pillagers like Jim Fisk and Jay Cooke had already demonstrated in the case of the Erie Railroad how far they would go in their relentless warfare and their callous exploitation of the public.

The topic was an ideal one for a young idealist with a bent for writing powerful expository prose. Soon Adams was turning out article after article on railroads, on railroad law, on the financing and public supervision of railroads and related matters. There was certainly no living to be made by producing such tracts, however instructive and well researched, so Adams began investing in railroads, in real estate, and, most successfully, in the Kansas City Stock Yards Company, which became, in the forty years he served as its president, the second largest such operation in the world. He was appointed to the Massachusetts Board of Railroad Commissioners, an agency created primarily as a result of his writing and lobbying. The other commissioners were far less well informed and Adams was soon running the commission to his own taste. Carl Schurz, secretary of the interior under Hayes, appointed Adams chairman of the Board of Government Directors of the bankrupt Union Pacific Railroad. In his new role Adams moved to Washington. "There," he wrote, "I had my experience in the most hopeless and repulsive work in which I was ever engaged—transacting business with the United States Government, and trying to accomplish something through Congressional action." The Senator on whom Adams must perforce rely was, in the New Englander's view, "an ill-mannered bully, and by all odds the most covertly and dangerously corrupt man I ever had the opportunity and occasion to observe in public life. . . . For that man, on good and sufficient grounds, I entertained a deep dislike. He was distinctly dishonest—a senatorial bribe-taker."

With his assignment completed, Adams accepted the presidency of the Union Pacific in 1884, succeeding Sidney Dillon, although "the concern was in bad repute, heavily loaded with obligations, odious in the territory it served," and, though Adams did not realize it, faced with financial collapse. Adams managed to get its finances in order, improve its service, and enhance its public image; but he could not reach a settlement with the government, and gradually the job became a nightmare to him. "I hated my position and its duties, and yearned to be free of it and from them. My office had become a prison-house. Loathing it, I was anxious, involved, hopeless." He was glad at last to relinquish it to Jay Cooke once more and free himself of his burden. He had made no friends among his fellow railroad barons. They looked on him as an odd bird, with his intellectual interests, upper-class Boston accent, and patronizing manners, and he found them "a coarse, realistic, bargaining crowd."

Yet Adams, who, as a critic, reformer, and historian of the Erie and, for six years, the frustrated president of the Union Pacific, knew the operations of the railroad barons from both sides, was deeply impressed by their accomplishments. "The simple truth," he wrote, "was that through its energetic railroad development, the country was then producing real wealth as no country ever produced it before. Beyond all the artificial inflation which so clearly foreshadowed a catastrophe, there was also going on a production that exceeded all experience." In Adams's rather Darwinian view of the matter, "a great, quiet natural force was at work"; it carried on in its own irresistible way while legislators and economists entertained the illusion that they, by their "meddling" with the tariff or "their jugglings with paper money," were shaping or controlling it. "While socialists talked, however, the locomotive was at work, and all the obstructions which they placed in its way could at most only check but never overcome the impetus it had given to material progress. . . ." His brother Henry might raise what doubts he wished about the larger forces of history and reflect on the tragedy of a generation that worshiped the dynamo rather than the Virgin, but Charles Francis plainly felt himself swept along by "a natural force" the immediate practical workings of which he understood well enough to make him a wealthy man.

Lester Ward, the sociologist, unlike Charles Francis Adams and like most of the intellectuals of his era, was a champion of the public ownership of the railroads, the land, and municipal utilities. In the midst of a chapter on education in his *Dynamic Sociology*, he made a substantial digression to argue the case for government ownership of railroads. "That unrestricted private enterprise cannot be trusted to conduct the railroad system of a rapidly growing country," he wrote, "may now be safely said to be demonstrated." Ward listed among the more conspicuous failures of the railroads: "Lines are built where they are not needed, rates are lowered below the power to cover expenses, the sense of losing makes the officers and directors indifferent to the proper service of the public, negligence causes disasters to passengers, and at length a crisis is precipitated and all the lines are suspended or absorbed by some one, or thrown into litigation. Railroad wars are followed by railroad monopolies, and it is difficult to tell through which the public suffers most." Germany had demonstrated that "government-owned or controlled railroad lines could function far more efficiently and safely than privately-owned lines," Ward concluded.

Between Americans and their railroads there existed what was probably history's most famous love-hate relationship. The railroads were symbols of American progress, of technology, of power. The parlor car epitomized elegance in motion; the diner, a combination of movement and gastronomical bliss, silver and gleaming linen and deferential waiters in starched white jackets; the sleeper invited dreams of the flight of angels.

At the same time the railroads represented everything ruthless and criminal in American capitalism. The most spectacular robber barons were the railroad barons and princes and kings and dukes, who treated their subjects more arrogantly than any real tyrant dared treat his. So the railroads were hated by perhaps the majority of Americans, certainly by those who suffered from their exactions, with a fierce and particular hatred. Virtually every attack on American capitalism focused on the iniquities of the railroads. Tom Watson, the Georgia populist, expressed the ambivalent feelings that railroads roused. "I never in my life watched a train of cars," he declared, "without some thrill of pleasure—so instinctive and typical is it of man's power and skill and success! Yet when I see the railroads used to crush out this city and build up that; to bottle up this great harbor and develop that; to help the monopoly (like the Standard Oil Company) to beat down its competitor; when I see them bringing newspapers, and Senators and Representatives to aid them in perpetuating wrongs upon the balance of the community, then it is that I find it impossible to refrain from denouncing the manner in which the magnificent blessing of the railroads is sometimes turned into a blasting curse."

The railroads were primary. If a single image or artifact had to be chosen to symbolize the Age of Industrial Capitalism, capitalism regnant and rampant, it would surely be a steam locomotive. It was the insatiable appetite of the railroads for steel and iron and coal that was the principal stimulus to those industries. Railroads spawned towns as trout spawned fingerlings. They made the astonishing growth of cities possible by carrying food and fuel to them in their freight cars, and they made large-scale agriculture possible by transporting its products, its corn and wheat and hogs and cattle, to the cities. The railroads worked everywhere to develop new markets, find new passengers, transport new and exotic freights, open up new regions for exploitation. The well-being of millions of Americans came to rest, to an alarming degree, on the decisions made by the directors of railroads strung across the country in a network of steel.

The names of the railroads rang like bells, evoked geographies, adumbrated landscapes. One could summarize the country in the litany of their names—the Southern Pacific, the Union Pacific, the Northern Pacific, the Burlington, and the Chesapeake & Ohio; they evolved into songs—"The Atchison, Topeka and the Santa Fe."

The railroads transported Americans in groups and clusters, in bunches and companies. They whirled them through space (Ralph Waldo Emerson felt like a swallow, skimming verdant fields, on his first train ride) *together*, hundreds of them neatly arranged in trains made up of passenger cars with evocative names on their sides. They were a highly convivial form of transportation and thus well suited for an age in which the predominant form of social organization was still the small town.

So it must be said that, vulgar, crude, predatory, and corrupt as many of the railroad barons were, they created an irresistible world of movement, of power, of speed, of comfort, of glamour. We have spoken earlier of the peculiar joys of being borne along on a canal barge with only the sounds of lapping water, the songs of the birds in the trees along the banks of the canals, and the creaking of the harnesses of the horses or mules that provided the propelling power. The railroad locomotive and its ornate cars were at the other extreme of the spectrum of movement. Noise and rush and power and the endless stream of images: cows and barns and towns and mountains and rivers, factories and mansions and hovels, a dizzy kaleidoscope. Man had never traveled so before.

7

The New Technology

To Henry Adams the story of the age was the story of the creation and utilization of energy, and energy which seemed to him to be dangerously out of control, an energy which, indefinitely multiplied, would, he predicted, someday blow up the world.

We have already noted Adams's views on the role of the railroads as producers and distributors of energy in myriad forms. Another striking form of energy was electricity. Indeed, it might be argued that the most serious rival to the railroads was the generation and distribution of electricity.

The growth of the telegraph was complementary to the growth of the railroads. By the outbreak of the Civil War it had proved itself an extremely valuable adjunct of the railway system.

Of the 12,000 telegraph offices, 9,000 were in railway stations, and when Norvin Green became president of Western Union in 1878, there were already 76,955 miles of wire. Green, a classic jack-of-all-trades, had started life as a grocer, gone to medical school, and mixed in Kentucky politics. As president of Western Union he set out to drive the competition out of business and make his company the exclusive conveyer of telegraphic messages. His principal rivals were the American Union and the Atlantic and Pacific. Green raised Western Union's capitalization to $80,000,000 and simply bought the two companies out. "Successful competition with your company," Green told his directors, "is improbable if not impossible." The company had attained "such magnitude and strength that it is no longer necessary to buy off any opposition," he continued. "Competition may be a popular demand, and it may be good policy on the part of your company to indulge competing lines between principal points. This would not materially interfere with remunerative dividends. . . ."

Green's prescription for creating a monopoly might be taken as the credo of those nineteenth-century capitalists who, like him, headed giant corporations the primary purpose of which was to rationalize the processes of production by driving the competition from the field. By 1883 Western Union owned 400,000 miles of telegraph wire, over which it sent 40,000,000 messages a year; profits rose in a five-year period from $3,500,000 to $7,000,000.

When the telegraph operators went on strike for higher wages in July, 1883, *Harper's Weekly* noted: "The function of the telegraph in our highly organized commercial and social life has come to be as general and as important as that of the mail. In some respects it is even more of a necessity. . . . Not only is it an indispensable instrumentality in ordinary exchanges, but it is absolutely necessary for the safe and sure administration of the railways themselves." The editor chastised the company for showing in its dealings with the operators "something of the same grasping and unscrupulous spirit that it has betrayed in its stock operations." Indifferent to public opinion, or convenience, Western Union refused to negotiate with the strikers, and the strike was broken. One result was a chorus of demands from unions and farmers' organizations that the telegraph system be nationalized. A number of bills were introduced into Congress to place the telegraph companies under the postal system, a move applauded by the postmaster general, who declared: "The mail and telegraph are the life current of business, and to a large extent of social life, and the private monopoly of either system must result in creating a preferred class, to which high rates may not be objectionable. The humbler citizen must do without. . . . The telegraph goes where it can find paying business only; and so it falls out that only a sixtieth part of the people of the United States, owing, not to need, but to the inconvenience and charges, employ the telegraph. . . . The fact is that in some respects the telegraph seems to get farther and farther away as the capital and power of the corporation increase." The invulnerability of Western Union to attacks by champions of the public interest was not diminished by the fact that it extended the privilege of free messages to all Congressmen and many state and municipal politicians.

One of the electrical marvels of the age displayed at the Centennial Exhibition in Philadelphia in 1876 was a telephone, invented by Alexander Graham Bell. When Bell tried to sell his invention to Western Union, it was dismissed as a "toy." Bell and his backers organized their own company and found an ideal manager in Theodore Newton Vail, only thirty-one years old. Vail, born in Ohio, was the cousin of Alfred Vail, who had worked with Samuel F. B. Morse to develop the telegraph and had received the first message on May 24, 1844—"What hath God wrought!" Theodore Vail had entered the Post Office Department in 1873, after having sought his fortune in Iowa and Nebraska. A year later his improvements in the efficiency of the railway mail service had won him promotion to assistant general superintendent of railway mail. Taking charge of the newly formed Bell Telephone Company, Vail made it, in nine years, the most successful of a host of new companies crowding into the field. Western Union, having scorned Bell's toy, turned to another inventor, Elisha Gray, formed the American Speaking Telephone Company, and undertook by every devious and underhanded method to prevent the general adoption of Bell's lines. Political pressures were brought to bear to prevent communities from franchising the Bell system, and bribes and threats were freely employed. Vail brought legal action against the American Speaking Telephone Company for infringement of Bell's patent, and in 1879, in the face of a court decision upholding the Bell patent, the Western Union subsidiary agreed to go out of business and sell its system of 56,000 telephones in fifty-six cities to Bell.

It tells a good deal about the nature of high finance in this period that 587 lawsuits were brought against Bell by individuals and companies anxious to get into the act. Thirteen went as far as the Supreme Court. Although Bell won all the suits, 125 companies were started under the cover of the legal action, and stock to the value of $225,000,000 was sold to gullible purchasers.

Perhaps Vail's most significant accomplishment was his creation of a department devoted to what we call today research and development to improve the instruments and the methods of transmission. He also was an innovator in his insistence on polite and considerate treatment of customers. He introduced the practice of putting telephone wires underground. The use by the Bell Company of copper rather than iron wire, again at Vail's instance, meant that sounds could be transmitted over much greater distances. As a consequence, the use of "long distance" lines, the first one between New York and Boston, soon became common. Virtually every innovation by Vail was resisted by the directors and stockholders of the company. Theodore Vail certainly belongs in the ranks of enlightened businessmen. Every aspect of the company's business he turned his hand to showed the effects of his bold imagination. By the time of his first retirement from the American Bell Telephone Company at the age of forty-two he had created one of the great new corporations that were to dominate the American scene for the next century.

The telegraph and the telephone used relatively little electricity but the development of many other new devices was frustrated by the difficulty of generating electricity in substantial amounts. Charles Brush was a Ohio farm boy whose obsession with chemistry and physics induced his father to send him to the University of Michigan. Later Brush went to Cleveland and set himself up as a chemist in his own laboratory. After four years devoted to improving iron technology, Brush became absorbed in the problem of designing a dynamo that would generate enough direct current to light a number of arc lamps. It was said that Brush, then twenty-six years old, solved the generator problem in two months and then a few weeks later developed an arc lamp that produced an intense light. In a contest among various recently developed dynamos held at Philadelphia's Franklin Institute in 1877 Brush's machine outclassed all others, and the merchant John Wanamaker immediately commissioned him to put his new lights in the windows of Wanamaker's handsome department store on Chestnut Street. Called the Blue Moon because of the color of the arc light, the invention was soon being installed in every progressive community. Cleveland put up two towers 250 feet high to light the central part of the city at night. While the towers were being built in Cleveland, Wabash, Indiana, was persuaded to install the arc lights in place of gas lamps. Four 3,000 candlepower lights were installed on the dome of the courthouse. The effect was described by a reporter for the *Chicago Tribune*, who wrote that he had mounted the courthouse dome, "where he beheld a scene of magnificent splendor. For a mile around, the houses and yards were distinctly visible, while faraway the river flowed like a band of molten silver. . . . Wabash enjoys the distinction of being the only city in the world lighted by electricity," he added. A few spoilsports who suggested that the newfangled lamps produced *too much* light were ignored in the general euphoria.

Elihu Thomson, born in Manchester, England, had been brought to the United States by his parents when he was five. After graduating from Central High School in Philadelphia, he had been given a position as teacher of chemistry at the school, and there he carried on his experiments in electricity, designing a small dynamo that proved a serious rival to Brush's invention. One of his fellow teachers at Central High School was Edwin Houston, who had established the practice of laboratory training in science that distinguished Central from other high schools in Philadelphia and indeed in the country. A group of eager financiers organized the American Electric Company around the two young high school instructors in 1880 (Thomson was twenty-six, and Houston was thirty-two). When the organizers of the new company proved less vigorous in promoting their invention than the two young men wished, they joined forces with a Lynn, Massachusetts, shoe manufacturer named Charles Coffin under the name of the Thomson-Houston Electric Company. An initial capitalization of $250,000 grew to $10,000,000 in a period of nine years.

Thomas Alva Edison had already made a name for himself as an inventor. Born in 1847 in the small Midwestern town of Milan, Ohio, Edison had been an indifferent student but a boy with an intense interest in chemistry and an almost equally precocious business instinct that had him selling newspapers and candy on the railroad trains that passed through Port Huron, Michigan, before he was out of short pants. He was a telegraph operator at the age of sixteen and went to work for the Boston office of Western Union at the age of twenty-one. A year later he patented his first invention, an electrographic vote recorder, which was followed soon afterward by an improved stock-ticker. Lured to New York by the hope of making his fortune, young Edison found two congenial spirits with similar interests and started an electrical engineering business. When he sold out his interest two years later, he had money enough to set up his own laboratory with a group of young experimental scientists and engineers. They all were talented and ambitious young men, well aware of the relationship of practical research to the rapidly expanding world of industrial technology. A whole series of inventions and improvements flowed from the laboratory at Menlo Park, New Jersey, including a carbon transmitter for the infant telephone and, a year later, Edison's most famous invention, the phonograph.

Neither Brush nor Thomson-Houston arc lamps were suited for indoor illumination. An incandescent light had already been invented, but it was severely handicapped by the fact that no long-lasting filament had been developed. Edison set himself to solving this problem. "I have let other inventors get the start of me in the matter somewhat," he told a reporter, "because I have not given much attention to electric lights, but I believe I can catch up to them now." The offhand words were the perfect expression of the ethic of the new age. "If you can make the electric light supply the place of gas, you can easily make a great fortune," the reporter said. To this Edison gave a classic reply: "I don't care so much for a fortune as I do for getting ahead of the other fellow." That was the American spirit! Edison was both the last of the tinkerer-inventors who triumphed through sheer persistence and one of the first representatives of organized research. It is also evident that he had an instinctive gift for discreet self-promotion. He was ready-made to be the archetypal hero of the new age.

On the eve of the election of 1880, Edison hung a string of his improved electric lights in front of his house and told an assistant: "If Garfield is elected, light up that circuit. . . ." When news of James Garfield's election was received, the lights blazed out. With such evidence, the banking house of Drexel, Morgan & Company organized the Edison Illuminating Company. The first use of incandescent lights came in New York City on September 4, 1882, in what was known as the Pearl Street Station, the name of the generating plant that provided the electricity. Edison supervised every detail of the installation of the system as well as designed most of the elements in it and then, at the appointed moment, "swallowed my heart," he later wrote, "and gave the word." The system worked. Brush now had a serious rival. Edison's incandescent lamp was far more versatile than Brush's arc lamp. Both ran on direct current, which could be transmitted for the distance of only a mile or so from a generating plant. New York needed, for example, some sixty generating stations. A French inventor named Gaulard had discovered that, with the use of secondary "generators" or transmitters, electric current could be sent a considerable distance. Elihu Thomson, hearing of this development, set to work designing an "alternating-current dynamo," a notion which so appealed to the inventor of the railroad air brake, George Westinghouse, that he immediately became an exponent and financial backer of the new system.

Westinghouse, son of a prosperous manufacturer of farm implements, was another boy genius. He had served at the age of sixteen in both the Union army and the navy. After the war he went to work for his father and at the age of nineteen obtained his first patent for a rotary steam engine. There followed a series of inventions, most designed to improve the safety of railroad operation, culminating in the air brake, patented when he was twenty-three. Backing for the Westinghouse Air Brake Company was readily available, and Westinghouse followed his initial patent with dozens more, solidifying his position both as a practical inventor and as a genius at organization and production. As ingenious as Eli Whitney, he set about to make all air brakes standard and interchangeable. To develop a system of railroad signals, he organized the Union Switch and Signal Company.

The moment when George Westinghouse joined forces with Elihu Thomson to promote alternating current was as significant, in its own way, as that famous instant twenty-two years earlier when Morse had sent his first message from Washington to Baltimore. To prove that alternating current with its much higher voltages was dangerous to the public, the direct current advocates conducted public demonstrations at which horses and calves were electrocuted before enthralled audiences. In Westinghouse's words, "the struggle for the control of the electric light and power business has never been exceeded in bitterness by any of the historical commercial controversies of a former day. Thousands of persons have large pecuniary interests at stake, and, as might be expected, many of them view this great subject solely from the stand-point of self-interest." The future was with Westinghouse. There were 8 central alternating current power stations in 1881; by the end of the century there were almost 3,000.

The next field to attract inventors and investors was the electric street railroad. Both Edison and Thomson turned their attention to the problem without notable success. It was left for an Englishman named Leo Daft and a Belgian immigrant named Charles Van Depoele to make the most practical electric cars. In Chicago in September, 1883, Van Depoele gave a demonstration "of a spring pressed under running trolley," the electric motors of which were driven by electricity drawn from an overhead wire. It was Daft, however, who installed the first working system in Baltimore two years later. Soon orders poured in from towns and cities anxious to be in the forefront of the new method of urban transportation.

Frank Julian Sprague, born in Thetford, Connecticut, and graduated from the Naval Academy in Annapolis, had demonstrated a precocious interest in the practical uses of electricity, especially the improvement of electric motors. After working for a few months in Edison's laboratory, Sprague organized the Sprague Electric Railway and Motor Company. In 1887 he got an opportunity to try out his own ideas for an electric railway in Richmond, Virginia, on a route twelve miles long. Sprague, who had just turned thirty, put a successful line using forty cars into operation in less than a year. Boston followed Richmond, and the age of the electric trolley was born. The Edison

Company bought out the Sprague Electric Railway and Motor Company, and the Thomson-Houston Electric Company bought out Van Depoele. (It was Van Depoele who suggested the use of carbon in the blocks of electrical engines, an innovation which Elihu Thomson generously called "the most important invention ever made in the electric railway field.")

The first use for crude oil, the reader may recall, was for medicinal purposes. A brand called Seneca Oil was advertised as follows:

> The healthful balm, from nature's secret spring
> The bloom of health and life to man will bring
> As from her depths the magic liquid flows,
> To calm our sufferings and assuage our woes.

Railroads and electric power companies found a rival in the oil and gas industry. The use of electricity for lighting, indoor and out, developed slowly. Meanwhile, the demand for gas grew astronomically as more and more uses were developed for it. Wells were discovered in such abundance that a single well drilled near Pittsburgh produced gas equal to 1,200 tons of coal a day. Six hundred miles of pipe carried natural gas from the wells to Pittsburgh and Allegheny City. The gas running to waste within piping distance of Pittsburgh was estimated at 70,000,000 cubic feet a day.

Sam Fox, an in-law of Sidney George Fisher, had invested $200 in an oil company and sold his shares a year later for $44,000. "The oil of Penna.," Fisher wrote, "has added immensely to the wealth of the state, almost as much as coal or iron. It has been discovered in many places west of the mountains, hundreds of companies have been formed to make wells, many of which have been successful & some individuals have made enormous fortunes."

Andrew Carnegie and several of his associates bought a farm, on which oil had been found, for $40,000. The partners decided to dig a pond to hold 100,000 barrels of oil, all they assumed the well could produce. There was far more oil than they had calculated. The value of the farm rose to $5,000,000, and in one year it paid "cash dividends of $1,000,000." For a time there was a glut of oil. There were indeed not enough tank cars to move it. Pipes were laid, and by 1884, sixty-two hundred miles of pipe carried oil from more than 200 wells. A barrel could be pumped from the Pennsylvania oil fields to an Atlantic port at a cost of ten cents a barrel. The field was yielding 70,000 barrels a day in 1884, and the value of petroleum products *exported* up to January, 1884, had exceeded $625,000,000 in value. So it went in virtually every mineral resource: iron ore, silver, zinc, lead, coal (it was estimated that the United States contained 300,000 cubic miles of coal, three-quarters of all the coal in the world). Recounting such figures, Andrew Carnegie, in *Triumphant Democracy*, added, "Thank God, these treasures are in the hands of an intelligent people, the Democracy, to be used for the general good of the masses, and not . . . turned to the base and selfish ends of a privileged hereditary class. . . . The weakest nation may rest secure . . . for the nature of a government of the people is to abjure conquest, to protect the weak neighbor from foreign aggression if need be; never to molest, but dwell in peace and loving neighborliness with all."

Since we have attended to men and women in every sphere of American life who have shown unusual devotion to the public good, it seems incumbent to find a capitalist hero, and no nineteenth-century tycoon has better claim to such laurels than Andrew Carnegie. Starting out as a young immigrant working as a bobbin boy in a textile factory at $1.50 a week, Carnegie rose, in the course of eleven years, to the office of the assistant to the superintendent of the western division of the Pennsylvania Railroad with the substantial salary of $2,400 a year. In the interval, by shrewd investments, he had acquired an additional yearly income of $47,860. Most of his money was invested in iron foundries since the railroads were insatiable in their demand for iron to construct bridges. In 1872 Carnegie observed the Bessemer process of making steel and had a minor revelation. The day of iron was over, and the day of steel had arrived. Carnegie built a steel mill which he called the Edgar Thomson Steel Works. A few years after it had begun operation, the mill was earning as much as 40 percent a year on Carnegie's original investment. By 1880 it and an adjacent iron mill brought in more than $2,000,000 a year. Carnegie prided himself on his paternalistic attitude toward his workers. More important, he listened to them and took their grievances seriously. One of the most persistent complaints of factory and railroad workers was that they were paid on a monthly basis and often very irregularly at that. One of Carnegie's employees told him: "I have a good woman for wife who manages well. We go into Pittsburgh every fourth Saturday afternoon and buy our supplies wholesale for the next month and save one third. Not many of your men can do this. Shopkeepers here charge so much. . . . If you paid your men every two weeks, instead of monthly, it would be as good for the careful men as a raise in wages of ten per cent or more." Carnegie, who had already instituted the eight-hour day, did as his workman suggested and, in addition, helped the men in his plants organize cooperative stores and sold them coal for their own use at cost.

While Carnegie talked in a relatively enlightened fashion about the welfare of his workers, he applied to them the same policy of cost control that he insisted on in all elements of the process of production. He bought iron ore mines in the Mesabi Range, railroad lines, coke and limestone furnaces, and Great Lakes ore ships. He was, in all his relations, highly opportunistic. While many of his rivals or fellow entrepreneurs fought *on principle* to bar unions or break strikes, Carnegie's question was invariably "How can I handle this crisis in such a manner as to cause the least interruption in production and the least loss to the company?" Perhaps the only exception to this policy was in his disavowal of the use of scabs or strikebreakers. Ironically, it was the attempted use of strikebreakers by Carnegie's general manager, Henry Frick, that precipitated the Homestead warfare of 1892, one result of which was the destruction of the Amalgamated Association of Iron and Steel Workers.

Carnegie's attention to every detail of plant operation meant that year after year through good times and bad the Edgar Thomson Steel Company (reorganized in 1881 into Carnegie Brothers and Company, Ltd.) and its associated enterprises showed large profits and issued generous dividends when his rivals lost heavily or went bankrupt.

By 1900, when he reorganized the companies simply as the Carnegie Company, the value of his properties had risen 500 times from his initial investment in 1873. In the decade from 1890 to 1900 annual profits increased from $5,400,000 to $40,000,000.

Carnegie's genius lay in developing in iron and steel production the same kind of interrelationships between different units of production that were being developed so effectively in the oil business by John D. Rockefeller. He also had his own sources of funds from his partners and associates, from bond issues, and from his own capital accumulation. In addition, he was endlessly resourceful in lowering the costs of production (a drive which was, of course, in sharp opposition to his avowed purpose of treating his workers fairly). In thirteen years he lowered the cost of producing steel rails, for example, from $57 per ton to $28. "If there be in human society," he wrote, "one truth clearer and more indisputable than another it is that the cheapening of articles ... insures their general distribution. ... Now the cheapening of all these good things ... is rendered possible only through the operation of the law, which may be stated thus: Cheapness is in proportion to the scale of production."

Carnegie's plant manager told a group of touring British steelmakers, astonished at the superior productivity of the American mill to its British counterparts, that the plant's success was due, in large part, to the speedy adoption of the latest European discoveries in metallurgy; the high morale of the workers, who were ambitious young men of a variety of nationalities; and the institution of an eight-hour day. As we have noted, Carnegie led the way in the use of the Bessemer process, and the output of that steel made in the United States increased from a mere 30,500 tons in 1870 to 850,000 tons ten years later. As distinguished from the virtually monopolistic conditions in the oil industry brought about by Standard Oil's domination, hundreds of steel mills sprang up all over the country, 1,005 according to the census of 1880. The closest the steel industry came to a monopoly was through Carnegie's acquisition of Henry Frick's coke ovens in the Connellsville region of Pennsylvania. Frick, to whom Carnegie turned over the management of his American interests, was the antithesis of Carnegie. While the ebullient Scotsman overflowed with high spirits and philanthropic impulses, Frick was the prototype of the cold, calculating capitalist, hostile to the claims of his workers, secure in his conviction that God had appointed him and his fellows to run the United States in their own best interests.

Iron was produced principally in Pennsylvania, primarily around the Pittsburgh area, and in New York and Michigan. In the 1880s Charlemagne Tower, a Philadelphian, opened up new fields in the Vermilion Range in Minnesota, and soon Texas, Wyoming, Missouri, California, and Colorado were producing large quantities of iron and coal. In Birmingham, Alabama, the discovery of large deposits of coal, iron ore, dolomite, and lime led to the founding of eight new companies involved in the manufacturing of iron products, and, increasingly, steel. By 1884 America produced one-fifth of the world's iron and one-fourth of its steel. In the manufacture of Bessemer steel the United States led the world—1,250,000 tons annually.

Brooks Adams picked 1897 as the most decisive date in modern history because it was then, by his interpretation, that the American steelmakers, meeting in Pittsburgh, established the hegemony of the United States iron and steel industry over the rest of the industrialized world. It was the moment of the inauguration of "the New Empire."

In 1874 the invention by Joseph Glidden of an improved form of barbed-wire fencing created another vast industry and changed the economy and, eventually, the geography of the West. John W. ("Bet-a-Million") Gates was one of the enterprising spirits who was determined to get in on the barbed-wire bonanza. By 1898 Gates had formed the American Steel and Wire Company of New Jersey, capitalized at $90,000,000 and including the greater portion of the wiremakers. J. Pierpont Morgan followed suit with the organization of the Federal Steel Company, capitalized at $100,000,000.

In textiles the story was much the same—constantly growing production with products to the value of billions of dollars. While the number of mills increased, the size of the average mill grew much more rapidly, and the productivity of the individual worker was much increased through the use of improved machines. Carpetmaking was one of the fastest growing of all industries. In 1860 the United States had imported most of its carpets; twenty years later the carpet manufactured in and around Philadelphia alone exceeded the output of Great Britain.

In the shoe and boot industry the improvement of machines made it possible for one man to turn out 300 pairs of shoes a day; one Massachusetts factory produced as many boots in a year as the 32,000 bootmakers of Paris. Again the movement was unmistakably toward larger units of production. In 1870 there were 3,151 bootmaking establishments employing 91,702 workers. Ten years later the number of factories had declined to 1,951 and the number of workers had increased by 20,000. More efficient machines resulted in an increase in production of 41 percent while the increase in the number of workers was only 20 percent.

If the industrial and railroad barons were predominantly from New England and the Eastern and the Middle Atlantic states, especially such cities as New York and Philadelphia, the mining barons or Bonanza Kings, as they were commonly called, were much more diverse in their origins. A study of the origins of 222 leading entrepreneurs in various fields ranging from railroads to steel mills in the period of 1870–1879 showed that 89 percent were of New England or Middle Atlantic origins (57 percent New England, 32 percent Middle Atlantic, and only 3 percent from the South). A similar study of the origins of "mining leaders" showed 54 percent from the New England-Middle Atlantic region and 23 percent from the South. Many of the Bonanza

Kings had origins that could accurately be described as poor. The reason was, at least in part, that a miner might start out, and often did, as an individual prospector and placer miner. If he found a promising lode, the possibilities of obtaining capital to develop it were reasonably good. The commonest way was perhaps through the issuance of stock. It can be safely said that in an age of wildly fluctuating stock, mining stock underwent the most remarkable fluctuations of all. Stock issued at $10 a share (a high price) might drop to $1 a share with word that the productivity of a mine had been greatly overestimated or zoom up to $700 or $800 a share if the mine looked like a bonanza. Jesse Knight was a Utah Mormon who became one of the richest silver miners in the country. As a boy Knight "knew nothing much but hardships such as herding cows barefoot, gathering pigweed and sego roots as a help toward the family's meager food supply," and wearing "coarse homespun cloth, sacks and madeover clothes of all kinds." Although Joseph De Lamar's father was a banker, he had died when Joseph was six, and Joseph had had to make his way in the world from an early age. Half of the forty-seven leading miners whose origins were studied by the historian Richard Peterson had started to earn their livings by the time they were fifteen. An exception was James Haggin, whose partnership with George Hearst laid the base for two great fortunes; Haggin was the son of a Kentucky lawyer and had attended college in a day when relatively few Americans had that opportunity.

It was clearly not in prospecting that the hope of riches lay. The prospectors themselves were classic individualists, restless, nomadic types who, if they made a strike, were disposed to sell it for whatever they could get and move on. The Bonanza Kings were, almost without exception, men of a very different stripe, men whose talents were organizational, men of the new age, shrewd, enterprising, often ruthless, increasingly well versed in the newest methods of large-scale mining and knowledgeable about the dramatically developing field of metallurgy.

More common was what we might call the mining developer, who bought up various claims in what might appear as a promising area, combined them, and brought in the capital to establish a large-scale mining operation employing the most up-to-date technology. In 1872 George Hearst, who had prospered in California and then moved his operations eastward to Utah and Nevada, purchased the Ontario mine at Park City, Utah, for $27,000. After Hearst had extinguished adjacent claims, he began large-scale production, and in fourteen years the mine paid out $12,425,000 in dividends, a major part of which found its way into Hearst's own coffers. In addition, Hearst acquired the Ophir mine in Nevada, the Homestake in South Dakota, and, eventually, the Anaconda copper mine at Butte, Montana.

Thomas Kearns worked for Hearst's Ontario Mining Company at Park City for six years as a shiftman, meanwhile studying geology and mineralogy. Then, with a partner, he contracted to run an exploratory tunnel for the Woodside Mining Company. In the course of excavating the tunnel, he discovered a vein that led into a claim owned by the Mayflower Mining Company. He then secured a lease on that claim and soon found silver and lead in substantial quantities. In working the Mayflower mine, Kearns and his partners found that the main vein went in the direction of the Silver King mine. They immediately bought a controlling interest in Silver King, which became one of the great bonanza mines of the West. If Kearns did not, strictly speaking, steal his millions in silver and lead, he certainly acquired them by ethically dubious means, yet the methods, however questionable, were those of the region and those of the age.

Dennis Sheedy began his mining career as a placer miner, working a claim which brought him $300 or $400 a day until, tired of the unceasing toil, he sold it for $2,200 and took up the life of a merchant and freighter. When he decided, in the late 1880s, to go back into mining, he undertook, by his own account, "three years of incessant study. . . . I read every book upon the subject obtainable, gaining a technical as well as a practical knowledge of the business." Organizing the Globe Smelting and Refining Company, Sheedy took over a mining operation that was bringing in to its investors some $200,000 a year and by improved methods of smelting increased its yearly output to $16,000,000 in less than two decades.

Some of the Bonanza Kings, of course, began their careers by grubstaking dirt miners in return for a share of whatever ore they might discover. Horace Tabor and his wife began their life in Leadville, Colorado, in this fashion. Tabor grubstaked two prospectors to $64 worth of credit in return for one-third interest in whatever their prospecting might turn up. In 1878 they hit a vein of silver ore which came to be known as the Little Pittsburgh mine. Tabor bought out the prospectors and after two years of mining sold the Little Pittsburgh for $1,000,000.

When four Irishmen bought up the stock of the Consolidated Virginia mine in 1871, it was selling at $2 a share. They acquired the mine for $80,000 and sank shafts at 500 and 1,167 feet. When one vein ran into the nearby holding of the California Mining Company, the stock of which was selling at $37 a share, they acquired control of that mine, whereupon its stock rose to $780. The so-called Big Bonanza produced in nine years silver worth $105,168,859. The sixty or so mines that made up the Comstock produced in a twenty-year period almost $300,000,000 in ores.

It is impossible to convey an adequate sense of the chaotic conditions in mining in regard to disputed claims. A whole legal industry grew up around the cynical and systematic corruption of the courts through false claims that were in effect a form of blackmail. Many mineowners found it cheaper to pay off such claims than to litigate them before judges of highly questionable honesty. Litigation over conflicting claims on the Comstock lode cost more than $10,000,000 in legal fees alone. In the words of a newspaper editor: "The trouble was really not so much that they [the judges] were corrupt, for that was a point of which all parties were only too ready to take advantage, but that they would not stay bought—a fact that entirely demoralized the game and made it the most chancy one ever known, whereas litigants felt there should be some certainty even in buying judges. There was no effected coyness or shyness on the part of the judges. They sent out their brokers and demanded a specific amount as the price of a favorable decision." Witnesses were also bought and sold. "No facts were so clear and well established," wrote one observer, "that they could not be controverted by a troop of hired liars. . . ."

Rival mineowners hired undercover agents to work for their competitors and steal whatever information they could about their production methods and hired Pinkerton agents to spy on their own workers and report those who seemed disposed to make trouble for the owners by demanding higher wages or less hazardous working conditions. A mineowner named Clement wrote to a partner: "I have not yet made terms with the . . . witnesses—I offered them $1,000—for their testimony, but would not accept—I expect they will come to terms after a while." Clement was indignant when he discovered that the witnesses had been offered more by his adversary and complained about the "depraved moral state of the country: Who is it that you can trust," he wrote plaintively, "but after receiving your money is ready to sell you to the next man?"

Of all the ways in which men have served Adam's punishment for disobedience in the Garden—"in the sweat of thy face shalt thou eat bread"—none has been stranger than that of the miner who descends into the depths of the earth, the land in classical mythology of departed spirits, a place of darkness, gloom and often terror.

The Rise of the Trusts

The greatest problem encountered by the "national" industries that sprang up like mushrooms to take advantage of the new technologies and the new materials and methods of marketing available was the instability of prices. The development of a new product for which there was a widespread public demand meant that hundreds of entrepreneurs rushed into the field, eager to make their fortunes or increase fortunes already made. The result was frequently a glut of products and a consequent disastrous fall in prices. Since combinations were forbidden by law, certain industries began to form "pools" of the principal manufacturers with an eye toward limiting production and maintaining high price levels. The best-known pool (all conducted their marketing and price-fixing agreements in secret) was the Michigan Salt Association. Actually the association was a kind of management and holding company the purpose of which was to stabilize (at the highest acceptable level) the price of salt. Because the enterprise was efficiently and fairly managed, it had the effect of lowering the current price of salt while preventing the fluctuations in price that had plagued the industry. The salt association was thus a classic example of an effort by producers to rationalize the methods of production and, more important, of marketing. With the development of national markets, made possible by the extension of railroad lines to every corner of the country, the pressure within particular industries to take such measures grew stronger with every passing year. It was evident that there were, as in the case of the Michigan Salt Association, prospective benefits to the consumer as well as to the producer. The danger was that once prices had been stabilized, constituting in effect a monopoly, the manufacturers would set them at a level which gave them excessive profits at the expense of the consumers and protected inefficient producers as well, thereby imposing an invisible tax on the users of the product. Equally important, the practice violated the venerable principle of free competition, constantly proclaimed as the heart and soul of the American economic system. As we shall see, the dilemma was not resolved then or later. In every decade giant national corporations have conspired to maintain prices at levels higher than those which would result from free competition, and Congress or its appointed agencies have taken belated and often reluctant action to prevent such agreements or to punish (usually mildly enough) those who were parties to them.

What had been done in the salt industry was soon attempted by the manufacturers of cordage, wallpaper, and paint. The Distillers and Cattle Feeders Trust was another effort to form an industry-wide combination. The National Biscuit Company came to control 90 percent of the crackers of the country. Cottonseed and linseed oil trusts were also formed, along with a sugar trust. Of the latter, a U.S. district court judge declared that it "can close every refinery at will, close some and open others . . . artificially limit the production of refined sugar, enhance the price to enrich themselves and their associates at the public expense, and depress the price when necessary to crush out, and impoverish a foolhardy rival."

But it was John D. Rockefeller who blazed the trail, followed by those shrewd and ruthless enough to emulate him. His instrument was the Standard Oil Company of Ohio, and his means were the buying up and squeezing out of rivals by every device at hand—legal or illegal—until Standard Oil had acquired at least seventy-four refineries and controlled in 1878 more than 90 percent of the oil production of the country. In addition to controlling the refineries, Rockefeller controlled the pipelines through which the oil flowed from the wells to the refineries. In 1879 he and seven of his associates were indicted for conspiracy to create a monopoly; but the case bogged down in legal wrangles, and Rockefeller got off scot-free. He at once turned his attention to forming a trust as a means to circumventing the prohibitions against pools. Under the terms of the trust, the various components of the parent company agreed to be governed by nine trustees to whom all the stock of the affiliated companies was consigned and who received in return "trust certificates."

The principal challenger of the Standard Oil Company turned out to be the Tidewater Pipe Line Company, which undertook to lay a pipe over the Allegheny Mountains from the Bradford oil field to a railhead of the Reading Railroad, a distance of 109 miles. Standard Oil fought Tidewater Pipe Line every mile of the way, and by 1883 the smaller company, its resources exhausted, had been absorbed by Rockefeller. What is perhaps worth noting about the long and, for the most part, sordid story of Standard Oil's fight to drive all competitors from the field was that it displayed, more dramatically (and successfully) than any other such struggle the strength of the impulse to rationalize and integrate all aspects of production. It was, indeed, as though a kind of natural law were at work, a law, as the tycoons themselves, of course, liked to think, akin to, or perhaps even a manifestation of, the Darwinian law of survival. Not only did the strongest, the most ruthless, and, it might be said, the most brilliant survive, but centralization seemed to have its own strange momentum. So much did that appear to be the case that Brooks Adams, pondering on a "law of civilization and decay," decided that the tendency of all great civilizations was toward the centralization of all political and economic power. The process of centralization created new quantums of power, which power in turn led to the illusion of omnipotence and thereby to arrogance, decadence, bureaucratic inefficiency, impotence, and destruction by newer and more vigorous invaders or rivals. Adams wrote a book to make the point.

The disposition of the trusts to form was initially counterbalanced by the determination of the states to thwart such efforts. New York, for example, sued a branch of the sugar trust that operated in the state for violating its antitrust laws, and the state court, deciding in favor of "the people of the State of New York," declared that there should be "no partnerships of separate and independent corporations, whether directly or indirectly, through the medium of the trust" but that "manufacturing corporations must be and remain several, as they were created. . . ." The response of the sugar trust was to find another corporate structure so that two years later, under the name of the American Sugar Refining Company, it controlled some 85 percent of the nation's sugar production.

The attorney general of New York, David Watson, decided that the Standard Oil Company of Ohio was also in violation of the state's antitrust laws. Every effort was made by Standard Oil to prevent Watson from bringing the case to trial, including, it was said, bribes and intimidation. Joseph Choate, the foremost corporation lawyer of his day, was counsel for Standard Oil. He based his defense on "the absolute innocence and absolute merit of everything we have done within the scope of the matters brought before the court. . . ." The court found against Standard Oil. In a verdict that carried an echo of William Manning's doctrine of original sin, the judges declared: "Experience shows that it is not wise to trust human cupidity where it has the opportunity to aggrandize itself at the expense of others. . . . A society in which a few men are the employers and a great body of men are merely employed or servants is not the most desirable in a republic; and it should be as much the policy of the laws to multiply the numbers engaged in independent pursuits, or in the profits or production, as to cheapen the price to the consumers." Like the directors of the sugar trust, the nine men who ran the affairs of Standard Oil quickly found a way around the court's decision by assuming the name of "liquidating trustees," under which rubric they continued to run the twenty-some identifiable entities that constituted Standard Oil of Ohio.

The effort to introduce an element of predictability and control into an essentially chaotic situation was an understandable one, welcomed by all those units to the operations of which it brought a degree of order and stability. At the same time the concentration of so much power and the opportunity it brought to increase profits by manipulating prices often proved irresistible. The fact is that "busting the trusts" may have been, like the long and bitter contention over tariffs and the war between the advocates of cheap and of hard money, a false issue in the sense that trusts or combinations in one form or another were simply a necessity if many industries were to survive.

A new development followed on the formation of huge corporations that periodically needed access to large amounts of capital. Not surprisingly, the bankers and financiers now came to the fore in what might be called Phase II of the history of nineteenth-century capitalism. It was perhaps inevitable that those who controlled the money supply should come in time to exercise a strong and often predominant influence on the corporations they financed. The result was that the entrepreneurial daring which had distinguished Phase I gave way to fiscal conservatism. When the Depression of 1893 put the Westinghouse Electric Company in jeopardy and Westinghouse applied for a loan, the bankers tried to tell him how to run his company and chastised him for putting too much money into experimentation and the buying of patents. Westinghouse rejected the bankers' interference and finally secured money with no strings attached from August Belmont. But the moment was heavy with portent. Other entrepreneurs less determined or less fortunate than Westinghouse found that they were, increasingly, dictated to by the "moneymen."

While the states had been active since the 1870s in passing legislation designed to restrain the more predatory of the trusts, Congress had been slow to act, in large part, it was said, because the Senate belonged to the "interests." Certainly it was true that time after time legislation drafted in the House to clip the wings of the great corporations and trusts was defeated in the Senate, and it was this fact, more than any other, that gave rise to demands that the Senators, like the Representatives, be elected directly. Many reformers saw direct election as the only hope of retrieving the upper house from the grip of Standard Oil et al.

In 1888 Senator John Sherman of Ohio introduced a bill "to declare unlawful trusts and combinations in the restraint of trade and production." He did not intend his legislation to inhibit the states in imposing their own constraints, he insisted. The state courts were "limited in their jurisdiction to the state," he pointed out, "and, in our complex system of government, are admitted to be unable to deal with the great evil that now threatens us." Senator George Hoar, a member of the Senate Finance Committee, undertook to rewrite the bill, which emerged in 1890. The resulting legislation was more Hoar's than Sherman's. That Hoar was disconcerted at having Sherman's name attached to it is clear from his complaint: It was called "the Sherman Act for no other reason that I can think of except that Mr. Sherman had nothing to do with framing it whatever." To Hoar "the accumulation in this country of vast fortunes in single hands" was a "grave evil" and "the most important question before the American people demanding solution in the immediate future." When he wrote his autobiography in 1902, it seemed clear that his bill had not accomplished its intended purpose: "[The] evil has increased rapidly during the last twelve years," he wrote.

After the passage of the Hoar-Sherman Act twenty-five new trusts were formed within five years.

Coincident with the rise of the trusts and the emergence of the great banking houses with their inherent conservatism that placed a far greater emphasis on profits than on technological innovation, there developed what we might call the ideology of capitalism, a set of theoretical propositions which, in simplest terms, sought to give moral justification for the economic and financial activities of capitalists. Inherent in the ideology of capitalism was the conviction that the "dangerous classes," primarily the rapidly growing company of industrial workers, an increasing proportion of them immigrants, were inferior beings, fortunate to receive whatever meager wages their employers chose to give them. Any effort on the part of workers to join forces in an effort to raise their wages or improve their commonly horrendous working conditions was at once denounced as a conspiracy (usually attributed to foreign communists) designed to deprive employers of the free use of their property. James McCosh, professor of philosophy at Princeton, wrote in *Our Moral Nature*, published in 1892: "God has bestowed upon us certain powers and gifts which no one is at liberty to take from us or interfere with. All attempts to deprive us of them is theft. Under the same head may be placed all purposes to deprive us of the right to earn property or to use it as we see fit."

Mark Hopkins, president of Williams College, took much the same line. "The Right to Property," he wrote in 1868, "reveals itself through an original desire. The affirmation of it is early and universally made, and becomes a controlling element in civil society. . . . Without this society could not exist. . . . The acquisition of property is required by love, because it is a powerful means of benefiting others. . . ."

Sidney George Fisher the elder was dismayed by his brother-in-law Charles Ingersoll's support for making "8 hours a legal day's work." The whole notion seemed to him "ludicrously absurd. . . . In 'old times' it was 15, then 12, more recently 10, and now the laboring people, stimulated by high wages and the consciousness of power caused by the great demand for labor in all departments, ask 8 hours with the same wages paid for 10. They demand a law to this effect and denounce any one who opposes them as a monarchist and an enemy to Republican Liberty." In Fisher's view, it was clear that "high wages are generally a curse, not to society merely but to the laborer. Their effect is idleness, dissipation, insolence to employers, riots, and violence. Very few are found to save their earnings and accumulate property, but they spend recklessly and at the end of the year are as poor as ever."

According to the journalist and reformer, Frederic Howe, the businessman's creed ran something like this: "By the superior intelligence of the employer a certain amount of wealth is produced, of which capital gets less if labor gets more. Without the employers labor would starve. Organized labor is the enemy of capital. Strike-leaders must be gotten out of the way, by bribery or otherwise. Free immigration provides a labor surplus. Immigrants can be worked twelve hours a day; by mixing nationalities they can be hindered from organizing; when they are maimed or worn out, others take their places. They need not be supported during hard times; when injured they can be sent to hospitals for repair. . . . Shorter hours in the factory mean longer hours in the saloon. When men drink they come late to work on Monday or do not come at all. They spend less time in the wholesome atmosphere of the steel-mill and the coal mine. The saloon is a menace to efficiency; therefore it should be closed."

A writer in the generally liberal *Atlantic Monthly* noted in the depression years of the 1870s: "When we consider the enormous shrinkage that has taken place in the value of almost all kinds of property . . . we see no evidence that labor has suffered disproportionately to other interests. . . . It is divinely ordained that man, in common with other animate beings, shall struggle for existence . . . the relations of capital and labor must necessarily conform to the divine scheme."

Jay Gould was said to have declared that his solution to the labor problem would be to dare "one half of the working class to kill the other half," and a conservative spokesman told a sympathetic audience at Chicago's Union League that working-class Americans needed to cultivate more of "the quiet submissiveness of the Chinese to offset nihilism!" Asa Candler, a pioneer manufacturer of soft drinks, loved to see little children at work. "The most beautiful sight we see is the child at labor; as early as he may get at labor the more beautiful, the more useful does his life become."

Andrew Carnegie, the celebrator of all things American, was, not surprisingly, an ardent exponent of capitalism, but he confessed himself troubled by the increasingly bitter war between capital and labor. "The problem of our age," he wrote in an article that appeared in the *North American Review*, "is the proper administration of wealth, so that the ties of brotherhood may still bind together the rich and the poor in harmonious relationship." Life had been "revolutionized" in the preceding centuries. "The contrast between the palace of the millionaire and the cottage of the laborer . . . to-day measures the change that has come with civilization." Much had undoubtedly been lost, but it was, Carnegie told his readers, futile to lament. What had happened had happened as the result of certain "laws" which could no more be evaded than the march of the seasons. The old relations between master and apprentice had been torn asunder. "We assemble thousands of operatives in the factory, in the mine, and in the counting-house, of whom the employers can know little or nothing, and to whom the employer is little better than a myth. All intercourse between them is at an end. Rigid castes are formed, and, as usual, mutual ignorance breeds mutual distrust . . . often there is friction between the employer and the employed, between capital and labor, between rich and poor. Human society loses homogeneity."

Similarly society paid a high price for the "law of competition," but the rewards were greater than the costs, "for it is to this law that we owe our wonderful material development, which brings improved conditions in its train. . . . While the law may be sometimes hard for the individual, it is best for the race, because it insures the survival of the fittest in every department." Great inequality of income, the concentration of business in the hands of a few, and competition between these were thus not only "beneficial but essential for the future progress of the race." Various substitutes had, to be sure, been proposed, but to Carnegie, "the Socialist or Anarchist who seeks to overturn present conditions is to be regarded as attacking the foundations upon which civilization itself rests." The right of the workman to his $100 was as sacred as the right of the millionaire to his millions. "To those who proposed to substitute Communism for this intense Individualism the answer, therefore, is: The race has tried that. All progress from the barbarous day to the present has resulted from its displacement." Those who favored cooperation as opposed to competition in effect favored "the destruction of Individualism, Private Property and the Law of Accumulation, and the Law of Competition; for these are the highest results of human experience, the soil in which society has produced the best fruit." The real question then was not how to change the system that had produced such benefits but, rather, "the administration of wealth" in such a way as to make it a force for public good and a means of reconciliation of the poor to the rich. The way to accomplish this was clearly for the wealthy to use their millions, over and above what was needed for living in a comfortable but not ostentatious style, for the common good. Instead of leaving great fortunes to their children, which would only corrupt them, millionaires should, like Peter Cooper, use their wealth to raise the moral and intellectual level of the masses. Carnegie applauded the "growing disposition to tax more and more heavily large estates left at death" as a "cheering indication" of a change in public opinion. "By taxing estates heavily at death the state marks its condemnation of the selfish millionaire's unworthy life." Such a policy, Carnegie argued, was far superior to the remedies proposed by communism which could not in any event work because they were against the fundamental "laws" which governed the progress of society. Of the rise of the new philanthropy, Carnegie wrote: "We shall have an ideal state, in which the surplus wealth of the few will become, in the best sense, the property of the many, because administered for the common good, and this wealth, passing through the hands of the few, can be a much more potent force for the elevation of our race than if it had been distributed in small sums to the people themselves."

In Carnegie's view, a friend of his who gave a quarter to a beggar was defying the principles of Herbert Spencer and thus doing incalculable damage—one of "the very worst actions of his life." Carnegie offered as models for millionaires Peter Cooper; Enoch Pratt of Baltimore, who gave the city a library; Senator Leland Stanford, who gave California a college, and "others, who know that the best means of benefiting the community is to place within its reach the ladders upon which the aspiring can rise—parks and means of recreation, by which men are helped in body and mind; works of art, certain to give pleasure and improve the public taste, and public institutions of various kinds, which will improve the general condition of the people;—in this manner returning their surplus wealth to the mass of their fellows. . . ."

Many things can be (and have been) said about Carnegie's solution to the inequities in American society produced by the rise of industrial capitalism. Certainly it had little to do with the desperately marginal lives of millions of American workingmen and women. Their first cry and need was for decent wages and conditions of employment—hours of labor, above all. No idealistic prescriptions by public-spirited tycoons could ease the pain or assuage the rage that periodically boiled over in bitter and bloody strikes and riots. James Madison and John Adams would doubtless have replied something to the effect that money is power, and power, in the long run, is always abused. If a few millionaires, arrogant in the confidence of their own judgment, disposed of unneeded dollars "for the public good," it was *their* notion of the public good, not the public's, and it was, therefore, as patronizing as the largess of any of Carnegie's despised dukes or earls. Furthermore, Senator Stanford had acquired his millions by practices that ruthlessly exploited the citizens of his state as well as his employees. He had in effect bought his seat in the United States Senate and there joined forces with the most reactionary of his colleagues to thwart every effort to pass legislation favorable to the interests of the "mass of his fellows" for whom Carnegie expressed what was doubtless a genuine solicitude. What Carnegie did not even try to deal with was the most critical issue of all: the temptation for owners and managers to hold down wages by whatever means lay at hand in order to increase profits. To that basic conflict there would prove to be no swift or ready solution.

Having made his pile, Andrew Carnegie retired to a castle in Scotland, leaving his American interests in the hands of Henry Frick. In Great Britain Carnegie bought several newspapers to disseminate his views about monarchy, concentrating his fire on the House of Lords and drawing invidious distinctions between American democracy and British aristocracy. "The best king or family of kings in the world is not worth one drop of an honest man's blood," he declared from his modernized castle at Skibo in Scotland, where eighty-five servants attended on his imperial needs and a ninety-foot swimming pool seemed to some visitors ostentatious. Woodrow Wilson, who visited there when he was the president of Princeton University, was impressed at being awakened by a Scottish bagpiper outside his door. Organ music was played during breakfast, trout and salmon fishing was available on twenty miles of the steelmaker's private streams, golf was played on his golf course ("I never found my business any more than mere play," he declared; "golf is the only serious business of life"), and guests browsed in his library of 25,000 volumes chosen by Lord Acton, the foremost British historian of the day, famous for his aphorism, "Power tends to corrupt and abolute power corrupts absolutely."

Perhaps Carnegie's greatest satisfaction was buying the Scottish seat of the duke of Buccleuch, from whose estate his family had been strictly excluded when he was a boy. He made it a public park for the workingmen of Dunfermline.

The ideologists of capitalism included clergymen as well as tycoons and corporation lawyers. All commonly rested their case on "laws," natural and divine. Darwinism provided them with the model of ruthless competition in which only the "fittest" survived. It thus followed logically that the richest entrepreneurs were the fittest. But many capitalists, like John D. Rockefeller, preferred to be "the most pious." For them William Lawrence, the Episcopal bishop of Massachusetts, was a godsend.

Lawrence deplored "a certain distrust on the part of our people as to the effect of material prosperity on their morality. We shrink with some foreboding at the great increase of riches and question whether in the long run material prosperity does not tend toward the disintegration of character." The "lessons of history" were often pointed to by those who distrusted material wealth for confirmation of their views, but Lawrence argued that "while wealth has been a source of danger, it has not necessarily led to demoralization." He himself was convinced "that neither history, experience, nor the Bible necessarily sustained the common distrust of the effects of material wealth on morality." He was confident that "in the long run, it is only to the man of morality that wealth comes. . . . We, like the Psalmist, occasionally see the wicked prosper, but only occasionally. . . . Godliness is in league with riches. . . . To seek for and earn wealth is a sign of a natural, vigorous, and strong character." The man blessed, as a result of his piety and faith, with riches "uses all that he has . . . in the wisest way, for the relief of the poor, the upbuilding of social standards, and the upholding of righteousness among the people. . . ." Material prosperity was helping "make the national character sweeter, more joyous, more unselfish, more Christlike. That is my answer to the question as to the relation of material prosperity to morality. . . ."

Such sentiments made Lawrence one of the favorite ecclesiastics of the capitalists and brought into the coffers of his diocese the largesse that made possible the erection of Trinity Church in Boston, the nation's most striking example of the union between religion and wealth.

William Makepeace Thayer, a Congregational clergyman and author of numerous rags-to-riches stories, like Lawrence tied success to piety. "It is quite evident," he wrote, ". . . that religion requires the following reasonable things of every young man, namely: that he should make the most of himself possible; that he should watch and improve his opportunities; that he should be industrious, upright, faithful, and prompt; that he should task his talents, whether one or ten, to the utmost; that he should waste neither time nor money; that duty, and not pleasure or ease, should be his watch-word. And all this precisely what we have seen to be demanded of all young men in reliable shops and stores. . . . We might say that religion demands success." With such qualities failure was "impossible."

Another important element in the ideology of capitalism was a residue of classical economics, the notion that an "invisible hand" somehow directs economic behavior in the best interests of the society as a whole, provided only that there is no heavy-handed interference by government. Derived in large part from Adam Smith's *Wealth of Nations,* in which it was presented as an argument against the policies of eighteenth-century mercantilism, it was combined with the more modern doctrines of Darwinism to reinforce the contention that capitalism should be free of any constraints or controls. Simply stated, the proposition was that, if everyone pursued his own economic interests, these would, in the aggregate, produce the highest level of general prosperity. Economic laws, in this reading, were as immutable as the law of gravity. They were embedded in Protestant Christian dogma to give them more durability and readier acceptance by the pious.

In brief, then, the ideology of capitalism rested on the notion of the sanctity of private property (the doctrine that the state should keep hands off all individual or corporate property) and the more recent Darwinian proposition that those who "succeeded" were the "fittest" in the merciless struggle for survival that characterized the animal and human existence.

Needless to say, many reform-minded Americans indignantly rebutted the ideology of capitalism. More important, workingmen and women resisted it by all the resources at their command. The consequence was a prolonged struggle—what came to be known as the war between capital and labor.

9

The Darwinians

If Darwinism, in one form or another, was an important ingredient in the ideology of capitalism, it entered directly or indirectly, as we have noted, into virtually every aspect of American thought and consciousness. Allied to Darwinism or integral to it was science, or "scientism," the claim of Science with a capital S to replace religion both as an explanation of ultimate reality and, perhaps even more important, as a "method," a means of asserting lesser truths.

The real issue was thus not whether science would dominate the age—it was already doing that—but whether it would establish itself as the exclusive explanation of the natural and the human world.

Among the multitude of those who preached the new testament, the most conspicuous were William Graham Sumner, a professor of sociology at Yale, and his ideological adversary, Lester Ward, whom we have already encountered as one of the founders of the National Liberal League.

Sumner, born in Paterson, New Jersey in 1840, was a year older than Ward. He grew up in Hartford, Connecticut, graduated from Yale, and studied ancient languages and history at Göttingen and Anglican theology at Oxford. Thereupon he was elected tutor at Yale and several years later became first a deacon and then rector of a series of

Episcopal churches. In 1872 Sumner was appointed professor of political and social science at Yale College, one of the first such appointments in the country.

Sumner's theological background did not prevent him from applauding the divorce of metaphysics from science. "Each of the sciences," he wrote, "which, by giving to man greater knowledge of the laws of nature, has enabled him to cope more intelligently with the ills of life, has had to fight for its independence of metaphysics." Sociology was only the most recent science to engage in the struggle. Since it claimed as its field of investigation "an immense range of subjects of the first importance," the struggle was bound to be severe. "Sociology," to Sumner, "is the science of life in society. It investigates the forces which come into action whenever a human society exists. It studies the structure and functions of the organs of human society, and its aim is to find out the laws in subordination to which human society takes its various forms and social institutions grow and change." Since the "practical utility" of sociology lay in "deriving the rules of right social living from the facts and laws . . . it must . . . come into collision with all other theories of right living which are founded on authority, tradition, arbitrary invention, or poetic imagination. . . . Sociology is a science which deals with one range of phenomena produced by the struggle for existence, while biology deals with another."

Sumner accepted the basic propositions of Malthus and Ricardo and the classic economists. "Constraint, anxiety, and possibly tyranny and repression" characterized all social relations. It was "when the social pressure due to an unfavorable ratio of population to land becomes intense that the social forces develop increased activity. Division of labor, exchange, higher social organizations, emigration, advance in the arts, spring from the necessity of contending against the harsher conditions of existence which are continually reproduced as the population surpasses the means of existence. . . . The law of population, therefore, combined with the law of diminishing returns, constitutes the great underlying condition of society. . . . Progress is a word that has no meaning save in view of the laws of population and the diminishing return. . . ." Those two "laws" were "the iron spur which has driven the race on to all which it has ever achieved. . . ." In Sumner's view "more energy, more intelligence and more virtue" would be needed simply to prevent disaster to the race, but in the mustering of that additional energy and intelligence a certain kind of progress was also involved.

Sociologists of the "progress" school like Ward seemed merely "sentimental" to Sumner—the most unkind designation that he could have devised—since they started from the principle "that nothing is true which is disagreeable. . . . The laws which entail upon mankind an inheritance of labor cannot be acceptable to any philosophy which maintains that man comes into the world endowed with natural rights and an inheritor of freedom. . . . The whole retrospect of human history runs downwards towards beast-like misery and slavery to the destructive forces of nature." Suffering and toil had been the great teachers of mankind. It was self-evident to Sumner "that if we should try by any measures of arbitrary interference and assistance to relieve the victims of social pressure from the calamity of their position we should only offer premiums to folly and vice and extend them further." Any "artificial social organization" spelled disaster.

The sentimental sociologists and reformers believed "that we can bring about a complete transformation in the economic organization of society and not have any incidental social and political questions arise which will make us great difficulty, or that, if such questions arise, they can all be succinctly solved by saying: 'Let the State attend to it'; 'make a bureau and appoint inspectors'; 'Pass a law.' " But the fact was that "the higher the organization of society, the more mischievous legislative regulation is sure to be."

Sumner's speculations had no such optimistic note as Ward's. The laws of evolutionary development were merciless: The strong survived; the weak went down. Through this process of natural selection the race survived and improved. To aid the weak was to contaminate the gene pool and produce a negative effect on the evolutionary process. In an essay entitled "What the Rich Owe the Poor?" Sumner's emphatic answer was "nothing."

Since "experiments" could not be devised with human subjects as in the "natural" sciences, it followed that sociology required a "special method," and the sociologists, in consequence, an especially long and arduous training. Like Ward, Sumner was dismayed by the casualness with which those who presumed to cure the diseases of society set about devising remedies.

Sumner was impatient with what he conceived to be the romantic and sentimental notion of "liberty," which held that "natural man," the savage, was free and that government and its laws inhibited man's natural freedom. The point was somewhat similar to the argument that John Adams had had with Jefferson and Tom Paine. Paine had declared government the "badge of lost innocence," implying that man was freer and better off without it, and Jefferson had been of the same persuasion. Adams and Madison (at least till the latter fell under the spell of Jefferson) believed that man was free only by virtue of just laws, firmly enforced (why, otherwise, have a constitution at all?). "There is . . . no liberty," Sumner wrote, "but liberty under law. . . . Civil liberty must . . . be an affair of positive law, of institutions and of history." It was not a "natural" right but it was "unstable and always in jeopardy, and . . . maintained only by virtue and diligence." *That* was Jeffersonian enough, but not the next sentence, which linked liberty with property: "[The] truth is that liberty and property go together and sustain each other in a glorious accord. . . ." In Sumner's view, the prosperity of the United States was not the result of "democracy" or "equality." By the colonization of America a new continent was won "for the labor class," and "this effect," Sumner wrote, "was not distinctly visible until the nineteenth century, because this new patrimony of the labor class was not available until the arts of transportation were improved up to the requisite point at which the movement of men and products could be easily accomplished." The claims of "philosophers and resolution-makers" that American principles of government were responsible were "totally false." They themselves were "but the product of the forces, and all their philosophies and resolutions . . . as idle as the waving of banners on the breezes. Democracy itself, the pet superstition of the age, is only a phase of the all-compelling movement. If you have an abundance of land and few men to share it, the men will all be equal. . . . Social classes disappear. . . . The mass of men, apart from laziness, folly, and vice are well off. No philosophy of politics or ethics makes them prosperous. Their prosperity makes their political philosophy and all their other creeds." But all these will be short-lived when the land fills up; then philosophies justifying quite different forms of action will be "discovered" and proclaimed. "Civilization," Sumner wrote, "has been of slow and painful growth. Its history has been marked by many obstructions, reactions, and false developments. Whole centuries and generations have lost their chances on earth, passing through human existence, keeping up the continuity of the race, but, for their own part, missing all share in the civilization which had previously been attained, and which ought to have ascended to them. It is easy to bring about such epochs of social disease and decline by human passion, folly, blunders, and crime. It is not easy to maintain the advance of civilization . . ."

In a splendid Burkean sentence, Sumner declared: "We are inheritors of civil institutions which it has cost generations of toil and pain to build up, and we are invited to throw them away because they do not fit the social dogmas of some of our prophets. . . . Every successful effort to widen the power of man over nature is a real victory over poverty, vice, and misery, taking things in general and in the long run. . . . The social philosophy which has been in fashion for a century past," he wrote, "has educated us in the notion that we ought all to be 'happy' (as the phrase goes) on this earth, and that, if we are not so, we ought to cry out, and then somebody is bound to come and take care of us. . . ." But in trying to remedy ills, social philosophers and politicians might well make things worse. "We should hold this ever in mind. It is exactly the reason for distrusting our wisdom and for 'letting things alone.' "

Sumner ended his essay on "Sociology" by reaffirming his conviction that misplaced sentiment was far more dangerous than leaving society to its own "laws" of development. "The old classical civilization fell under an irruption of barbarians from without," he wrote. "It is possible that our new civilization may perish by an explosion from within. The sentimentalists have been preaching for a century notions of rights and equality, of the dignity, wisdom, and power of the proletariat, which have filled the minds of ignorant men with impossible dreams. The thirst for luxurious enjoyment has taken possession of us all." That thirst, combined with the "notions of rights, of power, and of equality, and dissociated from the notions of industry and economy, produces the notion that man is robbed of his rights if he has not everything he wants . . . and that he is a fool if, having the power of the State in his hands, he allows this state of things to last. Then we have socialism, communism, and nihilism . . ." and the danger of being "trampled underfoot by a mob which can only hate what it cannot enjoy."

Sumner and Ward agreed at least on the negative consequences of religion. Science was so ruthless and so systematic that it must come inevitably into conflict with religion. There was another "form of phantasm" which did great harm: "faith in ideals. . . . Every ideal is a phantasm; it is formed by giving up one's hold on reality and taking flight into the realm of fiction."

William Graham Sumner believed that "the concentration of wealth is indispensable to the successful execution of the tasks which devolve upon society in our time." All the institutions in the society required such concentrations of resources. Concentrations of wealth and control were "not merely a matter of industrial power, or social sentiment, or political policy," they were "a universal societal phenomenon" with the character of natural laws. The age was "befooled" by talk of democracy. The form of industrial organization which had emerged was attacked by "democratic dogmas" which were simply irrelevant to the real situation. "The strongest and most effective organizations for industrial purposes which are formed nowadays," Sumner wrote, "are those of a few great capitalists, who have great personal confidence in each other and who can bring together adequate means for whatever they desire to do." He did not deny that it was "proper to propose checks and safeguards" on aggressive capitalism, "but an onslaught on the concentration of wealth is absurd and a recapitulation of its 'dangers' idle. . . ."

Sumner was a dogged defender of capital and capitalists, but he drew the line at plutocrats. Plutocracy was "the most sordid and debasing form of political energy known to us. In its motive, its processes, its code, and its sanctions it is infinitely corrupting to all the institutions which ought to preserve and protect society." But capital, attacked by the democracy "in the most ruthless fashion," was forced to defend itself by "resorting to all the vices of plutocracy." It was the major issue which menaced modern society "and which is destined to dispel the dreams which have been cherished, that we are on the eve of a millennium," Sumner wrote.

"Hard work and self-denial (in technical language, labor and capital)" were the only elements that really counted in advancing "the welfare of man on earth." These were best expressed in the effort to earn an honest living, to accumulate capital, and to bring up a family of children to be industrious and self-denying in their turn. "I repeat," Sumner wrote, "that this is the way to work for the welfare of man on earth." We might thus call Sumner the sociologist of Puritanism. The fact that he was "bred" in the Puritan heart of New England may well have had a decisive influence on his sociological notions. Ward, with his far freer and more expressive life, with the intense eroticism of his pre- and postmarital relationship with Lizzie Vought, escaped that stern and austere environment. The "organism" that was Ward responded to an environment that was far more expressive of the general American consciousness.

Sumner's principal solicitude was for what he called the Forgotten Man (what we today call the silent majority)—the middle-class American who "works, . . . votes, generally he prays—but he always pays—yes, above all, he pays." The Forgotten Man and the Forgotten Woman were "the very life and substance of society. . . . They are always forgotten by the sentimentalists, philanthropists, reformers, enthusiasts, and every description of speculator in sociology, political economy, or political science."

Sumner was an outspoken enemy of imperialism. He wrote angrily of the "earth hunger" that seemed to possess the world. To him it was clear that colonial ventures were entirely inconsistent with the basic principles on which the American Republic, for better or worse (it was not clear which), had been founded. "There is no place for them in the system," he wrote, "and the attempt to hold and administer them would produce corruption which would react on our system and destroy it."

Patriotism was to Sumner a phantasm, a "root of non-reality" and a cause of endless trouble. "The patriotic bias is hostile to critical thinking," he wrote in "The Scientific Attitude of Mind." Sumner's suspicion of patriotism and his theory that mankind is engaged in a perpetual war against nature made him a harsh critic of war: "[When] we quarrel among ourselves we lose the fruits of our victory [over nature] just as certainly as we would if she were a human opponent. All plunder and robbery squander the fund which has been produced by society for the support of society." At the same time he was willing to concede that "the wars and revolutions" that overthrow "the old institutions which have outlived their usefulness and become a cover for abuses and an excuse for error," were "a comparative good."

To the charge that he was a pessimist Sumner replied: "Pessimism includes caution, doubt, prudence, and care; optimism means gush, shouting, boasting, and rashness."

Sumner's rival, Lester Ward, is an especially compelling figure because of his passionate "modern" romance with Lizzie Vought. As a young man in Towanda, Pennsylvania, Lester Ward, determined to learn French, began a diary in that language in July, 1860. The diary is notable for the candor with which Ward discusses his infatuation with Lizzie. Having taken her to church, he fell instantly in love with her. "What a charming girl," he thought; "if I could . . . press my lips on hers and draw from them my soul's satisfaction." Visiting her house after church, he could no longer restrain himself. "Leaning forward," he wrote, "I received her sweet and tender form in my arms and in an instant her face was covered with kisses. What a sublime scene. . . . There we bathed ourselves in the passion of love until the crowing of cocks announced that it was day." "Darling, love, come let us drown together, loving, kissing."

Interspersed with accounts of their lovemaking is constant mention of Ward's anxieties about money. "I have great plans and ideas for the future, great ambitions," he wrote in his diary. "But I suppose they will all vanish for the lack of money." He was determined, one way or another, to acquire an education. In addition to studying French, Ward read every book he could get his hands on: Shakespeare's plays; works on physiology and chemistry, theology and philosophy. He studied "Geometry, Algebra, Latin, Greek and Bookkeeping." His days were spent in making and, more commonly, trying to sell, wheel hubs, and his nights in reading or making love to Lizzie. "Sometimes I am so stirred by love for my girl that I become almost mad; on such occasions my heart seems to rise into my throat; everything which passes me I embrace." He wrote: "She gave me her heart and her body, asking nothing more in exchange than my own. But with what tenderness and humility she said, 'I am afraid I am doing something I shouldn't in putting my hands on your bare breast.' " He kissed her "almost all over . . . kissed her on her soft breasts, and took too many liberties with her sweet person, and we are going to stop. It is a very fascinating practice and fills us with very sweet, tender and familiar sentiments, and consequently makes us very happy. . . . But the difficulty is that we might become so addicted in that direction that we might go too deep and possibly confound ourselves by the standards of virtue."

As we have noted often, middle- and upper-class sexual mores, at least in Eastern cities, did not tolerate overtly sexual relations between a suitor and his beloved. Indeed, indications of strong sexual feelings were believed to be "bad" and to reflect on the woman toward whom they were directed. Either Lester Ward and Lizzie Vought were exceptions to the prevailing "rule," or, what seems more likely, on the frontier and in rural communities a quite different code prevailed, one much more like that of early New England, where intense physical relations between couples intending to get married were accepted as a natural manifestation of youthful ardor.

Ward found a job teaching in a country school and tried his best to control his unruly charges with kindness and exhortation rather than, as was the common practice, with a whip. But he found it hard going. His pupils liked him but had no compunction about taking advantage of his good nature. Soon the word got about among the parents that he was unable to preserve order, and he was dismissed, a "terrible blow to me," he wrote. "I don't know what to do. What can I do?"

Dazzled by love and preoccupied by his perpetual financial stringency, Ward noted Lincoln's inauguration only in passing. He had much more to say about playing football and about his concern over the state of his soul. He joined a debating society which discussed such topics as "Resolved: that the Negroes have more cause for complaint than the Indians." He soon excelled in debate, but his soul remained in peril. His friend and Greek tutor "Professor" S. reminded him of his duty to God. "Supplicated . . . admonished and . . . prayed," Ward noted. It was all in vain. Ward got down on his knees and tried to pray, *but I did not know how.*" He wept in frustration and despair.

More than 200 young men left Towanda to enlist as soldiers in the Union army amid "many tears and much weeping," but Ward, tied to Lizzie and determined to marry her, read Xenophon's *Anabasis* in Greek, debated, played football, and began teaching Lizzie Latin. Shortly after his twentieth birthday he wrote a commencement address for his graduation entitled "Aspiration." Since Lester Ward was to become the Father of American sociology, his commencement address is of more than casual interest. Conceding that there was a "difference among men in natural capacity," Ward declared that "the great lack of intellectual abilities among men is the result of a contracted and inferior range of thought. Every mind," he added, "is so constituted as to admit of almost infinite expansion. There is, strictly speaking, no limit to the development of a normal and sane mind." It was not a "lack of natural talent as much as a lack of high, aspiring sentiments" that kept so much of mankind in poverty and ignorance." The critical question was "how is this world of comparative ignorance to be illuminated by the glowing light of intelligence. Some great and popular lecturer and reformer" might do much. But the real task "devolves upon ourselves individually. We are the ones who are expected to bring about this reform." The mental capacity was there, "in vast amount lying latent and undeveloped." All that was needed was "one grand moving power, the will."

The speech contained a number of familiar strands: the undeveloped potential of all human beings; the efficacy of the development of the "mental powers" through education, a proposition deeply rooted in the Secular Democratic (Enlightenment) notion of man as a rational creature; echoes of the Puritan reliance on the "will"; and, finally, the apotheosis of the Emersonian "individual." The path to individual and social redemption was through mind and will.

Ward found another teaching position, and he and Lizzie were secretly married, tasting "the joys of love and happiness which only belong to a married life. . . . My heart's darling whom I have loved so long, so constantly, so frantically, is mine! . . . The day for setting out for the war is here. . . . I must leave the sweetness of her company for the difficulties and fatigues of military camp. Terrible change!"

Ward's experiences as a soldier were those we are familiar with from other soldiers' letters and diaries: long marches; freezing rain; hunger; discomfort; boredom; the camaraderie of one's fellows; and, in Ward's case, serious wounds. At Chancellorsville he was wounded above his knee and in both thighs by shrapnel, and he lay for months in an army hospital before Lizzie got sick leave for him.

Back in Towanda with Lizzie to dress his wounds, he spent his first night with her "talking, telling little stories, and laughing until two in the morning, without being sleepy." Assigned to the army hospital in Alexandria, Ward sent for Lizzie and once more enjoyed the ecstasies of married love . . . "I loved her marvelously." Lizzie became pregnant, "but she took an effective remedy. . . . It did its work and she is now out of danger," Ward wrote.

Lester and Lizzie Ward studied together diligently—more Greek and Latin, French and Italian—and joined a temperance society which gave Ward an opportunity to make stirring speeches on the evils of alcohol. Ward having been discharged when it was judged that his wounds incapacitated him for further service, the Wards moved to Washington, and he began a persistent campaign to get a job as a clerk in a government office. He wrote to President Lincoln, asking for his support. "My necessities are great," he wrote; "I have no regular home, am an orphan, have no trade, am physically disqualified for any laborious occupation, and have been out of employment nearly all Winter. . . . For seven years I have struggled against every form of adversity, till, by my habits of hard labor, hard study, economy and integrity, I found myself prepared for college." He had given up this dream to serve his country, and he now asked "that Country to give me honorable employment . . . that I may . . . renew my chosen course."

Finally, after months of importunings and disappointments, Lester Ward got his coveted government clerkship and was soon making enough money to buy and furnish a small house with Lizzie. In June, 1865, Lizzie gave birth to a boy, to the delight of both parents, and

Ward found himself "busy almost all the time . . . in cooking, washing dishes and sweeping so that I cannot study much." Nonetheless, he was ecstatic. "Surrounded with all the good things of life," he wrote, "good work, good lodging, enough money and a prospect of being some day able to pursue my studies, to enter college, finish my elected profession, to establish myself with my lovable family somewhere on the beautiful new lands of the West where I can live and grow with the people and enjoy marvellously my life with my sweet wife and my superb son, and make myself wise and useful." Contending with periodic nosebleeds that seemed related to the strain of his manifold duties as government clerk, scholar, and father-husband, Ward urged himself on with such admonitions as "Henceforth work and study! Forward!" He joined a debating club, enrolled in the Columbian (now George Washington) College in Washington, plunged into the study of the sciences and became increasingly a freethinker—that is to say, a radical critic of the established churches and of orthodoxy in politics, social thought, and religion. "Freedom and independence of thought and opinion is one of the surest tests, as well of a sound intellect as of a proper education," he declared in one of his debates. "When all shall learn to take truth and facts and principles for their guides, instead of following after the leadership of other men and gulping down their dogmas and sophistries, then . . . disaffections and riots and insurrection and wars will cease," and "prejudice and passion" be overthrown.

More and more, Ward concerned himself with social questions. "Street beggary is the result of an imperfect state of society," he wrote. "Let all be educated, fed, clothed, well treated and taught to labor, and before another generation shall pass away, . . . the great evil of beggary [will be] utterly removed from our lands."

The study went on. Lizzie enrolled at the new predominantly black institution, Howard University, and Lester plunged into "freethinking" literature: Thomas Paine and Voltaire. He studied "analytical rectilinear geometry" and zoology, and more and more of his time went into establishing a secret society of freethinkers. Lizzie played her new piano, and Lester his violin, and they read Longfellow's "Hiawatha" together and played with their son. Lizzie became more and more involved in the fight for women's suffrage, and Lester was an enthusiastic recruit to the cause. In the debating society Ward took the affirmative of the proposition that literature had done more for civilization than Christianity had. Now Christianity is not simply ignored. It has become, in fact, the villain of the historical piece, the representative of superstition, the "most powerful enemy of progress whether in science, in art, or in ethics . . . in learning, in law and in politics . . . The most powerful defender of human slavery has been the Christian Church," Ward concluded. "It has clung to it with the tenacity of a drowning man and was the last to relinquish its loathsome idol."

In the midst of this idyll Lizzie became sick and died after a short illness. Ward was devastated. To forget his grief, he plunged more intensely than ever into his studies. He read widely in the various fields of science and found a kindred spirit in John Powell, the explorer of the Colorado River and head of the Geological Survey. Under Powell's sponsorship Ward produced his epic work, *Dynamic Sociology*, published in 1883. *Dynamic Sociology* (in two huge volumes) was one of those seminal works that capture the spirit of an age. Henry George had labored to free "political economy" from the grip of the classical economists. Ward, believing that *Progress and Poverty* was an unscientific, "popular" tract, set out to establish the study and "amelioration" of society on a basis as scientific as physics or biology. The degree to which he appeared to his contemporaries to have succeeded is suggested by the fact that, when *Dynamic Sociology* was published, there were no chairs in sociology in American universities and few, if any, courses offered in the subject. By the time the second edition of Ward's tome was published in 1896, he was able to write with obvious pride: "To-day there is no higher institution of learning in which sociology is not taught, and in many it is taught by that name, while a number of the leading ones have special chairs of sociology. . . . In the United States . . . there is already a small army of active professors of sociology . . . it bids fair to become the leading science of the twentieth century, as biology has been that of the nineteenth."

The Academy of Political and Social Science was founded in Philadelphia in 1890, and five years later the University of Chicago began the publication of the *American Journal of Sociology*. Ward could not, of course, claim credit for all these developments. Sociology or "social science," the scientific study of human society, was in the air. If science was the new god of the age, it was inevitable that "social" science should be advanced as a rival or companion to "natural" science.

Lester Ward began *Dynamic Sociology* with a challenge to the conventional scholarship of the day. "A growing sense of the essential sterility of all that has thus far been done in the domain of social science has furnished the chief incentive to the preparation of this work," he wrote. What Ward called "theo-teleology"—a religious explanation of "final causes"—was an archaic metaphysical ontology. The explanation of the inner nature of reality by reference to a non- or transphysical dimension of experience—transcendentalism in practical fact—was, in Ward's view, mired in futility because it "builds on pure ideas." Even "the philosophy of evolution" was sterile since it denied that society could be modified by the application to it of scientific principles which "constitutes the only practical value that science has for man." The hard-core evolutionists, influenced by an increasingly deterministically inclined Herbert Spencer and finding an American spokesman in William Graham Sumner, limited the possibilities of social evolution to millennia-long processes of intellectual development through selective breeding among humans. Such a notion was in every respect repugnant to Ward. "The real object of science is to benefit man," he wrote. "A science which fails to do this, however agreeable its study, is lifeless. Sociology, which of all sciences should benefit man most, is in danger of falling into the class of polite amusements, or dead sciences."

What Ward proposed was a dynamic sociology of progress and change. He shared with George, though in a different manner, a distaste for a "natural" process of which man was the object rather than the shaper and modifier, the meliorist. To the "law . . . of Evolution proper" Ward opposed "the law of Aggregation," which stressed the cumulative character of human knowledge. In Ward's view, "social forces" could be brought under the "guiding influence of the intellect, embodying the application of the Indirect Method of Conation and the essential nature of Invention, of Art, and of Dynamic Action." Heretofore governments, controlled by self-interested elites, had imposed their will on the mass of the population by force to further their own ends. In the new age the "Indirect Method of Conation," which was, in essence, universal education, would enlighten people on their own best interests and the means of achieving them. In referring to "the superiority of Artificial, or Teleological, Process over Natural or Genetic, Processes," Ward meant to say that society did not have to surrender to some notion of evolutionary biology or to "genetics" but that it had the "Artificial" (as opposed to "Natural") means to direct the human race toward socially desirable ends. This would be done primarily by "the equal and universal Distribution of the Extant Knowledge of the world, which . . . is the crown of the system itself." There was, in Ward's view, enough intellect already available. The woes of the industrial world were due not to human incapacity for thought but rather to the failure to make knowledge available to everyone without distinction as to class or economic status.

Ward sounded like some odd melding of the Enlightenment philosophers, such as Rousseau and Condorcet, with our old friend William Manning, who in 1790 deplored the disposition of the wealthy and powerful to maintain their control over the "laboring classes" by restricting access to education and the means of communication. "The strange truth thus comes up for our contemplation," Ward wrote, "that, instead of having been guided and impelled by intellect and reason throughout all the years of history, we have been ruled and swayed by the magnetic passions of epileptics and monomaniacs." Much of the fault for this state of affairs, Ward placed, as we might have guessed, at the door of religion. "Objectively viewed," he declared, "society is a natural object, presenting a variety of complicated movements produced by a particular class of natural forces. The question, therefore, simply is, Can man ever control these forces to his advantage as he controls other, and some very complicated natural forces?" The champions of laissez-faire had objected that "society has always done better when let alone; that all efforts to improve the moral or material conditions of society by legislation and kindred means have not only been inoperative, but have in the majority of cases done positive harms, often to the very cause they were intended to subserve." The reason was not hard to find. What was needed if society was to be improved, was "invention," the same kind of ruthlessly scientific examination of the true facts that characterized the natural or physical sciences. But legislators "as inventors have proved mere bunglers; because they have known nothing of the laws of society; because they have been ignorant of the forces over which they have sought to exercise control." The legislators must, therefore, accept the guidance of social scientists or become such themselves.

The model was always the physical sciences. "Physical realities," Ward wrote, "have, one by one, been stripped of their masks, and dragged before the light. Once caught, they have been tamed, trained, and put to man's service." While spectacular results had been obtained in the field of the natural sciences, "society as a whole has undergone no improvement"; indeed, it could be argued that in some respects it had regressed. But "knowledge which can exert no influence is not scientific. Science is dynamic. Whatever it touches is transformed. The only object in knowing is by means of it to do something." It was a stern doctrine that allowed no room for lightness, for play, for knowledge as an end in itself.

"All governments thus far," Lester Ward wrote, "have been devised, and established by, and for the benefit of, those desiring to govern. A true government would be demanded, created, and put in force by, and for the benefit of, those desiring to be governed." Traditionally the purposes of government had been: (1) restraint, (2) protection, and (3) the accommodation of the people. There was, however, a fourth purpose not yet fulfilled: "the direct improvement or amelioration of society." This belonged "to the art when it shall have reached its scientific stage. . . ."

Ward distinguished between "prohibitive" legislation and "attractive" legislation. The former forced obedience, while the latter won people to its support by "attraction," by the obvious advantages they enjoyed in consequence of its passage. Society, "possessed for the first time of a completely integrated consciousness, could at last proceed to map out a field of independent operation for the systematic realization of its own interests, in the same manner that an intelligent and keen-sighted individual pursues his own life-purposes. . . ."

A long section of *Dynamic Sociology* was devoted to demolishing the pretensions of religion to have any positive influence on individual or social life. "Instead . . . of considering what morality owes to religion," Ward wrote, "it may yet become a question how far natural morality has been lowered by such an association with supernatural belief . . . [and] it is a fair speculation how much higher the human mind would have risen in its efforts to comprehend the natural universe, had no such explanation as a spiritual being or a personal god ever suggested itself." From the rise of science "religion had nothing to gain and everything to lose; and it has, in fact," he concluded, "been constantly losing from the first, and must continue to lose to the last."

Among the most powerful and irrational forces moving man and woman in society are the "love-forces" and the "fear-forces," Ward argued. The "fear-forces" are physical: the fear of death or bodily harm; "the fear of inanimate nature"; "the fear of spiritual beings"; "the fear of disease"; and, often most crippling of all, "the psychical fear-forces," which Ward blamed primarily on religion. What must be avoided at all costs was "a return of the odious theological *regime*." Once it had thrown off the constraints of theology, "science had achieved a complete triumph over all the fields of inorganic nature, and the reign of law had been demonstrated throughout the domain of mechanical and physical forces."

Ward insisted that the progress of society depended on breaking the monopoly of the dominant class on knowledge: "The progress of society must depend on the progress of the intellect. . . . Human happiness, which is the ideal end of all social effort, can only be secured by the elevation and expansion of the reasoning powers of man. . . .

"The problem of dynamic sociology," Ward wrote, "is the *organization of happiness*." What would Thomas Jefferson have said? Everything in the United States had been organized: the railroads; the factories; education; even religion—i.e., "organized religion"—with, certainly, mixed results. So it was marvelously American to set out to organize happiness. The fact was that happiness was clearly what Americans wanted. Unhappiness was due, in large part, to wrong conduct, and "most of the wrong conduct is due to defective judgment, i.e., defective correspondence between organism and environment. . . . Knowledge, therefore, is the end to be more directly pursued, since through knowledge comes the entire succession of desirable objects—right conduct, progress, happiness." But only "right" knowledge brought such desirable results, knowledge that "adapts the organism to the environment, knowledge that reveals the relations of man to the universe," "truly practical" knowledge.

"The present enormous chasm between the ignorant and the intelligent, caused by the unequal distribution of knowledge," Lester Ward wrote, "is the worst evil under which society labors. . . . The large number deprived of the *means* of intelligence, though born with the capacity for it, are really compelled by the small number, through the exercise of a superior intelligence, to serve them without compensation. . . . For it is not the idler, but the toiler, the real producer of wealth, who has none: while the man who has wealth is usually a man of leisure."

In 1873 Lester Ward wrote a "treatise," as he called it, on education. It constitutes the last 100 pages of his *Dynamic Sociology*, and it might be argued that the preceding 1,100 pages are simply an introduction to that chapter. "The final object which Dynamic Sociology seeks," Ward wrote, "is the organization of happiness." This, as we have seen, it intended to achieve through the organization and distribution of knowledge. Such an education must be based on the "generalization" of the basic laws governing progressive social development and on "invention" in the sense in which that word is used by scientists. As knowledge was more widely distributed, it followed that "invention" would increase proportionately. This invention would be rapidly incorporated in the generalizations which [make] a corresponding increase in general happiness: "Instill progressive principles, no matter how, into the mind, and progressive actions will result. . . . The impulse to prosecute original research would be strengthened and widely extended, while, at the same time, the relative productiveness of the efforts thus expended would be immensely increased."

Ward proceeded to discuss (and dismiss) four existing forms of education—of experience, through discipline, for culture, and for and through research. The education of experience was, of necessity, partial and incomplete. Education through discipline seemed to be based on some vague notion of the "modification of brain-tissue" by routine intellectual tasks—intellectual gymnastics, Ward called it scornfully. Education for culture was the education of the refined upper classes, to whom cultivation was both a salable commodity and the stamp of their superiority over the common herd. About education for and through research, which one might have assumed would have been Ward's ideal, he was equally caustic. While it was true that "the education of *research* . . . assumes that the great aim should be to discover truth," it frittered away its resources in trivial and unproductive investigation which was far removed from the needs and interests of students and served to advance the careers of the researchers rather than to "originate" ideas for the common good of the society.

It is abundantly clear that the origins of *Dynamic Sociology* are far less in the observation of scientific data than in the author's moral outrage at the manifold injustices evident in the society around him. "Instead of trying to dissuade men from taking away the property of others," Ward wrote, much in the spirit of the Founding Fathers, "society must render it impossible for them to do so. The proper way to induce men to desist from unjust action is to make it for their own interest to do so. . . . This is the work of intelligence and education." He emphatically rejected the notion that the cause of poverty was the indolence of the poor. The only remedy for the capitalistic excesses that in Ward's view caused poverty was for labor to "retain possession of its products, and only transfer them to the consumer, making the processes of distribution wholly dependent upon and subservient to those of production."

We now approach one of the central theses of *Dynamic Sociology*:

Applied science is not neutral or objective after all. It is "essentially humanitarian," and "applied sociology must be especially so. . . . A society as a whole must seek its collective welfare. . . . It is the duty of society, in its collective capacity, so to regulate the phenomena of the social aggregate as to prevent, as far as possible, the advancement of a small class at the expense of a large one."

One of the most important aspects of Ward's tome was his insistence that the sum of human happiness could be substantially and, indeed, indefinitely increased by conscious choices and decisions made by informed experts, most notably by highly trained legislators and public officials chosen by an enlightened electorate—salvation, in brief, by government.

Dynamic Sociology, large and expensive as it was, made its way around the world. It was favorably reviewed in liberal Russian journals, translated into Russian, and ordered burned by the Council of Ministers in 1891 as a dangerous and subversive work. George Kennan, a journalist, an explorer, and an expert on Russia, wrote to Ward: "I heartily congratulate you. In this prosaic, indifferent age it is not every man who achieves the distinction of having his books burned by order of a Council of Ministers in the mightiest empire on earth! . . . You are evidently a very dangerous man. . . ." *Dynamic Sociology* was also banned by the state censors in Poland. The book made Ward famous and led to a professorship at Brown University.

Lester Ward was, of course, no more "scientific" than Sumner. They both were, in their respective ways, idealists, a species they both denounced. Sumner's ideals were incorporated in the industrious, pious, hardworking father of a family; Ward's, in the ideal of universal education. They both comprehended an important element of the truth. Sumner's skepticism or, as he preferred to call it, his "pessimism" preserved him from some of the naïvetés that characterized Ward's writings, but at the same time it diminished his vision and circumscribed his humanity. Still, he is an antidote to Ward's optimism about the benign character of the state. He indignantly rejected his rival's notion that "the state should take any measures that will 'make better men.'" Sumner declared: "A state can never make men of any kind; a state consumes men. New-born children are not soldiers, or taxpayers, or laborers. Years of cost of production must be spent upon them before they can be any of these contributors to society. It is the work of the family, the church, the school, and other educational institutions to bring them up and make them as good men as possible, and then turn them over to the state as citizens. The state, therefore, does not make them; it uses them up. . . ."

The irony was that in the dialectical tension created by their opposing views one found a resolution or synthesis. Ward was right—or, to use his own "method," was influencing his environment as an "originator"—in developing his theory of the distribution of intellect as the vector of progressive or "dynamic" social change. But he was wrong in much of his "sociology" or at least in his assumptions that man, by exercising control over nature, primarily through universal "scientific" education, would inevitably produce progress and happiness. Ward was wrong or weak on those very aspects of human experience—tragedy, suffering, and conflict—that Sumner insisted on emphasizing. On the other hand, Sumner was surely wrong in arguing that nothing should or could be done by the intervention of society collectively to alleviate the poverty, suffering, and misery in which most men and women (and children) lived in the modern industrial world. The liberal (or radical) and progressive spirit of Ward is far more congenial to us than Sumner's pessimistic determinism, yet we find ourselves in the last decades of this century painfully aware of the fact that the course of history since the early years of the century has done as much to vindicate Sumner as to verify Ward.

One of the things most notable about the relationship of the ideas of Ward to those of Sumner is that the universal system of education Ward considered essential to the proper evolutionary and progressive development of society has been very nearly achieved in the United States, but the sociology taught in these institutions of more or less higher education is much closer to that of Sumner than to Ward's doctrines. That is to say, while there are still a number of competing schools of sociological theory, most of them (the neo-Marxists being perhaps an exception) are "static" rather than "dynamic"; they study social phenomena "objectively" and "scientifically" to describe them rather than undertake actively to change them. Even "applied" sociology in the form of social work is devoted primarily to taking care of "cases" rather than to effecting substantial transformations in society.

Ward and Sumner are invaluable spokesmen for the two forms of consciousness we have stressed throughout this work. Ward gathered all the optimistic, progressive, and millennial spirit that was an essential element in the Protestant passion to redeem the world, secularized it, combined it with the Jeffersonian-rationalist-French Enlightenment vein, and gave it a "scientific" gloss, thereby exemplifying the Secular Democratic Consciousness.

Sumner, with his skepticism about "reason," "reform," "progress," and all such liberal catchwords, became a spokesman for the Classical-Christian Consciousness, which saw history as a slow, painful struggle against man's baser instincts. Undoubtedly Sumner's theological training and experience as a minister of the Gospel gave him his Classical-Christian view of man's life on earth and persuaded him that "every chance for accomplishing something better brings with it a chance of equivalent loss by neglect or incapacity."

The Darwinians certainly had numerous and vocal critics, most notably in the ranks of the Christian Socialists. Henry George, while he sought to make economics "scientific," was an avowed enemy of "social" Darwinism. For some theorists, among them William James, the enemy was not "science" or "Darwinism" but "materialism," the notion that the physical world was the only reality. John Fiske was determined to bridge the Darwinian world and the Christian world.

Two years younger than Sumner and a year junior to Lester Ward, Fiske was born in Hartford, Connecticut. As a boy, living with his grandparents in Middletown, he determined to become a famous philosopher, and he was soon conspicuous in the town as a dangerous freethinker who already questioned the creeds the town lived by. At Harvard he encountered Darwin and alienated a number of his teachers by his outspoken criticisms of the education he received there. After a brief term at the Harvard Law School Fiske set out to become a journalist in the new style. With Herbert Spencer as his model, Fiske became an expositor and modifier of the Englishman's *Synthetic Philosophy*. Invited by Eliot to deliver a series of lectures at Harvard, Fiske lectured on Darwinism and three years later produced his famous *Outlines of Cosmic Philosophy*. The book, which appeared in 1874, was the first large-scale exposition of Spencer's theories published in the United States, and as such it had a great vogue and wide influence on younger scholars. To Fiske the "law of evolution" had "precisely . . . the universality claimed for the law of gravitation." While he began his work with reflections on the origin of the universe, his main preoccupation was on the evolution of human consciousness and the social development of man. His main contribution to the developing social sciences, primarily the fields of sociology and anthropology, was to emphasize the significance of the prolonged period of nurture in humans as opposed to animals and to point to this as an essential element in the development of human intelligence. This extended period allowed for the *"continuous weakening of selfishness and the continual strengthening of sympathy,"* or "altruism." Fiske was careful to leave a place for a "Causal Agency" in the whole process, "a Power which is beyond Humanity and upon which Humanity depends. . . ." This was "the God of the Christian, though freed from . . . illegitimate formulas." Evolution was, for Fiske, a theory "in which science and religion find their reconciliation." The career that Fiske now launched was in many respects unique. He soon felt the resistance of the academic establishment to intellectual free-lancers ("popularizers" was the approbative term), but he continued to turn out a stream of books and articles ranging across the spectrum from American history to theology. In 1885 he published *The Idea of God as Affected by Modern Knowledge.* "At no time since men have dwelt upon the earth," Fiske wrote, "have their notions about the universe undergone so great a change as in the century of which we are now approaching the end. . . . Time-honored creeds are losing their hold upon men; ancient symbols are shorn of their value: everything is called in question. . . . Religion itself is called upon to show why it should any longer claim our allegiance. There are those who deny the existence of God." And there are many more who, without thinking of themselves as atheists or materialists, "have nonetheless come to regard religion as practically ruled out from human affairs." Having thus stated the case, Fiske went on to describe the development of the idea of God from earliest times, concluding that "from the crudest polytheism we have thus, by slow evolution, arrived at a pure monotheism,—the recognition of the eternal God indwelling in the universe, in whom we live and move and have our being." Thus "the glorious consummation toward which organic evolution is tending is the production of the highest and most perfect psychical life." The "germs of this conclusion existed in the Darwinian theory as originally stated." It was at first hardly noticed, but as its implications were "more fully studied in its application to the genesis of Man, a wonderful flood of light has been thrown upon the meaning of evolution, and there appears a reasonableness in the universe such as had not appeared before." Each subsequent book of Fiske's stated with increasing fervor the compatibility of evolution and Christianity.

In *The New Era*, published in 1893 and frequently reprinted, Josiah Strong, a liberal Congregational minister, captured the spirit of the times as well as any of his contemporaries. His was a simple formula, which drew directly on Christian redemptionism while reconciling it to the new Darwinian science. The new era was to be one in which the ancient barriers separating civilizations were broken down and a universal worldwide society was established. This would be progressive, Christian, mildly socialistic. The keynote would be change, disconcertingly rapid but ultimately salutary. "The discontent of labor," Strong wrote, "has gained such a hearing that there has been awakened within a few years an unprecedented interest in industrial and all sociological questions. . . . Advocates of the reorganization of industry on a cooperative instead of a competitive basis have made many disciples. The word Socialism is growing less obnoxious to Americans. . . ." American socialists pointed to the fact that the German government had insured German workers against illness, accidents, and old age; similar measures had been proposed in France and Hungary.

The two major themes of the new era, Strong wrote, must be "consolidation"—both factories and farms were growing larger—and "the development of the individual," with opportunities for the ordinary citizen to have a fuller and more rewarding life. "Many," he continued, "expect violent revolution."

Strong took the position of many liberal ministers that "Science is . . . as truly a revelation from God and of God as are the Scriptures. . . . This new evangel of science means new blessings to mankind, a new extension of the kingdom [of God]." Moreover, by embracing science as the latest manifestation of the Almighty, the Christian world must inevitably convert the heathen. "The opening of the heathen world to the power of the Gospel and the quickening forces of modern life" was the great task that lay ahead. The world of the future would be "composed of persons of perfect individuality, each enjoying perfect liberty and yet all in perfect harmony with the divine." Strong was convinced that "when the social conscience, properly enlightened, . . . actually rules the organized life of men, social wrongs will disappear, the strifes of classes and of races will cease, and wars will be no more."

John Bates Clark, professor of economics at Columbia University, responded to the challenge posed to the orthodox Christian community with a somewhat different emphasis. Writing in the *Independent*, the journal founded by Henry Ward Beecher, Clark foresaw continued growth and prosperity for the United States. "We shall improve agriculture and get our living more easily," he wrote in 1901, "but we shall make larger gains in producing comforts and luxuries. . . . Machines will become more deft, powerful, rapid and automatic. They will get their power from cheap and abundant sources, and there will be little left for the workers who use them except to touch the buttons that set them moving. Dwellings and furnishings will improve, and vehicles will multiply till the amount of labor that is now the equivalent of a nickel will give a poor man a longer and more interesting drive than a costly equipage now gives a rich man."

One of the early champions of "consumerism," Clark insisted that "an abundance of products" must be not only created but "created by and for the workers themselves. The distribution of wealth must be as satisfactory as the production of it is fruitful." The price for such progress would be "an enormous increase of inequality of outward possessions; but this very change will bring with it a continual approach to equality of genuine comfort. The capitalist may become too rich to sleep, while the laborer becomes so relatively rich that he can live in comfort and rest in peace."

Oddly enough, one of Sumner's most formidable opponents was the philosopher Charles Sanders Peirce. Peirce, who has often and rather misleadingly been accounted the Father of Pragmatism—of the philosophy of what "works" as the test of truth—was, in fact, a defender of Christian humanism. His prose style was as vigorous as Sumner's, and his indignation as deep. Peirce, in his attack on Sumner, quoted the Gospel of St. John: "God is love. . . . God sent not the Son into the world to judge the world; but that the world should through him be saved." Thus "Evolutionary philosophy" taught "that growth comes only from love . . . from the ardent impulse to fulfil another's highest impulse . . . this is the way the mind develops. . . ." As with the mind so with the cosmos. But the new doctrine of what might well come to be called the Economical Century had a different "formula of redemption. . . . It is this: 'Intelligence in the service of greed ensures the justest prices, the fairest contracts, the most enlightened conduct of all the dealings between men, and leads to the *summum bonum*, food in plenty and perfect comfort.' Food for whom? Why, for the greedy master of intelligence." Such philosophers were ready to concede that "Love is all very pretty: 'no higher or purer source of human happiness exists.' . . . But it is a 'source of enduring injury,' and, in short, should be overruled by something wiser." Some of the philosophers of the "greed" school allowed a bit of space for certain moral impulses. The philosopher of this persuasion, Peirce wrote, "wants his mammon flavored with a *soupçon* of god." If Peirce included in his net sociologists of the Ward school, he was clearly speaking of Sumner when he spoke of the theorists who termed all those who wished to improve the lot of the poor sentimentalists. "What after all is sentimentalism?" Peirce asked rhetorically. "It is an *ism*, a doctrine, namely, the doctrine that great respect should be paid to the natural judgments of the sensible heart. This is what sentimentalism precisely is; and I entreat the reader to consider whether to condemn it is not of all blasphemies the most degrading." Such insolence was enough "to provoke the very skies to scowl and rumble. Soon," Peirce added, "a flash and quick peal will shake the economists quite out of their complacency, too late. The twentieth century, in its latter half, shall surely see the deluge-tempest burst upon the social order,—to clear upon a world as deep in ruin as that greed-philosophy has longed plunged it into guilt. No post-thermidorian high jinks then!"

"In the same spirit," Peirce wrote, "it has been strongly maintained and is to-day widely believed that all acts of charity and benevolence, private and public, go seriously to degrade the human race. . . . Here, then, is the issue. The gospel of Christ says that progress comes from every individual merging his individuality in sympathy with his neighbors. On the other hand the conviction of the nineteenth century is that progress takes place by virtue of every individual's striving for himself with all his might and trampling his neighbor under foot whenever he gets a chance to do so. This may accurately be called the Gospel of Greed." Darwinism, Peirce believed, despite all its accomplishments, had brought with it an "unlovely hardness."

10

The Great Strikes

The resistance of "labor" to "capital" took a variety of forms, and it is these forms that make up a substantial portion of this volume. Indeed, as we have said earlier, virtually everything that transpired in the era under consideration was directly or indirectly related to the "war."

Among the working class the war took the form of union activity and/or political radicalism, specifically some form of Marxism, socialism, or anarchism. Among the middle-class enemies of capitalism (a group that included a large number of farmers) it took the form of a kind of indigenous socialism, most commonly Christian socialism, and what was called individualist anarchism to distinguish it from such foreign importations as syndicalism, which accepted various forms of cooperative action. "American" socialism, moreover, was generally nonrevolutionary and expressed the belief that socialism could be achieved without violence and through democratic processes. In addition to Christian socialism, the most popular domestic brand, Henry George's "single tax" socialism and Edward Bellamy's "National" socialism attracted thousands of middle- and upper-class adherents.

As early as the "hard times" of 1819, the first serious American depression, economists, politicians, and reformers had made various proposals for ameliorating the lot of the workingman. Direct relief was opposed by many on the ground that it could encourage idleness and dependence. What was done to relieve suffering and poverty, especially that caused by economic slumps, was largely done by private philanthropic groups, primarily Christian relief organizations run by women. The 1830s saw the establishment of numerous utopian socialist or communist communities by men and women who were dismayed by what seemed to them the excessively competitive and inequitable character of American society. If the most famous of these was Brook Farm, the longest-lived were the experiments in Christian socialism, such as John Humphrey Noyes's Oneida Community. At the same time an incipient union movement began to take form, a movement the guiding light of which was the English radical Frances Wright. A number of unions were formed, national conventions were held, some strikes were successful, and workingmen began to take an active role in politics. Their principal aims were to secure a nine- or ten-hour day and free public education. The Panic and Depression of 1837 were a severe setback to all efforts at improving the condition of skilled workers (little attention was given to the unskilled), and the virtual collapse of the movement was underlined by the return of Frances Wright to England.

The period of industrial expansion that followed the Civil War, especially the building of the railroads, marked a new phase in American labor history. The tide of immigration, halted by the Depression of 1857 and subsequently by the war, now reached flood stage as hundreds of thousands of Irish, Germans, and, finally, Italians poured into Eastern seaports. Among the German immigrants were a number imbued with the ideas of Karl Marx and his coadjutor, Friedrich Engels, as well as dozens of other revolutionary theorists. In addition, an older generation of German and Irish immigrants, many of whom had fought in the Union army, were more militant than they had been formerly. The same was true of those native Americans who as veterans of the Civil War found it increasingly difficult to find jobs. In addition, there was the inescapable fact that the situation of the average laborer (and farmer as well) was constantly deteriorating. Wages and working conditions were, in general, worse than they had been forty years earlier. The railroads were identified by many workingmen as the principal culprits. In a perpetual state of insolvency themselves, the railroads were often in arrears in wages; in bad times the first impulse of the tycoons who ran them was to cut the already abysmally low wages of their employees, while continuing to receive enormous salaries themselves and issue high dividends to stockholders. In the pre-Civil War era the Supreme Court had declared in the Dred Scott decision that black Americans had no rights that the courts—i.e., white Americans— must respect. Now it seemed increasingly evident that workingmen had no rights that their employers were required to respect.

The end of the war brought a flurry of union activity. The railroad car drivers struck in April, 1866, and held a mass meeting in New York City's Union Square. George Templeton Strong heard "one of their orators, an unwashed loon. He spoke grammatically, fluently, and sensibly, and with good manner and action." In Chicago, in August, 1867, the National Congress of American Labor met and called for a militant labor movement. But progress was dishearteningly slow.

The International Workingmen's Association—the "Red" International—was a Marxist union committed to achieving a socialist state in which the "workers" owned "the means of production" and to accomplishing this by violent revolution. Its appeal in the United States was primarily to foreign-born workers, and it was overwhelmingly German in its modest membership. Victoria Woodhull and her sister, Tennessee C. Claflin, had founded Chapter 12 of the IWA in 1872 (and published *The Communist Manifesto* in their weekly), but Marx, indignant at the sisters' free-love principles, had canceled the union's charter.

Mikhail Bakunin, the leading Russian anarchist, pulled his followers out of the International in 1872, proclaiming his motto, "Buy lead and you'll get bread." He established the Black International (opposed to Marx's Red International) and declared: "I demand the destruction of all States, national and territorial, and the foundation on their ruins of the International State of the Workers."

Novices in Marxism received a red card, identifying them as students of Marxist theory. When they passed an examination on socialist principles, they received a white card. The officers and officials of the party carried blue cards. New recruits were assured that the International Workingmen's Association was neither anarchistic nor committed to the use of force to achieve its goals.

To the charge that the socialists planned to "overthrow the present government by force," the Red Internationalists replied, "No, we predict by the light of science merely that an armed conflict between the insolent rich and the ignorant poor is near at hand; that the battle will end in chaos unless at the proper time the socialists interfere and by their aid secure a just system of society; and when they do interfere they propose to do so effectively." Members were exhorted "to grasp the whole situation as it now stands and endeavor to fit yourself for a leader in the revolution and a scientific organizer of the new society." The year predicted for the "downfall of the competitive system" was 1889. England, as the most industrially developed country, would doubtless be the first to experience the "outbreak," followed by France, Germany, and Spain.

That there had not been serious labor trouble in the United States was undoubtedly due in large part to the terrible depression that began in 1873 and lasted four years. When there was little work to be had and hundreds of thousands of hungry and desperate men were looking for any job that might put food in their families' mouths, there was little disposition to militant labor activity. Certainly there had been numerous indications of dissatisfaction in labor ranks. William Sylvis, an iron molder, had organized the Iron-Moulders International Union in Philadelphia as early as 1859. After the war he called a labor congress in Baltimore and was elected president of the National Labor Union, a precursor of the Knights of St. Crispin. Sylvis wished to combine the National Labor Union with Marx's First International. "Our case," Sylvis wrote to the officers of the International Labor Congress, "is a common one; it is a war between poverty and wealth. . . . Our late war resulted in the building up of the most infamous moneyed aristocracy on the face of the earth. This moneyed power is fast eating up the substance of the people. We have made war upon it, and we mean to win. If we can, we will win through the ballot box; if not—then *we will resort to sterner means*. A little *blood letting* is sometimes necessary in desperate cases."

Although the Depression of 1873 put a serious crimp in the union movement, it encouraged the spread of radical principles. The Workingmen's Party, avowedly communist, put down roots in many of the larger cities. In New York an army veteran named John Swinton headed the party and proclaimed its principles in a journal called *John Swinton's Paper*.

The Workingmen's Party of the United States endorsed the basic principles of the International. In its own statement of purposes it declared: "Political liberty without economic freedom is but an empty phrase. . . . We repudiate entire connection with all political parties of the propertied classes. . . . We demand that all the means of labor, (land, machinery, railroads, telegraphs, canals, etc.) become the common property of the whole people, for the purpose of abolishing the wages system and substituting in its place co-operative production with a just distribution of its rewards." With such far-reaching goals went a series of much more practical measures "to improve the condition of the working classes." These included an eight-hour day, "sanitary inspection of all conditions of labor. . . . Establishment of bureaus of labor statistics in all States as well as by the National Government. . . . Prohibitory laws against the employment of children under fourteen years of age in industrial establishments. . . . Gratuitous instruction in all educational institutions. Strict laws making employers liable for all accidents to the injury of their employees. Gratuitous administration of justice in all courts of law. Abolition of all conspiracy laws. . . . All industrial enterprises to be placed under the control of the Government as fast as practicable and operated by free co-operative trade unions for the good of the whole people."

A long accumulation of grievances on the part of American workmen toward those who employed them burst forth with frightening violence in the summer of 1877. While the initial acts were directed against the railroads, the spontaneous outbreaks revealed that the bitterness reached far beyond any particular industry.

At the beginning of July the Baltimore & Ohio Railroad notified its employees that it would make substantial cuts in their wages, reducing the pay of firemen from $1.75 per day to $1.58 and other wages correspondingly. For men who could hardly feed their families at the existing wage scale, the news brought a reaction first of despair and then of rage. Indignant workers began to meet. A committee was appointed to intercede with the officers of the company, but they refused to receive the delegation of workers. There was sentiment among many of the men for a strike but little organization and deep anxiety about how a strike could be sustained. When July 16, the date set for the wage cuts, came, employees at Camden Junction, near Baltimore, walked out. Some forty firemen left their engines and persuaded a number of brakemen to join them. Elsewhere reports began to trickle into the railroad's headquarters that similar, apparently spontaneous actions were taking place at different points along the B&O lines. The strategy hit upon by the strikers was to halt all freight traffic. Growing numbers of railroad employees were soon joined by the canalboatmen. In Baltimore other workers, union and nonunion, left their jobs—canmakers, boxmakers, and sawyers among them. By the morning of the seventeenth virtually all freight on the line was at a standstill. In the words of a contemporary historian of the strike, "the control of the immense property of the Baltimore and Ohio Railroad

Company had passed out of the hands of the officers and was held by the strikers . . . the greatest labor strike yet known was now fairly inaugurated."

A major strike center was Martinsburg, West Virginia; the officers of the railroad sent an urgent message to the governor of the state asking for militia to protect B&O property and start the trains running. When the militia company arrived at Martinsburg, it found itself vastly outnumbered by angry strikers. A militiaman, acting on orders from his captain, tried to prevent the throwing of a switch to sidetrack a westbound freight. One of the strikers fired at him, and he returned the fire, wounding the striker. When the captain ordered the strikers to disperse, they hooted and jeered, and the militiamen, who had friends and relatives among the strikers, joined forces with them. Cars in the Martinsburg yard were uncoupled, and the links and pins in the connections were destroyed or hidden.

Word came over the telegraph lines throughout the day that workers on other roads all across the country were going out on strike with the same tactics—tying up the freight lines and refusing to let locomotives and cars leave the railroad yards.

The president of the Baltimore & Ohio refused to meet with the strikers or discuss their grievances. Instead, he besieged President Hayes with demands that volunteers be called up and that the full force of the government be used at once to protect the property of the railroad—in effect to break the strike. Rumors circulated that it was Secretary of State William Evarts who prevailed on the President to avoid extreme measures. Hayes issued a proclamation, ordering "all persons engaged in . . . unlawful and insurrectionary proceedings to disperse and retire peaceably to their respective abodes . . . and I invoke the aid and cooperation of all good citizens thereof to uphold the laws and preserve the public peace." Some 250 regular soldiers were rounded up in various military posts in and about Washington and dispatched to Martinsburg. Meantime, a committee of strikers at Baltimore circulated a statement of their grievances, which did much to create public sympathy. With Federal troops standing by to preserve order, the B&O officials attempted to get their trains moving, but they could not find men to operate them, even with contingents of soldiers on the trains. The strikers, meanwhile, were treated to increasingly inflammatory speeches by their leaders. In the words of J. A. Dacus, a newspaper reporter, "It was a widespread belief among a large class of people in the lower ranks of society, who were reduced almost to starvation, that they had been wronged and oppressed beyond all endurance, that made the scenes witnessed in some many of the great cities of the country possible."

Word of strikes and wild demonstrations came from Philadelphia, Columbus, Ohio, Chicago, Cincinnati, and St. Louis. The initial success of the strikers in stopping the movement of freight and the apparent incapacity of the railroads, the militia, and even the Federal troops to get the trains moving emboldened the strikers. As the railroads stepped up their efforts to force trains through, the strikers, many of them now armed, threw engineers from their cabs. According to Dacus, the strikers on the outskirts of Baltimore began to be joined by "unemployed and vicious persons of the city, in sympathy with the strikers." The Maryland National Guard, the "Dandy Fifth," was called out to deal with the strikers at Cumberland, Maryland, but, as the militiamen assembled, they were surrounded by jeering crowds "of all ages, and both sexes." The Baltimore armory was pelted with rocks and stones, windows were broken, and shots fired. By now the city was in a turmoil, the streets jammed with restless groups of men and boys augmented, in Dacus's words, by "thieves, professional ruffians . . . drunken loafers, tramps," all "drawn into the seething mass of grimy workmen and odorous thieves." The city authorities were now thoroughly alarmed, and the mayor, fearful that order could not be maintained in the city, ordered the 6th Regiment called up.

The general air of alarm was increased by the tolling of the city's alarm bells, calling additional militia to duty. As the 6th Regiment made its way through the crowded streets, the nervous soldiers, hooted at and pelted with stones, opened fire on their tormentors. Twice more before they reached Camden Station, the guardsmen stopped and fired volleys into the crowd. When the regiment made contact with the beleaguered 5th, the combined forces attacked the mob and drove it back, but throughout the night of July 19 much of the city, including the shops and warehouses of the B&O, remained in the hands of the mob. Ten persons had been killed, and many more wounded. The governor of Maryland appealed to Hayes for Federal troops to help restore order. The 5th and 6th regiments were in a virtual state of siege at Camden Station. Dacus's history of the "Great Strikes," published a few months after their end, was plainly intended to place the blame for the violence that occurred on the "Internationalists," who, he insisted, were everywhere "behind the scenes, manipulating the populace, and organizing the rioters."

In Dacus's somewhat perfervid account of the progress of the strike, he wrote that "the whole country was in an uproar . . . no human foresight could determine that a reign of devastation and death, such as had never before afflicted the world, might not commence at any time." What was most alarming was that, in Dacus's words, "Behind the strikers men beheld a more dreadful force. It was the awful presence of that socialism, which has more than once made Europe tremble on account of its energy, its despotism, its fearful atrocities. . . . The Commune had found a place in America."

At nightfall a crowd estimated at more than 10,000, including, according to observers, a number of women and girls who urged "the men on to acts of outrage and bloodshed," filled the streets, but a hastily augmented force of police dispersed the crowd, arresting some 50 people. The *Baltimore Sun* commented, not unsympathetically, on the role of women in the strike. "The singular part of the disturbances," a correspondent of the *Sun* wrote, "is the very active part taken by the women, who are the wives and mothers of the firemen. They look famished and wild, and declare for starvation rather than have their people work for the reduced wages. Better to starve outright, they say, than to die by slow starvation."

President Hayes, by now thoroughly alarmed, called his Cabinet into a virtually permanent session. There were indications that the country might be on the verge of a full-scale revolution such as that which seven years earlier had tumbled Napoleon III from his throne, and it was decided to dispatch no more Federal troops but to gather them in Washington for the defense of the city. Some were posted at the Treasury building and others at the Capitol. Even in Washington the appearance of the soldiers was greeted with groans and hisses by scattered groups of strikers.

The situation in Pittsburgh, the headquarters of the Pennsylvania Railroad, was especially volatile. That city had a long history of labor unrest and of repressive actions by employers. It harbored a contingent of extreme radicals who considered themselves Marxists of one variety or another—anarchists, socialists, communists, or, not infrequently, all three. At Pittsburgh a major grievance, in addition to a 10 percent wage cut, was the Pennsylvania Railroad's new policy of "double headers," the effect of which was to require twice as much work of trainmen for the same pay. The tactics of the strikers were similar to those used three days earlier by the railroad workers at Martinsburg. No freight train was allowed to move in or out of the city. Three regiments of state guards arrived in Pittsburgh on the twentieth, but the strikers and their supporters hooted at the order of their commander to disperse and answered him with cries of "We want bread." When the officer in command of the guard regiments stated his determination to get the trains running, he was told he would be shot if he persisted. Soon there were twenty miles of freight cars collected on sidings. The guardsmen pitched camp along the tracks, interspersed with the fires and encampments of the strikers. Rumors that the officers of the Pennsylvania Railroad were determined to force a freight train through the blockade brought out a crowd estimated at 10,000, most of them in a defiant mood.

Two Gatling guns—rapid-fire machine guns—were ordered sent to Pittsburgh with 3,400 rounds of ammunition, along with a number of Philadelphia guard units, many of them made up of socially prominent young men of that city. "Great masses of people thronged the streets," Dacus wrote, "men and women, old and young, persons belonging to all classes, and occupying every station in life came out, and rushed back and forth with nervous, objectless haste." Sympathy with the strikers was predominant, and the militiamen "were everywhere execrated and treated with derision by the people." Again newsmen were surprised at the large number of women in the crowds and at their militancy. Dacus wrote: "Strange to say, there was a large element in the population of Pittsburgh, who had the reputation of being respectable people—tradesmen, householders, well-to-do mechanics and such, who were witnesses of the progress of the turbulent mob, who not only did not protest against their proceedings, but openly mingled with them, and encouraged them to commit further deeds of violence. . . . The fiendish spirit of the Commune had taken possession of an incredibly large proportion of the people of Pittsburgh. . . . Never before in the history of the United States had scenes such as those now witnessed arrested the attention of the people."

By July 21 the number of national guardsmen, or militia as they were still more commonly called, in Pittsburgh had reached several thousand. Efforts were made to identify and arrest the ringleaders of the mob, which like that in Baltimore was made up by now of far more than the railroad workers. Such efforts proved unsuccessful and indeed added to the tension already evident. When the sheriff of the county, backed by several regiments of Philadelphia militia, proceeded to a "general rendezvous" of the strikers, he was defied, and the militia jeered as "a pack of sneaks and cowards." When one of the men for whom the sheriff had a warrant was identified, he rushed forward, waving his hat and shouting to the crowd, "At them boys! at them! give them hell!" Apparently at this point the general in command of the militiamen ordered them to fire. Sixteen people were killed in the first volley, and many others badly injured. The crowd fell back in the face of the fire, taking its wounded with it, and word spread rapidly through the city.

A reporter for the *New York Herald* wrote: "The sight presented after the soldiers ceased firing was sickening. Old men and boys attracted to the [scene] . . . lay writhing in the agonies of death, while numbers of children were killed outright. Yellowstone, the neighborhood of the scene of the conflict, was actually dotted with the dead and dying; while weeping women, cursing loudly and deeply the instruments which had made them widows, were clinging to the bleeding corpses."

The Pittsburgh militia, stationed nearby, threw down their arms and joined the mob. An already excited populace flared up in wrath. There were proposals for attacking and exterminating the outnumbered militia. The fact that the units that had fired were from Philadelphia and contained many individuals far more sympathetic to the railroad companies than to the strikers added fuel to the fire. Outnumbered ten to one, the Philadelphia militia withdrew to the railroad roundhouse.

The mob meanwhile raided all the stores in the city known to sell guns and carried off some 400 Winchester and Henry rifles and as many revolvers. Dacus estimated that in all some 2,000 weapons, not including swords and knives, were seized, in addition to large quantities of ammunition. Thus armed, two columns of some 4,000 men were formed up into a semblance of military order and, followed by a vast crowd that included numerous women and children—Dacus refers to "the shrill screams of the women, the cries of the children, and the curses of men"—headed for the roundhouse, where they put the militia under siege, firing volley after volley into the windows without receiving any fire in return. Again in Dacus's words: "Three thousand armed militia, infantry, artillery, and cavalry, the police force of some hundreds, the constabulary, all were powerless in the presence of the armed and enraged multitude of many thousands." Soldiers found outside the roundhouse were killed, and the sheriff, trying to turn back a body of rioters bent on setting fire to railroad cars, was shot and killed. Systematic efforts were now made to destroy by fire as much of the property of the Pennsylvania Railroad as possible. Strings of freight cars on sidings in the railroad yards, in addition to workshops, sheds, offices and buildings of all kinds, were set afire. The mob, frustrated at being unable to get at the Philadelphia militia, decided to try to burn them out. A piece of artillery was found, loaded, and fired at the roundhouse, making a breach in its walls, but an attack by the mob was beaten back. Finally, oil was poured on a train full of coke, which was set on fire and run up against the side of the roundhouse, which quickly ignited, pouring out clouds of black smoke. At that point the 800 or so militiamen inside prepared to fight their way out of the city. Fortunately for them, their attackers were diverted by a more spectacular fire in another section of the city, and the badly demoralized guardsmen were able, under the cover of a Gatling gun, to make their escape, although they were fired at from housetops as they marched out along Pennsylvania Avenue. By five o'clock in the afternoon they arrived, badly battered, at Claremont, some twelve miles from the city. Eight soldiers had been killed, and a number wounded during the retreat. Their flight left the city in the hands of the rioters, who proceeded with their incendiary tasks. Burned were 125 locomotives, along with hundreds of tons of coal and coke and the 3,500 cars that carried them. Two hotels; a grain elevator; the Union Depot; the Pittsburgh & St. Louis freight depot covering half a dozen blocks; and hundreds of smaller buildings were also set on fire. Indeed, it seemed for a time as though the whole city might go up in flames. By the afternoon of July 23 a "continuous line of fire, flame, mouldering ruins and smoke extended along the tracks a distance of three miles." Burned-out and abandoned buildings were soon being looted. In Dacus's description: "Here a brawny woman could be seen hurrying away with a pair of white kid slippers under her arms; another, carrying an infant, would be rolling a barrel of flour along the sidewalk, using her feet as the propelling power; here a man pushing a wheelbarrow loaded with white lead. Boys hurried through the crowd with large-sized family Bibles as their share of the plunder, while scores of females utilized aprons and dresses to carry flour, eggs, dry goods, etc. Bundles of umbrellas, fancy parasols, hams, bacon, leaf lard, calico, blankets, laces and flour were mixed together in the arms of robust men, or carried on hastily constructed hand barrows."

Around the state not only were railroad terminals and depots affected, but mills, coal mines, factories, and foundries all were also swept up in an outburst of violence. It had, after all, been only a few years earlier that Pennsylvania coal fields had been gripped by the Molly Maguire episode, the culmination of years of violence, murder, and cruel repression in the fields. Sunbury, Altoona, Meadville, Lehigh, Lebanon, and Summit Hill all were for a time in the hands of strikers. Trains were stopped, and mines closed. At Summit Hill the strikers carried bread on poles as the insignia of their need and demanded that the company pay those whose wages were in arrears. In many places strikers included as one of their principal demands that they be paid on a specific agreed-upon day rather than whenever the company was disposed to do so; some strikers went so far as to demand that they be paid their wages weekly or at least biweekly rather than monthly.

By July 30 the entire Lackawanna coal mining region was idle. At Johnstown, when a trainload of United States regulars arrived, there ensued a fight in which a number of people were killed and several soldiers wounded. One of the bloodiest (and most unnecessary) episodes took place in Reading, Pennsylvania. The freight trains of the Philadelphia & Reading line had been stopped by strikers, but there had been no rioting and no violence in the town. The commander of the Pennsylvania guard nonetheless dispatched Brigadier General Frank Reeder to Reading with the 4th and 16th regiments, the 4th being made up of the so-called Easton Greys, another of the gentleman units from Philadelphia. The Greys arrived in Reading, formed up, and marched to the town square, where, apparently without provocation, they opened fire on a peaceable gathering of citizens which included a number of policemen. Thirteen persons were killed, five policemen were wounded, and twenty-seven others were also wounded, a number of them seriously. That night the Lebanon Valley Bridge, which crossed the Schuykill at Reading, was burned down, closing off contact with Harrisburg and the West. Men of the 16th Regiment declared that they would not fire on the people of the town under any circumstances. In the words of their spokesman, "We will not shoot workingmen, whatever the Easton Greys may do. They are our brothers, and the only one we'd like to pour our bullets into is that damned Frank Gowen" (superintendent of the Philadelphia & Reading Railroad and a man notorious for his role in the prosecution of the Molly Maguires).

The Easton Greys soon found themselves under attack by infuriated strikers, and the problem became, as it had been at Pittsburgh, how to evacuate them from the town. The battle cry of the strikers became "Wage and revenge," and a series of clashes took place between the strikers and the Easton Greys before the soldiers could be extricated.

Meanwhile, the Great Strikes, as they were now being called, spread like wildfire. In New Jersey the principal trouble spots were at Trenton and Newark. At the latter city the policemen expressed themselves as being in "full sympathy" with the strikers. Several of the guard companies took the same line. They themselves were workingmen, and they would not fire upon their fellows. Most newspapers were critical of the strikers. "The mob is a wild beast and needs to be shot down," the *New York Herald* declared, while the headlines of *The New York Times* proclaimed that Chicago was "in Possession of Communists." Tom Scott, the head of the Pennsylvania Railroad, urged that the strikers be given "a rifle diet for a few days and see how they like that kind of bread." In an editorial in the *Tribune*, Whitelaw Reid urged the owners and the government not to yield an inch to the strikers. "It is the business of the government to end such disorders," the *Tribune* announced, "and it will be a mercy to the strikers themselves and to all concerned to end this business quickly, whatever the cost." In another editorial the paper asked: "What is society to do when, with egregious folly, a mob is run against it, except to shoot, arrest, imprison, sentence and in capital cases, hang?"

The *Tribune* blamed the strike on a too lenient public opinion ruled more by a sentimental sympathy for the lot of the workers than for hardheaded, scientific assessment of the situation. "Public opinion," the paper declared, "slaughtered men and burned buildings in Pittsburgh. . . . For years we have been fostering a spirit of Communism in these United States." One of those caught up in the strikes was a young reporter for the *New York Tribune* named Jacob Riis. Driven out of Elmira by the striking railroad workers there, who suspected him of being a company agent, Riis and a friend headed for Philadelphia, but at Scranton the rails were torn up and the train halted. Mingling with an angry mob in the center of the town, Riis and his friend found themselves facing a line of armed men protecting the switching yards. When a brick hit the major who was exhorting the crowd to disperse, a command was given and the guns blazed. A man standing beside Riis fell, bleeding profusely. "There was an instant's dead silence," Riis wrote, "then the rushing of a thousand feet and wild cries of terror as the mob broke and fled. . . . In all my life I never ran so fast," Riis added.

Henry Ward Beecher spoke to a crowded audience at the Plymouth Church in Brooklyn on the significance of the strike. As *The New York Times* reported the meeting, after eulogizing the "working classes and . . . particularly . . . the industry, sobriety, and heroism of the railroad employees," Beecher expatiated on the theme of the necessity for cooperation between capital and labor. A workman had a "perfect right" to say to an employer that he would not work for him, but he had no right to interfere with the right of the next man to work. By taking such a position, the strikers "had put themselves in an attitude of tyrannical opposition to all law and order and they could not be defended. The necessities of the great railroad companies demanded that there should be a reduction of wages. There must be a continual shrinkage until things come back to the gold standard, and wages, as well as greenbacks, provisions and property, must share in it. It was true that $1 a day was not enough to support a man and five children if a man would insist on smoking and drinking beer." What was required was more training in "self-denial." A prudent family "may live on good bread and water in the morning, water and bread at midday, and good water and bread at night (continued laughter)." There might be cases of genuine hardship, "but the great laws of political economy could not be set at defiance." The strike must be defeated. A few days later, as the strike continued, Beecher warned in his Sunday sermon against the "importation of the communistic and like European notions." They were "abominations," which, if unchecked, must have the effect of destroying "the individuality of the person," in which case "individual liberty" must also be lost.

The *Chicago Daily News* took the part of the strikers, declaring: "For years the railroads of this country have been wholly run outside the United States Constitution. . . . They have charged what they pleased for fares and freight rates. They have corrupted the State and city legislators. They have corrupted Congress employing for the purpose a lobby that dispensed bribes to the amount of millions and millions. . . . Their managers have been plundering the roads and speculating on their securities to their own enrichment. Finally, having found nothing more to get out of the stockholders . . . they have commenced raiding not only upon the general public but their own employees."

Meanwhile, Hayes and his Cabinet officers received the latest reports of uprisings and discussed the proper strategy for restoring order. In one twenty-four-hour period, when much of Pittsburgh was in flames, the Cabinet met three times. Finally, on July 24, it was decided to treat the strike as an insurrection and use Federal troops wherever they were needed to restore order. General Winfield Scott Hancock was dispatched with a contingent of troops to Pittsburgh. There the citizens had already organized "vigilance committees" to put a stop to looting and arson when Hancock and his army regulars arrived. The Great Strike at Pittsburgh, the most lurid and violent riot in our history, was at an end. Dacus insisted, as he did in his account of rioting in other cities, that the strikers were honest, law-abiding men with genuine grievances who enjoyed the support of the respectable citizens of the city but had been led astray by the "communistic mob."

With Washington's garrisons reinforced and "unlawful gatherings" prohibited, attention was focused on such potential trouble spots as Chicago and St. Louis, critical rail junctions through which flowed much of the nation's essential goods.

A few lines avoided involvement in the strike by granting the strikers' demands. In New York City the Long Island Rail Road met with a committee of engineers and agreed to "endeavor to make arrangements providing in future for a fixed day in every month upon which to pay the engineers and other employees." The critical point in New York seemed to be passed when the mayor and the city officials agreed to allow a mass meeting at Tompkins Hall. A number of socialist speakers were present, and although they were bitter in their denunciation of capitalism, the general tenor of the meeting was one of moderation. "Keep on the side of law, and keep the law on the side of laborers," one speaker urged. John Swinton, editor of *John Swinton's Paper* and described by Dacus as "in point of education and culture entitled to the rank of leader of the New York Communists," told his audience: "You are as good as Henry Ward Beecher's congregation, and I think the comparison is rather in your favor. I think the Police Commissioners did well and wisely in permitting this meeting to take place, and Mayor [Smith] Ely has won imperishable laurels by saying there is no power in the constitution to prevent a meeting like this from taking place. And now . . . what is this social volcano that has brought us here together,—this power that has one hundred thousand Americans and one billion dollars within its grasp?" Swinton asked.

"On one side we see the movement of workingmen anxious only to restore the rate of wages to which they are justly entitled . . . and on the other we see the steady and relentless disposition on the part of capital to cut men's wages down so low as to make life a choice between starvation and suicide. Glory to the militia who refused to fire on the strikers. (Great applause.) Glory to the Sixteenth Pennsylvania, that refused to be accomplices of the murderers of innocent men, women and children at Pittsburgh." Swinton assured the strikers of the active support of the Workingmen's Party of New York, adding, "We consider all legalized charter corporations, such as railroad, banking, mining, manufacturing, gas, etc., under the present system of operations, as the most despotic and heartless enemies of the working classes. That their acts of tyranny and oppression have been the cause of demoralizing thousands of honest workingmen, thereby driving them to acts of madness, desperation and crime that they would not otherwise have been guilty of had they been justly dealt by." The Workingmen's Party, Swinton declared, was dismayed at the influence that business interests exerted over all branches of the government and believed that if this process was not reversed, "the government will become totally demoralized, the rights of the masses destroyed, and, instead of the voice of the people, the power of the almighty dollar will become absolute and supreme." The workingmen of the country must form their own political party, for "nothing short of a political revolution, through the ballot box, on the part of the working classes will remedy the evils under which we suffer."

If New York City escaped serious convulsions, the same could not be said for Syracuse, Albany, and Buffalo. There were riots and violence in the three cities. At Buffalo 700 militiamen were attacked by a mob, and 17 soldiers wounded. There again many of the militia sympathized with the strikers and refused to fire on them. Again all railroad shops were ordered closed, and freight trains blocked from leaving the city. For three days the strikers and their supporters were in complete control of the city.

In Ohio and Illinois there was a much stronger disposition on the part of the railroads to avoid serious trouble by at least temporarily acceding to the strikers' demands, while on the part of the workers themselves there seemed less disposition to violence. The Cincinnati, Hamilton, and Dayton Railroad Company accommodated some of the workers' demands, as did the Little Miami Company. In Cincinnati the strikers offered to protect railroad property and to keep passenger trains as well as the mail moving. No freight trains, however, moved through Cincinnati. Federal authorities there remained out of things, undoubtedly contributing to the preservation of order.

At Fort Wayne, Indiana, the freight trains were stopped, and all shops and factories in the city shut down. In Terre Haute by the twenty-fourth the strikers had taken control of all the railroads running through the city without any acts of violence. When some drunken section hands headed for the city, presumably to stir up trouble, heavily armed strikers turned them back. Strikers also took over the Pittsburgh, Fort Wayne, and Chicago railway, providing their own engineers, conductors, and superintendents to run the passenger trains and using two handsome parlor cars as their headquarters.

If there was to be a general uprising in a major city of the country, Chicago must be its center. In J. A. Dacus's words, "Chicago is great as being the seat of more startling and sensational developments than any or all other American cities. . . . Its great population is, perhaps, as much of a conglomerated mass, of as many races, kindreds and tongues, as the inhabitants in any other city in the world can be. . . . Chicago was long ago noted as having an unusually large number of Socialists, Internationalists, Spiritualists, and other peculiar people, among its inhabitants. It was the first city in this country, in which communism had the boldness to come out and avow itself openly. It was known generally, that the so-called 'dangerous class' were proportionately numerous in Chicago. . . ." Chicago was thus "regarded as a place where the most serious consequences of the Great Strikes should be expected."

Here again, as in Cincinnati, concessions were made by the owners of many of the railroad companies running into the city; therefore, Dacus observed, "the chances for Chicago to escape pillage and destruction were good, notwithstanding the immense number of visionary men, professional thieves, and idle and vicious characters to be found there, who were interested . . . in inaugurating a reign of terror."

Despite the concessions made by the various railroad companies, by July 24 only one line had any freight trains moving out of the city, and many of the larger plants and factories had been shut down by persons sympathetic to the broader goals of the strikes. Crowds of people, ready at any provocation to turn into a mob and then into "rioters," roamed the streets, engaging in clashes with small bands of police. As in New York City, substantial numbers of soldiers—15,000 guardsmen (highly unpredictable in their loyalties) and Federal troops—were brought to the city and placed as inconspicuously as possible at strategic points. The merchants met and organized a "body of special police," and the mayor ordered "idlers and curious people" to keep off the streets.

One reason that the more active members of the Workingmen's Party failed to take full advantage of the Great Strike in Chicago was that it did not fit into any recognizable ideological framework. While, according to the Marxist dialectic, the inconsistencies between capitalism and industrialism were bound to produce in time a proletarian revolution and the overthrow of capitalism, that revolution was generally considered to be, like the Second Coming, sometime in the fairly distant future. It was supposed to be not sudden and spontaneous but rather the culmination of a long process of education—raising, as we would say today, the consciousness of the workers and preparing for the dictatorship of the proletariat. There must have been frantic meetings of the officers and ideologues of the Workingmen's Party and all associated and affiliated socialist/communist groups to try to understand what was happening and determine what their reaction should be. As Dacus put it, "Even the workingmen and the Internationalists seemed to have been surprised by the suddenness and evident momentum of the popular movement in Chicago." Far from fanning the flames, some of the leaders, like John Swinton in New York, were disposed, while using the already familiar rhetoric of the class struggle, to caution against acts of violence that might give the authorities an excuse to arrest radical leaders and cripple the labor movement.

The Executive Committee of the Workingmen's Party took the practical rather than the ideological line and let it be known that it would consult with all discontented workers "to lay out a plan how to work to better their situation." At a mass meeting called by the committee, a number of speakers addressed a large and attentive crowd. A wounded veteran of the Union army held up a crippled hand and declared that he had been promised "a life of honor and emolument in case he should be wounded in his country's services." Now he was a cripple expected to live on $6 a month. Other speakers were eloquent in their accounts of the injustices done to workers everywhere in the country. After a series of ringing resolutions the meeting broke up peaceably.

Following three or four days of uncertainty, during which time it appeared that the city would be spared serious violence, a fight broke out at the Halsted Street Viaduct. There were injuries but no deaths, and the police dispersed a large angry crowd that had gathered. The next night word was spread about the city that workingmen and their adherents should gather at the viaduct to protest the action of the police in driving them off the night before. By nine o'clock in the evening of the twenty-sixth a crowd of some 10,000 had gathered at Halsted Street near the viaduct. Sixty policemen, sent to break up the rally, rushed on the crowd, apparently firing blank cartridges. After a brief panic the crowd, now perhaps properly to be designated as a mob, re-formed, and counterattacked the vastly outnumbered police. Soon the police were in full flight, pursued by the mob, at which point 50 mounted police appeared to rescue their fellows and began firing at the mob, killing 2, one a young boy. The battle was joined, the crowd hurling paving stones, bricks, and whatever missiles they could lay hands on, the police firing back. Five persons were killed, and more than 13 badly wounded. To Dacus, one of the most disturbing features of the riots was, as in Baltimore and Pittsburgh, the large number of women involved. "Taking up positions in their houses," he wrote, "they encouraged the male members of the mob to attack the police, and were excessively abusive. . . . Many of them provided themselves with heaps of stones, pans of mud, and other dangerous and unpleasant munitions of war, and vigorously hurled them from the windows of houses on the officers contending in the streets below." Some were armed with pistols and fired them at the police. Finally, the combination of military force and concessions by employers, as well, undoubtedly, as general exhaustion, brought the rioting to an end. Chicago had emerged from its ordeal less scarred than many had feared.

In St. Louis the strikers took control of the relay depot, where all through trains had to switch tracks, and shut down all freight in or out of the city. There, despite the prompt appearance of General Jefferson C. Davis, a veteran Union officer, with 400 regulars, events followed a familiar pattern. The strikers prevailed on other workers in the city and in East St. Louis to walk off their jobs and, despite the concessions made to the strikers by the Pacific Railroad, which employed a large number of men, crowds of restless and angry workmen roamed through the city. An open-air meeting called at Lucas's Market by the Workingmen's Party on July 23 brought a large turnout. Two days later rioting broke out.

In San Francisco fires that threatened to engulf the city were started, and, in the fighting that resulted from clashes between soldiers and rioters, a number of firemen, policemen, soldiers, and rioters were killed or wounded and a number of buildings were set afire. A Committee of Safety, formed of prominent citizens, took effective control of the defense of property in the city, and orders were given to shoot any one caught demolishing property or interfering with the efforts of the fire department to extinguish fires.

Finally, after almost two weeks of turmoil that spread through most of the major cities of the nation from East to West, the Great Strikes flickered out, leaving a heavy toll of dead and wounded and property damage in the hundreds of millions of dollars.

One of the most notable aspects of the strikes was that in instances in which local and state officials acted with restraint, the strikers usually did likewise. In addition, they showed a remarkable degree of self-discipline by preserving order in their own ranks. There were few accounts of drunken or riotous behavior that could be traced to the strikers themselves. Although somewhere between 100 and 200 people were killed, and perhaps 1,000 wounded, when one considers how widespread the strike was and how numerous the riots, the wonder is that the loss of life was not far higher. For this, it seems, the strikers deserve a major share of the credit, although it is certainly the case that many public officials behaved with wisdom and restraint.

At the end of the strike *The New York Times*, its apprehensions about communists abated, made a more temperate assessment of its consequences: "The workmen have here and there compelled compliance with their demands, and in other instances they have attracted popular attention to their grievances, real or alleged, to an extent that will render future indifference impossible. . . . The balance of gain is on the side of the workmen."

The ambivalence that many Americans of liberal persuasion felt about the events that together were known as the Great Strikes is clear in J. A. Dacus's hastily assembled account of the dramatic events of the last two weeks of July. He wished to make clear that his sympathies were completely with the legitimate grievances of the strikers and that he was by no means uncritical of the economic system which more radical theorists insisted was the inevitable result of the contradictions inherent in capitalism. "A policy that increases the number of poor, that depresses the condition of the working people is unwise," he wrote, "and must inevitably end in the destruction of the social order and the ruin of the country." But Dacus believed that there were alternatives to such a "policy" and that cooperation between capital and labor was the best hope for social and economic justice. At the same time he reprobated violence and insisted, not always entirely convincingly, that the violence that flared up in the various manifestations of the Great

Strikes was the work of "tramps," "riotous boys," the unemployed, and "evil-minded persons"—in short, the "dangerous classes," whose volatile emotions were cleverly played upon by the "Internationalists," "Communists," and "socialists," many of them foreigners and most of them followers of Karl Marx and the ideologues of the Paris Commune. Yet Dacus never stopped to speculate about the social origins of the "tramps" and the desperate unemployed or the significance of the rage among the dispossessed to which the strikes gave expression. It seemed evident beyond serious question to Dacus, "that the popular sympathies were without doubt with the strikers, but not with the vicious rabble that gathered in every city—with no other motive than to pillage and burn down houses and committ [sic] other deeds of violence."

Despite a tendency to blame the communists and "Internationalists" for some of the turmoil, Dacus was at pains to make it clear that he believed that "the strength, the fearful power, which stopped the wheels of commerce, closed the marts of trade and threatened to engulf all wealth, institutions, social organizations,—everything in the vortex of ruin, was not the offspring of a conspiracy, was not generated by elaborate planning, and did not result from mature deliberation. And in this very fact, the man of calm reflection discovers, not far ahead, the rocks on which the ship of State is likely to be driven—on which every hope of mankind may be wrecked. If it had been a deliberately planned and concerted movement; if those engaged in it had exhibited evidence of organization, then its failure would have given a better promise of enduring peace and order. But the spontaneity of the movement shows the existence of a widespread discontent, a disposition to subvert the existing social order, to modify or overturn the political institutions, under which such unfavorable conditions were developed. Somewhere, there must be something radically defective either in the system, or in the manner of its control. Such spontaneous demonstrations by large masses of the people, as we have witnessed in the United States in the year 1877, do not take place without a sufficient cause."

Knowledge of the event and, even more, awareness of its significance exist so dimly in our collective memory that it is necessary to dwell a bit on the nature and meaning of the Great Strikes.

First of all, there is the essential point emphasized by Dacus: that the strike or strikes were spontaneous. Events on such a scale are rare in history. The so-called Great Fear in France at the beginning of the French Revolution was just such a phenomenon. Like the Great Strikes, it did not originate in some center of political unrest and activity, specifically in Paris, but rather in isolated and unconnected acts of violence in the countryside against the cruel exactions of landlords. Such acts took place spontaneously all over France. So with the Great Strikes. To those relatively few Americans familiar with the course of the French Revolution it was an alarming parallel. Dacus was certainly correct in stating that "such spontaneous demonstrations by large masses of people . . . do not take place without a sufficient cause." The second point is that to the spontaneous strikes were immediately added spontaneous riots and demonstrations in which many more people than the strikers joined, all profoundly dissatisfied with their place in the American "system." It is also clear that the much-abused "Internationalists" were caught off guard by the strike and the consequences which flowed from it. Although they hastened to try to place themselves in the van of the "movement," their influence was, if anything, on the side of moderation; although their rhetoric was violent, their advice was cautionary. Marxist doctrine called for the working of historical dialectic, a slow, inevitable movement in the course of which the "workers" would become organized, self-conscious, and educated in revolutionary theory. The Great Strikes in no way conformed to such a blueprint and thus must have seemed as eccentric and bizarre to the leaders of the Workingmen's Party as it did to the embattled capitalists.

The effect of the Great Strikes on the consciousness of middle- and upper-class Americans—not to mention the capitalists—is not easy to assess, but it seems safe to assume that it was enormous. To some it suggested that revolution and "socialism" were just down the road. The strike had revealed such a depth of bitterness and hostility that it could hardly be imagined that those feelings would soon be dissipated. It seemed far more likely that it would be followed by even more serious outbreaks, especially since nothing substantial had been done to meet the grievances brought to the surface by the upheaval. To be sure, some Americans gave themselves more ardently than ever to the cause of social reform or at least to the amelioration of the most flagrant inequities. But the majority simply suppressed the fears and anxieties that had been raised by the strikes; they were too busy trying to maintain or improve their own status to worry overlong about the needs of the laboring class. Important residues nonetheless remained. Fear of the working or "dangerous" classes (to some minds the terms were virtually synonymous) grew stronger, as concomitantly did anxiety about foreign agitators, about communists, socialists, and internationalists. There would never be a decade in the next 100 years in which millions of Americans would not have their slumbers disturbed by the specter of international communism in one form or another. Certainly the impact on the literary imagination registered unmistakably in a series of popular novels dealing with the theme of an ongoing and dramatic conflict between capital and labor.

Unquestionably a perplexing question for the student of American history is why there was no aftermath to the Great Strikes. Instead of being the beginning of a genuine American labor movement, it was, in fact, its high point. The beginning was also the end. There would never be another moment when the future of the country seemed to tremble on the verge of widespread social upheaval, a time when 60,000 Americans—militia, U.S. regulars, and civilian vigilantes (that, at least, was Dacus's estimate)—were mustered up to defend property and ensure, if not the orderly functioning, at least the preservation of the forms of government, a time when hundreds of thousands of Americans, many of them armed with guns, pistols, clubs, and paving stones, challenged authority.

There would certainly be other violent and bloody clashes between workingmen and their bosses—Haymarket, Homestead, Pullman, hundreds, perhaps thousands of episodes, many of them far better known—but they were only the dimmest reprise of the Great Strikes. So we find ourselves with two problems in regard to the Great Strikes. First, why was it not the opening act in a long-running revolutionary drama? Second, why does the knowledge or historical memory of it exist so marginally in our consciousness? The latter question is obviously related to the first. It was easy to forget the Great Strikes because the anxieties they generated were not fulfilled; moreover, it is human to suppress what we wish to forget. The story of the Great Strikes is incompatible with the "image" of America we have generally wished to project—one of "freedom and justice for all." As for the first question, why it was the end and not the beginning, that is somewhat more difficult to answer, but we will address ourselves to the question from time to time throughout this work.

One of the consequences of the strike was a lively debate in Congress on the subject of army appropriations. Some members argued for "a large army, and a very large army, in order to put down impending strikes." A New York Congressman took issue with the proposition. "It is not in accordance with the theory of this government that the United States is to maintain an army for the purpose of restraining any portion of its citizens in their just right. No man can coerce another to do his will. It is just as sacred a right as the right to employ. . . . The wisdom of strikes is quite another matter." Among the supporters of the right to strike was James Garfield, who declared that the right to strike was "a right as broad and universal as American history," but it was the refusal to work coupled with organizing to prevail on others not to work that, in Garfield's view, threatened the foundations of society. In the words of the Congressman from Ohio, "When I unite with others, and by force and violence prevent you from working, I have violated your right as a laborer and as a man. . . . That has been the mischief of American strikes." Nathaniel Banks, an ex-Union general, challenged Garfield. "How is it," he asked, "with capitalists who combine with other capitalists against the employed?" That, Garfield replied, was "as great a violation of the law . . . deserving of . . . greater condemnation." It was not the strike, "not the proper and lawful refusal of laborers to be oppressed by capitalists, that threatens the public peace; but . . . the spirit of unlawful interference with the rights of laborers, the spirit of mob violence and misrule,—a spirit not born on our soil, nor in harmony with our traditions; it is 'the red fool-fury of the Seine' transplanted here, taking root in our disasters, and drawing its life only from our misfortunes which has lately threatened, and may still more seriously imperil, the stability of our institutions." Waving a stack of telegrams which he declared had been sent by the governors of ten states requesting the assistance of the United States military forces to preserve order, Garfield insisted that 50,000 soldiers were needed to preserve law and order in the face of foreign agitation. "I therefore say boldly," he concluded, ". . . against all comers I am for the reign of law in this republic and for an army large enough to make it sure."

From a modern perspective the use of soldiers of the regular army to restore or maintain order during the Great Strikes was the most controversial aspect of that event (or those events). The fact that the strike rapidly deteriorated into massive riots, of course, complicates the issue, as does the disposition of the militia to be, on the one hand, too punitive in their reactions to popular demonstrations, thereby displaying the class bias of some of the upper-class militia units like the Easton Greys, and, on the other, disposed to sympathize with the grievances of friends and relatives and of a class with which many of them identified. To use Federal troops to protect property and preserve order was one thing. To use them as in effect strikebreakers was certainly another. The difficulty in the Great Strikes was to distinguish between those two functions. It was a distinction never very clearly made. The strikers, by allowing the mail to be moved along with passenger trains, clearly hoped to avoid giving the Federal government an incentive to intervene on behalf of the railroads. But there is little reason to believe that even without the "riots," which were in many instances provoked by the unnecessarily aggressive behavior of the police or militia, the Federal troops would not in time have been used to ensure that the freight trains ran. Indeed, in a number of instances regular army soldiers were used for exactly that purpose, thereby depriving the strikers of their most effective weapon and becoming in effect strikebreakers.

But to concentrate on the role of the military is to obscure the most essential point of the Great Strikes. It was, and was perceived by the vast majority of Americans to be, in its essence an at least prospectively revolutionary upheaval that threatened traditional American institutions.

E. L. Godkin wrote in the *Nation*: "It is impossible to deny that the events of the last fortnight constitute a great national disgrace, and have created a profound sensation throughout the civilized world. They are likely to impress the foreign imagination far more than the outbreak of the Civil War. . . ." For fifty years or more there had been "throughout Christendom a growing faith that outside the area of slave-soil the United States had—of course with the help of great natural resources—solved the problem of enabling labor and capital to live together in political harmony, and that this was one country in which there was no proletariat and no dangerous class." The strikes had shattered that illusion. One consequence had been to weaken "the fondly cherished hopes of many millions about the future of the race. . . . We have had what appears a widespread uprising, not against political oppression or unpopular government, but against society itself. . . ."

Godkin's sympathies were clearly not with the strikers. In his view, "the kindest thing which can be done for the great multitudes of untaught men who have been received on these shores . . . and who are torn perhaps even more here than in Europe by wild desires and wilder dreams" was to demonstrate unmistakably to them that the United States society, based on "individual freedom of thought and action," was "impregnable" and could "no more be shaken than the order of nature." It must be made clear to the strikers that "day laborers of the lowest class" could not suspend, "even for a whole day, the traffic and industry of a great nation, merely as a means of extorting ten or twenty cents a day more wages from their employers." Godkin laid much of the blame for the strikes on "reformers and philanthropists," who had talked irresponsibly about "all things as open to discussion, and every question as having two sides. . . . Some of the talk about the laborer and his rights that we have listened to on the platform and in literature during the last fifteen years," Godkin wrote, " . . . has been enough, considering the sort of ears on which it now falls, to reduce our great manufacturing districts to the condition of the Pennsylvania mining regions, and put our very civilization in peril."

When John Swinton looked back from the perspective of the 1890s, it seemed to him that the Great Strikes had been a landmark. "Dread are the memories associated with the transcendent and portentous strike of 1877. . . . It was a case in which the loss of life and destruction of property far surpassed those that had occurred in any previous uprising of labor, or that have marked any one since then." Only those "who lived amid its scenes can truly know what it meant," Swinton concluded.

John Hay was one of those upper-class Americans who had been indignant at the failure of the authorities to suppress the strikers more rigorously. He wrote to his father-in-law, the wealthy Amasa Stone: "Since last week the country has been at the mercy of the mob, and on the whole the mob has behaved rather better than the country. The shameful truth is now clear, that the government is utterly helpless and powerless in the face of an unarmed rebellion by foreign workingmen, mostly Irish. There is nowhere any firm nucleus of authority. . . . The army has been destroyed by the dirty politicians, and the State militia is utterly inefficient. Any hour the mob chooses, it can destroy any city in the country—that is the simple truth." In the opinion of Hay, much of the trouble could be laid at the door of the Democrats, who had "tried to curry favor with the rioters. . . . These are the creatures which manage our politics," he added. Even the Republican candidate's "sympathies are with the laboring man, and none with the man whose enterprise and capital give him a living. . . . The prospects of labor and capital both seem gloomy enough. The very devil seems to have entered into the lower classes of workingmen, and there are plenty of scoundrels to encourage them to all lengths."

"Colonel Hay," William Roscoe Thayer, Hay's biographer, wrote apologetically in 1908, "like the rest of the world . . . had theorized on the likelihood of war between 'Capital and Labor' but he had reassured

himself by the comfortable assumption that under American conditions—equal opportunity for all, high wages, equal laws, and the ballot-
box—no angry laboring class could grow up." The riots convinced Hay
that the ballot box, instead of weakening the hostility of labor toward
capital, had strengthened it by encouraging the ambitions of the lower
classes. "Hay held," Thayer wrote, "as did many of his contempories,
that the assaults on Property were inspired by demagogues who used
as their tools the loafers, the criminals, the vicious,—Society's dregs
who have been ready at all times to rise against laws and government.
That you have property is proof of industry and foresight on your
part or your father's; that you have nothing, is a judgment on your
laziness and vices, or on your improvidence. The world is a moral
world; which it would not be if virtue and vice received the same
rewards. . . . So an attack on Property becomes an attack on Civilization."

Hay's solution was to write a novel "which should serve as a warning to those sentimentalists who were coquetting with revolutionary
theories, and to those responsible officials who, through cowardice or
self-seeking, were tolerant of revolutionary practices." *The Bread-Winners*, written in the winter of 1882–83 and published serially and anony-
mously in the *Century* magazine, became "the novel of the year," so
well did it comport with the feelings of those Americans who bought
and read books. Indeed, its success was greater than any novel published since the Civil War. In Thayer's summary, the thesis of the book
which was received so sympathetically was, in brief, "that 'honest' Labor
has nothing to complain of; that socialistic and anarchistic panaceas,
instead of curing, would poison Society; and that those persons who
engineer a social war are either actual or potential criminals, having
the gullible masses for their dupes. The moral is obvious—Society must
protect itself against the faction which plots its destruction." The "bread-
winners" were the factory owner and his loyal employees. The villain
of the novel was a demagogic and dishonest labor leader named Offitt,
in love with a beautiful factory worker named Maud. Offitt waylays,
robs, and almost kills the enlightened factory owner, Alfred Farnham
(who also is in love with a high-minded young "operative"), and pins
the crime on one of his naïve disciples, a young Irishman named Sleeny.
The message is that union leaders are villains not to be trusted, that
the only real hope of the workers is their kind and benign employers,
who have the workers' interests at heart far more than their false
friends the unionizers, whose desire is to exploit the workingman or

woman. It was ironic that the author of *The Bread-Winners* had been the confidant of Abraham Lincoln and, with John G. Nicolay, was to be his biographer.

Albery Whitman, the black poet, wrote a poem deploring both the Great Strikes and the hardships endured by the poor.

> Whenever Communism's snaky head
> Is raised against the heel of Capital,
> I want it crushed 'neath Law's majestic tread,
> And yet would heed poor honest labor's call . . .

Americans, Whitman declared, must not let their dismay at the strike blind them to the needs of the working class.

> While pride upon her easy finger wears
> The bread of thousands in a brilliant stone,
> The eyes of Wretchedness must stream with tears,
> And groaning labor be content to groan.

One of the results of the strikes was an effort in the case of the more thoughtful and humane (or more practical) tycoons to meet some of the more flagrant inequities. In the aftermath of the Great Strikes the Baltimore & Ohio instituted a program to assist the families of the victims of disabling accidents. The Relief Association, adapted from British models, was a form of insurance into which workers paid a regular fee that provided for them and their families in case of injury, illness, or death. Four years later the company set up a pension plan which guaranteed a retirement income at 50 percent of the worker's average monthly salary. By 1934 the Baltimore & Ohio had paid out $50,000,000 in retirement benefits to its employees. N. O. Nelson, a Norwegian who manufactured plumbing and building supplies, instituted a bonus incentive system whereby all profits after the payment of a 6 percent dividend were divided among his employees. In some instances plans designed originally for the benefit of the workers grew, in time, to be ingeniously exploitative. The Pullman Palace Car Company purchased 4,000 acres near Chicago on which to build an ideal workers' community. Following in the spirit of Robert Dale Owen's model industrial town, George Pullman engaged outstanding landscape architects to design the town and its environs. Neat brick houses were built, and two-bedroom apartments rented at $4 a month. Garbage was collected, in itself something of an innovation, and the streets were swept. A shopping center or arcade housed a number of shops, and the town contained a playhouse, hotel, and gymnasium. Health services were provided as well, and after the first few years of its existence the company boasted that the mortality rate at Hyde Park—the name of the village—was a third of that for the average town. On the negative side, the company rules governing the conduct of the workers and their families were strictly enforced, and the resident workers had no part in running the town. The result was a growing disenchantment on the part of the workers with what George Pullman believed to be a benign and philanthropic enterprise.

Undoubtedly the most important consequence of the Great Strikes was not so much the rapid growth of labor unions, although they did indeed enter the modern era of the union movement, as the development of a labor consciousness, an awareness of the power of labor, and, with that awareness, a new militancy.

There was still another notable consequence. A "failed" printer and editor who had known poverty and hardship at first hand began, in the aftermath of the strikes, to write a book that, published two years later, would be entitled *Progress and Poverty*.

Progress and Poverty

Henry George was born in Philadelphia on September 2, 1839, the son of devout Episcopal parents and the eldest of ten children. His father was one of that company of small-business men who suffered a constant buffeting from an often wildly unstable economy. The senior George published Sunday school tracts for the Episcopal Church. George himself had little formal schooling, finding it, in his own words, "for the most part idle, and wasted time." Sunday school and the Franklin Institute were the poles of his intellectual life.

The George household was a pious one. The splendid cadences of the Book of Common Prayer helped shape young Henry's literary style, and his family life, with several affectionate younger sisters, seems to have been warm and happy. When George was in California trying to make his way, one sister wrote him: "You have just passed your nineteenth birthday. Did you think of it, or were you too busy? If you had been home we would have had a jollification. What a kissing-time there would have been, playing Copenhagen and so forth. Hen, kissing is quite out of fashion since you left; no kissing parties at all, I believe."

George's childhood diary records the usual preoccupations of boys: skating and sledding in the winter; building a ship; playing boys' games. He was a member of the Lawrence Literary Society, and one of his

friends wrote him in later years: "Can you or I forget the gay, refresh-
ing and kindred spirits that formed that association . . . its sympathy
with ghost stories, boxing-gloves, fencing-foils and deviltry . . . its test
of merit and standard of membership, to drink red-eye, sing good
songs and smoke lots of cigars?"

At sixteen George went to sea on an old East Indiaman called the
Hindoo. On his return he decided to follow in his father's footsteps as
a printer, editor, and writer, but he began his career in the Depression
of the mid-1850s, when jobs were hard to come by, and wages at the
starvation level. He found employment where he could, becoming in
time a journeyman compositor and printer. Discouraged with the situation in Philadelphia, he tried Boston with no more success. Back in
Philadelphia, he wrote a friend: "The times here are very hard and
are getting worse and worse every day, factory after factory suspend-
ing, and discharging its hands. There are thousands of hard-working
mechanics now out of employment in this city." He decided to heed
Horace Greeley's injunction and found a place as storekeeper's assistant
on a side-wheeled lighthouse tender bound for California via the Strait
of Magellan.

In San Francisco times were as hard as they had been in Philadelphia. George had no coat; a newfound friend lent him one. He
could find no work as a printer. He worked briefly as a sailor on a run
from San Francisco to Victoria, tried the Oregon gold fields, worked
as a weigher in a rice mill until it shut down. "The only difference
between my sleeping and my waking costumes," he wrote his sister,
"was that during the day I wore both boots and cap, and at night
dispensed with them." Not only was there no fortune to be made, but
it was difficult in the extreme to keep body and soul together. An entry
in George's diary in February, 1865, read: "I have been unsuccessful
in everything." And again: "I am in very desperate plight, Courage. . . . Don't know what to do." He finally found a job with a weekly
paper; but the paper was soon sold, and he was out of work once more.
He and a friend started a newspaper of their own. "I worked," he
noted, "until my clothes were in rags, and the toes of my shoes were
out. I slept in the office and did the best I could to economize, but
finally I ran in debt thirty dollars for my board-bill." As though feeding
himself were not enough of a challenge, George married Anna Fox,
an Australian orphan, against the wishes of her guardian.

Anna had a wide, firm mouth and direct gaze that seemed to belie
her love of dancing and her gift for creating an atmosphere of play-

fulness and delight in the midst of perpetual scarcity. Her grand-daughter, the dancer Agnes De Mille, recalled her "drollery, caprice, and delicate conceits to make all family occurrences festivals of charming invention . . . the crown of wild flowers at a birthday breakfast; the crèche at Christmas time; the puddings and black fruitcake . . . the fine sewing and embroidery with silks; the incredible doll's clothes made exactly as her own reception gowns; the chic and wit of hats with holes for Teddy-bear ears . . . the tiny picture books one inch square. . . ." In her daughter's words: "She was small, barely five feet in height and tiny boned. Beautifully formed, she had exquisite shoulders and little patrician hands. . . . She danced like a fairy." On one famous occasion she made a bet that she could wear out her male partner dancing. She wore out not only him but also two others and the orchestra. Like George himself, there was a strong vein of the mystical in Anna Fox. When she sailed from Australia to the United States as a child, the ship she was on encountered a terrible storm and seemed in imminent danger of sinking. The captain of the ship, learning that Anna had been born with a caul over her face and believing the sea lore that no person born with a caul could be drowned at sea, lashed the five-year-old child to a mast while each member of the crew passed by and touched her head. "She never forgot the episode," Agnes De Mille wrote. Her granddaughter believed that it gave her "a sense of strength and protective force" that others felt and that made them turn to her "in moments of extreme crises for reassurance, for the talisman touch that would prevent their being swept away."

George worked as a substitute typesetter in San Francisco and then moved to Sacramento, where he put in exhausting hours. He got an odd job one evening collecting tickets for a modestly attended lecture in Sacramento by an itinerant comedian who called himself Mark Twain.

A year after his marriage George's first child was born. He tried the salesman's line—magazines and clothes wringers—and then a partnership in a job printing house. He and his partners lived in George's rented house with his wife and infant. They had no fire for heat and scant food. The day after Christmas, George went from woodyard to woodyard, trying to trade printing jobs for firewood. "I came close to starving," he wrote years later, "and at one time I was so close to it that I think I should have done so but for the job of printing a few cards which enabled us to buy a little corn meal. In this darkest time in my life my second child was born." In desperation George stopped a prosperous-looking stranger on the street and demanded $5. The man asked why he wanted the money. To save his wife and children from starvation. The man gave him the money. "If he had not," George wrote later, "I think I was desperate enough to have killed him."

George was obsessed with the theme of "success." He wrote his sister: "I am constantly longing for wealth. . . . It would bring me comfort and luxury which I cannot now obtain; it would give me more congenial employment and associates; it would enable me to cultivate my mind and exert to a fuller extent my powers; it would give me the ability to minister to the comfort and enjoyment of those I love most. And therefore it is my principal object in life to obtain wealth, or at least, more of it than I have at present. . . . It is evident to me," he added, "that I have not employed the time and means at my command faithfully and advantageously as I might have, and consequently that I have myself to blame for at least part of my non-success. . . ."

Henry George had been in California for almost four years when he received word that his sister Jennie, whom he adored, had died suddenly. When he told his wife, Anna, he burst into tears and paced the floor, repeating over and over, "There is another life! There *is* another life after this! I shall see my sister again!" A few years later he wrote to his mother on the death of her sister: "The older I grow and the more I think, the more fully I realize the wisdom and benefice that pervade the universe. . . . As we were born so we die. As there were others here to receive us, so must there be others there to meet us, and the Christian faith promises that the wise and good in all ages have believed that death is but a new birth. . . . Our little life, what is it, our little globe, what is it, to the infinity that lies beyond?"

It seemed to George, as he reflected upon his manifold misfortunes and the misfortunes of his friends, that there was something radically amiss in a society in which a few enjoyed great wealth while the mass of the people lived in poverty. He began to write articles and "pieces," reflecting on the causes of such striking inequities. They were printed by editors glad to fill space and themselves feeling that things were not as they should be. His writings were at first little more than familiar denunciations of the ruthless exploitations of the capitalists. He criticized the dispositions of a society "to resolve itself into classes who have too much or too little." He and his wife joined the Monroe League, a company of young men (Mrs. George was the only woman) pledged to go to Mexico and fight with Benito Juárez against Maximilian, but the filibusters were turned back by a United States revenue cutter.

Finally, in 1866, in a brief spell of postwar prosperity, George got a job as compositor on the *San Francisco Times*. Soon he was doing some reporting and writing an occasional editorial (many of his anonymous pieces were signed "Proletarian"). Two years later he joined a paper that was just starting. The new venture found itself in trouble because it could not get Associated Press news. The paper's owner decided to try to start a news service of his own. He sent George to New York to explore the possibilities, but in New York George found out that Western Union was in cahoots with Associated Press and would not carry a competing service on its lines.

In his five months' stay in New York George saw poverty far worse than he had encountered in California, and it gave fresh stimulus to his efforts to understand how poverty could exist in conjunction with such wealth. He came to the conviction that the key lay in the private appropriation of land that "belongs in usufruct to all. . . . To permit a few individuals to take for their aggrandizement this wealth that is created by the community thereby forces the community to levy exactions upon labor and thrift for the maintenance of its services. The very process, while thus penalizing labor and thrift, offers rewards to the few for withholding land for use to the many rewards that accrue to the speculator, the profiteer in that which is absolutely necessary to human life. . . . Here," George added, "were the fundamental reasons for the increase of poverty along with the increase of wealth. . . . I then and there recognized the natural order—one of those experiences that make those who have them feel thereafter that they can vaguely appreciate what mystics and poets have called 'ecstatic vision.'"

In 1871 he published a pamphlet entitled *Our Land and Land Policy*. In it George's basic notions of land tenure and rent were stated. After a succession of editorships, from some of which he was ejected because of his "radical" principles, George found himself, in the Panic of 1873 and the onset of the depression that followed it, once more out of work. This time he turned to a political sinecure. He had been instrumental in electing a Democratic governor of California on a reform platform, and he asked for a state job, "where there was little to do and something to get, so that I might devote myself to some important writing." The governor appointed George to the post of the state inspector of gas meters, which, George wrote, "yielded, though intermittently, a sufficient revenue to live on, and which required very little work."

In 1875 George, afire with his plans for reordering society, began a career as a public speaker. Eleanor Marx Aveling described him as "a little man, with exceedingly clear blue eyes that seem exceedingly honest, a straight-cut mouth, red beard, and bald head. In manner he is sharp, quick but not abrupt, and outspoken." He had a strong voice and an engaging manner as a lecturer, illustrating his remarks with anecdotes and humorous asides. Beginning as a stump speaker for Samuel Tilden in the election of 1876, George was invited to lecture on his economic theories at Berkeley. In San Francisco a group which called itself the Land Reform League of California was formed under George's general auspices. Sponsored by the league, he traveled about the state, attacking "the selfish greed that seeks to pile fortune on fortune, and the niggard spirit that steels the heart to the wail of distress. . . . Shall the ploughers forever plough the backs of a class condemned to toil? Shall the millstones of greed forever grind the faces of the . . . poor?" he asked.

In a speech in behalf of Tilden's candidacy for president, he described graphically the economic conditions of the country: "See seventy thousand men out of work in the Pennsylvania coal fields; fifty thousand laborers asking for bread in the City of New York; the alms-houses of Massachusetts crowded to repletion in the summertime; un-employed men roving over the West in great bands, stealing what they cannot earn. . . . It is an ominous thing that in this centennial year, states that a century ago were covered with primeval forest should be holding conventions to consider 'tramp nuisance'—the pure symptoms of that leprosy of nations, chronic pauperism. . . . What can any change of men avail so long as the policy which is the primary cause of these evils is unchanged?"

George found himself much attracted by the idea of becoming a college professor. Here at last he might find a life more secure and, equally important, more prestigious than that of a peripatetic lecturer and sometime newspaper editor. The state of California had just es-tablished a new university at Berkeley. Some of George's friends and political allies, among them William Swinton, brother of the radical journalist John Swinton, and President John LeConte, were on the faculty. George let them know of his ambition, and they arranged for him to give a lecture to a gathering of faculty and students. It was entitled "The Study of Political Economy." Political economy, George told his audience, was a branch of learning which "concerns itself with matters which among us occupy more than nine tenths of human efforts, and perhaps nine tenths of human thought." Mastery of the field would enable students to correct social ills which were the result of selfishness and ignorance. The solution to "social weakness and disease" lay in neither wild dreams of red destruction nor weak projects for putting [workingmen and women] in leading-strings to a brainless abstraction called the state, but in simple measures sanctioned by justice." The true law of social life was "the law of love, the law of liberty, the law of each for all and all for each . . . the highest expressions of religious truth include the widest generalizations of political economy." We do not know the intellectual predilections of the faculty members in George's audience, but it seems reasonable to assume that they were not stirred by reference to "the highest expressions of religious truth."

But George did not let the matter rest there. He went on to indict the academic community for its addiction to impractical and untested theories. "For the study of political economy," he told the students, "you need no special knowledge, no extensive library, no costly laboratory. You do not even need textbooks or teachers, if you will but think for yourselves. . . . All this array of professors, all this paraphernalia of learning cannot educate a man. Here you may obtain the tools; but they will be useful only to him who can use them. A monkey with a microscope, a mule packing a library, are fit emblems of the men—and unfortunately they are plenty—who pass through the whole educational machinery and come out but learned fools, crammed with knowledge that they cannot use. . . ." It was not a speech designed to cheer up the professors who heard it, whatever the students may have thought. Indeed, the professors may have wondered why, if George thought no better of "this paraphernalia of learning," he was so anxious to be identified with it. In any event no invitation to join the fledgling faculty was forthcoming, fortunately for George since it is much to be doubted if he would have found the time or been disposed as a member of the faculty of the University of California to have produced *Progress and Poverty.*

The years of public lecturing and of debates, spoken and written, with champions of orthodox economics, widened and extended George's own theories. Finally, in September, 1877, two months after the Great Strikes, he curtailed all his activities and immersed himself in what was to be his great work, a revelation of the true causes of worldwide depressions and social and economic injustice and, most important, the remedy. He worked like a man possessed, neglectful of his appearance, of his family and its needs, resistant to anything that might divert him from his task, which was, in his view, no less than the salvation of the world.

It became clear to George, as he thought about his great work of redemption, that he had two tasks: He must demolish the Malthusian-Ricardian-Smithian economics; he must utterly destroy the hydra-headed monster. And he must put in its place a new system whereby "progress" would produce not riches for a few and poverty for most but a common, shared level of comfort and well-being. "The present century has been marked," he wrote, "by a prodigious increase in wealth-producing power. The utilization of steam and electricity, the introduction of improved processes and labor-saving machinery, the greater subdivision and grander scale of production, the wonderful facilitation of exchanges, have multiplied enormously the effectiveness of labor." It had been natural to expect "at the beginning of this marvelous era" that "labor-saving inventions would lighten the toil and improve the condition of the laborer; that the enormous increase in the power of producing wealth would make real poverty a thing of the past."

Certainly that would have been the assumption of the Founding Fathers of the Republic, men like Franklin and Jefferson, if they would have seen "the forest tree transformed into finished lumber—into doors, sashes, blinds, boxes or barrels, with hardly the touch of a human hand," or "the great workshops where boots and shoes are turned out by the case with less labor than the old-fashioned cobbler could have put on a sole. . . ." They would have seen "arising, as necessary sequences, moral conditions realizing the golden age of which mankind have always dreamed. Youth no longer stunted and starved; age no longer harried by avarice; the child at play with the tiger; the man with the muckrake drinking in the glory of the stars. Foul things fled, fierce things tame; discord turned to harmony! For how could there be greed where all had enough? How could the vice, the crime, the ignorance, the brutality, that spring from poverty and the fear of poverty, exist where poverty had vanished?"

Instead of a new age of general prosperity and social justice, "disappointment has followed disappointment," George wrote. ". . . From all parts of the civilized world come complaints of industrial depression; of labor condemned to involuntary idleness; of capital massed and wasting; of pecuniary distress among business men; of want and suffering and anxiety among the working classes. All the dull, deadening pain, all the keen, maddening anguish, that to great masses of men are involved in the words 'hard times,' afflict alike the world today. . . . In factories where labor-saving machinery has reached its most wonderful development, little children are at work . . . amid the greatest accumulations of wealth, men die of starvation, and puny infants suckle dry breasts; while everywhere the greed of gain, the worship of wealth, shows the force of the fear of want. The promised land flies before us like the mirage. . . . Material progress does not merely fail to relieve poverty—it actually produces it. . . . This association of poverty with progress is the great enigma of our times. It is the central fact from which spring industrial, social, and political difficulties that perplex the world, and with which statesmanship and philanthropy and education grapple in vain. . . . It is the riddle which the Sphinx of Fate puts to our civilization, and which not to answer is to be destroyed. So long as all the increased wealth which modern progress brings goes but to build up great fortunes, to increase luxury and to make sharper the contrast between the House of Have and the House of Want, progress is not real and cannot be permanent."

George wished to give "political economy" the "certitude of a true science," realize "the noble dreams of socialism," and, finally, the most important, "identify social law with moral law." That is to say, he wished to make the point beyond refutation that there was no conflict between the idea of a moral order in the universe and the social and economic behavior of men. In order to accomplish this, he had to demolish the "old" science of Malthus reinforced by Darwin. The "law" of the old science was that the population inevitably outran the food supply; human beings multiplied faster than the supply of food, population increasing geometrically while the food supply at best increased arithmetically. The masses must therefore always press against the limits of available food. The poor must starve or live on the verge of starvation or die in sufficient numbers in natural or man-made holocausts to keep the population in rough balance with food. The Darwinian gloss on this was that only the fittest could survive in the life-and-death struggle for the limited resources of the planet. Those who survived were the "fit"; those who perished were the "unfit." A psychologist might suspect that the hostility of the upper classes (of which Malthus was inevitably a member) against the "dangerous classes," the poor and the powerless, was at least an ingredient in Malthusian reasoning. What cannot be questioned is the fact that it was hailed as true science (as opposed to religious "sentimentalism") and became an article of faith among the supporters of capitalism. Capitalism, it was argued with astonishing ingenuousness, was the exemplary political and economic expression of Malthusian-Darwinian science. That some people should grow richer and richer while others grew poorer and poorer appeared to be the perhaps regrettable but nonetheless inevitable result of the inexorable working of those natural laws the first and most spectacular manifestation of which was Sir Isaac Newton's law of gravity.

One of the corollaries of Malthusian-Ricardian-Smithian economics was that *capital preceded and created labor*. If this were indeed the case, capitalists were justified in ruling the world. It was *their* capital that made everything else possible: technological innovation; progress; even "work." All depended on the capitalists. The obligation of the capitalist toward his worker stopped with *paying the worker the lowest wage that would command his labor*. It thus followed that the more the workers available to compete for a limited number of jobs, the lower the wage scale could be driven and the higher, presumably, would be the profits to the capitalists, enabling them to invest in more productive facilities, thereby creating more jobs and ensuring more "progress." But the progress, it appeared, must be accompanied by the continuing or increasing degradation of the worker. A kind of debased religious imprimatur was inserted, as we have noted before, which took the line that the rich were those who had been the most faithful stewards of the Lord's bounty; the poor were, correspondingly, those whose faith was weak. Like the foolish virgins of the parable, they had failed to trim their lamps. They had allowed, in good capitalist fashion, the talents that the Lord gave them to rust instead of multiplying them. So it seemed that Christian dogmas reinforced scientific principles. That thought helped to give the greediest capitalist a good conscience as well as encouraging him to share his profits with the established churches and their affiliated organizations—colleges, hospitals, and missions.

To George, the exclusive possession of "that which nature provides for all men" was the stumbling block for a true progress. "If one man can command the land upon which others must labor," he wrote, "he can appropriate the produce of their labor as the price of his permission to labor. . . . To improvements, such an original title can be shown but it is a title to the improvements, and not to the land itself." Until private property in land was abolished, George insisted, there was no true freedom; "Declarations of Independence and Acts of Emancipation are in vain." He wrote of Malthus: "The great cause of the triumph of this [Malthusian] theory is that, instead of menacing any vested right or antagonizing any powerful interest, it is eminently soothing and reassuring to the classes who, wielding the power of wealth, dominate thought. At a time when old supports were falling away, it came to the rescue of the special privileges by which few monopolize so much of the good things of the world, proclaiming a natural cause for the want and misery which, if attributed to political institutions, must condemn every government under which they exist."

One of Malthus's most effective arguments had been by analogy from the animal kingdom. A particular terrain could accommodate only a certain number of animals. Anything in excess of this number must be driven to a new habitat or perish one way or another in the struggle for existence. The analogy seemed defective to George. "Give more food, open fuller conditions of life, and the vegetable or animal can but multiply; the man will develop . . . in higher forms and wider powers. Man is an animal; but he is an animal plus something else. He is the mythic earth-tree, whose roots are in the ground, but whose topmost branches may blossom in the heavens! . . . In other words, the law of population accords with and is subordinate to the law of intellectual development, and any danger that human beings may be brought into a world where they cannot be provided for arises not from the ordinances of nature, but from the social mal-adjustments that in the midst of wealth condemn men to want."

In this sentence as much as in any in the book (and there are, of course, many to the same effect) lies the key to the book's power. It freed man (scientifically) from the iron "laws of nature" into which Malthus and Darwin had thrust him and allowed free play to all his more generous instincts. Of the book's roughly 500 pages, almost half are devoted to the refutation of the Malthusian-Darwinian system.

The orthodox economists had announced that depressions were due to overproduction or, conversely, underconsumption. But the fallacy of such explanations was obvious. How could there be overproduction when millions of people were in desperate need? Another tenet of orthodoxy was that the war between capital and labor was what made the economic system work—the struggle of the capitalist to get his labor at the lowest wage and that of the workingman to get the highest wage he could command. The orthodox economists ignored the unequal nature of this warfare, in which all the decisive weapons were in the hands of the employer. It was such inequities that led to the clamor for cheap money issued by the government or to the demand that the government provide work when work was lacking. Such wild notions brought the masses of men under the influence of "charlatans and demagogues."

George's task, he told his readers, was "to seek the law which associates poverty with progress" and in the "explanation of this paradox . . . find the explanation of those recurring seasons of industrial and commercial paralysis which . . . seem so inexplicable. . . . Upon us is the responsibility of seeking the law, for in the very heart of our civilization to-day women faint and little children moan."

Some of Henry George's most deeply felt pages are concerned with the terrible feelings of financial insecurity incident to American life. "Poverty is the open-mouthed, relentless hell which yawns beneath civilized society. And it is hell enough. . . . For poverty is not merely deprivation; it means shame, degradation; the searing of the most sensitive parts of our moral and mental nature as with hot irons . . . the wrenching of the most vital nerves. . . . From this hell of poverty, it is but natural that men should make every effort to escape. . . . Many a man does a mean thing, a dishonest thing, a greedy and grasping, an unjust thing, in the effort to place above want, or the fear of want, mother or wife or children." Freed from this insatiable anxiety, this debilitating dread of poverty, men and women would disclose new powers and potentialities, "the springs of production would be set free, and the enormous increase of wealth would give the poorest ample comfort. Men would no more worry about finding employment than they would worry about finding air to breathe. . . ."

More than 170 pages into the text, George presented his principal thesis. As population increases, the pressure of that population, competing for a limited space, drives up the cost of land, both its purchase price and its rent. "The increase of rent which goes on in progressive countries is at once seen to be the key which explains why wages and interest fail to increase with increase in productive power." Rent, rising faster than either interest or productivity, absorbs that increment of increased productivity that would otherwise go into increased wages. Moreover, underdeveloped land, on which no improvements have been made, rises in value by virtue of the fact that adjacent land 'has been developed and thus provides its owner with an unearned increment of value that is the consequence of the efforts of others. "What proportion of the produce is taken as rent must determine what proportion is left for wages. Rent is thus an invisible tax on enterprise. Commonly included in capital, it is not capital but a tax on capital as well as on wages.

"White parasols and Elephants Mad with Pride are the flowers of a grant of land." The words were from a Brahmin text that George used at the beginning and end of Book V, entitled "The Problem Solved." The section begins with the statement: "A consideration of the manner in which the speculative advance in land values cuts down the earnings of labor and capital and checks production leads . . . irresistibly to the conclusion that this is the main cause of those periodical industrial depressions to which every civilized country, and all civilized countries together, seem increasingly liable. . . . That land speculation is the true cause of industrial depression is, in the United States, clearly evident."

It was not, of course, merely the speculative use of land that caused the devastating depressions that periodically racked the industrialized "progressive" nations. The fact that the currency contracted when expansion was most needed was an important contributing factor. In addition, "the protective tariffs which present artificial barriers to the interplay of productive forces" had an important role "in producing and continuing what are called hard times."

"Poverty deepens as wealth increases, and wages are forced down . . . because land, which is the source of all wealth and the field of all labor, is monopolized. To extirpate poverty, to make wages what they should be, the full earnings of the laborer, we must therefore substitute for the individual ownership of land a common ownership. Nothing else will go to the cause of the evil—in nothing else is there the slightest hope. . . . *We must make land common property.*" George pointed out: "A house and the lot on which it stands are alike property, as being the subject of ownership, and are alike classed by lawyers as real estate. Yet in nature and relations they differ widely. The one is produced by human labor, and belongs to the class in political economy styled wealth. The other is part of nature, and belongs to the class in political economy styled land.

"We should satisfy the law of justice," George wrote, "we should meet all economic requirements, by at one stroke abolishing all private titles, declaring all land public property, and letting it out to the highest bidders in lots to suit, under such conditions as would sacredly guard the private right to improvements. . . . Let the individuals who now hold [land] still retain if they want to, possession of what they are pleased to call *their land*. Let them continue to call it *their* land. Let them buy and sell, and bequeath and devise it. We may safely leave them the shell, if we take the kernel. *It is not necessary to confiscate land; it is only necessary to confiscate rent*. . . . In form the ownership of land would remain just as now. No owner of land need be dispossessed, and no restriction need be placed on the amount of land any one could hold. For, rent being taken by the State in taxes, land, no matter in whose name it stood, . . . would be really common property, and every member of the community would participate in the advantages of its ownership."

George also believed that "businesses which are in their nature monopolies are properly part of the function of the State, and should be assumed by the State. There is the same reason why Government should carry telegraphic messages as that it should carry letters; that railroads should belong to the public as that common roads should."

At the end of *Progress and Poverty* George turned from the "problems of social life" to the "problem of individual life." The two must intersect. You could not, finally, talk about one without speaking of the other. The paramount problem of the individual was the meaning of human existence. "The yearning for a further life," George wrote, "is natural and deep. It grows with intellectual growth, and perhaps none feel it more than those who have begun to see how great the universe is and how infinite are the vistas which every advance in knowledge opens before us." In the enlightened atmosphere of the times, when science appeared to rule supreme and human beings were mere expressions of vast and imponderable forces, it often seemed "impossible to look on this yearning save as a vain and childish hope, arising from man's egotism, and for which there is not the slightest ground or warrant, but which, on the contrary, seems inconsistent with positive knowledge." But George would not concede it to be so. He knew he must be reconciled in some other dimension of experience with his adored sister Jennie.

It was thus in a sense to create a space in which man's faith in the immortality of the soul could live once more that George had composed his book. Men like Malthus and Darwin had produced what professed to be "scientific interpretations" which had the effect of reducing "the individual to insignificance" and destroying the idea of a moral order in the universe. "It is difficult," George wrote, "to reconcile the idea of human immorality with the idea that nature wastes men by constantly bringing them into being where there is no room for them. It is impossible to reconcile the idea of an intelligent and beneficent Creator with the belief that the wretchedness and degradation which are the lot of such a large proportion of human kind result from his enactments. . . ." By making it evident that "the waste of human powers and the prodigality of human suffering" did not "spring from natural laws but were the consequence of ignorance and selfishness," George had banished "from the modern world" the "nightmare" notion that human life was without larger meaning than the merely social. Political economy had been called "the dismal science, and as currently taught, *is* hopeless and despairing." But there was a better and truer political economy, one in which "we see that human will is the great factor, and that taking men in the aggregate, their condition is as they make it; . . . we see that economic law and moral law are essentially one. . . ."

Science described, far in the future, "a dead earth, an exhausted sun—a time when clashing together, the solar system shall resolve itself into a gaseous form, again to begin immeasurable mutations. What then is the meaning of life," George asked, "of life absolutely and inevitably bound by death?" To him it seemed "intelligible only as an avenue and vestibule to another life. And its facts explainable only upon a theory which cannot be expressed but in myth and symbol. . . . Lo! here, now, in our civilized society, the old allegories yet have a meaning, the old myths are still true. . . . Shall we say that what passes from *our* sight passes into oblivion? Far, far beyond our ken the eternal laws must hold their sway. The hope that rises is the heart of all religions!"

When he had written the last lines late in the night, Henry George threw himself, weary and expended, on his bed and wept in relief and exultation. He had affirmed his conviction that he and Jennie would meet in some future state and in the process had written a book that would make him one of the most famous men of the age. He had not lost her after all; he had found himself. It seems safe to say that *Progress and Poverty* is the only work on economics that ends with reflections on the immortality of the soul. It was theological tract as much as an essay on economics, and the response that it received suggested that the age hungered for some reassertion of essentially religious perceptions against the brutally mechanistic formulations of the classical economists.

To his father George wrote: "It is with deep feeling of gratitude to Our Father in Heaven that I send you a printed copy of this book. . . . It represents a great deal of work and a good deal of sacrifice, but now it is done. It will not be recognized at first—maybe not for some time—but it will ultimately be considered a great book, will be published in both hemispheres, and be translated into different languages. This I know, though neither of us may ever see it here. But the belief that I have expressed in this book—the belief that there is yet another life for us—makes that of little moment."

The book was *not* at first much recognized. George had 500 copies printed up at his own expense and sent them to the major publishers with the hope that one of them would agree to publish it. Appleton finally did so, somewhat hesitantly. The book was generally favorably reviewed, most notably perhaps in the London *Times*, but its sales were modest. George had substantial debts and little income other than that from his lecturing. He went East in the summer of 1880, "afloat at forty-one," as he wrote a friend, "poorer than at twenty-one. I do not complain but there is some bitterness in it." In California his wife took in boarders to make ends meet, and his older son, Henry George, Jr., found work with a printer.

George threw himself into the Garfield-Hancock campaign, giving free trade talks that alarmed Garfield's conservative supporters. He was eased out of the political lecture circuit but he picked up some work with Abram Hewitt, the department store tycoon who was a member of Congress and needed someone to write up a report for him. While he was working for Hewitt, George wrote a pamphlet entitled *The Irish Land Question*. The long and bitter conflict between the Irish and their British overlords had flared up into one of its periodic crises. His pamphlet immediately became a weapon in that war. In the words of the literary critic Albert Jay Nock, before George quite knew what he had done, "a prodigious rabble of charmed and enthusiastic Irish had hoisted him on their shoulders and borne him into worldwide fame." In doing so, they drew attention to *Progress and Poverty*.

To every advocate of Irish rights (and there were hundreds of thousands of them in the United States, not confined to the Irish by any means, and tens of thousands in Great Britain), George was an instant hero. He visited Ireland and England. He gave lectures by the dozens to audiences of thousands. An enthusiastic philanthropist bought 1,000 copies of *Progress and Poverty* and placed them in public libraries around the country. He followed this gesture of munificence by paying off a considerable accumulation of George's debts. In time *Progress and Poverty* would rival the Holy Scriptures in popularity, selling more than

2,000,000 copies in the United States. It was translated into a dozen languages and was read wherever people could read.

Much of the effectiveness of *Progress and Poverty* can be attributed to George's style. He combined a direct, homely storytelling manner with appeals to his readers' deepest religious and humanitarian instincts. That the book is a marvelous exercise in logical argumentation cannot, I think, be denied. (Tolstoy wrote: "People do not argue with the teaching of George; they simply do not know it. He who becomes acquainted with it cannot but agree.") Whether, in fact, it is true is another question and fortunately somewhat beside the point in the context of this work. We are concerned less with its truth than with its consequences. On one level it was certainly "true"—that is to say, it corresponded to the needs and to the admittedly limited and partial perceptions of the majority of its readers, and it discovered readers by that very fact. It made room for larger and more generous "truths" about the economic and social relations of human beings to each other. So it was, at heart, a religious tract, sailing unabashedly under the flag of a scientific work in political economy.

John Jay Chapman was "startled" at the utopian tone of the last chapters of *Progress and Poverty* "with fruit trees growing in the streets— no courts—no crime—no poverty. . . . He is rapt. He is beyond the reach of the human voice. He has a harp and is singing—and *this* is the power of the book. It is preposterous. It is impossible. It is a romance—a rhapsody—a vision—at the end of a long seeming scientific discussion of rent, interest, and wages. . . . This burst of song, being the only lyric of this commercial period, is popular."

It turned out that not just Americans but people all over the modern world wished to believe in two things preeminently: the "scientific" rearrangement of the world and the old song of redemption through a higher power in the universe.

The message was simple enough: Man *is* important; there *is* a moral order in the universe; mind, following the precepts of the moral order, can and indeed must affect the process; there is some form of existence beyond the Valley of the Shadow of Death; life is a drama of incomprehensible richness and beauty as well as tragedy; we have only to be equal, to work together, to cooperate, to hold the land in common to experience God's bounty. Henry George's *Progress and Poverty* was the lineal descendant of John Winthrop's "A Modell of Christian Charity." It belongs with those prophetic works—the liter-

ature of redemption—which entered so profoundly into the conscious-
ness and the conscience of Americans that they changed our history:
Tom Paine's *Common Sense*, Harriet Beecher Stowe's *Uncle Tom's Cabin*,
Ralph Waldo Emerson's "The American Scholar," Walt Whitman's
Leaves of Grass.

There were, of course, practical as well as emotional reasons why
Progress and Poverty entered so powerfully into the consciousness of the
time. George pleased the socialists by referring to their "noble" aspirations. He comforted those friends of reform who feared socialism
as the agent of violent revolution by proposing the transformation of
society without violence. Collectivists were charmed by his insistence
that in true equality and cooperation lay the seeds of the new order.
Individualists were attracted by George's emphasis on the *individual*,
by the fact that he rescued the individual from the blind workings of
evolution. The pious were delighted to see religion and economics
reconciled, albeit in so vague a fashion as not to offend devout agnostics. Finally, his style was irresistible, combining, as it did, elements
of Emerson, biblical overtones, and the simple expository manner of
John Bunyan's *Pilgrim's Progress*.

The fact was that Americans had lived, from the beginning, in
the hope of universal redemption. It was the energizing principle, the
motive power, that drove the strange, crude, unwieldy vehicle that
became the United States on its dangerously accelerating course. Constantly threatened by disaster, it had survived by luck and pluck and
faith in history as a divinely ordained process of redemption. The
notion of life on earth—animal and human—as a ruthless and bloody
struggle for survival was profoundly alien to America and its deepest
traditions. If that was the "scientific" explanation, Americans would
live with it as best they could—but on the whole resentfully and unhappily. They turned as the thirsty to water, the starving to food to
the trumpet tones of the new prophet. *Progress and Poverty* insinuated
itself into inner recesses of the minds and souls of hundreds of thousands of Americans and worked there as a kind of antidote to mechanistic and materialistic doctrines. More conspicuously it inspired a
substantial number of the ablest among its readers to move heaven
and earth to give effect to its doctrines. It did so not only in the United
States but in Britain, in Denmark, in Sweden, in Australia and New
Zealand—indeed, all over the civilized world.

Alfred Russel Wallace, the great naturalist, wrote to Charles Darwin: "I am doing what I rarely if ever have done before—reading a

book through a second time immediately after the first perusal. I do not think I have ever been so attracted by a book, with the exception of your *Origin of Species* and Spencer's *First Principles and Social Statics*." George had undertaken to refute Malthus's *Principles of Population*, Wallace noted, "to which both you and I have acknowledged ourselves indebted." George "illustrates and supports his views with a wealth of illustrative facts," Wallace added, "and a cogency of argument which I have rarely seen equalled, while his style is equal to that of [historian Henry T.] Buckle and thus his book is delightful reading. . . . It is the most startling novel and original book of the last twenty years, and if I mistake not will in the future rank as making an advance in political and social science equal to that made by Adam Smith a century ago."

George Bernard Shaw acknowledged the influence of George on the Fabian Socialists of Great Britain. "My attention was first drawn to political economy as a science of social salvation," Shaw wrote, "by Henry George's eloquence and his *Progress and Poverty*, which had an enormous circulation in the early 'eighties, and beyond all question had more to do with the Socialist revival of that period in England than any other book. . . . When I was swept into the great Socialist revival of 1883, I found that five sixths of those who were swept in with me had been converted by Henry George."

As far away as China, Sun Yat-sen, the "George Washington of the Chinese Revolution," was so moved by George's book that he wrote: "I intend to devote my future to the promotion of the welfare of the Chinese people as a people. The teachings of Henry George will be the basis of our program of reform."

Single tax clubs sprang up all over the country, and soon George's disciples numbered in the hundreds of thousands. Capitalists read *Progress and Poverty* and became single tax reformers. Political economists were converted to George's theory. The Henry George "movement," centered in New York, was, in the opinion of Eleanor Marx Aveling and her husband, directed at too narrow an issue. The notion of nationalizing the land by a "single tax" had a great appeal for middle-class reformers, but it stopped short of addressing the most serious shortcomings of capitalism. Like the Knights of Labor, it was interesting primarily because of "its spontaneity and Americanness."

When the Conference of Labor Associations asked George in August, 1886, what principles he espoused in his campaign for mayor of New York, he declared that he was strongly opposed to "those general conditions, which, despite the fact that labor is the producer of all wealth, make the term workingman synonymous with poor man. . . . The party," George continued, "that shall do for the question of industrial slavery what the Republican party did for the question of chattel slavery . . . must be a working-man's party. . . . I have seen the promise of the coming of such a party in the growing discontent of Labor with unjust social conditions. . . . There is and there can be an idle class only where there is a disinherited class." George's future seemed to the Avelings to depend on his decision whether to "go forward with the labor party resolved on nationalization, not of land alone, but of raw material, machinery, means of credit, capital, or fall back towards the ranks of the old parties. . . ."

Karl Marx was one reader of *Progress and Poverty* who was not captivated. Marx described George as having "the repugnant arrogance and presumption which inevitably mark all such panacea breeds." The book was "the capitalists' last ditch," he said contemptuously. George, for his part, called Marx "a most superficial thinker, entangled in an inexact and vicious terminology," and "the prince of muddleheads."

12

The Conditions of Labor

Industrial capitalism was the starting point, the thesis in Hegelian terms. Labor was the anti-thesis. If capitalism was quite clearly the sum total of the capitalists, the corporate executives, the railroad and steel magnates, the bankers and financiers, those utilizing vast amounts of capital, labor was a far more ambiguous (or comprehensive) term. It covered a multitude of skins—white, black, yellow—and races and even classes. It comprehended, indeed, all those Americans, farmers, workers, intellectuals, reformers of every variety and denomination who were the victims, or merely the opponents, of capitalism. In the famous war between capital and labor they all were enlisted under the banner of "labor."

"Nature abhors the weak," Brooks Adams wrote in a cynical variation on the more familiar aphorism. So, indeed, it seemed in this era. The labor force, the men and women and children employed by the capitalists, worked under conditions hardly conceivable in a later, if not necessarily more enlightened, age. While conditions of labor were almost uniformly deplorable in good times, they were truly desperate in "hard times"—i.e., any of the periodic depressions that plagued the country.

The Depression of the 1870s had devastating effects on the Pennsylvania coal miners. One worker described the condition of Connellsville miners as "one of unmitigated serfdom. Life is scarcely worth having under such circumstances. . . . They suffer from the engrafted old world aristocratic tyranny. They are the slaves of anti-Republican corporations. In all directions these corporations have usurped the authority and perpetuated the tyrannies once confined to the despotisms of Europe. . . . Within the past three years we have been crippled so unscrupulously that today we are barely able to hold body and soul together. . . . Gentlemen, beware! Hunger knows no wrong." A local newspaper editor's comment was, "What a spectacle is offered by the quietness and perfect order of people thrown out of work and all but starving . . . patiently waiting during the past summer. . . . The chief influences of American life are wholesome and vital, and tend to national prosperity."

In 1886 Karl Marx's daughter Eleanor Marx Aveling and her husband, Edward, visited the United States to make a general survey of labor conditions and to talk with socialists and labor leaders around the country. They were struck by the activity in the labor movement generally, both in unionization and in radical political action on the part of various socialist and anarchist groups. In their opinion, the condition of workingmen and women in the United States was in every important respect as bad as that of the British working class. In addition, unionization in America was twenty or thirty years behind that in Britain. On the other hand, there were far more labor newspapers and journals in the United States than in Britain. The Avelings counted ninety-seven, including one entitled the *Woman's World* and excluding most of the foreign-language socialist and labor journals. Wherever the Avelings went they addressed large crowds of working-class people with a substantial admixture of middle- and upper-class reformers. In a twelve-week tour they visited thirty-five cities and towns as far west as Kansas. The meetings were, the Avelings wrote, "with the very rarest exceptions, largely attended. In many places hundreds of people were unable to gain admission. . . . We have never spoken to any audiences like the American audiences for patience, fairness, anxiety to get at the meaning of the speaker," they added. The Avelings found an enormous curiosity about the doctrines of socialism, which heretofore had been preached largely by Germans for German immigrants. "And in every town we met, both in private and in public, the leading men and women in the various working-class organizations."

In the view of the Avelings, British laborers still believed that "there is a community of interests between them and their employers. . . . But in America this mutual deception is nearly at an end. The workingmen and the capitalists in the majority of cases quite understand that each, as a class, is the deadly and inexorable foe of the other. . . ." The capitalists believed the struggle must end "in the subjugation of the working class," while the workingmen were equally convinced it would end "in the abolition of all classes."

Above all, the Avelings found vast ignorance in the United States about the true nature of socialism. Many of these people were, in their term, "unconscious socialists." They wrote: "Large numbers of persons finding at last that Socialism does not mean equal division of property, nor the application of dynamite to capitalists, nor anarchy, have in town after town, by hundreds upon hundreds, declared, 'Well if that is Socialism we are Socialists.'" Much of the Avelings' time was taken up, especially in the aftermath of the Haymarket bombing of 1886, in explaining the difference between socialism and anarchism.

The Avelings called on their readers to compare the accounts of working conditions in England in Marx's *Capital* with the state of affairs in the United States. Friedrich Engels's book *The Condition of the Working Class in England*, written in 1844, could be applied to America forty-odd years later by simply substituting "America" for "England" on page after page. The Avelings were also struck by the degree to which the labor commissioners of the various states in their statistical reports revealed a profound sympathy for the workingmen and women of their states. The report of the Massachusetts commissioners on conditions in Fall River, for example, noted that "every mill in the city is making money . . . but the operatives travel in the same old path— sickness, suffering, and small pay. . . . There is a state of things that should make men blush for shame."

In state after state the testimony of workers in different industrial crafts was monotonously the same. Things were getting worse with each passing year. "Times are harder now than I ever knew them before," a laborer in Kansas declared, while another said, "The condition of the laboring classes is too bad for utterance, and is rapidly growing worse." The testimony was also uniformly to the effect that "the rich and poor are further apart than ever before." A coal miner reported that he had had to move five times during the year to find employment. In Michigan a worker in a shoe factory testified: "Labor to-day is poorer paid than ever before; more discontent exists, more men in despair, and if a change is not soon devised, trouble must come. . . ."

The Avelings were convinced by their reading of the reports of the state labor commissioners and their own observations that, hours and wages aside, the physical demands placed by American employers on their workers were much more severe than those prevailing in Britain. American laborers started to work at an earlier age than their British counterparts, worked more strenuously, and died, on the average, almost a decade earlier. Thus the life expectancy of a British iron molder was fifty years and eleven months, while "the American moulder dies before he reaches the age of forty. . . ."

Employers and foremen practiced innumerable small deceits: short measures in the cloth mills; short weights in the mines; fines for the mildest infractions of innumerable restrictive rules governing every action of the worker. Blacklists and intimidation were common. Many workers reported to the Avelings that they were afraid to be seen talking to them for fear of losing their jobs and being thereafter black-listed as troublemakers, radicals, or union sympathizers. Workers were threatened with loss of their jobs simply for voting for political candidates antithetical to their employers. It was common practice for newly employed workers to be required to take an "ironclad oath" to belong to no working-class organization. Even subscription to a labor journal or newspaper could be cause for dismissal. Western Union, for example, required an oath which read, "I, ———, . . . hereby promise and agree . . . that I will forthwith abandon any and all membership, connection, or affiliation with any organization or society, whether secret or open, which in any wise attempts to regulate the conditions of my services or the payment therefor. . . ." The Knights of Labor, which became the first major union in the country, was often specifically proscribed. The employees of the Warren Foundry were required immediately to "free [themselves] from a combination in hostility to the company. . . . If they are not willing to do so, we request them to leave our premises. . . ."

Employers often required their workers to accept in whole or in part company script in lieu of money, which script, needless to say, could be redeemed only at the company store. Companies commonly deducted from their employees' pay—in addition to advances from the company store—money for the salary of a doctor or nurse, rent for a company house, and coal given out by the company on credit.

Thus it was not unusual for workers at the end of the year to find themselves actually in debt to the company that employed them. The reports of the New Jersey labor commissioners in 1884 contained numerous instances of workers who ended a year of labor in debt to the company. A worker in Paterson reported, "My actual earnings last year were but 100 dollars, while the cost of living was 400." A silk worker in the same town reported a 50 percent reduction in wages over a three-year period. A railroad employee told the Kansas commissioners: "A man . . . has to wait 50 days before he receives a cent of wages, and then only gets paid for 30 days, leaving the proceeds of 20 days' labor in the company's hands until he quits their employ."

Of a sample of 520 Michigan workers, 146 were paid weekly, 32 biweekly, 177 monthly, and 28 on demand, while 137 had no regular payday. Of the 137 with no regular payday, a number reported waiting 60 to 90 days for their pay. Only two-fifths of Michigan's factory employees were paid weekly, while two-fifths were paid monthly. As for hours, of 65,627 mill and factory "hands" in the state, 76 percent worked 60 hours a week or more. Moreover, 12 percent of the men, 22 percent of the women, and 34 percent of the children worked more than 10 hours daily.

Ironically, the men, better organized, worked on the average fewer hours than the women and children (the last worked longest of all). Tram drivers in Fall River, Massachusetts, worked an average of 15 hours a day, while for streetcar conductors in Kansas, 16 and 17 were standard. In New York bakers averaged $16^2/_3$ hours, six days a week. In the Pennsylvania coal mines 14 to 18 hours a day were typical, and one witness before the labor commissioners reported, "I know that some [men] go into the mines on Sunday, trying to make a living and cannot, while their employers own Sunday-schools, churches, preachers, Government bonds . . . with yachts, steamboats, orange plantations, and are very rich."

Along with low pay and long, long hours, workers in most trades and industries had to contend with extended periods of unemployment. In Topeka, Kansas, in 1885, of 660 skilled workmen, 156 worked part-time and 108 had no work at all. During the year 1 out of 5 skilled and unskilled workers was unemployed.

A constant complaint voiced to the Avelings on their tour in 1886 was that hundreds of thousands of men had been displaced by machines, a fact confirmed by one Philadelphia manufacturer, who told the Avelings that in a thirty-year period "machinery has displaced 6 times the amount of hand labor formerly required." In carpets, weaving, spinning ten to twenty times fewer workers were required; in spinning alone seventy-five times fewer. In the milling of flour one person did the work done by four a few decades earlier, while in machine tooling "one boy can produce as much as was formerly produced by 10 skilled men." In mining the story was similar. In the Hocking Valley of Ohio, improved machines enabled 160 men to do the work of 500.

The housing conditions of working-class men and women had deteriorated to an alarming degree. In New York City in 1883 there were 25,000 tenement buildings containing 1,000,000 inhabitants. Some 19,000 tenements accommodated 50 or more persons each, and families of 6 to 8 people living in a single room were not uncommon. The New York labor commissioners noted that the tenants "cook, eat, and sleep in the same room, men, women, and children together. Refuse of every description makes the floors damp and slimy, and the puny, half-naked children crawl or slide about it."

At Fall River sixteen houses occupied by more than 500 human beings used the same privy, and the odor was hardly to be endured in summer. In Lowell "the tenants of a single block had to carry their refuse of all kinds, and human excrements . . . into Austin Avenue for deposit." In another block in Lowell, commissioners counted thirty-six tenements containing thirty-six families and 396 persons. Such "excessively filthy," "unsanitary," "foul," wretched, and dirty lodgings were the property of the millowners, whose workers were often required to live in them as a condition of employment.

In cigarmaking operations, often carried on at home, "I see women," one witness reported to the New York labor commissioners, "surrounded by filth with children waddling in it, and having sores on their hands and faces and various parts of the body. . . . They are all the time handling this tobacco they make into cigars." Every industry had its own peculiar health hazards. "Sewing machine girls are subject to diseases of the womb," a report noted, "and when married mostly have miscarriages. In tobacco factories women are mostly affected with nervous and hysterical complaints, consumption and chest ailments. . . ."

"We have lived in English factory towns," the Avelings wrote, "and know something of English factory hands; but we may fairly say we have never in the English Manchester seen women so worn out and degraded, such famine in their cheeks, such need and oppression, starving in their eyes, as in the women we saw trudging to their work in the New Hampshire Manchester. What must the children born of such women be?" A consequence of the starvation wages paid women workers and the uncertainty of their employment was that many of them were driven to part-time prostitution or, as the New York labor commissioners' report put it, "*quasi* prostitution. . . . When out of work they cohabit with one or two men, but when work was obtained dropped such associations." In addition, many women complained to the commissioners that they were taken advantage of sexually by their bosses or employers. In Kansas City and Indianapolis two clergymen told the Avelings "of the fearful state of women forced to choose between starvation and prostitution" in those "flourishing towns."

It was also evident to the Avelings that wherever possible men were replaced as factory operatives by women and children, who were paid far lower wages. The criterion in replacing a man with a woman or child was simply whether the latter had the strength to operate a particular machine.

The New Jersey labor commissioners noted: "Woman and child labor is much lower priced than that of men . . . the hours of labor are longer and the rate of wages less, women never agitate, they merely 'toil and scrimp, and bear.' " However, those women who joined the Knights of Labor received the same wages as the men. Tens of thousands of women worked in what later came to be called sweatshops as seamstresses paid by piecework. The New York labor bureau report for 1885 noted that an expert at crocheting shawls could make no more than 12 to 15 cents a day. Seamstresses, in addition, were required to pay for the machine and for the thread they used. A sewer earned $1.50 per dozen for trousers. Vests were 15 cents apiece; gloves, 90 cents a dozen. An experienced "tailoress" earned no more than $3 or $4 a week. Less skilled millinery workers made 12 cents a day and were paid every two weeks. While the law required that chairs be provided for women workers, they were frequently not allowed to sit down. Of 1,322 women studied in a survey of the New York clothing industry, 27 earned $6 per week and 534 earned $1 a week. Fines were exacted, such as 25 cents for being five minutes late (two days' wages for a millinery worker); $1 for eating at the loom; 25 cents for washing hands; for imperfect work, for sitting down, for taking a drink of water, and so on.

The rooms in which women worked were foul, poorly ventilated, dirty, and badly lighted. It was a common practice to lock the workers in their rooms, thereby risking lives in case of fire. "One hundred women and small girls work in a cellar without ventilation, and electric light burning all day," the New York commissioners reported. Workers often suffered crippling injuries and sometimes incurable diseases. A woman who made artificial flowers found that her hands had been "poisoned" by the coloring she used. When she could not work, she was discharged, and the labor commissioners had to bring suit against her employer to collect 50 cents in back wages.

Increasingly child labor competed with schooling. A report of the New Jersey labor commissioners of 1885 noted that of an estimated 343,897 children of school age in the state, 89,254 attended no school, and of these, the majority worked in factories or in mines. In New York, out of 1,685,000 children and young people between the ages of five and twenty-one, only 1,041,089 were listed as enrolled in the "common schools," and average daily attendance was 583,142. In other words, on any given day an average of 1,101,958 children was *absent from school*. Even allowing for a number educated in private schools, the figure seemed to the commissioners "almost incredible." They declared: "An army of uneducated and undisciplined children is growing up among us."

Each year saw an increase in the numbers of children laboring. In Michigan statistics indicated that seventy-one "establishments"— factories and businesses—in forty-six towns and cities employed 350 boys and girls between eight and fourteen years of age. In New Jersey there were twice as many children employed in factories in 1880 as there had been ten years earlier, while the increase of women was 142 percent in the same time. In Detroit in 1885, ninety-two businesses employed 372 boys and girls at 50 cents a day for the boys and 31 cents for the girls. In Connecticut, out of a factory labor force of 70,000, 5,000 were children under fifteen.

In the mills of Yorkville, in New York City, children under fourteen worked an eleven-hour day, while in the cigar factories, which employed many children, the workday was ten hours. "In the smaller bakeries," the Avelings reported, "children of from 9 to 13 start work at eleven at night and go on until 4 in the morning."

The Pennsylvania mines were dangerous places for boys. Thousands were killed or maimed each year without compensation or aid of any kind except that which might be provided by some local charitable group. The *Luzerne Union* reported in January, 1876: "During the past week nearly one boy a day has been killed, and the public has become so familiar with these calamities, that no attention is given them after the first announcement through a newspaper or a neighbor." A Sunday school convention that met in Scranton in 1874 was taken on a tour of the nearby mines, where they saw the "bare-footed, black-faced urchins . . . picking slate from the dusty diamonds" and then heard a lecture on the "wonders of the Great Creator"—that was to say, on fossils.

A Fall River textile worker named Thomas O'Donnell told a Senate Committee on Labor-Capital Relations in 1883: "I have a brother who has four children besides his wife and himself. All he earns is $1.50 a day. He works in the iron works at Fall River. He only works nine months out of twelve. There is generally three months of stoppage . . . and his wife and family all have to be supported for a year out of the wages of nine months—$1.50 a day for nine months to support six of them. It does not stand to reason that those children and he himself can have natural food and be naturally dressed. His children are often sick, and he has to call in doctors." O'Donnell himself earned $133 a year with which to feed a family of four. He dug clams and scavenged wood and coal.

Two seven-story factory buildings in Rochester, New York, one employing 150 and the other about 270 women, had only one stairway each. An Ohio fire inspector, describing similar conditions, wrote that "it is somewhat difficult to speak with calmness of men who, while liberally insuring their property against fire, so that in case of such a visitation —a danger always imminent—their pockets shall not suffer, will not spend a dollar for the security of the lives of those by whose labor they profit."

A Massachusetts labor commissioner sounded more like a reformer than a bureaucrat when he wrote at the end of a report describing the conditions of child labor in that state: "I plead for the little ones. . . . In these days of legislative interference, when the shield of the State protects the dumb beast from the merciless blows of his driver; when the over-worked horse is remembered and released from his work . . . it would seem pitiable if childhood's want of leisure for rest of body and education should be denied them. Massachusetts . . . goes on regardless of the consequences, protecting the strong, forgetting the weak and poor . . . under the false plea of non-interference with the liberty of the people. The children have rights that the State is bound to respect. Their right is to play and make merry; to be at school, to be players not workers."

Quite by accident the Avelings discovered one of the most exploited groups in the United States: cowboys. Taken by their hosts in Kansas City to a Wild West show, they got into conversation with a handsome, blue-eyed cowboy named Broncho John, who, with encouragement from the Avelings, described vividly the manner in which ranchers exploited their hands. "To our great astonishment," the Avelings wrote, "he plunged at once into a denunciation of capitalists in general and of ranch-owners in particular. Broncho John estimated that there were at least 10,000 cowboys"—the Avelings believed there were many more—and "no class is harder worked . . . none so poorly paid for their services" because "they have no organization back of them" while their employers had "one of the strongest and most systematic and, at the same time, despotic unions that was ever formed to awe and dictate to labor." Listening to Broncho John, the Avelings, confident that "a Cowboy Assembly of the Knights of Labor or a Cowboy Union is sure to be started in the near future," devoted a whole chapter in their study *The Working-Class Movement in America* to the hardships of the cowboy.

Mary ("Mother") Jones, whose labors on behalf of miners made her a legendary figure among those who labored in the earth, wrote a vivid account of a coal miner's life: "Mining at best is wretched work, and the life and surroundings of the miner are hard and ugly. His work is down in the black depths of the earth. He works alone in a drift. There can be little friendly companionship as there is in the factory; as there is among men who build bridges and houses, working together in groups. The work is dirty. Coal dust grinds itself into the skin, never to be removed. The miner must stoop as he works in the drift. He becomes bent like a gnome. His work is utterly fatiguing. Muscles and bones ache. His lungs breathe coal dust and the strange, damp air of places that are never filled with sunlight. His house is a poor makeshift and there is little to encourage him to make it attractive. . . . Around his house is mud and slush. Great mounds of culm, black and sullen, surround him. His children are perpetually grimy from play on the culm mounds. The wife struggles with dirt, with inadequate water supply, with small wages, with overcrowded shacks."

The breaker boys, who picked flint and rocks out of the coal, Mary Jones wrote, "did men's work and they had men's ways, men's vices and men's pleasures. They fought and spit tobacco and told stories out on the culm piles of a Sunday. They joined the breaker boys union and beat up scabs." Mother Jones lamented to her death that there was "still too little joy and beauty in the miner's life"; the end of the "long, long struggle" was not yet.

Lumbering was akin to mining in the type of man it attracted and the arduous and highly hazardous nature of the work involved. John W. Fitzmaurice, who worked in lumber camps, told the story of them in *The Shanty Boy*, a kind of documentary which painted a vivid picture of the cruelly hard and dangerous conditions. He quoted the foreman of one such camp as declaring, "It's saw-logs we're after out here," and Fitzmaurice added, "it is saw-logs men are after in the woods, and in the rush, push and crush to get them, God help the sick or wounded!" The men were pitted against each other in merciless competition for the number of logs cut in a day. At the end of each day the tally was made. "As each speaks the others listen nervously, and with ill-concealed jealousy, to the men with the big figures. . . . This hurry and rush brings to the surface the 'survival of the fittest,' and the weakling or debauched fall out by the way. Consequently, the hospital business never lags." The larger camps had bars and prostitutes as standard adjuncts.

In every industry the story was monotonously the same: paupers' wages; the constant fear of dismissal; wretched and unsanitary working conditions; ten-, twelve-, and even fourteen-hour days (sixteen for bakers); six- and sometimes seven-day weeks; erratic pay; little or no compensation for injuries or fatalities; a constant increase in the number of women and children employed under such conditions; and, worst of all, the widespread conviction that workingmen and women (not to mention children) had been losing ground ever since the end of the Civil War.

Under such circumstances it is hardly surprising that the number of strikes increased year by year following the Great Strikes of 1877. In 1881 there were 471 strikes affecting 2,928 companies and 129,521 employees. Five years later the number of strikes had risen to 1,411, involving 9,861 companies and almost half a million employees. Roughly half (46 percent) of the struck companies acquiesced in the principal demands of the strikers. Over 3,000 more strikes were partially successful, and 40 percent of the strikes, involving 50 percent of the strikers, were judged "failures."

But the formation of unions was dishearteningly slow. The fierce competition between mine operators was one factor impeding effective unions. Marginal operators, struggling, especially in depression years, to stay solvent or at least existent, saw unions as dangerous enemies. Even more significant was the constant turnover of workers themselves. In such circumstances it was difficult for able leadership to emerge and to develop loyalty among a transient population. Every mining village had a nucleus of professional men, storekeepers, mine officials, and a few "old families," but the workers themselves came and went through the middle years of the century with bewildering rapidity. Rather than endure the rigors of long strikes, miners would simply decamp. The mineowners suffered from this phenomenon almost as much as the workers themselves. One deplored the fact that "the best men have of course gone," while the least enterprising and capable remained. In the Pennsylvania coal fields the widely varying national origins of the workers were another deterrent to common action. Welsh, Irish, English, and Germans had provided the initial cadres. During and more dramatically after the Civil War, Italians, Poles, and Slovaks began to come in increasing numbers. Italians were especially in demand as strikebreakers in the bituminous coal fields of Pennsylvania. Race wars were common. Particular traits were attributed by employers to each ethnic group. The Welsh, for example, were described by one mineowner as "a little tricky, & [apt] to lie a little more or less gently, as it suited their purposes," and as "bearing malice, and . . . being clannish." The larger towns where different ethnic groups lived were divided into sections or neighborhoods called by such names as "Scotch Hill, Welshtown, Shanty Mill or Cork Lane or Paddy's Land, Nigger Hill, Dutch Hollow, . . . Little Italy, Hungarian Hill, Polander Street." Each ethnic group had its own social customs, from the exuberant Polish wedding to the Welsh eisteddfod and the German *Turnverein* or *Sängerfest*. The different nationalities often could not even converse with each other, let alone work together to improve conditions.

When the Sage Foundation put out a report on the conditions in the Carnegie steel mills, it emphasized the role of immigrant labor. Slavs and Italians were given preference in employment, the report stated, "because of their docility, their habit of silent submission . . . and their willingness to work long hours and overtime without a murmur. Foreigners as a rule earn the lowest wages and work the full stint of hours. . . .

"Many work in intense heat, the din of machinery and the noise of escaping steam. The congested conditions of most of the plants in Pittsburgh add to the physical discomfort . . . while their ignorance of the language and of modern machinery increases the risk. How many of the Slavs, Lithuanians and Italians are injured in Pittsburgh in one year is unknown. No reliable statistics are compiled. . . . When I mentioned a plant that had a bad reputation to a priest he said: 'Oh, that is the slaughter-house; they kill them there every day.' . . . It is undoubtedly true, that exaggerated though the reports may be, the waste in life and limb is great, and if it all fell upon the native-born a cry would long since have gone up which would have stayed the slaughter."

With the slaves freed, Wendell Phillips, as we have seen, devoted a portion of his reformist energies to the plight of the Indian, but he had more than enough left for the workingman. He had watched the postwar business and financial interests, the growth of the railroads, and the first stirrings of modern industrialism with growing alarm. In October, 1871, at the Boston Music Hall, he expressed his indignation with the "capitalists." A few months later, addressing the International Grand Lodge of the Knights of St. Crispin, Phillips urged his listeners to "get hold of the great question of labor, and having hold of it, grapple with it, rip it open, invest it with light, gathering the facts, piercing the brains about them . . . then I know, sure as fate, though I may not live to see it, that *they will certainly conquer this nation in twenty years.* It is impossible that they should not." Phillips stressed the importance of organization. "I welcome organization," he declared. "I do not care whether it calls itself trades-union, Crispin, international, or commune; any thing that masses up a unit in order that they may put in a united force to face the organization of capital; anything that does that, I say amen to it. One hundred thousand men [the number of members claimed by the Knights of St. Crispin]. It is an immense army. I do not care whether it considers chiefly the industrial or the political question; it can control the land if it is in earnest." The abolitionists had been only a handful, but they "knew what they wanted, and were determined to have it. Therefore they got it." It was the same with the struggle of workingmen for decent conditions and decent wages.

Phillips offered his listeners a larger vision than simply higher pay and shorter hours. When he looked "out upon Christendom, with its 300,000,000 of people," he saw that a third of them did not have enough to eat. "Now, I say," he declared, "that the social civilization which condemns every third man in it to be below the average in the nourishment God prepared for them" was ordained from below, by greedy and sinful men, rather than from above. "Now I say that the civilization that has produced this state of things in nearly the hundredth year of the American Revolution did not come from above."

Long hours, poor food, and hard work brutalized a man and crowded him "down to mere animal life, . . . eclipsed his aspirations, dulled his senses, stunted his intellect, and made him a mere tool to work. . . . That is why I say, lift a man; give him life; let him work eight hours a day; give him the school; develop his taste for music; give him a garden; give him beautiful things to see and good books to read. . . . Unless there is power in your movement, industrially and politically, the last knell of democratic liberty in this Union is struck; for, as I said, there is no power in the State to resist such a giant as the Pennsylvania road. . . . From Boston to New Orleans, from Mobile to Rochester, from Baltimore to St. Louis, we have now but one purpose, and that is, having driven all other political questions out of the arena, the only question left is labor—the relations of capital and labor."

Unions

The Knights of Labor, originated in 1869 as a secret society, was dedicated to advancing the cause of labor but was at first primarily a fraternal order, strong on temperance and Christian piety. It came to bear the imprint of its second president, Terence Powderly, who wished to unite all workingmen in a great universal redemptive enterprise. Love, not hatred or hostility, must be its goal.

The Knights' declaration of principles dated back to the National Labor Union of 1866. Eight years later the Industrial Brotherhood adopted almost the same articles in its constitution, and when survivors of that effort met in Reading, Pennsylvania, in January, 1878, to found the Knights, they drew on the earlier declaration.

The preamble of the constitution of the Knights of Labor read: "The recent alarming development and aggression of aggregated wealth, which, unless checked, will inevitably lead to the pauperization and hopeless degradation of the toiling masses, render it imperative, if we desire to enjoy the blessings of life, that a check should be placed upon its power and upon unjust accumulation, and a System adopted which will secure to the laborer the fruits of his toil; and as this much-desired object can only be accomplished by the thorough unification of labor, and the united efforts of those who obey the divine injunction that 'In the sweat of thy brow shalt thou eat bread,' we have formed the [association] with a view of securing organization and direction, by cooperative effort, of the power of the industrial classes; and we submit to the world the objects sought to be accomplished by our organization, calling upon all who believe in securing 'the greatest good for the greatest number' to aid and assist us. . . ." Included among the society's aims was "the establishment of cooperative institutions, productive and distributive . . . weekly pay (in lawful money), equal justice through the courts for working man and capitalist, a prohibition of child labor, mechanic liens for wages, the abolishment of the contract system, the establishment of state bureaus of labor statistics, and the substitution of arbitration for strikes." The constitution called for the eight-hour day, "so that laborers may have more time for social enjoyment and intellectual improvement." Finally, the constitution called for equal pay for "both sexes . . . for equal work." Anyone but a "banker, stockbroker, gambler (with cards), lawyer, and alcoholic . . ." might be admitted as a member.

Among all the various testaments of our history, none surely is more idealistic or more American than Powderly's aspiration for the "Knights" of Labor. Powderly, who had been as dismayed by the Great Strikes as E. L. Godkin or John Hay, decided that the mission of the Knights of Labor was to intervene in the war between capital and labor as peacemaker and reconciler. To do this, a single great union, he concluded, was necessary.

Powderly was an Irishman, born in 1849 into a family of twelve children. At the age of thirteen he entered the labor market as a railroad switch tender in Scranton, Pennsylvania. Before he was out of his teens, he was active in the Machinists and Blacksmiths Union, for which he was fired and blacklisted. After knocking about the state trying to organize railroad workers, he returned to Scranton and was elected mayor of the city in 1878 on the Greenback-Labor ticket. The same year he became Grand Master Workman or, more simply, head of the new union.

To Eleanor Marx Aveling and her husband the principles of the Knights of Labor, at least in 1885, were "in the main socialistic," as indicated by Article 19, which stated it was the intention of the Knights "to establish cooperative institutions, such as will tend to supersede the wage system, by the introduction of an industrial cooperative system." The Avelings added: "Now this is pure and unadulterated Socialism." Powderly himself was described by the Avelings as "conservative, reactionary," and essentially "capitalistic" in his approach to the problems of labor. They also suspected a disposition to subordinate the interests of the laborer to those of the Roman Catholic Church. Nonetheless, the results were encouraging. Spurred by the recession of 1884, which resulted in widespread unemployment and the reduction of wages in many industries, membership reached 700,000 by 1886.

The Knights of Labor struck Jay Gould's Missouri Pacific in 1885 over an unannounced cut in wages. With the intervention of the governors of Missouri and Kansas, the strike was successful, the pay cuts were restored, and the men were given time and a half for overtime. Another strike some months later over discrimination against members of the Knights was also successful. Encouraged by these successes, Martin Irons, the militant leader of the Southwest Knights, called his men out over the firing of a foreman for alleged incompetence, declaring that the purpose of the strike was to chasten "these contemptible and blood-sucking corporations and their governmental allies. . . ."

Some 9,000 railroad workers went out on strike and attempted to stop the movement of trains on 5,000 miles of track running through four states. Many of the locomotives were sabotaged. This time public sympathy for the strikers was notably missing. The aims of the strikers went beyond what many people believed were reasonable limits. Irons refused the good offices of the governors of Kansas and Missouri. Powderly intervened to try to help settle the strike, but the accumulated grievances and the bitterness of the workers precluded any agreement. Gould, aware that the strikers had alienated public opinion, was determined to break the power of the union. He succeeded; the defeat was a devastating setback to the Knights, and Powderly admonished his "assemblies": "While I, as the chosen mouthpiece of the Order, am proclaiming to the world that the Knights of Labor do not advocate or countenance strikes until every other means has failed, the wires from a thousand cities and towns are bearing the news of as many strikes by the Knights of Labor, in which arbitration and conciliation were never hinted at. . . . In some cases these strikes were entered upon against the advice of the General Executive Board. It is claimed by our members that arbitration is one-sided . . . but the voluntary concessions made to us within the past three months prove most conclusively that the just claims of labor will be listened to if we go forward the way we started."

The problem was, in part, that radical talk was in the air. Many workingmen were attracted by talk of the necessity and, indeed, inevitability of communism or socialism. Eminently respectable people discussed such matters in private and public, and many individuals and groups in the incipient labor movement were affected by ideas which, after all, had been around for decades, albeit they had expressed themselves primarily in the relatively innocuous form of Christian communist communities.

If Powderly's conservatism put him at odds with the more militant Knights, his simple faith in universal brotherhood infuriated others. For example, he invited a black official of the union, Frank J. Ferrell, to introduce him at the union's general assembly in Richmond, Virginia. In introducing Powderly, Ferrell stated, "One of the objects of our Order is the abolition of those distinctions which are maintained by race or color. I believe I present to you a man above the superstitions which are involved in these distinctions. . . ." The result of Ferrell's appearance was a near riot in Richmond. Powderly defended himself against newspaper attacks and reaffirmed his union's commitment to "personal liberty and social equality." He wrote: "Southern labor, regardless of color, must learn to read and write. Southern cheap labor is more a menace to the American toiler than the Chinese, and this labor must be educated."

One of the principal bones of contention in the Knights of Labor was Powderly's strong temperance stand and his determination to make the Knights a kind of union-cum-temperance organization. No organizer or officer of the Knights could be a man "addicted to the use of strong drink," and "total abstainers" were given preference. One of the rules of the Knights specified: "No Local or other Assembly or members, shall directly or indirectly, give, sell, or have any ale, beer or intoxicating liquors of any kind at any meeting, party, sociable, ball, picnic or entertainment whatever. . . ." Powderly often seemed more dedicated to temperance than to unionism. Many workingmen, on the other hand, saw the temperance movement as an effort by blue-nosed middle-class reformers to deprive them of a consoling pint of ale or bottle of rum.

Undoubtedly Powderly's vision was too extravagant for the resources he could muster. In line with his belief in cooperative enterprises, he encouraged chapters of the union to establish cooperative stores and businesses. A local in New York set up a cigar factory, a factory to manufacture watch cases, a leather shop, and a printing plant. Almost all such ventures failed. In addition, Powderly found he could not control the more militant members of his union, who believed that employers could be prevailed upon to improve conditions only by such means as strikes and boycotts.

Victoria Woodhull had thrilled the woman suffrage convention in New York in May, 1872, by declaring, "We are plotting revolution; we will overthrow this bogus Republic and plant a government of righteousness in its stead." So, it might be said, talk of revolution was in the air. It infected the more militant members of the women's movement, and it is not surprising that it infected the Knights of Labor as well. Powderly was reported to have advised the lodges of his union to be "provided with powder and shot, bullets and Winchester rifles, when we intend to strike. If you strike, the troops are called out to put you down. You cannot fight with bare hands. You must consider the matter very seriously, and if we anticipate strikes, we must prepare to strike and use arms against the forces brought against us." Powderly, it should be said, denied that he had ever given such advice. The odds are that it was given by one of his militant lieutenants under his name. Certainly it is true that while Powderly's weight was almost invariably exercised on the side of restraint, there was constant talk of revolution.

The more militant Knights perceived that power was the real issue. What they did not take sufficiently into account was the fact that sympathy and support of the Eastern middle and upper classes for the workingman were thin at best and often, as we have suggested, nonexistent. The workingman was thought of as a crude, illiterate Irishman, a German, or, more recently, an Italian immigrant, not entirely American. Many saw him as the principal threat to the traditions on which the Republic had been founded.

In 1882 Johann Most came from Germany to the United States via England. He had spent a number of his thirty-six years in prison for radical activity. When he arrived in New York, Most came as a representative of Karl Marx's International Workingmen's Association, which already, as we have noted, had a number of chapters in the United States. In London he had published *Die Freiheit*, a journal espousing revolutionary anarchism. He resumed publication of *Die Freiheit* in the United States.

A reporter for the *New York Tribune* described Most as "a small, slender man about five feet four inches in height, with light hair and a full beard and mustache." He was disfigured by a swelling on the side of his face.

Most's first public appearance was at Cooper Union to a standing-

room-only audience, which greeted the German revolutionary enthusiastically. Through an interpreter he told his listeners that he had
come to advance the cause of socialism. He brought them the greetings
of the workers of Europe. In reporting the event, the *New York Tribune*
declared in its editorial columns: "The influence of the Socialists in
this country is plainly growing weaker. . . . It is with difficulty that the
Socialists of this city have been able to keep themselves before the
public. . . . Yesterday they . . . paraded the streets flying red flags as if
the public were a bull to be goaded into madness. They excited, however, only derision and laughter, even among the workmen. . . .
The occasion of the demonstration was the arrival of the German
agitator John Most. This man's sole claim to notoriety seems to be that
he is a foreigner who has been in jail about a dozen times."

Most's tour was a success in that large and generally sympathetic
crowds turned out to hear him speak, and the Socialist Labor Party
gained thousands of recruits. In the March, 1883, issue of *Die Freiheit*
Most published a portion of the *Revolutionary Catechism*, which declared
that for the revolutionist "there is only one pleasure, one comfort, one
recompense: the success of the revolution. Day and night he may cherish only one thought, only one purpose, viz. inexorable destruction.
While he pursues this purpose without rest and in cold blood, he must
be ready to die, and equally ready to kill everyone with his own hands,
who hinders him in the attainment of his purpose. . . ." A subsequent
issue gave information on how to manufacture dynamite.

Most's efforts encouraged the formation of a unified group called
the Information Bureau of the Socialist Federation of North America.
Affiliated socialist groups were formed in some twenty cities, including
chapters in New York, Philadelphia, Baltimore, Omaha, Kansas City,
St. Louis, Cincinnati, Cleveland, Detroit, and Chicago. A national "congress" was planned for October, 1883, calling on all socialists, "who
should be the pioneers of Labor in the great Social War," to meet to
consider the conditions of the American worker, conditions which, the
call to the meeting declared, were getting worse by the month. It was
thus necessary to push ahead boldly for "the furtherance and pro-
mulgation of our ideas and the formation of organizations to prepare
that force which is destined to abolish the infamous institutions of
oppression of today, and class-rule in whatever form it may appear."
The movement had heretofore been riddled with dissension. "Let us
put an end to this state of affairs. Let all those who have the cause of

their oppressed class at heart . . . meet in council and agree upon a uniform, practical and effective organization and agitation."

Twenty-six delegates from as many various groups gathered in Pittsburgh on October 1, 1883. All but 2 were of German extraction, and of the perhaps 4,000 or 5,000 members of the various revolutionary socialist groups they represented, the vast majority were German immigrants. The delegates were emphatic in rejecting the goal of improved working conditions—better pay and shorter hours. These were seen simply as sops offered by the capitalists to dampen revolutionary ardor. In the spirit of anarchism all efforts at centralization were resisted in favor of a loose federation to be called the International Working People's Association (IWPA).

The congress declared that the trade unions must constitute the "army of the oppressed and disinherited." They could hardly have made a worse choice. The trade unions, with their strong emphasis on improved working conditions and higher pay, were the least susceptible of all labor groups to the siren song of revolution. Finally, the delegates issued a "manifesto," which began by quoting from the Declaration of Independence. It was the right of the people "under absolute Despotism . . . to throw off such government and provide new guards for their future security." The United States had come to be just such a despotism—"the exploitation of the propertyless class by the propertied." The manifesto went on to expound Marx's labor theory of value and his argument that capitalism was committed to keeping wages at a subsistence level in order to increase its own profits. Since capitalism was international, the only way to overthrow the tyranny of capitalism was through international action. Victory "in the decisive combat of the proletarians against their oppressors can only be gained by simultaneous struggle along the whole line of the bourgeois (capitalistic) society. . . ." The "implements of labor, the soil and other premises of production, in short, capital produced by labor," must be changed into "societary property. . . . Only by this pre-supposition is destroyed every possibility of the future spoilation of man by man.

"The political institutions of our time," the manifesto continued, "are the agencies of the propertied class; their mission is the upholding of the privileges of their masters. . . . That they will not resign their privileges voluntarily we know . . . there remains but one recourse— FORCE! . . . By force our ancestors liberated themselves from political oppression, by force their children will have to liberate themselves from economic bondage. It is, therefore, your right, it is your duty, says Jefferson—'to arm!' "

The manifesto ended by quoting Marx: "Workmen of all countries, unite! You have nothing to lose but your chains: you have a world to win!" Although, as one historian has put it, "The Pittsburgh Manifesto was an unintegrated product of various schools of revolutionary thought, and failed to present a consistent and well-rounded body of principles," it did dramatize the most radical European political thought, and that thought, or those slogans, have been with us, in one form or another, ever since. They were, indeed, to have an immediate and alarming consequence.

While the Pittsburgh congress and the manifesto that resulted from it can hardly be said to have created a mass movement, some of the ideas expressed began to percolate through the more radical fringes of the labor movement. Perhaps most influential, since it corresponded with an emotional disposition on the part of many workers, was the doctrine of violence and the talk of armed resistance to "the police forces of capitalism." The Information Bureau of the Socialist Federation of North America was located in Chicago, as were many of the more radical workingmen's groups. The IWPA sponsored numerous meetings, some of which drew 1,000 or more people. In the fall of 1884, 3,000 turned out for a Thanksgiving Day rally to hear a series of inflammatory speeches and then paraded through the city, carrying signs with such sentiments as "Private capital is the reward of robbery"; "Our capitalist robbers may well thank *their* Lord, we their victims have not yet strangled them"; "The proletariat must be their own liberator."

Although the organized socialist groups remained largely German in their membership, some chapters of English-speaking workers were formed. Reflecting this fact, seven of the journals of the socialist movement were in German, only two in English: the *Alarm* and the *Nemesis*. The *Alarm*, edited by Albert Parsons, carried a number of articles by a leading woman radical, Lizzie Holmes. The *Alarm* attacked the "wage system" as the heart of exploitative capitalism and looked forward to a day, soon to come, when all products necessary to a wholesome life would be distributed free to those who needed them. "Capital," Parsons wrote, "being a thing, can have no rights. Persons alone have rights. . . . The International defiantly unfurls the banner of liberty, fraternity, equality, and . . . beckons the disinherited of the earth to assemble and strike down the property beast which feeds upon the life-blood of the people." As we have noted, IWPA journals published instructions for bombs and supplemented these with tactics of street fighting and advice on how to hide out from the forces of law and order after a violent deed had been committed. "Dynamite!" ran one article in the *Alarm*, "of all the good stuff, this is the stuff. Stuff several pounds of this sublime stuff into an inch pipe (gas or water-pipe), plug up the ends, insert a cap with a fuse attached, place this in the immediate neighborhood of a lot of rich loafers who live by the sweat of other people's brows, and light the fuse. A most cheerful and gratifying result will follow." Assassination was also advocated. "Assassination properly applied," one author wrote, "is wise, just, humane, and brave. For freedom all things are just." Even those labor journals which rejected force and violence as policy were often inclined to applaud the expression of such sentiments on the grounds that they at least served to terrorize the capitalists.

In the face of growing pressure from the public to suppress such writings, the mayor of Chicago, Carter Harrison, declared: "The constitution of the land guarantees to all citizens the right to peaceably assemble, to petition for redress of grievances. This carries the right to free discussion. . . . Some fear an organized resistance to authority. I do not. I do not believe that there is in our midst any considerable body of men mad enough to attempt such folly. . . ."

A West Coast counterpart to the International Working People's Association was the International Workingmen's Association, started in San Francisco on July 15, 1881, by Burnette Haskell, a lawyer disenchanted with his profession. The IWA was an instructive contrast with the IWPA. Since there were relatively few Germans or, indeed, European immigrants in California in 1881, the IWA had a very different emphasis. "The cause of all misery, vice, poverty and crime," it declared, "is the system which denies to each worker the full value of what that worker produces." Placing a strong emphasis on education and self-help, it called for a "scientific system of governmental cooperation of the working-people," in place of competitive capitalism. The IWA, while acknowledging that violence might be the accompaniment of "a universal revolution from the throes of which the NEW WORLD will be born," warned its members, who came to number more than 6,000, that premature violence would fatally compromise the cause. Dynamite might be used "collectively for the revolution when it comes," but as a means of creating sympathy for the oppressed it was distinctly counterproductive.

While Haskell headed the Pacific Coast Division of the IWA, Joseph Buchanan in Denver directed the activities of the Rocky Mountain Division. The official voice of the West Coast IWA was *Truth*, edited by Haskell, while Buchanan put out the *Labor Enquirer* from his Denver headquarters. Many leaders in the Knights of Labor were also active in Haskell's and Buchanan's movement, and despite substantial ideological differences, close ties were maintained between the IWPA and the IWA. "Neither branch," an IWA official wrote, "believes in the possibility of obtaining labor's emancipation by peaceable methods, and both know that industrial slaves have no political power; all are brothers; comrades in the same underlying cause, and all . . . look forward with eager anticipation to the universal social revolution."

In Chicago a number of cells of the Black International procured arms and began to drill in anticipation of the revolution; they were followed by the Detroit Rifles and, in Cincinnati, the Rifle Union. Half a dozen similar units drilled and practiced target shooting, but a judgment by the Supreme Court in the case of *Presser* v. *the State of Illinois*, which upheld an Illinois law prohibiting "all bodies of armed men excepting the regular State militia . . . from associating, drilling or parading with arms," soon forced them underground.

Chicago was the hotbed of labor radicalism, and many of that city's principal unions, such as the Progressive Cigar Makers Union No. 15, were avowedly socialist. When the Central Labor Union was formed in 1884, among its 12,000 members were what were to be called in a later age fellow travelers of the IWPA. As strikes spread, more and more employers hired small armies of Pinkerton agents and brought in strikebreakers as a routine matter. Often such measures led to violence on the part of the strikers, at which point the police and, in extreme cases, the state militia were ordered out by authorities to prevent damage to private property. It is important to keep in mind that there were many instances of spontaneous labor violence that owed nothing to the direct influence of the Black or Red Internationals but were the consequence of a profound sense of grievance and an abiding hostility on the part of workers toward their working conditions and their employers. Many businessmen, feeling uncomfortably beleaguered and aware that workers were arming and drilling, formed their own paramilitary organizations and even enlisted white-collar employees. Parsons's *Alarm* informed its readers: "Although the fact is not generally known even in this city, in one large business house alone there is an organization of 150 young men who have been armed with

Remington breech-loading rifles and pursue a regular course of drill-ing. . . . This is by no means an isolated case."

On the conservative side the Knights had to face a rival union, the Federation of Organized Trades and Labor Unions of the United States and Canada, which in 1886 changed its name to the American Federation of Labor. The AFofL, as it soon came to be known, was organized on the level of tightly knit craft unions. The leading figure to emerge in the union was Samuel Gompers. Gompers's approach was highly practical: more or less autonomous unions directing their attention to such practical goals as higher wages, shorter hours, and benefits for disabled workers. Gompers himself was a classic self-made man, born in London, the son of a cigarmaker—the cigarmakers had one of the strongest British unions. His family had come to New York when Samuel was thirteen. He attended Cooper Union in his after-work hours, thereby joining the considerable company of ambitious young workingmen who utilized the school that Peter Cooper had founded for just that purpose. At the age of eighteen Gompers was involved in a strike by the cigarmakers' union against an effort to introduce laborsaving machinery. The strike was defeated, and Gompers later wrote: "From that time I began to realize the futility of opposing progress." He also decided that the labor movement should eschew politics, especially radical political schemes such as those that had a strong attraction for many of the members of the Knights of Labor. He thus set about to make the cigarmakers' union a model for "trade" unions. As other unions were formed, they came in under the wing of the federation. In 1884 Gompers announced as one of the federation's principal objectives the establishment of the eight-hour day and launched an intense publicity campaign which stressed the argument that the eight-hour day would actually result in higher pro-ductivity (studies showed that there was a sharp decline in worker pro-ductivity in the last hours of a ten- or twelve-hour workday). May 1, 1886, was the day set by Gompers for a general strike to win an eight-hour day. Powderly refused to join the AFofL in its campaign for an eight-hour day ostensibly because he thought it was a political issue that could best be achieved through legislation. A strike, in his opinion, would be defeated, and the movement thereby set back.

The leaders of the IWPA were, like the Knights of Labor, though for very different reasons, opposed to Gompers's campaign. In their view, since capitalism was a decadent and doomed system, any accommodation with it would simply have the effect of dampening revolutionary sentiment and delaying the revolution itself. August Spies, one of the leaders of the IWPA, used the talk of an impending strike to force employers to accept the eight-hour day as an opportunity to warn workers that employers would use force to resist any such concession and that they in turn must be prepared to defend themselves. But as the deadline of May 1 approached, the IWPA, doubtless in response to strong feelings among laboring men generally and with the desire to make whatever hay it could out of the armed confrontations that it had predicted, trimmed its sails and announced that it was wholeheartedly in support of the strike. Meanwhile, the country debated the issue. The debate was, on the whole, thoroughly one-sided. What we might call today the establishment press, the influential big-city newspapers whether traditionally "liberal" or "conservative," was virtually as one in denouncing the eight-hour movement, primarily on the ground that it infringed the worker's right to work as long as he wished. A subsidiary concern, expressed by many, was that, given an eight-hour day, the emancipated worker would spend his spare hours in bars or in robbing his more prosperous fellow citizens. The *New York Tribune*, edited by Whitelaw Reid, supported the eight-hour day as a generally desirable goal but took the line that each worker must be free to bargain with his employer for reduced working hours. The *New York Post* argued that a compulsory eight-hour day would violate the most fundamental American principles by forcing laborers who wished to work ten or twelve hours to work no more than eight. The "individual agreement" argument was especially appealing to newspaper editors. It demonstrated their humanitarian impulses while effectively precluding any possibility of actually achieving an eight-hour day. The "Grand Chief Engineer" of the Brotherhood of Locomotive Engineers denounced the movement on the ground that "two hours less work means two hours more loafing about the corners and two hours more for drink." The *Independent*, which under Henry Ward Beecher had supported so many radical causes—abolition, the rights of women, justice for the Indians—characterized the eight-hour movement as "a charitable scheme for the benefit of saloon keepers."

A highly controversial issue was the question of whether a worker should get ten hours of pay for eight hours of work. Outside of the unions themselves (and by no means all the unions concurred), there was general horror at the thought that workingmen were so greedy and unscrupulous as to wish to cheat their employers out of two hours of work by collecting the same pay for eight hours as for ten or twelve. The unions' counterargument was that the worker did more work and did it better in an eight-hour day than in a ten- or twelve-hour one. It followed that if a worker did as much in eight hours as he had in ten but received pay for only eight hours, the employer was more the beneficiary of the eight-hour day than the worker, who, if he had two more hours in which to get drunk or make mischief, had two hours' less wages on which to indulge his bad habits and/or support his family.

Much of the negative reaction in substantial segments of the population to the agitation for an eight-hour day can be traced back to those American attitudes toward work of which we have spoken earlier. As we have seen, work, especially manual labor, had been endowed with a quasi-religious redemptive character primarily by those who did not work themselves, at least in the sense in which William Manning used that word. They—the doctors, lawyers, teachers, preachers, businessmen, and journalists—lived not by physical labor but by their wits; thus they seemed to ordinary working stiffs to have escaped the curse that an angry Jehovah had imposed on the children of Adam for his disobedience in the Garden—"in the sweat of thy face shalt thou earn thy bread." No sweat for the business and professional classes, although, as we have seen, they often did not like what they did to earn a living any better than the wielders of pick and shovel did.

To those Americans who looked on work—on physical labor—as God's appointed path to salvation (for others) and, perhaps equally important, as the measure of a man's character, the movement for an eight-hour day seemed an assault on one of the most essential verities. Beyond that, one suspects it roused in middle- and upper-class bosoms latent suspicion of and hostility toward—even fear of—the working class, a complex set of attitudes in which racial prejudices combined with a profound distaste for the freer, less inhibited life of workingmen, for their crudity and, above all, their *differentness*.

Certainly there were papers and journals and numerous individuals that gave strong support to the eight-hour day on humanitarian grounds. President Grover Cleveland endorsed the idea of an eight-hour day, and a number of Senators and Congressmen expressed similar views, prominent among them the reform-minded Senator from Massachusetts Henry Dawes. In the churches those who inclined toward the doctrines of Christian socialism supported the eight-hour day and the other demands of labor. As a consequence of an eighteen-month-long campaign led by Gompers and the American Federation of Labor, the attention of the nation was directed to May 1, 1886.

Actually the eight-hour-day campaign enjoyed conspicuous success before the May 1 deadline. Around the country many employers granted a nine- and, in some cases, an eight-hour day before the strike deadline. In Philadelphia 12,000 workers accepted a nine-hour day rather than strike. All in all, it was estimated that some 150,000 workers were given reduced workdays without striking.

Haymarket

While tension existed in many cities, the situation was especially volatile in Chicago. The winter of 1885–86 had been extremely cold. Thousands were unemployed. "Bread lines increased," Mary Jones recalled. "Soup Kitchens could not handle the applicants. . . . On Christmas day, hundreds of poverty stricken people in rags and tatters, in thin clothes, in wretched shoes paraded on fashionable Prairie Avenue before the mansions of the rich, before their employers, carrying the black flag [of anarchism]." To Mother Mary Jones and other labor leaders the parade seemed a reckless move that served only to increase the employers' fear and hostility.

The previous year had seen unsuccessful strikes by the lake seamen, dock laborers, and street railway workers. A leader in breaking the strikes had been the chief of police, John Bonfield, who was, in the words of Mary Jones, "a most brutal believer in suppression as the method to settle industrial unrest." Bonfield lost no opportunity to attack meetings of strikers or to break up picket lines. The result was a kind of seething unrest among the working-class population of Chicago. A number of newspapers and conservative spokesmen denounced the movement for the eight-hour day as the work of traitors and anarchists. The *Illinois State Register* complained of "Communistic

Germans, Bohemians and Poles, representing the lumber-yards, coopers, bakers, the cigar shops, the breweries, and the International Workingmen's Association."

Mary Jones noted that business interests of the city took the position that "the foundations of government were being gnawed away by the anarchist rats. . . . The city was divided into two angry camps. The working people on one side—hungry, cold, jobless, fighting gunmen and police clubs with bare hands." The situation was made to order for the anarchists, and large crowds gathered to hear them attack the cruel inequities of the capitalist system.

The weeks preceding May 1 were devoted to skillfully orchestrated public meetings throughout the city. A gathering, sponsored by the Labor Assembly, brought out a crowd estimated at more than 20,000; a week later a Central Labor Union rally and parade of 4,000 workers attracted some 20,000 spectators. As August Spies and Albert Parsons became increasingly conspicuous in such rallies and demonstrations, the *Chicago Mail* fulminated: "There are two dangerous ruffians at large in this city; two sneaking cowards who are trying to create trouble. . . . These two fellows have been at work fomenting disorder for the past ten years. They should have been driven out of the city long ago. They would not be tolerated in any other community on earth." The police were on alert, and 1,350 militia, trained to deal with riots, were also on hand on the eve of May 1. There was bad blood between the workers of the city and the police, who did not hesitate to break up workers' meetings and hustle the leaders off to jail. In the words of one reporter, the police "sometimes blundered, dispersed gatherings that were perfectly orderly and unobjectionable. . . ."

The McCormick Harvester Company plant had been struck several months earlier over a unionization issue, and Cyrus McCormick had locked out his workers; then, with the aid of Pinkertons and several hundred police, he had hired new workers, denounced as scabs by those locked out of the plant. As a consequence, the area around the McCormick factory buildings took on somewhat the character of a battle zone with frequent skirmishes between workers, scabs, police, and "Pinks," as the Pinkerton men were called.

When May 1 dawned in Chicago, some 30,000 men struck, and there were numerous marches and demonstrations through the city; but there were no violent confrontations and no bloodshed as many had predicted there would be. The following day—Sunday—was also quiet. Monday saw a revival of labor activity. A meeting was called for Black Road, near the McCormick plant, and Spies was asked to speak. Some 6,000 men had already gathered when he arrived. Some of those present protested his being allowed to speak on the ground that he was a notorious socialist agitator. His talk was surprisingly sober and low-key, urging that the strikers stand fast. As he was finishing, the gates of the McCormick plant swung open and the scabs emerged to enjoy a half-day holiday (occasioned by McCormick's acceptance of the eight-hour day). Spies's audience, which included a number of men locked out of the McCormick factory, began to drift off to harass the strikebreakers. The angry workers drove the scabs, protected by a handful of policemen, back into the plant. Plant windows were smashed and shots exchanged and the police called for reinforcements. Soon 200 or more police arrived and attacked the strikers with their billies, firing at some of the more conspicuous figures. Before the crowd dispersed, one striker had been killed, six seriously wounded, and a number injured. Six police had also been injured. Spies, receiving garbled reports and rumors, believed that six men had been killed, and he rushed back to the offices of the *Arbeiter Zeitung* to write a broadside for circulation among the workers of the city. It was head-lined "REVENGE! WORKINGMEN! TO ARMS!" It read: "Your masters sent out their bloodhounds—the police—they killed six of your brothers at McCormick's this afternoon. They killed the poor wretches, because they, like you, had courage to disobey the supreme will of your bosses. They killed them because they dared to ask for the shortening of the hours of toil! They killed them to show you 'free American citizens' that you must be satisfied and contented with whatever your bosses condescend to allow you, or you will get killed!" Spies ended his piece by calling on the workers of Chicago to "destroy the hideous monster that seeks to destroy you."

Only 2,500 copies of Spies's "call to arms" were printed, and no more than half distributed. The next day there were encounters between police and strikers with numerous casualties but no deaths. Meanwhile, a call went out for a meeting to protest police brutality, the meeting to be held that evening, May 4, at Haymarket Square. Flyers were distributed in the workingmen's sections of the city. They read: "Attention Workingmen! Great Mass Meeting. . . . Good Speakers will be present to denounce the latest atrocious act of the police, the shooting of our fellow-workmen. . . . Workingmen arm yourselves and appear in full force!" Spies insisted that the injunction to "arm yourselves" be omitted, and only 200 or 300 of the 20,000 flyers printed contained those inflammatory words.

The meeting at the square was slow to start. Scheduled for 7:00 P.M., it was 8 before Spies began to address a modest gathering of a few hundred men. He opened moderately enough, stating that the purpose of the meeting was to counteract the misrepresentations of the "capitalistic press." But he was soon denouncing McCormick for "the murder of our brothers," stating: "The families of twenty-five or thirty thousand men are starving because their husbands and fathers are not men enough to withstand and resist the dictation of the thieves on a grand scale. . . . You place your lives, your happiness, everything in the arbitrary power of a few rascals. . . . Will you stand that?"

Spies had spoken for some twenty minutes when Albert Parsons arrived and was introduced to the augmented crowd, which by then numbered several thousand. It was almost nine o'clock when Parsons began to speak, and some of the Germans among his auditors, whose grasp of English was slim, soon drifted off. After reviewing the world-wide history of the labor movement and declaring that socialism held the only cure for the ills that capitalism had foisted on the working-man, Parsons went on to excoriate the Pinkerton agents, the police, and the militia. "I am not here for the purpose of inciting anybody," he declared, "but to speak out, to tell the facts as they exist, even though it shall cost me my life before morning. . . . It behooves you, as you love your wife and children, if you don't want to see them perish with hunger, killed or cut down like dogs in the street, Americans, in the interest of your liberty and your independence, to arm, to arm your-selves. (Applause and cries of: 'We will do it, we are ready now.')"

At ten o'clock another speaker stepped forward, the main burden of his address being that there was no hope of improving the condition of workingmen through legislation; it must be through their own ef-forts. As he started to speak, a wind blew up, and it began to rain, causing many in the crowd to seek shelter. The speaker hurried to a conclusion, but at that point a company of 180 police officers entered the square and headed for the wagon body that had served as a speak-ers' platform. The captain in charge called on the meeting to disperse, "in the name of the people of the State of Illinois." At that moment someone threw a bomb into the ranks of the policemen gathered about the speakers. After the initial shock and horror the police opened fire on the 300 or 400 people who remained, and they in turn fled for their lives. One policeman had been killed by the bomb, and more than 60 injured. One member of the crowd was killed by police fire, and at least 12 were wounded. The newspaper accounts of the episode were, not surprisingly, lurid in the extreme. "NOW IT IS BLOOD," headlines in one Chicago paper proclaimed. The story that followed reported rumor as fact: "The anarchists of Chicago inaugurated in earnest last night the reign of lawlessness which they have threatened and endeavored to incite for years. They threw a bomb into the midst of a line of 200 police officers, and it exploded with fearful effect, mowing down men like cattle. Almost before the missile of death had exploded the anarchists directed a murderous fire from revolvers upon the police as if their action were prearranged and as the latter were hemmed in on every side—ambuscaded—the effect of the fire upon the ranks of the officers was fearful. . . . The collision between the police and the anarchists was brought about by the leaders of the latter, August Spies, Sam Fielden, and A. R. Parsons, endeavoring to incite a large mass meeting to riot and bloodshed."

The *New York Tribune*'s account stated that the incident was triggered by the cry "Kill the . . . ," whereupon "three bombs were thrown from near the stand into the midst of the officers. . . . The explosion of the bombs was terrific, and they were instantly followed by a volley from the revolvers of the policemen. The rioters answered with theirs. . . . The mob appeared crazed with a frantic desire for blood and holding its ground poured volley after volley into the midst of the officers." The effect of the stories that appeared in newspapers all over the country was to obscure the largely accidental nature of the encounter and convey the impression that the events were part of a carefully calculated anarchist-socialist-communist plot to murder a number of Chicago policemen. In Chicago, according to one observer, "the air was charged with anger, fear and hatred."

Nationwide the popular reaction was similar. The *Albany Law Journal* deplored the fact that "the lives of good and brave men, the safety of innocent women and children, and immunity of property should be, even for one hour, in a great city, at the mercy of a few long-haired, wild-eyed, bad-smelling, atheistic, reckless, foreign wretches, who never did an honest day's work in their lives. . . . There ought to be some law . . . to enable society to crush such snakes when they raise their heads before they have time to bite."

Everywhere editorial writers fulminated against communists, anarchists, and radicals in general. Since several of the leaders and many of those in the crowd at Haymarket Square were Germans, the hostility directed against German-Americans was especially evident. The *Chicago Herald* called for the immediate crushing of "Anarchism" and "Communism"; otherwise residents of the city "must expect an era of anarchy and the loss of their property if not their lives." The organ of the Knights of Labor hastened to dissociate that movement from the events of May 4. "Let it be understood by all the world," the journal proclaimed, "that the Knights of Labor have no affiliation, association, sympathy or respect for the band of cowardly murderers, cutthroats and robbers, known as anarchists, who sneak through the country like midnight assassins, stirring up the passions of ignorant foreigners, unfurling the red flag of anarchy and causing riot and blood shed. . . . They are entitled to no more consideration than wild beasts."

Six more wounded policemen died in the weeks following the bombing, each death adding to the level of public indignation. Perhaps *The New York Times* was not far from the mark when it observed: "No disturbance of the peace that has occurred in the United States since the war of the rebellion has excited public sentiment through the Union as it is excited by the Anarchists' murder of the policemen in Chicago. . . ." It was the hope of the *Times* that the "cowardly savages who plotted and carried out this murder shall suffer the death they deserve." *Harper's Weekly* ran lurid and highly imaginative illustrations of the bombing and called it "an outburst of anarchy; the deliberate crime of men who openly advocate massacre and the overthrow of intelligent and orderly society."

John Swinton's Paper was one of the relatively few rational voices raised in the aftermath of the Haymarket Affair. While deploring the bomb throwing, Swinton pointed out that the police had done much to provoke it by their last-minute efforts to break up a peaceable meeting. Unfortunately the episode would be used to shore up resistance to the legitimate demands of labor. The bomb was thus "a godsend to the enemies of the labor movement," Swinton wrote. "They had used it as an explosive against all the objects that the working people are bent on accomplishing, and in defense of all the evils that capital is bent upon maintaining."

In a similar spirit the *Topeka Citizen* asked if, rather than simply denounce anarchists, it might be well to inquire: "Is there no sane reason for these outbreaks? . . . The killing of a few rioters . . . does little or nothing toward stopping the spread of Anarchistic ideas. The proper way would seem to be to lay all prejudice aside and inquire into the cause of the growth of Anarchism. . . . It is not right to condemn ideas without first inquiring into the causes which produce them."

Few Americans of any class or persuasion failed to be emotionally affected by "Haymarket." When the bomb went off, Theodore Roosevelt was ranching in the Badlands. He wrote his sister: "My men are hard-working, labouring men who work longer hours for no greater wages than many of the strikers;—but they are Americans through and through. I believe nothing would give them greater pleasure than a chance with their rifles at one of the mobs. . . . I wish I had them with me and a fair show at ten times our number of rioters." Like virtually all members of his class, William James had little interest in or sympathy for "labor" or unions. He referred to the Haymarket Affair in a letter to his brother Henry as the "senseless 'anarchist' riot . . . which has nothing to do with the 'Knights of Labor,' but is the work of a lot of pathological Germans and Poles."

The police response was to round up all the "anarchists" and "socialists" who could be identified, starting with August Spies and Samuel Fielden. Everything was done to rout out and destroy all radical organizations in the city. One of the socialist leaders, a man named William Holmes, wrote to William Morris, the English reformer: "One week ago freedom of speech and of the press was a right unquestioned by the bitterest anti-Socialist. . . . Today all this is changed. . . . Socialists are hunted like wolves. . . . The Chicago papers are loud and unceasing in their demand for the lives of all prominent Socialists. To proclaim one's-self a Socialist in Chicago now is to invite immediate arrest." Socialist papers were shut up, and twenty-three printers, writers, and staff members of the *Arbeiter Zeitung* arrested.

Albert Parsons was still at large, but he decided to turn himself in, later explaining, "I never expect while I live to be a free man again. They will kill me, but I could not bear to be at liberty, knowing that my comrades were here and were to suffer for something of which they were as innocent as I. . . . " Parsons, scion of a distinguished family, had fought in the Confederate army as a boy of thirteen and after the war had been an assessor for the Internal Revenue Bureau and then secretary of the Texas Senate. Coming to Chicago to work as a compositor, he became active in the typographical union, a prominent member of the Knights of Labor, and, finally, an active socialist, who was blackballed by employers for his role in the Great Strikes of 1877.

Thirty-one radical leaders were indicted for being accessories before the fact to the murder of the police. Of those indicted, eight were recommended for trial for murder (the only native American among them was Albert Parsons). These the jury found guilty of having conspired to carry out the bombing. "We have," the foreman of the grand jury declared, ". . . found true bills only against such persons as had in their abuse of [the right of free speech] been more or less instrumental in causing the riot and bloodshed at the Haymarket Square. . . ." The words "more or less" in the verdict were revealing. No evidence was presented to the jury to indicate that any of the accused had any direct involvement in making, throwing, or causing to be made or thrown the bomb itself. The jury's verdict, it should be said to its credit, was at pains to emphasize that the so-called "anarchist conspiracy had no real connection with the strike or labor trouble." The jurors also reassured the public that "the total number of anarchists in this country from whom danger need be apprehended is less than one hundred." There were perhaps, in addition, "two to three thousand men, variously classed as socialists, communists, etc. . . . but who are not necessarily dangerous . . . to the peace and welfare of society. . . ."

A group of eminently respectable Chicagoans of socialist sympathies and German antecedents immediately established a fund for the defense of the accused men and retained William Perkins Black, a highly respected lawyer, to undertake their defense. Black was described by Eleanor Marx Aveling as a "physical and mental giant . . . pure American. . . . Fully six feet in height, and built in perfect proportions, with long, quite white hair, a darker moustache and imperial, and very strong, keen eyes, such as only kings and queens among men have, a man who would discuss the future of the working-class movement with a contagious fire," a great storyteller with a fine baritone voice, much given to singing "The Battle Hymn of the Republic."

In the trial the presiding judge, Joseph Gary, repeatedly made decisions that were prejudicial to the defendants (he overruled, for example, a defense challenge to a prospective juror who was related to one of the policemen who had been killed by the bomb). All the defendants pleaded not guilty. Louis Lingg, only twenty-two, confessed to making bombs for use against the police if members of the IWPA were attacked.

Despite the lack of evidence indicating a conspiracy in any proper meaning of that word, the jury, after three hours of deliberation, returned a verdict of guilty with hanging for seven of the defendants and fifteen years in the penitentiary for the eighth. The verdict was acclaimed by the great majority of newspapers with such headlines as

"Seven of the Indicted Found Guilty of Murder and Worthy of Death"; "The Scaffold Waits—Seven Dangling Nooses for the Dynamite Fiends. . . ." The *Chicago Inter Ocean* declared: "Anarchism has been on trial ever since May 4; and it has now got its verdict. . . . The verdict . . . is unquestionably the voice of justice, the solemn verdict of the world's best civilization. . . ." The *Chicago Tribune* considered the verdict "a warning to the whole brood of vipers in the Old World—to the Communists . . . the Socialists . . . the Anarchists . . . the Nihilists . . . —that they cannot come to this country and abuse its hospitality and its right of free speech . . . without encountering the stern decrees of American law. The verdict of the Chicago jury will, therefore, check the immigration of organized assassins in this country."

In the same spirit a Chicago businessman was reported to have said: "No, I don't consider those people to have been guilty of any offense, but *they must be hanged.* I am not afraid of anarchy; oh, no; it's the utopian scheme of a few, a *very* few, philosophizing cranks, who are amiable withal, but I do consider that the *labor movement should be crushed!* The Knights of Labor will never dare to create discontent again if these men are hanged."

The *New Orleans Times-Democrat* exulted over the "final tableau" that would disclose "a row of gibbetted felons, with haltered throats and fettered hands and feet, swinging to and fro, in the air; then it will be rung down again, and the people will breathe freer, feeling that anarchism, nihilism, socialism and communism were forever dead in America!"

When the nature of the "evidence" on which the accused men had been convicted became generally known, many labor organizations began to have second thoughts about their out-of-hand condemnation of "anarchists, socialists, and communists." The *Labor Leaf* spoke for many union members when it wrote: "That someone threw a bomb is certain; that it killed and wounded a large number of policemen is also certain; that the police were there without just cause, and for the express purpose of attacking the crowd, is certain; but that the eight men now under sentence had done a single act which justified their arrest and conviction has not been proved by any evidence yet produced."

In addition to growing doubts about the fairness of the trial itself, many people, sympathetic to labor, were deeply impressed by the demeanor and, even more, by the eloquence of the convicted men in their traditional addresses to the court. Spies was especially impressive.

It was anarchism, not the defendants, he declared, that was on trial. If the court was determined to sentence him to death for being an anarchist, they must do so, "for I am an Anarchist. I believe that the State of castes and classes—the state where one class dominates over and lives upon the labor of another class . . . is doomed to die, and make room for a free society, voluntary association, or universal brotherhood, if you like. You may pronounce the sentence upon me, honorable judge, but let the world know that in A.D. 1886, in the State of Illinois, eight men were sentenced to death because they believed in a better future. . . . If death is the penalty for proclaiming the truth, then I will proudly and defiantly pay the costly price! Call in your hangman! Truth crucified in Socrates, in Christ, in Giordano Bruno, in Huss, Galileo, still lives—they and others whose number is legion have preceded us on this path. We are ready to follow!"

Oscar Neebe, thirty-six years old, against whom the state's case was flimsiest of all and who had been sentenced to fifteen years in the penitentiary, gave one of the shortest and most moving addresses: "There is no evidence to show that I was connected with the bomb-throwing, or that I was near it, or anything of that kind. So I am only sorry, your honor—that is, if you can stop it or help it—I will ask you to do it—that is, to hang me, too; for I think it is more honorable to die suddenly than to be killed by inches. I have a family and children; and if they know their father is dead, they will bury him. They can go to the grave and kneel down by the side of it; but they can't go to the penitentiary and see their father, who was convicted of a crime that he hasn't had anything to do with. That is all I have to say."

Adolph Fischer declared: "You ask why sentence of death should not be passed upon me. I will only say that I protest being sentenced to death because I have committed no crime. I was tried in this room for murder, and convicted of anarchy. . . . However, if I am to die on account of being an anarchist, on account of my love for Liberty, Equality and Fraternity, I will not remonstrate. . . . This verdict is a death-blow against free speech, free press and free thought in this country."

An appeal was immediately prepared by Black to the State Supreme Court, and he was joined in the appeal by Leonard Swett, a friend and law associate of Lincoln's. The court, after a lengthy hearing and long consideration, upheld the verdict of the lower court, and the case was thereupon appealed to the United States Supreme Court.

With the decision to appeal to the U.S. Supreme Court, that curiously mercurial figure Benjamin Butler, sometime Congressman, Senator, general, and commander of occupied New Orleans, now a Democrat, entered the picture as one of the attorneys for the convicted anarchists, and along with him Roger Pryor, who had gained fame as the attorney for Theodore Tilton in his suit against Henry Ward Beecher. To those who asked why he had involved himself in such an unpopular cause, Pryor replied, "I have not the least doubt that our application for a writ of error will be granted. . . . Indeed, the records show so many errors in the ruling and in the trial that I cannot see how our application can be denied." Denied it was, however, and the attention of the country now shifted to the governor of Illinois, Richard James Oglesby, an ex-Union general, who alone had the authority to pardon the convicted men or to commute their sentences.

Soon a formidable coalition of liberal intellectuals and radical labor leaders was besieging Oglesby with petitions to show clemency for the condemned men. Matters were complicated by the fact that three of the seven in effect recanted and asked for clemency. Spies, Michael Schwab, and Fielden signed a letter to Oglesby asking for mercy and deploring "the loss of life at the Haymarket, at McCormick's factory, at East St. Louis, and at the Chicago Stock Yards." Louis Lingg, Adolph Fischer, George Engel, and Albert Parsons were adamant in their refusal to request the commutation of their sentences from hanging to imprisonment. "I regret the petition for imprisonment," Parsons wrote, "for I am innocent. . . . In the name of the American people I demand my right . . . to liberty."

William Dean Howells, famous as the editor of the *Atlantic Monthly*, who had socialist leanings, took the lead in rallying the nation's intellectuals. Samuel Gompers wrote to Governor Oglesby, asking for clemency for the Haymarket anarchists. "If these men are executed," he declared, "it would simply be an impetus to this so-called revolutionary movement which no other thing on earth can give. These men would, apart from any consideration of mercy or humanity, be looked upon as martyrs. Thousands and thousands of labor men all over the world would consider that these men have been executed because they were standing up for free speech and free press. We ask you, sir, to interpose your great power to prevent so dire a calamity."

Of course, anarchist papers, like *Die Freiheit, Arbeit Zeitung,* and *Truth,* were bitter in their attacks on the American system of justice. "What they are to suffer," Johann Most wrote, ". . . is not for the death of the police officers who fell on the Haymarket. The spirit of the new times is to be strangled on the gallows." George Francis Train, the eccentric millionaire whose causes had included everything from women's rights and sexual liberation to communism, went on a lecture tour, inveighing against their conviction. "You hang those seven men," he told a Chicago audience, "and I will head twenty million working men to cut the throats of everybody in Chicago."

Among the leaders in the fight for amnesty was Samuel Mc-Connell, a highly respected Illinois lawyer. He drew up a petition asking for amnesty and took it to old Lyman Trumbull, one of the founders of the Republican Party, the man who had beaten Lincoln for the Senate seat from Illinois in 1855 and who was himself a former member of the State Supreme Court. Trumbull, now seventy-four years old and veteran of hundreds of political battles, read the petition, "buried his face in his hands and said, 'I will sign. Those men did not have a fair trial.'"

Although Henry George believed that "No well-informed lawyer can defend the conviction upon legal grounds," he also believed that "it was proved beyond a doubt that these men were engaged in a conspiracy as a result of which the bomb was thrown, and were therefore under the laws of Illinois as guilty as though they themselves had done the act." Yet he sent word to "the boys in jail that I am in full sympathy with them, and they may count on me to do all in my power to set them free." A number of prominent ministers joined in the call for clemency, but organized labor remained sharply divided on the issue. The Knights of Labor, already accused of radical leanings and deeply concerned about the effect of the bombing on public attitudes toward the labor movement in general, was especially anxious to affirm its loyalty to basic American principles and constitutional government. One of its journals, the *American Labor Budget,* declared: "Socialism, anarchism, and murder find no defenders in the K. of L. . . . The Knights of Labor . . . are friends of the law and of order. . . . Down with socialism and anarchy. Up with education and equality." In the view of Powderly, the bomb "did more injury to the good name of labor than all the strikes of that year, and turned public sentiment against labor organizations." But the fact was that the more liberal or radical elements in the labor movement (or those that simply read the record of the trial more carefully) rallied in increasing numbers to the side of the condemned men. By the fall of 1887 fourteen prominent labor leaders, with Samuel Gompers at their head, issued an "appeal to the working class," stating: "Under the misguiding and corrupting influence of prejudice and class-hatred, these men have been condemned without any conclusive evidence as accessories to a crime the principals of which . . . are unknown. The execution of this sentence would be a disgrace to the honor of our nation, and would strengthen the very doctrines it is ostensibly directed against." Their execution, the signatories insisted, would be nothing more than "judicial murder, prompted by the basest and most un-American motives. . . ." The appeal ended with a call for "a great public demonstration to be held simultaneously in this and in all other cities of the Union on or about the 20th of October. . . ."

On the day appointed such meetings were indeed held, and thousands of signatures calling for clemency were collected. At Cooper Union, Samuel Gompers was among the speakers who addressed a crowd estimated at 4,000. Daniel De Leon, a young lecturer at Columbia, also spoke, declaring, "I come here deliberately and for the good name of our beloved country that its proud record shall not be blood-stained by a judicial crime as the one contemplated in Chicago."

In the face of a flood of petitions from a wide variety of groups, Governor Oglesby found himself in a dilemma. As labor groups came in increasing numbers to plead for clemency, a countercampaign was hastily organized by business interests calling for the prompt execution of the convicted men.

Worldwide attention was focused on the trial and the appeals and subsequent efforts to win clemency for the convicted anarchists. In England especially there was strong sentiment for the seven men. At a mass meeting in London, George Bernard Shaw, William Morris, and Annie Besant were among the speakers, and 16,405 English workingmen joined in a protest "against the murder of the labor leaders."

As the date for the executions approached, the state's prosecutor, Julius Grinnell, and the trial judge, Joseph Gary, wrote to Oglesby asking for clemency for Fielden and Schwab.

One of the more dramatic events in Chicago in the weeks preceding the execution was a meeting of businessmen. Governor Oglesby had told those working for clemency that if a substantial number of the city's businessmen would come out in support of clemency, it would make it easier for him to commute the sentences to imprisonment. Some fifty Chicago bankers, manufacturers, and businessmen were assembled and seemed favorably disposed to join the requests for clemency until Marshall Field, the richest and most powerful man in Chicago, rose to express his opposition. Lyman Gage, the banker who arranged the meeting, told Henry Demarest Lloyd: "Afterwards many of the men present came around to me singly, and said they agreed with me in my views and would have been glad to join in such an appeal, but that in the face of opposition of powerful men like Marshall Field they did not like to do so, as it might injure them in business or socially, etc."

At this point the discovery of four small bombs in Louis Lingg's cell introduced a new element. There were immediate charges of a police "plant," but the effect of the discovery was a severe setback to the campaign for clemency. A few days later Lingg set off a dynamite cap in his mouth that blew away part of his face and resulted in his death at almost the moment Oglesby announced his decision: to commute the sentences of Schwab and Fielden to life imprisonment. He could not consider commuting the sentences of Spies, Fischer, Parsons, Engel, and Lingg because they had specifically refused such commutation and demanded "liberty or death." Subsequently the governor told James Quinn, one of the leaders in the fight for amnesty, "that for every petition for mercy received from the friends of the condemned men, he could produce hundreds from business men and reputable, law-abiding citizens all over the country requesting him to remain steadfast in supporting the decision of the courts. . . . The business men were all unanimous that the men should all be hanged."

On November 11, 1887, Spies, Engel, Fischer, and Parsons were led to the gallows. Spies spoke from beneath the hood over his head: "There will come a time when our silence will be more powerful than the voices you strangle today!" Fischer called out, "Hurrah for anarchy," and Engel's last words were: "This is the happiest moment of my life!" Before Parsons could do more than shout, "Let me speak . . . Let the voice of the people be heard!" the trap was sprung.

There were no outbreaks of violence; but it was estimated that 6,000 people followed the coffins to the cemetery, and from 150,000 to 500,000 lined the streets to watch the funeral procession pass by. William Black, who had labored so valiantly to see justice done, reminded the mourners at the graves that they were not "beside the caskets of felons consigned to an inglorious tomb. We are here by the bodies of men who were sublime in their self-sacrifice and for whom the gibbet assumed the glory of a cross."

There was a considerable measure of truth in Henry Demarest Lloyd's observation that the Chicago anarchists had been killed "because property, authority, and public believed that they came to bring not reform but revolution, not peace but a sword."

In the view of Mary Jones, "Foreign agitators who had suffered under European despots preached various schemes of economic salvation to the workers. The workers asked only for bread and a shortening of the long hours of toil. The agitators gave them visions. The police gave them clubs."

The long travail which had deeply divided the country was over. But the Haymarket Affair, in all its ramifications, was one of those events that leave an unmistakable imprint on history. Perhaps the most notable was a kind of paralysis that seized the labor movement as all its attention for some eighteen crucial months was riveted on the fate of the convicted men. Whatever its leaders might say in condemnation or exoneration of the anarchists, the practical consequences were devastating. The Knights of Labor suffered most, in large part because Powderly's leadership was hopelessly discredited and Joe Buchanan, his rival, who espoused the cause of the condemned men, was unable to take his place as the leader of a united movement. Gompers, whose union was far less tainted by charges of radicalism was, by his forthright endorsement of the principle of clemency, able to strengthen his own leadership of the American Federation of Labor. Thus, rather paradoxically—since Powderly refused to oppose their execution while Gompers did—the conservative wing of the labor movement benefited. Radicals of all persuasions could point to the outcome of the long-drawn-out Haymarket Affair as fresh evidence that workingmen could not get justice in capitalist America. In terms of the practical goals of labor agitation—higher wages, shorter hours, better working conditions—these undoubtedly suffered a severe setback at a time that was crucial for the labor movement as a whole.

To the radical left, and to millions of workingmen and women all over the world, the executed anarchists became, as Gompers had predicted they would, martyrs. (Big Bill Haywood, the organizer of the International Workers of the World, left instructions that his ashes be divided between the Red Square in Moscow and the burial site of the anarchists.) They were remembered in a song—the "Haymarket Song":

> Toiling millions now are waking
> See them marching on

> All the tyrants now are shaking
> Ere their power's gone.

In almost every other way Haymarket was a disaster. It vastly augmented the already considerable paranoia of most Americans in regard to anarchists, socialists, communists, and radicals in general. It increased hostility toward "godless foreigners," a phrase that the prosecutor, Grinnell, had used frequently in referring to the defendants. It caused a serious impairment of freedom of speech in every part of the country, especially in regard to unorthodox political views (and indeed to a host of other matters). As William Holmes noted in his letter to William Morris, before Haymarket the principle of free speech had been widely honored (by, among others, the mayor of Chicago); afterward it took a brave man to defend that classic right. It divided and demoralized the labor movement and hastened the demise of the Knights of Labor, then at the height of its membership and influence.

At the union's convention in 1886 Powderly had tried to suppress the question by declaring that the real issue was monopoly, "for anarchy is the legitimate child of monopoly. . . . He is the true Knight of Labor who with one hand clutches anarchy by the throat and with the other strangles monopoly!" Powderly's damning of both capitalists and anarchists did not satisfy many of the members of his union. Finally, after angry debate, a motion was made opposing the execution of the anarchists on the ground that capital punishment was "a relic of barbarism." Still there was general dissatisfaction. Powderly was challenged for ruling that a motion supporting the anarchists was out of order, and in a long, emotional speech he ended: "[For] anarchy I have nothing but hatred, and if I could I would forever wipe from the face of the earth the last vestige of its double-damned presence. . . ." Many factors contributed to the disintegration of the Knights. The central one was Powderly's own temperament, especially the old-fashioned paternalistic and authoritarian spirit in which he ruled *his* union, but Haymarket fanned the smoldering conflict in the Knights into a blaze of dissension and the Grand Master Workman's angry attack on the convicted men accelerated the process of disintegration in the nation's first "big union."

After the collapse of the Knights of Labor, the closest thing to an industry-wide union was the United Mine Workers, founded in 1890, which originally affiliated with the AFofL but soon found itself in conflict with the Federation's craft orientation. The American Railway

Union, started by Eugene V. Debs in 1893, was another effort at transcending the limitations of the craft-union pattern favored by Gompers. The United States Strike Commission, established to investigate the causes of the spread of crippling strikes, described the philosophy of the American Railway Union as holding to the theory "that the organization of different classes of railroad employees upon the trade union idea has ceased to be useful or adequate; that pride of organization, petty jealousies and the conflict of views into which men are trained in separate organizations under different leaders, tend to defeat the common object of all and enable the railroads to use such organizations against each other. . . ." Debs was convinced that the power of the railroad tycoons was such that only a union of the 850,000 railroad workers without regard to subdivisions of "crafts" could counterbalance it.

15

Free Love

A popular aphorism declares that there is nothing so powerful as an idea whose time has come. For a brief, if intoxicating, moment it appeared that in the early 1870s the time had come to talk candidly about sexual matters, particularly the sexual exploitation of women by men. *Woodhull and Claflin's Weekly* and other radical journals (among them, of course, the journal of the National Woman Suffrage Association—*Revolution*) made their appearance in various parts of the country. Forbidden subjects were debated from public platforms; respectable newspapers made cautious (and largely hostile) references to the "movement." Political radicalism was in the air. Speakers came forward to declare that "capitalism" had failed and must be replaced by a more just and humane social and economic system. Stephen Pearl Andrews won supporters for his doctrine of universology and his proposals for a socialist state.

Thoughtful young men *and* women like Lester and Lizzie Ward joined debating societies made up, in the main, of "liberals," "free thinkers," "positivists," and "socialists." Various forms of anarchism found favor, and "freedom" became a magic and talismanic word. Everyone was to be *free*—women, children, blacks, immigrants, even husbands and wives. Perhaps it was inevitable that in this context the "sex question" should be a central issue in the postwar ferment of new ideas and old ideas revived. What was astonishing was the boldness with which the subject was attacked, the defiance of convention, and, for a time at least, the enthusiasm of the public response. The answer lies in part in the fact that many of the most radical social and political notions appeared initially under the rather misleading banner of spiritualism, a movement with a long history and a substantial degree of respectability. "The first female lecturers and public speakers were spiritualists," a Methodist writer noted, "and in the spiritualists' church, so-called women are the high priests; and the spiritual teachings in regard to the relation of men and women and their duties are reversed."

In addition, many of the proclaimers of the new creeds came out of the abolitionist movement, which had, after all, captured the country and brought about the greatest revolution in the nation's history. It was not surprising that former abolitionists like Stephen Pearl Andrews, emboldened by success, projected new utopias. Andrews had undertaken, the reader may recall, to create a "Universal Science" and a common language, developing shorthand in the process. He subscribed to spiritualism (he first encountered the Claflin sisters in their active spiritualist phase), health food, free love, and communism (he helped found the communist colony *Modern Times* on Long Island), and he wrote a succession of books on his philosophy of universalism. In addition, he learned Chinese, wrote a book in that language, married a woman physician, and took a medical degree at the New York Medical School. Finally, he became the principal guru for a troupe called the Pantarchy, who espoused state socialism and "free alliance," or free love, as it was more commonly called.

Marriage and the family were, it was soon evident, the real issues. It was widely declared, Abba Woolson wrote in *Women in American Society* in 1873, that marriage was "coming to lose much of its sanctity and honor in the eyes of the modern world." The frequency of divorce was pointed to as evidence of the decline of the institution. Woolson was, at heart, like the vast majority of marriage reformers and free love advocates, a romantic. What she deplored was not marriage but loveless marriages, marriages of convenience, marriages *on any principle except love*. When degrading, unequal, selfish marriages were replaced by unions of men and women of "equal culture and similar objects of thought," surely there would be fewer divorces. Woolson's friend John

Greenleaf Whittier identified himself with her views by writing an introduction to her book.

By "free love" Victoria Woodhull explained she meant that no marriage should be binding or necessarily permanent. Women should be free to give their bodies to whomever they chose, rather than submit to the sexual tyranny of a single man, denominated a "husband." The consequence of such a break with tradition would be that superior women, uncoerced by society, would give themselves only to superior men, producing in turn, superior offspring. "Her intercourse with others," Woodhull added, "will be limited, and the proper means taken to render it unprolific. . . ."

In Tennessee Claflin's words, "If to advocate freedom is 'free love' and contra indicated from *forced love*, then by all means do we accept the appellation. If there is one foul, damning blot upon woman's nature and capacities, it is this system that compels her to manifest and act a love that is forced; this kind of love is all the prostitution there is in the world." The marriage of "two pure, trusting, loving equal souls" was the only true marriage. So far were the advocates of free love from wishing to "reduce the relations of the sexes to common looseness" that many of them aligned with the so-called exclusionists, who insisted that love could exist only between two people at a time, so to speak. The varietists, as their name implied, took the line that love was a general sentiment and might thus be shared with anyone for whom an "affinity" existed. "Affinity" was a critical word for both varietists and exclusionists.

"Affinity" was a spiritual state, an "aura." Those with complimentary "auras" were "natural mates," married in the realm of the spirit whether or not they were married in the eyes of the state. Spiritualism, in turn, professed to be based on the new science of electricity. The means by which the spirits of the dead communicated with the living was through a form of electricity not dissimilar to that which was carried over the telegraph wires.

Victoria and Tennessee believed that since science was the god of the new age, scientific principles should be applied to human as well as to animal mating. To use "scientific principles" in mate selection was no more than the duty of every woman of conscience. "Mothers of humanity," Claflin wrote, "yours is a fearful duty, and one which should in its importance lift you entirely above the modern customs of society, its frivolities, superficialities and deformities, and make you realize that to you is committed the divine work of perfecting humanity." This commission made marriage "a thousand times more sacred than you or any other has ever regarded it. So fearfully sacred should it be that it should never be consummated until the researches of science and the teachings of wisdom are exhausted in the effort to prove that it will be a benefit to humanity." As Harriet Beecher Stowe was dedicated to making the home a physically and morally improving environment, so the Claflin sisters, seizing on the notion of "natural selection," wished to consecrate the physical relationship of men and women to the scientific improvement of the race. The home, they argued, was growing increasingly arid, spiritually and intellectually, because the husband and the wife were not friends and companions but slaves to the same outmoded convention. The home could not hold the husband, who fled to masculine enclaves for his games, his drinking, and even his furtive lecheries. Women in turn were forced to imitate the men with their own exclusively feminine circles for tea, cards, and gossip. "Thus the distance between man and woman, as the husband and wife, is gradually widening, and the home of the family every year becomes less and less the central point of attraction for all concerned. This . . . indicates a revolution in domestic life, such as the world has never known. Does woman comprehend whither she is floating? Does she realize that as a sex she is becoming estranged from man? Does she understand what the estrangement of the sexes means for her?"

To Claflin, the reason for the widening gap between the wife and her husband was "the growing aversion on the part of women to bearing children." Evidence was to be found in the increased use of contraceptives and the rising rate of abortion. "The means they resort to for their prevention is sufficient to disgust every natural man," she wrote, "and to cause him to seek the companionship of those who have no fear in this regard." The fault was the woman's since "Man does not wander from home, wife, and, perhaps, children for no cause." On the other hand, it was men who forced such unhappy strategies on women. "So long as women are the mere slaves of men," she wrote, "forced by the laws of marriage to submit their bodies to them, whenever and wherever they may so determine, and by thus being subjected are still further and more barbarously forced to become the unwilling mothers of unwished-for children, so long will the millennium days be delayed."

It was the "private prostitution" of marriage that must be abolished. The prostitute was paid for the use of her body and could withhold it if she wished. "Men under the new *regime*," Claflin wrote, "will become the companions of women instead, and will receive [a woman's sexual participation] as a special favor if so permitted to be."

Americans had sought redemption wherever they could find it—in vegetarian diets, in abolition, in temperance, in utopian communities, in religious revivals. Now they were to seek it in the feminine spirit, the anima. "Woman, as a whole," Tennessee Claflin insisted, "is possessed of a healthful, saving, purifying power that is needed everywhere. The basest sensualist bows and worships in the presence of a pure and holy woman, and loses the power to think of such a being falling to his level. And this is the saving element that is required by the body politic, to arrest its present tendencies to complete corruption." So that was it! The terrible conflicts and dilemmas of American society sprang from sexual exploitation, the exploitation of women by men, most strikingly in marriage. Small wonder that Harriet Beecher Stowe and her sister felt such anxieties about the state of the home. Although they did not dare approach the subject as boldly as the Claflins, their prescriptions for better ventilation, more sunshine, and more Christian zeal may well have veiled similar apprehensions.

But could politics be purified by "scientific" mating, by "the researches of science and the teaching of wisdom"? How were only *wanted* children, "benefits to humanity," to be parceled out to husbands and wives joined in a new companionship that did not cancel sexuality but fulfilled it? Once women were granted full equality with men, the drinking saloons, gambling halls, houses of prostitution "would soon disappear." To hasten the millennium, the mating of perfect companions must be followed by the scientific rearing of the offspring of such unions. It was these children who must be "the basis of future society." They might indeed be raised in "the proper kind of industrial institutions," thereby growing into "better citizens, better men and women." Victoria Woodhull and her sister compared the "Woman Question" with the "Negro Question." Victoria wrote: "The Negro question vitalized the Republican Party, because there was a principle involved in it; so, too, will the Woman Question vitalize the party that shall become its champion. . . . It is meet that the country which was almost the last to abjure slavery should be the first to enfranchise women."

Victoria Woodhull was in great demand as a public lecturer on spiritualism in the early 1870s. Her most popular topic was "The Sacred-Cows of Sexual Freedom." At Vineland, New Jersey, and at many other towns and cities across the nation (she reached San Jose, California, on her tour in 1872) she told her audiences that the legal safeguards placed around the family, primarily in the form of strict divorce laws, made the American town "a community of hot little hells." Far from wishing to break up the family, she wished to purify and spiritualize it by freeing it from all coercive elements. "In a perfected sexuality shall continuous life be found. . . . So shall life not come to an end when its spring shall not cease to send forth the vitalized waters of life, that earth's otherwise weary children may drink and live. . . . Then shall they, who have in ages past, cast off their mortal coils, be able to come again and resume them at will; and thus shall a spiritualized humanity be able at will to throw off and take on its material clothing, and the two worlds shall be once more and forever united." Such was the vision to be achieved "through the sexual emancipation of woman, and her return to self-ownership and to individualized existence."

"Spiritualized humanity" could "at will . . . throw off and take on its material clothing, and the two worlds . . . be once more and forever united." Behind those fervent words lay a strange concatenation of American dreams—the promise once more of the millennium, of heaven on earth; John Humphrey Noyes's notion of a perfected humanity and the end of man's sexual tyranny; the notion of personal autonomy and control over one's own life and, as a corollary, control over the natural world of which one was a part; the desire to be "individualized," to experience God in self. There were echoes and intimations of Josiah Warren's philosophical anarchism, of Emerson and the transcendentalists (very strong intimations there), and of Whitman's "Song of Myself." Most important of all, perhaps, was the very evident impulse to escape the terrible material reality of the United States, a condition of existence so painful as to seem often beyond bearing. A uniquely American amalgam, it touched the deepest yearnings of the crowds who turned out to hear Victoria Woodhull's startling new doctrine. Sex, darkly desired, hidden, evil and unclean, insatiable, insistent, relentless, a barrier, an obstacle, a stumbling block for both men and women; could it be that sex was to be the avenue to redemption, to a purified and a spiritualized humanity, to, literally, heaven on earth?

The spiritualists, most of them pious and upright men and women, themselves were alarmed at Victoria Woodhull's espousal of free love and even more at the scandals that hovered about her beautiful head. At a meeting of the American Association of Spiritualists, when questioned by someone in the audience about her personal virtue, Victoria replied defiantly: "If I want sexual intercourse with one or one hundred men I shall have it . . . and this sexual intercourse business may as well be discussed now, and discussed until you are so familiar with your sexual organs that a reference to them will no longer make the blush mount to your face any more than a reference to any other part of your body." The proper performance of the sexual act, especially on the part of the man, was not a casual matter in which he could satisfy his own impatient desires and leave his wife "unfulfilled . . . to breed nervous debility or irritability and sexual demoralization. . . . This involves a whole science and a fine art, hardly yet broached to human thought, now criminally repressed and defeated by the prejudices of mankind. . . ." The fact was, of course, that women were not supposed to have strong sexual desires or indeed to need or expect "fulfillment" in intercourse. Such feelings were not ladylike. Were a wife, through some happy mischance, to become sexually aroused by her husband during coition, she might seriously alarm him by sowing the suspicion in his mind that she was not as chaste and pure as she should be. The odds, of course, were all against such an untoward happening since respectable women had had it dinned into them since childhood that *any* "excess of animal spirits," especially any overtly sexual response, was unthinkable in a lady. The vast majority of middle- and upper-class women were thus unaware of their capacity for orgasm. The determination to be ladylike in bed was indistinguishable from the desire to be ladylike in the parlor.

The potency of the free love movement was made evident by the enthusiastic response it initially received from Elizabeth Cady Stanton and Susan B. Anthony as well as many of their followers. At the time of the second convention of the newly formed National Woman Suffrage Association in January, 1871, Victoria Woodhull, who had been denied the status of a delegate, turned up in Washington and prevailed upon the susceptible chairman of the Judiciary Committee of the House of Representatives to allow her to present a memorial to that body on the issue of suffrage for women. Outmaneuvered, the officers of the association delayed the opening of the convention and went to hear Woodhull's testimony. They were charmed, and that night, when the convention formally opened, Victoria Woodhull was seated on the speakers' platform, from which vantage point she read her memorial once more.

To the objections of some of the more conventional members of the association at the recognition given a woman of such notoriety, Susan B. Anthony replied that, however flawed Victoria Woodhull's character might be, it was certainly as good as that of most Congress-men, to which there was, of course, no answer. "Go ahead doing," Susan B. wrote to Woodhull, "bright, glorious, young and strong spirit, and believe in the best love and hope and faith of S. B. Anthony." Elizabeth Cady Stanton was as entranced by Victoria Woodhull as aus-tere Susan B. was. To her Woodhull was "a deliverer," the bearer of a revelation. "I have worked thirty years for woman suffrage," she wrote after attending one of Woodhull's lectures on free love, "and I now feel that suffrage is but the vestibule of Woman's emancipa-tion. . . . The men and women who are dabbling with the suffrage movement should be at once . . . and emphatically warned that what they mean logically if not consciously in all they say is next social equality and next Freedom or in a word Free Love, and, if they wish to get out of the boat, they should for safety get out now, for delays are dangerous."

At a great suffrage meeting held in the Apollo Hall in New York in May, 1872, Woodhull declaimed: "If the very next Congress refuses women all the legitimate results of citizenship we shall proceed to call another convention expressly to frame a new constitution and to erect a new government. . . . We mean treason; we mean secession, and on a thousand times grander scale than was that of the South. We are plotting revolution; we will overthrow this bogus Republic and plant a government of righteousness in its stead. . . ."

When Roxy Claflin, the sisters' mother, initiated a suit against Colonel James Harvey Blood, who professed to be Victoria's husband, it came out in court that Victoria's former husband, Canning Woodhull, was living in the family with a younger sister, Polly, and children by several marriages, including an afflicted son named Byron and a daughter named Zulu Maude. To attacks on her morals, Victoria replied in the *Weekly:* "Mrs. Woodhull will always appear when justice calls. . . . She is a life-long spiritualist and owes all she is to the education and constant guidance of spirit influence. . . . She also believes in and advocates free love in the high, the best sense . . . as the only cure for the immorality, lewdness and licentiousness which may corrode the holy institution of the Sexual Relation."

Another disciple of Stephen Pearl Andrews was Marie Stevens Howland, born in 1836, in Lebanon, New Hampshire. Marie Stevens moved to Lowell, Massachusetts, at the age of fourteen to work in the famous mills with the "Lowell girls" in order to support her two younger sisters, orphaned by their mother's death. She found conditions far from the idyllic picture so often painted. The young women worked long hours, breathing the lint-filled air, and lived highly regimented lives in company boardinghouses. By the age of twenty-one Stevens had risen to the rank of supervisor, educated herself, for which the libraries and educational facilities of the mills deserved credit, taught school in the notoriously tough Five Points area of New York, attended normal school, and been appointed principal of a primary school. At that point she paused long enough to marry a young lawyer of radical inclinations, Lyman Case, whom she met at one of the many organizations that Stephen Pearl Andrews formed—The Club, which met over Taylor's Saloon at 555 Broadway. Its members were described by a reporter as "bloomerites in pantaloons and round hats, partisans of individual liberty late of Modern Times, atheists, infidels and philosophers" mingling with "perfumed exquisites from Gotham," the latter phrase suggesting that a number of more radically inclined socialites were included in the essentially middle-class membership of The Club. Many of its members were former abolitionists. Jane Cunningham Croly was the "mistress of ceremonies" at The Club. It was Croly who had earlier organized the women's club Sorosis and the Women's Parliament.

Lyman Case taught Marie Stevens "speech, manners, movements, etc., etc." as well as Latin. Discovering a "spiritual" or "passional" affinity with Case, she moved with him into Unitary House. This was a kind of urban commune situated in a row of houses on Fourteenth Street in New York and made up of some twenty individuals who shared a common dining room. The rather sympathetic account in *The New York Times* noted: "The Free Lovers . . . have invented a large programme, and . . . some of them, at least, have begun to do what Mr. Charles Fourier, and the philosophers of Brook Farm after him, vainly attempted to accomplish . . . introduce into the heart of New York, without noise or bluster, a successful enterprise based on Practical Socialism." By the time the house proved not notably unitary and disbanded a few years later, the *Times* had become much more hostile. Identifying the spiritualists as the source of all the trouble, the newspaper declared: "The spirits, besides being unmistakable blockheads, are as prurient as Peter Dens himself. . . . They were not in the field five years till they sought a 'fusion' with the Free-Lovers, began to assail the marriage relation, invent new causes of difference between man and wife, and find excuses to satisfy the consciences of bigamists, adulterers and fornicators." The paper termed the experiment "a positive triumph of lust."

At the end of the Unitary House experiment, Marie Stevens formed a new affinity with Edward Howland, another free love advocate and anarchist, and the two spent several years in European communes.

Actively involved with the Claflin sisters, Victoria and Tennessee, and committed to communism, Marie Howland—she married Edward—helped them organize Section 12 of the International Workingmen's Association and was active in its affairs until Marx had the section expelled. Howland thereafter found her way to the famous Topolobampo commune in Mexico, where she joined forces with Albert Kimsey Owen. Born in Chester, Pennsylvania, Owen was an engineer who had identified himself with various radical causes, including the Knights of Labor and the Greenback Party. Howland wrote that the Social Palace (the living unit containing from 2,000 to 3,000 people), as it was to be called, must emphasize child care and training and that "the freeing of woman from the household treadmill must be effected before she can cultivate the powers so vitally needed in the regeneration of the race." After the failure of the Topolobampo colony in 1893, Marie Howland moved to Alabama and lived in the Fairhope single tax colony until her death at eighty-five.

Any exoticism might be expected in New York City, of course, but there were also free lovers in Massachusetts, in Kansas and Iowa, Illinois and Minnesota, and, of course, in California. In part this diffusion could be accounted for by the fact that free love was a plank in the platform of the anarchists, who were sprinkled liberally throughout the farming communities of the Middle West. But there was an identifiably distinct grass-roots strain in the movement, in which rural and small-town women were predominant and which focused directly and, in some instances, exclusively on the radical reform of conventional attitudes toward the whole issue of sexuality—the philosophy, the techniques, the role of sexuality in family life, and, above all, the necessity for sex education.

The free love movement was closely connected with a decidedly American form of anarchism, two of the major prophets of which were Henry David Thoreau and Thomas Paine. The rural free love, free thought movement was centered in the small farming towns of the Midwest, especially Kansas and Iowa. In Valley Falls, Kansas, the family of Moses Harman published the *Kansas Liberal*, which was soon transformed into *Lucifer* (the name Lucifer, the fallen angel or the devil, was in itself a challenge to Christian orthodoxy). *Lucifer's* most basic commitment was to free speech, the right to print whatever it wished. Free love was the cause it subscribed to most enthusiastically. Since there were almost as many interpretations of that alarming term as there were advocates of the doctrine itself, the pages of *Lucifer* were open to any and all proponents of radical sexual doctrines. The object of *Lucifer*, Harman declared, was to promote "free press, free rostrum, free mails . . . , free land, free homes, free food, free drink, free medicine, free Sunday, free marriage and free divorce. . . . In short we advocate the Sovereignty of the Individual or Self Government. We would have every man and every woman the proprietor of himself or herself."

Lillian Harman, Moses Harman's sixteen-year-old daughter, "married" Harman's young assistant, Edwin Cox Walker, in a deliberately illegal ceremony. Harman read a "Statement of Principles in Regard to Marriage"; Walker thereupon announced that he considered public marriage ceremonies "essentially and ineradicably indelicate, a pandering to morbid, vicious, and meddlesome elements in human nature. . . . Lillian," he declared, "is and will continue to be as free to repulse any and all advances of mine as she has been heretofore. In joining with me in this love and labor union, she has not alienated a single natural right. She remains sovereign of herself, as I am of myself, and we . . . repudiate all powers legally conferred upon husbands and wives." To which Lillian responded: "I retain, also, my full maiden name, as I am sure it is my duty to do. With this understanding, I give to him my hand in token of my trust in him and of the fidelity to truth and honor of my intentions toward him."

When Lillian and Edwin were arrested and charged with "lewd and lascivious cohabitation," the case became something of a national issue. Advocates of free love all over the country were joined by liberals and radicals in support of the couple. They were tried, found guilty, fined, and sentenced to serve prison terms—Lillian four months; Walker, six.

Another case that attracted wide public attention was that of Moses Hull (it was perhaps worth noting that two of the most ardent freethinkers and free love advocates were named Moses) and Mattie Sawyer. Hull was the editor of a free thought journal called *Hull's Crucible*, which supported every radical cause. He announced that he found monogamy painfully restrictive; with the consent of his wife, Elvira, he "humbly and prayerfully" abandoned himself to "diviner impulses." Elvira then further shocked public opinion by announcing that he had become a better companion in consequence. She nonetheless dissolved their marriage, and soon afterward Moses Hull and his fellow lecturer on free love, anarchy, and spiritualism, Mattie Sawyer, began living together.

The Hunt family of Ohio and later Kansas was notable for its dedication to free love. Hannah Hunt was a sex reformer, as were her sister Lizzie, her brother C. F. Hunt, and her daughter Lillie. All of them wrote for Moses Harman's *Lucifer*. Lillie Hunt became a leading Populist in the first stirrings of that movement. She was far more radical politically than most of the irate farmers with whom she worked. "Woman," she wrote, "has always been taught that her highest happiness lies in a correct step to the music of pots and kettles, a mastery over the ingredients and process of making palatable bread, butter, pie, and pickles, and general devotion to the loves and duties of home." In this world of material things, "philosophy, science, literature and art, lose its charms for her, and she finally has no ability or desire to enter in. . . . For one thing in my life I am truly grateful," she added, "I have never been guilty of being a good housekeeper. . . . Why is it necessarily any more a woman's place to wash dishes, scrub floors, make beds, etc., than it is a man's? Why not teach our boys to do all these as well as our girls?" Motherhood brought with it "duty, submission, self-repression . . . pain, suffering, unappreciative devotion and unresponsive affection. To be the 'queen of home,' means drudgery and imprisonment. It is to be a galley slave to the appetites and needs of her family." Such sentiments did not prevent Lillie Hunt from marrying and becoming a mother.

One of the most influential of the free love duos was Ezra Heywood, a Presbyterian minister, and Angela Tilton. In contrast with many of the free love alliances, Angela took Ezra's name and was his partner and the dominant force in editing their free love journal, the *Word*. Heywood described his reform activities as "negro emancipation, peace, woman's enfranchisement, temperance, labor and love reform." Both he and his wife did not hesitate to evoke Christian ideals when it seemed appropriate (Heywood called the Bible "a labor reform book of the most radical kind"), and their journal was dedicated to the "abolition of speculative income, of Woman's slavery, and war government." The Heywoods' house, Mountain Home, in Princeton, Massachusetts, became a center for kindred spirits. The New England Free

Love League was founded there in 1873. Several years earlier Heywood had started the New England Labor Reform League in Worcester, Massachusetts, a hotbed of radical ideas, as it had been in the days when John Adams taught school there. The Free Love League took the year of its founding as Year One of the Year of Love or Y.I.

In 1875 Heywood published an attack on conventional marriage called *Cupid's Yokes*, subtitled *The Binding Force of Conjugal Life: An Essay to Consider Some Moral and Physiological Phases of Love and Marriage, Wherein Is Asserted the Natural Right and Necessity of Sexual Self-Government*. Only twenty-three pages long, it immediately became a source book for the free love movement, constantly quoted and referred to. The purpose of the work was to "promote discretion and purity in love by bringing sexuality within the domain of reason and moral obligation." It called for "the expulsion of animalism, and the entrance of reason, knowledge, and continence," so that the "sexual instinct shall no longer be a savage, uncontrollable usurper but be subject to thought and civilization."

In 1878 the National Defense Association, a group pledged to defend the right of free speech under the First Amendment to the Constitution, was formed, and it found one of its first causes in the prosecution by Anthony Comstock, the crusader against "vice," of Ezra Heywood for publishing *Cupid's Yokes*. A rally in support of Heywood was held in historic Faneuil Hall. In a place and amid an atmosphere that recalled to many members of the audience the days of militant abolitionism, the meeting, 6,000 strong, passed resounding resolutions supporting the principle of free speech and Ezra Heywood specifically. The abolitionist atmosphere was accentuated by the fact that one of the heroes of the movement, seventy-four-year-old Elizur Wright, who had served in 1833 as secretary of the newly formed American Anti-Slavery Society, chaired the meeting. (Wright, in addition, had laid the groundwork for the reorganization and regulation of the life insurance business.) In the aftermath of the meeting, the National Defense Association dispatched Laura Cuppy Kendrick, a radical feminist, to Washington to petition President Hayes to pardon Heywood, as he did.

If Lillian Harman was the down-to-earth realist in the free love movement, Angela Heywood was its most lyric and impassioned voice. In temperament she resembled Victoria Woodhull most closely. To her the act of lovemaking was the most exalting and enchanting of all human relationships. One of her Pantarchy friends, Lucien V. Pinney, an associate of Stephen Pearl Andrews, wrote of her: "She has visions, hears voices, and dreams dreams, and she is at times a whirlpool of words, delivered with startling effect. She is naturally musical, and instinctively dramatic, loves the lights, colors and rhythmic sounds of the theatre, loves Art in action . . . but she is in nothing frivolous."

To Angela men were as much the victims of existing attitudes toward the relations between the sexes as women; she sought their liberation as well as that of her own sex. Love could not be free, she argued, until all the existing taboos on "sexual" words had been banished. Thus the word of the *Word* was "Fuck." She wrote: "Verily, how hath Natural Modesty forgotten herself if the Penis and the Womb be not elegant organs of the Human Body, equal in ability to entertain us with eyes and tongue. . . . Sexuality is a divine ordinance, elegantly natural from an eye-glance to the vital action of the penis and the womb, in personal exhilaration or for reproductive purposes." And again: "The Penis and the Womb, the Outer and the Inner are sublimely worthy peers in body faculty; their attentions, purposes, capacities, demands, supplies,—moved by Brain and Heart are the pith and glory of Being." Men and women were related sexually. Rather than that being a cause of shame and guilt, "let us face the glad fact with all its ineffable joys." Some women sex reformers took the line that women could get along very well without men except for impregnation when they wished a child, but Angela Heywood saw the matter in a very different light. The woman's "lady-nature knows it is the very great *everything* she wants to do *with* man." If she "duly gives to man who cometh in unto her, as freely, as equally, as well as he gives her, how shall she be abashed or ashamed of the innermost. . . . Nature can put Madame Intellect behind the door further than you can think while she revels with a man to her heart's content." She deplored the fact that she was forced to use the term "generative sexual intercourse" in her public lectures. "Three words, twenty-seven letters to define a given action . . . commonly spoken in one word of four letters that everybody knew the meaning of," she wrote. "Such graceful terms as hearing, seeing, smelling, tasting, fucking, throbbing, kissing, and kin words, are telephone expressions, lighthouses of intercourse centrally immutable to the situation; their aptness, euphony and serviceable persistence make it impossible and undesirable to put them out of pure use as it would be to take the oxygen out of the air."

Like Victoria Woodhull and indeed all the free love reformers, Angela Heywood called for "sincere thought and transaction" and denounced what she called "the physical force code of domestic, commercial, educational, church-and-state *heisms.*" She "used to think Passion was something *bad,* and was taught, by those who did not know, that Lust is the opposite of Love; I was mistaken, for the antithesis of Love is *hate*; while Lust means full, glowing, healthy animal heat." She acknowledged that love and physical passion were distinguishable one from the other. A man might love a woman yet not feel strong physical attraction to her, but "when a man gives his Passion to a woman she feels he *must* love her; else he *could not* yield it to her. . . . Can he be otherwise than dear to her?" Nor would she ally herself with the more extreme opponents of marriage. To her the words "husband" and "wife" represented the two sides of a "plural unity." Being a "wife" meant an "equality with man in the realm of Service; never," she added, "did I feel demeaned by so accepting the term wife, or the fact of wifehood." She had four children—Psyche, Angela, Vesta, and Hermes—and a notably happy marriage.

Angela Tilton Heywood was almost alone among free love theorists in celebrating the delights of sexual intercourse and insisting that a woman's capacity for sexual pleasure was equal to or greater than that of a man. The great majority of sex reformers accepted without serious question the notion that men's sexual appetites were excessive and basically insatiable while those of women were far more moderate. Many of their doctrines were thus directed toward appeasing or moderating the male's sexual drives, primarily by what today is called foreplay but without actual consummation and, above all, by helping men sublimate and control those drives. Also involved was the notion that the discharge of semen meant a loss of vital energy and a potentially dangerous thinning of the blood. Such notions were nonsense in Angela Heywood's vigorously expressed opinion.

The double standard of sexual behavior and the social code that granted the man sexual dominance the Heywoods referred to as the "Penis Trust." They proposed, in opposition to the "Penis Trust," a "Fucking Trust"—that is, "a collective effort to bring the moral, social & physical uses of sex-meeting into the domain of reason and moral obligation."

The notion of sexual play short of intercourse was advocated as a way of suppressing one's "lower" nature—unrestrained sexual appetites—in favor of one's higher or spiritual nature. Alice B. Stockham wrote a book entitled *Karezza: Ethics of Marriage* in 1896. The book stressed the theme of "spirituality" in marriage and also provided some practical birth control information. Another very influential book among the sex reformers was *Diana: A Psycho-physiological Essay on Sexual Relations for Married Men and Women* by Henry Parkhurst. Parkhurst divided the sexual urge into a general "magnetic attraction," produced by "sexual batteries" in men and women and the "generative" impulse to produce offspring. When the batteries became overcharged, Parkhurst argued, they involuntarily discharged their surplus "electricity." The only remedy was the "full satisfaction of the affectional mode of activity by frequent and free sexual contact"—that is to say, by "nongenerative" sexual relations, which, of course, necessitated some form of contraception. Yet it was clear that even Parkhurst had ambivalent feelings about sexual intercourse. He, too, ultimately came out for sexual intimacy as a way of developing self-control. Husband and wife, he maintained, should learn "to be together, seeing each other, and embracing each other without the intervention of clothing, and enjoy such caresses disassociated from passional feelings. . . ." Then there would be "little danger of sexual excess," and the "spiritual side" of the relationship could develop, unhampered by the "evil effects" of orgasms.

One consequence of the widespread theory that the emission of male seminal fluid dangerously thinned the blood and destroyed vital energy was the alarm, even among sex reformers, over "self-abuse" or masturbation. The term "self-abuse" was revealing. Many sex reformers came, reluctantly, to support intercourse for pleasure between men and women joined by "spiritual affinity" because it seemed a lesser evil than masturbation. Thus Stephen Pearl Andrews wrote: "The only obscenity there is is the unnatural uses to which natural capacities are compelled by the denial of their natural use. Thus self-abuse is obscene, and all its effects horrible; but sexual intercourse, where there is legitimate natural desire, is not obscene and no pure-minded person can ever conceive it to be so."

Among the more prominent figures in the free love movement was an ex-Quaker named Elmina Drake. Wishing to get married at the age of twenty-six, she put an ad in the *Water-Cure Journal* and chose Isaac Slenker out of sixty respondents. Homely and with a cleft palate, Elmina Slenker became one of the most active free thought, free love journalists, writing for Moses Harman's *Lucifer* and advocating such advanced notions as that of making contraceptives available to women free. She even produced a free thought magazine for children entitled the *Little Freethinker* and a book, *Little Lessons for Little Folks*. She lectured and wrote on Darwinism and on Herbert Spencer's sociology. One of her principal targets was alcohol. Religion and liquor and masculine domination were the causes, she argued, on numerous public platforms, for all of society's ills. Elmina Slenker seemed determined to alienate almost everyone, even her poor husband, who, when she was jailed by Comstock's forces, refused to post bail. Elmina was an "Alphaist"—that is to say she aligned herself with that wing of the free love movement which believed that coition should be prohibited except for the purposes of procreation. She shared the conviction of Eliza Farnham that women were the superior sex. "If there be a higher and better life yet to come," she wrote somewhat cryptically, "that race will no doubt be mainly of the feminine sex." It was her hope that science would discover a technique by means of which women could reproduce without the intervention of male partners.

Like Angela Tilton Heywood and Elmina Slenker, Lois Waisbrooker poured out a stream of books and pamphlets: *Suffrage for Women: The Reasons Why; Helen Harlow's Vow: or Self Justice; The Fountain of Life: or the Threefold Power of Sex; A Sex Revolution; The Occult Forces of Sex*, and a number of others. *A Sex Revolution* was a novel in which the heroine, Lovella—i.e., the loving one—urges women to strike against men's wars. "Who of you," Lovella asks a group of women, "are willing to yield up your sons to fight the sons of other mothers. . . . Man's method must be reversed . . . love guided by wisdom shall take the place of brute force."

Ezra Heywood, meeting Waisbrooker for the first time in 1875 at a spiritualist convention in Boston, wrote: "I . . . met what seemed to be a Roman Sibyl, Scott's Meg Merrilies, enacted by Charlotte Cushman, Margaret Fuller, and Sojourner Truth rolled into one. I sat in a pew looking into her eyes and listening to what seemed to be her talking, awhile, when she rose, went up the aisle, mounted to the platform, and the tall, angular, weird, quaint kind of a she Abraham Lincoln was introduced to the audience as 'Lois Waisbrooker.' " Ezra Heywood was not the only one to make the Lincoln analogy; the fiery Populist leader Mary Elizabeth Lease called her "the female Abraham Lincoln." Writing to praise *A Sex Revolution*, Lease added: "I wish every woman in the land could read your little book. You gave expression to my thoughts so clearly that it almost startled me. I have been organizing the women to war for peace, paradoxical as this may seem; now that I have your help in this most helpful book of yours I shall work with more certainty of success."

Lois Waisbrooker, in sharp contrast with Angela Heywood, rejected a primarily domestic role for women. Born, in her words, into the "lower strata of life," she had "worked in other people's kitchens year in and year out when I never knew what it was to be rested." Finally she got enough schooling to qualify her to teach children in a rural school. A dedicated abolitionist, she had taught in black schools prior to the Civil War and after the war took to the lecture platform to speak on spiritualism and free love. Like so many other woman orators, she was a direct and powerful speaker, drawing on the experiences of her own hard life and leavening her sermons with humor. "When I first began to act as an itinerant speaker," she wrote, "my work was mostly done in back neighborhoods in school houses among people who could gather in my life force but could give me very little in exchange."

Waisbrooker's humble origins made her particularly sensitive to proposals for population control that seemed to her to be aimed at reducing the numbers of the lower classes. "I hardly think the work of sex reformers is teaching how to limit propagation among the working people that there will be just enough of them to furnish servants for the rich, and to produce what these same rich people want," she wrote. She, like Elmina Slenker, had serious reservations about the eventual effect on the moral fiber of "sex for pleasure" and was, in consequence, hesitant to endorse contraception. She saw money as the "ruling love" of both men and women in American society. It was woman's love of money that had made it possible for men to dominate and control her. The connection between sex and money must be severed, Waisbrooker argued: "Woman must be free to use her sex functions only at the promptings of her love, and then her material of which the throne of the money god is built and sustained will no longer be manufactured. . . . We are rebels in the fullest sense of that word. We are determined to overthrow the ruling power [of money], to dethrone it and to place the Christ of love—existing in woman's soul—upon the throne."

Lillian Harman did not agree with Lois Waisbrooker that women should be subsidized by the state simply on the ground that they must be free of financial dependence on men, but she did suggest that couples associated in some more or less permanent free love alliance draw up a contract under the terms of which the woman would be paid a salary for her housework.

Dora Forster, a British sex radical who had considerable influence on Charlotte Perkins Gilman, concentrated on "the mix up of love and cookery," what Gilman called, more trenchantly, "cupid in the kitchen." Women used cookery as a major element in attracting and holding the male, Forster pointed out. One result was that meals were often heavy, greasy, and unhealthy, and the cook's sexual responses inadequate. In this view, wives, anxious to avoid sexual encounters with hasty, aggressive, and often brutal husbands, tried to buy their way out by stuffing their spouses with oleaginous dishes. Charlotte Perkins Gilman's solution was communal kitchens ruled by dietitians serving scientifically prepared food. The relationship between food and sex, like the relationship between sex and money, was obviously deep and enduring. We have already observed that of all America's vaunted "freedoms" the freedom to eat vast quantities of rich and indigestible food was perhaps the most important for immigrants who had come from countries where the working classes commonly lived on the edge of hunger and, in bad times, of starvation. Certainly there is considerable visual evidence that in present-day America what we might call co-eating is the tie that binds many husbands and wives.

There was, by modern standards, a considerable degree of naïveté among the most radical sex reformers. Lois Waisbrooker noted that she was forty-eight years old before she learned of oral sex acts. "I shall never forget the horror I felt when I first learned . . . that such a thing was possible," she wrote. To her it was a "diabolical perversion."

A by-product of the free love movement was free love communities. We have already mentioned Modern Times, Unity House, and The Club, all started by Stephen Pearl Andrews. The free love community of Memnonia, Ohio, founded by Thomas and Mary Nichols, flew a banner which proclaimed: "Freedom, Fraternity, Chastity." The Nicholses believed that sexual intercourse between a man and a woman was acceptable only when prompted by "intense spiritual affinity" and for the purposes of procreation. They issued a directory with the names of "affinity seekers" all over the nation. Another free love community was established at Berlin Heights, Ohio.

A major strand in the sexual revolution was eugenics, scientific breeding (or natural selection) to improve the race. Eugenics flirted with, where it did not actually become, racism. But where it touched the women's movement and feminism most closely was in the notion that women must have control over their own bodies and be free to select and to a substantial degree control their sexual partners. The International Woman's Council, which met in Washington in 1888, declared that "the only rational hope for human improvement, and for the abolition of vice, crime, pauperism and misery is through better conditions of heredity and maternity, and that superlatively the most important of these conditions is the self-ownership of woman." Moses Harman was of the same persuasion. Until the laws governing marriage and paternity were changed so that women could control the reproductive process, "the vast majority of children [will] be born mental and moral imbeciles," he declared, "fit for nothing else than to be ruled and exploited by the cunning, the capable, the narrowly selfish few."

In his own perverse way Anthony Comstock left the imprint of his character stamped as indelibly on the age as any public figure. The self-appointed guardian of the morals of Americans, he was a one-man vice squad of formidable and unsleeping vigilance. He was secretary of the Society for the Suppression of Vice and an agent of the Post Office. Generously supported by such tycoons as J. P. Morgan and Samuel Colgate, the shaving cream magnate, he prevailed upon Congress in 1873 to pass the Comstock Act prohibiting the sending of obscene material through the U.S. mails. The bill in essence left it to law enforcement agencies themselves, advised and, indeed, led by Comstock and his lieutenants, to determine what constituted obscenity. Comstock soon made clear that any material that discussed matters pertaining to sex in any but the most indirect and evasive terms was, prima facie, obscene, and, backed by the power of the courts, he set out to suppress, almost single-handedly, any discussion of the sexual aspects of human experience in the United States. It was a big task but one to which Comstock, who was apparently otherwise an agreeable man, proved equal.

Comstock was, to be sure, soon sustained by a small army of vice hunters. States and municipalities passed laws and ordinances in unprecedented numbers to suppress vice in all its forms. Nothing vaguely similar had happened in the United States before or, indeed, in any other country with the exception of Victorian England, seized by the same fury of repression. It can be said with some confidence that whatever its origins or ingredients, "Puritanism" was not among them. A more tenable proposition is that the inclination displayed by Americans to assert control over both themselves and their environment, an inclination evident from the earliest colonial days, asserted itself with disconcerting vehemence in the closing decades of the century, in large part because things suddenly seemed in danger of getting out of control. The repressive instincts were not, of course, limited to the matter of sex. They became increasingly evident in the areas of political expression and political behavior. In a certain sense the suppression of vice was a by-product of the war between capital and labor. By far the greater part of the vice suppressed was the "vice" of poor people: cheap sex; vulgar entertainment; bars and saloons. The vices of the rich remained, in large part, undisturbed; indeed, there is ample evidence that they waxed.

It is worth noting that Comstock did not pursue his victims without arousing strong opposition from individuals and organizations that placed a high value on the American tradition of free speech.

The National Defense Association was formed in 1878 primarily to combat Comstock. One of its founders was Dr. Edward Bliss Foote. Foote and his son, Edward Bond Foote, were leaders in the movement to demystify, as we would say today, medicine. In their efforts to make sensible medical practice available to the general public they recall Benjamin Rush's efforts in the early years of the Republic to democratize medicine. The elder Foote's first work, *Common Medical Sense*, sold more than 250,000 copies and made him a prosperous man. An enlarged volume, entitled *Plain Home Talk*, was another best seller. He supplemented it by a magazine called *Dr. Foote's Health Monthly*, published first in 1876 and thereafter for twenty years. He reached a juvenile audience with *Science in Story: or Sammy, the Boy-Doctor*. Perhaps the most notable aspect of *Plain Home Talk* was the information on contraception cautiously but firmly conveyed. One section of the book was devoted to a discussion of the sex organs and a general history of marriage. Another section was entitled the "Improvement of Popular Marriage." His purpose, Foote wrote, was to produce a work "comprehensible alike to the rustic inmate of a basement and the exquisite student of an attic studio." He soon became an industry with a four-floor office on Lexington Avenue in New York and his own mail-order pharmaceutical operation and publishing house. He was a tireless moralizer, admonishing his female readers that "in the eyes of God, respectable prostitution, such as marrying for homes and wealth, is no better than that practised by abandoned women. . . ." Women should do all in their power to become "less dependent upon their 'legal protectors,' and be enabled to live lives of 'single blessedness,' rather than unite themselves to the disagreeable masses of masculine blood and bones, for the mere sake of escaping from poverty and starvation." There was "no position in social life where the wife's labors are not," he wrote, "valued in dollars and cents, worth as much as those of her husband." Foote was also an advocate of contraception, on the ground that the population growth that was taking place all over the world had to be slowed dramatically, or millions of people would starve to death in coming generations. He also offered birth control advice, warning against the use of the "French male safe," made from sheep or hog intestines, "more or less permeated by oleaginous or fatty matter," and consequently "a nonconductor of the magnetism of the sexes." He recommended his own "Membraneous Envelope" made from the bladders of fish caught in the Rhine River as much safer and more sensitive, and he urged married men, many of whom were "proverbially promiscuous" and therefore often diseased from their contact with prostitutes, to use condoms in intercourse with their wives.

Dr. Foote had, of course, a substantial vested interest in free speech. Comstock had done his best to have his books and journals declared obscene. In 1878 Foote and eight others organized the National Defense Association, and he served as its first secretary. In addition to rallying public support for Ezra Heywood, the association, which included among its directors a successful publisher, John P. Jewett, and the well-known biblical scholar Albert Rawson, came to the aid of Walt Whitman's *Leaves of Grass* when Boston officials tried to suppress it in 1882, and assisted in the defense of Elmina Slenker four years later, when Comstock had her arrested for mailing obscene letters.

But nothing could deter Comstock. He pursued the Heywoods relentlessly and hauled Ezra into court on charges of publishing and disseminating obscene material. (He left Angela alone, perhaps sensing that she was too formidable an opponent.) Angela continually denounced him and the law that had given him such power over "the American woman's genitals." She suggested, as a countermove, that every American male should have his penis tied up with a piece of wire and periodically inspected by a female Comstock. Any man whose penis was not properly bound up would be tried by a jury of twelve women and subject to a ten-year prison sentence.

Heywood was tried and convicted of publishing obscene material. This time there was no presidential pardon. Now sixty-two, he served two and a half years in the Charlestown State Prison. During his prison term Harman's *Lucifer* published much of the material that would have appeared in the *Word*. To Heywood the alliance with the Harmans in Kansas recalled the old abolitionist days when Massachusetts and Kansas were allies in the antislavery cause. "Woman is the negro of today," he wrote, "whom Mr. Harman and I are befriending; it is Massachusetts and Kansas over again."

Moses Harman had long been Comstock's bête noire. Now Comstock turned his attention to Harman and *Lucifer*. Harman was indicted and convicted but not without becoming a martyr in the eyes of champions of free speech. When *Christian Life,* the journal of the National Purity Association, came to Harman's defense, a furious Comstock had its editor arrested and charged with obscenity for publishing two articles by Harman. Harman was convinced that Comstock's reaction was based on his alarm at having a leading Christian magazine take up Harman's cause.

Benjamin Flower, editor of the radical Christian journal the *Arena,* called Moses Harman a "venerable martyr" who "spends his money and life energies to secure what he believes to be a wider need of justice for women, and what he believes will lead to a higher and purer civilization, [and] is made the victim of a postal bureaucracy essentially Russian in character and essence. . . . To imprison such a man is to place a blister on the brow of the republic." The *Woman's Journal,* speaking for the conservative American Woman Suffrage Association, declared: "No one can have less sympathy than the editors of the *Woman's Journal* with some of the views advocated in *Lucifer;* but on one point Mr. Harman's views are perfectly sound, and that is on the right of a wife to the control of her own person."

With Harman under attack by Comstock's forces for obscenity— "marital rape" had been discussed in the pages of *Lucifer* (one letter from a female reader asked if it was just that a man could have "killed a woman with his penis" and go free when he would be indicted for murder if he had used a knife)—eleven women, representing ten states, drew up a "Remonstrance and Petition" praising Harman for calling public attention to the true situation of women and urging the judge to find him not guilty.

Harman had support from as far away as England, where a young playwright named George Bernard Shaw had followed with interest the careers of American sex radicals on the other side of the Atlantic. Shaw declined all invitations to visit the United States. He was, he wrote, "afraid of being arrested by Mr. Anthony Comstock and imprisoned like Mr. Moses Harman. . . . If brigands can, without any remonstrance from public opinion, seize a man of Mr. Harman's advanced age, and imprison him for a year under conditions which amount to an indirect attempt to kill him, simply because he shares the opinion expressed in my *Man and Superman* that 'marriage is the most licentious of human institutions,' what chance should I have of escaping?"

Shaw, if he did not venture to risk the "Unholy Inquisition" of the Post Office Department, did send £20 to Harman, with a note referring to his imprisonment as "quite the most monstrous achievement of 'the Nation of Villagers' within recent years. Unfortunately," Shaw added, "there is one subject on which Americans seem invincibly ignorant; and that one subject is America. They never know of anything that happens in their own country until an Englishman writes a book calling their attention to it. Nothing else can penetrate their chronic ecstacy of self-satisfaction in which they tolerate the welter of official despotism and unofficial anarchy which so revolts foreigners who know what really happens in the United States of America."

Harman was found guilty, and with appeals and retrials, his case dragged on for almost ten years before he served his jail sentence. He was seventy-five years old.

Lois Waisbrooker, editing *Lucifer* during Harman's prison term, reprinted a Department of Agriculture report on horse-breeding techniques, with its references to horses' penises, and asked her readers to reflect on the fact that the breeding of horses could be freely discussed while all efforts to discuss human reproduction were judged obscene.

After Harman's death Shaw wrote his daughter, Lillian: "It seems nothing short of a miracle that your father should have succeeded in living for seventy-nine years in a country so extremely dangerous for men who have both enlightened opinions and the courage of them. . . . I hope that now that he is dead, and can no longer shock Mr. Comstock and the rest of the American idols, some little sense of shame at the way he was treated may find expression in America."

All of this was certainly true, but what Shaw, being then a comparatively young man, did not perhaps take sufficiently into account was the invigorating effect of outraging public sentiment; its effect on the system, barring overt physical injury, appears to be almost entirely salutary, a fact which doubtless contributed to Shaw's own longevity. Indeed, when one surveys the life histories of the principal reformers of the nineteenth century, it is clear that they were a remarkably long-lived group; this might suggest that the best prescription for a long life is a career as a reformer of almost anything.

It turned out that free love was an idea whose time had most definitely not come. The forces of "decency," the defenders of morality and purity, of the home, of Christian values, of everything-as-it-is-and-so-far-as-possible-as it-was rallied to beat back, to discomfort, to harass, and, where necessary, to jail the prophets of the new freedom. Free love received their special attention, and eventually the tide turned. Elizabeth Cady Stanton and Susan B. Anthony abandoned that "bright brave spirit," the advent of which they had hailed so enthusiastically. Victoria Woodhull abandoned herself, took to the Bible, married an aristocratic English banker, and presided over a London mansion. She even returned, quixotically, to the United States to try to prevail upon newspapers to remove from their files the accounts of her lectures on the joys of free love. But before she lapsed completely into British upper-class respectability, she wrote and published at her own (or her husband's) expense one of the most remarkable tracts of the nineteenth century (a century of remarkable tracts), entitled *The Human Body, the Temple of God.* In it she proposed that the Bible be read as the story of the resurrection of the body, the temple of God. Understood in this light, sexual intercourse was revealed as a holy sacrament to be performed as reverently as any other sacrament. The sexual organs must be free from any connotation of evil or any encumbrances or repression or inhibition.

Strangest of all, when Elizabeth Cady Stanton came to write the *History of Woman Suffrage* she omitted any mention of its most dazzling star, the woman whom at one time she had credited with opening her eyes to the true nature of the women's movement. Public opinion is volatile in the extreme. The phenomenon of respected leaders' being abused and reviled for persevering in unpopular opinions (especially, of course, in the case of opposing a popular war) has been commented on by virtually every close observer of American life from Tocqueville on, but the rapid "closure," the response of repression directed most specifically at the sexual segment of the complex of radical ideas which surfaced in the aftermath of the war, is something of a puzzle.

In one light sex reform can be seen as the last gasp of Enlightenment rationalism. It was the fervent and avowed intention of the sex reformers to make sex rational and scientific. If the most powerful and mysterious force in life could not be tamed and domesticated, there was in the long run little hope for the triumph of reason over instinct and superstition.

It is clear also, in reviewing the history of the free love movement, that we must reassess the importance of spiritualism. Its more bizarre aspects—table rapping and séances—and the more notorious practitioners have distracted attention from its important consequences. We have already mentioned its relationship to transcendentalism and to abolitionism. It obviously served many people as an alternative to formal denominational religion by creating a kind of quasi Christianity, a religion free of institutional dogmas and constraints, of middle- and upper-middle-class conventions, and, increasingly, of a grimly repressive attitude toward sexuality. Spiritualists, moreover, were convinced that they could establish, through the study of electromagnetism, a material basis for the existence of the soul. It was this conviction that attracted them to free thought. The positivists, on the other hand, supported free thought for just the opposite reason: that it would, in time, prove conclusively that there was only a material basis for the universe.

Aside from the hard-core freethinkers, it was sometimes difficult to distinguish, on the basis of rhetoric and style, a spiritualist from a more or less orthodox Christian. The difference was often in the spiritualist's more lyrical and impassioned prose style, a style that not infrequently erupted into poetry. Many of the spiritualists' perceptions about social and economic relations in American society were basically sound; many are commonplaces today.

In the absence of spiritualism as a kind of organizing "center" it is difficult to see how the various reforms and reformers could have acquired the feeling of a common purpose that seems to be an essential ingredient in what we might call sustainable reform. Denied the sense of being part of a wider fellowship with similar beliefs (however vague) and goals, the individual reformer cannot persevere without degenerating into harmless eccentricity. Spiritualism, more than any other "ism," with the possible exception of socialism, provided that connective tissue. It drew together free lovers, freethinkers, free speakers, Bellamyites, single taxers, anarchists, Populists, vegetarians, communists, socialists, every strange breed of theological cat that grew so abundantly in the wilderness of America. Perhaps most important of all, it was classless. At a time when the churches were increasingly "capitalistic," spiritualism, like abolitionism, was "no respecter of persons." It reached from Fifth Avenue to Berlin, Ohio; Valley Falls, Kansas; and Home, Washington. Not all freethinkers and free lovers, not all socialists or anarchists, of course, were spiritualists, but spiritualism was, in a sense, the medium in which all floated and which helped sustain them.

16

From Free Thought
to Anarchism

Free thought, as we have seen, was closely related to (and often synonymous with) free love and anarchism, although both latter movements had substantial Christian divisions. Free thought was not, of course, new. Jedidiah Morse had warned against its pernicious influence in the election of 1800. Abner Kneeland had founded the *Boston Investigator* in 1831 as an explicitly free thought journal. But free thought had smoldered away without much public attention for decades before it burst into flame in the period following the Civil War. Part of its potency was doubtless due to the fact that orthodox Protestantism had grown more repressive in the face of what it viewed as the defections of the liberal denominations—the Unitarians, Episcopalians, Methodists, and Congregationists (who were hardly to be distinguished from the Unitarians).

One historian has estimated that between 1880 and 1895 there were at all times no fewer than six and sometimes as many as twelve national journals devoted to the cause of free thought. There were, in addition, at least five Liberal League newspapers in Kansas alone.

The principal organization for the dissemination of free thought doctrines was the National Liberal League and the principal organ was Moses Harman's *Lucifer*. In 1883, when the *Kansas Liberal* became *Lu-*

cifer, Harman wrote: "The God of the Bible had doomed mankind to perpetual ignorance—they would never have known Good from Evil if Lucifer had not told them how to become wise as the gods themselves. Hence, according to theology, Lucifer was the first teacher of science."

One of the favorite ploys of the freethinkers (who, it must be said, did all they could to outrage public opinion) was to publish excerpts from the Old Testament that contained words that had been judged obscene when they had appeared in newspapers or magazines. The millionaire reformer and self-proclaimed communist George Francis Train in 1872 invited Comstock's wrath by printing such passages in his journal the *Train Lique.* After he had been five months in the Tombs Prison awaiting trial, Train was declared insane. Almost twenty-five years later the forces of decency were still at it. J. B. Wise of Clay Center, Kansas, was arrested and confined to Leavenworth Prison for four months awaiting trial for mailing a postcard with a verse from Isaiah. He was found guilty of obscenity and fined $50. Liberal Jews (who preferred to be called Israelites) were active in the National Liberal League and the Free Religious Association, one of the founders of which was Isaac Wise, editor of the *American Israelite.* In 1879 Moritz Ellinger, editor of the *Jewish Times,* and Wise were vice-presidents of the National Liberal League.

The Kansas chapter of the National Liberal League was dominated by women advocates of free love. The convention's slate of officers in 1891 was made up entirely of women and was heavily tilted toward free love. Etta Semple, who organized the convention, recommended to the delegates: "[Bring] your trunks with blankets and luncheon and live in the Park" during the three days of the meeting at Ottawa, Kansas.

Edwin Cox Walker was a typical Middle Western Liberal Leaguer. Starting as a schoolteacher and farmer, he organized chapters all over the state of Iowa and advanced to every young man's dream: becoming a lecturer and journalist—in this case, a voice of Iowa freethinkers. He began writing articles for Benjamin Tucker's journal, *Liberty,* an organ published in Boston and devoted to promoting anarchy and radical causes in general. *Liberty* was dedicated to pointing "to the evils existing in individual life, society and government" and laboring for their elimination.

Annie Diggs, who lived in Lawrence, Kansas, was secretary of the Kansas Secular Union (the successor to the National Liberal League) and also a sometime assistant to Moses Harman. A vigorous freethinker, Diggs soon became a leader in the growing Farmers' Alliance as well as a prominent member of the Woman's Christian Temperance Union and a Fabian socialist. Prohibition posed an especially thorny problem for freethinkers and free lovers. To prohibit anyone from drinking (no one argued about admonition and exhortation; prohibition was the sticky point) ran counter to liberal principles. On the other hand, the mainstream of sex reform, feminism, or whatever one wished to call it had come to view male drunkenness as one of the most intolerable burdens that women had to bear. It was closely related to the rape syndrome since it was widely held that intoxicated males were the most common offenders in forcing their sexual attentions on their wives.

In 1879 freethinkers from all over the Middle West met at Bismarck Grove, Kansas. Wagons and tents made a small city which had somewhat the air of an old-time revival. There were speeches on every conceivable subject of radical reform, entertainers, singers, and activities of various kinds that lasted from morning until midnight.

In 1883 Valley Falls, Kansas, the home of Moses Harman's *Lucifer*, played host to a meeting of the National Reform Association, an organization devoted to "Christianizing" the Federal government. The "religionists" were followed a few weeks later by an equally fervent convention of freethinkers—the Liberal League—displaying such slogans as "No Mental Popery on This Platform" and "Individual Sovereignty and Social Order Are Parent and Child."

The former governor of Kansas, Charles Robinson, was a member of the Liberal League and a popular lecturer on everything prefixed by "free." Robinson was especially critical of the efforts of the National Reform Association to have God officially proclaimed head of the United States government. "Will he want a salary," Robinson asked, "& if so how much? Will taxes be higher or lower?" Robinson was also an active supporter of Moses Harman and *Lucifer*.

The Liberal Leaguers listened to lectures on such topics as "Orthodox Religion a Fraud upon Humanity and a Slander on God," by O. Olney, editor of *Thinker*, and "There Is No Hell," a lecture by Professor Peck. Professor Peck and his wife, Mrs. H. S. Lake, were practitioners of "free marriage." Mrs. Lake gave a talk on woman suffrage which was described by a friendly reporter as "radical and brilliant."

The *Christian Statesman*, the official organ of the National Reform Association, reported that the Valley Falls meeting had been a "gratifying success, considering it was the hardest field we have yet found. . . . It is the headquarters of Liberalism. A radical infidel sheet called the 'Kansas Liberalist' is published there, and the town is noted as a godless place, a center of immorality. Several murders have recently been committed in and around the town."

Just as free lovers and freethinkers often overlapped (many free lovers were avowed Christians), freethinkers were not uncommonly "American" or "individualist" anarchists. Anarchism, indeed, seemed full of contradictory ideals. Piotr Kropotkin, the prophet of "collectivist" or "European" anarchism, had written: "Read these words with love. . . . Plant these truths wherever you can. Every slave is a man, and every man a hero when his weapon is love and truth. . . . With these weapons there must be a free world." Perhaps the most notable differences between native American anarchism and the imported variety was that the American strain made the individual conscience the final judge of whether to concur in governmental policy or to resist it, whereas in its European form anarchism focused on the needs of freeing the mass of men from social and economic injustice.

In 1883 an anarchist convention meeting in Pittsburgh with delegates from twenty-six states declared that its goal was "the destruction of the existing class government by all means, i.e., by energetic, implacable, revolutionary and international action." Associations of anarchists from France, Italy, Britain, Spain, and Mexico sent fraternal greetings.

Moses Harman and Benjamin Tucker, the editor of *Liberty*, were classic individualist anarchists. While Harman rejected the "collective anarchists" as imposing the authority of the group on the individual members, he was an enthusiastic supporter of violence when it was deemed necessary or expedient. He hailed fire and dynamite as the classic weapons of the weak, the "equalizers" that might force the wealthy to share their wealth and power with the poor. "Then welcome the Age of Dynamite!" he wrote in 1883, three years before the Haymarket dynamiting. ". . . this latter age promises to be one of fierce convulsions . . . it will be marked by sudden, and, for the time being, disastrous changes. . . . The law of force against force, or the gospel of dynamite will not usher in the millennium of anarchy, but it will help prepare the way for that blessed era."

Like Harman's *Lucifer*, Tucker's *Liberty* seemed to one friendly critic to preach an excess of individualism. George Bernard Shaw wrote to a friend: "Tucker is a very decent fellow; but he persists, like most intellectuals, in dictating conditions to a world which has to organize itself in obedience to laws of life which he doesn't understand any more than you or I. Individualism is all very well as a study product; *but that is not what is happening.* Society is integrating, not individualizing. . . ."

Emma Goldman, a collectivist anarchist, visited Kate Austin, an anarchist writer who lived in a small Missouri town, Caplinger Mills. Goldman was deeply impressed by Austin's struggle to rear her eight brothers and sisters, orphaned after their mother's death. Struck by the range of knowledge displayed by Austin's articles in leading anarchist journals, Goldman asked her how she had educated herself. "From reading," Austin replied, "at first Ingersoll's works, later of *Lucifer* and other radical publications."

Undoubtedly the most exotic of the female anarchists was Voltairine de Claire (she changed her name to Cleyre). Beautiful, a gifted writer, wildly romantic, she was the daughter of an immigrant French-Catholic-socialist tailor, Hector de Claire, who came to the United States in 1854 at the age of eighteen. Two weeks before Fort Sumter, Hector de Claire had married Harriet Elizabeth Billings, whose father, Pliny Billings, had been an agent on the underground railroad. In the aftermath of Sumter De Claire enlisted in the Union army and fought throughout the war. Hector, an admirer of Voltaire, had wanted a son; he named his youngest daughter, born in 1866, Voltairine. Voltairine showed a precocious talent as a poet, attended a Catholic convent, emerged as a freethinker, became a member of Lester Ward's National Liberal Reform League, heard Clarence Darrow speak, and became a convert to socialism. To Voltairine, "It was my first introduction to any plan for bettering the condition of the working-classes which furnished some explanation of the course of economic development, and I ran to it as one who has been turning about in the darkness runs to the light." In abandoning her Catholicism, she wrote:

> And now, Humanity, I turn to you;
> I consecrate my service to the world!
> Perish the old love, welcome to the new—
> Broad as the space-isles where the stars are whirled!

She gave temperance lectures, free thought lectures, and free love lectures more or less indiscriminately, depending on the audience and the occasion. She recited her poems and made young male freethinkers dizzy with desire. "A young girl," someone recalled, "queerly dressed and with two long thick plaits of hair hanging down her back. When on a platform she wore a sort of Roman toga, and the effect was queer and unique."

The Haymarket Massacre of 1886 made De Cleyre an ardent anarchist. She was a friend of August Spies, who was executed for his role in the event and who had thrilled anarchists by declaring: "We are the birds of the coming storm." Voltairine took the sentence as the epigraph of her poem to Matthew Trumbull, one of the attorneys for the anarchists. Her goal, as she put it, was "to print the force of my will . . . on the movement towards human liberty." She wished to become a famous anarchist poet. Not surprisingly, her love life was usually a mess. She fell madly in love with a handsome young radical named T. Hamilton Garside, who treated her abominably. She had a brief romance and a child with feckless James Elliott and a more enduring romance with a much older fellow anarchist, Dyer Lum. Dyer Daniel Lum was an interesting figure in his own right. His great-grandfather had been a Minute Man at Lexington, and his grandfather was one of the famous Tappan brothers of abolitionist fame. Lum himself had been an abolitionist and had enlisted in the Union army at the outbreak of the war, being promoted from private to lieutenant for bravery and mustered out as a captain. Like so many ex-soldiers with similar ideals, he had watched the course of postwar America with growing dismay, convinced finally that the war had resulted in no more than "a limited gain for the negro and an unlimited loss for the white man."

Lum ran for the office of lieutenant governor of Massachusetts on the Greenback ticket with Wendell Phillips as the candidate for governor in 1876 and then worked as secretary for Samuel Gompers. The Great Strikes of 1877 made Lum a socialist. After a stint as secretary of a congressional committee appointed to look into the "depression of labor," Lum became a close friend of Albert Parsons and, soon after, an avowed anarchist.

It was allegedly Dyer Lum who smuggled into prison the dynamite capsule that Louis Lingg, one of the men arrested after the Haymarket Massacre, used to kill himself. By the time the trial was over and the anarchists were executed Lum was apparently thoroughly committed to violence as a tactic in the war against the capitalist state. A friend saw him walking along a Chicago street, oblivious to everything about him, "soft felt hat carelessly slung on one side, blue flannel shirt and red necktie, a suit of well worn homespun clothes, a pair of well worn shoes, and a large bundle of papers and writings under his arm, looking at no one, caring for nothing save the propaganda of Anarchism." The year was 1892, and Lum, hero of the Civil War, was the prototype of the radical intellectual of the coming century. Voltairine de Cleyre, lecturing in the Midwest, worried at news that her friend was drinking heavily and taking sleeping potions. She wrote him a poem entitled "You and I," which read, in part:

> You and I, in the sere, brown weather,
>   When the clouds hang thick in the frowning sky,
> When rain-tears drip on the bloomless heather,
>   Unheeding the storm-blasts will walk together,
> And look to each other—You and I. . . .
>   . . .
> You and I, when the years in flowing
>   Have left us behind with all things that die,
> With the rot of our bones shall give soil for growing
>   The loves of the Future, made sweet for blowing
> By the dew of the kiss of a last good-bye!

Not many months later Lum took his life by poison. Voltairine wrote of him: "His genius, his work, his character was one of those rare gems produced in the great mine of suffering and flashing backward with all the changing lights the hopes, the fears, the gaieties, the griefs, the dreams, the doubts, the loves, the hates, the sum of that which is buried, low down there, in the human mine."

On a trip to Europe Voltairine de Cleyre met Prince Kropotkin, the revered father of European anarchists. Back in Philadelphia, teaching English to Jewish immigrants, she encountered Samuel Gordon, a young Jewish anarchist and cigarmaker, who, five years her junior, progressed from being her pupil to being her lover. She managed to put him through medical school; but they often fought bitterly, and she rejected his proposals of marriage. (Most of her lovers distressed Voltairine by pressing her to marry them. Even the most dedicated anarchists and free lovers were not immune to the desire to make her permanently theirs.)

Voltairine de Cleyre estimated there were about 500 anarchists in Philadelphia by the end of the 1890s; there were some 145 active members, including 75 Russian Jews, 40 Americans, 24 Germans, 3 Italians, and 2 Cubans. Of the 145, only 19 were women. On November 11, 1900, more than 600 people turned out in Philadelphia to commemorate the Haymarket anarchists, listening to speeches in five languages. Among the prominent Philadelphia anarchists were Thomas Earle White, a lawyer, and Margaret Perle McLeod, one of the founders of the Ladies Liberal League.

In addition to avowed individualist and collectivist anarchists—ranging as we have seen from Moses Harman to Emma Goldman—there were numerous other "communitarians," men and women determined to establish alternatives to capitalism. Some wrote books; others established communities.

Bradford Peck, a self-made businessman who owned a department store in Lewiston, Maine, set out to "regenerate America along more efficient and altruistic lines." He put forth his proposals in a book with the engaging title *The World a Department Store*. His department store was distinguished by a cooperative restaurant and grocery store, a reading room, and a library. The same kind of efficiency and cooperation that had made his store a success could, he was convinced, be applied to all the problems of the larger society. Like most reformers, he lived to a splendid old age, dying at eighty-two in the midst of the Great Depression of the 1930s.

Perhaps the most imaginative vision of the future was that of a young traveling salesman named King Camp Gillette. Gillette had been born in 1855 at Fond du Lac, Wisconsin. In 1894 he published *The Human Drift*, a prospectus dedicated grandly "to all mankind." Competition, Gillette argued, was the source of all the evils in American life. He offered a plan "whereby the people gradually absorb and eventually come into complete possession of the world and its wealth." Large corporations owned by the people would take over the principal industries. By eliminating waste, corruption, and profits, men and women would need to work for only a five-year period in order to acquire enough credits to allow them to spend the rest of their time in the pursuit of culture and learning. The population of the country would be organized into a single huge city called Metropolis, with 60,000,000 or more people living in circular glass-domed apartment houses, many stories high. The concentration of the living quarters of the population in high-rise buildings would allow ample space nearby for parks, playgrounds, amusement centers, and educational facilities. The typical living unit of a family of four to eight members would have four windowless bedrooms (for the proper control of ventilation), four large bathrooms, four sitting rooms, a library, music room, and veranda. The central atrium of the glass-domed buildings would serve as a common hall where the residents could dine amid fountains and "exquisite paintings." Gillette's weekly magazine, *Twentieth Century*, offered its readers a five-volume package containing George Bernard Shaw's *Fabian Essays* and Edward Bellamy's *Looking Backward*, along with one of Ignatius Donnelly's works.

While Gillette was busy organizing Twentieth Century Clubs across the country and laying the groundwork for a campaign that would rally the nation to his scheme, he discovered that he could make a new kind of "safety" razor much less apt to knick the shaver than the commonly used straight razor. He thus began one of the more spectacular careers in the history of that capitalism of which he was such a severe critic. But it must be admitted he did so without abandoning his socialistic dreams. His razor and his competitive edge made him the richest socialist in the world.

Among the communities of the socialist-anarchist-free love-free thought-spiritualist category was the Kaweah Colony. Burnette Haskell, an early graduate of the University of California, had formed a secret society called first the Invisible Republic and then the Illuminati Foundation in much the same spirit as Lester Ward's National Liberal Reform League; its purpose was to fight superstition, especially religion as the most virulent form of superstition. Haskell assumed the editorship of his uncle's labor journal *Truth*, the masthead of which carried the slogan "Truth is five cents a copy and dynamite is forty cents a pound." Haskell urged his readers: "Arm to the teeth! The Revolution is upon you." He was a vigorous promoter of Edward Bellamy's nationalism, writing a book entitled *What Nationalism Is, the American Cure for Monopoly and Anarchism.* In 1886 he founded the Kaweah Colony, as the "purest and most radical democracy," located where Sequoia National Park was later established. One of the giant sequoias which rose so majestically in the colony was named the Karl Marx Tree. When the colony died, in part because of the bitter opposition of the lumber companies, the tree was renamed the General Sherman Tree.

G. H. Walser founded the town of Liberal, Missouri, as a free thought community, designed to demonstrate the superior character of free thought over religion, but the community split up when the Replogles, Georgina and Henry, began to push their free love doctrine in their paper, entitled *Equity*. The heretics were driven out of town by an angry mob of freethinkers.

A Polish count, Charles Bozenta Chlapowski, and his wife, Helena Modjeska, started near Anaheim, California, an agricultural commune, the most famous member of which was Henryk Sienkiewicz, the author of *Quo Vadis,* one of the best-selling novels of the day. When the commune collapsed after less than a year, the count returned to Poland, but Helena Modjeska learned English, remained behind, and became one of the most renowned actresses in America.

Perhaps the most bizarre of the new-wave communes was that founded in Northern California by a Swedenborgian minister, Thomas Lake Harris, who came West with some 2,000 followers to found Fountain Grove. Its dogma was contained in the notion of a bisexual deity incorporating the principle of masculine love and feminine truth. Harris issued instructions to the faithful in the form of daily poems. His notion that exuberant play held the key to a healthy life has a decidedly modern ring, and one of his poems declared:

> If you would slay the Social Snake
> That brings the Bosom grief and ache
> Dance while you may
> For heaven comes forth in Social Play.

He crowned himself Primate and King and undertook to muster "vortical atoms" to overcome evil in the world. He would, he told his infatuated followers, join the Lily Queen in heaven. Meantime, he chose his sexual partners on a more earthly plane, became immortal, as he announced, and joined his friend and disciple, Edwin Markham, in New York. At the time of Harris's death, in 1906, Markham and Harris's wife waited for three days for him to rise from the dead, but he failed to do so.

The most important (and most difficult) question for the historian is to assess the importance of grass-roots anarchism in the post-Civil War period. Was it the preoccupation of a few eccentrics, half-deranged characters, their brains addled by abolition and free love? Or did it represent a significant stratum of American political thought and social protest, a bold anticipation of the future? Did it become an element in that new consciousness that we have argued was taking form? The answer obviously depends in part on the perspective of the historian raising the question. First of all, there is the fact *that it existed.* It enlisted the energies and, in many instances, the lives of thousands of Americans who dreamed the perpetual dream of a redeemed and ennobled republic. In some areas, especially in the realm of freedom of the press and the right of women "to control their own bodies," to vote, to be free of masculine domination—goals which seemed at the time wicked, not to say mad—have, in fact, been achieved.

In some areas their fiercely held convictions appear no longer relevant. What is certainly clear is that political and social radicalism has been an old and deep-seated American tradition that reached its apogee in the last half of the nineteenth century. It is also clear enough that "the Sovereignty of the Individual," as Moses Harman called it, is one of the strongest currents in our history. One can trace a line from Jefferson (and Jackson) through Emerson, Whitman, and Thoreau, thence through the "individualist anarchists"—men like Josiah Warren, Stephen Pearl Andrews, and Andrew Jackson Davis, to name only a few—to a whole congeries of modern self-help, self-realization, self-fulfillment doctrines. In all these the words "self" and "individual" are the determining ones.

Equally important, aside from the hard-core anarchists, freethinkers, free lovers, free speakers, etc., a large number of less intellectually adventuresome Americans sympathized with many of the ideals of the radical theorists. One suspects there was at least a touch of freethinker in many small-town newspaper editors, a wistful attraction to the tantalizing visions of the prophets of free love in millions of young American women (and perhaps even a few American males). It can be said with considerable confidence that in the Midwest at least, editors of thoroughly respectable newspapers not infrequently expressed support for their beleaguered colleagues caught in the snares of Comstock and his battalions of vice hunters. The editor of the *Kansas City Sun,* writing in Benjamin Tucker's *Liberty,* noted sympathetically: "*Liberty* attacks the State, the *Truth Seeker* attacks the Church, the *Word* attacks Madam Grundy, but *Lucifer* is not content . . . without attacking all three."

Perhaps the final point is that with all its "frees," America has been wilder and freer than historians have informed us.

17

The James Family

Oswald Spengler, author of *The Decline of the West*, declared that the true meaning of an era is to be found nowhere but in the history of its elites. I subscribe, of course, to no such theory. It seems to me, to the contrary, that all the great movements of history are, of necessity, mass movements, but it is, at the same time, certainly true that intellectuals, artists, and, perhaps less clearly, politicians play an important and sometimes crucial role in the unfolding drama of history. If it were not the case that the most sentient individuals of an age provide us with invaluable clues to the inner spirit of that age as well as, not infrequently, help shape the future, we would be well advised to close up our universities and lock our libraries, indeed eschew thought entirely. This is an age of romance about "the people," and that, on the whole, is a good thing, for the people have been commonly ignored by the historians of earlier eras in preference for "big names," so there is much to be done in redressing the balance. At the same time it would be fatuous to tilt, out of ideological rigidity, too far the other way. Intellectuals, scholars, philosophers, and journalists are people, too.

This is all so obvious as, in another time, hardly to require comment; but we live in this time, not another time, and in this time we find ourselves slightly defensive about attention to "high culture." Too "bourgeois," a small voice whispers. The risk of overemphasizing high culture is one I cheerfully run. The two families discussed here were, beyond question, two of the most remarkable in our history, members of an elite if we have ever had one. One we know well already, the Adams family, starting with John, the second president. The other, the James family, is new to us although we have encountered the first William James as a major contractor on the Erie Canal and a featured speaker at its dedication ceremonies. The second William James, often referred to as the Father of Pragmatism, was the best-known philosopher-scholar of the age, while his brother Henry was its most esteemed novelist.

There is another rationale for introducing these two families more formally to the reader. It is a major premise of this work that families have a particular and perhaps unique importance in American history in part because, in the absence of a formal aristocracy or an array of traditional institutions suitable for transmitting values, the American family in successive generations has been the essential agency of such transmissions. To it, more than any other organ of society, has fallen the responsibility for defining and, especially in the generation we are concerned with in this volume, redefining the meaning and the mission of America. The American family has thus borne a double burden. It has been responsible for both continuity and change. "The family," Joyce Carol Oates has written, "is the deepest mystery, deeper than love or death."

The James and Adams families in this era offer an instructive contrast. Each had five siblings—four males and one female. The children of the austere Charles Francis Adams, United States ambassador to Great Britain during the Civil War, were Charles Francis, Jr., the Union cavalry officer; Henry, his father's secretary during the war; John Quincy; Brooks; and Louisa Catherine. The children of Henry James, Sr., were William, Henry, Garth Wilkinson, Robertson, and Alice.

The differences in the character of family life in the two famous clans is suggestive. The senior Charles Francis Adams was the classic stern puritanical father. His ideal had been to emulate the "iron mask" of *his* father, John Quincy, which never revealed his feelings. That he succeeded only too well is indicated by the junior Charles Francis's listing of his father's "seven errors" (sending him to Harvard was one; not teaching him to sail or ride a bicycle was another). Clearly what he missed above all was love. While Henry and Brooks came to be devoted brothers, it was a relationship that developed in their mature years. There was no indication of family closeness—Henry once wrote to Brooks in reference to Charles Francis: "I understand I have a brother." Charles Francis and John Quincy, it is true, were closely associated in making their hometown of Quincy a model community, but the Adamses' stiffness and reserve were always evident in their relationships with each other and with the world.

The Jameses, on the other hand, were, like the Beechers, a family full of love, of play and good humor. In notable contrast with the formality that characterized domestic relations of that era, the James children always addressed their father as Daddy and their mother as Mammy.

The first William James at the dedication of the Erie Canal in 1825 had declared: "It is the distinguishing attribute of man to be excited by what is grand, beautiful, and sublime in nature, or what is beneficial in the combinations of intellect and art. . . . We therefore rejoice this day for the extension of the population, liberty and happiness of man. . . . At this moment, I feel an indescribable emotion, something like a renewal of life." It was that William James who established the family fortunes that enabled his son Henry and his grandchildren to live, in a substantial degree, on their inheritance. He married three times and had fifteen children. Of those, eleven reached maturity, but seven died before they were forty. "Our father's family," Henry, Jr., wrote, offered "a chronicle of early deaths, arrested careers, broken promises, orphaned children." F. O. Matthiessen, the historian, described the family members as, "variously genial, charming, dissipated, or unstable." It was apparently with his own family in mind that Henry James wrote, in *The Wings of the Dove,* of "an extravagant unregulated cluster, with free-living ancestors, handsome dead cousins, lurid uncles, beautiful vanished aunts, persons all busts and curls."

The first William's eldest son, the senior Henry, father of Henry and William, was one of the more arresting figures of his generation, a friend of Emerson and William Dean Howells, a Swedenborgian, a man determined to infuse the education of his talented children with "spirit," "enthusiasm," and substantial amounts of the "sensuous." He had lost a leg at the age of thirteen from an infection that resulted from stamping out a fire caused by a friend's hot-air balloon, and he used an artificial limb until old age. Howells described "his white bearded face, with a kind intensity which at first seemed fierce, the mouth humorously shaping the mustache, the eyes vague behind the glasses; his sensitive hand gripping the stick on which he rested his weight to ease it from the artificial limb he wore." He had a notable flair for high life—stylish clothes and good food—that seems always to have been an element in the life of Princeton undergraduates.

After a brief term in a theological seminary James married the sister of a Princeton classmate and two years later had a nervous collapse while he was in England, a profound crisis which he described vividly in his book *Society the Redeemed Form of Man.* He had up to that point in his life held to an "audacious faith in selfhood." He wrote: "When I sat down to dinner on that memorable chilly afternoon in Windsor, I held it serene and unweakened by the faintest breath of doubt; before I rose from the table, it had inwardly shrivelled to a cinder. One moment I devoutly thanked God for the inappreciable boon of selfhood; the next, that inappreciable boon seemed to me the one thing damnable on earth, seemed a literal nest of hell within my own entrails." Convinced of "the nothingness of selfhood," James emerged from this crisis a confirmed Swedenborgian and devoted the balance of his life to lectures and articles on the Swedenborgian view of a world dominated by spiritual forces and to the education of his children, about which he had a number of novel and unsettling ideas. He was obsessed with the problem of evil (he grew disenchanted with Emerson because the Concord philosopher seemed unwilling to face its implications). To James evil was the instrument of the Lord in bringing the soul to salvation. "We have walked the weary road we have walked, and suffered the bitter things we have suffered, not because God hated or condemned us, or even had the faintest shadow of a quarrel with us, but solely because He loved us with unspeakable love, and wooed us in that unsuspected way out of the death we have in ourselves to the embrace of His own incorruptible life." The elder James was a friend of that prince of American eccentrics the Texas exile, antislavery champion, and advocate of free love Stephen Pearl Andrews. Annoyed by James's refusal to join his utopian colony on Long Island, Modern Times, the devotion of which to free love repelled James, Andrews termed him one "of the class of purely ideal reformers, men who will lounge at their ease upon damask sofas and dream of a harmonic and beautiful world to be created hereafter."

To Henry James, Sr., the family was not simply a warm and loving unity, but an essential part of his theological system. He wrote that "the only spiritual Divine end which has ever sanctified the family institution and shaped its issues, is the evolution of a free society or fellowship among men; inasmuch as the family is literally the seminary of the race, or constitutes the sole Divine seed out of which the social consciousness of man ultimately flowers." To James it followed that "in so far as you inconsiderately shorten [the] period of infantile innocence and ignorance in the child, you weaken his chances of a future manly character."

An anecdote may best suggest the quality of life in the James household. James believed that God was incarnate in the physical world, and so he instructed his offspring. Henry recalled: "I remember a little boy [William?] once saying to his father at [the] dinnertable: 'Father, you say that God is pure spirit of life, and consequently that He alone is or lives in all existence. Now I want to know if He is in this chicken on my plate?' " On an affirmative reply, the "little sceptic" answered, " 'Very well then if God is in this chicken which I am eating, then I am now eating God.' " No, God is only there in the sense that He is responsible for everything that nourishes our bodies. Silenced for the moment, the "brave little man" brought his cap to his father's study after dinner and inquired if God was in the cap as well. Yes, the father replied. Then the child placed the cap on the ground and sat on it. "Now tell me, if you can, that I am not sitting upon God." No, God was not in the actual material of the cap but only in "its living use to cover your head and protect it from the summer's heat and the winter's cold." Since the indwellingness of God was only in the cap-as-cover, the young James could sit upon God only by sitting on his own head. He was not even "using" the cap by sitting on it, only "*ab*-using it." Certainly such metaphysical exercises were not the family's only or even primary form of entertainment and instruction, but the story suggests the atmosphere of the James household, where dialectics were as commonplace as porridge.

Convinced that several years abroad were essential to his children's education, Henry James, Sr., could hardly wait to shake the American dust off his feet and abandon a country divided into three classes, as he put it: "the busy, the tipsy, and Daniel Webster."

The strains and stresses of being the offspring of Henry, Sr., seem to have manifested themselves most acutely in the three youngest children. Garth and Robertson, psychologically separated from their siblings by the fact that they had fought in the Civil War (Garth had been an officer in Robert Shaw's black regiment), committed themselves without reservation to the cause of the free blacks. After the war they asked their father for money to buy a cotton plantation in Florida in order to demonstrate the competence of free black labor. They found themselves so threatened by hostile whites that the enterprise was imperiled from the first. They were insulted on the streets of Gainesville, and armed men prowled about their plantation. After many months of harassment and danger the enterprise failed, and the defeated brothers went to Milwaukee, where they got jobs with the St. Paul Railroad. Garth James, in his broken middle age, recalled the figures that came and went in the family home: Charles Dana, editor of the *Sun*, George Ripley, Bayard Taylor, "Uncle Edward . . . and Uncle Gus . . . Grandma James—her silk dress—peppermints, lace mittens and gentle smile. . . . The only thing to say of it is that it was a beautiful and splendid childhood for any child to have had, and I remember it all now as full of indulgence and light and color and hardly a craving unsatisfied." Crippled by his war injuries and weakened by drink and dissipation, Garth Wilkinson James died in 1883, a year after his father.

A brilliant talker, high-strung and morbid, Robertson James suffered acutely from both the defeat of the Florida venture and the degradations that, in his view, a ravenous capitalism had imposed on the Union that he had fought to preserve. The railroad, Robertson wrote Howells, "was a great (and is) tomb to which the young men go down and in which the many bury and have to bury every emotion and desire which can glorify life." He had been the confidential secretary of the manager of the St. Paul Railroad, "one of the most successful and unscrupulous Railway Barons this continent has ever seen. . . ." Fifteen years "of penniless ill health and self-contempt" were the principal fruits of Robertson James's association with the St. Paul. "I had never been required *to do* the felonious things this management fattened on, but I was obliged *to know it* and keep still." Subject to periods of terrible depression, an intermittently heavy drinker, a Swedenborgian, a spiritualist, and, finally, a prospective Catholic, Robertson was, like his father and his older brother, a seeker, but his unhappy and tormented spirit never recovered from the shocks it suffered in the war and the war's aftermath. He had, he wrote Howells, finally "kicked myself into acquiescence with destiny." He had come to believe that "one unselfish emotion of the human heart—one act of self-sacrifice done in the darkness of doubt—can open heaven wider" than all Emersonian precepts. "So at night when one lies awake and thinks of things, or perhaps the one thing you've wanted on earth and couldn't get, the soft sense of a melting heart comes upon you and you begin to dimly feel for the first time the *truth of love*. Truth has no existence apart from love. . . . Since father died, who is the only being on earth I ever cared for deeply, that loss has built up in me out of the ignominy of drink and debauchery what seems to me of late to be becoming one long day in which I see nothing but the faces of Seraphs smiling." The experience made him vow that he would not "surrender to the passing darkness."

But Robertson's seeking for truth and longing for love remained unfulfilled. It was not until 1910, at the age of sixty-one, that he was relieved "of all the darkness and pain of his stormy life," in his brother Henry's words.

Alice James was another—what is one to say?—casualty of that intense world. The morbidity evident in her brothers flowered in her. Talented in her own right and the author of a remarkable diary, she suffered a variety of mysterious ailments from childhood and was plainly neurotic. She contemplated suicide, and when she questioned her father on the ethics of self-destruction, he replied mildly that he did not consider it wicked. The only question was a practical one: Did the act cause undue hardship and suffering to others? A biographer of Alice James suggests that by this response her father closed the door to suicide for her. In any event, when her mother died, she rose from her invalid bed and kept house for her father, and when she discovered that she had cancer, she greeted the news almost ecstatically. Now she would be released from a life that had been an unbearable burden to her and to others.

Of the dominance of the senior James in the lives of his children there can be not the slightest question. William wrote his father near the end of the latter's life that he was for him "still the central figure. . . . All my intellectual life I derive from you. . . . What my debt to you is goes beyond all my power of estimating. . . ." When he came to edit Henry Sr.'s writings, he expressed his regret that his father had been born in a period so inhospitable to theologizing, "for he was a religious prophet and genius, if ever prophet and genius there were. He published an intensely vital view of our connection with him." His eccentric theology had for his son "many and diverse affinities. It was optimistic in one sense, pessimistic in another. Pantheistic, idealistic, hegelian. . . . Dualism, yet monism; antinomianism, yet restraint; atheism (as we might almost name it,—that is, the swallowing up *of* God in Humanity) as the last result of God's achievements." He could not admit, "even as a possibility, that the great and loving Creator, who has all the being and the power, and has brought us as far as *this*, should not bring us *through*, and *out*, into the most triumphant harmony."

To the elder James "the only true or philosophic conception of creation,—namely the abandonment of yourself to what is not yourself in a manner is intimate and hearty, as that you henceforth shall utterly disappear within the precincts of its existence. . . . What I crave with all my heart and understanding,—What my very flesh and bones cry out for,—is no longer a Sunday but a weekday divinity, a working God, grimy with the dust and sweat of our most carnal appetites and passions, and bent not for an instant upon inflating our worthless pietistic righteousness, but upon the patient, toilsome, thorough cleansing of our physical and moral existence from the odious defilement it has contracted, until we each and all present at last in body and mind the deathless effigy of his own uncreated loveliness."

Far more than an act of filial piety, William James's editing of his father's writings was a labor of love and, undoubtedly, of propitiation and self-examination as well. It is difficult, perhaps impossible, to understand William James without reading his introduction to his father's writings, so numerous and obvious are the referents to William's own life and thought. Remarkable as he was, loving as he was, it is clear the elder James was never an *easy* parent. He placed on his children moral and intellectual obligations too heavy to carry, too essential to be abandoned. Rather like the Creator he was so preoccupied with, he created a separate universe of the mind and spirit which he and his family occupied. The very intensity and isolation of it imposed heavy burdens on his children's respective psyches. William James's labor, one must suspect, was a necessary liberation from his father's loving and demanding spirit. It marked a turning point in his own thinking. Henceforth it would be more directly concerned with "life" and less with "philosophy" in the formal sense. William Dean Howells was among those who were well aware of the affinity between the work of the father and the work of the son. "Those who know the rich and cordial properties of Henry James the elder," he wrote, "will find a kindred heartiness in the speculations of his son, and will be directly at home with him."

The volume was also a kind of release for Henry, who read it with "great filial and fraternal joy. . . . And how beautiful and extraordinarily individual (some of them magnificent) are all the extracts from Father's writing." While Henry could not "enter into" the senior Henry's "whole system," "can't be so theological, nor grant his extraordinary premises, nor throw myself into his conceptions of heavens and hells, nor be sure that the keynote of nature is humanity, etc.," he could at least "enjoy greatly the spirit, the feeling, and the manner of the whole thing. . . ." Both he and William James spoke, significantly, I think, of "poor Father." Henry affirmed that "poor Father, struggling so alone all his life, and so destitute of every worldly or literary ambition, was yet a great writer." William, replying to a letter from a fellow philosopher about the book, wrote: "Anything responsive about my poor old father's writing falls most gratefully upon my heart." He had been "unresponsive" to his father's thinking during the latter's lifetime. Now he was offering "a sort of atonement."

William James was thus described by his son William: "He was of medium height (about five feet eight and one-half inches), and though he was muscular and compact, his frame was slight and he appeared to be slender in his young, spare in his last years. His carriage was erect and his tread was firm to the end. Until he was over fifty he used to take the stairs of his own house two, or even three, steps at a bound. . . . In talking he gesticulated very little, but his face and voice were unusually expressive. . . . He talked in a voice that was low-pitched rather than deep—an unforgettably agreeable voice, that was admirable for conversation or a small lecture-room. . . . His speech was full of earnest, humorous and tender cadences."

William James's first love was art. He showed a precocious talent in drawing, and when he was eighteen he began the study of painting with William Hunt, one of the leading painters of the day. Henry James recalled "W.J.'s image . . . at its most characteristic" as "drawing and drawing, always drawing, especially under the lamplight . . . ; and not as with a plodding patience . . . but easily, freely, and, as who should say, infallibly. . . ."

After graduating from Harvard College, James entered the Lawrence Scientific School at Harvard, where one of his teachers was Charles Eliot, then professor of chemistry. Eliot wrote later of James that "he liked experimenting. . . . I received a distinct impression that he possessed unusual mental powers, remarkable spirituality, and great personal charm." James, on the other hand, confided to his family that he could not believe that Eliot "is a *very* accomplished chemist," adding cautiously, "but can't tell yet." Jeffries Wyman taught James comparative anatomy, introduced him to Darwinism, and imbued him with the scientific spirit.

After two years of study at Lawrence, James entered the Harvard Medical School. He dropped out in 1865 to accompany Louis Agassiz on a botanizing trip to the Amazon. He described the great biologist as a "popularly impressive type . . . so commanding a presence, so curious and enquiring, so responsive and expansive, and so generous and reckless of himself and his own, that everyone said immediately, Here is no musty *savant* but a man, a great man, a man on the heroic scale, not to serve whom is avarice and sin." The hours that he spent with Agassiz taught James "the difference," he later wrote, "between all possible abstractions and all livers in the light of the world's concrete fullness," a lesson he was never able to forget.

Filled with uncertainty about his own career, James alternated between periods of obsessive work and intervals of idleness. His health, which was often bad, became a major preoccupation—he was to have tendencies toward hypochondria throughout his life—and he decided to go to Germany to learn the language and study the new science of psychology. He found Berlin "a bleak and unfriendly place. . . . The inhabitants . . . rude and graceless. . . ."

During his year in Germany James experienced a psychological crisis. In one of the most famous passages in his *The Varieties of Religious Experience,* he describes, in thinly veiled terms, his own dark night of the soul. It came upon him, much as it had upon his father, "without any warning . . . a horrible fear of my own existence. Simultaneously there arose in my mind the image of an epileptic patient whom I had seen in the asylum, a black-haired youth with greenish skin, entirely idiotic, who used to sit all day on one of the benches, or rather shelves, against the wall, with his knees drawn up against his chin, and the coarse grey undershirt, which was his only garment, drawn up over them, enclosing his entire figure. He sat there like a sort of sculptured Egyptian cat or Peruvian mummy, moving nothing but his black eyes and looking absolutely non-human. This image and my fear entered into a species of combination with each other. *That shape am I,* I felt, potentially. . . . There was such a horror of him, and such a perception of my own merely momentary discrepancy from him, that it was as if something hitherto solid within my breast gave way entirely, and I became a mass of quivering fear. After this the universe was changed for me altogether. I awoke morning after morning with a horrible sense of dread at the pit of my stomach, and with a sense of the insecurity of life that I never knew before, and that I have never felt since. It was like a revelation; and although the immediate feeling passed away, the experience made me sympathetic with the morbid feelings of others ever since." James was convinced that "this experience of melancholia . . . had a religious bearing. . . . I mean that the fear was so invasive and powerful that, if I had not clung to scripture-texts like *The eternal God is my refuge,* etc., *Come up to me all ye that are heavy-laden,* etc., *I am the Resurrection and the Life,* etc., I think I should have grown really insane." To the end of his life James experienced "waves of terrible sadness," and as late as 1896 suicide was still much on his mind. He wrote to a friend: "I take it that no man is educated who has never dallied with the thought of suicide." What kept him from committing suicide more than anything else, he wrote to his friend Thomas Ward, was the thought that "by waiting and living, by hook or crook, long enough I might make my *nick,* however small a one, in the raw stuff the race has got to shape, and so assert my reality." There again was that mysterious sense of unreality that one encounters again and again in the most intimate confessions of upper-class young Americans—Sidney George Fisher, Charles Francis Adams, George Templeton Strong, and a number of others—so often, indeed, that one must suspect it is a peculiarly American response to the world. In America the most "nervous" constitutions are constantly threatened by the illusion of unreality. The real world is in constant danger of dissolving into the imaginary one; the material universe becomes as immaterial as a dream.

From Germany, James wrote Ward that he had been "All last winter . . . on the continual verge of suicide." He had come finally to the conviction that he had a will and belonged to "a brotherhood of men possessed of a capacity for pleasure and pain of different kinds." If one had to "give up all hope of seeing into the purposes of God, or to give up theoretically the idea of final causes, and of God anyhow as vain and leading to nothing for us, we can, by our will, make the enjoyment of our brothers stand us instead of a final cause." The sentence is a revealing one. If there was no God, there were at least friends "instead of a final cause." So friendship became for James and for many members of his class and time a kind of substitute for religion. Letters became scriptures—long, witty, brilliant letters to friends. Eastern upper-class circles, we might say, developed a cult of friendship designed to fill up the emptiness left by the withering away of conventional faith and the spiritual vacuum of America. If one could believe in nothing else, one could believe in friends. Moreover one was bound in a kind of fellowship with one's predecessors, who had made the world what it was. One could find friends among *them*. "Every thought you have and every act and intention," James wrote to Ward ("My dear old Thomas"), "owes its complexion to the acts of your dead and living brothers. *Everything* we know and are is through men. We have no revelation but through man."

For James it followed that "sympathy with men as such, and a desire to contribute to the weal of the species, which, whatever may be said of it, contains All that we acknowledge as good, may well form an external interest sufficient to keep one's moral pot boiling in a very lively manner to a good old age."

It was, finally, "loving affections" that gave life its deepest meaning. For the rest of his days James would make "loving affection" the center of his life—with his family, his friends, his students, his colleagues. Love was integral, and it must be expressed, freely and openly. Playfulness was an essential part of friendship, part of all loving relationships because it enlivened the world and raised the spirits. A sense of playfulness was in everything he wrote from his most formal papers to his most personal letters. It was in his letters to his colleagues, his children, his wife, his many female correspondents, as much a part of him as his springing step and erect carriage. It was one of the things that most put off his serious-minded fellow scholars. They thought it merely frivolous. (He wrote his young son Alexander: "Your Ma thinks you'll grow up into a filosopher like me and write books. It is easy enuff, all but the writing. You just get it out of other books, and write it down.")

When James returned from Germany after eighteen months, the course his life was to take was no clearer to him. In the words of his son, "without any definite responsibilities" he seemed "to be declining into a desultory and profitless idleness." He sank into a classic "American" nervous depression, awaking on many mornings with a sense of "horrible dread." On February 1, 1870, he wrote in his diary: "Today I about touched bottom, and perceived plainly that I must face the choice with open eyes: shall I frankly throw the moral business overboard, as one unsuited to my innate aptitudes, or shall I follow it, and it alone, making everything else the mere stuff for it?"

What tormented James and, it must be said, many of his contemporaries was the difficulty in believing in a purpose and goal to life in the face of an apparently mechanistic universe, devoid of a wise and loving deity and of a moral order ordained by him. That was, of course, the overriding intellectual-moral-spiritual dilemma of the age. (James told his students that a genuinely moral universe would be one in which not a single cockroach "would feel the pangs of unrequited love.")

Some young men and women had made the transition from a theistically oriented world, saturated with the yearning for and belief in redemption, individual and social, to a world dominated by "process" with hardly a qualm, indeed with a sense of relief. Charles Francis Adams, Jr., had read John Stuart Mill and Auguste Comte and dropped all vestiges of traditional religion as lightly as he might have discarded a badly worn-out suit of clothes. But Charles Francis had experienced Christianity as a cold Unitarian system of moral rectitude and interminable sermons. James had experienced it as freedom and love through his remarkable father. For James the war between science and religion, between Christianity and Darwinism, was also a contest between the new mode of thinking and his father's faith. Beyond that it was the classic puzzle of free will versus determinism. To adhere to Darwin meant, in a real sense, to reject his father. That James suffered acutely in that struggle was a measure of the power of his father in his life.

A few months later James wrote again in his diary: "I think that yesterday was a crisis in my life. I finished the first part of Renouvier's second Essai and see no reason why his definition of free will—'the sustaining of a thought because I choose to when I might have other thoughts'—need be the definition of an illusion. At any rate, I will assume for the present—until next year—that it is no illusion. My first act of free will shall be to believe in free will."

If man was in truth free, "then the only possible way of getting at that truth is by the exercise of the freedom which it implies," James wrote. In this process the "act of belief and the object of belief coalesce, and the very essential logic of the situation demands that we wait not for any outward sign, but, with the possibility of doubting open to us, voluntarily take the alternative of faith."

James's own career took on a more specific direction when he was appointed an instructor in anatomy and physiology by Harvard's new president and his old chemistry teacher Charles Eliot. He found his job a "God-send." He wrote: "It is a noble thing for one's spirits to have some responsible work to do."

The Harvard of the early 1870s was at the beginning of an extraordinary period of growth that was to lift it, largely through the efforts of Eliot, from a small provincial college to one of the world's great universities. It was still without those institutional rigidities that are apparently inseparable from size and maturity. When James's own intellectual interests shifted, he was able to teach psychology and while doing so write the *basic* work on the subject, his *The Principles of Psychology.* (James referred to the two-volume work as James and to a one-volume abridgment of it as Jimmy.)

Two years later he was appointed assistant professor of philosophy. He now devoted his energies to the principal intellectual task of the age: trying to reconcile science and religion.

When James arrived at Harvard, the reigning deity of the philosophy department was George Herbert Palmer, "a kind, a holy, and a gloomy man," John Jay Chapman wrote. His rooms were as gloomy and sanctified as he, "darkened by large, distressing steel engravings of the great philosophers—Locke, Kant, Hegel, and the rest, into whose company Palmer lured the serious-minded youths and charged them with capsules of religious poetry." There was, Chapman wrote, "a wellspring in him," but it was "hidden, blocked up . . . filled with the junk of philosophic thought and moralism." It was to clear away the accumulated philosophic "junk" that James took up his duties. He had, by the time of his appointment as assistant professor of philosophy, been a member of the Harvard faculty for eight years. In that period he had, through the publication of his *The Principles of Psychology,* achieved somewhat of an international reputation. He had also demonstrated, in his shift from physiology to psychology to philosophy, both the intellectual openness of Harvard and his own restless spirit, which could not be contained within any conventional disciplinary boundaries but constantly found new ranges to explore.

His special relationship with Eliot gave him far more power than a relatively junior faculty member could hope to exercise (he was, after all, thirty-eight at the time of his appointment as assistant professor of philosophy, not exactly an academic spring chicken). More important were his own personal qualities. James was charming in the best sense of that abused word—gentle, kind, gracious. People of widely varying backgrounds were drawn to him. His expressiveness, his intellectual vitality, his remarkable gift for friendship made him irresistible. If one were to search for a single word to describe him, it might well be "generous." He clearly had a generosity of spirit that was expended with that selflessness that the senior James had declared to be God's and man's noblest attribute.

James's remarkable gifts of mind and spirit enabled him to create something rare in American intellectual history: a company of friends united in the pursuit of truth. James had met young Josiah Royce, brilliant and shy and irredeemably Western, at Johns Hopkins, and the two young men, startlingly different, had found themselves drawn to each other. Royce, it seems, was rather overwhelmed by James's freely given friendship. Where he had encountered among his peers a certain wariness and reserve, prompted, he was sure, by his Western oddness, he found in James a wholly unaffected friendliness. James, for his part, was rather awed by the formidable erudition of the younger man and his brilliance in dealing with traditional philosophic problems. Royce was all system; James, all inspiration. Most important of all, Royce was laboring over *the* problem, the same question that intrigued and tormented James—the relation of science to religion. James was already plotting to re-create the Harvard department of philosophy, and he determined to add Josiah Royce at the first opportunity. Royce had meanwhile to go into exile in California as an instructor in English at Berkeley, but in 1882 James took a year's leave of absence, undoubtedly part of his plot to bring Royce to Cambridge, and prevailed on Eliot to appoint Royce in his place. Although it was clearly a temporary appointment at a very modest salary and James advised Royce to leave his wife and infant child in California, Royce pulled up stakes and moved East, bag and baggage, determined to escape from his durance in the uncivilized West.

When James returned, other academic chores were found for Royce until his appointment to a "regular" academic post as instructor in philosophy. The two foundation stones of the great era of American academic philosophy were now in place—James and Royce. They were to work in friendly rivalry for more than twenty years, to dominate the Harvard philosophy department and philosophical thinking in America, and to exert a broader influence on the country's intellectual life than any of their contemporaries.

There was a third, absent member of their company—Charles Sanders Peirce. While even James's sponsorship was insufficient to overcome Peirce's personal eccentricities and secure him a post at Harvard, Peirce was an important, if infrequent, lecturer at Harvard and, through James's friendship, a kind of adjunct member of the Harvard department on what might be considered extended leave to Milford, Pennsylvania. If he was lacking in stability and in predictable behavior and was hopelessly bohemian in his dress and manners, Peirce had many of the qualities of mind evident in James. Above all, he had a marvelous style when he chose to use it, James's gift for making complex ideas comprehensible to a "lay" audience, and the conviction that to do so was not only consistent with serious intellectual aims but his responsibility as a seeker after truth.

In 1878, in an article in the *Popular Science Monthly* entitled "How to Make Our Ideas Clear," Peirce took the line, in James's paraphrase, that since "our beliefs are really rules for action . . . to develop a thought's meaning, we need only to determine what conduct it is fitted to produce: that conduct is for us its sole significance. . . . The tangible fact at the root of all our thought-distinctions, however subtle, is that there is no one of them so fine as to consist in anything but a possible difference of practice." Peirce called the test of experience pragmatism. For twenty years the idea, indeed the word, lay where Peirce had dropped it, while Peirce, James, and Royce tested one another's philosophic formulations, all designed, in a manner of speaking, to solve the dilemma of faith and science. Could an individual, wholly committed to science and the scientific method also, logically (and philosophically) believe in God? Royce and Peirce believed that such a conjunction was possible, and each in his own way devoted remarkable intellectual powers to "proving" the proposition. James subjected each "proof" to the test of his own skeptical, questing spirit and announced: "unproved!" Somewhere there was a flaw, a fallacy that closed the door that had appeared so invitingly open. It was a remarkable game that drove Royce farther and farther in the direction of defender and apologist for Christianity until in *The World and the Individual* he concluded with a chapter on "The Union of God and Man" that ended: "We have dealt with the nature of God, with the origin and meaning of man's life, and with the union of God and Man. Our result is this:— despite God's absolute unity, we, as individuals, preserve and attain our unique lives and meanings, and are not lost in the very life that sustains us and that needs us as its own expression. This life is real through us all; and we are real through our union with that life. Close is our touch with the eternal. Boundless is the meaning of our nature. Its mysteries baffle our present science, and escape our present experience; but they need not blind our eyes to the central unity of Being, nor make us feel lost in a realm where all the wanderings ofttime mean the process whereby is discovered the homeland of eternity."

In 1906 at Professor George Holmes Howison's Philosophical Union at the University of California in Berkeley, James retrieved Peirce's word and definition of pragmatism. It proved to be a word and idea whose time had assuredly come. In his Lowell Lectures nine years later James noted: "On all hands we find the 'pragmatic movement' spoken of sometimes with respect, sometimes with contumely, seldom with clear understanding. It is evident that the term applies itself conveniently to a number of tendencies that hitherto have lacked a collective name, and that it has 'come to stay.' " The pragmatist, James said, "turns away from abstraction and insufficiency, from verbal solutions, from bad *a priori* reasons, from fixed principles, closed systems, and pretended absolutes and origins. He turns towards concreteness and adequacy, towards facts, toward actions, toward power." That meant the abandonment of rationalism and empiricism. "It means the open air and possibilities of nature, as against dogma, artificiality, and the pretence of finality in truth." As for religion, pragmatism, as opposed to materialism or positivism, was neutral on the subject, or, a better word, "open." Just as dogs and cats have "ideals" that "coincide with our ideals . . . so we may believe, on the proofs that religious experience affords, that higher powers exist and are at work to save the world on ideal lines similar to our own."

Of his formulation of pragmatism, James had high hopes. "I believe it to be something quite like the protestant reformation," he wrote his brother Henry. And to John Dewey he wrote that "it is the philosophy of the future, I'll bet my life." Although the word is hardly used today (except to suggest a thoroughly practical temper) and is merely referred to in courses of philosophy, there was a substantial measure of truth in James's prediction. If it virtually disappeared as a formal "philosophy," it did become one of those "invisible molecular moral forces" that James wrote of in another context, "that work from individual to individual, stealing through the crannies of the world like so many soft rootlets. . . ." It became something far more important than a philosophy, it became a habit of mind, a quality of the general public consciousness. Politicians and journalists and ordinary citizens spoke of America as a "pluralistic" society with less and less notion of where the word came from. More and more Americans relinquished their faith in "absolutes" and, outside academic walls at least, were ready to judge ideas by their consequences rather than by some abstract formula. The consequences were by no means all salutary. If "pragmatism" and "pluralism" meant a new openness and tolerance, a willingness, in common parlance, "to live and let live," an erosion of dogmatism, and a decline in religious and racial prejudices, they also meant an often bewildering absence of certitude, a sense of confusion and even abandonment. Pragmatism might thus be called religious, "if you allow that religion can be pluralistic or merely melioristic in type"—

in other words, if it does not have to be "true." To compare human beings to dogs and cats in their perception of meaning in the universe was cold comfort to the pious, but it was as far as James's rectitude would permit him to go.

Later, George Santayana, who had been a student of both Royce and James, was added to the Harvard philosophy department—bringing with him the unmistakable flavor of his own exotic origins, half New England Puritan, half Spanish hedonist—and then Hugo Münsterberg, whose Teutonic manners and remarkably wide-ranging interests gave a touch of the bizarre to the whole enterprise.

Santayana was, for the most part, a detached and skeptical observer of the Royce-James great debate. James, reading Santayana's *Interpretations of Poetry and Religion,* considered it philosophically speaking "a perfection of rottenness" in its Platonism, but, as he wrote a friend, "I have literally squealed with delight at the imperturbable perfection with which the position is laid down on page after page; and grunted with delight at such a thickening up of our Harvard atmosphere." With Royce's "voluntaristic-pluralistic monism," Münsterberg's "dualistic scientificism and platonism," Santayana's "pessimistic Platonism," and James's own "crass pluralism"—"so many religions, ways of fronting life"—". . . we should have a genuine philosophic universe at Harvard," James wrote a colleague. "The best condition of it would be an open conflict and rivalry of diverse systems."

James's teaching and his thinking were intertwined. He treated his students as colleagues, fellow searchers for the always elusive truth, a humor which the best of them found irresistible. As *his* son Henry James wrote: "He helped them by example as well as by precept, for it was plain to everyone who knew him or read him that his genius was ardently adventurous and humane." Certainly he could never have comprehended the notion that there was some kind of gulf or chasm between "scholarship" on the one hand and "teaching" on the other, and that the "scholarship" was the real task and contending with immature minds a chore. So he warmed into new life the cold flesh of Harvard instruction that Charles Francis Adams and dozens of others had complained of in the 1840s and 1850s; made the dry bones live.

In the view of William James, "the best use of our colleges is to give young men a wider openness of mind and a more flexible way of thinking than special technical training can generate. . . ." By the same token philosophy was important in the curriculum because "philosophic study means the habit of always seeking an alternative, of not taking the usual for granted, of making conventionalities fluid again, of imagining foreign states of mind. In a word, it means the possession of mental perspective. . . . It says, Is there space and air in your mind, or must your companions gasp for breath whenever they talk with you?" Doctrines were of little consequence. What students must catch from their teachers was "the living, philosophic attitude of mind, the independent, personal look at all the data of life. . . ."

That James's best students responded enthusiastically to such stimulus is abundantly evident. Numbered among them were many of the most brilliant spirits of the coming age—W. E. B. Du Bois, the Hapgoods, Walter Lippmann, and, perhaps the most brilliant and eccentric of all, John Jay Chapman. Chapman was the great-grandson of John Jay, the Founding Father and first chief justice of the Supreme Court, and the grandson of William Jay, the well-known abolitionist and pacifist. The relationship between Chapman and James became especially close. James sensed intuitively the intimate connection between love and courage, how courage grows out of love, that we are most courageous when most loved—and in a kind of loving network he found his own indomitable courage and gave courage to others. Equally important in an age of formal expression and formal relationships, he valued and achieved a remarkable *expressiveness,* a quality that was his greatest charm, the magnet that drew people to him. Clearly he passed it on to many of his students. "Every year I hear more about you," Chapman wrote James after his graduation from Harvard, "and I know you have put life into your whole science all over this country. I see the younger generation—run across them in one way or another—and trace back their vitality to you."

Increasingly James's own concerns turned back to the nature of religious experience. He wrote in 1900: "The problem I have set for myself is a hard one: *first,* to defend (against all the prejudices of my 'class') 'experience' against 'philosophy' as being the real backbone of the world's religious life—I mean prayer, guidance, and all that sort of thing immediately and privately felt, as against high and noble general views of our destiny and the world's meaning; and *second,* to make the hearer or reader believe . . . that, although all the special manifestations of religion may have been absurd (I mean its creeds and theories), yet the life of it as a whole is mankind's most important function." The work in which James undertook to illuminate if not "solve" the problem he had set for himself was *The Varieties of Religious Experience.*

Read in one way, *The Varieties of Religious Experience* is a kind of lament for James's inability to accept religious orthodoxy and his compassionate feelings for those who had. Indeed, by examining and rejecting the "materialist" arguments against religion—such as that it was simply evidence of a neurotic dependency—James perhaps did more for the faith than an ostensibly religious work could have done. "Few of us," he wrote, "are not in some way infirm, or even diseased; and our very infirmities help us unexpectedly. In the psychopathic temperament we have the emotionality which is the *sine qua non* of moral perception." (James may well have been thinking of his brother Robertson when he wrote the sentence; certainly he was aware of his own desperate struggle for sanity and poise.) "*Religion,*" he wrote at another point, ". . . *makes easy and felicitous what in any case is necessary;* and if it be the only agency that can accomplish this result, its vital importance as a human faculty stands vindicated beyond dispute. It becomes an essential organ of our life, performing a function which no other portion of our nature can so successfully fulfill."

At the end of *The Varieties of Religious Experience,* James listed the beliefs that distinguished "the religious life," concluding with those characteristic of the experience of conversion: "A new zest which adds itself like a gift to life, and takes the form either of lyrical enchantment or of appeal to earnestness and heroism. An assurance of safety and a temper of peace, and, in relation to others, a preponderance of loving affections." It was the "preponderance of loving affections" that most impressed others in James himself. So it is perhaps not too much to say that he created by his remarkable capacity for friendship, for "loving affections," a department and a school of philosophy. It was also the case that by his invention of pragmatism he, in a real sense, terminated classical philosophy. It would, of course, linger on, embalmed in departments of philosophy, but its real life was over. It had committed itself without reservation to solving a problem which, it turned out, could not be solved or, when solved, appeared to be irrelevant. But meantime it created, or, more accurately, James created, the high point of American intellectual life and bestowed on a Harvard that was constantly in danger of confusing growth with greatness its richest legacy of generous intellect and inspired teaching.

Henry James became the most accomplished novelist of his day and America's most famous expatriate. He joined the company of literary figures, beginning with James Fenimore Cooper and Washington Irving, who could not endure the crudity of American life. He settled in England. He and William kept up a warm correspondence, and William visited Henry whenever he crossed the ocean. "Harry," he wrote on a visit to London, is "as nice and simple and amiable as he can be," adding, "He has covered himself, like some marine crustacean, with all sorts of material growths, rich sea-weeds and rigid barnacles and things, and lives hidden in the midst of his strange, heavy alien manners and customs; but these are all but 'protective resemblances,' under which the same old, good, innocent and at bottom very powerless-feeling Harry remains, caring for little but his writing, and full of dutifulness and affection for all gentle things. . . ." He described his brother's English house as "a most exquisite collection of quaint little stage properties, three quarters of an acre of brick-walled English garden . . . old-time kitchen and offices, paneled chambers and tiled fire-places. . . ."

When Henry decided after twenty years abroad to return to the United States, William warned him of the disagreeable experience for which he must be prepared as well as "the sort of physical loathing with which many features of our national life will inspire you." The American voices, "the *vocalization* of our countrymen," William wrote, was "ignobly awful . . . incredibly loathsome." Henry should try to avoid the banality of the Eastern cities and travel "to the South, the Colorado, over the Canadian Pacific to the coast. . . ."

What made Henry James such a compelling figure to his contemporaries was that he, more than any of his predecessors, played self-consciously the role of the "writer as artist"—that is to say, the sustained, wholly serious, uncompromising literary craftsman. By the fortunate fact of his inheritance he was able to devote his entire life, free of such distractions as earning a living (he had no wife or children to provide for), to his "art." The fact that he practiced his craft in England and there enjoyed the status of a literary lion further enhanced his reputation in the sight of the predominantly Anglophilic reading public in the United States. In a time when traditional values, ideals, and, as we might say today, "life goals" were in the process of disintegration, the life and role of the "artist" were increasingly attractive. More young men (and women) than ever wished to be writers, and some of them at least hoped to be artists, "serious" writers or "great" writers, as opposed to those who simply made a living. For many of them Henry James became an ideal, if not a model. James's life was "novel," a kind of novel in itself—a long-running drama entitled "The Life of the

Artist as Lived by Henry James." The growing sophistication of literary criticism was especially congenial to the kind of novel James wrote and the subtle and intricate social problems that he dealt with. The great figures of the 1840s and 1850s—Emerson (who, of course, continued to be *the* oracle), Whitman, Thoreau, Melville, and Hawthorne—were prophets and moralists. What they had to say dictated the form in which they said it. They had little to say about style. No child of Henry James, Sr., could write without some attention to moral themes, but in James such themes were muted and diffuse. New World innocence and Old World sophistication and corruption were the principal subjects of his attention, and each year his writing grew more intricate and artful and, some (his brother William among them) said, more dense and impenetrable.

Despite his lifelong exile, James had a streak of pride in him at being an American. He wrote a friend: "We young Americans are (without cant) men of the future. . . . We are Americans born. . . . I look upon it as a great blessing, and I think that to be an American is an excellent preparation for culture. We have exquisite qualities as a race, and it seems to me that we are ahead of the European races in the fact that more than either of them we can deal freely with forms of civilization not only our own, can pick and choose and assimilate and in short (aesthetically and culturally) claim our property wherever we find it." Meantime, however, James preferred to live in England.

A Dash for the Timber. Painting by Frederic Remington, 1889.
(*Courtesy of Amon Carter Museum, Fort Worth, Texas*)

Sunset in the Yosemite Valley. Painting by Albert Bierstadt, 1868. (*Reproduced through the courtesy of The Haggin Museum, Stockton, California*)

Indians near Fort Laramie. Painting by Albert Bierstadt circa 1858. (*Courtesy of Museum of Fine Arts, Boston. M. and M. Karolik Collection*)

Biglin Brothers Turning the Stake. Painting by Thomas Eakins, 1873.
(The Cleveland Museum of Art. The Hinman B. Hurlbut Collection)

The Daughters of Edward Darley Boit. Painting by John
Singer Sargent circa 1882. (*Courtesy of Museum of Fine Arts,
Boston. Gift of Mary Louisa Boit, Florence D. Boit, Jane Hubbard
Boit and Julia Overing Boit in memory of their father.*)

Madame X (Mme. Gautreau). Painting by John Singer Sargent, 1884. (*The Metropolitan Museum of Art, Arthur H. Hearn Fund, 1916.*)

Fox Hunt. Painting by Winslow Homer, 1893.
(*The Pennsylvania Academy of the Fine Arts*)

The Race Track or Death on a Pale Horse. Painting by
Albert Pinkham Ryder circa 1910. (*The Cleveland Museum of
Art. Purchase, J. H. Wade Fund*)

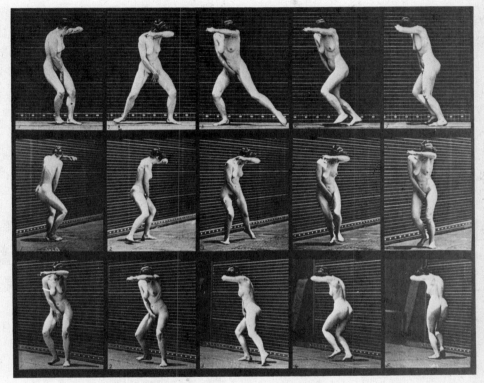

Turning Around in Surprise and Running Away, plate 73,
Animal Locomotion, by Eadweard Muybridge, University of
Pennsylvania, 1887 (*Courtesy of Stanford University Museum of
Art. Stanford Family Collection*)

Transportation Building, World's Columbian Exposition, 1893.
Photograph by C.D. Arnold. (*Courtesy of Chicago Historical Society*)

The Adamses

The Jameses and the Adamses were of the same social class; they were acquaintances, if not friends. They were graduates of Harvard, scholars, intellectuals in every sense of that rather amorphous word. They inherited the capital without which no nineteenth-century male was independent. Both William James and Henry Adams were Harvard professors (Adams relatively briefly). Both men were brilliant writers. Yet as to temperament two men could hardly have been more different.

Where William James, despite his innate skepticism, was all passionate involvement in life, Henry Adams was cynical detachment. Where James was firmly rooted in Cambridge, Adams was all his life a footloose wanderer, a homeless Ishmael, roaming the globe in a restless search for distraction.

Yet when one probes deeper, there are some striking affinities. Both suffered periods of deep depression; both were intermittently suicidal. Both were tormented by the question of religion or, more specifically, by their inability to believe. Both sought for some principle or order, some system in the universe. Both tried to found their lives on friendship. Both were highly dependent on women as friends and correspondents. With all this, James's life was a triumph over crippling skepticism and persistent neurosis, while Adams, pursuing the will-o'-the-wisp of science, gave full rein to that self-pity which generation after generation seemed almost a genetic trait with the Adamses. Yet we can hardly call a failure a man who wrote the nation's best history and its most brilliant autobiography. What we must attend to, however, was Henry Adams's own conviction that he was a failure, an obsolete man in the new capitalistic age. He wrote of himself in *The Education of Henry Adams*: "Had he been born in Jerusalem under the shadow of the Temple and circumcised in the Synagogue by his uncle the high priest, under the name of Israel Cohen, he would scarcely have been more distinctly branded, and not much more heavily handicapped in the races of the coming century, in running for such stakes as the century was to offer. . . ." On the other hand, he clearly enjoyed certain advantages in "being, so to speak, ticketed through life, with the safe-guards of an old, established traffic."

It seemed to Adams, "For him, alone, the old universe was thrown into the ash-heap and a new one created. He and his troglodytic Boston were suddenly cut apart—separated forever. . . . He [Adams] felt nothing in common with the world as it promised to be. He was ready to quit it. . . ."

We are already familiar with the youth and early manhood of Henry and Charles Francis Adams; Brooks, ten years younger than Henry, was always in his shadow, rather more like the son Henry never had than like a brother.

During the Civil War Henry Adams had written to his cavalry officer brother Charles Francis from England, speculating on how they and like-minded young men might join forces to direct the destiny of the Republic along the lines of enlightened reform. The old Puritan spirit of redemption was evident in Henry's speculations. But they were to come to little or nothing. Henry Adams returned to a country he hardly knew, a country which had no place for him in any way commensurate with his notion of what his role should be or, indeed, with his very real talents. He found himself, like so many of his fellow Americans of all classes, without a job, and he turned naturally and instinctively to the government—which was to say, to his friends in Congress and in the administration of Andrew Johnson—for a position. In doing so, he found himself in competition with thousands of other middle- and upper-class young men. The job seekers were innumerable, many of them wounded veterans like Lester Ward with presumably stronger claims to their country's gratitude than Adams. Few, to be sure, had Adams's connections, but minor diplomatic posts and undersecretaryships were all that were available. Another job seeker was John Hay, Lincoln's private secretary. Hay and Adams, whose wartime careers had certain striking parallels—both private secretaries, both intimately involved in the most dramatic political events of the war—shared literary interests and ambitions (both wished to be writers). Adams belonged to the highest caste—perhaps a better word than "class"—in the Republic. Hay, as a Midwesterner, belonged to no class. Both found a sponsor in Sarah Whitman, who conducted the country's most famous salon. Adams shared William James's obsession with friendship and with that noble ancillary activity common to his class and generation, letter writing. He and John Hay chose to be each other's "best" friend, the archetype of all their other friendly relations. They took long walks together, traveled together, talked and entertained together, and, when necessity forced them to be apart, wrote long, adoring letters to each other. When their respective marriages brought new "friends" into their relationship, they built adjacent houses and lived as much in each other's house as their own.

Among the intellectual bonds that tied them was their common disillusionment with and, eventually, hostility toward the United States that took shape after the war. It provided no field for their talents or their desire to serve the common good, or none at least that they could discern, none in the mode of gentlemen politicians, educated, high-minded, and intelligent young men, anxious to serve the public good. Rude newcomers pressed themselves to the fore. Political bosses, devoid of moral scruples, dominated city, state, and even Federal government.

Hay found employment on the *New York Tribune,* increasingly under Whitelaw Reid's control, writing editorials and "brief pieces." In addition he turned out stories, essays, and articles for the *Atlantic Monthly, Harper's Weekly,* and *Lippincott's Magazine,* but even with his multiple literary outlets he found it difficult to make ends meet. The solution to this dilemma proved to be an advantageous marriage to an heiress, Clara Stone of Cleveland, Ohio, who had a very rich papa and an indignant mama who stoutly opposed the marriage of her daughter to an impecunious young journalist. Hay wrote to his fellow secretary under Lincoln, John Nicolay, of his fiancée: "She is a very estimable young person—large, handsome and good. I never found life worthwhile before." Soon there was a baby. "It is painful, but I must tell you," the proud father wrote Reid, "my wife says, when you come to the house, that you have got to hold the baby."

Although Hay suffered from various physical disorders, including the "nervousness" common to American males, he and Nicolay began a biography of Lincoln. Increasingly Hay and his wife traveled for his health—to Colorado, to Wyoming and, more and more frequently, to Switzerland and the rest of the continent.

After several footloose years Henry Adams welcomed an appointment as Harvard's first professor of American history. Although he was a popular lecturer, he found the students generally dull and unresponsive and was glad to accept the additional task of editor of the *North American Review,* an office which he held for six years and which gave him a wide acquaintance in the literary world.

In 1872 Adams, seemingly a confirmed bachelor at the age of thirty-four, married Marion Hooper, whose sister was married to a Harvard colleague of Adams, Ephraim Gurney, and whose brother Ned was a close friend. Marion Hooper was one of those nineteenth-century American women who had extremely close relationships to their fathers (her mother had died when she was five, and her father had been both father and mother to her). He had encouraged her diverse intellectual interests and been, in a real sense, her teacher. She was a skillful horsewoman, who loved horses and dogs, and an accomplished photographer. She read Greek and Latin and spoke French, German, and Italian. When she married Adams, she was twenty-eight and still lived with her family in Brookline, Massachusetts. One sensed a kind of fragility of spirit in her. Susceptible as her new husband was to a whole range of feminine qualities and dependent on the feminine anima throughout his life, he seems to have acquiesced readily and indeed gratefully in her assumption of the role of accomplished housewife and hostess.

Like James, Adams had a number of future luminaries among his students. Theodore Roosevelt was one; Henry Cabot Lodge was another, and Adams encouraged him to consider if not a formal academic career—Lodge, like Adams, had inherited a comfortable income—at least the profession of historian. To the question of whether such a profession would "pay either in money, reputation or any other solid value," Adams replied in the affirmative. No one of their class, he reminded Lodge, "has done better and won more in any business or pursuit than has been acquired by men like Prescott, Motley, Frank

Parkman, Bancroft, and so on in historical writing; none of them men of extraordinary gifts, or who would have been likely to do very much in the world if they had chosen differently." What they did, he added, "can be done by others."

But teaching palled. "A teacher," Adams wrote, "affects eternity; he can never tell where his influence stops. A teacher is expected to teach the truth, and may perhaps flatter himself that he does so, if he stops with the alphabet or the multiplication table, as a mother teaches truth by making her child eat with a spoon; but morals are quite another truth and philosophy is more complex still. A teacher must either treat history as a catalogue, a record, a romance, or as an evolution; and whether he affirms or denies evolution, he falls into all the burning faggots of the pit. He makes of his scholars either priests or atheists, plutocrats, socialists, judges, or anarchists, almost in spite of himself. In essence incoherent and immoral, history has to be taught as such— or falsified." Adams wanted to do neither. "He had no theory of evolution to teach, and could not make the facts fit one. He had no fancy to tell agreeable tales to amuse sluggish-minded boys, in order to publish them afterwards as lectures."

When, in the fall of 1877, the Adamses took up quarters at 1501 H Street in Washington, Adams felt as though he had in some sense come home. "The fact is," he wrote a friend, "I gravitate to a capital by a primary law of nature, this is the only place in America where society amuses me, or where life offers variety. Here, too I can fancy that we are of use in the world, for we distinctly occupy niches which ought to be filled."

Adams wrote that he "held no office, and when friends asked the reason, he could not go into long explanations, but preferred to answer simply that no President had ever invited him to fill one." It was a revealing sentence, which expressed Adams's sense of grievance that he had not been able to follow in the political footsteps of his ancestors. "The American politician was occasionally an amusing object," Adams added.

The Hay family established itself nearby. Their houses became works of art, the Adams home remodeled for them by its owner, William Wilson Corcoran, a famous old philanthropist and art collector. Henry and Marion (whose nickname was Clover) went to Paris to buy the furnishings, which included several Turner watercolors. George Bancroft, the now ancient historian, lived a few blocks away. At a dinner given by President Rutherford Hayes in honor of Bancroft, Adams startled the President by declaring: "Our system of government has failed utterly in many respects. The House is not what it was intended to be, a deliberative body. The majority can't control its action. . . . Our army is as it ought to be, a mere police. It ought to be called a police! Our navy is nothing. In all ages the difficulty has been to decide who shall be ruler. It is the same here. No means has yet been discovered of doing it peacefully. We have not got it. Our reliance is on the people being so as to need no government. When that is the case we are safe."

The Hay and Adams houses became meeting places for artists, architects, writers, and such gentlemen politicians as passed scrutiny. Augustus Saint-Gaudens and his wife, Gussie, were frequent visitors, as were the John La Farges and John Singer Sargent when he was in the United States. Senator Henry Cabot Lodge was within the pale, as were the younger Roosevelts, Teddy and Alice. Admitted to the inner circle, almost as close to Hay and Adams as they were to each other, was Clarence King, one of the exotics of the age. King was a polymath whose knowledge seemed to reach everywhere. In the words of Adams: "King had everything to interest and delight Adams. He knew more than Adams did of art and poetry; he knew America, especially west of the hundredth meridian, better than anyone; he knew the professor by heart, and he knew the Congressman better than he did the professor. He knew even women; even the American woman; even the New York woman, which is saying much. . . . He knew more practical geology than was good for him, and saw ahead at least one generation further than the text-books," an oblique reference to and excuse for the fact that King had lost everything he had in mining speculations. "His wit and humor; his bubbling energy which swept everyone in the current of his interest; his personal charm of youth and manners; his faculty of giving and taking, profusely, lavishly, whether in thought or in money, as though he were nature herself, marked him almost alone among Americans. . . . Whatever prize he wanted lay ready for him,—scientific, social, literary, political,—and he knew how to take them in turn, . . . The men worshipped not so much their friend, as the ideal American they all wanted to be. The women were jealous because, at heart King had no faith in the American woman; he loved types more robust."

This "ideal American" did indeed love men more than women, suffered like Adams and Hay and so many others of his class and preceding generations from terrible spells of incapacitating depression, spent his last years in poverty in Arizona living with a black woman, and finally committed suicide at the age of fifty-nine. By the time he became a member of the Hay-Adams coterie King was famous for his remarkable surveying expedition from eastern Colorado to the California boundary with Mexico, conducted between 1867 and 1877 and resulting in a seven-volume *Report of the Geological Exploration of the Fortieth Parallel,* a classic work which made his reputation. It was King who invented the contour lines that distinguish every large-scale topographical map. In 1878 Congress placed all the Western geological surveys under King and created a new agency—the U.S. Geological Survey.

The Hays and the Adamses plus Clarence King constituted themselves the Five of Hearts Club and had a tea service with five hearts engraved on it and stationery with the same emblem. They joined forces to help Adams write an anonymous popular novel, *Democracy,* an exposé of Washington politics, published in 1880. The years in Washington were happy, productive years, but in the brilliant talk and hectic social life there was an edge of desperation, as at a prolonged party where gaiety must be sustained at all costs. Clover Adams's long, witty, sardonic letters to her father suggest that all was not as right as it seemed. Too much cynicism corrodes the soul; the Five of Hearts in their madcap pace seemed more and more remote from the deeper currents of the life around them, a life which, for the most part, they scorned. It was only *friends,* a few select kindred spirits, cousins and nieces, literary and artistic allies, who counted.

Clover Adams was subject to periods of deep depression. She had had such an attack during a trip on the Nile in 1872 and again just before her marriage, and there is a suspicion that one of the purposes of the intense social life was to distract her.

With Hay preoccupied with the Lincoln biography, Henry Adams turned his attention to an act of extended filial piety: a mammoth nine-volume history of the administrations of Jefferson and Madison. The work dealt only indirectly with his great-grandfather John Adams, but it was unsparing in its scrutiny of his successor. The Jefferson that emerged from its pages was a far cry from the idealized figure revered by the Democrats as the exemplar of democratic principles and the party's guiding light.

Adams's experience as his father's secretary and his life on the fringes of Washington politics as well as his cool and detached view of life in general made him ideally equipped to write the first "modern" history of the United States. He was an ironist with a style and an intelligence that American historians have seldom brought to their labors. The result was a brilliant portrait of an age, a work which ranged far beyond the conventional confines of history. The Adamses from the time of John all had been immersed in history, the reading, the writing, and the making of it. If Henry Adams had little to do with making it, he achieved a kind of vicarious fulfillment by writing it better than any American before or since.

In 1884 Adams and Hay commissioned their friend Henry Hobson Richardson, who had just completed his great Trinity Church in Boston, to design two adjacent houses in the Romanesque style for which Richardson was famous, fronting on Lafayette Square across from the White House. No pains or expense were to be spared; the houses were to symbolize the union of hearts of the Hays and Adamses.

There was a kind of calculated defiance in the site and the structures; the two handsome houses together presented a façade that did not suffer from comparison with their neighbor across the square. If the government could find no appropriate use for the name and talents of the most conspicuously gifted Adams of his generation, the descendant of presidents and statesmen, he, Adams, and his friend John Hay, almost equally neglected, would establish a capitol of the intellect, where true culture and true politics would flourish, where parties and conversations would take place that would far outstrip anything the presidential mansion could offer, where often savage mockery vied with satiric thrusts at the ruthless and venal men who had preempted the stage of national politics.

There were difficulties and delays in completing the defiant mansions, problems with contractors, misunderstandings with Richardson. In the midst of the confusion attendant upon such an ambitious undertaking, Clover Adams's father died. Soon she slipped into the always threatening depression. One morning after breakfast she withdrew to her room, ostensibly to develop photographs she had taken. Instead, she drank the poisonous developing fluid and died in agony. Adams was shattered. He wrote to E. L. Godkin that "fate at last has smashed the life out of me; but for twelve years I had everything I wanted on earth. I own that the torture has made me groan; but as long as any will is left, I shall try not to complain," and to his friend and publisher Henry Holt he wrote: "How we do suffer! And we go on laughing; for, as a practical joke at our expense, life is a success."

With La Farge as a traveling companion, Adams fled from the

still incomplete house to Japan, Tahiti, the Pacific islands. Hay wrote to him: ". . . oh! the misery of the empty house next door."

When Adams returned after almost five years of wandering to his house and his friend Hay, he returned with the ardor of a lover, but nothing was the same. He and Hay were still inseparable, but their relationship was shadowed by the possibility that Henry's devotion to Hay might have resulted in some deficiency in his love for Clover that contributed to her death. Clearly Adams could not have taken her father's place or found the means to woo her from that disastrous attachment. "Existence," he wrote in the *Education of Henry Adams,* "was, on the whole, exceedingly solitary, or so it seemed to him. He loved solitude as little as others did; but he was unfit for social work, and he sank under the surface."

After his wife's death Adams's visits to his Washington home were usually brief, mere intervals between visits to friends at St. Helen in Georgia, his summer place at Beverly Farms in Massachusetts (as close generally as he cared to come to Boston), London, Paris, Rome, and much farther afield—Yellowstone Park, Japan, Samoa, Mexico City. In Washington melancholy replaced boredom. Life, he wrote John Hay, "seems strangely unreal and weird on this ill-balanced perch. One can easily drop out." Perhaps the image of himself that Adams cherished most was that of a man out of his time, a "useless and superfluous" man, "like Joseph, in pictures of the Nativity, always holding or leading the donkey."

His English friend Cecil Spring-Rice wrote of Adams in the years following his wife's death: "He is queer to the last degree, cynical, vindictive, but with a constant interest in people, faithful to his friends and passionately fond of his mother and of all little children ever born; even puppies." To Spring-Rice, it seemed evident that Adams's life had been radically altered by one of those "griefs so great that after them one is independent of joy and sorrow or the respect of men." Besides Hay and La Farge (King drifted, or rushed, in and out of his life), Adams depended most heavily on women friends: the beautiful and fascinating Elizabeth Sherman Cameron, the niece of John and William Tecumseh Sherman, and a number of nieces who were like surrogate daughters, especially Mabel Hooper La Farge. He became a wanderer on the face of the earth, restless, bored, endlessly pursuing an elusive vision, living, as he said, more and more in the past. Yet everywhere he went, he saw people and things that delighted him and wrote irresistible letters to the innumerable nieces and, above all, to Hay ("Dearly Beloved," "Dear Heart," "My Adored One"); the two old men exchanged love letters like juvenile sweethearts, albeit epistles glittering with brilliant conceits and, one suspects, somewhat stylized despair.

"I am satisfied," Adams wrote to Francis Parkman, "that the purely mechanical development of the human mind in society must appear in a great democracy so clearly, for want of disturbing elements, [and] that in another generation psychology, physiology and history will join in proving man to have as fixed and necessary development as that of a tree; and almost as unconscious."

At the Chicago World's Columbian Exposition Adams had contemplated the dynamo. It became to him "a symbol of infinity. . . . He began to feel the forty-foot dynamos as a moral force, much as the early Christians felt the Cross. The planet itself seemed less impressive, in its old-fashioned, deliberate, annual or daily revolution, than this huge wheel, revolving within arm's-length at some vertiginous speed, and barely murmuring. . . . Before the end one began to pray to it; inherited instinct taught the natural expression of man before silent and infinite force." Two years later Adams accompanied the Hays and the Lodges on a trip to Normandy, and there he saw, for the first time, Mont St.-Michel. He was overwhelmed by the beauty and power of the idea of the Virgin. It was in her name that the greatest achievements of the human imagination had taken form. Against the virtually incomprehensible richness and mystery of the Virgin the modern age offered the dynamo. The dynamo and the Virgin became, for Adams, the poles of the human spirit; his emotional and intellectual response was unqualifiedly to the Virgin. Indeed, she invaded the austerely masculine heart of Calvinism and freed him from that long servitude. But he found another master in the second law of thermodynamics— the dissipation of energy—which he gleefully applied to human history.

"It's a queer sensation," Adams wrote, "this secret belief that one stands on the brink of the world's greatest catastrophe. For it means the fall of Western Europe, as it fell in the fourth century. It recurs to me every November, and culminates every December. I have to get over it as I can, and hide, for fear of being sent to an asylum." In 1901 he gave "the present society" fifty years to "break its damn neck. . . . Either our society must stop or bust, as Malthus would say. I do not myself care which it does. That is the affair of those who are to run it. . . ."

Henry apparently found his brother Brooks disputatious and difficult. Brooks tired him with his intensity. "We are too much alike and agree too well in our ideas," Henry wrote him, but he encouraged his speculations about the forces in history and amended his style.

The principal tie between the brothers was their efforts to free themselves from their Puritan heritage (while at the same time validating their ancestors) and their common search for the "laws" of history (they discovered different "laws," but the laws of each anticipated a world cataclysm). Brooks began his own emancipation with a history of New England entitled *The Emancipation of Massachusetts,* the first direct scholarly assault on the sacred ark of Puritanism. Published in 1887, Adams's volume was a startling departure from the conventional piety which had surrounded the Puritans and the leaders of the Revolution. As Brooks Adams told the story, the revered clergy of New England were raging fanatics who hated the British crown and sought from the earliest days of the colonies to throw off the yoke of England. Sam Adams was their willing and ingenuous tool, "a fanatical and revolutionary demagogue," who did his best, in the wake of the Boston Massacre, "so to inflame the public mind that dispassionate juries could hardly be obtained."

But Samuel Adams worked to purposes other than he knew. In tumbling down the power of Great Britain, he tumbled down also the repressive rule of the clergy, "for no church can preach liberality and not be liberalized. . . . In the next generation the great liberal secession from the Congregational communion broke the ecclesiastical power forever." Hence the "emancipation of Massachusetts," freed for her final mission to lead in the "battle against the spread of human oppression" in "the form of slavery . . . for it is her children's heritage that, wheresoever on this continent blood shall flow in defence of personal freedom, there must the sons of Massachusetts surely be."

It was *The Emancipation of Massachusetts,* according to Brooks, that started him off on his search for a "law" of "civilization and decay," and this search took him "in succession to England, to France, to Germany, to Algeria, to Italy, to Egypt, to Syria, to Turkey, to India, to Russia, to the West Indies and to Mexico." It prompted him to tell his fiancée, Anna Lodge, "that I was eccentric to the point of madness, and that, if she married me, she must do so on her own responsibility and at her own risk."

In some ways, Brooks Adams's best-known book—*The Law of Civilization and Decay,* the book on which his rather too modest fame rests—

is his least successful. Published in 1895 and obviously a product of the Panic and Depression of 1893, it gave a long and scholarly analysis of the consequences throughout history of "centralization" of power and of currency and the almost inevitable degeneration that followed that movement. (When his brother Henry warned that it would draw more attacks than *The Emancipation of Massachusetts,* Brooks replied that he had "no ambition to compete with Daniel Webster as the jackal of the vested interests.")

The Law of Civilization and Decay is perhaps most notable for the fact that it was one of the first efforts to interpret all human history "scientifically," to discern in it certain overriding uniformities that were so apparent as to constitute laws. Heretofore, as we have seen, American historians had assumed, overtly or covertly, that history was the working out of God's plan for the universe. At least they had refrained from directly challenging that assumption. Darwinism had, to be sure, made extensive inroads on that traditional view (if it had not, for all practical purposes, destroyed it). At the heart of *The Law* are several crucial propositions: The success of civilizations is proportionate to the amount of human and material energy available; the velocity of social change is proportionate to energy and mass; centralization is proportionate to velocity. Fear dominates societies in their earlier stages and produces religious, military, and artistic types whose principal function is to alleviate various forms of fear. In later stages fear yields to greed, and economic organization dominated by the capitalist manifests itself. Economic life brings competition, and competition brings degradation. The earlier types—the farmer, the religious man, the artist—give way to the financier and industrialist. The producer—the worker and the farmer—sinks into poverty and virtual servitude. Woman becomes the parasite of the "economic man" or constitutes a "biologically function-less third sex."

In a revised conclusion, written for the New York edition, Adams wrote: "Men do not differ in any respect from other animals, but survive, according to their aptitudes, by adapting themselves to exterior conditions which prevail at the moment of their birth, and it is perhaps the history of international exchanges, gauging the economic relations of the different races of the world, which permits us best to follow this process of natural selection."

The book ends on a falling note: "No poetry can bloom in the arid modern soil, the drama has died, and the patrons of the arts are no longer even conscious of shame at profaning the most sacred of ideals. The ecstatic dream, which some twelfth-century monk cut into the stones of the sanctuary hallowed by the presence of his God, is reproduced to bedizen a warehouse; or the plan of an abbey . . . is adapted to a railroad station." Everywhere "consolidation . . . seems to presage approaching disintegration."

Theodore Roosevelt, who had been a student of Henry Adams and was a personal friend of both the brothers, wrote a long and generally favorable review of *The Law* which revealed as much about Roosevelt's own thought as about that of Brooks Adams. Any thoughtful reader, Roosevelt noted, must agree "that there is grave reason for some of Mr. Adams's melancholy forebodings. . . . There is no use blinding ourselves to certain tendencies and results of our high-pressure civilization. . . ." Among these were the urban poor, constituting "a standing menace, not merely to our prosperity but to our existence." But on the matter of hard money versus soft Roosevelt was entirely orthodox, and he rejected Adams's gloomy prognostications of degeneration and decay.

Brooks Adams's greatest achievement was undoubtedly to direct the historian's attention to the economic basis of nations and the forms of competition they engaged in to increase their power vis-à-vis that of their rivals. Geography and economics were, in his view, the sister disciplines of history. The movement of trading caravans by land or merchant vessels by sea was more important than the histories of dynasties and wars in understanding the course of history. The production and, even more important, distribution of food, for example, were a central element in all history. "Life," he wrote, "may be destroyed as effectually by peaceful competition as by war. A nation which is undersold may perish by famine as completely as if slaughtered by a conqueror. . . . Nature abhors the weak."

If Brooks and Henry Adams chose lives of letters, of leisurely scholarly pursuits, of travel and inquiry into the roots of historical development, their brother Charles Francis opted for a life of action. To be sure, he, like his younger brothers, indeed like every ambitious young American, wished above all to be a writer, but he chose for his research and writing the relatively mundane field of railroad reform. He made himself in effect the first serious professional writer on the subject of railroads and the measures necessary to establish some control over them "as the most developing force and the largest field of the day."

In the words of Henry Cabot Lodge, Charles Francis Adams awakened "his public to the vast importance of the railroad system growing and spreading rankly over a continent without either regulation or control. . . . He demonstrated the need of action in the public interest." In Lodge's words, "The idea, the theory, the principles, were all his. . . . It is not going too far to say that no single man produced by his own unaided thought and effort so great an effect upon our economic development, with all its attendant political manifestations, so far as it was involved in transportation by rail, as did Charles Francis Adams when he brought about the establishment of the Massachusetts Railroad Commission." In addition to establishing himself as an expert on railroads, Adams plunged into speculations in Western lands and businesses, investing very successfully in a Kansas City stockyard among other enterprises. Under the circumstances it was perhaps inevitable that he and his brothers should find less and less in common.

Charles Francis and John Quincy had fought in the Civil War, while Henry had remained his father's faithful amanuensis in London and Brooks had been too young to join the army. The fact that John Quincy and Charles Francis had been soldiers may have well determined their subsequent careers as, respectively, a moderately successful state politician and a highly successful businessman-scholar, both men of action.

Charles Francis found time to write *Three Episodes of Massachusetts History,* a work of impressive quality, and, with Henry, an account of the Erie Railroad scandal, entitled *Chapters of Erie,* a work which remains the best history of the subject. He wrote in addition a biography of his old friend Richard Henry Dana as well as a series of essays on the military and diplomatic history of the Civil War, published in book form with the title *Studies: Military and Diplomatic.* The most interesting book he wrote was his *Autobiography.* Although by any normal standard, Charles Francis Adams was a very successful man, a reformer, businessman, scholar, and philanthropist, he considered himself (a disposition common to all the Adamses) a failure.

Each Adams, in his own fashion, struggled with the burden of history—of the Adams family and the residue of New England Puritanism. Some of the less attractive residues included a joyless social conformity, a fear of displaying emotions, and, perhaps above all, continuing acute sexual anxieties, which, while by no means an integral element in the Protestant Passion, had come to be identified with it and, indeed, in some ways to be seen as its most essential element. Charles Francis Adams's *Autobiography,* slight as it is, derives much of its fascination from the evidence it gives of Adams's own ambivalence about his clan and his class. It is striking in its obvious Freudian intention of "killing" the father, poor Charles Francis, Sr. Besides carefully enumerating the seven errors that his father committed in rearing him, thus warping and crippling him for life, Charles Francis missed no opportunity to disparage his parent. All this may have less to do with his father than with Charles's need to remove the weight of being an Adams from his back. When you are the grandson and great-grandson of presidents of the United States, success is measured by an impossibly exacting standard. "Failure" is defined as failure to be president.

Under the urgings of his father Charles Francis had kept a diary through his college years and his term as a law apprentice with Dana, but he tells in the *Autobiography*, with obvious relish, of how "it went into the fire; and I stood over it until the last leaf was ashes." In burning the volumes to the last leaf he had clearly performed an essential ritual: the escape from his past, from his father, grandfather, great-grandfather, from Boston and Harvard and Boston Latin School and Quincy, Massachusetts.

John Quincy Adams, his grandfather, had been Henry Adams's bête noir. He could not forgive him for clinging to the outworn shreds of his religious faith, and he could not forget him. Much of his adult life consisted of a buried dialogue with his long-dead grandfather. His hero was his father, a man perfectly balanced, free of the fanaticisms of *his* father (Charles Francis, Sr., had found John Quincy every bit as difficult a parent as Henry found him a grandparent; Charles Francis performed the traditional act of family piety by editing the papers of *his* grandfather, John Adams, with whom he clearly felt more at home than with his own parent). And so they went on, the various generations of Adamses, choosing up sides, so to speak, among their ancestors. Charles Francis II not only rejected his father but attributed to him all the failures and disappointments of his own life, from not encouraging him to engage in games to sending him off to four miserable years at Harvard.

It is difficult not to suspect that the differences between the temperaments *and* philosophies of the Jameses and the Adamses were rooted in the characters of their respective fathers. The senior Henry James had escaped from the world of Calvinist orthodoxy into a freer and more open realm and taken his children with him. Charles Francis Adams, Sr., was still locked in that narrow, airless universe; his children paid the price.

19

Immigration

It would not come as a surprise to the American Indian that the history of the United States was the history of immigration. Generation after generation, hundreds of thousands of nonnatives came to America. We are already reasonably well acquainted with the early classes of immigrants—the British, Irish, Germans, Swedes, Norwegians, and Danes. They continued to predominate in numbers, but different nationalities now appeared, most conspicuously the Italians and Eastern European Russians and Poles or Russian/Polish Jews. By the end of the century the influx included almost every race and nationality in the world, among them Austro-Hungarians, Czechs, and Greeks.

Capitalism, it turned out, had an insatiable appetite for cheap labor. Its agents scoured the four corners of the earth. In the 1870s, for example, the Inman Steamship Company dispatched 3,500 agents throughout Europe to sell tickets to the United States to relatives of immigrants. The tide of immigration, which had swelled to as many as 250,000 a year in the 1850s, predominantly Irish and German, had been slowed by the Civil War. From a high of 251,000 in 1857 immigration dropped to 91,000 in 1862, before it shot up to almost 400,000 in 1870. In that year more than 100,000 immigrants came from Great Britain, 57,000 from Ireland, and 30,000 from Scandinavia. Germany led, as it had for many years, with 118,000. Even before the war a trickle of Italian immigration had begun, and after the war this grew to first a stream and then a torrent. The vast majority of immigrants listed themselves as having no occupation or as laborers (undoubtedly most of the "no occupations" became laborers on Western railroads or factory workers).

The Panic and Depression of 1873 reduced the numbers of immigrants coming to the United States; only 138,500 came in 1878. But four years later the tide swelled to 789,000, and in the decade of the eighties more than 3,000,000 immigrants arrived at American ports of entry. Immigration from Italy, which had never exceeded 9,000 in a single year and averaged closer to 5,000, rose to 32,000 in 1882, stayed near that figure until 1895, and almost tripled to 100,000 by the end of the century. Immigration from Canada, which had run between 3,000 and 5,000 a year from the early decades of the century, rose to an average of 40,000 a year.

Behind each new wave of immigration were complex causes having to do primarily with economic conditions and the emigration policies of the immigrants' home countries, with wars and conscription in the homeland and job opportunities in the United States. The chancelleries of Europe vacillated in their attitude toward emigration, generally encouraging it when times were bad and resisting it when workers were needed to man industrial plants. Thus in the era of Bismarck and the unification of Germany immigration from that country dropped sharply; by 1895 it had fallen to a tenth of its high point in 1882.

The consequence of the continuing high rate of immigration from Great Britain, Ireland, and Germany was that the great majority of the laboring population in the first phase of postwar industrialism was Northern European in origin. Only a small portion of the work force was from Central or Southern Europe, areas that were to supply a large part of the industrial work force by the last decade of the century.

A substantial portion of the German, British, and Scandinavian immigrants were farmers, and they found their way in large numbers to the northern tier of Midwestern and Great Plains states—Wisconsin, Illinois, Minnesota, Nebraska, and the Dakotas—to join the hundreds of thousands of their compatriots who had preceded them. Large numbers of nonfarmers settled in the great industrial cities of the East and made their way as far west as the manufacturing towns of Ohio and Michigan and Chicago. German immigrants, as we have seen, made up the most radical segment of the industrial labor force (they imported

their own radical leaders, so to speak), but English and Irish workingmen were not far behind.

Andrew Carnegie had an ingenious method for calculating the
value to the United States of the new arrivals. They were certainly
worth $1,500 apiece, as much as a slave had been worth before the
Civil War. In addition, each one brought with him an estimated $125.
It thus followed that the value of the immigrants arriving in the United
States in the year 1882 was in excess of $1 billion, more than all the
country's gold and silver mines had produced in the same period.

The most exotic addition to the stream of immigrants was the
Chinese. In 1854, 13,000 Chinese had been brought to the United
States to work on the Pacific Coast railroads and in the Western mines.
Each subsequent year between 3,000 and 5,000 Chinese arrived until
1869, when the number increased to more than 12,000, rising in 1882
to nearly 40,000. By the mid-1870s there were roughly 100,000 Chinese,
concentrated in railroad building and mining.

Wendell Phillips had warned of "four hundred millions of Chinese"
ready "to pour their surplus into our Western veins, a race as bold, as
indomitable, as indestructible as the Yankee." That new wave of immigration would be the greatest challenge of all. "The shock," Phillips
declared, "will strain to the utmost the capacity of Republican institutions. The very thought of it has scared from its seat the faith of
many an American in self government."

His concern proved more than justified. It is arguable that of all
the immigrants who came to the United States, the Chinese suffered
the most hostility and persecution. Frederick Law Olmsted was appalled at the treatment of the Chinese in Mariposa, California. They
were robbed, beaten, lynched, and otherwise mistreated with the con-
nivance of the authorities. As for opium smoking, which so alarmed
the natives, there seemed to Olmsted "to be less essential vice in opium
smoking than in our national excitements. If they have learned anything of white men except vice and wickedness, I can't think by what
means it has been. I never heard of the slightest effort or purpose on
the part of any white man, woman or child to do them good."

Henry George was strongly opposed to Chinese immigration. He
described the Chinese in California as "utter heathens, treacherous,
sensual, cowardly and cruel. . . . Their moral standard is as low as their
standard of comfort. . . . They practice all the unnamable vices of the
East . . . generally apparently cleanly, but filthy in their habits. Their

quarters reek with noisome odours, and are fit breed-places for pestilence." Mark Twain, on the other hand, took a more enlightened view of the race. In *Roughing It* he wrote: "They are a kindly-disposed, well-meaning race, and are respected and well-treated by the upper-classes, all over the Pacific Coast. No Californian gentleman or lady ever abuses or oppresses a Chinaman under any circumstances. . . . Only the scum of the population do it, they and their children; they and, naturally and consistently, the policemen and politicians likewise, for these are the dust-licking pimps and slaves of the scum, there as elsewhere in America." In defense of George, it must be said that a huge Chinese laundryman had tried to attack his wife, and George had come home late one night to find her "quivering with fright."

Anti-Chinese feeling was not limited to the West. Jacob Riis, the champion of New York City's immigrants, had nothing good to say about them in that metropolis. To Riis the Chinese of Mott Street were at the bottom of the social scale. Their manners, their religion, their withdrawn interior life, their opium dens, and their enticing of young white women, since they had few women of their own, into the recesses of Chinatown clearly outraged him. "Between the tabernacles of Jewry and the shrines of the Bend," Riis wrote, "Joss has cheekily planted his pagan worship of idols, chief among which is the celestial worshipper's own gain and lust. . . . I state it in advance as my opinion, based on the steady observation of years, that all attempts to make an effective Christian of John Chinaman will remain abortive in this generation; of the next I have, if anything, less hope." Even the proverbial cleanliness of the Chinese offended Riis. "Mott Street is cleaned to distraction," he wrote. "Stealth and secretiveness are as much part of the Chinaman in New York as the cat-like tread of his felt shoes." From their cellar fantan dens came "the pungent odor of burning opium and the clink of copper coins on the table." The curious got glimpses of "the white slaves of its dens of vice and their infernal drug . . . girls hardly yet grown to womanhood, worshipping nothing save the pipe that has enslaved them body and soul."

In 1879 Congress forbade the importation of foreign laborers under contract, a law aimed primarily at Chinese immigration. Constant agitation in California against the Chinese had resulted in a clause in the state Constitution of 1879 that barred corporations from hiring Chinese and forbade their employment on any public works. The Treaty of 1880 with China gave the United States the right to "regulate, limit, or suspend" but not "absolutely prohibit" Chinese immigration. But in 1882, responding to pressure from the Western states, Congress suspended all immigration of Chinese for ten years.

New York and Chicago were the collecting stations for the new wave of Southern European immigrants. In 1870, 3,000 Italians were settled in New York City; thirty years later the number had swelled to 145,433. The number of Irish had declined slightly, while Austro-Hungarians had increased from 5,227 to 180,000, the greater part coming in the 1890s. The Germans, with 322,343 foreign-born in 1900, were still by far the largest single immigrant group in the city, and of all immigrant groups they proved most adept at assimilation. A German population of 187,972 in 1870 was large enough to absorb as many again in a thirty-year period without the severe traumas and dislocations that characterized most other immigrant groups (the British and the Canadians being perhaps the most notable exceptions).

The earliest Italian immigrants were from northern Italy, the region from Milan to Trieste; many were *artigiani* (artisans), shopkeepers, and fruit vendors. These pioneers were followed by the *contadini* from the overcrowded and impoverished areas of southern Italy. Among the latter were substantial numbers of *giornalieri*, or unskilled laborers, and a scattering of middle-class *prominenti*, some of whom came to exploit their fellow countrymen, and *padroni*, or labor contractors. Exploitative as he might be, the *padrone* performed an important function for Italian immigrants from rural areas who could speak no English. He found them jobs and took a portion of their salaries. Saloons or shops served as the *padroni's* headquarters, and they performed hundreds of essential services for their countrymen, from assisting in the emigration of relatives to helping Italians in legal difficulties or finding a flat. The more benign became "Papas," individuals of considerable moral and political weight.

The principal reason for the rising tide of Italian immigration was the population explosion in Italy, which brought widespread unemployment there. In addition, the burden of taxation weighed most heavily on the poorest farmers. For Italians the family and the home district were more powerful realities than nationality. Northern Italians looked down on their compatriots from the south, and loyalty to Rome or Verona was often stronger than a sense of Italianness. As Chicago became the American capital of Polish immigrants, so New York was the capital of Italian immigrants; they settled in large numbers on the Lower East Side, creating a Little Italy which came to be more fiercely

Italian in many ways than the homeland. One might say that immigrants from that country, recently welded into a nation by the efforts of Giuseppe Mazzini, had first to become thoroughly Italian (as contrasted with being Perugians, Milanese, or Romans) before they could become Americans.

By 1881 there were 20,000 Italians living in the area of Mulberry Bend and Mott Street in New York City. "Many of the most important industries of the city are in the hands of Italians as employers and employed, such as the manufacture of macaroni, of objects of art, confectionery, artificial flowers," a reporter noted. ". . . The fruit trade is in the hands of Italians in all its branches." In winter the fruit merchant "roasts chest-nuts and pea-nuts, and in summer dispenses slices of watermelon. . . ." Second-generation Italians often passed for Americans "and prefer to do so, since a most unjust and unwarranted prejudice against Italians exists in many quarters, and interferes with their success in their trades and callings," the reporter added.

Eighty percent of the Italian immigrants, the vast majority of whom had been farmers in their homeland, settled in cities. They had little sentimentality about farming. In Italy it had meant for them tenancy on some rich landlord's estate or grinding poverty and ruinous taxes. To escape to city life was a liberation. An Italian-American journalist attributed most of the problems of Italians in the United States to overcrowding in the cities. "Families of seven or more members crowd into houses containing only two rooms, one of which is the kitchen. This mode of existence, apart from the fact that it is fruitful in the development and extension of diseases, renders the people vile in their personal habits, and . . . makes them appear repulsive to the Americans. . . . But the influence of this agglomeration of the Italians goes still farther, for, besides the evils already spoken of, it furnishes an effective stimulus for the developing and deepening of moral corruption." In such circumstances individuals with no strong family or village attachments "find in the swarming Italian quarters of the large American cities fruitful fields in which to exercise their baneful powers for the despoliation of their countrymen, who, ignorant and ingenuous, become their ready victims. In the guise of agents, solicitors, or journalists, they extort money. As founders of gambling dens and houses of ill-fame, they organize schemes of blackmail and other crimes."

Italians in New York's Mulberry Bend—the Italian section—lived with other immigrants from the same villages; the patron saints' name days were their local holidays. "Between the vendetta, the mafia, the ordinary neighborhood feuds," Jacob Riis wrote, "and the Bend itself, always picturesque if outrageously dirty, it was not hard to keep it [Mulberry Bend] in the foreground. . . . The Bend is a mass of wreck, a dumping-ground for all manner of filth from the surrounding tenements. . . . The numerous old cellars are a source of danger to the children that swarm over the block. Water stagnating in the holes will shortly add to the peril of epidemic disease." Riis's predicted cholera epidemic did indeed occur.

Many of the Italian immigrants were involved in a recycling process. There were rag and bone and bottle pickers by the hundreds and they sorted through the city's refuse, removing those items they could convert to cash.

The Italian community of Chicago was described by an Italian-American journalist as made up of "newspaper-men, bankers, publicans, employment agents, lawyers, interpreters, midwives, musicians, artisans, laborers, sweaters' victims, grocers, bakers, butchers, barbers, merchants, etc., all of which are necessary to one another and cannot bear separation without disorganization. It is a town within a town, a stream, a rivulet in the ocean, of such intense force of cohesion that it cannot be broken, as the mighty ocean cannot break the Gulf Stream. The immigrant Italians are lodged by Italian innkeepers, and fed by Italian restaurateurs. Italian publicans quench their thirst, Italian employment agents or 'bosses' find them work, and group them and take them to the country, where, in the majority of cases, they board them, and act as interpreters between the contractor and them. Italian agents or bankers send their money to their families in Italy." The same journalist defended Italians against the charge of "filthiness." In Italy they were conspicuously clean, whitewashing their houses each year before Easter, but in Chicago and New York City, crowded into noisome tenements, they were overcome by the unhealthy and fetid character of their surroundings.

In Boston the Italians congregated in the North End near the home of Paul Revere. In that city the number swelled from slightly more than 1,000 in 1880 to 18,000 fifteen years later, by which time they constituted 11 percent of the foreign-born in that city. The Genoese, or northern Italians, with a heavy mixture of the Teutonic in their blood, were often fair and taller than their southern cousins, the Neapolitans and Calabrians. The Sicilians, small and swarthy and making up less than a fifth of the Italian population, were inclined to hold themselves apart. Two common charges against the Italian immigrants by their critics were that they were disposed to loaf and to quarrel and fight excessively. There was some truth to both charges. Italian culture condoned (and condones) for its males considerable leisure. The reflective imbibing of wine, animated conversation over cups of steaming coffee in streetside cafés, and spontaneous bouts of singing were abandoned with understandable reluctance in a new world of feverish bustle. Quarreling, by the same token, was a form of cultural communication, as prized by Italians as noserubbing among Eskimos. A more serious charge was that of criminality, leveled especially against Sicilians, who were accused of preying primarily on their own countrymen and ruling the Little Italys of various cities through intimidation.

An example of the tensions between immigrants of different nationalities may be found in the case of the Italian Labor Company, organized in New York City to contract Italian workers to mines and railroads. The use of Italians in the Pennsylvania bituminous coal fields as strikebreakers was naturally attacked by prolabor journals, which condemned the members of the company as "the dupes of unprincipled money sharks" and "tools to victimize and oppress other workingmen." The Italians were, however, warmly defended in the *New York Sun* as a valuable antidote to strikes. The mineowners had no hesitation in referring to the Italians as allies in the war between capital and labor. One mineowner declared to a newspaper reporter: "They understand there is a strike . . . and the sentiment among them is to work and to fight if necessary. . . . Each will have a musket and will be able to defend himself if called on to do so."

Not surprisingly, there was soon open warfare in a number of the mining communities between the "old miners" and the newcomers. Shots were exchanged; men were killed and wounded. Yet when Henry Frick brought in a force of Italians, guarded by special police, to break a strike in the Clearfield County mines, the effort was unsuccessful, and when Italians were brought into the Mahoning Valley for the same purpose, they took the part of the "old miners," one of whom wrote to a friendly newspaper: "The Italians in this valley are firm as a 'brick' and are willing to stand for their rights as long as they can get anything to eat. . . . The Italians told [the operators] . . . that they had 'black-legged' once, not understanding it, but would not do so any more."

The immigrant communities, varying remarkably in their character, were ingenious in developing their own countercultures and ethnic or fraternal organizations, from burial societies to "protective" associations. These existed independently of the official public agencies under which the immigrants lived; sometimes they cooperated with the official departments and bureaus of the various governmental agencies; sometimes they were, in effect, counteragencies which pursued their own ends invisible to those authorities. What is of paramount interest to the cultural historian is the richness of the affective and expressive life of the immigrant groups. They often brought their native costumes, their songs, their festivals, their marriage and burial customs with them. These they practiced, largely unnoticed by the somber, nervous, and repressed members of the establishment (as we would say today), who, if they noticed such goings-on at all, regarded them with amused tolerance, suppressing the uneasiness caused by such uninhibited behavior, accompanied, as it invariably was, by the consumption of substantial quantities of wine (Italian) and beer (German). In a rational, orderly, planned, and increasingly scientific world, the colorful "folkways" of the immigrants confirmed the natives' sense of their own superiority.

As a sympathetic writer in the *Atlantic Monthly* put it, the members of his class were, for the most part, "anxious plodders who did everything by rule; a thrifty, grave set, whose ideal was respectability, and their universal test common sense—formalists, utilitarians, who ate, walked, transacted business, married and died, with little apparent emotion, and in a perfectly decent but extremely uninteresting way." By contrast even the simplest and poorest Italians suggested by the way they walked and dressed, by their attire and "body language" that "there was an absolutely enjoyable vein in the mere act of living . . . a possible art of being happy."

Despite their crowded and unhealthy living conditions and often abject poverty, the immigrant communities were like islands of vivid life in the midst of the larger sea of "straitlaced" Americans, whose dark clothes, stiff collars, foursquare hats, and black high-laced shoes bespoke a diminished emotional life and an obsessive concern with manners and appearances. It was small wonder that the two Americas had little contact with each other. Perhaps the principal one was through immigrant women, who served as domestic servants to middle- and upper-class families and in that role absorbed what they could of American values and ideals. The men impinged on the consciousness of the upper classes primarily as vendors, barbers, tailors, gardeners, and, most dramatically, strikers, when working conditions became so unbearable as to bring on an often futile strike.

Robert Park, a liberal reformer, expressed a characteristic concern about the immigrants' dogged efforts to preserve elements of their native customs when he wrote: "Both consciously and unconsciously they might be expected to center the immigrant's interest and activities in Europe and so keep him apart from American life." Immigrants were a special problem for urban reformers since it was clear that much municipal corruption depended on a complex exchange of favors for political support based on the needs of unassimilated immigrants. In the impenetrable world of Little Italy, family clearly was a more pressing reality than nation, and certainly more important than "reform," which to immigrants seemed most often directed at making their lives bleaker by prohibiting liquors of all kinds.

The obsession of many Americans with eugenics, with "improving the race" by suppressing undesirable traits, worked to the disadvantage of immigrants, who were widely regarded as a threat to the nation's "racial purity." Joseph Rodes Buchanan, an eccentric California physician, recommended the castration of inferior males—"hereditary burglars" and the like. "Castration," he wrote, "is the supreme remedy for a diseased and bestialized race." His "New Education" would be supplemented by "the surgeon's knife" to help carry humanity to still higher levels. "What would our vineyards and orchards be without pruning?" he asked. The same proposal was made in regard to immigrants, who, it was argued, made up the greater part of the criminal classes.

If the immigrants who settled in such large numbers in the industrial cities of the East and Midwest were the most accessible, closely observed, and best known (as well as the source of most anxiety about the foreign-born), it would be a mistake to ignore the hundreds of thousands of immigrants who settled in rural communities of the Middle West and the Great Plains states. Germans, in substantial numbers, had emigrated to Texas before the Civil War in an area running northwest from San Antonio and New Braunfels to Fredericksburg and beyond, a distance of some 100 miles. German Zwinglians, Calvinists, Pietists, Lutherans, Catholics, and a handful of freethinkers settled in the hill country as farmers and artisans. Preserving the architecture of their homeland, their games and common celebrations, they resisted acculturation, remaining stubbornly German generation after generation.

Czech migration to the Great Plains began in the 1880s, and by the end of the century one out of every five American Czechs lived in Nebraska, Kansas, the Dakotas, Oklahoma, or Texas. Approximately half were farmers who homesteaded under the Morrill Act. Others became artisans or small-business men. As with virtually all immigrants, a substantial number became journalists. Every Czech community needed its own Czech-language newspaper. Hardworking and resistant to authority, many of the immigrants were determined freethinkers. In the words of one historian, "They . . . brought a suspicion of duly constituted authority and a tradition of political radicalism, including varieties of socialism as well as freethought and strongly libertarian views." The first Czech newspaper in Nebraska was founded by Edward Rosewater, a Czech Jew who had become a prominent Omaha businessman. The Union Pacific Railroad took ads in his paper urging Czechs to settle along the railroad's right of way. After six years the paper was bought by Jan Rosicky and transformed into a free thought weekly, making Omaha a center for both free thought literature and Czech publishing. Rosicky himself became a newspaper czar, with as many as fourteen Czech-language journals emanating from Omaha, among them the *Husbandman*, directed at Czech farmers, with a circulation of almost 30,000. Czech poets and novelists described the beauty and the hardships of prairie life. Bartos Bittner, editor of the magazine *Imp*, wrote:

> Brave pioneers, view now what was that wilderness
> Into which you came homesick and with empty hands!
> From "Father of Waters" to the Rockies' Cloudy crests
> Prosperity, like sweet streams, flows over prairie lands.
>
> Success so crowns your harsh, back-breaking labor there
> That none begrudge your having viewed with joyful pride
> How skillful hands gave works a countenance fair.
> Thus we wish you well; may success with you abide!

By 1900, 53 percent of all Czechs in the United States were to be found in twelve counties of the Great Plains states. Central to the life of the Czech communities were the so-called free schools, taught for the most part by volunteers, which concentrated on Czech history, language, and literature as well as on "free thought," and the sokol, or gymnastic society, which had its national center in Omaha.

Another group of immigrants to the Great Plains in the late nineteenth century were the so-called Volga Germans, Germans who had migrated to Russia more than a century earlier, attracted by Catherine the Great's promises of free land and religious toleration. The Russian migration had proved a disaster. One colonist wrote: "The dark winter days and the long nights seemed never to end. We were separated from all mankind, and we lived miserably and in the greatest need." Nonetheless, the immigrants showed remarkable capacity for adaptation and came in time, by skill and hard work, to thrive. In the early 1870s, when Czar Alexander II began a policy of forced assimilation, including compulsory military service in the Russian Army, the Volga Germans, spurred by crop failures, began a migration to the Great Plains states. Kansas and Nebraska were the goals of the first party to pull up stakes (almost invariably communities of rural immigrants tried to find a landscape and climate resembling those of their own region, often passing up more fertile and readily cultivable land in the process). Before purchasing land, one Volga German farmer chewed a portion of soil to test if it "tasted after grain." The settlers followed their ancient practice of building their houses around the "church square" (much as the settlers in early New England had done) and walking or riding to their outlying fields; grazing lots were held in common.

Almost half the Volga Germans chose city life, working in factories in Chicago, Denver, and Lincoln, Nebraska, but even in the cities they preserved their cultural identity, not just as Germans but as Volga Germans, with remarkable success. As late as the 1930s a writer noted a "closed colony" of Volga Germans in Chicago.

Another group of Germans who had lived for several generations near the Black Sea, the so-called Black Sea Germans, made their way to the Dakotas, where the great majority became farmers. German immigration was unique both in numbers and in the speed of the immigrants' "disappearance." That is to say, they did not so much assimilate, although hundreds of thousands clearly did, as disappear into the limitless reaches of interior America.

20

The Promised Land

The immigrant group that perhaps more than any other seemed "destined" to come at last to America was the Jews of Poland and Russia. In the twenty-year period 1880–1900 roughly half a million Eastern European Jews, estimated at one-third of the Jewish population of Europe, the great majority of them from Russia and from Russian-controlled Poland, came to New York City. In Russia, Poland, Lithuania, Rumania, and Moravia the Jews lived within the pale, ghetto sections of the larger cities, where they enjoyed a degree of immunity denied their coreligionists who lived "beyond the pale" and were in consequence subject to constant harassment. When the pogroms came, the pale proved a fragile barrier against forces of persecution. "Czar" in Hebrew meant "oppressor." In the words of a Jewish writer, "The only hope for the Jews in Russia is to become Jews out of Russia."

Mary Antin (her Anglicized name), who emigrated from Polotsk in Russia to Boston, Massachusetts, with her parents at the age of twelve, recalled the restrictions and the constant insecurity under which she and her family and friends lived in Russia. That Gentile children threw mud at her and spit on her she came to accept as a matter of course. The charge that Jews used the blood of murdered Christian children in their Passover festivals was harder to endure. Stories circulated in the Jewish community of Jews in other parts of Russia who had been physically attacked by furious peasants "with knives and clubs and scythes and axes," had been tortured and killed, and had had their houses burned down. Some refugees, with ugly wounds, reached Polotsk. On Christian holidays the Jewish families of the town locked their doors, shuttered their windows, and kept off the streets. Tales were told of Jewish boys and girls who had been seized by Catholic priests and baptized as Christians against their will. It seemed to Mary Antin the most terrible thing that could happen to her. Compulsory military conscription was another bane, for it meant being exposed to Gentile prejudices with no protection and the requirement to drill and work on the Jewish Sabbath, a terrible desecration.

Always beleaguered, always excruciatingly vulnerable, Mary Antin and her friends developed whatever protective coloring they could. "I knew how to dodge and cringe and dissemble," she wrote, "before I knew the names of the seasons." Most painful to a people who treasured learning and scholarship above all else was the fact that education was denied the great majority of Russian Jews. At the high school in Polotsk only 10 Jewish children were admitted out of every 100 pupils, and for the universities the ratio was 3 Jews to every 100 Gentiles. Jews were subject to "especially rigorous examinations, dishonest marks, or arbitrary rulings without disguise. . . . Pent up within narrow limits, all but dehumanized, the Russian Jew fell back upon the only thing that never failed him,—his hereditary faith in God." The study of the Torah was the basis and support of that faith; talmudic learning, the key to life. "In the phrase of our grandmothers," Antin wrote, "a boy stuffed with learning was worth more than a girl stuffed with bank notes." The one sure way for a poor, low-caste Jew to rise in the world by acquiring a well-endowed wife was for him to make a name for himself as a scholar. It all came to that. The Jews were, after all, God's Chosen People. "Though I went in the disguise of an outcast," Antin wrote, "I felt a halo resting on my brow. Set upon by brutal enemies, unjustly hated, annihilated a hundred times, I yet arose and held my head high, sure that I should find my kingdom in the end, although I had lost my way in exile; for He who had brought my ancestors safe through a thousand perils was guiding my feet as well. God needed me and I needed Him, for we two together had a work to do, according to an ancient covenant between Him and my forefathers."

That Jews should come at last in vast numbers to the United States seemed to many Jews and some non-Jews as well the fulfillment of history. The first white settlers in New England had fled, like the Jews of the Diaspora, from religious persecution. Imbued with Old Testament theology and, even more, imagery, they had founded "covenanted" communities and consciously tried to model themselves after the "Children of Israel." They had spoken of seeking "a promised land," "a Zion in the wilderness." They had called their experiment a New Jerusalem. They had named their towns Bethel and Zoar and Salem, quoted the Hebrew prophets, worshiped the Jehovah of the Jews, and even tried to translate Mosaic law and the laws of Deuteronomy into civil laws. To them England had been "the land of Egypt," and New England a new Canaan. They had their own priestly class and their own prophets—Richard, Increase, and Cotton Mather; Thomas Hooker; Anne Hutchinson; Roger Williams; and later Jonathan Mayhew. Now, 200 years and more later, there was a new migration.

To many European Jews the United States, since its birth, had appeared as a kind of promised land. The relatively few Jews, the great majority of them Spanish, or Sephardic, and German, who had found their way to the United States had indeed found it a new Canaan, a land where the classic Jewish traits of thrift, piety, and hard work were so honored as to be generally denominated Protestant. The feeling that the United States might be the promised Jewish homeland grew decade by decade in the face of a rising tide of harassment and persecution in Europe, above all, in Poland, Rumania, and Russia, the only flaw in the title being the fact that the "homeland" was occupied by a notably aggressive breed of Gentiles. As long as the majority of European Jews were safe within the pale from the grosser forms of harassment and persecution, they preferred to stay where they were, but when the immunities of the pale and the ghetto began to break down, hopes and dreams turned toward America. *The Promised Land* was the title of Mary Antin's autobiography. She wrote that Polotsk was seized by "the emigration fever," that " 'America' was in everybody's mouth. Business men talked of it over their accounts; the market women made up their quarrels that they might discuss it from stall to stall, people who had relatives in the famous land went around reading their letters for the benefit of less fortunate folks . . . children played at emigration. . . ." A few who had returned told fabulous tales. "One sad fact threw a shadow over the splendor of the gold-paved, Paradise-like fairyland. The travelers all agreed that Jews lived there in the most shocking impiety."

The emotions felt by Mary Antin on her arrival in America in the

1890s were undoubtedly similar to those of many immigrants. Everything was, at least for a child, an object of wonder and astonishment. "Everything was free, as we had heard in Russia. Light was free; the streets were as bright as a synagogue on a holy day. Music was free; we had been serenaded, to our gaping delight, by a brass band of many pieces. . . . Education was free." That was "the essence of American opportunity, the treasure no thief could touch, not even misfortune or poverty. On our second day I was thrilled with the realization of what this freedom of education meant." A little child from across the alley appeared and offered to conduct Mary Antin and her sister to school. Mary was astonished. "This child who had never seen us till yesterday, who could not pronounce our names, who was not much better dressed than we, was able to offer us the freedom of the schools of Boston! No application made, no questions asked, no examinations, rulings, exclusions; no machinations, no fees. The doors stood open for every one of us. The smallest child could show us the way."

To Mary Antin her first day of school was the most memorable day of her life. The impressions would stay with her always with a special vividness. She had, to be sure, an unusual intelligence; "none the less," she wrote, "were my thoughts and conduct typical of the attitude of intelligent immigrant children toward American institutions." Accompanied by her father, Mary Antin and her sister were taken to Miss Nixon, who greeted them kindly. To Miss Nixon Mary's father surrendered the precious certificates designating them as pupils in the school. "I think she divined," Antin wrote, "that by the simple act of delivering our school certificates to her he took possession of America." A special class was constituted under Miss Nixon for the half dozen Jewish immigrant children from the ages of six to fifteen.

With their distinctive garments and exotic styles, the Jewish immigrants were highly conspicuous. While men wore the shtreimel, a cap edged with fur, the *peyes* (earlocks), and the caftan, a long gabardine coat, and the young Jewish brides the *sheitel* (wig), the children were permitted, for the most part, to dress American-style. "We had to visit the stores and be dressed from head to foot," Mary Antin wrote of her arrival in Boston, "in American clothing; we had to learn the mysteries of the iron stove, the washboard, and the speaking-tube; we had to learn to trade with the fruit peddler through the window and not be afraid of the policeman; and, above all, we had to learn English." To the newly arrived immigrant, a social worker appeared—a beautiful young woman dressed in expensive clothes who, like a fairy godmother, "led us to a wonderful country called 'uptown,' where, in a dazzlingly beautiful palace called a 'department store,' we exchanged our hateful homemade European costumes, which pointed us out as 'greenhorns' to the children on the street, for real American machine-made garments, and issued forth glorified in each other's eyes." With "our despised immigrant clothing" the Antin girls shed "our impossible Hebrew names." A committee of friends earlier on the scene advised on American equivalents. Mary Antin's name being Maryashe in Hebrew, she was assigned Mary.

A guidebook written for immigrant Jews cautioned: "Forget your past, your customs, and your ideals. Select a goal and pursue it with all your might. No matter what happens to you, hold on. You will experience a bad time but, sooner or later you will achieve your goal. If you are neglectful, beware for the wheel of fortune turns quickly. You will lose your grip and be lost. A bit of advice for you: Do not take a moment's rest. Run, do, work and keep your own good in mind. . . . A final virtue is needed in America—called cheek. . . . Do not say, 'I cannot; I do not know.'"

One of Mary Antin's discoveries was that American children had a longer period of grace, of play, and she reveled in the discovery. It was as though she had been "let loose in a garden to play and dig and chase butterflies," only occasionally "stung by the wasp of family trouble; but," she added, "I knew a healing ointment—my faith in America." Through all the setbacks that her impractical, if hardworking, father experienced, his daughter consoled herself with this thought: "My father had come to America to make a living. America, which was free and fair and kind, must presently yield him what he sought." America's greatest virtue was a simple one. "America is not Polotsk" was one of her father's favorite sayings. In America, he told his children, "all occupations were respectable, all men were equal. . . . It is true," Mary Antin wrote of her father, "that he had left home in search of bread for his hungry family, but he went blessing the necessity that drove him to America. The boasted freedom of the New World meant to him far more than the right to reside, travel, and work wherever he pleased; it meant the freedom to speak his thoughts, to throw off the shackles of superstition, to test his own fate, unhindered by political or religious tyranny. . . . He was hungry for his untasted manhood."

For immigrant women, especially the young women who experienced it most powerfully as freedom from centuries of subordination, the experience of being American was perhaps less ambiguous than for the men. "I was so fond of the American way," Mary Antin wrote, "that it seemed to me a pitiful accident that my sister could have come so near and missed by so little the fulfillment of my country's promise to women [her sister, a few years older, had to go to work to help support the family and accepted a conventional Jewish marriage]. A long girlhood, a free choice in marriage, and brimful womanhood are the precious rights of an American woman." Mary Antin testified that her path had been smoothed at every step by upper-class American women—first her teachers and then college classmates and friends—"because I was their foster sister. They opened their homes to me that I might learn how good Americans lived. In the least of their attentions to me, they cherished the citizen in the making."

In the Yiddish theater a whole category of plays dealt with the problem of the Jewish woman who wished a wider and more stimulating intellectual and cultural life for herself. In *East Broadway*, *The Beggar of Odessa*, and *Broken Chains* heroines contended with imperceptive and materially oriented husbands. Several popular dramas ended with the heroines committing suicide.

A young immigrant woman, Minnie Louis, wrote a poem stating "What It Is to Be a Jew." Two of its sixteen verses read:

> To wear the yellow badge, the locks,
> The caftan-long, the low-bent head,
> To pocket the unprovoked knocks
> And shamble on in servile dread—
> 'Tis not this to be a Jew.

The Jew must divest himself of such alien emblems and then:

> Among the ranks of men to stand
> Full noble with the noblest there;
> To aid the right in every land
> With mind, with might, with heart, with prayer—
> *This* is the eternal Jew!

Jewtown, as the center of Jewish life was called in New York City, was, like the Bend, dirty and, at least to Gentile nostrils, malodorous, the most crowded section of the city—330,000 inhabitants to the square mile—and the home of the sweatshops. The Orthodox Jewish men, Jacob Riis wrote, "with queer skull-caps, venerable beard, and the outlandish long-skirted kaftan . . . elbow the ugliest and the handsomest women in the land. . . . Thrift is the watchword of Jewtown. . . . It is at once its strength and its fatal weakness, its cardinal virtue and its foul disgrace. . . . Money is their God. Life itself is of little value compared with even the leanest bank account." But if one inquired what the thrifty Jews did with their precious money, one discovered that a very substantial part of it went to assist their coreligionists in illness or in want or to help successive waves of Jewish immigrants get settled in their new homes.

On Ludlow Street and Hester Street in the so-called pigmarket, there were no pigs, but, Riis noted, "there is scarcely anything else that can be hawked from a wagon that is not to be found, and at ridiculously low prices. Bandannas and tin cups at two cents, peaches at a cent a quart, 'damaged' eggs for a song, hats for a quarter, and spectacles, warranted to suit the eye, at the optician's who has opened a shop on a Hester Street door-step, for thirty-five cents; frowsy-looking chickens and half-plucked geese, hung by the neck . . . are the great staple of the market." Hats and pants and suspenders beyond counting or accounting for. The cloakmakers had their busy season in the late summer. Seventy-five cents for an "all complete" cloak of cheap plush was an average price. A workweek from six in the morning until eleven at night brought two brothers between $7.58 and $9.60 a week. The cheapest apartment cost $13 a month. In the Hester Street area many tenement houses doubled as cigar factories, three or four members of a family working at the trade in a single close room without adequate light or ventilation.

Mary Antin described the ghetto slums as "the quarter where poor immigrants foregather, to live, for the most part, as unkempt, half-washed, toiling, unaspiring foreigners; pitiful in the eyes of social missionaries, the despair of boards of health, the hope of ward politicians, the touchstone of American democracy . . . a house of detention for poor aliens, where they live on probation till they can show a certificate of good citizenship."

Being only human, Jacob Riis had his favorites among the immigrant groups he described so vividly in *How the Other Half Lives*. The Italians, with their infectious vitality, their tumultuous and gregarious style of living, their colorful attire as they flocked through the Bend, were close to his heart. The substantial black population of the city also appealed to him, but, as we have seen, he chastised the Jews for their preoccupation with money. Against Riis's indictment we might oppose Mary Antin's defense of her people. "The Gentiles had their excuse of their malice," she wrote of their life in Russia. "They said our merchants and money-lenders preyed upon them, and our shopkeepers gave false measure. People who want to defend the Jews ought never to deny this. Yes, I say, we cheated the Gentiles whenever we dared, because it was the only thing to do. . . . When there are too many wolves in the prairie, they begin to prey upon each other. We starving captives of the Pale—we did as do the hungry brutes. But our humanity showed in our discrimination between our victims. Whenever we could, we spared our own kind, directing against our racial foes the cunning wiles which our bitter need invented. Is not that the code of war? Encamped in the midst of the enemy, we could practice no other. . . . To be a Jew was a costly luxury, the price of which was either money or blood. Is it any wonder that we hoarded our pennies? What his shield is to the soldier in battle, that was the ruble to the Jew in the Pale." The instinct did not die out in America. In some ways it was augmented. A poor Jew was nobody, doomed to suffer contempt and hostility; a rich Jew or even a prosperous Jew could buy immunity from the grosser forms of prejudice. If money was an obsession with most Americans of whatever ethnic background, it was a lifeline for Jews mired in the poverty and filth of the ghetto, the only path to dignity and, if not acceptance, at least a degree of toleration. So what money was to Americans in general it was in spades to Jews; not simply physical comfort, nourishing food, fashionable clothes, "success," it was the essential basis of a feeling of personal worth, the means of procuring small decencies of life, freedom from degradation, from almost daily humiliations. It was life itself. So parents and children alike labored, "sweated," wore their frail lives away, bent over the needle, the cutting knife, the sewing machine, in order to enter more fully into the heritage of freedom.

The most spectacular area of economic growth involving Eastern European Jews was to be found in the clothing industry. From 1880 to 1890 the number of "places," from factories of one or two rooms to much larger establishments, increased from 236 to 740, and capitalization fivefold. In the 1890s the number of clothing factories increased from 736 to 1,554. Shops manufacturing fur goods increased from 60 to 232 in the decade of the 80s, and value of the goods rose from $4,474,018 to $10,665,997. What the figures reveal is an astounding expansion of garmentmaking. All this was made possible by the availability of low-cost labor-intensive enterprises, requiring very modest amounts of capital to get started, low wages and high profit margins, at least in good times. Moses Rischin notes that in 1889 "a single Bowery firm sold 15,000 suits priced at $1.95 that were produced at a cost of 1.12\frac{1}{2}$." Ready-made suits were rapidly replacing tailor-made suits, and in the process the more enterprising tailors became manufacturers of the new garments. By 1913 there were 16,552 "factories" in New York City employing 312,245 employees, or an average of 19 employees per factory. Since the larger factories employed as many as 100 or more workers, it is clear that most were much smaller operations, employing from a half dozen to 10 or 12 "sweaters." While the initial cadres of workers in the garment industry had been Germans, Irish, and German Jews, the balance swung sharply by the turn of the century to Eastern European Jews, especially in the sweatshops.

Jews made up 80 percent of the hat- and capmakers, 75 percent of the furriers, 68 percent of the bookbinders and tailors. They were also concentrated in the printing, baking, blacksmithing, and building trades.

The American public school was, of course, the principal agency of assimilation for immigrant children and the children of immigrants. It was as though the urban public school had been invented for the benefit of Jewish children. It was love at first sight, a romance extending over generations, perpetually renewed. If the school was an enchanted world for Mary Antin, her beloved conductor through that world was Miss Dillingham, the teacher who understood and nourished the potential in her small, dark, intense little pupil. "I have never heard," Antin wrote, "of any one who was so watched and coaxed, so passed along from helping hand to helping hand as I was. I always had friends. They sprang up everywhere, as if they had been waiting for me to come."

For Mary Antin the process of her "Americanization" was indissolubly connected with her infatuation with George Washington. When she and her classmates came to study the history of the American Revolution, it seemed to her "that all my reading and study had been idle until then." When it was her turn to recite, she was overcome with emotion. "I could not pronounce the name of George Washington," she wrote, "without a pause. Never had I prayed, never had I chanted the songs of David, never had I called upon the Most Holy, in such utter reverence and worship as I repeated the simple sentences of my child's story of the patriot. I gazed with adoration at the portraits of George and Martha Washington until I could see them with my eyes shut." Washington was a citizen of the United States—the "First Citizen"—and now Mary Antin felt herself "a Fellow Citizen." She wrote: "It thrilled me what sudden greatness had fallen on me; and at the same time it sobered me, as with a sense of responsibility. I strove to conduct myself as befitted a Fellow Citizen. . . . As I read how the patriots planned the Revolution, and the women gave their sons to die in battle, and the heroes led to victory, and the rejoicing people set up the Republic, it dawned on me gradually what was meant by *my country*. . . . For the Country was for all the Citizens, and *I was a Citizen*. And when we stood up to sing 'America,' I shouted the words with all my might. . . . Naturalization, with us Russian Jews, may mean more than the adoption of the immigrant by America. It may mean the adoption of America by the immigrant." Transported, Mary Antin wrote a poem about the "luckless sons of Abraham":

> Then we weary Hebrew children at last found rest
> In a land where reigned Freedom, and like a nest
> To homeless birds your land proved to us, and therefore
> Will we gratefully sing your praise evermore.

She wrote an essay on George Washington. She took it to the *Boston Herald*, which printed it, and she found herself a celebrity in the Jewish community of Chelsea. She was called upon to read it aloud in school and then to give a repeat performance at another school, so great was her fame. Eventually she became an atheist and an author. "I am glad," Mary Antin wrote, "that American history runs, chapter for chapter, the way it does; for thus America came to be the country I love so dearly."

The feeling, as is said, was mutual. For the young "native" intellectuals, the journalists of liberal persuasion, who flocked to New York and Chicago from small Midwestern towns with their rigid orthodoxies and repressive ethos, the richly expressive cultural life, the radical politics, the devotion to things of the intellect so apparent in the Jewish ghettos of the great cities were irresistible.

"I had become as infatuated with the Ghetto," Lincoln Steffens observed, "as eastern boys were with the wild west, and nailed a mazuza on my office door; I went to synagogue on all the great Jewish holy days; on Yom Kippur I spent the whole twenty-four hours fasting and going from one synagogue to another. . . . The tales of the New York Ghetto were heart-breaking comedies of the tragic conflict between the old and the new, the very old and the very new; in many matters, all at once: religion, class, clothes, manners, customs, language, culture." Added to the normal generational gap was "an abyss of many generations; it was between parents out of the Middle Ages, sometimes out of Old Testament days hundreds of years B.C., and the children of the streets of New York today." Among the brilliant young journalists that Lincoln Steffens attracted to the *New York Commercial Advertiser* were Norman Hapgood and his brother Hutchins, as well as Neith Boyce (who married Hutchins). When Hutchins Hapgood began writing about the ethnic ghettos of New York, especially about the Lower East Side Jews, his older brother, Norman, had already started to explore the rich vein of Italian, German, Chinese, and Yiddish theaters. One of the brightest young reporters on the *Commercial Advertiser* was Abraham Cahan, and Hutchins Hapgood, through his friendship with Cahan, got access to the Jewish ghetto that centered on Hester Street.

Norman and Hutchins Hapgood, scions of old New England families, had been born and reared in, respectively, Chicago and Alton, Illinois, the town made notorious by the lynching in 1837 of Elijah Lovejoy, the abolitionist editor. The Hapgoods disliked Alton, with its poky, narrow-minded ways, as intensely as tens of thousands of other bright and ambitious young men had disliked the similarly inhibiting atmosphere of the small towns in which they had grown up. The brothers broke loose from Alton to reclaim their New England heritage by attending Harvard College. Hutchins Hapgood's health had been bad as a child and he had been an introspective and somewhat morbid boy. In his own words, "the extraordinary role which the state of being crippled, or disadvantaged, or oppressed or suppressed, plays in the movement toward fuller life . . ." became one of his major preoccupations. At Harvard both brothers blossomed through the friendship and intellectual stimulus provided by William James. "There," the younger Hapgood wrote, ". . . the clouds finally lifted. . . . I became really free of myself or at least sufficiently so to be constantly cheerful and buoyant. It was then, for the first time in my remembered life, that I could relax my mind. . . . I found freedom of the spirit all about me. It was an indescribable cool pleasure to come into contact with emancipated intelligence, with men of real culture and power . . . who moved about freely in the world of intuition and thought. . . . To my surprise I discovered that men other than half-idiotic epileptics and German gardeners [his principal confidants in Alton] were capable of intuitions; that learned and respectable men were yet human in impulse and thought."

Hutchins's newspaper pieces on the Lower East Side Jews represented the best spirit of the new journalism. Witty, affectionate, perceptive, they were, above all, "reconciling"—that is to say, they presented their subjects in such a light as to make them appear engagingly human and recognizable. As such they played no small part, along with similar pieces by Cahan and Steffens, in stimulating the interest and sympathy of the New York establishment. In the swarming tenements of the Lower East Side, Hapgood sensed something that he had desperately missed in his own lonely and unhappy childhood: the marvelously sustaining spirit of a true community. Wildly exotic as the life of the Jewish immigrants appeared by the standards of middle-class America, it throbbed with exultant laughter and tears and arm-waving rage; all forms of expressive life abounded. In characteristically American fashion Hutchins Hapgood saw the ghetto as more than a collection of colorful individuals; more, indeed, than a close-knit community of faith and love. To him it offered the hope of redemption for the larger American society. It recalled the spiritual unity of the covenanted communities of New England and John Winthrop's "A Model of Christian Charity" with its heavily Old Testament orientation. To Alton, Illinois, and all its sister towns filled with the temper of denial and repression, the naysaying "Thou shalt nots" of decayed Puritanism, the "spirit of the ghetto" gave a new vision of human solidarity. "What we need at the present time more than anything else," Hapgood wrote, "is a spiritual unity such as, perhaps, will only be the distant result of our present special activities. We need something similar to the spirit underlying the national and religious unity of Jewish culture." Neith Boyce saw the power of her husband's newspaper essays and collected them to form a book—*The Spirit of the Ghetto*. After thirty publishers had rejected it, Funk and Wagnalls published it in 1902. The picture it painted of East Side Jews was so remote from the stereotype that had been created even by relatively sympathetic reporters like Jacob Riis that it was received with some skepticism.

"The Spirit of the Ghetto," Hapgood wrote in his introduction, "is the spirit of seriousness, of melancholy, of a high idealism, which, when interpreted by the sympathetic artists, illuminates even the sweatshop, the push-cart market, and the ambitious business of man. . . . The invisible east side helps you to see the limitations of respectability. . . . It wears away the unnecessary, calls aloud for justice, for truth, and for beauty, of the human being who has reached the 'limit' and is therefore reduced to fundamental ideals.''

The romance of American intellectuals with the immigrant Jews of the ghetto was not limited to reforming journalists. John Jay Chapman wrote: "There is a depth of feeling in the Jew, that no other race ever possessed. . . . These Jews are more human than any other men. It is the cause of the spread of their religion—for we are all adopted into Judah. The heart of the world is Jewish. . . . We admire the Pyramids and the Egyptians, but the history of the Jews is the most remarkable, the most notable thing on the globe. Their sacred books and chronicles and traditions and history make the annals of every other people mere rubbish—and I feel this same power in the Jews I know. They are the most humane and strongest people morally and intellectually and physically. . . . I'm glad I'm a Jew. [Chapman spoke metaphorically.] I believe that's the reason why this paper-faced civilization impresses me so little. . . ." William James wrote to a Baltimore friend: "The Scotch are the finest race in the world—except the Baltimoreans and the Jews."

Voltairine de Cleyre, the dramatic prophetess of anarchism, was similarly enthralled with the Jewish immigrants to whom she taught English in Philadelphia. "In those twelve years that I have lived and loved and worked with foreign Jews," she wrote, "I have taught over a thousand, and found them, as a rule, the brightest, the most persistent and sacrificing students, and in youth dreamers of social ideals. While the 'intelligent American' has been cursing him as the 'ignorant foreigner,' while the short-sighted workingman has been making life for the 'sheeny' as intolerable as possible, silent and patient the despised man has worked his way against it all. . . . Cold, starvation, self-isolation, all endured for years in order to obtain the means for study; and, worse than all, exhaustion of body even to emaciation—this is common."

The Protestant Passion found an echo in what we might call the Judaic Passion for redemptive social action. In the Jewish community that passion took two principal forms. For those Jews who struggled out of the desperately hard conditions of the ghetto to become "rich Jews," with all that implied of armor against a hostile world, there was the classic road of philanthropy, for their own people first but for an infinite number of good causes as well.

One of the sharpest tensions in ghetto life arose from the attacks on Jewish Orthodoxy by "Reformed" Jews, who wished to abandon the more conspicuous paraphernalia of Orthodoxy, which distinguished them from the larger culture, and propound a religion more in keeping, in their view, with democratic ideals. Even more "beyond the pale" were those younger Jews who embraced infidelism—socialism, anarchism, and various forms of free thought. More and more the Yiddish theater became the vehicle for their secular ideals. The Ethical Culture Society was an invention of Felix Adler and liberal Jews who wished to preserve some of the historical and cultural life of the Jewish people along with an "ethical" culture but without traditional religious forms. Not confined to Jews but preponderantly Jewish, the Ethical Culture Society was an important agency of reform as well as secularization.

The young atheists ridiculed Jehovah as an Egyptian god and made fun of Yom Kippur. Johann Most, the anarchist leader, was called one of the "new rabbis of liberty." Most, they announced, would lead the "music, dancing, buffet, Marseillaise and other hymns against Satan." It was this spirit that Abraham Cahan tried to capture in his paper the *Jewish Daily Forward.* "The *Forward,*" Cahan wrote, "is the working men's organ in their every righteous fight against their oppressors; this struggle is the body of our movement. But its soul is the liberation of mankind—justice, humanity, fraternity—in brief, honest common sense and horse sense."

In their tendency to romanticize the ghetto some of the journalists overlooked the tragedy of the generational conflict that characterized ghetto life, especially among those nationalities most disposed to "assimilate" rapidly. In the highly traditional societies from which the immigrants had come, youth was subordinate to age, children to parents. Without any form of retirement or old age pension, parents depended wholly on their children when they were no longer able to work. Even when both parents and children worked, the children were expected to turn over all or the better part of their wages. A survey of 200 Jewish working girls in Chicago revealed that only 5 percent had the use of the money they earned; 62 percent gave everything they earned to their parents; the others were allowed to keep some of their wages.

But the economic side may well have been the lesser area of stress. More crucial, especially for immigrant Jews, were traditional religious observances and such ancillary matters as respect for elders. Lincoln Steffens noted in Hester Street that the sight of slouching Jewish boys, sitting on the steps of a synagogue, smoking cigarettes, would be too much for a father dressed in black, with his beard and temple curls, to bear, and he would seize and shake one for impertinence. The boy might strike the older man, and a "riot" would follow with "all the horrified elders of the whole neighborhood and all the sullen youth." The police would be called, and the men in blue "would rush in and club now the boys, now the parents, and now, in their Irish exasperation, both sides, bloodily and in vain. I used to feel that the blood did not hurt, but the tears did, the weeping and gnashing of teeth of the old Jews who were doomed and knew it. Two, three, thousand years of continuous devotion, courage, and suffering for a cause lost in a generation."

Paradoxically, the infatuation of the intellectuals with immigrant Jewish life and culture was accompanied by a rising tide of anti-Semitism, some of it Jewish. When Lincoln Steffens undertook to write a series of articles on the East Side ghetto Jews, he experienced the anti-Semitism of the "Uptown" Jews. The vivid life of the ghetto was "a queer mixture of comedy, tragedy, orthodoxy, and revelation," Steffens wrote, but accounts of that life made prosperous uptown Jews uneasy or angry. One Jewish woman complained that the *Post* gave too much space "to the ridiculous performances of the ignorant, foreign East Side Jews and none to the uptown Hebrews" and tried to have Steffens fired.

For upper-class Jews, intensely proud of their German cultural heritage, to which they had made such conspicuous contributions, the appearance on the scene of hordes of poor immigrant, religiously fundamentalist Jews was rather akin to the emotions of middle-class Northern blacks who found their efforts to advance their status and to integrate with the middle-class white community threatened by the migration of poor and illiterate Southern blacks, bringing with them a rich but thoroughly alien black culture in sharp contrast with the middle-class white culture that the "old" urban black families were striving to emulate.

The older generation of German Jews had prospered, in some instances exceedingly. By 1890 there were 2,058 Jewish firms with a Dun credit rating, and of these almost 25 percent were capitalized at over $125,000. Kuhn, Loeb & Company was one of the great financial houses of New York; the Speyers and the Seligmans were not far behind. The Guggenheim financial and industrial empire stretched across the country to Denver and the West Coast and counted extensive holdings in Latin America as well. Of 1,103 New York millionaires in

1892, Jews numbered 60. Jewish financiers like the Rothschilds and the Lazard Frères had become increasingly prominent in international financial circles, generally, to be sure, in conjunction with Gentile financial houses like Morgan's. Men like Brooks and Henry Adams could see no reason to suppress their hostility toward international bankers simply because they were Jews. Rather the reverse. It was clear that Jewish capitalists were more offensive than Gentile capitalists, in part at least because of the assumption that they did each other favors and exploited Gentiles. Henry Adams wrote John Hay from London in 1895 that the British "talk of making a new Ghetto. They secretly encourage the Anti-Semite movement. After all, the Jew question is really the most serious of our problems. It is Capitalistic Methods run to their logical result. Let's hope to pull their teeth."

The "Jewish capitalist" came to haunt American dreams in somewhat the same fashion as the "Irish Catholic." Like the "Irish Catholic," the "Jewish capitalist" was loyal to a dread foreign power. At the beginning of the century Jedidiah Morse had inveighed against the Illuminati, the Freemasons and freethinkers whose atheistic doctrines (of which he considered Jefferson the apostle) threatened orthodox Christianity. The Irish Catholics, most Protestant Americans were convinced, received their orders from the Pope through his network of archbishops and priests; Jewish capitalists, by the same token, were loyal only to Judaism and each other. Gentiles—goyim—were prospective victims.

The consequence was that there were two distinct forms of anti-Semitism: the anti-Semitism of rich German Jews toward poor Russian Jews and the anti-Semitism of men like Henry and Brooks Adams against the rich "international banker" Jews.

However, when all is said and done, it would be grossly unfair not to acknowledge that many wealthy, philanthropic Jews did a vast amount to assist their poor coreligionists. The Hebrew Immigrant Aid Society, founded in 1881 to assist Jewish refugees, provided immigrants with temporary lodging and helped them find jobs. Several dozen agencies, public and private, Jewish and non-Jewish, served the needs of the Lower East Side Jews—from the Beth Israel Hospital on Rutgers Square through the Forward Building, where the leading Yiddish newspaper was published, to the Henry Street Settlement, the Hebrew Sheltering House, the Home for the Aged, the Yiddish theater, the Hebrew Charities Building, and, not least in importance, Cooper Union at the junction of Fourth Avenue and Broadway. In the ghetto there were libraries, schools, hospitals—all the appurtenances of a small city, including some thirty public bathhouses.

Jewish leaders and philanthropists, sensitive to the charge that Jews could exist only in an urban setting where their reputed proclivity for financial exploitation of Gentiles could have free rein, were anxious to encourage agricultural settlements of refugee immigrant Jews. Such rural communities would give the lie to the proposition that Jews were somehow deficient in those qualities presumed, since the days of Thomas Jefferson, to be characteristic both of farmers in general and of American civilization in particular. It was not surprising that the most prominent supporters of agricultural settlements for their coreligionists were Jewish bankers, men like Jacob Schiff, Mayer Sulzberger, and the great European financier Baron Maurice de Hirsch. Rabbi Isaac Wise was another enthusiastic supporter, who declared: "America is our Zion and Washington our Jerusalem." There was, in addition, both a historical and theological dimension to the plan for agricultural communities. The Hebrews of the Old Testament had been an agricultural people, and much of the rhetoric and imagery of the Talmud derived from farming. To establish farm communities would be also to revive some of the deepest racial memories. It was thus that the Jewish Agricultural Society became the sponsor of the colonies of Alliance, Carmel, and Rosenhayn near Vineland in New Jersey and an agricultural settlement in Utah. Four hundred Jews settled the first colony at Alliance in 1882. Actually the colonies were less small democracies run by the settlers than principalities ruled by the philanthropic organizations that put up the money to establish them, but the ties were close between the Jews of Philadelphia and New York and the colonists. In the words of one historian, from the cities "came visiting rabbis, philanthropists, preachers, lecturers, Christian missionaries, Yiddish entertainers, small businessmen, radicals, labor union organizers, vacationers, do-gooders, and . . . new immigrants."

Bernard Palitz, an exponent of "Jewish agrarianism," wrote: "The energies of the immigrant must be directed not to petty trades, not to the push-carts, or the pack on the shoulders, not to the tailor shop, but to the free, health-giving, ennobling, invigorating and plenteous farm life." The foremost representative of this spirit among the refugees themselves was Am Olam, translated as "Eternal People" or "People of the World." The Am Olam movement was directed primarily to finding new homelands for Jewish refugees from Russia, but it placed strong emphasis on agrarian ideals. The Am Olam established colonies in Kansas, the Dakotas, Iowa, Michigan, Colorado, and the Pacific Coast states. In Kansas the Beersheba Colony near Cimarron received encouragement and support from Jews in Cincinnati.

Georg Brandes, a member of the Jewish Relief Committee, described parties of Jewish refugees in Silesia on their way from Russia to the farm colonies of New Jersey. "Each has its own leader, usually a student; all group members take a vow to share all they own. And it must be understood that they pledged themselves to a full communal existence; to work on the land which they would receive in America through joint ownership of tools; all income would belong to the group as a whole. They swore that no one would engage in commerce; only the managing committee would sell their produce, on a collective basis. In this, there is a mixture of Old-Russian and modern socialist ideas, with a wonderful infusion of national aspirations." A student leader with whom Brandes talked was determined "to wipe away the old slur that Jews are capable only of trading and that they desire only to accumulate money." Would their socialism flourish in the New World? Brandes asked. "Will they be able to maintain their cooperative spirit in a society where all is based on individualistic designs? . . . It is but common sense to predict that, sooner or later, the groups will disband. But at least for the first-generation agrarian colonists the socialist orientation seems well suited."

Jewish socialists were generally contemptuous, comparing the movement to the utopian socialist communities that flourished before the Civil War and then rapidly faded away. They charged that the colonies were a capitalist plot to disperse those Jews who might otherwise form important cadres for the socialist revolution. Ironically, the fate of the agricultural colonies, started with such high hopes, appeared in the long run to confirm the argument that modern Jews were not an agricultural people. Of all those started in the last decades of the nineteenth century, only the New Jersey communities survived. Doubtless one of the principal reasons for the survival of the Vineland colonies was their relative proximity to both New York and Philadelphia, great centers of American Jewry, able to provide material support and cultural reinforcement.

From 1870 to 1897 farm prices fell almost continuously. The number of independently owned farms constantly declined, while the number of tenant-occupied farms rose. In 1896 farm prices reached the lowest level in the country's history. Under such circumstances it is not surprising that the Jewish farm communities failed.

It was a strange double world, the world of the slums, of the ghettos. The outside stared in, puzzled and uneasy, made apprehensive by the richness and vitality of lives it could not comprehend. Compelling and repellent in varying degrees to the "natives," the immigrants enacted a drama rich beyond the telling of it. They in turn, the noisome and the unhealthy, looked out from the squalor of their "detention house," waiting to be advanced to the affluent society that surrounded them, that both helped them and obstructed them; they looked out, plotting the means of their escape—most commonly through their children, cousins, nephews, uncles—those fortunate enough to have already escaped. They fretted over the loss of the old ways, the weakening of clan and family ties, the lack of respect of children for their parents, the constantly weakening ties of religion, more evident among the Jews than the Catholics.

The avenues of escape from the ethnic ghettos of large cities varied widely. For some it was the mastery of an art, most commonly music. For others it was through the mastery of words, through journalism. For still others success in a business bought a way out by movement to a "better neighborhood," abandoning a tenement to the next wave of immigrants. The fact that immigration was continuous, that it grew year by year, meant that the earlier arrivals had practical knowledge to sell to the newcomers. They prospered by catering to the needs of later arrivals—or by exploiting them. Simply by their superior "know-how," the previous knowledge of how one became an American, many prospered and were borne upward by those below.

At the same time it is important to distinguish between the various immigrant groups in the process of assimilation. The Jews, for example, assimilated most quickly and most easily. As soon as their religion had abandoned its most exotic elements, it proved more an asset than an obstacle to assimilation. Reform Judaism and Liberal Protestantism discovered much in common, most strikingly a shared zeal for reforming the world. Those immigrant groups that were Roman Catholic in religious affiliation showed a strong disposition to hold fast to the ways of the Old World cultures from which they came. The Irish and the Italians, if they assimilated readily on certain levels, remained stubbornly ethnic, as we would say today. The fact that the Jews came from a dozen different countries and brought with them, in addition to their common religious faith, already changing under the pressure of modern life, many of the manners and customs of their adopted homes undoubtedly helped in the relative ease of assimilation. But in the long run "Jew" proved a far more enduring and identifiable category than "Irish" or "Italian."

With Italians, Irish, Poles, and other Central European immigrant nationalities, their Catholicism worked from both directions to preserve their nationality. That is to say, it worked to make them more resistant to assimilation, just as it created a barrier of prejudice imposed by the larger non-Catholic society. The fact that Catholic immigrant groups established their own educational institutions from elementary school through college meant that the most potent agent of assimilation— public schools—was rendered nugatory. The mentality of ethnic Catholics had in it, for understandable reasons, a substantial element of the "beleaguered"; the Jewish mentality, by contrast, sought to possess America as, if not the final "homeland," the next best thing to it. Those immigrants who, like the Italians, collected by the towns or cities from which they had come were apt to make out better than those who came as individuals, without friends or relatives to attach themselves to. By the same token those, like Henry Villard, Carl Schurz, and Jacob Riis, who came to make their own way in the larger American society were very readily assimilated, especially if they were persons of unusual intelligence and ambition.

Mick, bogtrotter, paddy, kraut, wop, dago, kike, yid, sheeny, greaser, spik, bohunk, polack, chink—they all came with various hopes and expectations to the land of the free. Here, in a process, or a hundred processes, of infinite drama and complexity and heartache, they became that strange hybrid, Americans.

21

The City

All the ambiguities and cruel paradoxes of American life found their symbolic center in the city—all that was most disheartening and all that was most hopeful: desperate poverty and ostentatious wealth; corruption and reform; crime and culture; the "dangerous classes," made up in large part of immigrants living in crowded and malodorous tenements; the industrious and pious middle class; the growing party of intellectuals, of writers, journalists, and scholars.

New York and Chicago were the prototypes, the most vital and colorful cities on the globe; they drew the bright young men and women like magnets. The cities were profoundly challenging and problematic. If America were to explode in violent revolution, it would start in the cities, where the contrast between wealth and poverty grew more intolerable each year. If there were to be a fairer, more just and humane America, it must be created in the city.

In 1874 almost 61 percent of all American exports were shipped from the wharves of New York City. By 1884 nearly 70 percent of all imports were unloaded on its docks. The city was also unquestioned as the financial capital of the country. In a twenty-year period its banking resources increased by almost 250 percent, as opposed to 26 percent for the nation. Of the country's 185 largest industries, 69 controlling

2,416 plants around the country had their headquarters in New York. The odoriferous leather district was located near Brooklyn Bridge. Newspaper Row was near the Fulton Fish Market, the largest in the world. The garment industry was rapidly expanding north and west from the Lower East Side. Between 1870 and 1915 the population of Manhattan doubled, while that of Queens, The Bronx, and Brooklyn increased nine, four, and sixteen times respectively. Between 1895 and 1898 Greater New York was completed by the annexation of Queens, Brooklyn, and Staten Island (Richmond).

Oswald Garrison Villard remembered a New York in 1877 of filthy and unlighted streets, "so unsafe after nightfall that no well-dressed woman dared to go out alone. . . . The purpose of the city's rulers was not to make a great city, or to render life easier and richer for its citizens, but to rob and exploit all of the weaker groups. There were gangs in plenty. . . . The docks and the water front were dreadfully run down, and the horrible slums through which ocean travelers drove to reach the inadequate hotels . . . made a most dismal and discouraging impression upon all foreigners . . . few people realize how degraded, dirty, and provincial Manhattan was. . . ."

To John Jay Chapman, a New Yorker born and bred, the city was not a civilization (like Boston); it was a "railroad station." He wrote: "There are epochs of revolution and convulsion—times of the migration or expulsion of races, when too much happens in a moment to permit of anything being either understood or recorded. Such times have no history. They are mysteries and remain mysterious. Such an epoch has been passing over New York City ever since I have known it. The present in New York is so powerful that the past is lost. There is no past. Not a book-shelf, nor a cornice, nor a sign, nor a face, nor a type of mind endures for a generation, and a New York boy who goes away to boarding-school returns to a new world at each vacation." The street on which the boy and his companions used to play is taken over, let us say, by Germans. When he returns from college, they have been replaced by Italians. When he reaches law school—"Polish Jews to the horizon's verge."

Between 1881 and 1895 murders, most of them committed in the larger cities, increased six times as rapidly as the population; they were from ten to thirty times as numerous as in the countries of Northwestern Europe—Britain, Germany, and France. In New York City gangs of toughs acted as extortionists. The Hell's Kitchen Gang and the Rag Gang, among others, levied charges on small merchants for "protection," and if the storekeeper balked, his store was blown up.

Juvenile crime was a major scandal. Children, in the words of Jacob Riis, "began before kindergarten age with burglary and till-tapping. 'Highwayman' at six sounds rather formidable, but there was no other name for it." In Riis's precinct seven housebreakers and two thieves of seven and eight years of age were arrested in one year. A boy and four girls ten years old were apprehended as thieves, two of them charged with assault and one with forgery; four eleven-year-old burglars—two thieves with prior records, and two boys charged with assault, one with highway robbery—were jailed. One was a suicide. So it went, a constantly increasing number of criminals of every age category.

If the city was the symbol of the unresolved contradictions of American life, the tenement building came to be the symbol of the city's failure to cope with the problems thrust on it by the unprecedented and uncontrollable flood of humanity that poured into it from foreign lands. As Jacob Riis pointed out, three-fourths of the population of New York—more than 1,200,000 people—lived in 37,000 tenements. The "suffering and sins of the 'other half' " were, in Riis's view, "a just punishment upon the community that gave it no other choice. . . ." The tenements were "hot beds of the epidemics that carry death of rich and poor alike; the nurseries of pauperism and crime that fill our jails and police courts; that throw off a scum of forty thousand human wrecks to island asylums and workhouses year by year" and half a million beggars and 10,000 tramps. That the tenement was "the child of our own wrong does not excuse it," Riis wrote, "even though it gives it claim upon our utmost patience and tenderest charity."

A commission to inspect tenements described a typical structure in this fashion: "It is generally a brick building from four to six stories high on the street, frequently with a store on the first floor, which when used for the sale of liquor, has a side opening . . . ; four families occupy each floor, and a set of rooms consists of one or two dark closets, used as bedrooms, with a living room twelve feet by ten. The staircase is too often a dark well in the center of the house, and no direct through ventilation is possible. . . . Frequently the rear of the lot is occupied by another building of three stories high with two families on a floor." In one tenement the police had counted 101 adults and 91 children. Riis appealed to his readers for help to relieve "that vast army of workers, held captive by poverty. . . ."

Some of the tenements had cellars that extended three floors belowground. "Hence," George Templeton Strong wrote, "more crowding, less air-space, more of whatever fosters pestilence." In the basements of many tenements were "cruller" bakeries, turning out cheap doughnuts. It was a perilous arrangement, and a number of tenements burned down when the grease-filled kitchens caught fire.

The first modest reform of tenement structures came in 1869, with an order from the board of health that every tenement bedroom must have a window. The not entirely unambiguous result was the air shaft and 46,000 new windows in New York tenements. The air shaft became in time an interior depository of every conceivable filth and garbage so that air that rose above it was foul with pollution. "If we could see the air breathed by these poor creatures in their tenements," a physician declared, "it would show itself to be fouler than the mud of the gutters."

The infant death rate in Mulberry Bend, the Italian ghetto, in 1888 was 325 per 1,000—one-third of all the babies born there in that year died. Ninety-four of the worst tenements were seized in 1888; the death rate in them had been 62.9 per 1,000, contrasted with 24.63 for the city as a whole.

The Children's Aid Society, founded "as an emphatic protest against the tenement corruption of the young," in Riis's words, had sheltered 300,000 "outcast, homeless, and orphaned children and found homes in the West for 70,000 more." One of the saddest aspects of the lives of children in the tenement districts was that of child beating and abuse. The Society for the Prevention of Cruelty to Children had come to the assistance of 138,891 "little ones" abused by their parents, rescued 25,000 battered children, and "convicted nearly sixteen thousand wretches of child beating and abuse." There were 15,000 dependent children in New York public asylums and institutions. In addition, one must count the foundlings—infants abandoned by their mothers in the hallways, alleys, and doorways or on the steps of Fifth Avenue mansions. The police collected 3 or 4 a night.

Of 508 babies born at or brought to Randall's Island Hospital in 1889, 333 died. Of the 170 picked up in the streets, more than 80 percent succumbed within a few weeks. In the same year 72 babies were found dead in the streets. The Foundling Hospital of the Sisters of Charity on Sixty-sixth Street, known as Sister Irene's Asylum, had a crib just inside its front door in which mothers who were unable or did not wish to keep their children could leave them, provided only that the mother consented to nurse her child and one other before she slipped away. The Sisters of Charity had a much lower mortality rate among their infants than the Randall's Island Hospital; among 1,100 infants only 19 percent died, "remarkably low for a Foundling Asylum," Riis noted. The hospital had received 20,000 infants by 1889. When they were old enough, children were either "sent West" to be adopted by childless couples (or by farm families anxious to have more hands to share the work) or sent to foster homes, where the city paid a sum for their care. Such children were known as pay babies, and, although efforts were made to see that proper care was taken of children so dispersed, the system was clearly open to serious abuse.

Lodging House, founded in 1855, had sheltered more than 250,000 boys and girls by 1890. Those who stayed there were required to work on the premises for their board and lodging, kept clean, and taught skills such as dressmaking and typing for the girls and bootpolishing for the boys. In 1889 alone more than 12,000 boys and girls found lodging there.

Of 82,200 persons arrested by the police in 1889, 10,505 were under twenty years of age. The number of men and women admitted to all the jails, public hospitals, workhouses, and asylums in the city in 1889 was 138,332. The cost to the city was well in excess of $2,300,000, and the total "cost of maintaining our standing army of paupers, criminals and sick poor," Riis wrote, ". . . was last year $7,156,112.94. . . . The 'dangerous classes' of New York," Riis added, ". . . are dangerous less because of their own crimes than because of the criminal ignorance of those who are not of their own kind. The danger to society comes not from the poverty of the tenements, but from the ill-spent wealth that reared them, that they might earn a usurious interest from a class from which 'nothing else was expected.' . . ." The usurious landlord was the real criminal in Riis's eyes—"the man with the knife," preying on the poor and the weak.

Modest and unsystematic as aid was for the impoverished, there were tens of thousands of the indigent who lived off handouts of various kinds. The Charity Organization Society was a consortium of various charitable organizations that tried to deal with the "deserving poor." A survey conducted by the society in 1888 of 5,169 sample "cases" showed 327 "worthy of continuous relief," 6.4 percent; 2,698 in need of work, 52.2 percent; 875 unworthy of relief, 17 percent— what would be called today welfare cheaters. The last category was made up of tramps, Gypsies, "beats," and those dedicated to living by their wits rather than by honest labor. In a nation that prided itself on sharp dealing and unscrupulous financial transactions—"Smart and Slick Incorporated," as Moritz Busch, the German journalist, called us—the wonder was that the figure was not higher. The percentage of paupers in the city was suggested by "the prevalence of pauper burials," in Jacob Riis's terms. In the five years preceding 1888 the percentage of burials in potter's field was 10.03 of all burials. The proportion of those who died in hospitals as opposed to almshouses was one in five. One of Riis's most persistent arguments was the enormous cost of poverty.

Chicago had one clear advantage over New York. It had burned down in 1871 in the most destructive fire in the nation's history and had to be rebuilt. It was a "new" city, bursting with people and vitality. But it shared all the problems of its Eastern rival—crowded ghettos, "dangerous classes," crime, prostitution, and corruption on a grand scale.

William Kent, a recent graduate of Yale who was to become a pioneer in the development of "testing laboratories" for businesses, described Chicago as "a great, lank, sordid, stoop-shouldered country boy. Possibilities immense or nil. Greedy days of '49 are here outdone. Everyone has struck pay dirt, or could have struck it. Backbone is the backbone of Puritanism, but how altered! All lines of caste are thrown away; nothing but money counts in real social life, and money is quite as good as any other snobby reason for exclusiveness. There is no line in business relations neither character nor success nor anything else. . . . Almost every real estate man is a thief. Shady transactions are entirely overlooked and forgotten. . . ." The city was a "seething caldron of the world—the abode of . . . crime riot and damnation. The home of conceit and dissatisfaction, individual liberty running into license and resultant tyranny. A happy go lucky town where everyone steals for himself and forgets that his neighbor has stolen in his turn . . ."

Louis Sullivan, the architect, was not exactly a small-town boy when he arrived in Chicago in 1872 at the age of eighteen, but his emotions must have been similar to those of many emigrants from small towns. Describing the city in his third-person autobiography, he wrote: "Louis thought it all magnificent and wild; a crude extravaganza, an intoxicating rawness, a sense of big things to be done. . . ." The city had decided to "raise itself three feet more out of the Mud" of Lake Michigan. "His soul declared that this resolve meant high courage; that the idea was big; that there must be big men here . . . there was stir; and energy that made him tingle to be in the game."

When William Stead, the famous English reformer, visited Chicago, Ray Stannard Baker interviewed him about social conditions in the city. Stead had already smelled out a number of unsavory matters, ranging from police corruption to flagrant prostitution. "What do you think [Christ] would do [if He came to Chicago]?" Stead asked the startled young reporter. "Walking about and looking at things as they are today—the poor, starving, derelicts who tramp the streets, the rich men, yes and the rich churches, that will not hear their cries. What do you think He would say and do if He walked down through the Custom House place and saw the houses of ill-fame in that neighborhood?" The editors of the *Record* refused to publish Baker's interview, and an angry Stead decided to publish his own exposé of the city under the title *If Christ Came to Chicago.* When Stead's book appeared, it displayed on its cover a picture of a militant Christ driving the moneychangers from the temple. The moneychangers had the faces of "some of the richest and most notable business and political leaders" of the city, men who were notorious for their thieveries. The frontispiece was a map of the city's red-light district with the brothels in red and the saloons in black, along with the names of the madams who ran the whorehouses. Seventy thousand copies were printed, and all were sold the day the book appeared. The most tangible result was the formation of the Civic Federation of Chicago, a citizens' organization dedicated to reform. To Stead, the hope of the so-called new journalism in the United States was a brilliant young editor-publisher named William Randolph Hearst, son of George Hearst, the great Bonanza King of Western mining. Stead exhorted Hearst to give a "soul" to "sensational journalism," by which, according to Baker, he meant a "moral purpose in some social movement or political reform."

The cities were run, if one could use that word to describe their chaotic life, by an alliance of predatory capitalists and venal bosses. "Both political government and business government were run on the same lines," Lincoln Steffens wrote, "both had unofficial, unresponsible, invisible, actual governments back of the legal, constitutional 'fronts.'" The capitalists were men like Charles Tyson Yerkes, one of the shrewdest and most unscrupulous financiers of the age. Much of his money came from mergers and stock manipulations involving Chicago streetcar lines. He left his wife to take up with a beautiful, if shady, young lady, lost a fortune, and made another. Pressed to the wall by rumors that his financial empire was on the point of collapse, Yerkes went to pious William Rainey Harper, who had won his educational spurs as head of Chautauqua, and made him an offer he couldn't refuse. He would contribute a $1,000,000 telescope to the University of Chicago's observatory on condition that the gift would be announced at once but that he would be allowed to provide the money sometime in the future. Harper acquiesced, and the announcement of the gift saved Yerkes's credit.

On the occasion of the city's celebration of the Great Fire, Mr. Dooley ruminated: "We've had manny other misfortunes an' they're not cillybrated. Why don't we have a band out an' illuminated street cars f'r to commimerate th' day that Yerkuss came to Chicago? An' there's cholera. What's the matter with cholera?"

Samuel Insull was another of the master manipulators. Brought in to reorganize the Chicago Edison Company, he did so with ruthless efficiency. "My experience," he said on another occasion, "is that the greatest aid to the efficiency of labor is a long line of men waiting at the gate." Men like Insull were able, in Frederic Howe's words, "to capitalize something that they could not capitalize in other businesses; they capitalized population, growth, sanitary demands, and then sold out the capitalized value to the public."

Philip Armour was one of the most appealing of the "barons." For one thing he ground out striking aphorisms almost as readily as his plants ground out sausages. "Most men talk too much," he said. "Most of my success has been due to keeping my mouth shut." Armour was one of the pioneers in cornering—buying cheap, holding on until the demand and price rose, and then selling dear. In his case it was hogs. By 1892 Armour had a work force of 20,000 in his meat-packing houses. "Through the wages I disburse and the provisions I supply," he declared, "I give more people food than any man living." He had a practical man's scorn of professors and heavy thinkers. "If there were fewer theorists in the world there'd be more success. Facts can be discounted at any bank but a theory is rarely worth par. Stick to facts!"

When his hegemony in Chicago wheat and hog markets was challenged by young Joseph Leiter—whose father, Levi, had given him $1,000,000 for a trip around the world—Armour fought back in one of the most famous financial coups of the age. Leiter used his million to corner the wheat market and buy up futures. The Great Lakes were frozen over, and Armour could not meet Leiter's call for wheat. He offered to settle at a sum that would have given Leiter a handsome profit. But Leiter, scenting a sensational victory, refused, and Armour sent icebreakers to cut a path for cargo vessels, brought in tons of wheat, broke the market, and left Leiter with debts calculated at $20,000,000.

The political bosses were of two principal brands: city bosses and state bosses. Thomas Platt was the boss of New York State. When he was elected to the United States Senate from New York, E. L. Godkin referred to him as "probably the most despised [man] in the community . . . who has neither character nor intelligence fit for legislative purposes." He was a man "popularly believed to be the most of his time engaged in bribery and corruption," who had no knowledge of government "except as may be necessary for the purchase of officials."

Frederic Howe described Matthew Quay, the boss of Pennsylvania, more charitably. Quay, he wrote, had "welded the railroads, the iron and steel interests, oil, the coal-mining industry and manufactures into a political system. To these were added the saloons and commercialized vice. . . . He was a real ruler, dictator of an economic soviet, made up of the big business interests of the state in league with the saloon and with vice." Personally he was "a lovable sort of man. His followers were devoted to him. . . . He controlled the press. Churches, saloons, and brothels worked with him. No voice was raised against the crime of selling out the State."

One of the principal bosses of New York State was Chauncey Depew, of whom Oswald Garrison Villard wrote: "Probably no man in American life did more to debase the politics of his State. . . ." Depew had been involved in a number of shady deals, and a suit had been brought against him by the attorney general of New York for fraud. On his death the eulogies poured out. The banker Thomas Lamont declared: "For three generations he has had a place all his own in the esteem and affection of his countrymen. They had been inspired by his optimism and humor, . . . inspired by his fine and straightforward political life." Myron Taylor, president of the United States Steel Corporation, declared Depew "an outstanding example of the highest standards and an inspiration to the professional and business life of the country . . . a fine type of the courteous Christian gentleman."

The city bosses—the aldermen and councilors—played a somewhat different and more utilitarian role. They were responsible for delivering the votes of their generally foreign-born constituents to the party machine—in the case of New York to Tammany.

In Chicago, Jane Addams, the founder of Hull House, was one

of the first to observe and describe the relationship of the big-city boss to the immigrants and working-class people of the city. In an article entitled "Why the Ward Boss Rules" she described his function perceptively and sympathetically. Such essentially simple people as the southern Italian peasants who made up such a large part of the Nineteenth Ward of Chicago "deep down in their hearts admire nothing so much as the good man," Addams wrote. To them the good man was one who helped those who were in need. The boss took money in the form of bribes and kickbacks from the bloated corporations that ran the municipal utilities, from the contractors and speculators who wished favors, and distributed it to those of his constituents most in need of assistance. If, in the process, a substantial portion stuck to his own fingers, the beneficiaries were the last to complain. Hence their skepticism or indifference when indignant upper-class reformers denounced the corrupt bosses. A man who stood by his friend when he was in trouble was admired. It seemed "entirely fitting that his alderman should do the same thing on a larger scale—that he should help a constituent out of trouble just because he is in trouble," Addams wrote, "irrespective of the justice involved." Indeed, the whole system of justice appeared to be something owned and manipulated by the well-to-do in their interest and to the disadvantage of the workingman and woman. It was remote, expensive, and, above all, utterly unpredictable. It did unjust things in the name of justice, such as telling underpaid and overworked textile workers or steelworkers that they could not strike for higher wages and better working conditions or, if they struck, that they could not picket. In an unfriendly and alien world only the political boss appeared to have their interests at heart. He attended funerals, weddings, and christenings, dispensed largess at Christmas, helped spring a constituent in jail on a charge of drunken and disorderly behavior.

The alderman of the Nineteenth Ward in Chicago distributed one Christmas six tons of turkeys and four or more tons of geese and ducks, each one handed out by himself or one of his lieutenants with a "Merry Christmas." In return "the constituent," the immigrant worker, dutifully and gratefully gave him the only thing he had to give, his vote, and when upper-class reformers told him, in refined accents, that his friend and advocate the boss was a bribe taker and no better than a common criminal and that he must no longer vote for him, the constituent was confused and demoralized.

In Jane Addams's words, "because of simple friendliness, the

Alderman is expected to pay rent for the hard-pressed tenant when no rent is forthcoming, to find jobs when work is hard to get, to procure and divide among his constituents all the places he can seize from the City Hall." The alderman of the Nineteenth Ward boasted that he had placed 2,600 residents of the ward on the public roll. "An Italian laborer," Addams wrote, "wants a job more than any thing else, and quite simply votes for the man who promises him one." In effect the alderman took money from those who had more of it than they often knew what to do with and distributed it among those who desperately needed it. In the face of this, all "good government" reforms were merely temporary, all talk of "cleaning up" the city was specious. Moreover, the boss distributed the largess at his disposal without requiring the filling in of forms or questioning the motives and the morals of those who applied for it. His advice was usually limited to admonitions to stay out of jail. "What headway," Jane Addams asked, "can the notion of civic purity, of honesty of administration, make against this big manifestation of human friendliness, this stalking survival of village kindness? . . . Such a man understands what the people want, and ministers just as truly to a great human need as the musician or the artist does."

When Lincoln Steffens met the boss of New York, Dick Croker, he found him "a sweet-faced man . . . all iron grey; his hair, his hat, his neat suit of clothes were of one tone of dark grey. His eyes were kind, and . . . a winning smile spread from his lips to his eyes." He would not talk to Steffens, he told him, as a reporter, but—"the sweet smile came back to his kind old face"—"I will talk to you as man to man. . . . I will tell you anything you want to know." Steffens, in the name of advancing his political education and his search for the relationship between ethics and politics, acquiesced. Why, he asked his new mentor, "must New York, with a mayor and city council, have a boss?" Because it had such an array of municipal officials. "Government is nothing but a business," Croker told him, "and you can't do business with a lot of officials, who check and cross check one another . . ." Business was business in America, but so was everything else: "politics . . . and reporting—journalism, doctoring—all professions, arts, sports—everything is business."

Croker was "worth a whole university" to Steffens. Through the boss he began to unravel the strange equation of which William Marcy Tweed had been such a consummate master: the uses of political and economic power in an essentially ungovernable modern metropolis;

the relationship between conventional morality and practical politics; finally, the relationship between "respectable" business and disreputable politics. "There was," Steffens concluded, "no more science in society than there was in the universities; there was no political science, no science of economics and no understanding of the psychology of 'bribery and corruption'; no thought-out plan for municipal reform."

22

The New Journalists

The most urgent question facing the nation was how to check the accelerating slide into chaos, so evident in the cities, and once that was done, how to transform the city from a hell to a heaven. It was, as it turned out, to be done essentially as an act of imaginative compassion by men and women of a new order of clerisy who called themselves journalists.

I have argued in an earlier volume of this work that the United States, more than any other nation in history, was "talked into existence." The debates in the convention in 1787 to frame the Constitution were the most remarkable example of sustained intellectual discourse in history. They were followed by the often equally brilliant debates in the thirteen different state conventions that met to ratify the newly drafted Constitution. Those debates defined the nature of the relationship of a people to the agencies of its government. In the national legislature the great debate continued, decade after decade, ringing the stops on the now familiar theme. In the chambers of the Supreme Court the most learned lawyers of the day exhausted their most impassioned eloquence on the subject, and Chief Justice John Marshall, in the decisions of "his" court, spelled out the more arcane meanings and implications of the Constitution. These were the bones of the body

376

politic; the flesh was sermons, orations, political disquisitions, lectures, newspapers, and journals. One gropes for the proper analogy. Words were the nation's tissue, its nervous system, the corpuscular blood circulating in its veins.

Decade after decade the words went on multiplying: explaining, justifying, exhorting, admonishing, defining, and redefining the essence of a people, a chaotic and disorderly nation having order imposed on it by words. By the last decades of the century the words, compounded by the new technology of printing, threatened to inundate the nation. As the crisis of the 1890s grew more and more acute, the words swelled to a vast torrent—confused, bitter, angry, prophetic words. As much as it was any other "age," it was the age of journalism.

Frances Willard, who was by way of being a journalist herself, considered journalism the most promising career for a young man or woman. It, she declared in 1889, was a wide and challenging field, and, she added, "it will be a larger field to-morrow than it is today, and nine tenths of our literary aspirants, if they have the divine call of adaptation and enthusiasm, will enter there." It was her conviction, moreover, that it was an ideal field for women. "Newspapers," she wrote, "need women more than women need newspapers. Fewer tobacco cobwebs in the air and brain and a less alcoholic ink are the prime necessities of the current newspaper." Despite the sordidness of much of the daily press, she believed that "the journalistic temperament is almost the finest in the world—keen, kind, progressive, and humanitarian. Take away the hallucination of nicotine and the craze of alcoholic dreams, and you would have remaining an incomparable set of brother-hearted men, whose glimpses of God would be not at all infrequent. Anchor alongside these chivalric-natured experts, women as gifted as themselves, and free from drug delusions; then, in one quarter century, you will have driven pugilists and saloonkeepers, ward politicians and Jezebels from the sacred temple of journalism, and the people's open letter from the great world shall be as pure as a letter from home."

When Jacob Riis wavered in his determination to be a journalist, thinking his calling might be that of a preacher, his bishop told him, "No, no, Jacob, not that. We have preachers enough. What the world needs is consecrated pens."

Young Ray Stannard Baker copied out of Thomas Carlyle's *French Revolution* what was to become his own credo: "Great is journalism. Is not every Able Editor a Ruler of the World, being a persuader of it;

though self-elected, yet sanctioned by the sale of his Numbers? Whom indeed the world has the readiest method of deposing, should need be: that of doing *nothing* to him: which ends in starvation." Baker also cherished a line from *Leaves of Grass*: "For facts properly told, how mean appear all romances." Trying years later to recapture the spirit of "exposure" journalism, Baker wrote that "we were ourselves personally astonished, personally ashamed, personally indignant at what we found, and we wrote earnestly, even hotly."

While Whitman had called for inspired poets—"a divine literatus"—he had also perceived journalism as "a source of promises, perhaps fulfillments, of highest earnestness, reality, and life."

What reporters and journalists had to make clear before they could awaken a general temper of reform in the readers of their journals was that the ignorance, poverty, crime, and vice for which the immigrants were so universally condemned were not genetic traits but the result of the conditions in which they lived and, above all, of their exploitation by rent-racking landlords and callous employers.

As Lincoln Steffens wrote later, when he and his fellow journalists began their "investigative reporting," the "educated citizens of cities said, and I think they believed . . . that it was the ignorant foreign riffraff of the big congested towns that made municipal politics so bad." When Steffens's exposé of graft and corruption in St. Louis appeared, for example, the *Boston Evening Transcript* observed editorially that municipal corruption really had nothing to do with ordinary Americans, "who were a highly moral and industrious people." It was the doing of degraded immigrants. Steffens and his fellows destroyed that illusion.

It would be a serious mistake, of course, to suggest that the American press—newspapers as a whole—was an enthusiastic advocate of reform. The facts were otherwise. There were, to be sure, liberal newspapers, Democratic and Republican, and even a few radical ones, but the overwhelming majority of newspapers were, as we have noted before, dedicated upholders of the *status quo*. In response to a toast to "the independent press" at a meeting of the New York Press Association, John Swinton replied: "There is no such thing in America as an independent press unless it is in the country towns. You know it, and I know it. There is not one of you who dare express an honest opinion. If you express it you know beforehand that it would never appear in print. I am paid $150 per week for keeping my honest opinions out of the paper I am connected with. Others of you are paid similar salaries for doing similar things. . . . The business of the New York journalist is to distort the truth, to lie outright, to pervert, to vilify, to fawn at the feet of Mammon, and sell his country and race for his daily bread; or for what is about the same thing, his salary. You know this, and I know it; and what foolery to be toasting an 'independent press.' We are tools, and the vassals of rich men behind the scenes. We are jumping-jacks. They pull the strings and we dance. Our time, our talents, our lives, our possibilities, all are the property of other men. We are intellectual prostitutes."

One of the earliest and most influential of the reform journalists was Jacob Riis. Son of a Danish schoolteacher, Riis, trained as a carpenter, came to the United States in 1870 at the age of twenty to make his name in the world. He found it, as so many before and after, tough going. Motivated by "a strong belief that in a free country, free from the dominion of custom, of caste, as well as of men, things would somehow come right in the end," he found a world very different from what he had imagined and for a time felt such despair that he contemplated suicide.

Since he had read in Denmark of the wild and woolly nature of America, his initial act was to buy himself a large pistol. His first job was building huts for miners at Brady's Bend Iron Works on the Allegheny River. After that he tried mining but found it too exhausting and dangerous. Riis's fortunes went from bad to worse. He pawned his pistol to buy food and then "joined the great army of tramps, wandering about the streets in the daytime with the one aim of somehow stilling the hunger that gnawed at my vitals, and fighting at night with vagrant curs or outcasts as miserable as myself for the protection of some sheltering ash-bin or door-way." Too proud to beg, Riis often went hungry in the richest city in the world, subsisting for days on refuse from Delmonico's restaurant. He roamed Mulberry Bend, already the center of a rapidly growing Italian population, and the notorious Five Points, the most crime-ridden section of the city, where no gentleman dared venture.

Prodded from a bench or doorway by a policeman's billy, Riis sought in vain for work, sometimes spending unusually cold or rainy nights in the crowded, filthy sleeping quarters provided for the homeless at police stations. When he had a nickel, he paid to sleep with several dozen other men in a flophouse. Dirty and unkempt, he realized that he was too shabby to get work even if there had been work to get. A night in the Church Street police station proved the last straw. There he got into a fight with "a loudmouth German" about the Franco-Prussian War and had his last possession, a gold locket, stolen and his dog killed. He himself was thrown out of the police station when he complained. Furious and disconsolate, he exchanged the muck of New York for the mud of the open road and became for a time a tramp, riding freight trains, living in hobo enclaves, learning which towns to avoid. He found himself "on the great tramps' highway, with the column moving south on its autumn hegira to warmer climes."

Riis had little sympathy with the tramps, most of whom seemed to him shiftless, lazy fellows. Making his way to Philadelphia, where Danish friends lived, he subsisted on apples from orchards along the way.

In Philadelphia the Danish consul took young Riis in, provided him with new clothes and fresh hope, and sent him off to a fellow Dane in Jamestown, New York, where there was promise of work. He felled trees, worked in a furniture shop that failed, trapped muskrats and sold their pelts for twenty cents apiece, gave lectures on astronomy and geology in the evenings, worked as a hired hand on a farm, milking recalcitrant cows. He was employed as a cabinetmaker in a factory full of small, precarious enterprises. As part of his salary he was allowed to live on the top floor of the building. Thrown out of work by the failure of the furniture company, Riis joined a crew to build a railroad bridge over a dry creek bed near Coonville in Cattaraugus County. He worked on a Lake Erie steamer and then as a traveling salesman of furniture, a patented flatiron, and, most ironic of all, a fancy edition of Dickens's *Hard Times*. The times were as hard as the title; the country was in the throes of the Depression of 1873.

When Riis accumulated a modest capital, he took a course in telegraphy, but his money ran out before he completed his study. More and more the conviction grew that he must be a reporter, the highest and noblest of all callings. "No one could sift right from wrong as he, and punish the wrong," he wrote. "The power of the fact is the mightiest lever of this or any other day." Only by choosing that profession could he bring to the attention of the prosperous middle- and upper-class Americans the wretched and inhuman conditions in which the urban working class lived. "Some one had to tell the facts," Riis wrote; "that is one reason why I became a reporter. . . . I don't care two pins for all the social theories that were ever made unless they help to make better men and women by bettering their lot." Riis had no patience with those "social scientists" who told him that he was "doing harm rather than good by helping improve the lot of the poor; it delayed the final day of justice we were waiting for. . . . Those are the fellows . . . who chill the enthusiasm of mankind with a deadly chill, and miscall its method science. The science of how not to do a thing. . . ."

When an opportunity came to edit a paper designed to puff the political careers of two ambitious politicians, Riis seized it eagerly. "I was my own editor, reporter, publisher, and advertising agent," he wrote. "My pen kept two printers busy all the week, and left me time to canvass for advertisements, attend meetings, and gather the news." He collected the edition from the press and carried it onto the Fulton Street Ferry and then by trolley down Fifth Avenue to cajole newsboys to distribute it. He had also to fight off the "beats" who harassed him. When the politicians, elected to office, had no more use for the paper, they sold it to Riis on credit. He made such a success of the venture that he was able to pay off his indebtedness within a year, sell the paper for twice what he had paid for it, and depart for Denmark to marry his fiancée, for whose consent he had waited six years.

Back in New York with his bride, Riis got a job as a reporter for Charles Dana's famous *Sun*, but he soon found it was impossible to live on a beginning reporter's salary and once again he despaired of his future. Just when he was about to abandon his career as cub reporter, his city editor assigned him to the police beat in Mulberry Bend, the toughest section of the city. It was a grand prize for a young reporter, with a substantial increase in pay to $25 a week.

Riis, with his foreign accent, was much resented by the veteran police reporters from other newspapers assigned to the same post. To Riis it was, in a curious way, like coming home. He had known Mulberry Bend from the underside, lived there and despaired there, and now he was back to find his "lifework," reporting on that strange and exotic world and trying with might and main to change it. Riis's first target was the police station lodgings, such as the one on Church Street where he had been robbed and beaten not many years before—"dens" he called them. "I resolved to wipe them out, bodily, if God gave me health and strength," Riis wrote. It took ten years and the support of the new police commissioner Theodore Roosevelt. Riis's other cause soon presented itself to him—the dangerous and unhealthy condition of the buildings, the tenements, in which masses of immigrants lived. The churches had started the campaign against the tenements and their owners, and after five years of agitation by reformers, there was formed the Tenement House Commission, "which first brought home" to the general public "the fact that the people living in the tenements were 'better than the houses.' That was a big milestone on a dreary road," Riis wrote. "From that time on we heard of 'souls' in the slum."

At first there was considerable resistance to Riis and his message. People simply did not want to hear it, especially the part that laid the blame at the door of respectable owners of tenements and demanded action to remedy the evils. He found the doors of his own church closed to him, and those of many others as well. He had to rent a theater for his lectures, illustrated with slides. Josiah Strong supported him. Henry Ward Beecher's Plymouth Church opened its doors, and the reform minister Dr. Charles Parkhurst welcomed him as an ally.

Riis recalled an interdenominational meeting of ministers "who were concerned about the losing fight the church was waging among the masses" at which a man stood up and called out, "How are these men and women to understand the love of God you speak of, when they see only the greed of men?" Decent housing could be built for poor people, he declared, if builders were willing to take 7 percent and save their souls rather than 25 percent and lose them. Thinking of the speaker's challenge, Riis wrote down the title of a book he would write, *How the Other Half Lives,* and copyrighted it. He was equally impressed by Dr. Parkhurst's eloquence. Parkhurst told the ministerial assemblage, "We have got to give not our old clothes, not our prayers. Those are cheap. You can kneel down on a carpet and pray where it is warm and comfortable. Not our soup—this is sometimes very cheap. Not our money—a stingy man will give money when he refuses to give himself. Just as soon as a man feels that you sit down alongside of him in loving sympathy with him, notwithstanding his poor, notwithstanding his sick and debased state, just so you begin to worm your way into the very warmest spot in his life."

Riis's editors tolerated his obsession in part because it sold newspapers. The Grand Jury on its tours observed the conditions that Riis reported so graphically. "The City Hall felt the sting and squirmed." Riis, in the face of the massive immobility of the city's officials, persevered year after year. The public "simply needed to know, I felt sure of that. . . . But it takes a lot of telling to make a city know when it is doing wrong." When nothing seemed to budge, Riis watched a stone-cutter hammering away at his rock; he thought of the story of Joshua's seven-time march around the walls of Jericho before they fell. In New York City it took almost twice seven years before the walls of Mulberry Bend fell and a park replaced a portion of that slum—fourteen years and Teddy Roosevelt and the good government club boys and a reform mayor. In the meantime, Jacob Riis's remarkable energy never flagged or wavered.

"We used to go in the small hours of the morning into the worst tenements to count noses and see if the law against overcrowding was violated and the sights I saw there," Riis wrote, "gripped my heart until I felt that I must tell of them, or burst, or turn anarchist. . . ."

Riis found it slow, hard work. Flashlight powder had just been invented, enabling photographers to take pictures indoors and in bad or uncertain light. The flashes were fired in a pistollike instrument which frightened the subjects, but Riis realized at once how much pictures added to a merely verbal description. He got permission from his editors to hire a photographer to accompany him on his nocturnal expeditions through the Bend and along Mott Street, up alleys and into malodorous lodgings. When the photographer balked at such ungodly hours, Riis taught himself the new technique, including developing the plates. He devised a less threatening pan for the flashlight powder, and, as he had anticipated, his photographs gave a vivid reinforcement to his word pictures. "Twice," he wrote, "I set fire to the house with my apparatus, and once to myself. I blew the light into my own eyes on that occasion and only my spectacles saved me from being blinded for life."

Riis railed when reformers closed the houses of prostitution and drove the prostitutes off the streets; they took refuge in the tenements and plied their trade there to the demoralization of the younger inhabitants of both sexes and the shame of the older tenement dwellers. The Tenement House Building Company was financed with private capital in 1885 to build a series of model tenements, well lit and well ventilated. Two years later whole blocks of tenements were torn down. That was the year, Riis wrote, "I began to grow stout, and honestly, I think it was the tearing down of tenements that did it. Directly or indirectly, I had a hand in destroying seven whole blocks of them. . . . I wish it had been seventy."

He had his title; finally he had his book. *How the Other Half Lives* was published in 1890 and became an immediate best seller. Theodore Roosevelt called it "an enlightenment and an inspiration," and young Frances Perkins, destined to become the first woman Cabinet member forty-odd years later, read it and "straightaway felt that the pursuit of social justice" must be her calling. Riis, with his arresting photographs and text, had, in fact, produced the first American documentary, in-

vented a genre that was to become universal; moreover, he had pioneered the new journalism that was to dominate the coming era of
reform.

One of Jacob Riis's junior colleagues among the police reporters
of the city was Lincoln Steffens. Steffens's own life was a kind of
prolonged romance. Born and brought up in Sacramento of prosperous and cultured parents, he graduated from the University of California and then set out, like so many of his class, for a year abroad,
with particular emphasis on Heidelberg and the "art student life" of
Munich. Acquiring a wife and a mother-in-law in Europe, Steffens
returned to the United States and settled down in New York, determined to be a journalist or, as he put it, "a reporter." His ambition
was to master the "theories of ethics" and contrast the theories with
the "actual conduct of men in business, politics, and the professions."
Starting on the *Evening Post*, "a conservative three-cent evening newspaper," Steffens was soon reporting the Wall Street news and, in the
process, making himself an authority on the dealings of the nation's
money capital. He quickly learned that the master manipulators of
trusts who frequently trespassed into criminal territory loved to boast
of their exploits to awed young reporters. James B. Dill, who managed
the merger of J. P. Morgan and Andrew Carnegie into the United
States Steel Corporation, gave Steffens "a picture of such chicanery
and fraud, of wild license and wrong-doing" that he was too startled
to write it all down. Dill pressed him to write it up—"it is your duty
to describe what is done under these [laws, which Dill had pushed
through the New Jersey legislature] and if your editor shows any hesitation, you may tell him to call me up on the phone; I will stand back
of whatever you print." Steffens had learned his first lesson in democratic politics. He found that the principal criminals were not only
shameless but secure in the knowledge that most of what they told
would never find its way into print because the readers of the nation's
newspapers *did not wish to know it*. Steffens also discovered that the
politicians and businessmen who joined forces so readily to rob the
public were, almost invariably, fine, cheery, friendly fellows who carried on their villainies with a disarming charm. When newspapers
recounted the illicit transactions of such men as Dill, "you were advertising our business—free," the irrepressible Dill gleefully informed
Steffens.

From Wall Street, Steffens found himself drawn, rather unwittingly, into the reform efforts of the Reverend Charles Parkhurst and

Jacob Riis. In Steffens's opinion, it was Parkhurst, more than anyone else, who inaugurated the era of municipal reform. His exposures of police corruption forced the New York state legislature to appoint a commission, the famous Lexow Committee, to investigate his charges. The investigation "proved and exposed the police and Tammany corruption, caused the election of a reform administration, and led up to the whole period of muckraking and the development of the Progressive party. . . . Such a service," Steffens added, "is not the kind that is appreciated by public opinion and history. . . ." To Steffens, Parkhurst was a far more interesting man than the stereotyped image of the grim-lipped reformer: "a man of strength, who was 'wise' in the slangy sense and otherwise wise. He never told or preached half of what he knew." When disgruntled individuals came to Parkhurst with their stories of scandal and corruption, the minister set a team of attorneys and detectives to work tracing down the leads; Steffens and Riis followed close on their heels to report to their readers.

One of Dr. Parkhurst's agents was a young journalist named Frederic Howe. Parkhurst appointed Howe captain of an assembly district that included Greenwich Village, and gave him the mission of reporting vice, especially illegal hours in saloons. "The saloon," Howe wrote, "was the source of political power. It bred the gang, was the training school of the boss. It gathered its tribute from the underworld and provided a club for the immigrant and the Irish leaders who ruled the city of New York." Howe found in the saloons' cheerful and sudsy environment a haven of friendship and boozy conviviality. He discovered, rather to his dismay, that he liked the saloonkeepers more than he liked Dr. Parkhurst and his lieutenants. The saloons gave "free lunches, salads, fried oysters, and other delicacies that went with a five-cent glass of beer." The free food was much better than the food at Howe's boardinghouse. He could study in a warm corner of the local bar better than in the law library. Jerry, the bartender, lent a kindly ear and provided free therapy for his regular customers. When Howe chided Jerry for breaking the law—for staying open after hours and keeping upstairs rooms for prostitutes—Jerry defended himself by asserting that if he kept the laws, he would be forced out of business. To survive, in the face of the heavy taxes imposed by the city, it was necessary to break the law. In order to break the law and operate, saloonkeepers had to pay bribes to the police. Persuaded by the arguments of Jerry and his fellows, Howe resigned his job as captain of the Vigilance League and wrote Dr. Parkhurst his reasons. "You and

I," he told Parkhurst, "are in partnership with the saloon." By placing a punitive tax on the saloons, the lawmakers encouraged violations of the law. "The laws," Howe argued, "make the police grafters. An honest policeman cannot keep his job. If a patrolman fails to come through to his sergeant at the end of the week, he is sent to the woods, to a lonely beat on the edge of town." The people who made such laws, Howe continued, "are our kind of people. They are in your congregation. They take millions out of the saloon-keeper, and he in turn takes these millions out of the poor. . . . He ruins homes. Finally he corrupts the politics of the city as well. You and I profit out of the ruin. . . . We don't have to pay as much taxes as we otherwise would."

Howe found the Irish the most congenial element in New York City. They lived in a world of "political reality," far different from the world of idealistic illusion in which Howe's Johns Hopkins teachers like Woodrow Wilson and Albert Shaw lived. "Here politics was part of everyday life, part of the family, of religion, of race. Politics was daily work." Howe's head was full of abstractions taught him at Hopkins. "To me," he wrote, "politics meant disinterested service. To the people of the East Side it meant getting something for themselves and their friends. . . . To the poor, politics meant bread and a circus. . . . The God the priest talked about was nearer the people than the God I would have had them worship. . . . Betrayal of the boss or the clan was an unforgivable offense. Everybody, everybody understood it. The judge sympathized with it. The policeman was the creature of it. . . . These practical East Side politicians . . . were kindly, tolerant; good companions. Their system was human and simple, something any one could understand. It took graft and it gave graft. It took graft from the saloon-keepers, prostitutes, contractors, and big business interests as naturally as its members took help and gave help to neighbors when sick or in need. . . ."

The reformers, needless to say, were not of Howe's mind. Dick Croker, the boss of New York, found to his honest astonishment that new forces were at work. Reform suddenly became fashionable. Arrayed against him were the "honest Republicans, the fine old aristocratic Democrats, the reformers called goo-goos after their Good Government Clubs, the 'decent' newspapers, and the good people generally." William Strong ran on the reform ticket and was elected mayor in 1895. Now the question was: Could Strong withstand the ancient forces of corruption or would he, too, succumb? Everyone was aware that the most crucial appointment was that of president of the police board. Jacob Riis was confident that it had to be young Theodore Roosevelt, who had run for mayor on the reform ticket four years earlier. "God will attend his appointment," Riis told Lincoln Steffens, who wrote: "Roosevelt it was. Riis came running out into the street shouting out the news and close after him came T.R., yelling, waving his arms to reporters and dashing up the steps of police headquarters."

Like an excited schoolboy elected president of his class, Roosevelt held a hasty meeting with the other commissioners (one of whom was Frederick Dent Grant, son of the general), ushered them out, and then steered Steffens and Riis into his office, closed the door, and exclaimed: "Now, then, what'll we do?" When the two reporters had gotten TR "calmed down, we made him promise to go a bit slow, to consult with his colleagues also."

The arrival of Theodore Roosevelt on the scene seemed to Riis a kind of miracle. Roosevelt had an energy to match Riis's, and the reporter became his guide and alter ego. Together the two men roamed the night city, catching policemen sleeping on duty or loitering in saloons, hobnobbing with known criminals. One night Riis took the new commissioner on a tour of the police lodging rooms for vagrants. It was two o'clock of a rainy night when they got to the Church Street station, the scene of Riis's humiliation, the sore spot he had sworn almost fifteen years earlier to see obliterated. Riis led the president of the police board down the dank cellar steps. "It was unchanged—just as it was the day I left there. Three men lay stretched at full length on the dirty planks, two of them young lads from the country. Standing there," Riis wrote, "I told Mr. Roosevelt my own story. He turned alternately red and white with anger as he heard it." And then he "struck his clenched fists together," and declared, "I will smash them to-morrow." Within a week the order was given to close the doors of the police lodging rooms on February 15, 1896, and never to open them again. For his midnight tours with Riis, Roosevelt was nicknamed Haroun al Roosevelt and more derisive names.

Riis was convinced that his friend's destiny was to become president of the United States. When Steffens pooh-poohed the notion, the impulsive Riis burst into Roosevelt's office to ask him outright. According to Steffens, "T.R. leaped to his feet, ran around his desk, and fists clenched, teeth bared, he seemed about to strike or throttle Riis, who shrank away, amazed. 'Don't you dare ask me that,' T.R. yelled at Riis. 'Don't you ever put such ideas into my head. No friend of mine would ever say a thing like that, you—you—' " Then, calming down a bit, Roosevelt told the two startled men, "Never, never, you must neither of you ever remind a man at work on a political job that he may be president. It almost always kills him politically. He loses his nerve; he can't do his work; he gives up the very traits that are making him a possibility. I, for instance, I am going to do great things here, hard things that require all the courage, ability, work that I am capable of, and I can do them if I think of them alone. But if I get to thinking of what it might lead to—" Then, aware of how much his outburst had revealed of the nature of his own ambition, he stopped, "with his face screwed up into a knot," and said slowly, "I must be wanting to be President. Every young man does. But I won't let myself think of it; I must not because if I do, I will begin to work for it, I'll be careful, calculating, cautious in word and act, and so—I'll beat myself. See?"

Riis and Steffens were at once Roosevelt's agents and preceptors. He often summoned them from his office window at police head-quarters by giving his "famous cowboy, 'Hi yi yi.'" What Roosevelt was really doing in his nocturnal jaunts, Steffens wrote, "was to talk personally with the individual policemen and ask them to believe in him, in the law, which they were to enforce. T.R. knew, he said, the power they were up against, the tremendous, enduring power of organized evil. . . ."

"I loved him," Riis wrote, "from the day I first saw him; nor in all the years that have passed has he failed of the promise made then. No one ever helped as he did. For two years we were brothers in Mulberry Street. When he left I had seen its golden age. . . . That was it; that was what made the age golden, that for the first time a moral purpose came into the street. In the light of it everything was transformed."

When Roosevelt resigned as police commissioner in 1897 to accept an appointment as assistant secretary of the navy, John Jay Chapman wrote in his *Political Nursery*: "He was false to his character as a fighter only in this, that he threw up the sponge eight months before time was called, and left the field to the knave who betrayed him and the fool who opposed him. . . . His departure was the cowardly act of a brave man."

"The effect of the exposure and reorganization by the Roosevelt board of police was to reform the methods of corruption and graft," Steffens noted. "The reformers did not learn much, but Tammany and the vice interests did. . . ." Moreover, the honest policemen were left to deal as best they could with their enemies after the reformers had withdrawn or departed.

Steffens's first real opportunity to break out of "reporting" into "journalism" came with the purchase, by Henry Wright, of the *Commercial Advertiser*, the oldest newspaper in New York, a paper which, in Steffens's words, "looked like a wretched old streetwalker . . . when 'we' got hold of it in 1897." It had a circulation of some 2,500 at the time Wright acquired it. He staffed it with the brightest young men (and women) he could find—Steffens, Hutchins Hapgood, Abraham Cahan ("an East Side Russian socialist"), and Neith Boyce, "an unsentimental, pretty girl, who ran a romance through the city room by editing Hutch and his copy till he fell in love with and married her"— Steffens called her "quiet, golden, sharp, quick and whimsical." For the rest, Wright followed a policy of hiring out of the graduating classes of Harvard, Yale, Princeton, and Columbia "not newspaper men, but writers. . . ." Steffens wrote: "We preferred the fresh, staring eye to the informed mind and the blunted pencil."

If Jacob Riis, a penniless Danish immigrant, laid the foundations of exposé journalism, another immigrant, an equally impecunious Irishman, would make it the nation's most powerful engine of reform.

S. S. McClure was born in Northern Ireland in a two-room cottage, the son of a farmer-carpenter. The teachings of the common school were supplemented by *Pilgrim's Progress*, Foxe's *The Book of Martyrs*, and the Bible. When McClure was eight, his father, working in the shipyards at Greenock, Scotland, was killed in an accident. His mother, left with three small children, was unable to manage the farm and decided to come to the United States, where two brothers and two sisters lived in Indiana. At Valparaiso, Indiana, young Sam McClure heard his first Fourth of July oration from a Democratic candidate for Congress. "He talked about the land of freedom," McClure recalled, "of popular institutions, and unbounded opportunities. I had never heard such a speech before. All these sentiments were new to me and moved me very deeply, . . . I felt that, as he said, here was something big and free—that a boy might make his mark on those prairies. Here was a young country for Youth." The children were farmed out to relatives. McClure's mother worked as a maid and then, determined to keep her family together, as a washwoman, washing and ironing for $1.75 a day. In the hard times that followed the war, the McClure family felt actual want. The only work his mother could get paid $2 a week. "I remember the hardship," he wrote years later, "of having to eat frozen potatoes boiled to a kind of grey mush. I did not thrive on this nourishment," he added. "Before the winter was over I had become so weak that my hands were very unsteady and I could not carry a glass of water without spilling it." Sam's principal intellectual nurture as well as his entertainment came from reading newspapers and magazines, among the latter the *Century Magazine* and *St. Nicholas Magazine*.

When Mrs. McClure remarried, she began a modest business making butter. "Besides milking and making butter for market," McClure recalled, "my mother did all the housework, the cooking and washing and ironing and caring for the children." She bore four more children, three of whom died in infancy. At the age of fourteen Sam McClure set out to fend for himself. With $1 in his pocket he decided to work his way through high school in a nearby town. He found an employer who gave him room and board in return for chores—making the fire in four stoves every morning at five-thirty, milking the cow and feeding the horses before he left for school. After school there was another round of chores until suppertime. On Monday morning he rose at one o'clock to help with the family wash. Without money, McClure was unable to replace his worn clothing or even buy an overcoat against the bitter winter chill. When it was cold, he ran. "Speed was my overcoat." At the age of sixteen Sam and a friend opened a butcher shop, trusting their customers to pay at the end of the month. Few did, and the boys soon found themselves bankrupt. They tried getting a job grading for the Baltimore & Ohio Railroad, and then, unable to save enough to return to school, Sam McClure got a job in Valparaiso in the Kellogg iron foundry at $4 a week. When the Depression of 1873 closed the factory and left McClure without a job, he became so discouraged that he "began to think of throwing up everything and taking to the road as a tramp." Indeed, he escaped being a tramp, he was convinced, "so narrowly that I have always felt that I know exactly what kind of one I should have been," he wrote years later.

Graduated from the Valparaiso High School after frequent interruptions to sustain body and soul, McClure decided to go to Knox College in Galesburg, Illinois. Arriving at Galesburg penniless, he lived for the first month on bread, soda crackers, and grapes. Once more he began the slow and laborious process of working to pay for his food and tuition, enrolling until his funds were exhausted and then dropping out to find another job and accumulate a little cash. So it went, month after month and year after year, enlivened for McClure by the fact that he fell in love with Harriet Hurd, the beautiful and accomplished daughter of his classics professor, who used every resource at his command to discourage the romance. After a visit with his mother to the old country, McClure returned to Knox, visited Harriet, and asked her "whether, if I turned out to be a good man, she would marry me in seven years." Harriet, who was a senior at Knox with a brilliant academic record (McClure was a sophomore), said she would, and McClure went away "feeling that the most important thing in my life was settled."

The constant expedients, the hard work, the long hours took their toll on young McClure. By the time he was twenty years old he had developed a strong aversion to manual labor of any kind. "I had always hated chores, and I had been a chore boy since I was eleven years old," he wrote. "Now my patience was exhausted." He redoubled his efforts at Knox, convinced that the only path out of a life of unremitting physical labor lay through its portals. Half-starved and more than half-frozen, he studied every moment he could spare. Harriet Hurd's father gave her $5 for a birthday present; she gave it to McClure, and he bought half a ton of coal with it. Surviving the school year, he got a job peddling an improved coffeepot. Next came a restaurant and then a stint as a grocery clerk. Finally, he got a job as a traveling salesman selling microscopes. To McClure it was one of the happiest summers of his life. He and a young companion "lived in the open, in the woods and groves, near the little towns in which we peddled and traded and bought our food. When we tired of one neighborhood, we would board a convenient freight-car and go on." At Knox, McClure helped run the school newspaper, the *Knox Student*. It was the beginning of one of the notable careers in American journalism. Before the year was out, McClure had written and printed a pamphlet entitled *The History of Western College Journalism*. The only cloud in his sky was the fact that he had not seen Harriet Hurd for five years. During the course of his senior year Harriet returned from a teaching post at the University of Nebraska, and their friendship resumed as though it had never been interrupted.

McClure's commencement oration was on "Enthusiasm." It lasted five minutes. In it the young orator declared "that the men who start the great new movements in the world are enthusiasts whose eyes are fixed upon the end they wish to bring about—that to them the future becomes present. It was when they believed in what seemed impossible," McClure added, "that the Abolitionists did most good, that they created the sentiment which finally did accomplish the impossible. . . . It is not the critical, judicial type of mind . . . that generates the great popular ideas by which humanity rights itself." McClure, reprinting his oration, added a poignant aside: "I had looked forward for eight years to graduating, and I had always thought that when I graduated I would be tall, that I would know a great deal, and that I would have all the plans made for my life. Here I was no taller, no wiser and with no plans at all. The future was an absolute blank ahead of me."

Sam McClure, no taller or wiser, decided to go East to find out why he had not heard from Harriet and to seek his fortune. Rebuffed by Harriet in an "interview almost too painful to describe," he found a temporary refuge with his former elocution teacher from Knox College, who lived near Boston. There he went to the Pope Manufacturing Company, which turned out bicycles. It was run by Colonel Albert Pope, a genius in advertising, whose maxim was "Some advertising is better than others, but all advertising is good." When McClure applied for a job, Pope, only thirty-nine himself, instantly recognized in the handsome, enthusiastic young man a kindred spirit. The only job open in the company was the temporary one of teaching prospective riders to ride at a nearby bicycle rink. McClure had never ridden a bicycle or "even been very close to one; but," he recalled, "I was in the predicament of the dog that had to climb a tree." In a few hours he learned to ride and was soon teaching others. The next day he was paid $1, and although he was not told to return, he did so, and while he was not exactly "engaged," he was not exactly fired either. At the end of the week Pope put him in charge of one of his rinks. A few months later he called him into his office and asked him if he would be interested in editing a magazine on bicycling, the *Wheelman,* that he planned to start primarily to promote his bicycles.

The first issue of the *Wheelman* came out two months after McClure had graduated from Knox. Up to this point, McClure noted later, he had lived in the future. Now he had "attached himself to something vital, where there was every possibility of development. I was in the big game, in the real business of the world; and I began to live in the present." Many times in the future, when he passed the recessed door of the Pope Manufacturing Company, McClure reflected that it was there that he had said good-bye to his youth. "When I have passed that place," he wrote, ". . . I have fairly seen him standing there—a thin boy, with a face somewhat worn from loneliness and wanting things he couldn't get. . . . When I went up the steps, he stopped outside; and now it seems to me that I stopped on the steps and looked at him, and that when he looked at me I turned and never spoke to him and went into the building. I came out with a job, but I never saw him again, and now I have no sense of identity with that boy; he was simply one boy whom I knew better than other boys. He had lived intensely in the future and had wanted a great many things. It tires me, even now, to remember how many things he had wanted. He had always lived in the country, and was an idealist to such an extent that he thought the world was peopled exclusively by idealists. But I went into business and he went back to the woods."

In S. S. McClure's disarmingly simple memoir of his early life, his reflection on the boy he left behind is the only portion that rises to true eloquence. It could stand as the archetypal expression of innumerable ambitious, idealistic young Americans who, in every generation, put aside the dreams of youth and entered into the serious business of the world, few, to be sure, as brilliantly as Sam McClure.

Bicycling was the first outdoor sport to seize the imaginations of Americans. Suddenly bicycling was all the rage. American men, it was pointed out, led sedentary lives and suffered from lack of clean air and wholesome exercise. Young Sam McClure, editing the *Wheelman* for Colonel Pope, found himself inundated by articles from bicycling enthusiasts, who, he wrote, "sent us articles on everything that had to do with bicycling." Many were accounts of extended "tours" made through the countryside and illustrated with photographs taken by the travelers. The magazine soon had a department devoted to clubs, meets, and races. The well-known poetess Harriet Spofford was engaged by McClure to write for the *Wheelman*. The magazine flourished, and he resumed his siege of Harriet Hurd's affections. She succumbed at last, and they were married in Galesburg, "seven years lacking three days from the date of our first boy-and-girl engagement," McClure wrote.

From the *Wheelman* McClure went on to the *Century Magazine*. While he was working for the *Century Magazine* in a comparatively humble capacity, the notion of syndicating articles for magazines and newspapers hit him with the force of revelation. He already prided himself on an instinct about what sorts of articles and stories would have the widest appeal to prospective readers. It seemed eminently logical to commission well-known writers to write such pieces, which could be sold to numerous journals rather than to one and sold for sums small enough to be afforded by newspapers of modest size. If enough such papers could be prevailed upon to sign up with the "syndicate," authors could make as much money as (or indeed, more money than) they could make writing for the best-paying journals like the *Century* and the *Atlantic Monthly*. Logical as it seemed, the notion was not an immediate success. It took McClure vast labors and considerable money, much of it borrowed, and several anxious years before his syndicate was on firm financial ground. Authors as well known as the short story writer Frank Stockton were joined by Robert Louis Stevenson, Rider Haggard, Conan Doyle, James Barrie, and Rudyard Kipling.

The idea of syndication was as brilliant as it was obvious. The existing conservative and old-fashioned journals took the line that there was a strictly limited supply of good writers and, in consequence, of good stories and articles. These they competed for discreetly. Sam McClure's notion that there was, in fact, a virtually unlimited supply seemed to them as bizarre as the suggestion that money grew on trees. McClure's genius was to apply to literary production the classic principles of supply and demand. Demand produced supply. The development of modern industrial capitalism had depended on new methods of distribution; the railroads solved that problem, enabling industrial capitalism to burgeon. Syndication was to the literary world what the railroad and the assembly line were to the world of industrial capitalism. With a vast new market, literary production (or at least journalism) doubled and then tripled and quadrupled. "Literature," it turned out, was not much different from sewing machines or bicycles; it, too, could be mass-produced. Alexis de Tocqueville, in the 1830s, had predicted a democratic literature. What Sam McClure stumbled upon or intuited was that every red-blooded middle-class American youth—women, it turned out, as well as men—wished above all else to be a writer and thus avoid "work" and all its attendant stresses and strains.

But McClure's ambition was to be an editor. Syndication was simply a stepping-stone. With borrowed capital McClure and two college friends, John S. Phillips and Edgar Brady, launched *McClure's Magazine* in the fall of 1893. Not long after the magazine had published its first issue (it went through the period of chronic crisis that seems to have marked virtually every successful publishing enterprise in its infancy), McClure received an article on "the paving of the streets of Paris," an unpromising topic by an unknown writer named Ida Tarbell. When

McClure read it, he said to John Phillips, "This girl can write. I want to get her to do some work for the magazine." McClure tracked Tarbell down in Paris, where a twenty-minute appointment turned into a three-hour intellectual feast. As soon as McClure could scrape together the money, he offered Ida Tarbell an editorial position on his magazine. Thus began the most fruitful alliance in the history of American journalism.

Born in Hatch Hollow, Pennsylvania, in 1857, Ida Tarbell had graduated from nearby Allegheny College, taught school in Ohio, and then gone to work for the *Chautauquan*, a journal of the reform-minded Chautauquans. After some years on that journal, at the age of thirty-four Tarbell left for Paris. There she attended the Sorbonne and did research on the role of women in the French Revolution.

Ida Tarbell's serialized "Life of Napoleon" raised *McClure's* circulation from 40,000 to 80,000 within a few months. She followed it with a "Life of Lincoln." Again circulation had a meteoric rise—120,000, 175,000, and then, five months after the series had started, 250,000, by far the largest circulation of any magazine in the country, greater than the combined circulation of its principal rivals—the *Century*, *Harper's*, and *Scribner's*. The enormous increase in circulation threatened to ruin the magazine. Its advertising rates had been based on a circulation of 60,000, but with increased printing and distribution costs far exceeding the returns from the new subscriptions, *McClure's* found itself $285,000 in debt at the end of the year. "I was thirty-nine years old," McClure wrote, "had been out of college fourteen years, and I had never been out of debt."

But he weathered the crisis. Soon the magazine was making handsome profits. In addition to Ida Tarbell, McClure hired Ray Stannard Baker, who had already made a name for himself as a reporter for the *Chicago News-Record*. The staff of *McClure's* was young when Baker joined the magazine. McClure himself was forty-one. Baker was twenty-eight. Benjamin Franklin Norris, called Frank by his friends, was the same age. Most of the authors published by *McClure's* were also young. Stephen Crane was twenty-seven. A promising Kansas journalist and editor named William Allen White was under thirty. Jack London, a West Coast writer, was twenty-three. Booth Tarkington, whose novel *The Gentleman from Indiana* was published serially in *McClure's* (Baker called it "a fresh breath of life: a book full of the America of the Middle West"), was twenty-nine. Kipling, one of *McClure's* "regulars," told him,

"It takes the young man to find the young man," as sound an editorial principle, one suspects, as any ever enunciated. Certainly it was true in McClure's case.

The daily luncheons at the Ashland House were full of excited and exuberant talk and often supplemented by distinguished visitors whose stories or articles had been published in *McClure's*. Kipling, querulous and solemn, was a decided disappointment, but Admiral Peary, Bliss Perry, and Hamlin Garland were interesting additions to the company of young journalists.

S.S., as he was called by his associates, was "all intuition and impulse, bursting with nervous energy," in Baker's words. He was also bursting with ideas for new magazines and new publishing ventures. His alter ego was John S. Phillips, his college-mate. If McClure was "all intuition and impulse," Phillips was all system and order. "I got into this precarious world of the printed word," Baker wrote years later, "largely as a result of his perfected art of editorial midwifery."

McClure may have been chronically short of funds, but he was never lacking ideas. He threw them off as a pinwheel throws off sparks. *McClure's* initiated a series of interviews "with noted men about their life and work" that proved enormously popular. They were called the "Human Document" series, a name suggested by the French author Alphonse Daudet, who exclaimed when the idea was described to him (and he was asked to grant an interview illustrated with photographs), *"Véritables documents humaines!"* With the "Human Document" series, McClure penetrated a kind of psychological frontier. He invented, as it were, a new way of perceiving public figures. They had been known hitherto by their works. To try to penetrate their personal lives, their human foibles and eccentricities would have seemed to an earlier generation an impertinence bordering on indecency. The very notion that a famous public figure had a private life raised, by extension, troubling questions about the relation of a writer or artist to other individuals and to the larger society. An individual had been conceived of as a person responding to certain clearly stated moral imperatives or mores. The "Human Document" series revealed a new notion of human personality far more richly colored, even on occasion eccentric.

The magazine also pioneered in a "new method of dealing with the latest discoveries of science. . . . It gave the reader himself the sense of exploration in an undiscovered country which the editors called 'The Edge of the Future.'" Professor Marie Curie discovered radium, and *McClure's* hastened to inform its readers of the new miracle. It had been preceded by Professor Wilhelm Roentgen's discovery of X rays. "In some ways," Ray Stannard Baker wrote, "this seemed the most astonishing of all recent discoveries. . . ." *McClure's* "made much of photographic illustrations taken *through* animals and even human beings."

McClure's was the first magazine to assign a writer to do a story in depth, as we would say today: to commission him or her to take weeks or months, if necessary, to track down all the pertinent facts about a particular person or event. As McClure put it, "I decided to pay my writers for their study rather than for the amount of copy they turned out—put the writer on such a salary as would relieve him of all financial worry and let him master a subject to such a degree that he could write on it, if not with the authority of a specialist, at least with such accuracy as could inform the public and meet with the cor-roboration of experts . . . they were the first accurate studies of this nature that had then appeared in a magazine in America. To secure this accuracy, to make such studies of value, I had to invent a new method of magazine journalism." The "exposure articles," Baker wrote, "demanded special care as to accuracy and fairness. . . . But what a boon to the writer! To be able to take his time, saturate himself with his subject, assure accuracy by studying the subject at first hand and consulting every possible expert. . . ."

The most serious rival to Sam McClure as a journalistic innovator was young Edward Bok. Bok had come to the United States from Holland in 1870 at the age of seven. The Boks belonged to a prosperous middle-class Dutch family, but business failure had forced the elder Bok to come to the United States to try to re-establish himself. Young Edward was acutely aware, especially after his father's early death, of his mother's decline in worldly fortune, and he set himself, at a tender age, the task of restoring her to the standard of living to which she had once been accustomed. He divided his time rigorously among helping his mother with the household chores, doing odd jobs to aug-ment her very modest income from taking in boarders, and applying himself conscientiously to his studies. As he put it in his third-person autobiography *The Americanization of Edward Bok*, "the American spirit of initiative had entered deep into the soul of Edward Bok."

At the age of thirteen Bok left school and became an office boy of the Western Union Telegraph Company, then owned by Jay Gould, at $6.25 a week. He read in *Appleton's Cyclopedia* about all the great merchant princes of the United States who had started life as poor as he and by thrift and industry had in time become millionaires. He walked five miles to work to save bus fare and put away his lunch money to buy improving books. He began writing to prominent public figures, Emerson among them, to solicit their advice and collect their signatures. His goal in life soon took shape. He would be a journalist, despite discouragement from his mother and from the great Gould himself. Finding a job as stenographer with the publishing house of Henry Holt (with a helping hand from Henry Ward Beecher), Bok started the Bok Syndicate Press. In this role he turned his attention, "for the first time, to women and their reading habits. He became interested in the fact that the American woman was not a newspaper reader. He tried to find out the psychology of this" and, after considerable research and cogitation, concluded that "the absence of any distinctive material for women was a factor." His inspiration was a syndicated column called "Bab's Babble." Unable to locate a suitable "Bab," Bok at first wrote the column himself. "It was," he noted later, "an instantaneous success, and a syndicate of ninety newspapers was quickly organized." Ella Wheeler Wilcox, one of the popular novelists of the day, was next enlisted to do a column under her own name, and this led in turn "to the idea of supplying an entire page of matter of interest to women. . . . The young syndicator now laid under contribution all the famous women writers to write on women's topics," and so one of the most spectacular journalistic careers of the age was launched. Bok was eighteen. He was soon summoned by Cyrus Curtis, head of the Curtis Publishing Company and publisher of the *Saturday Evening Post,* to assume the editorship of a magazine entitled the *Ladies' Home Journal,* started by Curtis's wife and with a solid subscribership of 400,000 in 1890. "He had found every avenue leading to success wide open and certainly not overpeopled," Bok wrote. "He looked at the top, and instead of finding it overcrowded, he was surprised at the few who had reached there; the top fairly begged for more to climb its heights." At every advance in his career and salary young Bok's first thought was to provide more amply for his mother. "She was the only woman he really knew or who really knew him. His boyhood days had been too full of poverty and struggle to permit him to mingle with the opposite sex. . . . He did not dislike women, but it could not be said he liked them," he wrote. They had never interested him. Of women, therefore, he knew little; of their needs less. Nor had he the slightest desire, even as an editor, to know them better or to seek to understand them." As editor of the *Ladies' Home Journal,* however, he overcame his natural repugnance for women, his mother excepted, sufficiently to employ "an expert in each line of feminine endeavor," with the single condition that she answer every letter addressed to her in her character as a writer for the *Journal*. To advise those women whose problems were too delicate to discuss in the pages of the *Journal*, Bok hired Mrs. Lyman Abbott, wife of the famous preacher, to respond personally and authorized her to create a network of qualified women in every part of the country to give assistance to those women in need of it. In addition, Bok offered college scholarships to young men and women who sold the largest number of subscriptions to the *LHJ*, "the complete offer being a year's free tuition, with free room, free board, free piano in their own room, and all traveling expenses paid." By 1919, 1,453 such scholarships had been awarded.

It was soon apparent to Bok that young American women were, through the prudishness of their mothers, woefully unprepared for motherhood—"in desperate ignorance." He hired qualified doctors and nurses to write for a regular department of the magazine with practical information. One of his most successful innovations was a series devoted to "the daughters of famous men." Finally, Bok was the first editor of a major magazine to devote large sums of money—$400,000 in one year—to advertising feature articles in upcoming editions of the *LHJ*. Soon the *Ladies' Home Journal* became a kind of Bible to millions of American women.

In 1901 McClure hired Lincoln Steffens away from the *Commercial Advertiser*. Steffens's major preoccupation was the relationship between corrupt politicians and private business that was painfully evident in very large American cities.

If McClure was the untidy genius of the magazine and Phillips the method and system, Ida Tarbell was the reigning queen, a brilliant editor as well as writer. "It was Miss Tarbell," Steffens wrote, "a devoted friend of S.S., a devoted friend of all of us, who with her tact . . . found a way to compromise and peace. . . . Sensible, capable, and very affectionate, she knew each of us and all our idiosyncrasies and troubles. She had none of her own so far as I ever heard. When we were deadlocked we might each of us send for her, and down she would come to the office, smiling, like a tall, good-looking young mother, to say, 'Hush, children.'" McClure's dependence on her was abundantly evident. "If you enjoy a story," he told Steffens, "I am confident that 10,000 readers will like it. If Miss Tarbell likes a thing, it means that fifty thousand will like it. That's something to go by. But I go most by myself. For if I like a thing, then I know that millions will like it. My mind and taste are so common that I'm the best editor."

Tall, handsome (one thought at once of the word "regal" to describe her bearing), Tarbell was discreetly seductive and at the same time reassuringly motherly. "It is difficult for me to express the growing admiration and affection I have felt for her down through all the years," Ray Stannard Baker wrote in his old age. ". . . She is beautiful with virtue—so generous, so modest, so full of kindness, so able, so gallant—and yet with such good sense and humor. . . . So fearless a writer, so honest, so interesting, with such ability to infect her pages with her own shining love of truth."

Ida Tarbell suggested to Lincoln Steffens that an interesting article might be written about "certain admirable aspects of the city government of Cleveland." So Steffens departed for the Ohio city "with no definite idea in his mind." On the way he got diverted to St. Louis. What he found there astonished him and the country, not to say the world: a network of municipal graft and corruption on such a scale as to boggle the mind. The "shame" of St. Louis would, in time, become the initial episode in *The Shame of the Cities.*

Americans had lived, since the early days of the Republic, a kind of schizophrenic existence, as we have had occasion to point out. On one level they constantly proclaimed the glory, the untarnished splendor of the United States of America, exemplar of justice, equality, liberty, freedom, the Chosen of the Lord, the saving Remnant of Humanity in general. On another level they experienced an often quite different reality: slavery; injustice, crudity, violence; the debauching of the Indians; intolerance of Catholics, of the Irish, of the Germans, of immigrants in general; chronic depressions and devastating failures; defeated hopes; lives warped by unending toil. Since the nightmare of the Civil War industrial capitalism had added another dark chapter, a new slavery of exploitation and corruption that seemed beyond comprehension and control. McClure's young editors set out to explore the no-man's-land between the illusion and the reality. It was to become the great intellectual exploration of modern times.

What most Americans who lived in large cities "knew," at least on one level of their consciousness, and took for granted or otherwise suppressed, was now out in the open. Stories of skulduggery in high places have an irresistible appeal under almost any circumstances, but the reaction of Americans to the revelations that now followed those of St. Louis, one upon another, may also have been received with a sense that at last the façade of rectitude had been stripped away and the ideal had been forced to confront the real. McClure wrote in his memoir: "When I came to this country, an immigrant boy, in 1866, I believed that government of the United States was the flower of all the ages—that nothing could possibly corrupt it. It seemed the one of all human institutions that could not come to harm." Most Americans shared his feelings to a greater or lesser degree. McClure was inclined to take the line that municipal corruption was, to a large degree, a consequence of the general demoralization produced by the war, but, as we are well aware, municipal (and state and even Federal) corruption has a long history, extending back to the early years of the century. What is interesting about McClure's observations is that they reveal the disposition of Americans to assume that the corruption that they saw about them in every generation was a recent phenomenon, that there had been an earlier, incorruptible age before morals had declined. Periodically episodes such as Boss Tweed's pillage of New York forced themselves on the attention of the public by their sheer magnitude; but the clamor soon died away, and such occurrences were, in any event, treated as aberrations, exceptions to the rule in a generally honest and pious society. Now the exposé journalists were piling up irrefutable evidence that wholesale corruption was as American as apple pie. It was both a rude shock and titillating. In addition, it provided radical critics of American capitalism and more cautious civic reformers with fresh ammunition. Soon it was all the style; new magazines sprang up with new revelations. Respectable old journals got into the business in self-defense.

It became evident, in Baker's words, "that a large number of thoughtful Americans were growing increasingly anxious or indignant about the lawless conditions existing in so many walks of our life." In his autobiography Baker headed the chapter in which he told of joining *McClure's* with the title "I Discover the Great American Renaissance." He wrote years later: "Looking back, I have thought of the period in America, including the last few years of the nineteenth and the early years of the twentieth, as the American Renaissance, even the Great American Renaissance." What came to Baker with the force of revelation was that America and Americans "were not absolutely perfect." As a member of the staff of *McClure's* Baker found himself "suddenly and joyously, in this new world, full of strange and wonderful new things, and I at the heart of it."

Another young reform-minded journalist was George Creel, who came from a small town in Missouri. Creel's first job was with the *Kansas City World*. Then he set off for New York to "take up where Edgar Allan Poe had left off." He arrived in that city, half-starved and looking more like a hobo than an ambitious young journalist from the skeptical state. After weeks of increasingly desperate searching he found he could sell humorous sketches to a number of papers at $2 per joke and so kept body and soul together. William Randolph Hearst's *American* offered Creel a job on the staff of the paper's comic supplement. He thus found himself deep in the *Katzenjammer Kids, Foxy Grandpa,* and *Buster Brown.* He saw Hearst, "very Western in his black, broad-brimmed Stetson." Creel also came to know the genius of yellow journalism, Morrill Goddard, "a gaunt, nerve-wracked man with a pair of mad eyes." Goddard confessed that his ideal was to have "the reader reel back after one look at the first page" of a typical edition, screaming, "My God! Oh, my God!"

Arthur Brisbane was the son of Albert Brisbane, the promoter of the Fourier Communes in the 1830s and 1840s. Brisbane had been the brilliant and unscrupulous editor of Joseph Pulitzer's *New York World* and had engaged in a circulation battle with Hearst's *Journal.* He had just joined Hearst, "zooming the circulation of the *Evening Journal* up to dizzy heights." Creel noted that Brisbane hammered on an old typewriter and talked into a recording machine at the same time.

It has been observed that the first generation of young exposé journalists and editors was, almost without exception, from the Midwest or Far West, although the meaning of this has been less generally commented on. Their appearance in the East (some remained identified with Chicago and the Middle West) signified the displacement (or replacement) of the New England literary establishment by a wholly new and fundamentally more "American" type. There had been earlier arrivals like William Dean Howells and, in a somewhat different mode, John Hay. But they had been domesticated by the reigning lords of literature. They took their intellectual clues from such men as Thomas Wentworth Higginson and James Russell Lowell. Now there was an invasion of young men with very different views and perspectives. They had no piety toward class or caste. They did not depend on dividends from giant industries or privately owned municipal utilities. They stood outside what we would call today the old-boy network. They had not grown accustomed to looking away from unpleasant sights or suppressing misgivings. As outsiders they saw everything freshly. Their native intelligence and imagination, coinciding with the rapid development of "media technology," enabled them to capture the attention of the country in a wholly unprecedented manner and in time to help alter the consciousness of their fellow Americans and change the way they perceived the nation.

In traditional societies the information that its members need is conveyed by a complex network of cultural artifacts—by institutions, ceremonies, myths, folktales, and religious forms. American society was too diverse, unformed, chaotic, and, above all, *new* to have developed such agencies—other than the Constitution itself (a document, estimable as it was, that left untouched large areas of American life). The nation had, therefore, to develop or adapt and vastly alter agencies and methods for disseminating essential information at all levels of the society. Newspapers had performed this function from colonial days to a degree unprecedented in other societies. They had, to be sure, performed it on the whole badly, commonly in the spirit of partisan rancor that so disgusted Charles Dickens and other foreign visitors. But in a remarkable demonstration of the adaptation of popular institutions to democratic needs, they performed it superbly in the last decades of the old century and the first decade of the new. Indeed, they did it so well that they created what was, in effect, a new form of expression (and protest). The newspapers or, more accurately, the magazines and the journalists that wrote for them first described the facts and then led the way in proposing remedies for them. So one feels that the nation, ready at any instance to fly apart or simply to disintegrate into its disparate and warring elements, was held together, not by politics but by words, torrents and rivers and oceans of words, describing, explaining, and, in the last analysis, reconciling Americans to each other and to the United States of America.

23

Jane Addams and Hull House

We have noted that an important variant of reform was the notion of "settling" among the immigrant poor to share their lives and to try to understand their own interior worlds, their cultures and traditions. Hutchins Hapgood, the author of *The Spirit of the Ghetto*, wrote: "We must love before we can make laws." It was in that spirit that Jane Addams founded Hull House on Halsted Street in the Nineteenth Ward of Chicago in 1889.

Jane Addams was born in 1860 in the town of Cedarville, Illinois, the youngest of eight children. Her mother died when Jane was scarcely three years old and her father, John H. Addams, was the central influence in her life. An ardent abolitionist, he was also a successful businessman who owned a mill and a bank and served as a Republican state senator. Indeed, he was the very model of the supportive father who appears in the background of virtually every female "achiever" in the nineteenth century.

John Addams, as a dedicated abolitionist and early Republican, was a friend and confidant of Abraham Lincoln, who called him "My dear Double-D'ed Addams." Jane was five years old when she came home to find her father weeping. "The greatest man in the world has died," he told her. His friend Lincoln had been assassinated.

Jane Addams attended Rockford Female Seminary, devoted primarily to turning out missionaries, and then prepared to study medicine at the Woman's Medical College in Philadelphia. Her father had taught her "to be honest with yourself inside, whatever happened," and to hold fast to "mental integrity above everything else." His death in 1881 left Addams bereft to the point of nervous collapse but with an inheritance sufficient to pursue her education. She dropped her medical studies because of a chronic spinal condition and for seven years searched restlessly, between periods of severe depression, to find her calling. She traveled in Europe with her stepmother to acquire "culture." In the course of her travels she met other young women who, like her, had graduated from one of the increasing number of women's colleges and, like her, were now drifting about Europe with their mothers or attentive chaperones. Most of them seemed to Jane Addams to suffer from her own malady—nervous depression and a general feeling of futility. Religion was for her, as for so many of her generation, a major preoccupation. While she could not accept the narrow "late Calvinism" which prevailed in the small-town Midwest from which she came, she could not wholly escape it. She wrote a friend: "If you have a God you are a Deist, if you more clearly comprehend that God through Christ then you are a Christian."

In London Addams was shocked at the conditions of the poor. She saw them fighting for decayed vegetables. "Their pale faces," she wrote later, "were dominated by that most unlovely of human expressions, the cunning and shrewdness of the bargain-hunter who starves if he cannot make a successful trade, and yet the final impression was not of ragged, tawdry clothing nor of pinched and sallow faces, but of myriads of hands, empty, pathetic, nerveless and workworn, showing white in the uncertain light of the street, clutching forward for food which was already unfit to eat." The scene haunted Addams. She could never after see even children's hands waving in a classroom without "a certain revival of memory, a clutching at the heart reminiscent of the despair and resentment which seized me then . . . I carried with me for days at a time that curious surprise we experience when we first come back to the streets after days given over to sorrow and death, we are bewildered that the world should be going on as usual and unable to determine which is real, the inner pang or the outward seeming. In time all huge London came to seem unreal," to Addams, "save the poverty in its East End."

Her pursuit of "culture" seemed shallow and intolerable in the face of such misery. She was reminded of the observation that "conduct not culture is three fourths of human life." In her "Weltschmerz," or "world pain," there was mingled "a sense of futility, of misdirected energy," along with a growing conviction that "the pursuit of cultivation would not in the end bring either solace or relief." She became convinced that "the first generation of college women had taken their learning too quickly, had departed too suddenly from the active, emotional life led by their grandmothers and great-grandmothers . . . that somewhere in the process of 'being educated' they had lost that simple and almost automatic response to the human appeal, that old healthful reaction resulting in activity from the mere presence of suffering and helplessness; that they are so sheltered and pampered they have no chance even to make 'the great refusal.' " In the college classroom the natural feminine disposition to aid the needy "had, as it were, become sublimated and romanticised" into essentially passive "cultivation." She heard one young college graduate explain to her mother, "I am simply smothered and sickened with advantages. It is like eating a sweet dessert the first thing in the morning."

Addams revolted against the notion that "the sheltered, educated girl has nothing to do with the bitter poverty and social maladjustment which is all about her, and which, after all, cannot be concealed, for it breaks through poetry and literature in a burning tide which overwhelms her." Yet Addams herself was passionately romantic. She fell under the spell of Mazzini's writings, and, arriving at the outskirts of Rome, she insisted that her bewildered traveling companions "enter the Eternal City on foot through the Porta del Popolo, as pilgrims had done for centuries."

The winters Jane Addams spent with relatives in Baltimore marked the "nadir" of her "nervous depression and sense of maladjustment. . . ." Although she attended lectures at Johns Hopkins, she became "much disillusioned . . . as to the effect of intellectual pursuits upon moral development." She went through a period of being strongly drawn to the positivists' conception of a "Supreme Humanity" and conviction of "human solidarity," based on secular values, but she came finally to feel that the most compelling model for her own venture was that of the early Christian community. She decided to become a member of the Presbyterian church in her hometown of Cedarville and took upon herself "the outward expressions of religious life with all humility and sincerity." More than ever "she longed for an outward symbol of fellowship, some bond of peace, some blessed spot where unity of spirit might claim right of way over all differences." In addition, she felt growing within her "an almost passionate devotion to the ideal of democracy," nowhere "so thrillingly expressed as when the faith of the fisherman and the slave had been boldly opposed to the accepted moral belief that the well-being of a privileged few might justly be built upon the ignorance and sacrifice of the many. Who was I," she wrote, "with my dreams of universal fellowship, that I did not identify myself with the institutional statement of this belief, as I stood in the little village in which I was born, and without which testimony in each remote hamlet of Christendom it would be so easy for the world to slip back into the doctrines of selection and aristocracy?"

Jane Addams thus began with two miseries, in a manner of speaking: the misery of the first generation of privileged young college women who could find no final satisfaction in the pursuit or acquisition of "culture" and the misery of the poor and neglected. It was her perception that *they needed each other*. That conviction led her to the notion of a place where they might meet free of all the inhibitions associated with formal charity. She realized that she was typical of those young people who believed that "somewhere in Church or State are a body of authoritative people who will put things to rights as soon as they really know what is wrong. Such a young person," Addams wrote, "persistently believes that behind all suffering, behind sin and want, must lie redeeming magnanimity. He may imagine the world to be tragic and terrible, but never for an instant occurs to him that it may be contemptible or squalid or self-seeking."

What was needed, Jane Addams decided, was a "Cathedral of humanity . . . capacious enough to house a fellowship of common purpose" and "beautiful enough to persuade men to hold fast to the vision of human solidarity." The result was Hull House. To it she hoped to attract "young women who had been given over too exclusively to study" and who might there "restore a balance of activity along traditional lines and learn of life from life itself; where they might try out some of the things that had been taught and put truth to 'the ultimate test of the conduct it dictates or inspires.' "

In 1889 Hull House became a reality. "It represented no association," Addams told a meeting of the Ethical Culture Society at a meeting in the summer of 1892, "but was opened by two women [Addams and her friend Ellen Gates Starr], backed by many friends, in the belief that the mere foothold of a house easily accessible, ample in space, hospitable and tolerant in spirit, situated in the midst of the large foreign colonies which so easily isolate themselves in American cities, would be in itself a serviceable thing for Chicago." It was her hope that "wherever educated young people are seeking an outlet for that sentiment of universal brotherhood which the best spirit of our times is forcing from an emotion into a motive," others would establish similar communities.

The upper-class young woman, recently graduated from college, found herself "besotted with innocent little ambitions, and does not understand this apparent waste of herself," Addams wrote, "the elaborate preparation, if no work is provided for. There is a heritage of noble obligation which young people accept and long to perpetuate. The desire for action, the wish to right wrong and alleviate suffering, haunts them daily. Society smiles at it indulgently instead of making it of value to itself." Such young men and women heard constantly "of the great social mal-adjustment, but no way is provided for them to change it, and their uselessness hangs about them heavily." The best of the young people realized that "art when shut away from the human interests and from the great mass of humanity is self-destructive. They tell their elders with all the bitterness of youth that if they expect success from them in business, or politics, or in whatever lines their ambition for them has run, they must let them consult all of humanity; . . . they must let them find out what the people want and how they want it."

Hull House was situated on South Halsted Street, near the stockyards and the shipyard. Between Halsted Street and the river lived some 10,000 Italians—Neapolitans, Sicilians, and Calabrians primarily. To the south were many Germans and, spreading out in side streets, Polish and Russian Jews. Farther south there was a huge Bohemian colony which qualified Chicago as the third largest Czech city in the world. To the northeast there were numerous French-Canadians, and there were sprinklings of many other nationalities throughout the city. There were also large numbers of Irish, most of them second-generation Americans but still strongly clannish. Hull House was located in the Nineteenth Ward. In the ward, Jane Addams wrote, "the streets were inexpressibly dirty, the number of schools inadequate, factory legislation unenforced, the street-lighting bad, the paving miserable and altogether lacking in the alleys and smaller streets," while hundreds of houses were unconnected with the street sewer. The principal livelihood of the inhabitants of the ward came from sweatshops given over to finishing clothing. "Back tenements flourish," she wrote; "many houses have no water supply save the faucet in the back yard; there are no fire escapes; the garbage and ashes are placed in wooden boxes which are fastened to the street pavements." There were 250 saloons, one saloon for every twenty-eight voters, and the saloon was "the center of the liveliest political and social life of the ward." The ward had seven Catholic parochial schools, enrolling 6,244 children, while three Protestant schools cared for 141.

It seemed to Jane Addams that the situation of the immigrant in Chicago had a kind of curious analogy to the fragmented social experience of Americans in general, even, indeed, the experience of the educated upper-class young women for whom she felt a special concern. The immigrants "live for the moment side by side, many of them without knowledge of each other, without fellowship, without local tradition or public spirit, without social organization of any kind. . . . The chaos is as great as it would be were they working in huge factories without foreman or superintendent. Their desires and resources are cramped." Cities like Chicago were divided into "rich and poor, into the favored, who express their sense of the social obligation by gifts of money, and into the unfavored, who express it by clamoring for a 'share'—both of them activated by a vague sense of justice."

Addams was obsessed with the conviction that the "blessings— we associate with a life of refinement and cultivation" must be made universal if they were to be permanent, "that the good we procure for ourselves is precarious and uncertain, is floating in mid-air, until it is secured for all of us and incorporated into our common life. . . .

"We may make foreign birth a handicap to [immigrants] and to us, or we may make it a very interesting and stimulating factor in their development and ours." Anthropologists had maintained that in ancient times contacts between different cultures had "produced a curious excitement that often resulted in the creation of a new culture that had never existed before." Jane Addams was convinced that Americans "may get, and should get, something of that revivifying and up-springing of culture from contact with the groups who come to us from foreign countries, and that we can get it in no other way."

It seemed evident to Addams that "a certain *renaissance* [was] going forward in Christianity. The impulse to share the lives of the poor," she wrote, "the desire to make social service, irrespective of propaganda, express the spirit of Christ. . . .

"The spectacle of the [early] Christians loving all men was the most astounding Rome had ever seen. They were eager to sacrifice themselves for the weak, for the children and the aged. They identified themselves with slaves and did not avoid the plague. They longed to share the common lot that they might receive constant revelation. It was a new treasure which the early Christians added to the sum of all treasures, a joy hitherto unknown in the world—the joy of finding the Christ which lieth in each man, but which no man can unfold save in fellowship." There was, she felt, "a distinct turning among many young men and women toward this simple acceptance of Christ's message" and a rejection of the notion, embedded in the conventional denominations, that Christianity was "a thing to be proclaimed and instituted apart from the social life of the community." As she told the (one must assume) rather disconcerted members of the Ethical Culture Society, "I believe that this turning, this renaissance of the early Christian humanitarianism, is going on in America, in Chicago, if you please, without leaders who write or philosophize, without much speaking but with a bent to express in social service, in terms of action, the spirit of Christ." There were, in her view, three primary forces behind the settlement house movement: "first the desire to interpret democracy in social terms; . . . the impulse . . . urging us to aid in the race progress; and . . . the Christian movement toward Humanitarianism."

To Jane Addams, true education was "deliverance." Young men and women must be "delivered from all constraint and rigidity" before their faculties could be effectively used. She quoted Mazzini with approval: "Education is not merely a necessity of true life by which the individual renews his vital force in the vital force of humanity; it is a Holy Communion with generations dead and living, by which he fecundates all his faculties." She called Hull House a settlement. The word "house," added by others, rather spoiled or obscured the point. A settlement was a community; a community, or settlement, was made up of equals bound together by trust and love, pursuing together, in a spirit of mutual discovery, "the delights of knowledge." For her a settlement "is a protest against a restricted view of education"; it made it "possible for every educated man or woman with a teaching faculty to find out those who are ready to be taught." Half the race was engaged in a "starvation struggle"; to shut oneself away from that half of the race, the most vital part, was "to live out but half the humanity which we have been born heir to and use but half our faculties."

The settlement house, Jane Addams wrote, "stands for application as opposed to research; for emotion as opposed to abstraction, for universal interest as opposed to specialization. . . . A settlement would avoid the always getting ready for life which seems to dog the school, and would begin with however small a group to accomplish and to live."

Addams was a skillful and attentive anthropologist. She understood the perplexities of the immigrant families, many of them from rural peasant backgrounds, trying desperately to adjust to the wholly alien life of the city. Different nationalities came to Hull House on different days. Saturday evening was reserved for Italians. Entire families came, and national holidays were observed. The Italians, Addams wrote, "came to us with their petty lawsuits, sad relics of the *vendetta*, with their incorrigible boys, with their hospital cases, with their aspirations for American clothes, and with their need for an interpreter." Fridays were devoted to Germans, who enjoyed "that cozy social intercourse which is found in its perfection in the 'Fatherland,' " Jane Addams wrote. They sang a great deal "in the tender minor of the German folksong or in the rousing spirit of the Rhine. . . ." Addams and her fellow workers at Hull House were especially anxious to instill in the immigrants a pride in the customs and culture they had brought with them. It seemed to her that the best way to instill in the often contemptuous children of immigrants a respect for their parents was to respect and encourage those domestic arts and folkways that the parents commanded. She sought to "bring together the old life and the new, a respect for the older cultivation, and not quite so much assurance that the new was the best. . . ." She wished "our foreigners" to "project a little of the historic and romantic into the prosaic quarters of our American cities." In addition, the house was headquarters for numerous clubs: the Young Citizens' Club and the Hull House Columbian Guards, who helped make the streets safe.

More than 200 students or apprentices in social work were associated with Hull House and lived within a radius of six blocks. A handful of residents attended to the running of the house. College extension courses were offered in a wide variety of subjects, practical and cultural; sometimes as many as thirty-five were going on concurrently. Without endowment or capital and depending entirely for its support on sympathetic friends, Hull House was able to act as a critically important mediator between individuals and the large charitable institutions of the city, most of which were laced up "in certain formulas" and thus in constant danger of "forgetting the mystery and complexity of life." The house worked closely with the Visiting Nurses' Association, the health department, City Hall, the Hebrew Relief and Aid Society, the Children's Aid, the Municipal Order League. Five bathrooms in the rear of Hull House were open to the neighborhood, and in one typical month 980 baths were taken. There was also a day nursery for the children of working mothers and a diet kitchen to teach proper nutrition and the preparation of wholesome food. There was a coffee-house adjacent and nearby a cooperative boardinghouse for young workingwomen, run by the residents themselves. Jane Addams was thoroughly sympathetic to the movement for women's unions, especially in the garment industry, and four women's unions met at Hull House in its early years: the bookbinders, the shoemakers, the shirt-makers, and the cloakmakers. The Working People's Social Science Club met weekly with the purpose of raising the consciousness, as we would say today, of working people as to the need for common action to improve both the conditions of employment and the general character of their lives through cooperative action. There was no proposal for social and economic reform too radical to receive a hearing. Some of the wilder notions were tempered by discussion and debate. Economic conferences of workingmen and businessmen sponsored by the house resulted in better understanding of the respective sides of the war between capital and labor. Here single taxers debated socialists, and members of the Personal Rights League crossed swords with anarchists and Republicans. At one meeting workingmen had an opportunity to tell the chief of police what they thought of the treatment by the police of the city's poor. The average number of people who came to Hull House in the course of a week, Addams wrote, ran around 1,000. In a Hull club of 24 Russian-Jewish boys, all children of immigrants, 11 went on to graduate from universities or from professional schools.

The police kept a close eye on Hull House, and the newspapers especially directed hostile attention toward a spot that they described as "a nest of anarchists." A policeman, observing a heated political debate among immigrant radicals, said to a member of the Hull House staff, "Lady, you people oughtn't to let bums like these come here. If I had my way, they'd all be lined up against a wall at sunrise and shot."

Democracy and Social Ethics was a deceptively simple title for a book of remarkable subtlety and insight. The fact was that Jane Addams did for the working-class poor, largely immigrant, what Harriet Beecher Stowe had done for the slaves of the South; she gave her readers a sense of the human reality of a class of people who had previously existed quite outside the consciousness of middle- and upper-class Americans. Her book did not, of course, reach nearly so wide an audience as did *Uncle Tom's Cabin*, but the audience that it did reach was a critically important one, containing a disproportionate number of the leaders and shapers of public attitudes, liberal and radical reformers of a wide variety of persuasions.

What Addams perceived most clearly was that the conventional moral attitudes of the middle and upper classes, of "old" Americans— whom we have come to refer to as white Anglo-Saxon Protestants, or WASPs—imposed an often insurmountable barrier between them and the working class, the immigrant and the poor or generally deprived. In order to overcome this barrier, it was necessary to understand the "culture" of the underprivileged classes; how poor people and alienated people thought and felt; how they perceived the world; how their codes of behavior were as "moral" and as appropriate to their social situations as the very different values of those who stood higher on the social and economic scale; how, indeed, the poor, in their mutual sympathy and dependence on each other, often came closer to the ideal of Christian brotherhood than their "betters." What poisoned all relationships between the more benevolent members of the upper classes and the poor was that the conduct of the upper classes had "hardened into customs and habits" which determined their intellectual formulations, or images of the world. When their emotive lives—their feelings and sentiments—prompted them to acts of kindness and generosity toward those less fortunate members of society, they often found themselves acting in contradiction to what they believed to be their principles, or, in following their principles, they did violence to the generous impulses of their hearts. The result was that they suffered, in Addams's words, "from the strain and indecision of believing one hypothesis and acting upon another." Americans' "estimate of the effect of environment and social conditions" had "shifted faster than our methods of administering charity have changed." It had once been believed that "poverty was synonymous with vice and laziness, and that the prosperous man was the righteous man. . . ." Then charity could be administered "harshly with a good conscience"; it was, in any event, better than the subject deserved. The benefactor felt that his charity was a measure of his own moral superiority.

The poor, on the other hand, had a different view of the world.

They understood very clearly that life had dealt them a cold deck; the entire system bore mercilessly upon them. In their own misfortunes they helped their friends and neighbors as best they could, neither questioning nor judging the basis of their need. Thus they were puzzled or outraged by the behavior, public or private, of those agencies established to assist them. These agencies plainly viewed them as seriously deficient, as actual or potential loafers and deadbeats. They established elaborate and humiliating procedures to determine if they were genuinely "needy" or "worthy." Such behavior appeared to the poor "as the cold and calculating action of a selfish man . . . they do not understand why the impulse which drives people to 'be good to the poor' should be so severely supervised. They feel . . . that the charity visitor is moved by motives that are alien and unreal." Their disposition is to ask: "What do you want, anyway? If you have nothing to give us, why not let us alone and stop your questionings and investigations?"

The charitably inclined upper-class visitor, Jane Addams found, was particularly upset at the disposition of poor working-class girls to spend their meager wages on frivolous clothes rather than save their money. "Her income goes into her clothing, out of all proportion to the amount which she spends upon other things," the "charitable visitor" complained—another instance of the shiftlessness of the poor. If social advancement was the working girl's aim, Jane Addams replied, buying clothes was the most sensible thing she could do with her money since "she is judged largely by her clothes." In this, as in innumerable other such matters, the college-educated upper-class young woman "discovers how incorrigibly bourgeois her standards have been. . . ." She realizes that she cannot "insist so strenuously upon the conventions of her own class, which fail to fit the bigger, more emotional, freer lives of working people." The phrase is a striking one—"the bigger, more emotional, freer lives of working people." Obviously it was a vision of life that had great attraction for Addams herself, one that she had won at the cost of much thought and close acquaintance with despair.

Perhaps above all, the upper-class young woman anxious to do good had little notion of "the most awful element of poverty, [the] imminent fear of starvation and a neglected old age." It was this latter anxiety that drove immigrant parents to rear their children under a fearful discipline in which they were viewed as the only bulwark against such a fate and which in turn prompted the children to rebel against such a harsh regimen and denounce it as an outmoded residue of the Old World, as indeed un-American.

"Nothing is more certain," Addams wrote, "than that each generation longs for a reassurance as to the value and charm of life, and is secretly afraid lest it lose its sense of the youth of the earth. . . . One generation after another has depended upon its young to equip it with gaiety and enthusiasm, to persuade it that living is a pleasure. . . ." So had it been since the times of the Greeks. "Only in the modern city have men concluded that it is no longer necessary for the municipality to provide for the insatiable desire for play." The "stupid experiment of organizing work and failing to organize play" had brought revenge in the form of "gin-palaces" and commercialized vice of every kind. The need for play could not be met by sermons admonishing moral rectitude. The floozy with "the self-conscious walk, the giggling speech, the preposterous clothing . . . the huge hat, with its wilderness of bedraggled feathers" was simply announcing "to the world that she is here. She demands attention to the fact of her existence, she states that she is ready to live, to take her place in the world." The towns were no better than the cities. It seemed to Addams that the eyes of upper-class city dwellers were blind "to the mystic beauty, the redemptive joy, the civic pride which these multitudes of young people might supply to our dingy towns."

Jane Addams shared the determination to make the cities beautiful and harmonious. "We cannot afford," she wrote, "to be ungenerous to the city in which we live without suffering the penalty which lack of fair interpretation always entails." She wished to "rectify and purify" the city until it was free of its "grosser temptations. . . . The spontaneous joy, the clamor for pleasure, the desire of young people to appear finer and better and altogether more lovely than they really are, the idealization not only of each other but of the whole earth which they regard as but a theater for their noble exploits, the unworldly ambition, the romantic hopes, the make-believe world in which they live, if properly utilized, what might they not do to make our sordid cities more beautiful, more companionable?"

William James called *Democracy and Social Ethics* "one of the great books of our time." James told Addams: "The religion of democracy needs nothing so much as sympathetic interpretation to one another of the different classes of which society consists; and you have made your contribution in a masterly manner. . . . The fact is,

Madam, that you are not like the rest of us who seek the truth and try to express it. You inhabit reality."

The San Francisco reformer Fremont Older wrote: "It was not until I read your 'Democracy and Social Ethics' that I was able to understand how wrong I had been in condemning the masses of the people for what I deemed to be a low moral standard. Your psychology of the minds of the poor has been by far the most helpful aid I have ever known."

Despite her rejection of the academic world's divorce of theory from experience, Jane Addams sought out the assistance of scholars and professionals in all relevant fields. The settlement, she insisted, must call on the sociologist and the psychiatrist as well as on "the services of artists, economists, gymnasts, caseworkers, dramatists, trained-nurses. . . ." To her it should unify and universalize human experience in a way that the colleges and universities with their rigid departmental divisions could not or were not willing to do. In practical fact, Hull House, as it grew through numerous modifications and additions, contained virtually all the new principles of cooperative living: nurseries, playgrounds, a library, a theater, a gymnasium—all tracing their lineage to the work of earlier reformers.

Hull House was a center of radical reform. Ellen Gates Starr worked to cultivate a love of beauty among slum children. Alzina Stevens was an outspoken Populist. Henry Demarest Lloyd became chairman of the Literature Committee of the Arnold Toynbee Club of Hull House and helped plan the programs for the Labor, Cooperative and Single Tax congresses of the World's Fair Auxiliary. Among those attending the exposition were Sidney and Beatrice Webb, who visited Hull House in 1893 with John Altgeld and Clarence Darrow and prevailed on Jane Addams to smoke a cigarette. Henry Demarest Lloyd perhaps gave Hull House its most enduring accolade: "While others speculated and theorized and patented complicated mechanisms for the perpetual motion of social harmony, this simple and living impulse offered itself as a sacrifice to prove that all men needed to do was to live together, and that it was no sacrifice, but delight, and honor and safety."

In addition to Jane Addams and Ellen Gates Starr, Hull House (not to mention its numerous progeny of settlement houses) attracted some of the most remarkable women of the day. One of Julia Lathrop's ancestors had come to the Massachusetts Bay Colony in the early seventeenth century, just missing the *Mayflower* because he had been jailed for denouncing the Church of England. The Lathrops moved West in subsequent generations until Julia's parents ended up in Rockford, Illinois. William Lathrop, Julia's father, had been an abolitionist and one of the founders of the Republican Party in Illinois. He encouraged his daughter to develop her mind by reading widely and pursuing her education. (He took a woman, Alta Hulett, into his law office to help draft a bill that would permit women to practice law in Illinois, and when it was passed, Hulett became the first woman admitted to the Illinois bar.)

Julia enrolled at Rockford Female Seminary and, when it became apparent that she was not adequately prepared for admission to Vassar, her father hired tutors to repair Rockford's deficiencies. She graduated from Vassar in 1880, while the college was still in the first exciting flush of its founding, and then went into her father's law office. In 1889 at a Rockford meeting, Julia Lathrop met Jane Addams and Ellen Gates Starr, who had come back to Addams's alma mater to recruit workers for a "settlement house" which would open in the fall. Julia Lathrop returned to Chicago with them and became one of the pillars of Hull House. She made mental hygiene, the establishment of juvenile courts, and the health of children her specialties and became the first woman member of the Illinois State Board of Health.

Florence Kelley was the daughter of William Kelley, an early Republican and abolitionist, who had started life as a printer at the age of eleven and gone on to become a highly successful lawyer and judge. Kelley's enthusiasm for high tariffs on pig iron gave him the name of Pig Iron Kelley. He was one of the classic "supportive fathers," encouraging Florence to pursue her education, to read widely, and to interest herself in public affairs. As important an influence on Florence Kelley's life was her great-aunt Sarah, a Philadelphia Quaker and friend of John Stuart Mill, free trade, and equality for women.

Admitted to Cornell at the age of sixteen, Florence Kelley wrote a brilliant thesis on laws dealing with child labor, but she was refused permission to enroll at the University of Pennsylvania's school of law. She studied at the University of Leipzig for a year and was denied a degree. During a trip to England she, like Jane Addams, was horrified at the conditions of labor. Back in Germany she discovered Karl Marx and translated Engels's *The Condition of the Working Class in England in 1844*. She married a radical Polish-Russian physician named Lazare Wischnewetsky and had three children by him. Now members of the Socialist Labor Party, she and her husband moved to New York, where

Florence was expelled from the party because of doubts about her doctrinal purity. Her expulsion was one of the strains that caused her marriage to Wischnewetsky to break up. She moved to Illinois, sued for divorce, won custody of her children, and resumed her maiden name. She joined Hull House a year after it had opened. Her children were lodged at Henry Demarest Lloyd's spacious home in Winnetka. When she turned up at Hull House on a December morning, Florence Kelley found Henry Standing Bear, a Kickapoo Indian, on the doorstep. Jane Addams opened the door carrying the cook's baby.

As a resident of Hull House Kelley turned her attention once again to the issue of child labor. After working for a special congressional committee appointed to investigate "the Slums of the Great Cities," she went on to report on the conditions of the Chicago sweatshops in the garment district, arguing that they were even worse than those of New York City's notorious Lower East Side. In John Altgeld's administration of the state of Illinois, she became the investigator of child labor. In 1893 the combined efforts of the Chicago reformers resulted in the passage of the Illinois Factory Act, which became a model for reformers in other states. When Kelley couldn't get a local district attorney to prosecute a company in which a young boy had lost his arm because he had been using a poisonous substance to gild picture frames, she earned a law degree so that she could argue such cases herself.

In 1895 an important new recruit appeared at Hull House. Alice Hamilton had grown up in Fort Wayne, Indiana, part of a large family that included seventeen cousins. Her mother, a quiet and rather withdrawn woman, was an enthusiastic disciple of Frances Willard, who often stayed at the Hamilton house on her lecture tours. Alice's father, Montgomery Hamilton, an ardent abolitionist, had dropped out of Princeton to enlist in the Union army. He was, his daughter recalled, obsessed with theology and was an indefatigable reader. Gertrude Hamilton instilled in her daughter the conviction that "There are two kinds of people, the ones who say, 'Somebody ought to do something about it, but why should it be I?' and those who say, 'Somebody must do something about it, then why not I?' " Both father and mother had been nurtured in the antislavery tradition.

The Hamilton daughters, Alice among them, were shipped back East to Miss Porter's School in Farmington, Connecticut. Upon graduating, Alice enrolled in the premedical program at the University of Michigan, one of the first universities to accept women as medical students.

At the New England Hospital for Women and Children in Boston, Alice Hamilton was exposed to the conditions under which working-class women lived. She was appalled. Back in Fort Wayne she discussed the conditions she had witnessed in the Boston slums with her sister Norah and her cousin Agnes Hamilton, a follower of Henry George and of Richard Ely's new economics. At this propitious moment Jane Addams appeared in Fort Wayne, lecturing. The Hamilton girls went and were enthralled. After a disappointing stint in Germany Alice, still uncertain where her life's work lay, accompanied her sister to Baltimore, where Norah went to become headmistress of Bryn Mawr School Alice enrolled at the Johns Hopkins Medical School, just coming into its great days with men like William Welch, Simon Flexner, William Osler, and John Finney on the faculty. The Women's Medical School of Northwestern University in Chicago then offered her a position teaching pathology. She accepted and asked Jane Addams if she could live at Hull House and participate in its work.

It appears to be the case that every movement that is to have power in the world must become, to a degree, fashionable. Obviously the settlement house movement touched a very responsive chord in middle- to upper-class bosoms. It became fashionable, and dozens of settlement houses were established by young men and women inspired by Jane Addams's example.

John Jay Chapman and his second wife, Elizabeth Chanler, were drawn into "settlement work." Chapman was especially preoccupied with the education of children. He wrote and directed a number of children's plays and was never so happily occupied as when he was involved with children, teaching or playing. The Chapmans rented a store in the section of New York City known as Hell's Kitchen and fixed it up as a clubhouse for young people with instruction in basket weaving, sewing, and furniture making. The neighborhood children, largely Irish Catholics, proved an unruly and intractable lot. There was an unexpected degree of hostility rather than the gratitude that the Chapmans had expected. While they were full of good intentions, they belonged to a class and species—upper-class Protestant—that the Irish children knew as the "enemy." To Elizabeth Chapman, trying to run the "club" was like "heavy surf-bathing with a bad undertow." Two boys, whom Chapman had evicted for bad behavior, returned with mouths full of kerosene, which they sprayed on Chapman's beard (an obvious symbol to them of his upper-class status) and then tried to set fire to it. After a year the club was closed; Elizabeth Chapman's doctor felt she was imperiling her health.

"The social settlement," Jacob Riis wrote, "starting as neighborhood guilds to reassert the lost brotherhood, became almost from the first the fulcrum . . . whence the lever for reform was applied. . . . If parks were wanted, if schools needed bettering, there were at the College Settlement, the University Settlement, the Nurses' Settlement, and at a score of other such places, young enthusiasts to collect the facts and to urge them, with the prestige of their non-political organization to back them. The Hull House out in Chicago set the pace. . . ."

Frederic Howe took his turn in settlement house work, and his judgment was more severe. "Residents at the settlement house had good food and comfort-rooms," he noted; "they enjoyed a certain distinction because of their good works." Having joined the young men and women in a Chicago settlement house, Howe found himself invited out to dinners, asked to make speeches about immigrants, on politics, on cleaning up the city. Somehow the situation seemed false to him. "As a friendly visitor to the tenements," he wrote, "I felt uncomfortable. . . . I did not enjoy dancing with the heavy-footed mothers of many children who were lured from the tenements to our parties." Howe was asked to be a trustee of the Charity Organization Society, which exercised a dictatorial rule over the private charities of the city, certifying the respectable and freezing out the dubious. "Personal charity was out of date." The new mode was "scientific." Howe wrote: "Pleas for help were subjected to an acid test before relief was given; there must be no drinking, there must be evidence of willingness to work." The latest managerial practices were instituted. Applicants were card-indexed; files were kept on them. "People," in Howe's words, "were 'cases.'" Efficient and self-confident young women trained as "social workers" ran things. Businessmen sat on the board of trustees. Like the vigilance committees of Dr. Parkhurst, the social workers seemed most concerned with redeeming prostitutes and closing saloons. Once again Howe resigned with a letter declaring that he did not believe in the organization of charity. It could not be organized like the steel trust and "run by paid clerks" without losing the very essence of charity which meant love. "When you do away with personal charity," Howe told the trustees, "you do away with love. . . . Your society, with its board of trustees made up of steel magnates, coal operators and employers is not really interested in charity," he concluded. "If it were, it would stop the twelve-hour day; it would increase wages and put an end to the cruel killing and maiming of men. It is interested in getting its own wreckage out of sight." Which was only to say that that which starts as love inevitably becomes institutionalized.

Whatever its shortcomings may have been, the settlement house movement more than justified its existence by enlarging the consciousness of the upper classes as to the true situation of the urban masses.

24

The Farmers' Revolt

In our preoccupation with the city it is important to keep steadily in mind the fact that the most acute pressure point in the society was, in the last analysis, the farm. Every year the farmer produced vast new quantities of food—wheat and corn, hogs and cattle—and each year his economic situation grew more grim, and he more desperate and more disenchanted with capitalism.

The first thing to say, then, about the American farmer was that he was astonishingly productive. The statistics were awesome. Pigs to the number of 56,750,000 were slaughtered every year, more than one per inhabitant of the country. "It was much the same with our four-footed domestic beasts. Were the live stock upon Uncle Sam's estate," Andrew Carnegie wrote, "ranged five abreast, each animal estimated to occupy a space five feet long, and marched around the world, the head and tail of the procession would overlap." Pork was one of the largest items of export. In 1880, $50,000,000 worth went to England alone. In addition to 1 billion pounds of butchered meat, more than 500,000 livestock were sent to Europe in 1884.

In 1880 it was estimated that only 15 percent of the total arable land in the United States was cultivated but that 15 percent produced 30 percent of the grain of the world. Three times as much capital was invested in agriculture as in manufacturing. Out of roughly 4,000,000 farms, some 3,000,000 were owned by the farmer who worked them, while 1,000,000 were rented or worked on shares, but this number constantly increased. Two-thirds of the private holdings were between 50 and 500 acres in size. Only 91,000 farmers owned more than 500 acres. Of the farms not owned by those who farmed them, the great majority were worked on shares, and the greater portion of these were in the South.

The most notable improvements in agriculture had been brought about by the increasingly widespread use of machinery. As early as 1850 farm machinery was valued at $450,000,000. By 1880 more than 3 billion bushels of grain were reaped in the United States, of which almost 2 billion (1,700,000,000) was corn; $50,000,000 worth was shipped abroad. In 1885, 500,000,000 bushels of wheat were produced; Great Britain imported $175,000,000 worth. Andrew Carnegie, in *Triumphant Democracy*, was enthralled by large-scale farming. A certain Dr. Glin of California had 45,000 acres in wheat, he noted. Machines did much of the labor that had before been done by field hands; each threshing machine threshed, winnowed, and bagged sixty bushels of wheat a day. "Notwithstanding this," Carnegie wrote, "it is pleasing to know that not even with the advantage here implied are these gigantic farms able to maintain the struggle against the smaller farms owned and cultivated by farmers." Carnegie's optimism proved ill-founded; many small farmers, unable to capitalize on the new agricultural technology, abandoned their farms each year. A constant process of consolidation went on, but the principal factor in rising productivity was the uninterrupted process of putting new land under cultivation. In Kansas alone more than 220,000 new arrivals had flooded the state in a period of six years: 1881–1887. The miles of railroad track more than doubled in the same period, and the number of farms had increased by almost 20,000.

To foreign visitors interested in the remarkable productivity of American agriculture, much of the explanation lay in the Department of Agriculture. In the words of one observer, "The present condition of crops in California or in Egypt; the degree of cloudiness in Dakota or Maine; the number and condition of hogs in market at Kansas City, or in transport to Chicago; the appearance of grasshoppers in Georgia; the wheat in store at Duluth or New York; the number of bales of cotton at Bombay or Mobile . . . a drought in Arkansas; the southward flight of cranes in Dakota . . . the relative cloudiness of the planet Mars— these and a thousand and one other matters, as diverse as can be

imagined, are noted, docketed and labeled, every change being recorded as soon as it takes place."

The department, only a few decades old, employed some 10,000
people to make regular reports on crops, prices, cost of transportation,
weather conditions, and so on throughout the continent and the world.
"Thus the American farmer or merchant can always ascertain the amount
of acreage in particular crops; the condition of the crops as regards
growth, maturity and probable yield. . . ." The department maintained
an experimental garden in which crops from other parts of the world
were tested for their suitability for cultivation in America. Here Chinese
sorghum was first introduced, as was the Bahia orange, which,
transplanted into California, in ten years had produced crops of
greater value than the cost of establishing and maintaining the entire
department.

But the most important element was undoubtedly the enterprise
and ingenuity of the farmer himself. In many nations of the world
farmers were, in essence, rural workers or tenants, commonly called
peasants. Even in countries like Italy and more notably in Japan, where
farmers enjoyed high status (they ranked above merchants and craftsmen and only below the samurai), they were highly traditional and
conservative in their farming practices.

In America the situation was strikingly different. The farmer
generally owned his farm (though it was often heavily mortgaged and
tenancy increased dramatically in this period); he was an entrepreneur
in his own right, a rural capitalist with a substantial investment in land,
draft animals, and, more and more commonly, farm machinery. He
was as anxious as any manufacturer to improve his techniques and, he
hoped, his profits, but in dramatic contrast with the manufacturer-
capitalist, the farmer-capitalist's increased productivity lowered his profits and not infrequently obliterated them entirely. The manufacturer
and financier, it seemed to the farmer, were inordinately rewarded for
productivity while he was penalized.

The principal enemies of the farmer were the railroads, the banks,
and the weather. In addition to devastating depressions, the farmer
had the elements to cope with. In 1887 drought came to all the Great
Plains—the Dakotas, Kansas, and Nebraska—and corn production fell
from 126,000,000 bushels in 1886 to 76,000,000 in 1887. Many homesteaders sold their thin cattle for what they would bring, abandoned
their claims, and returned to their homes and relatives in the East,
completely defeated. "All that fall," John Ise wrote, "the discouraged

settlers trekked out of the drought-stricken country. Day after day they passed by, grizzled, dejected and surly men; sick, tired and hopeless women. . . ."

In 1881 corn sold for 63 cents a bushel; nine years later it sold for 28 cents. The price of cotton dropped from 15 cents in 1873 to an average of 8 cents from 1886 to 1889. The number of mortgaged farms increased year by year until by 1890, in Kansas, for example, 64.4 percent of the farms were mortgaged up to 38 percent of their value. Every month saw numerous foreclosures. In the words of one lament:

> My husband came from town last night
> Sad as a man could be,
> His wagon empty, cotton gone,
> And not a dime had he.
>
> Huzzah-Huzzah
> 'Tis queer I do declare:
> We make the clothes for all the world,
> But few we have to wear.

At the heart of the economic distress of the farmers was the fact that the yearly value per acre of the ten principal crops had declined from $14.70 in 1870 to $9.71 in 1893. In the same period average freight costs increased each year.

In such circumstances the harried Georgia farmer or the hog raiser of southern Minnesota bore little resemblance to Jefferson's romanticized independent "yeoman" farmer. His post-Civil War descendant was far from independent. He was hopelessly dependent on unpredictable markets, domestic and foreign alike. He was dependent on the money supply and the interest rates (often usuriously high), on the weather (that at least was nothing new), and, above all, on the railroads. The *Nation* reported the situation of the farmer accurately enough: "Increased nominal value of land, higher rents, fewer farms occupied by owners; diminished product; lower wages; a more ignorant population; increasing number of women employed at hard, outdoor labor . . . and a steady deterioration in the style of farming—these are the conditions described by a cumulative mass of evidence that is perfectly irresistible."

Jefferson had acclaimed his beloved farmers as "the chosen people of God, if ever He had a chosen people, whose breasts He has made

His particular deposit for substantial and genuine virtue. . . ." Andrew Carnegie in *Triumphant Democracy* echoed the Jeffersonian vision when he wrote: "Free institutions develop all the best and noblest characteristics, and these always lead in the direction of the golden rule. These honest, pure, contented, industrious, patriotic people really do consider what they would have others do to them. They ask themselves what is fair? These are the people of rural America."

In fact, the farmers were, as much as any city dweller, stockholders in Slick and Smart Inc. Furthermore, they suffered individually and collectively from what we might call a diminished image problem. As the city became the most potent symbol of growth and progress, the farmer appeared as a "rube," a "hayseed," a "hick," chained to the farm because he wasn't "smart" enough for city life. For this reason (and presumably numerous other more practical reasons), he suffered a high degree of stress and had a short life expectancy and an alarmingly high rate of suicide and insanity. As for his morals, it must be said, regretfully, they seemed to have been no better than anyone else's.

When Emma Goldman visited a "native" anarchist, Kate Austin, who lived in the farm community of Caplinger Mills, Missouri, Austin gave Goldman a grim picture of rural life. "You have no idea what the sexual practices of these farmers are," she told her urban sister radical. "But it is the result mostly of their dreary existence . . . no other outlet, no distraction, no colour of any kind in their lives . . . the farmer has nothing but long and arduous toil in the summer, and empty days in the winter. Sex is all they have." It was no wonder that their sex lives were brutal and sometimes bizarre. "How should these people understand sex in its finer expressions, or love that cannot be sold or bound?" she asked Goldman.

Abba Woolson was eloquent on the narrow and exacting life of a farm wife. However hard the farmer's life might be, working with little help "upon a soil whose productive qualities have been well-nigh exhausted," he had "a season of rest," but his wife's duties never ceased. So it was with farm daughters as well. "Labor in the proper amount might seem a duty and a delight; but the narrow and cheerless future that is offered them at home appears stripped of everything which can render life desirable." In New England sheep could not be kept on account of wild dogs. Pasture was too meager for beef cattle. The result was an excessive dependence on hogs and pork, the least healthful of animal meat, in Woolson's opinion. This was supplemented by large quantities of indigestible fried food. Wholesome homemade bread had been replaced by "abominable compounds, whose chemical ingredients are ruinous to both teeth and stomach." Instead of walking, everyone preferred to ride. "A horse and wagon must be brought to the door if the distance to be traversed is but half a mile . . . excessive toil, lack of diversion, unhealthy food, and ill-aired rooms, submitted to partly from necessity and partly from ignorance as to their results, cannot but seriously impair the health of all who experience them."

Young men and women fled from the bleakness of such towns "for the eager life of crowded cities." All the old holidays and seasonal festivities had been abandoned, one by one. Especially missed were the militia muster days; even the Fourth of July and Washington's birthday were seldom observed. (One should note here that Woolson was speaking primarily of New England towns, which had suffered a notable loss of morale in the years immediately preceding and following the Civil War.) With the traditional holidays only sporadically observed, there was "absolutely nothing" that provided "for that necessity of human nature for spontaneity and fun." In the country schools no more notice was taken of the beauty and instruction afforded by adjacent nature than if the pupils inhabited the grimmest urban landscape. It was as though country towns had fallen into a long, debilitating slumber. Those who could escape at least found in the crowded, hectic cities *life*, vivid, pulsating, corrupt and often overwhelming as it might be.

Edwin Cox Walker, associate editor with Moses Harman of *Lucifer* and Harman's son-in-law, having been one, had no romantic illusions about the farmer. "We are accustomed to boast of the purity and devotion to liberty of the country's populace," he wrote. But the fact was less alluring. "If ignorance and mis-education regarding natural law are purity, then indeed are the masses of farming population pure; while their conception of liberty is that embodied in a majority despotism which lays its hand upon and controls every private concern of the individual." The plight of the farm wife, as Walker described it, was especially deplorable. "She has no time for recreation, and her nearest neighbor may be a mile away. Who shall wonder then," he added, "that she often knows nothing outside of the details of her housework and the latest neighborhood gossip? Who shall wonder that the statistics of our insane asylums show a larger relative proportion of demented from the class of farmers' wives than from any other?"

Farmers were, very generally speaking, either temperance men or drunkards. In the isolated and lonely conditions of farm life, drinking in moderation was a demanding discipline. They and their wives were commonly pious Christians—Baptists and Methodists mostly, with an increasing number in the ranks of the Holiness or Pentecostal churches, especially in the South. Many were Christian Socialists, who combined political radicalism with fundamentalist religious doctrines.

Conditions of living varied from arduous to desperate. In western Kansas, Nebraska, and the Dakotas most of the settlers, in the absence of trees, lived in sod huts or dugouts. The matted prairie sod was cut into squares and piled between framing timbers to form a substantial, if commonly damp, house. Even the roof was of sod. Henry Ise brought his bride, Rosie, to his newly constructed dugout in western Kansas only to find that heavy rains had caved in part of the roof and that there was a foot of water in the house.

The Ises suffered in the summer from baking heat and dry winds that blew away their topsoil and their crops and in the winter from numbing cold. In one period of three months a rabid wolf spread terror along the river, biting domestic animals and people indiscriminately before it was finally shot; a mother and her two young children drowned trying to cross a rain-swollen creek on their way home from a neighboring farm; and another farmer was killed when a heavy timber he was using to build a barn fell on him.

Henry and Rosie Ise had scarcely buried an infant daughter when they had their first encounter with grasshoppers—"millions, billions of them—soon covered the ground in a seething, fluttering mass, their jaws constantly at work biting and testing all things . . . making altogether a low, crackling, rasping sound, like the approach of a prairie fire." They consumed the corn in the fields, vegetables in the family garden. Ropes in the barn were cut through, portions of saddles and bridles consumed; the paint on the wagon was partially eaten. They invaded the cabin itself and "flew into the water, into the milk pans, and into the kettles cooking on the stove. They ate holes in the curtains on the windows, and the clothes hanging on the wall." For a week they lingered on, a terrible plague, and they departed only when every iota of greenery had been consumed. In their wake came searing drought and terrible heat.

Sickness—cholera, ague, and pneumonia—laid people low, especially the very young and the old. There were the ever present Indians lurking about, ready to steal a horse, chickens, or a pig. There were bandits and rustlers and, in the dry summers, the constant threat of grass fires. There were grasshoppers, tornadoes, floods, dust storms.

After the torrential storms of 1871 the creek banks were lined with the carcasses of cattle. "So thickly did they cover the round," Rosie Ise recalled, "that one might have walked upon them for a half a mile, stepping from one to another and never touching the ground." Finally, when all these natural disasters had been survived, there was in a sense the cruelest disaster of all—a man-made one: the unpredictable market, where prices dropped year after year until it cost more to grow an acre of wheat or corn or bring a steer to slaughter than the farmer or rancher was paid for his product. Fiercely idiosyncratic and stubbornly individualistic by nature, the farmer came slowly and, on the whole, reluctantly to accept the necessity for common action to redress his grievances.

Farmers were notoriously hardworking, famously productive, pious, and God-fearing. From having been the exemplars of American democracy they now found themselves its victims. Small wonder they grew more rebellious with each passing year. Almost to a man they believed that their troubles stemmed from a rigid and inadequate money supply. The political response of farmers to their progressively deteriorating economic situation was a series of increasingly militant farmers' organizations, culminating in the most radical (and the shortest-lived) political party in our history. In the process the farmers developed a remarkably articulate group of leaders and produced a body of critical and exhortatory literature without precedent and without succession.

The revolt of the farmers was not long in coming. The National Grange of the Patrons of Husbandry was started by Oliver Hudson Kelley with six others in December, 1867. Modeled on the Masonic Order, there were seven degrees and four categories: Laborer, Cultivator, Harvester, and Husbandman. The categories for women were Maid, Shepherdess, Gleaner, and Matron. The Pomona or Hope degree was the fifth stage for masters. Patrons of the sixth degree made up the National Council. The final degree was that of Demeter (Faith). The preamble of the constitution of the Patrons read: *The soil is the source from which we derive all that constitutes wealth. . . .*" Kelley was a man with a mission, and that mission carried him up and down the land, east, west, and south, until by 1874 local chapters counted a million and a half members.

Edward Martin's *History of the Granger Movement; or, the Farmers' War Against Monopoly* was a battle call to farmers who had endured the exactions of the railroads. "The Grange," he wrote, "seeks to array the agricultural class, nearly one half of our whole population, as a compact body against the evils." Soon there were numerous "front" organizations: the Producers Convention, the Railroad Committee, and the Anti-Monopoly Party. The farmers, through the legislatures of their states, proved formidable opponents of the railroads. For a decade the war raged in courts, in newspapers, in pamphlets, and even in literature. A farmer-poet, named Leonard Brown, active in the Granger movement, wrote a poem entitled "Iowa, Land of the Prophets," which called for a great uprising of the people:

> The few grow rich the many poor
> And tramps are dogged from door to door
> The millionaire would have his word
> And e'en his very whisper heard
> And Congress bow before his nod
> And Presidents cry "Gold is God!"

When the capitalists were overthrown, when "grasping Greed and Avarice drown/ And War and Poverty go down":

> Love, Equality and Peace
> Shall bless for aye the human race
> True Christianity restored,
> Mammon no longer is adored—
> All in one common brotherhood,
> The good for all the greatest good.

Brown and militant farmers evoked the dream of the faithful community where Christian cooperation would take the place of competition. In the spirit of John Winthrop's "A Modell of Christian Charity," Brown called for the unions and the granges to educate Americans "up to a higher and truer level of brotherhood. . . . Societies and lodges will be merged into the great society—the State—of which all are members, and brethren; a society of mutual helpfulness, of mutual benefits, of mutual love and good will, wherein my neighbors' children will be as dear to me as my own . . . then will each man be indeed a very Christ of love, radiant with the spirit of the Divine Teacher." Money—capital—was at the root of all the injustices and inequality in American society. Those who had money used it not to help their brothers and sisters but to oppress them. "The laws," he wrote, "are framed to help the rich. . . . Money increases by its own growth, so to speak. . . . 'Ten percent interest will eat the world up.' This is a great wrong."

In Iowa Dudley W. Adams, master of the Union County Grange, declared in 1872 to an audience of receptive farmers: "What we want in agriculture is a new Declaration of Independence. We have heard enough, ten times enough, about the hardened hand of honest toil, the supreme glory of the sweating brow, and how magnificent is the suit of coarse homespun which covers a form bent with overwork. . . . I tell you, my brother tillers of the soil, there is something in this world worth living for besides work. We have heard enough of this professional blarney about the honest farmer, the backbone of the nation. We have been too much alone. We need to get together to rub off the rough corners and polish down the symmetry. We want to exchange views and above all we want to *learn to think*. . . ." The words ran back in a direct line to Shays's Rebellion and William Manning's *Key to Libberty*.

The struggle that followed was intense, bitter, and prolonged. Many of the state laws passed by farmer-dominated legislatures in the Midwest were hastily drafted and inequitable. The railroads fought them in the courts, and the courts, after initial decisions supporting the so-called Granger Laws, began to retreat and return judgments favoring the railroads. In the mood of defiance the farmers generated a frenzy of cooperative activities: stores, marketing cooperatives, and even companies run on cooperative principles to manufacture farm equipment.

Most of the cooperatives failed, and under severe pressure from the railroads, which in some instances canceled train service to recalcitrant farm communities, the farmers were driven back, and the Patrons of Husbandry suffered a sharp decline in both its membership and its political clout. Brief as its heyday was, it nonetheless revived the tradition of Christian radicalism.

Eleanor Marx Aveling and her husband were highly critical of the pragmatic orientation of the granges, which they described as endeavoring "to make farms self-sustaining, to diversify crops, to discountenance the credit and mortgage system, to dispense with a surplus of middle men, to oppose the tyranny of monopolies. . . . But," they complained, "there is an air of vagueness about laboring for the good of mankind, developing a better manhood, fostering mutual understanding, suppressing prejudices." The Granger movement was a grass-roots organization which, if it waned almost as rapidly as it had waxed, laid the foundations for a new element in American politics, an aggressive farmers' political party. A host of successors sprang up to carry on the work: the Farmers' Alliance, the Farmers' Union, the Brothers of Freedom, the Farmers' Mutual Benefit Association, the Agricultural Wheel, the Greenbackers, and the Cooperative Union of America.

In the South the Texas Alliance, the Louisiana Farmers' Union, and the Agricultural Wheel were organized in the 1870s and 1880s. A clue to their principal grievances can be found in the Cleburne Demands, issued by the convention of the Texas Alliance in 1886, designed, according to preamble, to "secure to our people freedom from the onerous and shameful abuses that the industrial classes are now suffering at the hands of arrogant capitalists and powerful corporations." The first demand was for "the recognition by incorporation of trade-unions, co-operative stores, and such other organizations as may be organized by the industrial classes to improve their financial condition, or to promote their general welfare." The tenth demand called for an increase in the coining of gold and silver "and the tendering of the same without discrimination to the public creditors of the nation. . . ." The same article called for a national currency controlled by the United States Treasury in such a manner as to give the country "a per capita circulation that shall increase as the population and business interests of the country expand."

Still another demand was for the "passage of an interstate commerce law, that shall secure the same rates of freight to all persons for the same kind of commodities, according to the distance of haul, without regard to amount of shipment." Finally, the Texas Alliance recommended "a call for a national labor conference, to which all labor organizations shall be invited to send representative men, to discuss such measures as may be of interest to the laboring classes."

The National Agricultural Wheel assembled in 1887 at McKenzie, Tennessee, and laid out what were to become the general aims of the farmers' movement, starting with the demand that "The public land, the heritage of the people, be reserved for actual settlers only—not another acre to railroads or speculators. . . . That measures be taken to prevent aliens from acquiring title to lands in the United States [it was estimated that British investors owned some 21,000,000 acres of land in the U.S.] . . . that Congress shall . . . prevent dealing in future of all agricultural and mechanical productions . . . a graduated income tax . . . the strict enforcement of all laws prohibiting the importation of foreign labor under the contract system . . ." and "that all means of public communication and transportation shall protect the Chickasaws and Choctaws, and other civilized Indians of the Indian Territory, in all of their inalienable rights, and shall prevent railroads, and other wealthy syndicates, from over-riding the law and treaties now in existence. . . ."

By a process of consolidation the National Farmers' Alliance and Industrial Union took form in the late 1880s and came to be known as the Southern Alliance. An important adjunct was the Colored Farmers' National Alliance and Co-operative Union. One of the measures popular with the Alliance was the so-called subtreasury plan in which the farmer, rather than surrender his crop to bankers to speculate on, would store his nonperishable crops in government warehouses and receive low-interest loans on them. Initially the Alliance turned to Democratic candidates to carry its proposals to Congress. But it was soon evident that Democrats, once in office, displayed little concern for Alliance objectives.

A major obstacle to reform in the Midwest generally was that, in the words of an Iowa Republican, J. P. Dolliver, the state "would go Democratic when hell went Methodist." In 1889 it went Democratic, but it might have saved itself the trouble as far as any improvement in farm conditions was concerned. The pleas for relief from farmers were met on the floor of Congress with the taunt "What you want is to talk less and work more." Charles A. Boutelle of Maine shouted at a farm state Congressman: "Quit howling and go to work."

One of the more remarkable works to emerge from the fever of populism was by a young farmer-journalist (how often the two went together) from Hardy, Arkansas. W. Scott Morgan, who had been active in the establishment of the Arkansas chapter of the Agricultural Wheel, wrote a vast work published in 1889 entitled *History of the Wheel and Alliance, and the Impending Revolution*. He began his book with an analysis of the relationship between capital and labor. "The natural law of labor," he wrote, "is that the laborer is entitled to all the fruits of his toil. There is no variation to this rule. It is fixed upon the universal law of nature. . . ." In any other political system "the selfishness of those who have unjustly . . . acquired capital . . . , [by] robbing labor of its profits, would have ere this produced a revolution," Morgan declared. But a "spirit of forbearance" inherited from the "fathers of the Revolution" had averted such a catastrophe. Nonetheless, the world was "approaching a crisis without a parallel, in some respects, in all its

434 / THE RISE OF INDUSTRIAL AMERICA

past history." Anyone who doubted its imminence must be "densely ignorant of the ominous import of such widespread dissatisfaction among the producing classes throughout the world. The fires of discontent are burning on both continents. . . . To assume that there is no just cause for all this uprising on the part of labor would be equivalent to national suicide."

Put simply, Morgan's beliefs were as follows: "First—Man is naturally disposed to take pleasure in remunerative employment. Second—He is justly entitled to the fruits of his own labor. Third—Any violation of this natural law will breed social disorder, and universal violation will bring national calamity."

Morgan described the tactics of the "regular" politicians: "Vote 'er straight. Don't kick. Help us this time. If you don't see what you want in our platform, ask for it. Wait until we get there, and we'll show you how 'tis done. Whoop 'em up down in your neighborhood. Use dynamite and lay it on the other party. Use whisky. Vote 'em wherever you find 'em, niggers and all. Cry negro domination; low tariff; high tariff; radical; reconstruction; Power Clayton [carpetbag governor of Arkansas]; rebel; liar; thief; scoundrel; anarchist; bloody shirt; war; rebellion; blood and thunder. Anything to get up excitement, and rouse men's passions. If you can't carry your point that way, buy voters, bribe judges, stuff, steal and burn ballot boxes. It's all right. The other fellows do it, and we must get there this time or the country will go to the dogs. . . . No country in the history of the world has ever been cursed with so many and such gigantic monopolies as free (?) America. Free, only in name. Free, only in the fact that we still have a glimmering hope of crushing this monstrous system of robbery by an intelligent use of the ballot; that failing, all hope is lost, except that last fearful resort, revolution. May the God of our fathers prevent it." The voters, especially farmers and laborers, must be made aware of the fact that the major parties were more interested in perpetuating their power than in responding to the real needs of the people. "On every vital issue of the day they occupy a position with the capitalist," Morgan wrote. "This condition must be changed. These policies must be dropped or the masses of the people will be forced into poverty. . . ." Morgan closed his book with a ringing appeal: "Laboring men of America! The voice of Patrick Henry and the father of American Independence rings down through the corridors of time and tells you to strike. Not with glittering musket, flaming sword and deadly cannon: but with the silent, potent and all-powerful ballot, the only vestige of liberty left.

Strike from yourselves the shackles of party slavery, and exercise independent manhood."

Milford Howard, a Congressman from Alabama, was especially eloquent on the means by which the two established parties played off the poor voters of the North and West against their counterparts in the South. "In the North the shibboleth has been, 'vote as you shot.' In the South it has been, 'down with the carpet-bagger and Yankee.'" By such tactics the politicians had tried to obscure the fact that the nation's poor had common cause against the capitalists. While the followers on one side "shout at the top of their voices, 'Nigger, nigger!' . . . the wily old plutocrats get together and determine which candidate must be elected, and at once go to manipulating and wire-pulling. . . ."

Tom Watson of Georgia was another conspicuous leader of the farmers' movement in the South. Watson was an ardent supporter of close ties between farmers and industrial laborers. Speaking to the Brotherhood of Locomotive Firemen at Augusta, Georgia, he detailed the steps by which the "evils of our present system" could be remedied: "By co-operation among laborers. You must organize, agitate and educate. Organize to get the strength of unity; agitate the evils and cause thereof to arrest public opinion. . . ." Work for "a radical change in our laws . . . we must have legislation which either takes from the tyrannical power of capital or adds to the defensive strength of labor. We must make capital lay down its pistol, or we must give labor a pistol, too. When each man knows that the other has a 'gun' and will use it, they get exceedingly careful about fingering the trigger." There must also be a "change of public opinion, which will bring the irresistible power of moral support to the side of labor as against the unreasonable exactions of capital. Every pulpit, every newspaper, every leader of thought in every profession, should give to this question earnest attention and then speak out. I dwell on this because I regard public opinion as omnipotent. . . . The bravest man quails before the silent aversion of hostile public opinion. The stoutest leader weakens before its frowning face. It changes policies, customs, manners. It enforces an unwritten law, and the criminal who violates it swings from a limb. . . . You think you hold your life at the mercy of the law! You do nothing of the kind. You hold it at the mercy of public opinion." That opinion then must be reformed. Watson himself had known want and hunger. He had gone "weary up and down your streets asking for work and finding none. . . . The horror of that dreadful time I shall never forget. It has left its mark on my mind and on my heart. It has shaped my convictions and controlled my feelings."

Watson was equally eloquent about the conditions of workers in the mines of Pennsylvania, the mills of New England, and "those bent and feeble sewing men of New York City, crouched in dreary garrets and plying their needles":

> Stitch-stitch-stitch
> In poverty, hunger and dirt;
> Sewing at once with a double thread
> A shroud as well as a shirt.

"They tell us the country is suffering from overproduction of food. Then why," asked Watson, "do men go hungry through your streets? Overproduction of goods? Then why do shrinking women and feeble children go shivering down icy sidewalks so scantily clad that suffering speaks in every line of pinched and haggard features? Overproduction? I will tell you where the overproduction is. It is in the cold-hearted and hard-hearted men who will not see anything which does not belong to their class. It is in the men who consider the mere getting of gold the gospel of life; it is the men who have grown proud and cruel because they possess capital (the thing which was labor yesterday), but utterly despise the labor of today."

John Swinton was a labor leader who pressed for an alliance between workers and farmers. "In recent years," he wrote in *Striking for Life* (1894), "the political ideas of the farmers of the West have been away ahead of those of the battered masses in our cities. They have acted with more independence than the denizens of cities; they have displayed a clearer judgment; they have been far less subservient to the old party hacks who domineer over the cities; they have not been afraid to elect Governors and Legislatures which represent them. . . ." They were far from being as radical as Swinton would have wished, but he was convinced that "we of the cities must clasp hands with the men of the fields in a new campaign for human rights and for freedom."

Among the labor leaders anxious to form a farm-labor alliance were the Vrooman brothers of Kansas City, who edited a labor newspaper. When the Avelings spoke there (and signed up forty new members for the Socialist Labor Party), they met Walter Vrooman, "the boy-orator," who was only seventeen but already a well-known public speaker. Once he was arrested after a speech the police considered subversive; a crowd gathered to free him, and the police, fearful of a riot, let him out of jail the back way. Walter and his brother, Harry, nineteen, edited the *Labor Inquirer*. The Avelings found them "quite boys still and with a keen sense of fun." In New York City Walter was a "huge sensation" as an orator.

The path of the organizers of the farmers' movement was far from smooth. A rise in the price of grain in 1887 brought numerous defections, and Jeremiah ("Jerry") Simpson, a Kansas radical, was so disheartened by the collapse of the Union Labor Party in 1888 that he wrote: "I know that for the man who sees the evils of the time—the want, ignorance and misery caused by unjust laws—who sets himself so far as he has the strength to right them, there is nothing in store but ridicule and abuse. The bitterest though, and the hardest to bear, is the hopelessness of the struggle, 'the futility of sacrifice.' But for us who have taken up the crusade, there shall be no halting; and as our ranks grow thin by death and desertion, we should close up, shoulder to shoulder, and show an unbroken battle line to the enemy."

The forty-six-year-old Simpson had been a farmer, rancher, local politician, Great Lakes sailor, and soldier in the Union army. He settled in Kansas in 1879, attracted by the "boom." Like many others, he lost all his savings in the drought and bust of 1887 and found himself deeply in debt. But a new wind was stirring over the plains, and a few months later he wrote in an euphoric mood: "Our meetings are growing; at first they were held in country school houses while the other parties held theirs in the open air; now ours are outside, and the other parties are never heard of at all." Simpson found that in his various adventures he had acquired a wealth of experience that now stood him in good stead as he went about the state, speaking to men and women who, like him, had seen their hopes vanish under a pile of debts.

William Allen White "deeply respected" Simpson. "He was smart," White wrote. "He had read more widely than I, and often quoted Carlyle in our conversations, and the poets and essayists of the seventeenth century. His talk, as we rode together on trains or sat in hotel lobbies, or loafed in hotel bedrooms, was full of Dickensian allusions, and he persuaded me to Thackeray, whom I had rejected until then. Jerry Simpson was not a sockless clown. He accepted the portrait which the Republicans made of him as an ignorant fool because it helped him to talk to the crowds that gathered to hear him. . . . He was Yankee to the core of his bones, a tough-skinned man, brown and bronzed with crow's-feet at the corner of his eyes. . . . He wore gold-rimmed glasses that fastened over his ears, and he beamed through them with benevolence and wisdom. His hands were big and gnarly, and he shook hands with warmth and sincerity." Simpson ran against a corporation lawyer, nicknamed Prince Hal for his elegant ways and lavish style of living. In the Kansas Seventh Congressional District, Sockless Simpson won comfortably. "The real Jerry Simpson," White added, "profited by the fame of his own effigy."

As the movement gathered momentum, Tom Watson put out a handbook for stump speakers, full of damning facts about capitalists and capitalism. It was crammed with statistics listing the minimal taxes paid by tycoons, the interest rates they collected on dividends, the acres of public lands given to railroads, the nature of the "rings" and "pools," the activities of the "Standard Oil Magnates, Coal Barons, Rail Road Kings, Sugar Trust Operators, Steel and Iron Combiners." One section detailed the arguments in favor of income taxes, which "would discourage the accumulation of enormous fortunes and would afford a legal method of checking the growth of concentrated wealth." The handbook detailed the favors of the government to bondholders, adding, "Consider it a moment and then collapse and go to bed." The critical point was that control of the monetary system must be wrested from the bankers and their corporate allies. "Why is it," Tom Watson asked, "that in strikes and lockouts the military is always called out to protect the interest of capital, but never to protect the toilers? . . . We must . . . declare that it is treason for capitalistic combinations to hire armies and equip them with muskets and revolvers for the purpose of slaughtering our citizens. . . . There is only one Government in the country that must and should be respected. The Pinkerton Government must be abolished and outlawed. It has no status under the Constitution of the United States. No corporation in its charter is clothed with power to declare war and raise armies."

Another section of Watson's handbook put forward the arguments for public ownership of the railroads, among them that "it would remove the causes of hatred of the people to the Roads and harmonize all interests" and "put into the hands of the people a weapon with which they could destroy any Combine among Capitalists in any Article of Commerce." Finally, "it would be a giant stride in the direction of equality and manhood rights and the destruction of our Class System of Special Privilege, Shoddy Aristocracy based on Commercial Spoils

and advancing through the dirty lanes and perils of bribery and corruption."

What was to be done? Watson did not hesitate to say that "we
must give them the bayonet," although it was not clear whether he was
speaking literally or metaphorically. "It is always the same. Petitions
are rejected: remonstrances spurned: complaints laughed aside: protests silenced: resistance stamped out with an iron heel. All these things
are done as long as it is supposed they can be safely done. It is only
when Tyranny sees danger that it hears reason. . . . The Congress now
sitting is one illustration. Pledged to reform, they have not reformed.
Pledged to Economy, they have not economized. Pledged to Legislate,
they have not legislated. . . . Drunken members have reeled about the
aisles—a disgrace to the Republic. Drunken speakers have debated
grave issues on the Floor and in the midst of maudlin ramblings they
have been heard to ask, 'Mr. Speaker, where was I at?' " Undeserved
suffering was a cruel burden. "As the Nobleman said to the King, the
night the Bastille fell, 'No, sire, it is not a Revolt, it is a Revolution.' . . . To restore the liberties of the people, the rule of the people,
the equal rights of the people is our purpose; and to do it, the revolution in the old system must be complete. We do not blindly seek to
tear down. We offer the good Law for each bad Law; the sound rail
for every rotten rail. We work in no spirit of hate to individuals. We
hate only the wrongs and the abuses and the special privileges which
oppress us. . . . We call on God above to aid us. For in the revolution
we seek to accomplish, there shall be law and order preserved in-
violate."

Thomas Nugent, the nominee of the People's Party for governor
of Texas in 1892 and 1894, was a power in the state and one of the
most engaging political figures of the era. A college graduate and an
ex-district judge, he was an avowed Christian Socialist. Like many of
his fellow Alliance members, he based his social criticism on the Scriptures and the writings of the Founding Fathers. Swedenborgian in his
leanings, a student of Emerson, he had imbibed with his mother's milk
those semimystical yearnings characteristic of the American psyche. In
the words of one historian, "He looked upon the whole human race
as being conjoined to the Lord—and this conjunction he called the
Divine Humanity. All things were to him a One. Each part of an organic
whole whose soul God is, and whose body is man." In one of his
speeches during the gubernatorial campaign Nugent sounded what

was a frequent note in his political addresses: "Great men no longer lead the old parties because great men are men of soul, of humanity, of genius, of inspiration. They are never machine men."

In Nugent's rhetoric "Wall Street" was the symbolic villain, "the big bankers and moneylenders, the stock jobbers, the men who bull and bear the market." Nugent, while strongly opposed to protectionism, insisted that it was not the real issue. The advantages of low tariffs, like the advantages of high tariffs, would accrue not to the workingmen and women of the country but to the capitalists. The real problem was the "distribution of wealth." The tendency of men was always toward conservatism, Nugent argued. "We learn to love what we are accustomed to, and misguided affection makes us cling with death-like tenacity to social and political institutions long after they have ceased to be useful or serviceable to the human race—yes, long after they have become the instruments of injustice and oppression." Only the appearance of the reformer had checked the downward movement of society: "whenever and wherever evil conditions have brought suffering and distress to earth's despairing multitudes, then and there the reformer has reappeared with the same devotion to the cause of humanity, the same self-abnegation, the same boundless confidence in his schemes of relief; and his reappearance has ever been signalized by the same outpouring of derision and contempt, the same misconstruction and opposition."

While Nugent praised Christian socialism, he was careful to distinguish that variety from, in his words, "those extreme socialistic schemes which seek by the outside pressure of mere enactments or systems, to accomplish what can only come from the free activities of men. . . . The social brotherhood is slowly growing among the people as breast after breast thrills responsively to the sound of that 'calling.' " If human selfishness were ever transcended, "glorified industries will arise in orderly unity and harmony like the 'City of God.' . . ." Nugent was convinced that "the national banking system, like Carthage, must be destroyed, and the national government must no longer be permitted to farm out its credit to corporations to be used for private gain. . . . The Populists favor the free and unlimited coinage of gold and silver at the present ratio, and the emission of incontrovertible paper to supply any lack of circulation, thus to make the entire volume of money sufficient to supply the demands of trade."

Of all the populist and radical leaders of the Midwest, none was more colorful or eccentric than Ignatius Donnelly of Minnesota. A

Shakespearean "scholar" who believed that Lord Bacon had written the plays attributed to Shakespeare, a seer and mystic who wrote a book on the lost continent of Atlantis and speculated on the origin of the earth, Donnelly involved himself in every reform movement of the age and, in addition, wrote several antiutopian novels predicting an age of degeneration and destruction for the United States. His best-known work, *Caesar's Column* (1891), carried on the title page a passage from Goethe: "The true poet is only a masked father-confessor, whose special function it is to exhibit what is dangerous in sentiment and pernicious in action by a vivid picture of the consequences." He was not, Donnelly assured his readers, an advocate of the overthrow of the American civilization that he described; nor was he an anarchist. "I seek to preach into the ears of the able and rich and powerful the great truth that neglect of the sufferings of their fellows, indifference to the great bond of brotherhood which lies at the base of Christianity, and blind, brutal and degrading worship of mere wealth, must—given time and pressure enough—eventuate in the overthrow of society and the destruction of civilization. . . ." Addressing the churches on their mission, he wrote: "The world to-day clamors for deeds, not creeds! for bread, not dogma; for charity, not ceremony; for love, not intellect." Honest observers of modern civilization were forced to concede "that life is a dark and wretched failure for the great mass of mankind. The many are plundered to enrich the few. . . . The rich, as a rule, despise the poor; and the poor are coming to hate the rich. The face of labor grows sullen; the old tender Christian love is gone; standing armies are formed on one side, and great communistic organizations on the other. . . . They wait only for the drum-beat and the trumpet to summon them to armed conflict." Donnelly's plea was "for higher and nobler thoughts in the souls of men; for wider love and ampler charity . . . for a renewal of the bond of brotherhood between classes; for a reign of justice on earth that shall obliterate the cruel hates and passions which now divide the world."

There are notable passages in *Caesar's Column*, among them those that depict an increasingly hollow and meaningless society. Describing a modern metropolis, Donnelly wrote: "The truth is, that, in this vast, over-crowded city, man is a drug,—a superfluity,—and I think many men and women end their lives out of an overwhelming sense of their own insignificance;—in other words, from a mere weariness of feeling that they are nothing, they become nothing." In the novel a public agency exists to help people, those weary of life, to commit suicide as painlessly as possible. Gabriel, the protagonist, accompanies his friend Maximilian into the "Under-World" of a modern city. Maximilian describes the city as "hollow and rotten to the core."

"What do you mean?" Gabriel asks, horrified.

"What I mean is that our civilization has grown to be a gorgeous shell; a mere mockery; a sham; outwardly fair and lovely, but inwardly full of dead men's bones and all uncleanness. To think that Mankind is so capable of good, and now so cultured and polished, and yet all below is suffering, wretchedness, sin and shame . . . civilization is a gross and dreadful failure for seven-tenths of the human family . . . seven-tenths of the backs of the world are insufficiently clothed; seven-tenths of the stomachs of the world are insufficiently fed; seven-tenths of the minds of the world are darkened and despairing, and filled with bitterness against the Author of the universe."

Gabriel felt that he was "witnessing the resurrection of the dead; and that these vast, streaming, endless swarms were the condemned, marching noiselessly as shades to unavoidable and everlasting misery." When their wretched lives were over, they were disposed of in vast furnaces.

Gabriel, observing such human suffering, came to the conclusion that only the intervention of government could moderate the injustice. "Government, government—national, state and municipal—is the key to the future of the human race." The "city of the future" must take over the role of the family and the small community. "The city . . . must furnish doctors for all; lawyers for all; entertainment for all; business guidance for all. It will see to it that no man is plundered, and no man starved, who is willing to work."

The Golden Bottle was another one of Donnelly's political tracts in the form of a novel. The hero is Ephraim Benezet, a Kansas farmer who discovers an alchemist's bottle and with the gold that he is able to make becomes president of the United States and sets out to put the Populist platform into effect. An era of cooperation and fellowship ensues, and the downtrodden of the world rise up against their oppressors.

World government is established, and universal peace follows. Underpinning all is a reawakened Christianity. The centerpiece of *The Golden Bottle* is Benezet's inaugural address as president: "*Keep the land in the hands of the many.* [Cheers.] Limit the amount that any man may own. [Cheers.] See to it that the workingmen obtain homes. [Great cheers.] *Use the powers of government for the good of the governed.* [Cheers.]"

Wealth is to be accumulated through a national system of savings and the capital so accumulated is to be lent out to "the farmers and working-men on real estate security, at two percent per annum, to enable them to save or obtain homes . . . and prevent the transformation of this country from a republic into a despotism. [Tremendous applause.]"

One of the earliest and most influential figures in the emerging People's Party was James B. Weaver. Weaver had been born in Dayton, Ohio, in 1833. A lawyer of abolitionist sentiment at the outbreak of the war, he had enlisted as a private in the 2d Iowa Infantry. Charles Edward Russell, the reforming journalist, wrote of Weaver's Civil War career: "I think there never was a braver man. He rose to be second lieutenant, first lieutenant, captain, major, colonel, and brigadier general, and each promotion was won by daring or skill, or both, on the battlefield. He was one of those strange birds, a Christian soldier." To Weaver the enemies of American democracy were "the swift advance of corporate power . . ." and the menace, quite as great, that lay in the control of the world's finances by a group of bankers and large bond-holders. In the campaign of 1876 he had been denounced as a communist. "Nihilist" and "anarchist" were also common epithets applied to him by the conservative press. Russell described Weaver as "about the average height, notably erect and soldierly in his bearing, spare as an Indian, one of those wiry, tireless, alert, but notably self-controlled men that seem to carry about them a certain unescapable aura of power and distinction. . . . His aquiline, high-bred features, commanding gray eyes, curling gray hair, closely trimmed military mustache were parts of the total impression of him. . . . He had an excellent voice, mellow and yet of great carrying power . . . here was a man essentially a Puritan, rigid as iron in his faith . . . and yet having an exquisite sense of humor. He could cut and sting in debate; he was a master of the sardonic and the absurd."

Weaver broke with the Republicans over the paper money issue and was elected to Congress from Iowa in 1878 as a Greenbacker. Growing more radical with each passing year and more disillusioned with the monetary policies of the two parties, he ran for president on the Greenback ticket in 1880, receiving 307,306 votes. The fruit of his political radicalism was *A Call to Action*, a volume of more than 400 pages, devoted to a scathing critique of American capitalism. It was Weaver's exegesis of the principles of populism, and as such it deserves a close reading. But it also stands on its own as one of the most thorough and thoughtful works of political economy produced by an American author, worthy of a place beside such classics as *The Federalist Papers*. In his introduction Weaver set the tone of his work. "We are nearing a serious crisis," he wrote. "If the present strained relations between wealth owners and wealth producers continue much longer they will ripen into a frightful disaster. This universal discontent must be quickly interpreted and its causes removed. It is the country's imperative Call to Action, and cannot be longer disregarded with impunity. . . . A bold and aggressive plutocracy has usurped the Government and is using it as a policeman to enforce its insolent decrees. . . . The public domain has been squandered, our coal fields bartered away, our forests denuded, our people impoverished, and we are attempting to build a prosperous commonwealth among people who are being robbed of their homes. . . . The corporation has been placed above the individual and an armed body of cruel mercenaries permitted, in times of public peril, to discharge police duties which clearly belong to the State." Weaver then went on to analyze the instruments of the plutocracy: the Senate; the courts; the legal fraternity. The Senate received the heaviest blows. It was crowded with millionaires and the lackeys of millionaires. There was "not a single great leader in the Senate . . . not one who is abreast of the times, or who can be truthfully said to be the exponent of American civilization or the active champion of reforms made necessary by the growth and changed relations of this century. . . . They are stifled by their surroundings and dwarfed by their parties. One and all, they stand dumb and aimless in the presence of the mighty problems of the age."

It seemed clear to Weaver that "the moral, intellectual and political leaders during the twenty years immediately following the war, with the single exception of Wendell Phillips, failed to comprehend the problems which confronted them." They had stopped with the overthrow of slavery, not realizing that labor was equally enslaved. Now there was a new class of "slave drivers" who "plied their cruel vocation among all the families of men. To overthrow them," Weaver wrote, "is the grand work of the new crusade." With the growth of corporations, "the relation of the legal profession to the people and to the administration of public justice has undergone a frightful change. . . ." The law, intended as a bulwark against oppression, had been subverted to the service of the plutocracy. Such was the opinion of one of the last liberal jurists of the Supreme Court, David Davis, appointed by Lincoln. "The rapid growth of corporate power of all classes and grades," Davis had told Weaver in the spring of 1880, "and their corrupting

influence at the Seat of Government . . . filled me with apprehension."
Davis was convinced "that the corporations were maturing their plans
to gain complete control of the Supreme Court. . . ." If he were blind,
he could "still hear enough to alarm me. It is not lawful for me to utter
many things which I have heard, because I get them in my private and
confidential relations every day; but this is my chief concern. If we
lose the Courts, we lose all."

Davis's concerns had proved to be well founded. As each justice
of liberal persuasion died, he was replaced by a jurist with a background
in corporate law. In the decade of the 1880s seven justices of the
Supreme Court died or retired; no decade of our history has seen so
many justices replaced. The transformation of the Court was thereby
complete, and its reactionary decisions were anticipated. The corporations now held the nation in far severer thrall than the "slave power"
had ever done.

Not all corporations were vicious, but the fact was that the corporate structure as it had evolved since the Civil War had "the power
to do wrong . . . without the possibility of accompanying restraint,"
Weaver wrote. Human beings had, over the centuries, displayed the
capacity to "evolve about all the evil that humanity can bear," and now
there was a "supplementary harvest of injustice and wrong doing which
results from the creation of a horde of artificial persons [corporation],
who are void of the feelings of pity and the compunctions of conscience. . . . Are we still an asylum for the oppressed of all nations,"
Weaver asked, "or are we about to become the policemen for the
monarchs and despots of the old world—a despicable international
slave-catcher, under a world-wide fugitive slave law—engaged in the
business of arresting and returning to their cruel task-masters the poor
slaves who are fleeing hither? . . . A century of experiment has shown
that our economic system is utterly unsuited to an increasing population, to the unerring laws of nature and to the fundamental wants
of the human race. Think of the barbaric savagery of a system which
permits a single generation to appropriate to itself the whole planet
upon which it lives, in defraud of all who are to come after them!"

The rage and anger of the people, "which are daily manifesting
themselves in strikes, lock-outs and incipient riots," were "simply the
picket firing which precedes the general conflict, if the people of America refuse much longer to listen to the voice of reason. If our troubles
of to-day are serious, what will be our peril twenty years from now
with our population grown to a hundred millions?"

It was a scandal that, in Weaver's words, "Our supply of raw material is abundant, and our facilities for manufacturing without a parallel. We have every variety of climate with fruits and cereals ample to supply the wants of the world," but "instead . . . we find that discontent, debt and destitution exist throughout every state and territory in the Union. . . . We find millions of people homeless and out of employment; millions more in danger of losing their homes, and still more millions working for wages scarcely sufficient to sustain life and respectability and so meager as to shut out all hope for the future. . . . It is certainly the duty of statesmen, philosophers, philanthropists and Christian people to search out the real causes of these distressing evils."

The Alliance leaders made the constant analogy between the exploitation of labor and the institution of slavery. A Kansas farmer, writing to Ignatius Donnelly, urged that the unemployed be put to work clearing the slums of the great cities, "recognizing the Slums of our great cities as a disgrace to the nation, the existence of which should mantle our brows with a deeper shame than ever did the institution of American Slavery."

What is striking about all the writings of the Populists is the breadth and range of their critiques. They are far more than mere inventories of farmers' grievances. Indeed, all of them devote as much, if not more, attention to the plight of the industrial worker as to that of the farmers, commonly seeing the farmers' distress as a kind of by-product of the exploitation of the industrial worker. W. Scott Morgan told his readers of Ann Fullmon of New York City, who "finishes pantaloons for a living, sews on buttons, makes buttonholes, puts on straps, buckles and presses them for 13 cents a pair; averages $2 a week for self and family," and of Kate Crowley, who "makes men's drawers at 10 cents for a dozen pair. She can finish two dozen pairs in a day by working from 6 A.M. to 9 P.M., and gets 20 cents for her day's labor."

Moreover, most of the works are written out of a remarkably sophisticated historical consciousness. They trace the changing economic conditions brought about by the rise of the industrial era; some go back to classical times to discuss the antecedents of the modern world. They are familiar with Adam Smith, Malthus, and Ricardo, with conditions in Britain and on the Continent, in Germany and Russia. Not surprisingly, a prophetic and evangelistic vein runs through their work, sometimes more and sometimes less explicitly Christian. Finally, the Populists were in general distinguished by an attitude toward black Americans far in advance of the time.

Tom Watson was determined to form an alliance between white and black farmers. He declared: "The Negro Question in the South has been for nearly thirty years a source of danger, discord, and bloodshed. It is an ever-present irritant and menace." Both parties had raised the cry of "Negro domination . . . until they have constructed as perfect a 'slot machine' as the world ever saw. Drop the old, worn nickel of the 'party slogan' into the slot and the machine does the rest. You might beseech a Southern white tenant to listen to you upon questions of finance, taxation, and transportation, you might demonstrate with mathematical precision that therein lay his way out of poverty into comfort; you might have him 'almost persuaded' to the truth, but if the merchant who furnished his farm supplies (at tremendous usury) or the town politician (who never spoke to him except at election times) came along and cried 'Negro rule!' the entire fabric of reason and common sense which you had patiently constructed would fall. . . ." It was in the South that the black man "is founding churches, opening schools, maintaining newspapers, entering the professions, serving on juries, deciding doubtful elections, drilling as a volunteer soldier, and piling up a cotton crop which amazes the world." If the South were ever to free itself from its exploiters, "there must be a new policy inaugurated, whose purpose is to allay the passions and prejudices of race conflict. . . ."

Watson did not stop with political rhetoric. On at least one occasion he offered sanctuary to a black politician pursued by a mob bent on lynching him. He was merciless in castigating the Democrats. "They have intimidated the voter," he declared in 1892 as the elections drew near, "assaulted the voter, murdered the voter. They have bought votes, forced votes and stolen votes. They have incited lawless men to the pitch of frenzy which threatens anarchy. They have organized bands of hoodlums of both high and low degree to insult our speakers, silence our speakers, rotten-egg our speakers, and put our lives in danger."

The same spirit was evident in the Louisiana People's Party, meeting in convention in October, 1891. It produced an "Address to the People of the State of Louisiana. . . . Irrespective of Class, Color, or Past Political Affiliation." Of the 171 delegates attending the party's nominating convention a few months later, 24 were black. Two were nominated for the state legislature but declined the nomination on the ground that they would hurt the ticket and were appointed to the party's state executive committee. "We declare emphatically," one of the planks of the platform read, "that the interests of the white and colored races in the South are identical, but that both would suffer unless the undisputed control of our government were assured to the intelligent and educated portion of the population. Legislation beneficial to the white man must, at the same time, be beneficial to the colored man."

The same stand was taken by the People's Party in Alabama, where a Populist leader denounced the fact that black votes were persistently "stolen or miscounted . . . with the excuse that it was for the security of the white man's government. Now the votes of both white and black are stolen in the interest of a white rascal's government! The whole moral tone of society from Statesmen to the rum seller is blighted with the curse of this crime."

In 1894 Watson was still pleading for political equality for blacks and denouncing intolerance: "No country ever thrived under it; no people ever improved under it. Tyranny used it as a prop; malice uses it as a deadly weapon. Wherever its iron hand has ruled, progress has been halted, mental achievement ceases and human happiness disappears. . . . Whenever any people has been cursed with intolerance, either political or religious, its ruinous effects can be traced in the history of national decay and death. . . . It takes brave men to make a country great. And to have brave men the community must not combine to crush the individual who dares to have personal independence."

The Ocala, Florida, convention of the Farmers' Alliance in December, 1890, was a landmark in the formation of a national farmers' movement by virtue of the fact that it brought together leaders of the agrarian organizations from all sections of the country under the leadership of Leonidas Lafayette Polk. It was Polk, a North Carolina farmer and newspaper editor, who took the lead in turning the Southern Alliance into a national organization. The Ocala Convention was not yet ready to try a third-party experiment, but a year later a convention in Cincinnati boldly declared that "the time has arrived for a crystallization of the political reform forces of the country and the formation of what should be known as the People's Party of the United States of America." Added force was given to the declaration of the Cincinnati conference by the spread of hard times.

The Southern Alliance in 1890 drew up a program calling for the unlimited coinage of silver, subtreasuries to make credit easier for farmers to secure, laws prohibiting stock market speculation, strict regulation of railroads or government ownership, popular election of U.S. Senators, and a graduated income tax. While the East cried "socialism," the Grange, the Colored Alliance, and the Northern Alliance adopted similar platforms and vowed not to vote for any candidate for public office who did not endorse their demands.

Kansas became a hotbed of agitation led by one of the most remarkable women of the age, Mary Lease. Mrs. Lease had been born in Pennsylvania in 1853, educated in New York, and gone to Kansas when she was nineteen. She studied to become a lawyer and was admitted to the bar in 1885. She soon discovered that she had a natural gift for public speaking that reminded the older generation of Anna Dickinson. She joined the Farmers' Alliance Lecture Bureau and during the winter and fall of 1890 made more than 160 speeches. "Mary Lease," William Allen White wrote, "was the complete antithesis of Jerry Simpson. I have never heard a lovelier voice than Mrs. Lease's. It was a golden voice, a deep rich contralto, a singing voice that had hypnotic qualities." Her speeches, White recalled, were often routine political harangues, "but she could recite the multiplication table and set a crowd hooting or hurrahing at her will." She was built like a tree, six feet tall with a small head set on her large body. "Her skin was a pasty white; her jowls . . . a little heavy," but her eyes were "capable of everything except spoken language." With her hair in a bun on the top of her head she was a formidable figure, the powerful expositor of the hopes and fears of her audiences.

"What you farmers need to do," she told enraptured audiences, "is to raise less corn and more HELL! . . . We wiped out slavery and by our tariff laws and National Banks began a system of white wage slavery worse than the first. Wall Street owns the country. It is no longer a government of the people, by the people and for the people, but a government of Wall Street, by Wall Street and for Wall Street. The great common people of this country are slaves, and monopoly is the master. The West and South are bound and prostrate before the manufacturing East. . . . The parties lie to us and political speakers mislead us. . . . We want money, land and transportation. We want the abolition of the National Banks, and we want the power to make loans direct from the Government. We want the accursed foreclosure system wiped out. . . . The people are at bay, let the blood-hounds of money who have dogged us thus far beware."

Such words had a splendid ring to them. Suddenly the farmers took hope; they made it clear that they could indeed raise hell as well as corn. Ignatius Donnelly, who had served three terms in Congress as a Republican, had the enthusiasm of a convert. He was as inspiring a speaker as Mary Lease and drew large crowds wherever he spoke. In Nebraska the farmers joined forces with Terence Powderly's Knights of Labor to capture the state legislature. Kansas voted in five Congressmen and a Senator pledged to Alliance principles, and when the leading farm organizations and the Knights called a conference in Cincinnati in 1891, 1,400 delegates showed up in a militant mood. The spirit that hung over the hall where the delegates met was reminiscent of the exciting days of 1852, when the Republican Party was formed from all the miscellaneous elements of reform in the country. It was enough to frighten the business interests of the country half to death. This time the delegates organized the People's Party, drew up a platform based largely on that of the Southern Alliance a year earlier, and adjourned, flushed with the conviction that the future belonged to them.

A fierce struggle now ensued in the farm states between the Cleveland or hard money Democrats and the increasingly radical free silver wing of the party. Eastern hard money men like Henry Villard worked closely with their Midwestern counterparts to stifle the insurgents. Villard, who had strong ties to German leaders, played skillfully upon the anxieties produced among the foreign-born by the activities of the American Protective Association, yet another manifestation of a nativism that seemed unsuppressible. Villard, who had extensive holdings in the Middle West, visited the region in 1891 and came home convinced that radical farmers were ruining the country. They had gained control of many state legislatures, he noted, and were creating "an epidemic of dishonesty . . . manifesting itself in the most outrageous legislative violence to railroads and the free coinage of silver infatuation."

In this spirit, with the depression deepening and with farmers and industrial workers joining in talk of revolution, the nation approached the presidential elections of 1892.

Just as historians have been disposed to depict the black politicians of the Reconstruction Era as illiterate and corrupt buffoons, they have been inclined—with laudable exceptions, of course—to treat the Populist leaders as colorful and somewhat clownish figures. Nothing could be further from the truth. Many of them, it is true, used the techniques of the spellbinding public orator. James H. Davis was an Alliance speaker who often mounted the speakers' platform carrying ten volumes of Jefferson's collected works and quoted copiously from them, and Mary Lease told her farmer audiences to raise less corn and more hell. But their books (of which there were an extraordinary number) and their articles and speeches reveal a highly sophisticated grasp of social and economic fundamentals.

25

Politics

We have deliberately scanted the earlier political developments of this era on the ground that they were, if not precisely irrelevant, at least subordinate to the larger issues to which politicians of both parties responded, for the most part, with reactionary incomprehension.

While it was true that essentially nonpolitical events produced certain reflexive political actions, those actions appear, in retrospect, largely meaningless. Nevertheless, since our system is manifestly political, we must pick up those threads.

Politics, like virtually every other aspect of American life in this era, was in large part a by-product of the war between capital and labor, especially if we include farmers in the latter category. When William Sinclair wrote *The Aftermath of Slavery*, he had reference primarily to the legacy of racial prejudice left by that malodorous institution. But it left another oppressive legacy, as we have seen—states' rights. In addition, it fixed the two parties in rigid molds which held them in thrall for the next half century. Those individuals and segments of society that were most disposed to radical alteration in the American economic system were "fixed" in the Republican Party, which came increasingly to be under the domination of the capitalists. In

Meadville, Pennsylvania, Frederic Howe recalled, there was "something unthinkable about being a Democrat—Democrats, Copperheads, and atheists were persons whom one did not know socially. As a boy I did not play with their children. The Republican Party and the Methodist church divided our allegiance."

The case was only slightly different with the Democrats. The postwar agrarian South was a hotbed of radical political ideas. The People's Party put down its deepest roots there. But to vote Republican in the South was often literally to court death. Thus the reformers in the North and the radicals in the South were prevented from forming an alliance by the fact that ancient animosities left them locked in to parties dominated by the most conservative elements in both sections. So, as the Farmers' Alliance discovered, it made little difference which party was in power. As it became clear that the Republican Party was irredeemably the party of reaction, some of the more realistic Midwestern radicals turned to the Democrats, but here again they were thwarted. Virtually everywhere the Democratic Party remained securely in the hands of the business interests.

Making any realistic response to the nation's most pressing problems virtually impossible were two issues that, while they had little to do with the economic well-being of the country, completely dominated national politics from the end of the war to the end of the century. They were, of course, hard money versus soft money and the tariff question. The amount of political rhetoric and human energy expended on those two issues is beyond calculation. Or endurance. It is staggering and depressing, and the story had best be told as simply and briefly as possible. Money was alternately hard and soft without any clear correlation to the nation's economic situation. If cheap money prevailed at the time of one of the periodic depressions, the depression was blamed on cheap money. If the depression came when money was hard, it was blamed on hard money. The only thing that can be said with reasonable certainty was that the hard money-soft money-greenback-free silver-gold controversy was a class and sectional issue. The capitalists wanted hard money, and their practical reasons were, as we have noted in earlier volumes, reinforced by a general conviction that hard money was moral and soft money immoral.

The tariff issue was less clear. Tariffs went up and down (mostly up) without any clear evidence that they materially affected the general state of the economy. It was clear, however, that high tariffs put millions of dollars in the pockets of the owners and stockholders of protected industries. It follows from all this that the most bitterly contested issues of the period were in large part illusory. Hard money and tight credit certainly hurt farmers grievously. On the other hand, it was presumably possible to go too far in the other direction. Under the circumstances it is hardly to be wondered that politics itself had an ever greater air of unreality about it. The quadrennial madness produced undistinguished, if not outright deplorable, candidates for the presidency, who had no more notion of the real problems of the country or how to solve them than the electorate in general.

In the decades between the presidency of Andrew Jackson and the Civil War we had witnessed a similar phenomenon. Since slavery was the only issue of any consequence and no political candidates prior to Lincoln dared address the issue directly, political life had a dreamlike unreality about it, and a series of eminently forgettable presidents held office. In the postwar period the war between capital and labor was *the* issue, but again it could not be dealt with directly, at least on the national level. So once more we had a series of forgettable presidents: Rutherford Hayes, who stole the office from Samuel Tilden (the office was so diminished in influence at that point that it was hardly more than petty larceny); James Garfield, who was shot before he could demonstrate his ability; Chester Arthur, a hack politician with a shady record in the pits of New York politics; Grover Cleveland, a cut above the rest; Benjamin Harrison, who looked presidential and evoked the memory of an earlier and presumably better time; courageous Cleveland again, grown even more conservative in his years out of office; and then, finally, William McKinley, the "Major," a decent if undistinguished man, manufactured by Mark Hanna.

While the familiar hoopla attended every election and the voters were assured that the future well-being, if not the very existence, of the country depended on voting for this candidate or that, things went on much as before. This state of affairs—the unwillingness or inability of the two parties to deal with the realities of American life—produced the Populist Party (much as the refusal of the Whigs and the Democrats to come to grips with slavery had produced the Republican Party) and, in 1892, the most exciting (indeed, alarming) election since that of 1860.

It is hard to dispute Henry Adams's observation that "no period so thoroughly ordinary had been known in American politics since Christopher Columbus first disturbed the balance of American society." The Grant administration, Adams wrote, "drove him, and thousands of other young men, into active enmity, not only to Grant, but to the system or want of system, which took possession of the President. . . . Work, whiskey, and cards were life." Even the press was not exempt from the general feeling of debilitation and moral slackening. "No editor, no political writer, and no public administrator," Adams wrote, "achieved enough good reputation to preserve his memory for twenty years. . . . On the whole, even for Senators, diplomats, and Cabinet officers, the period was wearisome and stale."

But that was clearly only half (or indeed much less than half) of the story. Titanic forces were at work, and it is not surprising that to men of the temperament of Henry Adams those forces appeared to be working in a blind and largely destructive way. The fact was, as Adams reiterated rather tiresomely, the politicians of the period were either corrupt or uncomprehending and commonly both. Jane Adams perceived there was a vast gap between the relatively comprehensible world of the first half of the century and the bewilderingly complex society that seemed to spring into existence at the end of the war. The set of mental images, of symbols, of social "signs" and intellectual formulations that had at least appeared to conform, in some modest degree, with the realities of the perceivable world were entirely inadequate for the "new phase," as Henry Adams called it. It was an era that recalled the period immediately following the initiation of the Federal government under the newly drafted Constitution. Then, with the fieriest and most inflammatory rhetoric, Americans chose sides with the revolutionary French or the counterrevolutionary British and breathed fire and destruction on their opponents until, judging from the rhetoric alone, one would have assumed that the infant Republic was in the midst of revolution as violent and sanguinary as that of the French. In retrospect it seems clear that the same kind of process was at work in the last half of the nineteenth and the first decades of the twentieth century—changes too intricate and complex to be understood, and the adjustment of the public imagination (or consciousness) to a new and unanticipated set of political and social realities. In such periods democratic politics take on a particularly unreal air, and politicians yield the stage to poets, artists, novelists, and intellectuals of one variety or another, whose task it becomes to build bridges between the old consciousness and the new, between a dying world and one "waiting to be born." The election of Andrew Jackson marked the emergence of modern democratic politics. Ironically, it also marked the triumph of a kind of people's capitalism, a *laissez-faire* policy of unhampered economic individualism distinctly at odds with John Quincy Adams's far more "modern" vision of a government which would use its powers for the economic, social, and cultural benefit of all its citizens. In addition, and not for the last time, the parochialism of states' rights triumphed over the larger vision of a unified and truly "united" people.

One consequence of the Great Strikes was the Greenback-Labor Party, formed at a convention in February, 1878. Some 800 delegates from twenty-eight states met at Toledo, Ohio, and drafted a platform calling for an eight-hour day, the free coinage of silver at parity with gold, and the restriction of Chinese immigration. "To admit sympathy with the detestable Greenbackers was to be ostracized socially, commercially, and culturally," Charles Edward Russell wrote. "Respectable men refused to speak on the street to Greenbacker acquaintances, brothers and sisters withdrew the hand of fellowship at the prayer meeting and it was seriously debated whether a Greenbacker ought not to be expelled from the church."

In the congressional elections of that year the Greenback-Labor Party won fourteen congressional seats and a total of 1,060,000 votes. It was an impressive showing, and it seemed to promise a successful future. James B. Weaver of Iowa emerged as the spokesman of the new alliance. The party's leaders looked forward to the presidential elections of 1880 with high hopes. The party convention of that year in Chicago adopted a platform endorsing women's suffrage, a graduated income tax, and Federal regulation of interstate commerce. Weaver was the party's presidential candidate.

The Republicans, also meeting in Chicago, were faced with a contest between two charming and corrupt rivals: James G. Blaine, a perennial candidate, and Roscoe Conkling, boss of the New York State political machine. (The Democrats, of course, controlled New York City through Tammany.) "General" James A. Garfield of Ohio was the convention's dark horse. With the delegates deadlocked over Blaine and Conkling, Garfield was chosen on the thirty-sixth ballot, and Chester Arthur, a Conkling henchman, was nominated for vice-president. The party's platform called for civil service reform, veterans' benefits, the limitation of Chinese immigration, and a protective tariff.

The Democrats nominated General Winfield Scott Hancock, whose reluctance to protect the rights of freedmen in the Reconstruction period had endeared him to Southern Democrats. The only significant difference between the Democratic and the Republican platforms was on the tariff issue. In one of the closest elections in our history, Garfield collected 4,449,053 popular votes to 4,442,035 for Hancock—a difference of only 7,018 votes. Weaver received 308,578, and Neal Dow, the Prohibition candidate, 10,305. In electoral votes Garfield had a comfortable margin—214 to 155. The election was decided by a few thousand votes in New York and Indiana. Garfield was shot by Charles Guiteau four months after he took office. The assassin, who was clearly insane, was convicted of murder and executed. The most notable consequence of Garfield's assassination by a disappointed job seeker was the belated passage of a civil service reform bill. Garfield was succeeded by Chester Arthur, who, to virtually everyone's surprise, extricated himself from the control of the Republican machine, vetoed an $18,000,000 pork-barrel rivers and harbors bill, pushed civil service reform, and prosecuted the spectacular mail frauds of the star routes, thereby ensuring himself a modest place in history as a reformed crook.

The dominant issue of Arthur's presidency was the tariff. The high tariff faction included the coal producers, who wanted high tariffs on coal, the wool growers, who wished high tariffs on wool, the manufacturers of nickel, who, of course, wanted high tariffs on nickel. In the words of the head of the nickel trust, "It is meet that we should declare to the country that we will support no party and no candidate who cannot be depended upon . . . to protect and defend home labor. It is fitting for us to call 'hands off' to those who are itching to tear our tariff laws to shreds; . . . to call upon the representatives of all other American industries to stand by us as we will stand by them in resisting all changes in the tariff laws and all tariff-making by treaty until these laws can be carefully and prudently revised by a Congress or a commission known to be devoted to the interests of the nation."

When a congressional committee began hearings in 1882 on a revised tariff schedule, all nine members were avowed protectionists, and four were allied with the iron, sugar, steel, and wool industries. A parade of witnesses to the number of 600 appeared before the committee, many of them urging higher tariffs and a number appearing to argue for new industries that had never benefited from protective tariffs and thought it was time they should.

The commission's relatively enlightened report recommended cuts of 20 to 25 percent in most tariffs on the ground that improved machinery and methods of production enabled most manufacturers to compete with foreign imports. President Arthur added his support, declaring: "The present tariff system is in many respects unjust. . . . I recommend an enlargement of the free list . . . a simplification of the complex and inconsistent schedule of duties upon certain manufacturers, particularly those of cotton, iron and steel, and a substantial reduction of the duties upon those articles and upon sugar, molasses, silk, wool, and woolen goods."

The antiprotectionists (they could not be called a party since they were found in both parties, though most conspicuously in the Democratic Party) were rather an odd bag. They included liberal and radical friends of the farmer and workingman and such doctrinaire free-traders as William Graham Sumner. They included hard money men and soft money men. Among them were Carl Schurz and Sunset Cox of Ohio, who had proposed, facetiously, taxing the sunlight because it competed with gaslight.

Despite the report of the commission and the urgings of the President, the "interests," referred to commonly as the "third house of Congress," managed by relentless lobbying with those legislators dependent on them to make an unholy hash of the actual tariff legislation that resulted. John Sherman, who subscribed to the general principle of protection, was himself outraged and wrote in his memoirs that "the tariff act of 1883 laid the foundations of all the tariff complications since that time." Certainly it made abundantly clear who ran the country and for what purpose.

The presidential election of 1884 was hailed by farmers and reformers as ushering in a new era. The Democrats had a hero in Grover Cleveland, the reform governor of New York. Cleveland not only looked encouragingly presidential, but had a forthrightness, integrity, and courage unhappily rare in democratic politicians. In a fiery nominating speech Wisconsin Congressman E. S. Bragg hurled out the sentence that became Cleveland's principal campaign slogan when he declared that he loved him "for the enemies he had made."

The Republicans finally capitulated to Blaine—"the continental liar from the state of Maine," as his opponents were to chant. The mysteriously expiring National Greenback-Labor Party, meeting in Indianapolis in May, nominated Benjamin Butler, the "beast of New Orleans," as its presidential candidate. This time there was a defection of independent Republicans reminiscent of the revolt in 1872 against Grant. Such old-line liberal Republicans as Carl Schurz (who had led the revolt in 1872), George William Curtis, E. L. Godkin, and Charles Francis Adams, Jr., appalled at the nomination of Blaine and charmed by the Cleveland "character," led a band of the Mugwumps—Republicans with Democratic principles—into Cleveland's camp. John Jay Chapman, not the most charitable of critics, wrote that Cleveland was "about the best man I ever met . . . perfectly unselfish and a very religious sort of person who knows human nature and thinks hard all the time."

The campaign that followed was a strong contender for the most scurrilous in our history, which is certainly saying a good deal. To the charge that Cleveland had had a child by his housekeeper and the accompanying bit of doggerel, "Maw, Maw, where's Paw/ He's in the White House, haw-haw-haw," Senator George G. Vest of Missouri replied, "What of it? We did not enter our man in this race as a gelding."

Many Republicans who viewed Blaine with suspicion despite (or because of) his charm, suppressed their misgivings about his political morality and voted for him in the hopes that they could "wring one more President out of the Bloody Shirt." The phrase "waving the bloody shirt" is one of the more familiar slogans of our history, so much so that we hardly comprehend its full meaning. The implication is that the Democrats were so tarred with the brush of treason by virtue of the Civil War and Copperheadism that the Republicans, despite their manifold shortcomings, were able decade after decade to retain political power by virtue of reminding the voters, often in lurid prose, of the sins of the Democrats. Herein lay the greatest negative political legacy of the war.

The Tammany machine was especially active against Blaine in New York City. The state was crucial to Blaine. The Reverend Samuel Burchard called on him with a delegation of clergy at the Fifth Avenue Hotel a few weeks before the election. Burchard was quoted by an attentive newspaper reporter as referring to the Democrats as the party of "Rum, Romanism, and Rebellion." The Democrats seized joyfully on Burchard's unforgettable aphorism and used it to discredit Blaine. Again the popular vote was close. Fewer than 100,000 votes separated the two candidates. Butler and the National Greenback-Labor Party polled somewhat more than half of Weaver's total, and the Prohibition Party vote rose spectacularly from Dow's 10,000 four years earlier to 150,000. In the electoral vote Cleveland led, 219 to Blaine's 182, a relatively narrow margin. The Democrats carried the crucial state of New York by 1,149 out of 1,125,000 votes cast, making Cleveland the first Democratic president since Buchanan, twenty-eight years earlier. It took a major defection from Republican ranks and a serious faux pas to effect the change. Farmers and critics of capitalism voted for Cleveland in the hope that a Democratic president would impose some checks on tariffs and on capitalist depredations in general.

Cleveland sounded encouragingly liberal in his inaugural address. There should be economy and simplicity in government. Washington's Farewell Address and the Monroe Doctrine would continue to guide foreign policy. The Indians must be treated fairly and honestly, and "polygamy in the territories destructive of the family relationships and offensive to the moral sense of a civilized world, shall be repressed"— reference, of course, to the Mormons. Civil service reform must be carried forward as well. These modest objectives could be achieved only with divine aid.

Cleveland urged congressional legislation to arbitrate disputes between capital and labor, declaring: "The discontent of the employees is due in large degree to the grasping and heedless exactions of employers and the alleged discrimination in favor of capital as an object of governmental attention. It must also be conceded," Cleveland added, "that the laboring men are not always careful to avoid causeless and unjustifiable disturbance."

Perhaps the shrewdest analysis of the coming four years was that of a farm leader who wrote to Ignatius Donnelly: "Cleveland is elected . . . yet I do not look for much relief for the masses, for the same monopolies that run the Republican party run the Democratic party."

Cleveland devoted his attention to issues it was as hard to object to as "home and mother" and honesty, among them a disavowal of the government's right to interfere on behalf of any segment of the society. His administration would do nothing, he declared, to benefit corporations or their victims. Everyone was on his own, rich and poor alike. Beyond that, Cleveland gave considerable attention to strengthening the Democratic Party. To that end he was zealous in appointing Democrats to every available post, taking care, at the same time, that the men appointed should be "sound" men, good conservative types, not ranters and radicals like Ignatius Donnelly. The distribution of patronage in the Middle Western states was thus placed in the hands of corporation lawyers and railroad executives like William Vilas and J. Sterling Morton. It seemed only common sense to recruit corporation lawyers for, as Vilas remarked, "great corporations always secure . . . the best legal talent to protect their interests and in this they show much shrewdness and economy."

James J. Hill soon emerged as one of Cleveland's most trusted advisers on financial matters. Among those Democrats frozen out was Donnelly, whose labors in behalf of the party had been heroic. Patrick Kelly, a wholesale grocer in St. Paul, to whom Donnelly appealed for a recommendation as surveyor general, indicated which way the political winds were blowing when he refused Donnelly's request, observing that "your appointment . . . would bring about more disaffection and trouble than I care to encounter." He would try, however, to get him a consular post abroad, thereby, of course, getting him out of Minnesota politics. In the words of one antimonopoly Democrat, "The millers' ring runs the Republican party and the railroad ring runs the Democratic party."

Melville Fuller was an active conservative Democrat in Chicago. A highly successful corporation lawyer with no judicial experience, Fuller was appointed chief justice of the United States by Cleveland. In the opinion of the *Philadelphia Press*—and many others—Fuller was the most obscure and inexperienced man ever appointed to that exalted office. He knew how to vote on the corporate side of every issue, however, and he remained on the Court for twenty-two years.

Lucius Quintus Cincinnatus Lamar, Cleveland's secretary of the interior, had drafted Mississippi's ordinance of secession in 1860. As Congressman from that state he had joined his Georgia colleague Alexander Stephens in opposing the Civil Rights Act of 1875. A fair and moderate man, he was also an unequivocal supporter of states' rights.

With Cleveland in office, Henry Adams suffered profound disillusionment. He considered the Cabinet a scandal of mediocrity, and as for the Democratic Congress, "so ignorant and stupid a body of men never took charge of a great country before, and already corruption has begun . . ." he wrote to E. L. Godkin.

The result of the "popular clamor" over the exactions of the railroads was a so-called Interstate Commerce Act passed in 1887. James Weaver spoke of it contemptuously. "Having been a pretty close student of the Bible," he told a political rally in Lima, Ohio, "I will state before this audience here to-night that it will be no harm for you to worship it, for it is not like anything in the heavens above, or in the earth beneath. The law says, speaking of the long and short haul,— and that is about all there is in the law,—that they shall not charge more for a short haul than for a long one. Well, this is remarkable, is it not?" Then the law added, "under substantially similar circumstances over the same line in the same direction." Weaver commented: "I defy all the lawyers in Lima to tell me; there is no one under the sun that can tell me what it means. . . . Just imagine the Great Law-Giver, when He gave the ten commandments: Thou shalt not kill; Thou shalt not steal under substantially similar circumstances and conditions over the same line in the same direction. (Loud and tumultuous applause)."

The potency of the Interstate Commerce Commission is perhaps best indicated by the fact that in the first decade of its existence the freight rates on the transportation of wheat (the principal grievance of the farmers) virtually doubled while the price of wheat fell.

Courage Cleveland had in abundance (that, it turned out, was unfortunate). He refused to sign a succession of bills providing, in his view, excessive pensions for veterans, including a bill to pay pensions to those invalided for what we would call today nonservice-connected disabilities. But he also vetoed a bill to provide seeds for farmers devastated by a Texas drought on the ground that he did "not believe that the power and duty of the General Government ought to be extended to the relief of individual suffering which is in no manner properly related to the public service or benefit. . . . The lesson should constantly be enforced that though the people support the Government the Government should not support the people."

Toward the end of his term Cleveland once again demonstrated his courage, if not his political acumen, by attacking the protective tariffs. His principal concern in lowering the tariffs was his conviction that the high surplus in the United States Treasury worked to depress business and tempt Congress to make pork-barrel appropriations.

But even while the Republican Party anticipated a return to power in 1888, the fall elections of 1887 gave indications of incipient revolt against both parties. In Iowa 49 out of 100 members of the state House of Representatives were farmers. William Larrabee, the Republican governor, aware of where the wind was blowing, sounded almost as radical as Donnelly or Lloyd.

In 1888 the Republicans nominated the kind of harmless nonentity for president that political managers adore (and a disconcerting number of whom have been elected). The principal claim to fame of Senator Benjamin Harrison was perhaps the fact that he was the grandson of President William Henry Harrison, whose ineptness was obscured by the fact that he died a few weeks after taking office. The Republicans fervently endorsed the principle of protective tariffs and dealt with the constantly growing treasury surplus by declaring that they would sooner see "the entire repeal of internal taxes rather than surrender any part of the protective system."

Joseph Medill, Republican editor of the *Chicago Tribune* and an advocate of tariff reform, was horrified by the tariff plank in the Republican platform in the election of 1888, but he felt the party could hold the traditional Republican states of the Midwest in spite of it. "We have lots of Republicans deeply dissatisfied with that rabid, unrepublican . . . plank," he wrote a political ally, "but they have been kept from bolting from the strength of the old party ties . . . and the scare cry of free trade against the Democrats, and they have barely concluded to vote for Harrison on the assurance that the Republican Senate was framing a better reform bill than the Democratic House had done."

The Republican charges against Cleveland ranged from his agreeing to return the Confederate battle flags (a generous offer he was forced to renege on) to his vetoing of the veterans' pensions. A planted letter to the British minister to the United States, Lionel Sackville-West, soliciting his advice about whom to vote for drew the desired response: Cleveland. The notion so enraged Irish voters that they defected in substantial numbers, and Benjamin Harrison was elected with 233 electoral votes to Cleveland's 168, although Cleveland had almost 100,000 more popular votes.

The disenchantment of many voters was suggested by the fact that the Union Labor Party and the United Labor Party both nominated presidential candidates (along with the Prohibition Party). The candidate of the Prohibitionists, Clinton Fisk of New Jersey, received 250,125 votes, 100,000 more than his predecessor, while the Union Labor Party polled 146,897.

While Harrison himself exercised little leadership, his administration witnessed the elevation of the Department of Agriculture to the status of a Cabinet post (a belated sop to angry farmers) and the admission of the Dakotas, Montana, and Washington to statehood. The Republicans, who had run on a platform of generosity to veterans, passed the Dependent Pension Act, extending benefits to all veterans unable to work whether their incapacities were service-connected or not. It was an important step because it established the principle of government responsibility for a necessitous segment of the population.

It was followed by the Sherman Antitrust Act and the Sherman Silver Purchase Act. (Senator John Sherman had a special talent for getting his name attached to important bills.) The Antitrust Act was a toothless piece of legislation, more show than substance. Under its genial supervision, the number of trusts increased sharply. The Silver Purchase Act was mild enough, but it was stubbornly opposed by the goldbugs and passed only with the support of Congressmen elected by the farm alliances and through the appearance of the Congressmen from the new states. It required the Treasury to purchase 4,500,000 ounces of silver a month at prevailing prices and issue legal tender treasury notes redeemable in gold or silver.

In the middle of Harrison's administration the great British financial house of Baring in London failed, helping trigger a worldwide depression. Each month saw new failures in banks and financial houses. Everywhere one looked there were storm clouds. The numbers of unemployed mounted. Relief agencies were strained to the limit to provide for the hungry. Angry farmers were threatening revolution if their demands were not met. Socialism was everywhere in the ascendancy; ministers, scholars, farmers, union men, reformers—all were embracing some variation of socialism or anarchism. The railroads and corporations, alarmed at the turn of affairs, fought back. An ally of Donnelly's in Rochester, Minnesota, wrote to him in May, 1890, that he was "under the ban of the Chicago and North Western Railroad. This town is the headquarters of the Railroad and Wheat ring and these corporations hold us with an iron grip. They have influence upon every church and every organization that has taken hold of the Lecture business. About one half the town, the money lenders and merchants, are violently opposed to me from my action against the Railroad and Wheat ring. The working men are with me to a man."

The Panic of 1890 destroyed a number of fortunes, and even those families, like the Jameses and the Adamses, whose capital was in real estate and well-established commercial ventures felt the shock. One of the more spectacular failures was that of the Union Pacific. Clarence King was also a victim. Five of his mining partners died, and "each in his agony kicked over a full pail of milk which King had been a year in drawing," Hay wrote Adams, adding that "worst of all, that coal arrangement which he had cooked up with your brother Charles, and which he looked forward to as a provision for his declining years, has gone to Hades with the revolution in the Union Pacific."

In the midterm congressional elections of 1890 young William Jennings Bryan, a friend of Sterling Morton's, ran for Congress in a campaign that stressed his antiprotection views. When one of Omaha's old-line Democrats asked Morton, "Who the hell is Bryan?" Morton replied rather primly, "Mr. Bryan is able, eloquent and of most pure and untainted character. His election, which I consider quite probable, will do honor to every citizen in this District. And to elect him I am doing all that is in my power to do." As Bryan campaigned, he found that free silver was virtually the only thing on people's minds. When a voter asked him what his arguments were in favor of free silver, Bryan replied, "I don't know anything about free silver. The people of Nebraska are for free silver and I am for free silver. I will look up the arguments later."

Signs of revolt were evident everywhere. Nebraska went Democratic for the first time in its history. In Wisconsin the Democrats swept the state. John McCauley Palmer, a Minnesota refugee from the Republican Party, was elected to the Senate.

All that Congress could come up with was further tampering with the tariff. What emerged was the McKinley Tariff, the highest ever. One important new principle that came from the debate over the tariff, largely through the efforts of aging James Blaine, was that of reciprocity. The president was authorized to raise or lower tariffs in response to the raising or lowering of such barriers by nations with which the United States carried on trade. Objecting to a tariff on South American hides, Blaine argued that it would add to the cost of every piece of leather goods bought by Americans, for the profit only of slaughterhouses. "Such movements as this for protection," he declared, "will protect the Republican party only into speedy retirement."

The McKinley Tariff aroused a storm of protest, especially among farmers and in the Democratic and Populist press. The *Chicago Times* wrote of it: "The trick tariff committee . . . express deep sympathy with the struggling farmer. They tell him that the principal reason he suffers is because he is subjected to ruinous competition with the pauper tillers of the soil of other lands. . . . " The facts were very different. Professing to protect the farmer by imposing duties on imported agricultural products, thereby, according to the committee's calculations, saving the farmers some $45,000,000, the bill raised tariffs on other items that the farmer must buy, thereby adding $105,000,000 to his projected expenditures. The fact was nobody knew what to do. Everything that was attempted proved useless or worse. Only the Populists had a program, and that program, to most Americans of conservative leanings, was socialism, plain and simple.

As the election year of 1892 approached, the conservative Democrats, aware that Republican ranks were in disarray, began a feverish search for a presidential candidate. Cleveland had returned to the practice of corporation law and, with the assistance of Wall Street friends, made a comfortable fortune, despite the general financial distress. The Sherman Silver Purchase Act had produced a violent reaction among the moneymen, notably on Wall Street. If Cleveland would take a strong stand on hard money, he could be his party's standard-bearer once more. In February, 1891, more than a year before the presidential nominating conventions for the election of 1892, he publicly denounced "the dangerous and reckless experiment of free, unlimited, and independent silver coinage."

The breadth of Cleveland's appeal to the capitalists was suggested by Andrew Carnegie's support. "You know," he wrote Cleveland, "that for several years my chief anxiety in public matter had been in regard to the 'silver question' and that I stated in the North American Review that if I were called upon to vote for a Free Trade Democrat who supported sound money, or a Tariff Republican who was not sound upon money, I should vote for the former."

The Republicans were clearly stuck with Harrison. They replaced vice-president Levi Morton, the New York banker, with Whitelaw Reid, the New York publisher, whose greatest political asset was that he was *not* a banker. Cleveland was nominated by the Democrats, who swallowed his goldbug principles without a hiccup.

The delegates of the People's Party gathered in Omaha to draft a platform and nominate a candidate for president of the United States. They met with the fervor of a religious revival. Ignatius Donnelly wrote the preamble to the most radical platform ever presented to the American electorate by a major party. ". . . We meet in the midst of a nation brought to the verge of moral, political, and material ruin. Corruption dominates the ballot-box, the legislature, the Congress, and touches even the ermine of the bench. The people are demoralized. . . . The newspapers are largely subsidized or muzzled; public opinion silenced; business prostrated; our homes covered with mortgages; labor impoverished and the land concentrated in the hands of the capitalists. The urban workmen are denied the right of organization . . . a hireling standing army, unrecognized by our laws, is established to shoot them down. . . . The fruits of the toil of millions are boldly stolen to build up colossal fortunes for a few, unprecedented in the history of mankind; and the possessors of these, in turn, despise the republic and endanger liberty. From the same prolific womb of governmental injustice we breed the two great classes of tramps and millionaires." To the earlier call for government ownership of railroads, the Populists, as they were soon called, added telephones and the telegraph. The spirit animating the Omaha Convention was reminiscent of the birth of the Republican Party at Philadelphia years earlier, the same odd assortment of native dissenters of every variety—temperance men, vegetarians, single taxers, utopians of various hues, all animated by the vision of a redeemed America and a new day. James Weaver was nominated by acclamation.

The Socialist Labor Party nominated its own candidate, Simon Wing of Massachusetts, and the Prohibitionists named John Bidwell of California. Aside from Weaver, Bidwell was by far the most interesting and able of the presidential candidates (as well as the oldest—seventy-three). Born in 1819 and reared on the Missouri frontier, Bidwell had been in the first immigrant train to California, had been a leader in the fight for the Bear Republic, had discovered gold on the Feather River, and had become the best known agriculturist in the state.

Since the Democratic platform supported silver and its candidate was an avowed gold man, the country was treated to the odd spectacle of a candidate running on a platform the principal plank of which—on silver—he had explicitly rejected. The Democratic platform denounced the McKinley Tariff as "the culminating atrocity of class legislation" and demanded the importation of raw materials duty-free, with much lower tariffs on manufactured goods. Tom Johnson and Henry Watterson joined forces to nail the plank in the platform against Cleveland's angry protests.

As the prospects for Cleveland's election improved, a fierce struggle developed among the Midwestern Democrats for control of the party. The Democratic boss of Wisconsin was Edward C. Wall. At Villard's suggestion he drew up a currency plank for the state's Democrats and sent it to Villard to be sure that it met with Cleveland's approval. A grateful Villard contributed $40,000 to the Wisconsin Democrats and activated his "German Bureau" to help get out the vote. The German Bureau covered the states of New York, Wisconsin, Illinois, and Indiana, all with large German populations. Two Democratic politicians with a firsthand knowledge of German matters were assigned to each state to direct political activities; they were assisted by Germans imported to run a "literary department"—in other words, to grind out campaign literature. The *New York World* also contributed $70,000 to be distributed among foreign-language newspapers where it would do the Democratic cause the most good; the Milwaukee brewers gave $21,500 to support antiprohibition candidates. The danger of religious bigotry was constantly emphasized, especially as it threatened parochial schools. Free silver was played down as much as possible. William Freeman Vilas wrote: "Demagogues love to thrum our eardrums with their clamor of the wrongs the agriculturist suffers, and stir a spirit of unrest." The fact was that it was business corporations which had made the country great; "corporate powers and corporate values," he insisted, "have advanced with a more rapid step than the invention of our statesmen and law-makers." He added: "Time and genius" would relieve their "inconveniences." He agreed with the necessity for civil service reform. "The Augean stables must be cleaned of long accumulated corruption," he told more than one audience, "our public trusts set utterly above the reach of political beasts of prey, our trade made free of taxes which rob the general people, our commerce to ride the waves of every sea. . . ." Vilas gave considerable attention to strengthening his alliance with the conservative Tilden wing of the Democratic Party in New York State.

Another increasingly active Democrat was James J. Hill, fashioner of the Great Northern Railroad. When the Democrats nominated Cleveland in 1884, Hill had wired Tilden, "What about this man Cleveland?" and when Tilden gave him the OK, Hill had sent $5,000 to Cleveland's campaign manager. Levi Leiter, a Chicago merchant, chipped in $10,000, and Isidor Straus was generous. It was clear that businessmen saw no threat to their interests in the Democratic candidate.

26

Homestead

Even as the delegates of the newly formed Populist Party met in Omaha, 1,000 miles away in Homestead, Pennsylvania, the war between capital and labor assumed alarming proportions.

Andrew Carnegie had founded the town of Homestead not far from Pittsburgh as a model community to house the workers of the Carnegie Steel Company, placed the operations of the plant in the hands of his protégé Henry Frick, and retired to Scotland to live like a Scottish laird and write *Triumphant Democracy*. As we have seen, he prided himself on being a model employer. He specifically rejected the use of scabs or strikebreakers. "The right of the workingmen to combine and form trade unions" was "no less sacred than the right of the manufacturer to enter into associations . . . with his fellows," he wrote. The public should understand "the terrible temptation to which the working man on strike is sometimes subjected. To expect that one dependent on his daily wage for the necessaries of life will stand peaceably and see a new man employed in his stead is to expect too much . . . . There is an unwritten law among the best workmen: Thou shalt not take thy neighbor's job."

When the miners of the Frick Coke Company, in which Carnegie was the major investor, went on strike in 1887, Frick was determined to show the miners who was boss. He prepared to bring in strikebreakers, but when word reached Carnegie at his Scottish castle, he directed Frick to settle the strike. An angry Frick accused Carnegie of "a prostitution of the Coke Company's interests in your determination to promote your steel interests." A few months later, when Carnegie decided to stop his eight-hour shift plan at the Edgar Thomson plant near Pittsburgh and establish a sliding scale of wages tied to steel prices, the workers walked off the job. When a committee of workers came to negotiate, Carnegie beguiled them with stories and anecdotes and pieties about the nobility of labor. "We will never try to fill our works with new men," he assured them, ". . . we could never get such good men as you are. It is the scallawags who are idle and looking for work when there is a strike. . . . No one will ever have your places here. We like you too much." After five months Carnegie fearlessly attended a meeting of strikers to respond, he said, to genuine grievances. His appearance amid the strikers and his confident and indomitable manner disarmed the men, and they went back to work without achieving their demands. In the operation of his own mills and factories Carnegie kept ruthless pressure on his executives to cut costs and improve production. Those unable to do so he fired, some fifteen of his top aides in all.

Henry Frick was one of the least interesting of the tycoons. A native of Pennsylvania, he had made $1,000,000 by the time he was thirty, processing coke. Carnegie took him on as manager of his steel company at Homestead. Frick had none of Carnegie's interest in the workingman and the conditions of labor. His single preoccupation was profits.

In 1892, in the face of the deepening depression and a drop in the price of steel, the contract of the Amalgamated Association of Iron, Steel and Tin Workers came up for renewal. Carnegie, as we have said, had earlier worked out an agreement with the union under the terms of which wages rose as prices rose and correspondingly fell, though at a lower rate, when prices fell. In place of the expired contract Frick offered the union a reduction in wages to a minimum of $22 a month. The union asked for $24; Frick offered $23 and refused to negotiate further. As the date—June 30—for the expiration of the existing contract approached, tension mounted in Homestead. Frick was not popular with the workers in the plant, and they suspected that he anticipated in a strike the opportunity to break the union. Certainly he took elaborate security precautions at the plant, stringing three miles of barbed wire around the buildings. When some of the men hanged

Frick in effigy, he shut down the plant and brought in hastily deputized sheriffs to guard it. The union leaders were affronted by Frick's actions, insisting that they were capable of protecting the plant. They ordered the outnumbered deputies to depart. Frick countered by dispatching two boatloads of Pinkerton agents, armed with rifles, up the Monongahela River to occupy the mills. The by now thoroughly aroused workers barricaded themselves and opened fire on the Pinkertons. The detectives fought back. On the second day of the battle the workers got possession of a small brass cannon and did their best to sink the boats. Unsuccessful, they next poured oil into the river and set it afire. With twenty men wounded and seven dead, the Pinkertons surrendered with the understanding that they would be given safe-conduct back to Pittsburgh. In spite of that assurance, they were roughly handled by the angry mob, which had seen a number of workers and onlookers killed or wounded. The governor of Pennsylvania ordered the state militia into Homestead to restore order.

On July 21 Frick was shot by a young anarchist named Alexander Berkman. Berkman was a handsome young Russian immigrant. Through the influence of an uncle he had become a nihilist in Russia when he was still in his teens and then, under danger of arrest, had fled to the United States. Here he became a friend and disciple of Johann Most, who represented the most radical wing of the American anarchists. Berkman lived in a commune in Worcester, Massachusetts, with his Russian friend Fedya and "the Girl," a young Lithuanian woman, also an anarchist, twenty-three-year-old Emma Goldman. Berkman and Goldman ran a restaurant which catered to working-class men and women of radical persuasion.

Emma Goldman, full of the same romantic revolutionary ardor, had arrived in the United States in 1885. To Berkman and Goldman, the violence at Homestead offered an irresistible opportunity to hasten the dialectic by which the workers' revolution must, inevitably, topple capitalism. Berkman was possessed with that terrible lust of revolutionary idealism from which modern political terrorism springs. As he recalled July 6, he and Fedya were in their "little flat" when "the Girl" entered. "Her naturally quick, energetic step sounds more than usually resolute," he wrote. "As I turn to her, I am struck by the peculiar gleam in her eyes and the heightened color.

" 'Have you read it?' she cries, waving the half-opened paper.

" 'What is it?'

" 'Homestead. Strikers shot. Pinkertons have killed women and children' . . . Her words ring like the cry of a wounded animal, the melodious voice tinged with the harshness of bitterness—the bitterness of helpless agony."

Immediately it appeared to Berkman that the opportunity had presented itself to carry out one of the basic principles of anarchist doctrine—the *attentât*, or political assassination. Faith in the *attentât* as an instrument of the workers' revolution was one of the distinguishing differences between the most radical anarchists and the majority of Marxian socialists or communists. By assassinating a hated exploiter of the workers, the anarchist leaders believed that they could demonstrate the self-sacrificing devotion of intellectuals and theorists to the cause of the people and thereby help create a revolutionary temper among the lower classes.

As important as the act itself, with its consequent worldwide publicity, would be the trial and execution that must inevitably follow it. The trial would give the assassin the opportunity to proclaim, in the glare of public attention, the principles of revolutionary action and thereby raise the consciousness, as we would say today, of the workers of every modern industrial nation. The *attentât* was thus the supreme act of sacrifice for "the People." As insistently as it had been proclaimed in anarchist journals and pamphlets, it had yet to be practiced in the United States. When the news came that the strikers had defeated 300 Pinkerton "janizaries" and forced them to surrender, Emma and Alexander were ecstatic. "What a humiliating defeat for the powers that be!" Berkman wrote. ". . . Well may the enemies of the People be terrified at the unexpected awakening. . . . The People, the workers of America, have joyously acclaimed the rebellious manhood of Homestead. . . . The toilers . . . had defied the oppressor. They were awakening. But as yet the steel-workers were only blindly rebellious. The vision of Anarchism alone could imbue discontent with conscious revolutionary purpose; it alone could lend wings to the aspirations of labor." Berkman began to prepare feverishly for the *attentât* of Henry Frick: "Loudly called the blood of Mammon's victims. . . . Loudly it calls. It is the People calling. Ah, the People! The grand, mysterious, yet so near and real, People. . . . What a supreme joy to aid in this work! This is my natural mission. I feel the strength of a great undertaking. . . . To the People belong the earth—by right, if not in fact. To make it so in fact, all means are justifiable; nay, advisable, even to the point of taking life. . . . To remove a tyrant is an act of liberation, the giving of life and opportunity to an oppressed people."

Emma Goldman was inspired by the example of Sonya in Dostoyevsky's *Crime and Punishment* to work as a prostitute in order to make money to buy a pistol for Berkman to use in his *attentât*. "My cause," she wrote, ". . . was Sasha . . . his great deed . . . the people. But could I be able to do it, to go with strange men for money? The thought revolted me. It took several hours to gain control of myself. When I got out of bed my mind was made up."

Alexander Berkman and Emma Goldman belonged to that strange company of middle- and upper-class revolutionaries who are still abroad in the world. Berkman eulogized them as "those men and women, the adored, mysterious ones of my youth, who had left wealthy homes and high station to 'go to the People,' to become one with them, though despised by all whom they held dear, persecuted and ridiculed by the benighted objects of their sacrifice." The theological tones are unmistakable. Since they could no longer believe in a benign and omnipotent God in whose name one performed acts of sacrifice, those high-minded and romantic young men and women became worshipers at the altar of that new "divinity"—the People—whose prophet had been Jean Jacques Rousseau, whose word became flesh in the fires of the French Revolution.

Arriving in Pittsburgh on the way to Homestead on his mission of assassinating Frick, Berkman noted the "thick clouds of smoke . . . shrouding the morning with somber gray. The air . . . heavy with soot and cinders; the smell . . . nauseating. In the distance, giant furnaces vomit pillars of fire, the lurid flashes accentuating a line of frame structures, dilapidated and miserable. They," he added, "are the homes of the workers who have created the industrial glory of Pittsburgh, reared its millionaires, its Carnegies and Fricks." The sight strengthened his resolution. There could be no compromise with a system "that turns the needs of mankind into an Inferno of brutalizing toil. It robs man of his soul, drives the sunshine from his life, degrades him lower than the beasts. . . ."

At Homestead the streets were filled with grim-faced men, many of them carrying Winchester rifles. There were signs of the recent battle everywhere: dismantled breastworks, empty artillery shells, broken furnace stacks, and smoldering cinders. Berkman heard a strike leader named Hugh O'Donnell address the crowd of strikers. The sheriff had warned them that the state militia was on the way to restore order. "Brothers," O'Donnell began, "we have won a great, noble victory over the Company. We have driven the Pinkerton invaders out of our city."

"Damn the murderers," from the crowd.

"You have won a big victory, a great significant victory, such as was never before known in the history of labor's struggle for better conditions." Vociferous cheering. "But you must show the world that you desire to maintain peace and order along with your rights. The Pinkertons were invaders. We defended our homes and drove them out; rightly so. But you are law-abiding citizens. You respect the law and the authority of the State. Public opinion will uphold you in your struggle if you act right. Now is the time, friends!" Then louder: "Now is the time! Welcome the soldiers. They are not sent by that man Frick. They are the people's militia. They are our friends. Let us welcome them as friends."

O'Donnell's speech was followed by applause and boos. Another speaker followed O'Donnell and denounced the soldiers as tools of Frick and the capitalist interests of the state. "The scoundrel of a Sheriff . . . asked the Governor for troops, and that damn Frick paid the Sheriff to do it, I say!"

It seemed for a time as though the strikers, excited by the unidentified speaker, were determined to resist the militia as they had resisted the Pinkertons. But one of the most respected strike leaders, "Honest" McLuckie Burgess, "a large-boned, good-natured-looking working-man," urged moderation, saying, "I don't see how you are going to fight the soldiers. There is a good deal of truth in what the brother before me said; but if you stop to think on it, he forgot to tell you one little thing. The *how*? How is he going to do it, to keep the soldiers out? . . . I'm afraid it's bad to let them in. The black-legs [strikebreakers] *might* be hiding in the rear. But then again, it's bad *not* to let the soldiers in. You can't stand up against 'em: they are not Pinkertons. And we can't fight the Government of Pennsylvania."

Berkman made his way to Frick's office at the mill. Handsome and well dressed, he passed the unsuspecting guards. As the door of Frick's office opened to admit one of his aides, Berkman caught a glimpse of a "black-bearded, well-knit" figure seated at a desk—certainly Frick himself. Berkman presented his card to a black doorman, who vanished into the office and returned to say, "Mistah Frick is engaged. He can't see you now." He handed Berkman's card back to him. Berkman turned as though to leave and then brushed the attendant aside and strode into Frick's luxurious office. There were two men at the end of a long table. Berkman started to call out Frick's name, but as he wrote later, "the look of terror on his face strikes me speechless. It is the dread of the conscious presence of death. 'He understands,' it flashed through my mind." Berkman drew and aimed his pistol. Frick tried to rise and then averted his head as his would-be assassin pulled the trigger wondering as he did so if Frick had an armored vest beneath his coat. Frick gave a cry of pain and fell to the floor. As Berkman advanced toward Frick to be sure he was dead, Frick's companion grappled with him, and Frick himself, to Berkman's dismay, began to cry, "Murder! Help!" thus indicating that he was far from dead. Berkman fired once more, but his shot was deflected. As Berkman wrestled with Frick's aide, he managed to wrench loose long enough to aim again at Frick; but the gun failed to go off, and just then a carpenter, who had come running in response to the sounds of the shots and the cries for help, entered the room and hit Berkman over the head, stunning him. Half-conscious, he continued to try to close with Frick, drawing a dagger and stabbing at his legs. Finally he was overpowered by a crowd of police, clerks, and workmen. A policeman pulled Berkman's head up by the hair, and his eyes met those of his victim, supported by two men. "His face," Berkman wrote, "is ashen gray; the black beard is streaked with red, and blood is oozing from his neck. For an instant a strange feeling, as of shame comes over me; but the next moment I am filled with anger at the sentiment, so unworthy of a revolutionist."

In jail Berkman was subjected to days of interrogation. The same question was asked a hundred times: "Why did you attack Mr. Frick?" Always the answer was the same: "He is an enemy of the People." As soon as he could, Berkman singled out the only striker in prison, a tall, bold, sturdy young man, the beau ideal, in Berkman's mind, of the heroic worker. The man's name was Jack Tinford, and Berkman tried to explain to him that he had attempted to assassinate Frick for him, Tinford, and his fellow strikers. Tinford greeted this revelation with stony silence. "Jack," Berkman declared, "it was for you, for you people that I—"

"You better not talk that way in court, they'll hang you," Tinford replied. The mad act would harm the steelworkers far more than it could help them. "They don't believe in killing; they respect the law . . . the mill-workers will have nothing to do with Anarchists." The strike, Tinford said, was none of Berkman's business.

Tinford's reaction was a terrible blow to Berkman, but he comforted himself with the thought that it could not be typical. "The People could not fail to realize the depth of a love that will give its own life for their cause. To give a young life, full of health and vitality, to give all, without a thought of self; to give all, voluntarily, cheerfully; nay, enthusiastically—could anyone fail to understand such a love? . . . This first act of voluntary Anarchist sacrifice will make the workingmen think deeply." Even more than Haymarket, his attempt on Frick's life would "educate labor to its great mission."

Frick lived, and Berkman was denied his hoped-for martyrdom. Instead of death, he was "buried alive" in Western Penitentiary, sentenced to twenty-two years in prison. He discovered, sadly, that his fellow inmates thought him mad; they were deplorably lacking in class consciousness, and they listened to him with amusement and derision, mixed with a growing respect for his passionate idealism and his humanity toward his companions. After serving fourteen years of his sentence, Berkman was released, rejoined Emma Goldman in what was to be a lifelong union unblessed by capitalist legalities, and wrote a remarkable account of his experiences in prison entitled *Prison Memoirs of an Anarchist*. As Jack Tinford had predicted, the assassination attempt did nothing for the cause of the strikers, or labor, or "the People"; it served no other purpose than to discredit further the radical movement in the United States.

When Johann Most turned on Berkman and denounced him for his attempted assassination of Frick, Emma Goldman, who had been Most's lover, decided to punish him. She concealed a whip under her cloak, went to one of his lectures, leaped onto the stage, and whipped him. "Repeatedly I lashed him across the face and neck, then broke the whip over my knee and threw the pieces at him. It was all done so quickly that no one had a chance to interfere."

A torrent of denunciation for the use of the Pinkerton agents poured out in the nation's newspapers. The *Topeka Advocate* called the Pinkertons "a band of hired Hessians," used, along with the state militia, "not for the purpose of restoring peace and arresting the treasonable organization of Pinkerton thugs, but for the purpose of intimidating the union workingmen, protecting capital and crowding down wages through the introduction of non-union men . . ." A County Alliance chapter in Kansas passed a resolution expressing support for the Homestead strikers. "We heartily sympathize with the union laborers at Homestead, Pa.," the resolution read, "in their determined, just and sacred efforts to be protected as wage earners as fully as the protected manufacturers, and condemn our present industrial system which subjects the laborer in the field, in the shop or mine, to the merciless and soulless moneyed corporations as to what he is to receive for the products of his labor. . . ."

Mary Lease had her own fiery reflections on Homestead. "The world stands aghast," she declared, "at the murderous attempt of a Scotch baron entrenched and fortified by Republican legislation, to perpetuate a system of social cannibalism, and force, by the aid of Pinkerton cut-throats, the American laborers to accept starvation wages. . . ." A farmer named W. H. Bennington wrote to the *Topeka Advocate* apropos of Homestead: "Capital has been waging war on labor for years. . . . We shall continue to hope for a peaceable solution of these differences, but we fear the haughty tyranny of capital will persist in its resort to war measures by the use of Pinkertons and militia beyond the point of endurance." An Alliance meeting in Texas passed a resolution stating: "We regard the Pinkerton Detectives as an armed mob, under the employ of the money power of the U.S. for the purpose of intimidating labor. Therefore be it resolved, That we call upon our representative in Congress to legislate them out of existence." The *Lincoln* (Nebraska) *Alliance-Independent* on July 28, 1892, spoke for much of the agrarian Midwest, in voicing support for the strikers. "The capitalists," the journal's editor wrote, "have determined on a war to the death against [the union]. The laborers will resist this warfare with all their power. . . . They realize that their only protection against the tyranny of capital lies in their union. Once this is broken up, the capitalist will only have the individual laborers to deal with."

As the full extent of public indignation at Frick's strikebreaking efforts became evident, Carnegie began to waffle. He wrote an associate: "Matters at home *bad*—such a fiasco trying to send guards by boat and then leaving space between River & fences. . . . We must keep quiet and do all we can to support Frick and those at the Seat of War."

An English newspaper declared that the events in Homestead revealed Carnegie's *Triumphant Democracy* to be "a wholesome piece of satire," and the *St. Louis Post-Dispatch* announced: "Count no man happy until he is dead. Three months ago Andrew Carnegie was a man to be envied. Today he is an object of mingled pity and contempt. In the estimation of nine-tenths of the thinking people on both sides of the ocean he has not only given the lie to all his antecedents, but confessed himself a moral coward." Where a "grain of consistency" would have called for him to take charge of an explosive situation, he had "run off to Scotland out of harm's way to await the issue of the battle he was too pusillanimous to share. A single word from him might have saved the bloodshed—but the word was never spoken. . . . Ten thousand 'Carnegie Public Libraries' would not compensate the country for the direct and indirect evils resulting from the Homestead lockout. Say what you will of Frick, he is a brave man. Say what you will of Carnegie, he is a coward."

Carnegie wrote to a friend shortly after the strike: "This is the trial of my life (death's hand excepted). Such a foolish step—contrary to my ideas, repugnant to every feeling of my nature. Our firm offered all it could offer, even generous terms. Our other men had gratefully accepted them. They went as far as I could have wished, but the false step was made in trying to run the Homestead Works with new men. It is a test to which the workingmen should not be subjected. It is expecting too much of poor men to stand by and see their work taken by others." To another correspondent he wrote: "The pain I suffer increases daily. The Works are not worth one drop of human blood. I wish they had sunk." He offered some of the strike leaders who had lost their jobs pensions. After his retirement he established a relief fund for Homestead workers and wrote: "No pangs remain of any wound received in my business career save that of Homestead. . . . I was the controlling owner. That was sufficient to make my name a byword for years."

What is perhaps most worth noting about the Homestead strike is the fact that public opinion was, at least initially, so strongly on the side of the workers that Carnegie, one of the most popular public figures in the country, his fame apparently sealed by his libraries and his apotheosis of "the Democracy," telling Americans everything they wished to hear about themselves without a single shadow to mar the splendid luminosity of the picture, fell at once from grace and, indeed, never regained the exalted status he had enjoyed before that grim event.

The strike marked the beginning of an increasing coolness between Carnegie and Frick, and it also brought a strong reaction against the use of Pinkerton agents. Senator J. M. Palmer of Illinois was one of a number of prominent political figures who condemned Frick's use of the Pinkerton men. "The army raised and commanded by the Pinkertons," he declared, "is as distinctly known in this country as is the regular army of the United States. . . . The commander in chief of this army, like the barons of the Middle Ages, has a force to be increased at pleasure for the service of those who would pay him or them. . . . They have been employed in New York, and have shed the blood of citizens of that State. They . . . have shed the blood of citizens of Illinois." The great corporations, Palmer insisted, "must . . . be understood to be public establishments in the modified sense . . . and the owners of these properties must hereafter be regarded as holding their property subject to the correlative rights of those without whose services the property would be utterly valueless." Palmer had been one of the founders of the Republican Party and a major general in the war. Switching to the Democrats in 1872, he insisted that giant industries were in effect public agencies with clear responsibilities to their employees as well as to the general public.

Meanwhile, a wave of bitter strikes swept the mining states. The formation of the Executive Miners' Union in Coeur d'Alene, Idaho, in 1889 came as a result of the introduction of new machinery and a cut in the miners' wage from $3.50 to $3 for a ten-hour day. The union struck the mine, and the owners capitulated; but they soon joined with other owners to form the Mine Owners Protective Association, which had the twofold function of concerting action against the railroads and their arbitrary freight rate increases as well as against the efforts of mine workers to raise their wages and/or secure a shorter working day. Among the owners in the Coeur d'Alene area were William Crocker, of the San Francisco family; Cyrus McCormick, of Chicago, who had made his fortune in agricultural equipment, specifically reapers; and John Hays Hammond, who took the lead in trying to break the union by organizing a lockout, importing nonunion workers, and protecting them with armed guards. In 1892, when the union discovered a Pinkerton spy in its midst, the members expressed their outrage by dynamiting one of the mills, taking over the machinery of two of the mines, and forcing the surrender of guards and scabs. The governor of Idaho thereupon declared martial law and sent in the national guard, and President Harrison authorized the use of Federal troops. Union men were rounded up and imprisoned in stockades, and the strike as well as the power of the union was broken for the moment.

One aftermath of the violent clash at Coeur d'Alene was the formation of the Western Federation of Miners the following year in the copper town of Butte, Montana. As many as 5,000 miners were enrolled as members of the federation, in the words of Big Bill Haywood "the greatest single social force of the working class in the western part of America." John Hays Hammond called the union "a gang of Irish-Austrian-Italian anarchists."

Mining strikes were not confined to the Western states. Mary ("Mother") Jones, an organizer for the United Mine Workers, arrived at the Dietz coal mine in Virginia to be greeted by a frightened young miner who informed her that the superintendent of the mine "told me that if you came down here he would blow your brains out." Jones replied: "You tell the superintendent that I am not coming to see him anyway, I am coming to see the miners." No one in the town of Norton would rent the miners a hall in which to hold a union meeting. Finally the black residents of the community agreed to let the miners use their church, but just as the meeting was about to start, the black warden appeared with word that the coal company had given the church the land it stood on. "They have sent word that they will take it from us if we let you speak here," he told Mother Jones. The meeting was held at "the four corners of the public road." Mother Jones and the union leaders were tried for disturbing the peace, fined, and threatened with imprisonment if they persevered.

At Arnot, Pennsylvania, where a strike had been going on some four months, Mother Jones was called in to strengthen the resolution of the miners. When it became clear to her that the mineowners had hired thugs with instructions to shoot any strikers who attempted to interfere with the owners' use of scabs, Mother Jones organized the women of Arnot into a force 3,000 strong, armed with mops and buckets, and marched them to the mine head. There they attacked the scabs with their mops and raised such a racket by beating on the buckets that the mine mules were frightened away. That night the manager of the modest hotel at which Mother Jones was staying appeared at eleven o'clock to announce that the mine owned the hotel and he had been told that he would have to oust her or lose his job. A miner, assigned to guard Mother Jones, took her to a miner's house to spend the balance of the night. The next morning she was awakened by the miner's weeping wife. "Mother, you must get up. The sheriff is here to put us out for keeping you. This house belongs to the Company." Mother Jones recalled: "The family gathered up all their earthly belongings, which weren't much, took down all the holy pictures, and put them in a wagon, and they, with all their neighbors, went to the meeting. The sight of that wagon with the sticks of furniture and holy pictures and the children, with the father and mother and myself walking along through the streets turned the tide. It made the men so angry . . . they determined not to give up the strike until they had won the victory." But it was the women who closed down the mine. "From that day on," Mother Jones wrote, "the women kept continued watch of the mines to see that the company did not bring in scabs. Every day women with brooms or mops in one hand and babies in the other arm wrapped in little blankets, went to the mines and watched that no one went in. All night long they kept watch. They were heroic women."

The turning point in the strike came when the farmers in the countryside, who had been turned against the strikers by company agents, were persuaded by Mother Jones to support the strikers. Finally, in the face of the miners' determined resistance, the company capitulated, and the miners held a joyful victory celebration. "Old and young talked and sang all night long . . ." Mother Jones wrote.

The story of the strike, of Mother Jones's role, and of the action of the women spread through the coal mines as far as Kentucky, and Mother Jones was in constant demand as an organizer and strike director.

27

1893

It was against a background of deepening depression and accelerating violence that the election of 1892 took place. Revolution was in the air. Or at least talk of it was commonplace.

In March, 1892, an Illinois correspondent of the *Farmers' Alliance*, published in Lincoln, Nebraska, noted that "Illinois has two classes of men who are ripe for socialism: the poor of the cities," of whom it was estimated there were 300,000 in Chicago alone, and "the farm renters . . . These men, too, are fast, very fast ripening for socialism. The line between land lord and tenant is being forcibly put as the line of demarkation is now drawn in the cities between boss and employee."

Frances Willard, the head of the Woman's Christian Temperance Union, was not afraid of the label "socialist." She was frank to say in innumerable speeches that the fate of the Republic rested on its ability to make a fairer distribution of the wealth which flowed so abundantly into the coffers of the rich. "If this is socialism," she told an audience of women in the South, "so be it." Willard was dismayed at the failure of the farmers and the industrial workers to form an alliance, and she urged Henry Demarest Lloyd to organize a prohibitionist-farmers alliance that would take a strong position in favor of the rights of non-farm laborers.

Radicalism grew more radical and conservatism more conservative, and as both sides girded for Armageddon, Christian Socialists
sounded as militant as the Marxist variety. The *Churchman*, a Presbyterian journal, declared: "There are a thousand evidences that the
present state of things is drawing to a close, and that some new development of social organization is at hand." The New York chapter
of the Christian Socialist Club met with the Bellamy Nationalist Clubs
and heard addresses by leading reformers. In Detroit a Conference of
Applied Christian Workers and Social Reformers debated how best to
infuse industrial society with the ethics of Christian socialism, and
Henry Demarest Lloyd, giving the principal address, reaffirmed his
faith in the "Co-operative Commonwealth." Another such gathering
was the Crosbyside Conference of Social Gospel, attended by various
leaders in reform, including several college presidents, Richard Ely
and several of his students, Edward Bellamy, Henry George, William
Dean Howells, Jane Addams, Frances Willard, Samuel Gompers, Lyman
Abbott, and "a squadron of Social Gospel clergy led by B. Fay Mills."

Of the Christian Socialist evangelists, George Herron was the most
sensational. Iowa College (later Grinnell), under the presidency of
George Gates, was the "capital" of Christian socialism, and Herron was
its prophet. His sociology lectures were so popular that the only space
large enough to hold the students was the college chapel.

On lecture tours he aroused similar enthusiasm. At the University
of Michigan, Herron drew 3,000 people, one of the largest audiences
ever gathered at Ann Arbor. He was equally successful at the Union
Theological Seminary, at DePauw University, Indiana State, and Princeton. Students seemed eager to absorb his vision of a redeemed America
and a Christianized world. When he lectured in Montreal, "a reporter
compared the sensation to the explosion of a bomb in a public square
of the city." Herron told the jam-packed audiences that flocked to hear
him: "The church was not sent to be an institutional dominion, but a
sacrificial and redemptive life in the world." The country was faced by
revolution because it had failed in faith. "Revolution," he declared, "is
caused by seeking to substitute expediency for justice. . . ." America's
"stupid national conceit" had blinded it to "the wicked moral blindness
of our industrialism. . . . This social strain, this winter of unemployment and want, is without excuse to a righteous reason. There is no
war; no pestilence; no failure of harvests. There is an abundance in
our land for the people. Yet this richest nation of the world, in the
midst of a material prosperity so marvelous as to become the object of

political worship, suddenly finds a vast population face to face with famine, dependent upon some quality of public philanthropy. . . ."

The intensity of feeling, the sense of mounting crisis can perhaps best be measured by Grover Cleveland's margin in popular votes, 364,000, the largest since Grant. Cleveland had 277 electoral votes to 145 for Benjamin Harrison. Weaver was a distant third with 22. "However they studied it," Henry Adams wrote of the election, ". . . neither Hay, King, nor Adams knew whether they had attained success, or how to estimate it, or what to call it; and the American people seemed to have no clearer idea than they. Indeed, the American people had no idea at all; they were wandering in a wilderness much more sandy than the Hebrews had ever trodden about Sinai. . . ."

The Populists startled everyone by their strength in the farm states. Weaver polled almost 40 percent of the vote in Nebraska, 11.5 in Minnesota, and 4.5 in Iowa. Individual Populists did much better, and a number of state legislatures fell to them. Lorenzo Lewelling was elected governor of Kansas on the Populist ticket, as was Davis Waite in Colorado. Waite had been editor of the *Aspen Union Era*, a teacher, lawyer, and secretary of a local chapter of the Knights of Labor. He was convinced that Colorado was involved in a war "which must be waged against oppression and tyranny to preserve the liberties of man— the eternal warfare of monarchy and monopoly against the rights of the people to self-government."

The most striking figure to emerge in the election of 1892 was John P. Altgeld. Altgeld had been born in Germany in 1847. He was thus forty-five years of age in 1892. He had grown up in Missouri and been involved early in the Granger movement. In 1875 Altgeld moved to Chicago to practice law. Running for Congress in 1884, he was defeated by a Republican, but his charm and eloquence and his out-spoken advocacy of the cause of the farmers and workingmen drew attention to him and marked him as a promising politician. He was soon campaigning for the compulsory arbitration of labor disputes in Chicago and writing for the *Chicago Mail* about the deplorable con-ditions of labor. After a term as a municipal judge, Altgeld became a protégé of "King Mike" McDonald, the boss of the Democratic machine in Cook County, and in 1891 he received the endorsement of the Cook County Democrats for governor of Illinois. Using the greater part of his own fortune, amassed in real estate speculations, Altgeld conducted a classic handshaking campaign, traversing the state in a systematic search for voters. In the words of the *Chicago Inter Ocean*, "Judge

Altgeld has visited more families, kissed more babies, inspected more dairies and helped set more hens than any man before who wanted to be Governor." He did not neglect businessmen, and he found a warm response among the Illinois Germans.

That Altgeld was no radical disturber of the social order was indicated by his comment that the "really influential men in America are the successful private individuals—positive men, earnest, conscientious, thoroughgoing men. Take successful business men, successful manufacturers, leading railroad men, lawyers, physicians, and even preachers when they have sufficient independence to develop any individuality—they are the men who mould public opinion . . . secure legislation and shape the policy of the country." This was Altgeld in 1891. Under the persuasive counsel of Clarence Darrow, who became one of his closest friends and advisers, and in the face of the growing economic crisis, Altgeld moved substantially to the left—to the quasi socialism of Henry Demarest Lloyd and prolabor sympathies of Darrow himself. When he was governor, Altgeld's most courageous and controversial act was pardoning the Haymarket anarchists. "None of the defendants," he wrote, "could be at all connected with the case. The jury was picked. Wholesale bribery and intimidation of witnesses was resorted to. The defendants were not proved guilty of the crime charged under the indictment." When she read Altgeld's reasons for pardoning the anarchists, Voltairine de Cleyre wrote her mother: "Brave man! He has killed himself politically to save the poor working men! And in the ages he'll get it too—as Paine is getting his now—after 100 years."

In the interval between the election in November and Cleveland's inauguration, almost four months later, the nation's drift to disaster continued unchecked. A general panic was set off by the failure of the Philadelphia & Reading Railroad, which had gone through several receiverships. On February 25, 1893, the trustees of the railroad declared bankruptcy. Three months later the rope trust, the National Cordage Company, collapsed. A series of railroads followed suit—the Erie, the Union Pacific, the Northern Pacific, which had weathered a number of financial storms. As trusts and corporations failed, hundreds of thousands of workingmen lost their jobs and, without unemployment compensation of any kind, joined the growing company of the unemployed.

John Swinton's Paper described the situation: "In our land of plenty, we have seen millions of people passing into the valley of hardscrabble.

"In our busy land, we see a million men and women looking daily for work.

"In our land of workers, we see wages forever tending to the level of slavery.

"In our land, that offers welcome to all mankind, we see the growth of a horde of paupers, beggars, and tramps.

"In our land, where all men are said to be born equal, we see the upspringing of a ruling class of millionaires.

"In our land of free soil, we see the people's heritage falling into the hands of rack-renting landlords.

"Under our Constitution, that prohibits special privilege, we see privileged corporations all over the land.

"In our Congress and our Legislatures, established as agencies of popular power, we see capital holding the reins and running the machine."

All these issues came together in one single issue: the proper use of the country's resources and the proper enforcement of the people's rights. It was the question which could not be shirked. "The American people," Swinton wrote, "have always had some great work in hand, from the old days of pioneering and revolutionism to the later times of abolitionism and reconstruction. They worked their way through them all. When they take hold of the new question they will work their way through that, somehow or other.

"It is about time to begin. Every year of delay it will be harder and more dangerous."

In somewhat of a panic Brooks Adams sent for Henry to return home from his eternal peregrinations, and home Henry came to be what help he could. He found Boston, he wrote, "standing on its head, wild with terror, incapable of going to bed and brushing its weary old tusks in the morning; all of this because no one could get any money to meet his notes." He took a kind of grim satisfaction in the collapse of the English money markets. "My belief," he wrote, "is that the old bully will go on her knees. . . . We have never seen such a prolonged or so intense a pressure since our society existed. It will be nip and tuck with us to keep order if it lasts over the year. What strains our social arrangements to the dangerous point, ought to break Europe all up." Ann Lodge, Adams reported, was at Nahant, "where gentlemen daily commit suicide off her rocks by walking into the water with their clothes and hats on."

"If I live forever," Brooks Adams wrote a quarter of a century later, "I shall never forget that summer. Henry and I sat in the hot August evenings and talked endlessly of the panic and of our hopes and fears, and of my historical and economic theories, and so the season wore away amidst an excitement verging on revolution." It seemed clear to Brooks that "throughout the ages it had been the favorite device of the creditor class first to work a contraction of the currency, which bankrupted the debtors, and then to cause an inflation which created a rise when they sold property which they had impounded." Adams found a long series of precedents, "beginning with the panic at Rome under Tiberius. . . ."

The only remedy that suggested itself to Cleveland was a special session of Congress, convened in August, 1893, to repeal the Sherman Silver Purchase Act. In the debate in the House, William Jennings Bryan held even the hard money men spellbound for a time as he described the "imperious, arrogant, compassionless" corporations aligned against "that unnumbered throng, which gave a name to the Democratic party, and for which it has assumed to speak. Work-worn and dust-begrimed, they make their sad appeal . . . their cries for help too often beat in vain against the outer wall, while others less deserving, find ready access to legislative halls."

William Vilas, indignant at the opposition to repeal, wrote to a friend that the majority for repeal was composed of "patriotic men" of opposing parties while "the opponents of repeal are composed not only of similar elements from both of the old political parties, but with a third party which is almost, in its principles, like the advance guard of a French Revolution."

Terence Powderly did not hesitate to charge that many Democrats had been subverted to vote for repeal by "Federal Patronage." Senator Henry Moore Teller of Colorado was bitterly opposed to repeal, declaring that Westerners "do not disguise the fact that we are to go through the valley and the shadow of death. We know what it means to turn out our 200,000 silver miners in the fall of the year." Colorado was a test case for the agrarian-labor split within the Populist ranks. All that held them together was a conviction that the salvation of the state (and the nation) required the free coinage of silver. "Put up the price of silver by legislative remonetization," a Populist leader declared, "and dollar wheat will follow fast." There was little sympathy among the farmers for the efforts of the railroad workers to improve their wages and reduce their hours of work; a farmer, after all, worked from sunup to sundown. "We must insist on better regulations of interstate commerce," one prominent Populist editor wrote, "without stopping to consider the comparatively insignificant proposition of wages." A Colorado editor, who resented Davis Waite's prolabor position, wrote: "He forgets that one good Colorado farmer pays more taxes than dozens of these miners who are making so much fuss and expense to the state." The strikes should be outlawed. "Amid the widespread industrial troubles, farmers are serene and content."

When the Sherman Silver Purchase Act was finally repealed on October 30, 1893, Vilas wired Cleveland that it was a "personal triumph" for the President. Jacob Schiff, the head of Kuhn, Loeb & Company, the great financial house, and investor in a hundred ventures across the country and across the world, assured Cleveland that repeal was all that was necessary to restore the badly battered economy. It would, he wrote, "restore confidence at home and abroad . . . and insure a return to prosperity in the not far future."

Henry Adams was more skeptical. He admitted, in a letter to Hay, that "the amiable but quite lunatic gold-bug had ended by making me a flat-footed Populist and an advocate of fiat money. This is clever of them. I had not thought they could do it. . . . For a thorough chaos I have seen nothing since the war to compare it with. The world surely cannot long remain as mad as it is, without breaking into acute mania. Everyone looks on his neighbor as a dangerous lunatic. . . . The single lofty figure of noble sanity is that of Grover; but as I happen not to be sane, but to disagree with him on every possible point, and as the Democratic party is also insane and disagrees with him, he has no true admirers and supporters except the two Republican senators from Massachusetts. . . . Cleveland has smashed my party into smithereens and is pretty well smashed in return. . . . Every debate is a four-sided fight; the republican attacks the democrat; the eastern democrat flies at the throat of the western democrat; all three then attack Cleveland." John Sherman bitterly denounced J. Pierpont Morgan and Senator David Bennett Hill of New York while they in turn "were rolling around, gouging each other; and all of them wild to burn Cleveland alive. . . . Oh, cock-a-doodle-doo!" Adams added that "if I were not a pessimist and a fatalist, a populist, a communist, a socialist, and the friend of a humanist [Hay], where would I be at?" He could see nothing but "universal bankruptcy before the world, whichever way it turns, and whatever standard it prefers in which to reckon the balance-sheet of its insolvency. I take little stock either in gold, silver or paper, except that I want all I can get of them all." The most conspicuous casualty among Adams's close friends was Clarence King, who went to a private asylum. Adams himself was "suspended . . . over the edge of bankruptcy. . . . By slow degrees the situation dawned on him that the banks had lent him, among others, some money—thousands of millions . . . for which he, among others, was responsible and of which he knew no more than they." He could only laugh; but other men "died like flies under the strain, and Boston grew suddenly old, haggard, and thin."

Lorenzo Dow Lewelling, the governor of Kansas, attracted national attention by his "Tramp Circular," which he sent to all the police boards in the state, instructing them to be especially lenient in their treatment of the itinerant unemployed. Lewelling began with a brief history lesson on the abuse of the "incorrigible vagabonds" of Elizabethan England by royal officials. The poor of Kansas must receive no such treatment. "Those who sit in the seats of power," he wrote, "are bound by the highest obligation to especially regard the cause of the oppressed and helpless poor. The first duty of government is to the weak. Power becomes fiendish if it be not the protector and sure reliance of the friendless. . . ." The rockpile and the bull pen were not to be used as a form of harassment for those wanderers who came within any of the police jurisdictions of the state.

One of the responses to Lewelling's "Tramp Circular" was a letter from a farmer which read: "Whatever may be the opinion of the plutocrats, the aristocrats and all the other rats, God and the people will bless you for this brave word." Another letter writer declared: "The very people & party, that made the conditions that gives us this army of unemployed, or 'tramps,' if you will, are the first to denounce your courageous & manly words. If this is anarchy, then I am an anarchist."

In Colorado Davis Waite issued a Thanksgiving Proclamation in November, 1893, which, in its sardonic humor, gave characteristic expression to the spirit that animated the People's Party. After a perfunctory thanksgiving that "no war, famine or pestilence" had vexed the land, Waite reminded his fellow citizens of the 45,000 silver miners "who in a land of boundless natural resources, have been deprived of employment by tyranny and by corrupt and unconstitutional legislation" as well as of "the agriculturists . . . whose crops cannot be marketed for the cost of production" and were, in consequence, daily losing their homes "to increase the inordinate riches of extortioners whose avarice and greed, aided by legislation, have grasped in the hands of thirty thousand people more than half the wealth in the United States, and are fast reducing to pauperism the common people of the world."

The accumulating pressure for radical solutions was evident at the AFofL annual convention in Chicago, where Samuel Gompers had to use all his guile to prevent the socialists from taking control of the union convention. Addressing the convention, Henry Demarest Lloyd supported the "principle of collective ownership and control of all the means of production. "Democracy," he declared "must be *progressive* or die . . . the *general welfare* . . . is the object of society," and unions must take the lead in creating this "*new democracy of human welfare.*" By the end of the year there should be a "grand international constitutional convention" to draft a new bill of rights "to guide and inspire those who wish to live the life of the commonwealth." In the meantime, there must be planning and education to prepare for the day of international cooperation. Lloyd's speech was greeted with enthusiastic applause, and 20,000 copies were ordered printed and distributed throughout the chapters of the union. Gompers praised it, and Altgeld wrote: "It has the imprint of genius on every line." The Populists and liberal academics were equally enthusiastic.

The principal issue before the union delegates was how far to go in endorsing the principles of socialism pushed by Gompers's principal rival, Tom Morgan. In his autobiography, *Seventy Years of Life and Labor*, written long after the tumultuous events of the 1890s, Gompers was at pains to dissociate himself from the socialists who had been so active in the American Federation of Labor. Socialism was then in bad odor, and it was hard to believe that thousands of Americans had been proud of that designation a few decades earlier. "I know Socialists from practically every approach," Gompers wrote; "I think I have met a representative of every one of the fifty-seven varieties. Some of my early shopmates were zealous Socialists of the Marxian school." There were two principal types: those willing to work within the union movement to strengthen it and those who simply wished to appropriate the unions to their own political ends. The latter were "Socialists who were profoundly pessimistic about existing society. They started many organizations to supplant trade unions, and all failed." Nonetheless, "socialism" in a rather vague non-Marxist sense was very evident in all union gatherings and in much labor literature, as Henry Demarest Lloyd's speech to the AFofL convention made evident. Indeed, when Morgan tried to place the union squarely in the socialist ranks, Gompers warmly denied the charge that he was antisocialist. "I say here, broadly and openly," he declared, "that there is not an inspiring and ennobling end that [the socialists] are striving for that my heart does not beat in response to. But our methods are different. The Socialist Party and Trade Unions are different; inherently do they differ in their methods." Gompers welcomed socialists in the AFofL but only as union members. But a year later his socialist rival, Morgan, was back trying to accomplish by referendum what he had failed to achieve on the floor of the convention, which was firmly under Gompers's control. The year that followed was a time of intense struggle within the federation between the Morgan-led socialists and Gompers and his lieutenants. At stake was nothing less than the future direction of the American labor movement.

The Panic of 1893 marked for Henry Adams the renewal of his education. He was delighted to find that his brother Brooks was preoccupied with much the same problem that engaged him: the tendency of capitalism to self-destruct, as we would say today, to move inevitably and uncontrollably toward greater and greater concentrations of money and people until the whole compact mass began to disintegrate. "Everything American, as well as most things European and Asiatic, became unstable by this law, seeking new equilibrium and compelled to find it."

The year 1893 was to have more to distinguish it than financial panic and deepening depression. It was also the year of the Chicago World's Columbian Exposition, to give the event its proper title, the most remarkable display of the achievements of triumphant capitalism ever assembled. The coincidence of the fair's opening in the depth of the nation's worst depression since 1837 was not lost on capitalism's numerous critics, but planning for the fair had begun, of course, several years earlier, when Chicago outbid New York for the privilege of putting it on and Frederick Law Olmsted was hired to select and design the site.

The fair itself, as the tangible evidence of American power and progress, was to be the most spectacular of all the world's fairs that had become so popular in the preceding decades. In addition to displaying the awesome technical achievements of industrial capitalism, it was to demonstrate the cultural sophistication of the American Renaissance; Augustus Saint-Gaudens declared, rather flamboyantly, that such an assemblage of artists had not been on display since fifteenth-century Florence.

Culture was an especially tender subject with upper-class Americans. The European critics of democracy seldom failed to point out that if the Republic had outstripped the Old World in railroad building or the production of steel, in the realm of the aesthetic, of the things that really mattered to "cultivated people," it lagged far behind Europe.

So a major preoccupation of the fair's directors was to put that canard to rest by making it inescapably evident that culture and democracy (or capitalism) were compatible. No cost was to be spared. The motto of the fair was "I Will." What could have been more appropriately American? Richard Morris Hunt, a master of the Neo-Renaissance style, increasingly favored by tycoons and politicians for private and public buildings, was chosen as the principal architect for the exposition. He and other Eastern architects and artists approached to work on the fair were at first plainly suspicious of the taste and general cultural sophistication of a city that had grown famous slaughtering hogs.

The center of the fair was the Grand Basin, a lagoon 2,500 feet long and 250 feet wide. In the middle was Frederick MacMonnies's marble boat containing a number of allegorical figures. At the eastern end of the lagoon was Daniel Chester French's 65-foot-high statue of the Republic. Richard Morris Hunt had done the Administration Building, with its spectacular golden dome. McKim, Mead & White had designed the Agricultural Building, which also had a gilded dome crowned by Augustus Saint-Gaudens's statue of Diana. The Manufacturing and Liberal Arts Building (a rather awkward conjunction) covered 30 acres—it was the largest structure in the world under a single roof. Electricity Hall had walls that stretched for 70 feet, with Corinthian columns 42 feet high. Louis Sullivan had designed the Transportation Building. The Palace of Arts, designed by Charles B. Atwood, had a glass transept and, like the Agricultural Building, a dome, on top of which an enormous lady spread her wings. The Horticultural Building, with a crystal dome 113 feet high, was 1,000 feet long, and the statues that decorated its interior had been done by Lorado Taft, the mentor of many of the young women sculptors at the Chicago Art Institute. Daniel Burnham, the supervising architect for the entire fair, had stipulated that all the buildings must be white—simulated white marble or granite—and the final effect was dazzling, especially at night, when thousands of electric lights gave the "White City" an ethereal quality that captivated the most sophisticated or cynical visitors. The lagoon, with skiffs and gondolas gliding over its surface, was also a sensational success.

Bertha Palmer was the queen of Chicago, beautiful, rich, intelligent, and ambitious. She was determined that the exposition should make evident to every visitor the talents and accomplishments of the "new" American woman. The bill passed by the Illinois legislature authorizing the fair provided for a Board of Lady Managers. Many women objected to the term "lady" as implying that the women interested in the fair were "idle women of fashion," whereas in fact, the board included "doctors, lawyers, real-estate agents, journalists, editors, merchants, two cotton planters, teachers, artists. . . . " Two members of the board, Catherine Van Valkenburg Waite and Myra Bradwell, had studied law with their husbands. Active in the founding of the Illinois Woman Suffrage Association, both Bradwell and Waite had graduated from the Union Law School, and both edited law periodicals. A cousin of Susan B. Anthony, Dr. Frances Dickinson, was one of the leading ophthalmologists in the city, which counted some 200 women doctors in the late 1880s. Another prominent Chicago reformer was Corinne Brown, wife of a banker. Her strong labor sympathies induced her to become corresponding secretary of the International Labor Congress.

When a competition was announced for the design of the Women's Building, thirteen women entered the lists. Twenty-three-year-old Sophia Hayden won first prize for a Renaissance-style Museum of Fine Arts that she had submitted for her MIT thesis. It was chosen by the judges primarily because "with its balconies, loggias, and vases for flowers, it was the lightest and gayest in its general aspect and consequently best adapted for a joyous and festive occasion." Lois Howe won second prize.

Enid Yandell, a handsome and self-confident young woman of twenty-two from Louisville, Kentucky, was assigned to fashion the figure of the caryatids which were to line the roof garden of the Women's Building. Bertha Palmer was soon conducting tours of Yandell's studio for important visitors, among them Julia Dent Grant, the widow of General Grant, who told Yandell bluntly that in her opinion a woman's place was in the home.

"So you do not approve of me, Mrs. Grant?" Enid Yandell asked.

"I don't approve of those women who play on the piano and let the children roll about on the floor," the old lady declared, "or who paint and write and embroider in a soiled gown and are all cross and tired when the men come home and don't attend to the house or table. Can you make a better housewife for your cutting marble?"

"Yes," replied the doughty Yandell, "I am developing muscle to beat biscuit when I keep house." Beaten biscuit being a classic Southern delicacy, Mrs. Grant seemed slightly mollified. For determined Miss Yandell the Chicago exposition was the beginning of a long and successful career as a sculptor.

A formal competition was held for the main sculptural pieces to surmount the Women's Building. The winner, among seventeen entrants, was nineteen-year-old Alice Rideout of San Francisco. It proved extraordinarily difficult to prevail upon Miss Rideout to come to Chicago to supervise the execution of her two pieces. It took an imperious order from Bertha Palmer to move her, but once there she was an instant hit. A reporter described her as "very girlish and unassuming. Perhaps her unconsciousness of her own ability is one of her greatest charms. There is no doubt as to her possessing this ability. . . ."

Among the sixteen unsuccessful entrants was seventeen-year-old Kühne Beveridge, who went on to study with Rodin and exhibit at the Royal Academy in London and many lesser places. Merle Meres submitted a clay model of a handsome woman entitled "Genius of Wisconsin," which was eventually rendered nine feet high and placed in front of the Wisconsin Building.

Bitter controversies surrounded the interior design and decoration of the Women's Building. Sophia Hyden, whose views were ignored by Bertha Palmer, had a nervous breakdown, and it was said that she had become hopelessly insane. She recovered enough to marry an artist named William Bennett, but she abandoned the field of architecture, apparently with relief. Alice Rideout, after her remarkable triumph, apparently never set chisel to marble again (her sculptures for the fair, to be sure, were rendered in plaster, not in marble). She returned to Marysville, California, the small town where she had grown up. Her one experience of the larger world seems to have sufficed.

Vinnie Ream Hoxie was perhaps the best known of American women sculptors. She did a standing more-than-life-size statue of Lincoln for the Capitol, the first work of a woman commissioned by Congress. Her statue of Admiral Farragut was also a commendable, if pedestrian, piece. Hoxie herself, her pixielike face framed by masses of blond curls, was many people's notion of what a female artist should look like. When Mrs. Hoxie's work was rejected for the Women's Building by Bertha Palmer, she tried to win acceptance in the general arts category for her allegorical figure entitled "The West." It is a credit to the good judgment of the art jury that it was turned down, but it was installed in the Women's Building after all.

One of the most influential figures in the American art world was Sara Hallowell. She had assembled a remarkable collection of American paintings including the works of James Abbott McNeill Whistler, John Singer Sargent, and Eastman Johnson for the Chicago Interstate Industrial Exposition in 1885, and five years later she introduced Chicagoans to the work of the French Impressionists at the same exposition. She was also adviser on acquisitions for Mrs. Palmer and for a number of newly established municipal and private museums. But despite the fact that she had the unqualified backing of Bertha Palmer, the male fair committee was unwilling to see the important post of director of fine arts go to a woman. Montague Marks of the influential *Art Amateur* wrote: "Certainly she has done more for the art education of Chicago and the West generally than all your millionaires who have been buying costly old masters and exhibiting them at the Art Institute. Furthermore, she is a good judge of modern paintings, has remarkable executive ability, and is on the most friendly terms with artists at home and abroad." The job went to Halsey Ives, director of the St. Louis Museum of Fine Arts, and he appointed Sara Hallowell his secretary, in which role she soon became the de facto director, collecting paintings from all the important private collections in the United States and from dealers abroad. Isabella Gardner of Boston contributed from her famous collection, and Alexander Cassatt, whose sister, Mary, was living in Paris, also lent from his collection of French Impressionists. From the West Coast came important paintings from the collections of Collis Huntington and William Crocker.

While Sara Hallowell was in Paris rounding up additional works, Bertha Palmer wrote her that the commissioning of two large panels, fifty-eight by twelve feet, had been authorized and suggested that she offer the commission to the American painter Elizabeth Gardner, living in Paris. Gardner, a New Hampshire-born painter of considerable reputation, was one of a number of American women working in Paris, but she declined the commission on the ground of ill health. When Bertha Palmer and her husband arrived in Paris on fair business, Sara Hallowell introduced Mrs. Palmer to Mary Fairchild MacMonnies, the talented wife of the sculptor Frederick MacMonnies, who had already been commissioned to do the centerpiece of the exposition, a huge fountain group. Mary Fairchild had been born in New Haven in 1858 and worked in Paris in the atelier of Pierre Puvis de Chavannes. Bertha Palmer was impressed with her work and commissioned her on the spot to do one of the murals. Hallowell then introduced her patron to Mary Cassatt, a student and friend of Edgar Degas, who had exhibited in Paris and Rome. Cassatt was commissioned to do the second mural for the Women's Building.

Mary Cassatt was nearly fifty years old at the time. She was one of those women of her generation who had decided to put their careers ahead of conventional marriages. She was, her mother wrote somewhat disapprovingly, "intent on fame and money. . . . After all, a woman who is not married is lucky if she has a decided love for work of any kind and the more absorbing the better." Rather than mount a ladder, Cassatt had a deep trench sixty feet long dug, and she raised and lowered her canvas so that she could work at ground level.

One of the most gifted women painters displayed in the Gallery of Honor in the Women's Building was Cecilia Beaux. Born and reared in Philadelphia, Beaux was a brilliant portraitist whose work was compared to that of Whistler and Sargent. In the Paris Salon of 1896 she had the unusual honor of having six of her portraits hung in a group.

The exposition opened on May 1, 1893. Cleveland was on hand to press the button on what would signal its official beginning. At 12:08 the President, in the company of a throng of dignitaries, foreign and domestic, including the queen of Spain, and surrounded by a sea of humanity numbering, the police estimated, a quarter of a million, performed his appointed task. Thousands of flags were simultaneously unfurled from the roofs of the buildings around the lagoon, bands broke into music, and the MacMonnies fountain threw jets of water high into the air. "At that instant," a report notes, "the drapery fell from the golden figure of the 'Republic,' backed by the classic peristyle, she stood forth in radiant beauty welcoming the world."

Cleveland gave a short speech, hailing "the stupendous results of American enterprise and activity . . . the evidences of American skill and intelligence. . . . We stand today in the presence of the oldest nations of the world and point to the great achievements we here exhibit, asking no allowance on the score of youth." The United States was pleased at the opportunity to view the interesting, if clearly less impressive, accomplishments of other nations, the President implied, "while in appreciative return we exhibit the unparalleled advancements and wonderful accomplishments of a young nation, and present the triumphs of a vigorous, self-reliant and independent people. We have built these splendid edifices, but we have also built the magnificent fabric of a popular government, whose grand proportions are seen throughout the world. We have made and here gathered together objects of use and beauty. . . . We have also made men who rule themselves." The deeper meaning of the exposition, the President declared, was "the advance of human enlightenment; and . . . the brotherhood of nations."

After the luncheon that followed the President's address, Bertha Palmer and the members of the Board of Lady Managers adjourned hastily to the Women's Building for the opening of their building. The ceremony took place in the spacious Hall of Honor, where the World's Fair chorus sang songs composed by women. Among the honored women guests were delegates from Russia, Brazil, Sweden, Siam, and Britain. (Mrs. Charles Dickens was one of the British guests.)

Bertha Palmer gave the official welcome. She was frank to acknowledge that there had been "tedious delays and . . . dark clouds" in the planning of the Women's Building, but the Board of Lady Managers had been sustained by "the spontaneous sympathy and aid" which had reached it "from women in every part of the world." For her, the exposition, especially the Women's Building, symbolized the "unity of human interest, notwithstanding differences of race, government, language, temperament and external conditions." Splendid as had been the technical achievements of the modern industrial nations during the course of the nineteenth century, they had not "afforded the relief to the masses which was expected. The struggle for bread," she declared, "was as fierce as of old. We find everywhere the same picture presented—overcrowded industrial centers; factories surrounded by dense populations of operatives; keen competition; many individuals forced to use such strenuous efforts that vitality is drained in the effort to maintain life under conditions so uninviting and discouraging that it scarcely seems worth living. It is a grave reproach toward enlightenment that we seem no nearer the solution of many of these problems than during feudal days." It was especially appropriate to mention such matters at the opening of the Women's Building since they touched on "the compensation paid to wage earners, and more especially that paid to women and children. . . . Of all existing forms of injustice there is none so cruel and inconsistent as is the position in which women are placed in regard to self-maintenance— the calm ignoring of their rights and responsibilities which has gone on for centuries." She denounced "the theory which exists among conservative people that the sphere of woman is her home—that it is unfeminine, even monstrous, for her to wish to take a place beside or compete with men in the various lucrative industries. . . ." The result was that women were actively discouraged from taking a larger role in the world while working-class women were cruelly victimized. "These," she told her responsive listeners, "are the real heroines of life, whose handiwork we are proud to install in the Exposition, because it has been produced in factories, workshops and studios under the most adverse conditions and with the most sublime patience and endurance." Women were determined to play an active and useful role in the world. They had "no desire to be helpless and dependent. . . . This is entirely in conformity with the trend of modern thought, which is in the direction of establishing proper respect for human individuality and the right of self-development. Our highest aim now is to train each to find happiness in the full and healthy exercise of the gifts bestowed by a generous nature."

What is perhaps most worth noting about Bertha Palmer's address is the fact that she and the women delegates to the International Congress of Women, which took place in conjunction with the exposition, were the only people to give serious attention to the severe social and economic conflicts that were being, at that instant, dramatically highlighted by the deepening depression. Those men who, like the President, had occasion to deliver public addresses dwelt almost exclusively on the glorious achievements of American enterprise; on, in Andrew Carnegie's phrase, "triumphant democracy," as though nothing clouded that happy and self-congratulatory vision.

Alice Asbury Abbot, a Chicago journalist, wrote: "It is well that art and architecture have done so much for the fair grounds. If it were not for the lovely exteriors and enchanting landscapes, the tremendous force of the materialism expressed by the exhibits would oppress beyond belief. To the multitude there is but one building, and that is the woman's, which stands for an idea." Kate Field, the editor and publisher of Kate Field's Washington, a weekly newspaper with a national circulation of more than 10,000, wrote: "If popularity be a sign of approval, the Women's Building outranks all others. I never entered its portals, without being oppressed by an overflow of humanity. Every woman who visited the Fair made it the center of her orbit. Here was a structure designed by a woman, decorated by women, managed by women, filled with the work of women. Thousands discovered women were not only doing something but had been working seriously for many generations. . . . Many of the exhibits were admirable, but if others failed to satisfy experts, what of it?" she concluded defiantly.

Following the example set by Frances Willard's WCTU, Susan B. Anthony and Elizabeth Cady Stanton called together, in conjunction with the fair and under the aegis of the National Woman Suffrage Association, the International Congress of Women to celebrate the forty-fifth anniversary of the Seneca Falls Convention. The primary purpose of the meeting was to "rouse women to new thought . . . intensify their love of liberty, and . . . give them a realizing sense of the power of combination." To reassure apprehensive males, the convenors declared that they were of a common mind on one principle . . . "namely, man's sovereignty in the State, in the Church, and in the House." (Yet there was an edge of defiance of masculine authority in the rhetoric of the convention.) "Much is said," the call to the meeting declared, "of universal brotherhood, but, for weal or for woe more subtle and more binding is universal sisterhood." When the speakers talked of freedom, it was clear enough that freedom must be won in the face of masculine resistance and obtuseness.

Delegates came from Great Britain (by far the largest representation), France, Denmark, Norway, Finland, and India, plus "thirty-one different associations of moral and philanthropic reforms." The convention opened with a religious service in which six ordained women ministers participated, including the first woman to be ordained in the United States, Antoinette Brown Blackwell. The Reverend Anna Shaw delivered a sermon on "The Heavenly Vision." The women's movement, she reminded her listeners, had been born out of the antislavery movement, out of women's "longing for the liberty of a portion of the race": enslaved Americans of African descent. Now God was revealing to women the world over "the still larger, grander vision of the freedom of all human kind."

Elizabeth Cady Stanton then recalled for the delegates the remarkable progress that had been made in the status of women since the stirring days of the Seneca Falls gathering. Women's "rights of person and property were under the absolute control of fathers and husbands. They were shut out of the schools and colleges, the trades and professions, and all offices under government . . . and denied everywhere the necessary opportunities for their best development. Worse still women had no proper appreciation of themselves as factors in civilization, like the foolish virgins in the parable, women everywhere in serving others forgot to keep their own lamps trimmed and burning, and when the great feasts of life were spread, to them the doors were shut. . . . The true woman," Stanton told her listeners, "is as yet a dream of the future. . . . A just government, a humane religion, a pure social life await her coming. Then, and not until then, will the golden age of peace and prosperity be ours."

There were sessions—we would doubtless call them workshops today —on the special problems of women, but most were on the wider social needs to which women must address themselves if they were to reform society: on child labor, on the working conditions of industrial laborers, especially women; on prostitution, temperance, politics, and philanthropy. In short, the focus was on action rather than on introspection.

A special general session honored the pioneers in the women's movement—Susan B., Elizabeth Cady, Lucy Stone, and Nettie Blackwell. The most prominent male pioneer was Frederick Douglass, his fierce, proud face now crowned by a coronet of white hair. There had been no record kept of his birth date. By his own best calculation he was in his seventy-first year.

Eighty-one separate meetings were held, and an estimated 150,000 people attended the sessions. Eight hundred and thirty women joined in planning the congress or in chairing or lecturing at the various sessions, which ranged from scholarly ("Assyrian Mythology") to scientific ("Cholera in Hamburg") to feminist ("The Glory of Womanhood," the "Financial Independence of Woman," "Complete Freedom for Women"). Julia Ward Howe, at seventy-four the *grande dame* of American letters, presented a paper on women in Greek drama. Several sessions dealt with clothes reform and exercise as a means of improving the admittedly wretched health of women. Many concerned themselves with the status of women (invariably deplorable) in other parts of the world—Turkey, Egypt, India, Italy, Bohemia. Here missionary women were prominent, and the congress paid them a special tribute for their labors in improving the condition of women all over the world.

Cara Reese, a reporter for the *Pittsburgh Commercial Gazette*, irritated many of the delegates by warning women ambitious for a career that their first responsibility was as wives and homemakers. "The dusty parlor, the cluttered kitchen, the half made beds, the hurried meals are familiar objects," she noted, "in homes where women have gone over to the hustling world." She urged her listeners to keep their homes "in true gospel fashion" rather than become "money-making" women. She presented herself as the champion of "the unappreciated homemakers of today, and, and, oh men and brothers, how many there are! who watch the career of the wage-earning women with hungry eyes. . . . Both are discontent and in that discontent lies the leaven that will work future destruction."

Martha Cleveland Dibble offered reflections on "The Nervous American," in this case primarily the American male. Americans had accomplished great things through the expenditure of vast amounts of nervous energy. In this sense "nervous" meant agile, restless, quick, and active. But the other side of the coin was nervous-"ness." This was the price exacted by ambition and the struggle to get ahead in a cruelly competitive society. "How many of our men live, or seem to live," Dibble asked, "only to do business? The man seems submerged under its exactions. The thing he created to serve him as a means to an end is transformed into the master, to which he is chained. He no longer seeks amusements; home sees little of him; wife and children are small incidents in his daily life; friendship is an almost forgotten word; general reading is out of the question; and the grind of the counting room or office goes on year after year, till the wheels stop, utterly worn out. . . . Does money-making—for that is the incentive in most cases—does this constitute the only legitimate and worthy employment of time? Is there not today a large field in philanthropy, science, art, literature, and healthy recreation of many kinds, which can profitably and agreeably occupy one's powers . . . ?" American men died early, "killed by overwork . . . the victims of nervous exhaustion," leaving no "grand old men," full of years and wisdom, to guide the youth and strengthen the councils of the nation. If such tendencies were not checked, they would result in "feeble offspring" and a rising rate of mental breakdown and insanity. Martha Dibble's remedy was a modest one: "rowing and running and tennis and bowling, riding, swimming and base-ball." If the Republic were to be preserved, young men must be "virtuous and temperate."

Anna Julia Cooper of Washington, D.C., the corresponding secretary of the Colored Women's League, gave a talk on the aspirations of her sex, the tone of which awakened memories of abolitionist days. "Let woman's claim be as broad in the concrete as it is in the abstract," she declared. "We will take our stand on the solidarity of humanity, the oneness of life, and the unnaturalness and injustice of all special favoritisms, whether of sex, race, country, or condition. If one link of the chain is broken, the chain is broken. . . . Least of all can the woman's cause afford to decry the weak. . . . The colored woman feels that the woman's cause is one and universal; and that not till the image of God, whether in parian or ebony, is sacred and inviolable; not till race, color, sex and condition are seen as the accidents and not the substance of life . . . not till then is woman's lesson taught and woman's cause won— not the white woman's, not the red woman's, but the cause of every man and every woman who has writhed silently under a mighty wrong. Woman's wrongs are thus indissolubly linked with all undefended woe, and the acquirement of her 'rights' will mean the final triumph of all right over might, the supremacy of the moral force of reason, and justice, and love in the government of the nations of the earth."

In the face of strong protests from black leaders that the contributions of their race to American history were being ignored, the managers of the exposition set a Colored People's Day and invited Frederick Douglass, now American minister to the Haitian Republic, to give the principal address. Many Chicago blacks viewed the "Day" as an unsatisfactory substitute for a proper recognition of the role of black people in the nation's history and urged their fellows to boycott it. Douglass nonetheless gave a militant and moving speech to an audience of several thousand black men and women.

When Ida Wells, one of the militant young blacks who had boycotted the "Day," read Douglass's speech, "a masterpiece of wit, humor, and actual statement of conditions under which the Negro race of this country labored," she and her friends recanted and apologized to the "grand old man." It was Douglass's last major public address, and many listeners were deeply moved by the contrast of age and youth in the principal speaker and the young poet who followed him: Douglass in his seventies and Paul Laurence Dunbar, twenty-one. Dunbar, who worked as an elevator operator, had just published his first book of poetry, *Oak and Ivy*, raising the money for the printing from the passengers on his elevator. Soon his poems and short stories of black life made him one of the country's better known young writers. Dunbar's short stories featured the dialect of Southern blacks, and many of them gave a comic picture of black life not dissimilar to the minstrel show stereotype; but his poetry dealt more directly with black aspirations for dignity and brotherhood.

Whenever Frederick Douglass visited the exposition, he was immediately surrounded by throngs of admiring whites who wished to shake his hand or tell him of their role in the abolitionist movement.

The World Labor Congress, also held in conjunction with the World's Columbian Exposition in 1893, revealed some of the divisions among radical reformers. Edward Bellamy had been scheduled as a principal speaker, but when he demanded that a whole day be devoted to his "Nationalism," he was promptly dropped by Henry Demarest Lloyd, who was in charge of the program. Sidney Webb was there, discussing the philosophy of the British socialist movement; Jane Addams talked about sweatshops, as did Beatrice Webb. Richard Ely lectured on "Public Ownership of Agencies to Supply Public Needs." A delegation of British labor leaders met with their American counterparts to explore common concerns and tactics. Meantime, the Depression of 1893 continued, touching most distressingly the lives of the workingmen and women and their children. The Chicago Relief Aid Association and its counterparts in other industrial cities and towns were inundated by the needy. Homeless people slept in parks, under bridges, in alleyways, in saloons, and even in police stations. A mass meeting at the Central Music Hall in Chicago listened to British Lib-Labs (Liberal-Laborites) and then voted to organize a civic federation that would bring together all reform groups to stamp out municipal corruption and work to improve the condition of labor. The Chicago Civil Federation was formed, headed by Lyman Gage, a liberal banker.

The depth of the divisions in the Democratic Party of the Midwest was indicated by Sterling Morton's angry attack on the Populists at the opening of the Congress of Agriculture, convened in conjunction with the exposition. Morton was Cleveland's secretary of agriculture, and he thus spoke as the official voice of the administration. "The most insidious and destructive foe to the farmer," he announced, in what was tantamount to a declaration of war on the radical wing of his own party, "is the 'professional' farmer who, as a 'prompter' of granges and alliances, for political purposes, *Farms the Farmer. . . .*" The farmers and the agitators who stirred them up were advised by Morton to read Adam Smith's *Wealth of Nations*, which was "to political economy as the New Testament is to the Christian religion."

Henry Adams, in the midst of somber speculations about the "laws" of decay and decline, set off for the fair, where he found "matter of study to fill a hundred years." Now his education must encompass chaos. "Indeed, it seemed to him as though, this year, education went mad. . . . When one sought rest at Chicago, educational game started like rabbits from every building, and ran out of sight among thousands of its kind before one could mark its burrow. The Exposition itself defied philosophy. One might find fault until the last gate closed, one could still explain nothing that needed explanation. As a scenic display," Adams added, "Paris had never approached it," but the astonishing fact was that it was there at all. Not since Noah's Ark and the Tower of Babel had such oddly incongruous objects been collected in one spot on the globe. Even if one could accept it as "a step in evolution" bizarre enough to startle Darwin, "a sort of industrial, speculative growth and product of the Beaux Arts artistically induced to pass the summer on the shore of Lake Michigan," there was something ineffably exotic about it. Adams sat down under Richard Hunt's dome to reflect. "Here was a breach of continuity—a rupture in historical sequence." The question it raised in Adams's mind was that his artist friends—John La Farge, Hunt, Richardson, Saint-Gaudens, McKim, and Stanford White—might, after all, be the dominant figures of a new age in which aesthetic considerations dominated mercantile concerns. The artists themselves were skeptical. Their art, they insisted, was, to the tycoons of the Midwest "a stage decoration; a diamond shirt-stud, a paper collar." The massed artifacts of industrialism were simply overpowering. Adams lingered among the dynamos, "for they were new, and they gave to history a new phase." He decided "that the American people probably knew no more than he did; but that they might still be driving or drifting unconsciously towards some point in space. . . . Chicago was the first expression of American thought as a unity; one must start there." He "revelled in all its fakes and frauds, all its wickedness that seemed not to be understood by our innocent natives," Henry Adams wrote to John Hay, "and all its genuineness that was understood still less. I labored solemnly through all the great buildings and looked like an owl at the dynamos and steam-engines." The fair appeared to Adams as a kind of monument to the goldbugs, the capitalists and the tycoons. While his friends wanted to "torture" the goldbugs before ceremoniously drowning them in the pool of the Court of Honor, Adams, more humane, "would only drown them without torture, or electrocute them with their own dynamos, painlessly."

The exposition was full of ancillary delights. George Washington Gale Ferris, a civil engineer, had been commissioned to devise some spectacular diversion, something to rival the Eiffel Tower of the Paris Exposition of 1889. Ferris's response insured him immortality. He constructed a giant wheel, 250 feet in diameter. It carried thirty-six glass-enclosed cars, each with a capacity of 40 passengers. All told, 1,440 people could ride it at the same time. It was supported by towers 140 feet high and weighed 1,200 tons. It paused six times in its revolution for passengers (who paid 50 cents for a ride) to view the exposition grounds, the city beyond, and the glistening Lake Michigan from different elevations.

And then there was the Midway. One of its main attractions was a young magician named Erich Weiss, who changed his name to the catchier Harry Houdini. Little Egypt gyrated despite Anthony Comstock's efforts to close her down, and there were other even less salubrious diversions. A young black piano player named Scott Joplin from Texarkana excited audiences with a new kind of music that he called ragtime. A thousand "chair boys" pushed elderly or indolent or ailing visitors about the fairgrounds in wheelchairs. One of the chair boys was a student at Atlanta University, James Weldon Johnson, already writing poetry and prose based on racial themes.

Throughout the summer 27,000,000 people visited the Chicago exposition. It was a triumphant moment for the Middle West, a declaration of independence of the West from the East, a statement of equality, if not of superiority (certainly the East had done nothing to rival it); it ratified the position of Chicago as the "capital" of the Middle West.

Oswald Garrison Villard wrote that it was "one of the great milestones in our national life. Its beneficial effect on our architectural development can never be measured; as an educational institution it was a tremendous success. Its beauty, especially at night, was beyond adequate description."

At least three or four novels were written with the exposition as their setting. Detailed reports of every aspect of the grand event filled journals and newspapers all over the country for those unfortunates who could not afford to attend. Innumerable towns and cities, inspired by the Columbian Exposition, had their own more modest versions. It was as though the exposition had suggested to America a way to escape, for an enchanted moment, the grim realities of daily life in a nation racked by the war between capital and labor and by a devastating depression.

Back in the United States in the fall of 1893 after a summer in Europe, William James saw America with new eyes—"force and directness in the people, but a terrible grimness, more ugliness than I ever realized in things."

In New York City fiery young Emma Goldman became a popular speaker at labor rallies. At a demonstration in Union Square in the summer of 1893 she saw "a dense mass before me, their pale, pinched faces upturned to me. My heart beat, my temples throbbed, and my knees shook." She cried out: "Men and women, do you realize that the State is the worst enemy you have? It is a machine that crushes you in order to sustain the ruling class, your masters. Do you not see the stupidity of asking relief from Albany with immense wealth within a stone's throw of here? Fifth Avenue is a citadel of money and power. Yet you stand, a giant, starved and fettered, shorn of strength. Cardinal Manning long ago proclaimed 'necessity knows no laws' and that 'the starving man has a right to a share of his neighbor's bread.' . . . Well, then, demonstrate before the palaces of the rich; demand work. Demand bread. If they deny you both, take bread. It is your sacred right!"

Police in the crowd arrested Goldman. In court she was defended by old Abraham Oakey Hall. Hall had been Boss Tweed's coadjutor in the high tide of municipal corruption. His slim elegance had been caricatured in dozens of Thomas Nast's scathing cartoons. But in the twenty years or so since the downfall of the Tweed Ring, Hall with his impeccable tailoring and upper-class connections had experienced a kind of conversion, emerging as "a man of liberal ideas." Now he came forward as Emma Goldman's defense lawyer. In Goldman's admiring words, he was "tall, distinguished-looking, vivacious," much younger-looking than his white hair indicated. He told Goldman that he had taken her case in part because of his knowledge of police corruption— "he knew how easily they swear away a man's freedom and he was anxious to expose their methods. . . . The issue of free speech would bring his name before the public again." So Oakey Hall emerged from relative obscurity, borne aloft by Emma Goldman. But his efforts proved unavailing. Goldman was sentenced to a year on Blackwell's Island for inciting to riot. She denounced capitalist justice and went off to serve her sentence, refusing to allow an appeal. Her indomitable spirit proved impervious to the rigors of prison life. She became a nurse to the unfortunate women who made up the prison population and at the end declared it her "best school." She wrote: "Here I had been brought close to the depths and complexities of the human soul; here I had found ugliness and beauty, meanness and generosity. . . . The prison had been the crucible that had tested my faith. It had helped me to discover strength in being, the strength to stand alone, the strength to live my life and fight for my ideals, against the whole world if need be."

If we except 1861 and the beginning of the Civil War, the year 1893 was the most dramatic in our history. While Congress dithered and fiddled, the United States was drained of $87,000,000 in gold. Faced with disaster, the capitalists demonstrated, in Brook Adams's words, an unsuspected "intellectual flexibility" by improvising the trust, "the highest type of administrative efficiency . . . which has, as yet, been attained." It was the trust that, in Adams's opinion, saved the nation's economy by utilizing the Western mines and their mineral resources to the full.

28

Coxey's Army

When the Chicago World's Columbian Exposition closed in the fall of 1893, the country slumped back into the depression; the magic illusion was dismantled, and hungry men and women roamed the city's streets or gathered to hear anarchists and socialists denounce capitalists. Samuel Gompers estimated that 3,000,000 men and women were unemployed countrywide. One alarming manifestation was the companies of tramps, numbering, it was estimated, tens of thousands, that roamed the country, begging or stealing food and terrorizing whole communities. James Weaver called particular attention to "vast armies of homeless tramps ever wandering alongside of vacant land held for speculation. . . ."

Congress could think of nothing better to do than fiddle with the tariffs again. Henry Adams described that body as "Poking the tariff with a stick to make it mad." "Winter is here," he wrote Hay, "and my perpetual miracle is that people somehow seem to go on living without money or work or food, or clothes, or fire. One or two million people are out of work; thousands of the rich are cleaned out to the last shoe-leather; not one human being is known to be making a living; yet on we go. . . . But it can't last."

One man had a notion. He believed in the eccentric idea that

Congress not only could take actions to relieve the general distress but had the moral obligation to do so. In Massillon, Ohio, in the spring of 1894, Jacob Coxey planned a march on Washington to dramatize the plight of the unemployed millions and plead for some action on the part of the government to relieve suffering. Ray Stannard Baker, then a fledgling reporter for the *Chicago News-Record,* was assigned to report on Coxey's march.

Coxey was a prominent citizen of the little community, jack-of-all-trades, a farmer and horse breeder as well as the owner of a quarry that produced silica sand, a product used in making steel. He lived with his wife and daughter in a large, comfortable farmhouse which served as "General" Coxey's GHQ for the planning and organization of his projected march. A small, mild-looking, bespectacled middle-aged man with a straw-colored mustache, who had fought in the Civil War, he was a classic American type. Behind his innocuous exterior burned the ardent heart of a utopian reformer. A devout Christian, Coxey wished to see the United States at last converted into a true Christian commonwealth. Although he had certainly never read John Winthrop's "A Model of Christian Charity," he was animated by the same desire to redeem the times.

He had a most unlikely coadjutor in Carl Browne from Calistoga, California. Browne was a large, flamboyant man who dressed in fringed buckskins with silver-dollar buttons and sported a spectacular flowing beard parted in the middle. To Baker he looked like a salesman of Kickapoo Indian medicines. Browne handed Baker a card with his written signature and the words "The pen is mightier than the sword."

He also showed Baker a large portrait that he had painted of Jesus Christ, which bore a striking resemblance to Browne himself. He was a Theosophist, and he told the young reporter that when people died their souls and bodies went into separate reservoirs to make new human beings. He had within him a portion of the soul of Christ and of the Greek historian Callisthenes. Around the painting of Christ, Browne had written: "PEACE ON EARTH Good Will toward men! He hath risen!!! BUT DEATH TO INTEREST ON BONDS!!!"

Browne had painted a considerable array of banners and signs. One banner showed Coxey dosing "the sick chicken of honest labor" from a bottle of "eye-opener," the Coxey plan for the "resurrection of the nation." Other banners bore such slogans as "We workmen want work, not charity: how can we buy at the stores on charity and cast-off clothes?"

The two oddly assorted leaders informed the skeptical Baker that they intended to start from Massillon on Easter Sunday with 20,000 marchers and on May Day reach Washington and there present a petition to Congress demanding that something be done to relieve the distress of unemployed and destitute Americans. Coxey had received thousands of letters of encouragement and many contributions of money from individuals, labor unions, and Populist organizations. He called the projected march "a petition in boots."

To Baker's queries on how Coxey intended to feed his "army," the leaders replied with handbills which proclaimed: "Fall in, let everybody send or bring all the food they can . . . join the procession, you who have bring to those who have not. . . . We are acting from inspiration from on high. We believe that the liberty-loving people comprising this indivisible and undividable American Union will respond in such numbers to this call of duty that no hessian Pinkerton thugs . . . can be hired for gold to fire upon such a myriad of human beings, unarmed and defenceless, assembling under the aegis of the Constitution. . . ." Coxey quoted Elbert Hubbard's prophecy of an Armageddon where "the brute nature and immortal soul of man" would close "in final contest, which shall herald the dawning of the era of love and tenderness, when nations shall know the fatherhood of God and live the brotherhood of man."

While the preparations for the march went ahead, Mrs. Coxey gave birth to a baby, who was promptly named Legal Tender Coxey, and Browne gathered recruits in nearby towns by fiery speeches at torchlit rallies denouncing the "Money Power" and the "Octopus of the Rothschilds." Browne also composed a song for his enthusiastic listeners to sing to the tune of "After the Ball."

> After the march is over,
> After the first of May,
> After the bills are passed, child,
> Then we will have fair play.

Coxey and Browne found unwitting allies in the reporters who soon swarmed around Massillon, writing colorful and often mocking accounts of the preparations for the march. If more sophisticated readers smiled at the bizarre accounts, hungry and desperate men in cities and towns felt a surge of hope. Newspaper editorials that denounced the march as dangerous and revolutionary served only to heighten public interest in it and win more recruits for the army. One of the recruits was Dr. Cyclone Kirkland, a little man in a silk hat whose métier was predicting hurricanes through astrology. He began writing an epic poem on the march in the style of the *Odyssey*. Kirkland told Baker it would be a "hummer in a cyclonic way." A black minstrel singer named Professor C. B. Freeman, who claimed to be the loudest singer in the world, had left his wife and children to "follow de Gen'l." Another recruit, who arrived by Pullman car, was "The Great Unknown"; he subsequently turned out to be "Dr." Pizarro, a traveling medicine man who was usually accompanied by a band of Indians. There was even a brass band, the "Commonwealth of Christ Brass Band—J. J. Thayer, Conductor."

The cynical reporters, sure that the march would never start, debated the idea of hiring 100 unemployed roustabouts from a nearby defunct circus to march for a day or so with Coxey and Browne so that their papers would at least have a story. But astonishingly, as Easter approached, grim, ragged men began to appear, dropping off freight trains, arriving in farmers' wagons or on foot. Soon there was indeed the nucleus of an army. The people of Massillon, doubtless pleased at their town's sudden fame, turned out to provide food and shelter for the recruits. At eleven o'clock on Easter morning Windy Oliver, the bugler, riding a horse with a red saddle, sounded attention. Browne, on one of Coxey's finest horses and wearing a dashing sombrero, joined the general at the head of the column, the Commonwealth of Christ Band struck up a tune, and the march began. At the head of the strange column rode Jasper Johnson Buchanan, a black man, carrying the United States flag. Conspicuous among the marchers was Hugh O'Donnell, one of the leaders in the Homestead strike.

The Three Graces—Faith, Hope, and Charity—were female relatives of Coxey's. Mrs. Coxey accompanied the march in a carriage with Legal Tender, and the general's son, Jesse, wore a blue and gray uniform, symbolizing the unity of North and South in the fight for social justice. A huge crowd had assembled to witness the beginning of the march, and the army, counting perhaps 400, set off for Canton, its first day's march, to the accompaniment of shouts of encouragement.

No one was more surprised by the spectacle than the newspaper reporters, themselves grown into a small army. "The whole enterprise had seemed preposterous; it couldn't happen in America," Ray Stannard Baker reflected. Other "armies" were recruited elsewhere around the country, some from as far away as California.

The reporters who had been covering the preparations for the march were convinced that it had to end in disaster because of the difficulty of supplying any considerable number of marchers with food, but, as Baker noted, "instead of beginning to disintegrate immediately, as we had anticipated, the army grew in numbers and at each stopping place the crowds were larger and more enthusiastic. . . . Coxey had started with only enough in his wagons for a day or two, but at each town where a stop was scheduled, there appeared an impromptu local committee, sometimes including the mayor and other public men, with large supplies of bread, meat, milk, eggs, canned goods, coffee, tea—a supply far more generous and varied than even Coxey and Browne had expected or imagined." It was clear that the good wishes and hopes of large numbers of ordinary Americans marched with Coxey's tatterdemalion band.

When the army reached Pittsburgh, a city often racked by labor troubles, the humbler citizens, many of whom had vivid memories of the Great Strikes of 1877, turned out in a tumultuous welcome. Bands, delegations of marchers from unions, schoolchildren, and socialists packed the streets to cheer the marchers and join in what took on the character of a victorious parade. "I shall never forget as long as I live," Baker wrote, "the sight of that utterly fantastic, indescribably grotesque procession swinging down a little hill through the city of Allegheny singing with a roar of exultation Coxey's army song to the tune of 'Marching Through Georgia.' "

> Come, we'll tell a story, boys,
> We'll sing another song,
> As we go trudging with sore feet,
> The road to Washington;
> We shall never forget this tramp,
> Which sounds the nation's gong,
> As we go marching to Congress.

Baker, increasingly sympathetic to the strange procession and its eccentric leaders, walked with the marchers and talked with them. "I had known just such men in my boyhood," he wrote. "To call them an army of 'bums, tramps, and vagabonds,' as some of the commentators were doing, was a complete misrepresentation. A considerable proportion were genuine farmers and workingmen whose only offense was that they could not buy or rent land . . . or find a job at which they could earn a living." Baker became convinced that "there could have been no such demonstration in a civilized country unless there was a profound and deep-seated distress, disorganization, unrest, unhappiness behind it—and that the public would not be cheering the army and feeding it voluntarily without a recognition, however vague, that the conditions in the country warranted some such explosion." He wrote to the editor of his paper: "It seems to me that such a movement must be looked on as something more than a huge joke. It has more meaning than either Coxey or Browne imagines." But the editor, reprinting Baker's letter as part of an editorial, drew from it conclusions opposite to those intended by his young correspondent. To the editor, "the continual turning of the people to Washington for aid . . . is pathetic and portentous. The country," he concluded, "is sick just to the extent that its people try to lean on the government instead of standing upright on their own feet."

The editor's view was shared by the great majority of middle- and upper-class urban Americans, who could discover little sympathy for the armies that threatened to converge on Washington with their demands for congressional action to relieve the widespread suffering. Coxey's Army and those auxiliary armies forming—by one journalist's calculations—in at least eleven different towns and cities aroused the never distant anxiety about the "dangerous classes" that was such a persistent element in the consciousness of the upper classes. John Hay professed to believe that revolution was just around the corner. Coxey and his army would soon be in Washington, and Hay hoped the mob would spare his house, as he wrote Henry Adams, "because it adjoins yours. You, of course, are known throughout the country as a Democrat and an Anarchist and an Unemployed. Your house will be safe anyhow; so you might as well stand on my steps while the army passes, and shout for 'Chaos and Coxey' like a man."

As the army approached Washington, it found the going increasingly arduous. There were cold spring rains and even snow to contend with. The residents of the towns through which the army passed were far less hospitable; food and fuel grew scarce; toll roads barred the marchers' way, and tolls were demanded for every "soldier" in the now-depleted force. Beyond Cumberland, Maryland, the roads were so bad that Coxey chartered canalboats on the Chesapeake & Ohio Canal at the charge for "perishable freight" of fifty-two cents a ton. For three days the army made its way down the canal past "the dogwoods and judas trees in bloom, and innumerable wild flowers on the hillsides." The marchers sunned themselves on the decks; the general hammered out "orders" and "resolutions" on a battered typewriter, and Browne wrote poems celebrating the great journey. At Williamsport, Maryland, the army debarked and was joined a few days later by two converging armies, one from Philadelphia, led by a man in a high silk hat named Christopher Columbus Jones.

At last, on a blisteringly hot day, the combined armies approached the Capitol itself, marching down Pennsylvania Avenue. Coxey's daughter Mame, dressed in red, white, and blue, on a handsome white horse and representing the goddess of peace, led the procession. Large crowds lined the streets, and the police were out in force to block any effort to invade the congressional chambers. In front of the Capitol Browne dismounted, and Coxey, leaving his carriage, kissed his wife to the cheers of the onlookers.

Browne then made a dash through the police lines, apparently with the intention of entering the Capitol. The police overtook him and clubbed him to the ground. Coxey, meanwhile, reached the steps of the Capitol, but before he could read his prepared address to the crowd, the police dragged him away, too. He was arrested and charged with walking on the grass. The marchers were scattered by mounted police, and the Commonwealth of Christ was no more.

Coxey's "Address of Protest" was read in Congress by a sympathetic Populist legislator. It declared that the Constitution guaranteed to all citizens the right to petition for redress of grievances. "We stand here to-day to test these guarantees. . . . We choose this place of assemblage because it is the property of the people. . . ." They were there to protest "the passage of laws in direct violation of the Constitution" and "to draw the eyes of the entire nation to this shameful fact. . . . Up these steps the lobbyists of trusts and corporations have passed unchallenged on their way to committee rooms, access to which we, the representatives of the toiling wealth-producers, have been denied. We stand here to-day in behalf of millions of toilers whose petitions have been buried in committee rooms, whose prayers have been unresponded to, and whose opportunities for honest remunerative, productive labor have been taken from them by unjust legislation, which protects idlers, speculators, and gamblers; we come to remind the Congress here assembled of the declaration of a United States Senator, 'that for a quarter of a century the rich have been growing richer, the poor poorer, and that by the close of the present century the middle class will have disappeared as the struggle for existence becomes fierce and relentless.' " In the name of justice "and in the name of the commonweal of Christ, whose representatives we are, we enter a most solemn and earnest protest. . . . We have come here through toil and weary marches, through storms and distresses, over mountains, and amid the trials of poverty and distress, to lay our grievances at the doors of our National Legislature and ask them in the name of Him whose banners we bear, in the name of Him who pleaded for the poor and oppressed, that they should heed the voice of despair and distress that is now coming up from every section of our country, that they should consider the conditions of the starving unemployed of our land, and enact such laws as will give them employment, bring happier conditions to the people, and the smile of contentment to our citizens."

If the Eastern newspapers were contemptuous of the remnants of Coxey's ragged army that reached Washington, they had many supporters in the Midwest and among workingmen and women. The *Topeka Advocate* observed: "These men have as much right to go to Washington and demand justice at the hands of congress as bankers, railroad magnates and corporation lawyers have to go and lobby for measures by which to plunder the public; and if their rights are not respected there will be trouble; rest assured of that. Let the powers that be beware how they treat the Coxey army." The *Wealth Makers*, published in Lincoln, Nebraska, noted apropos of Coxey's march: "For our part we wish that all the destitute, wretched, miserable millions of American citizens which unjust legislation has made, could camp around the Capitol at Washington and form an ever present conscience-arousing spectacle for our national lawmakers to face."

Annie Diggs, a Kansas Populist, urged the passage of legislation that would form the unemployed into an "industrial army" to be "employed on works of public improvements, such as canals, rivers, and harbors, irrigation works, public highways, and such other public improvements as Congress . . . shall provide."

In fact, the so-called good roads bill (also known as the Coxey Bill) was introduced into the Senate by William Alfred Peffer, a Kansas newspaper editor, turned Populist politician. The bill called for the printing of $500,000,000, the money to be used to employ the jobless on the construction and improvement of the "general county-road system of the United States." The pay should be not less than $1.50 a day for an eight-hour day, and "all citizens of the United States making application to labor shall be employed."

Three days later another Coxey Bill was proposed to allow any "State, Territory, county, township, municipality, or incorporated town or village" to issue noninterest-bearing bonds, the proceeds from which were to be used to make "public improvements."

Former President Benjamin Harrison took the occasion of an address to the Republican State Convention in Indiana to support protective tariffs, declaring: "The times are full of unrest, disaster, and apprehension. I believe today that all the tumult of this wild sea would be satisfied, as by the voice of Omnipotence, if the industrial and commercial classes of this country would know today that there would be no attempt to strike down protection in American legislation."

Larger than Coxey's Army was that of a thirty-two-year-old printer named Charles Kelley. Kelley's Industrial Army, recruited primarily in California, numbered some 1,500, among them Jack London. One of the "soldiers" was a young miner-cowboy named William Haywood, called Big Bill by his friends because of his size. Haywood remembered the "march" as one of the "greatest unemployed demonstrations that ever took place in the United States." At Council Bluffs, Iowa, Kelley's Army was turned out of the railroad cars that had brought them East and forced to exist as best they could in the rain while the people of the town brought them food. After a week they continued their march on foot, but hungry, weary, and discouraged, the "Industrial Army" melted away.

In Montana a group of 650 miners, led by "General" Hogan, captured a Northern Pacific train at Butte and ran it themselves. When a trainload of railroad deputies overtook them at Billings, there ensued a sharp fight in which the railroad men were routed. At this point troops were called up from a nearby Federal fort, and the train was surrounded. The men surrendered and were dispersed, a handful finally making their way to Washington.

Although fewer than 1,000 or so men of the various armies that set out for Washington arrived there and although their reception was unvaryingly cold—hostility mixed with ridicule—the episode was an unsettling one for the world's greatest democracy. For each of the ragged, hungry, and defiant men who reached the nation's capital in symbolic protest there were thousands who shared his bitterness and, perhaps more, his confusion and disillusionment, who wished to know what had happened to the dream of "liberty and justice for all." To a contemporary journalist named M. J. Savage, the marches were a symptom. "Symptoms," he wrote, ". . . mean always internal disturbance, they mean the possibility of diseases that may threaten the vitals."

29

Pullman

Companies pressed to the wall by the depression cut wages sharply. This led in turn to a new outbreak of strikes by increasingly militant workers which, before the year was over, involved more than 750,000 men.

The Pullman Palace Car Company laid off more than half its work force and cut the wages of the rest by 25 percent. In fairness to Pullman, it must be said that in order to keep even his reduced work force employed, he apparently accepted orders at loss. On the other hand, he rejected the workers' argument that the rents on company-owned houses should be reduced proportionately to the reduction in wages. To this request Pullman replied that "none of the reasons urged as justifying wage reduction by it as an employer can be considered by the company as a landlord." Three of the committee of workers who had asked Pullman to reduce rents in line with wages were fired the following day. As it turned out, they belonged to the American Railway Union, formed by Eugene V. Debs to include all railway workers born of white parents. The American Railway Union resembled the Knights of Labor in that it aspired to include all railway workers in "one great brotherhood" rather than in craft or trade unions.

The union called a strike to protest the firings, and Pullman in turn laid off all the workers and closed the plant, taking the position that the action of the union relieved him of the responsibility of providing for employment at a loss. A month later the union proposed arbitration; but the company refused, and the union responded by declaring that no union member would function on a Pullman car on any line until the company accepted the principle of arbitration. The roads struck were essentially those that belonged to a group called the General Managers' Association, twenty-four lines extending over some 41,000 miles of rails in the Midwest. The Federal commission subsequently appointed to investigate the circumstances surrounding the Pullman strike called the General Managers' Association "an illustration of the persistent and shrewdly devised plans of corporations to overreach their limitations and to usurp indirectly powers and rights not contemplated in their charters and not obtainable from the people or their legislators." The refusal of the railroads that made up the association to negotiate was branded by the commission "as arrogant and absurd when we consider its standing before the law, its assumptions, and its past and obviously contemplated future actions."

Although Governor John Altgeld of Illinois insisted that he was capable of handling the situation, President Cleveland responded to the pleas of the railroad directors for protection of their property by authorizing the swearing in of 3,600 special deputies. The men (whom the Chicago superintendent of police described as "thugs, thieves and ex-convicts") were selected, armed, and paid by the General Managers' Association. They were in effect the armed forces of the railroads, operating under the authority of the United States government. Even the Pinkertons had never managed to achieve that status. The reaction of the strikers to this move was direct and vehement. Rioting, provoked by the "deputies," broke out in Chicago. The unemployed, the angry, and the embittered joined with the strikers, recalling the Great Strikes of 1877.

Richard Olney, Cleveland's attorney general, was unequivocally in support of the General Managers' Association. From the early days of the strike he had tried to prevail upon a reluctant Cleveland to use U.S. troops to restore the movement of trains. The President, a strict constitutionalist, was troubled by the fact that he could find no constitutional basis for intervention since Altgeld refused to request it. It was Olney's inspiration to prevail on Cleveland to appoint a special counsel to the U.S. attorney in Chicago. The plan was that this counsel, whose appointment was initially proposed by the General Managers'

Association, would secure an injunction in a Federal court against the strikers, in the enforcement of which Cleveland could then order troops into the city. The association offered the name of Edwin Walker, an attorney for the Chicago, Milwaukee & St. Paul.

Walker was immediately appointed, and Olney instructed him to do all he could to kill the strike in Chicago, thereby making it "a failure everywhere else" and preventing "its spread over the entire country." Walker was told to explore and exhaust all legal remedies, thus preparing the way for Federal intervention. The recently passed Sherman Antitrust Law might well be invoked on the ground that the strike was an illegal combination in restraint of interstate trade. Another avenue to be explored was the argument that the strikers were committing a "public nuisance." Since obstructing a public highway was an example of a public nuisance, it could be argued that a railroad was a "public highway."

On July 2 an injunction against Debs and the strikers was obtained in a Federal court. Under the terms of the injunction any striker could be arrested and "summarily dealt with for contempt of court," as *The New York Times* put it. Factories were shutting down because of lack of coal, and cattle cars were unloading at way stations to prevent the death of the cattle by starvation. In Sacramento a crowd of 3,000 had interrupted a rail movement.

On July 2 at the Rock Island tracks a large crowd refused to disperse when ordered to do so by a Federal marshal. One deputy was stabbed, and the sheriff knocked down. "I am here at Blue Island," Walker wired Olney. "Have read the orders of the court to the rioters here and they simply hoot at it. . . . We have had a desperate time here all day and our force is inadequate. In my judgment it is impossible to move trains without having the Fifteenth Infantry from Fort Sheridan moved here at once. There are 2,000 rioters here and more coming." Press reports gave a very different picture of the situation at Blue Island, and the mayor of Chicago insisted that things were well in hand. Olney, for his part, wanted an even darker report as a basis for sending in troops, and the Federal officials of the city promptly obliged, one of them wiring that "it is my judgment that the troops should be here at the earliest possible moment. An emergency has arisen for their presence in the city."

Armed with the telegram, Olney appeared at a Cabinet meeting to urge the immediate use of Federal troops, even though General Nelson Miles, commander of the Western Department, had expressed the opinion that there was no need for troops in Chicago. On the Fourth of July infantry, artillery, and cavalry were brought into Chicago and posted about the city. Olney telegraphed the Federal attorney, Thomas Milchrist, to convene a grand jury to indict Debs and other union leaders, and he announced to inquisitive reporters that "we have been brought to the ragged edge of anarchy, and it is time to see whether the law is sufficiently strong to prevent this condition of affairs. If not, the sooner we know it the better, that it may be changed."

Debs responded angrily, declaring: "The first shots fired by the regular soldiers at the mobs here will be the signal for a civil war. I believe this as firmly as I believe in the ultimate success of our course. Bloodshed will follow, and ninety per cent of the people of the United States will be arrayed against the other ten per cent." Whether because of the arrival of the troops or because popular passions had reached a boiling point, widespread looting and destruction of property began on July 5. For several days it seemed as though Debs's prophecy had come true, in Chicago at least. The rioters were similar to those described in press accounts of the Great Strikes of 1877 in Pittsburgh: juveniles, women, drifters or "tramps," and what we today would call street people, augmented by "a low class of foreigners," whoever they might be. Hundreds of trains were burned, buildings set afire—among them six large structures from the Columbian Exposition—and stores gutted. More soldiers poured into the city, and on the seventh the inevitable clash took place between rioters and soldiers. The mob threw bricks and stones at the soldiers, and some shots were fired. The soldiers fired back, and seven persons were killed and dozens wounded. Altgeld called up 5,000 militia to assist the regulars in trying to establish order.

The emotions of Ray Stannard Baker were not dissimilar to those felt by many Americans of his class and generation. It seemed, on the one hand, that the workingmen, left by the government, by the churches, and even by the majority of reformers to their own devices, had no recourse except to strike to try to obtain a modest degree of economic justice or, more simply, a wage sufficient to feed, clothe, and shelter themselves and their families, "and yet," on the other hand, Baker wrote, "when I saw huge mobs running wild, defying the officers of the law, attacking non-union workers, putting the torch to millions of dollars' worth of property—I was still more perplexed. Could such anarchy be permitted in a civilized society? . . . I was deeply stirred, and these more or less clumsy questionings were the best I could do at the time."

On the morning of July 8, 1894, Baker was present at the railroad yards in Hammond, Indiana, outside Chicago. There he saw the mob trying to overturn a Pullman car. As men tugged on the hawser, a train appeared down the track, there was a popping noise like fire-crackers, and Baker saw a spectator standing near him slump to the ground, blood spurting from his chest. The approaching train was filled with soldiers, who were firing indiscriminately. A bullet just missed Baker as he ran for cover behind a freight car. Others fell nearby, and when the firing ceased, one man had been killed and seven wounded, none of them strikers. In Baker's view it was that "battle," which was hardly a battle in any proper sense, that broke the strike. Debs and other union leaders were immediately arrested. Baker went with a man named Hogan, president of the American Railway Union, to see Debs in prison. Debs came out of his cell, "a tall stooping figure in shirt sleeves," put his arms around Hogan, and kissed him. The imprisoned labor leader was as optimistic and cheerful as ever, convinced that the union must win the strike.

Public attention focused on the two adversaries—Debs and Pullman. To Ray Stannard Baker, freshly radicalized by Coxey's Army, Debs resembled the humorist Bill Nye: "He had the same gangling height, the same thinning hair and blue eyes . . . was somewhat awkward, with an embarrassed gentleness of manner and a gift of explosive profanity." James Whitcomb Riley had described him:

> And there's Gene Debs—a man 'at stands
> And jest holds out in his two hands
> As warm a heart as ever beat
> Betwixt here and the judgment seat!

In Debs's own words, "I have a heart for others and that is why I am in this work. If I rise, it will be *with* the ranks, not *from* them." More than once imprisoned, he wrote "My Prison Creed":

> While there is a lower class I am in it;
> While there is a criminal element I am of it;
> While there is a soul in prison I am not free."

Emma Goldman described Debs as "very tall, very lean [a man who] stood out above his comrades in a more than a physical sense.

What struck me most about him was his naïve unawareness of the intrigues going on around him." His disarming innocence was, in a curious way, Debs's greatest strength. In a world full of wolves and tigers, of ambitious manipulators and fierce rivals for power, his simplicity of spirit was irresistible.

Pullman was a mild, benevolent-looking man with soft, innocent eyes, luxurious chin whiskers, and good intentions. He had built a model town for his workers and made it pay as well; he was immovably stubborn in the conscious rectitude of his position.

"The contest," Debs declared, "is now on between the railway corporations united solidly on the one hand and the labor forces on the other." The country chose sides—the strikers or the railroads. The *New York World* called the strike a "war against the government and against society . . . iniquitously directed by leaders more largely concerned to exploit themselves than to do justice or to enforce the right." But Pullman's obduracy caused widespread sympathy for the strikers, and the mayors of Chicago and Detroit presented Pullman with telegrams from mayors of fifty some cities urging him to accept arbitration. Even Mark Hanna, a spokesman for corporate interests, was indignant with Pullman and denounced him in that citadel of conservatism the Union Club of Chicago as "a damned idiot." When a defender of Pullman argued that Pullman was a benefactor of the workers and had built them a model town, Hanna replied, "Oh, hell! Model—! Go and live in Pullman and find out how much Pullman gets sellin' city water and gas ten per cent higher to those poor fools." Bertha Palmer, a strong supporter of unions (she helped organize the seamstresses of Chicago), crossed Pullman off her guest list.

The facts of the strike were commonly distorted by newspapers hostile to the union movement, especially to the American Railway Union. Reporters often found their stories rewritten to reflect unfavorably on the strikers or their leaders. Some stories were simply manufactured. The *Chicago Tribune* of June 30 announced, "MOB IS IN CONTROL," and the following day, "MOB BENT ON RUIN—DEBS STRIKERS BEGIN WORK OF DESTRUCTION"; another headline read: "GUNS AWE THEM NOT—DRUNKEN STOCKYARD RIOTERS DEFY UNCLE SAM'S TROOPS—MOBS INVITE DEATH." On July 7 the headline of the *Inter Ocean* blared: "UNPARALLELED SCENES OF RIOT TERROR AND PILLAGE"; "ANARCHY IS RAMPANT." Other newspapers took their clue from the antilabor papers in Chicago. The *Washington Post* carried a story with a Chicago dateline that began: "The situation tonight is more alarming than at any time since the trouble began. War of the bloodiest kind in Chicago is imminent, and before tomorrow goes by the railroad lines and yards may be turned into battlefields strewn with hundreds of dead and wounded. Lawlessness of the most violent kind was the order of things today. . . . Chicago was never before the scene of such wild and desperate acts as were witnessed today and tonight . . . tonight it came to the knowledge of the Federal authorities here that the anarchists and socialist element made up largely of the unemployed, were preparing to blow up the south end of the Federal building and take possession of the millions in money now stored in the treasury vaults."

An editorial in *The New York Times* recommended announcing that all workers who quit their jobs to express sympathy for the strikers should be declared criminals. Debs himself was a "lawbreaker at large, an enemy of the human race. . . . Debs should be jailed, if there are jails in his neighborhood, and the disorder his bad teaching has engendered must be squelched." *Harper's Weekly* declared that in attempting to break the strike, "the nation is fighting for its own existence just as truly as in suppressing the great rebellion. . . . Until the rebellion is suppressed all differences of opinion concerning its origin, or the merits of the parties to the dispute out of which it grew, are irrelevant to the issue of the hour, and must wait the future."

While many clergymen expressed sympathy for the strikers and their aims and the Christian Socialists pledged their strong support, the Reverend Herrick Johnson, professor at the Presbyterian Theological Seminary in Chicago, sounded a more belligerent note. "The time has come," he declared, "when forbearance has ceased to be a virtue. There must be some shooting, men must be killed, and then there will be an end to this defiance of law and destruction of property. Violence must be met by violence. The soldiers must use their guns. They must shoot to kill."

Unquestionably many Americans, Olney and Cleveland among them, were anxious to smash the strike lest it spread. James J. Hill of the Great Northern spoke for like-minded men when he wrote to a Cabinet member during the strike: "The present labor strikes throughout the country have prostrated business beyond anything that has ever occurred. The panic of last year is nothing compared with the reign of terror that exists in the large centers. Business is at a standstill, and the people are becoming thoroughly aroused. Their feeling is finding expression about as it did during the War of the Rebellion . . . the public without reference to party lines, are unanimous in approving and supporting the action of the President." Minnesota Senator Cushman Davis declared that Debs had "called from the caves and dens of Chicago the professed criminal, the idly vicious, the anarchist. Everyone who is conspiring to put down modern civilization is now moving under the mask of this strike and taking knife and destroying property in its name." The word "anarchism" recurred with monotonous frequency in editorials and comments on the strike.

Many papers questioned Debs's sanity, charging him with being a dipsomaniac whose memory had been impaired by excessive drinking. "Those who know Debs well," *The New York Times* editorialized, "believe that his present conduct is in large measure, if not wholly, due to the disordered condition of his mind and body, brought about by the liquor habit, for which he was under treatment such a short time ago."

Papers favorable to the strikers' cause—and there were a number of them, mostly Democratic—tried to deflate the sensational and exaggerated stories. "The mass of people," the *New York World* declared, on July 9 "evidently do not bother about the strike. . . . Of mob rule and riot, in the sense in which it is usually understood—that of reckless and wanton destruction of life and property—there has been a deplorable lot of it, but the tales of its extent have been greatly exaggerated."

Hostility toward the strikers did not imply sympathy with George Pullman. The *Chicago Times* described him as a "cold-hearted, cold-blooded autocrat. . . . He wears no mask. His character is reflected in his countenance. He has a fat pudgy face. . . . A pair of small piggish eyes gleam out from above puffed cheeks, and the glitter of avarice is plainly apparent in their depths." While few papers were as rancorous as the *Times*, the criticism of Pullman was widespread. An article in the *North American Review* declared that the United States had become a plutocracy "far more wealthy than any aristocracy that has ever crossed the horizon of the world's history. . . ." The new rulers did not fight for their country's liberties "but for its boodle; their octopus grip is extending over every branch of industry; a plutocracy which controls the price of the bread we eat, the price of the sugar that sweetens our cup, the price of the oil that lights our way, the price of the very coffins in which we are finally buried."

The *Chicago Times* gave wholehearted support to the strike, calling it "absolutely justifiable." The editor considered "the strike and the boycott the only weapons left to those who have neither land nor capital, but only strong hands and a willingness to work. This strike is worth to the nation ten times what it has cost. It has set the people thinking. It may have widened the breach between capital and labor, but it has helped to unify wage-earners. It has also demonstrated the essentially public character of the railroads that the movement for their nationalization has been advanced by ten years in thirty days. . . . It has shown the Federal Administration to be on the side of the corporation, and has taught the plain folk that if industrial liberty is to be won corporation Presidents must not be elected."

Debs was as much a hero to many Midwestern Populists as he was to the beleaguered ranks of labor. The *Lincoln* (Nebraska) *Alliance-Independent* described him as an enemy to tyranny.

To a Kansas farmer the Pullman strike was "of stupendous importance in the widest possible sense. . . . Unquestionably, nearly, if not quite, all Alliance people are in fullest sympathy with these striking men. . . ." The *Advocate*, a Populist journal, declared: "Thousands of people to-day see the absolute necessity of government ownership and operation of railroads who never saw it before." The strike had also made abundantly evident the fact that "the republican and democratic parties are on the side of capital, and the press of both parties has been solidly arrayed against labor. . . . It has become apparent in this contest that in any difference between capital and labor the courts and all the civil and military authorities are at the service of organized capital. Labor," the editor added, in words that echoed the Dred Scott decision, "has no right that capital or its allies are bound to respect."

Jane Addams, who knew and liked Pullman, wrote a remarkable essay on the strike, an essay directed especially at the irony of George Pullman, hailed as a philanthropist and benefactor of the workingman, becoming, in the eyes of many, the villain of the strike. She compared Pullman to King Lear and his workers to Lear's faithful daughter whom he rejected. Pullman's great failing, Addams wrote, was that he had imposed his own benefactions on his workers. He had failed to involve them directly, "to call upon them for self-expression"; he assumed that he knew their needs better than they did. Like Lear, thinking of himself "as the noble and indulgent father . . . he has lost the faculty by which he might perceive himself in the wrong. . . . A movement had been going on about him and in the souls of his working men of which he had been unconscious. . . . Of the force and power of this movement, of all the vitality within it . . . this president had dreamed absolutely nothing." The movement of which Pullman had been so unaware was a stirring of the "proletariat," who "had learned to say in many languages that 'the injury of one is the concern of all.'" Philanthropy, Addams argued, was a negative influence in society unless it was animated by "that great faith which perennially springs up in the hearts of the people, and re-creates the world." This was the faith in the solidarity of all races and classes. Pullman, she argued, represented an obsolete ethic. The fact was that the best spirit of the age was "directed toward the emancipation of the wage-earner, that a great accumulation of moral force is overmastering men and making for this emancipation as in another time it has made for the emancipation of the slave; that nothing will satisfy the aroused conscience of men short of the complete participation of the working classes in the spiritual, intellectual and material inheritance of the human race." The workers, on the other hand, had, like Cordelia, failed to include their employers in the scope of their own salvation. Unless they did so, they would encounter "many failures, cruelties and reactions." How far Jane Addams was ahead of her time may be judged by the fact that it was eighteen years before "A Modern Lear" was finally published.

At the height of the strike Debs asked Samuel Gompers, whom he knew well in his role as an officer of the Brotherhood of Railway Carmen, to call for a general strike in support of the American Railway Union. Gompers and the officers of the AFofL responded with a telegram to President Cleveland, asking him to come to Chicago and "give us your aid so that the present industrial crisis may be brought to an end. . . ." The telegram was not answered, and under continued pressure from Debs, Gompers drew up a lengthy statement on the strike, admonishing AFofL members *not* to strike, while condemning Pullman and the General Managers' Association. The trade union movement, Gompers declared, was one "of reason, one of deliberation . . . democratic in principle and action, conservative in its demands. . . ." It had its "origin in economic and social injustice . . ." and was the "protector of those who see the wrongs and injustice resultant of our present industrial system, and who by organization manifest their purpose of becoming larger sharers in the product of their labor. . . ." Through "our intelligence and persistency, the earnestness of our purpose, the nobility of our cause," the federation would "work out through evolutionary methods the final emancipation of labor."

Gompers and the federation recognized "in this strike of the American Railway Union . . . an impulsive vigorous protest against the gathering growing force of plutocratic power and corporate rule." Yet the fact was that the General Managers' Association had managed to rally to its side "the Federal Government, backed by the United States marshals, injunctions of courts, proclamations by the President, . . . sustained by the bayonets of soldiers and all the civil and military machinery of the law. . . . Against this array of armed force and brutal moneyed aristocracy, would it not be worse than folly," Gompers asked, "to call men out on a general or local strike in these days of stagnant trade and commercial depression?"

Gompers's statement displayed its author's skill in steering a middle course. It denounced the "plutocratic wreckers," expressed strong sympathy with the strikers, urged restraint, and spelled out the strategy of the federation itself. The federation was committed to "evolutionary methods," to "larger shares," and, finally, to wresting control of the country from the "brutal moneyed aristocracy" and placing it "in the hands of the common people." In effect Gompers took advantage of the strike to lay out the guiding principles of the American Federation of Labor for the rest of its natural life, thereby charting a characteristically, if not uniquely, American course.

As the strike dragged on through the summer, Ray Stannard Baker found himself more and more emotionally involved with the strikers and their families, many of them deeply in debt and on the verge of starvation. His stories of hunger and need in the *Record* brought in a flood of contributions, and soon Baker was acting as a kind of one-man relief committee to distribute food to the families of the neediest strikers. Finally the newspaper itself took over the work of charity, "a merciful duty" for the "hungry and distressed people of Pullman." Baker was "thrilled" by the "extraordinary idealism and patience with which these poor men and women came to their own help. They had to suffer everything, not only the loss of their jobs, but literally hunger and cold, in forming any organization at all." The strike was broken, the leaders were blacklisted, and the men returned to work thoroughly defeated.

"Debs' Rebellion," Baker wrote, "was one of the greatest industrial conflicts in the history of the country—perhaps the most important of all in its significances. The issues it raised were carried through to the Supreme Court of the United States with a resulting decision that had a profound influence upon the labor movement in America. It led to the rapid growth of the Socialist party. . . ."

One consequence was a renewed effort on the part of Tom Morgan and socialists to take control of the AFofL. Gompers was equally determined to resist such a move. Both factions did their best to secure the election of delegates favorable to their side of the issue. The first nine planks proposed by Morgan at the union's conclave in Denver in 1894 were adopted with only a few modifications. Plank 10, calling for "the collective ownership of the means of production and distribution," brought on a bitter floor fight. Gompers's strategy was to kill the plank by a series of amendments, perhaps the most telling of which stated that the collective ownership should be instituted "as rapidly as the people of the United States shall declare in favor thereof by means of initiative and referendum." For five days the fight continued while the socialists held meetings to try to bring pressure to bear on the delegates. But once again Gompers held the union fast; Plank 10 was defeated by a two-to-one margin, and the socialists had to get what satisfaction they could from ousting Gompers from the presidency of the union, a coup which lasted only a year.

Historians continue to argue about the role of the Federal troops in provoking rioting since it seems plainly the case that there had been relatively little disorder prior to their arrival. What is evident is that in 1894, as in 1877, there was deep and widespread bitterness and dissatisfaction among a great many American workingmen. That it did not spread far beyond Illinois or, indeed, much beyond Chicago seems to have been more the result of chance and a lack of worker solidarity than anything else. With the decline of the Knights of Labor, caused at least in part by the failure of that body to support the Haymarket anarchists, there was no organization that presumed to speak for the whole of labor. It seems reasonable to assume that even if Gompers had called for a general strike, the call would likely have been ignored, and certainly Gompers was shrewd enough to suspect as much.

There was much less public sympathy with the strikers than there had been at the time of the Great Strikes. The other important point to make, of course, is that the Great Strikes had been spontaneously "general." The Pullman strike was called by the union leaders and began over what might be called a jurisdictional issue—the firing of three union members. It thus seemed to the public to be in the nature of a struggle for power between labor and capital, a struggle in which most Americans were caught in the middle. In addition, the generally bad times, which the strike allegedly was making worse, lessened sympathy for the strikers. If Pullman had not behaved in such an autocratic manner, there would have been even less sympathy with the strikers.

The ease with which a relative handful of strikers tied up a substantial part of the business of the country alarmed many people since it disclosed the vulnerability of the economy to what many people felt was the irresponsible action of a union leader. Although "foreign agitators" had much less to do with the Pullman strike than with a number of its predecessors, it is notable that the level of paranoia was much higher than before. Coincident with the beginning of the strike, Sadi Carnot, the president of France, had been assassinated by an anarchist, and this fact was made much of in connection with the supposedly revolutionary bent of the strike leaders.

Among the consequences of the strike was the discrediting of Debs and the notion of a great union embracing all workers and a substantial strengthening of Gompers's trade union approach. At the same time Cleveland did not escape sharp criticism for infringing states' rights. And if the outcome of the strike was generally popular, it had the effect, as Baker wrote, of swelling the ranks of those who called themselves socialists. Ten thousand men and women met at Cooper Union to protest the use of Federal troops, and Henry George, one of the principal speakers, declared: "I yield to nobody in my respect for the rights of property, yet I would rather see every locomotive in this land ditched, every car and every depot burned and every rail torn up, than to have them preserved by means of a federal standing army."

Whatever else is obscure, it can be said with confidence that Olney and Cleveland welcomed the opportunity to demonstrate their determination to use the powers of the Federal government wherever necessary, or perhaps wherever possible, to suppress militant union activity. The use of troops not only served to inflame popular feeling and thus to increase the danger of violence but also, in practical fact, broke the strike. Underlying everything that happened was an adversary psychology on the part of Olney and Cleveland, well expressed in the President's comment, "If it takes the entire army and navy of the United States to deliver a postal card in Chicago, that card will be delivered."

Undoubtedly one factor complicating the strike issue was the desperate state of the nation's economy and the fear that a prolonged strike would seriously retard recovery—or hasten revolution. By the end of 1894, 642 banks were defunct, and 22,500 miles of railway, enough to traverse the country more than seven times, were in receivership. One-quarter of the nation's industrial plants were closed down, and hundreds of thousands of workers were jobless. From 1891 to 1895 the index of farm produce dropped precipitously from a value of $14.70 in 1891 (already a depressed figure) to $9.71 in the latter year. Wheat cost more to grow than the farmer received for it. Only the freight rates went up. James Hill, self-appointed adviser to Cleveland (as he had been adviser to Harrison and would be to McKinley with a splendid indifference to party labels), noted that in a "careful inquiry along over five hundred miles of our lines as to the ability of the farmers to find the necessary money to pay for their binding twine, and the little they need for harvest help," they had turned out to be destitute. "The panic of last year," he wrote to Daniel Lamont, secretary of war and ex-aide to William Whitney in his street railway ventures (he would become Hill's business associate after his term of office), "is nothing, compared with the reign of terror that exists in the large centers. Business is at a standstill, and the people are becoming thoroughly aroused. Their feeling is finding expression about as it did during the War of the Rebellion."

The economic revival promised by hard money men had not come by the fall elections of 1894. Things were worse; the country had sunk deeper than ever into depression. The voters made clear their disenchantment with both parties. Democrats by the tens of thousands abandoned their party's standard. Books analyzing the evils of capitalism poured from the presses. Radical magazines and radical proposals sprouted like mushrooms.

In the Nebraska gubernatorial elections the voters of that distressed state, always in the van of radical politics, freed themselves of the conservative Democrats, whose candidate polled only 6,985 votes. The Republican candidate had 94,113 votes, and the fusion candidate, who appealed to the disenchanted in both parties, 97,815. Bryan narrowly missed being chosen as Senator.

The general disillusionment with Cleveland brought a resurgence of Republicans in Congress, but the agitation for tariff reform continued. Senator William Lyne Wilson, ex-professor of ancient languages and formerly president of West Virginia University, took the lead in drafting a bill to lower the tariff schedule substantially, but the bill suffered grievously in committee. Arthur Pue Gorman, Senator from Maryland and a tycoon in his own right, restored many of the cuts, most strikingly in the case of sugar. H. O. Havemeyer, head of the sugar trust, it turned out, had made generous contributions to both parties in the election of 1892. He insisted, with disarming candor, that "the American Sugar Refining Company has no politics of any kind."

"Only the politics of business?" an unfriendly member of the Senate committee asked.

"Only the politics of business" was Havemeyer's classic reply. The debate over the Wilson bill was given heightened drama by the disclosure that a number of the Senators were speculating in sugar stocks at the very time they were considering a bill to protect the sugar refining industry. Senator Quay of Pennsylvania freely confessed in a defiant statement: "I do not feel that there is anything in my connection with the Senate to interfere with my buying or selling the stock when I please; and I propose to do so." The Senate made 634 changes in the Wilson bill, and the tariff on refined sugar was raised to a higher rate than it had had under the McKinley Tariff, all of which prompted a query from the bill's original author: "Is this a government by a self-taxing people or a government by trusts and monopolies? The question is now, whether this is a government by the American people for the American people, or a government of the sugar trust for the benefit of the sugar trust."

Milford Howard, the Alabama Populist Congressman, who wrote a number of articles and several books denouncing capitalism, published in 1894 *If Christ Came to Congress*, a novel in which the venality of Congressmen was vividly portrayed. In *The American Plutocracy*, which appeared the next year, Howard described the war between plutocracy and democracy. "I do not mean the Democracy of Grover Cleveland," he wrote, "for it is only plutocracy masquerading in a stolen costume. I mean the Democracy of Thomas Jefferson, Andrew Jackson and Abraham Lincoln. The issue is now clearly defined and it is to be the greatest, the most stupendous struggle of all the ages. It is the uprising of the people against the money power."

Like many other Populist orators, Howard compared the wage slaves of industrialism to the chattel slaves of pre-Civil War days. The new masters demanded that "the toilers of the nation, those who work with brain and brawn, be made slaves to this libidinous plutocracy." (The Populist implication of sexual licentiousness often accompanied the charge of greed for money.) For the moment, Howard declared, the battle was a battle of ballots, but if they failed to bring about the necessary reforms, "if constitutional methods will not avail . . . this continent will be shaken by a mighty revolution. . . . The spirit of avarice is devouring the great heart of this nation. The greed for gain gets such possession of men's souls that they become demons. They rush into the maelstrom of money-getting, and soon lose all fear of God and love for their fellow-men. . . ."

The defeat of the American Railway Union, the imprisonment and discrediting of Debs, Gompers's success in keeping the AFofL from going socialist—all were part of a pattern of reaction. Everywhere alarmed Republicans and conservative goldbug Democrats rallied their forces and dug deep into their purses to finance political campaigns aimed at incumbent Populists.

In Kansas mineowners launched a campaign to break the power of the unions in Cherokee and Crawford counties, two Populist strongholds. The owners' tactic was to "provoke the miners to strike," in the words of Lorenzo Lewelling. "Having accomplished this purpose, the operators . . . proceeded to erect private forts, garrisoned with conscienceless mobs armed with Winchester rifles, intended to commit murder in resisting mere trespass upon lands; an offence which, under the statutes, constitutes manslaughter."

In Colorado the *Rocky Mountain News*, at least nominally Populist, lined up against Davis Waite, charging that his "fantastic, selfish, and lawless course . . . has already driven thousands from the Populist party and held the state up to ridicule and contempt."

On the Republican side "law and order" became the watchword, and Waite was attacked as "socialistic and anarchistic." The *Denver Republican* editorialized in the fall of 1894: "Let the Populist party triumph in the approaching election, and capital will shun Colorado as people avoid a city stricken with plague. Our reviving mining interests will be stunted in their growth, and Colorado men will appeal in vain to Eastern and European capitalists for money with which to develop any of our natural resources or to embark in new industries." The Republican candidate for governor accused populism of being "false to its promises of reform . . . controlled by demagogues and cranks. Populism is really socialism." The law must be supreme.

The Colorado election of 1894 was the first state election in which women could vote, and Waite's opponents appealed for the women's vote. "How can any earnest, self-respecting Christian, man or woman, vote for the blasphemous, Sabbath-desecrating, Christ-libelling candidate for governor whom the populists have on their ticket?" asked the *Greeley Sun*. If Waite was reelected, "all over the east women will be put down as being cranks and unfit to cast a ballot with reason."

The American Protective Association, an anti-Catholic nativist organization, worked assiduously behind the scenes to spread the notion that Waite was pro-Catholic and that Catholics would benefit from a Populist victory. The Citizens' Alliance, a kind of vigilante band of union-busting businessmen, was also active. Waite was defeated by a Republican nonentity, and the women's vote was blamed by many for his defeat. A woman supporter wrote Waite: "God help me, I was never so near hating my own sex as I am tonight when the news of your defeat comes to me. Ingratitude, thy name is Woman!"—a reference to the fact that Waite had been an early champion of woman suffrage.

In Colorado, encouraged by the Republican victory, the mineowners determined to break the power of the unions. That decision marked the beginning of almost twenty years of warfare in the silver and coal fields of the Rocky Mountain region, a war in which many lives were lost, most of them by striking miners, and infinite misery was endured. When word reached the mines that the operators had agreed to break the unions, an Irish miner announced defiantly: "The moment they announce that as their object they will sign their own death warrant, as you will find that the labor unions will all organize rifle clubs and will be operated something on the plan of the Molly Maguires." A spy in the employ of the Thiel Detective Agency reported that such comments were heard among union men as "The s——s of b———s brought a lot of cutthroats in here to shoot us down like dogs, and after the strike was over those of us who were not murdered by the cutthroats could not get a day's work in the camp. Do you think such s——s of b———s are fit to live?"

The *Miner's Magazine* printed a poem that expressed common sentiments:

> Only a man in overalls, lay him anywhere—
> Send for the company doctor—we have no time to spare
> Only a little misfire, only a miner crushed,
> Put another one on, for from dark till dawn
> The smelter must be rushed.

The feeling of being on the defensive was already evident in the Populist Convention in 1894 at Chicago. The most dramatic moment of the convention came with the speech of Lyman Trumbull, Lincoln's friend and rival, now eighty-one years old. Trumbull told the cheering delegates: "If the accumulation of fortunes goes on for another generation with the same accelerated rapidity as during the present, the wealth of this country will soon be consolidated in the hands of a few corporations and individuals to as great an extent as the landed interests of Great Britain now are. Neither strikes of the laboring classes, which array against them the moneyed power and the governmental power which it controls, nor the government control of the great railroad and other corporations, will remove the existing conflict between labor and capital which has its foundation in unjust laws, enabling the few to accumulate vast estates and live in luxurious ease, while the great masses are doomed to incessant toil, penury, and want." Trumbull went on to denounce "these Federal judges, like sappers and miners," who had "for years silently and steadily enlarged their jurisdiction. . . ." Unless checked by legislation, they would "soon undermine the very pillars of the Constitution and bury the liberties of the people underneath their ruin."

The fall congressional elections of 1894 brought serious losses for the Populists and substantial gains for the Republicans.

Reflecting on the events of 1894, Henry Adams saw them as a signal victory for capitalism. It seemed to him that the country had oscillated throughout its history between a kind of democratic industrialism and capitalism, the latter "centralizing, and mechanical." The issue had come to a head in 1893, and the majority, in accepting the single monetary—gold—standard, had "at last declared itself, once for all, in favor of the capitalistic system with all its necessary machinery. All one's friends, all one's best citizens, reformers, churches, colleges, educated classes, had joined the banks to force submission to capitalism; a submission long foreseen by the mere law of mass. Of all forms of society or government, this was the one he liked least. . . . A capitalistic system had been adopted, and if it were to run at all, it must be run by capital and by capitalistic methods. . . . " The alternative was to try to run it by an alliance of farmers and city laborers. This, Adams suggested, had been tried in 1800 by Jefferson and in 1828 by Jackson and had ended in disaster in both instances. The "mechanical consolidation of force, which ruthlessly stamped out the life of the class into which Adams was born . . . on the other hand created monopolies capable of controlling the new energies that America adored." That was, at least to Adams, the heart of the matter. Only capitalism could create and control the complex network of mechanical energy that was necessary to provide the inexhaustible cornucopia of products, or objects, that Americans lusted for, that was to them as rain on a parched cornfield was to the farmer.

William Dean Howells wrote a poem for *Harper's Magazine* entitled "Society":

> I looked and saw a splendid pageantry
> Of beautiful women and lordly men,
> Taking their pleasure in a flowery plain,
> Where poppies and the red anemone,
> And many other leaf of camoisy,
> Flickered about their feet . . .
>
> I looked again and saw that flowery space
> Stirring, as if alive, beneath the tread
> That rests now upon an old man's head,
> And now upon a baby's gasping face,
> Or mother's bosom, or the rounded grace
> Of a girl's throat; and what had seemed the red
> Of flowers was blood, in gouts and gushes shed
> And now and then from out that dreadful floor
> An arm or brow was lifted from the rest,
> As if to strike in madness, or implore
> For mercy . . .

30

The Election of 1896

In the summer of 1895 Henry Adams wrote to his brother Brooks, who was pursuing his search for the meaning of history in India: "Cleveland and Olney have relapsed into their normal hog-like attitudes of indifference, and Congress is disorganized, stupid and child-like as ever. Once more we are under the whip of the bankers." Adams could not decide if the United States was "on the edge of a new and last great centralization, or of a first great movement of disintegration." There were arguments to be made on both sides.

The principal obstacle to any action by the government to alleviate the nation's suffering was the conviction that the government could constitutionally do nothing other than tinker with tariff schedules and the ratio of gold to silver or, for the goldbugs, establish a gold standard.

When William Hope Harvey, the author of *Coin's Financial School*, a book of popular financial advice with a strong soft money bias, urged Senator Vilas of Wisconsin to propose legislation for the Federal assumption of farmers' debts, with a repayment period of twenty to thirty years at an interest rate of 3 or 4 percent, Vilas replied with the query as to what article of the Constitution would permit such action. Harvey's answer was notable: the same article that gave Congress the right to "lend hundreds of millions to the Union Pacific Railroad; to give away nearly $2,000,000 in pensions . . . or to establish protective tariffs for special industries; or to appropriate money for the Louisiana and Alaska purchases; or to pay bounties to sugar growers. . . . In short when you ask for a Constitutional right to extend the credit of the government to the distressed land owners of the United States . . . I am inclined to reply, 'Oh, cease your fooling.' " For fear of doing too much, the Cleveland administration did nothing.

There was, of course, one area where it was clear the President could act with a wide degree of latitude: foreign affairs. He was now, doubtless to his relief, afforded an opportunity to give evidence of his famous courage, so often exercised in the face of public sentiment. Great Britain and Venezuela had been bickering over the boundary line between British Guiana and the latter country for years. A British proposal in 1840 to establish the so-called Schomburgk Line was rejected by Venezuela. When gold was discovered in the area in the mid-1880s, Great Britain reneged on its earlier offer, and Venezuela thereupon broke off diplomatic relations and asked the United States to arbitrate the issue. The United States responded affirmatively, but the British government in 1887, at the end of Cleveland's first term as President, refused the offer. The refusal rankled in the President's substantial bosom, and in his second tour of duty, with Great Britain hinting at action to punish Venezuela for its intransigence, Cleveland once again proposed arbitration. The British government once more refused.

Richard Olney, who as attorney general had been so enterprising in breaking the Pullman strike, now as secretary of state produced a refurbished version of the Monroe Doctrine that in effect dared the British to take armed action against Venezuela. In one of the roughest notes in the history of U.S. relations with Great Britain, Olney declared: "The United States is practically sovereign on this continent and its fiat is law upon the subjects to which it confines its interposition. . . . Why? It is not because of the pure friendship or good-will felt for it. It is not simply by reason of its high character as a civilized state, nor because wisdom and equity are the invariable characteristics of the dealings of the United States. It is because in addition to all other grounds its infinite resources combined with its isolated position render it master of the situation and practically invulnerable against any and all other powers."

Olney's dispatch took its place with the Ostend Manifesto as a monument to American self-righteousness. It demonstrated, beyond any reasonable doubt, that the United States could be as insufferably arrogant as the British themselves. The Eastern Anglophiles howled as though *their* tails had been twisted. Cleveland was delighted. He called the impolitic message "Olney's twenty-inch gun," designed to blow the British out of the water, and he fired a volley of his own. In a special message to Congress on December 17, he declared: "It will, in my opinion, be the duty of the United States to resist by every means in its power as a willful aggression upon its rights and interests the appropriation by Great Britain of any lands . . . which after investigation we have determined of right belongs to Venezuela." In Congress "the President's vigorous expressions were cheered to the echo," a reporter noted. It also brought an enthusiastic response from Theodore Roosevelt, who wrote to his friend Senator Henry Cabot Lodge: "I am very much pleased with the President's, or rather, with Olney's message. . . . I do hope there will not be any backdown among our people. Let the fight come if it must; I don't care whether our seacoast cities are bombarded or not; we would take Canada." The most charitable thing that can be said about this strange effusion (and a number like it) is that on the subject of war, Roosevelt was more than a little dotty.

That, certainly, was the view of the editor of the *Nation*, E. L. Godkin, who wrote: "The situation seems to me this: An immense democracy, mostly ignorant and completely secluded from foreign influences and without any knowledge of other states of society, with great contempt for history and experience, finds itself in possession of enormous power and is eager to use it in brutal fashion against any one . . . who comes along . . . and is therefore constantly on the brink of some frightful catastrophe. . . ."

It may be assumed that the *Journal of Commerce* echoed the feelings of the business community when it observed: "What is the occasion for all this militant insanity we do not know. Some of it is probably due to the fact that a generation has elapsed since we have had a war, and its unspeakable horrors are largely forgotten. Undoubtedly the reconstruction of the navy has done much in this direction. . . . There is no necessary connection between a reasonable naval policy and jingoism, but unquestionably naval officers are impatient to use their new fighting machines. . . ."

William Graham Sumner was caustic about the "Monroe fetish." He wrote: "We should do our best to declare our emancipation from all doctrines, to do our own thinking on all our own questions, and to act according to our own reason and conscience, not according to anybody's traditional formula." Those who were constantly "shouting 'Monroe' at us," Sumner added, "all drop the Monroe doctrine" when it no longer served their purposes. John Hay wrote to his brother-in-law: "It is incumbent on all sane men to be very careful how far they commit themselves to the support of one in so disturbed state of mind as the President at this moment. The man who could write so headlong a message, and follow it a few days later with that panicky cry for help from Congress . . . is a most unsafe guide to follow."

On the other hand, Congressman Thomas Paschal of Texas was delighted with Olney's twenty-inch gun. "You are right, now go ahead," he wrote enthusiastically, "turn this Venezuela question up or down . . . and it is a 'winner' . . . morally, legally, politically, or financially: Your attitude at *this* juncture is the trump card. It is, however, when you come to diagnose the country's internal ills that the possibilities of 'blood and iron' loom up immediately. Why, Mr. Secretary, just think of how angry the anarchistic, socialistic and populistic boil appears on our political surface, and who knows how deep its roots extend or ramify. One cannon shot across the bow of a British boat in defense of this principle will knock more pus out of it than would suffice to inoculate and corrupt our people for the next two centuries."

That such was not Cleveland's intention was demonstrated by his stubborn resistance to another clamor—the call, especially in his own party, for war with Spain over Cuba that came in the last year of his administration. If his intention in the Venezuela affair had been to pander to public sentiment, a similar belligerence over Cuba would doubtless have ensured him of his party's nomination in the upcoming presidential election and, in all probability, another term as president. The fact was that Olney's twenty-inch gun, regrettable as its tone may have been, did bring the British to their senses. Arbitration of the boundary paved the way for a new era of harmony between the two countries.

The Cuba situation, meanwhile, deteriorated. As though the government and people of the United States, in the midst of a devastating depression (which was, to be sure, worldwide), did not have enough to do to put their own house in order, they undertook to straighten out the world and take up the "white man's burden," heretofore borne by European imperialism. The nation's impotence at home, where the threat of revolution evoked the response of repression, may well have contributed to the impulse to act decisively in those areas where its power could be directly and uninhibitedly expressed.

Provoking wars abroad to distract the people at home from the grievousness of their own situation was not a new notion. Nor, indeed, is there any indication that it was the policy of Cleveland's administration or that which followed it. The matter was rather the reverse. It was the citizenry that cried out for action, and its demand was undoubtedly based, in large part, on genuine moral indignation.

Reinforcing moral indignation were less worthy inclinations, among them a growing spirit of what for want of a better word was called imperialism. Imperialism in turn had three major components. Undoubtedly the most prominent was what we might call Christian imperialism, the ancient conviction—as old as John Winthrop's "A Modell of Christian Charity"—that it was the mission of the United States as a redeemed and redeemer nation to carry the message of universal peace and brotherhood to every corner of the globe. The stronghold of Christian imperialism was the Midwest. It was congenial to the Populist temper. Josiah Strong's immensely popular book *The New Era* made the classic case for Christian imperialism. Strong described Anglo-Saxon Americans as "this race of unequalled energy, with all the majesty of numbers and the might of wealth behind it—the representative . . . of the largest liberty, the purest Christianity, the highest civilization—having developed peculiarly aggressive traits calculated to impress its institutions upon mankind. . . ." When this race had spread itself over the earth, "can any one doubt that the result of this competition of races will be the survival of the fittest. Is it not reasonable to believe that this race is destined to dispossess many weaker ones, assimilate others and mould the remainder, until in a very true and important sense, it has Anglo-Saxonized mankind?"

Christian imperialism was supported by corporate imperialism, which intended to integrate the rest of the world in the American economic system. Cuba, Hawaii, the Philippines, Puerto Rico should, like Colorado and Wyoming, become colonies of Wall Street.

Henry Cabot Lodge, one of the most scholarly of our legislators, former student of Henry Adams, and amateur historian, was the spokesman for corporate imperialism. To those Americans of the British "Manchester School" of free trade and anti-imperialism, Lodge declared defiantly: "We have a record of conquest, colonization and expansion unequalled by any people in the Nineteenth Century. We are not to be curbed by the doctrines of the Manchester school, which . . . as an importation are even more absurdly out of place [here] than in their native land. . . . From the Rio Grande to the Arctic Ocean there should be but one flag and one country. . . . For the sake of our commercial supremacy in the Pacific we should control the Hawaiian Islands and maintain our influence in Samoa." When a canal is built across the isthmus, "the island of Cuba, still sparsely settled and of almost unbounded fertility, will become to us a necessity," Lodge concluded.

There was, in addition, the vague general feeling that imperial possessions were one of the requirements for being a "Great Nation." Vast stretches of land, incalculable natural riches, a "vigorous and industrious people," technical know-how, and, above all, "progress" might not be enough. The influential *Review of Reviews*, generally "liberal" in its leanings, announced that although "Conquest is not desired by any group or party in the United States, . . . the annexation of Hawaii, the undivided control of the Nicaragua Canal, the acquisition of a strong naval station in the West Indies, and the emphatic assertion of certain principles regarding European interference in the affairs of Central and South America would form a moderate and reasonable American policy."

Finally, there was the fashionable new doctrine presented by Admiral Alfred Thayer Mahan in his highly influential book *The Influence of Sea Power upon History, 1660–1783*. Mahan argued that on a largely aqueous planet, a powerful "two-ocean" navy was essential to protect a nation's commercial interests and, as we say today, national security. The new coal-fired battleships required frequent refueling. It followed, therefore, as the night the day, that a "great power" must dominate the seas or at least be able to contest them, and to do this, it must have fueling stations scattered about the world so that its battleships could range freely and cruise where the nation's interests dictated.

How all these matters related to Cuba is our immediate concern. The infatuation of Americans with Cuba and its neighboring islands went back to the years before the Civil War. It was then the South—Southern Congressmen and Southern filibusters—that seemed determined to add that large and potentially rich island to its slaveholding empire. Narciso López, a Spanish general, had led a movement for independence from Spain. Expansion-minded James Polk in 1848 had put out feelers to see if the Spanish might be prevailed upon to sell the island for $100,000,000. The reply had been discouraging. Spain "sooner than see the island transferred to *any power* . . . would prefer seeing it sunk in the ocean." Fleeing Cuba, López found refuge in the United States and here recruited hundreds of American invaders. The invasion turned out to be a fiasco. López was captured and garroted, and George Templeton Strong wrote that the so-called liberation movement was no more than "a lust after another people's productive coffee-estates, a thirst for personal property, specie, jewelry, and the like, owned by somebody else, the desire of being on the winning side in a grand period of confiscation, and larceny on a large scale." Polk's successor twice removed, Franklin Pierce, had continued to express an interest in acquiring Cuba, and *his* successor, James Buchanan, was one of the authors of the infamous Ostand Manifesto, produced in 1854, which spoke sympathetically of the Cubans "now suffering under the worst of all possible governments, that of an absolute despotism." If Spain, "dead to the voice of her own interest, and actuated by stubborn pride and a false sense of honor," refused to sell Cuba, the United States in its concern for justice to the Cuban people as well as for "self-preservation" would be justified, "by every law, human and divine, in wresting it from Spain . . . upon the very same principle that would justify an individual in tearing down the burning house of a neighbor if there are no other means of preventing the flames from destroying his own home." It was a striking, if addlebrained, analogy. Pierce's plans came to naught; but Cuba continued to burn, and the Spanish colony continued to be one of the United States' most lucrative markets. By the late 1880s the clamor for intervention in Cuba on behalf of the Cuba Libre, or Free Cuba, movement had become a national political issue.

The real nature of the Cuban struggle for independence was often difficult to unravel, and it was made more so by the biased and inflammatory reports of newspaper correspondents, especially those from Hearst's *Journal* and Joseph Pulitzer's *World*, engaged in a no-holds-barred battle for circulation in New York City. Those who opposed American involvement were quick to express their fears that the real motive behind the cries for intervention was the primarily larcenous desire, as Strong had put it, for other people's property: greed masquerading as benevolence. That argument scanted the disposition of Americans to align themselves, sometimes too impetuously, with those who were fighting for "freedom." The capitalists were, in fact, apprehensive about the whole notion of war with Spain, which, it was feared, would alarm the stock market and further depress the economy. Cleveland, for his part, was determined to avoid war with Spain by any honorable means. The *New York Sun*, which had long coveted Cuba, editorialized: "The good-will of the Cleveland adminstration is reserved for monarchists; it has no fellow feeling for republican revolutionists." But a new Republican-dominated Congress could, the *Sun* assured its readers, be counted on to come to the aid of the Cubans, "and if the President shall try to thwart them he will be roughly disciplined."

The American response to the Venezuela incident clearly indicated a growing militancy. In the next session of Congress bills galore were introduced by Senators and Congressmen vying with each other in patriotic zeal. Senator William Eaton Chandler of New Hampshire brought in a bill calling for $100,000,000 to strengthen the armed forces. Senator Watson Squire of Washington demonstrated the patriotism of the West Coast by presenting a bill to spend $87,000,000 for coastal defenses, while Senator Lodge proposed spending $100,000,000 for the same purpose.

Lodge reminded his fellow Senators that "our immediate pecuniary interests in the island are very great. They are being destroyed. Free Cuba would mean a great market for the United States; it would mean an opportunity for American capital invited there by special exemptions; it would mean an opportunity for the development of that splendid island. . . . "

At this point public opinion was further inflamed by the appearance in Cuba of General Valeriano Weyler y Nicolau, dispatched by the Spanish ministry to complete the subjugation of the rebels. The tactic Weyler settled upon was well calculated to intensify sympathy for the insurgents. He undertook to "reconcentrate" a considerable portion of the population of the island in closely guarded camps. The conditions in these camps, bad to begin with, soon became worse. They appeared to many observers to be little more than a means of exterminating Cubans. If much that was reported in American newspapers was inaccurate or simply false, fashioned out of rumors and whole cloth, much was true. In the disillusionment that followed the wildly emotional intrusion of the United States into Cuba in 1898, there was a disposition to blame the shooting war with Spain on the newspaper war between the *Journal* and the *World*, but the fact was that, lurid and grossly inflated as the newspaper accounts were, Cubans in large numbers were fighting and suffering in a war against colonialism of a peculiarly cruel and bloody kind. The fact that Butcher Weyler, as he was soon called, did not commit most of the atrocities credited to him, should not obscure the fact that reconcentration was a brutal and inhuman policy. If Spain had done nothing more, it would have fully merited the hostility directed against it.

Before Olney's term of office expired with the end of Cleveland's administration, he made a positive contribution to the Cuba crisis that, if fate had decreed a different course of events, might well have resolved the issue short of war. He challenged Spain to give some indication that its sole concern was not simply with repression of the insurgents and a "return to the old order of things" but that it was capable of instituting reforms which would meet the most obvious inequities—"an authentic declaration of the organic changes that are mediated in the administration of the island with a view to remove all just grounds of complaint."

Olney's advice was coincident with a change in the Spanish government and the accession to power of a more liberal faction, which immediately recalled Weyler and dispatched a new governor with instructions to pursue a less draconian policy.

Stimulating to the public passions as they were, Venezuela and Cuba were at root only diversions. As the presidential election of 1896 approached, talk of revolution was still very much in the air. To many Americans—Henry and Brooks Adams among them—the Republican sweep of the 1894 congressional elections marked a final defeat in the decade-long struggle to subordinate capitalism to democracy through the electoral processes. The Marxian socialists who argued that there could be no negotiated peace in the war between capital and labor were correspondingly strengthened.

The Midwestern Democrats had suppressed their misgivings and supported Cleveland in 1892 despite the accumulation of evidence that his heart belonged to the Eastern capitalists. As the date for the 1896 Democratic nominating convention approached, party leaders in the Western states began their search for a candidate true to the silver cause. A name frequently mentioned was that of young William Jennings Bryan. Bryan had served two terms in Congress and drawn favorable attention by his eloquence, his piety and rectitude, his engaging manners, and his consistent advocacy of silver. He had hoped to ascend to the Senate in 1894. He had been the clear choice of the Democratic party leaders in Nebraska; but the state reverted to Republicanism, and Bryan, finding himself out of office, took over the editorship of the *Omaha World-Herald* and used the paper to broaden his political base and disseminate his form of old-fashioned political revivalism, compounded of Christian egalitarianism, free coinage of silver, and hostility to Eastern bankers. He also traveled from state to state as a Chautauqua lecturer, meeting Democratic leaders and making political alliances. Few people who met the young Democrat with his open, friendly manner and mellifluous voice failed to be impressed.

Bryan had been born in 1860 in Salem, Illinois, the son of Silas Lilliard Bryan, of Irish ancestry, and Mariah Elizabeth Jennings Bryan. Silas Bryan was a lawyer, a state senator, and a circuit court judge. William was one of nine children, four of whom died before they reached maturity. When William Allen White spoke patronizingly of Bryan's "fine Fourth Reader views of the relations of life," the "Reader" he was referring to was, of course, that of William Holmes McGuffey, the greatest producer of schoolbooks in our history. The *Readers*, as we have earlier noted, presented a simple doctrine of Christian service and uplift.

Bryan went to Illinois College, founded in 1829 by one of the famous "Yale band" of missionary educators who came West to bring cultivation to the frontier. Julian Monson Sturtevant was still president when Bryan attended, and Greek and Latin were still the heart of the curriculum. It may indeed be suspected that the education available to Bryan and his classmates was at least the equivalent of that dispensed to the scions of upper-class families at Harvard and Yale.

In any event Bryan blossomed there and became somewhat of a luminary as a collegiate debater. A group photograph taken in 1880 shows him at an intercollegiate debate contest with eight other male debaters and one woman—Jane Addams, thin and intent-looking. The same age as Bryan, she was a student at the Rockford Female Seminary. After a relatively brief career as a lawyer, Bryan, now a resident of Lincoln, Nebraska, was elected to Congress in 1890 at the age of thirty.

Traversing the Midwestern states of Iowa, Illinois, and Kansas in the months preceding the 1896 Democratic Convention, Bryan hit upon a phrase that never failed to evoke a warm response in his audiences, a sentence which referred to "the cross of gold and the crown of thorns." He filed it away "for a suitable occasion."

On the Republican side, Marcus Alonzo Hanna had made his large fortune as a wholesale grocer and coal mine operator. He believed devoutly that the welfare of the Republic rested on protection. Frederic Howe's devotion to reform made him a merciless critic of Mark Hanna, who, he wrote, enriched himself "without compunction, believing that the State [of Ohio] was a business man's State. It existed for property. It had no other function. . . . Great wealth was to be gained through monopoly, through using the State for private ends: it was axiomatic therefore that business men should run the government and run it for their personal profit. Men who questioned this idea were disturbers, Socialists, anarchists, or worse." To men like Hanna all life was subsumed under the heading of "business." Howe wrote: "They had no other enthusiasms. They talked business, loved business, judged all men and all measures in business terms. The political state existed for their benefit. Lawyers, ministers, teachers were employees, vassals. Farmers and working men were a servile class. . . . He made war," Howe wrote of Hanna, "not to bend men but to break them. He treated the State in the same way. It must be broken to his will."

A variety of techniques were used by Mark Hanna and his lieutenants in and out of the legislature to prevent bills they opposed from passing. Open bribery was exceptional; the distribution or withholding of favors and offices was the safer and more common method. Some of the more intractable "were compromised by prostitutes brought on from Cleveland and Cincinnati for that purpose. Indiscreet seekers after pleasure were made obedient by fear of exposure and blackmail. . . . Ohio, in short, was not ruled by the people. It was ruled by business . . . by bankers, steam-railroads, public-utility corporations. . . .

"Ohio, like Pennsylvania," Howe wrote, "was corrupt and contented. . . . It hated any challenge, political, moral, or religious, to the system." Hanna was "a colossus astride of the country." He decided on important legislation and made presidents.

Hanna decided to groom for the presidency a man of impeccable protectionist sentiments. The man he chose was a modest hero left over from the Civil War, Major William McKinley. McKinley, born in Ohio, had enlisted in the Union army at the age of eighteen and been promoted to major for gallantry under fire. After the war he had practiced law in Canton, Ohio, and served fourteen years in Congress. It was he, indeed, who had been in large part responsible for Harrison's undoing by drafting and shepherding through Congress the tariff bill of 1890. McKinley was a good-natured man, ruled by simple notions; if not a party hack, he was certainly a party war-horse.

The first step in McKinley's elevation was his election to the governorship of Ohio, a feat managed by Hanna and his allies in 1892.

When McKinley was faced with a default on a $100,000 note that he had endorsed for a friend, Hanna set out to raise the money to free his candidate from the onus of bankruptcy proceedings. (Among the contributors to Hanna's fund was John Hay.) Hanna then orchestrated what may have been, at least up to that time, the most skillfully managed promotional campaign for a presidential candidate: He flooded newspapers and journals all over the country with stories of McKinley's virtues—his achievements were relatively modest—his heroism, as hardly more than a boy, under Confederate fire, and his irredeemably bland utterances on every issue. McKinley had the gift, invaluable to a politician of narrow vision and limited understanding, of emitting sonorous platitudes as though they were recently discovered truths.

Republicans met in St. Louis on June 15 and dutifully nominated the candidate manufactured by Mark Hanna. William Roscoe Thayer, John Hay's biographer, called McKinley's nomination "the most grotesque episode in American politics." The Republican platform contained a plank calling for a gold standard, high protective tariffs, and U.S. "control" of Hawaii. The Silver Republicans thereupon bolted.

The Socialist Labor Party gathered in New York City on the Fourth of July and nominated Charles Matchett for president.

When the Democrats assembled in Chicago in the middle of July, the leading candidates for the Democratic nomination were Richard Parks Bland—a long time Missouri Democrat, coauthor of the famous Bland-Allison Act of 1878, and champion of free silver—and Horace Boies, who had switched from the Republicans. Boies did not "drink whiskey, nor use tobacco," wore an old-fashioned Prince Albert coat, and a "Mona Lisa smile on his affidavit face," and had a golden tongue.

Bryan coveted the office of chairman of the Resolutions Committee or chairman of the convention. His ambitions were evident, but his support was limited to the Nebraska delegation and the delegation from the Oklahoma Territory.

Bland's managers, aware of Bryan's oratorical powers, did their best to prevent him from addressing the convention. However, through a series of happy coincidences (and some skillful maneuverings) Bryan found himself in the position of "cleanup hitter" in a debate before the delegates on the silver issue. As he began to speak, his powerful and compelling voice reached the farthest corners of the hall. The air was electric with anticipation. At each carefully timed sentence, Bryan recalled later, "the audience seemed to rise and sit down as one man. At the close of a sentence it would rise and shout, and when I began upon another sentence, the room was still as a church. There was inspiration in the faces of the delegates. . . . The audience acted like a trained choir—in fact, I thought of a choir as I noted how instantaneously and in unison they responded. . . ." "Church" and "choir" were highly appropriate words for the essentially religious zeal awakened in Democratic breasts as the thrilling words, with their promise of freedom and redemption, rang out like exultant bells.

Finally, with the delegates already in an ecstatic state, Bryan gave the great pretested words: "Having behind us the producing masses of this nation and the world, supported by the commercial interests, the laboring interests, and toilers everywhere, we will answer their demand for a gold standard by saying to them: 'You shall not press down upon the brow of labor this crown of thorns, you shall not crucify mankind upon a cross of gold.' "

Pandemonium! Ray Stannard Baker decided "then and there that [Bryan] was the greatest popular orator I had ever heard." After the speech Baker tracked Bryan to his hotel room, "literally crowded to the doors with excited followers . . . bronzed farmers and ranchmen of the Middle West rubbing elbows with red-faced city politicians . . . standing on every chair in the rooms, even on the sofas and desks." Called on to speak, Bryan balanced precariously on a huge "bridal" bed of black walnut. "What a picture he made there in that smoke-befogged room with the crowd all around him yelling and stamping like Comanche Indians," Baker wrote. ". . . I thought I had never seen a handsomer man; young, tall, powerfully built, clear-eyed, with a mane of black hair which he occasionally thrust back with his hand." Among "old friends, stanch supporters out of the West, loyal men he loved," Bryan talked with "an intimacy of feeling, a fire of devoted emotion, an imparted sense of complete dedication to a sacred cause. . . ." It seemed to Baker that he had, in surpassing degree, the ability to speak directly to the hearts of his listeners.

No speech in our history, it must be said parenthetically, had such an unmistakable impact on the nation's future or at the very least on the future of a major political party. Bryan and his followers did not rout the goldbugs, but Bryan, by his speech, nailed his party, it must be said, to a cross of silver which the party had to bear through three successive presidential elections—1896, 1900, 1904—long after the issue even vaguely corresponded to any practical economic or political reality. "An assembly, or a party, which allows itself to be the victim of such a metaphor," William Roscoe Thayer wrote, referring to Bryan's Cross of Gold speech, "is as much to be pitied as the children whom the Pied Piper conjured, without return, into the mountain."

Bryan, Frederic Howe observed shrewdly, was "pre-eminently an evangelist." He told Howe that if he were younger, he would abandon politics and "dedicate his life to foreign missions; the nations that knew not Christ were lost. . . . He thought as the Middle West thought. More than any one I have known," Howe wrote, "he represented the moralist in politics. He wanted to change men. He was a missionary; America was a missionary. . . . He was the *vox ex cathedra* of the Western self-righteous missionary mind."

To a group of Silver Republicans nursing their wounds after their party's endorsement of gold and contemplating a bolt to the Democratic Party, word came over the ticker tape of Bryan's nomination. It killed all hope. One of the group cried out: "Marat, Marat, Marat, has won," referring to the murderous demagogue of the French Revolution. Defection was no longer to be considered. "Socialist" was the least of the epithets directed against Bryan; "nihilist" and "anarchist" were commonly used. Young William Allen White, editor of the *Emporia* (Kansas) *Gazette*, besieged by Populists, wrote the most famous editorial of the age: "What's the Matter with Kansas?" A delighted Mark Hanna had millions of copies broadcast throughout the nation as a McKinley campaign document.

The principal planks in the Democratic platform called for "the free and unlimited coinage of silver at the ratio of 16 to 1 for gold" and condemned protective tariffs, monopolies, and the use of injunctions in labor disputes. One plank took the Supreme Court to task for declaring the income tax unconstitutional.

The nomination of Bryan presented the Populists with an insoluble dilemma. Bryan was now so clearly and irredeemably the candidate of the people—of the common man, the farmer, and, less clearly, the industrial worker (who did not respond, it must be noted, with such rapture to the free silver issue)—that it would be folly to run a Populist candidate who might drain away enough votes to elect the Republican candidate. Ignatius Donnelly described their dilemma. "Shall we or shall we not endorse Bryan for president?" he wrote a friend; " . . . I like Bryan but I do not feel we can safely adopt the Dem. Candidates. I fear it will be the end of our party."

A fellow Populist, writing to Donnelly, also expressed opposition to such a move. "Let the old Rotten Democrat machine with its camp followers, gold bugs, place hunters, straddle bugs, humbugs, demagogues, etc., etc., go to the devil."

When the Populists met at St. Louis, the delegates were deeply divided. The Illinois delegates were determined to extricate the party from the control of the "silver Populists." They wished to weld together the champions of government ownership, the Bellamy nationalists, the radical trade unionists, and the Fabian socialists, but the convention was firmly in the hands of the silverites, who were determined to endorse Bryan. Henry Demarest Lloyd's effort to get a government ownership plank included in the platform was squelched. Lloyd told Richard Ely that the convention had been "the most discouraging experience in my life." The radicals, frustrated by the compromise with the advocates of free and unlimited coinage of silver, "would go into one or the other of the socialist parties," and the "Populist movement would become increasingly conservative and anti-labor," Lloyd predicted. He blamed the defeat of the radical, prolabor Populists on the "silver-mining millionaires," who had used the silver issue as "the Cowbird of American politics . . . to take possession of the social reformers' nests . . . in order that he may use these reformatory movements to enrich himself at the expense of his dupes and victims." Lloyd told a friend that he would vote for Bryan as "the Knight of the Disinherited, like Ivanhoe, but he will not be the next President and I am content."

The Lloyd wing of the party tried to salvage something by nominating Tom Watson for vice-president (the Democrats had chosen one of those rare birds, an Eastern silver man, Garret A. Hobart).

The Democratic goldbugs seceded from their party and held a "National" Democratic convention at Indianapolis, where they declared against free silver and protective tariffs and nominated Senator John McAuley Palmer, former governor of Illinois, an able man who deserved a better fate.

The Prohibitionists nominated Joshua Levering of Maryland (there was never a dearth of able Prohibitionists candidates, despite the fact that, or perhaps because, it was a lost cause). Even the Prohibitionists split on the gold/silver issue. When the delegates nominated a gold Prohibitionist, the "silver Prohibitionists" nominated their own candidate, Charles Bentley of Nebraska.

The stage was thus set for what may well have been the wildest presidential campaign of all. The business interests, the goldbugs, the protectionists, the Eastern establishment, and Wall Street seemed continually on the verge of hysteria. Money poured into McKinley's campaign coffers until Hanna had accumulated ten times the war chest available to Bryan. Fourteen hundred Republican speakers fanned out across the country, warning of death and destruction if Bryan was elected. The triple specters of communism, socialism, and anarchism were evoked. Voters were bullied and threatened. Workers were told they would lose their jobs if the Democrats won.

It was a war of the East against the West: the farmers against the railroad tycoons and bankers; the workers against the industrialists; gold against silver; plutocracy against democracy. John Jay Chapman called "Bryanism . . . nothing but a revolt on the part of the poorer classes against the exploitation of the country by the capitalist. . . . 'Something must now be done for me,' says the laboring man, and the mine owner says 'Silver.' The appeal is by a little manipulation worked up into a craze, with the result that property is made unsafe."

A kind of doomsday mentality spread about the country. No one was certain, Henry Adams wrote Hay, whether the outcome would be "revolution or rout." Henry and Brooks resumed their continuing debate on the question: "Resolved: history (and the United States) is rushing to a violent conclusion."

Walter Hines Page was thoroughly pessimistic. He noted in the *Atlantic Monthly* that if Bryan were elected, "the paralysis of industry would be something frightful. . . . During the four months between Mr. Bryan's election and his inauguration the panic would produce such disastrous effects that the whole country would suffer a violent revulsion of opinion."

It was clear where Theodore Roosevelt's sympathies lay. He wrote a friend: "I am a good American, with a profound belief in my countrymen, and I have no idea that they will deliberately lower themselves to a level beneath that of a South American republic by voting for the preposterous farrago of sinister nonsense which the Populistic-Democratic politicians at Chicago chose to set up as embodying the principles of their party, and for the amiable and windy demagogue who stands upon that platform."

William Allen White, interviewing Bryan for *McClure's* magazine, found him "too definitely conscious that he was an extraordinary personality," who "knew too well that he had many graces. In short, he was dramatizing himself with a skillful art as William Jennings Bryan," a "shirtsleeved, folksy, hail fellow, a bit of a back-slapper and hand-shaker, cordial, even lovable. . . ." Mrs. Bryan, on the other hand, was all business. In White's view, she was "a born Phi Beta Kappa, a student, an introvert who surveyed . . . everyone around her husband with a fishy eye of distrust."

McKinley's "campaign" consisted of sitting on the porch of his modest home in Canton, Ohio, and receiving delegations of Republican politicians. The Grand Army Band met incoming trains at the railroad station and conducted the visiting dignitaries to McKinley's house to be greeted by the candidate. A speedy messenger, Joe Smith, was also at the station. He ascertained the salient facts about the newest delegation and bicycled back to McKinley's home-headquarters so that the information could be integrated into the candidate's speech of welcome. Depending on the home territory of the dignitary or delegation, the band might play "Marching Through Georgia" (for Union veterans) or "Dixie" (for visitors from the South) or "Onward, Christian Soldiers" (for the pious).

In August, John Hay was confident that McKinley, the "major," must win with ease. Bryan was, to be sure, making a stir, but Hay assured a friend that "he will drop into congenial oblivion next November."

"The Boy Orator makes only one speech—but he makes it twice a day," John Hay wrote to Henry Adams. "There is no fun in it. He simply reiterates the unquestioned truths that every man who has a clean shirt is a thief and ought to be hanged; that there is no goodness or wisdom except among the illiterate and criminal classes; that gold is vile; that silver is lovely and holy. . . . He has succeeded in scaring the Goldbugs out of their five wits. . . ." And later, after he had talked to McKinley in Canton and been "more struck than ever with his mask . . . a genuine ecclesiastical face of the fifteenth century," he wrote to Adams: "The Majah has a cinch—and don't you forget it."

John Hay proved an accurate forecaster. When the votes were polled, McKinley was clearly the winner—7,035,638 and 271 electoral votes to 6,467,946 and 176 for Bryan. The Prohibition candidate polled that party's persistently loyal 140,000 or so, while the "gold Democrat," John Palmer, tallied 131,529, and Charles H. Matchett, the Socialist, 36,454. The Republicans held both houses, which they had won in 1894.

The *New York Tribune* editorialized: "There are some movements so base, some causes so depraved, that neither victory can justify them nor defeat entitle them to commiseration. . . . The wicked, rattlepated boy, posing in vapid vanity and mouthing resounding rottenness, was not the real leader of that league of hell. He was only a puppet in the blood-imbued hands of Altgeld, the anarchist, and Debs, the revolutionist, and other desperadoes of that stripe. But he was a willing puppet, Bryan was—willing and eager. None of his masters was more apt than he at lies and forgeries and blasphemies and all the nameless iniquities of that campaign against the Ten Commandments."

Henry and Brooks Adams took the result as confirmation of Brooks's law of decay. "I am extremely well satisfied with the way it works out," Henry Adams wrote, "and look forward to much amusement in seeing your formulas tested in serious history. . . . I am pleased by McKinley's triumph, as he was the true logical outcome, and presents exactly the unintelligence of the situation. . . . Altogether, nothing could have gone truer to our stellar theories." Disaster was accelerating, as the brothers had concluded it must.

The election of 1897 swept the New York reformers out of office—Roosevelt had already retreated to the job of assistant secretary of the navy—and the Tammany candidate for district attorney, Asa Gardner, set the tone of the campaign by shouting, "To hell with reform," to the enthusiastic cheers of his listeners.

As for the retiring incumbent President—Cleveland—a Princeton professor of jurisprudence and political economy wrote a fitting epitaph. "Men have said," Woodrow Wilson observed, "that he was stubborn because he did not change and self-opinionated because he did not falter. He has made no overtures to fortune, has obtained and holds a great place in our affairs by a sort of inevitable mastery, by a law which no politician has ever quite understood or at all relished, by virtue of a preference which the people themselves have expressed without analyzing."

31

Religion

I t is a major premise of this work that religion is not simply a topic
among topics but the driving force of American history, that without
close attention to Protestant Christianity it is impossible to make sense
of our past. Beginning with that Ur document of our past, John Winthrop's "A Modell of Christian Charity," English America has been in
large part defined by the doctrines and dogmas of Protestantism. What
I have chosen to call the Protestant Passion, the insatiable desire to
redeem mankind from sin and error, starting with Americans but by
no means ending there, has been manifest in a variety of forms, both
in institutions—that is to say, denominational churches and dissenting
sects—and in individuals. The distinction is important. While the great
majority of professing Christians belonged to particular sects or denominations—such as Methodists, Baptists, Presbyterians, Congregationalists, and Episcopalians—many were stoutly and sometimes stridently
opposed to the churches. This was perhaps most strikingly the case
with the abolitionists. The battle fought by the abolitionists against
slavery was fought unequivocally in the name of Christian brotherhood. Granted that the antislavery warriors ranged from such marginal
Christians as Unitarians and transcendentalists to Baptists and hard-
line Presbyterians, I have discovered no prominent abolitionist, black

554

or white, who was an avowed freethinker, atheist, or agnostic. Most abolitionists indicted churches for their failure to give their whole-hearted support to the case.

The point to be stressed is that the motivation behind all the great reform movements of the first half of the nineteenth century was the Protestant Passion, which might or might not be made evident through the organized churches. The denominational churches sustained the foreign and domestic mission movement and were deeply involved in most facets of urban reform, particularly, though not exclusively, in the founding of hospitals for the poor and in the distribution of charity. Generally speaking, however, their weight fell on the side of political and social conservatism. The theological emphasis was on personal piety, good works, and individual salvation. The tendency was to ratify the existing order and support, without qualification, the sanctity of private property. The churches represented what Henry James, Sr., referred to as "the God of the orthodox. . . . Against this lurid power—half-pedagogue, half-policeman, but wholly imbecile in both aspects—I . . . raise my gleeful fist, I lift my scornful foot," he wrote. George Herron, also a Christian Socialist, took the same line. While the churches were guilty of "the wicked folly of fancying that the building of many and great churches, the lengthening of church rolls" were "the getting of Christianity into the world, the multitudes," Herron charged, "are as sheep without social shepherds, devoured by ravenous political and industrial wolves." The churches stood for "respectability and property, but not for Christ's law of sacrifice and association; they stand for benevolence," he wrote, "not for the justice of the kingdom of God." Some congregations actually owned tenements and thus "participated directly in one of the great evils of the day. . . . If there were nothing for the church beyond Protestantism, as we see it now, then the church would be a decadent institution, and Christianity would have to find another universal organ. The horrid blasphemy, the religious anarchy, the social selfishness, the theological wickedness, of this divided Protestantism, affronts every sense of sacrifice and order which man has received from God," he thundered.

In the period covered by this volume, Protestant Christianity in all its forms, orthodox or aberrant, underwent its severest trial. The war between science and religion was as fierce and unrelenting in its own way, though not of course so bloody, as the war between capital and labor. Those were the great "wars" of the age, and not surprisingly they intersected at a number of points. There had been skeptics and heretics aplenty in earlier periods of our history, but there had been no organized and sustained attack on the basic assumptions of Protestantism. Lester Ward's National Liberal Reform League, with its secret membership rolls and appeal to all "positivists," "materialists," socialists, and assorted "freethinkers" to rally to the attack on religious obscurantism and superstition in the name of reason and reform, was a straw that showed the way the wind was blowing. To pious Christians it seemed as though "freethinkers" were springing up everywhere, like dragon's teeth. No small town was without its "village atheists"; no city, without its associations of freethinkers, as they preferred to call themselves. Free thought magazines sprouted by the score, and Colonel Robert Ingersoll made himself one of the most famous men of the day by challenging God to strike him down on innumerable lecture platforms. For those, like Henry and Brooks Adams, too sophisticated to swallow Darwinism whole, there was the terrible prospect of living without a faith, bereft of that form of consolation.

The psychic cost was high. Henry Adams confessed "his aching consciousness of a religious void" and wondered whether "any large fraction of society cared for a future life, or even for the present one. . . . Not an act, or an expression, or an image, showed depth of faith or hope." He wrote: "Of all the conditions of his youth which afterwards puzzled the grown-up man, this disappearance of religion puzzled him most. The boy went to church twice every Sunday; he was taught to read the Bible, and he learned religious poetry by heart; he believed in a mild deism; he prayed; he went through all the forms; but neither to him nor to his brothers or sisters was religion real." He never entered a church to worship in his adult life. "That the most powerful emotion of man, next to the sexual, should disappear," Adams added, "might be a personal defect of his own; but that the most intelligent society, led by the most intelligent clergy, in the most moral conditions that he ever knew, should have solved all the problems of the universe so thoroughly as to have quite ceased making itself anxious about past or future . . . seemed to him the most curious phenomenon he had to account for in a long life."

One is tempted here to make a big city–small town distinction. Liberal and radical Christianity was primarily urban. In the towns a decayed Calvinism soured the air and chilled the soul. The testimony of those who experienced it was virtually unanimous. Edward Bellamy recalled that as a child he had been "taught to believe that he was a grievous sinner, accursed from God with whom he must make peace or suffer the most terrible consequences."

At the heart of the problem of loss of faith was the fact that the Protestant Passion, the "Thou shalt" which was the armor of the faithful in taming a wild continent, had shrunk to the negative injunction "Thou shalt not": not enjoy, not celebrate, not delight in God's creation.

"All through my childhood, how I disliked Sunday," Charles Francis Adams, Jr., wrote. "I remember now the silence, the somber idleness, the sanctified atmosphere of restraint . . . Lord! that going to Church! . . . I passed so many weary, penitential hours in those winter months in 'the forties.' . . . Those New England Sabbaths actually embittered my youth. It required the drastic war education to emancipate me from them."

Oswald Garrison Villard recalled his neighbors the Cochrans, who closed every blind in their house on Sunday. "Usually they sat indoors; if they ventured out on the porch . . . they seemed to speak in muffled tones. Twice each Sunday they went to church, swathed in deepest black . . . to return to the gloomy house for endless prayers. . . ."

Religion in Meadville was, to young Frederic Howe, much the same: "a matter of attending church, of listening to long and tedious sermons, of irritable, empty Sunday afternoons, church sociables, and Wednesday-evening prayer meetings." His Sunday school, also attended by Ida Tarbell, was little better. Howe had "been brought up on a kind of hair-shirt morality, the assumptions of which were that one ought to be doing what one liked least; that suffering is good for character and that distasteful work is an excellent and profitable thing." Although he did his best to cast off the religion that he had inherited, he came to believe, as he grew older, that "this particular brand of evangelistic morality became bone of my bone, flesh of my flesh. It was a morality of duty, of careful respectability. It was the code of a small-town. . . . I had no rights to my own life; danger lurked in doing what I wanted. . . . One's desires were to be suspected; they were in some way related to lustful things, and lust in thought was as bad as lust in deed." One could be sharp in business or corrupt in politics, "but one could not forget that life was a serious business, that duty was always before one's eyes, that one should be diligent in things distasteful. . . ." Above all, one must avoid "even the appearance of careless morals, drinking or association with men of questionable opinions. . . . The important thing was to live as other men lived, to do as other men did, avoid any departure from what other men thought. Not to conform was dangerous to one's reputation."

The narrator of E. W. Howe's *The Story of a Country Town* notes: "My father's religion would have been unsatisfactory without a hell. It was a part of his hope in the future that worldly men who scoffed at his piety should be punished, and this was as much a part of his expectation as that those who were faithful to the end would be rewarded. Everybody saved, to my father's thinking, was as bad as nobody saved, and in his well-patronized Bible not a passage for pleasurable contemplation which intimated universal salvation was marked, if such exists. . . . Religion was a matter of thrift and self-interest as much as laying away money in youth and strength for old age and helplessness. . . ."

William James, in a somewhat apologetic introduction to his father's writings after the latter's death, described the intellectual climate of the times: "This is anything but a theological age, as we all know; and so far as it permits itself to be theological at all, it is growing more and more to distrust all systems that aim at abstract metaphysics in dogma. . . . The conventional and traditional acquiescence we find in the older dogmatic formularies are confined to those who are intellectually hardly vitalized enough either to apprehend or discuss a novel and rival creed." Most persons with serious intellectual pretensions were, in James's words, "full of bias against theism in any form, or if we are theistic at all, it is in such a tentative and supplicating sort of way that the sight of a robust and dogmatizing theologian sends a shiver through our bones."

James, himself unable to believe, wrestled with man's apparent "will to believe" and the "varieties of religious experience" that, however diverse, displayed an unshakable conviction in a transcendent or "spiritual" dimension to life. Every area and every aspect of American life were affected by this "war." Economists, historians, educators, reformers, even politicians (not to mention the clergy) joined one side or another—there were certainly many sides and numerous alliances and internecine wars. Philosophy was almost totally absorbed by the issue. Some philosophers, like John Fiske and Josiah Royce, manned the barricades for their form of Christianity. Charles Sanders Peirce devoted his remarkable talents as a logician to creating a "space" within which religion could be "justified" and did it without ever making quite clear what he was about. William James, taking his cue from Peirce, devoted his lesser talents but far greater powers of persuasion and personal influence to defending the right to believe, if not the necessity for believing, though he himself could not believe in anything more orthodox than love.

James's friend Henry Adams considered himself a "Darwinist" because "it was easier to be one than not," despite the fact that he found the literal Darwinism of many of his contemporaries absurdly unscientific. "Unbroken Evolution under uniform conditions," Adams wrote, "pleased everyone—except curates and bishops; it was the very best substitute for religion; a safe, conservative, practical, thoroughly Common-Law deity . . . the idea was seductive in its perfection; it had the charm of art. . . . In geology as in theology," it could only be proved that "Evolution . . . did not evolve; Uniformity . . . was not uniform; and Selection did not select." To the orthodox Darwinians, though not to Darwin himself, "Natural Selection seemed a dogma to be put in place of the Athanasian Creed; it was a form of religious hope; a promise of ultimate perfection." In that respect it was not strikingly dissimilar to the eighteenth-century Enlightenment's faith in the perfectibility of man through reason. In the earlier case the perfection was to be achieved by the conscious use of human reason; in the latter it was to be achieved by an inevitable "process," as fixed and irresistible as any divinely ordained natural law. It was, indeed, an up-to-date version of natural law. Finally, Adams wrote, "He was a Darwinian for fun."

Stated in its simplest terms, the problem was how to reconstruct the ruins of the old theistic world; how to build a new scientific world that would meet the deepest needs of the human heart, or, conversely, how to defend the old theistic scheme against the new heresies. The life-and-death nature of that struggle dominated the mental world of Americans—no one of more than the most rudimentary intelligence would entirely escape it—in the decades following the Civil War. Everybody and every institution defined or, in some cases, redefined himself, herself, itself in relation to that issue. There were, for example, the new religions or sects generally grouped together as "New Thought" or "Science of the Mind": the old transcendentalists; the old and new spiritualists; the free lovers, freethinkers, free speakers, freeloaders; the Christian and non-Christian socialists; the anarchists, communal and individualist. It was, in effect, all "religion," the old religion of Protestant Christianity or the new religion of "Science"; the rehabilitation of the old consciousness or the creation of a new one. What would emerge, of course, would not be clearly and unmistakably one or the other.

As we have noted, Darwinism and "Science," with their notions of evolutionary development, contributed to a rising tide of what we might call scientific racism. But a major tenet of Protestant theology in the post-Civil War period was the doctrine of the Fatherhood of God. The abolitionists had fought slavery primarily on the basis of that doctrine. God was the Father of all peoples without regard to caste or color. Therefore, all men were brothers and must love one another and seek to bear each other's burdens. Washington Gladden gave classic expression to the doctrine. "If God is the Father of all men," he wrote, "all men are therefore brethren; and there can be but one law for home and school and shop and factory and market and court and legislative hall. One child of the common Father can not enslave another, nor exploit another; the strong and the fortunate and the wise can not take advantage of the weak and the crippled and the ignorant, and enrich themselves by spoiling their neighbors; each must care for the welfare of all, and all must minister to the good of each. This is the law of brotherhood, which is beginning to be seriously considered all over the world, as the only solution to the problems of society."

One of the most successful formulations of the response of the "new theology" to Darwinism was that of Newman Smyth, a graduate of Bowdoin College who had served in the Union army, then attended Andover Theological Seminary and studied theology at the University of Berlin. In *Old Faiths in New Light*, Smyth "began by accepting loyally the results of scientific research into the present constitution of things. We trust our senses, and the logic of the senses, just so far as human understanding can work out a positive science. We admit that the course of visible nature can best be summed up in some general law of evolution. We do not question, and have no moral interest in questioning, a physical evolution, and a mechanism coextensive with the bounds of nature. . . . Our objection to evolution is not that it may not be true, but that, if proved true, it is only a half-truth. We dare not put a part for the whole. . . . A philosophy worthy of the name must admit both sciences—the science of the natural and the science of the spiritual which transcends nature,—or its conclusions will be only half-truths. Physical evolution finds its complement only in a higher truth. The one thought of the Creator is expressed in two parts of speech, a noun and a verb. . . . Nature . . . is not a mere collection of specimens preserved for our dissection; and philosophy still has a higher task to fulfil than to keep the doors of a world-museum. There is an 'inner life of things,' and a unity of the spirit in the creation."

Lyman Abbott, Henry Ward Beecher's successor at the Plymouth Congregational Church, was also editor of the *Christian Union*. "Up to a recent date," he wrote in 1885, "industrial competition, even when producing suffering and death, was the best condition which existing circumstances would permit. It represented the normal tendency of commerce and society. It involved invention and discovery, and made the unnumbered improvements upon which modern life is based. Under its auspices the growth of civilization has gone on from the rudest state to its present development. . . . We cannot move a foot, stir a step, to purchase or sell, but we find the great genius of capital, the friend of man under our feet, by our side, at our back."

But at hand was a new era, when the positive elements of capitalist invention and imagination were overshadowed by the tendency of capital to accumulate in the hands of a few powerful and often unscrupulous men. "The application of new principles to industrial life" was needed, Abbott believed, "in order that competition may cease and diffusion begin. For, with all the good that competition has wrought, the principle is now a destructive one." Under Abbott's direction the *Christian Union* set forth the "new principles" of cooperation and more equitable income distribution that must characterize the new order. Abbott was active with Henry Codman Potter, the Episcopal bishop of New York, in founding, in 1887, the Church Association for the Advancement of the Interests of Labor; that organization's monthly journal, the *Hammer and the Pen*, had a decidedly radical tinge. Among other measures, the CAAIL proposed to churchgoers that they give their printing business only to printers who subscribed to fair labor practices. The CAAIL was also active in efforts to arbitrate strikes, appointing the New York Council on Mediation and Conciliation to settle the electrical workers' strike in 1895.

Washington Gladden was an early representative to what would come to be called the Social Gospel. He preached applied Christianity. "Society," he wrote in a book with that title, "results from a combination of egoism and altruism. Self-love and self-sacrifice are both essential; no society can exist if based on either of them to the exclusion of the other. Without the self-regarding virtues it would have no vigor; without the benevolent virtues it would not cohere. But the combination of capitalists and laborers in production is a form of society." To Gladden, "the attempt of the present system is to base this form of society wholly on competition, which is pure egoism. It will not stand securely on this basis. . . . To bring capitalists and laborers together in an association, and set them over against each other and announce to them the principle of competition as the guide of their conduct . . . is simply to declare war, a war in which the strongest will win." Gladden gave wholehearted support to the movement to form labor unions. To do otherwise was to leave the workers without power to defend themselves against their exploiters. "Combinations, whether of capital or labor," Gladden wrote, "are generally made these days for fighting purposes. And war is a great evil—no doubt of that. But it is not the greatest of evils. The permanent degradation of the men who do the world's work would be a greater evil . . . the present state of the industrial world is a state of war. And if war is the word, then the efficient combination and organization must not all be on the side of capital. . . . If war is the order of the day, we must grant to labor belligerent rights. The sooner this fact is recognized, the better for all concerned."

One of the touchiest aspects of Christian theology as it applied to the war between capital and labor was the nature of sin. It cut both ways. Were the poor, as the Darwinians suggested, simply those punished by personal weakness—by bad habits and natural improvidence—or were they, in Christian terms, more sinned against than sinning? Correspondingly were the capitalists who exploited their workers and the public in general "sinners" or simply able, ambitious (and often pious) men who were involved in a "sinful system"? In order to align Christianity on the side of radical social reform, it was necessary to attack the idea of sin as a strictly individual matter. As early as 1874 Horace Bushnell had pointed out "that evil, once beginning to exist, inevitably becomes organic, and constructs a kind of principate or kingdom opposite to God. . . . Pride organizes caste, and dominates in the sphere of fashion. Corrupt opinions, false judgments, bad manners, and a general body of conventionalism that represent the motherhood of sin, come into vogue and reign. And so, doubtless, everywhere and in all the worlds, sin had it in its nature to organize, mount into the ascendant above God and truth and reign in a kingdom opposite God." To Bushnell, the real task was not the defense of Christian orthodoxy against the assaults of skeptics and freethinkers but the extension of the teachings of Christianity ever wider into the world. "The world," he wrote, "is still too coarse, too deep in sense and the force-principle, to feel, in any but a very small degree, the moral power of God in the

Christian history. Slowly and sluggishly this higher sense is unfolding . . . and we may anticipate the day, when there will be a sense opened wide enough, for Christ, in his true power, to enter. . . ."

Walter Rauschenbusch, often (and clearly mistakenly) taken to be the Father of the Social Gospel, expressed the same view several decades later. "The permanent vices and crimes of adults," he wrote in 1907, "are not transmitted by heredity, [but] by being socialized. . . . Just as syphilitic corruption is forced on the helpless foetus in its mother's womb, so these hereditary social evils are forced on the individual embedded in the womb of society and drawing his ideas, moral standards, and spiritual truths from the general life of the social body." Thus it was the mission of the Christian churches to break into that closed world of socially organized "sin," validated though it might be by "public opinion."

The most original and most influential of the Christian Socialists was George Herron, who began his evangelical career, as we have noted, in the Panic and Depression of 1893. Born in 1862 in Montezuma, Indiana, Herron was an autodidact with little formal education, but he managed to become an ordained Congregational minister and was soon a leader among radical ministers. His piety and emotionalism derived from the frontier revival and from the radical millennial spirit of the "Valley of Democracy," the Mississippi Valley; his "socialism," from the age-old Christian yearning for the true community.

In 1890 his address to a Congregational club on "The Message of Jesus to Men of Wealth" brought him instant notoriety. After a year as pastor of a church in Burlington, Iowa, the young minister (he was not yet thirty) acquired a wealthy supporter, Mrs. E. D. Rand, who did all in her power to forward his career; she endowed a chair at Iowa (now Grinnell) College, the president of which, George Gates, shared Herron's radical Christian views and hoped to make the school the center of a nationwide rebirth of Christian zeal.

Herron's own experience of conversion, of being "born again," was a classic one. "I saw the selfishness, the pride, the absolute unholiness of my heart until I could bear the revelation no longer," he wrote. ". . . I groped in that horror of darkness . . . I knew that nowhere had I an inch of standing ground save in the mercy of God. . . ." His spiritual mentors he considered to be John Ruskin, Calvin, Savonarola, Leo Tolstoy, and the historian George Bancroft. To Herron, the essence of the Christian message was sacrifice—"the sacrifice of Christ upon the cross as the unquenchable call of all Christians to sacrifice."

He declared: "Religion is not something besides life, not a withdrawal of life from fellowships, but the pouring out of life as a sacrifice to God in the service of man." Above all, Herron's message was related to the rise and prospective triumph of populism. His magazine the *Kingdom* declared: "The new social movement springing out of the soil of the Western States is assuming a Socialistic aspect. . . . I look to see out of the Western States the greatest religious movement since the reformation. It will be a revival of faith closely akin to primitive Christianity."

Herron accepted the basic postulate of Protestant Christianity in America, that "God created and sent our nation to be an example and a witness of the power and wisdom of Christ unto the political salvation of the world. He appointed and anointed this nation," he wrote, "to seek and fulfill the righteousness of his kingdom." But America had failed. "We have betrayed our trust, and forsaken our mission. God is disappointed in this nation. We are a fallen nation, an apostate people. . . . We have used the liberty wherewith [our fathers'] sacrifice made us free to rob and oppress one another. . . . The hurt of this people cannot be lightly treated, or easily healed. The nation is sick at heart, and the body politic full of disease and corruption. Except our nation repent, turning from political sin to social righteousness, it cannot be saved, and will lose its divine place in the earth."

A series of Herron's lectures were published under the title *The Christian Society*. "In an age which mammon rules," he declared, "when property is protected at the expense of humanity, when the state regards material things as more sacred than human beings, the gospel of the kingdom of God . . . needs to be terribly preached as the judgment of love to the industrial despotism. . . ."

Political freedom was dependent on "industrial freedom." This, indeed, was the essence of socialism. "The life of man is objectively an economic life," Herron wrote. "In the sphere of production and distribution is the common life fulfilled. Production is communion with God; the producer is God's co-worker. . . . The people must finally own and distribute the products of their own labor. . . . The condition of competition is inconsistent with both Christianity and democracy. . . . Industrial freedom through economic association is the only Christian realization of democracy. . . ." The existing system was desperately hard and unfair. "No thrift or integrity, no faithfulness to work or uprightness of character, can guarantee men against loss of employment in the present system of competitive industrialism, issuing in social irresponsibility and absolutism of the strongest competitor." In addition, "our competitive order intellectually dwarfs and morally distorts the successful as well as the unsuccessful."

Herron, like Henry Demarest Lloyd and indeed like virtually all the leading reformers, had faith in the state as the instrument of the people's collective will. If democracy were made real, the state must become its servant. "The state," he told his listeners, "is the only organ through which the people can act as one man in the pursuit of righteousness . . . it must be the organized faith of the people; the manifestation of the highest right of which the people have knowledge in common; the organ of their common consciousness of God. . . . If there is purpose in history, the state must be the organ for the accomplishing of that purpose. . . . Except the state be born again, except it be delivered from pagan doctrines of law and government, from commercial and police conceptions of its functions, from merely individualistic theories of freedom, it cannot see the divine social kingdom, without which it cannot itself endure and increase." Moreover, the nation was "under the same obligation to sacrifice itself for the redemption of the world that Jesus was."

Nor was the path easy. Herron reminded his listeners that "every great reform has been won at unreckonable cost. A Calvary is the tribute Freedom always claims from men. Every commercial privilege which an American enjoys was purchased on Golgotha." Social justice was the paramount issue. To Herron history could be understood only as the progressive realization of the implications of Christ's sacrifice upon the cross. "The commercial and political supremacy of the Anglo-Saxon peoples," was, for example, "largely due to the faith of Calvin and Cromwell in the divine government of the world."

Herron's journalistic "voice" was the *Kingdom*, which at its height had a readership of 20,000. One by-product was the Christian Commonwealth Colony in Georgia. Motivated, in the words of one historian of the movement, by "a curious mixture of ideas drawn from Karl Marx, St. Francis and Jesus," the colonists undertook to "organize an educational and religious society whose purpose is to obey the teachings of Jesus Christ in all matters of life, and labor, and the use of property." All property was owned in common, and all persons were welcome. During the life of the Georgia Commonwealth, as it was called, Ralph Albertson, a member of the community, began to publish a journal called *The Social Gospel, a Magazine of Obedience to the Law of Love*. The magazine was an immediate success and helped muster financial support for the colony.

Sociology and economics were identified by Christian theorists as the two new academic disciplines most in need of being "Christianized." The dividing line between the more ardent Social Gospelers and the Christian Socialists was often a fine one. The economic and political crises of the late 1880s and early 90s pushed many Christians over that line. In 1889 William Dwight Porter Bliss, a Congregational minister whose father, Edwin Elisha Bliss, had been a famous missionary to the Turks and Armenians (it is interesting to note that many of the more radical Christian ministers were the children of missionaries), founded the Society of Christian Socialists and the Social Reform Union. The latter was a group of Christian Socialists who organized the College of Social Science to teach the Christian sociology that George Herron argued was the only "scientific" sociology. The mainstays of the faculty of the College of Social Science were two professors, Edward W. Bemis and Frank Parsons, recently fired from the Kansas State Agricultural College.

In 1899, when the *Kingdom*, compromised by Herron's increasing radicalism, expired, it was succeeded by a journal published in Chicago by the National Christian Citizenship League and entitled the *Social Forum*, committed to "stand for all *The Kingdom* stood for," more specifically that "the only true economic and political outcome of Christianity is socialism . . . an essential part of true religion." During its brief life the *Social Forum* absorbed the *Truth Teller*, published in Lincoln, Nebraska, and the *Conscience*, "another fine organ of applied Christianity," published in Berthold, North Dakota. Charles M. Sheldon's *Capitol*, published in Topeka, Kansas, was another self-proclaimed voice of Christian socialism.

The South was not without its own journals of Christian socialism. In the Bible Belt the Reverend James Converse of Morristown, Tennessee, published the *Christian Patriot*, advocating the "socialism of Jesus Christ," as well as the regional best sellers *The Bible and Land* and *Uncle Sam's Bible, or Bible Teachings About Politics*, both of which advocated public ownership of land, of railroads, and of the means of production.

Herron found an ally and disciple in J. Stitt Wilson, mayor of Berkeley, California, who, influenced by Herron's teachings, formed a group of Christian Socialists who called themselves the Social Crusade and preached the gospel of Christian socialism on street corners. Their journal, the *Social Crusader*, which referred to Herron as "the Isaiah of our times," found a ready readership, and the Crusaders boasted that they had held fifty meetings in a single month, supplemented by conferences in a number of Midwestern towns and cities that had succeeded "beyond our hopes." Herron continued preaching his brand of the evangelistic socialism and was one of the nominators of Eugene V. Debs for president on the Socialist ticket in 1900; but the audiences diminished, and it became increasingly clear that the movement had failed to create the tide of Christian socialism on which it had set its hopes.

Meanwhile, Herron, like so many radical Christians, was strongly drawn to the free love movement. Herron and Carrie Rand, the daughter of his benefactress, had been attracted to each other since Burlington days. Carrie had been appointed dean of women at Grinnell, and Herron began dividing his time between his legal wife and Carrie. Mrs. Herron, unwilling to embrace the doctrine of free love that had attracted her husband, won a divorce in 1901. The Grinnell Congregationalists deposed him from his ministry; the *Social Crusader* went out of business; Herron and Carrie Rand were "married" and departed for Italy with Carrie's mother. The trio returned to New York in 1906 to found the Rand School, but for all intents and purposes, Herron's spectacular career as a Christian Socialist evangelist was over by 1901. With him went the sustaining zeal of the crusade. The retreat of its "Isaiah" was a blow to the movement, but its decline was clearly related to larger issues, such as the resuscitation of the American economy and a growing spirit of conservatism throughout the country. A substantial portion of the American people came down to earth with a thud. Like drunks after a wild bender or drug takers in the aftermath of a hallucinogenic trip, they woke to find that their extravagant visions had vanished in the cold light of day. McKinley was reelected president in 1900; business was still in the saddle, more confident and arrogant than ever. For those millions who had anticipated a millennium of one kind or another—political, social, religious, or, in the case of the Christian Socialists, all three—there was a kind of collective hangover. In such a setting Herron's own personal disgrace seemed part of the ruin of popular democracy.

Besides the Darwinian assault on orthodoxy, traditional Christianity had to cope with "biblical scholarship," most of it emanating from Germany. The biblical scholars, approaching the Bible in the spirit of modern scientific investigators, cast serious doubt on the traditional attribution of various books of the Bible to particular authors, e.g., Moses did not write the Pentateuch, or Ezra write the Chronicles. Solomon did not write the Song of Songs, or Daniel the Book of Daniel. The Synoptic Gospels of the New Testament were examined in the same ruthless spirit, and their conventional authorship questioned as well. Was there, after all, a "historic" Jesus, a real person, whether human or divine? Were the Gospels written during the lifetime of Jesus by his disciples or later by writers who drew on traditions or on a common document since lost? Protestant ministers and theologians had to fight on two different fronts. One attack was directed specifically at the biblical account of Creation. The second, and in a sense more difficult to deal with, was the question of whether Jesus Christ was human or divine.

Charles Briggs, a Presbyterian minister and member of the faculty of the Union Theological Seminary, scandalized his church by attacking what he called Bibliolatry. "The Bible," he declared, "has no magical virtue in it, and there is no halo enclosing it. It will not stop a bullet. . . . It will not keep off evil spirits any better than a cross." What higher criticism had destroyed was not the Bible but "the fallacies and conceits of theologians. . . ." In the uproar that followed Brigg's talk, he was suspended from the Presbyterian ministry.

Still another response to the war between capital and labor and the assault on traditional values was a revival of the millennial vein so long evident in Protestant Christianity. The Millerites, disappointed in their expectation of the millennium in 1843, had formed the Adventist Church based on what might be called a continuing expectation of the millennium. Apocalypticism, with its emphasis on individual salvation by withdrawal from an ungodly (and increasingly unmanageable) world in anticipation of the Second Coming, had two variations. The premillennialists believed that Christ would come to initiate 1,000 years of peace and harmony on earth; the postmillennialists believed that He would come at the end of such a period for the final judgment and the end of the world. A strong element of postmillennialism has been evident in American Christianity from its earliest days, and it fitted well with the Social Gospel's call for the Kingdom of God on earth. The so-called Prophetic Conference, an interdenominational premillennial gathering at the Holy Trinity Episcopal Church in New York in 1878, indicated how far that movement had penetrated the conservative old-line denominations. Though both shared the same suffix, post-

and premillennialism were poles apart. The postmillennials were eager to reform the social order in the 1,000 years prior to Christ's return. The premillennials believed the time was too short for any such ambitious plans; they wished to put their own souls in order in the time that remained.

In somewhat the same spirit as the premillennialists was the group founded by Charles Taze Russell, a Congregationalist turned Adventist, who announced that Christ had already returned to earth—in 1874—invisibly. He would return visibly to judge the living and the dead. By an interpretation of Scripture only 144,000 souls from the beginning of time could hope to be carried to heaven; the rest could be no more than witnesses, hence the name Jehovah's Witnesses. It was the duty of the pious Christian simply to suffer as Christ had suffered for the sin and evil of the world. All political and social institutions, Russell taught, were corrupt, and no allegiance should be given by a Witness to any temporal power. No government, no laws could command more than the passive acquiescence of the faithful. Russell told his followers that "the best and the worst of earth's nations are but 'kingdoms of this world,' whose lease of power from God is now about expired, that they may give place to their ordained successor, the Kingdom of Messiah, the Fifth Universal Empire of earth . . . and it will do much to establish truth and to overthrow error."

As in previous severe depressions, old-fashioned evangelical revivalism carried from small towns and frontier communities to the cities flourished. The master of the urban revival appeared on the scene dramatically. Vast of bulk, with a remarkably melodious voice and striking charisma, Dwight Moody and his singing sidekick Ira Sankey became the most famous revivalists of the age. Born on a Massachusetts farm in 1837, Moody was such a success in business by the age of twenty-three that he decided that his mission in life was to spread the word of Christ. Beginning with a Methodist Mission Band and an active role in the Young Men's Christian Association, Moody discovered his real gift as a touring revivalist from 1873 to 1875 in Great Britain. There, with Sankey singing hymns while he preached, Moody developed the techniques of advance publicity and promotion that became standard practices in revivalism.

The support of local ministerial associations was always solicited by Moody in advance. The revivals were aggressively nondenominational, and the message was a simple one that millions of Americans seemed desperately eager to hear: God loved them. In sermons sprinkled with simple homilies and anecdotes Moody reiterated the theme. "To-day God calls you to come under His banner of love. Legions of angels will help you, and God Himself will protect and keep you." *But* "if you die in your sins, there is not in the Bible one ray of hope to show that there will be opportunity to repent hereafter. Now is the accepted time of salvation. . . . May you come to-night and be saved." The vexing problems of doctrine and responsibility of Christians for promoting social justice Moody left to other, more sophisticated evangels; he concentrated on saving souls. Moody did not stop with the revivalistic exhortation. He organized a platoon of aids who met troubled individuals in the "inquiry room" to counsel and advise. He prided himself on reviving "Biblical Christianity," family prayers, and expressive forms of worship—mass hymn singing and the escorting of the repentant to the glory seat. Cards were distributed to the converted for their names and religious preferences, and these were in turn passed on to local ministers to follow up. The problem was that many of those who had been swept up by the enthusiasm generated by Moody and Sankey found the established churches disappointingly cold and formal in their modes of worship.

If Moody's urban revivals were the most spectacular such events, the most common were the classic revivals in rural towns which continued to be a major element in small-town life. College-age youth was especially susceptible to the revival spirit. The winter revival meetings at Allegheny College in Meadville, Pennsylvania, took the form of long walks of freshmen and sophomores with seniors who "inquired about our souls," Frederic Howe recalled. "Night after night they herded us into the Stone church. There the revivalists prayed, worked on our fears, made us feel that we were eternally damned if we went without their particular brand of religion." Under such pressure Howe succumbed and "crept forward to be prayed for by strangers for sins of which I was ignorant and for a salvation that seemed at best dreary."

Revivalists, modernists, liberals, "new theologians," and old Bible thumpers, Social Gospelers and Pentecostals, millennialists of various brands, and the ever-present spiritualists could not satisfy the need of Americans, especially, it seemed, chronically insecure middle-class Americans, for some form of "spiritual" or quasi-religious experience. There thus appeared a new and potent phenomenon which was termed, loosely, New Thought. New Thought claimed to be "scientific." It placed its principal emphasis, as its name implied, on the *mind*. Critics described it as a modern form of the ancient Christian heresy of gnosticism, a denial or diminution of the material world in favor of the world of the spirit. The world existed most powerfully not in the physical body, not in concrete objects of the external world, but in the mind-spirit. Unhappiness, despair, failure in the practical world, even illness were all "in the mind" and could all be cured by one's thinking right thoughts. Perhaps more than any other form of "religious" consolation, New Thought suggested the vast ocean of doubt and confusion that threatened to engulf the lonely individual American ego, detached from class or community, even, to a degree, from race. Descended from transcendentalism and spiritualism most conspicuously, it flirted with, if it did not entirely embrace, many of the altruistic impulses of the day. It shared with free love persistent anxiety about sex and assured its adherents that one of the promises of the life hereafter was that there should be neither male or female. Indeed, the mind was asexual, the realm of basically sexless spiritual affinities. Racism, class animosities, the hates and prejudices that seemed to spring up so abundantly in American life—all these might be dispelled by proper thought.

William James discussed the "mind cure movement" in his *The Varieties of Religious Experience*. The "leaders of this faith," James wrote, "have an intuitive belief in the all-saving power of healthy-minded attitudes as such, in the conquering efficacy of courage, hope, and trust, and a correlative contempt for doubt, fear, worry, and all nervously precautionary states of mind. . . . Mind-cure might be briefly called a reaction against all [the] religion of chronic anxiety which marked the earlier part of our century in the evangelical circles of England and America."

James knew whereof he spoke. In the winter of 1887 he had paid "ten or eleven visits to a mind-cure doctress, a sterling creature, resembling the 'Venus of Medicine,' Mrs. Lydia E. Pinkham, made solid and veracious-looking," he wrote his sister. "I sit down beside her and presently drop asleep whilst she disentangles the snarls out of my mind. She says she never saw a mind with so many, so agitated, so restless, etc. She said my *eyes*, mentally speaking kept revolving like wheels in front of each other and in front of my face, and it was four or five sittings ere she could get them *fixed*." James wrote to E. L. Godkin: "Whatever one may think of the narrowness of the mind-curers . . . they are proving by the most brilliant new results that the therapeutic relation may be what we can at present describe only as a relation of one person to another person. . . ." To James the mind cure sects had demonstrated "that a form of regeneration by relaxing, by letting go . . . is within the reach of persons who have no conviction of sin and care nothing for . . . theology."

In such works as Henry Wood's *Ideal Suggestion Through Mental Photography* and R. W. Trine's *In Tune with the Infinite*, both works that sold by the tens of thousands, readers were assured that they could get in touch with "that Divine Energy we call God" and that when they tapped that "spirit of infinite life and power that is back of all" through the use of their minds, they would experience this "Divine inflow," and all worry, anxiety, and fear would cease. "To recognize our own divinity," Trine wrote, "and our intimate relation to the Universal, is to attach the belts of our machinery to the power-house of the Universe. One need remain in hell no longer than one chooses to; we can rise to any heaven we ourselves choose."

Mind cure placed much emphasis on meditation in tranquil and harmonious surroundings. The apostles of New Thought called this entering the silence. "The time will come," Trine wrote, "when in the busy office or on the noisy street you can enter into the silence by simply drawing the mantle of your own thoughts about you and realizing that there and everywhere the Spirit of Infinite Love, Wisdom, Peace, Power, and Plenty is guiding, keeping, protecting, leading you."

Far and away the most successful of the Science of Mind/mind cure/New Thought sects was that devised by Mary Baker Eddy. A moody, rebellious, neurotic girl, constantly at odds with her domineering father, who held to an old-line hellfire and damnation Calvinism, Mary was an able student who learned Greek, Latin, and Hebrew from her adored older brother Albert. She taught Sunday school while still a girl, and a childhood friend recalled: "She always wore fine clothes we admired. We liked her gloves and fine cambric handkerchief. She was, as I have come to understand, exquisite, and we loved her particularly for her daintiness, her high-bred manners, her way of smiling at us, and her sweet musical voice."

Her brother Albert Baker, nominated to Congress, died at the age of thirty-one, a devastating blow to Mary. Not long after her brother's death she was courted by George Washington Glover, a contractor from Charleston, South Carolina, some years her senior. They were married in 1843, and Mary moved to Charleston, where she began a campaign to persuade her husband to free his slaves. Before he could comply, he was stricken with yellow fever and died. Although his slaves constituted an important part of her husband's estate, Mary gave them their freedom.

The young widow then returned to her parents' home, gave birth to a boy named George, and lapsed into chronic invalidism. The child was sent to foster parents. As her health improved, Mary Baker Glover began to write articles, many of them on the subject of slavery, for the *New Hampshire Patriot*. After an unsuccessful effort to start a kindergarten, she became involved in spiritualism. Living with her married sister Abigail, Mrs. Glover had another nervous collapse. Finally, after nine years of widowhood, she married a big, blustering sometime dentist and promoter, named Dr. Daniel Patterson. In the words of her official biographer, "Mrs. Glover's invalidism interested him." In 1856 the Pattersons moved to Groton, New Hampshire, where he practiced dentistry fitfully and his wife, attended by a blind girl, followed the calling of a full-time invalid. The village gossips had it that there was nothing wrong with Mary Patterson; she simply used ill health as a means of controlling her roving husband. In any event Mary consoled herself by reading the Bible and pursuing her study of spiritualism. Finally, her husband, no doubt desperate, introduced her to an eccentric ex-clockmaker and "healer" named Phineas Quimby, "a nervous, shrewd little man with a piercing black eye and determined mouth." Mary Baker Glover Patterson fell under Quimby's spell. He cured her, and she became convinced that "there is cause and effect in the spiritual world as in the natural. . . . I know there is a science of health, a science of life, a divine science, a science of God." Cured herself, she discovered a gift for curing others.

Mrs. Patterson finally broke away from Quimby and moved, bag and baggage and somewhat reluctant husband, to Lynn, Massachusetts, even then a dreary industrial seacoast town north of Boston, famous as a shoe manufacturing center. In Lynn, Dr. Patterson became increasingly restive, running off, perhaps to the relief of his wife, who clearly had other things on her mind, with a young married woman. When he returned contritely, she gently turned him out. Sex, like health, was, after all, merely a state of mind, the result of improper or unhealthy thoughts.

"In the year 1866," Mary Baker wrote, "I discovered the Christ Science, or divine laws of Life, and named it Christian Science. God had been graciously fitting me, during many years, for the reception of a final revelation of the absolute divine principle of scientific being and healing." The truths revealed were "that all real being is in God, the divine Mind, and that Life, Truth, and Love are all-powerful and ever-present; that the opposite of Truth,—called error, sin, sickness, disease, death,—the false testimony of false material sense—of life in matter. . . . " By mind one could control matter.

"Mind-Science," Sibyl Wilbur, Mrs. Eddy's biographer and follower, wrote in 1910, "has begun to abolish the necessity of surgery, healing of itself the lame, the blind, the deaf; teaching mothers to bear children without pain, children to grow normally without malfunction, men and women to abandon evil habits which bring consumption, scrofula, leprosy; nations to abandon wars which slaughter and cripple. . . . " This revelation, according to Wilbur (and of course Mrs. Eddy), was the result of a serious fall which required that she heal herself.

Mary Baker subsequently divorced Patterson (after having forgiven him) and began to make her living as a healer, accepting patients but, more important, teaching others how to be healers at the Metaphysical College, where tuition was a stiff $300 for a course of instruction that lasted "twelve half-days." One of her students was Asa Gilbert Eddy, "a grave, sweet-tempered man, to whom children were devoted," a traveling salesman for a sewing machine concern. Eddy was ailing, and Mrs. Patterson cured him, persuaded him to enroll in the college, and quietly married him in 1877, apparently more to quell a jealous uprising among her disciples than from any overwhelming attraction to Eddy himself. "To him was the special duty given of guarding her against the onslaughts of the envious and ambitious who pressed too close with their human desires," thus presumably interfering with the untrammeled exercise of mind. When Eddy fell ill, his wife was presented with a dilemma. Since illness was in the mind, not the body, it would hardly do to treat his illness by conventional methods (he apparently had heart trouble). Mrs. Eddy concluded that he had been poisoned by "a secretion engendered by the working of hatred. . . . Not material poison but mesmeric poison." So it was mind after all. She nursed him patiently but to no avail, and he passed on to the world of pure mind in 1882.

A few years later Mrs. Eddy founded the Church of Christ, Scientist, and it grew astonishingly, proving that she had touched a responsive chord in many middle-class Americans who found the material world too much for them. Her followers, in words quoted by Sibyl Wilbur, believed her to be "patient, gentle, loving, compassionate, noble-hearted, unselfish, sinless—a profound thinker, an able writer, a divine personage, an inspired messenger." The words were Mark Twain's. He was clearly fascinated by Christian Science (he called it "the Standard Oil of religion"), but he was Mrs. Baker's deadly enemy. Twain wrote a curious book on Christian Science, "a religion which has no hell; a religion whose heaven is not put off to another time . . . but begins here and now, and melts into eternity." He insisted that Mrs. Eddy's doctrines were the stolen fruits of Phineas Quimby, who, of course, was just Twain's cup of tea.

Ironically, while the postmillennial doctrines encouraged social reform, the premillennial spirit was most evident in missionary activity; to bring light to the heathen *before* the millennium not only was the duty of the Christian but would hasten the millennial day. If the churches grew cold and formal (or remained so) and secular thought challenged the religious ethos—the Protestant Passion—that had been the dominant theme of earlier history, the foreign missions grew and flourished. Missionary men and women labored on in India, Africa, and the Near East, carrying the "good news" of God's redeeming love, and great new fields were opened for the Lord's work, notably in China and Japan. China's millions could absorb all the missionaries the Western world could muster. It was soon evident that the vast, disintegrating nation had an irresistible appeal to many Americans who felt the missionary call.

Japan, with its rigid feudal structure, was a special case. For ten years after Matthew Perry's visit in 1853, a fierce struggle took place between the shōgun, now little more than a figurehead, a puppet of the most powerful and reactionary daimyo, or lords, and the lesser lords who saw in the appearance of Westerners a chance to overthrow the shōgun. Into these troubled waters came a remarkable diplomat, Townsend Harris, a man who seemed to have an instinctive feeling for the intricacies of Japanese court intrigue. He waited patiently for months for the shōgun to receive him. Finally he began the journey to the capital at Edo, along roads freshly swept for his passage, while the residents of the villages through which he passed prostrated themselves on the ground. On December 7, 1859, Harris was received by the shōgun in a ceremony centuries old. Meanwhile, missionaries from various Western countries, most conspicuously from the United States, assembled at Yokohama, awaiting permission to venture forth into the interior of the country to preach the word of the risen Christ as the redeemer of the world. As they waited, year after year, while the desperate struggle for supremacy went on among the feudal lords and the issue of "Westernization" hung in the balance, they improved the time by acquainting themselves, in one degree or another, with the Japanese language and to a modest degree with Japanese culture. A handful of young Japanese students were permitted to study with missionary teachers in Yokohama. Perhaps the most notable early success was that of Captain L. L. Janes, a devout graduate of West Point, whose influence was so strong that in 1871 thirty-five of his students became converts to Christianity. Much the same thing happened in the newly founded agricultural school at Sapporo, headed by Dr. W. S. Clark. Once again a whole class of students requested Christian baptism. Dōshisha University in Kyoto, founded by a Japanese Christian, Shimeta Niishima, experienced a revival in 1886 so intense that regular classes were suspended and 200 students baptized. By 1888 there were more than 450 missionaries in Japan, the majority of them Americans, and 25,000 declared Christians. The result of almost ten years of internal struggle was the resignation of the shōgun and the crowning of young Emperor Meiji. It was 1889 before the Japanese received an official decree of religious freedom. In the constitution drafted that year Article 28 provided that "Japanese subjects, within the limits not prejudicial to peace and order, and not antagonistic to their duties as subjects, shall enjoy freedom of religious belief." The qualifications were, prospectively, formidable.

Americans came later to the missionary field than the British in China and remained more or less in their shadow until the end of the century, but by 1900 there were more than 1,500 Protestant missionaries in China, a third of them American men and women. There were 500 missionary stations in the various provinces and approximately a half million "adherents," 80,000 of whom were in regular communion. At this point—June 24, 1900—the dowager empress evoked the Righteous Harmonious Fists movement or the Boxer Rebellion, as it came to be known, urging *mieh yang* ("destroy the foreigner"). In the massacres that followed, many Chinese Christians were killed. Among the missionaries, 188 men, women, and children died. The uprising was severely suppressed, but its consequences were surprising. The missionary population and the Christian churches in China grew remarkably. By 1919 there were 5,462 Protestant missionaries in China and several million converts. The Chinese Revolution, led by Sun Yat-sen, a Christian educated by missionaries, broke out in 1911. When asked to what he attributed the success of the revolution, Sun replied: "To Christianity more than any other single cause. Along with its ideals of religious freedom, it brings a knowledge of western political freedom, and along with these it inculcates everywhere a doctrine of love and peace. These ideals appeal to the Chinese; they largely caused the Revolution, and they largely determined its peaceful character."

In the words of John Fairbank, an outstanding Sinologist and himself the son of missionary parents, "The very ideas of reform that they [Chinese who came into close contact with Christian missionaries] picked up . . . inspired them . . . to become Chinese nationalists, eager to save China by modernization, or even, as it then seemed, by Westernization. . . . At first the Christian teaching seemed to be the key to Western power." The price was high. Again in Fairbank's words, "Missionaries who took on the burden of changing China from within suffered at first a high mortality, and those who did not die or leave sometimes knew despair, fear, or even rage along with the hope and charity more customary in their calling." They were "foreign devils" to the native Chinese, and when they ventured out of their missionary compounds, small children often ran along beside them, shouting, "The foreign devils are coming!" Yet missionary service clearly had its rewards. Besides a vivid sense of serving the Lord, often under the most dangerous and arduous conditions, the missionaries lived in a world singularly of their own creating.

India remained the largest American missionary field, with China a close second. Significantly, by 1890 women predominated in every mission field, from India, where they outnumbered men nearly two to one, to Africa, where the margin was slight. In the Near East the ratio of women to men was more than two to one. In China there were 198 men to 314 women, and in Japan women outnumbered men, 283 to 146.

The hearts of young women at Vassar and Wellesley were heavy with yearning to carry the words of God's love to their sisters in every darkened corner of the world, to embrace them with assurances that God had sent His Son to spread the message that God the Father loved all, black and white and yellow, rich and poor, men and women, without discrimination, that all mankind and womankind were brothers and sisters. Indeed, if there was a discriminatory element in God's love, it was in that He loved best the poor, downtrodden, and oppressed.

Isabel Trowbridge Merrill, of the class of 1900, addressed herself to "The College Girls of America," assuring them that "the life of a missionary is the happiest, most joyous, most satisfying one I know. . . . A college girl's whole training is toward activity and what else can give her so much pleasure and satisfaction as to be in an environment that calls out all her powers, and gives her a chance to live a vital life that tells? Oh, girls, it pays so many times over. And if *we* do not take Christ to the women and girls in Turkey, *who will*?"

The missionaries sent out by the Woman's Union Missionary Society of New York employed twenty women in eight stations as well as eighty "Bible women," native women who could read the Bible to their sisters, and had opened twenty-five schools for girls. Fifty years after the founding of the women's board of missions it had contributed more than $10,000,000 to mission work. The editor of the *Missionary Review*, a journal for women missionaries, wrote: "That today oriental women are taking a great part in the revolutions of life and thought that are transforming Asia is due primarily to the faith and effort of unknown and unappreciated women missionaries. It was these women who gathered together little groups of untaught girls, and in spite of opposition of fathers and husbands, yes and even of missionary men themselves, taught them to read."

The situation of the missionaries was, to be sure, ambiguous in the extreme. They entered basically hostile soil. Their freedom to preach the Christian Gospel and indeed their physical safety were often insured by the guns and bayonets of United States soldiers or marines (in the case of China by British soldiers). They were everywhere bitterly opposed by native leaders, especially, of course, by the scholarly and priestly class in China and Japan, which did all it could to arouse the animosity of the people toward them and frustrate their efforts at conversion. Small wonder, since they were filled with socially subversive doctrines, such as the equality of all men and women, as well as the political principles of liberal democracy. As we have seen, they concentrated their efforts as much on the education and health of the peoples to whom they came as on their conversion. But while the numbers they converted were never large, they were uncommonly influential. Since upper- and middle-class individuals were most accessible to the missionaries, these made up the greater portion of their converts, and they in turn often became the intellectual and political leaders of their people. The missionaries were thus the conduits through which Western ideas in their most appealing form reached non-Western peoples. One very important by-product of the rapid expansion of missionary schools was the stimulus they provided for the establishment of public education by native governments alarmed at the growing influence of Western ideas.

The missionaries and their converts lived in communities of the faithful that were reminiscent of those of the early church, where race and nationality were triumphed over by brother- and sisterhood, lives often of singular grace and beauty.

But the converted native lucky or unlucky enough to travel to America was in for a severe shock. That was the experience of a Japanese Christian, Uchimura Kanzō, who came to the United States in 1884, expecting to find a "lofty, religious, Puritanic" America. So strong, he wrote, "was my confidence in what I had read and heard about the superiority of the Christian civilization over that of the Pagan" that "the image of America as pictured upon my mind was that of a *Holy Land*. . . . " Instead, he found "a land of mammon-worship and race-distinction!"

Transcendentalism had opened the door to an appreciation of other world religions, and liberal Protestantism passed through it with enthusiasm. Stimulated by the rapid growth of the missionary movement in Japan and China and development in Japan of comparative religion, initiated by the missionaries themselves, ministers of different denominations took the opportunity afforded by the World's Columbian Exposition in Chicago in 1893 to organize the Parliament of Religions.

Helena Blavatsky arrived in New York in 1873 and founded the Theosophical Society with Colonel H. S. Olcott and William Q. Judge. *Isis Unveiled*, Madame Blavatsky's statement of the society's principles, appeared four years later and she herself became a U.S. citizen in 1878. Blavatsky's aim was to establish a new syncretistic religion, made up of elements of Hinduism, Buddhism, and Christianity.

Hinduism as an element in New Thought attracted much attention. The star of the Parliament of Religions at the Chicago exposition of 1893 was a young Hindu swami, Vivekananda. Vivekananda called for a general recognition of the spirituality of the Eastern religions without efforts at conversion and thereby won numerous converts, especially among ladies from Boston.

William James was drawn to yoga. It seemed to him that "the Yoga discipline . . . in all its phases" might be "simply a methodical way of *waking up deeper levels of will-power than are habitually used*, and thereby increasing the individual's vital tone and energy." He had "no doubt whatever that most people live, whether physically, intellectually or morally, in a very restricted circle of their potential being. They *make use* of a very small portion of their possible consciousness, and of their soul's resources in general, much like a man who, out of his whole bodily organism, should get into a habit of using and moving only his little finger. . . . " James speculated that "the so-called 'normal man' of commerce . . . the healthy philistine, is a mere extract from the potentially realizable individual whom he represents, and that we all have reservoirs of life to draw upon, of which we do not dream." To a correspondent who exhorted him to try yoga, James replied that he was such "a dry and bony individual, repelling fusion, and avoiding voluntary exercise" as to be a poor subject, but he promised to try fasting and deep breathing.

The church of the "other America," the Roman Catholic Church, remained on the defensive. If non-Catholic Americans were bitterly divided on scores of issues—silver versus gold, towns versus cities, science versus religion, whites versus blacks (and reds and yellows)— they were as one in their fear and hatred of the Catholic Church and, generally speaking, of Catholics in the abstract, if not always in the particular. Pious Protestants still thought of the Pope as the Antichrist, the enemy of the faith, the Beast of the Apocalypse. To the atheists, agnostics, and freethinkers, the Catholic Church was the symbol of authoritarianism, perpetuating superstition and keeping the "masses" in ignorance. Benjamin Orange Flower, descendant of several generations of idealists and reformers, opponent of slavery, advocate of free love, friend of the freedman, editor of the radical journal *Arena*, hated Catholicism more than conventional marriage, indeed, as much as he hated capitalism.

In the census of 1880 the Methodists were listed as the largest denomination with 3,286,158 members, followed by the Baptists with 2,430,095 and the Presbyterians with 885,468. The Catholics claimed 6,832,954 of that faith, almost as many as the seven principal Protestant denominations combined. The church itself had three major ethnic divisions by the end of the century: Irish, German, and Italian. The church hierarchy, the ecclesiastical establishment, was firmly in Irish hands. The Irish were as adept at churchly politics as they were at the secular variety. The ward boss and the priest shared a wisdom born of shrewd endurance in the face of harassment that stopped short of open persecution primarily because they knew so well how to use the levers of power. American history, abundant in ironies, has few to equal the symbiotic relationship between big-city Catholic Irish bosses and Protestant capitalists. It was only common prudence reinforced by scriptural injunction that the Children of Light—the Irish—should be as cunning as the Children of Darkness—the Protestant heretics. It was often difficult to tell who was victim and who was victimizer.

The papacy, it must be said, did little to appease those essentially unappeasable Protestant anxieties of America. In 1870 the Vatican Council promulgated the doctrine of papal infallibility (a doctrine, it should be said, strongly opposed by American delegates to the council). It was the proverbial red flag to Americans, the text for thousands of sermons on the iniquity of Rome.

Twenty-one years later Pope Leo XIII issued an encyclical, *Rerum novarum*, perhaps best translated as "On Modern Ideas." While the tone of the encyclical was moderately liberal by Catholic standards, its indictment of radical politics offended the champions of reform and reinforced the image of the Catholic Church as an institution basically opposed to social reform and committed to the status quo. Particularly resented by many Americans was the encyclical's denunciation of socialism and its defense of private property. On the other hand, *Rerum novarum* defended the rights of labor and called for the solution of social and economic conflict by the extension of Christian love. The church—"We" of the encyclical—acknowledged the seriousness of the "Social Problem" but claimed jurisdiction over it: "Doubtless this most serious question demands the attention and efforts of others besides Ourselves—of the rulers of States, of employers of labor, of the wealthy, and of the working population themselves for whom We plead. But We affirm without hesitation that all the striving of men will be vain if they leave out the Church. . . . "

The dilemma of Catholic prelates of the church in America was that while the upper classes were the mainstays of the church in Europe, in the United States the church—at least the dominant Irish portion of it—was overwhelmingly working-class. The church in the United States could not, therefore, avoid being involved directly in the war between capital and labor. In that war the church had few soldiers in the capitalist camp. It was thus forced to press constantly for a more liberal policy in Rome if it was to maintain its hold on the faithful. The crucial figure in this prolonged contest between the inherent conservatism of the Holy See and the American church was a remarkable man, James Gibbons. Born in Baltimore in 1834, Gibbons, a small, mild-mannered man, soon attracted attention for his administrative and diplomatic talents. He had attended the Vatican Council of 1870 (and opposed the dogma of papal infallibility) and as archbishop of the Archdiocese of Baltimore, he involved himself in a wide range of civic reforms. Political to his fingertips, he proved the ideal person to act as intermediary between Pope Leo XIII and the American Catholic and Protestant communities. More than any other individual in the American Catholic hierarchy, Gibbons shaped the character and course of American Catholicism.

He succeeded, for example, in his firm but tactful campaign to prevent the placing of *Progress and Poverty* on the church's index of works forbidden to the faithful and persuaded the Pope to abandon his plan to condemn the Knights of Labor as a "secret society." In 1886 Gibbons was given the red cap of a cardinal, only the second American so honored, and his status as the nation's foremost Catholic was thereby confirmed.

Archbishop John Ireland of St. Paul was a liberal spirit who rivaled or exceeded Gibbons in his desire to democratize the American church. In 1889 he gave his support to a proposal for a gathering of Catholic laymen in conjunction with a convention of the clergy. Gibbons, uneasy "at the mixed character of the convention," went along. "Laymen," Ireland declared, in his opening sermon, "are not anointed in confirmation to the end that they may merely save their souls and pay their pew rent. . . . They must think, work, organize, read, speak, act, as circumstances demand," and avoid "too much dependence upon priests." This was dangerously Protestant talk, but Ireland was much impressed by the capacities of the 1,500 lay delegates. He was embarrassed, he declared, "that I was not conscious before of the power existing in the midst of the laity and that I have done nothing to bring it about. . . . Say to your fellow Catholics that there is a new departure among Catholics of the United States. Tell them henceforth you are going to do great things." But the Pope was not in favor of "new departures," and Gibbons found himself obliged to sprinkle cold water on Ireland's efforts to increase the role of the laity. When plans were being drawn up for the World's Columbian Exposition at Chicago in 1893, a number of prominent Catholic laymen called for a Catholic Columbian Congress in conjunction with the exposition. Gibbons, alarmed by the call for cooperation with Protestants "in general philanthropic and reformatory movements," called on Ireland to help him suppress the congress. It took place nonetheless, but fourteen months later Pope Leo XIII vetoed the notion of ecumenical action on social issues, declaring that "Catholics ought to prefer to associate with Catholics."

Nevertheless, American Catholics, with their disposition to take liberal stands on controversial issues, were a constant source of anxiety to the Pope. In the often wild ferment of social reform in the 1890s many American Catholics showed a marked disposition to gravitate to the liberal end of the political spectrum. In addition, certain influential priests undertook to try to heal the Catholic-Protestant schism by emphasizing those doctrines held in common by both "religions" and playing down the differences. This Leo felt he could not condone, and in January, 1899, he issued the encyclical *Testem benevolentiae*, which was understood to be a rebuke to the liberal tendencies in the American church or, more simply, to "Americanism." In addition to condemning all efforts to "modernize" Catholic doctrine in the spirit of reconciliation, the Pope warned against overemphasizing the power of the Holy Spirit to work in the individual, a decidedly Protestant notion. "The rule of life which is laid down for Catholics," the encyclical declared, "is not of such a nature as not to admit modifications, according to the diversity of time and place." These must emanate from the Holy See, not from the initiative of individual Catholics. "Hence," the encyclical concluded, "from all that We have hitherto said, it is clear, Beloved Son, that We cannot approve the opinions which some comprise under the head of Americanism. . . . For it raises the suspicion that there are some among you who conceive of and desire a church in America different from that which is in the rest of the world." That was clearly impossible, without undermining the authority of the church.

That the relationship between the Holy See and the Catholic Church in America should have been a tense and difficult one was no less than might have been expected. What was remarkable was that the Holy See retained its authority in the United States uncompromised to any serious degree and that the United States in turn exercised a liberalizing influence on the papacy to the conspicuous benefit of the church. The man to whom principal credit for this achievement must go was James Cardinal Gibbons, unquestionably the most influential ecclesiastical figure of nineteenth-century America. With instinctive tact, irresistible charm, and unswerving devotion to his far-flung flock, Gibbons, over the span of forty years, guided and shaped American Catholicism.

The hostility of non-Catholic Americans toward their Catholic compatriots remained a conspicuous feature of American life. Typical of the anti-Catholic books that abounded was *Romanism and the Republic* by a Methodist minister and educator named Leroy Vernon, who had delivered the book in the form of eighteen sermons in the Salem Square Congregational Church in Worcester, Massachusetts, to standing-room-only crowds.

The chapter headings suggest the sermons' contents: "The Pope the Enemy of Civil and Religious Liberty"; "Romanism Antagonistic to the Constitution and the Laws"; "The Purpose of Romanism to Destroy Our Public Schools" (three separate chapters); "Shall Romanism Teach a Pagan Morality to American Youth?" (also three chapters). The situation, Vernon warned his readers, was desperate: "Vanity parades, ambition climbs, business hastens to be rich. The press panders, the politicians trim, the preachers doze; the priests sow tares. The country drifts, drifts, drifts," unaware that the Jesuit assassins, under orders from Rome, are bent on its destruction. At the end of 435 pages of the church's iniquities, the author assured his readers that he had "only touched on the beginnings of its actual wickedness, and of the ruin which it works." If the Lord spared him for the work, he promised a sequel wherein his readers might see "in all its horrors, the beastly immorality of priests and people, of Popes, Cardinals and bishops, of men, women and children, as the result of this wicked, ungodly, unscriptural, and unchristian system of auricular confession."

In the year of the Chicago exposition anti-Catholic feeling manifested itself with startling ferocity. The familiar spirit of nativism, stimulated perhaps by the rising tide of predominantly Catholic immigration, cropped up in unexpected places. Anti-Catholic secret societies were formed; arms and ammunition, collected in anticipation of a Catholic war on Protestants. A patently forged document called "Instructions to Catholics," reputed to be issued by the Pope, received wide circulation, printed in presumably respectable newspapers and distributed in leaflet form. Among its more sensational "instructions" were such as these: "We view with alarm the rapid spread of educated intelligence, knowing well that wherever the people are intelligent the priest and prince cannot hope to live on the labor of the masses whose brains have been fertilized by our holy catechism. . . . We view with alarm the rapid diffusion of the English language. . . . In order to find employment for the many thousands of the faithful who are coming daily to swell the ranks of the Catholic army, which will in due time possess the land, we must secure control of all the cities, railways, manufactories, mines, steam and sailing vessels—above all, the press— in fact, every enterprise requiring labor, in order to furnish our new- comers employment; this will render it necessary to remove or crowd out the American heretics who are now employed. You need not hes- itate. It is your duty to do so. You must not stop at anything to accom- plish this end."

Washington Gladden was among the Protestant clergy who tried to expose the fraud and quiet the panic; but hundreds of clergymen and lay Christians rushed to get on the bandwagon, and thousands maintained a discreet silence. Knowing the "Instructions" to be false, they apparently felt that any stick that was handy might be employed to belabor Catholics.

The anti-Catholic societies used the forged "Instructions" as the basis for a campaign to remove Catholics from private employment and public office. The state of Ohio seemed particularly susceptible to the yahoos. Stories circulated that Catholics were importing armed soldiers hidden in coffins and crates, that they were drilling in the basements of churches. No rumor was too preposterous to find willing dupes. A Protestant minister declared from the pulpit that he was buying a rifle to defend his wife and children from armed Catholics. The forged "Instructions" were followed by a forged papal encyclical which declared that "on or about the feast of Ignatius Loyola, in the year of the Lord 1893, it will be the duty of the faithful to exterminate all the heretics found within the United States." "Such," wrote Wash- ington Gladden, "was the epidemic or unreason and bigotry which was raging in free and enlightened America, during 1893 and 1894."

In addition to the rising tide of immigration, the catastrophic depression which began in 1893 caused widespread anxiety about jobs. But these were just triggering events at best; beneath them lay gen- erations of bitter hostility toward the Roman Catholic Church and all its works and members. Crude and violent in the lower levels of Amer- ican society, it was far more discreet but no less strong among the educated and the well-to-do. Among scholars and intellectuals of an increasingly secular disposition, it was simply another manifestation of an animosity toward religion in general. Catholicism as a more "au- thoritarian" religion was perceived as a greater threat to "freedom" than the more disorderly legions of Protestantism. Finally, there was the fact that the corrupt political machines that controlled most big cities in an alliance with business interests drew their political strength and relative immunity from reform efforts from the predominantly Catholic working class, German and Irish and, more recently, Italian.

Since man is clearly a "believing" rather than a "rational" animal, most Americans adapted such elements of Darwinism as suited them. In many instances they accepted the major propositions of Darwinism *and* the major propositions of Christianity. To use the phrase of the British economic historian R. H. Tawney, these divergent ideas lived together in their minds in "vigorous incompatibility." Catholics, predominantly immigrants and hyphenated Americans—Irish-Americans, Italian-Americans, German-Americans—by and large ignored the whole question and went serenely on, secure and untroubled in their faith.

The more orthodox of "fundamental" Christians were forced to deny specifically the Darwinian system. While the old main-line Protestant denominations grew more liberal or "colder" over the years and accommodated themselves without great difficulty to the main elements of Darwinism (and geology)—that is to say, they argued that the account of Creation in the Book of Genesis had long been understood by enlightened Christians to be a myth or a parable of the beginnings of human life on earth and was not to be taken literally—the orthodox insisted on the "fundamentals" of Christianity.

In the diverse and often contradictory responses of Christian theorists and activists to the challenge of "Science," primarily the form of Darwinian evolution, it must be held clearly in mind that what Henry Adams called "this disappearance of religion," a phenomenon that puzzled him, was the common experience of American intellectuals in this era. Many, to be sure, embraced some form of spiritualism and/or mind cure/New Thought as a substitute, but the old orthodoxy crumbled, and out of its lumber a new consciousness was constructed.

32

Education

As we have had occasion to note from time to time, whatever Americans differed on they were as one in their faith in the efficacy of education; more than the efficacy—the redemptive power. Whatever was wrong with American life could, it was almost universally assumed, be remedied by education. It was a secular form of grace, a sacred institution, the alchemist's stone that might be depended on to change immigrants into 100 percent Americans (whatever *they* were); freed slaves into middle-class Americans with incidentally black skins; Indians ditto; racially prejudiced Southern (and Northern) whites into champions of black equality; drunkards into teetotalers, and so on, virtually *ad infinitum*. Education was akin to religious conversion, to being reborn from sin into salvation. There were, to be sure, sharp differences of opinion on what constituted an education and how the young should be taught. An argument as old as the Republic—Benjamin Rush and John Adams were the principal antagonists in its initial phase—was whether education should be "scientific and practical" or "liberal-classical."

As everything in this time period had the prefix "new," so, too, did education. The "old" education was generally perpetuated, and the "new" education tirelessly theorized about. Most experts agreed that "new" meant "scientific," but just what "scientific" meant was not so clear.

The first educational area to be made "scientific" was that of graduate studies, and it was, indeed, the rise of graduate studies that most clearly characterized the new education and the new consciousness. "Scholarship" and "research" joined "science" as talismanic words. In the struggle over the nature of education a kind of uneasy compromise was reached. Undergraduate education was allowed to remain essentially "liberal," while graduate education became "scientific."

Sidney George Fisher was, not surprisingly, a champion of the "old" education. Fisher deplored the more practical bent of the colleges. "The colleges of the country," he wrote, "are sinking in tone, lower & lower, in accordance with the opinion & manners of the people— I mean of what is considered even the best educated portion of the people. Practical ability, physical science, knowledge that may promote success in the great & absorbing ambition of all—making money—are now immensely prised & preferred to literature, philosophy, & art. Parents wish to see their sons successful men of business, not scholars & gentlemen, & to gratify this desire the colleges are reducing their standards of excellence & admitting the natural sciences to the foremost place among the studies prescribed."

It was also the age of the college preparatory school—the prep school or private secondary school modeled after the British public school. These came in two varieties: country day and boarding. Their unabashed purpose was to prepare their upper-class pupils for admission to Harvard, Princeton, Yale, Williams, or Amherst while teaching them a bit of Latin and Greek and shaping their characters. The emphasis was on personal piety and muscular Christianity. Mildly educated and discreetly snobbish, the graduates of Groton, Andover, Exeter, Deerfield, St. Andrews, and half a dozen other bastions of the Eastern upper crust constituted the nearest thing to an American aristocracy. Self-assured, their values securely "internalized," as the sociologist David Riesman has put it, they formed the cadres of the ruling class—the bankers, lawyers, politicians, and reformers who largely controlled the levers of power.

The private school that young Oswald Garrison Villard attended in New York was "conventionally barren," he recalled. Its master "had no other thought than to teach the customary classical course. We had no laboratory, no chemistry, the merest smattering of physics, and the usual inadequate instruction in modern languages."

John Jay Chapman described his preparatory school as "a mysterious and gloomy whirl of things, a vast, complex, factory-building of clocks, bells, and automata. The meals were dreadful and the friendly attentions of the masters mortifying; and besides, there was never enough to eat. . . . I cannot bear to pass a town high school in an automobile." Yet Chapman helped start St. Andrews, an Episcopal preparatory school in Rhode Island.

With the general emphasis on childhood and on producing a "finer race" through better breeding practices, it was doubtless inevitable that pedagogy should receive considerable attention. Lester Ward, as we have seen, hoped to guide and accelerate the evolutionary process through education. Many other reformers had similar expectations. John Dewey became the prophet of the new pedagogy.

The enrollment of pupils in public elementary schools increased from 8,869,000 in 1876 to 14,984,000 in 1900, but only 519,000 pupils attended high school. In 1876 only 20,000 high school students were graduated—11,000 women and 9,000 men. By 1900 the number had more than quadrupled—to 95,000—and the ratio of women graduates had increased substantially; almost two-thirds were women.

In 1880 it was estimated that 62 percent of all white school-age children attended school, as opposed to 34 percent of "Negro and other races." By 1900 the percentage for whites had *dropped* sharply to 53 percent, apparently because of the influx of immigrants, and for blacks and "others" to 31. While the percentage of students enrolled declined, the average daily attendance doubled, and the length of the school year increased from 133 days to 144. Male and female teachers had been fairly evenly balanced in 1876—110,000 men to 150,000 women—but by the end of this period the ratio was 127,000 men and 296,000 women. Public elementary and secondary school education had become overwhelmingly feminine.

The rate of illiteracy dropped sharply. In 1870 20 percent of the population was judged illiterate; by 1900 the number was down to 10.7 percent, only 2 percent of whom were native whites (down from 8.7 twenty years earlier); 13 percent of the foreign-born were classed as illiterate, as were 23 percent of all blacks.

In 1876 there were some 600 "colleges," many of them colleges only by courtesy and most of them highly ephemeral. The One-Study College of Mastersville, Ohio, offered one course of study at a time to its students—a half year of math, for example, followed by a similar period devoted exclusively to literature or geography. The transitory nature of many colleges is suggested by the fact that the census of 1890 listed a thousand "Institutions of Higher Education" in the country, a spectacular increase from 600 in 1876, but the next census in 1900 showed a decline to 977, many doubtless the victims of the depression of 1893. An especially significant figure was the proportion of male college faculty members to female in 1880—7,358 men and 4,194 women. Twenty years later—1900—the census listed 19,151 men as opposed to 4,717 women. The dramatic shift in the proportion of male to female "professors" and "instructors" in a twenty-year span measured the increasing "professionalization" of college teaching and a growing emphasis on advanced degrees as a prerequisite for teaching positions. This was a development highly unfavorable to women. By the constant extension of the period of graduate study and stress on scholarship as opposed to teaching, the entry of women into college teaching was discouraged. The modern organization of colleges and universities into departments, a reform brought from Germany decades earlier by George Ticknor, was also discouraging to women because it effectively placed the control of faculty appointments in the hands of the various departments rather than, as traditionally, in the hands of the president and trustees.

In 1870 there were only 52,000 degree candidates enrolled in 563 "institutions of higher learning" (IHLs). They represented 1.1 percent of the college-age youth of the nation. By 1900 the number had more than quadrupled—235,000—but it represented only 2.3 percent of the college-age population. In 1870 9,371 bachelor degrees were conferred; 8,000 to men and 1,371 to women. In 1900 roughly 22,000 degrees were awarded, 5,237 to women. While college enrollment had more than quadrupled, the number of students receiving bachelor degrees had slightly more than doubled. In 1900, 1,583 master's degrees, a figure fairly constant since 1885, were awarded. In 1876, 32 Doctors of Philosophy (Ph.D.s) were awarded (rising from 1 in 1870), and by 1900 the number had risen to 382, only 23 of which had been given to women, substantially less than 10 percent. The vast majority of women faculty members were to be found in women's colleges and state colleges and universities, where they were concentrated in the newly created departments of domestic science, physical education, and public health and where they were increasingly looked down on and patronized by their colleagues in the more conventional academic disciplines, such as literature and chemistry.

While the number of institutions of "lower learning"—public elementary and secondary schools specifically—increased substantially and the percentage of students attending schools declined throughout the period, the professionalized, scholarly segment of the IHLs grew by leaps and bounds or, more accurately, by a vast proliferation of scholarly books and programs of advanced study.

As important as how many students attended school was what those students learned. On the whole very little: to read and write and do some modest arithmetical calculations. Those fortunate enough to have the McGuffey *Readers* absorbed a good deal of estimable literature and many improving moral precepts, but most learning was by the dreariest rote. The evidence that the total experience of school was disheartening in the extreme is largely unchallenged by those who bothered to reflect upon their school days. From Richard Henry Dana to George Templeton Strong there is no dissent from the soul-deadening effects of such instruction. Certainly there must have been good schools scattered about, and there were certainly able and often inspiring teachers. The reforms that Horace Mann had instituted were widely adopted in the decades following his death in 1859, and the efforts to make teaching a profession were stimulated by the founding of teachers' colleges and normal schools. In rural one-teacher schools a good teacher might mean an excellent education, but such a teacher, as we know from the experience of Lester Ward, labored under severe constraints. When Ward tried to teach in a more stimulating and imaginative way than the dull routines prescribed by tradition, he was promptly fired by an indignant school board.

Especially in the larger towns and cities the improvements in facilities—in buildings, classrooms, and science laboratories—were notable. The shift from men to women teachers apparently brought with it a considerable improvement in the quality of teaching. In New York City, Jacob Riis devoted almost as much of his reforming zeal to securing playgrounds for schools as to rehabilitating tenements. Indeed, when all was said and done, the now taken-for-granted playground may well have been the most notable educational reform of the era.

On one level the public schools were an unambiguous success. For the Jewish immigrants from Eastern Europe, with a long tradition of respect for learning, the American public school with its universal access and informal democratic ways was a dream come true. One has only to recall the experience of Mary Antin, the young Polish-Russian Jew who emigrated to Boston in 1891.

The model and exemplar of the new research and learning was, as we have noted frequently, science. Harvard, with men like Louis Agassiz, Asa Gray, and Benjamin Peirce, had been a beacon light in the development of a scientific curriculum. At Yale Benjamin Silliman made important geological discoveries. James Dwight Dana, a cousin of Richard Henry Dana, was a student of Silliman who pioneered in the field of metallurgy and wrote the classic *Manual of Geology*, published in 1862. "Geology," Dana declared, "is not simply the science of rocks, for rocks are but incidents in the earth's history." He conjectured that the history of the earth could best be understood in terms of time periods. He named the first of these the Archeozoic era, which, he calculated, began some 1.5 billion years ago. The Pleistocene epoch, he estimated at 40,000. In a long career of research and writing at Yale, Dana produced 215 books and articles, making him one of the most prolific as well as one of the most brilliant and influential American scientists.

It is noteworthy that much of the best scientific work was done under the auspices of Federal agencies such as the Army Corps of Engineers, the Signal Corps, and the Federal Meteorological Service. The most notable figure in the realm of what we might call public science was Joseph Henry, who started his adult life as a surveyor and a teacher of chemistry and physics at the Albany Academy, in New York. Henry's tireless tinkering began to adduce important new information about electricity. Appointed to a faculty position at the College of New Jersey—Princeton—Henry worked with Morse on his telegraph. As secretary of the newly formed Smithsonian Institution, he made it the "incubator of American science," encouraging researchers in virtually every area of applied science, prominent among them weather forecasting, and joining with Dr. William Redfield to help found the American Association for the Advancement of Science. Redfield, a saddler turned paleethnologist and student of meteors, was also a businessman who established the first barge line on the Hudson River.

Despite the increasingly impressive achievements of scientists holding academic chairs, the sciences remained distinctly subordinate enterprises in most IHLs, inadequately funded, carried on in poorly equipped laboratories often located in basements and spaces for which no better use could be found. The newly appointed president of the University of California, Daniel Coit Gilman, called, in his inaugural address in 1872, for more attention to the sciences, especially to the need for increasing the scientific sophistication of nonscientists. This was a task that fell in large part on the state universities and on the small denominational colleges, where one or two inspiring faculty members might attract several generations of students to their field. While the best-known scientists were to be found, increasingly, in the larger colleges and universities, the small denominational colleges turned out a much higher proportion of distinguished scientists. Again it was the institutions of the Midwest and, to a lesser extent, Far West that led the way. The fact was that compared with the achievements of the great European scientists, especially those of Britain and Germany, the accomplishments of American scientists were comparatively modest.

The growth of professional schools rivaled the growth of IHLs in general. Medical schools increased in number from 75 in 1870 to 160 in 1900, although many were medical schools only by a generous interpretation of that phrase, and by the end of the century the shoddy character of some had become a public scandal. Dental schools showed a sharp increase in the period as more Americans were able to afford beguiling smiles. While the majority of lawyers were still apprenticed, a number of law schools were founded, many as adjuncts of state universities.

Harvard was, at the beginning of this period, a model of all that was most retrograde about higher education in America. Because a disproportionate number of famous Americans attended it, a general notion that it was a superior institution got about. Unfortunately some of those famous graduates told quite a different story. "No one," Henry Adams wrote, "took Harvard College seriously . . . as far as it educated at all, [it] was a mild and liberal school, which sent young men into the world with all they needed to make respectable citizens, and something of what they wanted to make useful ones." Four years of it "resulted in an autobiographical blank, a mind on which only a water-mark had been stamped. . . . It taught little and it taught that ill, but it left the mind open, free from bias, ignorant of facts, but docile." Adams recalled his classmates as "quietly penetrating and aggressively commonplace," notably without enthusiasms. It seemed easy to "stand alone . . . when one has no passions; easier still when one has no pains."

Charles Francis Adams, Jr., thought little better of Harvard than did Henry. He considered his class ('56) distinguished chiefly for the fact that two of its graduates ended up in the state prison. He found the instruction and the atmosphere stultifying. "In one word," he wrote, "the educational trouble with Harvard in my time was the almost total absence of touch and direct personal influence as between student and instructor. The academic, schoolmaster system prevailed; and, outside of the recitation room, it was not good form—it was contrary to usage—for the instructors and the instructed to hold personal relations."

Of his stint as a professor of history at Harvard, Henry Adams noted that most of his students were dullards; some outstanding ones gravitated to the young teacher, who taught with an atypical enthusiasm and showed a keen interest in those undergraduates capable of responding to his own ideas and interests. There was no "department" of history at Harvard; as far as American history was concerned, Adams was it. "My rage for reform is leading me into an open war with the whole system of teaching," he wrote a friend. "Rebellion is in my blood, somehow or other." Like his colleague William James, Adams rebelled against the merely formal contact of teachers with their students. He invited Henry Cabot Lodge, Edward Channing, Albert Bushnell Hart, and Henry Osborn Taylor to his house for evening seminars. In 1876 they produced a collaborative study, *Essays in Anglo-Saxon Law*. Three of them received Ph.D.s, among the first awarded by Harvard.

All that was destined to change radically, if not always clearly for the better. In 1854 Charles William Eliot was hired as a tutor in mathematics. Harvard then had 18 faculty members. Fifteen years later, when Eliot was made president, the faculty had increased to 27, and there were, in addition, 64 instructors and administrators. At the time of Eliot's retirement in 1909, the faculty and staff numbered more than 700.

Eliot was the Andrew Carnegie of the educational world, and it is not surprising that the two men found a natural affinity. Both thought *big*. Eliot's intention was to make Harvard the greatest university in the United States. His ideas on how to accomplish this were, to be sure, mundane. They consisted of attracting distinguished scholars, paying comparatively generous salaries, improving facilities, and establishing professional schools. This all needed money, and Eliot proved an inspired fund raiser. He loved hobnobbing with the rich and was able to persuade a substantial number of them that there was no better use for their money than bestowing it upon Harvard. The university thus grew in company with, and, in general, in harmony with, capitalism. Eliot made Harvard famous by introducing, with considerable fanfare, the elective system, which cynics declared was simply the intellectual equivalent of political *laissez-faire*, a charge that Eliot was not disposed to deny since he was a conservative in politics and a champion of the *laissez-faire* principle. He plainly believed in private enterprise in education as well as in business and denounced governmental support for education as the beginning of "the military, despotic organization of public instruction which prevails in Prussia."

By the 1890s the Harvard faculty, in large part as a consequence of Eliot's efforts, included such figures as Alexander Agassiz, son of a famous father, in the science department and Horatio Greenough in classics; George Kittredge, Barrett Wendell, and Charles Eliot Norton in English; Edward Channing and Albert Bushnell Hart in history; Frank Taussig, son of a German immigrant father, in the "new" economics. Edward Charles Pickering was at the midpoint of a distinguished career as head of the Harvard Observatory. With the exception of James and his colleagues in philosophy and the more distinguished scientists on the faculty, Harvard was still very much the center of what has been called the genteel tradition in American letters. The faculty was conservative in its politics and in its social attitudes. The tradition of educating gentlemen in the classics was still dominant. The average undergraduate, while given more help and direction than in earlier years, was fortunate to make contact with any of the faculty "stars." The classes were often too large to permit close contact between faculty and students.

The atmosphere was intensely snobbish. When Albert Bushnell Hart offered Oswald Garrison Villard a position as an assistant in his history course, the flattered Villard thought it was because of his intellectual promise, but Hart told Villard "that he had selected me because of my social standing, the fact that I wore nice clothes, and was a member of a couple of good clubs. He was tired, he said, of having to pick 'greasy grinds,' . . . because they so often lacked the appearance and ability necessary to win the . . . respect of their students."

The undergraduates were preoccupied far more with social than with intellectual matters. "Practically nobody in the class was interested in world events," Villard wrote of his classmates. They sneered at Norton's scholarly asides and slept through Nathaniel Shaler's geology lectures. Norton and Shaler were popular because they taught "snap" courses, courses that required little outside work and could be easily passed, especially with the aid of a tutor or a trot. In Villard's class were a number of "rich young fashionables" who idled their way through college "before going on with lives of ease."

The education available at other IHLs was not substantially different. Frederic Howe's five years at Allegheny College had been "very nearly barren . . ." he wrote. "The inflexible pattern of American collegiate life left almost no impress on my mind. It had neither variety nor inspiration; it stimulated neither revery nor inquiry. What was offered was not what I wanted. It was not what any one wanted. . . . My real life was outside of the classroom, in politics, fraternity life, in journalism and ephemeral college activities. . . . Professions of faith were rather more important than scholarship." Revival meetings were the great events of the winter. The professors were pious, amiable, well-meaning men, many of them retired preachers or missionaries. "None of the subjects stirred in me the least enthusiasm," Howe recalled.

When Lincoln Steffens entered the University of California, he found the situation much the same. He came with a set of passionate enthusiasms to which the routine work of the classroom seemed to have little relation. "No one ever developed for me," he wrote, "the relation of anything I was studying to anything else, except, of course, to that wretched degree. Knowledge was absolute, not relative, and it was stored in compartments, categorical and independent. The relation of knowledge to life, even to student life, was ignored, and as for questions, the professors asked them, not the students; and the students, not the teachers, answered them—in examinations. . . . It was not assumed that we had any curiosity or the potential love of skill, scholarship, and achievement or research."

Ray Stannard Baker was "bitterly critical of the educators I had had in college. Why," he wrote, "hadn't they told me about, or at least referred me to, the books that would have helped me in understanding the things I was seeing." He had had first-rate courses in the physical sciences at Michigan State, "but the study of human relationships, whether sociology or economics, was then practically unknown. . . . As for the world of business and industry, I understood, dimly, that it was operated according to the immutable gospel of Adam Smith. 'Enlightened selfishness' would solve all the problems."

Education was a major industry in the Middle West, the pathway to a professional career and a channel of redemption. In Jacksonville, Illinois, for example, there was the Whipple Academy (attended by William Jennings Bryan), Illinois Women's College, Illinois College, Jacksonville Female Academy, and the state schools for the blind and the deaf. The business of Jacksonville was plainly education.

In 1816 George Ticknor had written in considerable elation to Thomas Jefferson to tell of his discovery of German scholarship, which had brought the German universities "forward more in forty years as far as other nations have been three centuries in advancing & which will yet carry them much further." Such advances were, in large part, due to the "unwearied & universal diligence among their scholars. . . ." Ticknor's friend and fellow scholar George Bancroft had a similar reaction. He wished to transplant German historical scholarship to the United States and there "unite it with a high moral feeling." Learning would "go to school with religion" and thus be put into the service of society rather than pursued for its own sake.

Now the day had come to introduce the rigors of Germanic scholarship into the intellectually unassuming atmosphere of the American IHLs. This was to be done primarily through the institution of the German graduate seminar, at which carefully chosen advanced students of exceptional promise met with the most learned scholars in small informal groups to discuss their researches. Johns Hopkins in Baltimore was the American prototype. Its president, Daniel Coit Gilman, lured from the University of California in Berkeley, where he had helped guide that institution's first modest steps, undertook to assemble the most outstanding scholars in the country.

In the words of Frederic Howe, Gilman "selected as instructors men of enthusiasm, of independence, of courage." The university itself was "very badly housed in a group of old lofts and residences on Howard Street, close by the business section of the city." There were no playing fields, no chapel, no clubs or fraternity houses. In place of the traditional rows of seats, the instructor and his students sat informally in comfortable old chairs around a long table. "Teachers and students alike felt a dignity and enthusiasm in their work," Howe wrote. "Johns Hopkins, in my time, and in the first quarter of a century after its founding, was as free as a privately endowed university could be. . . . I wondered at the intimacy between professors and students, at the possibility of meeting distinguished teachers as human beings." Religion had dominated everything at Allegheny. At Johns Hopkins it was "completely overlooked"; its "taboos were disregarded." The students, aware that they were part of a unique enterprise, compared Hopkins to the medieval universities of Paris, Padua, or Bologna. Ira Remsen was a famous chemist; Basil Gildersleeve, a famous Greek scholar; Herbert B. Adams, one of the country's foremost historians. Yet each of these men met with students as with fellow scholars. In this atmosphere the students lived and worked together like members of a medieval guild.

One of the most popular lecturers was Woodrow Wilson. Howe

described Wilson as "a child of Calvinistic forebears, of Virginia background, of university enthusiasms." He was a "brilliant conversationalist," who "spent most of his time in his room by himself preparing his lectures and writing." The ideal with which he attempted to imbue his students was that of "disinterested statesmanship, of government by *noblesse oblige*." Walter Bagehot, the English political theorist, had been his model; British statesmen, in Wilson's view, should be emulated. Drawn from the best families and "trained from youth for the service of the state . . . they had no private ends to serve." In Howe's words Wilson "loved England as the mother of civil liberty and of parliamentary government." The writings of the Founding Fathers— Jefferson, Madison, Hamilton—and *The Federalist Papers* were essential documents to which he directed his students, along with the debates on the framing of the Constitution. In Howe's words, "Woodrow Wilson the President is to be found in these early influences. He never outgrew them. He lived in a world of dreams rather than with men. His reveries were of English and American statesmen, himself among the number.—He loved Virginia, the Mother of Presidents, and esteemed great documents as the most enduring of deeds."

Another influential professor was Richard Ely, whose Chautauqua lectures had attracted Howe to Hopkins. Ely was born in a small town in upper New York State in 1854. He graduated from Columbia and then spent three years studying economics at a number of German universities. In 1881 he returned to the United States and was appointed to the faculty at the recently founded Johns Hopkins. Ely became the champion of what was soon called the new economics, which took the novel ground that economic principles were not immutable but must change as the society changed to reflect the needs of its members. One of the few Americans bold enough to criticize his countrymen's primary faith in individualism, Ely suggested that excessive individualism imperiled society's capacity to protect its common interests. From this followed his espousal of such reforms as public supervision of factories to protect the life and health of the workers, support for unionization, and slum clearance.

The notion of a cooperative rather than a competitive society was one that Ely helped publicize, making common cause with the Christian Socialists. At the same time he was an advocate of a kind of managerial elite made up of specialists. Jefferson had earlier called for "a natural aristocracy" of talents. Ely's emphasis was on the growing need for a government staffed by highly trained individuals, the graduates of such advanced studies as those offered at Johns Hopkins.

From Ely, Howe learned "that the industrial system was not what I had assumed it to be in Meadville. . . . Employers, I now learned, were capitalists. They exploited their workers. In the new world that took shape for me at the university, industry was a grim affair of mines and mills, trusts and monopolies. . . . Little children were slaves in cotton-mills and sweat shops. . . . There was menace in the industrial system; there was need of change. . . . I came alive. I felt a sense of responsibility to the world. I wanted to change things. I was not very clear what I wanted to change or how I should go about it. It had to do with politics."

It was this feeling that gave the enterprise an air of special excitement: the sense on the part of the faculty and of the young men collected under its aegis that they might use the results of the new scholarship to resolve the war between capital and labor and reform the nation's badly battered and, for the most part, only nominally democratic institutions; the redemptive vision had a new form. It was, as Bancroft had hoped, a wedding of scholarship, of "disciplined study," and research, of refined methodology with "a high moral feeling." The students were a dedicated, almost monastic band, explorers in a new and unmapped land of the mind. Their common labors gave their friendships an added dimension. They graduated from Hopkins carrying with them the spirit engendered by those heady days when it seemed the world must yield to mind, when reason, through the agency of "scholarship," would at last vanquish the irrational, the unplanned, and the undirected "drift" that had characterized so much of human history. *First*, to "know," through research, what the real facts were and *then*, through the application of reason, to provide the solution. That was the new science.

The graduates became presidents of colleges and universities, chairmen of departments, reform-minded journalists, distinguished scholars, public servants, politicians. Charles Homer Haskins was a medieval historian and dean of the Harvard Graduate School, which he remade on the Hopkins model. Charles Hazen was a history professor at Columbia; Edward Ross was one of the pioneers in sociology at the University of Wisconsin. John Franklin Jameson taught at Hopkins for six years after he had graduated and then became director of the department of historical research at the Carnegie Institution in

Washington, D.C. Walter Hines Page distinguished himself as a journalist and diplomat. Looking back on Johns Hopkins from the perspective of almost forty years, Howe wrote: "It was as unlike the timid small college from which I came as it is unlike the universities of today [1924], which seek their presidents from among business men, lawyers, good money-getters, and in which freedom of teaching is being subordinated to the desire for a big endowment. The teachers, not the trustees, determined what was to be taught and how they should teach it. There was no placating of possible donors, no mirroring the views of an economic class. . . . There was a spirit of courage and restless inquiry communicated from instructors to students. . . . We were encouraged to be ourselves, to find our own lives, to make our own decisions. Education was not a thing of books alone, it was to be taken wherever one could find it." Students were encouraged to do part of their studies abroad, and Howe went to Germany for a year and returned more confident than ever that the future lay with "my own kind of people . . . educated, university people who read books and talked about them. I had a strong belief in the superiority of the Anglo-Saxon race. English-speaking people were the chosen people. . . ." The new world into which Howe was emerging was "still moralistic," he realized. "I got its new moralities," he added, "the moralities of educated men, of scholars, of intellectual reformers. . . . The people were hungry for guidance; of that we were clear—guidance which we, the scholars, alone could provide. . . . The Johns Hopkins motto was *Veritas Vos Liberabit*. Through the truth we would redeem the world. . . . I was initiated into a new order; the order of scholars whose teachings had changed me, would change the world. . . . This was the priesthood of my service."

Following Gilman's lead, the Massachusetts millionaire Jonas Gilman Clark lured G. Stanley Hall, who had studied in Germany under such luminaries as H. L. F. von Helmholtz and Wilhelm Max Wundt, away from Hopkins to head Clark University at Worcester. Like Gilman before him, Hall, a distinguished psychologist, assembled an "independent-minded and courageous" young faculty.

Hall had scarcely rounded it up when it was stolen by William Rainey Harper, president of the University of Chicago. Harper, who had learned his trade as head of Chautauqua, had the Rockefeller millions behind him. He also stole George Mead, the philosopher-psychologist, from the University of Michigan, thereby introducing the morals of the market, as exemplified by his sponsor, into the world of academe, not yet accustomed to intellectual raids and monopolies. Harper's other prize acquisition was John Dewey.

The standard college curriculum underwent dramatic changes in the spirit of the "new" education. Economics had already a secure place in most college programs, but the new and the old economics fought a fight to the death, a fight more bitter because it was more directly related to the war between capital and labor than any other academic "discipline."

Sociology, the study of society, gradually made its way into the curriculum of the more progressive institutions. Despite the insistence of George Herron (and others) that the only correct and scientific sociology was Christian sociology, that rather loosely defined field of study grew increasingly secular in character. Instead of setting out to change the world or, more specifically, the American social and economic system, it directed its attention to observing and studying society.

Psychology, following the lead of William James and Harvard, was also added to the IHL curriculum, as was anthropology, which might be said to have been the most unabashedly Darwinian of the new fields of study—the new "disciplines." Each discipline had its own "methodology" and, increasingly, its own special language. The anthropologists' "scientific" studies of race were alleged to confirm the propositions of Herbert Spencer. The anthropologists measured skulls and professed to find that the cranial capacity and general intelligence of white Anglo-Saxons were superior to those of aborigines, Asians, and blacks; that of men greater than that of women; and so on. (They did other things, of course, more intelligent and more useful as well as more accurate.)

Generally the new studies of man and his relation to other men were referred to as social science, the clear implication being that their methodology and hence the results of their investigations were, or soon would be, as precise as those of the natural sciences.

It may well have been the case that Daniel Coit Gilman's most assiduous pupil was, in the last analysis, the president of Harvard. The implications of Johns Hopkins were not lost on Eliot. He discerned that the future of higher education lay with "research," "scholarship," graduate study, professional schools, and, above all, science—all of which were expensive—and he bent his very considerable energies to wooing capitalists and advancing the "corporate university." John Jay

Chapman was especially offended by Eliot's chummy way with millionaires. At the dedication of the new Harvard Medical School, for which J. Pierpont Morgan had unloosened some of his millions, "Eliot goes about," Chapman wrote to William James, "in a cab with Pierpont, hangs laurels and wreaths on his nose, and gives him the papal kiss. Now what I want to know is this—what has Eliot got to say to the young man entering business or politics who is about to be corrupted by Morgan and his class? How eloquently can Eliot present the case for honesty? Can he say anything that will reverberate through the chambers of that young man's brain more loudly than that kiss? If Eliot is a great man, I want a small man."

But Chapman was, it turned out, a voice crying in the wilderness. As the demands of modern scholarship, of graduate study and, more particularly, the requirements of natural sciences became greater and much more expensive, the problem of making ends meet financially, especially for private colleges, became acute. The solution most commonly adopted was to appeal to the nearest capitalist; the reward was an honorary degree and the donor's name attached to a new science laboratory or gymnasium or music hall. The inevitable consequence was that some donors came to take a keen interest in what was taught in such areas as economics and political science, especially as it might reflect, directly or indirectly, on their motives and morals. An almost exactly corresponding sensitivity was evident on the part of IHL presidents and deans of the faculty. Capitalists were, for the most part, hard-boiled practical men who had no intention of granting money to critics. As the national debate over hard money versus soft, of gold versus silver, grew more and more acrimonious, the pressure on faculties to line up on one side or the other often became acute. Dissenting faculty members were summarily fired by imperious boards of trustees stacked with capitalists.

Henry Demarest Lloyd had argued in *Wealth Against Commonwealth* that the "merchantile aristocracy" had extended its domination over "State, Church, and School." Many other radical reformers had reached similar conclusions. Professors reckless enough to criticize the business interests that provided a major part of the funds to maintain the institutions at which they taught found themselves under heavy pressure to recant or keep silent and, failing to do so, often found themselves without jobs. Henry C. Adams, an opponent of *laissez-faire* economics and an advocate of "welfare democracy," was fired from Cornell as a result of pressure from Jay Gould and his associates, who had been generous contributors to the university. Often a word to the president of an institution, dependent on the largess of local tycoons, was sufficient to bring about the muzzling or ousting of a professor of heterodox opinions.

The University of Chicago was an extreme case of a captive institution of higher learning. It had been founded and was, in large measure, sustained by Rockefeller money. It was thus not surprising that the heretical opinions of economics professor Edward Bemis on such touchy subjects as the public ownership of municipal utilities and "natural" monopolies got him in hot water. Bemis was a protégé of Ely, who had made himself objectionable to conservative theorists by his doctrine of government intervention in the economy. In 1892 Ely had gone from Hopkins to the University of Wisconsin, then the vigorous academic center of reform sentiment in the nation, as director of the School of Economics, Political Science, and History. While Ely disavowed Marxian socialism, he flirted with Christian socialism and supported the right of workingmen to organize unions as well as to bargain collectively. In addition, he advocated the public ownership of such natural resources as coal, iron ore, and timber. E. L. Godkin, editor of the *Nation*, called for the firing of Ely as "a practical ethical socialist." Others joined in the attack (Carl Schurz expressed his apprehension) and the regents of the university appointed a committee to investigate the charges. Ely was cleared of the accusation of being a socialist, and the principle of academic freedom was confirmed and even rendered in bronze on a boulder in front of Bascom Hall.

Ely's exoneration at Wisconsin did not deflect the determination of President William Rainey Harper to expel Bemis from the University of Chicago by one means or another. One of Bemis's most popular courses was entitled "The State as an Agent for Social Amelioration," which gave an indication of the way the ideological wind was blowing. Walton Clark, general superintendent of the United Gas Improvement Company, a subsidiary of Standard Oil, allegedly told Bemis not long after his appointment to the university, "If we can't convert you we are going to down you. We can't stand your writing. It means millions to us." Harper's efforts to force Bemis to resign, thereby avoiding the scandal which must accompany his being fired for his heterodox opinions, were as ingenious as they were disreputable. Matters were brought to a head by the Pullman strike, in the course of which Bemis, attacking strikebreaking by injunction, addressed a large rally. Harper informed him that the speech had caused such indignation among the city's potentates that "it is hardly safe for me to venture into any of the Chicago clubs. I propose that during the remainder of your connection with the university you exercise great care in public utterances about questions that are agitating the minds of people."

The head of the political science department chimed in with a letter to Harper, declaring that Bemis "is making very hard the establishment of a great railway interest in the University. I know you have done what seemed best to stop him. . . . I do not see how we can escape . . . except by letting the public know that he goes because we do not regard him as up to the standard of the University in ability and scientific methods." Another member of the department, Albion Small, admitted to Bemis that he had no fault to find with his scholarship but criticized his involvement in "public questions." He himself, he told Bemis, had given up the subject of reform for the time being in his classes and was lecturing on transcendental philosophy "so as to be as far as possible from these reform movements and establish the scientific character of my department." When Bemis proved uncooperative in the matter of resigning his supposedly tenured position, Harper warned him that a fight would result in his being blacklisted so that he would not be able to get another academic post. Persisting in his recalcitrance, he was fired.

Seeking some justification for forcing Bemis out, Harper, in a talk entitled "The Public Work of Professors," argued that it was the duty of the professor to teach a subject, "not his opinions. . . . He must stand above party lines, and be independent of party affiliations." He might, of course, act as he wished in his capacity as a citizen, but any professor who confused "personal privilege with official duty" and substituted "popular pleading for scientific thought" should be expelled from the university. Harper's doctrine is worth lingering over since it became the standard of academic orthodoxy for the college and university for the following century. The older academic consciousness had not, as we have seen, been without its punitive aspects. Religious piety was often a requisite for appointment to a teaching position; not only piety but adherence to certain points of dogma were often required as well as membership in a particular denomination. Catholics, of course, were not even considered for appointment in Protestant institutions. Moral principles were assumed to underlie all fields of study, and adherence to the Christian religion was considered the best guarantee that those principles would be observed and taught. Now science had replaced morality as the rock on which all academic studies must rest. To be unscientific was the equivalent of being irreligious or immoral in the earlier era. Any strongly held political or social opinion was suspected of being unscientific, the result of emotion rather than of dispassionate investigation. There were two conspicuous consequences of this odd notion: Professors were trained to suppress, so far as that was possible, their "feelings" and "emotions" in deference to "objectivity," and those who deviated from this canon by becoming partisans of social causes or radical advocates of reform were denounced for being "unscientific" and not infrequently turned on by their own colleagues, as Bemis was.

In any event, the friends of Edward Bemis kicked up a substantial fuss over his being dumped by the University of Chicago. Lyman Abbott wrote in the *Outlook*: "The money power is not to be permitted to control our great universities, or their teaching. . . . It is impossible to maintain freedom of research and teaching without touching what are called 'burning questions.' . . . Freedom of teaching, in our judgment, is absolutely essential to the higher life of our universities, and colleges; to their vitality, their progress, and their integrity." The *Chicago Chronicle* noted wryly: "The Chicago University knows on which side its bread is buttered. Let us pour Standard Oil upon troubled waters." George Gunton, spokesman for the Rockefeller interests, wrote in his journal the *Social Economist* (founded by Rockefeller): "Why should an institution pay a professor to teach social doctrines which are contrary to the consensus of opinions of the faculty, the supporters of the institution, and of the general community?" In the midst of the Bemis controversy, Rockefeller advanced the most conclusive argument— $1,000,000 for the school's endowment and $2,000,000 conditionally upon the university's raising a matching sum. President Harper announced a holiday. Students and faculty sang songs to the glory of John D., and the vice-president of the trustees declared: "There was a man sent from God whose name was John."

At Brown University, E. Benjamin Andrews was fired for supporting William Jennings Bryan in the election of 1896 on the ground that "unsound financial doctrines" should not be taught at respectable institutions of higher learning. Rockefeller withheld a large contribution to Brown until Andrews was fired, and the trustees then selected Rockefeller's pastor as the president of the university.

J. Allen Smith, born in Pleasant Hill, Missouri, in 1860, had attended the University of Missouri, where he read Henry George's *Progress and Poverty* (despite a warning issued to students not to read it). After a brief period studying law, Smith decided to do graduate work in political economy at the University of Michigan. There he imbibed the heresies of Richard Ely and John R. Common. These caused him no problem in his first academic post at Marietta College in Ohio, the president of which was in thorough sympathy with populism and Christian socialism. However, when Smith voted for Bryan in 1896, the president could not protect him from the ire of the trustees, men whom Smith described as "partisan Republicans . . . interested in gas and other monopolies [who] would like to see the teaching in this college subordinated to their own private interests." When Smith was fired, he found a position at the Populist-dominated University of Washington in 1897.

Edward Alsworth Ross, a graduate of Coe College, Iowa, and Johns Hopkins, where he earned his Ph.D. in two years, accepted a full professorship in economics at the recently founded Stanford University at Palo Alto. Ross's espousal of liberal and radical causes so incensed Jane Lathrop Stanford, the widow of Leland, who had supplied the funds to start the university, that she insisted he be fired. His dismissal led to the resignation of seven other faculty members, among them Arthur Lovejoy, a promising young philosopher and former student of William James.

The doctrine of objectivity was used over the years to harass and often to silence professors with unorthodox political and economic views—socialists (and later communists) were, of course, particularly vulnerable. Ironically, professors in the main concurred with administrators and boards of trustees in insisting that true scholarship must be "objective."

From any rational perspective, the American college must appear as one of the more bizarre institutions created by the species in its ascent from primitive life. A distinguishing feature of that stage in the progress of the race which we have denominated civilization has been most commonly a learned, often priestly class—theologians, lawgivers, clerk-scholars. Calvin, in his protest against a decadent and authoritarian Rome, insisted that every Christian had an obligation to search out the truth of the Gospel for himself without priestly intermediaries. He must learn to read and interpret the Bible and, in doing so, develop all the talents that the Lord had given him. There must be, in a famous phrase, a priesthood not of a chosen few but "of all believers"—the common saints of the Lord. It was that doctrine which made the Puritans so determined to advance schooling in the American wilderness.

The Founding Fathers offered a more secular gloss on Calvin's proposition: A republican government was the most exacting of all forms of government. It would be maintained only by a virtuous and enlightened citizenry, a literate citizenry, filled with "civic virtue," a self-sacrificing concern for the good of the state as a whole, over and above all merely private and selfish interests. There was more to it, of course. The Enlightenment, the Age of Reason, which insisted that man was a rational creature and that progress depended on trained and refined reason, was a major factor which in time came to predominate as the primary rationale for general public education. That had been, the reader may recall, one of the bones of educational contention between John Adams and Thomas Jefferson. Jefferson wished to see nothing taught but the most up-to-date "science," while Adams insisted that the accumulated experience (and, he hoped, wisdom) of the race must be taught as well.

If we assume that the constantly expanding system of public primary and secondary school education produced a reasonably literate public (an assumption it is no longer safe to make), the proliferation of denominational "colleges" of uncertain credentials clearly had another function only vaguely related to "learning." Many, to be sure, were established for the ostensible purpose of training ministers and missionaries for their respective denominations, but as the century wore on, this function became strictly secondary. Whatever "learning" was dispensed was "learning" only in the most modest sense of the word. The majority of students who enrolled in colleges and, of course, more frequently in "universities" dropped out before completing the relatively undemanding work required for a degree. Of those who were graduated, only a handful could be called learned; even "educated" was, for most, a generous accolade. Most of those who merited such proud encomiums had earned them more through their own enterprise or the happy chance of an inspiring teacher than as a consequence of the curriculum they had been subjected to. The testimony of the great majority of students who went to college in the nineteenth century is virtually unanimous on this point.

Within these generalizations it seems clear that the institutions that had the most salutary effect on their students were those distinguished by zeal in a particular cause. In such institutions as Knox, Oberlin, and Grinnell learning seemed more directly related to life, and faculty and students shared common ideals and goals. Indeed, the small Midwestern colleges appear to have done considerably better by their students than the older and more traditional Eastern institutions, the Harvard of William James being the most notable exception.

To say that only slightly more than 2 percent of Americans attended college by 1900 is misleading. In many small towns, especially those that were the homes of colleges, a substantial portion of the town's high school graduates attended college, at least for several years. Those towns of the Middle and Far West colonized by New Englanders (and there were many such) clung to a tradition of learning as stubbornly as the Jews. If they could afford to, they sent their sons to Harvard (and later their daughters to Wellesley and Smith) to preserve the tie with the "motherland." If not, their sons attended the nearest college, and by the 1870s these served as staging areas for the bands of energetic and ambitious young men and women who invaded Chicago and New York and soon made those cities centers of intellectual life and social reform.

There was yet another educational realm that expanded remarkably in this era. That was what came to be called adult education. Americans remained people of "the word," whatever that word might be. Lecturing not only continued but proliferated exceedingly. The railroads helped by whisking lecturers all about the country until there was hardly an American so unfortunate as to be inaccessible to a lecturer bearing word of the latest scientific development or the newest promise of wealth or salvation. No one was apparently too rich or too exalted to go on a lecture tour or, at the very least, to lecture tirelessly within a reasonable radius of his or her home. Correspondingly, there was no one so humble or obscure as not, if he or she had some new powerful revelation to expound and a modicum of talent in expounding it, to find audiences willing to listen and, more important, to pay some modest sum for the privilege.

Close on the heels of freethinkers came Christian evangelists. Imperialists were followed by anti-imperialists; purity leaguers, by advocates of "affinity," physical and spiritual. The inventors of new religious sects were followed by speakers warning against their heresies. Socialists, communists, and anarchists, foreign and domestic, seemed in virtually limitless supply.

There came to be even a kind of holy city devoted to the sacred rites of lecturing. Chautauqua, on the beautiful lake of the same name in New York State, became the mecca of lecturer and lecturee alike.

Thousands flocked there every summer to hear the most famous Americans give their most learned lectures. To be invited to lecture at Chautauqua was to receive an envied accolade.

John Heyl Vincent, an ordained minister from Alabama, and his friend and fellow worker for Christ, Lewis Miller, joined forces to reform the Sunday school curriculum. Miller was the grandson of a German immigrant who had settled in Baltimore and enlisted in the Continental army. The family moved to Ohio, where Miller had grown up on a farm and become infected with the radical spirit so evident in the farming communities of the Midwest. An inventor and manufacturer of farm machinery, Miller moved to Akron, Ohio, where he became actively involved in educational reform. Among his "inventions" were the four-term college year (first adopted at Mount Union College) and the use of partitions in elementary and Sunday schools to allow for more flexible classrooms. In the words of Miller's son-in-law, Thomas A. Edison, "he seemed to be eternally making money in his factory in order to enable him to better carry on his schemes for education."

Their shared interest in Sunday school education brought Vincent and Miller together, and in 1875 they began in Chautauqua what we today might call a Christian retreat, in which polite entertainment was accompanied by sermons, prayers, religious reflections, and, increasingly, secular lectures. A Temperance Conference presided over by Frances Willard was held there, followed by a Scientific Congress. In 1886 Vincent published *The Chautauqua Movement*, an account of the ideals and founding of Chautauqua. By the time his partner, Lewis Miller, lost most of his fortune in the financial collapse of 1893, the Chautauqua was an enormously popular venture with dozens of permanent buildings spread over several hundred acres, featuring music instruction and a College of Liberal Arts.

Theodore Roosevelt was among those charmed by Chautauqua, calling it "the most American place in America," and in its combination of liberal piety and intellectual and aesthetic uplift it certainly had as good a claim to that designation as any other spot.

In his *Talks with Teachers*, William James commented rather wickedly on Chautauqua. "The moment one enters that sacred enclosure," he wrote, "one feels one's self in an atmosphere of success. Sobriety and industry, intelligence and goodness, orderliness and ideality, prosperity and goodness pervade the air. Here you have a town of many thousands of inhabitants, beautifully laid out in the forest. . . . You have a first class college in full blast. You have magnificent music. . . . You have every sort of athletic exercise from sailing, rowing, swimming, bicycling, to the ballfield. . . . You have kindergarten and model secondary schools. You have general religious services and special club-houses for the several sects. You have perpetually-running soda-water fountains, and daily popular lectures by distinguished men. You have the best of company, and yet no effort. You have no zymotic diseases, no poverty, no drunkenness, no crime, no police. You have culture, you have kindness, you have cheapness, you have equality, you have the best fruits of what mankind has fought and bled and striven for under the name of civilization for centuries. You have, in short, a foretaste of what human society might be, were it all in the light, with no suffering and no dark corners . . . [a] middle-class paradise, without a victim, without a blot, without a tear." As he emerged "into the dark and wicked world" from a solid week of such salubriousness, he found himself longing for "something primordial and savage, even though it were as bad as an Indian massacre, to set the balance straight again. This order is too tame, this culture is too second-rate, this goodness too uninspiring. This human drama without a villain or a pang. . . ." James was ready to take his chances "in the big outside worldly wilderness with all its sins and sufferings . . . there is more hope and help [there] a thousand times than in this dead level and quintessence of every mediocrity." All this was unanswerably true, but clearly only half the truth. What the railroad switching yards of Chicago were for the nation's transportation system, Chautauqua and its imitators became for the exchange of ideas and the flow of information. It was there, for example, that the "mother" of the new journalism, Ida Tarbell, learned her trade as an editor of the community's journal, the *Chautauquan*. The listeners came by families, most typically, to enjoy nature, to swim in and sail on the lake, to consume health food, scientifically prepared according to the latest theories of nutrition, and, above all, to learn the Truth, to be informed, uplifted, and improved, strengthened in mind and body.

The spreading estate on Lake Chautauqua was only the headquarters of a nationwide network—some 20,000, it was estimated, at the movement's height. A generation of talkers—ministers, professors, journalists, and politicians—augmented their incomes by traveling to every corner of the nation as Chautauqua lecturers.

The band of hardy Chautauquans who took to the lecture trail around the country, visiting Chautauquas in innumerable towns and cities, divided the circuit into the "Bed Bug Belt, the Cyclone Belt, the Broiling Belt, and the Hellish Hotel Belt." The Cyclone Belt, the journalist Charles Edward Russell decided, was the most dangerous, if not the most comfortable since Chautauqua meetings were commonly held in large tents singularly susceptible to unanticipated cyclones. One of the most seasoned veterans of the circuit gave his secrets to the novice Russell. According to Russell, "he explained that the first thing to remember was that no audience really wanted to hear anybody, but only went because it had to go. . . . The man that could make all those people forget the miseries of the hard benches and the heat could have their support and money every time." The formula to follow was to keep the speech relatively short and fill it with homilies. "Talk for ten minutes about the little red schoolhouse, then ten minutes on the value of early education and training in good habits, followed by reflections on the 'dear old parson of the little old church on the hill. . . .' Next get into the principles of success. This is what snatches them every time. Honesty, fidelity to duty, industry, specially industry, (go heavy on industry—every farmer has his hired man) have been the touchstones of your own success. Tell about early struggles and privations and ring in a lot about the poor poor farm boys that have become millionaires." The home was the final theme. "Say that it is the American home that has made America great." The talk must be larded with stories, and the stories must be old. "There is nothing an audience resents so much as a brand-new story." Another Chautauqua regular advised Russell to stick to home and mother; the next best line was to be "optimistic and reassuring. The banks like that and the banks run most of the Chautauquas."

The unrivaled star of the Chautauquas of interior America was William Jennings Bryan. One of Russell's most vivid memories was of the natural amphitheater at Ashland, Oregon, with a great crowd "waiting to hear Mr. Bryan for the nineteenth time." Many had traveled more than 100 miles to hear the famous orator. At Shelbyville, Illinois, some 30,000 turned out.

In the spread of adult education the cities were not neglected. In New York City in 1897 some 400,000 people attended more than 1,000 public lectures at the Metropolitan Museum of Art, Cooper Union, and the city schools' evening classes. The Young Men's Hebrew Association sponsored speeches by, among others, Theodore Roosevelt and Woodrow Wilson.

The People's Institute, organized by Charles Sprague Smith, pro-

fessor of German at Columbia, was a brilliant success. It tackled the
most difficult and controversial topics of the day, and its brand of
mildly Christian socialism drew large audiences to hear speakers such
as the English Fabian socialists Sidney and Beatrice Webb, and Father
Edward McGlynn, the Catholic priest whose activities in behalf of Henry
George's campaign for mayor of New York got him excommunicated
from the church. The institute sponsored a famous debate between
Gaylord Wilshire, a millionaire California socialist, and Professor Edwin
Seligman of Columbia, which drew an enormous audience, "crowding
aisles, entrances, and all vacant spaces, even clambering upon the platform, leaving only room there for the speakers."

One of the stars of "popular education" was Thomas Davidson,
who denounced the "unbrotherly, supernatural, world-despising religion of the churches" and called for a Christian society where "the
cruel distinction that has so long been drawn between civic and religious
life, between the service of man and the service of God, will be blotted
out, and it will be recognized that a noble civic life, which seeks the
good of all, is the most religious of all lives." He declared that "the
Jewish religion is far more rational than the Christian, and indeed,
Christians, as they advance, come nearer and nearer to Judaism."

Lester Ward, in his faith in education as the channel of worldly
redemption, spoke for a substantial company of liberal reformers. In
Ward's view the system of private education, "all things considered, is
not only a very bad one, but, properly viewed, it is absolutely worse
than none, since it tends still further to increase the inequality in the
existing intelligence, which is a worse evil than a generally lower state
of intelligence would be. . . . State education is far better for the
pupil. . . . The lowest *gamin* of the streets here meets the most pampered son of opulence on a footing of strict equality. Nothing counts
but merit itself." Finally, "any system of education which falls short,
even in the slightest particular, of absolute universality, can not proceed
from any true conception of what education is for, or of what it is
capable of accomplishing." It was in that spirit that the state universities
began their ascendancy.

What would in time come to be known as the knowledge industry
had its beginnings in this period—not only its beginnings but its "glory
days." At Johns Hopkins, at Clark, at the Harvard of William James,
at Wisconsin and Michigan and Indiana, even at the Rockefeller-dom-
inated University of Chicago, graduate education in the United States

enjoyed its Golden Age. Inspired by the conviction that "mind" could be put to the service of society; that "research" would provide the grounding for social justice; that the new economics, psychology, and "dynamic" sociology would be the instruments of reform, scholars, journalists, and budding politicians perceived a new promise in the world of scholarship.

33

Blacks

There was a world of irony in the fact that a sculptural group twenty-two feet high entitled "Emancipation," commissioned and paid for by freedmen and erected in Lincoln Park, was dedicated by Frederick Douglass on April 14, 1876, the anniversary of the fall of Sumter and of Lincoln's assassination. The hopes for black equality that had risen so high in the aftermath of the Union victory had been dashed in the years since Appomattox. Americans are so generally committed to the notion of "progress" in history that it always comes as something of a shock to us to realize how often, even in our own history (or perhaps especially in our own history), categories of Americans have lost ground in terms of the nation's original commitment to justice and equality. From the era of the American Revolution, for example, women, blacks, Indians, and, to an extent, immigrants lost ground, and suffered a slow erosion of rights and, equally important, status. (In the case of women, it was less legal rights that were lost than status.)

The emancipation of the slaves promised, as we have seen, a new dispensation for the freedmen and women of the South and for Northern blacks as well. Hundreds of thousands of blacks in the North and South alike came forward to claim their rights as American citizens, and thousands emerged as energetic and resourceful leaders of their people. Henry Turner, Robert Elliott, Jonathan Gibbs, the Cardozo brothers, the Lynches, Charles Caldwell, and many others were heroic fighters in the effort to make emancipation more than a promise.

The "bargain" of 1876, which in effect reestablished the dogma of states' rights with vast and, on the whole, deplorable consequences, was also a death sentence for the hopes of Southern blacks. The notorious Black Codes, passed by the Southern legislatures in the immediate aftermath of the war and under the aegis of President Andrew Johnson, had given unmistakable evidence of the intentions of the white South toward its former slaves—nothing less than complete and abject subordination. The South had claimed, in the period of Reconstruction, that it was the intention of the North to impose "black rule" on it as punishment for its intransigence. All the efforts of the South to suppress black political (or economic) activity were defended on the ground that its white men and women were simply struggling to protect themselves from domination by corrupt and illiterate black politicians. The black politicians responded reasonably enough that even if they wished to "rule" the South, they could not; they were substantially outnumbered in all Southern states except South Carolina and Mississippi. Their goal was never more than a fair share of political power and economic opportunity. To ensure a fair share, they must exercise their rights as citizens. But this the white South was unwilling to concede. It therefore began methodically to strip its black citizens of their citizenship, to ensure that they would play a diminishing and ultimately insignificant political role, that they should become, for all practical purposes, entirely without power to protect their interests, their rights, and even their lives. This process took time. It had been said and doubtless believed by many Southerners, men like Wade Hampton, that they bore no malice toward black people and that as soon as the freedmen had demonstrated their capacity for responsible political behavior through education and the development of "character," they would be admitted to all the rights and privileges of citizenship. But it proved otherwise in fact. The more blacks indicated both the disposition and the ability to participate in the political process, the more rigorously they were suppressed. In the aftermath of Reconstruction most of the initial black leadership was killed, intimidated, or driven out of the South.

The same treatment was accorded to any white politician who dared encourage black political activity. A typical case of intimidation of a white ally of blacks occurred in Copiah County, Mississippi. John

Prentiss Matthews, a white man, was the most powerful political figure in the county, which had a population of 5,000 divided almost evenly between blacks and whites. Matthews's father had owned thirty-five slaves before the war, and after the war Print Matthews, as he was called, had worked closely with the Republicans to make the transition to freedom easier for the county's black population. Matthews believed that if the blacks were to vote, their friendship and support would be essential to political success. The family lived in Hazlehurst; Matthews's sons attended the University of Mississippi, and Print and his brothers ran the largest general store in town as well as owning several plantations.

In the election of 1883 Print Matthews called together the supporters of his Fusion Independent Party, made up of black Republicans and white farmers favorable to the Greenback-Labor Party. The response of Democrats to this prospectively formidable alliance was an all-out campaign of terror. A hundred and fifty armed men roamed the county, pulling an artillery piece and firing intermittently into the air when no better target presented itself, at blacks when they were visible. Black cabins were visited, and the residents threatened with beatings and death if they dared vote. Tom Wallis, a black farmer who was a friend and ally of Print Matthews, was called on by the riders, who were described as "among the best men in the county, a good many of them planters and men of various professions." When he resisted a beating, he was shot and killed and his wife wounded. Frank Hayes and his wife, also known as supporters of Matthews, were shot, and a black church used for political meetings was burned to the ground. Most of the blacks in the county abandoned their homes in the days immediately prior to the election and hid in the woods. In the words of one of them, "Dar is a mighty big settlement of cullud people up our way, and de biggest part of dem laid out at night, for they dasn't stay at home. Some white men was in de woods, too, but dey was all Republicans. We all had to lay out like possums when de dogs are after dem."

Matthews was served with a notice warning him not to go near the polls on election day. It was signed: "Adopted by the citizens of Copiah County, this 5th day of November, 1883." He replied to the messengers who delivered the ultimatum: "I think I have as much right to vote as any of you. I have never done any of you harm. I have tried to be useful to society in every way that I could . . . you have got it in your power to murder me, I admit. But am going to vote tomorrow, unless you kill me."

When Print arrived at the polling place in his precinct the next morning, he encountered Ras Wheeler, a Democratic henchman who had been given the assignment of preventing Matthews from voting. Matthews exchanged a few words with Wheeler and then presented his ballot to an election official. Wheeler reached inside a nearby wood-box, took out a shotgun, and killed Matthews. Democrats greeted the news of the murder, it was said, with "extravagant demonstrations of joy." Jubilant Democrats from nearby towns converged on Hazlehurst, in the words of a Democratic newspaper, "like gallant and chivalrous Knights at ancient times to render assistance to their threatened brethren and, if need be, to defend the women and children with their lives." They came yelling and shouting like Indians. A handful of courageous blacks met at nearby Crystal Springs "and passed resolutions of sorrow" at the death of their friend.

The next day the Copiah Democratic Executive Committee met at the courthouse and passed a series of resolutions. The first warned that any attempt at avenging Print Matthews's death on the part of his family or friends would place them "without the pale and protection of the law . . . and . . . we will visit upon them certain, swift retribution. . . ."

The second resolution stated that "the welfare of all races and classes in this county" requires "that the Matthews family shall keep out of politics . . ." and, finally, that "no man or set of men shall organize the negro race against the whites in this county. . . . Resolved that we do hereby pledge ourselves, each to the other, our lives and fortunes and our sacred honor [words taken, ironically, from the Declaration of Independence], that we will . . . from hence forth, hold ourselves in readiness to enforce the foregoing resolutions. . . ." The Hazlehurst brass band was thanked for providing the music for the meeting.

The events in Copiah County were repeated, with variations appropriate to the setting, in virtually every county of the South where freedmen attempted to continue to exercise the civil and political rights they had enjoyed in the Reconstruction government.

A notable exception to those black leaders silenced or intimidated was John Roy Lynch, author of *The Facts of Reconstruction*. Lynch emphasized, as the reader may recall, the alliance between the old planter

aristocracy and the "mulatto" politicians who were very conscious of
their blood ties to the ante-bellum leaders. In many instances they were
the sons of the plantation owners. Lynch, indeed, was so confident of
the support of his white colleagues that he decided to run for Congress
in the Sixth District of Mississippi in 1880, four years after the end of
Reconstruction. He secured the Republican nomination in a convention in which black delegates outnumbered whites. When intimidation
of the voters and manipulation of the ballots gave the general election
to the Democratic candidate, the political handwriting as to the future
political prospects of black candidates for public office in Mississippi
was clear. With Republicans in control of the House, Lynch appealed
the results to the Committee on Elections and after two years of investigation—the length of his congressional term—the seat was awarded
to him by vote of the House. It was a hollow victory. He was forced
to run again immediately, and this time his Democratic opponent, a
popular white lawyer, defeated him by a margin of 800 votes. Lynch
remained, however, the chairman of the Republican State Executive
Committee as that body shrank in power to a distributor of Federal
patronage under a succession of Republican administrations.

A Mississippi newspaper wrote of Lynch: "He made and unmade
men, organized and disorganized rings and cliques, and directed and
controlled legislatures like a very autocrat. He is yet a man of power
and authority—yet a shining light in the Republican camp." Lynch
dealt in real estate, apparently profitably, owning at one time or another six plantations of various sizes; studied and practiced law; held
Federal office, and in the Spanish-American War accepted an appointment by McKinley as an officer and paymaster in the United States
Army. He and his second wife retired to Chicago in 1912, and it was
there that he wrote *The Facts of Reconstruction*. American historians, led
by the formidable James Ford Rhodes, were busy creating and extending the myth of black venality and incompetence in the period of
Reconstruction, and little notice was given to Lynch's book. Lynch
characterized Rhodes's history as "not only inaccurate and unreliable,
but . . . the most one-sided, biased, partisan, and prejudiced historical
work I have ever read." Certainly, as regards at least Reconstruction,
the charge was not far off the mark. Rhodes, for his part, refused to
attend to any of Lynch's specific criticisms on the ground that Lynch
was "a severely partisan actor at the time while I, an earnest seeker
after truth, am trying to hold a judicial balance and to tell the story

without fear, favor or prejudice." It was a remarkably unselfconscious, if sententious and self-congratulatory observation, conceivable only in the spirit of the new "scientific" and "objective" history. But one should not be too hard on Rhodes. His illusion that he knew the facts and understood the events better than the actors in it was one that would be shared by his fellow historians for decades to come.

Along with other Southern black Republicans, Lynch continued to be a delegate from his state to Republican national conventions. In the Republican Convention of 1884, two active, reform-minded young Republicans, Henry Cabot Lodge and Theodore Roosevelt, in a move to block the nomination of James Blaine, proposed Lynch for temporary chairman, thereby preventing the election of a Blaine supporter. In that role Lynch made the first keynote address given by a black politician at a presidential convention.

The destruction of the political power of Southern blacks was not easily or quickly accomplished. There was, indeed, reason for anxiety on the part of Democratic leaders about an alliance between blacks and poor white farmers. Populists and black Republicans were able to assert themselves in North Carolina in 1894 in dramatic fashion. Blacks were appointed to a number of public offices, funds for education were substantially augmented, and taxation was made more equitable. In 1896 George White, born a slave and a graduate of Howard University, was elected on the Fusion ticket to Congress. White had served eight years in the state legislature, and in Congress he promptly took up the cause of blacks. By 1898 the Democrats, through intimidation and fraud, had regained control of the state legislature, although White was reelected to Congress.

William Sinclair wrote, in *The Aftermath of Slavery*: "The ballot is the citadel of the colored man's safety; the guarantor of his liberty; the protector of his rights. . . . With the ballot the negro is a man; an American among Americans. Without the ballot he is a serf, less than a slave; a thing." Senator Benjamin Tillman, of South Carolina, "had recently advocated the killing of thirty thousand colored men in that state," Sinclair wrote. He had boasted in public lectures of the part he had taken in shooting "niggers." In Detroit, Michigan, it had been reported that Tillman said in a public lecture, "On one occasion we killed seven niggers; I don't know how many I killed personally, but I shot to kill and I know I got my share." Sinclair added: "Not one of these unfortunate colored people had committed, or had even been charged with, any offence. They simply attempted to exercise their rights as American citizens and cast their ballots. For this they were shot to death."

Tillman became the prototype of those politicians who made "nigger baiting" the basis of their political appeal. The South Carolina Constitution of 1868, in the drafting of which Robert Elliott had played such a prominent part, was an offense to Tillman. He backed a referendum to call a new convention for the avowed purpose of removing the "shame" of the "Radical rag" of 1868. The convention, which met in 1895, was dominated by Tillman supporters and included 6 black delegates out of 160. A proposed amendment to the Constitution restricted the suffrage to those who had paid a poll tax at least six months before the election and could read and write any section of the Constitution, to the satisfaction of the board of elections, or owned property assessed at $300 or more. Knowing they spoke in a lost cause, the black delegates nonetheless made angry speeches in opposition to the amendment. The most eloquent of the black delegates was Thomas Ezekiel Miller. Miller had been born a free black in South Carolina in 1848. He graduated from Lincoln University in Pennsylvania and was later school commissioner of Beaufort County. After one term in Congress he served in the state legislature. The amendment, Miller declared, struck "at the root of the tree of universal government." It was plain that the purpose of the convention was "to disenfranchise the Negro in the rice fields and his poor, uneducated white brother, who plows the bobtail ox or mule on the sandhills . . . to disenfranchise the Negro in every walk of life. . . . Call us aliens. We, *aliens*? The people who were the foundation of the American civilization, *aliens*? A people . . . who by their endurance, toil and suffering made it possible for our white neighbors to establish this government, the asylum of us all. . . . Then to whom can the term citizens be applied. . . . The Negro has borne the burden of toil, and for what? To plan a civilization from which he is to be forever excluded. No, no, no! We have purchased it with labor; we have purchased it with afflictions; we have purchased it with loyalty; we have purchased it with blood drawn at the point of the lash of the taskmaster; we have purchased it with blood spilt upon the fields of battle; it is ours by all the laws of right and justice. . . . We are no more aliens to this country or to its institutions than our brothers in white. We have instituted it; our forefathers paid dearly for it. . . . In the image of God, made He man, all equal, in the possession of inalienable rights, but at all times it has been the property-owning class who have sought to grind down, impoverish and brutalize their own blood if that blood was in the body of the poor and the weak. It is against this class legislation that I stand here and raise my voice, and in the name of the poor, struggling white man and the peaceful, toiling, loving Negro."

A reporter for the *Columbia Register* wrote: "Miller's speech Friday was an eloquent appeal on behalf of the Negro. While listening to his soaring flights, many of the delegates regretted they felt an inexorable determination not to accede to his plea, a determination born of stern necessity."

Economic discrimination went hand in hand, of course, with political discrimination. In the period immediately after the war and with the protection provided by Federal troops, blacks had substantially extended their range of jobs. John Mercer Langston, a black lawyer and general inspector of black schools in the South for the Freedmen's Bureau, reported to the bureau in 1872 that one-third of the blacks of North Carolina were craftsmen and artisans. Blacks working as wheelwrights, gunsmiths, blacksmiths, millwrights, machinists, carpenters, painters, shipbuilders, and stonemasons outnumbered their white counterparts six to one in Langston's judgment. In addition, a number were pilots and engineers. Ten years later the great majority of North Carolina blacks was confined to tenant farming and menial positions. The same was true of other Southern states. The Mississippi politician James Vardaman declared that black people had only one role: "That of a menial. That is what God designed him for and the white people will see to it that God's design is carried out."

The man who emerged as the leader and spokesman, first of Southern blacks and then of all blacks, was Booker T. Washington. As a student at Hampton Institute under the presidency of General Samuel Armstrong, Washington had attracted the general's attention by his energy and intelligence. Armstrong recommended Washington, then twenty-five years old, as head of the newly established teacher training school at Tuskegee, Alabama. With forty students and an abandoned shack, Washington began in 1881 what came to be known as the Normal and Industrial Institute. Hard work, simple living, healthy diet, cleanliness, and piety were the white middle-class values that Washington stressed at Tuskegee. He also revealed an unusual talent for diplomacy in dealing with that "other nation"—the Southern whites—and in attracting Northern capitalists, chief among them Andrew Carnegie.

In the mind of Washington (and many white leaders), the future of the South lay in entering the industrial age and thereby freeing that section of the country from the limitations of a solely agricultural economy. It was this exclusive dependence on an agricultural base—cotton and tobacco primarily—that had bound the South to black slavery and made the Civil War as well as the victory of the North inevitable. Now the South must cast off the chains of its bondage to the industrial North and establish its own industrial base. In this task the role of the freed black was essential. Just as he had provided the comparatively modest technical skills needed on a plantation—blacksmithing, carpentry, tailoring, etc.—he must now master the new industrial technology, thereby making himself a vital element in the creation of the New South. Washington quoted with approval the words of Collis Potter Huntington, the railroad tycoon: "Our schools teach everybody a little of everything, but, in my opinion, they teach very few children just what they ought to know in order to make their way successfully in life. They do not put into their hands the tools they are best fitted to use, and hence so many failures."

According to Washington, he frequently encountered black women who could "converse intelligently upon abstruse subjects, and yet could not tell how to improve the condition of the poorly cooked . . . meat and bread which they and their family were eating three times a day. . . . We want more than the mere performance of mental gymnastics. Our knowledge must be harnessed to the things of real life." Certainly "science, mathematics, history, language or literature" had an important place, but they must be secondary to training for those tasks which were most needed by black people. The foundation of black advancement must be laid on "habits of thrift, a love of work, economy, ownership of property, bank accounts." Washington quoted Frederick Douglass: "Every blow of the sledge hammer wielded by a sable arm is a powerful blow in support of our cause. Every colored mechanic is by virtue of circumstances an elevator of his race. Every house built by a black man is a strong tower against the allied hosts of prejudice. . . . Without industrial development there can be no wealth; without wealth there can be no leisure; without leisure no opportunity for thoughtful reflection and the cultivation of the higher arts." It was not Washington's intention to set limits of any kind to black achievement —"in arts, in letters or statesmanship"—but he believed that "the surest way to reach those ends is by laying the foundation in the little things of life. . . . I plead for industrial education and development for the Negro," he wrote, "not because I want to cramp him, but because

I want to free him. I want to see him enter the all-powerful business and commercial world."

Washington was proud of the fact that thirty-three "trades and industries" were taught at Tuskegee. Of the institute's sixty buildings, fifty-six had been built by the students themselves, and in one year alone they had manufactured 2,000,000 bricks. A slow, difficult road lay ahead. "Our pathway," Washington declared, "must be up through the soil, up through swamps, up through forests, up through the streams, the rocks, up through commerce, education and religion!"

Washington's speech at the Cotton States and International Exposition at Atlanta in 1893 earned him a national reputation. Widely reprinted by approving white newspapers, it marked the thirty-seven-year-old Washington as the spokesman of his race or at least that portion of it residing in the South. Washington reiterated the theme of hard work and thrift: "There is as much dignity in tilling a field as in writing a poem. It is at the bottom of life we must begin, and not at the top." Referring to an exhibition of black arts and achievements at the exposition, he assured his listeners that "we do not for a moment forget that our part in this exhibition would fall far short of your expectations but for the constant help that has come to our educational life, not only from the Southern states, but especially from Northern philanthropists, who have made their gifts a constant stream of blessing and encouragement. The wisest among my race," Washington continued, "understand that the agitation of questions of social equality is the extremest folly, and that progress in the enjoyment of all the privileges that will come to us must be the result of severe and constant struggle rather than of artificial forcing. No race that has anything to contribute to the markets of the world is long in any degree ostracized." Washington warned against the encouragement of foreign immigration into the South—"those of foreign birth and strange tongue and habits." White Southerners were exhorted: "Cast down your bucket among those people who have, without strikes and labor wars, tilled your fields, cleared your forests, built your railroads and cities, and brought forth treasures from the bowels of the earth, and helped make possible this magnificent representation of the progress of the South. . . . While doing this, you can be sure in the future, as in the past, that you and your families will be surrounded by the most patient, faithful, law-abiding and unresentful people that the world has seen . . . with a devotion that no foreigner can approach, ready to lay down our lives, if need be, in defense of yours, interlacing our industrial, commercial, civil and religious life with yours in a way that shall make the interests of both races one. In all things that are purely social we can be as separate as the fingers, yet one as the hand in all things essential to mutual progress."

He ended with a plea for the blotting out, with God's help, "of sectional differences and racial animosities and suspicions . . ." and "obedience among all classes to the mandates of the law. This, this, coupled with our material prosperity, will bring into our beloved South a new heaven and a new earth."

Rebuttals to Washington's speech by indignant blacks were not slow in coming. One of the most eloquent was that of John Hope. Son of a Scots father and mulatto mother, Hope had been witness at the age of eight to the Hamburg Massacre. In large part as a consequence of the massacre, his father moved to the North, and young Hope attended Worcester Academy, helping to pay his way by working as a waiter. Graduating from Brown University, he was appointed to the faculty of Atlanta Baptist College. Hope was particularly offended by Washington's frequent assurances that blacks were not seeking equality with whites. In a debate in Nashville on the occasion of George Washington's birthday, Hope delivered a scathing attack on all blacks who played down the issue of racial equality. "If we are not striving for equality," he asked his audience, "in heaven's name for what are we living? I regard it as cowardly and dishonest for any of our colored men to tell white people or colored people that we are not struggling for equality. If money, education, and honesty will not bring to me as much privilege, as much equality as they bring to any American citizen, then they are to me a curse, and not a blessing. . . . Let us not fool ourselves nor be fooled by others. If we cannot do what other free men do, then we are not free. Yes, my friends, I want equality. Nothing less. . . . Now, catch your breath, for I am going to use an adjective: I am going to say we demand social equality. . . . If equality, political, economic and social is the boon of other men in this great country of ours, of *ours*, then equality, political, economic and social is what we demand. Why build a wall to keep me out? I am no wild beast, nor am I an unclean thing.

"Rise, Brothers! Come let us possess this land. . . . Cease to console yourself with adages that numb the moral sense. Be discontented. Be dissatisfied. . . . Be as restless as the tempestuous billows on the boundless sea."

Another black politician who had been active in the period of

Reconstruction (he had been acting governor of Louisiana), Pinckney Benton Stewart Pinchback, was as outspoken as Hope. Pinchback was one of those blacks who retained substantial political power in their home states through close alliances with the Republican national organization and the power to distribute Federal patronage. He campaigned vigorously for McKinley's election and made, in that cause, a famous speech at Cooper Union. In it he argued the point that the Constitution specified that "The citizens of each state shall be entitled to all the privileges and immunities of citizens in the several states." These words, he declared, made the efforts of particular states to restrict the franchise, or pass "Jim Crow" laws, unconstitutional. It was "an insult and a wrong which should be resisted by the whole race with every lawful means at its command. . . . The ballot, in a government such as ours, is the palladium of the rights of the citizens. A voteless class has no rights that anybody is bound to respect. They are sure to become the footballs of demagogues and ambitious politicians to be kicked about hither and thither, and made the objects of contempt or ridicule. . . . Our cause is just and must prevail if we manfully, earnestly and judiciously appeal to the heart and conscience of the American people for redress of our grievances."

G. N. Grisham, principal of a high school in Kansas City, Missouri, took issue with what he believed to be Washington's implication that scholarship should be left to whites while blacks developed their "industrial" skills. He urged "the thinking Negro" to "contribute to magazines, write books and cooperate with learned societies . . . investigate and discover truths . . . attack evils, devise remedies and advocate reforms." In the past "detached" scholarship, pursued in ivory towers, might have been well enough, but the new scholarship had made itself an advocate of a wide range of social and economic reforms. "Scholarship," Grisham insisted, "cannot create and breathe in an atmosphere all its own. . . . The Negro scholar, untrammeled by traditional modes of thought and undazzled by glittering errors of the past, may be peculiarly fitted for that clear thinking and intellectual daring now demanded in the solution of the great problems of civilization."

A young black scholar who conformed almost ideally to Grisham's prescription was, at that moment, ready to make his appearance. William Edward Burghardt Du Bois grew up in Great Barrington, Massachusetts, a classic New England town, pervaded by the ethos of a gently decaying Puritanism. The Du Bois family were dark-skinned Puritans who accepted the values of the town without serious question.

They were, in fact, just those exemplary blacks turned white or white-blacks that New England missionaries had intended to produce when they went South.

Du Bois remembered Great Barrington as "a boy's paradise." There were mountains to climb and streams to fish in, frozen lakes for skating. His father was dead; his mother "brown and quietly persistent; the aunts and one uncle a bit censorious but not difficult to get on with; and then an endless vista of approving cousins." The members of his family were "small farmers, servants, laborers, barbers and waiters. They earned their way. I early came to understand that to be 'on the town,' the recipient of public charity, was the depth not only of misfortune but of a certain guilt." Restraint and control were admired attributes. "It was not good form in New England or in Great Barrington to express yourself volubly, to give way to emotion—people held themselves in," he wrote. "They were sparing even of their greetings." Du Bois learned the "habit of repression," and it stuck with him all his life, making him somewhat of an anomaly in the black South. The United States in the decades when he was growing up was, he observed, "an extraordinary country . . . reckless and prosperous, squandering its seemingly endless resources, tying east and west with railroads, exploiting coal and iron and oil and making fortunes for a new and ruthless caste of businessmen who were cashing in on the cost of the Civil War." Du Bois could see the results of the era in his own small town. "Wealth was the result of work and saving, and the rich rightly inherited the earth. The poor, on the whole, were to be blamed. They were lazy or unfortunate and, if unfortunate, their fortunes could easily be mended by thrift and sacrifice."

In 1885 at the age of seventeen, Du Bois received a scholarship to Fisk University in Tennessee. Despite the misgivings of his family about his venturing into the South, he found Fisk "an extraordinary experience, I was thrilled," he wrote, "to be for the first time among so many people of my own color or rather such various and such extraordinary colors, which I had not seen before, but who seemed close bound to me by new and exciting ties. I had never seen such beautiful girls in my life or men who gave themselves such merited airs. . . . The three years there were years of growth, strength, expanding ambition. I learned new things about the world. I came in contact for the first time with a sort of violence that I had never realized in New England."

Du Bois's first culture shock occurred in the black church service he attended. What most struck him in the manner of those approaching the plain little church was "the air of intense excitement" that possessed them. "A sort of suppressed terror hung in the air and seemed to seize us," he wrote in *The Souls of Black Folk*, "—a pythian madness, a demonic possession, that lent terrible reality to song and word. The black massive form of the preacher swayed and quivered as the words crowded to his lips and flew at us in singular eloquence. The people moaned and fluttered, and then the gaunt-cheeked brown woman beside me suddenly leaped into the air and shrieked like a lost soul, while round about came wail and groan and outcry, in a scene of human passion such as I had never conceived before."

Finally there was the "Frenzy or 'Shouting,' when the Spirit of the Lord passed by, and, seizing the devotee, made him mad with supernatural joy. . . . It varied in expression from the silent rapt countenance or the low murmur and moan to the mad abandon of physical fervor,— the stamping, shrieking, and shouting, the rushing to and fro and wild waving of arms, the weeping and laughing, the vision, and the trance." The study of Negro religion, Du Bois wrote, "is not only a vital part of the history of the Negro in America, but no uninteresting part of America. The Negro church of to-day is the social center of Negro life in the United States, and the most characteristic expression of African character. . . . Depravity, Sin, Redemption, Heaven, Hell, and Damnation are preached twice a Sunday with much fervor, and revivals take place every year after the crops are laid by; and few indeed of the community have the hardihood to withstand conversion. . . . Such churches are really governments of men. . . ." There was an organized black church for every sixty black families in the nation. Churches were the principal property owned by blacks.

The spirituals moved Du Bois profoundly. "Out of them," he wrote later in *The Souls of Black Folk*, "rose for me morning, noon and night, bursts of wonderful melody, full of the voices of my brothers and sisters, full of the voices of the past." If sorrow and despair marked them, they were also touched with hope.

Graduated from Fisk, Du Bois won a scholarship at Harvard, which had always been his goal. He entered those exalted precincts in the fall of 1888 as a junior. It was an intoxicating experience for a young man of intellectual bent. He was often a guest in William James's home. "Of all the teachers," Du Bois wrote, "he was my closest friend. I was a member of the philosophical club; I talked often with Royce and Shaler; I sat in an upper room and read Kant's *Critique* with

Santayana. . . ." In order to fill out their scholarships, Du Bois and a fellow black undergraduate, Clement Morgan, gave "readings" in hotels, parlors, and churches.

Even before he left Cambridge, Du Bois had begun speaking and writing on the "black question." As one of five students selected to speak at commencement, he chose the subject of Jefferson Davis, in order, as he later wrote, to face "Harvard and the nation with a discussion of slavery as illustrated in the person of the president of the Confederate States of America." The talk caused a mild sensation and led Episcopal Bishop Henry Codman Potter to write: "Here is what an historic race can do if they have a clear field, a high purpose, and a resolute will."

The talk was certainly a bold one. Du Bois described Davis as a decent and honorable man misled by the "Teutonic" notion of "the Strong Man." This archaic ideal turned him into a man who sought to advance civilization "now . . . by murdering Indians . . . hero of a national disgrace called by courtesy, the 'Mexican War'; and finally, as the crowning absurdity, the peculiar champion of a people fighting to be free in order that another people shall not be free." This "Strong Man" notion manifested itself as national policy. "The Strong Man and his mighty Right Arm has become the Strong Nation with its armies." The American's life could only be understood as the outgrowth of a philosophy which sought "the advance of a part of the world at the expense of the whole; the overweening sense of the 'I' and the consequence forgetting of the 'Thou.' "

Du Bois's next statement was directed at the Federal elections bill, introduced by another bright Harvard graduate in history, Senator Henry Cabot Lodge. Du Bois opposed the Lodge bill on the ground that its underlying assumption was false: "that if you have an evil in the community, all you have to do is pass a law against it, and presto, it is gone. We must ever keep before us the fact that the South has some excuse for its present attitude. We must remember that a good many of our people South of Mason and Dixon's line are not fit for the responsibilities of republican government. When you have the right sort of black voters you will need no election laws. The battle of my people in the South must be a moral one, not a legal or physical one."

For such sentiments Du Bois was taken to task by the able black editor of the *New York Age*, T. Thomas Fortune, who headed his rebuttal: "He Is Young Yet." Fortune dismissed Du Bois's argument as "humbug," adding, "Southern newspapers may praise Mr. Du Bois' remarks, but they represent simply the opinions of a very young man who will think and talk differently a few years hence."

Du Bois returned to Harvard after the obligatory year of study in Germany and earned his Ph.D. with a brilliant dissertation, "The Suppression of the African Slave Trade." He was offered a position as instructor in Latin and Greek at Wilberforce University in Ohio. There Du Bois, very much the dandy, with kid gloves and cane, began his academic career. There he met the poet Paul Laurence Dunbar, who came to Wilberforce to read his poems, and Du Bois, who knew his work, was delighted to find that he was black.

Wilberforce was a highly conservative black college the administration of which vetoed Du Bois's request to teach sociology and almost fired him for refusing to lead prayers in the college chapel. After two years at Wilberforce, Du Bois was appointed an instructor at the University of Pennsylvania. While there he was asked to undertake a study of the black Seventh Ward of the city of Philadelphia, which believed "that this great, rich and famous municipality, founded by godly Quakers was going to the dogs because of the crime and venality of its Negro citizens." He found the task an exacting one. "The Negroes," he noted, "resented being studied at all and especially by a colored stranger; the whites endured the study as a gesture toward an answer they already knew." Du Bois conceded that the rate of black crime had increased substantially since the war, but there were, he insisted, two explanations commonly overlooked by whites. Under slavery there had been, in effect, no black crime. All blacks of criminal tendencies were dealt with either on their own plantations or by a police system "designed primarily to control slaves," largely outside the law. Thus, with emancipation, blacks with tendencies to violence or theft suddenly appeared as crime statistics. In addition, the conditions of poverty and ignorance under which most urban blacks lived, debauched and preyed upon by white politicians, were such as to breed crime. The agencies of the law used primarily to intimidate them and impair their freedom appeared "as instruments of injustice and oppression," and many poor blacks looked "upon those convicted by them as martyrs and victims."

Perhaps most demoralizing of all to the great majority of blacks, in Du Bois's view, was the complete social segregation of the races. Gone was the close personal contact between blacks and whites that was part of everyday life under slavery. "In a world where it means so much to take a man by the hand and sit beside him, to look frankly into his eyes and feel his heart beating with red blood; in a world where a social cigar or a cup of tea together means more than legislative halls and magazine articles and speeches,—one can imagine the consequences of the almost utter absence of such social amenities between estranged races, whose separation extends even to parks and streetcars." Middle-class blacks especially suffered from the lack of "generous acknowledgment of a common humanity and a common destiny," where "the color-line comes to separate natural friends and co-workers." Ironically, it was only at the very bottom of the American society, "in the saloon, the gambling-hall, and the brothel," that the color line "wavers and disappears."

On the issue of work Du Bois sounded indistinguishable from Booker T. Washington: "Work, continuous and intensive; work, although it be menial and poorly rewarded; work, though done in travail of soul and sweat of brow, must be so impressed upon Negro children as the road to salvation, that a child would feel it a greater disgrace to be idle than to do the humblest labor. The homely virtues of honesty, truth and chastity must be instilled in the cradle. . . ." Equally important, "the better classes of the Negroes should recognize their duty toward the masses."

Du Bois addressed his readers in a poignant conclusion to his report on the Seventh Ward. "Two sorts of answers are usually returned," he wrote, "to the bewildered American who asks seriously: What is the Negro problem? The one straightforward and clear: it is simply this, or simply that, and one simple remedy long enough applied will in time cause it to disappear. The other answer is apt to be hopelessly involved and complex. . . ." It advances such bewildering questions "as to how far human intelligence can be trusted and trained; as to whether we must always have the poor with us; as to whether it is possible for the mass of men to attain righteousness on earth and then to this is added that question of questions: after all who are men? Is every featherless biped to be counted a man and brother? Are all races and types to be joint heirs of the new earth that men have striven to raise in thirty centuries and more?" The "still widening idea of common Humanity," Du Bois wrote, "is of slow growth and to-day but dimly realized." The Anglo-Saxon, the Teuton, the Latin all had been allowed within the pale; even the Celt and Slav admitted to its margins. It was half denied "the yellow races of Asia, but with the Negroes of Africa we come to a full-stop, and in its heart the civilized world with one accord denies that these come within the pale of nineteenth century

Humanity. This feeling, widespread and deep-seated, is, in America, the vastness of the Negro problems. . . ."

The result of Du Bois's researches was a remarkable work, running to more than 500 pages in print and meeting every criterion of the new scholarship. Supplemented by charts and statistics and by a detailed map of the area studied, it became an instant classic and remains a model of sociological inquiry. In Du Bois's words, "it showed the Negro group as a symptom and not a cause."

The problems that Du Bois examined in the black ghetto of Philadelphia—crime, poverty, ignorance, commercialized vice—were common, in varying degrees, to most large cities of the North and Midwest. They were, and would remain, the problems of the "black masses," where, paradoxically, all that is most characteristically "black" is also lodged.

From Pennsylvania, Du Bois was invited to Atlanta University, where he initiated studies of black urban life. To the idealistic young black man who had made his way in the white world, the problem of race relations was simply one of knowledge. Since man, whatever color his skin, was a rational creature, it followed that when white fallacies and misconceptions about blacks were proved false by scientific demonstration, prejudice would evaporate and the races would be reconciled. In Du Bois's words, "The Negro problem called for systematic investigation and intelligence. The world was thinking wrong about races because it did not know. The ultimate evil was ignorance and its child, stupidity. The cure for it was knowledge based on study." Du Bois was not unique, of course, in holding such views. They were the common stuff of intellectual discourse, the assumptions underlying the rapidly growing fields of sociology, history, anthropology, and economics—the social sciences.

A particular incident turned Du Bois away from his cloistered study. A black farmer named Sam Hose killed his landlord in a dispute over wages. Before he could be arrested and brought to trial, a mob lynched him. Du Bois, on his way to the *Atlanta Constitution* (the editor of which was then Joel Chandler Harris) with an article pleading for calm and for the observance of the processes of the law, was met with the grim news. Hose's knuckles were on display at a nearby grocery store. "I turned back to the university," he wrote, in recollection of the event. "I suddenly saw that complete scientific detachment in the midst of such a South was impossible." More and more Du Bois turned to the new journalism to present publicly, rather than in the small circle of academics, the cause of black Americans. His study *The Philadelphia Negro*, exemplary as it was, had done nothing to mitigate the condition of that city's black population. In addition, Du Bois had come to feel deeply that black culture had its own "soul," its own inner power and meaning. Its fate was not simply to be brushed aside or absorbed by white culture. It had an integrity that must be recognized and honored for what it was. The result was *The Souls of Black Folk*, an exploration of "the strange meaning of being black here at the dawning of the Twentieth Century . . . for the problem of the Twentieth Century is the problem of the color line." Du Bois sought to lift briefly "the Veil" concealing black life from the white world that surrounded and threatened to engulf it.

To Du Bois it was evident that the conversion of the slave into a free man had rendered "the white South . . . so much the more set and strengthened in its racial prejudice," which "crystallized . . . into harsh law and harsher custom" while the "marvelous pushing forward of the poor white daily threatened to take even bread and butter from the mouths of the . . . sons of the freedman." There was, in fact, a curious moral to be found in the rise of the "poor white," admittedly a loose category. It was this. The gentlemen rulers of the South held the poor white in perhaps greater contempt than they did the black slave, and the weight of this contempt kept the poor white in *his* form of servitude, poverty, and impotence. Once the power of the plantation aristocracy had been broken by the war and its aftermath, the poor white proved himself capable of making his way in a new society based on ambition and an eye for the main chance. Unimpeded by notions of what was appropriate for a gentleman to do, he turned his work-hardened hands to whatever tasks presented themselves—running a store, mining coal, cutting timber, following a plow—and in the process he exploited, with splendid impartiality, the old master class *and* the ex-slaves, whom he had always despised.

Du Bois listed as the distinguishing characteristics of black religion "the Preacher, the Music, and the Frenzy." The preacher was "the most unique personality developed by the Negro on American soil. A leader, a politician, an orator, a 'boss,' an intriguer, an idealist. . . ." The music was the soul of black folk, "the most original and beautiful expression of human life and longing yet born on American soil."

Du Bois believed that the role of the black preacher was a direct devolution from the tribal medicine man. He found his function on the slave plantation "as healer of the sick, the interpreter of the Unknown, the comforter of the sorrowing, the supernatural avenger of wrong, and the one who rudely but picturesquely expressed the longing, disappointment, and resentment of a stolen and oppressed people. Thus, as bard, physician, judge, and priest, within the narrow limits allowed by the slave system, rose the Negro preacher, and under him the first Afro-American institution, the Negro church." After the Civil War the African Methodist Church became "the greatest Negro organization in the world. . . ."

"In the Black World," Du Bois wrote, "the Preacher and Teacher embodied . . . the ideals of his people,—the strife for another and juster world, the vague dream of righteousness, the mystery of knowing. . . ." But such ideals "with their simple beauty and weird inspiration" were no longer sufficient; they were even an impediment to the psychological emancipation of black people.

The other crucial influence on Southern blacks was missionary teachers who had come South to open schools and to teach the freedmen and their children. The power of the missionary teachers, Du Bois wrote, was not simply or even mainly in the knowledge they brought but in their power to put their pupils in "sympathetic touch with the best traditions of New England. They lived and ate together, studied and worked, hoped and harkened in the dawning light. In actual formal content their curriculum was doubtless old-fashioned, but in educational power it was supreme, for it was the contact of living souls." From the seeds thus planted in love some 2,000 black graduates of both sexes had gone on to become teachers, ministers, doctors, and university professors, among many other occupations, and 400 won bachelor's degrees from Harvard, Yale, Oberlin, and seventy other leading white colleges and universities, in addition to those who graduated from black institutions. Fifty-three percent were teachers, Du Bois reported, "presidents of institutions, heads of normal schools, principals of city school-systems, and the like. Seventeen percent were clergymen; another seventeen percent were in the professions, chiefly as physicians. Over six percent were merchants, farmers and artisans, and four percent were in the government civil-service. . . . I cannot hesitate in saying," he added, "that nowhere have I met men and women with a broader spirit of helpfulness, with deeper devotion to their life-work, or with more consecrated determination to succeed in the face of bitter difficulties than among Negro college-bred men. . . ."

"They made their mistakes," Du Bois wrote, "those who planted

Fisk and Howard and Atlanta. . . ." But they were right "when they sought to found a new educational system upon the University; where forsooth, shall we ground knowledge save on the broadest and deepest knowledge? The roots of the tree, rather than the leaves, are the sources of its life. . . ." The founders overlooked the fact that not all blacks, as not all whites, had the mental capacities to absorb higher education. They failed to make necessary distinctions between those whose intellect was best suited to manual labor and those who were capable of advanced study. "The function of the university," Du Bois wrote, "is not simply to teach bread-winning [as Washington seemed disposed to argue] or to furnish teachers for the public schools or to be a center of polite society; it is, above all, to be the organ of that fine adjustment between real life and the growing knowledge of life, an adjustment which forms the secret of civilization."

Certainly the black colleges of the South supported by Northern churches made an impressive list; Berea College in Kentucky, Fisk University at Nashville, Atlanta University, Tougaloo University in Mississippi, Talladega College in Alabama, Straight University at New Orleans, and Tillotson College in Texas were all founded and maintained by the American Missionary Association.

"The worlds within and without the Veil of Color are changing, and changing rapidly," Du Bois wrote, "but not at the same rate, not in the same way, and this must produce a peculiar wrenching of the soul, a peculiar sense of doubt and bewilderment. Such a double life with double-thoughts, double duties, and double social classes, must give rise to double words and double ideals, and temper the mind to pretence or revolt, to hypocrisy or radicalism." Hypocrisy threatened black Southerners, who must be amiable buffoons or docile slaves in all but name, must fawn and flatter to survive. Radicalism was the refuge of the Northern black. "Driven from his birthright in the South by a situation at which every fibre of his more outspoken and assertive nature revolts, he finds himself in a land where he can scarcely earn a decent living amid the harsh competition and the color discrimination. At the same time, through schools and periodicals, discussions and lectures, he is intellectually quickened and awakened. The soul, long pent up and dwarfed, suddenly expands in new-found freedom. What wonder the tendency is to excess,—radical complaint, radical remedies, bitter denunciation or angry silence." Northern blacks despised "the submission and subserviency of the Southern Negroes" but had no better suggestions on any other means "by which a poor and oppressed minority can exist side by side with its masters."

Finally, and perhaps most tellingly, Du Bois described the essential quality of being a black American—black consciousness. The black American was a "sort of seventh son, born with a veil, and gifted with second-sight in this American world." He wrote: "It is a peculiar sensation, this double-consciousness, this sense of always looking at one's self through the eyes of others, of measuring one's soul by the tape of a world that looks on in amused contempt and pity. One ever feels his two-ness,—an American, a Negro; two souls, two thoughts, two unreconciled strivings; two warring ideals in one dark body, whose dogged strength alone keeps it from being torn asunder." The black man "would not bleach his Negro soul in a flood of white Americanism," Du Bois concluded, "for he knows that Negro blood has a message for the world. He simply wishes to make it possible for a man to be both a Negro and an American, without being cursed and spit upon by his fellows, without having the door of Opportunity closed roughly in his face."

Like all great books, *The Souls of Black Folk* is distinguished by a style of singular power and eloquence. Inspired in part by the black spiritual, it is a kind of song of sorrow and anger or the translation of a song (it ends with a chapter entitled "Sorrow Songs"), a litany, a lament. "The Nation has not yet found peace from its sins; the freedman has not yet found in freedom his promised land. Whatever good may have come in these years of change, the shadow of a deep disappointment rests upon the Negro people,—a disappointment more bitter because the untainted ideal was unbounded save by the simple ignorance of a lowly people." So it was song after all: "We the darker ones come even now not altogether empty-handed: there are to-day no truer exponents of the pure human spirit of the Declaration of Independence than the American Negroes; there is no true American music but the wild sweet melodies of the Negro slave . . . and, all in all, we black men seem the sole oasis of simple faith and reverence in a dusty desert of dollars and smartness. Will America be poorer if she replace her brutal dyspeptic blundering with light-hearted but determined Negro humility? or her coarse and cruel wit with loving jovial good-humor? or her vulgar music with the soul of the Sorrow Songs?" Song as it is, *The Souls of Black Folk* has all the requisite history in it as well. There are echoes of Whitman, tones of Emerson. "I have seen a land right merry with the sun, where children sing, and rolling hills lie like passioned women wanton with harvest." Beside the road sits a veiled and silent figure, waiting for "the unveiling of that bowed human heart. . . . The problem of the Twentieth Century is the problem of the color-line."

The *Souls of Black Folk* belongs with *Uncle Tom's Cabin* in the literature of the relations between the black and white races in America. Harriet Beecher Stowe's genius had been to enlarge white consciousness to include the common humanness of slaves and do it so vividly that those who read *Uncle Tom's Cabin* could never again think of black people as less than fully human. The genius of Du Bois was to create (or define) black consciousness for black people. His book became a Bible, a credo, a source text for American blacks; for black people everywhere in the world. James Weldon Johnson, the black poet and leader, wrote that it had "a greater effect upon and within the Negro race in America than any other single book published in this country since *Uncle Tom's Cabin*," and almost fifty years later the South African black writer Peter Abrahams noted that it had on him "the impact of revelation . . . a key to the understanding of my world."

The chapter that caused the greatest sensation at the time of the publication of *The Souls of Black Folk* was Du Bois's attack on Booker T. Washington. Although Du Bois at thirty-five was only twelve years younger than Washington, he spoke for a new generation of Northern blacks (one could not call them leaders, for few of them had a real constituency among the mass of blacks). "Easily the most striking thing in the history of the American Negro since 1876," he wrote, "is the ascendancy of Mr. Booker T. Washington." Washington had emerged, in Du Bois's view, "at the psychological moment when the nation was a little ashamed at having bestowed so much sentiment on Negroes, and was concentrating its energies on dollars. His programme of industrial education, conciliation of the South and submission and silence . . . was ideally suited to the post-Reconstruction mood of the South" and, indeed, of the country as a whole. "To gain the sympathy and coöperation of the various elements of the white South was Mr. Washington's first task; and this, at the time Tuskegee was founded, seemed, for a black man, well-nigh impossible." Yet Washington by "unlimited energy and perfect faith" had made his so-called program "into a veritable Way of Life." The result had been the "Atlanta Compromise," which made its author "the most distinguished Southerner since Jefferson Davis, and the one with the largest personal following."

But Washington in his success, Du Bois charged, learned "the speech and thought of triumphant commercialism, and the ideals of material prosperity" so thoroughly that he was ready to sacrifice all black aspirations for higher things. There was, Du Bois insisted, "among educated and thoughtful colored men in all parts of the land a feeling of deep regret, sorrow, and apprehension at the wide currency and ascendancy which some of Mr. Washington's theories have gained." The tacit bargain that Du Bois believed Washington had struck with the white South was that Southern blacks would acquiesce in the loss of their civil rights if they received in return "larger chances of economic development." Submission in such a policy had resulted in the loss of political power, the drastic curtailment of civil rights, and "the steady withdrawal of aid from institutions for the higher training of the Negro."

What Washington had failed to understand was that "it is utterly impossible, under modern competitive methods, for workingmen and property-owners to defend their rights and exist without the right of suffrage." The result of Washington's program of submission was that there were "two classes of colored Americans." Those in the class made up of militant blacks in the tradition of Denmark Vesey and Nat Turner "represent the attitude of revolt and revenge; they hate the white South blindly and distrust the white race generally. . . ." The one thing they agreed on was "that the Negro's only hope lies in emigration beyond the borders of the United States." But the long arm of American power had recently manifested itself in the suppression and killing of "weaker and darker peoples in the West Indies, Hawaii, and the Philippines," so that the question that radical black advocates of emigration had to ask was: "Where in the world may we go and be safe from lying and brute force?" The policy of submission was clearly a failure, Du Bois declared. It had simply facilitated the stripping away of all black rights. The time had come for a radically different policy. "Negroes must insist continually, in season and out of season, that voting is necessary to modern manhood, that color discrimination is barbarism, and that black boys need education as well as white boys." To keep silent was to encourage criminal behavior on a national scale; "it is wrong to aid and abet a national crime simply because it is unpopular not to do so." Worst of all, Washington's doctrines had tended to make "the white, North and South, shift the burden of the Negro problem to the Negro's shoulders and stand aside as critical and rather pessimistic spectators." The North could not buy out of its own guilt by contributions to black causes. The real question extended far beyond the desperate plight of black Americans. Simply put, it was: "Can the moral fiber of this country survive the slow throttling and murder of nine millions of men?"

It was now the duty of "the black men of America . . . to oppose a part of the work of their greatest leader. So far as Mr. Washington preaches Thrift, Patience, and Industrial Training for the masses," Du Bois concluded, "we must hold up his hands and strive with him, rejoicing in his honors and glorying in the strength of this Joshua called of God and of man to lead the headless host. But so far as Mr. Washington apologizes for injustice, North or South, does not rightly value the privilege and duty of voting, belittles the emasculating effects of caste distinctions, and opposes the higher training and ambitions of our brighter minds—so far as he, the South, or the Nation does this,—we must unceasingly and firmly oppose them." It was unfortunate that Booker T. Washington's reputation was embalmed in a work of such wide influence. While Du Bois was carefully respectful of Washington's accomplishments for black people, he was nonetheless unfair to Washington in several important respects. First, Washington was not opposed to "higher education" for bright young blacks; he did his best on numerous occasions to advance the careers of such young men. He took the line that in view of the actual situation of the mass of Southern blacks the teaching of practical skills was more important than a conventional liberal education. Beyond that he entered in good faith into a kind of compact with the white South. When Southern leaders assured Washington that the white South would accept blacks as their at least political and economic equals when, by thrift and industry, they had proved themselves worthy, Washington took their promises at face value. But, like so many others of his race, he underestimated the depth and intensity of white hostility. As it became more and more apparent to even the most casual observer that all such hopes for white acceptance were chimerical, Washington clung doggedly to his "programme." To renounce it would have been to call into question all that he had stood for and to admit that he had been gulled and betrayed by his white friends. Instead, Washington became increasingly defensive, fighting back with all the very considerable weapons at his command and not scrupling to use his friendship with rich and powerful whites—Roosevelt and Carnegie among them—to protect his own position. His power and his prestige were, in fact, remarkable. After the death of Douglass in 1895, Washington reigned supreme over black America.

If black intellectuals, following the lead of Du Bois, were increasingly critical and alienated, the vast majority of American blacks, North and South, clearly took great pride in his fame and bowed to his leadership.

The tragedy of Booker T. Washington was that a policy that in the context of the time when it was first conceived made considerable sense and may indeed have been the only possible program was, like virtually every other program or policy proposed by blacks or friendly whites to improve the situation of black people in America, rendered nugatory by the massive and impenetrable wall of white prejudice, which was evident with varying degrees of intensity in every part of the nation and at every level of American life.

There was clearly more to Tuskegee and to Washington's philosophy than mere accommodation and black "improvement." Washington argued that there was a worth and dignity in labor—"hand training"—which, when combined with "moral, religious, and mental education," need yield nothing in worth or dignity to traditional liberal education with its exclusive emphasis on training the intellect alone. Teaching rather than scholarship was the heart of Tuskegee, Washington insisted. Farming, mechanical drawing, blacksmithing, wood turning, construction, typesetting, furniture making, shoe and mattress making were the practical skills needed by black men and women in the South. As a graduate of Hampton Institute Washington had learned the satisfactions of working with his hands, of a well-planted vegetable bed and a well-cooked meal. Most of the black colleges started by Northern whites in the South offered their black pupils a curriculum indistinguishable from that of Northern liberal arts institutions—Latin and Greek, French and German, arithmetic and algebra, geography, art, instrumental music, and modern European history, subjects which in Washington's view served to increase the alienation of such schools' graduates from the needs and interests of their fellow blacks and to result in frustration for those graduates who tried to enter the white-dominated fields for which their education had presumably fitted them.

Critics of Washington have argued that he accepted too uncritically the individualistic success ethic of white America and paid too little attention to ideas of racial solidarity and cooperative action, but it must be said in his defense that he had little choice. As we have seen, the white South was disposed to resist to the point of violence any black effort at collective action. The facts of black life in the South were substantially as Washington described them. What he could not foresee or bring himself to accept, even as the evidence mounted on every side, was that the white South not only was unwilling to let able blacks rise but was determined to force them ever deeper into submission and subordination.

Much of the present-day discussion about Washington's educational and racial philosophy fails to take into account that he *had no alternative.* For the place and time his doctrine that blacks must win the confidence and friendship of whites in order to make even modest progress was unassailably true. Those who came to differ with him lived, almost without exception, outside the South. At the very least they did not have to protect an institution—Tuskegee—for which they had the primary, if not the sole, responsibility. The value of Washington's leadership can be measured, in the final analysis, only by the lives of the men and women who graduated from Tuskegee Normal and Industrial Institute (and in many instances went on to further study)— the teachers, preachers, lawyers, doctors, and black leaders generally who performed essential services for their people under the most discouraging circumstances.

The passage of time made Washington's policy increasingly reactionary, and it was essential that his spell over the mass of his people be, if not broken, at least challenged so that a new and more militant spirit could in time take its place.

Du Bois, being human, had limitations to his own vision. He was perhaps too wedded to the ideal vision of a liberal education that he had experienced at Harvard in that comparatively brief moment when the Harvard of James and Royce throbbed with intellectual life. His notion of leadership of American blacks passing from the hands of the autocratic Washington to "the talented tenth" of educated blacks, ignored the grass-roots nature of all viable democratic leadership and gave more weight to the role of intellectuals than a thoughtful examination of history would perhaps justify.

A striking fact of black life was the growing migration from the rural South to the West and to the cities of the North. Delayed for a time by the hopes engendered in the Reconstruction Era, the movement began in earnest in the 1870s with the support, at least initially, of many black leaders. In 1879 Frederick Douglass praised black Americans for eschewing violence and meeting repression in the South by "a simple, lawful and peaceable measure"—emigration, "the quiet withdrawal of his valuable bones and muscles from a condition of things which he considers no longer tolerable. . . . This Exodus has revealed to Southern men the humiliating fact that the prosperity and civilization of the South are at the mercy of the despised and hated Negro." Yet Douglass eventually came to believe the exodus was "ill-timed and in some respects hurtful." He was convinced that a kind of national change of heart favorable to the cause of black Americans was in the air: a curtailment of states' rights; a reassertion of constitutional/Federal authority to protect the lives and property of black people in the South and elsewhere. "National ideas," he declared, "are springing up all around us; the oppressor of the Negro is seen to be the enemy of the peace, prosperity and honor of the country . . . the sceptre of political power must soon pass from the party of reaction, revolution, rebellion and slavery, to the party of constitution, liberty and progress." In a time "so full of hope and courage" it was unfortunate to abandon the field of battle. Moreover, to leave the South would be to abandon that region forever to the Democratic Party with fateful consequences for the nation.

Richard Greener was a warm advocate of emigration or exodus. He had been born in Philadelphia, but his family moved to Boston when he was five. He was educated at Phillips Andover Academy and graduated first from Oberlin and then from Harvard, where, at the age of twenty-six, he received the first B.A. given a black man by that institution. Professor of metaphysics and logic at the University of Columbia, South Carolina, until it was closed at the end of Reconstruction, he became first law instructor at Howard and then dean; he resigned to practice law and to lecture. Greener was convinced that the emigration of Southern blacks would bring the South to respect the rights of those blacks who remained lest the whites be left without a labor force. He assumed "that the predominance of the Negro in politics in the South is gone for a generation at least. The South will not have it and the North has exhibited no very marked disposition to enforce it."

But Greener had the West in mind for the exodus rather than the Northeast, and the West proved thoroughly intractable. In a time when agricultural prices were falling constantly and tens of thousands of experienced farmers were being forced off the soil, it was utopian to believe that blacks, whose agricultural experience was limited in large part to a single cash crop, cotton, who had no capital and no "support system," could thrive or even survive. Where agricultural colonies of Russian and Polish Jews, of Italian peasants, and of German farmers failed by the score, the black exodus could hardly have done otherwise.

It soon shifted to Northern cities, at first a trickle and then a stream. To the warnings of black leaders and Southern whites, apprehensive at losing their labor force, one black journalist replied: "My relatives and friends who have gone North since the war tell a different story. They have held no offices, but they are free. They sleep in peace at night; what they earn is paid them, if not they can appeal to the courts. They vote without fear of the shot-gun, and their children go to school. It is true that the Northerner people do not love us so well as you did, and hence the mixture of races is not so promiscuous there as here. This we shall try to endure, if we go North, with patience and Christian resignation."

Henry Turner, minister in the Israel Bethel Church in Washington, D.C., had enlisted as chaplain in one of the first black regiments formed during the Civil War. He had been with Sherman in Georgia and after the war had moved to Georgia, first to start a school and then to play a prominent role in Reconstruction politics. He was a leading figure in drafting the Reconstruction Constitution of Georgia and one of the most powerful of all black orators. Embittered by the end of Reconstruction and the campaign against the rights of the freedmen in every Southern state, Turner took up residence in the North. It was as though he and his people had been given a glimpse of the promised land and then been turned back to wander once again in the wilderness of white America. When the Supreme Court, in a series of decisions starting with the Slaughterhouse Cases in 1873 through the so-called Granger Cases, made it evident that a majority of the justices were unequivocally committed to the doctrine of states' rights, Turner began to advocate black emigration from the United States and called on advocates of "African reparation or Negro nationalism elsewhere" to meet in Cincinnati. Opponents of emigration—Turner referred to them contemptuously as the "stay-at-home portion"—were in the majority. Turner, to preserve the appearance of unity, accepted a series of resolutions expressing the indignation of the delegates at the rising tide of racial prejudice in the country. Those present agreed to call a convention of the National Council of Colored Men to draw up a more formal protest against "the dreadful, horrible, anomalous and unprecedented conditions of our people in the United States" and, in reference to the rising tide of lynchings, against "the revolting, hideous, monstrous, unnatural, brutal and shocking crimes charged upon us daily . . . and the reign of mobs, lynchers, and fire fiends, and midnight and midday assassins. . . ."

The overthrow of the Civil Rights Act of 1875 had "decitizenized us," Turner declared. "The Goddess of Liberty, which ornaments the dome of our national capitol . . . has been transformed into a lying strumpet so far as she symbolizes the civil liberty of the black man. . . ." Congress and the Supreme Court had both "dumped the Negro." Turner declared: "Unless this nation, north and south, east and west, awakes from its slumber and calls a halt to the reign of blood and carnage in this land, its dissolution and utter extermination is only a question of a short time . . . the United States will never celebrate another centennial of undivided states, without a change of program. A Negro is a very small item in the politics of this country, but his groans, prayers and innocent blood will speak to God day and night, and the God of the poor and helpless will come to his relief sooner or later and another fratricidal war will be the sequel. . . ."

Was it remarkable, in the face of such rank injustice, that black leaders should support emigration? he asked. "I am abused as no other man in this nation," Turner declared, "because I am an African Emigrationist." It was not for that that he had risen to speak, however, and he was not without gratitude to "our generous-hearted friends of the North" or, indeed, to those white Southerners who had labored in the cause of justice for black people, but "to passively remain here and occupy our present ignoble status . . . would be to declare ourselves unfit to be free men. . . . For God hates the submission of cowardice." Outnumbered as they were, physical resistance was "literal madness." There were, furthermore, no grounds to "expect better times for the Negro in this country, but . . . to the contrary, we are being more and more degraded by legislative enactments and judicial decisions."

Some of the "emigrationists" favored "partial African emigration"; others preferred Mexico, Canada, or South or Central America. A small but vocal faction called for a portion of the United States to be set aside as a black nation.

After the lynching of three young blacks in Memphis, Ida Wells, the black woman editor, wrote in *Free Speech*: "The city of Memphis has demonstrated that neither character nor standing avails the Negro if he dares to protect himself against the white man or become his rival. There is nothing we can do about the lynching now, as we are out-numbered and without arms. The white mob could help itself to ammunition without pay, but the order was rigidly enforced against the selling of guns to Negroes. There is therefore only one thing left that we can do; save our money and leave a town which will neither protect our lives and property, nor give us a fair trial in the courts, but takes us out and murders us in cold blood when accused by white persons." Wells proposed that Memphis blacks refuse to ride on the city's handsome new electric railway or deal in white stores. "Business," she wrote, "was practically at a standstill, for the Negro was famous . . . for spending his money for fine clothes, furniture, jewelry, and pianos and other musical instruments, to say nothing of good things to eat." So effective was the boycott of the streetcars that the superintendent of the City Railway Company came to Ida Wells to ask her to use her influence to get Memphis blacks to ride on them once more. Wells urged the city's blacks to hold firm and took pains to enlist the support of the largest black churches in Memphis. In addition, many of those Memphis blacks who could afford to do so left the city, and others refused to work for white employers. Dismayed housewives found themselves without black cooks or maids. As the black evacuation grew in numbers, white newspapers, alarmed at the dwindling supply of cheap labor, published lurid stories of hardships in the West and, above all, the dangers from the Indians. Under such headings as "The New Promised Land, Unlike Old Canaan. It Doesn't Flow with Milk and Honey," the white newspapers tried to discourage emigration of blacks.

The principal result of the "exodus" was that the black sections of Northern cities—Philadelphia and New York most conspicuously—grew substantially. The tensions that developed between the older "respectable" middle-class blacks, who, in some instances had been living in the Northern cities for several generations, and the newcomers were reminiscent of the tensions between the German Jews and the Eastern European newcomers. What were referred to as the "black-and-tan" slums of Thompson and Sullivan streets in New York City were, in the words of Jacob Riis, a far cry from the "clear and orderly community . . . of colored people that is growing up on the East Side from Yorkville to Harlem." The black's "home surroundings, except when he is utterly depraved," Riis added, "reflect his blithesome temper. The poorest negro house-keeper's room in New York is bright with gaily-colored prints of his beloved 'Abe Linkum,' General Grant, President Garfield, Mrs. Cleveland, and other national celebrities, and cheery with flowers and singing birds. In the art of putting the best foot foremost, of disguising his poverty by making a little go a long way, our negro has no equal. . . ." Playing the numbers was his favorite recreation. "Penniless, but with undaunted faith in his ultimate 'luck,' he looks forward to the time when he shall once more be able to take a hand at 'beating policy.' "

One consequence of black immigration into the North was growing resistance on the part of unions to accepting black members or to working alongside members of black unions or simply beside blacks. When one of Frederick Douglass's sons, Lewis, who had learned the printing trade setting type for his father's newspaper, got a job in the Government Printing Office, the white printers walked off the job. His father wrote: "He is not condemned because he is not a good printer, but because he did not become such in a regular way, that regular way [union membership] being closed against him by the men now opposing him. There is no disguising the fact—his crime was his color."

In Baltimore shipbuilders employed more than 1,000 blacks in the yards; white workers struck to force their firing. One of the black workers, Isaac Myers, hit on the scheme of getting his fellow shipbuilders to buy a shipyard. By appealing to black churches, he raised $10,000, purchased a shipyard, and soon had more than 300 calkers and carpenters at work. Within five years, as the result of government contracts, the debts of the yard were paid off. Myers, a light-complexioned, powerfully built man with a walrus mustache, went on to form the black Maryland State Labor Union. In 1869 he was invited to attend a white trade union convention. There the delegates voted to support the formation of black unions which might then affiliate with the National Labor Union. Myers appealed to black artisans to "lay by a small sum weekly for the purchase of the necessary tools"; then, with his labor as capital, the black worker could "go out and build houses, forge iron, make bricks, run factories, work plantations, etc." Such unions could become promoters of "the moral, social, intellectual and industrial welfare of our people."

One of the principal sources of tension between white and black unions was that a number of the white unions, inspired by Karl Marx's International Workingmen's Association, had organized the Labor Reform Party to do battle with those employers they believed to be capitalist exploiters. The disposition of the black union leaders was far more conciliatory. Isaac Myers declared to a Richmond convention that the Colored National Labor Union wished "to establish the most friendly relationship between labor and capital, because we believe their interests to be inseparable." Myers knew of a shop where the workers received $3.25 per day and a percentage of their output. "The result is," he declared, "the shop turns out a third more work than any other establishment of the same kind in the State." Unless black workers organized, Myers warned, "in a few short years the trades will pass from your hands—you [will] become the servants of servants, the sweepers of shavings, the scrapers of pitch and the carriers of mortar." So far from trusting the good intentions of the white unions, Myers was convinced that behind their public declarations of a desire to co-operate they were "organized for the extermination of colored labor."

In 1870 Frederick Douglass was made president of the Colored National Labor Union, but even he was unable to make headway against the growing resistance of white unions and the doubts among educated blacks. Richard Greener was a spokesman for the latter group when he wrote to challenge Douglass for identifying himself with "a colored offshoot of the notorious *Internationale* which proposes to overthrow stable government in England and give us a mobocracy in America." Greener confessed that he had yet to read a clear statement of the union's objectives, "from its high priest, Karl Marx, down to Myers in America . . . ," but he suspected that they wished to do no more than to relieve themselves of the burden of doing an honest day's work. Under the circumstances it is not surprising that the Colored National Labor Union was short-lived, expiring in 1872.

Black efforts to unionize continued, and when an Alabama newspaper editor denounced "The Folly, Tyranny and Wickedness of Labor Unions," a black labor organizer replied that the unions in the state of Alabama were "intended to do for the laboring masses what they are not as individuals capable of doing for themselves—that is, they have men in whom they confide to investigate and supervise their contracts and see that their interests are not compromised." The black washerwomen of Atlanta, Georgia, formed a union in 1880, and 3,000 of them struck a year later. The strike was broken by the combined efforts of the police, who did not scruple to arrest picketing women, and the owners of the strikers' homes, who threatened to turn them out into the streets.

For those blacks of the exodus who went West, the story was little different. At the end of Albion Tourgée's *Bricks Without Straw*, the hero, Colonel Servosse, and his wife watch a band of former slaves setting out for Kansas. These were the famous "Exodusters," the nucleus of a black farming community. Some moved on to Nebraska to build the classic sod houses that marked that frontier state's treeless prairies. Benjamin Singleton, a hero of the underground railroad who organized much of the exodus to Kansas, declared, "I am the whole cause of the Kansas migration." The exodus caused a crisis in Kansas when thousands of penniless blacks of all ages began arriving. A hundred thousand dollars were collected from residents of the state to help the newcomers get established. Philip Armour, the meat-packing tycoon, collected money from fellow capitalists in Chicago and contributed meat from his plant as well. At the settlement of Nicodemus, a black colony suffered from repeated crop failures and the brutal winters that stripped away the topsoil. A band of 150 black settlers was driven out of Lincoln, Nebraska, but others fared better. Dr. M. O. Ricketts was an ex-slave who had graduated from the University of Nebraska College of Medicine. He and five other blacks were elected to the state legislature before the end of the century. It was axiomatic that those ex-slaves who found their way to communities with a strong abolitionist tradition were received hospitably. O. J. Jackson was one of the founders of the town of Deerfield, Colorado, and black homesteaders settled in some numbers in Cherry County, Nebraska. Denver had a black population, although the state Constitution, passed in 1865, denied the vote to blacks. Barney Ford built and ran the Inter-Ocean hotels in Denver and Cheyenne and was the first black man to serve on a Colorado grand jury, while his friend Henry Wagoner became a deputy sheriff in Arapahoe County, Colorado.

Other blacks became cowboys. Britton Johnson, "a shining jet black negro of splendid physique," as a contemporary described him, was known as the best shot on the Texas frontier. He and three other black cowboys were killed by a party of Comanche and Iowa Indians. Cowboy Jim Taylor was a well-known figure in Utah, where he married a Ute woman. Nat Love, known as Deadwood Dick to the readers of penny dreadfuls, was a familiar figure in Dodge City, a cowpuncher, an Indian fighter, and a friend of Bat Masterson and the Jameses. Cherokee Bill was one of the most feared outlaws and gunfighters in the Oklahoma Territory. Bill Pickett was described by a rancher for whom he worked as "the greatest sweat and dirt cowhand that ever lived—bar none." It was Pickett, a famous rodeo rider, who was credited with inventing bulldogging—leaping from a running horse to a steer's horns and throwing the racing animal on its back. Pickett became a rodeo performer with Tom Mix and Will Rogers, his assistants for a time.

The Oklahoma Territory, a refuge for Indians, attracted a number of black settlers as well. Indian and black farm families frequently intermarried. Year after year white settlers—boomers—led by the indefatigable David Payne, had tried to squat on lands given the Indians at the time of the Great Removal, and year after year they had been rounded up, often by the black 9th Cavalry, and escorted out. Finally, in 1889, the government had yielded to the unrelenting pressure and opened the unoccupied territory to settlers, some of whom, "sooners," had already scouted out prospective claims. The opening of the territory was doubtless the single most dramatic event of the closing decades of the century in the West. For weeks wagons and riders collected to await the firing of the cannon that would signal its official opening at noon on April 22, 1889. When the gun was fired, a mad stampede started to stake out claims. Among the thousands who poured into the land were an estimated 10,000 blacks. The number may be exaggerated; but within twenty years twenty-five black communities had been founded, and the state had a population of 137,000 blacks, the largest black population in any Western state, California excepted. Boley, Oklahoma, with a population of 4,000, seemed to Booker T. Washington an ideal black community when he visited it in 1905.

Uncle Jesse, the town poet, wrote:

> Say, have you heard the story,
> Of a little colored town,
> Way over in the Nation
> On such lovely sloping ground?
>
> • • •
>
> With not a thing but colored folks
> A-standing in the streets?
> Oh, 'tis a pretty country
> And the Negroes own it, too
> With not a single white man here
> To tell us what to do—in Boley

As long as Oklahoma was a territory, blacks enjoyed the protection of the United States government; but racial feeling ran high, and black leaders were afraid that with the coming of statehood they would be defenseless against the hostility of their white neighbors. The Western Negro Press Association meeting in Muskogee, Oklahoma, in 1902 wired President Roosevelt urging him to deny statehood to Oklahoma until its political leaders eschewed all laws directed at curtailing the rights of blacks. Roosevelt did not respond, and soon after Oklahoma entered the Union in 1907, it enacted the classic grandfather clause, adopted by other Southern states, which effectively disfranchised Oklahoma blacks. For black Oklahomans it was the end of their dream of equal citizenship; many, disheartened by the rising tide of prejudice and persecution and finding themselves sharecroppers on white land, slipping into a form of peonage hardly distinguishable from slavery, headed East for the large cities of the North, where prejudice, although present, was less obvious and less abrasive.

The most terrible manifestation of white hatred for blacks was the institution of lynching. Year after year hundreds of blacks of both sexes were lynched by white mobs. It must, of course, be noted that lynching was not invented for the benefit of blacks. Americans had been addicted to lynching, especially in the West, for generations. In the period of slavery whites had generally lynched each other since slaves were valuable property. After the Civil War Southern whites of the lynching disposition gave their more or less undivided attention to blacks.

William Sinclair, the black historian, wrote in 1905 that the refusal of the South to accept the freed black as fully human had resulted in an atmosphere where "mobs torture human beings and roast them alive without trial and in defiance of law and order; mobs shoot down women and children who have never been charged with crime, and against whom there is no suspicion,—it is enough that they are negroes. Mobs take possession of the streets of great cities and assault and shoot down innocent colored people, driving them from their homes and burning their property. . . . Mobs intercept and hold up the regularly constituted officers of the law, take prisoners from their possession and shoot them to death. Mobs break into jails and take out prisoners and hang them, sometimes in the jail yard, and riddle their bodies with bullets. Mobs even invade the sacred precincts of the court-room, and during the actual process of the trial, take prisoners from the custody of the lawful authorities and shoot them in the very temple of justice. . . . In one instance sixteen colored men were shot to death on the floor of the court-room in Mississippi, during the actual processes of the trial of two colored men charged with a minor offence."

In 1892, 235 "untried Negroes," to use W. E. B. Du Bois's words, were slaughtered by lynch mobs. The day after Sam Hose had been burned to death in Atlanta, Willis Sees, at Osceola, Arkansas, was hanged on suspicion of barn burning. In 1894, three women were lynched in three different Southern states. In February, 1898, at Lake City, South Carolina, a white mob broke into the home of the town's black postmaster, killed him and an infant child, seriously wounded his wife and three daughters and son, and then burned the post office and his house. Although the postmaster was a Federal official, McKinley's administration made no effort to punish the murderers.

In Palmetto, Georgia, a mob broke into the town jail and killed four alleged black arsonists and wounded four others. Alexander Walters, bishop of the African Methodist Episcopal Church, was moved by the episode to denounce the notion that all blacks had to do was prove themselves worthy in order to be accepted as equals by whites. "The real cause of our trouble," he declared in a talk at Jersey City, "is race hatred. Some years ago it was thought that as the Negroes became intelligent and cultured this race prejudice would disappear; but in some sections of this country it has only intensified this feeling. The passing of the Jim Crow-car laws in several of the Southern states; the disenfranchisement of Negroes, regardless of qualifications; the shutting-out of them from hotels, restaurants, and places of amusement, are all manifestations of race hatred. We are censored as a race for not exhibiting manly qualities and are considered 'impudent niggers' if we presume to assert our manhood. . . . In the name of almighty God, what are we to do but fight and die?"

Even United States soldiers were not immune. In Huntsville, Alabama, where the 10th Cavalry was stationed after its return from Cuba, some of the citizens of the town offered a reward for every black soldier killed. Two U.S. soldiers were murdered.

It was common, not to say routine, for a white woman charged with or even suspected of having had sexual intercourse with a black man to assert that she had been raped. The consequences were frequently a lynching without the pretense of a trial. In Texarkana, Arkansas, Ed Coy, a black man, was burned to death on suspicion of rape. Afterward, Judge Albion Tourgée established that the woman making the accusation had been forced to do so by a white mob and made to set the match to his pyre. White rapists who had blacked their hands and faces in order to throw blame on blacks were occasionally apprehended. Often the courts were little better than the mobs. Ed Aiken, a nineteen-year-old black, was sentenced to ten years on a Georgia chain gang for frightening a white girl by not getting out of her path quickly enough. The fact was, the Reverend D. A. Graham charged, that twenty black women were raped by whites for every white woman raped by a black man, yet Southern black women in such cases had no redress.

Between 1892 and 1898, 1,226 persons, the great majority blacks, were lynched in the United States. Less than a third had been accused of rape. In 1892, of 241 lynched, 46 had such a charge against them; in 1898, out of 131 lynched, only 24 were charged with assault or attempted assault. The story was much the same everywhere.

In the summer of 1900 the attention of the country was drawn to a particularly lurid event in New Orleans. Robert Charles was a young black man who had been a resident of Copiah County, Mississippi, when Print Matthews, leader of the Fusion Independents of that county, had been murdered at the polling place. He had drifted to New Orleans, where he worked at odd jobs and became increasingly militant over the city's systematic discrimination against blacks, especially the harassment of blacks by the police. He also became an agent for Bishop Henry Turner's *Voice of Missions*, a militant black journal. A large, powerfully built man and a natty dresser, Charles, like most of the city's blacks and whites, carried a revolver concealed in his clothes. On the night of July 23, while Charles and a friend waited to meet two women, they were accosted by three policemen, who had received a report of "suspicious niggers" loitering in a predominantly white neighborhood. The three officers approached the two black men. When Charles rose from the steps where he had been sitting, one of the officers "grabbed him." Charles tried to pull away, and the two men grappled while the policeman belabored Charles with his billy stick. Finally Charles broke loose and ran. The policeman pulled his gun and fired. Charles fired back. Both men were hit.

The uninjured police were joined by several more officers. Charles, meanwhile, had returned to his own room, where he had a rifle concealed. When five policemen arrived at Charles's house, he was ready to sell his life dearly. He killed two officers before the rest fled for their lives.

In the confusion occasioned by the shooting Charles escaped and found refuge with friends in the black section of the city. The public response to the shooting was a three-day race riot directed indiscriminately against blacks of all ages and both sexes. Some were shot; others, beaten. The sentiment of the baser white population can probably be gauged by an editorial which had appeared in the *New Orleans Times-Democrat* a few weeks before the shooting and subsequent riot: "He (the negro) calls no man 'massa' unless he had been tipped a quarter. He will call you God for fifty cents; and grovel at your feet for a dollar. He never did an hour's honest work in his life save when driven at the end of a lash, and that is now unhappily against the law . . . to glorify him is like glorifying unspeakable lust and bestial cruelty." Dr. Gustave Keitz, anticipating a racial war in the city, recommended that some blacks be forcibly shipped to the Philippines, and others castrated. When lynching was necessary, it "should be done with as much speed and as little pain as possible" in the name of humanity.

When Charles killed the policemen, Major Henry Hearsey, editor of a leading newspaper, took the occasion to play upon white fears. "Under the dark, seething mass of humanity that surrounds us . . . all appears peaceful and delightful," he wrote. "We know not, it seems, what hellish dreams are arising underneath; we know not what schemes of hate, of arson, of murder and rape are being hatched in the dark depths." The danger of the Charles episode was that it would lessen the blacks' fear of the police.

In the systematic hunting of blacks by armed whites, Baptiste Philo, a seventy-five-year-old black man, was shot from a distance. His assailant, coming up to finish him off, was heard to remark, "Oh, he's an old negro. I'm sorry that I shot him." It was the only such expression of regret recorded.

In the aftermath of the New Orleans riots the Reverend Newell Dwight Hillis, pastor of Henry Ward Beecher's Plymouth Church at Brooklyn, declared, "Just now the whole country is suffering from a reaction on the negro question, and the colored race have known a month of such depression and sorrow and heartache as they have not known in forty years. . . ."

When order was finally restored by the state militia, three black men and an elderly black woman had been killed by mobs, and fifteen others shot or badly beaten. Charles was still at large. Finally the police received a tip that the fugitive was holed up in a house on Saratoga Street. A police sergeant set out with three officers in a patrol wagon to arrest him. From his hiding place in a closet Charles watched the officers searching the building and then shot two of them. As word spread through the city, crowds converged on the house, and police and militia surrounded it. The beleaguered Charles had plainly decided to kill as many whites as possible before his death. By five o'clock in the afternoon on the 27th he had shot and killed seven persons, including four policemen, and had wounded another twenty, eight seriously. At last the building he was in was set afire, and Charles, doubtless already wounded a number of times, was shot trying to escape the flames. Lying in the mud of the street, he was shot and kicked by hundreds of spectators anxious to desecrate his body. Two more blacks were murdered by enraged whites that night in isolated incidents, but the presence of the militia prevented another full-scale riot from breaking out.

In Wilmington, North Carolina, whites engaged in a vendetta against blacks, and when order was finally restored, at least nine blacks were dead and twenty-five wounded. One of the survivors, the Reverend Charles Morris, described the episode before the International Association of Colored Clergymen, meeting in Boston. One man had been forced to run a gauntlet while he was shot at repeatedly. Another was shot twenty times in the back as he fled. Thousands of other terrified blacks fled from their homes into a chilling rain, among them "half-clad and barefoot mothers, with their babies wrapped in a shawl, whimpering with cold and hunger. . . . All this happened not in Turkey, nor in Russia, nor in Spain . . . but . . . in the best state in the South, within a year of the twentieth century, while the nation was on its knees thanking God for having enabled it to break the Spanish yoke from the neck of Cuba. This is our civilization. This is Cuba's kindergarten of ethics and good government. This is Protestant religion in the United States that is planning a whole missionary crusade against Catholic Cuba. This is the golden rule as interpreted by the white pulpit of Wilmington."

George White, a North Carolina black Populist who had been elected to Congress in the "Populist revolt" of 1896, introduced a bill in 1900, as he was about to leave Congress, making lynching a Federal crime. In presenting the bill, White reviewed the familiar record of prejudice and oppression culminating in the foulest crime of all—lynching—directed against black Americans and reminded his colleagues that some members of Congress "had undertaken the unholy task of extenuating these foul deeds, and in some instances, they have gone so far as to justify them. . . . Since January 1, 1898, to April 25, 1899," White told his colleagues, "there were lynched in the United States 166 persons, and of this number 155 occurred in the South. Of the whole number lynched, there were 10 white and 156 colored. The thin disguise usually employed as an excuse for these inhuman outrages is the protection of the virtue among white women." White's own investigations had revealed that 32 of those lynched were accused of murder, 17 of assault, 10 of arson, 2 with stealing, and 1 with being impudent to white women. In addition, 72 were lynched without any specific charges being made against them. "I tremble with horror for the future of our nation," White declared, "when I think what must be the inevitable result if mob violence is not stamped out of existence and law once more permitted to reign supreme."

The case of black women was significantly different from that of black men. The century's veneration for "womanhood" and "motherhood" extended, in a decidedly attenuated form, to black women as well as white. Southern white men of all classes continued to have sexual relations with black women without suffering disapprobation. In the post-Civil War period black women made up the majority of the household servants in Southern homes (the positions of butler, gardener, and/or coachman were reserved for black males, but these could be afforded only by the more prosperous families), and as maids, cooks, and nurses black women enjoyed a privileged status as so-called members of the family. "Josephine is like a member of the family," a white hostess would say of an old black cook or nurse. "She's been with the family since I was a girl. She still calls me Miz Ann." In fact, there was a special flow of sympathy and understanding between black women and their mistresses: They both had, after all, to put up with Southern males, with their sexual aggressiveness and general insensitivity. It was thus upper-class white Southern women who led the movement against lynching and dared speak out against the atrocities suffered by blacks.

In the North reform-minded white women who identified themselves strongly with the abolitionist tradition, conscious of their battle for their own rights, were far more responsive to the aspirations of their black sisters than their male counterparts were to the plight of black men. Moreover, black women had, generally speaking, more financial security than black men, and free of the most demoralizing and demeaning aspects of black-white relations, they often appeared as the stronger and more stable figure in the black family.

One of the most prominent leaders of the fight for black rights was Ida Wells, born in 1862 in Holly Springs, Mississippi, of slave parents, one of eight children. Her father was a skilled carpenter whose services were much in demand, and the Wells children grew up in modest but comfortable circumstances. From the time she was old enough to go to school, Ida, who was an exceptionally bright child, attended Rust "College" in Holly Springs, an all-purpose educational institution started by Northern missionaries. Orphaned by a smallpox epidemic that killed more than a tenth of the town's population, sixteen-year-old Ida cared for those of her brothers and sisters who survived. Traveling to Memphis to visit an aunt, she was told by the conductor that she would have to ride in the smoking car. She left the train at the next station and instituted a suit against the railroad which she won in the lower court but lost when the railroad appealed to the State Supreme Court. The twenty-two-year-old woman wrote: "I have firmly believed all along that the law was on our side and would, when we appealed to it, give us justice. I feel shorn of that belief and utterly discouraged, and just now, if it were possible, would gather my race in my arms and fly away with them. O God, is there no redress, no peace, no justice in this land for us? Thou has always fought the battles of the weak and oppressed. Come to my aid at this moment and teach me what to do, for I am sorely bitterly disappointed. Show us the way, even as Thou led the children of Israel out of bondage into the promised land."

Teaching school in Memphis, Ida Wells discovered a talent for journalism and was soon writing for church journals and black newspapers. After a year of free-lancing she was offered the job of editor on a Memphis paper called *Free Speech*.

The aftermath of her editorial denouncing lynchers was an attack on the offices of *Free Speech* by a mob that destroyed the press. Wells was in Philadelphia at the time attending a convention, or she might well have become another victim of the mob. Remaining in New York, she joined T. Thomas Fortune's *New York Age* and began to write and lecture in an effort to arouse public opinion against lynching. A lecture tour of Great Britain brought her into contact with a number of women reformers there (one result was the formation of an Anti-Lynching Committee in England), and when she returned to the United States, she organized the Women's Era Club in Boston and encouraged the formation of black women's clubs in a number of large cities. Again the emphasis was on publicizing the facts about lynching.

At the time of the Chicago exposition in 1893, a black schoolteacher named J. Imogen Howard appealed for attention to the achievements of black women. She was appointed to the New York Board of Lady Managers for the fair and worked for two years without salary to assemble an exhibit of the work of female "Afro-Americans." She began by collecting statistics on the work of black women. To this end she organized numerous subcommittees of black women, first in the state and then beyond it. Soon she had a nationwide network of black women. On the basis of Imogen Howard's labors, the board reported, it was found that black women had shown their capabilities as "teachers, authors, artists, doctors, designers, musicians, nurses, engravers, missionaries, lawyers, inventors, clerks, librarians, bookkeepers, editors, etc." It was an impressive, not to say astonishing, inventory. The average American of either color would hardly have imagined that black women could have made their way, to any significant degree, into professions that white women had only recently penetrated. What it suggests was that black women received positive aid and encouragement from their white sisters to venture into domains hitherto closed to women, regardless of race. In addition, black males were not in a position to place impediments in their way to the degree that the dominant white males did to women of their race. Finally, those white women who made their way in substantial numbers into occupations and careers hitherto closed to them were, in the main, women of liberal and, indeed, often radical social and political views. They were therefore especially disposed to lend a helping hand to ambitious black women.

Although black women had been represented in the planning of the Women's Building at the Chicago exposition, and their work included in the exhibitions, black men had been excluded, and Ida Wells joined with Frederick Douglass and other black leaders in writing a pamphlet entitled *The Reason Why the Colored American Is Not in the World's Columbian Exposition*. This was followed by *A Red Record*, the detailed statistical record of lynching in the United States in the years 1892–1894.

At the age of thirty-three Wells met and married Ferdinand Lee Barnett, a widower with two children and editor of the *Conservator*, a black newspaper in Chicago.

Anna Julia Cooper was born a slave in Raleigh, North Carolina, in 1858. She was graduated from Oberlin with a master's degree in 1887, taught school in Washington, D.C., and became the second female school principal in that city. Six years later she published *A Voice from the South, by a Black Woman of the South*. "One muffled strain in the Silent South . . . the one mute and voiceless note has been the sadly expectant Black Woman," she wrote in her opening pages. Much had been heard of the plight of the black man, but little of the black woman. "The feverish agitation, the perfervid energy, the busy objectivity of the more turbulent life of our men serves, it may be, at once to cloud or clog their vision somewhat, and as well to relieve the smart and deaden the pain for them." Cooper observed that "the American woman of to-day not only gives tone directly to her immediate world, but her tiniest pulsation ripples out and out, down and down, till the utmost circles and the deepest layers of our society feel the vibrations." But the white woman, dominant as she was, politely attended to and courteously treated, gave little thought to the fact that her black sisters of the South were treated far differently, ejected from trains and trolleys, abused, and discriminated against. "The colored woman of to-day," Cooper wrote, "occupies . . . a unique position in this country. . . . She is confronted by both a woman question and a race problem, and is as yet an unknown or an unacknowledged factor in both." Moreover, black women found their men apprehensive and resentful if they tried to step beyond the home—"as far as my experience goes the average man of our race is less frequently ready to admit the actual need among the sturdier forces of the world for woman's help or influence." They were deaf to the suggestion that "great social and economic questions" might profit from her "intermeddling," that she might "improve the management of school systems, or elevate the tone of public institutions, or humanize and sanctify the far reaching influence of prisons and reformatories and improve the treatment of lunatics and imbeciles." In Anna Julia Cooper's view, the black women of the South formed the core of the moral fiber that held their men true in the cause of black rights.

What took place in the last decade of the nineteenth century and the first decades of the twentieth was a kind of final campaign on the part of Southern whites to complete the subjugation of Southern blacks, a campaign met by a desperate struggle on the part of bolder blacks to preserve some shreds of personal dignity and freedom. Why the relations between the races reached such a degree of hostility in this era is not easy to discover. The most logical explanation seems to be a rising tide of racial animosity that affected every aspect of American life. Racism took on the habiliment of science and became respectable. It had been in the air since the early days of social Darwinism. Now, fanned by the anxiety resulting from the protracted war between capital and labor and the rising tide of immigration, racism asserted itself with a new insistence. Respectable sociologists and geneticists advocated the sterilization of undesirable immigrants from Central and Southern Europe lest the native gene pool be hopelessly contaminated by inferior stock. Since the Anglo-Saxon was to be the savior of the world, it was essential to guard "against the deterioration of the Anglo-Saxon stock in the United States by immigration," Josiah Strong wrote. "There is now being injected into the veins of the nation a large amount of inferior blood every day of every year." Such immigration must be checked, Strong insisted, not for America's sake but for the sake of that world which America alone could save. Strong did not imagine that an Anglo-Saxon was any dearer to God than "a Mongolian or an African"; it was merely that he was God's appointed instrument for their salvation. The survival of the Republic, it was announced, depended on improved principles of breeding. Anarchists and socialists, along with assorted radicals, free lovers, and marriage reformers, contributed unwittingly to the mood by their emphasis on improving the genetic inheritance of children. In the spirit of the age of science, the discoveries of Gregor Mendel made clear, it was argued, that only by scientific breeding could the race be improved and the millennium hastened. The apprehension of the dominant Anglo-Saxon whites of all political persuasions over the "pollution" of their blood became as intense as our present anxiety over the pollution of the atmosphere. In not a few instances it rose to a pitch approaching hysteria as "native" Americans rallied to fight off the fatal contamination. We can only speculate on the degree to which it intensified long-standing Southern fears of miscegenation. Certainly with the North preoccupied by the threat posed by the European immigrants, public indignation over the treatment of Southern blacks was muted, if not silenced.

While the most terrible manifestations of racial prejudice were evident in the South, there was abundant evidence of Northern prejudice at every level. In addition to James Ford Rhodes, the distinguished historians John W. Burgess and William Dunning expressed a patronizing or outright hostile attitude to blacks. Burgess wrote of Reconstruction: "There is no question now that Congress did a monstrous thing and committed a great political error, if not a sin, in the creation of this new electorate [the freed blacks]. It was a great wrong to civilization to put the white race of the South under the domination of the Negro race."

Dunning wrote in this same spirit in *Reconstruction, Political and Economic, 1865–1877*: "The negro had no pride of race and no aspiration save to be like the whites. With civil rights and political power, not won, but almost forced upon him, he came gradually to understand and crave those elusive privileges that constitute social equality. A more intimate association with the other race than that which business and politics involved was the end toward which the ambition of blacks tended consciously or unconsciously to direct itself." This desire for "social equality," Dunning wrote, led to the demand for "mixed schools" and for the absence of discrimination in "hotels and theaters, and even . . . the hideous crime against white womanhood which . . . assumed new meaning in the annals of outrage."

In 1896 the Supreme Court handed down a decision that seemed to seal the inferior position of blacks in the South. A man named Plessy, actually *one-eighth* black, had bought a ticket between two towns in Louisiana. A Louisiana law, passed in 1890, declared that "all railway companies carrying passengers in their coaches in this state, shall provide separate but equal accommodations for the white and colored races. . . ." Plessy set out to test the constitutionality of the law by insisting on riding in a coach reserved for whites on the ground that the accommodations provided for black passengers were not "equal." He was arrested, tried, and convicted, and he appealed through the state courts to the Supreme Court, which decided in favor of the state of Louisiana, Justice John Harlan dissenting. In his dissent, perhaps the most famous in the history of the Court, Harlan declared: "If a white man and a black man choose to occupy the same public conveyance on a public highway, it is their right to do so; and no government, proceeding alone on grounds of race, can prevent it without infringing the personal rights of each. . . . In my opinion, the judgment this day rendered will, in time, prove to be quite as pernicious as the decision made by this tribunal in the Dred Scott Case. . . . The destinies of the two races, in this country, are indissolubly linked together, and the interests of both require that the common government of all shall not permit the seeds of race hate to be planted under the sanction of law."

Among those applauding the Court's decision was J. P. Morgan, who declared: "Niggers are lazy, ignorant and unprogressive; railroad traffic is created only by industrious, intelligent and ambitious people."

Susie King Taylor, the ex-slave who had worked in Thomas Wentworth Higginson's black regiment as laundress and teacher, wrote in an autobiographical memoir in 1902: "Living here in Boston where the black man is given equal justice, I must say a word on the general treatment of my race, both in the North and South, in this twentieth century. I wonder if our white fellow men realize the true sense or meaning of brotherhood? For two hundred years we had toiled for them; the war of 1861 came and was ended, and we thought our race was forever free from bondage, and that the two races could live in unity with each other, but when we read almost every day of what is being done to my race by some whites in the South, I sometimes ask, 'Was the war in vain?' Has it brought freedom in the full sense of the word, or has it not made our condition more hopeless? In this 'land of the free' we are burned, tortured, and denied a fair trial, murdered for any imaginary wrong conceived in the brain of the negro-hating white man. . . . It seems a mystery to me. They say, 'One flag, one nation, one country indivisible.' Is this true? Can we say this truthfully, when one race is allowed to burn, hang, and inflict the most horrible torture weekly, monthly, on another?" Susie Taylor knew she would not live to see the day, but it must come. "God is just," she wrote; "when he created man he made him in his image, and never intended one should misuse the other. All men are born free and equal in his sight."

"We shall get it hammered into our heads one of these days," Washington Gladden wrote a few years later, "that this is a moral universe; not that it is going to be, by and by, but that it is moral now, moral all through, in tissue and fiber, in gristle and bone, in muscle and brain, in sensation and thought; and that no injustice fails to get its due recompense, now and here. The moral law admonishes us not to make our fellow man our tool, our tributary. 'Thou shalt treat humanity'—it is Kant's great saying—'ever as an end, never as a means to thine own selfish end.' Disobey that law, and the consequence falls." This most basic law of morality, Gladden declared, had been twice broken: in slavery and in the treatment of blacks in the post-Civil War period by white Americans, North and South. "On such a race," Gladden wrote, "there will surely fall the mildew of moral decay, the pestilence of social corruption, the blight of its civilization."

The Women

Women have appeared so frequently throughout this volume that it might be argued that they hardly need a separate consideration. Yet such is clearly the case since the most perceptive observers of the last quarter of the century believed that their startling emergence in virtually every area of American life was the most notable fact of the age.

We have already taken note of the appearance of the American woman as a new human type. A host of remarkable individuals—Lucretia Mott, Harriet Beecher Stowe, Fanny Kemble, Elizabeth Cady Stanton, Sojourner Truth, Margaret Fuller, and Dorothea Dix, to mention a few—were only the advance guard of what was to become, in the decades following the Civil War, a great army of aggressive and energetic women. The modes and organizations which they used to express their new role in American life (where adequate forms did not exist, they created them) were many and varied.

The women's rights movement split into two separate organizations with an attendant degree of bitterness and recrimination. What we might term loosely the New York wing of the movement focused attention on social problems: the vote for women, more liberal divorce laws, fair treatment of working people and immigrants, regulation of child labor, and even unionization. The New England wing remained, for the most part, true to its abolitionist faith. Such issues as divorce and a woman's "right to her own body" (a doctrine the more radical women were proclaiming) made the New Englanders nervous. More important, they felt an obligation to put black male suffrage before female suffrage. In the words of Lucy Stone, "woman has an ocean of wrong too deep for any plummet . . . and the Negro has an ocean of wrong that cannot be fathomed. But I thank God for the Fifteenth Amendment, and hope it will be adopted in every state. I will be thankful in my soul if anybody can get out of that terrible pit. . . ." And Julia Ward Howe was quoted by Frederick Douglass as saying, "I am willing that the Negro shall have the ballot before me," and, "I cannot see how anyone can pretend that there is the same urgency in giving the ballot to women as to the Negro." Frederick Douglass took the same view. He was quick to denounce those women who wished to push the vote for their own sex before the vote for the Negro or even to associate the two causes.

To Jane Addams the rationale for giving the vote to women was essentially the same as that for extending it to any voteless, powerless group in society. Only the group knows what are its own best interests. No one else, however well intentioned, is able to speak for it. Indeed, "speaking for" is simply the subtlest form of tyranny or condescension. "Women," she wrote, "have discovered that the unrepresented are always liable to be given what they do not need by legislators who wish merely to placate them. . . . The community, for instance, will never be made 'vividly aware' of the effects of chronic fatigue upon young working girls or upon children who divert their energy from growth to pasting labels on a box by men whose minds are fixed upon factory management from the point of view of profits."

But woman suffrage was delayed by two complementary anxieties. One was the concern of conservative politicians that women would vote on the radical side of issues (although it was the vote of women in Colorado that was said to have defeated the Populist governor of that state, Davis Waite). The other concern was that Catholic women might vote for corrupt city machines. Henry Blackwell noted that the introduction of woman suffrage in Massachusetts could once more "thoroughly Americanize" the state "by counteracting the Democratic vote." But the argument cut two ways. There was, of course, no assurance that the same priests who took their orders from Rome would not herd immigrant women to the polls to vote as the Pope directed, just as they presumably did with Catholic males.

The most important addition to suffrage organizations was the Woman's Christian Temperance Union. The Prohibition Party had been founded in the late 1860s to work for a constitutional amendment prohibiting the manufacture and sale of intoxicating liquors. The Woman's Christian Temperance Union was founded in 1873 in the town of Hillsboro, Ohio, where a group of women, inspired by Dr. Dio Lewis, met to pray and sing hymns. The movement spread to nearby Washington Court House, where the women formed a "Committee of Visitation" and appealed to local liquor dealers, "in the name of our town, in the name of God who will judge you and us, for the sake of our own souls which are to be saved or lost," to close their saloons. Church bells tolled, and women and children knelt in the snow, chanting and praying. The saloonkeepers capitulated and dumped the noxious stuff in the streets to loud hosannas. Frances Willard joined the WCTU in 1874, and her talents as an organizer, speaker, and writer resulted in her being elected president of the organization five years later. The WCTU enjoyed spectacular growth under Willard's leadership and extended its influence into virtually every aspect of reform affecting the lives of women.

Frances Willard took the line that it was the function of the WCTU, above everything else, to protect the home. This, in her view, was best done by running the home on Christian principles and excluding liquor from the premises. "To preserve the individuality, the privacy, and sanctity of home, while diminishing its cost and friction, is the problem that women in council must set themselves to solve," she wrote. Starting with the reform and protection of the home, women would find the world a home equally in need of reform and in no respect more than in the inequities from which they suffered. "A great new world looms into sight," she declared, "like some splendid ship long-waited-for— the world of heredity, of prenatal influence, of infantile environment; the greatest right of which we can conceive, the right of the child to be well born, is being slowly, surely recognized. Poor old Humanity, so tugged by fortune and weary with disaster, turns to the cradle at last and perceives that it has been the Pandora's box of every ill and the . . . casket of every joy that life has known. When the mother learns the divine secrets of her power, when she selects in the partner of her life the father of her child, and for its sacred sake rejects the man of unclean lips because of the alcohol and tobacco taint . . . then shall the blessed prophecy of the world's peace come true; the conquered lion of lust shall lie down at the feet of the white lamb of purity and a little child shall lead them." (All of which sounded remarkably like Victoria Woodhull and her friends.)

The WCTU's avowed objective was "the enthronement of Christ's spirit in the world—its customs, its habits, and its legislation." Under Willard's firm guidance it campaigned for kindergartens, police matrons, and child labor laws. It sought to eliminate prostitution, and, decidedly ecumenical in spirit, it called on Jews, Catholics, Methodists, Unitarians, and all others to join in "the one pulse, a protected home and a redeemed America." If liquor was the chief enemy of the home and of a redeemed America, the love of money was almost as great a menace. Money had "warped and minified more lives, turned more homes into small compacts of perdition, and defeated the Gospel's blessed purpose, more than all the other curses that ever crazed the human heart." Some of the more conservative members of the WCTU, alarmed at what they considered its socialistic leanings and its "do-everything policy," determined to be "divested of the radicalism" that was "destroying" the parent body, broke off and formed the more conservative National Woman's Evangelical Temperance Union, which proved short-lived.

Undoubtedly one of the principal appeals of the WCTU, especially to lonely and isolated women, was its lively meetings. The Thornton, Indiana, meeting in July, 1890, began by singing "All Hail the Power of Jesus' Name." Then came an "impressive and energizing prayer" and a reading from Scripture. An elocution and singing contest followed, featuring such topics as "Prohibition, the Hope of Our Country," "The Rumseller's Legal Rights," and "Save the Boy," interspersed with renditions by a mixed quartet of "Sleeping on Guard," "Lift the Temperance Banner High," and "A Child's Pleading."

A word must be said about the organization of the WCTU. Forty women, each with a helper in every state, officiated over forty departments and "ten thousand local unions." Although she was carefully apolitical, Frances Willard had a decidedly radical approach to social and economic problems. It was her conviction that in any just, humane, and Christian society, the incomes of all citizens should be roughly the same. The so-called industrial revolution must be made to benefit the workingman and woman as well as the capitalist. "If to teach this is to be a socialist," she declared, "then so let it be!"

In her autobiography Frances Willard claimed, with some justice, that the WCTU had "developed the brain of woman as no schooling ever did before, has broadened the sympathy of her heart until it takes in all humanity, has educated her will until it has become a mighty power, and has exalted to supreme heights her faith in God." Willard's English friend Hannah Whitall Smith, in her introduction to *Glimpses of Fifty Years: The Autobiography of an American Woman*, wrote of her: "She has done more to enlarge our sympathies, widen our outlook, and develop our gifts, than any man, or any other woman of her time. Every movement for the uplifting of humanity has found in her a cordial friend and active helper—and she has been essentially American in this, that she is always receptive of new ideas, without being frightened of their newness."

What cannot be sufficiently emphasized is that the abolition and temperance movements formed the basic cadres of reform, especially for women, throughout the greater part of the nineteenth century. Temperance was, in many instances, the parent of abolition and, of course, long survived it. We have insisted throughout this work that the temperance movement had two dimensions. Alcoholism was the major pathology of American society almost from its inception. One can only guess at the causes.

Dr. Mary Weeks Burnett, a delegate from the National Temperance Hospital and Medical College Association, at the national convention of the WCTU in 1880, undertook to analyze the causes of alcoholism. These included "the climate of America, its form of government, its mixed population and its numberless racial crossings, its exciting political and business life into which people are drawn as into a maelstrom." All these elements made Americans "a peculiar and complex people" especially susceptible to all forms of narcotics. To these "causes" we might add excessive individualism, the disintegrative effects of American life, extreme physical hardship, the loneliness of prairie farms, and the relative absence of festivals and celebrations common to traditional cultures. Above all, there was the nerve-racking sense that the individual was sustained only by prodigious efforts of the will. The same was true with communities, recently established and highly unstable. For every ambitious, upwardly mobile individual who "made it," a hundred or a thousand failed. For every town that grew into a city, dozens simply disappeared from the map, casualties of an unpredictable economy or failures of will. So it was with the nation itself. It was periodically racked with devastating depressions that not uncommonly wiped out in months the arduous labor of years. Indians threatened the frontier; angry workers and the desperate poor kept cities in turmoil. Farmers experienced chronic insecurity. All in all, there was ample cause for Americans to seek solace in spirituous liquors. But there was something more to the temperance movement surely than the problem of alcoholism, severe as that undoubtedly was. It was, among other things, a form of associational activity which promised redemption. Profoundly and persistently Christian (it was one of the few reform movements that did not become secularized by the end of the century), it constituted, like abolitionism, a kind of ecumenical church. Whereas the older Christian denominations became increasingly class- and section-bound, socially timid, and politically reactionary, temperance reached into every corner of the country, ignoring class lines, regional distinctions, rural and urban divisions. While its roots were primarily rural and its constituency was overwhelmingly middle-class, its mission was the salvation of the world by teetotalism. Decade after decade, generation after generation, it fought against the disintegrative effects of American life by attempting to integrate all Americans in its ranks. In somewhat the same manner that the abolitionists had dramatized the evils of slavery, the temperance movement dramatized man's struggle (it was almost invariably the man who was intemperate and the woman who was the victim).

In addition to the two major suffrage organizations and the WCTU, thousands of women became involved in the club movement. Florence Harriman started the Colony Club in New York, which became the model for many others. One of the Colony members declared, "I've waited for this evening all my life. I have just telephoned the boys, 'Don't wait dinner; I'm dining at my club.' My dear, I've been getting that message for years—now I'm giving it." The architect of the Colony Club was Stanford White. Mrs. Harriman described the club's "azalea-colored assembly room; the roof-garden with its white trellis work and climbing ivy, blue and white Italian porcelain, and fine old Italian stoves of green earthen ware that stood at each end of the sun parlor; the swimming pool sunk, white marble, with mirrored walls, and ceiling hung with an arbor of translucent glass grapes through which the yellow light streamed like late afternoon in Palermo . . . a beauty parlor, a rest room, where lunch could be fetched on a tray; the running track where I never saw a member, thick or thin; the eleven colonial bedrooms. . . ."

Most such clubs sponsored talks and lectures on the social issues of the day. Prominent among such issues were the duties and responsibilities of women as well, frequently, as their rights. Even those that were not started to support a cause soon found one or more to command the attention of their members. For many women the clubs were a kind of training ground, an intermediate step between the home and wider political concerns and activities. Florence Harriman described in her memoirs how she sought in social work "an antidote for all the frivolities in which I seemed plunged." She began "to learn to work and organize and to understand some of the problems of the working people of America. . . ." In time she became a King's Daughter, the Christian organization for social work among the immigrants on New York's Lower East Side.

In Chicago the Fortnightly Club was founded by Kate Newell Doggett, who "wore her hair short" and flirted with socialism. The club had 500 members divided into committees on reform, philanthropy, education, housekeeping, art and literature, science and philosophy. The topics discussed ranged from "Evolution of the Modern Woman" to "Should Emigration Be Restricted," "Co-Education," and "Dante and the Divine Vision." In the words of an English visitor, Beatrice Forbes-Robertson Hale: "No class in the world will so willingly listen to so many lectures as will these club women." Finding the Fortnightly Club too literary and little interested in social reform, Ellen Henrotin, wife of the head of the Chicago Stock Exchange, started the Women's Club in 1887. This club included women from a wide variety of social and economic backgrounds. Many of them were in business or held jobs. The club's influence extended everywhere; it took up the fight to establish juvenile courts and investigated and exposed the horrendous conditions in the Cook County Insane Asylum and the Poorhouse. An offshoot of the club—the Protective Agency—placed matrons in the police stations of the city to guard the rights of women and children charged with crimes. Through the club's efforts a police trial board was set up to hear women's complaints of mistreatment by the police. The Protective Agency also undertook, as its name suggests, to protect the legal rights of women: to prevent their eviction by unscrupulous landlords and assist in securing divorces from brutal husbands. It also prevailed on the state legislature to increase the penalties for rape. It came to the aid of women charged with prostitution as well. The list of the club's good works and reforms seemed endless: a manual training school for homeless boys; the sponsorship of legislation making schooling compulsory; the introduction of manual training and domestic science into the curriculums of the Chicago high schools; a scholarship at the newly formed Art Institute and scholarships in philosophy and sociology at the equally new University of Chicago.

Charlotte Perkins Gilman hailed the club movement as one of the "most important sociological phenomena of the century,—indeed, of all centuries,—marking . . . the first timid steps toward social organization of these so long unsocialized members of our race. . . . Now the whole country is budding into women's clubs. The clubs are uniting and federating by towns, States, nations; there are even world organizations. The sense of human unity is growing daily among women." Madame Blanc (the pseudonym of a French woman journalist) was equally impressed. The clubs were "a school in organization," everywhere well attended, hospitable, intelligent, and animated. Visiting one such club, she "admired the ease of manner shown . . . by all the ladies who spoke in turn, the precision of their opinions, the critical sense that they displayed." She was convinced that "periodical meetings of this nature have a strong influence on the mind of women, on their powers of conversation, banishing too frivolous and too personal subjects, accustoming them to listen attentively, to refute an argument logically."

Jacob Riis was generous in giving credit to the legions of reformminded women, especially in the field of education. "We should have been floundering yet in the mud-puddle we were in, had it not been for the women of New York," he wrote, "who went up to Albany and literally held up the Legislature, compelling it to pass our reform bill." In Albany "the women . . . prevailed by the power of fact. They knew, and the legislators did not. They received them up there with an indulgent smile, but it became speedily apparent that they came bristling with information about the schools to which the empty old Tammany boast that New York 'had the best schools in the world' was not an effective answer."

As we have seen, the home and family were the source of profound anxiety or, at the very least, ambivalence on the part of many American women. Catharine Beecher and Harriet Beecher Stowe joined their formidable forces to reform the American home, which they clearly considered a shambles. Their book *The American Woman's Home: or, Principles of Domestic Science, Being a Guide to the Formation and Maintenance of Economical, Healthful, Beautiful, and Christian Homes*, published in 1869, was a perennial best seller, one of the most influential books of the age. It was "affectionately dedicated" to "THE WOMEN OF AMERICA in whose hands rest the real destinies of the Republic, as moulded by the early training and preserved amid the maturer influences of home." Happy, airy, clean, economical, well-ordered homes were, of necessity, the authors implied, "Christian." Chapter One was summarized thus: "THE CHRISTIAN FAMILY: Object of the Family State—Duty of the elder and stronger to raise up the younger, weaker, and more ignorant to an equality of advantages—Discipline of the Family—The example of Christ one of self-sacrifice as man's elder brother—His assumption of a low estate—His manual labor—His trade—Woman the chief minister of the family estate—Man the outdoor laborer and provider—Labor and self-denial in the mutual relations of home-life, honorable, healthful, economical, enjoyable, and Christian."

Even the physical arrangement of the house must be Christian. "Necessity of economizing time, labor, and expense, by the close packing of conveniences—Plan of a model cottage—Proportions—Piazzas—Entry, Stairs and landings—Large room—Movable screens—Convenient bedsteads—A good mattress. . . . Closets, corner dressing-tables, windows, balconies, water and earth-closets, shoe-bag, piece-bag—Basement-Conservatories—Average estimate of cost." (For a comfortable house $1,600 was a reasonable estimate.)

From "Scientific domestic ventilation" the Beechers went on to "Health of Mind," "Care of infants," and "Care of the Homeless, the Helpless and the Vicious." There were diagrams and floor plans, pictures of the latest-model stoves, and engravings of the heart and lungs to illustrate the importance of proper ventilation.

Another "home reformer" was Alba Woolson. "Among all the jeremiads that we hear delivered upon the degeneracy of modern days," she wrote in 1873, "there is none more frequent or more bitter than the lament over the loss of housekeeping abilities among women." If the causes for such a state were uncertain (or even the truth of the assertion), Woolson was convinced that one of the principal ones was the passion of American women for fashion.

To the question "What is the chief end of man?" Woolson wrote that the Westminster Catechism replied: "To glorify God and enjoy Him for ever." But in the United States the answer to that ancient query appeared to be "that the chief end of man is to make money, and the chief end of woman is to get married." A woman's fate lay in her marriage. "This one irrevocable act determines her lot. Whether she is to be rich or poor, courted or ignored by the world about her, will depend almost entirely upon the income and the talents of the companion she may select." Thus she must become "a siren, and lure lovers and admirers to her side, finally selecting the most likely to succeed and thereby elevate her to a level she could not hope to attain on her own." Willy-nilly she must spend her days in husband hunting. She must suppress any sign of an independent will or lively intelligence and practice every artifice to trap a husband. The capable and intelligent woman with too much sense of her own worth to play games is ignored for the "helpless little noodle" who charms him with silly love songs. He marries the "little noodle," who becomes "an inefficient, weak-minded woman, while her husband grows and develops by contact with the world." Until women abandoned their role as "helpless little noodles" and demanded an education the equal of a man's, they would continue to be patronized and dominated by men.

Melusina "Zina" Fay Peirce shared the concern of the Beecher sisters and Alba Woolson with reforming the family, but her attention was directed more at what and how the family ate. Melusina was a member of the Fay and Gilman families, both distinguished in the history of New England. Her aunt Caroline Howard Gilman, wife of a Unitarian minister, Samuel Gilman, had been a dedicated abolitionist, reformer, writer, and poet. In 1834 Caroline Gilman had proposed that New England towns organize "grand cooking establishments" to relieve wives of cooking chores. She speculated that the meals could be cooked and delivered for less than individually prepared meals would cost.

Zina Fay was born in Burlington, Vermont, in 1836, one of nine children. She was very conscious of being descended from that early feminist Anne Hutchinson, who threw the Massachusetts Bay Colony into an uproar by challenging the authority of the clergy. Her father sent her to the Young Ladies' School in Cambridge, taught by Louis Agassiz. In Cambridge she met Charles Sanders Peirce, three years her junior. They were married in 1862, when Peirce, who had just joined the staff of the United States Coast and Geodetic Survey, was twenty-three. The marriage ended in divorce in 1883, and the scandal which attended it can be presumed to have had a good deal to do with Peirce's losing his job as professor of philosophy at Johns Hopkins. Zina Peirce was a remarkable woman in her own right. Initially involved apparently in some of her temperamental young husband's researches, she felt increasingly confined by the marriage. In 1868 she wrote of the "costly and unnatural sacrifice" of her own abilities. Even if a husband did not oppose his wife's desire for a career, "he thinks her unnatural, discontented, ambitious, unfeminine" and thus dampens her own enthusiasm. In consequence, "nobody gives her a helping hand; so that if she accomplishes anything it is against the pressure—to her gigantic—of all that constitutes her world."

To Zina Fay Peirce the solution was cooperative living arrangements, by means of which women would be freed from the drudgery of household chores. Cooperative apartments with common kitchens, laundries, and nurseries appealed to her. She believed it unjust that certain fortunate adults should be supported "by the extra toil of the rest of the community as educated women are now. . . ." Such a "state of things" was "entirely contrary to the natural division of labor [and] . . . the most fruitful source of disorder, suffering and demoralization. . . ." The ideal cooperative unit, Peirce thought, would be between twelve and fifty women and their families, organized to do their domestic work "collectively." The husbands would be required to pay for all domestic services at the rates paid skilled workers. The women would wear comfortable and convenient clothes and employ a general manager or overseer. These measures would bring "the whole moneyed and employed class among women into direct and responsible relations with the whole employed or industrial class." The poor would thus be encouraged to "become capitalists in a small way, and thereby bridging the now ever-widening chasm between the moneyed and the working classes. . . ." Peirce went so far as to lay out the floor plan of a cooperative apartment house with the "sales room, consulting-room and fitting-room" (for the manufacture of clothes for the community) on the first floor, the workrooms on the second floor, and the dining room, gymnasium, and reading room on the third floor. From cooperative apartment houses, Zina Peirce went on to design blocks and whole neighborhoods. "Think how much more beautiful city architecture will be now!" she wrote. "The houses, instead of being built around a square, could be set in the middle of it. . . . Every tenth block would contain the kitchen and laundry and clothing house; and for these domestic purposes the Oriental style could be adopted, of interior courtyards with fountains and grass, secluded from the street."

Encouraged by the response to her articles, Zina Peirce tried to organize a cooperative of Cambridge residents, primarily Harvard professors and their wives (including her father-in-law and mother-in-law, the senior Peirces)—the Cambridge Cooperative Housekeeping Society. Among those who turned up at the society's first meeting were William Dean Howells and his wife, Elinor, who was, it turned out, a niece of John Humphrey Noyes. The purpose of the society was more scientific than philanthropic: "to learn, by actual experiment, whether it is possible to apply to the Manufactures of the Household—namely, Cooking, Laundry-work, and the making of Garments—the methods which are found indispensable in every other department of modern industry—the combination of Capital, and the Division and Organization of Labor." A house was rented, and thirty-three women signed up. The husbands proved recalcitrant; at least Zina Peirce blamed them for the collapse of the experiment after little more than a year of operation.

The failure of the experiment did not dampen Zina Peirce's enthusiasm for the notion of cooperative living. She and Peirce separated, although, it should be said, she never accused him of directly discouraging her efforts, and in 1880 she published a book entitled *Cooperative Housekeeping: How Not to Do It and How to Do It, a Study in Sociology*. The book included a bitter passage on the despotism that husbands exercised over their wives and reflections on "the absolute obliviousness of women by men. . . . In view of all its incalculable consequences, it is the most colossal fact in history." The *New York Tribune* decried her "somewhat extravagant conclusions . . . and often hysterical . . . manner" but expressed the opinion that her more "sensible suggestions" might become "at no distant day the basis of a domestic reform."

Another woman prominent in the cooperative movement was Mary Livermore. During the Civil War she and fifty other women had organized a cooperative laundry. "Whenever women are dead in earnest about it," she wrote, "and *want* a cooperative laundry, then they can organize one." Actively involved in the women's movement, Livermore went with the more conservative National Woman Suffrage Association and became editor of that organization's *Woman's Journal*. By 1886 she had aligned herself with the cooperative movement, writing that "isolated housekeeping must be merged into a cooperative housekeeping." Chautauqua, with its common dining rooms and kitchenless cabins, became a kind of prototype for the cooperative living style of the future.

A younger disciple of Zina Peirce's was Charlotte Perkins Gilman. Her *Women and Economics*, published in 1898, is a witty, deadly serious exploration of the relation between economics and inequality and the means of redress—communal arrangements where cooking, dishwashing, and laundry are done cooperatively. Gilman, who had read and absorbed a degree of Marxism, depicted men as beings of "pride, cruelty, and selfishness," creatures of "destructive energy, brutal, combative instinct . . . intense sexuality." The real villain was an "over-sexed" society, in which sexual appetites that could not be satisfied in any normal way were ceaselessly stimulated. It was a society in which, as opposed to animal societies, the females of the species were entirely dependent on the males for food. In order to be fed, women had to exaggerate their own sexuality to attract and capture males. Such behavior disposed the aroused male to "a degree of sexual indulgence that directly injures motherhood and fatherhood." In one of the book's most brilliant phrases, she notes that "the feeding sex [the male] becomes the environment of the fed." In addition, the woman attempts to secure her position of dependence by overindulging the male with greasy, unhealthful food, a condition which she describes as the "cupid in the kitchen" syndrome. Women, as the disposers of men's incomes, become "priestesses of the temple of consumption." Matters were made worse by the overspecialization and overorganization imposed on society by males, while women, "confined absolutely to this strangling cradle of the race, go mad by scores and hundreds." They must be freed from the "clumsy tangle of rudimentary industries that are supposed to accompany the home"; only then will we have a world "of pure, strong, beautiful men and women, knowing what they ought to eat and drink . . . capable of much higher and subtler forms of association" than the individualistic and competitive models presently available. Thus will true science be applied to the domestic scene, in a domestic science as practical as chemistry or physics. Gilman anticipated the day "when human relationships will be based on mutual interest and affection instead of one great overworked passion . . . only kept from universal orgies of promiscuity by being confined in homes." Women, "specialized" in industry, "will develop more personality and less sexuality; and this will lower the pressure on this one relation in both women and men." Women will then shed their "childish, wavering, short-range judgment, handicapped by emotion."

The scientific laboratory was the model for one of the most influential "kitchen reformers, " Ellen Swallow Richards. One of the first graduates of Vassar, Richards had gone on to get a B.S. degree at MIT, where she then taught "sanitary chemistry." She believed the old-fashioned kitchen was hopelessly outdated, unsanitary, and inefficient, and she developed her Rumford Kitchen, installed at the World's Columbian Exposition, as a model of the new kitchen designed to be used "scientifically," with exact measurements of ingredients and food stored to prevent spoiling and contamination. Large-scale food preparation was the only practical way to ensure that wholesome and nutritious food was served to the average American of either sex, Richards believed, and her ideas received wide circulation through the *New England Kitchen Magazine*, which she edited.

As we have noted earlier, the bad health of American women was a fact commented upon by students of the social scene, both foreign and domestic. As early as 1810 Médéric L. E. Moreau de St.-Méry had commented on the tendency of American women "to nervous illness . . . which is extremely frequent." The reasons are not hard to guess; they include a whole set of restrictive conventions: physical confinement; constricting clothes; intellectual and sexual repression. There was a disposition in the whole matter of women's health to assume, as Americans of every generation have been inclined to do about every aspect of American life, that things had previously been much better. Sturdy old ladies were pointed to as evidence that the problem of poor health in women was a modern phenomenon. Catharine Beecher was so convinced that chronic illness was the lot of "the women of this generation" that she devoted the better part of her adult life to the problem, devising, in the process, "physical education." Her travels through many states revealed that there was "a terrible decay of female health all over the land." She herself had suffered from "extreme prostration of the overworked brain and nerves," to the point where she could not walk without crutches. She had exhausted all the popular remedies of the day. She had tried rhubarb, iron, and camphor and had been twice bled for "nervous excitement." She had experimented with food cures, water cures, electric cures, sulfur baths, Russian baths, chemical baths, Turkish baths, sun baths, the grape cure, the lifting cure for "internal displacement," various "breathing cures," and, finally and most successfully, the Swedish cure, consisting of fresh air and exercise. Catharine's sister Harriet had taken what may have been the Swedish cure or a combination of cures for nervous depression (or, as it was more commonly called, prostration), which required that she be away from home for more than six months. Isabella Beecher Hooker likewise suffered from periods of severe depression. Elizabeth Avery Meriwether was among the converts to a new "Hygienic" diet. After attending the Centennial Exposition in Philadelphia, she went to take Dr. R. T. Trall's "water cure" at his sanatorium in Florence Heights, New Jersey. The "Hygienic" diet eschewed all condiments and meat. Bread was made of whole wheat flour and contained no salt, butter, lard, or shortening. Apples, raisins, and nuts were featured, along with a little weak tea and an occasional egg.

Alarmed at the bad health of her women friends, Catharine Beecher decided to conduct a kind of crude poll by writing to friends in every town and city she had visited asking them to report on the health of the ten women in their communities that they knew best. Her respondents were given a scale that ranged from "perfectly healthy" through "feeble" and "delicate" to "sickly." Her Milwaukee informant gave her a depressing inventory of the health of the women she knew in that frontier metropolis. Their ailments ranged from "headaches," "very feeble," "chills" to "consumption," "pelvic displacements," and "coughs." Her correspondent wrote: "I do not know one healthy woman in the place." So it ran from Milwaukee, Wisconsin, to Essex, Vermont, and Peru, New York (which counted three "healthy" and two "pretty well" out of the ten). In Oberlin, long the home of radical politics and high thinking, of the ten wives best known to the respondent, none was healthy; in Wilmington, Delaware, and in New Bedford, Massachusetts, Beecher's respondents could think of "but one healthy woman in the place." In other towns and cities throughout the country the "habitual invalids" and "delicate or diseased" outnumbered the "strong and healthy" from four to one to ten to one.

Of Catharine Beecher's nine married sisters and sisters-in-law "all of them [were] either delicate or invalids, except two." She had fourteen married female cousins, "and no one of them but was either delicate, often ailing or an invalid. . . ." In more than 200 towns reached through her survey only 2 had a majority of healthy women. The report was the same from all regions of the country—North, South, West. In Boston, from her wide acquaintance, Catharine Beecher knew of only one married woman who was "perfectly healthy." Indeed, she professed herself unable to recall, in her "immense circle of friends and acquaintances all over the Union, so many as ten married ladies born in this century and country who are perfectly sound, healthy and vigorous." She was convinced that the same appalling statistics applied to the "industrial classes."

Alba Woolson confirmed Catharine Beecher's observations on the health of American women. In a chapter in her book entitled "Invalidism as a Pursuit," she noted that in her own wide acquaintance she knew of "but one or two [women] who have no physical ills to complain of. The majority everywhere are constantly ailing, and incapable of vigorous exertion." One encountered hordes of such women in summer hotels; too weak and ailing to walk a half a mile, they were "content to vibrate about the piazzas." Woolson had traveled enough abroad to be convinced that "this general invalidism among women is peculiar to the American people." Such women "appear," she wrote, "to subsist on quack medicine and herb teas. . . . With us to be ladylike is to be lifeless, inane, and dawdling. . . . Clear, vigorous speech, quick movements, and a ringing laugh, are things to be condemned and repressed as far as possible." But the fact was that such attitudes were not only foolish but un-Christian. God had ordained physical laws as well as moral laws, and it was as wicked to break one as the other.

In Woolson's view, the conventional training and education of women left them after marriage "inferior in mental culture, disingenuous in character, nervous, dyspeptic, and hopelessly broken in health, with a taste for display, a craving for compliments and adoration, and a love of crowded, characterless assemblies. . . ." One consequence of a male-dominated world was that although men "can tolerate no hint of evil in a woman, she must tolerate all things in them." Thus many a fashionable young man led the life of an "abandoned *roué*" and then, his taste for dissipation sated for the moment at least, selected some "modest, innocent girl" as his bride. "Such unions," Woolson wrote, "are a desecration of marriage, made in the name of Him who has given us but one code of morals, for both men and women to obey. . . ."

There was a growing awareness among more "advanced" women of the ways in which the idea of femininity or, in a modern phrase, the "feminine mystique" was used to limit and constrain women's role. In *The Ugly-Girl Papers*, Susan O. Power took the line that a woman's beauty was, in the last analysis, a reflection of her inner character. A happy, healthy young woman radiated a beauty that no finery or cosmetics could rival. If women wished to be beautiful, they must, first of all, have good nerves, and good nerves required "peace of mind." The nerves of American women were notoriously bad; "better things are before us," she wrote, "coming from a fuller appreciation of the needs of the body and soul, but the fact remains that this is a generation of weak nerves. It shows particularly in the low tone of spirits common to men and women." Adults should imitate the healthy "tumble and turmoil" of children and rather than quell "their riot . . . join it with them." They would find it "a blessing" and the first step toward good health and good spirits. Men and women in truth went mad for the lack of "bounding exercise" and open air; it made them "drunkards, gamesters, and flings them into every dissipation of body and soul." Men and women who led "repressed lives" often confessed to "a longing for some fierce, brief madness that would unseat the incubus of their lives. . . . They felt as if they would like to go on a spree, dance the tarantella or scream till they were tired." But they were alarmed by such impulses and suppressed them. How many sober clergymen and weary businessmen would be revived if they were to "leap, run, shout, and wrestle, and sing at the full strength" of their voices. A woman especially needed a tent on a lakeshore, "where she would have to leap brooks, gather her own fire-wood, climb rocks, and laugh at her own mishaps. . . . The nervous, capricious woman must be sent to swimming-school, or learn to throw quoits or jump the rope, to wrestle or to sing." For women whose nerves failed them, the remedies were simple enough. Warm baths, "sunshine, music, work, and sleep" were "the great medicine for women," Power concluded.

If we allow for some exaggeration (it is not uncommon for people troubled by some abnormality to see it too readily in others), clearly the picture that emerges is still a grim one. Seen in this light, the periodic depressions of Jane Addams in the 1880s and the chronic invalidism of Alice James seem "normal" for their time and class; Clover Adams's fits of depression and eventual suicide become part of a pattern rather than simply an isolated episode. The rough actuarial statistics available from the period make clear that the life expectancy of women was much less than that of men. So we are presented by another of those paradoxes in which history abounds. At the very time when women were emerging from dependent and subordinate status, discovering new powers and potentialities and exercising remarkable influence in a wide variety of heretofore untried fields, they were also suffering from an unprecedented array of physical and nervous disorders. One cannot help wondering about the effect of this long inventory of female disorders on the "congenial and devoted husbands." What proportion of female ailments and indispositions were the result of impossible clothes, overheated homes, and lack of exercise, and what portion caused by psychic disorders, by distress of mind and spirit? Of course, the two were by no means dissociated.

Alba Woolson was surely right when she wrote in 1873: "All the fervent discussion of the present day concerning woman, so earnestly written and so eagerly read, only proves a universal conviction that there is something wholly wrong about her as she is; and not only this, but that society is suffering sadly in consequence, and crying aloud for deliverance. It can never be set right till she is released from the tutelage she is so fast outgrowing, and led by man to take her place at his side as an honored companion and equal. . . ."

The growing velocity of the women's movement resulted in the founding of half a dozen women's colleges in the conservative East and the admission of women as students in the public universities that sprang up in virtually every state in the years following the Civil War. Smith College, established through a bequest from Sophia Smith, opened its doors in 1875 and soon established a reputation for simple living and high thinking. Mount Holyoke had been founded by Mary Lyon in 1837 as the Mount Holyoke Female Seminary. Although it called itself modestly a seminary, under Lyon's leadership it rivaled most of the men's colleges of the day in the intellectual and moral discipline it imposed, and exceeded many. The production of missionary women was its specialty for almost a century, and graduates of Mount Holyoke were to be found in the most remote and exotic corners of the globe, carrying the word of the Lord, founding schools and hospitals, and working to improve the status of native women.

In 1861 Matthew Vassar, an English immigrant who had made his fortune as a brewer, gave $800,000 to start Vassar College, which opened four years later dedicated to the most advanced and "scientific" principles of education and of living. Vassar was one of the first colleges in the country to offer its students instruction in music. It was also attentive to the doctrines of Catharine Beecher in regard to the importance of exercise for women, and it instituted one of the first collegiate programs of physical education, training corps of young women, who would in turn plant the seeds of physical education programs in institutions of higher learning all over the country and especially in the rapidly growing state universities. Vassar was noted for its department of euthenics (one of those new "scientific" words coined in such profusion). Euthenics was the science of wholesome living; proper diet, exercise, comfortable clothing, music, and dance all figured prominently in the new science.

Wellesley College admitted students in 1875, the same year as Smith, and it, too, was notably progressive. It was the first women's college to have well-equipped scientific laboratories. Its department of hygiene was as notable an innovation as Vassar's department of euthenics. It boasted a graduate school of physical education, and among the handsome buildings on its campus were a chapel, an art building, a museum, a notable music building (Billings Hall), and an impressive library. Wellesley's founder, Henry Fowle Durant, was one of the more interesting and eccentric figures in our history. Born Henry Welles Smith in Hanover, New Hampshire, and a graduate of Harvard, class of 1841, he became a highly successful lawyer and then underwent an experience of conversion, as a consequence of which he changed his name and became an evangelical minister, a dedicated abolitionist, and an enthusiast for the education of young women. As founder and treasurer of the college Durant gave it its initial character—pious and progressive—and its innovative curriculum. When he died in 1881, he was succeeded by Alice Freeman, making Wellesley one of only two women's colleges with female presidents (Mount Holyoke was, of course, the other). Alice Freeman was a graduate of the University of Michigan, who had served as head of the Wellesley history department. In 1887 she resigned to marry George Herbert Palmer, a Harvard professor of philosophy and natural religion.

In the late 1870s another Harvard professor, Arthur Gilman, and his wife began giving instruction to women in the community. They were joined by other professors, and in 1882 the Society for the Collegiate Instruction of Women was chartered. Known initially as the Harvard Annex, it was rechartered in 1892 as Radcliffe College in honor of the first woman to give an endowment to Harvard. Elizabeth Agassiz was president from its modest beginning in 1879 until 1903, when she was succeeded by a man.

Of course, Antioch College, founded in Yellow Springs, Ohio, in 1852 by devout abolitionists, had admitted women from the beginning, as had its sister college, Oberlin, founded in 1833. Knox College at Galesburg, Illinois, had opened its doors in 1841, a joint effort by Congregationalists and Presbyterians, with a strong abolitionist flavor. It, too, had been coeducational from its inception.

So while the principle of coeducation had been established, at least in the West, a generation earlier, the private men's colleges in the East kept their doors resolutely closed to women. It thus followed that if Eastern upper- and middle-class women were to have access to a "higher" education without venturing into the untutored and barbaric West, they must have their own institutions. The consequences of the resolute antifeminism of such Ivy League male bastions as Harvard, Dartmouth, Yale, Amherst, Williams, etc. were of very considerable intellectual and even social consequences. The new women's colleges were instant centers of lively intellectual life, of educational innovation and experimentation. The arts—considered the proper sphere for feminine sensibility—abounded and flourished. Hygiene, physical education, and euthenics (soon to become "domestic science" and then "home economics") defined themselves as separate and respectable fields of study. They were, foremost, avenues of access into academe for hundreds of professionally oriented women, barred, for the most part, from the more traditional academic fields such as history, philosophy, economics, and the sciences. At the same time it must be said that many able women in the traditional fields found positions in state universities, where the prejudice against women professionals was not as deeprooted as it was in the East. Leaving graduate study aside, the most intellectually vigorous institutions of higher learning in the United States in the last decades of the nineteenth century (and the early decades of the twentieth) were the newly established women's colleges of the Northeast: Mount Holyoke, Smith, Wellesley, Vassar, and Radcliffe.

One of the most conspicuous results of the new women's "Ivy League" was the development of a "women's curriculum," different in many respects from that which obtained in men's institutions or, indeed, in the large coeducational public institutions, primarily state universities. The fact that this new women's curriculum was on the whole more intelligent, more "progressive," and more humane than the corresponding men's curriculum mattered less in the long run than the fact that it served to perpetuate the notion that there were substantial differences in the qualities of male and female intelligence. Whether, in fact, this is the case, it was used in a variety of subtle ways to discriminate against women. Actually everyone, male and female, would probably have been better off if the typical women's curriculum had prevailed over the men's. For example, the present emphasis on the arts in virtually all institutions of higher learning, especially in such public institutions as junior colleges and state colleges, is at least two generations behind such emphasis in women's colleges. The women's curriculum, with its attention to the cultural and aesthetic aspects of experience, served to ratify the assignment of "culture" to women, and thus it furthered that "feminization" of American culture of which Henry Adams and others complained. Such a doctrine, or attitude, which consigned culture with a capital C to women's domain, led to a kind of deprivation of the affective, emotional, sensual life of the American male with unhappy consequences.

There were other consequences. The intellectual stimulus and excitement in the women's colleges were in large part generated by the conviction on the part of many of the students that they were embarked in a great new venture. To them, women's colleges were an important, if not essential, part of God's plan for the emancipation of their sex and the redemption of the world. On graduation, however, they came up against the hard facts of American life, where the vast majority of males still expected women to play conventional (and subordinate) roles as wives and mothers. The young women had, in fact, received two conflicting and more or less irreconcilable signals from their colleges and their teachers. One informed them that there was a whole, fascinating, virtually unexplored world into which only a few of their more determined sisters had yet ventured. This world had to do with the most fundamental questions—of power, of reform, in broader terms, of redemption. Hundreds of tasks, peculiarly suited to the loving, nurturing, caring nature of women cried out to be undertaken. The other message, and for a time at least the dominant one, was that "culture" —the practice of the arts and their encouragement— was the particular destiny of women. The history of art was the centerpiece of the women's curriculum. Ideally college was to be followed by a woman's version of the grand tour, with visits to all the great museums and art galleries of Europe. It was against this assignment that Jane Addams rebelled. She saw hundreds of young women like herself gazing with growing desolation on the classic monuments of Europe and wondering what they all had, finally, to do with the role of women in American society, which seemed to be heading toward some terrible Armageddon between capital and labor. An education should, after all, prepare the educated for a useful and happy life in the larger society. The hard-won, much-prized education acquired by more and more American women seemed destined to have no such outcome. In the opinion of Jane Addams it did nothing so much as cut them off from the satisfactions and rewards of traditional feminine roles. As in immigrant families, the continuity of generations was broken. It was not so much that daughters were set *against* their mothers and grandmothers (the former were typically the proud chaperones of their educated daughters); it was simply that they had been inducted into another world, a world that fitted ill with the "real" world. The result was predictable—confusion; frustration; often acute depression. Jane Addams became the therapist of the new class of educated women. She perceived that they could not live by "culture" alone. Hull House was created consciously by Addams to save her own soul (and intellect) and that of the hundreds and then thousands of young women who rallied around her there or started their own urban "settlements" modeled on it. So women's education bore fruit after all. It forced the creation of new forms and new agencies to utilize the energies which it released. Nonetheless, it was an ambiguous legacy. Not all educated women found new roles. For some, it must be suspected, the disappointment was acute, and the psychic dislocations were extreme.

In the West matters were somewhat different. There coeducation was the norm. There, where women were engaged daily with men in breaking the land, in planting homesteads, and starting new communities, the barriers and distinctions between the sexes were far less noticeable than in the East and, where they existed, had a practical, functional, rather than theoretical or legal, basis. Where heavy physical labor was involved in daily life, the more demanding physical tasks were commonly performed by men, although women on occasion carried on labors that would doubtless have caused their more refined Eastern sisters to faint. The consequence was that Western women enjoyed the political rights and social status of which their Eastern sisters only dreamed. After the Wyoming Territory had been organized, women were given the vote in 1869. The same was true in Colorado. Moreover, women were not uncommonly lawyers, doctors, and even judges and mayors. When Amelia Bloomer moved to Council Bluffs, Iowa, she, who had been so often abused and derided in the East, was greeted as a celebrity, invited to speak to "promiscuous" audiences of men and women, to lecture on woman suffrage at the Methodist Church, and invited to go to Omaha to give a talk on the same subject to the State House of Representatives. There she was escorted to the platform by "General" William Larimer, an early abolitionist and Republican, one of the leading figures in the state. The House had her speech published and passed a bill in favor of women's suffrage that died in the Senate.

Certainly for those women who considered themselves part of the new dispensation it was an exciting age. Their most basic emotion was that of "breaking free" and forming part of a universal sisterhood. Madame Blanc, the touring French journalist, wrote: "In no country are individual friendships nobler and more devoted." Upper-class women and their immigrant working-class sisters laboring in the same cause often became devoted friends. Mary Anderson, a Swedish immigrant who rose from domestic service to become secretary of a union of women shoemakers and later the first head of the women's division of the Department of Labor, was the "dear friend" of Mrs. Raymond

Robins, a member of Boston's elite. They visited each other, remembered birthdays and anniversaries, and concerted their efforts in the cause of improving the conditions in which immigrant women worked.

There were, of course, hundreds of thousands of women untouched by the often strident debate over women's proper role. The vast majority of immigrant women had no choice but to work to keep body and soul together. As Jane Addams perceived, they suffered the profoundest sense of alienation; torn from the familiar soil and rituals of the old country, they were cruelly battered by an unfamiliar world. Only the fact that they were settled in neighborhoods of immigrants with common backgrounds, where some vestiges of traditional ways and manners could be preserved, saved them from a kind of social autism.

Working as a midwife in the city's slums, Emma Goldman also came to have a deep awareness of the emotional life of immigrant women. "Most of them," she wrote, "lived in continual dread of conception; the great mass of the married women submitted helplessly, and when they found themselves pregnant, their alarm and worry would result in the determination to get rid of the unexpected offspring. It was incredible what fantastic methods despair could invent: jumping off tables, rolling on the floor, nauseating concoctions, blunt instruments. These and similar methods were being tried, generally with great injury. It was harrowing but it was understandable." She herself was constantly being beseeched to perform abortions, but she resolutely refused. Her interests "embraced the entire social problem, not merely a single aspect of it, and I would not jeopardize my freedom for that one part of the human struggle. I refused to perform abortions and I knew no method to prevent conception."

The bitterest blow experienced by immigrant women was the breaking of bonds between generations. In the cultures from which most of the immigrant women came, children were completely subordinate to their parents; the family was the central and essential social unit of the society. In America, travelers had been noting, since early in the century, the independence and, indeed, willfulness of the American child, who did not scruple to defy his parents from the time he could toddle, almost as though he bore a genetic disposition to rebellion. The children of immigrants picked up this American trait almost instantly. To the natural disposition of American children to question parental authority was added, in the case of immigrant children, the conviction that their parents' ways and values were hopelessly out of date, and, worse, un-American. At the same time young immigrant women experienced the United States as an exciting liberation. Virginia Pickett recalls the almost legendary story of her grandmother, who came to the United States with her family as a young girl. In the Polish-Jewish community of Warsaw, where she had been born, young women who became engaged to marry shaved their heads as a symbol of submissiveness to their husbands-to-be and wore wigs. Pickett's grandmother, when she became engaged to marry, refused to shave her head. There was a scandal in the immigrant Jewish community. Her fiancé was mocked and ridiculed; her parents were humiliated. The rabbi expostulated with her. She was adamant; she was now an American woman. She rejected any such self-abasement, no matter that it had centuries of tradition behind it, no matter the uproar. The story of her intransigence persisted in the family and came, in later life, to be told admiringly as an example of what it meant to become an American: a liberation.

The reformers of the home were in agreement that the family was the heart of any vigorous society. If its wives and mothers were victims of neurosis and a variety of physical disabilities, it had no prospects but decay and dissolution. Why, above all, Catharine Beecher asked, did she find so many "comfortably situated" wives "united to the most congenial and devoted husbands expressing the hope that their daughters would never marry"? That was indeed a sobering question. Why in an age that elevated the home and family to a status that seemed to partake of the divine, the subject of endless sentimental reflection and maunderings, did "comfortably situated" mothers express "the hope that their daughters would never marry"? That hope made them kin to their less respectable sisters, advocates of free love and the declared enemies of middle-class marriages. The fact was that a substantial number of the daughters of such unions did not marry, some from choice and others, one presumes, from necessity. If a young woman was determined to find a husband who encouraged and supported a more active role for his prospective bride than that of dutiful wife and mother, the range of choice was greatly narrowed. There were clearly not enough relatively enlightened young men to go around. The alternative was a single life and, given the prevailing sexual mores, for all but the boldest and most adventuresome, a celibate life: spinsterhood and old maidism. Nonetheless, in the last decades of the century more and more young women chose to defy convention, reject marriage, and pursue independent careers. This was especially the case with those who chose professions—doctors, academics, missionaries. In those ranks one found a high proportion of unmarried women.

Some 40 percent of the women who attended the newly established women's colleges in the East did not marry (in 1915 only 39 percent of the alumnae from eight women's colleges were married), most out of a conviction that they could not pursue the careers they wished under the confining conditions of matrimony. Many more initially expressed a determination not to marry but succumbed to the romantic impulses of their hearts and did indeed marry, many of them men who were sympathetic to their aspirations. Those who took vows of celibacy constituted a kind of order of secular nuns, a new phenomenon in history, women who had dedicated their lives to the vision articulated by Anna Julia Cooper, the secretary of the Colored Women's League: "the solidarity of humanity, the oneness of life . . . the supremacy of the moral force of reason, and justice, and love in the government of the nations of the earth."

The dislocations of sex were dramatized in appalling fashion by the number of prostitutes. The issue of prostitution was referred to discreetly as that of "social purity." It was estimated that there were 20,000 prostitutes in New York in the 1860s (London counted 60,000). Dr. Elizabeth Blackwell, sister-in-law of Lucy Stone and Nette Brown, was one of the first women to write specifically on the "social evil," informing women of "the hideous danger to themselves and their children" posed by the recourse of their husbands to prostitutes and the venereal diseases that resulted from such encounters. Born in England in 1821 (she died at eighty-nine), Elizabeth Blackwell was the first woman in modern times to receive a degree in medicine and a license to practice. Convinced that God had called her to be a physician, she graduated from Geneva College in New York State. She studied subsequently in Scotland and Paris and returned to New York to open an infirmary for women and children that included a medical school for women. Public health and preventive medicine were her special concerns. Her sister Emily, five years younger, followed in Elizabeth's footsteps. Rebuffed by a dozen medical schools, she finally graduated with honors from Western Reserve in Cleveland.

After several years of study abroad Emily joined Elizabeth in her New York infirmary. Always somewhat under Elizabeth's shadow, she took on the administrative duties of the infirmary and medical school and, like Elizabeth, wrote extensively on the "social purity" issue, on "Public Hygiene," and on medical education for women.

Elizabeth Blackwell noted that every effort throughout history to eradicate or even to control prostitution had been an "absolute failure . . . the evil and its consequences are as great and as uncontrollable as ever." What lay at the heart of the problem was the "relations of men and women." All efforts at reform had rested on "false principle of the inequality of men and women . . . to the almost universal belief that [sexual] license . . . is necessary to men, while Chastity is the one essential virtue of women. . . . This view," Blackwell wrote, "has come down to us as a relic of barbarism, from the old times when women were slaves. . . . This inequality of moral obligation in men and women is the last tract of the slavery of sex. . . . That wives and mothers should be pure, another class of women must have the whole balance of evil poured out upon them. The higher sense of mankind says that the family is the essential unit of the State. Our practice says the family plus prostitution is the essential unit." Seen in this light, prostitutes should be respected as performing an essential service for a society the basic mores of which forced such a distortion in the relationships between the sexes that the creation of a special class of women was necessary to compensate for that distortion; "instead of being made the scapegoat of a society and driven into the desert with the sins of a nation on its head," the class of prostitutes "should be regarded as an order vowed to sacrifice in obedience to a cruel social necessity; and their occupation should be regarded as legitimate and respectable, and should be surrounded by all the safeguards that may be required for its protection." Since men could not be expected to overturn a system that allowed them an indulgence denied to women, it must fall to women to take action to overturn the notion that there was one standard of morality for men and another for women. Sex, Blackwell insisted, had, like everything else in the United States, been made into a commodity: "Shrewdness, large capital, business enterprise, are all enlisted in the lawless stimulation of this mighty instinct of sex." While "immense provision is made for facilitating fornication," very little was done to encourage chastity. At the same time she ridiculed the notion that women were in some way less sensual or less sexual than men. She realized that "the attraction of sex does not cease [in women] with the physical inability to bear children; the soul of passion does not perish with physical decay. . . . In the attraction of one sex to the other, the young woman is unconsciously impelled, under the inexorable law of race perpetuation, toward the accomplishment of her special race-work, by a force out of proportion to her intellectual development or her worldly experience. She is led in the direction of this great mission of motherhood, not by the conscious craving of any abnormal appetite, but by the far stronger and more irresistible might of creative energy working through her. This energy renders her tremblingly susceptible to those influences which tend toward the accomplishment of her special work. This race instinct over-rides individuality to a degree. . . ." Actually motherhood, supported by "a strong and reliable attachment," freed a woman from her "undue burden of sexual instinct so that she may develop harmoniously as an individual." It was an arresting reflection. Since women were, in a sense, at the mercy of their own sexual drives, it was important for them to control and moderate those drives through marriage, motherhood, and a stable relationship with a man. Seen in this light, a woman's desire to marry was less a social convention than a protection against the abuse of her reproductive instinct.

The Blackwells believed that the successful fight against prostitution required two principal elements: First, the notion that there was an implied "absence of moral obligation on the part of men" must be destroyed, for until men accepted the same code of sexual morality as that imposed on women, laws intended to suppress prostitution would be completely ineffective, and secondly, middle- and upper-class women—"the wealthier, more educated, better placed women"—must enter into friendly social relations with the poorest and most friendless young women, the class from whom most prostitutes were recruited; "upon the ground of the equality of a common womanhood . . . every woman should feel bound to throw her help and influence into these efforts."

Another indefatigable worker in the social purity movement was Kate Bushnell, born in a small Illinois town in 1856. She earned her medical degree at the Chicago Woman's Medical College and departed for China as a medical missionary. When she returned to the United States three years later, she enlisted in Frances Willard's army of reform, the WCTU, and took up the management of the social purity department, organizing city missions for prostitutes and investigating Wisconsin lumber camps, where, it was alleged, young immigrant women were held in virtual slavery as prostitutes. In an essay Kate Bushnell compared the social opprobrium directed against a prostitute in American society with the hostility displayed in China toward someone struck by lightning, the view in that country being that lightning was divine punishment for an act of murder. To Bushnell's mind it was as absurd to despise and ostracize a prostitute for performing a function that society insisted upon as it was to brand a Chinese struck by lightning as a murderer. In both cases the denigrated individuals were the victims of false notions. Men who visited illegal houses of prostitution, far from being branded as criminals, did not hesitate "to boast openly of their exploits as libertines. . . . Think of it! Such liberty is not allowed to any other criminal." Statistics indicated that "the vast majority of murders and suicides have their provocation in illicit love, and thousands of times every year young innocent girls are brutally outraged. . . . Worse than all, this crime of crimes has to do with the ushering into existence of thousands of children yearly. . . ." Poorhouses and orphanages were filled with the offspring of such illicit unions. Some authorities had estimated that "eight tenths of all men are diseased from one form only of the disease resulting from early indiscretions, and their wives almost universally infected also." Men, Bushnell wrote, "are standing on our street-corners, sitting on our judicial benches, even kneeling among the worshippers in the house of God, who, when alone with men, find no richer topic of discussion than the stealing of the forbidden fruit of lust, and the memory of its flavor causes their vile mouths to water." Men resisted all alterations in a system that permitted them to be "bolder than women." Such a man took the line, "I can be aggressive enough to find out the moral stamina of any woman or girl with whom I associate, and can make the most of my opportunities . . . when I lead a girl away with me, the blame is put upon her for my action, I suffer no penalty. I like the moral teachers who say that when a woman falls she falls so much lower than a low man, for this doctrine, which makes me so much better than my victims, frees me from condemnation. . . . There are thousands upon thousands of homeless, disgraced girls lurking about the street-corners of our large cities at night. There are thousands of bad men and boys with them. But when the men and boys get tired of the streets they go reeling home to faithful wives and patient mothers. But when the girls get tired they must go to the brothel. . . ."

The White Cross Army upheld "the law of purity as equally binding on man and woman" and sought legislation to protect and defend "the comparatively innocent seduced girl" and to punish the seducer; Catharine Beecher proposed "mothergartens," where pregnant women could find refuge against "the lustful, selfish propensities in force and fury" of their husbands, against what was called, more boldly, "marital rape" or "matrimonial prostitution."

If American women were in a psychic prison, they were also confined in a far more practical prison: They were imprisoned in clothes. For Frances Willard, the clothes a woman was swathed in were a most appropriate symbol of her confined and dependent status. She remembered with acute unhappiness the precise moment when she was no longer allowed to race about with short hair and short skirts and old felt hats, "when my free, out-of-door life had to cease, and the long skirts and clubbed-up hair spiked with hair pins had to be endured. . . . I cried long and loud when I found I could never race and range about with freedom." It was the "date of my martyrdom." All her life long she recalled wistfully from the days of her childhood "the modest, simple, short dress, loose jacket, and broad-brimmed hat" and longed for a similar freedom. For an adult there were gloves, bonnets, compound shirts, muffs, wraps to fasten, shoes to button, "and then all of their burdens and constrictions to endure." Her cry was: "How long, O Lord, how long?"

While men's "informal" clothes grew more comfortable and practical—indeed, the "idea" of informal clothes appropriate to particular activities became more widespread—women's remained impossibly confining. They continued to be laced into corsets, in most instances laced more tightly than ever. Clothes reform had been a plank in the women's movement for thirty years—bloomers first made their appearance in the 1840s—but it was the least successful of all the myriad reforms that preoccupied Americans in the decades following the Civil War. Undoubtedly it was closely related to sexual repressiveness. Still, in the final analysis it was the women themselves who chose to be so attired, so laced and flounced. It is hard to suppress the suspicion that they at least subconsciously conceived of their complex assortment of skirts, corsets, and undergarments as a kind of armor against unwanted masculine intrusions while at the same time heightening the aura of sexuality. For many women, simply putting on such garments, especially with the assistance of a maid, was in itself an erotic experience. In the face of a mountain of evidence that sexual intercourse was often an unsuccessful ordeal for women, fraught with the complementary dangers of disease and unwanted pregnancy, it seems reasonable to assume that for many middle- and upper-class women, clothes were a kind of sexual surrogate. The intercourse was with the clothes rather than with human partners of the opposite sex. Of course, no properly brought-up young woman would even allow such a thought to cross her mind, but it is notable that the reform of women's clothing rested, in large measure, on a change in attitude toward the act of intercourse itself. When intercourse was established, by a few bold pioneers, as a mutually rewarding experience, women's clothes lost much of their cumbersome sexuality.

One of the shrewdest commentators on the social implications of women's dress was Thorstein Veblen, an energetic free lover who left scandal in his wake. Women, like architecture, Veblen wrote, conformed to "the canons of conspicuous waste, useless and expensive, and . . . consequently valuable as evidence of pecuniary strength . . . and under the guidance of the canon of pecuniary decency, the men find the resulting artificially induced pathological features attractive. So, for instance, the constricted waist. . . ."

Masculine attitudes toward women were, women insisted, part of their "environment," the bars and doors of the prisons they were bent on escaping. Those attitudes varied widely, of course, from strongly supportive to sportive, from admiring to hating to puzzled. On the whole, puzzled probably predominated. "The study of history is useful to the historian," Henry Adams wrote, "by teaching him his ignorance of women; and the mass of this ignorance crushes one who is familiar enough with what are called historical sources to realize how few women have ever been known. The woman who is known only through a man is known wrong . . . and all this is pure loss to history, for the American woman of the nineteenth century was much better, more interesting than the man."

Clearly, the most prescient men—Henry and William James, Brooks and Henry Adams, John Jay Chapman, and many others—seemed curiously and uniquely dependent on the psychic life of their women friends while at the same time puzzling over the destiny of this new creature, emerging from her ancient chrysalis in dazzling multiformity.

One school, as we might have anticipated, believed that the redemption of the United States, and eventually the world, would be achieved by women. Lester Ward belonged to that camp. He asserted that "it must be from the steady advance of woman rather than from the uncertain fluctuations of man that the sure and steady progress of the future is to come."

In *Democratic Vistas*, Walt Whitman called for a new breed or type of woman. "The idea of the women of America, (extricated from this daze, this fossil and unhealthy air which hangs about the word *lady*,) develop'd, raised to become the robust equals, workers, and, it may be, even practical and political deciders with the men—greater than man, we may admit, through their divine maternity, always their towering, emblematical attribute—but great, at any rate, as man, in all departments; or, rather, capable of being so, soon as they realize it, and launch forth as men do, amid the real, independent, stormy life."

Fathers and male friends were often highly supportive of not simply the "rights" of women but the full development of their human capacities. Husbands were the problem. The advice to Florence Jaffray from one of the city's social leaders when her engagement to marry Borden Harriman was announced was: "I give you one recipe, my girl, for a happy life with your husband. Mutual consideration and a good cook," and her father told her at lunch at Delmonico's, "If you want to hold your husband, never nag him. And never ask questions because if he wants you to know he will tell you and if he doesn't, perhaps he will lie."

Husbands were disconcertingly slow to surrender what they fancied were their prerogatives. When Frederic Howe married the beautiful young Unitarian minister Marie Jenney, she was better known than he was. Her church had grown impressively as she became "widely known as a speaker, as a leader in the suffrage movement, and in social activities." Although she wanted to continue in such work after her marriage, Howe, emancipated as he was in most respects, could not face having a wife who was involved in activities outside the home. "I wanted," he wrote, "my old-fashioned picture of a wife rather than an equal partner." In Howe's small-town view of the world "men and women fell in love, they married, had children; the wife cooked the meals, kept the house clean, entertained friends, spent as little as possible. . . . She cared for the family when sick, got the children ready for school and church, arranged the men's clothes . . . and during the winter made cakes and pies for the church sociables. She did not offend the opinions of her neighbors or of her husband, she was careful of her conduct, and only had an opinion of her own in a whisper. In so far as I thought of it at all women were conveniences of men. . . . Men were kind to them; they did not swear in their presence, they cleaned their boots before entering the house, gave them as good a home as they could, and were true to their marital vows. That was the most binding obligation of all. Men who failed in the latter regard were quite beyond the pale of the people I knew. . . . I spoke for women's suffrage," Howe recalled, "without much wanting it. And I urged freedom for women without liking it. My mind gave way, but not my instincts. . . . I hated privilege in the world of economics; I chose it in my own home."

Walter Hines Page in the *Atlantic Monthly* expressed the feelings of many American males when he wrote in the 1890s: "The decline in the character of our public life has been the national result of the lack of large constructive opportunities. . . . It has been a time of social reforms, of the emancipation of women, of national organizations of children, of societies for the prevention of minor vices and for the encouragement of minor virtues, of the study of genealogy, of the rise of morbid fiction, of journals for ladies, of literature for babes, of melodrama on the stage because we have had melodrama in life also, of criticism and reform rather than of thought and action. These things all denote a lack of adventurous opportunities, an indoor life, such as we have never before had a chance to enjoy; and there are many indications that a life of quiet may have become irksome. . . . Is it true that, a thousand years of adventure behind us, we are unable to endure a life of occupation that will not feed the imagination?"

A number of things might be said about Page's paragraph. One is the rather negative connotation he seems to give to "reform" in general (although it must be said, parenthetically, that Page considered himself a reformer), and another is his concern about the emphasis on the female side of society, "ladies," "emancipation of women," "children," "babes"—all grouped together and, at least by implication, contrasted with "hard" male activities, which were clearly on the decline. The latter, it should be noted, was a very general masculine anxiety. Individuals as diverse in their outlook as Henry Adams and William James expressed it.

Of course, emancipated women were not alone in their resistance to conventional marriage. To men of liberal or radical disposition who prized *their* freedom, the great majority of women appeared to be identified with the most conservative aspects of society. Seen in this perspective, women offered themselves as bait in a trap. In her discreetly manipulated sexuality, the woman seemed to promise her suitors what she could not in fact deliver: sexual delight. It was this aspect of women that alarmed Edward Bellamy. He wrote: "It is the misfortune of women that they are bound up with conservative ideas and the preservation of the status quo. Hence, a man must hate them when he rebels. Then it is that love is a chain." Bellamy, closely associated as he was with New Thought, anticipated a day in which "Love will be without tragic undertone, a cheerful comradeship only of people who suit but do not adore each other. Men and women will be broader and less intense correspondingly in their relations to one another, while a thousandfold more than now occupied with nature and the next steps of the race, i.e. that which is at present called the superhuman."

Finally, at the moment when many women and some men were expressing grave doubts about the health and soundness of conventional marriage, the apotheosis of motherhood took place. Whatever their other differences might be, Alphaists, Dianaists, advocates of birth control, free love, conventional marriage, or continence, on one point virtually all reformers (and certainly nonreformers) agreed: Motherhood was woman's highest and noblest calling. Heated discussions and often violent debates revolved around the question of how to protect, purify, and exalt motherhood; how to protect the prospective mother from brutal rape by a diseased husband; how to protect the pregnant mother from further male assaults; how to divert or modify the husband's lusts in the name of a "spiritualized" marriage and "scientifically" improved offspring.

Ellen Key, a Swedish writer and lecturer whose writings were widely read in America, was a prophet of the new motherhood. "Modern women," she wrote, "with their capacity for psychic analysis, with their physical and psychical refinement, are often repelled by the crudeness, the ignorance, or the importunities of man's nature." Thus they have lost the maternal instinct. Under the new dispensation it will be "regarded as a crime for a young wife voluntarily to ill-treat her person, either by excessive study, or excessive attention to sports, by tight-lacing, or consumption of sweets, by smoking or the use of stimulants, by sitting up at night, excessive work, or by all the thousands of other ways by which these attractive simpletons sin against nature." It was not clear whether the mother was the redeemer figure or the child. It was rather as though all that was left of the precepts and teachings of New Testament Christianity was "And a little child shall lead them." Some feminists raised this question: Was not too much expected of motherhood—the redemption of the world? With Ellen Key and a host of other feminist writers announcing that mothers were the only hope of a fallen world, those mothers who tried to keep abreast of the "state of the art" could be forgiven if they felt somewhat bewildered.

Beatrice Forbes-Robertson Hale, an English feminist, sounded an eminently sensible warning: "The insistence upon motherhood and child-care in the writings and speeches of leading feminists," she wrote, "is sometimes so intense as to almost endanger the claims of husband and father. . . . It is safe to say there has never been a time in which the child has received more than a fraction of the earnest care of mind and body bestowed on him by the educated mother of this generation. . . . The college-bred mother flies from her old faith in instinct to an extreme belief in science, and the boy that used to play in the mud now has his toys sterilized."

Angela Tilton Heywood and, later, Charlotte Perkins Gilman (both mothers) had similar warnings against "modern mother worship." The "dying soldier on the battlefield," Gilman wrote, "thinks of his mother, longs for her, not for his father. The traveler and exile dreams of his mother's care, his mother's doughnuts. . . ." The fact was that "human motherhood is more pathological than any other, more morbid, defective, irregular, diseased." It was clear to Gilman that "the human mother does less for her young, both absolutely and proportionately, than any other kind of mother on earth." She had too little knowledge of the world, of hygiene—of, in fact, anything—to be an adequate teacher of the young. She might indeed love her offspring, but "direct, concentrated, unvarying personal love is too hot an atmosphere for a young soul." American children were seared and shriveled by their mothers' love. The woman who worked was "usually a better producer" than the woman who did not. The revered and sentimentalized mother was, in fact, "erratic and pathological."

It is certainly true that for young males in most human societies the father had been the dominant figure and the most pervasive influence. Conversely, the mother-daughter (and grandmother) relation has been the most powerful one in traditional societies. In America those classic relationships were in large measure reversed. The great majority of powerful and active women in the nineteenth century had their closest relationship with their fathers or, at the very least, had strongly supportive fathers who encouraged them to develop their capacities to the fullest (I have, in fact, found none of whom this was not the case, from Lucretia Mott to Jane Addams). By the same token, more and more American "male achievers" came, as the century wore on, to credit their success in life to their mothers (the feelings of "low achievers" about their mothers are not so well recorded). That this was not the case in the early years of the Republic is suggested by the male descendants of John Adams, none of whom makes much more than passing, and often condescending, references to his mother.

"In theory," Henry Adams wrote to George Cabot Lodge, "my instinct rather turns to the woman than to the man of the future. In modern society, the man and his masculinity are at disadvantage. The woman is gaining on him. At least, it strikes me that she has literally driven his taste out of literature. Our magazines are wholly feminine. What," Adams asked rhetorically, "will the woman turn out to be? . . . The woman, as I have known her, is by no means the woman of sentiment. She is, if anything, less sentimental than the man. She is only beginning her career. What she will become is known only to the Holy Virgin. . . . A branch of the sex is sure to break off as an emancipated social class. If I were beginning again as a writer, I think I should drop the man, except as an accessory, and study the woman of the future. The American man is a very simple and cheap mechanism. The American woman I find a complicated and expensive one. . . . The American man is one-sided to deformity, and yet extraordinarily conceited, as far as literature reveals him. The American woman flatters him and rules him. He likes to be ruled. He is a peaceful, domestic animal, fond of baby-talk. I like him for he is helpless and sympathetic; afraid of himself, of his woman, of his children; yearning for love and doughnuts; shocked at automobiles and Trusts; proud and puffed up at riding a horse and shooting a bear; he is a gentleman whom I knew well; in fact, though it is not a thing I boast of, I was once an American man myself. Unluckily I was never an American woman. The American woman has not yet existed. She is still a study. She is all that is left to art."

35

The Empire of Reform

I f there were half a dozen "socialisms," there were hundreds of reforms. Many socialists were tireless reformers belonging to innumerable organizations dedicated to various schemes for saving their fellows from the consequences of their wickedness and folly. John Jay Chapman wrote of "a guerrilla warfare of reform."

We might divide the reform activities of this era into several basic categories (which, to be sure, often overlapped). First, there were those reforms directed at the individual or family—temperance; domestic economy; dress reform; nutritious eating habits; cooperative living. Under the tireless promptings of Catharine Beecher the American Women's Educational Association resolved: "That the science of domestic economy should be made a study in all institutions for girls. . . ."

Then there were social reforms—the fights against prostitution and crime; the movements devoted to public health, parks and playgrounds, etc.

Still another category consisted of organizations directed at protecting the constitutional rights of Americans. The Personal Rights League fought the American Protective Association (a "nativist" association) and all attacks on civil liberties. In addition, it took up the issue of adulterated food.

The most commodious category, as we have seen, was municipal reform, embracing dozens of specific reforms. In New York City Lillian Wald organized the Social Halls Association to provide entertainment for tenement dwellers. The model was Clinton Hall, which had restaurants, clubrooms, a bowling alley, a roof garden, and a dance hall.

The Children's Aid Society of New York was a model for other such institutions. From its founding in 1853 to 1885, it provided lodging for 30,000 homeless children. It sheltered an average of 600 children and ran an industrial and night school as well, helping in the process to feed and clothe more than 10,000 children a year. Many were transferred "to selected homes in the country, there being almost an unlimited demand for children's labor in this country," a somewhat chilling note.

Municipal reform which focused on the issue of public ownership of public utilities was called MO and referred to as "gas and water socialism."

A series of sweeping "political" reforms were proposed in New York City: The Brooklyn plan, put forward by Mayor Seth Low of Brooklyn, undertook to concentrate power in the hands of a single elected official—the mayor—who had the right to appoint and fire all the heads of the major departments: waterworks; streets and sewers; health. The power of the purse remained, however, with the City Council. The Galveston or Des Moines plan—both cities tried it—did away with the "entire fabric of municipal organization and combined all the executive and legislative powers in a five-man elected board." Even ministers were recruited in an effort to find honest public officials. In Columbus, Ohio, Washington Gladden, the outspoken reform minister, was elected to the City Council and helped thwart efforts to sell city franchises under terms excessively favorable to the utility companies. As Gladden put it, "if in any city there are ten or twenty or two hundred millions of dollars invested by private persons or corporations in public-service industries, these millions, as human nature goes, are directly interested in having bad government in that city."

Ohio led the nation in prison reform. It followed the increasingly popular practice of putting prisoners to work and selling the products of their labor. In Ohio a prisoner could, by good behavior, lessen the term of his sentence five days each month and, in addition, receive upon his release a tenth of the wages earned by his work in prison. No distinctive prison garb was worn, and no "degrading punishments" were allowed.

One of the most acclaimed reforms in the area of crime, its punishment and prevention, was the establishment of reform schools for boys and girls, who before had been confined with hardened adult criminals. There were, by 1874, thirty-four reformatories in the country with a total population of 9,000 reformees. Statistics indicated that 91,000 had passed through them, and by Jacob Riis's calculation, "nearly seventy thousand were reported as permanently reformed—saved!" A contemporary report declared: "These useful institutions are an immense advance on the prisons which preceded them. The youth is no longer confined with the mature criminal; the sexes are separated; and at night, as a general practice, there is but one child in each cell, or, if in a large dormitory, the children are carefully watched to prevent evil communications. They are all taught useful trades, and have regular day instructions in schools besides religious teaching on Sunday. After their term of sentence has expired, or previously if their good conduct permits, they are indentured with worthy and respected farmers and mechanics."

Such organizations as the National League for Promoting Public Ownership of Monopolies, the Bureau of Economic Research, the National Federation for Majority Rule, and the Anti-Trust League constituted still another class of reform activity.

Finally, there was a general category that had to do with major economic and political reforms of the society as a whole. This latter category was directed to *changing people's minds* as a prelude to the transformation of the larger society. Henry George's Single Tax Clubs clearly belonged in this category. Many religious and quasi-religious organizations combined programs of moral and spiritual redemption with calls for sweeping social and political transformations. Such was the case with Madame Blavatsky's Theosophists, who endorsed Edward Bellamy's Nationalism. New Thought devotees were often leaders in the fight for justice to blacks.

Every city and every town had debating and literary societies and these, like the club that Lester Ward belonged to in Washington, D.C., were often, in effect, fronts for radical social and political opinions.

The lyceums and Chautauquas circulated public lecturers all around the country. John Dewey and Henry Demarest Lloyd lectured at the Farmington School of Ethics in the spring of 1898. The Ann Arbor Summer School of Ethics was another stop on the lecturing tour, as was the Deerfield Summer School of History and Romance.

Three of the most influential reformers of the era were Henry

Demarest Lloyd, Edward Bellamy, and John Jay Chapman. The diversity of their backgrounds suggests the ubiquity of the reform spirit. Lloyd and Bellamy belonged to an older generation of reformers; Chapman, to the "last generation" of reformers.

Born in New York City in 1847, son of a Dutch Reformed minister who was a poor provider for his wife and four children and a mother descended from the early Dutch settlers, Lloyd was reared as a Jacksonian Democrat. He and his two brothers, poor but ambitious, attended W. Plenkeron's Academy. Henry Lloyd went on a scholarship to Columbia College and there became a leader in student literary activities and a devout Emersonian. After he graduated from Columbia, he won his reformer's spurs as a champion of free trade. Like so many of the ablest and most ambitious young men of his generation (and subsequent ones), Lloyd aspired to be a "Bowles . . . or Greeley or Bennett"—in short a journalist and editor rather than "the most successful lawyer or richest merchant or most brilliant author in America. I had rather raise myself to their height," he wrote a friend, "than be raised by others to the Presidency." Sounding thoroughly Emersonian, he wrote that he wished to be "all that is musical, humanitarian, muscular, imaginative, brainy, poetic, powerful with men and material. . . . All forms of money making I despise as pursuits in themselves for themselves, the law is too technical and traditional. I am too unconventionally and unaffectedly pious to be a minister," he added.

When Lloyd visited Chicago in behalf of the Free Trade League, a college-mate introduced him to Horace White, editor of the *Chicago Tribune*, whose publisher, William Bross, had been a founder of the Republican Party in Illinois and a friend of Lincoln's. Offered a job as a reporter for the *Tribune*, Lloyd was soon a suitor of Bross's daughter, Jessie. Jessie was a "new woman," a friend of Frances Willard, the vice-president of the Chicago Philosophical Society, a devoted admirer of Emerson, an heiress, and a leader in Chicago society. After a brief apprenticeship in the lower ranks of the *Tribune*, Lloyd was put in charge of the paper's "literary section" and not long after won the hand of Jessie Bross, thus assuring his position as an up-and-coming young capitalist. With Jessie's fortune and his own rapid rise on the *Tribune* (he was soon an editor), the Lloyds established two handsome houses, one in Chicago and one on the outskirts of Winnetka, and made them centers for reformers and political radicals of every description. Wayside, the Lloyd house at Winnetka, was described by a French newspaper correspondent as a place where "rich and poor, white and black, gentle and simple, college president and seamstress, artist and mechanic, divine and laymen" met "on the basis of liberty, fraternity and equality." Tom Morgan, the pillar of the American Railway Union, wrote of Lloyd: "With him I lost all my feeling of class distinction and antagonism, all doubt and bitterness was gone and in its place perfect confidence." A delegate at one of the innumerable conferences he attended described Lloyd "as the most picturesque man here with his seamed melancholy face and warm, quiet, gentle manners. . . . His language is picturesque, poetic, imaginative, illuminative. . . . He is as delicate, as fragile, as beautiful as a Sèvres vase, and intense and musical as a violin strung ready for the master's hand, as sympathetic as a woman."

One of the most horrendous episodes in the labor history of the 1880s occurred in Spring Valley, Illinois, a coal mining community. In the summer of 1889 the owners of the mines locked out their employees for protesting a 60 percent wage reduction. Lloyd was soon involved in publicizing the circumstances of the strike, attacking the owners and espousing the cause of the miners. The miners, he discovered, had been told at the end of a day's work that they should take out their tools, "as the mines would be closed until further notice. In one afternoon . . . all the miners in town were deprived of their livelihood. They had not struck; they had not asked for any increase in wages; they had made no new demands of any kind upon their employers. Simultaneously with the closing of the mines, the company's store was closed. . . . No explanation was vouchsafed as to when the mines would be re-opened. . . . They were locked out. It was a strike but it was a strike of the millionaires against miners. . . . It was a strike in violation of every pledge, tacit and expressed, which these rich men had given when they built their railroad, and sold land and opened the mines, and called in the men from other work far and near. . . . To 'make more money' disease and starvation were invited to come to Spring Valley, and they came." Lloyd wrote: "The story of Spring Valley" needs not many changes "to be a picture of what all American industry will come to be if the power of your Bourbons of business, such as you have shown yourselves to be at Spring Valley, develops at its present rate up to the end of the nineteenth century."

The articles exposing the actions of the mineowners were printed in the *Chicago Tribune* and reprinted in many other newspapers with labor sympathies. The editor of the *Tribune* wrote that "a Society which permits such inhuman outrages as that at Spring Valley is either asleep or in an advanced state of decay," and William Dean Howells wrote to Lloyd that he had read his account of the strike with "grief and rage."

Out of Lloyd's articles on Spring Valley came a book, entitled *A Strike of Millionaires Against Miners or the Story of Spring Valley*, which was, as much as anything else, an indictment of capitalism and of the ruthless indifference of the mineowners to the hardships and suffering of the miners. The strike itself dragged on for almost a decade. At one point 300 of the miners offered to become slaves if they were given food, clothes, and housing.

Lloyd fastened on John D. Rockefeller as the symbol of all that was wrong with American capitalism. It is not too much to say that the oil tycoon became Lloyd's obsession. "He is," he wrote of Rockefeller, ". . . a depredator . . . not a worshipper of liberty . . . a Czar of plutocracy, a worshipper of his own Money Power over mankind. He will never sacrifice any of his plans for the restraints of law or patriotism or philanthropy. . . . His greed, rapacity, flow as a Universal solvent wherever they can, melting down into gold for him, private enterprise, public morals, judicial honor, legislative faith, gifts of nature. He will stop when he is stopped—not before." In 1889 Lloyd decided to write a book, "a full, and absolutely and documentarily accurate" history, that would focus on Standard Oil as "the most characteristic thing in our business civilization . . . the most threatening for the future," emphasizing "the moral, social, and industrial displacements and perversions that have followed from the appropriation by the strong and clever of the lion's share of the power and wealth created by modern machinery."

It seemed to Lloyd that "the mania of business has reached an acuter and extremer development in America than elsewhere because nowhere else have bounteous nature and free institutions produced birthrights and pottages so well worth 'swapping,' but," he added, "the follies and wickedness of business have nowhere been so sharply challenged as in free America." A free people had pursued "their depredators" into every nook and cranny of the national life.

What followed from Lloyd's reflections on the iniquities of capitalism was his most important and successful book, *Wealth Against Commonwealth*. It was distinguished from hundreds of denunciations of capitalism by Lloyd's style. A close student of Emerson, Lloyd combined his master's gift for epigrammatic sentences with that reforming zeal of which Emerson was so wary. The result was one of the most eloquent and widely read indictments of capitalism produced in the nineteenth century. The beginning was classically Emersonian: "Nature is rich; but everywhere man, the heir of nature, is poor." The reason was the practices of the monopoly capitalism—"the syndicates, trusts, combinations." With people starving they raised the cry of "overproduction. . . . holding back the riches of earth, sea, sky from their fellows who famish and freeze in the dark, and declaring to them that there is too much light and warmth and food. They assert the right, for their private profit, to regulate the consumption by the people of the necessaries of life, and to control production not by the needs of humanity, but by the desires of a few for dividends. . . . Liberty produces wealth, and wealth destroys liberty." That was the paradox that must be solved if the nation and the world were not to be engulfed in disaster. "Our size," Lloyd wrote, "has got beyond both our science and our conscience. . . . Captains of Industry 'do not know' whether the men in the ranks are dying from lack of food and shelter; we cannot clean our cities nor our politics; the locomotive has more man-power than all the ballot-boxes, and mill-wheels wear out the hearts of workers unable to keep up beating time to their whirl."

Lloyd's particular enemy was social Darwinism. "The man who should apply in his family or his citizenship this survival of the fittest theory as it is practically professed and operated in business would be a monster, and would be speedily made extinct, as we do with monsters." Indeed, the whole model of competitive individualism was obsolete, Lloyd insisted. "For a hundred years or so our economic theory has been one of industrial government by the self-interest of the individual. Political government by the self-interest of the individual we call anarchy." Those who denounce it in politics, however, do not hesitate to practice it in industry.

Henry Demarest Lloyd inveighed against a society in which "childhood is forbidden to become manhood and manhood is forbidden to die a natural death," a society featuring "mausoleums in which we bury the dead rich, slums in which we bury the living poor. . . . A really human life is impossible in our cities," he declared, "but they cannot be reconstructed under the old self-interest. . . . We are very poor. The striking feature of our economic condition is our poverty, not our wealth. We make ourselves rich by appropriating the property of others by methods which lessen the total property of all. . . . Modern wealth more and more resembles the winnings of speculators in bread during famine—worse, for to make the money it makes the famine."

Lloyd gave particular attention to the increasing impersonalization of capitalist society. Men did not own their own tools, their farms, the mills and mines and stores they worked in. Indeed, it was often difficult to tell who owned them; not an individual but a corporation that claimed the rights of an individual even as it robbed real individuals of their rights.

Individualism had done its service—"we have overworked the self-interest of the individual"—and it was now evident that cooperative endeavors and the general good of the society were paramount considerations. "Priests, voluptuaries, tyrants, knights, ascetics—in the long procession of fanatics a new-comer takes his place; he is called 'the model merchant'—the cruelest fanatic in history. He is the product of ages given to progressive devotion to trading . He is the high-priest of the latest idolatry, self-worship and self-interest. . . . One thing after another has passed out from under the regime of brotherhood and passed under that of bargainhood. The ground we move on, the bodies we work with, and the necessaries we live by are all being exchanged, by rules fetched with cupidity from heartless schools. . . . By these rules the cunning are the good, and the weak and tender the bad, and the good are to have all the goods and the weak are to have nothing. . . . It appears to have been the destiny of the railroads to begin and of oil to lubricate to its finish the last stage of this crazy commercialism. Business colors the modern world as war reddened the ancient world. Out of such delirium monsters are bred, and their excesses destroy the system that brought them forth. . . . Sincere as rattlesnakes, they are selfish with the unconsciousness possible to only the entirely commonplace, without the curiosity to question their times or the imagination to conceive the pain they inflict, and their every ideal is satisfied by the conventionalities of church, parlor, and counting-houses."

Our literature has no more devastating a portrait of a human type than Lloyd's "Captains of Industry"—"practical as granite and gravitation." Lloyd is at pains to make clear that such leaders who seem to have appeared "as by a law of nature" are in fact the consequence of "the false ideals of us who have created them and their opportunity." If Western civilization is destroyed, it will not be by barbarians from below, as the historian Thomas Babington Macaulay had predicted. "Our barbarians come from above. Our great money-makers have sprung in one generation into seats of power kings do not know. . . . Without restraints of culture, experience, the pride, or even the inherited caution of class or rank, these men, intoxicated, think they are the wave instead of the float. . . . They are gluttons of luxury and power, rough, unsocialized, believing that mankind must be kept terrorized. Powers of pity die out of them, because they work through agents and die in their agents, because what they do is not for themselves." Only when the friends of brotherhood and justice create a republic "in which all join their labor that the poorest may be fed, and the weakest defended" can the forces at work in capitalist society "which generate those obnoxious persons—our fittest" be reversed.

The problem was, in Lloyd's opinion, that Americans, believing man naturally good, had developed a naïve faith that the powerful would use their power for the benefit of all. There was a human disposition to trust "good men to do good as kings." But history proved abundantly that power corrupted the best and wisest of kings. "Identical is the lesson we are learning with regard to industrial power and property," Lloyd wrote. "We are calling upon their owners, as mankind called upon kings in their day to be good and kind, wise and sweet, and we are calling in vain. We are asking them not to be what we have made them. . . . Can we forestall ruin by reform? If we wait to be forced by events we shall be astounded to find out how much more radical they are than our utopias. History is the serial obituary of the men who thought they could drive men. . . . Ruin is already hard at work among us. Our libraries are full of official inquiries and scientific interpretations which show how our master-motive is working decay in all our parts. The family crumbles into competition between the father and the children whom he breeds to take his place in the factory, to unfit themselves to be fathers in their turn."

Lloyd called for "a thorough, stalwart resimplification, a life governed by simple needs and loves" as the "imperative want of the world." To him it was evident that America's "new wealth is too great for the old forms." Products cooperatively produced must be cooperatively enjoyed, and a new "tribal relation" created. The change would come not by scholarly tomes but by the disinterested actions of the principled. "All the sayings have been said. The only field for new effects is in epigrams of practice. . . . The change must be social, and its martyrdoms have already begun." There must be "honesty, love, justice in the heart of the business world," but there must also be "the forms which will fit them."

In the new order there "must be no private use of public power or public property. These are created by the common sacrifices of all, and can rightfully be used only for the common good of all—from all, by all, for all." Not only must there be a new social and industrial order in which all shared, but individual life would open out in marvelous new dimensions. "We can have all the rights we will create," he wrote. "All the rights we will give we can have. . . . A new liberty will put an end to pauperism and millionairism and the crimes and death-rate born of both wretchedness. . . . There can be no single liberty. Liberties go in clusters like the Pleiades. . . . In manners, in literature, in marriage, in church, in all, we see at work the saving ferment which is to make all things new by bringing them nearer to the old ideal. . . . We are to have a private life of a new beauty. . . . We are to become commoners, travellers to Altruria. We are to become fathers, mothers, for the spirit of the father and mother is not in us while we can say of any child it is not ours, and leave it in the grime. . . . And the little patriotism, which is the love of humanity fenced within our frontier will widen into the reciprocal service of all men." The prophets of the new age will "stimulate new hatred of evil, new love of the good, new sympathy for the victims of power" and help form "a new conscience."

Few of the new school economists went so far as to endorse government ownership of the trusts. The American Economic Association's journal did not condescend even to review *Wealth Against Commonwealth*. Those academics who did review the book took Lloyd to task for not being more impartial and scientific. The *Political Science Quarterly* described it as a tract rather than a scholarly work. It was, however, enthusiastically reviewed in liberal and prolabor journals. The Christian Socialist *American Fabian* called it "impregnable," and it enjoyed as much popularity in England as in the United States. Rockefeller was not slow to mount a counterattack. George Gunton, a conservative economist heavily subsidized by Rockefeller, undertook to refute Lloyd. When Gunton was appointed professor of economics at Columbia some ten years later, it was learned he had received $225,000 from Standard Oil interests in addition to a half million to underwrite his economics journal.

"Before every revolution marches a book," Lloyd wrote: "the *Contract Social, Uncle Tom's Cabin*." Lloyd's own book might be said to march before the revolution in social thought through which what we might call the Conscience State, a term more accurate and more appropriate than the "Welfare State," came into existence. Government control was "the great weapon, for the masses. Now that we've got the nation," Lloyd wrote somewhat overoptimistically after Cleveland's election, "let us use the nation. The only way to checkmate tendencies of individual selfishness and power, the aggressions of corporations, is by public

opinion acting through the provided organs of public government."
The new democracy could not be achieved by appealing to particular
interests. "The appeal must be made to the *community of interests*." Yet
Lloyd was aware that the capitalist could not be brought to heel by
appeals to his better nature. "Grant that it is the business of those who
have industrial spirit to combine," he wrote, "it is the business of those
who have public spirit to control combinations, and make them square
with the public good. This they will assuredly not do themselves." In
Lloyd's words, the new motto of the reformers must be "that government is best which governs most."

As director of the Brotherhood of the Co-operative Commonwealth (an organization inspired by his book), Lloyd became an advocate of the cooperative movement. The movement had its roots in
the early stages of populism, but it was strongly reinforced by ideas
imported from Britain, where the movement flourished. The Knights
of Labor had been much concerned with establishing cooperatives.
The World's Congress of Co-operation, held in conjunction with the
World's Columbian Exposition, gave fresh stimulus to those Americans
to whom agricultural and industrial cooperatives seemed a solution to
the evils of capitalism. A National Co-operative Congress was held in
St. Louis in 1896, concurrent with the Populists' nominating convention.
A leader in the cooperative movement was J. A. Wayland, editor of
the Christian Socialist journal *Appeal to Reason*. Wayland assisted George
Herron in setting up the Christian Commonwealth Colony in Georgia.
To Lloyd the establishment of the Georgia community seemed "the
most religious manifestation of our day," possible refuge against "the
troublous anarchy I fear is coming."

With the goal of establishing a colony on Puget Sound the Brotherhood of the Co-operative Commonwealth enrolled 1,200 members
and raised some $30,000. The result was the Equality Colony, dedicated
to the principles of William Morris and John Ruskin. Even Debs was
drawn to the movement and approached Lloyd to solicit his help in
organizing a colony for the American Railway Union. Although Lloyd
refused to assist Debs because he considered him too doctrinaire a
socialist, he laid the cornerstone of the Ruskin College of the New
Economy at Ruskin, Tennessee, and gave the principal address, in
which he hailed the formation of the "New Conscience," which would
not allow one class of men to exploit another. Each man should become
"a creator" working for "the Messianic democracy of a self-redeeming
people." It seemed to Lloyd that the cooperative movement contained

a "thoroughgoing program of a complete social reconstruction." No other scheme of reform "surpasses it in radicalism," he added; "no other approaches it in achievement, neither in its numbers of adherents nor solidarity of resources, in men, minds, and money."

A kind of corollary to the cooperative movement was that of so-called copartnership, in which an employer accepted his employees as copartners, sharing with them, as with his stockholders, the profits of the business. In some copartnerships the workers, in fact, replaced the stockholders. The movement had its origin in England, and a visit to such ventures convinced Lloyd that copartnership was a harbinger of better days to come for workingmen and women.

Lloyd also helped draw attention to the response of New Zealand to the dangers of capitalism. Under a Liberal-Labor regime, New Zealand had gained world prominence by its reforms. The railroads and telegraph and postal services were already owned by the government. In addition, the administration legalized trade unions and established procedures for compulsory arbitration of labor disputes. The prime minister, a former shepherd, took the lead in dividing large estates into small ranches and establishing "Village Settlements," leased for 999 years. Unemployment compensation was provided for those out of work temporarily, and old-age pensions were inaugurated. Lloyd set off to see for himself this wonder of "welfare democracy." The result was a book entitled, a little misleadingly, *A Country Without Strikes* and a set of new causes to publicize in the United States, the principal one being compulsory arbitration.

Lecturing in Chicago in December, 1891, at a protest meeting against police brutality in the disruption of a painters' union meeting, Henry Demarest Lloyd warned that the alternatives facing the United States were a "French Revolution" or "an Anglo-Saxon revolution of peace, compromise and progress." One of his impressed listeners was Clarence Darrow, a lawyer for the Chicago and North Western Railroad, who wrote: "It was *great*. In logic & law it cannot be disputed. It made me feel that I am a hypocrite & a slave and added to my resolution to make my term of servitude short."

Lloyd, in his constant fluctuations between competing social theories, represented the generally unsettled character of liberal reform. He moved from bimetallism to free silver to hard money; from cooperative communities to socialism and back again. He denounced the churches and organized religion in general, as fervently as he denounced the "materialistic and atheistical aspects of . . . modern thought."

He looked to the trade union movement for the achievement of "industrial democracy" and then looked away when it failed to respond to the broader social issues that concerned him.

Edward Bellamy was born in Chicopee Falls, Massachusetts, in 1850. His father, Rufus King Bellamy, named after the New York Federalist, was a Baptist minister, plump, easygoing, an indifferent provider. Bellamy's mother was "a thin, almost translucent wisp of a person . . ." with a will of iron. Bellamy was convinced that his father ate himself to death. His mother, by contrast, "never had any patience with self-indulgence. . . . She regarded the main purpose of life to be discipline of the heart, soul, and mind; and deprivation of sense gratification she regarded not as a misfortune, but as a blessing and a benefit."

It is not surprising that the offspring of such an incongruous mating should have resolved "to retain the child's zest for the pleasures of life, while possessing the stoic's power of renouncing them without a pang whenever it may be needful. . . ." On his twenty-first birthday Edward Bellamy's mother enjoined him to be a " 'living sacrifice' to your God and Saviour." But Bellamy read Karl Marx and Charles Darwin and decided to become "an infidel," as "a better way to serve his country."

Rejection by the West Point Military Academy put an end to Bellamy's dream of being an army officer. A voracious reader, he began to write reviews and articles for the nearby *Springfield Union*. He took a trip through Germany and England in 1868, and his glimpses of working-class poverty and degradation began his obsession with the issue of social justice.

Back in Springfield, Bellamy was overcome by a sense of failure and futility. "I had thought myself to be something greater than other men and I find that I am but after all a mediocre person. . . . I am weary and could wish to die, for good and all and over with it. If I am not more than other men I would be nothing."

Several years later, having tried the law, he decided to become a writer, one who would put his pen in the service of the exploited and deprived. Like Lester Ward, Bellamy became a freethinker and a member of the town lyceum, where he presented his political and social views.

In 1878 Bellamy published his first book, a novel entitled *Six to One*. His second, *Dr. Heidenhoff's Process*, was hailed by no less a critic than William Dean Howells as being worthy of Hawthorne. *The Duke of Stockbridge*, a sympathetic story about Shays's Rebellion, appeared a year later. In 1882, at the age of thirty-two, Bellamy married Emma Augusta Sanderson, eleven years his junior. His writing brought in barely enough money to keep food on the table, and Bellamy and his wife soon had additional mouths to feed.

In 1886, deeply troubled by the labor upheavals of that year which culminated in the Haymarket Affair, Bellamy began work on a utopian novel, *Looking Backward*. Julian West, the protagonist of *Looking Backward*, born in 1857, goes to sleep in 1887 and wakes in 1957 to find that the United States has become a utopian socialist society, a highly centralized and benignly autocratic state in which all material needs are provided for.

West's guides to this transformed society are Dr. Leete and his daughter, Edith. As Dr. Leete explains to West, the changes he observes were brought about by a crisis in the war between capital and labor. Capital "threatened society with a form of tyranny more abhorrent than it had ever endured." Americans "believed that the great corporations were preparing for them a yoke of baser servitude than had ever been imposed on the race, servitude not to men but to soulless machines, incapable of any emotion but insatiable greed. Looking back, we cannot wonder at their desperation, for certainly humanity was never confronted with a fate more sordid and hideous than would have been the era of corporate tyranny which they anticipated."

In 1957 Americans are organized into male or female divisions of the Industrial Army. Everything is carefully planned, and highly trained experts do all tasks from housecleaning to the preparation of food. The means of production are owned by the state, and the work of individuals is paid for by labor credits based on national productivity. "All problems growing out of the division of labor, and its results," Bellamy wrote, "have been solved by the union of the entire nation in a general business partnership, in which every man and woman is an equal partner. The conduct of the industries, commerce and general business of the country is committed by the national firm to a so-called army of industry, which includes all the able-bodied citizens . . . between the ages of 21 and 45. . . . All persons chose their occupations in the army of industry, according to natural tastes and gifts. . . . At the age of 45 all members of the industrial army . . . are discharged from further service, and remain absolutely free to occupy themselves as they will for the remainder of life."

The industrial duty of citizens was similar to military duty. Individuals were organized "for peace as at present for war. The people stand shoulder to shoulder . . . against hunger, and cold, and nakedness, every wrong and every want that human nature can repel; an invincible square, with the women and the children, the sick, the aged and the infirm in the centre." Every citizen accepted responsibility for his or her fellows—"mutual obligation of citizen to nation, and nation to citizen."

Bellamy's ideal society was a kind of "meritocracy" of experts. While everyone was paid the same wage, the more able and industrious were promoted and honored according to their deserts. Moreover, since no one would be "dependent upon the favor or patronage of any other or group of others . . ." they all can develop "a robust and unfettered individuality."

Women, earning their own credits (money has been abolished), are free to marry on the basis of "personal preference" rather than "sordid or prudential calculations." Crime has virtually disappeared with the elimination of money, and the general health of society is vastly improved. All this has been achieved peacefully by virtue of greater and greater concentrations of trusts and syndicates which "realized their manifest destiny by absorption in the great trust of the nation, the universal partnership of the people." Nationalism, Bellamy declared, was based on "the principle of fraternal co-operation."

Bellamy wrote of *Looking Backward*: "[It] is intended, in all seriousness, as a forecast, in accordance with the principles of evolution, of the next stage in the industrial and social development of humanity, especially in this country. . . ." To Bellamy "the dawn of the new era is already near at hand. . . ."

There are echoes of Plato's totalitarian state in *Looking Backward* as well as intimations of Marxian socialism, although Bellamy himself steered clear of the word "socialist." He wrote Howells: "It smells to the average American of petroleum, suggests the red flag and all manner of sexual novelties, and an abusive tone about God and religion. . . . What ever German and French reformers may choose to call themselves, socialist is not a good name for a party to succeed with in America."

The popular response to *Looking Backward* was comparable to the response to *Progress and Poverty*. "Of only one other book (Uncle Tom's Cabin)," his publishers noted, "have three hundred thousand copies been printed within two years of its publication. . . . The story of its remarkable popularity and influence will hereafter form a very interesting chapter in the history of American literature and sociology."

A reviewer in *The New York Times* noted: "Mr. Bellamy has achieved so brilliant and complete a success . . . that the reader is carried away by the development of the New Utopia. . . . [He] has succeeded in describing a thorough reorganization of society without demanding the least concession to unpractical fancy. . . . To produce such an effect is to rise to the plane of high art." To the reviewer the "changes" were not "fantasies but . . . possibilities. . . ."

The Nationalist Clubs, devoted to Bellamy's vision, were an even more remarkable phenomenon. Cyrus Willard, a cousin to Frances Willard (who, incidentally, called *Looking Backward* "a new evangel"), became a dedicated aide to Bellamy and a charter member of the Nationalist Clubs; he estimated in 1890 that there were, countrywide, more than 500,000 members. Among them were most of the leading reformers of the day.

Bellamy poured all his limited physical energies and modest resources into promoting his blueprint for a new social order. He began a work entitled *Equality*, published in 1897, and lived, meanwhile, on raw eggs, milk, and whiskey. Finally, it was determined that he had tuberculosis. He went to Denver for treatment, and there the doctors killed him. He was forty-eight.

Among those young Americans who felt the call to political activism and reform, one of the most gifted was John Jay Chapman, a graduate of Harvard and Harvard Law School. Chapman wrote his fiancée, Minna Timmins: "I think there are no more books that need to be written in the world just now. The world has got all the books it wants. . . . The time is for action and political organization. Better cast a vote than write a book. I am inclined to think that these people organizing charities and setting germs of self-betterment to sprout on a large or small scale are the important people."

Chapman's great-great-grandfather was John Jay, the Founding Father, member of the Constitutional Convention, author with Hamilton and Madison of *The Federalist Papers*, and first chief justice of the Supreme Court. His great-grandfather was William Jay, an abolitionist leader, and his grandfather was the reformer, pacifist, and abolitionist John Jay. Another grandparent, Maria Weston Chapman, had been a leader in both the antislavery movement and the women's rights movement. Perhaps only the Adamses could claim a more distinguished parentage. Chapman was, in addition, strikingly handsome and "wild," with a quality of passionate intensity that often alarmed and disconcerted his friends. While he was a student at Harvard, he imagined that a young woman with whom he had fallen in love without acknowledging the fact to himself, had been insulted by a classmate. Chapman sought out the student and attacked him with a heavy stick, inflicting a serious injury. When he found out shortly afterward that the man he had injured was innocent of any misdoing, Chapman held his hand over a candle until it was so badly burned that it had to be amputated. That the act had a profound effect on Chapman's life cannot be doubted. In the upper-class social circles of New York City and Boston in which he moved, the episode gave him a highly romantic reputation; he was often referred to as Mad Jack Chapman. The romantic element was enhanced by his idyllic courtship of beautiful Minna Timmins (whose honor he thought he was defending). Minna Timmins was half Italian and half Bostonian, as brilliant as Chapman and as passionate. They had as tempestuous a love affair as any novelist could conceive. The antithesis of his mentor, William James, in most respects, Chapman had James's capacity for love and friendship and a charm that few could resist. Dickinson Miller, a fellow student, wrote of him: "He is glowing and beautiful like fire, pure and purifying like fire, lambent, wayward, unshapeable like fire, uncontrollable like fire, destructive like fire, seeking heaven like fire."

That John Jay Chapman, like the Adamses and the Danas, was profoundly conscious of his family's tradition is certain. At the time of his grandfather Jay's death, he wrote: "The fact is that his name and the family tradition have been controlling ideas with me ever since I can remember—perhaps too much so. . . ." Chapman was very conscious of being an American "aristocrat," a "swell," a person somehow above the constraints of more ordinary men. "Come down to it and you find the paradox that only aristocrats are truly democratic in their social conduct and feeling," he wrote. "They only are simple—they only have nothing to gain and nothing to lose, and have the freedom and simplicity of human beings." Certainly the antislavery movement, with which Chapman identified strongly, constituted a genuine "moral aristocracy," a company of men and women who changed the course of our history by persisting generation after generation in their ideals.

After a period of skepticism and a serious nervous breakdown Chapman came to a "restoration" of his childhood religious faith. "I was no longer merely intellectual," he wrote, "I was religious, as I had been cut out by nature to be . . . . I was a unity. The rest was patience. . . . So far as the consciousness of being the creature of divine power goes, it has never left me."

The Chapmans moved to New York City and Jack Chapman threw himself wholeheartedly into the work of the City Reform Club. In a surprisingly short time he had enlisted a number of the city's most "solid citizens" in addition to a number of young "firebrands." Chapman and his fellow radicals made a heroic effort to try to persuade "artisans and laborers" to join the club, all to no avail. Edmond Kelly, one of the club's young Turks, thereupon resigned in despair and announced himself a socialist. Out of the City Club came the Good Government Club, a group of liberal Republicans determined to make their party the party of reform. They were soon known as goo-goos, and their efforts scorned by the party regulars. Chapman's principal political weapon was ridicule. "Denunciation is well enough," he wrote, "but laughter is the true ratsbane for hypocrites." Once during a political rally Chapman jumped from the cart on which he was speaking to grab a heckler by the coat collar. The heckler subdued, Chapman finished his speech and then took "the ruffian" for a drink, "all of which," he wrote, "was purely the result of excitement—but which had a romantic and courageous appearance, greatly enhanced by the fact of my having only one hand."

For four years—1897 to 1901—Chapman published *Political Nursery*, a more or less monthly journal of four pages devoted to his view of American politics. Its motto was: "Let break what must break, we shall soon see the way." It was Chapman's conviction, derived from his master, James, that "there is no such thing as an abstract truth. You must talk facts, you must name names, you must impute motives. You must say what is on your mind. It is the only means you have of cutting yourself free from the body of this death. Innuendo will not do."

"It is awful fun," James wrote a friend, recommending Chapman's *Political Nursery*. "He just looks at things, and tells the truth about them—a strange thing to even *try* to do, and he doesn't always succeed."

In *Practical Agitation* (1900), which James called "a gospel for our rising generation," Chapman traced the philosophical grounds for the reform movement. It seemed to him that a "subtle change" had been effected in the way the citizen thought of his "public duty." If the American "frame of government afforded no outlet" to the force of modern industrial capitalism, "had our ills been irredeemably crystallized into formal tyranny, we should perhaps have witnessed great revivalist upheavals, sacraments, saints, prophets, prostrations, and adoration. As it is we have seen deadly pamphlets, schedules, enactments, documents which it required our whole attention and our whole time to understand. . . . These horrid things they bring, these instruments forged by unremitting toil, technical, insufferable—they are the cure. With such levers, and with them only, can the stones be lifted off the hearts of men. They are the alternatives to revolution. . . . A few men have a desire, a hope of improving some evil. They stagger towards it and fall. The impulse is always good. The mistakes made are progressive. If you draw an arrow through them, it will point north." Seen in this light, reform was not a spasmodic response to a particular evil; it was simply recognition of the fact that the struggle against evil and indifference was perpetual.

The critic Edmund Wilson wrote that "perhaps no writer of his generation has dealt at once so realistically and with so much clairvoyance with the modern world. . . ." To Wilson, Chapman's *Practical Agitation* and *Causes and Consequences* (1898) marked "the turning of the tide in the open discussion of the relations between American public life and business." If this judgment is somewhat excessive in view of the labors of such journalists as Ida Tarbell, Steffens, the Hapgoods, and others, it is nonetheless a tribute to the unique influence that Chapman exerted and to the constantly widening circle of young men and women who were drawn to reform through his writings.

Oswald Garrison Villard wrote of Chapman: "He was nearer to genius, I think, than any writer I have known. . . . He was charming to fascination, had a wonderful sense of humor, was as brilliant in conversation as in his writing, and could see further through the shams of our social and political life than anyone I knew. His courage was without limit. . . . From his courage I gained courage. Through his eyes I learned to see much that I had not seen or understood. Partly because of his inspiration I gave a great deal of time to civic affairs." To Villard, Chapman's mind was an "electrical dynamo . . . that shed sparks every second."

In his self-conscious measuring of the social and political realities of his time against the standard of what would come to be called Christian neo-orthodoxy he was, if not unique, most unusual. Alone among the leading literary figures of the age, he reasserted the Classical-Christian Consciousness as a challenge to the Secular Democratic faith within the context of reform.

The organizations committed to reform of one sort or another were literally beyond counting. Conferences, congresses, lectures, debates—a vast ferment of earnest inquiry and often angry contention went on perpetually. The Hull House Social and Economic Conference, held in 1896, was attended by Henry Demarest Lloyd, Washington Gladden, and John Dewey among dozens of others. The conferees debated the single tax, Bellamy's Nationalism, Tolstoyan economics, the practical aesthetics of Ruskin, William Morris's new feudalism, reform of industrial society by the creation of a new form of money, cooperation and communalism, socialism and municipal ownership.

Chapman himself penned the best description of the soldiers in the Empire of Reform. "If anyone will turn over the pages of the Charities Directory or will stop for a moment in front of the Charities Building in Fourth Avenue," he wrote, "he will be impressed with the multiplication of benevolent agencies that has taken place within the last generation,—the number of hospitals, settlements, boys' clubs, girls' clubs, babies' clubs; small park associations and schools of philanthropy. Somewhere behind the bricks and mortar of these societies are the men and women whose insistence has brought them into being. . . .

"A whole society and social caste of workers has sprung into existence,—a galaxy and salvation army of militant benevolence . . . having an inner life and social atmosphere peculiar to itself, its tone and mission. There is an unconquerable religious spirit in these priests of humanity; though religion is a word at which many of them are offended. Suffice it to say here that . . . [they] cannot be cajoled or sidetracked; they are driven forward by a force behind or within them. They feel in themselves that they are right. These people very well fulfill Emerson's ideal of the individual or Nietzsche's theory of the superman. They are a law unto themselves. . . . It is only through the power of such beliefs on the part of writers and workers that things get written or done. It is common to hear these beliefs called illusions. If so, they are illusions in form only. One might almost say that the substance of them is religious truth itself."

36

The Literary Scene

A merican literature in the period under consideration appeared
in some ways to fulfill Tocqueville's prediction. "As soon as the
multitude begins to take an interest in the labors of the mind," he wrote
in 1832, "it finds out that to excel in some of them is a powerful means
of acquiring fame, power, or wealth. The restless ambition that equality
begets instantly takes this direction. . . . The number of those who
cultivate science, letters, and the arts, becomes immense." At the same
time Tocqueville warned that the greater part of the literature produced under such circumstances would be mediocre since writers could
"at a cheap rate [achieve] a moderate reputation and a large fortune. . . . The ever increasing crowd of readers and their continual
craving for something new ensure the sale of books that nobody much
esteems. . . . Democratic literature is always infested with a tribe of
writers who look upon letters as a mere trade, and for some few great
writers who adorn it, you may reckon thousands of idea-mongers."
That, of course, was not the whole story. For one thing, four of the
writers whose major works had been published in the remarkable decade prior to the Civil War—Emerson, Melville, Whitman, and Harriet
Beecher Stowe—survived well into the postwar era, although with, as
one might say, diminished capacity or at least output.

Herman Melville, obscure and without an audience, wrote some of his greatest short stories in this era, the most noted of which, "Billy Budd," was not published until long after his death. Ralph Waldo Emerson, who lived until 1882, wrote little after the war, and in his last years he was a virtual invalid, often vague and distracted. Nonetheless, his mere existence was experienced. For New England at least, he was a demigod, a hero beyond reproach who had helped shape the mind of a generation of Americans.

The poetry Americans liked after the war was the poetry they had liked before. William Cullen Bryant gives us our best clue to the poetic consciousness of the day with his highly popular 700-page anthology *The Library of World Poetry*. Bryant grouped the poems under categories so that the reader could find the verses appropriate to his or her immediate need. "Poems of Childhood" were divided into "infancy" and "youth" and followed by poems of "the affections," "friendship," "love," "marriage," "home," "filial and fraternal love," "disappointment and estrangement," "bereavement and Death." There were poems of "sorrow and adversity," "religion, nature," "peace and war," "temperance and labor," "sentiment and reflection," "tragedy," and, finally, "humor."

John Greenleaf Whittier (whom Frances Willard described as "the household poet of our abolition family. We knew more of him by heart, in all senses of that phrase, than of any other singer, living or dead") lived on, lamenting the materialism of the age:

> For art and labor met in truce,
> For beauty made the bride of use,
> We thank Thee; but, withal, we crave
> The austere virtues strong to save,
> The honor proof to place or gold,
> The manhood never bought or sold.

To Whitman, Whittier exemplified "the zeal, the moral energy that founded New England—the splendid rectitude and ardor of Luther, Milton, George Fox. . . ." Whitman himself, sixteen years Emerson's junior, continued to amend, to edit, and modestly to supplement *Leaves of Grass*. His poetry was not much read by decent people or widely admired (when John Jay Chapman gave his grandmother Whitman to read, the old lady rebuked him: "She said she had never seen so many different kinds of words in her life"), but he became one of the nation's literary monuments, visited by famous people as they visited Niagara Falls or Emerson himself. Fired from his government sinecure by a superior who considered his poems obscene, Whitman ensconced himself in Camden, New Jersey.

In *Democratic Vistas*, a collection of his prose pieces published in 1871, Whitman's optimism faltered. "I say," he wrote, "we had best look at our times and lands searchingly in the face like a physician diagnosing some deep disease. . . . Never was there, perhaps, more hollowness at heart than at present, and here in the United States. Genuine belief seems to have left us. The underlying principles of the States are not honesty believ'd in, (for all this hectic glow, and these melo-dramatic screamings,) nor is humanity itself believ'd in. . . . The spectacle is appalling. We live in an atmosphere of hypocrisy throughout. The men believe not in the women, nor the women in the men. . . . The depravity of the business classes of our country is not less than has been supposed, but infinitely greater. The official services of America, national, state, and municipal, in all their branches and departments, except the judiciary, are saturated in corruption, bribery, falsehood, mal-administration; and the judiciary is tainted. The great cities reek with respectable as much as non-respectable robbery and scoundrelism. In fashionable life, flippancy, tepid amours, weak infidelism, small aims, or no aims at all, only to kill time. In business (this all-devouring modern word, business) the one sole object is, by any means, pecuniary gain. . . . The best class we show, is but a mob of fashionably dress'd speculators and vulgarians. . . . Are there, indeed, *men* here worthy the name? Are there athletes? Are there perfect women, to match the generous material luxuriance? Is there a pervading atmosphere of beautiful manners? Are there crops of fine youths and majestic old persons? Are there arts worthy of freedom and a rich people? Is there a great moral and religious civilization—the only justification of a great material one?" All such hopes seemed "altogether in the future."

Having traveled to Boston to deliver a talk on Lincoln's birthday, Whitman lingered a week. He visited the "good gray poet" Longfellow, whom he came to resemble in appearance. Longfellow had visited Whitman in Camden three years earlier when Whitman had been crippled by a stroke, and now he felt it a duty as well as a pleasure to return the call. Longfellow was seventy-four; Whitman would not "soon forget his lit-up face and glowing warmth and courtesy." Whitman's critics had taken him to task for his "scorn and intolerance" of the New England poets, but Whitman rejected the imputation. "I can't imagine," he wrote, "any better luck befalling these States for a poetical beginning than has come from Emerson, Longfellow, Bryant and Whittier."

In 1878 Bryant, the dean of American nature writers, newspaper editor, abolitionist, and lifelong reformer, died. Whitman had felt close to Bryant. The older man had been "markedly kind" to him. They had walked together when Whitman lived in Brooklyn—long, talkative rambles "out toward Bedford or Flatbush." Whitman noted in his "specimen book": "And so the good, stainless, noble old citizen and poet was laid to rest amid the nature he loved so fondly, and sang so well her shows and seasons." Bryant had been born in the eighteenth century—1794, during Washington's second administration. He had grown up with the Republic, its first citizen-poet. Whitman wrote of him, "Pulsing the first interior verse-throbs of a mighty world—bard of the river and the wood, ever conveying a taste of the open air, with scents from hayfields, grapes, birch borders . . . with here and there through all poems, or passages of poems, touching the highest universal truths, enthusiasms, duties—morals as grim and eternal, if not as stormy and fateful, as anything in Aeschylus."

Whitman returned to New York City after an absence of many years. It was the city that had molded his aesthetic sensibility, given him the subjects for his earliest poems. Once more he roamed the streets he knew so well—"bubbling and whirling and moving like its own environment of waters—endless humanity in all phases," searching once again for the meaning of it. Defiant of "cynics and pessimists," he still found it "the directest proof yet of successful democracy, and of the solution of that paradox, the eligibility of the free and fully developed individual with the paramount aggregate. . . . In old age [he was fifty-nine], lame and sick," he added, "pondering for years on many a doubt and danger for this republic of ours—fully aware of all that can be said on the other side—I find in this visit to New York, and the daily contact and rapport with its myriad people, on the scale of the oceans and tides, the best, most effective medicine my soul has yet partaken, the grandest physical habitat and surroundings of land and water the globe affords—namely Manhattan Island and Brooklyn, which future shall join in one city—city of superb democracy, amid superb surroundings."

But another, more compelling experience awaited Whitman. In 1879 for the first time he set out by train to the West, the West that had always drawn his imagination so strongly, especially since the Civil War, when he had nursed so many of its sons. "In the sleeper," he wrote, "with our loud whinnies thrown out from time to time, or trumpet blasts into the darkness. Passing the homes of men, the farms, barns, cattle—the silent villages . . . as on and on we fly like lightning through the night. . . . "

Over the prairies, mile after endless mile, to the Rockies, Whitman's train sped, bringing him at last to Denver, which enchanted him. At the Kenosha Pass, he reveled in "all this grim yet joyous elemental abandon—this plentitude of material, entire absence of art, untrammeled play of primitive Nature—the chasm, the gorge, the crystal mountain stream, repeated scores, hundreds of miles—the broad handling and absolute uncrampedness—the fantastic forms, bathed in transparent browns, faint reds and grays, towering sometimes a thousand, sometimes two or three thousand feet high. . . . New sense, new joys, seem developed." The mountains were the "vertebrae or backbone of our hemisphere." As the anatomist had declared man essentially a spine, "topped, footed, breasted, and radiated, so the whole Western world is, in a sense, but an expansion of these mountains." Above all, it was the intoxicating air—"delicious rare atmosphere"—that captivated. "Everywhere the aerial gradations and sky effects inimitable; nowhere else such perspectives, such transparent lilacs and grays. . . . What an exhilaration!—not the air alone, and the sense of vastness, but every local sight and feature."

Finally, it was the limitless prairies and the Great Plains that moved him most—"the inexhaustible land of wheat, maize, wool, flax, coal, iron, beef and pork, butter and cheese, apples and grapes—land of ten million virgin farms. . . . Day after day and night after night, to my eyes, to all senses—the aesthetic one most of all—they silently and broadly unfold. Even their simplest statistics are sublime." Experts told him that when they were properly irrigated, the prairies might easily grow "enough wheat to feed the world." Only the Western women were a disappointment. The women of Denver seemed like pallid imitations of their Eastern sisters, "all fashionably dressed . . . and generally doll-like."

In the early fall of 1881 Whitman returned to New England, to Concord, for what he may well have believed would be his last visit with Emerson. By the famous green, he sat with his mentor and old friend, "a long and blessed evening . . . in a way I couldn't have wished better or different." Bronson Alcott and his brilliant daughter Louisa were there, and much of the talk was of Thoreau. Whitman was content to listen and watch, rapt, his friend's face, "eyes clear, with the well-known expression of sweetness, and the old clear-peering aspect quite the same."

Seeing Emerson put Whitman in mind of their meeting, twenty-one years earlier, when Emerson had tried to persuade him to omit the overtly sexual poems—"Children of Adam"—from the newest edition of *Leaves of Grass*. Whitman had listened to Emerson's arguments—to most of which he had no rejoinder—and then found himself strangely strengthened in his own resolution.

A year later he was back to visit Emerson's grave, "without sadness—indeed a solemn joy and faith. . . . A just man, poised on himself, all-loving, all-enclosing, and sane and clear as the sun," well aware that an era in American letters or, more aptly, in American life was over with his friend's death.

Despite a series of paralytic strokes, Whitman kept a kind of journal which would finally appear as *Specimen Days and Collect*, a record of how one may, after all, grow old joyously in America. "Perhaps the best is always cumulative," Whitman wrote. "One's eating and drinking one wants fresh . . . but I would not give a straw for that person or poem, or friend, or city, or work of art, that was not more grateful the second time than the first—and more still the third." The beautiful head with its aureole of gray hair grew more beautiful with age—a national icon. Photographers came to photograph him; among them was Thomas Eakins, who took some splendid photographs and painted his portrait at the age of sixty-eight.

Frances Willard sought Whitman out at Camden and found him "about seventy years of age, attired in gray, from his soft gray overcoat to his old-fashioned gray mittens, with sparse gray hair, kind, twinkling gray eyes, and russet apple cheeks, the mildest, most modest and simple-hearted man I ever saw. . . . He has no ends to serve, no place to hold in the conversation, nothing to gain or lose. . . . What he really is I do not know. I only tell about him as he was to me, and his sense of God, Nature and Human Brotherhood struck me as having been raised to such a power, and fused in such a white heat of devotion, that they made the man a genius."

James Russell Lowell, born in 1819, was one of those Boston poets who grew old before their time. He continued to write poetry, prose, and critical essays and to play a central role in the postwar literary world. Fussy and irascible, he was clearly a survivor from an earlier age, rebuking worshipful Harvard undergraduates for using "will" instead of "shall" and displaying what seemed to one of them—John

Jay Chapman—a touching vulnerability. He was not happy as a Harvard professor. He wrote the sister of his friend Charles Norton: "I forgot for a few blessed hours that I was a professor, and felt as if I were something real." He hoped for release from his durance by selling some land that he had inherited. If he could do so and could thereby "slip my neck out of this collar that galls me so, I should be a man again," he wrote, adding, "I am not the stuff that professors are made of. Better in some ways, worse in others. . . ." The America that he had embraced at the end of the war had proved a fickle mistress. He wrote:

> Shall not that Western Goth, of whom we spoke,
> So fiercely practical, so keen of eye,
> Find out, some day, that nothing pays but God,
> Served whether on the smoke-shut battlefield,
> In work obscure done honestly, or vote
> For truth unpopular, or faith maintained
> To ruinous convictions, or good deeds. . . .
> Shall he not learn that all prosperity,
> Whose bases stretch not deeper than the sense,
> Is but a trick of this world's atmosphere. . . .
> Or find too late, the Past's long lesson missed,
> That dust the prophets shake from off their feet
> Grows heavy to drag down both tower and wall?

John Jay Chapman was uncharitable. "Too much culture," he wrote of Lowell, "—too many truffled essays and champagne odes and lobster sonnets, too much Spanish olives, potted proverbs—a gouty old cuss in his later essays." His early essays were clear and rapid, but his later prefaces were expressive chiefly "of hems and haws and creased literary trousers!"

In 1878, after his son had married one of Longfellow's daughters, Richard Henry Dana, dismayed by the rise of "an irresponsible, shifty, ephemeral oligarchy of speculators, corporation wielders, and caucus mongers," went into a kind of self-imposed exile, first in Paris and then in Rome. In 1881, on his deathbed, Dana "fought battles, made arguments, preached sermons & at last made painful journeys . . ." in his wife's words. Perhaps he recalled the imperishable journey of his youth, his "two years before the mast." He was buried in the Protestant cemetery in Rome, not far from the graves of Keats and Shelley.

Thomas Wentworth Higginson was another prominent figure on the literary scene. The *Atlantic Monthly* was his particular outlet. He turned out a stream of articles, essays, and stories for William Dean Howells and gave his name to every good cause. He wrote a history of the United States serially for *Harper's Magazine* and took Matthew Arnold about Boston on a sight-seeing tour. Although he had long been a pillar of the women's rights movement he could not bring himself to support its presidential candidate, rough, demagogic Ben Butler, and so fell out of favor, resigning under some pressure, as one of the editors of the *Woman's Journal*. He adored his daughter by his second marriage, took her bicycling on one of the new-model safety cycles then in vogue, lectured on "total abstinence," and reveled in middle-aged domesticity. What most clearly earned him the gratitude of posterity was his friendship with Emily Dickinson, which began in 1862, when she sent him some of her poems. After ten years of correspondence, when it was clear that Emily Dickinson could not be lured from her refuge at Amherst, Higginson traveled to that town to meet her. She appeared in a white piqué dress and blue shawl, carrying two lilies in her hand and talking nervously and, it seemed to Higginson, excessively. He found her disconcertingly plain and much too intense and was alarmed by her definition of good poetry—"it makes my whole body so cold no fire can ever warm me. . . . I feel physically as if the top of my head were taken off." He wrote: "I never was with anyone who drained my nerve power so much. Without touching her, she drew from me. I am glad I do not live near her." If Higginson remained wary, Dickinson continued to adore him, convinced that his response to her letters had saved her sanity. Although he had not encouraged the publication of her poems, feeling, he said, that they were too eccentric and "advanced" for the reading public to which they were addressed, he recognized her genius, and they continued to correspond until her death in 1886.

But if Higginson came further than most literary critics of his day toward an appreciation of Emily Dickinson, he found *Leaves of Grass* "nauseating." He denounced Whitman for failing to fight in the war and ridiculed his celebration of the common man on the incorrect ground that Whitman himself had never labored. Mark Twain seemed to Higginson no more than a light humorist, a literary comedian who pandered to the popular taste.

Like most of the intellectuals and literary figures of his day, Higginson was a socialist of sorts. Although he did not support the nationalization of all industries, he joined with Edward Everett Hale, Julia Ward Howe, Lucy Stone, and Howells to form the Boston Na-

tionalist Club, dedicated to advancing the "national" socialism advocated by Edward Bellamy. "I have made up my mind that the tendency
of events is now toward Nationalism—or State Socialism, if you please,"
he wrote in 1889, "—and am prepared to go a few steps farther, at
any rate, in that direction."

Thomas Wentworth Higginson's literary influence was often a
negative one inasmuch as his notions of what constituted literature
were in the main extremely conservative. His hegemony over American
letters was challenged by a newcomer, fourteen years younger and
from the West. William Dean Howells, with the sponsorship of the
New England literary establishment, notably Lowell, soon replaced
Higginson as, if not precisely the dean of American letters (he was still
too young for that accolade), at least, its most influential arbiter.

The arrival of Howells on the literary scene marked the formation
of a national literature, replacing the essentially parochial literature of
New England. With the exception of Melville (who had, after all, a
number of New England ancestors) and Whitman, *all* the important
literary figures of prewar America had been New Englanders, and
most of them Bostonians or Cantabrigians. The arrival of Howells was
a harbinger of a literary invasion from the Middle West.

Howells had been born at Martins Ferry, Ohio, on the Ohio River,
one of a large, affectionate family of eight children and innumerable
relatives. His father was a newspaper editor and printer and a fervent
abolitionist. If the senior Howells was a rather poor provider, having
in him a good deal of the small-town dreamer, he was very conscious
of his New England antecedents and passed on his literary inclinations
to his children, reading aloud to them from Robert Burns, Shakespeare, and Sir Walter Scott.

After a stint as news editor of the *Ohio State Journal*, during the
course of which he wrote a campaign biography of Lincoln, Howells
traveled to Boston to track down the literary lions—Emerson, Holmes,
Lowell, and the rest. He approached Boston as "the passionate pilgrim
from the West approached his Holy Land." Lowell was especially taken
with the intense young Middle Westerner, and his encouraging response marked the beginning of a warm friendship that lasted until
Lowell's death. At a literary dinner hosted by Lowell in a private dining
room of the Parker House, Oliver Wendell Holmes turned to Lowell
and, indicating Howells, said, "Well, James, this is like the apostolic
succession; this is the laying on of hands." Howells wrote later: "I took
this sweet and caressing irony as he meant it; but the charm of it went

to my head long before any drop of wine, together with the charm of hearing him and Lowell calling each other James and Wendell, and of finding them still cordially boys together."

It was doubtless through Lowell's intervention that Howells, too frail for a life of military service, secured a position as consul to Venice during the Civil War. As we have noted, a diplomatic post was the equivalent of a modern-day government grant for promising or established literary figures. Howells considered himself primarily a poet, but in Venice his "Letters," written for the *Boston Advertiser* and later published as a book, established him as a travel writer. After the war he was promoted by his new literary friends to the post of assistant editor of the *Atlantic Monthly*, a great prize for a rising young literary fellow. As assistant editor and then editor Howells became the most influential literary figure of the day.

The three major literary figures of the last quarter of the century were wildly disparate: Henry James, Mark Twain, and Emily Dickinson. James, as the self-conscious artist, was in his own time by far the most influential of the three. As both critic of and contributor to the new culture emerging in America, he had numerous imitators, especially among women novelists, such as Constance Fenimore Woolson.

Roderick Hudson, James's first "major" novel, appeared serially in 1876 and then in a three-volume edition four years later. In it a wealthy young patron of the arts, Rowland Mallet, undertakes to subvent the studies in Rome of a promising but impecunious young artist, Roderick Hudson, who captivates him with his energy and ambition. Hudson wishes to depict "all the Forces and Elements and Mysteries of Nature. . . . I mean to do the Morning; I mean to do the Night! I mean to do the Ocean and the Mountains; the Moon and the West Wind. I mean to make a magnificent statue of America!"

To observe the progress of his protégé, Mallet accompanies Hudson to Rome. There Hudson falls in love with a beautiful American expatriate, Christina Light, and when she marries an Italian prince, Prince Casamassima (the prince and princess appear in subsequent novels), Hudson either kills himself or, distraught, falls from a cliff. End of novel.

Rowland Mallet became the prototype of many of James's masculine protagonists. Early in the novel he declares: "Upon my word I am not happy! I am clever enough to want more than I have got. I am tired of myself, my own thoughts, my own eternal company. True happiness, we are told, consists of getting out of one's self; but . . . to stay out you must have some absorbing errand. Unfortunately I have no errand, nobody will trust me with one. I want to care for something or for somebody. And I want to care with a certain ardour; even, if you can believe it, with a certain passion." All this was expressed to an older female friend. Like James's own ancestors, Mallet's had "been brought up to think much more intently of the duties of this life than of its privileges and pleasures." Lacking "the simple, sensuous, confident relish of pleasure," he was given to alternate indulgences and fits of remorse, accompanied by "extreme melancholy," obsessed with the feeling that "he was neither fish nor flesh nor good red herring." Mallet (and James?) felt himself to be "an awkward mixture of moral and aesthetic curiosity," who would have made an ineffective reformer and an indifferent artist. It seemed to him that the glow of happiness must be found "either in an action of an immensely solid kind on behalf of an idea, or in producing a masterpiece in one of the arts." It was an effective statement on behalf of a class that no longer had a clearly defined role. No longer honored and deferred to as guiding intellects and exemplars of the moral law, James's class (and that of the Adamses, Danas, Higginsons, et al.) had to find new functions or perhaps merely "activities." "Culture" was the most congenial; many thus became a kind of fallen clerisy.

Settling in England, James produced what was perhaps his finest (certainly his best-known) novel, *The Portrait of a Lady*, in 1881. Three more novels followed in the decade of the eighties before James took a disastrous excursion into playwriting. By the end of the decade of the nineties he had produced several brilliant short novels, the most famous of which was *The Turn of the Screw*.

A theme to which James returned time and again was the encounter of American women with European culture (one is inevitably reminded of Jane Addams). This was a new form of the well-established theme of American innocence versus European sophistication. In this genre the "new" American woman, with her liberal social ideals and remarkable energy, was forced to come to terms with a cynical and decadent, or merely worldly-wise, European upper class. A lifetime of experience and reflection resulted in a gallery of female portraits; basic to them all was the image of women as the ingenious and often ruthless manipulators of men. In a series of stories and novels that grew more and more intricate and impenetrable as he grew older until even his brother protested, James made the drawing room and manor house the stage for the most subtle modulations of feeling.

What can be said, at the very least, is that James carried the genre as far as genius could carry it. He had a host of imitators and disciples but no peers, and his novels tell far more about the wearying refinements of a substantial part of the Eastern upper class to which he belonged than they do about an America of which he knew or cared little.

What appealed strongly to the literary critics of the day (and of subsequent days) was that James was purely and self-consciously the artist and craftsman. In that sense he may be said to have been the first American professional writer (although he could not have supported himself by writing alone, and a modest but comfortable inherited income made possible his writing as well as his exile), a writer for whom the "crafting" of a novel was the highest challenge. What mattered was not so much what you said, but the artistry with which you said it. That preoccupation, which grew into an obsession, made his style increasingly complex and obscure. Marcel Proust was doing much the same thing at roughly the same time—observing in infinite detail the decline of a decadent class—but Proust was, in the end, more successful, perhaps because he created an entire world which gave his masterpiece a coherence that James's novels lacked.

If Henry James became the beau ideal of the literary world whose sights were generally fixed on English letters, Samuel Clemens became the great American literary personality of the age. We last encountered him fleeing West with his brother to escape the nightmarish internecine warfare in his native Missouri. He found a job in Virginia City, a new mining boomtown, as a reporter for the town's paper. Using the pseudonym Mark Twain, he served an apprenticeship as a humorist with the famous Artemus Ward. Moving West to California, he encountered Bret Harte, and the two young men compared notes on the tribulations of being a writer in America. It was in California that Twain wrote the story that made him a minor national figure: "The Celebrated Jumping Frog of Calaveras County." After a spectacularly successful lecture at Cooper Union, Twain took a trip to Europe and the Holy Land and wrote of his experiences in a comic vein in *The Innocents Abroad*, published in 1869. At a time when Americans were just beginning that ubiquitous tourism that eventually would make them notorious, Twain captured perfectly the combination of awe and self-conscious superiority with which Americans have regarded the rest of the world—those poor peoples who have been unfortunate enough not to have been born in the United States or enterprising enough to have emigrated here.

The voyage was a turning point in Twain's own career. It helped, through the publication of *The Innocents Abroad*, to make him a "book-writer," as opposed to simply a journalist. While Twain had little good to say of the old masters, excoriating them as overrated and overvalued, he was charmed by many aspects of Europe, especially the leisurely pace of Italian life. "In America," he wrote, "we hurry—which is well; but when the day's work is done, we go on thinking of losses and gains, we plan for the morrows, we even carry our business cares to bed with us, and toss and worry over them when we ought to be restoring our racked bodies and brains with sleep. We burn up our energies with these excitements, and either die early or drop into a lean and mean old age at a time of life which they call a man's prime in Europe. . . . I do envy these Europeans the comfort they take. When the work of the day is done, they forget it. . . . They go to bed moderately early, and sleep well. They are always quiet, always orderly, always cheerful, comfortable, and appreciative of life and its manifold blessings." Americans were careful in their attention to "inanimate objects" but less careful of human beings. "What a robust people, what a nation of thinkers we might be," he rhapsodized, "if we would only lay ourselves on the shelf occasionally and renew our edges!"

The Holy Land was a disappointment, though that leg of the visit was given a certain piquancy by the presence of fierce Bedouins, "whose sole happiness it is . . . to cut and stab and mangle and murder unoffending Christians." One chapter was headed "We Miss Lot's Wife"; another, "Why the Whale Threw Up Jonah."

The Innocents Abroad was and remains a marvelously American book. Twain was unfailingly good-humored, shrewdly observant, determined not to bow down to false idols, richly romantic in the spirit of the age. Quite properly it made his name. William Dean Howells, already something of a literary power, reviewed it in the *Atlantic Monthly* and praised it warmly. With "all its sauciness and irreverence," it showed a good spirit.

Roughing It followed *Innocents* and exploited the growing interest in the romantic West of cowboys and ranchers. *The Gilded Age*, written with Charles Dudley Warner, followed a year later, 1872, and then came *The Adventures of Tom Sawyer*, a classic, if sentimental, picture of the life of a small-town boy which was enormously popular and established a genre of its own. In *Life on the Mississippi*, a book to go beside Richard Henry Dana's *Two Years Before the Mast*, the great river found its chronicler—Dana's ocean and Twain's river, the interior and exterior water passages of America.

Then, in 1884, came Twain's noblest work, *The Adventures of Huckleberry Finn*, a book that secured his place among the figures of world literature. That Twain felt deeply the terrible weight of injustice borne by black Americans is certain. He paid the tuition of a young black through Yale as a kind of propitiatory act, a symbol of the debt every white man owed every black, and his wife told him that he could save himself some grief if he considered every man black until he was proved white. In his remarkably uninformative, though wryly amusing, autobiography, Twain wrote of his clandestine visits as a child to the slave cabins on the outskirts of Hannibal and of Aunt Hannah, whom the boys of the town believed to be a thousand years old and to have talked with Moses. "All the Negroes," he wrote, "were friends of ours, and with those of our own age we were in effect comrades." Their "affectionate good friend, ally, and adviser" was "Uncle Dan'l ... whose sympathies were wide and warm, and whose heart was honest and simple and knew no guile. . . . It was on the farm," Twain added, "that I got my strong liking for his race and my appreciation of certain of its fine qualities." Sixty years later, Twain wrote in 1910, those feelings "have suffered no impairment. The black face is as welcome to me now as it was then."

It did not occur to Sam Clemens as a boy that slavery was wrong; it seemed part of the order of the universe. But he never forgot one poignant episode. A slave boy named Sandy, hired by the Clemenses from a Hannibal family, had been sold away from his home in Maryland. Cheerful and gentle, "the noisiest creature that ever was," he sang perpetually, and his singing got on young Sam's nerves. When Sam protested to his mother, Twain recalled the incident, "The tears came into her eyes . . . and she said something like this: 'Poor thing, when he sings it shows that he is not remembering, and that comforts me; but when he is still I am afraid he is thinking, and I cannot bear it. He will never see his mother again; if he can sing, I must not hinder it, but be thankful for it. If you were older, you would understand me; then that friendless child's noise would make you glad.' "

Twain warned the readers of *Huckleberry Finn*: "Persons attempt-

ing to find a motive in this narrative will be prosecuted; persons attempting to find a moral in it will be banished; persons attempting to
find a plot in it will be shot." The plot is the river; the moral is the
power of friendship, of love and trust that exist between those two
classic innocents, exposed to the chicanery and wickedness of the world;
the motive is to contrast that simple world of natural innocence and
of nature, beautiful and dangerous, with the manifold corruptions of
the world.

Huckleberry Finn was both a journey, the greatest fictional journey
in American literature, a journey taken forever, and an act of gratitude
to Uncle Dan'l and of reconciliation to his race. Huck and Jim—white
boy, innocent of all the powerful evil in the world, and runaway Jim,
his companion, protector, and friend—live in their eternal bond. The
book changed the direction of American fiction. Ernest Hemingway
wrote of it that "all modern American literature comes from one book
by Mark Twain called Huckleberry Finn." William Faulkner concurred—"all of us . . . are his heirs"—and T.S. Eliot, who came from
the region, noted that Twain discovered "a new way of writing," fash-
ioning "a literary language based on American colloquial speech." To
H.L. Mencken, Twain was the "true father of our national literature."
Such claims may be excessive; certainly the reproduction of "American
colloquial speech" was at least as old as Lowell's *The Biglow Papers* and
Stowe's *Uncle Tom's Cabin*—but what Twain did do was strip the novel
of all its self-conscious moralistic trappings and allow the narrative to
carry the reader along as effortlessly as the broad waters of the Mississippi carried the raft with Huck and Jim.

Finally, Twain was the nonpareil chronicler of the great American
"con," the trick, the fast shuffle, the shell and pea game, "Smart and
Slick Incorporated." Tom Sawyer's famous fence-painting con is re-
capitulated in Huckleberry Finn, in the Duke and King's con of the
bumpkins in the towns along the Mississippi. In a whole series of
Twain's short stories and sketches, slick characters cheat the innocent,
as in "On Raising Chickens"—"raising" them off their roosts at night
in a neighbor's henhouse and slipping them into a sack. The supreme
trickster was "the mysterious stranger"—Satan?—who corrupts the
incorruptible Hadleyburg. It was Twain's enduring parable and his
last word on the falsity of respectable small-town life. Only a disillusioned lover could have written such a bitter obituary of the town in
America. It was a judgment from which the town, in a sense, never
recovered.

In a real sense Twain himself, with his ice-cream suits and stagy presence, his ill-advised business ventures, the pessimism and rage beneath the humor, became the victim of his own artfully constructed image. His "greatness" was a close thing; if we subtract *Huckleberry Finn*, what is left is a brilliant humorist in a classic American vein, who concealed his bitterness and disillusionment with America. Like Cooper and Irving and Henry James, Twain could not stand much of America at a time. He traveled abroad constantly and spent the better part of the 1890s in Europe.

Only great lovers can know the kind of despair that Twain, caught in his public role, knew. I have spoken earlier of the basic schizophrenic quality of American life: professing one thing; practicing another; unable, except for a few rare souls like Hawthorne and Melville, to gaze into the pit. Those two did and made their art congruent with their own experience of life. Twain had the moral and intellectual equipment of an Aeschylus and Euripides, but success and wealth were clearly important to him. He never resolved his ambivalence about "capitalism"; hating its excesses, he nonetheless longed to be a capitalist. He told Frederic Howe, "All my life I have been a slave. I have had to get up in the morning, I have had to write an article or get ready for a lecture, I have been pursued by managers, publishers, and, worst of all, by dinners which I thought I wanted to go to when I accepted the invitation but which I hated when the evening came around. I have been a slave all my life—to engagements and to other people."

The other literary figure of the period we must attend to was undoubtedly the most exotic flower of American letters. Emily Dickinson was born, lived, and died in Amherst, Massachusetts. In her relatively brief lifetime of fifty-five years she hardly strayed from that town. Of Puritan ancestry, she was a classic small-town spinster. Born in 1830 in the house she died in, she and her sister, Lavinia, lavished their affection on their older brother, Austin, a lawyer, and on their father. She referred to her father as "My Heavenly Father." She wrote after his death: "His Heart was pure and terrible. . . ." Clearly he was one of those powerful but intimidating nineteenth-century fathers whose unflinching support of his daughters armed and spurred them to dare all. Emily spent a year at nearby Mt. Holyoke Female Seminary, recently founded by the formidable Mary Lyon and saturated with the Protestant Passion to redeem the world. She read the Brontës, George Eliot, and Elizabeth Barrett Browning. Emerson's writings were influential, as they were with virtually all women writers. She was also strongly, if indirectly, influenced by the growing women's movement, if not so much by its ideological predispositions as by the feeling it conveyed of a unique feminine mission in the world and a unique feminine sensibility capable of registering the unseen harmonies of the world in a distinctive mode. Dickinson seems to have had a succession of passionate, if entirely platonic, attachments to older men, the most important of whom was a Presbyterian minister named Charles Wadsworth, whose departure to take a church in San Francisco left her desolate. Thomas Wentworth Higginson was his distant successor.

Emily Dickinson's outlet for her ardent passions was poetry. The best poetry, I think we must assume, is poetry the person writes to save his or her life. Certainly this was the case with the flood of poems (sometimes one a day) that poured forth from Dickinson's pen. Often on the verge of a nervous breakdown or, as she felt, insanity, she staved off the darkness by her verse. There was more than a touch of the seer and mystic in her poems, more than a touch of madness. She became, as the years passed, a virtual recluse; she dressed in white and spoke of her Calvary. Helen Hunt Jackson, a childhood friend of Emily Dickinson's in Amherst and also a protegée of Higginson's, recognized her genius and urged her to allow some of her poems to be published, but she resisted the suggestion.

In her mid-forties Emily Dickinson fell deeply in love with an older man, a widower and former friend of her father's, Judge Otis Lord, and that love, returned, gave a splendid glow to her last years and the poems of those years. We have made the distinction among American writers between those bold enough to look into the chasm, into the "darker side" of human experience—Hawthorne, Melville, Poe, and Twain, in some of his later pieces—and those who wrote in a more characteristically American vein of sunny optimism—Emerson and Whitman, for example. Emily Dickinson belongs with Hawthorne and Melville. "Had we the first intimation of the Definition of Life, the calmest of us would be Lunatics!" She wrote: "Could we see all we hope—there would be madness near . . . the unknown is the largest need of the intellect." On the other hand, she wrote: "The mere sense of living is joy enough."

> To be alive—is Power—
> Existence—in itself—
> Without a further function—

Her poetry is an extraordinary and unique combination of darkness and light, of somber power and lighthearted playfulness. We feel continually the intensity of a passion only just under the control of the artist, and many of her best poems have an almost unbearable tension; they capture and captivate as the work of no other poet.

She called her poems "my letter to the World." They were, above all, love letters. She wrote to Samuel Bowles, third of that name and second to edit the *Springfield Republican*: "Please to need me."

> By a flower—By a letter—
> By a nimble love—
> If I weld the Rivet faster—
> Final fast—above—
>
> Never mind my breathless Anvil!
> Never mind Repose!
> Never mind the sotty faces
> Tugging at the Forge!

She was, in this sense, a precursor, an early prophet of the power of "loving affections," to use William James's phrase, of friendship and "spiritual" love. One of her most famous lines is "Parting is all we know of heaven, And all we need of hell." She was, in addition, a profoundly, if in no sense orthodoxly, religious poet.

> If "All is possible" with him
> As he besides concedes
> He will refund us finally
> Our confiscated Gods—

And again:

> How ruthless are the gentle—
> How cruel are the kind—
> God broke his contract to the Lamb
> To qualify the Wind—
>
> .   .   .
>
> I shall know why—when Time is over—
> And I have ceased to wonder why—
> Christ will explain each separate anguish
> In the fair schoolroom of the sky—

(The sardonic tone may have escaped some of her more pious readers.)

> Remembrance has a Rear and Front—
> 'Tis something like a House—
> It has a Garret also
> For Refuse and the Mouse
> Besides the deepest Cellar
> That ever Mason laid—
> Look to it by its Fathoms
> Ourselves be not pursued—
>
> .   .   .
>
> I like a look of Agony,
> Because I know it's true—
> Men do not sham Convulsion,
> Nor simulate, a Throe—
> The eyes glaze once—and that is Death—
> Impossible to feign
> The Beads upon the Forehead
> By homely Anguish strung.

The poems of Emily Dickinson demonstrate the power of a remarkable intellect, a philosophic intent, in the best sense of that word, when it is fused to a desperate passion.

After Emily Dickinson's death Thomas Wentworth Higginson traveled to Amherst for her funeral and there read Emily Brontë's "Last Lines," "a favorite with our friend who has now put on the Immortality which she seemed never to have laid off." "E. D.'s face a wondrous restoration of youth," he wrote later in his diary, "—she is 54 and looked 30, not a gray hair or wrinkle, and perfect peace on the beautiful brow." Higginson became a warm advocate of publishing a volume of her poems. When one of Emily Dickinson's friends, Mabel Loomis Todd, sent him a batch of Emily's poems, he wrote back enthusiastically: "I can't tell you how much I am enjoying these poems. There are many new to me which take my breath away & which also have *form* beyond most of those I have seen before. . . . " Higginson, as editor, made certain modest, if, to later and more scrupulous editors, outrageous, changes in Dickinson's poems to make them more "conventional" and, therefore, presumably more accessible to readers, and when the book was published in 1890, he wrote to Mrs. Todd: "Books just arrived—bound. I am *astonished* in looking through. How could we ever have doubted them." Soon it had gone through four editions. Another collection was planned at once, and Higginson wrote to Todd: "Let us alter as little as possible now that the public ear is opened." By 1895, 30,000 copies of Emily Dickinson's poems had sold in two collections.

It was remarkable that her poems found such an instantaneous public. Much too radical in form and disquieting in content for the taste of conventional literary critics, they evoked a strong response from literate readers. In the desert of essentially mediocre poetry and prose that flooded the country year after year, they bloomed like exotic flowers. Why? It would be agreeable to think that the readers, most of whom were women, read her with a "modern" appreciation of her greatness, but the fact was that she was writing entirely within the framework of the great "popular poets." Like Bryant (and the others), she wrote of death, of love and immortality, of God, of nature. If unorthodox in form, her poems were highly "moral" in content. Above all, they were inescapably the product of a remarkable intelligence and a feminine consciousness. It is important to keep in mind that two women—Mabel Loomis Todd and Helen Hunt Jackson—were the earliest champions of her work and that few male critics responded with enthusiasm.

Needless to say, there was a substantial gap between the three authors we have been concerned with and those lesser lights whose work constituted the great body of popular literature. When Eleanor Marx Aveling and her husband visited the United States in 1886, they commented on the fact that America's literary figures had not made the plight of the working class the subject of their novels. "We have portraits of ladies, of Daisy Millers, and so forth," Mrs. Aveling wrote. "But there are no studies of factory-hands and of dwellers in tenement houses; no pictures of those sunk in the innermost depths of the modern *Inferno*." She called for an "Uncle Tom's Cabin of Capitalism." Her judgment was unfounded. She was doubtless thinking of Charles Dickens, and while America produced no Dickens, it produced a veritable flood of "social protest" novels and short stories. Indeed, the short story and the social or "problem" novel became the two most conspicuous genres in the literary world, the latter reflecting the paramount importance of the war between capital and labor. George Herron, the

Christian Socialist, was convinced that the "social" novel was a major instrument of reform. "The fact that the novel is becoming more than the preacher the social teacher," he wrote, "lies in its dealing more with the common things and common experiences of life, and less in the imaginary romances of kings and their courts. The kingdom of God is the kingdom of the people and their work."

Albion Tourgée in his novel *Murvale Eastman, Christian Socialist* called for reform along socialist lines. Eastman, a young Episcopal minister, outrages his conservative congregation, especially its founder and richest member, Wilton Kishu, by preaching a sermon in which he asks why in an ostensibly Christian society are there two distinct classes, "the one Rich and the other Poor? . . . Are the Rich to grow richer forever, and the Poor to grow forever feebler and more dependent. . . . Are the Rich to be always regarded as the chief supporters of law and order, government, religion, society, and the Poor forever esteemed the nurslings of discontent and peril? . . . Is the dollar mark the real measure of human values?"

Instead of being expelled from his pulpit for such heresies, Eastman wins the congregation over at least to an acceptance of his right to speak his own mind and finally converts the capitalist Kishu.

Many novels were first printed as serials in the *Atlantic* or *Harper's*. The line between journalism and novel writing or between writers of fiction and nonfiction was very loosely drawn. Most journalists wrote a novel or two. All novelists wrote articles, essays, and, perhaps most commonly, travel accounts. Most of the novels written by the journalists drew on some area of social controversy with which they were familiar; there were novels of mills and mill girls, especially of workingwomen, of cattle barons and lumbermen, of factory owners who exploited their workers and ground the faces of the poor (one of the most popular subjects); there were novels about high life and low life; socialites and tramps, immigrants, steelworkers, strikers, and socialists.

Most of the novels written in the post-Civil War period were intended to be tearjerkers. They were supposed to move their readers to tears as remorselessly as calomel was supposed to move their bowels (weeping and being "regular" were considered basic requirements of a sensitive soul and a healthy body). The novel might be soberly realistic or wildly romantic, but tears from the reader were *de rigueur*. Only, of course, feminine tears; the ban on male tears remained in force, although occasionally a male reader confessed that a particularly moving passage might have brought an irrepressible tear to his eye. The new realism proclaimed by Howells professed to be dead set against such lachrymosity. At a dinner party in Howells's *The Rise of Silas Lapham*, one character asks another if he has read the immensely popular novel *Tears, Idle Tears*, adding, "It's perfectly heart-breaking with such dear old-fashioned hero and heroine in it, who keep dying for each other all the way through, and making the most wildly satisfactory and unnecessary sacrifices for each other." A down-to-earth guest replies sarcastically: "It ought to have been called, *Slop, Silly Slop*."

The formula was simple enough. The writer enlists the sympathies of the reader for the hero—handsome, courageous, gallant—and the blond, beautiful, virtuous heroine, and then kills off one or the other or, preferably, both. (It is, of course, a formula that still works its teary wonder: Witness the spectacular success of Erich Segal's *Love Story* as a book and movie.)

A random selection from *Harper's Weekly* of September, 1869, indicates the prevailing tone: "Chapter LIII." (Chapters were short and numerous in tales of this kind.) "The woman at his feet felt inexpressibly awed and humbled. Was this the husband who had gone mad for jealousy of her?—who had wrecked his whole life because of her sin? . . .

" 'Is it you, Stuart?' she moaned, as she still crouched at his feet. 'Are you the Stuart I knew—the Stuart who loved me. . . . Oh!' she murmured, as she tightened the fair coil of her arms around his throat. . . . His eyes lit up with sudden fire; his lips trembled. . . . 'Oh!' he groaned, 'you are a devil, woman—a devil sent from hell to wake a tempest in my soul. . . . Take your beauty from my sight, lest I curse it in the name of an utterly lost soul. Go, go! . . . I desire to be left with my God and my memory.'

"She arose humbly enough, and without one more wasted word or gesture, went straight to the door."

It was a prose heavily dependent on exclamation marks, full of sin and repentance, throbbing with a discreet sexuality.

A subdivision of the social novel, the conflict or tension of class in an avowedly classless society, was the novel of miscegenation. In these novels (and short stories) one of the characters discovers he or, again more typically, she has a black forebear and is thus irredeemably tainted. This was a theme favored by the most popular black writer of the era, Charles Chesnutt. In "Her Virginia Mammy" a handsome and talented young woman meets a black seamstress who the reader perceives is her mother, but the mother, to save her daughter's honor, conceals the facts from her and pretends to have simply been "Her Virginia Mammy." At the end of the story Clara marries the young white doctor to whom she is engaged, saved by her mother's discretion. When Chesnutt published a collection of his stories, the book was entitled *The Wife of His Youth, and Other Stories of the Color Line.*

Another subdivision of the reform or social issue novel was the utopian novel. Almost everyone took a turn at it. William Dean Howells checked in with *A Traveler from Altruria* (1894), the tale of a visitor from another planet, who is bewildered by the illogic and inequity of American capitalism. With the popularity of science and the talk of interplanetary travel by rocket, a growing number of the critical visitors to the United States in these novels were from outer space. There were two basic plots for the utopian novel: the Rip Van Winkle mode, in which the narrator or critic-hero wakes up X years in the future and finds the world "socialized" and improved beyond recognition (Edward Bellamy's *Looking Backward*); and the visitor-from-outer-space mode, in which the space traveler contrasts the far more highly "socialized" planet from which he has come with the chaos, irrationality, and injustice he finds on earth.

Howells's *A Traveler from Altruria* is a vision of the future sympathetic to the claims of socialism. The setting of the novel is a land where Christian socialism prevails, where there is no oppression or exploitation of one class by another, where housekeeping is done cooperatively and servants have disappeared—much the scenario that Zina Peirce had tried to effect in the Cambridge Cooperative Housekeeping Society.

Henry Olerich was born in the Wisconsin mining town of Hazel Green. He had been a classic jack-of-all-trades, a farmer, welldigger, hotelkeeper, schoolteacher, and principal, who also produced a design for an improved tractor, and drill press operator. Olerich was a small-town dreamer and visionary, an advocate of free love, equality for women, and a classless society. In *A Cityless and Countryless World*, published in 1893, he described his utopia on Mars. A Martian visitor, Mr. Midith, tells earthlings about the society of Mars made up of families of "a thousand or more men, women and children. . . . Years ago we had cities and towns, and a country similar to yours at the present time; but experience gradually taught us that it is not healthful to live in a crowded, smoky city and town. . . . We also found that a family of husband and wife and their children, living alone in a country home, are largely wasting their lives socially and economically." The Martians lived in "big-houses" of six residential wings, six stories high, a thousand to a "house."

The flood of utopian novels and the constant talk of reorganizing society along socialist lines prompted a number of satiric novels. Mary Bradley Lane wrote *Mizora: A Prophecy*, which appeared first in 1880 as a newspaper serial. In it Lane imagined a race of Amazons whose diet was made up of synthetic food. Anna Bowman Dodd's novel *The Republic of the Future* described New York as a socialist city in 2050 where "all family life had died out" and the word "home" had even disappeared from use. "Husband and wife are in reality two men having equal rights, with the same range of occupation, the same duties to perform, the same haunts and the same dreary leisure." Children were brought up in state-run nurseries, while food for the Socialistic City was pumped by electricity through "culinary conduits" from Chicago. One character announces: "When the last pie was made into the first pellet, woman's true freedom began."

Among the satires was that of a German writer, Eugen Richter, whose *Pictures of a Socialistic Future* gave a rather chilling description of a society in which the state cared for the young and the elderly; people were assigned one-room apartments by a state-run lottery, and public kitchens produced institutional meals consumed under the watchful gaze of police who held stopwatches.

Charles Dudley Warner was one of the better-known critics of the new capitalism. Born in Plainfield, Massachusetts, in 1829, he graduated from Hamilton College and became, as so many of his class, background, and generation, a lawyer, earning his degree from the University of Pennsylvania Law School. Disliking the law, he seized the first opportunity to become a journalist and editor of the *Hartford Evening Press*. His book of travel sketches, published in 1872, was a sensational success, catapulting him into the front ranks of American journalists and inducing Mark Twain to join him in writing *The Gilded Age*, a satirical romance about the rise of the new capitalists. Soon Warner was one of the prolific writers of the age, turning out twelve volumes of essays, nine books of travel, four novels, and two biographies. The most interesting of Warner's novels, at least to us, is *That Fortune*, published in 1899. The hero, Philip Burnett, is an ambitious small-town boy who dreams of being a famous soldier, a Congressman, a poet. His childhood friend and confidante is Celia Howard. She, like Philip, had ambitions. Before she was eleven, "her mother had listened with some wonder and more apprehension to the eager forecast of what this child intended to do when she became a woman, and already shrank from a vision of Celia on a public platform, or the leader of some metempsychosis club. . . . Indeed, this little sprout of the New Age spoke patronizingly of her hopelessly old-fashioned parent as 'little mother.' " Although trained as a lawyer, like Warner Burnett gravitates toward his first love, literature, and moves in the company of "the unconventional and illuminated, the 'poster' set in literature and art, wild-eyed and anemic young women and intensely languid, *nil admirari* young men, the most advanced products of the studios and of journalism. . . . The members were on a constant strain to say something brilliant, epigrammatic, original. . . . The women especially liked no writing that was not 'strong.' " Philip falls madly in love with the heiress to "that fortune," Evelyn Mavick, but Evelyn's ruthlessly ambitious mother is determined to marry her to a titled Englishman, Lord Montague. This plan is thwarted by Evelyn's stubbornness and the collapse of the Mavick fortune. With it goes all hope of the marriage to Lord Montague, who, it is now clear, cares only for the Mavick money. Philip, now a successful writer, and Evelyn are united in matrimony with the blessings of Celia Howard, who, a doctor in a Chicago clinic working with immigrants, has remained Burnett's staunchest friend. Three things are worth noting about the novel: the by now classic transition from lawyer to writer, from mundane drudgery to "art"; the hollowness of new fortunes and social climbing; and the woman friend—Celia—the object of nonerotic, sisterly love, who in her self-abnegation, rejects the conventional role of wife and mother, even while remaining a lifelong friend. Although marrying Evelyn, Philip loves the brilliant and unselfish Celia "more than ever."

Travel and "art" or "culture" were prominent themes in many novels, reflecting the preoccupation of upper-class Americans with those related topics. Much of James's popularity rested on his ability to combine them. The travel novel featured European settings—London and Paris and especially Italy. The characters visited the great museums, commented extensively and reverently on the work of the old masters (it was in mockery of this culture worship that Mark Twain in *The Innocents Abroad* derided the "old masters"), encountered expatriate Americans and upper-class "travelers" (contrasted with mere "tourists"), and hobnobbed with nobility. Lords and ladies glided through the pages of these works in numbers sufficient to populate a small principality.

Determined to be a "writer-editor," William Dean Howells turned out a series of essays, sketches, travel accounts, and novels of social life—such as *A Modern Instance*, in 1882—and a novel of the rise of a simple farmer, Silas Lapham, to become a millionaire. *The Rise of Silas Lapham*, published serially in the *Century* in 1884 and the following year as a book, is the work on which Howells's modest fame as a writer largely rests. The novel is less notable for its literary quality than for its development of what would become a classic American theme: the poor boy who fights his way up to wealth and prominence and the snubs and rebuffs he receives from the established elite on his way. Another of the "new" features of *The Rise of Silas Lapham* was the central role of a newspaper reporter, Bartley Hubbard, who serves as the initial narrator-commentator. Lapham's daughters, Penelope and Irene, rather than being conventional heroines, have many of the problems of the "new" woman—i.e., college followed by the question of domestic life or career. Toward the end of the novel this passage occurs: Irene "had toughened and hardened; she had lost all her babyish dependence and pliability; she was like iron; and here and there she was sharpened to a cutting edge." Penelope agrees to marry the highly desirable upper-class hero, Tom Corey, only after considerable vacillation and after it is clear to her that he respects her independence. The daughters, both of whom, incidentally, love Tom Corey, are the strongest individuals in the novel. Lapham does the honorable thing at the end and sacrifices his fortune to preserve his integrity. To the modern reader *The Rise of Silas Lapham* appears as little more than an old-fashioned romantic novel. That it was hailed for its realism tells more about the "state of the art"—the nineteenth-century American novel—than it does about Howells or, indeed, about the rise of the new rich. If it was an advance, it was, for a certainty, a very modest one. Henry Adams, a close friend of Howells, acclaimed it. Lowell wrote, somewhat ambiguously, to a friend: "It's the most wonderful bit of 'realism' (isn't that what you call it?)." William James was, if anything, more enthusiastic. He praised its "humanity and unflagging humor," adding that "if I mistake not [it] will last for all future time, or as long as novels *can* last."

Henry Kitchell Webster, who contributed to the social protest genre, was a classic Midwestern case. Born in Evanston, Illinois, of parents who had emigrated from New England, Webster went East to college and graduated from Hamilton College in New York State in 1897. For the next two years he taught rhetoric at Union College. His besetting ambition was to be a writer, and at the age of twenty-five, he and his friend Samuel Merwin set out to establish themselves in the literary world. They edited a magazine for boys called the *Boy's Herald* and wrote several operas and three novels, the most successful of which was about a battle for control of a railroad, entitled *The Short Line War*. Two years later Webster wrote *The Banker and the Bear*, an account of the fierce struggle between a banker, John Bagsbury, and a speculator who sets out to destroy him. Every unscrupulous tactic of lying, cheating, embezzling, and starting false rumors is used by the adversaries.

The most interesting aspect of Webster's novel is his attention to the effect on their wives and their home lives of the manipulations of the financiers and speculators. The wife of a speculator in the commodity market, old before her time, warns a young banker's fiancée not to inquire about her husband's affairs. "You don't want to know about such things; truly, you don't! If you are going to be happy with John, you mustn't know anything about his business—about what he does in the daytime. . . ." It was not just that businessman-husbands constantly did unscrupulous things that any self-respecting wife would be horrified to learn of; it was the fact that business was the "great purpose" in their lives, "the only thing that really counts. Everything else is only incidental to that." John, the dismayed Alice was assured, would succeed. "He isn't afraid of anything; and he won't lose his nerve; he can stand the strain. But you can't, and if you try your face will get wrinkled . . . and your nerves will fly to pieces, and you'll just worry your heart out." Complete ignorance will be her only armor. On the other hand, *Dick* Haselridge, John Bagsbury's niece, represents the "new woman." She is bright, independent, and forthright; she even dresses in a direct and emancipated style, scorning frills and fripperies. Her "friend" is Jack Dorlin, who constantly importunes her to marry him, but Dick is "too busy." Jack was "easily the best friend she had. To no one else could she show her thoughts just as they came. . . . He was—oh, he was the best of good comrades." She, as contrasted with poor Alice, understands her uncle's business very well, "for the active side of life, the exercise of judgment and skill, appealed to her very strongly."

William Morton Payne was born in Newburyport, Massachusetts, in 1858. A writer and critic, editor in 1892 of the now venerable *Dial*, Payne wrote his own exposé of big business—*The Money Captain*, published in 1898 and very similar in tone to Henry Webster's novel of big business chicanery. *The Money Captain* tells the story, with considerable boy-and-girl romance mixed in, of the struggle of Archibald

Dexter—the Duke of Gas—to retain control by whatever methods are necessary, of the enormously remunerative franchises for the gas and electricity needed to run Chicago. It also explores the connection between big business, in the person of the wealthy and respectable Dexter, and the corrupt city boss, Polka Dot Simpson, on whose support Dexter's fortunes rest. In a showdown Simpson threatens a supercilious Dexter: "That won't do. . . . We help you out and stand by you, and you've got to stand by us, or, by God! there'll be trouble. . . . We're in the same boat, and we don't propose that you're goin' to scuttle the boat. We won't have it." The confrontation ends in violence when the furious and drunken Simpson strikes Dexter, who, a few hours later, dies of an apparent apoplectic rage, leaving his vast fortune to his young housekeeper and companion. The implication is that she will run Consolidated Gas with unimpeachable honesty and a generous concern for the public welfare. And Dexter? Dexter, the author tells us, "for all his success, was a figure in the common democratic foreground of business; he was intimately and solely of the great everyday warp and woof of toil. He bore all his fruit at once—when he died," and passed his ill-gotten gains on to the high-minded young woman who had cared for him despite his failings.

Another category of the novel of social protest was the immigrant novel. An excellent example of this genre was *Joseph Zalmonah*, by a journalist named Edward King. Born in Middlefield, Massachusetts, in 1848, King had covered the Franco-Prussian War and the uprising of the Paris Commune for the *Springfield Republican*. Travel books were King's specialty, but in 1893 he produced *Joseph Zalmonah*, a realistic account of Russian-Jewish garment workers on New York's Lower East Side. In a chapter called "The Panorama of Suffering," King described the living conditions in a ghetto tenement and the working conditions in a sweatshop. Zalmonah, who believes that only a strong union can bring about any lasting improvements in the lives of the workers and their families, finds himself frustrated by the reluctance of the workers to join unions or to strike. "They had been seduced," he noted, "by the glittering descriptions of some mysterious social cataclysm, at the close of which they would be called upon the scene to divide up the vast riches of the millionaires of America." Finally, through "the Hebrew branch of the Socialistic Labor Union," Zalmonah is able to form a union of "knee-pants makers." From this others eventually follow, and he is able to gather the individual unions together in the United Hebrew Trades. Known as an agitator, he is fired and blacklisted from his trade. He throws all his energies into unionizing. Soon the "socialists" are as angry with Zalmonah as the sweaters—the owners of the sweatshops. By unionizing, they declare, he is simply obstructing the work for the revolution and the triumph of the socialist state. A crisis is created when thirty cloak manufacturers, determined to break the union movement, lock their workers out. Zalmonah organizes a protest march of the starving workers and their families. Faced down and intimidated, the manufacturers try to buy Zalmonah off while the militant socialists exhort him to use his influence with the workers and the passions of the moment to launch the revolution. The "procession of the hungry" has "made a tremendous sensation. The public is alarmed. The newspapers are talking about labor riots on a grand scale. . . . The capitalists are quaking in their palaces! . . . One push and we might topple the whole wall down. . . . Topple it down and bury the fat carcasses of the capitalists under it."

But Zalmonah is confident that "we . . . can win our cause by legitimate methods. . . . I am . . . little disposed . . . to go into the overturning business. . . ." His hopes are frustrated; he is arrested for inciting a riot, and Bathsheba, a young woman who wishes to seduce him, upbraids him for naïveté in believing that the sweaters will ever slacken their efforts to destroy the unions and grind the poor. She herself despairs of revolution. "The greedy manufacturers make the strong among the [immigrants] drive the weak! The ignorant are ground down in this land of liberty as they never were ground in the Pale! And what is your reward for all your efforts to bring order out of this hideous chaos, to let the light fall in upon this festering slave-market, to expel the oppressors and protect the helpless? What does a free land—a liberty-loving nation—give you for all this? A prison, and the name of a common malefactor!"

Even the ubiquitous tramp had his chronicler in a writer whose own career was more exotic than the stories he told. Josiah Flynt Willard, born in Appleton, Wisconsin, in 1869, was the nephew of Frances Willard. After a year of college he set out on a classic hegira—a stint as a farm hand in the Nebraska wheat fields, a period of "riding the rails," a shift as a reporter on a newspaper in Buffalo, New York (which ended when he was arrested and convicted of trying to steal a horse and buggy), and then another term of bumming around the country, stopping occasionally to write for small-town newspapers and then moving on before his past could catch up with him. Shipping on a freighter out of Hoboken, New Jersey, he made his way to Berlin;

studied political economy at the University of Berlin; met the play-wright Henrik Ibsen, among other literary figures; and decided to make the lives of tramps and criminals his special study. He did so in a series of exposé books.

There were, of course, novels, essays, articles, learned books, ser-mons, and plays championing the cause of capitalism. As we have noted, John Hay, indignant at the outbreak of strikes and the agitation for radical reform, wrote *The Bread-Winners* to celebrate the virtues of industry and thrift. John Forney's *The New Nobility*, published in 1881, was the most ingenious of the procapitalism school. The new nobility is the American manufacturers whose enterprise and skill have enabled them to rise from humble origins to become industrial leaders. Such is the hero, George Harris, whose "forge and anvil were his college." As a skilled mechanic young Harris "had been called upon by an agent of the Russian government . . . and invited to visit St. Petersburg, to undertake the equipment of a great Russian railroad; to construct the machine-shops, to build the locomotives . . . and to educate in skilled labor the youth of the Empire who might be the leaders of the next generation." Harris had performed the task so brilliantly that young as he was, he had acquired the beginnings of a fortune.

A millionaire several times over by mid-life, Harris goes traveling with his wife, daughter Mary, and his son Henry. In England the Harrises become acquainted with Earl Dorrington, who is convinced that Americans "amount to nothing. . . . They have no past; no great families; no great leaders; no literature and no gifts of governing. America is only an accident, and accidents are sudden and suddenly perish." Lord Conyngham, the earl's son, nonetheless falls in love with Mary Harris. Forney's response to the earl, meanwhile, is given by a mysterious American expatriate called simply the Old Gray—appar-ently Whitman—who declares that the United States, with all its faults, is "blocking out and dovetailing . . . the great democratic edifice of the coming world, not for or out of ourselves merely, but out of all races—British, German, Scandinavian, Spanish, French, Italian . . . the United States is merely a model in small for the United States of the World; the whole world, and all lands, and all good men and women are inextricably involved in our success. . . . We are a People, averaged, dilated, religious, sane, practical, owning their own homes—fifty mil-lions the next census will show—sublime masses, such as the world never saw before, faults enough there are, and miseries enough, and frauds, enough, and the poor and unemployed, no doubt. Yet where is Man so brought to the front? Where are the ideals of all enthusiasts, and all the past, already so realized?"

Old Gray's Whitmanesque eloquence is reinforced by Henry Harris, "his face bright, open, clear," who visits a workingmen's saloon where communist agitators called for revolution. Harris gives the company "one cure for your disease . . . one big pill for your ills—go to America. . . . you can get land over the water for next to nothing an acre. We Yankees are beginning to feed all Europe. Help us to do it. You will be well paid for it." Immigration, not revolution, is the answer. "More misery results from strikes, drinking, socialism, and communism in England and in Germany than from all other causes combined, hard times included," Harris tells the workers.

At the end of the novel, after adventures too bizarre to relate, Henry Harris and Lord Conyngham, who is now Mary Harris's fiancé and whose favorite expression is, of course, "By Jove!" receive a plan for reforming the world from George Harris. It is headed "The Work of the World." "*Africa*—Discover; build railroads; send missionaries of all sects; found and build up Christian nations. . . ." And so on down through "*America*—Establish civil service reform; bring South into lines of emigration and commerce; guard against partisan politics; prepare to meet and survive unparalleled trials, perhaps, catastrophes; maintain public schools against all foes; develop the power of the press; compel the world to conform to American example by sheer force of superiority. *Everywhere*,—Perfect light and force; heat as well as light every city from a common center within same; cook and wash also at same; if possible, navigate air; cut Isthmus of Panama; discover and invent as needs of men demand; abolish war and intemperance; reconcile labor and capital." The plan concluded: "With energy the above work should be done by the year 2000." Henry Harris notes, as he lays down the paper: "It is odd, but the year 2000 will be the seventh Sabbatical age of the world. It will be a remarkable coincidence if the six thousand years of work *is* done by then."

Mary, incidentally, makes clear to Lord Conyngham that she is "possessed with the purpose of being more than merely a loving wife." When her father asks her whence she got her "ambition," she replies, "I am an American girl."

Hamlin Garland was born in 1860 in a log cabin near West Salem, Wisconsin. The Garland family, New England in its origin, moved one step ahead of poverty, or, perhaps more accurately, in step with it, from Wisconsin to Iowa to the Dakota Territory in a desperate search for a farming livelihood. The period of Garland's childhood coincided with some of the grimmest years of falling prices and harsh weather in the prairie states, and Garland, struggling to break free from the cycle of backbreaking work and bankruptcy, determined to become a college teacher of literature. Turned down by Harvard, he made the Boston Public Library his college, enrolled at the Boston School of Oratory, and finally became an instructor there. Friendships with Holmes and Howells gave him a toehold in the Boston literary world, and he began to write articles for the *Boston Evening Transcript* and give public lectures. A convert to Henry George's single tax form of socialism, Garland returned to the Middle West in 1887 and collected and re-collected material for his *Main-Travelled Roads*, the first "realistic" picture of the bleakness and hardship of farm life on the middle border. *Main-Travelled Roads,* published in 1891, brought Garland a degree of recognition, and, stimulated by its success, he turned out three novels the next year, the most successful one being *A Member of the Third House*. The hero of the novel is a young newspaper reporter who unearths the scandalous corruption of the "Third House" of Congress, made up of railroad and utility lobbyists. The Consolidated Railroad is owned by the "Iron Duke," ruthless old Lawrence Davis, who buys and sells state legislators. Helene Davis, the Iron Duke's daughter, is the object of the affections of the young reform-minded reporter Wilson Tuttle. When Davis is threatened with exposure and ruin, he tries to bribe or threaten Tuttle to drop his investigation. One of the bought state senators, a man named Ward, exhorted by his daughter Evelyn, testifies against Davis, and the Iron Duke, his crimes exposed, shoots himself. The novel is a slight one; the story is simply told. The purpose is clearly more reformist than literary. The message is that the "Third House" must be dissolved by an aroused citizenry if the state is to have honest government.

One of the briefest and most brilliant literary careers of the century was that of Stephen Crane. Crane, born in Newark, New Jersey, in 1871, served his apprenticeship as a journalist under his mother, Mary Helen Crane, a devout Methodist, president of the local chapter of the WCTU, and a successful journalist and lecturer. Crane was a fascinated observer and commentator on the streets of New York City. As a reform-minded journalist he ranked with Jacob Riis, Lincoln Steffens, Ray Stannard Baker, and Hutchins Hapgood. His interest in the lives of the city's prostitutes inspired *Maggie: A Girl of the Streets*, published under a pseudonym in 1892 when Crane was twenty-one.

Three years later *The Red Badge of Courage* was published. Crane was twenty-four. He had never experienced war directly, but *The Red Badge of Courage* is one of the great classics of warfare, a remarkable achievement of the imagination. Before his death of tuberculosis in 1900, he had written nine more books, scandalized the public by living with his common-law wife, Cora Taylor, gone on an abortive raid with Cuban revolutionaries, and served as a war correspondent in Cuba, where he experienced what he had previously only imagined.

Establishing himself in England, he became the friend of Joseph Conrad, H. G. Wells, and Henry James. The realism that Howells called for but never achieved was evident in all of Crane's writing, despite his passionately romantic temper.

The reason for the enormous popularity of the short story in America was simple enough. The remarkable proliferation and popularity of literary magazines provided an almost inexhaustible market for short stories (and, of course, essays and articles as well). Most of the short stories had an unexpected or surprise ending. Typical was an early Henry James story entitled "A Landscape Painter," which appeared in the *Atlantic Monthly* of February, 1866. In it an apparently impecunious young painter who marries a poor but beautiful and intelligent young woman for love discovers that she had known all along of his great, though concealed, wealth and has cold-bloodedly married him for his money. "It was the act of a false woman," the indignant painter protests. "A false woman?" his deceiver replied. "No, simply of a woman. I am a woman, sir." And with a smile: "Come, *you* be a man!" The story is both a classic of the surprise-ending genre and a suggestive clue to James's view of women as creatures of artful duplicity.

Regional and local color short stories had a great vogue. In these, which had masculine and feminine "divisions," so to speak, dialect was a prominent feature. Joel Chandler Harris wrote his enormously popular Uncle Remus stories for the *Atlanta Constitution* in 1880 and followed them with a series of short stories, the best of which appeared in two collections, *Mingo and Other Sketches Black and White* and *Free Joe and Other Georgian Sketches*. Most of Harris's stories deal with the postwar relationship between the old aristocracy and the rising class of poor whites and the latter's relationship to the ex-slaves. "Mingo," for example, treats both themes sympathetically. Mingo, who used to be a slave on the plantation of a family now reduced to poverty, works for a prospering "poor white" woman and reflects on his divided loyalties.

Harris was a fascinating figure in his own right. Ray Stannard Baker, a fellow journalist, wrote of him: "I liked him on sight. His face bore the seal of good humor and good health and a pleasant outlook on the world. Around his eyes the years had worn little wrinkles of amusement. . . . He seemed to me one of the simplest and most genuine human beings I had ever met." Harris introduced Baker to some of the old black men and women who had been the sources of his wonderful stories of Br'er Rabbit and Br'er Fox. Harris had come from a "poor white" family, "with little or no education except what he himself got from an old Southern classical library." He had begun work in a country printing office at the age of eleven, "becoming wise in the best and most curious knowledge of Negroes, of dogs, of horses; of the way of the red stream in the swamp; of the folk of the woods. . . . Success such as Harris has had," Baker wrote, with, as he put it, "a wistful thought of the serious problems I was myself facing, often sends a young writer flying to New York where he is promptly petted, befooled and stimulated into an over-production that shortly ends him." Harris was "possessed, centered, absorbed." He had "a kind of tranquil assurance and contentment" that Baker yearned for.

George Washington Cable was born in New Orleans in 1844 to parents who had moved from Lawrenceburg, Indiana, bringing with them their antislavery sentiments. Not part of the city's close-knit aristocracy, Cable's father lost his fortune when his son was five years old, and the family experienced hard times. Cable's father found work as a river boat pilot, and after his death in 1859, young George, then fourteen, went to work to help support the family—his mother and numerous siblings. With the city occupied by Federal troops after Butler's invasion, Cable ran off and enlisted in the Confederate cavalry. After the war he found himself drawn increasingly to the career of a writer and journalist. By 1870 he was writing for the *New Orleans Picayune*. Soon his sketches of New Orleans life, especially of its Creole culture, were appearing in *Scribner's Monthly*, and in 1879 they appeared in a book entitled *Old Creole Days*. Increasingly Cable's efforts were directed toward a wide range of social reforms, the most conspicuous being prison reform and racial justice. Cable was drawn to the theme of miscegenation. To him it represented all the hypocrisy of the "color line," and New Orleans was its capital. More and more he attempted in his stories and in the novel *The Grandissimes*, which dealt with the history of a proud Creole family, to convey the horror of slavery and its legacy of repression and injustice. Howells called *The Grandissimes* "a noble and beautiful book, including all the range of tragedy and comedy; and it made my heart warm towards you while I had the blackest envy in it." As his writing gained prominence, Cable found himself under bitter attack from New Orleans Creoles, who accused him of betraying his city for Northern gold, displaying a "disguised Puritanism," and "assuming the fanatical mission of radical reform and universal enlightenment. . . ." An anonymous writer called him "a buzzard, glutted with carion . . . an unnatural Southern growth, a bastard sprout."

In a commencement address delivered at the University of Mississippi, at Oxford, Cable challenged his indignant listeners to forsake myth and face the realities of the postwar South. He called "the plantation idea . . . a semi-barbarism. It is the idea of the old South with merely the substitution of a negro tenancy for negro slaves. . . . Landlordism kept the South poor one century, and just as sure as it survives it will keep her poor another." The "southern mind clung to outmoded notions of the relations between human beings," Cable declared. "Is the 'southern instinct' not cunning enough," he asked, "to snuff out the stupid wickedness of exalting and abusing our fellow humans class by class and race by race instead of man by man?"

Mark Twain became one of Cable's admirers. "You know," he wrote to Howells, "when he comes down to moral honest, limpid innocence, and utterly blemishless piety, the Apostles were mere policemen to Cable. . . ." The warmth of his reception in the North (he was invited by Daniel Coit Gilman to give six lectures at Johns Hopkins) and the growing hostility toward him in the South (one of the petty forms of harassment he suffered was having his property evaluations and tax assessments raised sharply) determined Cable to move North and take up his residence with his family in Northampton, Massachusetts. He and Twain had become the closest of friends, even to undertaking a lecture tour together. The only thorn in their friendship lay in the fact that Cable was notably pious and Twain an avowed freethinker. In Washington, D.C., with Twain, Cable wrote his wife triumphantly: "I got him out to church at last!" It didn't take, however. Twain remained stubbornly unconverted. He wrote to Howells at the end of his tour with Cable: "You will never, never divine, guess, imagine, how loathsome a thing the Christian religion can be made until you come to know and study Cable daily and hourly. Mind you, I like him; he is pleasant company; I rage and swear at him sometimes, but we do not quarrel; we get along mighty happily together; but in him and his person I have learned to hate all religions. He has taught me to abhor and detest the Sabbath-day and hunt up new and troublesome ways to dishonor it."

Another literature that was of considerable importance in and of itself was children's literature. Although *The Century of the Child*, the title of the book of the Swedish reformer Ellen Key, referred to the twentieth century rather than the nineteenth, the title was more appropriate, as it would turn out, for the earlier century—at least if we measure the volume and quality of writing devoted to children. The phenomenon was not, of course, confined to the United States, nor did it reach its highest form here. The Grimm brothers in Germany and half a dozen Englishmen from Robert Louis Stevenson to Lewis Carroll were outstanding practitioners. But most of the "serious" American writers either began by writing books for young people or supplemented their incomes throughout their careers by writing books for boys and girls. Not surprisingly, this was especially true of the generation of women writers born in the decade of the 1850s. Hawthorne turned out a great number of books and stories for children, among them a children's history of the United States. So did Mark Twain (*The Prince and the Pauper, The Adventures of Tom Sawyer,* and *The Adventures of Huckleberry Finn*). *The Rover Boys* roved everywhere in innumerable volumes, Louisa May Alcott wrote her famous book, and later the *Nancy Drew* books demonstrated that girls could have as many adventures as boys. If life were longer, and this book larger, we could traverse the mountain of children's literature that accumulated in the last half of the century. What is important to note in passing is the fact that it represented, above all else, a new attitude toward children and childhood. Children were increasingly seen not just as small adults but as strange and even exotic creatures inhabiting a unique world of their own, as complex as, and in many ways far more compelling than, the world of adults. Also involved in the focusing of attention on children was, as we have noted, the conviction that they were to be the uncorrupted bearers of the new consciousness.

Frank Munsey, the publisher of half a dozen magazines, also found time to write books for boys full of improving moral precepts. As he explained in the preface to *The Boy Broker*, published in 1888, the book was intended to make its readers "more manly, more self reliant, more generous, more noble and sweeter in disposition." The young hero, Herbert Randolph, is a Vermont farm boy who "proposed to make his way in New York—to become what is known as a successful man, to make a name for himself—a name that would extend to his native State and make his parents proud of their brilliant son." Like the heroes of all such stories, Herbert was "a great reader. Biography had been his favorite pastime. He knew the struggles and triumphs of many of our most conspicuous merchant princes." Munsey was at pains to make apparent the obstacles to be overcome by any such ambitious youth. Only one out of a hundred who came to the city seeking their fortune succeeded, he warned.

The Boy Broker carried the inscription "To My Dear Father, whose rigid New England discipline, seemed to me as a boy severe and unnecessary, this volume is affectionately dedicated with the grateful acknowledgement that he was right and I was wrong."

To the growing ranks of black journalists, whose audience was almost exclusively black, were added black poets and novelists whose work was intended to be read by primarily white readers. Two of the earliest such writers were Albery Whitman and Charles Chesnutt. Whitman was born a slave in 1851 in Kentucky. Left an orphan, he managed to acquire an education and became a schoolteacher and an elder and pastor in the African Methodist Episcopal Church, finally securing a position as general financial agent at Wilberforce University in Ohio, an institution the primary mission of which was "the preparation of Christian Teachers for Southern fields of labor."

In 1877 Whitman published a volume of his verse entitled *Not a Man and Yet a Man*, dedicated "to those who loved the negro in mankind, and pitied him, and stooped to help him in his low estate, assailed by fierce opinions . . . to those . . . looking forward, the full fruition of their bright hopes see, the nations of all earth forever free. To those, the Abolition Fathers. . . ." Whitman's poems celebrated the struggle of black people for freedom and their contributions as blacks to American independence: "And can we then forget that patriots, patriots, black, / Marched with white brothers to the dread attack?" He wrote a series of Indian poems clearly modeled on Longfellow's *The Song of Hiawatha*—Whitman's hero was Nanawawa—with the American Revolution as the historical background. The poem ends with the black narrator's vowing to "rise above by *toiling* from below."

> Free schools, free press, free speech and equal laws,
> A common country and a common cause,

Are worthy of a freeman's boasts—
Are Freedom's *real* and intrinsic costs.
Without these, Freedom is an empty name,
And war-worn glory is a glaring shame.
Soon where yon happy future now appears,
Where learning now her glorious temple rears,
Our country's hosts shall round one interest meet,
And her free heart with one proud impulse beat,
One common blood thro' her life's channels flow. . . .
And soon, whoever to our bourne shall come,
Jew, Greek or Goth, he here shall be at home.
Then ignorance shall forsake her crooked ways,
And poor old Caste there end her feeble days.

Paul Laurence Dunbar, the black poet, was born in Dayton, Ohio. He had edited his school paper, and with his friend Orville Wright, already preoccupied with the notion of flying, he published his own short-lived journal called the *Tattler* and wrote the class song on his graduation in 1891. A teacher of Dunbar's persuaded the chairman of the Western Association of Writers, meeting in Dayton in the summer of 1892, to invite Dunbar to deliver the opening remarks. Dunbar chose to do so in the form of a poem which declared:

A welcome warm as Western wine,
And free as Western Hearts be thine.
Do what the greatest joy insures,
The city has no will but yours.

The poem, and, above all, the fact that the poet was black created a minor sensation. Dunbar sent his poems off to a number of magazines. One caught the eye of the Bard of the West, Indiana's James Whitcomb Riley. Riley, unaware that Dunbar was black, wrote him, praising the poem and calling him "a singer who should command wide and serious attention. . . ." In another letter Riley wrote Dunbar: "Certainly your gift . . . is a superior one, and therefore its fortunate possessor would wear it with a becoming sense of gratitude, and meekness—always feeling that for any resultant good, God's is the glory. . . . Already you have many friends. . . ." In 1893 Dunbar published his first book of poems, *Oak and Ivy*, with the assistance of white friends.

Not only had Boston to share the literary scene with New York and Chicago (New York, indeed, *replaced* Boston as the literary hub of the universe), but San Francisco advanced its own claim to a significant place in the literary scene. The most spectacular figure in what might be called the Pacific coast renaissance was Ambrose Bierce. Bierce had enlisted in the Union army as a drummer boy at the age of eighteen, immediately after the fall of Fort Sumter. Wounded at Shiloh, he was promoted to lieutenant and later mustered out of the army as a brevet major. A strikingly handsome man, he declared that his role as associate editor of the *Argonaut* was "to purify journalism in his town by instructing such writers as it is worth while to instruct, and assassinating those that it is not." Few targets escaped his acidulous pen—"bloated bondholders," bigoted union leaders, suffragists, socialists, religion. Of the last he wrote: "No sane man of intelligence will plead for religion on the ground that it is better than nothing if it is not true. Truth is better than anything or all things; the next best thing to truth is absence of error."

The epitome of his black humor was his *The Devil's Dictionary*, containing such definitions as:

"Politics, n. A strife of interests masquerading as a contest of principles. . . .

"Radicalism, n. The conservatism of tomorrow injected into the affairs of today. . . .

"Realism, n. The art of depicting nature as it is seen by toads. . . .

"Religion, n. A Daughter of Hope and Fear explaining to Ignorance the nature of the Unknown. . . .

"Saint, n. A dead sinner, revised and edited."

To Upton Sinclair, who felt the sharpness of his tongue, Bierce was "a great writer, a bitter black sinner, and a cruel, domineering old bigot."

At the age of seventy-one Bierce visited the battlefields of the Civil War he had known so many years before and then departed for South America. He wrote to Lora Bierce: "Goodby—If you hear of my being stood up against a Mexican stone wall and shot to rags, please to know that I think it a pretty good way to depart this life. It beats old age, disease or falling down the cellar stairs. To be a Gringo in Mexico—ah, that is Euthanasia!"

We may see Bierce as a representative of a generation of Union soldiers who fought in the Civil War, believing that out of it would come a new and better America and a fairer human order, and who were bitterly disillusioned by the chaos and rancor that split the country into hostile classes and sections. Certainly his Civil War stories are his most brilliant achievement and have earned themselves a respectable place in our literature. Bierce's return in his last years to the scenes of the battles of his youth reinforces the notion that he could never rid himself of the hold that the war had on him or reconcile himself to the nation that emerged from the war. Undoubtedly his sardonic temper was the consequence of a conjunction of the personal and historical, but whatever that mix may have been, Bierce's agonized life serves to remind us of a fact that is beyond dispute: that the Civil War marked the generation that fought it in ways too deep ever to yield fully to the historian's inquisitive eye. Bierce brooded over his difficulties in finding publishers for his books and finally disappeared into Mexico to an unknown death under circumstances as strange as those of any of his stories, which so often ended in death.

Edwin Markham was an active participant in the literary life of San Francisco and Oakland. Markham, born in 1852 in Oregon, had had a bitterly hard childhood. He had spent lonely years as a sheepherder and a failed farmer. A fiery Populist and later socialist, he had been a spiritualist and follower of mad Thomas Lake Harris, the founder of the Fountain Grove commune. Inspired by Jean François Millet's "The Man with the Hoe," which he saw in Charles Crocker's art gallery on Nob Hill, Markham, in 1899, wrote a poem with the same title. More famous than any other single poem in the nation's history, with the possible exception of Longfellow's *Hiawatha*, Markham's "The Man with the Hoe" made his name known not only in the United States but around the world. Translated into forty languages, it brought him more than $250,000 in royalties before he died and made him the "poet of the people," the poet of social protest and radicalism. The poem caught perfectly the sentiment and the radical mood of the decade's end.

> Bowed by the weight of centuries he leans
> Upon his hoe and gazes on the ground,
> The emptiness of ages in his face,
> And on his back the burdens of the world.
> Who made him dead to rapture and despair,
> A thing that grieves not and that never hopes,
> Stolid and stunned, a brother to the ox?
> Who loosened and let down this brutal jaw?
> Whose was the hand that slanted back his brow?
> Whose breath blew out the light within his brain?

Was this, Markham asked, the creature to whom God gave dominion over sea and land? He was a symbol of the world's "blind greed," "humanity betrayed," a "protest that is also prophecy." The poet called on "the lords and rulers in all lands" to "straighten up this shape;/ Touch it again with immortality. . . / Make right the immemorial infamies. . . ."

> How will the Future reckon with this man?
> How answer his brute question in that hour
> When whirlwinds of rebellion shake all shores?
> How will it be with kingdoms and with kings—
> With those who shaped him to the thing he is—
> When this dumb terror shall rise to judge the world,
> After the silence of the centuries?

37

American Literature:
Women's Division

Women played such a conspicuous, if not dominant, role in American letters in this period that it seems appropriate, if not indeed necessary, to consider them a separate category. In the words of a British visitor, James Fullerton Muirhead, "All down the literary ladder . . . we find a considerable part of every rung occupied by the skirts appropriate to the gentler sex. . . ."

When Henry Adams complained of the "feminization" of American literature, it is doubtful if he had Harriet Beecher Stowe specifically in mind, but she, more than any other woman of the nineteenth century, had laid the foundation for that development. When in 1882, on the occasion of her seventy-first birthday, her publisher gave a party for her, some 200 of the nation's principal literary lights attended to honor the diminutive woman who had not only written the most popular literary work of the century but established the genre of the small-town short story, which was to become, if it had not already become, the particular domain of women writers. Whittier wrote a poem for the occasion, as did Oliver Wendell Holmes, the unchallenged master of "occasional poetry." Henry Ward Beecher made a brief speech, praising their parents and especially his mother.

Whittier's poem ended with the lines:

The waves that wash our gray coast lines,
The winds that rock the Southern pines
Shall sing of her; the unending years
Shall tell her tale in unborn ears.
And when, with sins and follies past,
Are numbered color-hate and caste,
White, black, and red shall own as one,
The noblest work by woman done.

Holmes wrote of her world fame:

Briton and Frenchman, Swede and Dane,
Turk, Spaniard, Tartar of Ukraine,
Hidalgo, Cossack, Cadi,
High Dutchman and Low Dutchman, too,
The Russian serf, the Polish Jew,
Arab, Armenian, and Mantchoo
Would shout, "We know this lady."
It was she who found the Archimedian "place to stand on,"
Her lever was the wand of art,
Her fulcrum was the human heart,
Whence all unfailing aid is;
She moved the earth! Its thunders pealed,
Its mountains shook, its temples reeled,
The blood-red fountains were unsealed,
And Moloch sunk to Hades.

There were other poems and piles of letters and telegrams. Judge Albion Tourgée, who had made a valiant attempt to do for Reconstruction what Mrs. Stowe had done for slavery itself, gave a short address. Harriet Beecher Stowe, who had watched postwar America go so sadly awry and had seen blacks losing all they seemed, for a time, to have gained, told her friends: "If any of you have doubt, or sorrow, or pain, if you doubt about this world, just remember what God has done; just remember that this great sorrow of slavery has gone, gone by forever. . . . Let us never doubt. Everything that ought to happen is going to happen."

She was to live for another fourteen years, slipping slowly and gently into a kind of twilight, comforted by the "inconceivable loveliness of Christ," attended by adoring friends and relatives, nieces and nephews by the dozen, unarguably the greatest of a century of remarkable women.

One of the pioneers of what we might call the feminist social reform novel was Elizabeth Stuart Phelps Ward. Born in Boston in 1842 of a long and distinguished New England ancestry, she showed remarkable precocity. When she was only twenty-four, she wrote *The Gates Ajar*, a highly sentimental "religious" novel which became an instant best seller, indeed, one of the all-time best sellers, and made her world-famous. Three years later *The Silent Partner* was published. It was a sharp attack on the exploitation of workers in the mill towns of New England. The heroine, Perley Kelso, is the selfish, pampered daughter of a wealthy millowner. She has a chance meeting with a young woman mill hand named Sip Garth, and her conscience is stirred by the encounter. She gets to know Sip, discovers the dreadful working conditions in the mills and the pinched and desperate lives of the workers. When her father dies, Perley resolves to become a silent partner in the mill in order to reform it. She breaks her engagement with the young man who, as part owner of the mill, refuses to consider the reforms she demands, and she also rejects the hand of the young superintendent of the mill, who shares her dream of reform. When her fiancé quotes Adam Smith to her to prove that the marketplace, not sentiment, must govern the conditions of labor in the mill, she replies that "he is too learned, and you are too lazy. . . . But, Maverick, there *is* something in this matter which neither of you touch. There is *something* about the relations of rich and poor, of master and man, with which the state of the market has nothing whatever to do. There is *something*, a claim, a duty, a puzzle, it is all too new to me to know what to call it,—but I am convinced that there is *something* at which a man cannot lie and twirl his mustache forever."

Maverick derides her concern for the workers: "When you are in genuine difficulty, they will turn against you. . . . There is neither gratitude nor common business sense among them. There's neither trust nor honor. . . . They would ruin us altogether for fifty cents a week." Perley's reply is that if they are treated fairly and honestly, as she intends to treat them, they will respond with loyalty and trust. The novel's denouement comes when, in bad times, the workers threaten to strike over a reduction in their wages. Perley assures them that the company is on the verge of bankruptcy and that it can survive only by reducing wages. The workers accept her assurances, and a disastrous strike is averted. But Perley now sees that her lifework is to improve the conditions of labor and that this can be done only by Christianizing the principles and the hearts of millowners and workers alike. "The fact is," she tells her suitor, "that I have no time to think of love and marriage. . . . That is a business, a trade, by itself to women. I have too much to do. . . . I cannot spare the time for it."

Sip Garth, converted to Christianity, becomes an evangelist, particularly successful with the millworkers because she speaks their language and knows their hearts and, finally, because "the religion of Jesus Christ . . . is the only poor folks' religion in all the world."

Rose Terry Cooke, one of the founding mothers of the New England small-town short-story genre, belonged more to the generation of Harriet Beecher Stowe than to the new age. Born in 1827 in Hartford, Connecticut, Rose Terry attended Emma Willard's Hartford Female Seminary, taught school, worked as a governess, and married an iron manufacturer named Rollin Hillyer Cooke. Her first published efforts were religious poems published in Charles Dana's *Sun*. Soon her sketches of New England town life were being published in *Harper's* and the *Atlantic Monthly*. They were, for the most part, unabashed sermonettes, the moral of which was that piety and hard work were the only path to salvation. *Root-Bound and Other Sketches*, a collection of short stories, was published in 1885. The character of the work can best be judged by the title story, the theme of which is the notion that flowering plants and shrubs with roots closely contained in small tubs or barrels produce more luxuriant blooms than those that are unconfined. Hence in the small town neighborliness, love, faith, and trust flourish as they cannot in the wildness and disorder of the city.

The oldest of that generation of women writers who came to their maturity in the postwar years was Sarah Orne Jewett, born in South Berwick, Maine, in 1849. What is perhaps most striking about Jewett's carefully fashioned stories is the sense that she adapted to a specifically feminine perspective on the world the most advanced storytelling techniques, techniques gleaned primarily from such French masters as Flaubert, Balzac, and Maupassant. Indeed, she wrote of the restless and unhappy Madame Bovary: "If she could have taken what there was in that dull little village! She is such a lesson to dwellers in country towns who drift out of relation to their surroundings. . . ." Jewett's father, a doctor, had been a disciple of Emerson and the most important figure in her childhood, teaching her to observe carefully everything about her, especially the world of nature, and encouraging her ambition to be a doctor. It was soon evident that her health was too frail; she suffered from arthritis and fits of nervous depression. For a virtual invalid marriage was out of the question. At the age of seventeen she began writing poems and short stories for children (a path, incidentally, that many women writers followed). Soon she was writing stories for adults. The *Atlantic Monthly* accepted one, and William Dean Howells became her enthusiastic advocate. A collection of her Maine stories under the title *Deephaven*, published in 1877, not only brought her considerable fame but helped define the new category of local color writers. By the end of the century she had produced twelve volumes of "sketches," the best known of which is *The Country of the Pointed Firs*, and three rather unsuccessful novels, and her reputation, if not precisely worldwide, extended far beyond her native land. She likened her technique to nibbling "all around her stories like a mouse." Flaubert's maxim was her guide: "Write of ordinary life as one writes history."

"Green Island," a sketch from *The Country of the Pointed Firs*, describes the tidy, carefully cared-for female household that became, in the work of all the New England women writers, a symbol of their determination to create and preserve a simple domestic order in the face of the chaotic and disintegrating larger society. The narrator accompanies a Mrs. Todd with her son, William, to visit Mrs. Todd's fiercely independent old mother, who lives by herself on Green Island. Slowly and lovingly the author, the "I," unfolds the small world of Green Island: the house, with its modest but immaculate furnishings, the garden, the fields, and the patch of forest. The three eat, pick vegetables, have tea, sing old familiar songs. William's voice is "a little faint and frail, like the family daguerreotypes" but "perfectly true and sweet," as pleasant a surprise as the fish hawk's nests that he had pointed out on their walk about the island and the late-blooming linnaea they had come upon "in an open bit of pasture at the top of the island." At the end of the day, "with a generous freight of lobsters and new potatoes which William had put aboard, and . . . a full 'kag' of prime number one salted mackerel," the visitors pushed off for shore. That was it. No twists, no surprise ending, no moral except the small gifts of daily life that fill up the world like a benediction.

Mary Wilkins Freeman was born in 1852 and spent most of her youth in Brattleboro, Vermont, and Randolph, Massachusetts. She was, in her own way, as mysterious a figure as Emily Dickinson. Plainly influenced by Harriet Beecher Stowe, Wilkins set out to record the life of New England towns with the eye of an artist and the perceptions of a sociologist. Clearly she partook of the new consciousness. One of her stories (and the title of a collection of short stories) was "A New England Nun"; Freeman herself was a member of that new order of literary nuns who put their writing before the conventional female roles of wife and mother—she was fifty years old before she married a doctor, Charles Freeman. By the time her first book of stories—*A Humble Romance*—was published in 1887, when she was thirty-five, she had already acquired a reputation through the appearance of her work in numerous magazines, especially *Harper's Weekly* and the *Atlantic Monthly*. *A New England Nun* was published four years later to even more critical acclaim.

Many of the stories were tales of quiet feminine revolt against ancient masculine tyrannies. The most engaging of these is "The Revolt of 'Mother.' " Sarah and Adoniram Penn have grown old together in their taciturn New England way, living in a cramped, dilapidated little house, Sarah always in anticipation of Adoniram's promise of more adequate quarters. But Adoniram's passion is fixed more on the comfort and good housing of his cows than of his wife. When, with a new cow barn almost complete, he ventures off to buy another cow, Sarah employs local day laborers to convert the barn hastily into a spacious house and moves in bag and baggage before Adoniram returns, leaving the house for the cows. The delight of the story is in its telling, in the wit and charity of it and its affectionate observation of two stubborn people who talk little and feel much. But it is also a story about a woman's emancipation of herself, the more effective for being so understated.

To Freeman the old consciousness, the remnants of Calvinism, was a "chaotic deposit of flinty, fruitless irrelevancies"; the survivors bore "the traces of those features of will and conscience so strong as to be almost exaggerations and deformities." New England had been forged in the relentless fires of Puritan "will." Now that flinty will, no longer directed to survival in the wilderness, turned in upon itself and fed on fierce contests with the wills of others over matters of no consequence in the strangely ritualized personality struggles that characterized New England villages. In the tradition of Mrs. Stowe, Wilkins probed gently into the dimmer recesses of her characters' psyches. In "A Conquest of Humility," Lawrence Thayer and Delia Caldwell are to be married, but Lawrence refuses to go through with the ceremony. The guests reclaim their wedding presents, and Delia goes home, humiliated. The "other woman" is pretty Olive Briggs, who works in the milliner's shop. She in turn jilts Lawrence, and he has to endure the jeers and rudeness of the town as Delia had to endure its sympathy. In the end Lawrence and Delia are reconciled and married. It is all disarmingly artless and profoundly artful with that quality of condensed emotion and economy of expression common to the best fiction.

In "A New England Nun," Louisa Ellis and Joe Daggett are to be married after a courtship of fifteen years. During fourteen of those years Joe has been away, roaming the world. Returned, he visits Louisa dutifully every week, invading her "delicately sweet room," where every object has its established, sacred place and where he feels like a bull in a china shop. Firmly set in the ways of an old maid, Louisa comes to dread her impending marriage, and when she inadvertently discovers that her fiancé has come to love another woman (although he is determined to do the honorable thing by Louisa), she gratefully breaks off the engagement and resumes her familiar routines, "prayerfully numbering her days, like an uncloistered nun."

Mary Freeman's talent was not a major one, but it was perfect in its own way and, one suspects, enduring. Henry James read her stories with "enormous enthusiasm." Like Emily Dickinson, she spent a year in the restrictive atmosphere of the Mt. Holyoke Female Seminary. She acknowledged a debt not only to Goethe, Hawthorne, Emerson, and Thoreau but also to Sarah Orne Jewett, who had burst earlier on the literary scene. Freeman's output was measured at 7,000 words a day—the equivalent of a substantial short story—which must be very nearly a record for productiveness.

Louisa May Alcott, born in 1832 to Abigail and Bronson Alcott, was thirty-five when she began the book that would make her famous, if not immortal—*Little Women*. Daughter of one of the most eccentric Americans of the century (Bronson Alcott was an early and extremely vocal vegetarian; he offended Carlyle by eating potatoes and strawberries mixed together for breakfast), she had a difficult childhood in Concord, Massachusetts. Suffering from chronic ill health and periodic depression, Louisa May found solace in writing. By the time she wrote *Little Women* she had been supporting her improvident family for years, publishing secretly in Frank Leslie's magazine the most lurid romances full of suppressed sexuality. She had been a rebellious, headstrong child, whose father did his often unavailing best to make her conform to his ideal of an obedient, well-behaved young woman, warning her against her "anger, discontent, impatience, evil appetites, greedy wants, complainings, ill-speakings, vileness, headlessness, rude behavior." In *Little Women* Louisa May Alcott created, out of the often bizarre life of the Alcott family, an idyllic picture of American girlhood, a picture irresistible to successive generations of female readers, a remarkable tribute to her own artistic powers that doubtless served the deeper purpose of reconciling her to the disorder and disappointments of her own life (among the latter was her unspoken love for her neighbor Henry Thoreau). In a sense the tragedy of Louisa May Alcott lay in the fact that she was born in a kind of odd historical "seam"—the 1830s—too late for that calm assurance of divine favor that sustained Harriet Beecher Stowe through her long lifetime and too soon to be part of the generation of emancipated women born in the 1850s.

Alice Brown was born in 1856 in Hampton Falls, New Hampshire. Her long and often elaborately plotted stories frequently employed the device of a concluding commentary on the narrative. "A March Wind" tells the story of a spinster's late love for an itinerant mechanic— a "tramp," to the indignant townspeople—who stops by to do a job of work for her and remains to marry her. It is one of the few fully realized, more or less conventional love stories in the corpus of New England short stories.

"All the writing of this country has been done by New England-ers," John Jay Chapman wrote his wife, "and they are unconsciously accustomed to incense burning, fumes of self-appreciation. . . ." But that, of course, was not quite the whole story. The New England men who had, for all practical purposes, constituted, as Chapman suggested, the American literary establishment—Cooper, Irving, Melville, and Poe aside—now gave way to New England women, and they proved far less disposed to "incense-burning."

We are already familiar with Charlotte Perkins Gilman, who was born in 1860 in Hartford, Connecticut. She was the daughter of Fred-eric Beecher Perkins, a nephew of the formidable Lyman Beecher. An author, editor, and librarian, Frederic Perkins abandoned his family and left Charlotte, her mother, and her siblings to a life of genteel poverty. Charlotte displayed considerable talent as an artist, and by the time she was twenty she was earning more than her keep as a commercial artist. High-strung, "nervous," and unstable, she married a fellow artist named Charles Walter Stetson, a match that seems to have been a disaster from the first. Although she and Stetson had a child, she found herself overwhelmed by domestic responsibilities and had a nervous breakdown. By this time writing had replaced painting and drawing as her major preoccupation, but the "alienist" who treated her, the famous S. Weir Mitchell, himself a novelist of some reputation, insisted that she stop all writing since, in his view, it contributed directly to her nervous condition. (It is interesting to recall that Emily Dickinson's doctor took away her "Pen" during a period of nervous depression, presumably for the same reason.) Charlotte Stetson divorced her husband and fled to California, leaving her child with him. In California she visited the California poet Joaquin Miller and met intense young Hamlin Garland, whose *Main-Travelled Roads* had been praised by Howells as one of the first realistic pictures of Midwestern farm life (the other being E. W. Howe's *The Story of a Country Town*). She threw herself into the women's movement with a passion, reading the writings of the leading feminists, turning out a series of short stories and articles, and lecturing on women's rights, labor, and the cooperative movement. Her most significant contribution to feminism was her insistence that the basic cause of women's problems was their economic dependence. Strongly influenced by Zina Peirce, she argued that there could not be true freedom or equality for women until they had economic independence.

In the process of healing herself and counteracting the inept therapy of Mitchell, Gilman wrote one of the most haunting short stories in American literature, "The Yellow Wall Paper," a harrowing tale of a woman suffering deep depression who is driven ever closer to insanity by the bumbling efforts of her doctor husband to cure her. The standard treatment for such disorders was complete isolation and rest.

"The Yellow Wall Paper" is in the form of a secret diary. Her husband's patronizing attitude toward her illness, the diarist increasingly perceives, is its cause. "John laughs at me, of course, but one expects that in marriage. . . .

"John is practical in the extreme. He has no patience with faith, an intense horror of superstition, and he scoffs openly at any talk of things not to be felt and seen and put down in figures." In other words, he is the modern, rational, scientific American male.

"John is a physician," the patient writes, "and *perhaps*—(I would not say it to a living soul, of course . . .)—*perhaps* that is one reason I do not get well faster. . . .

"You see he does not believe I am sick! . . . [He] assures friends and relatives that there is really nothing the matter with me but temporary nervous depression—a slight hysterical tendency."

Gradually her husband's unconscious cruelty drives his wife deeper and deeper into what we would call today paranoid schizophrenia, the conviction that the world is conspiring against her and that she is slowly turning into the torn and peeling yellow wallpaper. (That she should be confined in such a room is testimony to her husband's insensitivity.) I suspect it is safe to say that no American writer has written a more haunting psychological study.

Helen Maria Fiske Hunt Jackson, the childhood playmate of Emily Dickinson and her warm advocate, was born in Amherst in 1830. She married in 1852, and after the deaths of her husband and children Thomas Wentworth Higginson encouraged her to try to support herself by writing. Soon she was turning out a stream of stories and essays, indistinguishable from the vast tide of such literature. In 1875, after her marriage to William Jackson, she moved to Colorado, where she wrote a novel based on the life of Emily Dickinson and became the most famous champion of the cause of the Indians with *A Century of Dishonor*, published in 1881, and her enormously popular novel *Ramona*, published three years later. *Ramona* utilized the Spanish-Indian culture of the Southwest for its sentimental romance, in which the plight of the Indians was largely obscured by the novel's complex plot. Helen Hunt Jackson died in 1885, at the age of fifty-five, a year after the publication of *Ramona* and a year before Emily Dickinson's death.

One of the unhappiest of female literary lives in this era was that of Constance Fenimore Woolson. A great-niece of James Fenimore Cooper, Woolson was a successful novelist in the style of her hero, Henry James. They corresponded constantly (her letters to James were substantially better than her novels). She and James had a series of odd meetings in London and in Rome, sometimes staying in the same hotel. In Rome, when Woolson killed herself by jumping from her apartment window, James hurried to her hotel and retrieved and later destroyed the letters he had written her (he missed a half dozen or so), but he did not attend her funeral. John Hay and his wife, who were visiting Rome, went, and Hay wrote Henry Adams that they had laid her down "in her first and last resting-place—a thoroughly good, and most unhappy woman, with a great talent, bedeviled by disordered nerves. She did much good and no harm in her life, and had not as much happiness as a convict."

The contrast between the Southern male writers like Thomas Nelson Page and their female counterparts was as striking as that between the male and female writers of the North. Kate O'Flaherty Chopin was a half a world away from her New England sisters, but she, too, was a master or mistress of the vivid "psychological" short story with the surprise ending. She had grown up in St. Louis, a member of that city's old French Catholic elite. Her father was an Irish immigrant who had prospered in business and married into an "old family." Despite a highly conventional upbringing, Kate O'Flaherty was sensitive to the currents of women's emancipation. At seventeen she wrote a sketch which she entitled "Emancipation: A Life Fable." It began: "There was once an animal born into the world, and opening his eyes upon Life, he saw above and about him confining walls, and before him were bars of iron through which came air and light from without; this animal was born in a cage." But one day, grown to maturity, it finds the cage door open. Despite its fear of the unknown world outside, the animal leaves its cage to suffer the dangers and joys of freedom.

At the age of nineteen Kate O'Flaherty married Oscar Chopin, a wealthy young Louisianian, and not long after the marriage accompanied him to New York, where he sought out the "Lady brokers of Broadway," the famous Claflin sisters, Victoria and Tennie C. Kate Chopin described Tennie C. as "a fussy, pretty, talkative little woman, who discussed business extensively with Oscar, and entreated me not to fall into the useless degrading life of most married ladies—but to elevate my mind and turn my attention to politics, commerce, questions of state, etc., etc. I assured her I would do so. . . ."

Settled in New Orleans, in the midst of the Creole culture that was her husband's, Chopin had six children and, as a handsome and brilliant woman, lived a vivacious social life. When her husband died in 1882, she returned with her children to St. Louis and soon thereafter joined the growing ranks of women writers, making the Creole life of New Orleans her special subject, as Mary Wilkins Freeman had made the New England town hers. A flood of stories and novels poured out in the years that followed, many of them having to do with the "new" marriage relationship that emphasized the rights and needs of both husband and wife. One of her early stories, "Wiser Than a God," concerns a young woman who refuses a conventional marriage and becomes a successful pianist. In "A Point of Issue" a young married couple have ideas about marital freedom similar to those of the free love advocates, but social pressures force them into a more conventional relationship. "Desirée's Baby" deals with the popular theme of miscegenation. Beautiful Desirée, married to a Creole aristocrat, has a child by him that has unmistakably black features. Her husband, Aubigny, coldly rejects the child. When Desirée cries, "What does it mean?" he replies "lightly": "It means that the child is not white; it means that you are not white." The rejected Desirée drowns herself and her infant.

Sifting through family papers after Desirée's death, the husband discovers, from an old letter, that the black blood is his. "Desirée's Baby" was just the kind of lurid tale that ladies loved to weep over. It was snatched up by *Vogue* magazine, which published eighteen more of Chopin's stories in the next ten years.

Bayou Folk, a collection of her short stories of Creole life, was the work that established Chopin's reputation as a local colorist, but many of her bolder stories, especially those dealing with sexuality and marriage, were rejected by editors fearful of offending their readers' sensibilities. In 1894 she wrote "The Story of an Hour," a brilliant study of a young wife's emotions on hearing of her husband's tragic and unexpected death in a railroad accident (Kate Chopin's father had died in a railroad accident when she was four years of age; her husband had died of typhus when she was thirty-one). After the first moment of desolation she is overwhelmed by a kind of joy. "When she abandoned herself a little whispered word escaped her slightly parted lips. She said it over and over under breath: 'free, free, free!' . . . She did not stop to ask if it were not a monstrous joy that held her. A clear and exalted perception enabled her to dismiss the suggestion as trivial. She knew that she would weep again when she saw the kind, tender hands folded in death, the face that had never looked save with love upon her. . . . But she saw beyond that bitter moment a long procession of years to come that would belong to her absolutely. And she opened and spread her arms out to them in welcome." The "twist," of course, is that the report of her husband's death proves, as Mark Twain said, "premature." Brently Mallard appears, "a little travel-stained," having taken another train. When his wife sees him, she dies of a heart attack, "of joy that kills," her friends all agree. A few weeks after having written the story, Kate Chopin reflected in her diary how detached she felt from the lives of her husband and her mother and how she gloried in her own growth. But if it were possible for her husband and mother to return to life, she assured herself, "I would unhesitatingly give up every thing that has come into my life since they left it and join my existence again with theirs. To do that, I would have to forget the past ten years of my growth—my real growth. But I would take back a little wisdom with me; it would be the spirit of perfect acquiescence." And later she wrote: "I am younger today at 43 than I was at 23. What does it matter. Why this mathematical division of life into years? Days are what count—not years."

The theme of women breaking away from conventional lives became one of the earmarks of Chopin's stories. Sometimes the break was a radical one. In "The Maid of Saint Phillippe" the heroine joins the Cherokee to live the life of a hunter. In her novel *The Awakening*, Kate Chopin struck the boldest course. Her heroine, Edna Pontellier, is married to an older husband chiefly interested in making money and has two small children. As a repressed Presbyterian, married into an exuberant and emotional Catholic family, Edna is dismayed at her inability to express affection freely and openly. Her female in-laws discuss matters no proper Protestant family would ever mention. While her husband is away on a business trip, Edna abandons herself to a suddenly aroused sexual desire and involves herself in two affairs, one with a known roué and one with a young musician; the latter turns into love. Edna flirts with the notion of running away, abandoning her children, and becoming an artist herself. She longs to live the life "which her empassioned, newly awakened being demanded." Foreseeing a succession of "affairs" occasioned by her sexual needs, unfulfilled in marriage, and coming to feel that her children were "antagonists who . . . sought to drag her into the soul's slavery for the rest of her days," she "eludes" them by drowning herself.

As interesting as the question of the motivation behind Kate Chopin's vivid stories of feminine discontent and aroused sensuality is that of the responses evoked in her readers. That one woman, or, as we have seen, thousands of women should have had such feelings was not remarkable, but that Chopin should find responsive readers by the tens of thousands was more notable. It suggests, at the least, that her readers experienced a kind of conspiratorial thrill at sentiments they must have sympathized with, if they could not wholly approve. As for the reactions of those men who may have ventured to read Mrs. Chopin's stories and novels, we can imagine their disquiet.

One of the pioneers among women novelist-journalists was Rebecca Harding Davis, born in 1831 in Washington, Pennsylvania. She lived in the South during much of her childhood and began to write when she was still in her teens. She was thirty years old when an article entitled "Life in the Iron Mills," published in the *Atlantic Monthly*, attracted attention to her work. Several years later she married L. Clarke Davis and began to rear a family, meanwhile working as an associate editor of Greeley's *Tribune*. Her novel *Margaret Howth* (1862) deals with slum life and tells the story of a manufacturer who chooses for his wife a working girl rather than a frivolous heiress.

Waiting for the Verdict, published in 1868, was the first novel of miscegenation (class distinctions were also an important element in the book). In the climactic episode of the novel the hero, a surgeon named John Broderlip, is asked to perform an operation that will save the life of a runaway slave, Nathan. Talking to Nathan, he realizes that the slave is his half brother. Broderlip is faced with a terrible dilemma. If he operates and saves his brother's life, he will be forced to acknowledge "the few black drops that made him kin to this creature. . . . There was no middle ground. Let him acknowledge the mulatto as his brother, and he stood alone, shut out from every human relation with the world to which he belonged. A negro—no wealth, no talent, no virtue could wash out that stain or put him on a level with the meanest servant in his house again." He is tempted to let Nathan die during the operation, but he overcomes the impulse and decides to cast his lot with his own people henceforth. He tells his fiancée that "he was born below the level of humanity," and when she protests, he continues, "My parents were clean, honest, pious Methodists. But they were black. The man lying yonder is my brother." His fiancée turns on him a "stunned, unforgiving stare" and coldly dismisses him. When her father protests, she declares, "John Broderlip is the son of a negro; there is not one of his hospitals or patients to-day would open their doors to him . . . ; there is not a club, church, theater or restaurant from which he would not be ejected like a felon. . . . No white man or woman would receive him to their table. If he married there would be no citizenship for him, no honor for his wife, no education for his children. They are the one class which the law and the white man are privileged to trample under foot." Broderlip goes off to enlist in a black regiment and fight for the Union.

Grace King was born in New Orleans in 1852. Like Kate Chopin, King wrote of the Louisiana Creole culture. She also dealt with the theme of miscegenation in "The Little Convent Girl," a story in which a girl drowns herself when she discovers that her mother is black. Her "Creole Sketches," published in the *New Princeton Review* in 1888, brought her wide recognition. While her stories lacked the feminist thrust of Kate Chopin's often mordant tales, they described what was clearly a woman's world. In the title story of *Balcony Stories*, published in 1893, the opening sentences set the tone of the book: "There is much of life passed on the balcony in a country where the summer unrolls in six moon-lengths, and where the nights have to come with a double endowment of vastness and splendor to compensate for the tedious, sun-parched days.

"And in that country the women love to sit and talk together of summer nights, on balconies, in their vague, loose, white garments,—men are not balcony sitters,—with their sleeping children within easy hearing, the stars breaking the cool darkness. . . . Experiences, reminiscences, episodes, picked up as only women know how to pick them up from other women's lives . . . and told as only women know how to relate them; what God has done or is doing with some other woman whom they have known—that is what interests women once embarked on their own lives,—the embarkation takes place at marriage, or after the marriageable time,—rather, that is what interests the women who sit of summer nights on balconies. . . . Each story *is* different, or appears so to her; each has its own peculiar pathos in it. . . . Sometimes the pathos and interest of the hearers lie only in this—that the relater has observed it, and gathered it, and finds it worth telling."

The passage was almost an analogue for what we might call the communications system that women were in the process of constructing by means of the innumerable magazines and newspapers through which they reached each other in an invisible feminine network.

Mary Noailles Murfree was born in 1850, near the town of Murfreesboro, Tennessee, named after the Scottish half of her family (the "Noailles" represented the more exotic French strain). Writing for publication had long been considered bad form in the South, For a woman to display serious literary interests was definitely infra dig. Perhaps that was the reason Mary Murfree chose the masculine pen name of Charles Egbert Craddock. Like her sister writers, she made her way and name through her short stories, which were published in a volume called *In the Tennessee Mountains* in 1884. To Mary Murfree must go the laurel for first discovering and "fixing" the literary image of the mountain folk, indolent, improvident, contentious, drinking, playing "kyerds," hunting deer and possum, and, above all, talking, talking, talking. The popularity of *In the Tennessee Mountains* indicated that she had hit a rich vein of local color ore. She continued to mine it through eleven more best-selling volumes.

As journalists, novelists, and, perhaps above all, short story writers, women confirmed the fact that they were a force to be reckoned with in American life. If they did not preempt the literary scene, they certainly left their unmistakable imprint on it.

38

The Arts

When George Templeton Strong's son, Temple, abandoned the comforts of his father's handsome house for a garret in which he could play his flute undisturbed, his departure could be taken to mark a representative moment in the relations of the arts to the Republic. Thousands of young men and, increasingly, young women would follow a similar path, seeking in the arts freedom from middle-class constraints and inhibitions. In time art would become synonymous with that elusive "freedom" and "independence" that young Americans of every generation sought as the knights of King Arthur's court sought the Holy Grail. We have seen how the desire to be a writer was a major obsession of such young men from the earliest years of the new nation. Now "writer" and especially the category "poet" became touched with the magic wand of "art." John Hay, William Dean Howells, and hundreds of others who found that poetry put no bread in their mouths went on, reluctantly, to write less exalted forms of prose.

Much of the desire to enter the realm of art through the portal of Polyhymnia was a residue of transcendentalism or, more accurately, of Emerson's apotheosis of the poet as the exemplary figure in society. The charms of Calliope, experienced by Temple Strong, were increasingly pursued. The visual arts trailed somewhere in the rear, impeded by the Protestant tradition of iconoclasm, an inheritance from the Reformation. Painting and sculpture profited from the fact that public manifestations of "culture" required visibility. A marble statue in the classical mode was much more evident than a book of poems on a library shelf. The arts also gained immensely by being associated with the rising tide of feminism. Since the arts were assigned to the American woman as her special province, they were conveyed upward in her ascent. It was, after all, at women's colleges that courses in the history of art were first introduced, and it was the graduates of women's colleges—among them Jane Addams—who made up the greater part of that company of American women touring the galleries and monuments of Europe in search of "culture" to bring back to a barren United States.

In addition, the "new nobility," the "dukes" of municipal utilities—figures of the "American Renaissance"—began to seek out, as the conspicuous appurtenances of power and wealth, expensive art objects, above all, paintings by the masters of the Italian Renaissance. Their agents scoured the great private collections of England and Europe. Henry Frick was a pioneer in such high-class banditry, and soon he had dozens of imitators. Frick spent his summers at Pride's Crossing in Massachusetts, and every year he had his priceless collection of paintings loaded in a steel railroad car, specially built to transport them, and brought them from New York to his Pride's Crossing estate. When Oswald Garrison Villard asked Frick if he was not afraid of the paintings being stolen or damaged in transit, he replied, "Oh, no. They are insured."

John Hay, with his wife's wealth, bought a Botticelli: "a beautiful thing—a picture of the first importance. I lie awake nights fearing it will warp. . . ."

Old masters became as much a part of the equipage of the tycoon as his tailor-made morning coat or his diamond stickpin. It was a development that drew the scorn of Henry Demarest Lloyd: "Art, literature, culture, religion, in America . . . feel the restrictive pressure which results from the domination of a selfish, self-indulgent, luxurious, and anti-social power [capitalists]. . . . Song, picture, sermon, decrees of court, and the union of hearts must pass constantly under stronger control of those who give their lives to trade and encourage everybody else to trade, confident that the issue of it all will be that they will hold as property . . . the matter by which alone man can live, either materially or spiritually."

The preoccupation of the new rich with old art was not, at least initially, much use to those young men and women producing new art, although in time, as we shall see, the largess of the conspicuous displayers enriched many of them. Those Americans bold enough to launch themselves on careers as painters or sculptors were usually, like their predecessors, the offspring of the wealthy upper-class families with assured incomes, who could afford to spend the required years of study in Paris or Rome and who, in a number of instances, simply moved abroad to work in an atmosphere considered more encouraging to artistic endeavor. Typical of this category was Abbott Henderson Thayer, member of a wealthy and distinguished Boston family. Born in 1849, Thayer studied with Jean Léon Gérôme in Paris and returned to paint statuesque ladies in diaphanous robes. He strove for "monumentality" in his female figures and achieved it. John Jay Chapman wrote of him: "Thayer . . . is a hipped egotist who paints three hours, has a headache, walks four hours, holds his own pulse, wants to save his light for the world, cares for nobody, and has fits of dejection during which forty women hold his hand and tell him not to despair—for humanity's sake . . . very selfish and spoiled—and of course he can't paint."

The most notable exception to this general rule was a largely self-taught painter, much in the tradition of George Catlin and Caleb Bingham. Winslow Homer was born in Boston, Massachusetts, in 1836, outside the charmed circle of that city's upper class. He acquired his love of drawing and painting from his mother, herself a painter of more than average talent. His father encouraged him to apprentice himself to a lithographer; the extraordinary popularity of illustrated magazines had created a demand for competent engravers and lithographers who, most commonly, rendered photographs which could not yet be reproduced, and paintings into plates for the printer. At the end of a two-year apprenticeship Homer moved to New York City, where he soon had all the work he could do as a free-lance illustrator. Much of his work went into *Harper's Weekly*, and when the Civil War broke out, he was commissioned as an artist-reporter for the magazine. The necessity of working quickly on the most direct and practical portrayal of the daily occurrences in the lives of soldiers from camp to battlefield helped Homer acquire both a remarkable technical facility and the capacity to render the movements of the body with an extraordinary fluidity.

After the war Homer turned more directly toward a career as a painter. He spent ten months in Paris at the period when the Impressionists were beginning their experiments with light and color and absorbed enough from them to affect his own work without deflecting it from its preoccupation with the common gestures of life. When he abandoned illustration in 1875, he was in every sense an accomplished painter. Like Audubon, he loved to hike and hunt, camp and fish, ranging the forests, the ocean shores, the mountains of the Adirondacks, and the islands of the Caribbean. Children were favorite subjects—weaning a calf, playing ball in the schoolyard, fishing, sailing, eating watermelon, "nooning," lolling in a field, picking strawberries, watching birds. So were women playing the popular new game of croquet, waiting on a headland for their fishermen husbands to come in from the sea. He painted ducks falling from the hunter's shot, trout jumping, the quietly expectant posture of the hunter or fisherman, the guide resting on his oars in a hushed moment, the powerful body of a black sailor on a demasted sloop with sharks circling—a mysteriously compelling scene that lingers in the mind's eye. No American painter, except perhaps Bingham, has given us such enduring images of ourselves in play and work, in action and repose, and, above all, in nature. What Whitman did in words, Winslow Homer did with brush and pen. Master of the American landscape and seascape as well, his private life, jealously guarded, was as mysterious as his art.

Thomas Cowperthwaite Eakins was eight years younger than Winslow Homer. Eakins's grandfather had been a weaver. His father, Benjamin, taught penmanship in Philadelphia, where Thomas was born. The family was in modest circumstances, and Thomas attended the public school—Central High School—recently converted, largely through the efforts of Thaddeus Stevens, from a charity school for the poor. Eakins revealed a precocious talent for drawing, displayed chiefly in the maps he drew at school. The curriculum was a severe one—Latin and Greek, French and German, trigonometry, calculus, and astronomy. Rembrandt Peale taught drawing. After Eakins had graduated from high school, he received encouragement from the members of the Sketch Club, who included Thomas Nast and Thomas Sully, and worked at the Pennsylvania Academy—a "free school of art." There was little instruction, but the aspiring artists who used the studio space helped each other as best they could. As important to Eakins as his painting was his enthusiastic participation in the newly discovered world of sports. Swimming, sailing, and sculling on the Schuylkill were all the rage, and Eakins was an enthusiastic athlete.

In 1866 Eakins left for Paris to seek admission into the world headquarters of the new art movement—the École des Beaux-Arts. Just how he financed his undertaking is not clear, but he was soon, like Thayer, working with Gérôme, the school's most renowned teacher. The students at the école were a rowdy lot, hazing newcomers and boxing and wrestling each other to determine the order of domination. It was at the école that Eakins first saw nude young men wrestling and worked extensively from nude models.

His schooling stretched out to four years, but when he returned to Philadelphia in 1870, he had developed the style that would characterize all his subsequent work. Like Winslow Homer, he was fascinated by the postures and movements of the body, especially as manifested in sporting activities—rowing, wrestling, sailing, boxing, swimming, skating. As we have noted, the post-Civil War era was the era of the discovery of the body in all its sinuous majesty, and Eakins, more than any other artist of the day, made himself the recorder of the body. This both alarmed his friends and irresistibly drew public attention, not all of it favorable by any means. The bodies that he reproduced were, moreover, not the conventional and largely sexless figures that had been allowed under the classification of "classical" but real, live human bodies of extraordinary, almost frightening physical potency. By the same token, his portraits, with their Rembrandt-like lighting, seemed to seize on the essence of his subjects in a way disconcerting to conventional critics. They brought to mind the best of Gilbert Stuart's portraits or Copley's early work before he was corrupted by stylish British portraiture.

Within a year after his return to Philadelphia, Eakins painted what was in many ways his greatest painting, a picture of his friend Max Schmitt, in a single scull (Schmitt was champion of the single scull; Eakins placed himself in a scull in the background). One thinks at once of Caleb Bingham's "Fur Traders Descending the Missouri," his first major painting and his most famous. There is the same quality of "stillness," a moment of rest in the vigorous activity of rowing, a moment which suggests the activity of rowing more acutely than any effort to catch movement itself could. The "Biglin Brothers Turning the Stake" was painted the next year (1873), and the famous scene of shooting the marsh birds called "rail," a year later. Three more paintings of scullers—friends of Eakins—were completed in the same period, constituting the most extensive coverage of any American sport by a single artist.

Eakins's fascination with the human body had the practical result of securing him a professorship of anatomy at the Pennsylvania Academy of Fine Arts and making him a warm supporter of one of the most eccentric characters in our history, Edward James Muggeridge.

Born in England in 1830, Muggeridge came to the United States in 1852, announcing to friends as he departed, "I am going to make a name for myself. If I fail, you will never hear of me again." He literally "made a name for himself"—the new name of Muygridge. In San Francisco he became a successful book dealer and photographer of paintings. Seriously injured in a stagecoach accident, he returned to England to recuperate and there, between 1861 and 1866, took up photography full time. When he returned to California, he had further modified his name to Edward Muybridge; now he called himself an "artist-photographer" and produced photographs for stereoscopes. He took a series of photographs of Yosemite which he described as "marvelous examples of the perfection which photography can attain in the delineation of sublime and beautiful scenery" and "the most artistic and beautiful photographs ever produced on this coast." In 1872 he met the railroad tycoon Leland Stanford, who commissioned Muybridge to take a photograph of his famous trotter Occident "at full speed," in an effort to settle once and for all the controversy over whether all four of a horse's feet are off the ground in a trot or gallop. Muybridge was able to take a dim picture which satisfied Stanford on the particular point, and Stanford encouraged him to continue his experiments and gave him his financial support.

Muybridge's experiments were interrupted by the discovery that his wife had been having an affair with a man who was, in fact, the father of Muybridge's "son." Muybridge promptly killed his wife's lover. A sympathetic jury acquitted him. After a respite, taking photographs in Guatemala, Muybridge returned to California to resume his efforts to take pictures of a horse in motion. This time he decided to take a series of photographs from a battery of cameras, triggered by the horse's movements through wires laid at twenty-one-inch intervals. At Stanford's Palo Alto estate in June, 1878, Muybridge took the pictures which were to make him world-famous (Stanford contributed $20,000 to fund the experiment). The *Spirit of the Times*, a California journal, hailed the achievement as establishing "a new era in photography, and instantaneous is no longer a misnomer." Before the summer was over, Muybridge had made 200 sets of "serial photographs comprising more than two thousand negatives of various animals in motion," but Stanford's mare Sally Gardner remained the most vivid, the archetypal image signifying the dawn of a new age of visual wonders. Within a year Eakins, using Muybridge's photographs, had "filled in" the intervals between the photographs to make a panel depicting continuous motion, one of the first "moving" pictures.

Muybridge himself, flamboyant and egotistical, departed on a European tour with lantern slides and his zoopraxiscope. In London, Tyndall, Huxley, Gladstone, and Tennyson, as well as the prince and princess of Wales, were in his audiences. Muybridge's name was increased for the occasion: He was now Eadweard Muybridge.

What Muybridge's audiences found most unsettling was that many of his photographs showed animals, especially horses, in what were then considered awkward, unbecoming, and ungraceful postures at some points in their movement. This was considered tantamount to an assault on art, whose formalized representations of motion had come, over the ages, to have the effect of law.

Although Stanford pulled the rug out from under Muybridge by publishing the early photographs without acknowledging Muybridge's central role—giving the impression that credit belonged to Stanford— Muybridge found sponsors for the project nearest his heart, photographs of the human body in motion, through Eakins and the trustees of the Pennsylvania Academy of Fine Arts.

It was one thing to take photographs of animals in motion; it was far more daring to take pictures of nude men and women in motion. It took all of Eakins's prestige and that of his friend and sponsor Farman Rogers, a wealthy gentleman scientist and patron of the arts, to win approval for the project. Undoubtedly the shock to the public sensibilities was lessened by the fact that Muybridge began his series with photographs of animals in the Zoological Gardens and progressed to human subjects only when the "scientific" nature of his experiments was well established. By the end of Muybridge's vast project more than 20,000 photographs had been taken with greatly improved camera and lens. The results, when published in an expensive limited edition of ten volumes in 1887, caused a great flurry. They were, quite simply, revelations of an aspect of nature hitherto hidden from the human eye. All in all, they constitute one of the most remarkable scientific achievements of a century of remarkable achievements.

The 530 plates of nude males in every conceivable posture and movement (many of the plates contained 30 individual images), most having to do with athletic endeavors, were complemented by 531 plates of nude females, some frankly erotic, such as the plates of women kissing each other, playing coyly with a fan, dancing together, getting into and out of bed. Many plates were of domestic activities—washing, ironing, cooking, making beds, carrying objects, dressing, and undressing. Most of the women were artists' models supplied by Eakins through the Academy of Fine Arts; many were strikingly handsome. To those carefully screened artists and students of anatomy allowed access to them, they were images of enormous erotic power, recorded and assembled under the magic aegis of science.

Muybridge had found in the United States the public and the sponsorship that enabled him to extend dramatically our vision of the natural world. Eakins took his own photographs of wrestlers and boxers who were the subjects of many of his later paintings, but there is no question that he learned a great deal from his contact with Muybridge's project.

If Winslow Homer and Thomas Eakins were the dominant figures in "Eastern art," "Western art" developed its own subject matter and its own stars, the most famous (and the most gifted) of whom was Albert Bierstadt. In Western art, one theme dominated everything, one theme determined technique and subject matter: the landscape and skyscape, with their almost incomprehensible vastness, sublimity, and majesty. As the West became settled and the frontier ostensibly closed, the grandeur of Western scenery began to possess the collective mind of the East. With its rough and unpolished ways, its scandalous preference for cheap money, its radical politics, and its general "wildness," the West seemed to the East a burden, an embarrassment, even a danger, but the scenery was something else. Many things contributed to the East's infatuation with the West: the growing awareness of the geologic age of the planet to which the West gave such dramatic emphasis; the Darwinian notion of the struggle for survival, which, it could be argued, the frontier demonstrated most strikingly; the romantic image of the cowboy as the exemplar of the "rugged individualism" that the capitalist insisted was the essential American type; the growing interest in the body, in sports, in hiking and camping and a vigorous outdoor life—"the strenuous life," the virtues of which Theodore Roosevelt would soon be trumpeting. Roosevelt was not precisely a capitalist (he lived on the proceeds of capitalism; his father was better described as a capitalist), but in his rather simpleminded infatuation with the West, especially with cowboys and Indians, he expressed perfectly the response of the capitalist to the West. The West validated the capitalism and sanctified the capitalist, although in actual, practical fact, Westerners perpetually denounced capitalists and capitalism and never tired of abusing Wall Street as the Mammon of Unrighteousness.

The point of all this as it refers to art is that huge landscapes of Western terrain, especially vistas of the Rockies, Yosemite, and the Grand Tetons, the last of which became, in time, a Rockefeller retreat, were much favored by capitalists, as were scenes of cowboys and Indians. Albert Bierstadt was the master of the first genre; the master of the latter was Frederic Remington.

The Bierstadt family had migrated from Düsseldorf, Germany, to New Bedford, Massachusetts, in 1832, when young Albert was two years old. (He was thus born in that vintage year for painters and writers—1830.) He grew up in the classic manner of a small-town boy in the fishing and whaling town. It was not a congenial atmosphere for a budding artist. Art was considered frivolous, the province of spinster ladies, but by the age of twenty Albert was bold enough to advertise himself as a teacher of "Monochromatic painting." He promised a new technique whereby pupils "are enabled to execute good pictures at their first attempt, far superior to their own expectations." It was perhaps a sign of the times that the young artist found two patrons, the prosperous Mrs. Hathaway and a local storekeeper named John Hopkins. Although his paintings impressed the culturally inclined citizens of New Bedford, Bierstadt was convinced that he had to study in Düsseldorf, then the art capital of Europe, if he hoped to perfect his technique. A consortium of New Bedford friends put up the money for his trip, and the twenty-three-year-old artist departed for study with one of the best-known painters of the Düsseldorf school. At Düsseldorf he found a friend in his compatriot Worthington Whittredge, ten years his senior, from Springfield, Ohio. Bierstadt financed his studies by shipping off paintings to New Bedford to be sold to interested friends and sponsors.

From Düsseldorf Bierstadt made his way to Italy, painting as he went. In 1857 he returned to New Bedford in the midst of the devastating depression of that year and found it difficult to make ends meet at a time when many people were reduced to the barest necessities. Bierstadt's first painting after his return was a striking portrait of an old Indian woman named Martha Simon, but his first "national" appearance was his enormous painting of Lake Lucerne displayed at the annual show of the New York Academy of Design, where it was distinguished by being the largest painting among the 635 exhibited.

A year later Bierstadt was on his way West to the regions that were to be thereafter most strongly associated with his work. He had mastered the rudiments of photography and took numerous photographs and made sketches and watercolors that were converted by engravers into plates for *Harper's Weekly*. South Park, the Platte River, the Wind River Mountains, and the Wasatch Range all were subjects for Bierstadt's sketch pad and camera, to be worked out after his return home into large paintings. In addition, he did a number of paintings "from life," perhaps the best being "Horse in the Wilderness" and a painting of a party of Indians near Fort Laramie.

Bierstadt realized that his best prospective market was in New York City. He and his brothers opened a photographers' shop in the so-called Studio Building, recently built by William Morris Hunt with the intention of providing studios for artists. Among Bierstadt's fellow artists in the building were Eastman Johnson, John Kensett, and the sculptor Augustus Saint-Gaudens. Bierstadt went West again in 1863, accompanied by one of the more exotic figures on the New York literary scene, Fitz Hugh Ludlow, who had recorded his addiction to hashish in a book entitled *The Hasheesh Eater*, hailed by one critic as a work of "unparalleled genius." Left behind was Ludlow's beautiful young wife, Rosa. This time Bierstadt reached Yosemite and visited Shasta and the Cascade Range. "The Rocky Mountains" and a series of extraordinary paintings of the Yosemite Valley were the products of the trip and marked Bierstadt's arrival on the art scene as a rival of Frederick Church. "The Rocky Mountains," exhibited at the National Academy of Design annual show, commanded attention by its size—six by ten feet. It was, in addition, a brilliantly painted picture in purely technical terms. As much as any single work it established the canon: what pictures of the Western landscape might aspire to be. It made Bierstadt rich and famous. Ludlow sank into hopeless addiction, a fate not uncommon to well-bred young men in that era. Rosa divorced him and married Bierstadt, thus completing the circle of his felicity.

Bierstadt continued to paint his remarkable canvases, which now sold for enormous sums. He married again after Rosa's death, and he and his new wife traveled extensively, with Bierstadt acclaimed everywhere as one of the great masters of painting. At the time of his death in 1902, Bierstadt was the most successful American artist of his day in dollars and cents. His reputation declined sharply thereafter. Art critics were no longer interested in the "grand" and the "sublime." The very size of his paintings put people off. It was as though he were trying not so much to paint a picture as to put the "outside" inside and place the viewer inside the outside. More recently art critics have discovered that Bierstadt and his numerous imitators and painters in the same vein are actually Luminist painters with a remarkable capacity for dealing with light and space and color, and his reputation has marvelously ascended. (The capitalists never wavered.) However that may be, Albert Bierstadt was a painter of extraordinary talent who helped to fix the image of the Western landscape in the minds of many who never saw the reality and to sharpen the reality for those who did.

If capitalists were charmed by Bierstadt's vast canvases, they were absolutely dotty over the work of Frederic Remington and his school of cowboy painters. In practical fact, the great chronicler of the cowboy, the rancher, the Indian, and the U.S. cavalry trooper was the son of prosperous parents from Canton, New York. His father, "Colonel" Remington, had been a cavalry officer in the Civil War. After the war he became a Republican newspaper editor, a sportsman, and a politician.

After military school Frederic Remington was admitted to Yale, where he played on the football team in a day when football was closer to legalized mayhem than to sport. Remington showed a youthful precocity in drawing. His favorite subject was soldiers. Yale had recently established an art school, but Remington recalled that the school had only two pupils and one "melancholy professor of drawing, a German who took little interest in his students or their work."

On a trip West, Remington made a number of sketches, one of which he sold to George William Curtis for *Harper's Weekly*. Inheriting some money on his twenty-first birthday, he bought a sheep ranch near Peabody, Kansas, and took up the life of a rancher, joining, in his words, "the great army of broken-down students and professional men" who had turned "their backs upon the bustling world to secure new life and vigor on these upland plains." The life proved far more rigorous than Remington had imagined, and the experiment lasted only a year. He retreated to Kansas City, Missouri, married his sweetheart from his college days, and spent much of his time sketching and horseback riding. It was not a remunerative combination, although *Harper's Weekly* took another sketch. The next line of retreat was to Brooklyn. Realizing that he would need more training if he were to have any prospect of making his living as an artist, Remington attended the Art Students League, a newly formed cooperative art school. Gradually his circle of magazines broadened—first the juvenile magazine *St. Nicholas* and then *Outing*, a new magazine of the outdoors, run by his Yale friend Poultney Bigelow. Bigelow was delighted with Remington's drawings. "Here," he wrote later, "was the real thing, the unspoiled native genius dealing with Mexican ponies, cowboys, cactus, lariats and sombreros. No stage heroes these, no carefully pomaded hair and neatly tied cravats; these were men of the real rodeo, parched in alkali dust, blinking out from barely opened eyelids under the furious rays of an Arizona sun."

By 1887 Remington, a chubby man with elegant manners, had begun to exhibit at the annual show of the National Academy of Design. Theodore Roosevelt was writing a series of articles on the West for the *Century*, and he asked to have Remington as an illustrator. The two New Yorkers, one a Harvard man and one a Yalie, thus joined forces to celebrate the Wild West, not, to be sure, the West of desperate farmers talking socialism and revolution or the West of the Guggenheim and the Rockefeller mining towns but a West that was already slipping away, a West of gunslingers and, above all, cowboys, the ultimate American individualists, the survivors. Magazine illustrations, particularly in *Harper's Weekly* and the *Century*, were Remington's bread and butter; it was only slowly that he began to envision himself as a full-time painter. Secure in New York's upper crust, he took regular trips West—a stint with a band of Apache, a visit to a cavalry post, stops at Comanche, Cheyenne, Kiowa, and Navaho reservations to paint and sketch. He became one of Eadweard Muybridge's earliest disciples, so infatuated with Muybridge's discovery that horses at the gallop intermittently had all feet off the ground that one searches in vain among his myriad of speeding steeds for a hoof touched to the earth. Remington's horses skim like swallows, and their suspension adds to the sense of swift and reckless motion that they convey.

The disheartening aridity of the cowboy and the Indian genre of Western painting that Remington to a substantial degree established should not blind us to the artist's genuine gifts. In hundreds of illustrations and his fine, bold, brilliantly painted canvases he helped fix the image of the West in the American imagination. That it was a negligible and highly transitory element in the total life of all the various "Wests" mattered less in the long run than its remarkable potency.

Whatever vicissitudes Remington's reputation suffered at the hands of art critics, the capitalists remained loyal. At this moment the largest collections of his work are in galleries established by the oil tycoons Amon Carter and Sid Richardson, friendly rivals in accumulating Western icons.

There were, of course, other accomplished "Western painters," Charles Russell and William Leigh prominent among them; few, if any, came from the West (Leigh was born in Virginia and lived in New York), and none seriously challenged Remington's preeminence. Remington himself went on to do a series of famous bronzes of horses and their cowboys.

Bierstadt fixed the setting, the "sublime" mountains and the awesome spaces, the now-acclaimed Luminism of the "big sky country." Against those backdrops Remington's cowboys, Indians, soldiers, and trappers are in perpetual motion, caught in intensely physical epiphanies of stress and violence. Finally, when there were "movies," they moved to the rhythms of Remington's captivating pictures and consummated the myth that two upper-crust New York friends had helped create. In the last analysis Remington, inheriting his father's equine obsession, was a passionate painter of horses. Horses dominate most of his major canvases and remind the viewer that whatever else may be in doubt, the subject of scholarly controversy or changing interpretations of the West, no one dare gainsay the centrality of the horse.

The major painters of the post-Civil War era come conveniently in pairs. Winslow Homer and Thomas Eakins are Eastern painters; Bierstadt and Remington are Western painters or, more accurately, Eastern painters of the West. Another pair were "high society" painters. James Abbott McNeill Whistler (his triple-barrel name suggested his aristocratic origins) was born in Lowell, Massachusetts, in 1834. His father, George Washington McNeill, was a civil engineer and, like George Harris in John Forney's novel The New Nobility, McNeill went to St. Petersburg in Russia to take charge of the construction of a railroad line. At the age of eleven the precocious James had a private drawing teacher. After his father's death James McNeill and his mother returned to the United States. Through friends of his father McNeill, who now took his mother's maiden name, Whistler, got an appointment to West Point. He was dismissed because of poor work in the sciences. He worked for a time for the United States Coast and Geodetic Survey and then, with the help of friends and relatives, left for France in 1855 to study art. In 1863 he moved to London, and, aside from a brief flight to Italy to escape his creditors, he remained in London until

1892. By this time he had an international reputation; his mannerist style and muted colors (he was even credited with inventing a color, a soft bluish green that became a kind of trademark) were perfectly suited to render slender, elegant ladies and gentlemen. A close study of the style, the posture and expression of the subjects, especially the women and children, gives the viewer a keen sense of the change in "sensibility" that was evident in the British and American upper classes.

Whistler made himself the premier recorder (his only serious rival was John Singer Sargent) of the international social set. If Winslow Homer was a kind of visual analogue to Walt Whitman, Whistler's paintings were a visual counterpoint to Henry James's novels. He shared James's conviction that the United States was an impossible place to live.

Whistler was certainly a brilliant painter. Not only was his excessively praised "Mother" done early in his long career, but two of his most memorable paintings—"Symphony in White No. I" (1862) and "Symphony in Flesh Color and Pink" (1873)—were completed well before he had achieved the fame of his later years. They had a shocking novelty about them that disconcerted critics.

John Singer Sargent's parents had already fled the United States for Florence when he was born in 1856. His parents were part of that company of wealthy Americans who drifted about Europe with large retinues of servants and governesses fighting off an ennui that threatened to consume them. By the age of twelve young John had decided on the career of an artist. After a stint at the École des Beaux-Arts, he exhibited his first important portrait at the Paris Salon. His portrait of Madame Gautreaux, a famous Parisian beauty, caused a sensation by its explicit sensuality. (It was said that Madame Gautreaux overhearing someone say some years later that she had lost her freshness, returned home, drew the curtains of her bedroom, and never ventured out again.) "Madame X," as Sargent chose to call it, is one of the most remarkable portraits ever painted. It was done when Sargent was only twenty-nine years old; it made him an instant celebrity and caused such a scandal in French artistic and social circles that he felt obliged to take refuge, as it were, in London.

In 1887 Sargent made the first of a number of painting "tours" in the United States, rather as Gilbert Stuart had earlier gone to Great Britain. Tycoons and socialites vied to have their portraits painted, and in Boston Sargent received a commission to paint murals for the newly built Boston Public Library, a classic Beaux-Arts structure in the popular neo-Renaissance style. The Boston Public Library murals are Gothic and bizarre in the extreme.

Sargent's portrait of Maria Louisa Davis, a social leader of Worcester, Massachusetts, and her son, Livingston, is one of the artist's happiest achievements. In the contrast between the mother's direct, handsome face, with its suggestion of candor and practicality, and her son's wide-eyed "softness," one is tempted to discover generational transformation echoed in many other representations of American upper-class life. The coming generation will lack the power and assurance of its predecessor, it seems to say.

It has been my contention throughout this work that the bizarre and macabre, the wildly eccentric and the slightly mad have been as much a part of the "American experience" as the rational and optimistic temper more commonly associated with our history as a people. Certainly there were more than traces of such a spirit in the work of Thomas Cole. David Gilmour Blythe's morbid gnomes were the antithesis of George Caleb Bingham's heroic figures. On the literary side, Poe, Hawthorne, Melville, and later Twain and Ambrose Beirce explored "the darker side."

Among the painters of the period, three identified themselves with the mysterious, the symbolic, the profoundly troubling. In this they were influenced by such European fantasists and mystics as Gustave Doré and William Blake. Elihu Vedder, Albert Pinkham Ryder, and William Rimmer all mined the fantastic and symbolic in their early work, with John La Farge, Henry Adams's close friend, a sometime practitioner.

Elihu Vedder, born in 1836, came from a lower-middle-class background not dissimilar to that of Albert Bierstadt. As soon as he was able, he headed for Italy and spent five years roaming Europe, studying where he could find a teacher. Vedder's "The Questioner of the Sphinx" (1863) and "The Lair of the Sea Serpent," done the next year, both are arresting works. His illustrations for the *Rubáiyát of Omar Khayyám* were strongly influenced by Blake.

After a brief period in the United States, where his work failed to win critical praise, Vedder went back to Rome and spent the greater part of his long life there, returning periodically to the United States, usually to execute some large classical mural for one of the "Renaissance" Beaux-Arts buildings that sprang up everywhere.

Albert Pinkham Ryder was born in New Bedford, Massachusetts, in 1847, not long before Albert Bierstadt departed for Düsseldorf. Ryder, who studied at the National Academy of Design, was one of the few painters—Frederic Remington was another—who did not feel obliged to spend a substantial time working in the ateliers of Europe. A highly private man with a private vision, he worked slowly over his dark, windswept landscapes. Storms, heavy with some portending disaster, are a common theme. Lonely, mysterious figures flee before a threatening Nature or before Death on a pale horse.

Finally, there is William Rimmer. Rimmer was another American original. He was born in Liverpool, England, in 1816, and while he was still a child, his parents emigrated to Massachusetts. Rimmer, like Cole and Durand, worked at a dozen different trades—as a shoemaker, a musician, a teacher of music, and finally a doctor of medicine. Always desperately poor, he had endless schemes for making a fortune so that he could devote himself to his painting and sculpture; all proved disasters, but his knowledge of anatomy finally enabled him to secure a position at the Boston Museum of Fine Arts teaching anatomy. His "Call to Arms," done in the year of his death, 1879, and his famous "Flight and Pursuit" are examples of his capacity for fantasy. At the end of his life he wrote: "Nature holds dominion, and Nature alone,—where the cold wind has no mercy, the storm no feeling; where all the elements do their will, and all the powers move at pleasure. We are but mites who live in spite of forces that do their spite as they are moved. . . . I believe in the existence of a spirit world and of immortality: but what good does that do us?"

One of Rimmer's students was John La Farge, and it may have been from Rimmer that La Farge acquired some of his own taste for the mystical. La Farge was born in New York City in 1835. His family was an upper-class French one, as his name suggests, and it maintained its ties with relatives in France, enabling the young La Farge to spend the virtually obligatory years studying in Paris. When he returned to the United States in 1858, he set up a studio at Newport, Rhode Island, with his friend William Morris Hunt. Magazine illustration helped sustain him, and his earliest paintings showed striking parallels to the work of the French Impressionists. Most important to his career, he belonged to that charmed circle of upper-class artists, architects, and intellectuals of which Henry Adams and John Hay and their respective wives were, for a time, the brilliant center.

As we have noted in discussing the Chicago World's Columbian Exposition, women were producers as well as consumers of art. Sarah

Choate Sears was a Boston Brahmin who began to paint eight years after her marriage and soon established herself as one of the best watercolorists in the country, winning prizes at a series of international art exhibitions. She was a friend of John Singer Sargent's, and one of his most engaging portraits was painted of her in 1889.

Bela Lyon Pratt, born in Norwich, Connecticut, was one of the first women to study at the newly established Yale School of Fine Arts and later at the Art Students League in New York. She worked as Augustus Saint-Gaudens's assistant and after 1893 taught sculpture at the Boston Museum School. Nude figures in a vaguely classical style and portrait busts were her specialty.

Edmonia Lewis, daughter of a black father and an Indian mother, was a capable sculptress. She specialized in busts of prominent political figures, and it was thought especially appropriate that she should do the bust of Charles Sumner for the Massachusetts State House. Her piece, entitled "Hiawatha's Wooing," was given to the Boston YMCA by the actress Charlotte Cushman.

It is evident from their photographs that the first generation of American women sculptors and painters, the "white marmorean flock," as Henry Adams called them, were a new breed. One perceives in their faces a certain openness, a directness of gaze, the air of a self-consciously *new* new woman. Art was, after all, to be the harbinger of the age, and these women were her votaries. They existed in an exalted realm inaccessible to men. In Greek mythology the arts had been born under the sponsorship of the Muses, all women. Now women would reclaim the arts as a symbol of their emancipation and their most appropriate and natural form of expression. Art and the reconstruction of society, the eradication of poverty, suffering, and injustice seemed somehow bound together.

Sculptors abounded. It was an age of public statuary, preferably equestrian figures commemorating great generals, and of neoclassical figures clothed in tons of marble drapery. Female figures represented everything from profane love to the Muses. Sentiment cloyed, and symbolism was rampant. It was as though the "new nobility" were determined to overawe their critics by the sheer weight of their riches transformed into art.

In the words of the painter-critic Kenyon Cox, "When the sculptors of today, following the lead of the painters who had already begun the movement, turned again to the independent study of nature, they naturally reverted to Renaissance models. . . . There only could they find the modern man with his pronounced individuality and his special development of character . . . and so, jumping over four hundred years, jumping over the inroad of academicism and all the subsequent degradation of art, the best sculpture of to-day is the legitimate successor to that of the fifteenth century." Another critic, John Van Dyke, enthused: "I hope I may live long enough . . . to see . . . on this new soil and under these bright skies, the greatest art the world has ever seen."

Augustus Saint-Gaudens was the exemplar of the "new" sculpture. Born in Dublin, Ireland, in 1848, of French and Irish parentage and brought by his parents to New York in infancy, he was trained as a cameo cutter and practiced the craft while he studied at the National Academy of Design and at Cooper Union. His craft also enabled him to support himself while he studied at the Beaux-Arts and later in Rome, where, with his charm and energy, he became the beau ideal of the young American artist of the new age. Back in the United States after a ten-year stint abroad, he won a commission to do a full-length statue of Admiral Farragut for Madison Square in New York City. He also became a fast friend of John La Farge and, through him, was inducted into the Hay-Adams circle. When the Farragut was unveiled in 1881, Saint-Gaudens, then thirty-three, was hailed by critics as America's most gifted sculptor. There followed a number of other commissions, including the memorial to Robert Shaw on the Boston Common and two statues of Lincoln for the city of Chicago, but his most famous work was the mysterious figure commissioned by Henry Adams as a memorial to his dead wife, Clover.

Henry Hobson Richardson, the architect of Hay's and Adams's adjoining mansions on Lafayette Square in Washington (he was just Adams's age) had won the competition for a new Trinity Church in Boston, in 1872, intended as a proper setting for the famous sermons of Phillips Brooks, the great Episcopal preacher. When the building was completed, Richardson commissioned his friend La Farge to do the murals and the interior decoration of the church, which immediately became (and remains) the most famous ecclesiastical structure in the United States.

Trinity Church represents the culmination in America of the craft tradition that originated in England with William Morris and John Ruskin and the Beaux-Arts movement that dominated American and European architecture until well after the end of the century. It secured

Richardson's reputation and enhanced that of La Farge. Cynics made themselves merry over the fact that Richardson progressed (or moved) from primarily ecclesiastical architecture to railway stations, thereby, it was suggested, demonstrating the triumph of material over spiritual values.

Mariana Griswold Van Rensselaer, the art historian and friend of Richardson who wrote a biography of the architect two years after his death in 1886, summed up his work as follows: "Strength in conception; clearness of expression; breadth in treatment; imagination; and love for repose and massive dignity of aspect, and often for an effect which in the widest meaning of the word, we may call 'romantic.'" At the same time there is a kind of desponding heaviness about his buildings to the modern mind. The endlessly repeated Romanesque elements pall. Nothing he did subsequently equaled his happy alliance with La Farge in Trinity Church.

The most brilliant and original of the rising generation of architects in the postwar years was Louis Henri Sullivan. He was also one of the youngest, born in 1856 to immigrant parents. His father, an Irishman, taught dancing. His mother, Adrienne Françoise List, had been born in Geneva. Her parents were members of a prosperous middle-class family that lost its money; they had come to the United States to try to recoup their fortunes. Much of Sullivan's youth was spent with his grandparents. His father was a disciple of the new cult of physical culture, and he put Louis through a merciless regimen of cold baths, running, and other outdoor sports. Like most American boys, young Sullivan hated school. When he was thirteen, his parents moved to Chicago, leaving him with his grandparents in order not to interrupt his schooling. At the age of fourteen he was admitted to the Boston English High School and there fell under the influence of Moses Woolson, a member of a classic New England family, who told his pupils, as Sullivan recalled: "You are as wards in my charge; I accept the responsibility involved as a high exacting duty I owe myself and equally to you. I will give you all that I have, you shall give me all that you have."

Sullivan, who wrote one of the most engaging autobiographies in our history, noted of his mentor: "Impartial in judgment, fertile in illustration and expedient, clear in statement, he opened to view a new world. . . . By the end of the school year he had brought order out of disorder, definition out of what was vague, superb alertness out of mere boyish ardor; had nurtured and concentrated all that was best in the boy; had made him consciously courageous and independent; had focussed his powers of thought, feeling and action; had confirmed Louis' love of the great out of doors as a source of inspiration; and had climaxed all by parting a great veil which opened to the view of this same boy the wonderland of Poetry." At the age of sixteen Sullivan entered the recently founded Massachusetts Institute of Technology's School of Architecture. He found the experience a disappointing and frustrating one, "a sort of misch-masch of architectural theology . . . it was not upon the spirit but upon the word that stress was laid . . . the sanctity of the orders Louis considered quaint; the orders were really fairy tales of long ago, now by the learned made rigid, mechanical and inane in the books he was pursuing wherein they were stultified, for lack of common sense and human feeling. . . ." His disillusionment was complete when he discovered that MIT was only a pale imitation of the École des Beaux-Arts in Paris.

He decided, nonetheless, to go to the source, but first he undertook to acquire some practical training as an architect. He did this by the expedient of looking for recently built buildings that he especially liked and then applying for work to the architect who had designed them. After a period in Philadelphia he moved on to Chicago.

Louis Sullivan was seventeen when he came to Chicago in the aftermath of the Great Fire. It was an ideal time to arrive. One architectural firm had designed five miles of building "fronts," another, more than three.

After two years as an apprentice in Philadelphia and Chicago, Sullivan felt that he was ready to try the École des Beaux-Arts. His dissatisfaction with the school derived from the fact that it presented architecture as a series of styles, rather than of problems to be solved. To Sullivan, the history of architecture was "not merely a fixation here and there in time and place, but . . . a continuous outpouring never to end, from the infinite fertility of man's imagination, evoked by his changing needs." The school, in his view, lacked "the profound animus of primal inspiration." He concluded that "solitary in his thoughts and heart-hungry . . . he must go his way alone, that the Paris of his delight must and should remain the dream of his delight. . . ." Back in Chicago, he found the city in the grip of the Depression of 1873 with little work for unknown architects, so he walked its streets day after day until he knew it as his own. He became infatuated with engineering, feeling that the engineers were the real heroes of America, the only men who faced practical problems of building without the inhibitions of tradition. He plunged into Darwin and Spencer and embraced the "scientific method" as it applied to architecture. The word "pragmatic" was not yet in vogue, but Sullivan was already thinking pragmatically about building structures. He asked less what "style" was called for than what purpose the building was to serve and how its function might dictate its form. He was far from a functionalist; ornament was to him integral, but he approached each building as a distinct and separate problem.

He met a brilliant young architect named Dankmar Adler, "a heavy-set, short-nosed Jew, well-bearded, with a magnificent domed forehead which stopped suddenly at a mass of black hair . . . a picture of sturdy strength, physical and mental," with a "mind open, broad, receptive, and of an unusually high order . . . the talk was brief and lively," Sullivan wrote. A year later the two men formed a partnership, and Sullivan "with the efficiency of a Moses Woolson and Beaux Arts training" (again in his words) was soon designing the buildings that would make him the most influential architect of the age. He was twenty-four years old. Iron framework buildings were in their infancy. The firm of Burnham & Root had just completed the first fireproof office building with an all-iron framework, the Montauk Building, and William Le Baron Jenney was also experimenting with multistoried iron frame buildings. In his autobiography Sullivan wrote that "a series of important mercantile structures came into the office, each one of which he [Sullivan] treated experimentally, feeling his way toward a basic process, a grammar of his own. The immediate problem was daylight, the maximum of daylight. This led him to use slender piers, tending toward a masonry and iron combination, the beginnings of a vertical system. . . . Into the work was slowly infiltrated a corresponding system of artistic expression, which appeared in these structures as novel, and, to some, repellent in its total disregard of accepted notions."

The challenge was to build up to the greater heights made possible by the invention and improvement of the elevator without increasing the thickness of the foundations and the bearing walls. The solution that Adler & Sullivan worked out over more than a decade was individual footings that were anchored by piers, above which rose cast-iron framing sections and "screen-walls" of masonry. These were the essential elements of the skyscraper, and with the substitution of structural steel for iron and, in most instances, glass for masonry, they are the same techniques used today in the construction of skyscrapers (we owe much certainly to the genius who coined the splendid word "skyscraper").

In their early years Adler & Sullivan designed four buildings for the steel tycoon Martin Ryerson. Together they trace a fascinating line of development as the architects tried to reconcile a totally new form with conventional elements of design. Like Richardson, Sullivan was addicted to the Romanesque arch; but he treated it much more lightly and ingeniously than the older architect, and throughout his buildings one finds a marvelous inventiveness and sense of play that seldom flag. His greatest triumphs were unquestionably the Auditorium Building, completed in 1889, an enormous ten-story complex which contained an auditorium seating more than 4,000 people, a large hotel, offices, and a tower that was for years the highest point in Chicago, and the Transportation Building for the World's Columbian Exposition.

Saint-Gaudens and La Farge also collaborated with their architect friends Stanford White and Charles Follen McKim.

McKim was born in Isabella Furnace, Pennsylvania, in 1847, graduated from the Lawrence Scientific School at Harvard, and then spent three years at the Beaux-Arts before returning to work in Richardson's office. (Florence Harriman wrote of McKim: "Being with him was like bathing in a crystal pool, mind and soul were purified.")

In 1878, McKim joined with William Rutherford Mead, one year his senior, and Stanford White to form the most famous architectural firm in our history. White was the youngest of the three (he was twenty-six at the time). The three young men won their laurels with the commission to build the house-apartment for Henry Villard on Madison Avenue. Saint-Gaudens designed the pink marble fireplace in the dining room (still extant in the Villard mansion, now part of a luxury hotel) as well as many other details of the interior decoration (La Farge did the murals for the music room). Villard's complex of apartments in a kind of modified Italian Renaissance style set off an epidemic of huge, portentous structures along Fifth Avenue. (Louis Sullivan heaped scorn on William Vanderbilt's "château" on Fifth Avenue. "You do not laugh?" he asked. "Have you no sense of humor, no sense of pathos?") Most tycoons had to have, in addition, country or resort mansions no less lavish and costly than their city abodes. The manifold accomplishments of McKim, Mead & White were crowned with the Boston Public Library, where, as we have noted, Sargent and La Farge were enlisted to decorate the walls and ceilings and design stained glass windows.

The marriage of art and architecture represented by the numerous collaborations among Saint-Gaudens, La Farge, and McKim's firm reached its apogee with the World's Columbian Exposition in 1893.

This was to be the triumphant demonstration of the coming of age of American art, an art which it was solemnly affirmed rivaled, if it did not surpass, the original Renaissance. Crude and vulgar as America might appear in European eyes, it was ready to place money in the service of art on a scale it dared the Old World to rival. Moreover, so vast were the nation's resources, its capital, that it would produce the illusion for a day. Capital would wave its golden wand, and like magic, a great white city would spring into being around a vast lagoon over the surface of which a marble ship with marble passengers would glide.

Architectural critics were surprised and impressed by the work of the young women who appeared as architects. It was as though the feminine temperament were especially suited to the rapidly expanding field of professional architecture. Robert Peabody, a member of the Boston firm of Peabody & Stearns, wrote to the director of the exposition praising the "remarkable ability shown by clever young women who had finished architectural courses in various Eastern institutes."

Louise Blanchard was a well-known woman architect. She had started her own firm in Buffalo, New York, in 1881 at the age of twenty-five and then married her partner, Robert Bethune. She and her husband had built a number of public structures in that city. In 1888 she had become the first woman member of the American Institute of Architects, and a year later a fellow. Cornell, MIT, and Cooper Union all accepted women as candidates for degrees in architecture. Frances Mahony won a degree from MIT in 1894. Perhaps the most exotic among the young women who began their training in architecture in the 1880s was Sophia Hayden, who had been born in Chile of a Spanish mother and grown up in the suburbs of Boston. After she had received a Bachelor of Architecture degree from MIT, she taught mechanical drawing. Her friend Lois Howe was also a graduate of MIT. Julia Morgan was one of the few women architects who held a degree in engineering (from the University of California). She had gone to France to study at the École des Beaux-Arts, the source of the grandiose neo-Renaissance style.

Another successful woman architect was Minerva Parker. She had graduated from the Philadelphia Normal School of Art in 1882 and worked for six years as a draftsman in the office of an architect named Frederick Thorn. After Thorn's retirement she succeeded him, married a Unitarian minister named Nichols, and built a number of houses and handsome public buildings, including two women's clubs and several factories.

Perhaps the most acute comment on the architecture of the Gilded Age was that of the acidulous young sociologist Thorstein Veblen, whose delight was to criticize the foibles of the rich. "The process of selective adaptation of designs to the end of conspicuous waste, and the substitution of pecuniary beauty for aesthetic beauty has been especially effective in the development of architecture," he wrote.

We dare not conclude this discussion of the arts without reference to America's greatest landscape architect, Frederick Law Olmsted. Olmsted was the author of the most comprehensive accounts of slavery in his *Journey in the Seaboard Slave States* and *A Journey Through Texas*. Much of what we know about Southern life and the institution of slavery we owe to his observations. His greatest monument is Central Park in New York City, which he designed and the construction of which he supervised.

Central Park marked the beginning of what was called the park movement, a worldwide phenomenon, and the park was copied by innumerable cities. Olmsted himself was puzzled by the ubiquity of the movement. "It did not run like a fashion," he wrote from the perspective of the end of the century; "it would seem rather to have been a common, spontaneous movement of that sort which we commonly refer to as the 'Genius of Civilization.' . . . Why this great development of interest in natural landscape and all that pertains to it; to the art of it and the literature of it?" For many of the parks the firm of Olmsted, Vaux & Company was the consulting architect. Chicago, Buffalo, Boston—all sought Olmsted's advice.

The movement toward semirural areas adjacent to large cities—suburbs—was an important development of the period. As cities became more hazardous to life and limb, many residents retreated to less crowded and dangerous zones.

To Frederick Law Olmsted, called in as a consultant in the development of a number of suburbs, the principle to be kept in mind in planning roads, walks, trees, and shrubbery was the central fact of the character of community, "the grand fact . . . that they are Christians, loving one another, and not Pagans, fearing one another. . . ." This was to be expressed in "the completeness, and choiceness and beauty of the means they possess of coming together, of being together, and especially of recreating together on common ground." This meant "no fences, wide curving drives, ponds, boat landings, and rustic pavilions." In 1886 Olmsted was commissioned to design the grounds of the Leland Stanford, Jr., University at Palo Alto, and four years later he began work on the plans for the World's Columbian Exposition in Chicago. The exposition was his last great undertaking, the climax of one of the most brilliant careers of the century. Olmsted's health and sanity declined rapidly (he was seventy-one when the exposition took place), and he was finally committed to the McLean Hospital in Waverly, Massachusetts—the grounds of which he had designed—in 1898, where he died five long, bitter years later. A dreamer, an idealist, a humanitarian and reformer from his days as an abolitionist to the end of his career, Frederick Law Olmsted was a singularly sweet and charming man who drew to himself the loving affection of those who knew him.

Consumers and producers of art, women were increasingly arbiters as well. As we have noted, Sara Hallowell advised the new nobility on art acquisitions for their personal collections and for galleries and museums and introduced her clients to the Impressionists. Mariana Griswold Van Rensselaer, one of the foremost art critics of the day, wrote of the "new" art: "Inspiration unsought and unquestioned is a thing of the past. Study, reflection, absorption, electricism,—these are the watchwords of the future." In the wake of the Centennial Exposition in Philadelphia "came the new band of native artists preaching a new artistic gospel . . . a like-minded, brotherly band to preach that the painter's first privilege, first task, first duty was *to learn the art of painting*. Our elder schools had been almost entirely absorbed in the subjects of their discourse . . . had forgotten almost entirely that in every form of human utterance when it turns to *art*, the language itself is of primary importance.

"With our new world restlessness, impatience, inexperience, we are too prone to forget that everything alive must go by steps. . . ." It was enough to learn what good painting meant. But the current generation had done much more. It had "already given us fruits as well as buds. . . ."

Van Rensselaer took a special interest in making art available to the poor. It was in large part her influence that resulted in the Metropolitan Museum of Art in New York City being open on Sunday for "working people."

What is indisputably the case is that art entered powerfully into the American consciousness in the decades following the Civil War. "Scores of artists—sculptors and painters, poets and dramatists, workers in gems and metals," Henry Adams wrote, "designers in stuffs and furniture . . . were at work, a thousand times as actively as ever before, and the mass and originality of their product would have swamped any previous age. . . ." But Adams was not sanguine about the result; "the effect was one of chaos. . . ." There seemed to him no ordering principle, no comprehensive vision behind the vast outpouring of creative energy. It was as passionate and disorderly as the society in which it existed and which it captivated.

As important historically as artists who created such vivid pictures of American life was the "explosion of images" that resulted from the new technology of printing. In the words of one historian, "The 19th century saw a complete revolution in the mechanical principles of printing; before it was over the foundation of all modern techniques had been firmly established." The new technology made possible an astonishing proliferation of magazines and journals by making the process of producing printed material remarkably inexpensive by traditional standards (it thus "democratized" printing) and gave birth to "illustration," to an explosion of images. The initial process of printing images was laborious in the extreme; sketches, paintings, photographs and decorations had to be engraved on wooden blocks. The engravers were master craftsmen who produced images of extraordinary potency that constituted a kind of subdivision of more formal art. When the hand-engraved woodblock was replaced by the photogravure method, the image to be reproduced was photographed on a copper plate, which was then dipped in acid.

The proliferation of words was merely an acceleration of a familiar medium—printing—but the explosion of images brought a critically important new dimension into the psychology of perception. How people saw (and experienced) the world around them was altered by the images which represented reality to them in a flood of popular illustrated magazines and journals. In the aggregate they constituted a new order of reality.

The West

The West was still the frontier, a land of infinite opportunity, and Americans flocked to it by the hundreds of thousands and, in time, by the millions, filling in its inhabitable spaces and many of its uninhabitable ones as well. In the words of William Smythe, the Western crusader for agrarian democracy and irrigation, "The war was over— the war had begun! . . . It remained to wage war on the forest, the plain, the desert, and the mountain, and to create a better civilization than the world had seen."

There were, of course, the territories—states-to-be, governed from Washington. The fact that the national government owned and was responsible for enormous tracts of land, tracts as large as countries, was the most powerful single incentive toward a "national" view of things and thereby an essential counterbalance to the tenacious doctrine of states' rights. The necessity for administering, in however modest a form, this vast empire trained the government, almost against its will, to think and act "nationally" rather than "federally." Eventually the "public domain" as a nationalizing force would be supplemented by an aggressive foreign policy that was also, of necessity, "national."

John Quincy Adams had seen in "internal improvements" and "internal resources" the great unifying nation-building themes of the

Republic. "Ages upon ages of continual progressive improvement, physical, moral, political, in the condition of the whole people of this Union," Adams wrote, "were stored up in the possession and disposal of these lands. . . ." He had "long entertained and cherished the hope that these public lands were among the chosen instruments of Almighty power . . . of improving the condition of man by establishing the practical, self-evident truth of the natural equality and brotherhood of all mankind, as the foundation of all human government, and by banishing slavery and war from the earth. . . ."

All discussion of "the West" is complicated, as we have seen, by the fact that there were at least six "Wests": the Mississippi Valley West (with Northern and Southern subdivisions), the Great Plains West, the Rocky Mountain West, the Great Desert West, the Northwest, and the Southwest. There was as little similarity between Oregon and New Mexico as there was between Vermont and South Carolina. The inhabitants spoke the same language, saluted the same flag, respected more or less the same Constitution (while interpreting it differently). But the only things common to the West were the facts that the various segments of it lay in the geographic western portion of the continental United States and that all the Wests shared a deep suspicion of the East. Whatever else might divide the West, it was as one in its hostility toward that part of the nation that lay east, generally speaking, of the Mississippi. When the Wests looked East, they saw snobs, dudes, Wall Streeters, city slickers, and a myriad of people who profited from their often desperately hard labor. They saw do-gooders and Indian lovers, "nigger" lovers, Chinese lovers, individuals and associations devoted to lecturing them on their crude and barbarous ways. When Easterners came West to inspect them, to condescend to them, to sport fancy accents and fancy clothes, they felt their collective hackles rise.

When the East looked West, it saw rugged, snow-capped mountains; prairies; natural wonders beyond counting, including the fabled Yellowstone, Estes Park and Colorado Springs, the Grand Canyon, the Teton Range, and, finally, the grandest and most awesome of all, the Valley of the Yosemite. Easterners saw cowboys and Indians, and the more practical of them saw dollars—gold and silver and timber in apparently inexhaustible amounts. They saw angry, radical farmers and desperate and dangerous workers who had absorbed some of the Western ethic of violence. They saw Populists, socialists, anarchists, freethinkers, and free lovers (such types were to be found, of course, in the East as well, but they seemed easier to contain, less threatening).

Above all, the East saw crudity and lawlessness, the taking of the law into the hands of those who had experienced its inequities.

The differences between Easterners and Westerners were many and varied; they ranged from clothes to accents. In both categories Westerners were far more informal than their Eastern cousins. They parted their hair differently and wore blunt, stubby shoes while the Easterners had more stylish footwear, usually of English manufacture or style. Easterners called each other by their last names even when they were close friends; Westerners preferred to address each other by their first names. But accents were perhaps the most conspicuous difference. An observant Westerner could, and usually did as soon as his bank account permitted, repair to an "Eastern" tailor or bootmaker, but he could not as easily put off his flat Midwestern voice in favor of the cultivated accents of the Eastern upper classes, distinguished in large part by "broad a's" as in "Hahvahd" or "tomahto." In the East the prevailing style in virtually all things from tennis togs to hacking jackets, from domestic furnishings to light opera remained decidedly British.

Beside the practical, inescapable fact of its size, the most compelling fact about the West was its growth in population in the years following the war. In the period from 1865 to 1890 Nebraska's population grew from 28,000 to 1,066,000; Iowa's from 600,000 to 1,600,000; and that of the Dakota Territory from 5,000 to 140,000 and then quadrupled in five years. The population of Minnesota increased 43 percent in five years, and Minneapolis grew in the same period from 47,000 to 130,000, while its sister city of St. Paul grew from 41,000 to 111,000. Flour from the mills of Minneapolis alone could provide twenty-five loaves of bread for every inhabitant of the United States. Kansas City had grown from 300 inhabitants in 1855 to 125,000 by 1885, and in ten years the number of bushels of grain processed in the city's mills increased more than tenfold. In the eighties and nineties more than 5,500,000 acres were homesteaded; the states just west of the Mississippi increased in population from 4,500,000 to almost 10,000,000 by the end of the century.

Oregon, accessible by two railroad lines, increased in population from 91,000 in 1870 to 414,000 thirty years later, while California almost tripled in population in the same period—to 1,485,000. Arizona, with 10,000 inhabitants in 1870, had jumped to 123,000 by 1900.

In a sense this all went on offstage, if we take the stage to be the great cities of the East. The financial interests of New York and Boston were certainly well aware of the profits to be made in Western lands and mines, especially in the rapidly growing cities of the Midwest. Charles Francis Adams's fortune was based on his ownership of Kansas stockyards, the business of which increased from $20,000 a year, when he took over the distant management of the company, to $1,000,000 twenty years later. There was a notable irony in the tie between a member of the latest generation of the Adams clan and Texas cattle butchered in Kansas City. Charles Francis Adams was, as a human type, as far from the world of Joseph McCoy, the founder of the Abilene cattle drives, as it was possible for two Americans to be. Yet McCoy's longhorns put dollars in Adams's pocket, thereby enabling the latter to be incorruptibly above the battle, pursuing the career of a Boston reformer and philanthropist.

As we have seen, the farm areas of the Near West or, as it was now commonly called, the Midwest—Kansas, Iowa, northern Illinois, Nebraska, and, to a lesser degree, the Dakotas—were centers of radical political and social thought and agitation. They were also, by no means coincidentally, the most "New England" of the Western states. Many towns were New England in all but locale. They had been colonized by bands of New Englanders, often by way of New York State's "burned-over region" (the western part of the state, swept by a succession of religious revivals and radical movements). Yellow Springs, Ohio, was founded by a colony of free love, free thought enthusiasts, who also espoused complete democracy; the goings-on there scandalized the countryside for miles around until an itinerant Methodist minister, braving the town's hostility toward all forms of organized religion, held a revival meeting and converted most of the town to Methodism— whereupon it became the most rigidly orthodox Methodist town in the state. The unconverted moved on in search of stauncher atheists.

Republicanism/abolitionism was a deep tie between New England and those of its sons and daughters who ventured West. In Mastersville, Ohio, the Masterses and Holmeses (cousins) subscribed first to Garrison's *Liberator* (storing each copy carefully away as though it were Holy Writ) and then, after the war, to the *Boston Evening Transcript* and Henry Ward Beecher's *Independent*. The fact was that a substantial part of the readership of the religious and literary periodicals that emanated in such numbers from Boston lay west of the Mississippi and kept the memories and the ideals of New England green in the scorched plains and bitter winters of Kansas, Iowa, and Nebraska.

Of all the Great Plains states Kansas was undoubtedly the most

"New England." It manifested in a hundred ways the trauma of its birth. In the struggle for Kansas that followed the passage of the ill-fated Kansas-Nebraska bill, the state filled up with those fiery souls of Calvinist persuasion who were determined to save the soul of America from the devil's work—slavery. William Allen White, the Emporia newspaper editor, was stating a basic fact when he declared that "as a state, Kansas has inherited a Puritan conscience." Indeed, Kansas was, in a real sense, early New England, risen like the phoenix in the prairie country of the Middle West. Every reform movement, every radical notion flourished there. It was virtually the home of the prohibition movement, as it was of populism. In the words of one historian, "Whenever a wrong was discovered, whether it was the common drinking cup or the waste resulting from labor disputes, the Kansan launched a crusade to eradicate the evil." In one of his most famous editorials, White wrote: "Kansas is a state of the Union, but it is also a state of mind, a neurotic condition, a psychological phase, a symptom, indeed, something undreamt of in your philosophy, an inferiority complex against the tricks and manners of plutocracy—social, political, and economic. . . . When anything is going to happen in this country, it happens first in Kansas." Reforms issued from Kansas "like bats out of hell. Sooner or later other states take up these things, and then Kansas goes on breeding other troubles. Why, no one seems to know. . . . There is just one way to stop progress in America; and that is to hire some hungry earthquake to come along and gobble up Kansas. But . . . that earthquake would have an awful case of indigestion for two or three epochs afterward."

William Smythe noted that "New England" was "no longer a mere geographical term. It is a certain spirit of civic pride and individual enterprise. . . . Its sons go forth to conquer the waste places. They plant their traditions, and raise a crop of institutions."

While the isolated farm (and, farther west, the ranch) was a conspicuous feature of the Great Plains region, the town was the characteristic social entity of the Middle West. An extremely precarious and vulnerable form of social organization, the town was a classic example of an organism sustained by the naked will of its inhabitants. It lacked, for the most part, all those ceremonies and occasions, those symbolic and mythic representations of reality that seem essential to sustain life or at least to endow it with sufficient grace and beauty to make it endurable. It had, thus, to be brought constantly up to the mark, lest it degenerate. One thinks of Dickens's despair over a society the principal ceremony of which was the lecture—and the principal form of emotional release of which, Dickens might have added, was the religious revival. The fact was such outpourings were essential to preserve sanity. We know that many towns fell into some fatal dissipation—alcohol was the most common; sexual aberrations were not unknown—and simply disintegrated. Kate Austen startled Emma Goldman with her reference to the bizarre sexual practices of Missouri farmers. A recent study of small towns in Wisconsin at the end of the nineteenth century disclosed an unsettling pattern of insanity, alcoholism, murder, perversion, and suicide—unsettling, that is, in terms of our sentimental and idealized notion of town life.

Alton, Illinois, appeared to Hutchins Hapgood, in retrospect, a town where "most people seemed . . . painful or benumbed slaves, where the intensity of life revealed itself only in ugly passion. . . ."

Edgar Watson Howe, who preferred the relative anonymity of the initials E. W., was editor of the *Atchison* (Kansas) *Globe*. In 1883 he published in an edition of 1,500 copies and at his own expense *The Story of a Country Town*, which he had written in the evenings by lamplight after his daily stint as editor of the *Globe*. In it Howe expressed his own bitterness at the harsh and narrow character of town life as he had experienced it and the forbidding nature of his preacher father. The town of Fairview was a grim little way station on the road West, one of numerous towns that "sprang up on credit, and farms were opened with borrowed money . . . where no sooner was one stranger's money exhausted than another arrived to take his place; where men mortgaged their possessions at full value, and thought themselves rich notwithstanding, so great was their faith in the country; where he who was deepest in debt was the leading citizen and where bankruptcy caught them all at last." Those who stopped in Fairview were "too poor and tired" to follow the trek West. "I became early impressed," Howe declared, "with the fact that our people seemed to be miserable and discontented, and frequently wondered that they did not load their effects on wagons again and move away from a place which made all the men surly and rough, and the women pale and fretful." The cant phrase, endlessly repeated, was that the settlers had moved West "to grow up with the country." In such bleak surroundings Howe's father, whose only disposition was to hard work, was "stern and silent," an unloving and indifferent parent whose attention was fixed on hell. Many Midwestern towns were started by two or three closely related families. The Holmeses and the Masterses were cousins who settled

Mastersville, Ohio, and dominated the life of the town for a generation or more. Ed Lemmon, a cowhand, wagon boss, trail rider, and range manager—"Boss cowman"—recalled a friend named Jack Wilson who landed in Pittsville, Missouri, in 1864 and married Miranda Pitts. At the election of 1880 "six hundred adult Pitts men voted at one polling place."

Another category of town was the immigrant community—German, Norwegian, Swedish, even, occasionally and unsuccessfully, Jewish. If life was often bitterly hard in the immigrant communities, it was relieved by ceremonies and customs which the immigrants brought with them, by their native dances and music, the gymnastics of the Germans, the marriage festivals of the Swedes.

In any event it was hard to gainsay Walt Whitman's observation during his Western excursion: "No one . . . begins to know the real, geographic, democratic, indissoluble American Union, in the present, or suspect it in the future, until he explores these Central States, and dwells awhile observantly on their prairies. . . ."

Farther West, in cattle and sheep country, the character of the people changed dramatically, but the facts and figures of growth were still astounding. The Dakota wheat crop in 1885 was 30,000,000 bushels, more than that of Egypt. Montana's population increased in a twelve-month period from 85,000 to 110,000, its cattle from 475,000 to 850,000, and its output in silver, gold, and other minerals from $10,000,000 to $23,000,000. Sheep raising slowly overtook and then passed cattle raising as the major agricultural activity of the state (mining, of course, aside). In 1885 there were some 600,000 sheep compared with 500,000 cattle. Ten years later the number of sheep had almost tripled. For one thing it took far less of a grubstake to get into sheep raising than into cattle—$2.35 a head for sheep versus $20 a head for cattle. By 1900 Montana was the principal wool-producing state in the Union with more than 6,000,000 sheep grazing (and often overgrazing) its hills. Fort Benton was the center of the sheep raisers' domain. Like many Western towns, Benton was a wild mixture of types and nationalities—Canadians, French, blacks, Mexicans, Indians, and refugees from many states of the Union.

British money and Eastern money came West with the pioneers. The census of 1886 revealed that residents of New York had $1,300,000 invested outside the state, and it was estimated that half of Nevada was owned by investors from other states. The Anglo-American Cattle Company was organized in England in 1879 with Harry Oelrichs, an

American, in charge. The third son of the sixteenth Baron Dunsany of Ireland came to Wyoming in the same year and started a ranch on a tributary of the Powder River. Two Harvard classmates, Frederic de Billier and Hubert Teschmacher, went game hunting in Wyoming and returned to establish a huge ranch on the North Platte. Soon the cattle boom was going full blast, aided by a book entitled *The Beef Bonanza or How to Get Rich on the Plains*. The Prairie Cattle Company was founded in Edinburgh in 1881 with a capital of more than $1,000,000, and the country swarmed with aristocratic young Englishmen as well as wealthy and adventurous young Americans. They made Cheyenne their headquarters (it was the state capital) and founded the Cheyenne Club, perhaps the toniest club in America, where the members wore white ties and tails which they called their Herefords, were served the finest wines and champagnes, and were fed by an imported French chef. At a dinner given by the British members for the Americans, forty-one guests polished off sixty-six bottles of champagne and twenty bottles of red wine in addition to copious amounts of whiskey. Moreton Frewen, a young British swell, appeared as agent for a number of wealthy English investors and built himself a castle, an elegant two-story log cabin with a carved mahogany staircase, at Traving; married Clara Jerome, the daughter of the New York financier, whose sister would marry Lord Randolph Churchill; and established her in the castle. Soon she was entertaining the 1880s equivalent of the jet set: Sir Samuel and Lady Baker, Lord Mayo, Lord Granville Gordon, Lords Manner and Donoughmore, many of them investors in the Powder River Cattle Company. Manner and another guest (the British passion for killing things was rivaled only by that of the Americans) "killed 95 wild duck, mallards, shovellers, widgeon and teal, within a mile of the house." More money was raised, and the ranch was extended southward from the headwaters of the Powder River for some ninety miles. On this vast expanse of land between 40,000 and 80,000 cattle ranged (no one was certain how many), and in the great roundups of 1883 and 1884 it was estimated that twenty outfits with 200 cowboys and 2,000 horses were involved in working some 40,000 head of cattle.

The states of the High Plain and Rocky Mountain West were acutely conscious of being economic colonies or dependencies of Eastern financiers. It was not too much to say that Rockefeller owned Wyoming and Colorado. The Guggenheims owned Utah; Bunker Hill and Sullivan owned Idaho; the Union Pacific and the lumber companies owned Oregon (the Union Pacific owned many of the lumber companies). In addition, Eastern families owned substantial portions of such Western cities as there were. Much of Milwaukee, St. Paul, Minneapolis, Detroit, Omaha, Denver, and points west were owned by Eastern investors and returned rents to them. Of course, not all states were owned by Eastern capitalists. California was owned by the Southern Pacific—by the Crockers, Stanfords, Huntingtons, Hearsts, etc.

Italian, Irish, German, Syrian, Mexican immigrants and a dozen other nationalities labored in the mines, extracting gold and silver and coal and copper and lead, making great fortunes for (largely) Eastern investors. It was one of the strangest juxtapositions of human beings in all history—the lords above and the workers beneath.

Butte, Montana, was the greatest copper-mining town in the world, and it, like Lincoln County in New Mexico and Johnson County in Wyoming, became the center of a bitter struggle for control of the economy and of the state in which it was located. The main antagonists were Marcus Daly, an Irish immigrant and a miner by way of Calaveras County, California, and William Andrews Clark. Daly bought the as yet undeveloped Anaconda mine for $30,000 in 1880 (he thought he was buying a silver mine). Three years later it shipped more than 25,000 tons of copper to Swansea, Wales, for smelting at a gross profit of $1,702,400. By 1890 copper led silver and gold with a value of $17,625,020, while silver was second at roughly $16,000,000. In the same period the population of the state increased from 40,000 to 143,000.

Daly's adversary was William Andrews Clark, a Pennsylvanian who had studied law at Ohio Wesleyan. For a time the politics of the state of Montana became a projection of the personal feud between Clark and Daly. Clark owned thirteen mines in Butte, a mine or two in Coeur d'Alene, and most of the rich United Verde Copper Company in Arizona, as well as City Street Railway Company of Butte, the Electric Light Company, the *Butte Miner* (a newspaper), and the Rocky Mountain Telegraph Company.

Along the western edge of the Great Plains and in the valleys of the Rockies and west to the Pacific, ranches and ranchers created a unique economy and life-style. The rancher was a baron, a kind of feudal lord often presiding over hundreds of thousands of acres, with the difference that he "worked" cattle with his ranch hands, riding the range, living in a ranch house that was usually no more than a glorified cabin. A millionaire with dirt on his hands, he was already clearly defined by the 1870s. Madame de Hegermann-Lindencrone, born Lillie Greenough of Cambridge, Massachusetts, has given us our most vivid portrait of "the Western rancher," Gary Cooper in anticipation. She encountered him—John Brent—at the castle of the Count of West-phalia in 1874. The young count had met Brent at the races at Wies-baden, and infatuated, as all the German aristocracy were, with the American West, he had brought him back in triumph to the family Schloss. Mr. Brent was, Lillie Greenough Hegermann-Lindencrone reported to her mother, "a big, tall, splendidly built fellow with the sweetest face and liquidest blue eyes one can imagine. He had a soft, melodious voice and the most fascinating manner, in spite of his far-Western language. Everyone liked him; my American heart warmed to him instantly. . . ." When the countess asked him, in her most velvety tones, " 'Do you take sugar, Mr. Brent?' 'Yes, ma'm, I do—three lumps, and if it's beety I take four. . . . I've got a real sweet tooth,' he said with an alluring smile to which we all succumbed." Even the countess, in-stead of being appalled by such informality, was charmed, while the count discussed horses and guns with Mr. Brent to his heart's content.

Lillie shuddered at the thought of what Mr. Brent's notion of dinner clothes might be, but he appeared "dressed in perfect evening dress, in the latest fashion, except his tie, which was of white satin and very badly tied." Everyone realized at once that their remarkable guest had struck just the right note.

The great hall of the castle had an enormous fireplace. "I suppose this is where the ancestors toasted their patriarchal toes," Mr. Brent said. When the countess asked him what his occupation was, he de-clared, "Oh, I do a little of everything, mostly farming. I've paddled my own canoe since I was a small kid." This information was received with a moment of perplexed silence. "Is there much water in your country place?" the countess inquired.

"Don't you mean country? Well, yes. We have quite a few pailfuls over there. . . ."

Mr. Brent was most impressed by the count's vast armory of weap-ons. He had never seen so many outside of "a shindy." What was a shindy? "Well, it's a free fight, where you kill promiscuous."

"Gott im Himmel!" cried his alarmed interrogator. "Do you mean to say that you have killed any one otherwise than in a duel?"

"I can't deny that I have killed a few . . . but never in cold blood. . . . You see, over there"—pointing with his cigar in the general direction of Colorado—"if a man insults you, you must kill him then and there, and you must always be heeled."

When the count informed Mr. Brent that the great hall was "a very good specimen of Renaissance style," Mr. Brent replied, "I don't know what 'rennysauce' means, but this room is the style I like . . . tomorrow I'd like to take a snapshot of it and all the company to show mother. . . ."

He had come "across the pond," he told the count and countess, "because the doctor said I needed a rest and change."

"I hope that you have had them both," the count replied.

"I got the change, all right; but the hotel-keepers got the rest."

The next day Mr. Brent examined the count's "horseflesh" with the eye of an expert. "This one is not worth much, and that one I would not give two cents for, but this fellow"—indicating the count's best racer—"is a beauty." Then, to the complete enchantment of the family and staff, "Mr. Brent walked to the paddock, asked for a rope, and proceeded to show us how they lasso horses in America." Finally he jumped bareback on one of the count's horses and rode it through its frantic plunges until it was "tame and meek."

When it came time for John Brent to depart for Colorado, there was universal grief. He held the beautiful Lillie's hand (she was an accomplished concert singer and had sung for him), sighed, and turned away his head (presumably to hide a tear). The Western hero, the young prince, was on his way back to his mother. "If you ever come to Colorado," he said, giving her hand an extra squeeze, "just ask anyone for Johnny Brent, and if I don't stand on my head for you it'll be because I've lost it." Cut cameras. Print take.

Before Brent left, the count took down one of his prize pistols from the wall and presented it to the American visitor with the words, "This will remind you of us, but don't kill anyone with it."

Johnny Brent had moved unawed through the splendor and glitter of the Westphalian court, his naturalness irresistible to every one who encountered him—the aristocracy of the New World mixing unselfconsciously with the Old.

In contrast, the life of the glamorized cowboy was brutally hard and miserably underpaid. Eleanor Marx Aveling in her report on the conditions of labor in the United States devoted a whole chapter to the exploited cowboy and the need for a cowboy union. Big Bill Haywood, who had worked as a cowhand and knew the cowboy's life at first hand, organized a union for rodeo performers, and in 1886 the cowboys working in the area of the Powder River went on strike for guaranteed wages of $40 a month. "Not a wheel turned," the *Rocky Mountain Husbandman* noted, "until the foremen submitted to the terms made up by a committee from the cowboys." The strike was broken by the Stock Growers' Association, and Jack Flagg, the leader of the cowboys, was blacklisted by all the ranchers. He thereupon homesteaded on the Red Fork of the Powder River and set himself up with his own brand—the Hat. Out of his break came the famous Johnson County War.

There were, in fact, numerous "wars" in the territories and new states—cattlemen against sodbusters (farmers); cattlemen against sheepmen; the big cattlemen against the little ranchers. The Johnson County War revolved around political and economic power—the small cattlemen (often accused by the large cattlemen of creating their herds with mavericks from the giant cattle corporations) versus the big-timers, who had joined forces to form the Wyoming Stock Growers' Association in an effort to put a stop to rustling. Mavericks were unbranded cattle—calves not yet branded or yearlings that had escaped the roundup. These were considered legitimate game by cowboys, ambitious to start their own herds. The ranchers whose cows had dropped such mavericks considered them their as yet unbranded stock. In addition, many rustlers—i.e., small cattlemen—added to their herds by altering the brands of a large corporate rancher with a "running iron," a simple iron without a brand on the end which, in the hands of an "artist," could be used to change one brand into another. It was said, with considerable truth, that all a cowhand needed to become a cattle rancher was a long rope with a running iron. A classic example was said to be the IC brand which was altered by an ingenious rustler or ambitious cowboy to ICU. This brand was further modified by *another* enterprising cowman to ICU2.

The Wyoming Stock Growers' Association, made up of powerful and arrogant men, agreed that they would hire no cowboys who had ranches of their own on the ground that such hands were the principal culprits in rustling, having the maximum of temptation combined with the maximum of opportunity. This naturally caused resentment among both the guilty and the innocent. Another stock growers' practice was to blacklist any cowhand suspected of rustling or of agitating against the measures of the association.

In April, 1892, fifty gunmen of the Wyoming Stock Growers' Association (twenty-five of them "hired guns" from Texas) surrounded a cabin on the Powder River which they believed was occupied by a group of rustlers and called on them to surrender. There were actually only two men in the cabin, and they refused to come out, firing at their attackers. Both were shot and killed. One of them was Nate Champion, the so-called king of the cattle thieves. A piece of paper bearing the words "Cattle Thieves, Beware" was pinned on Champion's vest, and the Johnson County War had begun.

When word of the killings reached Buffalo, the nearest town, it turned out that there was more sympathy for the "rustlers" than support for the Stock Growers' Association. Before long some 300 armed men had gathered at Buffalo and ridden off to besiege the besiegers at the TA ranch, owned by one of the association's leaders, while the territorial governor, described by one of the cattlemen as "a weak-kneed ass, inept and overly smart," dithered in Cheyenne. After the siege had run several days, Governor Barber telegraphed to President Harrison: "An insurrection exists in Johnson County in the state of Wyoming . . . against the governor of said state. . . . Open hostilities exist and large bodies of armed men are engaged in battle." Barber appealed to the President for Federal troops to put down the insurrection. The U.S. troops intervened on the third day of the siege, and the "war" was officially over.

The Lincoln County War was a struggle for control of New Mexico between two groups of businessmen and ranchers in the town and county of Lincoln. On one side were the entrenched and thoroughly corrupt partners, L. G. Murphy, J. J. Dolan, and J. H. Riley (all young men under thirty), who wished to preserve their control of the mercantile and banking business of Lincoln and their lucrative business selling beef and supplies to the nearby army post. On the other side were a newcomer, John Tunstall, a young Englishman, and his lawyer, Alexander McSween. Charges of cattle rustling helped increase the bitterness between the two factions, and after several of Tunstall's supporters—recruited principally from the smaller cattlemen who were enemies of the Murphy-Dolan-Riley faction—were shot, a "war" broke out; more than twenty men, Tunstall and McSween among them, were killed, and the town of Lincoln was kept in a state of siege for almost five days. William Bonney, Billy the Kid, received his baptism of fire in the Lincoln County War. When the United States soldiers were called in to restore order, they became involved in the controversy, and it took the arrival of a new territorial governer, the redoubtable Lew Wallace, author of *Ben Hur*, to put out the flames.

Life in the mining towns and lumber camps of the West was extremely hazardous to health. Fatal and crippling injuries and disease were endemic. The atmosphere was heavy with the continual threat of violence. Guns were everywhere. Men fought to avenge a real or fancied insult, or they fought out of boredom, or intoxication, or for the sheer, uninhibited pleasure of fighting.

On the other hand, one of the most attractive features of life in the Western mining states—primarily Colorado, Utah, Idaho, and later Nevada—was the openness of the society. Henry Wolcott wrote to his brother from Central City, Colorado, in 1870: "I should like to see you, Ed, out here, too. There are some splendid fellows here; plenty of good tobacco, good parties of the stag variety; good stories, good board, light air, lots of reading matter, lots of wood and oil; good shave (hot-water arrangement); good bed blankets, (no sheets); and I have a devilish smart 'dorg.' "

Confederate veterans and emigrants from the South carried with them the Southern code of honor and, in its name, democratized the duel and introduced the gunfight. Gunfighters became more famous than governors or legislators. Dodge City, Virginia City, Albuquerque—wherever there was a railhead for cattle or a terminal town on the cattle drives, gunfighters and would-be gunfighters collected. Bandits and murderers became folk heroes, provided only that they killed enough Indians, Mexicans, and fellow delinquents to gain a degree of notoriety. Billy the Kid, Doc Holliday, Wild Bill Hickok, their fame trumpeted by "westerns," became mythical figures, larger than life. Law officers, in some cases merely gunfighters on the right side of the law, became heroes as well, Pat Garrett and Bat Masterson prominent among them. In addition to the individual gunfighters walking down the main street of town at high noon, there were the Robin Hood-like bandits who pleased people by robbing the hated railroads and the banks. There were the Daltons and the Jameses—Frank and Jesse— Al Jennings, and Butch Cassidy and the Sundance Kid, holed up at Robber's Roost, outwitting the posses sent to track them down.

With cattle, as with people, the mortality rate was high. Julian Ralph, the journalist, wrote in 1893: "The cattle owners, or cowmen, are in Wall Street, the South of France, or in Florida in the winter, but their cattle are on the wintry fields where now and then, say once in four years, half of them, or 80% of them, or one in three (as it happens) starve to death because of their inability to get at the grass under the snow. . . . But the cowmen do business on the principle that the gains in good years far more than offset the losses in bad years." In the winter of 1886 one ranch, the Hashknife, placed its loss at 75 percent, while the Crosby Cattle Company lost 80 percent. The Turkey Track and EC ranches had 27,000 head of cattle at the beginning of the winter and 250 by spring.

If hardship and violence were part of the fabric of Western life, transience was another. Near Keokuk, Iowa, was New Philadelphia, which in 1850 had been a respectable city with churches and stores and a college that cost $100,000. When David Macrae visited it, a little more than ten years after its founding, it was already deserted. "Trade has taken a different direction," he noted; "the people have rushed after it; the deserted buildings are going to ruin, and the only students attending the college are the farmers' pigs, which roam at will through the college grounds, preparing to graduate in pork." As the Americans put it, New Philadelphia was "played out."

In Mariposa, California, Frederick Law Olmsted was dismayed by the extreme fluidity and transience that marked all social relations. There were no orderly, coherent, "covenanted communities" (outside of a handful of utopian communes). It was every man for himself. According to Olmsted, the basic social unit was "chums" or "buddies"— from two to ten individuals banded together for mutual protection and profit. In the two years that Olmsted lived in Mariposa he reported that there had been three district attorneys. "Three citizens previously engaged in other occupations have entered upon the practice of law. The principal capitalist, the largest merchant, and three other leading merchants have left the country; at least a dozen storekeepers have sold out and as many more come in. . . . In one case a mill has changed hands three times, in several others twice. The justice of the peace, the seven successive school committeemen, three out of four of the physicians, the five butchers, the five innkeepers, eight out of twelve tradesmen. . . . the blacksmiths, the two iron founders, the two barbers, the daguerreotypist, the bathing house keeper, the seven livery stable keepers, the three principal farmers, the three school teachers and about seventy out of one hundred miners and laboring men . . . have moved from one house, office or shop to another, or have left the country. . . ." he noted. Of eighty-seven persons Olmsted knew, eighty-five had changed their residence within two years.

Reading Olmsted's account of Mariposa, one is reminded of a kind of the mad acceleration of an America that Tocqueville had described fifty years earlier. In consequence of such mobility there was, according to Olmsted, no form or order, no trust or good faith in the dealings of people with each other. But there was "a rapid increase of freedom of thought, freedom of suggestion . . . and a rapid weakening of each man's habit and disposition to follow any course which society seems to have laid out for him in a persistent or consistent way." In one of his most interesting observations, Olmsted wrote: "The condition about which centers all there is here of peculiar conservatism and all that there is of peculiar recklessness is . . . that of Slipshod." The only thing that men were "systematic and intense" about, it seemed to him, was their determination to persist in their slipshod ways. Lynch law was a case in point. To Olmsted it appeared "nothing but an intense form of the common effort to get along without real and prolonged deliberation and system. . . . Just enough law, or show of law, to maintain the greatest degree of lawlessness under which men can have any use of neighbors."

In an age the dominant theme of which was the growth of industrial capitalism and the concomitant growth of cities, the Far West was virtually without cities. In the whole vast sweep of continent from Chicago to San Francisco, the only place that began to deserve the name of city was Denver (Salt Lake was, after all, a special case). In lieu of cities there was a wide variety of towns, vast ranches, and small farms. There were mining towns, lumber towns, cattle towns, and railroad towns (there were two types of railroad towns: towns colonized by the railroads to sell lands along their rights-of-way and towns established at junctures of rail lines and at railheads for switching yards and repair stations). Most of the towns were thus company towns, started and controlled by the corporations that owned the mines, the timber, the cattle, or the railroads. Crude and ephemeral as they were, they were not without efforts at some degree of civilization. Devoted women like Phoebe Apperson Hearst (in Coeur d'Alene) started libraries, temperance clubs, and reading societies and struggled to bring a touch of culture to scenes of desolation that might have been drawn from Doré's illustrations of Dante's *Inferno*. Under the circumstances it is not surprising that many more towns were started than survived.

Salt Lake City, the capital of the Deseret Empire from which Brigham Young intended to convert the world to the Church of the Latter-Day Saints in anticipation of Christ's Second Coming and the beginning of the millennium, dominated the state of Utah. If Young's ambitions proved excessive, the Mormons nonetheless spread their influence into the adjacent territories (and later states) and found themselves involved in a fierce fight over the issue of polygamy. The attacks on the institution were voluminous and bitter. It was a doctrine especially offensive to women. Conservative Christian women and radical feminists alike deplored it, the former on moral grounds, the latter on the ground that it was a practice demeaning to their sex. With the women of the nation aroused against it, the days of polygamy were numbered. Seeing the handwriting on the wall, so to speak, Brigham Young had a revelation which declared that polygamy was no longer acceptable for orthodox Mormons. After a bitter fight which split the church, monogamy prevailed.

We are by now familiar with the various Wests—the Fur West of the Yellowstone-South Park-Rocky Mountain West, the Far West of the Pacific coast states, the Southwest, etc. What we have not heretofore paid much attention to was a new West, the Great Desert West, thousands upon thousands of miles of sagebrush and thin grass, of alkaline soil or rock and sand. Desert America had been conceived of negatively—the last and most terrible obstacle before the golden coast; the graveyard of innumerable oxen and substantial numbers of emigrants.

Now it began to be perceived positively. It was not, as it appeared, a scene of desolation; it was an environment with a life of its own, hidden, intermittent, fragile, beautiful. The clear, dry air, the changing colors, and, when water was conveyed to it, its astonishing fertility were remarked upon. Seeds dormant since the glacial age burst into abundant life when watered. Idealists, dreamers, journalists, land speculators joined forces, albeit unwittingly, to transform the public's notion of the desert. To those reformers who believed that the nation's only hope lay in a strong national government working to develop the nation's resources in a democratic spirit for the benefit of all the people, the desert, with its promise of fertility through irrigation, seemed the perfect opportunity for such intervention. A leader among desert reformers was William E. Smythe, who lapsed into poetic rhapsodies at the prospect.

> *The Nation reaches its hand into the Desert*
> And lo: private monopoly in water and in land is scourged
> from that holiest of temples,—the place where men
> labor and build their homes:
>
> • • •
>
> *The Nation reaches its hand into the Desert.*
> That which lay beyond the grasp of the Individual yields
> to the hand of Associated Man. Great is the
> Achievement,—greater the Prophecy!

Smythe was born in Worcester, Massachusetts, in 1861, the son of a prosperous shoe manufacturer. To him the desert dictated forms of "associated action," forms of cooperation which could be models for the larger society. He envisioned communal efforts that did not have to work against the grain of the competitive, individualistic society of which they were a part but in which the economic viability of the undertakings depended on democratic cooperation. Smythe believed that only so could the land be rescued from the increasing encroachments of large farming corporations, which in their ruthlessly aggrandizing spirit forced small, undercapitalized farmers off their lands. Large-scale irrigation, the building of diversion dams and canals to utilize the waters of the great rivers—the Missouri, the Columbia, the Snake, the Colorado, the Yellowstone, the Platte, the Humboldt, all of which passed, in one region or another, through "arid" lands—was an undertaking beyond the capabilities of the great financial houses of Wall Street (and even if it were not, it must be protected from them). "The inspiring thing," Smythe wrote in the introduction of his testament, *The Conquest of Arid America*, "is that a point has been reached when the real builders of the world—the men who clear the brush, level the land, plow, plant, cultivate, and reap—can help in a practical way, because their speeches and books and proclamations are written on the face of the imperishable earth." If the national irrigation movement succeeded, "no imagination can set bounds to the achievement upon which we have entered nor picture the civilization which will arise in the waste places of the West."

In Smythe's words, "The first great law which irrigation lays down is this: There shall be no monopoly of land. This edict it enforces by the remorseless operation of its own economy. . . . A large farm under irrigation is a misfortune; a great farm, a calamity. Only the small farm pays. But this small farm blesses its proprietors with industrial independence and crowns him with social equality. That is democracy. . . . This is the miracle of irrigation on its industrial side." The limit of irrigated land per farmer was between twenty and forty acres. More could not be successfully cultivated. Thus "each four or five thousand acres of cultivated land will sustain a thrifty and beautiful hamlet, where all the people may live close together and enjoy most of the social and educational advantages within the reach of the best eastern town. . . . The great cities of the western valleys will not be cities in the old sense, but a long series of beautiful villages, connected by lines of electric motors. . . ." The models and exemplars of the new arid land agriculture were, not surprisingly, the Mormons. They proved that it could be done. In Smythe's words, "the man who wants to win an independence from the soil will accomplish more with a given investment of capital, energy, and time in the Irrigated West than anywhere else in the world. . . ."

In 1891 Smythe organized the National Irrigation Congress in Salt Lake City and founded the journal *Irrigation Age*. He later became a leader in the Little Landers movement, helping start Little Lander colonies at San Ysidro and later at Tujunga and Hayward, California, preaching the doctrine of the "New Earth," a respect for the land, and small-scale intensive agriculture.

Smythe joined forces with Frederick Haynes Newell, a hydraulic engineer who had served an apprenticeship with John Wesley Powell in the latter's exploration of the Colorado. Newell, known as the Father of Irrigation in the West because of his intelligent labors as a hydraulic engineer, wrote a report to Congress, submitted in 1894, which disclosed that there were more than 52,000 farmers and ranchers in the Great Desert Basin region who irrigated some 3,500,000 acres of land.

It was largely through these efforts of Newell and Smythe that the Newlands Act was passed in 1902, providing for government initiative in irrigating lands and limiting the amount of land so irrigated that could be owned by one farmer-rancher to forty acres.

Ray Stannard Baker, seeking to restore his health in Arizona, was infatuated with the "Desert . . . as a reality and as a symbol." He decided to write about "what could be done by bringing in the water to these desert wastes." Near Phoenix he saw this "marvel": on the one side land, "dry from the beginning of time; on the other a field of green alfalfa, luxuriant beyond belief, deeper than a man's thigh. . . . The great field . . . seemed to stretch for miles, the vivid green of it comforting and blessing one's weary eyes. It seemed a vision of infinite peace; the culmination of contentment after years of labor and of struggle." Tears came to his eyes.

But Smythe's (and Baker's) dreams of irrigated cooperative communities came, in the end, to nothing. In the words of Ida Tarbell, "every unsound and dishonest exhibit in the use of capital, common in the country, manifests itself in . . . irrigation schemes." Many settlers found that the contracts which they had understood to guarantee them water were written in such a way as to exempt the developers from any obligation to provide it. Some developers, having persuaded settlers to put up substantial sums of money and, frequently, to borrow heavily to buy land and secure access to water, foreclosed the mortgages and seized whatever modest improvements had been made on the land when water was unavailable and settlers could not repay their loans. In those states where access to water was essential to farming or ranching, efforts were made by the state legislatures to introduce some principle of order and equity into the picture. The most successful legislation was probably that of Wyoming. That state established a rule of thumb to gauge the amount of water needed to irrigate an acre of land, set guidelines for determining who had rights to what amounts of water, and appointed officials to supervise its proper distribution.

"Arid America," Joaquin Miller, who had been caught up by Smythe's dream, exclaimed, "we have watered it with our tears!"

In addition to the real West of corn and wheat, farms, cattle and sheep, and silver and gold, there was the West of romance and illusion; Fantasy West. Fantasy West was the West that existed in the imaginations of Easterners and tourists.

The man who helped create Fantasy West and constantly nourished it was a flamboyant buffalo hunter and Indian scout named Will Cody, otherwise known as Buffalo Bill. Fifty biographies were written about him, translated into a dozen languages. It has been estimated that 1,700 issues of pulp magazines were devoted to largely fictional accounts of his adventures. Perhaps his greatest achievement was the killing of more than 4,000 buffalo in eight months for the crews of the Kansas Pacific Railroad.

Beginning his theatrical career under the auspices of E. Z. C. Judson, better known as Ned Buntline, author of mountains of pulp fiction, Cody began acting in vapid "western" dramas written by Buntline. For a time another famous Bill, Wild Bill Hickok, was part of the act, but he grew bored with his roles and returned to the West, where he could shoot real people.

Taking off time from his acting career in 1876, Cody joined Colonel Merritt in a campaign against the Cheyenne and killed the chief Yellow Hand, adding considerably to his box-office appeal. In 1883 he and Buntline hit on the idea of a complete "Wild West" show, with cowboys, Indians, bucking broncos, trick shooting, the works. Launched at the Omaha fairground, it drew 25,000 spectators. The next step was a tour, and the *Hartford* (Connecticut) *Courant* expressed a common sentiment when it called Cody's production "the best open-air show ever seen."

Annie Oakley, "Little Sure Shot," joined the show in its second

year and immediately became a star in her own right, trouping for
seventeen years. Her accuracy in shooting a card out of her husband's
mouth gave her name to a punched, i.e., complimentary, ticket. By the
end of 1885, 1,000,000 spectators had seen the show. When the company sailed for its first British tour and a command performance for
Queen Victoria, it was made up of more than 200 performers, 180
horses, 18 buffalo, and 10 mules, as well as miscellaneous elk and deer.

Two years later, when Buffalo Bill and his troupe spent seven
months in Paris, Rosa Bonheur devoted long hours to painting horses
and buffalo as well as doing a famous portrait of the "Colonel." When
his horse died, Cody had the head stuffed and sent it to her. It still
hangs in her studio.

Yellowstone Park was established as the first national park in 1872
(Buffalo Bill built his ranch house near the entrance to the park), and
soon the park was a mecca for tourists, foreign and domestic. Colorado,
with its soaring peaks and spectacular scenery, was the tourists' favorite
state, and Estes Park rivaled Colorado Springs (called Little England
because of the English who settled there) as an attraction. An early
tourist—certainly the most colorful—to reach Estes Park was Isabella
Lucy Bird Bishop, that indefatigable world traveler, whose account of
her first trip to the United States in 1855 is so illuminating. She made
her way there with considerable difficulty in 1873, wearing a dashing
wide-brimmed hat, "Turkish" trousers, and boots. From Greeley, the
utopian temperance colony promoted by Horace, she went by freight
car to Fort Collins, noting in passing that "these new settlements are
altogether revolting, entirely utilitarian, given up to talk of dollars as
well as making them, with coarse speech, coarse food, coarse everything." Arriving finally at Estes Park, she met the notorious Jim Nugent, an Englishman by birth, Mountain Jim he was called, "a broad,
thickset man, about middle height, with an old cap on his head, and
wearing a grey hunting-suit much the worse for wear (almost falling
to pieces, in fact), a digger's scarf knotted about his waist, a knife in
his belt and 'a bosom friend,' a revolver, sticking out of the breast-
pocket of his coat; his feet, which were very small, were bare, except
for some dilapidated moccasins made of horse hide." He had a bristly
mustache and an "imperial," a goatee. One eye was gone. " 'Desper-
ado,' " she noted, "was written in large letters all over him." He had
lost his eye in an encounter with a grizzly and her cubs. Nugent became
her devoted guide and regaled Isabella with mountain lore. She had,
he told her, been preceded in her plan to scale Longs Peak by Anna

Dickinson, the famous abolitionist lecturer. Isabella and Jim made a climb together; Jim sang to her; they discovered a common interest in spiritualism, concluded they had "an affinity," and planned to meet later in the spirit world. Clearly they were in love. "I put it away as egregious vanity," Isabella wrote a friend, "unpardonable in a woman of forty." She wrote again: "I changed my horse for his beautiful mare, and we galloped and in the beautiful twilight, in the intoxicating frosty air. . . . Mr. Nugent is what is called 'splendid company.' Ruffianly as he looks, the first words he speaks—to a woman at least—place him on a level with educated gentlemen. . . . Shall I ever get away?" She escaped to more adventures, to the Continental Divide and South Park, leaving her heart with Mountain Jim. In a few weeks she was back. She found a repentant Nugent, whose better nature she had stirred and whose sins suddenly weighed unbearably on him. "My heart dissolved in pity for him," she wrote a friend, "and his dark lost self-ruined life. He is so lovable and fascinating and yet so terrible. I told him I could not speak to him, I was so nervous, and he said if I could not speak to him he would not see me again."

So they parted, after further unhappy sessions. Jim was shot by a jealous neighbor, and Isabella wrote another marvelous book about her experiences, *A Lady's Life in the Rocky Mountains*, a best seller that helped draw attention and, in time, millions of other tourists to Estes Park, none of whom, it seems safe to say, had an experience quite as exotic as Isabella Lucy Bird's.

Undoubtedly the most famous Western tourist (he would have resented the term) was a wealthy aristocratic young New Yorker, Theodore Roosevelt. Recently elected a New York state assemblyman, he met a naval officer named Henry Honeychurch Gorringe who owned a ranch in the Dakota Territory. Roosevelt wanted to shoot a buffalo. Gorringe assured him that they were still plentiful near his ranch and offered the use of it. Roosevelt arrived at Medora in the fall of 1883, equipped by Abercrombie & Fitch and loaded for buffalo. After weeks of fruitless hunting Roosevelt at last got his buffalo, jumped on it, and did a war dance of exuberance. Before he returned to New York, he had made plans with a "partner" to buy a ranch—the Maltese Cross—and 450 head of cattle. After the death of his mother and his wife on the same day, Valentine's Day, 1884, Roosevelt took refuge on his Dakota ranch. He hunted in the Badlands, joined in a roundup—where he astonished the cowboys by calling out, "Hasten forward quickly there," instead of "Head off them cattle!"—and even got into a saloon brawl when a drunken sheepherder taunted him as "four-eyes" and demanded that he set up drinks for the crowd. As one would expect of a future president of the United States, he knocked his tormentor cold. Or at least that was the way the story was told. This time he added another ranch, the Elkhorn, to the Maltese Cross and bought 1,000 cattle.

One consequence was a book, *Hunting Trips of a Ranchman*, the first of a series that would culminate in *The Winning of the West*. After a fall and winter of politics Roosevelt was back the next summer, no longer a dude but a rancher. A cowboy said of him, "He was not a purty rider, but he was a hell of a good rider." Roosevelt collected a band of cowboys and joined in the spring roundup at the juncture of Box Elder Creek and the Little Missouri. Increasingly he saw his future as that of a rancher. To him there was no life "more attractive to a vigorous young fellow than life on a cattle ranch. . . . It was a fine, healthy life, too; it taught a man self-reliance, hardihood, and the value of instant decision. . . . I enjoyed the life to the full."

Roosevelt even tracked down three thieves who stole a boat of his on the Little Missouri, captured them, and turned them over to the justice of the peace, a trek of almost 200 miles. But his future clearly lay elsewhere. He returned to New York, married a childhood friend, Edith Kermit Carow, and ran for mayor against Henry George and Abram Hewitt. The *Sioux Falls Press* took note of his campaign in words he treasured: "Theodore is a Dakota cowboy and has spent a large share of his time in the Territory for a couple of years. . . . When he first went on the range, the cowboys took him for a dude, but soon they realized the stuff of which the youngster was built."

Roosevelt's withdrawal from ranching was hastened by the terrible winter of 1886–1887, while he was on a delayed honeymoon in Europe with Edith. When his foreman rode over the range in March, he could find no live cattle. Roosevelt lost more than $60,000 in the destruction of his herd, but he had begun a romance which would last as long as his life. Campaigning for the vice-presidency in 1900, he traveled to Medora and told his audience of cattle hands and railroad men: "The romance of my life began here."

There was clearly a galaxy of Western "types," who ranged from the amoralists and free lovers of Kansas to the freebooters of Mariposa and Crippled Creek. William Smythe gave his own highly romanticized description of the Western and Eastern "temperaments": "The man with the Western temperament loves the unbuilt house and the virgin soil—the vast resources awaiting the conquest of human genius and human labor. He wants to live in a land where things are being done. . . . He wants to have a part in doing them,—wants to build the house, plant the ivy, turn the rivers out of their courses, drive the desert back inch by inch, carry railroads through unheard of mountain passes, write constitutions, found cities and states."

The man with the "Eastern temperament," on the other hand, "prefers his civilization ready-made. He loves the old home, the old familiar names and streets, the old associations. He loves the ivy, too, but wants to know that it was planted by his great-grand-father. . . . When this man gets West he is homesick. But his brother of the Western temperament works with fierce joy. He is worth ten times as much to himself and to society as he would have been if he had always remained on his native heath." If that sounded a bit severe, Smythe proved ready to accept many of his Eastern friends as honorary Westerners. All that was necessary was that, like Theodore Roosevelt, they adored the West. They didn't have to live there.

When he considered the men of the Pacific coast, Smythe waxed lyrical. "They were men of the Forward Look. They are clearing the intellectual forests, rooting up the social sage-brush, irrigating the arid wastes of politics and economics. Ah, what a harvest they are preparing for the future—the David Starr Jordans, the Benjamin Ide Wheelers, the George A. Gateses, and the rest of the big-brained, big-hearted brood who are training the rising generation in the bright sunshine of the Pacific Coast!"

Ray Stannard Baker felt divided loyalties. He was a Westerner, the son of pioneers, who had gone East. His father, a failure "as a merchant and as a small manufacturer . . . had lost his health and all his money." He had gone to the frontier "and there," Baker wrote, "he found great and satisfying work, as satisfying spiritually as it was materially. . . . For it seemed to him quite the greatest thing in the world to clear away the forests, root out the stumps and build roads, churches, schools, houses, for the eager people who were to come crowding in. . . . He seemed to me always a strong, sure man, self-directed, united within himself, and therefore a contented man. . . . What a different world I knew from that of my ancestors! They had the wilderness, I had the crowds. I found teeming, jostling, restless cities; I found immense smoking, roaring industries; I found a labyrinth of tangled communications. I found hugeness and disorder. I found after the clean forests and the open plains, confusion and dirt and poverty and crime. I found dishonest politics and greedy business men." While there had been evil on the frontier, "it was not concentrated and complex and overpowering." On the frontier was backbreaking, soul-destroying hardship, cruelty, and suffering in abundance. There was perpetual warfare with the Indians and sometimes terrible torture and death. It was not that life in the city was more arduous; it was, in fact, filled with creature comforts to a degree unimaginable on the frontier, and "work" was, at least for the middle and upper classes, far, far easier than work on the frontier. But it was the complexity of life in the city that was so confounding, that sent city dwellers fleeing to a tamed and domesticated West with splendid sunsets, vast, pellucid skies, snow-topped mountains, and endless ranges, where deserts without thirst and mountains without the desperate travail of traversing them were balm to the weary spirits of city dwellers. It seemed to Baker, as he thought about the frontier and the city, that "the supreme problem confronting mankind was the art of living in a crowded world." He decided that his best contribution to that problem as a writer was to become a "maker of understandings" so people might learn to live reasonably happily in a world too full of others. He decided to write a novel on the theme: "the Art of Living in a Crowded World." It occurred to Baker that John Muir might have the secret. He sought him out at his Contra Costa home, a vigorous sixty-three, "a wiry man, all muscles and sinew. . . ." Like Joel Chandler Harris, Muir was "all of one piece," one of those "possessed men, sure men, inwardly united, men who expend themselves fearlessly and utterly in some great cause, great exploration, great art." Baker went hiking with Muir in the hills around his Contra Costa home and became acquainted with Muir's animal friends—beavers and elk and deer, squirrels and marmots. Earlier Emerson had traveled to California and met Muir. It was a historic encounter—the aged prophet of nature and the younger man who had actually lived the life of which Emerson had written. Emerson declared Muir "the Sequoia of the human race." A man who turns to nature, Muir had declared, "must be humble and patient and give his life for light; he must not try to force nature to reveal her secrets, saying proudly, 'I am a great man! Trot out your wonders: I am in a hurry.' "

We are well aware of the invincible hatred of the North that the South clutched to its collective bosom; we are perhaps less aware of the mutual hostility of the West for the East, primarily the Northeast (the West felt itself in many ways in rapport with the South—both were essentially agricultural; both were exploited colonies of Wall Street). Theodore Roosevelt wrote to Henry Cabot Lodge on August 19, 1896: "The hatred of the East among many Westerners, and the crude ignorance of even elementary finance among such a multitude of well meaning, but puzzle-headed, voters, give cause for serious alarm throughout this campaign." For his part, William Graham Sumner believed that the West was a serious threat to the Republic. He deplored "the position and power of the Rocky Mountain states, which," he wrote in 1896, "are certainly as foreign to democracy as anything can possibly be."

William James's impressions were more mundane (he arrived in time for the San Francisco earthquake). He was surprised to find "servants almost unattainable (most of the house-work being done by students who come in at odd hours), many of them Japanese, and the professors' wives, I fear, having in great measure to do their own cooking." In James's opinion, Stanford's "geographical environment and material basis being unique," the university authorities "ought to aim at unique quality all through. . . . They might, I think, thus easily build up something very distinguished. . . ." by offering large stipends to well-known scholars. Instead, they seemed content to hire untried low-paid young academics, "whose wives get worn out with domestic drudgery. The whole thing *might* be Utopian," James added, "but it is only half Utopian. A characteristic American affair." He lectured three times a week, to 400 students, whom he found "earnest and wholesome," albeit "rustic."

We cannot leave the West without a thought for the region's original inhabitants. Several hundred thousand aborigines were scattered about the West on millions of acres of land—reservations—to which they adapted themselves as best they could.

There was one final Indian tragedy to be enacted. Word spread in 1889 among the Plains tribes—the Cheyenne, Arapaho, Sioux, Shoshone, and dozens of other tribes—of an Indian messiah. Among the Paiute of the Nevada desert was a young Indian named Wovoka, called Jack Wilson by the rancher in Mason Valley for whom he worked. James Mooney, the anthropologist who visited Wovoka, has given us the best account of the nature of what came to be called the Ghost Dance religion. The Indian messiah, an avowed Christian, declared that he had been taken up into heaven and had there received a revelation from God or the Great Spirit, informing him of an imminent renewal of the world, a millennial event in which most whites would be destroyed in a great flood, dead Indians would be resurrected, game would be replenished, and all tribes that followed the prescribed practices of the Ghost Dance would become immortal. As word spread of the messiah, representatives of various tribes made the long, arduous trek to Mason Valley to receive his blessing and instructions. In the Cheyenne version, Wovoka told the emissaries of that tribe: "When you get home you have to make dance. You must dance four nights and one day time. You will take a bath in the morning before you go to your homes. . . . I will give you a good cloud and give you a chance to make you feel good. I give you a good spirit, and give you all good paint." When Christ returned, "they were never die never cry, no hurt any body, do any harm for it, not to fight. Be a good behave always. It will give satisfaction in your life. . . . Do not tell the white people about this, Jesus is on the ground, he just like cloud. Every body is live again. I don't know when he will be here, may be it will be this fall or in spring. . . . There will be no sickness and return to young again. Do not refuse to work for white man or not make any trouble with them. . . ." The injunction "Do no harm to anyone" appears in all versions of the messiah's message. There was to be no warfare between the tribes and no acts of hostility against whites. Those who practiced the Ghost Dance would become invulnerable to the white man's bullets.

The millennial expectation was clearly borrowed from Christianity in an apocalyptic vision similar to that in the Revelation of St. John. Reports circulated that Wovoka was himself Christ, that he had declared that he had died for the white man (here displaying the marks of nails in his hands), that the white man had proved faithless, and that he had now returned to bring immortal life to the Indians. The Sioux in the Pine Ridge, Rosebud, and Wounded Knee reservations made their own more militant gloss on Wovoka's doctrines. They fashioned shirts of rough cloth which they assured converts to the new faith would repel soldiers' bullets.

As word of the dance, with its extreme emotionalism, spread among Indian agents and settlers, whites became increasingly alarmed. The dance was forbidden on most reservations, but the ban made the Indians only the more determined to practice it. Sitting Bull, back from exile in Canada, emerged once more as leader of the Teton Sioux. The Sioux had a host of practical grievances against the Federal government, the most serious being a sharp reduction in the food supplies guaranteed them by treaty. An effort by the Indian police to arrest Sitting Bull as a dangerous agitator resulted in a fight in which six policemen and eight Sioux, including Sitting Bull and his seventeen-year-old son, Crow Foot, were killed. General Miles, who knew him well as an adversary (Sitting Bull, like Chief Joseph, was not a chief but a medicine man), wrote of him: "His tragic fate was but the ending of a tragic life. Since the days of Pontiac, Tecumseh, and Red Jacket no Indian has had the power of drawing to him so large a following of his race and molding and wielding it against the authority of the United States, or of inspiring it with greater animosity against the white race and civilization."

The death of Sitting Bull threw the Sioux into turmoil. Fearing an attack by U.S. troops, they fled the reservation, pursued by several thousand soldiers. Surrounded at Wounded Knee, they were ordered to surrender all weapons. When they were reluctant to do so, a fight broke out. It quickly turned into a massacre as more than 300 Sioux, the majority of them women and children, were cut down.

Within two weeks the sporadic fighting that followed Wounded Knee was over, and the Sioux were back on their reservation, reassured by General Miles's restrained and tactful actions; but Wounded Knee was one more tragedy of misunderstanding to add to the long roll of such incidents. It was never shown that the followers of the Ghost Dance religion intended to attack whites. On the contrary, Wovoka had urged peace with the whites in anticipation of the millennium. The anger of the Sioux over short rations had combined with the Ghost Dance rituals to produce a highly volatile situation in which Sitting Bull's death set off a chain reaction that resulted in the massacre.

Elements of the Ghost Dance religion survived to merge, in many instances, with traditional millennial Christianity from which it had clearly been derived. During its lifetime it served to draw formerly hostile tribes together in a fashion never before achieved and thus might be said to have left a positive legacy.

North and South

We have made the point previously that the United States, besides being an often uneasy confederation of individual states—this fact most dramatically illustrated by the endlessly repeated litany about states' rights—was made up, even more emphatically, of sections: Northeast, South, and West. New England was perhaps the easiest section to define. The simplest designation was "Puritan ethic." New England was the stronghold of thrift, piety, and hard work, unwavering shrewdness, the sharp deal, wooden nutmegs, duty, moral rectitude, stiff manners, simple living and high thinking, temperance and reform in general; the land of repressed emotions, and archaic vestiges of Calvinism, literature, poetry, transcendentalism. The faint odor of decay, a certain moral mustiness clung to it; it seemed increasingly disposed to live in a glorious past.

In Boston, John Jay Chapman noted, history was ever present. You could stop the first person you met on the street and find in him "the influence of Wyclif or Samuel Adams." The spiritual life of New England had never been "luxuriant"; indeed, it was "one-sided, sad, and inexpressive in many ways." Now it seemed more pinched than ever. Boston was to Chapman a town distinguished by "a genial hum of interlocked families who had come down from colonial times with their *lares* and *penates*, ceremonies, festivals, traditions, and passwords, local oracles, stock-dignitaries, and licensed characters." So devoutly were the "gods" of New England worshiped that Chapman could recall "causing a chill that could be felt to run around a stately dinner table" by some impious remark about Hawthorne. Yet Chapman reveled in the city's hospitality and urbanity, "for life in New York is a steady fight, steady discomfort."

Henry Adams, as a Boston expatriate, was more severe. "Boston," he wrote, "horrified me. It is green with mental mould. Everyone says it, but all kick violently at anyone who tries to rub it off. It makes me sick to go around among people, as I would in a lunatic asylum, trying to say nothing for fear of an explosion."

Boston's State Street was, to be sure, second only to Wall Street as a financial center. Its interests reached across the continent. New England mills along the fall line of its rivers continued to turn out millions of yards of cotton cloth. Charles Eliot made Harvard the prototype of the "new" university, the faithful handmaid of the "new" capitalism.

Lowell, Holmes, and Higginson still dominated the literary scene, joined by their Midwestern recruit William Dean Howells. If the older, genteel tradition was clearly passing away with the appearance of a host of invaders from the Middle West and South, newcomers such as Mark Twain and George Cable were eager to settle within New England's sacred precincts. The spirit of reform so powerfully expressed in the abolitionist movement seemed on the wane. While there was no cause—education for ex-slaves, temperance, justice for the Indians, cooperative housing, rights for women, peace, the single tax, Bellamy's Nationalism, and socialism—that did not have its loyal adherents, if not its origins, in Boston, much of the old fire was gone. To Henry Demarest Lloyd, Boston was long on talk and short on action. Compared to a fever of reform activity in Chicago, the New England "capital" seemed like "an abandoned farm."

The New England character remained somewhat stiff and cramped; the moral rectitude, unbending and self-righteous (in Charles Francis Adams's opinion, "no Puritan by nature probably ever was companionable"), was much in evidence. The rest of the country might grumble about New England or deride it, but it could not be ignored. For better or worse the consciousness of Americans had been, in certain essential respects, shaped by that fierce New England will, by that redemptive passion that would not rest in its zeal for reforming the world, a passion that had its roots in the primary Reformation of the Geneva theologian John Calvin. Charles Francis Adams, Jr., recalled that both his father and his grandfather "were afflicted with the everlasting sense of work to be accomplished—'so much to do, so little done!' The terrible New England conscience implanted in men who . . . had largely outgrown Calvinistic theology."

The infatuation of Bostonians with all things British was not a trait confined to New England. It was shared by the Eastern upper class generally. It went deeper than a mere infatuation with English manners, English clothes and sports (and, of course, sports clothes), and muscular Christianity. It embraced and rested in happy bliss upon the notion of "Anglo-Saxon civilization" as the highest achievement of human beings in history, a kind of culmination of the evolutionary process. Thus, to cement good relations between the two nations was important not only in what we would call today geopolitical terms, but also in "racial" terms, as a bulwark against the barbarism of much of the rest of the world. For this task John Hay seemed to his admirers predestined. He was, to be sure, an upper-class Easterner by adoption, but that fact made him, if anything, more loyal to his new class and a faithful servant of its interests. At the onset of the war with Spain, Hay wrote urgently to his friend Henry Cabot Lodge, Senator from Massachusetts, "It is hardly too much to say that the interests of civilization are bound up in the direction the relations of England and America are to take in the next few months."

What was most alluring to Americans like Henry James and John Hay about England was that the "heaviness" of the "elder Victorians," their deadly moral earnestness which has sometimes been mistakenly called Puritanism (the Puritans were by comparison fun-loving), was being replaced by a new kind of social "play." "The spirits of the nineties were to be gregarious," Chapman wrote. The "true gift" of the British upper classes "lay in the discovery of how to enjoy life, and in this field they succeeded à merveille. . . . Self-dedication to an ideal was distinctly in the air, but the choice of a sphere was left free to all. One great lady would make very gifted drawings; another would visit the slums; a third affect ceramics; a fourth revived the needlework of Elizabethan draperies. The spirit of the game was in the air. Of course, the intermingling of the professional artists added glamor to the atmosphere. Social life became thrilling." It affected even the serious artists, expatriates like Henry James and Whistler, who "instead of plodding away before their easels and at their desks . . . were constantly talking about their art. Indeed, the spirit of play entered their studios."

Chapman "despised Americans for their social timidity and colorlessness. . . . It required years of experience and hard thinking," he wrote toward the end of his life, "for me to throw off my impressions of the English as a race of supermen, and I couldn't have done it alone." It had been his wife, Minna Timmins, who had shepherded him "through the underworld of ambition, selfishness, and savagery that lies, or used to lie, below the surface of social life in England."

The South was almost as easy as New England to sum up in a series of stereotypes or clichés, most of which mirrored reality. It was gracious living, leisure, indolence, "culture," easy, open manners, noblesse oblige (a less demanding form of duty), aristocracy, and Episcopalianism. The trouble was that those familiar clichés said nothing of the emerging class of poor whites (and some who failed to emerge) and, above all, of the presence of large numbers of black people who constituted the most basic Southern reality of all.

The South was as much a state of mind as a geographical region, perhaps more. The most conspicuous aspect of that mind (hatred of the Yankees aside) was nostalgia. Walter Hines Page, a Southerner who took refuge in the North, deplored the apparently ineradicable disposition of the Southerners to live in the past. It seemed to him that "the organization of society, of trades, of professions—of everything—[was] against improvement. . . . It is an awfully discouraging business to undertake to prove to a Mummy that it is a Mummy. You go up to it and say, 'Old Fellow, the Egyptian dynasties crumbled several thousand years ago; you are a fish out of water. . . . This is America. The Old Kings are forgotten, and this is the year 1886. . . .' " The South was such a mummy.

Page, who had gotten his Ph.D. from Johns Hopkins at the same time that Frederic Howe was a student there, tried "to free the Southern mind from its medieval theology and from the negro question." He bought a daily paper in Raleigh, North Carolina, one of the more liberal Southern cities. His paper had a substantial local following, a good portion of which Page immediately lost by ridiculing a controversy between the Presbyterians and the Baptists. He lost the rest by suggesting that the Democratic Party was not infallible. Thereupon he fled to New York and became a writer for the *Evening Post*.

George Creel recalled that in his childhood years in Independence, Missouri, Confederate "Colonels rocked on every porch, held forth in the courthouse yard on summer afternoons, delivered all the Fourth of July orations. . . . Fat colonels, lean colonels, blustery colonels, quiet colonels with faces like nicked sword blades, and swashbuckling colonels eager for a quarrel—all living in a past they refused to put behind them."

Creel's father, a planter impoverished by the war, had turned to farming to make his living, but at farming he was, in his son's words, "a flop from the beginning. Reared as a 'gentleman,' with all of its antebellum implications, he knew agriculture only from the back of a horse, and had neither training nor industry. Without slaves and an overseer to do the work, the farm proved a losing venture, and he went back to diligent drinking as an escape from his failure." A failure as a farmer, George Creel's father tried cattle raising with no more success. The next move was to Independence, Missouri, where Creel's mother kept the family going by the "dreary business" of taking in paying guests.

An essential part of the nostalgia syndrome was the myth of the "Lost Cause." One of the principal architects of the myth was Thomas Nelson Page. A fellow laborer in the vineyard was George Bagby, a physician and local colorist. His story "The Old Virginia Gentleman" was hailed by Page as "the most charming picture of American life ever drawn," and Bagby himself wrote: "In simple truth and beyond question there was in our Virginia country life a beauty, a simplicity, a purity, an uprightness, a cordial and lavish hospitality, warmth and grace which shine in the lens of memory with a charm that passes all language at my command." There was, of course, an occasional shadow: "Sorrows and cares were there—where do they not penetrate? but oh! dear God, one day in those sweet, tranquil homes outweighed a fevered lifetime in the gayest cities of the globe."

Before the war Virginia teemed with colorful life. "The young master, with his troops of little darkies, was everywhere—in the yard, playing horses; in the fields hunting larks or partridges; in the orchards, hunting for birds' nests . . . ; in the woods, twisting or smoking hares out of hollow trees. . . . 'Young Mistiss,' in her sun-bonnet, had her retinue of sable attendants, who, bare-armed and barefooted, accompanied her in her rambles through the garden. . . ." Then there was always " 'comp'ny' coming, Beaux . . . neighbors, friends, strangers, kinfolks—no end of them." Everywhere the loyal, obliging, obedient "darkies"—never "niggers"; that was white trash talk.

The interloper who had destroyed forever this circle of felicity was, of course, the Yankee. Left to themselves, Virginians, and presumably other Southerners as well, would, of course, have freed the slaves. "Let alone, the Virginian would gladly have made an end of slavery, but, strange hap! malevolence and meddling bound it up with every interest that was dear to his heart—wife, home, honor. . . ." By unlucky chance the issue of slavery was confused with "that buckler of State rights which [the Virginian] held up against the worst of tyrants— a sectional majority."

Father Abram Ryan, a Catholic priest and ex-Confederate chaplain, was one of the most effective contributors to the myth. "The Conquered Banner" became a kind of official poem of the South:

> Furl that Banner, softly, slowly!
> Treat it gently—it is holy—
>   For it droops above the dead.
> Touch it not—unfold it never,
> Let it droop there, furled forever,
>   For its people's hopes are dead!

A measure of the strength of the "Lost Cause" was the wild enthusiasm with which Southerners greeted a tour by Jefferson Davis in 1886, under the auspices of Henry Watterson, editor of the *Louisville Courier-Journal*. The response was such, one observer noted, "as no existing ruler in the world can obtain from his people."

In a book of essays entitled *The Negro: The Southerner's Problem* (1904), Thomas Nelson Page made a classic statement of the semiofficial Southern view of the war. "When the war closed," he wrote, "and the Negroes were set free, the feeling between them and their old masters was never warmer, the bonds of friendship were never more close. The devotion which the Negro had shown during the long struggle had created a profound impression on the minds of the Southern whites. . . . When the end of slavery came there was, doubtless, some heart-burning, but the transition was accomplished without an outbreak, and well-nigh without one act of harshness or even of rudeness. If there was jubilation among the Negroes on the plantation it was not known to the Whites."

To Thomas Nelson Page and other apologists for the South, it was essential to establish the fact, beyond question or dispute, that the Civil War was not fought to abolish or defend slavery. The fact was "that whatever may have been the immediate and apparent occasion, the true and ultimate cause of the action of the South was her firm and unwavering adherence to the principle of self-government and her jealous devotion to her inalienable rights. . . . Unless we possess strength sufficient to maintain [this view], the verdict of posterity will be against us," Page wrote.

Albion Tourgée commented wryly on the popularity of the "Lost Cause" literature. "A foreigner studying our current literature, without knowledge of our history, and judging our civilization by our fiction would undoubtedly conclude that the South was the seat of intellectual empire in America," he wrote, "and the African the chief romantic element of our population." In the preceding months, he noted, "every one of our great popular monthlies presented a 'Southern story' as one of its most prominent features; and during the past year nearly two-thirds of the stories and sketches furnished to newspapers by various syndicates have been of this character . . . it cannot be denied that American fiction to-day, whatever its origin, is predominately Southern in type and character" and "distinctly Confederate in sympathy."

Joel Chandler Harris, with his "red unkempt hair" and "freckled face and freckled hands," in the words of his fellow Southerner, the elegant Walter Hines Page, was the illegitimate son of an Irish workingman and a merciless critic of the pretentious. "The stuff we are in the habit of calling Southern literature," he wrote in the *Atlanta Constitution* in 1879, "is not only a burlesque upon true literary art, but a humiliation and disgrace to the people whose culture it is supposed to represent. . . . The truth might as well be told: we have no Southern literature worthy of the name."

The basic theme in all the writings of post-Civil War America was that America was a crass, materialistic society, coarse and vulgar, preoccupied with money, racked by bitter class and sectional animosities, derelict in every civic duty, indifferent to those graces and amenities which give life its principal charm. It was this brutal, blundering Yankee world that out of greed and envy, covered over with self-righteousness, had struck down the only real cultivation that the New World had produced and left in its place desolation. There was just enough truth in the picture of the postwar United States to give the myth an irresistibly romantic glow. Plainly America had lost something precious, something of great value, or at least it had failed of its highest hopes and expectations. Perhaps it was there, in the keeping of the Old Virginia gentleman or in the magnolia-scented plantations of Georgia or Louisiana, with happy black voices singing in the background.

That such a notion should have taken possession of the Southern consciousness is hardly surprising. That it should have made as easy a conquest of the imaginations of the "other Americans," the Yankees, is somewhat more of a puzzle. ("Carry Me Back to Old Virginny" was written by James Bland of Long Island, a descendant of slaves.) Perhaps the answer is to be found in the simple fact that none of us can stand much reality. In the flight from the generally grim facts of late nineteenth-century America, the ante-bellum South was a cheaper and more convenient refuge than London, Paris, or Rome. In a country starved for romance the mythologized South offered abundant services.

It seems clear enough that in the religious realm the old-time piety flourished undimmed. An English traveler, Sir William Archer, wrote: "The South is by a long way the most simply and sincerely religious country that I was ever in. . . . In other countries men are apt to make a private matter of their religion . . . ; but the Southerner wears his upon his sleeve." The revival remained an important fixture of American religious life. Sam Jones, a famous revivalist, expressed the spirit of such occasions. "When I get up to preach all I do is to KNOCK OUT THE BUNG and let nature cut her caper." The Methodists and the Baptists predominated. C. Vann Woodward notes that from 95 percent (in the Deep South) to 80 percent (in Virginia) of all Southerners belonged to those two sects, contrasted with 47 percent in the nation as a whole. In the words of the president of the University of Virginia, "The fancied home of the cavalier is the home of the nearest approach to puritanism and to the most vital protestant evangelism in the world to-day."

While Thomas Nelson Page and George Bagby lamented the lost glories of the South, spokesmen of the New South like Henry Grady and Henry Watterson called for the South to "out-Yankee the Yankee." For these Southerners "business" was the magic word. Mark Twain described them as "brisk men, energetic of movement and speech; the dollar their god, how to get it their religion." The Southern businessmen were described by a Northern journalist, A. D. Mayo, as the Third Estate of the South. "For the coming decade," Mayo wrote in 1890, "the place to watch the South is in this movement of the rising Third Estate. What it demands and what it can achieve in political, social, and industrial affairs . . . on these things will depend the fate of this important section of the country for years to come." Richard Edmonds, a Baltimore newspaper editor, announced that "the easy-going days of the South have passed away, never to return. . . . The South has learned that 'time is money.' "

J. D. B. De Bow's *Review*, revived after the war, became an ardent champion of industrialization. "*We have got to go to manufacturing to save ourselves,*" De Bow wrote. "We have got to go to it to obtain an increase of population. Workmen go to furnaces, mines, and factories—they go where labor is bought. Every new furnace or factory is the nucleus of a town. . . . Factories and works establish other factories and works."

Henry Watterson went all over the North with his crusade for Northern capital, orating wherever a handful of capitalists could be assembled. He assured the American Bankers Association at its convention in 1883 that the South was no different from any other section of the country. It would give "a guarantee of peace and order . . . and offers a sure and lasting escort to all the capital which may come to us for investment. . . . We need the money. You can make a profit off the development." The South was not a region of "lazy barbarians," but "a great body of Christian men and women, who have had a hard struggle with fate and fortune, but who have stood against the elements with fortitude that contradicts the characteristics formerly imputed to them."

Spokesmen for the South attempted to reassure Northern critics that the South was treating and intended to treat the ex-slaves fairly. Richard Edmonds, the Baltimore editor of the *Manufacturers' Record*, wrote in 1891: "The condition of the Southern Negro is one of progressive evolution from the darkness of slavery into the fullness of freedom. He is not only a man by the law of the land, but he is rising toward true manhood by the exercise of his physical and moral powers. In all history there has been no similar instance in which a ruling race has so nobly and unremittingly aided its former bondsmen to rise to the highest levels of which they were naturally capable."

The South, like the West, was tempting to foreign and Northern investors. The Louisville & Nashville Railroad was largely in foreign hands. It owned half a million acres in Alabama, and its lines connected thirty-two furnaces to iron and coal towns, with an investment of more than $30,000,000. English investors were rumored to have poured $10,000,000 into timber and mineral lands around Middlesboro, Kentucky. Northern capital was also much in evidence. Truman Aldrich and Daniel Pratt were New Englanders who became leaders in the Alabama coal and steel industries. A native Southerner, Henry Fairchild De Bardeleben, Pratt's son-in-law, owned 900 coke ovens and numerous coal and ore mines. "I was the eagle," he declared, "and I wanted to eat up all the craw-fish I could—swallow up all the little fellows, and I did it." Stunned by the Depression of 1893, De Bardeleben was eventually swallowed up by J. P. Morgan. Milton Hannibal Smith, president of the L&N for almost fifty years, created a major industrial complex in the South.

In the tobacco world, the same process of consolidation went on, accompanied by the same trumpetings of capitalist triumph. The Dukes and the Reynoldses fought for domination. "Let buffalo gore buffalo, and the pasture go to the strongest," declared the head of the Bull Durham Company. Bull Durham marketed 5,000,000 pounds of tobacco in 1883 and spent $30,000 to advertise his product on the sides of barns all over the United States.

Southern entrepreneurs, often with Northern capital, challenged New England's virtual monopoly of cotton cloth, building their own mills. Georgia, by 1880, was producing three times the admittedly modest prewar output. Mills in the South increased from 161 in 1880 to 400 in 1900; the first entirely electrified factory was built in the South. Indeed, the building of cotton mills became a matter of civic pride (as well as of enormous profits). By pushing the Northern cotton manufacturers into bankruptcy, by beating them at their own game, the South could exact a measure of revenge for its defeat in the war, for, according to the Southern mythology, it was Northern greed for Southern cotton that had been the real and efficient cause of the War Between the States.

The history of Big Lick, Virginia, was typical of the transformation of many Southern towns. It changed its name to a more dignified Roanoke and with infusions of Northern capital grew by 1892 into a substantial manufacturing town with a population of 30,000.

The New South, so tirelessly proclaimed by Henry Grady of the *Atlanta Constitution* and his black ally Booker T. Washington, was disconcertingly like the Old South. True, Atlanta became a busy, bustling, Northern-style city, a commercial and industrial center. Montgomery and Birmingham, Alabama, by virtue of coal deposits and Northern capital, became steel manufacturing towns. Cotton made a comeback.

Lumbering became an important industry. But economic progress was painfully slow and nowhere more so than on the marginal farms owned by poor whites and blacks or farmed on "shares."

With all the extravagant plans for an industrialized South and the millions upon millions invested in the region by Northern and British and even European speculators, the region remained stubbornly rural. The urban population had risen no higher than 10.3 percent in 1890, while in the North Central states it stood at 26 percent in that year and rose to more than 30 percent by the end of the century.

One of the unhappy legacies of the congressional Reconstruction was that in addition to opportunists and adventurers, many of the more liberal Southerners made a disinterested effort to cooperate with the Reconstruction governments. In doing so, they made themselves marked men; when the Reconstruction governments ended, their political careers ended with them. Whatever potential they may have had for moderate leadership was destroyed. Still, there were a few courageous spirits who dared raise their voices on behalf of the black people of the South. Lewis Harvie Blair was an outspoken advocate of black equality. It was only by granting blacks their full rights as citizens, he argued, that the South could rise after the devastation of the war. Born in Richmond in 1834, Blair belonged to a family of prominent Presbyterian ministers. One forebear held the first chair of theology at Princeton and was acting president there for two years. Blair was one of thirteen children of a charming and improvident man "of refined taste and good intelligence" who loved to play the flute. He had served in the Confederate army; in his words, "more than three years wasted in the vain effort to maintain that most monstrous institution, African slavery, the real tho' States Rights were the ostensible cause of the War." Blair wrote *The Prosperity of the South Dependent upon the Elevation of the Negro*, published in 1889, arguing that only integrated schools could achieve that goal. A student of Adam Smith and Herbert Spencer, Blair had been disappointed in his hopes of seeing a new South rise from the ashes of the old. "Instead of beholding the glorious South of my imagination," he wrote more than a decade after the end of the war, "I see her sons poorer than when war ceased his ravages, weaker than when rehabilitated with her original rights, and with the bitter memories of the past smoldering, if not rankling, in the bosoms of many." Father of twelve children, Blair found himself increasingly isolated by his conviction that the poverty and backwardness of the

South were the consequence of the repression of a major portion of the population—its black citizens. He argued that only integrated education could serve both races fairly and overcome the forces of prejudice. "The Negro must be allowed free access to all hotels and other places of public entertainment; he must be allowed free admittance to all theatres and other places of public amusement; he must be allowed free entrance to all churches. . . . In all these things and in all these places he must, unless we wish to clip his hope and crush his self-respect, be treated precisely like the white, no better but no worse." The South could not afford to maintain separate schools for white children and black. Segregated schools were the certain mode of dooming to perpetual ignorance both whites and blacks in thinly settled sections.

There was, finally, no rational basis for the racial attitudes of the South. "We can't defend color for a moment," Blair wrote toward the end of his treatise, "unless we contend for segregating every small portion of the human family, and decide in favor of reverting the civilized world to its original savage and barbaric elements, for 'color,' if carried out, leads logically and inevitably to this. . . . We can no more defend our attitude towards the Negroes than could the Algerian corsairs defend their attitude towards the Christian world; than can despots defend their attitude towards their subjects. . . ."

To Lewis Blair, the Northern merchants and manufacturers who through high tariffs ruthlessly exploited the agricultural states, among them the states of the South, were "blind to every consideration of justice and equity." They used "the legislative machinery of a common country to serve their own selfish ends."

George Cable, the writer and friend of Mark Twain, was a native of New Orleans. He shared Lewis Blair's conviction that integration of blacks and whites was the only solution to the problems of the South. He believed that "the day must come when the black race must share and enjoy in common with the white the whole scale of *public* rights and advantages provided under American government." In short stories and newspaper articles he supported the integration of schools. When he wrote an article for the *New Orleans Bulletin* arguing the case for integrated schools, the indignant editor wrote a detailed refutation, stating the orthodox view: "The only condition under which the two races can co-exist peacefully is that in which the superior race shall control and the inferior race shall obey. . . . African proclivities are towards savagery and cannibalism. . . . For our part we hope never to see the white boys and girls of America forgetful of the fact that negroes are their inferiors."

But voices like those of Lewis Blair and, in the Deep South, George Cable were increasingly rare, and those who dared speak out paid a heavy penalty in public hostility. Americans, as we have had occasion to note from time to time, have such a disposition to an optimistic and "progressive" view of history that it often comes as a surprise to find how often they have regressed rather than progressed. The persistent question is, of course: Why regression? First, there was the profound substratum of fear and hostility that the mere presence of blacks had aroused in whites of all classes and castes. The dream of black insurrection haunted Jefferson. Mary Chesnut cried out its truth when she heard of her old aunt murdered in her bed. In the plantation class the fear was obscured by the image of kindly masters and loyal slaves who "loved" each other. Since love pushed its way up in the most unlikely places, since people in daily contact with each other must love or die, there was enough truth in the proposition to give it a degree of credibility. But with the poor whites, the "sandhill tackeys" and the "red-necks," there was no such amelioration. They were free to hate without dissembling. Even here there were, of course, notable exceptions. Tom Watson identified himself with the poor white farmers and sought a political alliance with black farmers. For almost ten years he fought to include blacks in the Southern farmers' movements that culminated in the Populist Party. In part, the rising tide of prejudice coincided with the passing from the political scene of old aristocracy, men like Hampton and Stephens, part of whose code of honor was to do justice to the weak and defenseless, and the rise of a new breed of politician determined to seize political power by whatever expedients lay at hand. Free blacks feared and hated the new men. Moreover, Southern blacks, like liberal Northerners, had pledged undying fealty to the Republican Party. Wade Hampton's faith that the freedmen, free of the baneful influence of Northern Republican carpetbaggers, would become loyal Democrats proved groundless. The Republican Party meant freedom to Southern blacks, and Republicans the vast majority of them would remain. Because the white South was solidly Democratic, the fact that blacks were solidly Republican made them appear as a political threat.

Finally, as we have mentioned before, the whole Darwinian scheme, with its emphasis on "evolving" life, encouraged the always seductive notion that certain races were more "advanced" in the evolutionary scale than others. As the political power of blacks eroded in the aftermath of Reconstruction, the temptation to crush it entirely proved irresistible.

What was perhaps the decisive factor was that in large part through the efforts of men like Tom Watson, the fortunes of Southern blacks became tied to the fate of the Farmers' Alliance and, subsequently, the Populists. It seems as safe as any generalization to say that if the Populists had triumphed, black Southerners would not have been systematically deprived of their rights as American citizens. The reaction against the Populists as radical ranters and, on the race issue, as "nigger lovers" prepared the way for policies that affected the poor white farmer as well as the black. The New South, the South of factories and mills and coal mines, the "Third Estate" of business-oriented South, asserted its hegemony. Politically active blacks represented a volatile and potentially unmanageable element in the electorate. If the South were to enjoy an environment favorable to business investment, it must be able to guarantee, as Henry Watterson constantly asserted, "peace and order."

Other elements were mixed in: the continued hard times; the desperate struggle for survival in rural areas which pitted race against race and raised the general level of anxiety to a point where minor incidents caused major confrontations. Included was doubtless a motive of revenge that we have taken note of earlier. The white Republicans who, in the Southern view, had degraded and humiliated them by placing blacks in positions of power and influence had departed, leaving behind them their black allies to reap the whirlwind that they had sown.

All this could not, nonetheless, have happened had it not been for the fact that the Federal courts and, most important, the Supreme Court adopted the doctrine of states' rights as the nation's official creed, placing the Constitution squarely on the side of reactionary politics and rendering the Bill of Rights nugatory as regards the citizens of particular states. Moreover, the North grew increasingly indifferent. Indeed, as more and more blacks emigrated North, the level of discrimination rose there albeit at a slower pace. In the North the zeal for reform focused, as we have seen, on municipal corruption, on reform of the monetary system, and, perhaps most strikingly, on the "evils of capitalism" and the war between capital and labor. There was, in any event, little or nothing Northerners could do except admonish the South for its wicked ways.

The "damn Yankee" syndrome in the South certainly had its Northern counterpart: periodic denunciations, usually for political purposes, of the Southern "traitors" and "rebels." Whitelaw Reid, who had tried and failed in his own agricultural venture in the South, wrote in 1880: "To us the principles to which they [the Southerners] cling are heresies not to be entertained after such bloody refutation as they have had . . . no facts, no statistics, no arguments, can make them comprehend that the Northern masses are their superiors intellectually, physically, numerically, and financially."

Poverty, disappointment, and bitter frustration were the root facts of the postwar South. In his survey of the South in *The Souls of Black Folk*—of farms run like factories by Northern investors, of black counties and an occasional tough survivor of the old order—W. E. B. Du Bois gives dozens of unforgettable vignettes like that of the silent mansion of the Thompsons, who, ruined by the falling cotton prices of the eighties, simply "packed up and stole away." In another grove, "with unkempt lawn, great magnolias, and grass-grown paths," the "Big House stands in half-ruin, its great front door staring blankly at the street, and the back part grotesquely restored for its black tenant. A shabby, well-built Negro, he is unlucky and irresolute. He digs hard to pay rent to the white girl who owns the remnant of the place. She married a policeman, and lives in Savannah."

On another deserted plantation "an old ragged black man" told Du Bois the tale of "the Wizard of the North—the Capitalist—" who "had rushed down in the seventies to woo this coy dark soil. He bought square miles or more, and for a time the field-hands sang, the gins groaned, and the mills buzzed." Then the agent embezzled the funds, and the corporation that owned the land closed its business and abandoned the houses and machinery to rot and rust. The Waters-Loring plantation stood "like some gaunt rebuke to a scarred land."

To many Southerners, black and white alike, the issue was simply survival. Sidney Lanier, the poet, wrote to his brother: "Perhaps you know that with us of the younger generation of the South pretty much the whole of life has been merely not-dying."

41

Sports

If Americans in the period from the earliest settlements to the Civil War had been almost obsessively concerned with the state of their souls, they now became obsessed with their bodies. Foreign travelers had frequently commented on the sallow and unhealthy appearance of American males, notably businessmen and those who earned their living by sedentary pursuits. American "nerves" were, it was generally agreed, deplorable. Americans smoked like chimneys and drank like fish. They ate indigestible food soaked in fat; they lived too fast and died too young. With their lamentable habits, it did indeed seem as if their much-abused bodies were little more than the fragile envelopes of their souls. Charles Francis Adams, Jr., took his father to task many years after the latter's death for failing to teach him as a child how to skate or sail or swim. He wrote of his father: "Sports and games he held in horror; almost as much as for young men just out of college he held Europe in horror. . . . " Henry Adams recalled that in his youth "sport as a pursuit was unknown."

We have seen the ecstasy with which the younger Charles Francis discovered his physical self as a cavalry officer, not simply enduring but actually reveling in the hardships of military campaigning. Undoubtedly, for many young men of Adams's antecedents, the physical arduousness of the war came as something akin to a revelation. Sidney George Fisher, talking with furloughed officers, reported that "they like the adventure of novelty, the manly exercises & the companionship and soon get used to the privations & hardships of the camp & the march. A good result of the war," he added, "will be the formation of a taste for active & athletic pursuits, in which our young men are deficient, and the development of courage, temperance & the spirit of submission to just authority and of self-sacrifice."

Christian theologians began to speak of the "resurrection of the body" as having an immediate, this-worldly dimension. The body was a gift of God. To abuse it, they declared, was a form of blasphemy. Muscular Christianity found a home in the private college preparatory schools of New England and in the Young Men's Christian Associations. Frances Willard praised the founder of the Indian College at Carlisle, Pennsylvania, Richard Henry Pratt, as having "the root of the matter in him as a muscular Christian of the nineteenth century." Reformers and radicals generally, people like Stephen Pearl Andrews and Victoria Woodhull, began to talk insistently, even stridently, about the body. Feminists insisted that wives had rights to their own bodies that husbands could not violate. A major preoccupation of the free love movement was "the body." Victoria Woodhull in her essay "The Human Body the Temple of God" gave the most striking interpretation of the Bible as a metaphor for the body. Josiah Strong in his immensely popular book *The New Era*, published in 1893, declared: "The race can never be perfected until there is a much greater respect for the human body. Many who do not lack self-respect," he stated, "hold their bodies, or at least the laws which govern them, almost in contempt." Sounding rather like Victoria Woodhull, Strong wrote: "Ever since Christ dignified our human nature by assuming it, man's body has been the temple of God. Surely we cannot honor God by dishonoring his temple. . . . Yet multitudes who would shudder at the thought of committing sacrilege do not hesitate to desecrate this temple of the living God."

Florence Harriman believed it was "English influence" that made upper-class Americans so sports mad. "All New York aped the English. . . . New York society men, especially sportsmen, were slaves to the Prince of Wales to the last button on his coat." Americans reveled in British country life and, "having found it the most delightful existence in the world, decided to fashion their own upon it. . . . The flamboyant New Yorkers of the eighties, the bankers and the empire-minded railroad owners who were the economic power behind the new leisure class, looked for their fashion to England. And Britain gave them sports." In the 1880s Florence Harriman's father brought one of the first tennis sets from England to Irvington, New York, where the locals thought the nets were to catch birds. He built a wooden court on his lawn, and since there were so few tennis players, he had his English footman taught tennis so he could make a fourth for doubles in an emergency.

James Gordon Bennett imported polo from England, and it, too, like tennis and, a little later, golf, became all the rage. The Hurlingham team from England came to play at Newport and sold their ponies to take better Texas and Mexican ponies home with them. When women, Florence Harriman among them, sailed catboat races off Newport, no one thought of it as a new frontier in women's rights, but it nonetheless marked a substantial change in the status of upper-class women.

The first golf links at Newport were laid out in 1893 amid jokes about the fact that it took "whole cow-pastures to play it in" and that it was best suited for sedentary millionaires who hit balls "no larger than a parrot's egg."

In New York City the Coaching Club, founded in 1876, held annual meets. Some fifteen coaches would assemble at the Brunswick Hotel on Twenty-sixth Street and drive through Central Park. "The prettiest women in town, in crisp summer gowns and leghorn hats, with bouquets of cornflowers, daisies or buttercups, flowers to match the racing colors of the host, sat atop the coaches. The men," Florence Harriman wrote, "wore the Coaching Club uniforms, green coats with gray top hats and boutonnieres. Harlequin couldn't have designed a giddier and more delightful show as they dashed along. . . . "

Duck hunting was another upper-class vogue. John Hay was an avid duck hunter, and he wrote Adams from a hunting preserve in Ohio: "There are two or three old men from 80 to 90 . . . in whom every passion, lust, avarice, appetite and thirst, are all gone, and nothing is left but the inextinguishable love of killing ducks. They get up at daybreak and shoot until it is so dark they cannot see their last duck fall, and then limp in to supper groaning and whimpering, and nodding with sleep."

Even Henry Adams, city born and bred, went off with John Hay on a camping expedition to the Yellowstone. Hay found himself involved in buying elaborate camping equipment—guns and fishing tackle, reels and flies. From the Grand Canyon Hotel in Yellowstone

Park, Hay wrote his wife that he had never spent "a day so stuffed full of natural beauty and grandeur." They had made their way to that part of the canyon "which is called by the idiotic name of 'Inspiration Point.' . . . " A party of women tourists arrived with guides who had to hold onto them to prevent them from blowing away; two of their hats "went sailing down into the chasm a thousand feet below." The Depression of 1893 had emptied the hotels, and they were "in the depth of woe." At the "Mud Volcano" Hay and Adams saw "the most hideous and dreadful sight." Hay wrote: "We heard it grumbling and coughing. . . . To think that for ages and ages that hideous throat is expectorating that red sea of mud every other second." In two months the friends covered 500 miles on horseback "through trackless wilderness," dined "mostly on fish and game of our own purveying . . . and felt as remote and friendless as Grover Cleveland in Washington."

"The fun of these expeditions is the togs you bring," Chapman wrote to his wife from an Adirondack retreat. "Every man has two guns—patent shoes—peculiar gaiters, tarpaulins—caps—of arctic types—overcoats—undercoats—cartridge belts." One of Chapman's fellow campers was "loaded like a caravan to cross the Desert" with "eight waistcoats and sweaters and straps all over him."

The greatest sports craze of the era was bicycling. "At past fifty," Charles Francis Adams, Jr., wrote, he "solemnly and painfully learned to ride the bicycle." His brothers did the same. By 1882 it was estimated that there were 20,000 bicycles in the United States. Eight years later there were more than 100,000. In 1880 the League of American Wheelmen was formed in Newport, Rhode Island, by several thousand cyclists who had gathered there on Decoration Day. Four years later so many bicyclists attended a rally on the Boston Common that the cycling events that were scheduled had to be canceled. A cycling school in New York taught businessmen to ride, and a bold spirit named Thomas Stevens started off from Boston to pedal around the world on his high-wheeled vehicle. He crossed Europe, transfixing hundreds of thousands who observed his progress; pedaled through the Middle East, stopping to visit with the shah of Persia; and arrived in California in 1887, a national hero. Meantime, among less venturesome cyclists, casualties rose astronomically.

The most important innovation in cycling, as it turned out, was one introduced for the benefit of women cyclists, who hesitated, in their voluminous skirts, to rise so high above the earth. The safety bicycle had wheels of equal size and could be readily mounted by ladies without permanently compromising their character. Soon there were velodromes for races—the racers were called scorchers and much admired by small boys; they were employed by bicycle manufacturers to ride and plug their products. Next came the so-called six-day bicycle race, where cyclists tried to complete as many laps as possible in a six-day period. It was estimated that in 1902, $30,000,000 was spent on the sport by Americans, making it one of the country's major industries.

Close on the wheels of the cyclists came the roller skaters, who tooled around hardwood floors to the strains of calliopes. At the height of the roller skating mania, it was estimated that $20,000,000 had been invested in rinks.

In popular sports, baseball was unchallenged. The National Association of Baseball Players had been founded in 1858. At the beginning of the war the Brooklyn Excelsiors toured through the Middle Atlantic states, playing before as many as 15,000 spectators. Newspapers added sports sections to their daily offerings, and one newspaper noted: "Now men travel to great boxing contests on vestibule limited trains. . . . If they choose to stay home . . . they have the news relayed to them instantly by reporters sending their dispatches across the great wastelands via cable. Truly this is the age of electronic miracles."

In Washington, a team was formed with men who held nominal government jobs in order to be free to play baseball full time. They all wore uniforms of the same color and design and were accompanied by a band and a squad of Zouaves. One of the players wrote: "When we arrived in different towns we were always greeted by the mayor and by at least three brass bands. There were welcome signs everywhere. One English journalist covering our tour asked us, 'Why can't you be moderate in anything? Why must you always go mad?' There was no answer. America is mad for baseball."

In 1870 a "national championship" was advertised between the Brooklyn Atlantics and the Cincinnati Red Stockings. The result was "Atlantic eight; Cincinnati seven. The finest baseball game ever played," the enthusiastic president of the Red Stockings wired home. Starting as an amateur sport, with frequent payments under the table for stars, baseball moved swiftly and irresistibly toward professionalism. *The Lakeside Monthly*, which denounced the Red Stockings as a band of "shiftless young men, debasing a fine game with their open greed," admitted that more and more teams paid their players.

When the Red Stockings played sixty-six games without a defeat from Boston to St. Louis and San Francisco, it was clear that no team could match them without paying its players. Pitchers at first pitched underhand and were required to throw the ball until the batter hit it. To speed up the game, the hitters were allowed only three strikes, the pitchers four balls. In 1875 a Harvard player donned a mask to protect his face when he caught the pitcher's throws, and soon players were wearing gloves on both hands to protect them from hard-hit and hard-thrown balls. In 1876 a code of rules governing both the players on the field and, even more important, the rowdyism of the spectators, who were commonly drunk and disorderly during the games, was adopted by all the major teams. The National League was born and promptly gave evidence that baseball had come of age by producing a scandal when it was revealed that the Louisville Grays had accepted bribes to lose critical ball games to the Hartford Blues.

Black athletes suffered from discrimination in sports as they did in every other aspect of American life. In professional baseball, Moses Fleetwood Walker was the first famous black player. He was followed by his brother, Welday Wilberforce Walker. Some twenty black players were active in big league baseball in 1884, including George Stovey, a pitcher for the New York Giants. The owner of the Chicago team of the National League announced in that year that his team would not play against any team fielding black players. The other teams capitulated, and that marked the end of black players in professional baseball. They formed their own leagues and produced some of the greatest players of the era, prominent among them Cyclone Joe Williams, a Texan. The great Walter Johnson, the most famous pitcher of his age, wrote of Williams: "If his hair wasn't curly and his skin too bronze, this fellow Williams would be the very best there is. He was everlastingly breaking off a curve around a batter's knees. He works deliberately and never gets himself excited. It is a shame that these fine fellows and excellent athletes do not get a chance to show their wares in the same competition as the rest of us."

In the late 1880s and early 1890s the greatest jockey in the country was a black rider named Isaac Murphy who rode three Kentucky Derby winners, a mark that was not equaled for forty years and beaten by Eddie Arcaro only in 1950. In 1884 Murphy won the Derby on a horse trained by a black man, William Bird. William Simms, another famous black jockey, was the first American to win a horse race in England. Jim Winkfield won the Kentucky Derby in 1902. Thereafter there were few black jockeys.

It was against a background of growing popular obsession with sports that collegiate and then intercollegiate sports burgeoned. Competition in swimming and running was already common. In 1869 Princeton and Rutgers met in an improvised game that was a mixture of soccer and rugby with twenty-six players to a side. The team that first kicked six goals was to be the winner. Players could kick the ball and throw it, but they could not run with it. Five years later Harvard and McGill allowed players to run with the ball, more in the fashion of rugby. But the most decisive changes in the game came with the appearance on the scene of a Yale student named Walter Camp. Camp was a natural athlete who made the development of football his principal avocation. In 1878 at a convention held at Springfield, Massachusetts, Camp tried to impose uniform rules on a sport often played by rules determined immediately prior to a game. He proposed that each side be limited to eleven players (about the only thing that has remained constant in the evolution of the game). He also proposed that the rugby scrum be abandoned and a man designated as "a center" to pass or kick the ball backward to a "back." "If this rule is adopted," he declared, "it will guarantee possession of the ball and there will be a rapid development of stragetic plays designed to advance the ball." The next question to be solved was how long the team with the ball should retain possession. Some teams had run the ball a dozen times or more without advancing it. In a Yale-Princeton game Princeton had clung to the ball for an entire half without scoring. Camp suggested that "if on three consecutive fair tries or downs a team shall not have advanced the ball five yards, nor lost ten, [it] must give up the ball to opponents at the spot of the fourth down. When a team advances five yards, it will receive a first down and have as many tries as is required to progress the ball another five yards." Other rule changes governing scoring and kicking were made. But the rules were inadequate to modify seriously the organized mayhem that football soon became. Camp, who was a classic exemplar of muscular Christianity, insisted that the game was a splendid character builder. "When it comes to the football field," he wrote, "mind will always win over muscle and brute force. What a gentleman wants is fair play and for the best man to win. If he accepts these principles, he will find his own character greatly enriched. If your opponent takes trifling liberties with you, such as slapping your face, let all such action merely determine you to keep a close watch on the ball. . . . There is no substitute for hard work and effort beyond the call of mere duty. This is what strengthens the soul and ennobles one's character." Brutality proved more successful than gentlemanliness, and as casualty lists grew, Camp was dismayed. He proposed penalties for unsportsmanlike conduct—kicking or gouging. Woodrow Wilson, the Princeton coach, joined Camp in a fruitless campaign against the violence of the new sport, but spectators and students loved the mayhem. In nineteen years more than fifty players died of injuries received in the new sport. Outstanding players began to be recruited and paid. One man played, under various pseudonyms, at nine schools over a period of thirteen years.

James Hogan, a Yale player, was expelled when it was discovered that he had received meals and board, a $100 scholarship from the athletic department, and a nominal job as campus agent for the American Tobacco Company. Fired from Yale, he played at Pittsburgh, Allegheny, and Vanderbilt. High schools followed the lead of the colleges, and by 1899 it was estimated that there were 5,000 teams and 120,000 players. Football had become that classic of American life, "big business." It seemed to have a natural affinity for capitalism, and capitalism for it. Colleges with successful football teams drew handsome dividends in the form of benefactions from rich alumni. Champions of capitalism announced that the fiercely competitive character of football was a model of a system which stressed the survival of the fittest and divided the world into "winners" and "losers." Critics charged that the corruption, brutality, and loss of life that accompanied the spread of the game were an excellent paragon for capitalism. In Henry Kitchell Webster's novel of high finance and low morals *The Banker and the Bear* the heroine tells a male friend, "It's like a football game. If you're standing on the side lines, you aren't allowed to punch people's heads, or kick shins, but if you're running with the ball, why nobody minds if you forget to be polite." In other words, anything goes.

Even so dedicated an intellectual as Thomas Wentworth Higginson could not resist the lure of a Harvard football game on a crisp autumn afternoon. He wrote in his diary: "Nov. 22. Football game—very exciting. Harvard 22; Yale 0. When a young man attempts to kick a goal in such a game as to-day's he has 36,000 pair of eyes fastened with interest upon him. Is there any other such opportunity in life?"

"We have lost," Camp complained, "the Homeric thrill of human action, the zest of out-of-doors, the contest of speed, of strength of human intelligence, of courage. Unless steps are taken to reform the sport we shall discover that our precious football is being relegated to the ash heap of history. Brutality has no place in this sport. This is a game that must train its followers, its players and its spectators in the qualities of a successful character."

Reformers identified collegiate football as one of the aspects of American life seriously in need of reform. The dean of the Chicago Divinity School, Shailer Mathews, wrote: "Football to-day is a social obsession. . . . Football is a boy-killing, education-prostituting gladiatorial sport. It teaches virility and courage, but so does war. I do not know what should take its place, but the new game should not require the services of a physician, the maintenance of a hospital, and the celebration of funerals," and Nicholas Murray Butler, president of Columbia, denounced "this madness and slaughter."

But the butchery continued. Twelve players were killed in 1902, and the public outcry, fanned by sensational press exposés of hired players, threatened to force the abandonment of intercollegiate football entirely. At this point a longtime friend of the game intervened. Theodore Roosevelt had been too frail to play football at Harvard, but he adored the game, representing as it did to him the epitome of the strenuous, manly life (he was prone to football analogies such as "Hit the line hard!"). At this critical juncture, having recently succeeded to the presidency, he summoned athletic directors from Harvard, Yale, and Princeton to Washington and told them: "Do not report back to me until you have a game that is acceptable to the entire nation. You must act in the public interest. This glorious sport must be freed from brutality and foul play. The future of the republic is dependent on what you do. The character of future generations is in your hands."

The chastened representatives departed, and when they returned, they had a series of reforms designed to lessen the brutality of the game and lower the casualty rate (which had risen to seventy-one college, high school, and semiprofessional players in 1905). Football was saved, but whether the Republic was correspondingly strengthened or the savagery of the game substantially modified may be doubted.

It was clear to George William Curtis, who had begun his education at Brook Farm and concluded it as editor of *Harper's*, that sports had become the real purpose of the colleges. "The fact remains," he wrote in an essay entitled "Brains and Brawn," written in 1887, "that the true college hero today is the victor in games and sports, not in studies." That this was the case was "partly a reaction of feeling against the old notion that a scholar is an invalid and that a boy must be down in his muscle because he is up in his mathematics." But it did not follow from this that "because the sound mind should be lodged in a sound body . . . the care of the body should become the main, and virtually the exclusive interest of young men."

The response of undergraduate students in institutions of higher learning to football, a response far more passionate than their response to "learning," reinforced the conviction of cynical observers that whatever American colleges were *about*, scholarly and intellectual matters were unmistakably peripheral. In the tenacious survival and constant growth of collegiate and subsequently professional football, a lesson, if not a moral, may be found. Americans love violence with a disconcerting passion for a people pleased to describe themselves as "peaceful." In addition, they are highly inventive and resourceful. Walter Camp and his adherents developed a uniquely American game by a process of trial and error. Part of football's appeal came clearly from the fact that it met two profound American needs: violence and precision. It also evolved constantly in the direction of greater and greater specialization and more flagrant commercialization. It thus emerged, at last, as the ultimate American game.

In Springfield, Massachusetts, at a training school for YMCA athletic directors, James Naismith, who already instructed in boxing, wrestling, swimming, and canoeing, was asked in 1891 by his department head to devise a winter game with the fast action of football but without its brutality. His ingenious solution was a game in which opposing players tried to throw a soccer ball through a peach basket suspended high in the air at each end of a "court." In contrast with football and baseball, basketball quickly found its classic form, although it remained a relatively obscure sport for almost a generation after its invention.

In the upper class the relationship between sex and sports was clearly stated. Richard Henry Dana, Jr., wrote in his biography of his father that the elder Dana, that "cruiser" of red-light districts, has "warned me against picking up what usually amounts to misinformation on such subjects from other boys on street corners" and urged him to seek whatever knowledge he desired from him "or the family doctor if and when I needed further knowledge, and otherwise to dismiss such subjects from my mind by keeping it busy with interesting topics, whether of work or play." Much of the growing enthusiasm for sports was based on the notion that intense physical activity would moderate sexual appetites by exhausting the participants as well as by keeping them occupied for considerable periods of time. Any loss of semen by intercourse with a local strumpet or by masturbation was believed to weaken a boy dangerously on the eve of an athletic contest.

Masturbation, in addition, was depicted in lurid colors as grossly immoral, physically debilitating, and tending to produce a host of dismal side effects, including, but not limited to, insanity. Children too young to engage in organized sports were often, like the Dana children, "sent out for a short run . . . before breakfast."

In the realm of sports the new freedom that women enjoyed was dramatically represented. Kate Chopin has her heroine, Edna Pontellier, in *The Awakening*, learning to swim with a feeling of "exultation, as if some power of significant import had been given her to control the working of her body and her soul. She grew daring and reckless. . . . She wanted to swim far out, where no woman had swum before. . . . As she swam she seemed to be reaching out for the unlimited in which to lose herself."

If sports helped moderate youthful desires of the flesh, they had an equally important role in building character. Thus defeat could be even more important than victory. Young Richard Henry Dana won a place on the Harvard crew, but in a contest with Yale the Harvard oarsmen were defeated. Dana's father comforted him with the assurance that "My dear boy, it may be better for you in the end, not to have been victorious. It is a discipline to your moral character. Perhaps you may be able to thank God for some of these little disappointments and mortifications. An uniformly successful youth is not the best preparation for life." In addition, there was the fact that the Yale crew was reliably reported to be made up of "foul-mouthed blackguards," who contrasted sharply with the "self-command and dignity of Harvard."

The next year, when the Yale "blackguards" were again victorious, Dana offered what comfort he could. "Twice in succession," he wrote, "you have been deprived of years of patient thought, hard labor, self-denial, and self-restraint, by accident . . . and fraud of others. It is a great discipline and a great trial." Life was full of such disappointments, and an essential part of maturity was learning fortitude in the face of such grim setbacks as losing boat races to Yale "by accident . . . and fraud." Dana sent his disconsolate son on the required European tour, urging him to try to forget "boating." He must give himself "to the study of the political and social conditions of the countries you visit, and the conversation of the most intelligent men and women, and to the great works of art, in architecture, painting and sculpture, and the historic monuments." Then he might see the rowing losses to Yale in a better perspective.

In addition to muscular Christianity, an important element in the rapid growth of collegiate athletics was the preoccupation of the academic world with Greek civilization and the conscious effort of American academics to emulate Greek models (the trend was so marked that Henry Adams spoke of Athens as "the Professors' paradise"). The Greek injunction for a "sound mind in a sound body" became the rationale for the growing emphasis on sport. It was in this spirit that the movement was started to hold a modern "Olympic games," to which all the nations would send their amateur athletes to compete in the classic track and field events of the Greek games.

We have commented in earlier volumes on the disposition of Americans to turn everything into sport or entertainment—most conspicuously, politics. The impulse to commercialization was equally strong. Most peoples have a "national" game, invented or borrowed. In America's passion for sport we borrowed all the games we could lay our hands on, radically modified some—cricket and football—so far as to be virtually unrecognizable, and invented several—basketball and roller derbies for two.

Tocqueville, in his famous analysis of democracy, said nothing of substance about the "play instinct" in Americans, but it seems clearly an accompaniment of democracy. When "play" was separated from "work," and a constantly expanded time created for "leisure," boredom became the greatest threat to the psychic life of Americans, and sport became its principal antidote.

Beyond that there was a genuine expansion of affective life in the discovery of the body so strikingly manifest in sports. Americans extended the realm of perception and improved both their health and their longevity in the process. If the manifestations of the "play impulse" were sometimes brutal and not infrequently absurd, the impulse itself was sound.

42

The Upper Classes

The new rich competed with the old rich, and it was often difficult to tell, in their vulgar ostentation, the new from the old. Perhaps the most noticeable change in the life of the very rich was their "conspicuousness." In ante-bellum days the rich of New York or Philadelphia usually lived in houses the modest façades of which gave little hint of their occupants' wealth; that was displayed in luxurious ballrooms and lavish interiors. Now the rich built extravagant mansions that publicly proclaimed their wealth.

Henry Villard's Renaissance-style apartments on Madison Avenue in New York City set the tone and provoked a riot. It was as though, in the face of mounting criticism of capitalism and capitalists, the money lords and robber barons were increasingly defiant, determined not only to display their wealth but to flaunt it. Ward McAllister, the social arbiter of the city, declared that by the 1890s "being a millionaire had become a distinct calling or profession," and Ralph Pulitzer observed: "New York society consists of a whirlpool of tentative novices with a sediment of permanent members." In 1897 when $400 or $500 a year was comfortable income for hundreds of thousands of New Yorkers, Mrs. Bradley-Martin spent $360,000 on a ball, announcing that she was doing so to stimulate business during the depression. James Hazen

Hyde had an extravagant ball at Sherry's, the famous restaurant, and Harry Lehr put on a lavish dinner for dogs. Stanford White arranged a full-dress ball at the Academy of Design. The table was set with candelabra and "rare old tankards." A boar's head was the centerpiece, and stuffed peacocks spread their brilliant tails at the corners of the table. It was McAllister who uttered the famous dictum that there were only 400 people in New York worth taking social notice of, the number who, it was calculated, could fit into Mrs. Astor's drawing room.

One of the principal scandals of the day was the determination of Mrs. William Vanderbilt, Alva, recently divorced from her husband, to marry her daughter, the exquisite Consuelo, to an English title, Charles Spencer-Churchill, the ninth duke of Marlborough. Employing every stratagem, including threatening to shoot Consuelo's true love, the mother forced her daughter to marry the young duke, and they were united at St. Thomas Episcopal Church, while Walter Damrosch conducted a sixty-piece orchestra, in one of the most glittering social events of the century. The terms of the marriage were $100,000 a year to the newlyweds from the Vanderbilts, with an additional $2,500,000 to the duke in railroad stock.

The New York Yacht Club, which had been started a generation earlier, came into its own. Expensive yachts raced the waters of Long Island, and Newport entered its most luxurious days. "Men in frock coats and top hats and women in beautiful clothes appeared at the Casino at high noon, and listened to music. At three went to dinner," Florence Harriman recalled. Servants were put into livery, and house parties became the rage "with breakfast at any hour."

As the social hegemony of the old rich—the Astors, Vanderbilts, Roosevelts, etc.—was challenged by the vulgar assertiveness of the new rich (generally speaking, it took no more than a generation to age money in the United States), the ORs closed ranks and defined "society" in terms of those to be admitted to their balls and cotillions—and, most important of all, those whose daughters would be allowed to "come out" (all others presumably had to "stay in").

In New York Ward McAllister and Mrs. Astor devised what became the first *Social Register*, a catalogue of the elite. To be in it was to be blissfully *in*. To be out of it was, for the socially ambitious, a fate equivalent to, if not exactly worse than, death. Other Eastern cities followed suit—Baltimore, Philadelphia, Boston, and, finally, even such remote and semibarbarous metropolises as St. Louis. Silly as the whole notion was, it proved surprisingly successful and long-lived. In democratic America it was essential to know who was within the social pale and who was without. Jews and Catholics (except for a handful of old, old Catholic families like the Carrolls and O'Donovans) were emphatically without, as were those individuals of otherwise impeccable credentials who were divorced or involved in some scandal.

If you were rich and without, you spared no pains to get within. When reform activities became the fashion among the ORs, the surest path to social acceptance was by generous contributions of time and money to such causes as the prohibition of child labor or the unionization of seamstresses—Bertha Palmer's favorite cause in Chicago. (The Junior League was originally an association of reform-minded young upper-class women.)

The number of servants (or domestics) employed in a household was generally taken as a reliable index of a family's prosperity. Servants thus proliferated exceedingly (Charlotte Perkins Gilman called them "that silent, observing army"). One consequence was that wives, in charge of a corps of servants, were required to assume the managerial responsibilities of the owners of small businesses.

In imitation of the British even American upper-class families of modest means turned their children over to nurses, who were often, in shameless aping of the English originals, called nannies. A nanny—often an amiable Irishwoman—a cook, an upstairs and a downstairs maid, a waitress or butler, and a coachman or, with the advent of the automobile, a chauffeur were what prosperity required.

For the wealthy or truly rich—the Vanderbilts and the Astors, the Harrimans, the Villards and the Hills—the only limit to the number of servants was the resourcefulness of the master and mistress in conceiving of tasks to be performed occasionally. Andrew Carnegie had seventy-six servants and assorted flunkies in his Scottish castle. The Pulitzers, in their handsome New York mansion, had nineteen servants. When Pulitzer commissioned Stanford White to design a new house, he specified no frills. "I want an American home for comfort and use, not for show or entertainment. Keep it simple." An indoor swimming pool, ballroom, and music room suggested the limits of upper-class austerity.

The mere presence of servants, Charlotte Perkins Gilman noted, affected profoundly the atmosphere of the home. Certain kinds of behavior were inappropriate "in front of the servants"; certain things were not said or done. There was a particular tone of voice in speaking to servants and in their presence. Natural or spontaneous behavior was discouraged, if not entirely suppressed. On the other hand, the consequences were not entirely negative. Servant girls were, as we have noted earlier, often the amiable agents of the young males' initiation into the mysteries of sex. Often ties between the mistress of the house and her personal maid were warmer and more affectionate than those with her husband and members of her family.

In the words of Andrew Carnegie, "There is no palace or great mansion in Europe with half the conveniences and scientific appliances which characterize the best American mansions." Telephones connected the stables, gardeners' houses, and other outbuildings. "Speaking-tubes connect the drawing-room with the kitchen; and the dinner is brought up 'piping hot' by an elevator. Hot air and steam pipes are carried all over the house; and by the turning of a tap the temperature of a room may be regulated to suit the convenience of the occupant. The electric light is coming into use throughout the country as an additional home comfort. . . . One touch of the electric button calls a messenger; two touches bring a telegraph boy; three summon a policeman; four give the alarm of fire."

Of this whole arcane and archaic world of the "rich" we would add only one further observation. Silver might have been in dispute as a medium of exchange, but as a symbol of success it was unchallenged in the domestic setting. There the silver standard was supreme. Kirk and Stieff devised dozens upon dozens of domestic implements and eating utensils as specialized as the machines on a factory assembly line. There were, for example, an infinity of special spoons—spoons for nuts, spoons for dessert, spoons for soup, spoons for demitasse, spoons for salt, spoons for iced tea, spoons for conveying bonbons or peppermints from the silver dishes especially devised to hold them to the diner's plate. There were similarly forks for salad, forks for fish, forks for poultry, knives for butter, knives for carving, knives for cutting up fruit, silver dishes for vegetables, for salads, for roasts, for crackers, for hors d'oeuvres. There were silver hairbrushes and clothes-brushes and toothbrushes and engraved silver picture frames to place on the grand piano and display the handsome members of the family, especially brides.

The proliferation of implements for eating served several useful purposes. It enabled the rich to display their wealth conspicuously and in a manner that constituted a form of highly specialized social knowl-edge known only to the initiated. To know which implement went with each course or subcourse was to be one of the initiated; conversely not to know was to be an outsider.

Although the personal morals and behavior of the rich were generally bad, few achieved such spectacular effects as Jim Fisk (for the *arrivistes*) and Stanford White (for the socialites). Harry Thaw, the depraved young heir to the Thaw millions, was devoted to sadomasochism and whipped Evelyn Nesbit on their honeymoon. He also put Anthony Comstock on the trail of that aging libertine Stanford White out of a mad jealousy that his wife had been Stanford's mistress. And he shot White, thereby creating the greatest scandal of the day.

Elizabeth Drexel of Philadelphia, an heiress in her own right, married Harry Lehr, the most amusing man in New York, a socialite without money who lived by his wits. He assured his fiancée he was not "animal" or "emotional." After they were married, it turned out these were euphemisms for impotence. "I make a career of being popular," he told his startled bride. And later he declared: "I must tell you the unflattering truth that your money is your only asset in my eyes. I married you because the only person on earth I love is my mother."

Upper-class marriages began to break up at what seemed, at least to Brooks and Henry Adams, an alarming rate. Almost equally distressing was the spreading disease of more or less public infidelity.

Augustus Saint-Gaudens had a passionate affair with one of his models, the beautiful Davida, which resulted in a child. When Augusta Saint-Gaudens took her husband to task, he replied: "Dear Gussie, sweetness and kindness in a woman is what appeals mostly to men and a blessed charity for human failings makes one beloved." Mary Fairchild MacMonnies, who had painted one of the huge murals for the Women's Building at the Chicago exposition, had displayed toward "the gross actions" of her husband a "finer" attitude and had thereby won a "deeper respect." His own affair was, by comparison, a "mere peccadillo," which had, nonetheless, caused him great "misery of mind." Robert Peary, in his Arctic solitudes, took a handsome Eskimo woman, Allakasingwah, to his bed and had a child by her which she proudly showed to Peary's wife, Jo. William Travers Jerome, the New York millionaire and civic reformer, had a notorious affair with Ethel Stewart Elliot, the wife of a friend.

When the rich traveled they did so with interminable retinues and entourages: maids, valets, nurses, children, poor relations, and scores of trunks and suitcases (including often bed linen and towels). When Lord Russell, the British peer, visited Thorwood, the summer home of Henry Villard, he and his wife brought forty-five pieces of luggage with them. That was somewhat excessive, to be sure, but twenty or thirty were not uncommon when gentlefolk traveled, and to carry fewer than ten was to suggest straitened circumstances or a decided lack of style.

In the depths of the Depression of 1893, Henry Adams noted: "All my friends are going to Europe. . . . The Hays, Camerons, Lodges, Blaines, all start before mid-summer. . . . " Adams took a house on Lake Geneva for the summer. "The first effect of coming back," he wrote on his return to his Washington home, "is always a sense of great fatigue to me. . . . It is no fun to run and catch on a train moving like these U. States. A few days of effort exhausts me till I want to lie down and cry."

Certainly it gave a strange quality to life, those endless peregrinations, like small armies on campaign, to Rome, to Florence, to European spas, and, most desired of all, to English country homes. Henry James wrote: "Of all the great things that the English have invented and made part of the credit of the national character, the most perfect, the most characteristic, the only one they have mastered completely in all its details so that it becomes a compendious illustration of their social genius and their manners, is the well-appointed, well-administered, well-filled country house."

Traveling companions were as carefully chosen as wives or mistresses, indeed more carefully. As he grew older, Henry Adams complained that it was increasingly difficult to find "a tolerable companion," one with "youth, energy, humor, intelligence, and enthusiasm all in one." In all that ceaseless traveling there was commonly little joy. "We have driven in cabs through several towns," John Hay wrote to Adams from Italy. "We have smelt incense in many churches. We have gazed on several acres of spoiled canvas and seen some good pictures. . . . " Moreover, with each passing year one encountered in one's travels more and more Americans. "All America," Henry Adams wrote to Mabel La Farge in the summer of 1896, "is rushing wildly about Europe, as usual, making a weird spectacle and talking—God help us— such dreary, weary, bleary old rot, like their fathers and grandfathers and travelled Americans of all times and conditions, till they make me wish I lived in the time of St. Bartholomew. . . . " Adams traveled "through climates and geographies" until he thought he was "busted and dead." Europe was "rotten with worms,—socialist worms, anarchist worms, Jew worms, clerical worms,—God alone knows his own microbes."

In addition to the endless traveling, some wealthy Americans moved out bag and baggage. London, Paris, and Rome were the favored refuges. A friend of Henry Adams's, Elizabeth Warder Ellis, moved with her family to Rome, because, in Adams's opinion, "she was tired of fussing and squabbling." Henry Adams wrote to Mabel La Farge, who was planning to move with her husband and children to Paris, that "lots" of American women were there, "with nurseries and without; with money and without; with sense and without; and they seem to like it better than here."

Most of the tireless travelers were in agreement that the United States, unlivable as it might be and blemished as it might be, was still much to be preferred to that decadent Europe to which they so persistently fled. Taking the baths at Bad Nauheim during the Dreyfus trial, James wrote vehemently to a friend of the "treason, lying, theft, bribery, corruption, and every crime" on the part of those involved. "We must thank God for America," he added, "and hold fast to every advantage of our position. Talk about your corruption! It is a mere fly-speck of superficiality compared with the rooted and permanent forces of corruption that exist in the European states." While it was true that "millionaires and syndicates" in America had "their immediate cash to pay," they had no "intrenched prestige to work with, like the army sentiment, the aristocracy and royalty sentiment, the church sentiment, which here can be brought to bear in favor of every kind of individual and collective crime. . . ." American intellectuals, in James's view, "must all work to keep our precious birthright of individualism, and [of] freedom from these institutions."

The life of the rich was, of course, not all vulgar ostentation, licentiousness, or traveling in caravans. Some of it was simply fun. Florence Harriman recalled that "Fuss and Feathers" was her grandfather's "half-ironical blanket word for all the trappings and trimmings, the [social] comings and going of his granddaughters. Sometimes," she added, "society has seemed to me like pink frosting on a cake,—a cake in a world that hungered for bread. . . . But that is only a mood. On the whole I have loved balls, garden parties, and hunting, as a pony loves his paddock. I cannot be solemn about the snobbery and the wastefulness. . . . The truth is that snobbery is not so wicked,—it is usually very, very dull, and as for wastefulness, if one believes in private property at all, I think that the . . . Balls that added to the gaiety of nations and set money in circulation were far more pious enterprises than unostentatious hoarding." Harriman hunted with the Westchester hounds and danced the nights away.

One form of the revolt of the old rich against the vulgar new rich was bohemianism—the conscious adoption, in a crude and materialistic society, of the values of the aesthete.

William Sturgis Bigelow was the exemplar of the new aesthetic. He abandoned the faith of his Puritan fathers for Buddhism. He collected Japanese art and maintained a summer place on Tuckernuck Island, Massachusetts, where only his male friends were invited. There they enjoyed the luxury of wearing informal clothes, lounging about in their pajamas if they wished, provided only that they dressed for dinner in formal evening clothes. It was there that George ("Bay") Cabot Lodge, Henry's poet son, wrote his poetry and read it to appreciative listeners. Bay Lodge was a new type of poet-artist-philosopher. He had gone to Paris and lived in the Latin Quarter with his Harvard friend Joseph Trumbull Stickney, great-grandson of John Trumbull, the artist of the American Revolution. When the two young men met Henry Adams in Paris, they fell in readily with his *fin de siècle* spirit and formed the Conservative Christian Anarchist Party.

Dress was the symbol of the revolt against convention. Bay Lodge dressed rather like Walt Whitman, with a large sombrerolike hat, a gold chain around his neck, and a loose shirt. A friend recalled his appearance when he ventured into Boston: "He had a tall, well-built physique, heavily tanned, clad in beach slacks and a shirt open at the neck—the picture of a radical spirit at war with all the Brahmins on Beacon Hill."

Yet even bohemianism had its limits. John Jay and Minna Chapman prided themselves on their scorn of convention. Yet when Minna let down her long hair as they were walking on Fifth Avenue, Chapman was horribly embarrassed. She laughed at his discomfort, and he, in revenge, took off his coat. That was too much even for free-spirited Minna. She coiled up her hair and stuck it under her hat; he put on his coat.

The footsteps, or carriage tracks, of the rich were dogged by an observant hayseed from Minnesota who was so conspicuously poor that, too thrifty to buy garters, he pinned his socks to his trousers. Thorstein Veblen was the son of Norwegian immigrants; he attended Carleton

College and did graduate work at Johns Hopkins and at Yale. After seven grim years as a Minnesota farmer, Veblen was rescued by the offer of a faculty position at Cornell. There he began his sardonic study of the foibles of the rich, especially their devotion to vulgar and conspicuous display.

Among all the "ages" which we might designate as "the age of . . . " the "age of friendship" might well claim primacy, at least in upper-class circles. We have already noted the fact that figures as disparate as William James and Henry Adams made friendship—male and female—the central meaning of their lives. A corollary to friendship was letter writing; so from the age of diary and journal keeping we move to the age of letter writing.

Henry Adams wrote that "of all the mysteries that have perplexed my life and driven me to absinthe for relief, the greatest and most hopeless mystery has been my friends' friends, and the tie that unites my friends with their friends." Friendship became a passion and an art. Its unwritten rules were as set and formal as the relationship between a samurai warrior and his feudal lord. There were no overtly homosexual tones to such relationships, and the classic combinations were friendships of men with men—Henry Adams and John Hay and Clarence King—of women with women—Emily Dickinson and her beloved "Sue"—and, of course, platonic love between men and women. It was, in some ways, that relationship—the nonsexual love of a man and a woman for each other—that seemed most novel and compelling. It was, as we have noted, a theme in innumerable novels as well as a conspicuous reality in the lives of such men as the Adamses, John Jay Chapman, and William and Henry James. The literary by-product of such friendships was letters. Indeed, in American Letters, letters constituted a distinct, if minor, genre. There were no more great private diaries like those of the Adamses, Philip Hone, Sidney George Fisher, Richard Henry Dana, and George Templeton Strong. (Diaries, of course, continued to be kept by many people, but they were seldom as self-consciously literary and never as brilliant.) The brilliance poured into personal correspondence and made the last decades of the nineteenth century and the first decade or so of the twentieth the true age of letters.

Speaking of the Harvard faculty in the late 1880s, Oswald Garrison Villard wrote that "they were the product of the time of leisure and of good manners, when people wrote long letters to each other in their own handwriting to record their feelings and beliefs, to exchange experiences, and to match comments on happenings all over the world."

Letters were an essential dimension of William James's life. He wrote to Fanny Morse: "I, with my curious inertia to overcome, sit *thinking of letters*, and of the soul music with which they might be filled if my tongue could only utter the thoughts that arise in me to youward, the beauty of the world, the conflict of life and death and youth and age and man and woman and righteousness and evil, etc. . . . " Responding to a "long and delightful" letter from "Beloved Royce," James wrote that "you give birth to one young one only in a year, but that one is a lion. I give birth mainly to guinea-pigs in the shape of postcards. . . . I need not say, my dear old boy, how touched I am at your expressions of affection, or how it pleases me to hear that you have missed me. . . . You are still the center of my gaze, the pole of my mental magnet. When I compose my Gifford lectures mentally, 'tis with the design exclusively of overthrowing your system, and ruining your peace. I lead a parasitic life upon you, for my highest flight of ambitious ideality is to become your conqueror, and go down in history as such, you and I rolled in one another's arms and silent (or rather loquacious still) in one last death-grapple of an embrace." Between them they comprehended "the whole paradoxical physico-moral-spiritual Fatness, of which most people single out some skinny fragment. . . . "

To penetrate the essential life of a particular era may require that the historian read its diplomatic correspondence; for another, its military dispatches; for another, its sermons; another, its private diaries. For this era it is, above all, its letters. To John Jay Chapman, life was "nothing but passion. From the great passion of love to the regard for a passing stranger is all one diapason, and is the same chord." The most essential task was to break and batter down "the doors of silence once and forever . . . and go about the world escaped from that prison. . . . " For that gift Chapman thanked "the powers of Life." To write "openly . . . that is all there is. Everyone feels so in his heart." It was primarily through letters that a repressive age might learn to speak and write "openly."

With all this, the casualty rate was high. William Amory Gardner was a classmate and close friend of John Jay Chapman's, "the best educated man in the class of '84," and one of three brothers. Joseph, the wittiest, committed suicide as a young man; Augustus, Gus, worked himself to death in his middle years; Amory devoted his life to helping to found and nurture the Groton School for Boys.

We have mentioned the unhappy lives of William James's brothers Garth and Robertson. John Hay's son, Del, died in a mysterious fall from a window at his Yale reunion. The list of breakdowns, unexplained deaths, drug addiction, and alcoholism could be substantially extended. Clearly money was part of the problem rather than the solution to the more schizophrenic aspects of American life.

43

The New Empire

As we have seen, McKinley's election in 1896 was hailed by the Eastern upper classes as the salvation of the Republic, and McKinley himself, the creation of Marcus Hanna, was extravagantly praised. Henry Adams, his hopes of office reviving briefly, considered the new President "a very great man; perhaps the greatest we have known since the immortal Washington. . . . " Whitelaw Reid, also eager for office, wrote McKinley: "You have the greatest opportunity since Lincoln— as you have made the greatest campaign since his, and have had the greatest popular triumph." McKinley's words to his predecessor (they were, after all, not very different in their ideas and opinions) were reputed to have been: "Mr. President, if I can only go out of office at the end of my term with the knowledge that I have done what lay in my power to avert this terrible calamity [war with Spain] with the success that has crowned your patience and persistence, I shall be the happiest man in the world."

The President wanted Hanna in his Cabinet, but the latter was reluctant to surrender his base of power in Ohio for the uncertainties of Washington politics. He demurred. He preferred to be a Senator. But John Sherman was the highly respected longtime Senator from Ohio, one of the most powerful elders in that body. No matter. McKinley and Hanna prevailed on Sherman to resign his Senate seat to become secretary of state, and Hanna was appointed to the Senate in his stead. A disillusioned and indignant Henry Adams wrote: "Grant had done nothing that seemed so bad as this to one who had lived long enough to distinguish between the ways of presidential jobbery. . . . John Sherman, otherwise admirably fitted for the place, . . . was notoriously feeble and quite senile, so that the intrigue seemed to Adams the betrayal of an old friend as well as of the State Department."

But McKinley somewhat repaired the damage by appointing John Hay ambassador to Great Britain. Indeed, the election of the Ohio Republican brought with it a return from exile of a number of those upper-class individuals, like Whitelaw Reid and John Hay, who had been excluded from political life under the previous administration. McKinley "laid his hand heavily," Henry Adams wrote, "on this special group. In a moment the whole nest . . . was torn to pieces and scattered over the world. . . . Only the Lodges and the Roosevelts remained," and "even they were at once absorbed in the interests of power. Since 1861 no such social convulsion had occurred," Adams added.

Theodore Roosevelt was appointed assistant secretary of the navy, in which post he pressed ardently for war with Spain (or anyone else) and grieved his superior by his disposition to insubordination. He made his views perfectly clear in a public oration, declaring: "No national life is worth having if the nation is not willing, when the need shall arise, to stake everything on the supreme arbitrament of war, and to pour out its blood, its treasures, its tears like water rather than to submit to the loss of honor and renown." The *Washington Post* was charmed with such manly sentiments. "Well done, nobly spoken! Theodore Roosevelt, you have found your proper place at last—all hail!"

On the troublesome issue of Cuba Henry Adams wrote: "That we must recognize the independence of Cuba next winter, is, I think, as nearly inevitable as any matter of future policy can be." But Adams refused to believe that Spain would fight. "Anyway," he concluded, "we must do something for Cuba; and the precedents are all one way. That is, we must require an armistice, and enforce it."

Much of the sentiment for war with Spain was to be found in the Middle and Far West. Albert Beveridge, the Senator from Indiana, wrote: "We will establish trading posts throughout the world as distributing points for American products. We will cover the ocean with our merchant marine. We will build a navy to the measure of our greatness. Great colonies governing themselves, flying our flag and trading with us, will grow about our posts of trade. Our institutions will follow our flag on the wings of our commerce. And American laws will plant themselves on shores hitherto bloody and benighted, but by those agencies of God henceforth to be made beautiful and bright." Beveridge's sentiments were uttered at a moment when it was still possible to cherish the notion that the influence of the United States around the world could be only benign. Christian commerce seemed quite genuinely, to Beveridge, to be a channel of redemption for the less fortunate portions of mankind. The teachings of Christ wedded to American material prosperity would lift the world from pagan misery. That native peoples might have their own notions of freedom and justice did not occur to Beveridge. But he soon learned better what dangers and follies were inherent in such noble intentions and recanted.

McKinley, as we have seen, had previously declared himself entirely opposed to war. Mark Hanna, his gray eminence, was opposed. Tom Reed, the powerful Speaker of the House, was also opposed. A powerful antiwar faction in the Republican Party was headed by Carl Schurz, George Boutwell, ex-governor of Massachusetts, and Senator George Hoar, distinguished relics of the Civil War era.

A new regime in Spain promised, in the fall of 1897, "a total change of immense scope" in that country's Cuban policy. There began a series of complex negotiations between McKinley, hard pressed by the advocates of war, and the new Spanish ministers. The American minister in Madrid was General Stewart Lyndon Woodford, an enemy of war and a skillful diplomat. His rival, in a manner of speaking, was the American consul general in Havana, Fitzhugh Lee, an enthusiastic advocate of war. What followed was, in effect, a contest between Woodford and Lee, the one to prevent war, the other to bring it about. McKinley was the anxious and uncertain man in the middle.

Whenever Woodford's intelligent manipulation of the Spanish court offered the hope of peace, Lee or chance checked him. It was Lee who promoted the ill-conceived notion of having Captain Charles Sigsbee and the battleship *Maine* dispatched to Havana in anticipation of the collapse of Spanish authority and the consequent necessity of evacuating American citizens. Its appearance in Havana Harbor was in itself tantamount to a declaration of war, but Spain swallowed its pride and treated the intruders with careful civility. The new governor general of Cuba seemed genuinely committed to producing order on the island with a minimum of repression. Spain gave increasing evidences of a disposition to meet the insurgents' demand up to the point of autonomy.

Then the *Maine* blew up. Whether by an internal explosion or a mine was never to be determined. What can be said with confidence is that it was unlikely to have been the work of the Spanish since it brought about the one thing they wished above everything else to avoid—war. Out of a crew of 350 men and officers, 252 were killed in the explosion and 8 others died later. The Spanish did everything within their power to assist in the rescue of survivors and expressed what were undoubtedly their sincere regrets at the disaster.

Hearst's *Journal* issued an extra on February 18, 1898, with the headline "Whole Country Thrills with the War Fever yet the President Says 'It Was an Accident.'" During the week 5,000,000 copies of the *Journal* sold, with the *World* not far behind. Henry Demarest Lloyd offered a toast to William of Orange, "who struck the first great blow at Spanish despotism, and to William [McKinley] of the United States," who, he hoped, would strike the "last blow." To Lloyd the American occupation of Cuba would be a "great prelude to the fraternalization of the races" by having "*all* the inferior nations under the great protectorate of the greater one." It seemed to Lloyd mistaken to suppose that the United States could "progress from perfection to perfection while the Chinese ossified, and the Cubans and Philippine people were disemboweled. . . ."

Jacob Riis was among those who had no qualms or misgivings about war. "It was to me," he wrote, "a means, first and last, of ending the murder in Cuba. . . . It was time to stop it, and the only way seemed to wrest the grip of Spain from the throat of the island." Riis longed to go to war as a newspaperman "to tell the truth about what was going on in Cuba."

Oswald Garrison Villard and the *Evening Post* were "naturally in favor of the Cuban demand for self-government." Villard "sympathized with the rebels, and severely critized the Spanish offer of autonomy made in the fall of 1897, feeling certain that it 'could prove only a mockery and a source of fresh disaster to the Cubans.'"

Senator Redfield Proctor of Vermont added considerable fuel to the fire by his report on conditions there. He made a visit of inspection to Cuba and was appalled by what he saw. More than 400,000 Cubans were still in reconcentration camps. "Torn from their homes, with foul earth, foul air, foul water and foul food or none," he reported to his fellow Senators, "what wonder that one half of them have died and that one quarter of those living are so diseased that they cannot be saved?" It was not the alleged barbarity of Weyler but the "spectacle of a million and a half people, the entire native population of Cuba, struggling for freedom and deliverance from the worst misgovernment of which I have ever had knowledge" that horrified Proctor.

While the nation eagerly prepared for war with Spain and all attention was focused on Cuba, 7,000 miles away in the Philippines another revolution was in progress. Native Filipinos were in revolt against Spanish rule. Led by a brilliant guerrilla fighter named Emilio Aguinaldo, insurgents had for several years been carrying on a war for independence. It seemed to Lodge and Roosevelt that war with Spain would present a splendid opportunity for "freeing" the Philippines and adding those islands to the New American Empire. According to the Mahan doctrine, the United States required a naval base in the Pacific (or, preferably, several bases) if it was to have a global navy. The only obstacle was Aguinaldo and his army of liberation. The proponents of acquiring the Philippines felt confident that Aguinaldo would welcome American hegemony and that if he proved obdurate, he could be easily brushed aside.

While the secretary of the navy literally slept, his eager assistant took steps to ensure the capture by the Americans of the Philippines. Roosevelt had maneuvered the appointment of the aggressive Captain George Dewey as commander of the Eastern fleet presently in Hong Kong. In the event of war, Roosevelt informed Dewey, he was to head full steam for Manila Bay to engage the broken-down remnants of the Spanish fleet at anchor there.

The commission appointed to look into the cause of the explosion of the *Maine* decided on somewhat unsubstantial evidence (but all that existed) that the cause was external and the proponents of war, led by the *New York World* and the *Journal*, thereupon concluded that it was an act of war against the United States by Spain and clamored more loudly than ever for a war of liberation. E. L. Godkin expressed the indignation of the old-line journalists for the shenanigans of the newcomers. "Nothing so disgraceful as the behaviour of these two newspapers in the past week has ever been known in the history of journalism," Godkin wrote. "Gross misrepresentation of facts, deliberate invention of tales calculated to excite the public, and wanton recklessness in the construction of headlines . . . have combined to make the issues of the most widely circulated newspaper firebrands scattered broadcast throughout the community."

Meanwhile, the indefatigable Woodford labored to remove all cause of war by prevailing on the Spanish to make concession after concession. On February 26 Woodford wired McKinley: "I think that we have now secured the practical adjustment of every important matter that has been committed to me up to date. Autonomy cannot go backward. It must go forward and its results must be worked out in Cuba. . . . They cannot go further in open concessions to us without being overthrown by their own people here in Spain. . . . They want peace if they can keep peace and save the dynasty. They prefer the chances of war, with the certain loss of Cuba, to the overthrow of the dynasty."

Republican politicians, alarmed at the public hostility increasingly directed at McKinley for not declaring war on Spain, feared that the Democrats would use the President's pacific inclinations to oust Republicans from Congress in the coming elections of 1898. They therefore increased the pressure on the President to declare war. On Tuesday, March 31, Woodford was assured by the Spanish ministers that they were prepared to submit the issue of compensation for the *Maine* to arbitration, revoke the reconcentration decrees, push ahead with autonomy, and appropriate funds to return the peasants to their lands. A truce would be granted, and the good offices of the United States would be welcomed in trying to repair the ravages of the long struggle for independence. In addition, the Pope offered to mediate the points at issue, and the Spanish queen cabled the American President expressing her determination to do everything in her power to avoid war. "I believe," Woodford cabled, "that this means peace, which the sober judgment of our people will approve long before next November, and which must be approved at the bar of final history."

At this point McKinley, never a notably resolute man, crumpled. In the not entirely fair (or candid) words of Oswald Garrison Villard, the President "proved how easy it was for a foolish, weak, or unfaithful man in the White House to alter all by himself the whole policy of the country." Theodore Roosevelt wrote triumphantly to his friend Elihu Root on Monday, April 5: "Thank Heaven, this morning it looks as if the Administration had made up its mind to lead the movement instead of resisting it with the effect of shattering the party and humiliating the nation." The President, on April 11, transmitted to Congress a message calling for war and deftly obscuring the fact that no cause for war any longer existed.

"In the name of humanity, in the name of civilization, in behalf of endangered American interests which give us the right and duty to speak and to act, the war in Cuba must stop," McKinley declared. In order to stop it, another war must start. The President asked Congress to authorize him to "use the military and naval forces of the United States as may be necessary for these purposes." He reaffirmed the nature of Americans as "a Christian, peace-loving people."

McKinley's message put the issue in Congress's court and that body seemed possessed of "a spirit of wild jingoism." The Senate, not quite so militant as the House, accepted an amendment which asserted: "That the United States hereby disclaims any disposition to exercise sovereignty, jurisdiction, or control over said island, except for the pacification thereof, and asserts its determination when that is accomplished to leave the government and control of the island to its people." The so-called Teller Amendment was, in fact, a notable statement which served to reassure many opponents of American intervention in Cuba.

Referring to the April 4 telegram, Woodford told Oswald Garrison Villard: "When I sent that last cable to McKinley I thought I should wake up the next morning to find myself acclaimed all over the United States for having achieved the greatest diplomatic victory in our history—the surrender of the proud Castilian nation."

A week after the President's message the House of Representatives, in a scene that resembled "a political convention" more than a deliberative body, with the galleries crowded and the Congressmen, singing the "Battle Hymn of the Republic" and "Dixie" along with "Hang General Weyler to a Sour Apple Tree as We Go Marching On," passed a war resolution by a vote of 310 to 6. The margin was much narrower, 42 to 35, in the Senate. The resolution ordered Spain immediately to "relinquish its authority and government in the Island of Cuba and withdraw its land and naval forces from Cuba and Cuban waters." The Spanish, not surprisingly, refused. The "war" had begun. The nation was in ecstasy.

With war declared, tens of thousands of volunteers hastened to enlist. There was, it turned out, an insufficiency of nearly everything needed to equip an invasion force, most important of all, rifles. The national guard disliked and distrusted the regular army. Many guardsmen were reluctant or outright unwilling to serve under West Pointers, who were considered snobs and autocrats. The New York 7th Regiment, made up largely of "gentlemen," refused to serve at all. The 9th and 10th Cavalry, black units with distinguished records in the Indian wars, were hustled off to Tampa, the staging area for the invasion of Cuba, and units of the national guard and regular army began to assemble there. The guard units, led by officers elected by the men, were poorly disciplined and had little notion of proper sanitation. Soon there was an alarming incidence of illness.

The secretary of the navy, John Long, prodded by his impetuous and often close to insubordinate assistant, Theodore Roosevelt, wired to Captain Dewey: "War has commenced between the United States and Spain. Proceed at once to Philippine Islands. Commence operations at once, particularly against the Spanish fleet. You must capture or destroy." It thus came about that the first American military action was not in Cuba but in faraway Manila. Dewey arrived at that harbor and at once engaged a Spanish fleet better suited for the dry dock than for combat (the one new Spanish ship had not yet been fitted with its principal guns). Dewey steamed back and forth, firing at the Spanish ships through clouds of black smoke until they all were sunk or disabled. Dewey's immortal order was: "You may fire when ready, Gridley," a not especially stirring utterance, which nonetheless at once took its place with such classic sentences as "Don't fire until you see the whites of their eyes," "Don't give up the ship," "I have not yet begun to fight," and "Damn the torpedoes; full steam ahead." Somehow the navy always seemed to outstrip the army—whites of eyes excepted—when it came to memorable phrases.

The Spanish admiral surrendered what was left of his force. Two American officers and six men had been "very slightly" wounded. The chief engineer of the *McCulloch* died of a heart attack. Out of some 1,200 sailors and marines, the Spanish lost 381 killed and wounded. It was a glorious victory. News of it threw the country into a paroxysm of joy. Consul Oscar Williams wired a colorful account of the battle with emphasis on the bravery of the American sailors and officers. "With magnificent coolness and order, but with the greatest promptness our fleet, in battle array, . . . [they] answered the Spanish attack. . . . History has only contrasts. There is no couplet to form a comparison."

Commodore Winfield Scott Schley pronounced Dewey's victory at Manila as worthy to "take its place side by side with the greatest naval victories of the world's history." Certainly it was a candidate for the most one-sided. Victor Herbert wrote a song—"The Fight Is Made and Won"—which immediately became the hit song of the day. In the war between Hearst and Pulitzer, the war with Spain appeared as a kind of by-product; "each claimed the conflict as his own personal property," George Creel wrote, and "rivalry reached the stage of utter madness." The façades of the respective newspaper buildings were obscured by scaffolds, on which "singers, speakers, artists, and musicians . . . created pandemonium from morning until night." If the *World* had three bands, the *Journal* engaged six. In the wild competition one editor "went raving crazy."

Cooler heads took a somewhat different view of the matter. The declaration of war by Congress on Spain, William James wrote, "was a case of *psychologie des foules*, a genuine hysteric stampede at the last moment. . . . " Europe could not, of course, believe that America's "pretense of humanity, and our disclaiming of all ideas of conquest is sincere. It has been *absolutely* sincere!" James wrote a French friend. "The self-conscious feeling of our people has been entirely based on a sense of philanthropic duty, without which not a step could have been taken." James believed that "we shall never take Cuba . . . unless indeed after years of unsuccessful police duty there, for that is what we have made ourselves responsible for." But the matter was far less clear with Puerto Rico and the Philippines. "We had supposed ourselves," James wrote, "(with all our crudity and barbarity in certain ways) a better nation morally than the rest, safe at home, and without the old savage ambition, destined to exert great international influence by throwing in our 'moral weight,' etc. Dreams! Human Nature is everywhere the same; and at the least temptation all the old military passions rise, and sweep everything before them."

William Graham Sumner also denounced the Spanish-American War and predicted that the United States would soon be doing those very things which it had denounced the Spanish for doing; "the spirit of cruelty and oppression we had set out to exorcise by military force would in turn enter into our own souls." The whole affair strengthened Sumner's conviction that "men love war." This seemed to him the only conclusion that could be reached "when two hundred thousand men in the United States volunteer in a month for a war with Spain which appeals to no sense of wrong against their country, and to no other strong sentiment of human nature, when their lives are by no means monotonous or destitute of interest, and where life offers chances of wealth and prosperity, the . . . love of adventure and war must be strong in our population." What would come, Sumner asked, "of the mixture of sentimental social philosophy and warlike policy? There is only one thing to be rationally expected," he noted, "and that is a frightful

effusion of blood in revolution and war during the century now opening."

While the preparations for invasion of Cuba went ahead, bum-
blingly, the country considered how it should react to its unexpected
bonanza, the Philippines, which seemed ripe for plucking. An increasingly uneasy Aguinaldo watched as evidence piled up that the interests
of the United States were not entirely congruent with those of the
Filipinos themselves. For the Anglophiles the Philippines seemed to
offer the possibility of a stronger tie with Great Britain. Walter Hines
Page, one of the most enthusiastic of that breed, wrote to his friend
James Bryce, the foremost English interpreter of America: "We see
already the beginnings of an 'Imperial' party here. Indeed, I do not
see, nor do I know anyone who sees how we are going to get rid of
these islands [the Philippines], even if it were certain that we shall wish
to get rid of them. The possession of the Philippines and the Hawaiian
Islands will bring an overwhelming reason for as close an alliance as
possible with Great Britain. . . . There can be little doubt but a wider-
looking policy has come into our political life to remain."

The *Chicago Times-Herald* wrote: "We find we want the Philippines. . . . The commercial and industrial interests of Americans, learning that the islands lie in the gateway of the vast and undeveloped
markets of the Orient, say 'Keep the Philippines.'

"We also want Porto Rico. . . . We want Hawaii now. . . . We may
want the Carolines, the Ladrones, the Pelew, and the Marianna groups.
If we do we will take them. . . . Much as we may now deplore the
necessity for territorial acquisition, the people now believe that the
United States owes it to civilization to accept the responsibilities imposed upon it by the fortunes of war."

Consul Williams, ever the champion of civilization, suggested that
each American concern that established itself in the newly acquired
Philippines would "be a commercial center and school for tractable
natives conducive to good government on United States lines. . . . I
hope for an influx this year of 10,000 ambitious Americans and all can
live well, become enriched and patriotically assist your representatives
in the establishment and maintenance of republican government on
these rich islands. . . . "

Meanwhile, Secretary of the Navy Long was being driven to distraction by his energetic assistant. "He means to be thoroughly loyal,"
he wrote of Roosevelt, "but the very devil seemed to possess him yesterday afternoon." With Long away briefly, Roosevelt had taken a

number of high-handed actions, among them "authorizing the enlistment of unlimited numbers of seamen and ordering guns from the
Navy Yard at Washington to New York, with a view to arming auxiliary
cruisers which are now in peaceful commercial pursuit. . . . He has
gone at things like a bull in a china shop. . . . "

Roosevelt resigned his position and ordered a uniform from Brooks
Brothers—"a blue cravennet regular lieutenant-colonel's uniform without
yellow on the collar. . . . " His long-suffering superior noted: "His heart
is right, and he means well, but it is one of those cases of aberration-
vain-glory; of which he is utterly unaware. He thinks he is following
his highest ideal, whereas, in fact, as without exception every one of
his friends advises him, he is acting like a fool. And yet, how absurd
all this will sound if, by some turn of fortune, he should accomplish
great things and strike a very high mark."

Virtually all military movements are accompanied by an irreduc-
ible degree of confusion and mismanagement, misunderstood orders,
inadequate plans, faulty execution, but the assault by poorly equipped
and inadequately trained American soldiers on the island of Cuba had
more than its quota of ineptitude. The end of the war was already
anticipated in its beginning. There was no hope of Spain's retaining
its hold on Cuba, and the Spanish understood that fact very well. But
the drama had to be played out in the name of national honor. A
certain number of Spanish *and* American soldiers had to be killed or
maimed or, what turned out to be a much more common fate, die of
disease, for the sake of "honor" on the Spanish side and warlike bel-
licosity on the American.

At the embarkation camp in Tampa a story that drunken white
volunteer soldiers had used a black child as a target to practice their
marksmanship caused a riot that lasted several days and resulted in
the wounding of twenty-seven black soldiers and three whites. George
Prioleau, the chaplain of the 9th Cavalry, encountered Southern racial
prejudice for the first time and wrote to a Northern paper: "You talk
about freedom, liberty, etc. Why sir, the Negro of this country is a
freeman and yet a slave. Talk about fighting and freeing poor Cuba
of Spain's brutality; of Cuba's murdered thousands, and starving re-
concentradoes. Is America any better than Spain? Has she not subjects
in her very midst who are murdered daily without a trial of judge or
jury? Has she not subjects in her own borders whose children are half-
fed and half-clothed, because their father's skin is black. . . . ? Yet the
Negro is loyal to his country's flag . . . he sings 'My Country 'Tis of

Thee, Sweet Land of Liberty,' and though the word 'liberty' chokes him, he swallows it and finishes the stanza 'of Thee I sing.' "

The harbor and the city of Santiago de Cuba were chosen as the point of attack. What was left of the Spanish fleet that had steamed across the Atlantic to be ritually sacrificed eluded the American squadron dispatched to intercept it and found a temporary refuge in the harbor of Santiago. There it was blockaded while American soldiers landed below the city. Among the first ashore were Colonel Roosevelt's Rough Riders and the 9th and 10th Cavalry *sans* horses. Six regiments were under the command of the ex-Confederate general Fighting Joe Wheeler. There were, it seemed, almost as many newspaper reporters as soldiers. Their "general" was the dashing Richard Harding Davis, ace reporter and son of the well-known writer, Rebecca Harding Davis; splendidly equipped by Brooks Brothers, he was so handsome that it was said Charles Dana Gibson had chosen him as the model for the "Gibson man" to complement the "Gibson girl." Stephen Crane, whose style was more informal and whose prose was far better than Davis's, was also much in evidence. Roosevelt and his horseless Riders sang together:

> Rough, rough, we're the stuff,
> We want to fight, and can't get enough,
> Whoo-pee!

Santiago itself was well fortified and defended by some 17,000 seasoned Spanish soldiers. On the road to the city Wheeler and his men soon came under enemy fire. The Spanish, armed with Mauser rifles far superior in accuracy and rate of fire to most of the American arms, caused numerous casualties, most conspicuous among them Sergeant Hamilton Fish, grandson of Grant's secretary of state. Pinned down by the heavy fire, the Americans began to lose men at an alarming rate. At this point the Spanish abandoned their entrenchments, and General Wheeler, directly behind his men, cried out, "We've got the damn Yankees on the run!"—perhaps the most imperishable utterance of the war.

The dismounted Rough Riders were in the van of those who gained the summit of the hill and occupied the abandoned breastworks, and Richard Harding Davis was with them. Such was the Battle of Las Guásimas. Sixteen Americans had been killed, and fifty-two wounded.

Six days later the Americans reached the outer ring of defenses before the city of Santiago. The enemy strongpoint was San Juan Hill. Once again the advancing Americans were pinned down by heavy enemy fire. The 71st New York National Guard Regiment, demoralized by a high rate of casualties, refused to advance, and a number indeed retreated precipitously to safer ground. By late morning the American forces, numbering some 5,000 men, had been deployed to concentrate their fire on San Juan Hill, defended by approximately 500 Spanish soldiers. Casualties from heat prostration and enemy fire mounted to the point that the hastily assembled aid stations were unable to attend adequately to the wounded. A black soldier, Sergeant R. Anderson of the 10th Cavalry, wrote that "the heat from the sun was almost unbearable, and quite a number of men, officers and enlisted, fell on the way from its effects, and all the while the Spaniards were throwing volley after volley into us, and men of every rank fell at each volley. All this time we were unable to locate the enemy, being in a dense jungle. . . . " As the volume of fire mustered by the Americans increased, the Spanish volleys dwindled away. Again in Sergeant Anderson's words: "When a [Spanish] soldier put up his head to fire, sometimes as many as six of our bullets would strike his head at once. . . . This action on our part wholly destroyed the discipline of the enemy so that they would not show any part of their body, but would simply stick their rifles above their entrenchments and fire without aim. . . . " "For five days," Anderson wrote, "I had no coat, hardly any shirt, it being torn off by wire fences; no blanket; eat before day; no half rations; no coffee, wringing wet from wading streams, sweat and rain . . . I hope to see no more war."

At two o'clock in the afternoon the arrival of a battery of Gatling guns—rapid-fire or "machine" guns—put heart in the Americans and took heart out of the outnumbered Spanish. The Rough Riders and the 9th and 10th Cavalry rose from the tall grass and worked their way up the hill, a distance of several hundred yards, after the barbed wire blocking their advance had been cut by Sergeant Thomas Griffith of Troop C, 10th Cavalry. Arriving in the enemy entrenchments, Colonel Roosevelt gathered all the men within reach of his high-pitched voice and pursued the retreating Spaniards.

Again, Richard Harding Davis in his Brooks Brothers correspondence togs was there to record it all for the *New York Herald*. The Rough Riders, he wrote, "had no glittering bayonets, they were not massed in regular array. There were a few in advance, bunched together and creeping up a steep, sunny hill, the top of which roared and flashed with flame. . . . " From the point of view of the classic cavalry charge it was a distinct disappointment, but Davis was equal to the occasion. The "creeping" advance "was more wonderful than any swinging charge could have been."

A white veteran of the Battle of San Juan Hill wrote: "I am not a negro lover. My father fought with Mosby's Rangers and I was born in the South, but the negroes saved that fight." Stephen Bonsal wrote of the "superb gallantry" of the black soldiers, adding that "it is a fact that the services of no four white regiments can be compared to those rendered by the four colored regiments—the 9th and 10th Cavalry and the 24th and 25th Infantry. They were at the front at Las Guásimas, at Caney and at San Juan. . . . "

When the dust settled and night fell, the Battle of San Juan Hill had passed into legend. There had been, in the week since the Americans landed, two minor engagements in which Roosevelt and his Riders had played the most conspicuous role (if we except the black 9th and 10th Cavalry, which had done at least as well). It was all no great shakes militarily; but Roosevelt had given evidence of his courage and ambition, and, as it would turn out, that would be enough to make him president of the United States. Indeed, it might be said that was the only clear and unequivocal result of the Spanish-American War: It produced one of the most remarkable chief executives in our history.

After the fall of San Juan Hill the Spanish took up positions in the city of Santiago. There, it was clear, they could exact a very heavy toll on attackers, but they chose, with commendable prudence, to surrender instead. General Miles carried out swift and successful operations in Puerto Rico, and the Caribbean phase of the war ended for all practical purposes.

In the midst of the "war," the country was briefly distracted by the issue of Hawaii. The Sandwich Islands had long provided natives, "Kanaka," as sailors on American ships and whalers, and native women as mistresses for the sailors who made port in the islands. The islands had also been one of the most fertile grounds for missionaries. The sons of the missionaries had become pineapple tycoons and now, in effect, ran the islands. But the Germans, sniffing around for Pacific islands (the kaiser had read Mahan, too), seemed to pose a threat. Roosevelt had written to Alfred Mahan: "I suppose I need not tell you that as regards Hawaii I take your views absolutely, as indeed I do on foreign policy generally. If I had my way we would annex those islands tomorrow. . . . I believe we should build the Nicaraguan Canal at once, and in the meantime, that we should build a dozen new battle ships, half of them on the Pacific Coast; and these battle ships should have a large coal capacity and a consequent increased radius of action. . . . The Secretary also believes in building the Nicaraguan Canal as a military measure, although I don't know that he is as decided on this point as you and I are." The fact that Sanford Dole, President of Hawaii, was a strong advocate of annexation by the United States was a decided plus. The Foreign Relations Committee of the Senate recommended annexation enthusiastically (the *Nation* asked editorially: "What is Hawaii?" and answered its own question: "Sixty millionaires"). Acquiring Hawaii, the committee declared, was "a duty that has its origin in the noblest sentiments that inspire the love of a father for his children . . . or our Great Republic to a younger sister that has established law, liberty, and justice in a beautiful land that a corrupt monarchy was defiling. . . . We have solemnly assumed those duties and cannot abandon them without discredit." There was substantial opposition in Congress, but Hawaii was annexed by joint resolution of both Houses.

In Cuba disease began to decimate the ranks of the victorious invaders, and after several months of bureaucratic waffling most were evacuated to camps in the United States for demobilization. In quarantine at Montauk Point, their numbers considerably diminished by battle casualties and disease, but happily reunited with their horses, the Rough Riders galloped about for the edification of the reporters who swarmed around and, in general, behaved in a thoroughly undisciplined fashion. (Oswald Garrison Villard wrote that he had seen a "number of raw militia regiments but never a regiment so undisciplined and unmilitary as the Rough Riders.")

While the Rough Riders were enthusiastically acclaimed, the troopers of the black 9th and 10th Cavalry experienced a very different reception. George Prioleau wrote bitterly that although black and white soldiers had fought under the same flag, "these black boys, heroes of our country, were not allowed to stand at the counters of the restaurants and eat a sandwich and drink a cup of coffee, while the white soldiers were welcomed and invited to sit down at the tables and eat free of cost. You call this American 'prejudice.' I call it American 'hatred' conceived only in hellish minds. There are but few places in this country, if any, where the hatred of the Negro is not. You will find it in every department and walk of our country . . . if a Negro man marries, or even looks at a white woman of South Carolina, he is swung to the limb of a tree and his body riddled with bullets. It seems as if there is no redress in earth or Heaven. It seems as if God has forgotten us. Let us pray for faith and endurance to 'Stand still and see the Salvation of God!' "

Colonel Roosevelt wrote to his sister from Montauk Point: "My regiment will be mustered out in a few days and then I shall be foot-loose. Just at the moment there is a vociferous popular demand to have me nominated for Governor, but I very gravely question whether it materializes." Before they were demobilized, the Rough Riders gave their leader a bronze statue entitled "The Bronco Buster" by his friend Frederic Remington "as a very slight token of admiration, love and esteem in which you are held by the officers and men of your regiment." In reply Roosevelt expressed his pride in the regiment founded on "the cow puncher"; then, seeing the black troopers of the 9th and 10th Cavalry Regiments, men who were every bit as deserving of acclaim as the Rough Riders themselves, Roosevelt turned to them and praised them for their heroism. "The Spanish called them 'Smoked Yankees' but we found them to be an excellent breed of Yankee. . . . Outside of my own family . . . I shall never show as strong ties as I do toward you." He then shook their hands. It was a gracious and spontaneous gesture, of the sort of which Roosevelt at his best was uniquely capable. It was, in truth, about all the recognition the 9th and 10th Cavalry Regiments received.

Dewey worship was an index to the touching need of Americans for heroes, however modest their accomplishments. In addition to Victor Herbert's popular song, a brand of chewing gum was called Dewey's Chewies, and a laxative was named The Salt of Salts on the ground that it was the admiral's brand. The admiral noted in his diary: "Towns, children, and articles of commerce were named after me. I was assured that nothing like the enthusiasm for a man and a deed had ever been known."

September 27 to 30, 1899, were set aside for celebration, the central event of which was to be a parade up Fifth Avenue in New York City. A temporary triumphal arch 200 feet high of wood and plaster had been hastily erected; a more permanent memorial would come later. The Cincinnati Inquirer was headlined: "Dewey's White Triumphal Arch is Modelled After That of Titus. Was a Labor of Love for the Sculptors. . . . " A campaign was launched by Joseph Pulitzer and the World to persuade Dewey to run on the Democratic ticket for president. After first protesting his lack of qualifications, the admiral changed his mind. "Since studying the subject I am convinced that the office of the President is not such a very difficult one to fill, his duties being mainly to execute the laws of Congress," he announced. If he were chosen "for this exalted position," he would obey Congress in the same spirit in which he had "always executed the orders of my superiors." Dewey proved singularly evasive in response to questions on his party affiliation, referring queries to his wife. The Dewey boom declined, and Mr. Dooley observed: "When a Grateful republic . . . builds an arch to its conquering hero, it should be made of brick, so that we can have something convenient to hurl after him when he had passed by."

The end of the war brought with it revelations of blundering and inefficiency and a barrage of charges and countercharges, of wrangling between officers over the apportionment of praise and blame, recriminations between the army and the navy, and, most serious of all, accounts of breakdown in the medical and sanitary provisions with a consequent high rate of death by disease. By the end of 1898, 5,462 officers and men had died. Of that number, only 379 had been killed in fighting. The toll of death from disease in the four principal training camps in the United States was 917; the rest had died of disease in Cuba and Puerto Rico.

The long agony of the "pacification" of the Philippines kept the Cuban issue alive and provided the enemies of the war with an ample supply of ammunition to employ against the "imperialists." It was clearly a "democratic," not a "capitalistic," war; most of the "capitalists" were opposed or indifferent. The war had the ancillary effect of setting a number of thoughtful Americans like William James to reflecting upon what it was in the psychology of a presumably enlightened, and avowedly peace-loving people to bring them to such an act of belligerent folly.

It can also, I think, be said with some confidence that the Cubans (and the Puerto Ricans) profited on the whole from the American actions. Just as the road to hell may be paved with good intentions, the road to certainly not heaven but some place substantially better than hell may be paved with predominantly bad intentions. The clear losers, of course, were the Spanish and those Filipinos brave and foolish enough to resist the self-righteous might of the United States. There was another casualty in the view of Oswald Garrison Villard: American newspapers. Villard was convinced that "those months of unbridled sensationalism and the throwing off of any pretense of journalistic responsibility to the public left permanent marks upon almost the

entire press—certainly in the matter of typography." The "scare" headlines, lurid and often inflammatory, soon became a standard feature
of American newspapers.

In March, 1896, Theodore Roosevelt had written: "At present
the only hope of a colony that wishes to attain full moral and mental
growth is to become an independent state. . . . There is no chance for
any tropical colony owned by a Northern race." The war with Spain
gave Roosevelt a somewhat different perspective. In October, 1898,
he declared that while the war had not been a "great one . . . nevertheless
it was a war which has decided much for our destiny and which has
been of incalculable benefit to the country; a war because of which
every American citizen can hold his head high, for the nation now
stands as the peer of any of the Great Powers of the world, and we
who fought in it hope we have proved that we are not unworthy of
the men who so valiantly wore both the blue and the gray in the years
from 1861 to 1865."

What the war was of "incalculable benefit to" was the political
ambition of Roosevelt himself. It made him governor of New York
and, with some luck, president of the United States. In what respect
it made the United States "the peer of any of the Great Powers of the
world" is even more of a puzzle. All in all, the statement is a classic
Roosevelt utterance, showing him at his most fatuous.

John Hay's most famous (or infamous) letter was the one he wrote
to Roosevelt from London on July 27, 1898, after the "brilliant campaign" of the Spanish-American War: "It has been a splendid little
war; begun with the highest motives, carried on with magnificent intelligence and spirit, favored by that Fortune which loves the brave. It
is now to be concluded, I hope, with that fine good nature, which is,
after all, the distinguishing trait of the American character."

It is easy to satirize the Spanish-American War. In fact, it is almost
impossible not to do so. So it has proved great sport for historians,
especially those of the anti-Roosevelt persuasion. But it must be remembered that the outrage of Americans over the treatment by Spain
of the natives of Cuba was genuine. Despite the vainglorious and often
absurd statements that poured forth from pulpit and press, from politicians, professors, and preachers, there was an important substratum
of humanitarian zeal that we should not overlook or denigrate. The
forces opposed to war (as distinguished from those sympathetic to
ideals of the insurgents) were numerous and vocal. Without the unlucky and still inexplicable blowing up of the *Maine* it seems reasonable

to assume that there would have been no war; correspondingly, if McKinley had had a little more spine, there would have been no war.

The treaty ending the Spanish war was signed on December 10, 1898 and ratified by Congress in February. McKinley prayed devoutly over the proper course of action in the Philippines, but God was not responsive. It seemed to the President that the Filipinos "were unfit for self-government" and that if they were left to their own devices, "they would soon have anarchy and misrule over there worse than Spain's was. . . . " There was, sadly, nothing to do "but to take them all and to educate the Filipinos and uplift and civilize and Christianize them" (most of the Filipinos were Catholic, but that was worse than infidelity). In short, America must do its very best for them "as our fellowmen for whom Christ also died." It is easy enough, in a skeptical age, to mock the President's complacent ethnocentrism, but it would be a mistake to believe him anything less than sincere.

W. R. Day, succeeding John Sherman as secretary of state, expressed in a letter to the American consul a view undoubtedly shared by many of his compatriots. "This Government has known the Philippine insurgents only as discontented and rebellious subjects of Spain, and is not acquainted with their purposes. . . . The United States, in entering upon the occupation of the islands as a result of its military operations, . . . will do so in the exercise of the rights which the state of war confers, and will expect from the inhabitants . . . that obedience which will be lawfully due from them."

One of the principal arguments of the expansionists was that "American production has outrun American consumption and we must seek markets for the surplus abroad," in Henry Demarest Lloyd's words. Without new markets the American economy would wither on the vine. Other apologists for expansion pointed out that as rich as the United States was in natural resources, these were not inexhaustible, and in order to compete with other modern nations, it must ensure a supply of those raw materials which it lacked. Still another, less respectable argument was that colonial dependencies were necessary adjuncts of a "great power" such as the United States was or, at the very least, was in the process of becoming.

Such logic may have appealed to the "imperialists," but it failed to satisfy such men as Moorfield Storey, the able reform lawyer of abolitionist antecedents, who asked: "Why should Cuba with its 1,600,000 people have a right to freedom and self-government and the 8,000,000 people who dwell in the Philippine Islands be denied the same right? . . . It is said that there is a war necessity or that we need indemnity. Can we extract our expenses from the enslaved people whom we intervened to help? . . . Is the commandment 'Thou shalt not steal,' qualified by the proviso 'Unless it is necessary'?"

The "war" in the Philippines had hardly begun before we instituted the "concentration" camps for which we had recently denounced the Spanish. American troops not only burned Filipino towns and destroyed crops in the field but used the dreaded "water cure" torture they learned from the Spanish to gather military intelligence—i.e., where peasant guerrillas were hiding. More than eighty soldiers and officers were tried for torturing or abusing Filipino prisoners. Lieutenant Preston Brown, a Yale graduate, was found guilty of killing "an unarmed, unresisting Filipino . . . a prisoner in his charge." A court-martial sentenced him to dismissal and five years' imprisonment. Roosevelt, by then President, commuted the sentence to a loss of promotion rating, and Brown became in time a major general. Captain Cornelius Brownell was found guilty of killing a Catholic priest named Father Augustine by torture while trying to extract military information from him.

One of the particular ironies of the war was the prominent part played in it by black soldiers of the regular army. Sergeant Saddler of the 25th Infantry noted that the Spaniards called the black soldiers " 'Negretter Solados' and say there is no use shooting at us, for steel and powder will not stop us."

"I was struck," William Simms, a soldier in the 10th Cavalry, wrote, "by a question a little boy asked me, which ran about this way, 'Why does the American negro come . . . to fight us when we are much a friend to him and have not done anything to him. He is all the same as me and me all the same as you. Why don't you fight those people in America who burn Negroes, that make a beast of you . . . ?' "

A black soldier fighting in the Philippines wrote to a black newspaper to much the same effect: "Our racial sympathies would naturally be with the Filipinos. They are fighting manfully for what they conceive to be their best interests. But we cannot for the sake of sentiment turn our back upon our own country."

A Filipino physician told John Galloway, a soldier of the 25th Infantry, that he and his countrymen would much rather "deal with" black soldiers than white. "Colored soldiers do not push them off the streets, spit at them, call them damned 'niggers,' abuse them in all manner of ways, and connected race hatred with duty, for the colored soldier has none such for them." Patrick Mason, a sergeant in the 24th Infantry, sounded the same note. "You have no idea," he wrote the *Cleveland Gazette*, "the way these people are treated by the Americans here. . . . The poor whites [among the soldiers] don't believe that anyone has any right to live but the white American, or to enjoy any rights or privileges that the white man enjoys."

Under the circumstances it was not surprising that black journalists and newspaper editors were among the principal critics of the American invasion of the Philippines. The Reverend Charles Morris, who had been driven from his pulpit in Wilmington, North Carolina, in the notorious massacre there, questioned whether an America with such crimes on its conscience could "afford to go eight thousand miles from home to set up a republican government . . . while the blood of citizens whose ancestors came here before the Mayflower is crying out to God against her from the gutters of Wilmington."

The war in the Philippines dragged on until it became a national scandal. Sixty-five thousand men were dispatched to that island, four times the number employed in Cuba. Andrew Carnegie, champion of peace, wrote sarcastically to Whitelaw Reid: "It is a matter of congratulation that you seem to have finished your work of civilizing the Filipinos. It is thought that about 8000 of them have been completely civilized and sent to Heaven. I hope you like it."

The editor of the *San Francisco Argonaut* wrote sardonically that "the talk about benevolent assimilation" was "insufferable cant." He added: "We do not want the Filipinos. We want the Philippines. The islands are enormously rich, but, unfortunately, they are infested by Filipinos. There are many millions of them there, and it is to be feared that their extinction will be slow. . . . The development of the islands cannot be successfully done while the Filipinos are there. Therefore the more of them killed the better."

When liberal newspaper editors denounced the war and called for an end to it, they were attacked as "little Americans" and denounced as traitors for "giving aid and comfort to the enemy," thereby encouraging resistance and prolonging the war. The Cabinet seriously discussed bringing charges of treason against the offending newspapers.

William James was among those who made the cause of the insurgents his own. He joined the Anti-Imperialist League, spoke out publicly against McKinley's venture, and wrote to the *Boston Evening*

Transcript expressing his dismay. The fighting there and the reaction at home had demonstrated "by the vividest of examples what an absolute savage and pirate the passion of military conquest always is, and how the only safeguard against the crimes to which it will infallibly drag the nation that gives way to it is to keep it chained for ever; is to never let it get its start." The United States was engaged in "piracy positive and absolute." McKinley's position, according to James, was: "We are here for your own good; therefore unconditionally surrender to our tender mercies, or we'll blow you into kingdom come." To James it was all "horrible, simply horrible. Surely there cannot be many born and bred Americans who, when they look at the bare fact of what we are doing . . . do not feel this, and do not blush with burning shame at [its] unspeakable meanness and ignominy. . . . Could there be a more damning indictment of that whole bloated idol termed 'modern civilization' than this amounts to? Civilization is, then, the big, hollow, resounding, corrupting, sophisticating, confusing torrent of mere brutal momentum and irrationality that brings forth fruits like this." James was depressed by "the impotence of the private individual, with imperialism under full headway . . . " but he urged all those who shared his feelings to speak out. "The infamy and iniquity of a war of conquest must stop." The voice of the American people must be heard in Washington.

In the words of Oswald Garrison Villard, "Until Manila was captured we were all for the Filipinos; our officials encouraged and aided Aguinaldo and gave him every reason to believe that we were interested only in establishing a Filipino republic and turning over the country to its inhabitants." But after the Battle of Manila the Americans "ignored, abused, and exasperated Aguinaldo in every way." The war lasted three years and cost the United States $17,000,000 in addition to the American and Filipino lives. Villard was convinced that the war (which McKinley called "benevolent assimilation") was the necessary consequence of the nation's desire to become "an Asiatic power," like the other industrial nations.

"One shudders to recall the temper of the times as it found expression in the newspapers and in Congressional oratory," Washington Gladden wrote a decade later. In Gladden's view, McKinley had done "his best to restrain the rampant jingoism of Congress" and, but for Proctor's report on the conditions in the Cuban concentration camps, might have succeeded. "All kinds of motives," Gladden added, had mingled "to produce effective public opinion; the ferocity of the brute, the greed of the trader, the ambition of the self-seeker, the narrow patriotism of the jingo, the antipathies of race, the bigotries of religion, the passion for freedom, the hatred of cruelty, the sentiment of humanity,—all these were seething together in the public mind in those early days of 1898." The intervention in Cuba had a far more lasting significance. It drew the United States into "consultation and cooperation" with the other world powers, a step that was necessary, in Gladden's view, if there was to be any hope of peace and harmony in the world.

44

The End of
the Century

In the weeks following the end of the Cuban invasion, John Jay Chapman and the band of young Republican rebels of whom he was the leader settled on Theodore Roosevelt, flushed with his dramatic performance at San Juan Hill, as the reform candidate for governor of New York. In his *Political Nursery* Chapman wrote: "Now for a State ticket with Roosevelt at the head, and decent men from both parties behind him, men known to the whole state if possible . . . honest men in any case. . . . He is to be the instrument of the citizen destroying the Boss." The "Boss," of course, was Thomas Platt. Chapman and a friend, Isaac Klein, went to Montauk Point on August 24, 1898, to propose to Roosevelt that he run on the Independent ticket. Chapman wrote of the meeting: "I shall never forget the lustre that shone about him for I went to see him at Montauk Point, and my companion accused me of being in love with him, and indeed I was. I never before nor since have felt that glorious touch of hero-worship which solves life's problems by showing you a man. Lo, there, it says, Behold the way! You have only to worship, trust, and support him."

Roosevelt agreed to run on the Independent ticket. Then the regular Republican nomination was offered him. He could, the Independents agreed, run on both. But Platt would have no such straddling, and Roosevelt, under pressure from Platt, rejected the Independent nomination.

When the newspapers discovered that the reformer Roosevelt had gone secretly to see Boss Platt, Roosevelt asked Lincoln Steffens to tell him how he might extricate himself. Steffens replied, "There is no known literary form for denying a fact without lying." He advised Roosevelt to write his denial on a piece of paper and read it to himself until he believed it.

Chapman went to Oyster Bay to confront Roosevelt with his duplicity. It was a tense and unhappy session. "I unloaded the philosophy of agitation upon [him]," Chapman wrote, "and pictured him as the broken backed half-good man . . . the trimmer who wouldn't break with his party and so, morally speaking, it ended by breaking him." Roosevelt, Chapman added, "received all this with a courtesy, deference, and self-control that were absolutely marvellous. I never expect to see such an exhibition of good breeding as Roosevelt gave that night. We shook hands the next morning at parting, and avoided each other for twenty years."

The Reform Club, which had supported him, also asked for a meeting with Roosevelt. It took place on September 24 and Chapman, who missed the gathering, reported that Roosevelt received such a tongue-lashing by R. Fulton Cutting, "one of the most cultivated . . . and aristocratic of the reformers," that "Roosevelt could hardly walk when he left." When Roosevelt tried to protest his innocence, Cutting "cut him off like a French nobleman dismissing a lackey. . . ." He said: "Mr. Roosevelt, I don't think we need to discuss the matter further." Roosevelt had done what gentlemen were never supposed to do. Politicians were expected to lie to each other and to their constituents, but gentlemen politicians, rare species as they were, were not supposed to lie to *other gentlemen*. "No matter how long Roosevelt lives or what he does," Chapman wrote in the *Political Nursery*, "he can never again furnish such a terrible example of the powers of the boss as he did when he refused to allow his fellow-citizens to vote for him except on the Platt ticket."

To Steffens, the most astute student of TR, it seemed that his mind and his "hips" were constantly in conflict. His mind told him to take the advice and counsel of the reformers, but his hips inclined him to the bosses. "The make-up of his regiment—dudes and athletes from the east and gunmen from the west—showed what his hips preferred," Steffens wrote.

Venerable Carl Schurz led a movement to defeat Roosevelt, and the *Nation* supported it. The position of the *Nation* was that Roosevelt had "a boyish and unstable mentality." But Roosevelt was elected governor, and when he spoke out in support of the Philippine conquest, William James took his former student severely to task. James was repulsed by a presumably responsible political figure of allegedly liberal inclination who "gushes over war as the ideal condition of human society, for the manly strenuousness which it involves, and treats peace as a condition of blubberlike and swollen ignobility, fit only for huckstering weaklings. . . . To enslave a weak but heroic people, or to brazen out a blunder, is a good enough cause, it appears for Colonel Roosevelt. To us Massachusetts anti-imperialists, who have fought in better causes, it is not quite good enough. . . . 'Duty and Destiny' have rolled over us like a Juggernaut car."

The aged and ailing John Sherman had been replaced as secretary of state by William Rufus Day, an Ohio lawyer who was equally unqualified for the office. Now, however, McKinley appointed Day a peace commissioner to negotiate the treaty concluding the Spanish war and chose John Hay, then ambassador to Great Britain, to replace him as secretary of state.

Hay, an unabashed Anglophile, had done yeoman labor in developing a rapprochement with the British. In Great Britain his overtures had been responded to warmly inside and outside the government. The prominent liberal politician Joseph Chamberlain, whose wife was an American, asked, in a speech to the Birmingham Liberal-Unionist Association, "What is our next duty?" and replied, "It is to establish and to maintain bonds of permanent amity with our kinsmen across the Atlantic. There is a powerful and generous nation. They speak our language. They are bred of our race. Their laws, their literature, their standpoint upon every question, are the same as ours. Their feeling, their interests in the cause of humanity and the peaceful developments of the world are identifiable with ours. . . . I even go so far as to say that, terrible as war may be, even war itself would be cheaply purchased if, in a great noble cause, the Stars and Stripes and the Union Jack should wave together over an Anglo-Saxon alliance."

Henry Adams, remembering British policy during the Civil War, took a somewhat more cynical view of the rapprochement between Great Britain and the United States. "After two hundred years," he wrote in *The Education of Henry Adams*, "of stupid and greedy blundering, which no argument and no violence affected, the people of

England learned their lesson just at the moment when Hay would otherwise have faced a flood of the old anxieties. Hay himself scarcely knew how grateful he should be, for to him the change came almost of course." Adams believed that the conversion of England was due to "the sudden appearance of Germany as the grizzly terror which in twenty years effected what Adamses had tried for two hundred years in vain. . . ." England had been "frightened into America's arms," and Adams himself could "feel only the sense of satisfaction at seeing the diplomatic triumph of all of his family, since the breed existed, at last realized under his own eyes for the advantage of his oldest and closest ally."

In Hay's devotion to the British, he could see no evil on their part. When the Boer War broke out and Americans of all classes showed considerable sympathy for the insurgent Boers, Hay was furious, as he wrote Henry Adams, at "our idiotic public . . . snivelling over" the Boers. He apparently favored their extermination, deploring the fact that the British "have lost all skill in fighting; and the whole world knows it. . . ." That fact had serious implications for the British-U.S. alliance that Hay was trying to cement. "Germany arranged things," he added; "the balance is lost for ages." He wrote another friend: "What can be done in the present diseased state of the public mind? There is such a mad-dog hatred of England prevalent among newspapers and politicians that anything we now do in China to take care of our imperiled interest, would be set down to 'subservience to Great Britain.'" France was "Russia's harlot."

Notwithstanding his affinity for the English, Hay felt he must respond to his commander's call. In the words of Henry Adams, "the old habits of the Civil War left their mark of military drill on every one who had lived through it." It was thus, according to Adams, that Hay "shouldered his pack and started for home" to become McKinley's secretary of state when his disposition was to remain ambassador.

Adams would have been less than human not to have envied his friend's new position of authority. "For history," Adams had written, "international relations are the only sure standards of movement; the only foundation for a map. For this reason . . . international relation was the only sure base for a chart of history." That was the reality that John Hay, once Abraham Lincoln's personal secretary, now in his sixtieth year and in poor health, set out to master.

While the country slowly recovered from the worst effects of the depression, the United States found itself drawn into that tangled world of international politics that the first president had warned against. For almost 100 years the United States had been content to issue resounding pronunciamentos on the sacredness of the Monroe Doctrine while observing Washington's advice. Now it was to enter decisively, if not entirely single-mindedly, onto the stage of world history. It was, to be sure, a critical moment. The alliances and delicate balances of the Old World were coming apart at an alarming rate. In the fierce jockeying for colonial possessions, national tempers grew short.

A Germany united under busy Bismarck had already caused alarm by its seizure of Alsace-Lorraine from France, announcing in dramatic fashion its arrival on the scene of international banditry. In Germany, in the summer of 1896, it seemed to Henry Adams that chaotic as American politics were, the situation in Europe was far worse. "The only policy on which Germany, England and France are at one, republicans and monarchists, church and state, is to sustain every despotism in existence, and to prolong every atrocity and every rottenness in the world."

Indeed, the character and intentions of the "new Germany" were the subject of a vast amount of speculation. It was evident that among the ancient political entities coming unglued was the Austro-Hungarian Empire. Adjacent nations sat like vultures waiting to pounce on the carrion. In a reaction reminiscent of the phenomenon of "hybrid vigor" in the animal kingdom, the newly integrated Germany discharged remarkable outbursts of creative energy.

Ray Stannard Baker was dispatched to that nation by *McClure's Magazine* to discover the "secret" of Germany's industrial might, which threatened to eclipse that of England. What he found puzzled and impressed him. "I am trying hard," he wrote his wife, "to get clear ideas of the *meanings* of things over here; why Germany is making such progress; how much is due to her system of bureaucracy, how much to her splendid educational methods, how much to her natural resources." Science was the god of the modern age, and in science Germany had outstripped the world.

Baker took note of "the new impetus in scientific research and discovery." Part of that nation's success, he concluded, was due precisely to the fact that everything was run from the top down. The marvelously efficient and generally honest bureaucracy was in striking contrast with the chaos and corruption of democratic politics. In the United States, because business and politics were supposed to be divorced, their necessary relationships were usually illicit. In Germany the bureaucracy, operating on instructions from Bismarck and his successors, facilitated in every way the development both of scientific research and its application to industrial processes. "The Englishman," Baker wrote, "has gone to sleep content with his own commercial supremacy and greatness; the American is not yet fully awake to his own power; the Frenchman frets himself with visions of a greatness that is gone; but the German is fully alive to every world-condition, establishing banks and businesses in South America, buying islands of Spain . . . boldly taking the lead in the Chinese troubles, extending his colonies in Africa, preparing to absorb Austria and possibly Asia Minor— stretching the lines of his merchant marine around the world, and putting his manufactured products into the homes of every nation on earth."

In all this the older Germany of high culture, of Goethe and Beethoven, of poetry and philosophy and brilliant humanistic scholarship, was in large part obscured. The poet and musician had been replaced by the "great man of affairs, of world politics, of giant industries." At Stettin a navy to overshadow that of Great Britain was being constructed. Everywhere there was evidence of a militant nationalism. It seemed evident to Baker that the leaders of Germany "would establish a dictatorship from above, not a democracy laboriously built up from within; they would work by force of arms, not by reason and cooperation." With the injunction to be obedient to their superiors the German people appeared quite content. "This spirit," Baker wrote, "I found everywhere rampant in German life. . . . Having myself been brought up on the American frontier I had, in that most democratic of all democracies, breathed the bracing air of individual freedom, and I began actually, in Germany, to feel suffocated."

The real secret of German industrial progress, Baker believed, was the alliance between the professor's researches in his laboratory and the factory owner. "Were it not for the German professor," Baker wrote, "Germany would never have reached her present high place among the nations, either intellectually, industrially, or commercially. Delve into the history of any of the greatest business enterprises of the empire—for instance, the sugar-beet or coal-tar industries—and you will find a quiet, plodding, painstaking, preoccupied German professor; and if you seek for the causes for the astonishing perfection and economy with which many German factories are today operated, you will find the German professor with a staff of scientists working side by side with the men who operate the machinery, keep the books, sell the completed products." The great German scientist Ernst Haeckel told Baker, "Here in Germany the tendency is all toward the centralization of power in the government, the removal of individual responsibility, and the working together of large masses of men as one man. In America, the tendency has been different: there the individual is developed, he has great power and responsibilities—the man is the unit. Who shall say how these great influences will work out?"

Kaiser Wilhelm was much in evidence in Berlin, dashing about the streets with his retinue of guards and staff officers. He had declared the small but militant company of socialists enemies of himself and of the state and arrested and imprisoned them wherever he could discover a pretext.

John Jay Chapman had visited and observed that same Germany. His poem on the death of Bismarck—"At Midnight Death Dismissed the Chancellor"—had a prophetic ring, anticipating the Prussianization of Germany and its consequences:

> Organized hatred. Educated men
> Live in habitual scorn of intellect,
> Hate France, hate England, hate America.
> Talk corporals, talk until Napoleon
> (Who never could subdue the mind of France)
> Seems like some harmless passing episode,
> Unable to reveal to modern man
> What tyranny could encompass. Years of this
> Will leave a Germany devoid of fire,
> Unlettered, rebellious, impotent,
> Nursing the name of German unity
> And doing pilgrimage to Bismarck's shrine. . . .

The Germans would reap the crop Bismarck had sown and find "every seed a scourge. For on the heart . . . each envenomed throb/ Relentlessly records an injury, / While the encrusted nation loses health, / And like a chemical experiment / The crucible gives back its qualities."

Russia was also stirring its vast feudal bulk and making it clear that it intended to be as mischievous and troublesome in Eastern Europe as Germany was in the West.

The general unsettling of things in Europe was exacerbated by the appearance on the international scene of the Asian world, specifically Japan and China. Japan had proved an exceedingly apt pupil of the West. Acting on the injunction of Bismarck that any nation that aspired to greatness must prove itself by pillaging defenseless neighbors, the Japanese, in 1894, had performed a classic Oedipal act on the stage of international politics by attacking and defeating its huge, ailing "father," China. The European vultures promptly closed in to dispute the remains. In the words of William Roscoe Thayer, after the Japanese defeat of the Chinese armies, "China lay like a stranded whale, apparently dead, or dying, and the chief powers of Europe came, like fishermen after blubber, and took here a province and there a harbor, and were callous to the fact that their victim was not dead. They not only seized territory, but forced from the Chinese concessions for mines, railways, commercial privileges, and spheres of influence."

Such, in brief, was the world which Hay, as secretary of state, inherited, a world of increasing complexity and dangers. Among other headaches was the continuing Filipino insurrection; a situation in Cuba bordering on armed resistance; revolutionary upheavals in the so-called republics of Central America; and the revived issue of the Panama Canal.

A world traveler, scholar, journalist, sometime poet and novelist, with a subtle and sophisticated intellect, Hay had one serious failing: Both he and Adams had that contempt for practical politicians common among intellectuals. With Adams, who held no public office, it was a minor deficiency, if we can even call it that. But for Hay, who became secretary of state late in life, when set in his ways and in his thoughts, it was a far more serious failing. His contempt for most members of Congress was evident in much of what he did and said. He considered it "improper and undignified" to appear before congressional committees or even to send representatives to explain and argue for the passage of legislation that he considered essential for the well-being of the country. Indeed, he became obsessed with the Senate. "I can think of nothing but the Senate and talk of little else," he wrote Henry Adams.

High on Hay's list of things to be achieved was a canal across the Isthmus of Panama. This required negotiations with Colombia, of which Panama was part, and with Great Britain to redefine the terms of an earlier treaty, the Clayton-Bulwer Treaty of 1850, drafted at the time of the Mexican War; the United States had pledged then to permit access to the projected canal without discrimination to all the nations of the world, and the United States and Britain had agreed never to "assume or exercise any dominion . . . over any part of the Central America."

The treaty that Hay negotiated with Britain and sent to the Senate encountered instant opposition led, to Hay's indignation, by George

Hoar and Henry Cabot Lodge. The principal objection of the Senators was to a clause agreeing to keep the canal open to all belligerents during any armed conflict, even though the United States might be a party to the war. Hay wrote to Joseph Choate denouncing the "howling lunatics" in the Senate who dared oppose the treaty. "I have never struck a subject so full of psychological interest," he added, "as the official mind of a Senator." That was not the best mood in which to deal with recalcitrant legislators. Hay blamed the Senate's rejection of the treaty on the malice and ignorance of its members but, above all, on the "filthy newspaper abuse. . . ." Lodge wrote to Hay: "The American people can never be made to understand that if they build a canal at their own expense and at vast cost, which they are afterwards to guard and maintain at their own cost, and keep open and secure for the commerce of the world at equal rates, they can never be made to understand, I repeat, that the control of such a canal should not be absolutely within their own power. . . ." Lodge believed that a treaty which agreed that the United States would "maintain the neutrality of the canal as between belligerents when the United States itself was not engaged in war" would be accepted by the Senate. Also, the United States must have the right, denied it in Hay's draft, of fortifying the canal. With the concurrence of the Senate at last obtained under those terms, Hay proceeded to negotiations with the Colombian government.

The intent of the McKinley-Hay foreign policy was to bring Germany into a general European alliance while neutralizing Russia. "This," Adams wrote, "was the instinct of what might be called McKinleyism; the system of combinations, consolidations, trusts, realized at home, and realizable abroad." It was the "coal powers" against the "gun powers."

China and Japan were other "problems" that Hay had to deal with. They were, to be sure, very different issues. Hay set himself the very considerable task of preventing the dismemberment of China by European powers and Japan. In this task he found a wholly unexpected ally in Germany; it was, ironically, Germany's ambitions in China that had helped precipitate the crisis. Anti-British feeling, Hay believed, complicated all his efforts. "How can I make bricks without straw?" he wrote to John Watson Foster. "That we should be compelled to refuse the assistance of the greatest power in the world *in carrying out our own policy*, because all Irishmen are Democrats and some Germans are fools—is enough to drive a man mad."

The situation in China was brought to a crisis by the Boxer Rebellion of 1900. The Boxers were encouraged by the dowager empress Tz'u Hsi to rise up against the foreigners. A number of "foreign devils," including missionaries, were killed, and in June the Boxer Rebellion reached Peking, where foreign legations were besieged. Some 500 members of various European diplomatic corps took refuge in the British compound, and every Cabinet in Europe collapsed. In the face of general disarray in the chancelleries of Europe only the United States acted with speed and resolution. McKinley, at Hay's urging, declared his intention of landing an army to help the Chinese government suppress the Boxers and restore order. It was a move worthy of Oriental deviousness, since it was common knowledge that the Boxers had acted with the tacit approval of the dowager empress.

When word reached the kaiser that the German minister had been shot in Peking, he sent out a punitive expedition under Count Alfred von Waldersee, bidding his soldiers, in William Roscoe Thayer's paraphrase, "to give no quarter and to comport themselves so like Huns that for a thousand years to come no Chinese would dare to look a German in the face." (Thayer, like Roosevelt, was unabashedly hostile to the German emperor and to the Germans generally.) Hay set himself to check the German plans, arguing that to condone them would be to inflame the country further against all Westerners. In his program to reassert the principle of the Open Door, Hay first won the cooperation of Great Britain and then skillfully played off one European power against the other. In Thayer's words, "Hay, more than any other individual, persuaded England, in a world crisis from which was to issue the new adjustment of nations and races, of Occident and Orient, and of civilization even, that her interests, if not actually her salvation, called for a larger union with her American kinsmen."

Announcing the concurrence of Britain and Germany as "final and definitive," Hay turned his attention to France, Italy, and Japan. The Russian foreign minister, believing he had been had, was furious and for a time vowed he would not be party to any such agreement, but with the other powers solidly arrayed against Russia, that nation acceded.

"The moment we acted," Hay wrote later, "the rest of the world paused, and finally came over to our ground; and the German Government, which is generally brutal but seldom silly, recovered its senses, climbed down off its perch, and presented another proposition which was exactly in line with our position." The date was October 10, 1900. The policy of the United States, as Hay saw it, was "to take what we can and give nothing—which greatly narrows our possibilities." Hay admitted to Henry Adams that he would "rather . . . be the dupe of China, than the chum of the Kaiser." As Adams expressed it, "Hay suddenly ignored European leadership, took the lead himself, rescued the Legations and saved China. . . . Hay put Europe aside and set the Washington Government at the head of civilization so quietly that civilization submitted, by mere instinct of docility, to receive and obey his orders." In Adams's opinion, "Nothing so meteoric had ever been done in American diplomacy." History at this point "broke in halves"— by which Adams apparently meant that the United States had demonstrated that it could, in a sense, create its own history independent of Europe and Asia or that history must be recorded before and after Hay's diplomatic triumph.

Meanwhile, back at the White House, McKinley and the Republicans were preparing for the upcoming presidential elections, confident that for the first time since Grant an incumbent president would win reelection. Indeed, the prosperity that followed the Spanish-American War made McKinley virtually unbeatable. The principal Republican slogans were "Republican Prosperity" and "The Full Dinner Pail." The Republicans with little effort raised and spent more money than had ever been disbursed in a presidential campaign. "We'll stand pat!" Mark Hanna declared when a reporter asked him what the Republican campaign strategy would be. McKinley would run as "The Advance Agent of Prosperity," the man responsible for "Dollar Wheat," high wages, and high profits for business.

The first nominating convention was that of the Social Democratic Party (the Socialists), which met in Indianapolis on March 9 and nominated Eugene V. Debs for president and Joe Harriman of California for vice-president. The People's Party, made up of those Populists unwilling to join the Democrats under William Jennings Bryan, convened at Cincinnati early in May and nominated Wharton Barker, a Philadelphia banker, for president and Ignatius Donnelly for vice-president.

The Socialist Labor Party met in New York (its stronghold) on June 2. Its candidate for president was Joseph Maloney, a pillar of the party in Massachusetts.

Two weeks later the Republicans met in Philadelphia. Vice-President Garret Hobart had died, and the only uncertainty about the convention was who the vice-presidential candidate would be.

The young reform-minded Republicans wanted Theodore Roosevelt. Roosevelt had steered a skillful course through the shark-infested waters of New York politics. As Lincoln Steffens saw it, Roosevelt had been determined from the first to fight off all efforts to "use him up" politically. During his brief tenure as governor, the "bosses and the business interests" besieged him, "holding out offers of contributions and backing for the U.S. senatorship and even for the presidency.... 'They want the earth,' " Roosevelt blurted out one day to Steffens, " 'and they would destroy me and themselves and the earth to get it.' "

However much the independents and goo-goos (Roosevelt scoffed at the Good Government Club as "the idiot variety of 'goo-goo' ") wished him to be the vice-presidential candidate, Mark Hanna was dead set against him. To Hanna, Roosevelt represented the worst aspects of the Eastern upper class—a snob, a poseur, a reformer, almost lunatic in his enthusiasms. Hanna blamed Roosevelt for the Spanish-American War and was indignant at the artful manner in which he had used it to advance his own political prospects. But Roosevelt had a powerful supporter in Boss Platt. It was thus Boss Hanna of Ohio against Boss Platt of New York. It was widely said that Platt wished to get the unpredictable Roosevelt safely out of New York State, but it was also true that there was a close bond between the very different men. Roosevelt, as Steffens noted, always liked bosses better than reformers, perhaps on the same principle that pampered upper-class children enjoy playing with toughs (Steffens, incidentally, did, too).

In February, 1900, Roosevelt told reporters: "Under no circumstances would I accept the nomination for the Vice-Presidency . . . it seems to me clear that at the present time my duty is here in the State, whose people chose me to be Governor. Great problems have been faced and are being solved in this State at this time, and if the people desire, I hope that the work thus begun I may help to carry to a successful conclusion." He was "happy to add that Senator Platt cordially acquiesces in my views of the matter."

On the heels of Roosevelt's visit John Hay wrote a bit maliciously to Henry White: "Teddy has been here; have you heard of it? It was more fun than a goat. He came down with a somber resolution to let McKinley and Hanna know once for all that he would not be Vice-President, and found to his stupefaction that nobody in Washington except Platt had ever dreamed of such a thing." According to Hay, McKinley, the "Major," made it plain "that he did not want him on the ticket—that he would be far more valuable in New York—and

Root said, with his frank and murderous smile, 'Of course not,—you're not fit for it'. And so he went back quite eased in his mind, but considerably bruised in his *amour propre*."

By June Roosevelt had changed his mind, or Platt had changed it for him. He forced Hanna's hand by appearing at the Republican convention in his wide-brimmed Rough Rider hat. Immediately 20,000 delegates began chanting the most bewitching cry in American politics: "We want . . ." In this instance, of course, they all wanted Teddy, and the bosses bowed, while a dismayed Mark Hanna said to a friend, hastening to climb on the bandwagon, "Don't any of you realize there's only one life between this madman and the White House?" To McKinley, already leery of the manic New Yorker, Hanna said, "Now it's up to you to live." An uneasy McKinley observed to Lodge: "I want peace and I am told that your friend Theodore . . . is always getting into rows with everyone. I am afraid he is too pugnacious." The *Nation* wrote scathingly: "Ambition, combined with the dread of breaking with his party machine, was the magic ring" that Platt had only to rub, "in order to bring the rough-riding jinn obediently to heel, saying: 'Here am I!'" McKinley and Roosevelt seemed to William James, indignant at the direction of American foreign policy, "a combination of slime and grit, soap and sand, that ought to scour anything away, even the moral sense of the country."

That the vice-presidency was a notorious graveyard for presidential aspirants, Theodore Roosevelt knew as well as anyone. He was too decent a chap consciously to wish for the President's demise and too realistic not to realize that the odds on McKinley's death by illness or assassination were less than one in five—out of twenty-three presidents, two, Lincoln and Garfield, had been assassinated, and two more, William Henry Harrison and Zachary Taylor, had died in office. (An attempt had been made on Jackson's life.) Roosevelt reflected rather gloomily on his own future prospects. "If I get through the Vice Presidency," he wrote a friend, "I should like to get a position in a college where I could give lectures on United States history to graduates, and at the same time start to write a history of the United States." Law was another alternative.

Most important, from the Republican point of view, was the fact that Roosevelt, in his romantic infatuation with the West, reconciled that region to the East in the form of the Republican Party. He made the Rocky Mountain West a kind of personal fief. Where other presidents had looked from the Middle West to the East and from the East to Europe, Roosevelt looked West. Far more than specific economic programs, his unabashed enthusiasm for the West warmed Western hearts and won Western allegiance. The victim of this mutual attraction was, ironically, the authentic voice of the West, the boy orator William Jennings Bryan. It would not have occurred to Bryan to don buckskins and six-shooters or to dash off at the head of a company of cowboy "rough riders." (It must be admitted that although he opposed the Spanish-American War, Bryan had sought a colonel's commission to lead American soldiers, perhaps hoping thereby to counteract the negative political effects of his opposition to that highly popular conflict.) It took an Eastern aristocrat to upstage a Westerner born and bred.

The Democrats had fallen too deeply in love with Bryan to consider nominating any other candidate. He was the overwhelming choice of the party's convention, which met at Kansas City in July. Adlai E. Stevenson of Illinois was the nominee for vice-president.

The Democratic Party denounced American "imperialism," and at Bryan's instance the platform included a demand for the free coinage of silver. Older and wiser heads tried to prevail on Bryan to allow the plank to be omitted on the ground that it was no longer a viable political issue; large amounts of gold discovered in South Africa had, they argued, met the need for an increased money supply, but Bryan was adamant. He was a man of principle, and the principle was silver, so the party must go the last mile bearing the cross of silver. Once more the representative of the "common man," the West, the farmer and worker, the prophet of the radical democratic traditions of the nation ventured forth to face the torrent of hatred and abuse that poured out of the conservative press, especially that of the East.

The "pacification" of the Philippines became the major campaign issue. McKinley and Hay found themselves opposed by men who had been among the founders of the Republican Party, among them Carl Schurz and George Hoar. Humorous, worldly, and detached as Hay professed to be, he bitterly resented the criticisms of his policies. He wrote to Whitelaw Reid complaining about the "wild and frantic attack now going on in the press against the whole Philippine transaction. Andrew Carnegie really seems to be off his head." Carnegie wrote Hay "frantic letters" signed "Your Bitterest Opponent." A mob, he warned McKinley, would storm the White House if he persisted in his course and "the entire labor vote of America will be cast against us. . . ."

Hay also deplored the effect that "Bryan, roaring out his desperate appeals, to hate and envy" was having "on the dangerous classes. Nothing so monstrous has yet been seen in our history." Hay described Carl Schurz's support for Bryan as based on the conviction that it would "be best to elect a lunatic President, and trust to a sane Congress to keep him in order." He and Henry Adams, on the other hand, believed that it would be infinitely better to elect a "sane President, and have a lunatic Congress for him to control."

As the campaign progressed, William Randolph Hearst rarely missed a chance to take the side of the Filipinos, excoriate McKinley, and denounce imperialism. One item in the *Journal* read: "If bad institutions and men can be got rid of only by killing, then the killing must be done." It was never clear who the author of this homicidal item was; but it was in a long and dishonorable tradition of American journalism, and it was promptly resurrected when McKinley was shot not many months later. Ambrose Bierce, writing for Hearst's San Francisco newspaper, taking note of the murder of Governor William Goebel of Kentucky earlier that year, wrote:

> The bullet that pierced Goebel's breast
> Can not be found in all the West;
> Good reason, it is speeding here
> To stretch McKinley in his bier.

In the election McKinley polled almost 1,000,000 more votes than Bryan (who received fewer votes than he had four years earlier). The Prohibition candidate, John Woolley, polled 209,166, and Debs 94,768. McKinley's votes translated into 292 electoral votes, almost twice Bryan's 155. The Republicans controlled both houses of Congress.

The fact that the election of 1900 coincided with the end of the most "progressive" and chaotic century in the history of the race led to numerous reflections, many of them not encouraging. Indeed, so general was the mood of pessimism that McKinley in his second inaugural took the "prophets of evil" to task for their determined negativism. The nation, he declared, had not been founded by such fainthearted individuals. He compared the crisis faced by the country with the Revolution itself. The builders of the Republic "triumphed. Will their successors falter and plead . . . impotence . . . ?"

Not surprisingly, McKinley took credit for ending the depression which had gripped the nation through the first half of the decade just passed, although he and his administration had done no more, in fact, to cure it than his predecessor had done to cause it. He had, he assured his auditors, done all "that in honor could be done to avert the [Spanish-American War] but without avail. It became inevitable. . . . It imposed upon us obligations from which we cannot escape. . . ." He stated: "We are not making war against the inhabitants of the Philippine Islands. A portion of them are making war against the United States." The United States was simply giving "full protection" to the loyal Filipinos, to whom we owed "a government of liberty under law."

The President was not alone in chastising the doubters. Many commentators on the social scene—editors, journalists, ministers, and liberal politicians—deplored the country's "end of the century" temper, "blue with talk of degeneration in religion, democracy, society." Forbes Winslow wrote: "On comparing the human race during the last forty years, I have no hesitation in stating that it has degenerated, and is still progressing in a downward direction. We are gradually approaching . . . a near proximity to a nation of madmen. By comparing the lunacy statistics of 1809 with those of 1900 . . . an insane world is looked forward to by men with a certainty in the not far distant future."

Henry Adams wrote Brooks: "What took our breath away to foresee far ahead, has become admitted commonplace. I cannot pretend to see further. The whole situation is new." Still, there were those "arithmetical calculations from given data . . . from explosives, or electrical energy, or control of cosmic power." Either society must stop its mad expenditure of energy or "bust, as Malthus would say. . . . I apprehend for the next hundred years an ultimate, colossal, cosmic collapse; but not on any of our old lines. My belief is that science is to wreck us, and that we are like monkeys monkeying with a loaded shell; we don't in the least know or care where our practically infinite energies come from or will bring us to. . . . It is mathematically certain to me that another thirty years of energy-development at the rate of the last century, must reach an *impasse*." A few weeks later he wrote: "We are over the edge of Niagara." He was convinced that "the greatest catastrophe since the reformation is close on us, and we can't mention it without bringing it on faster."

To Adams, the election of 1900 was only a symptom. The true reading of history was to be made in the money markets of Europe and the fluctuations of the stock market. Not long after the turn of the year he wrote to Brooks: "The New York stockmarket goes on a complete drunk every day, and runs prices up without mercy. Consolidations go on wildly. We export huge volumes, and import less than ever; yet France takes our gold." Adams was convinced that "the world will break its damned neck within five and twenty years; and a good riddance. The country cannot possibly run it. I incline now to anti-imperialism, and very strongly to anti-militarism. I am inclined to let England sink; to let Germany and Russia try to run the machine, and to stand on our internal resources alone. . . . They cannot be shut out."

While Emma Goldman was in Chicago visiting a former patient, a young anarchist named Nieman from Cleveland sought her out. He was handsome and plausible, and Goldman was dismayed to hear that some of her fellow anarchists were wary of him, suspecting him of being a spy. Emma went on to Buffalo, where the President was scheduled to open the Pan-American Exposition. There Nieman, whose name in fact was Leon Czolgosz, shot McKinley on September 6, 1901. Czolgosz, it turned out, was not a foreign revolutionary. Born in Detroit, he was a lapsed Catholic whose hostility toward McKinley had been aroused by the campaign against Aguinaldo and the Philippine insurrectionists. He had bought the nickel-plated Iver Johnson revolver that he used to shoot the President for $3.10 from a Sears, Roebuck catalogue.

Czolgosz was convicted of McKinley's murder—he died largely as the result of an operation to remove the bullet, holding Mark Hanna's hand, it was said, and singing "Nearer, My God, to Thee"—and sentenced to be executed. Before Czolgosz's death he denounced the American actions in the Philippines and declared defiantly, if somewhat irrelevantly, "I am an anarchist. I don't believe in marriage. I believe in free love."

When arrested and questioned, Czolgosz had expressed admiration for Emma Goldman and her writings. In St. Louis, where she was visiting friends, she saw a headline which read "Assassin of President McKinley an Anarchist. Confesses He Was Incited by Emma Goldman. Woman Anarchist Wanted." Arrested in Chicago, she was subjected to a merciless police grilling. Finally she won over her interrogators by her obvious candor and forthrightness. Interviewed by reporters, she refused to condemn Czolgosz. "The boy in Buffalo," she declared, perhaps thinking of Berkman, "is a creature at bay. Millions of people are ready to spring on him and tear him limb from limb. He committed the act for no personal reasons or gain. He did it for what is his ideal: the good of the people. That is why my sympathies are with him. On the other hand, William McKinley, suffering and probably near death, is merely another human being to me now. That is why I would nurse him."

Voltairine de Cleyre also defended Czolgosz. "It was not anarchism but the state of society which creates men of power and greed and the victims of power and greed . . ." she wrote in Emma Goldman's *Mother Earth*. Both McKinley and Czolgosz were victims. "The hells of capitalism create the desperate; the desperate act—desperately!"

The fact was that within a period of three years three prominent political leaders had been assassinated by anarchists. Antonio Cánovas del Castillo, premier of Spain, was assassinated in 1897 by Michele Angiolillo, a young Italian anarchist who had seen the marks of torture and castration on Spanish anarchists mutilated by the police; King Umberto of Italy was shot and killed by an anarchist named Gaetano Bresci from Paterson, New Jersey, in 1900, not many months before McKinley's assassination.

William Allen White was treated to an extraordinary spectacle the day of McKinley's funeral. Thomas Reed, the gargantuan Speaker of the House, had been deposed by McKinley and Mark Hanna. Reed, White declared, had made it abundantly clear that he "could not go along with the kind of government which Hanna would establish—the open liaison between American politics and business, especially industrial business." Reed's political base lay with what was loosely called Wall Street, with the big bankers and financiers, specifically the Morgan interest. "Hanna," White noted, "was the apotheosis of industry rather than banking." Reed—"six feet of blubber," White called him—was a man of "wide erudition and culture—New England Brahminism blowing a hundred miles an hour." Now, on the day of the funeral, he gave vent to all his bitterness. "He cursed McKinley and Hanna for what they were. I have never heard such exquisitely brutal, meticulously refined malediction in all my life," White added. ". . . It was rage chilled into sarcasm and frigid contempt. The man's bleak glacial passion, New England understatement freezing in invective. . . ."

The shooting of McKinley had a curious psychological effect on many Americans. For thousands of reformers, Roosevelt's succession brought the hope of a better day. The bubble of revolution was pricked and the reformers—"prophets of evil," McKinley had called them—took heart. Something might, after all, be done to redirect the course of American history. If monuments were erected to assassins, unhappy Czolgosz would certainly deserve one. When McKinley was shot, Lincoln Steffens wrote, "we reformers went up in the air . . . took our bearings, and flew straight to our first president, T.R." Roosevelt could not conceal his delight at his good fortune. Put on the shelf by the regulars, fate had dealt him a winning hand. He was as exuberant as a boy.

"His offices were crowded with people, mostly reformers, all day long," Steffens wrote, "and the President did his work among them with little privacy and much rejoicing. He strode triumphantly around among us, talking and shaking hands, dictating and signing letters, and laughing. Washington, the whole country was in mourning, and no doubt the President thought he should hold himself down; he didn't; he tried to, but his joy showed in every word and movement. I think he thought he was suppressing his feelings." Several days after he had taken the oath of office, Roosevelt gathered up William Allen White and Steffens and took them for an ebullient walk, uninhibitedly exultant. "With his feet, his fists, his face and with free words he laughed at his luck. He laughed at the rage of Boss Platt and at the tragic disappointment of Mark Hanna; these two had not only lost their President McKinley but had been given as a substitute the man they thought they had buried in the vice-presidency. T.R. yelped at their downfall. And he laughed with glee at the power and place that come to him."

Hay revealed the shrewdness of his own political instincts (Congress aside) when he wrote "My Dear Roosevelt," congratulating him and evoking the memory of his dead father—"my old-time love for your father—would he could have lived to see you where you are! . . . With your youth, your ability, your health and strength, the courage God has given you to do right, there are no bounds to the good you can accomplish for your country and the name you will leave in its annals." Hay touched all the right notes and none more compellingly than his reference to the senior Roosevelt. Not surprisingly, the President insisted that Hay remain on as secretary of state.

After McKinley's funeral Hay wrote a friend: "What a strange and tragic fate it has been of mine—to stand by the bier of three of my dearest friends, Lincoln, Garfield and McKinley, three of the gentlest of men, all risen to the head of the State, and all done to death by assassins." Americans who knew of the Civil War only through their history books "were as familiar with political assassination as though they had lived under Nero," Henry Adams wrote.

At his swearing in the new President declared: "I will show the people at once that the administration of the government will not falter in spite of the terrible blow. . . . I wish to say that it shall be my aim to continue absolutely unbroken the policy of President McKinley for the peace, the prosperity, and the honor of our beloved country."

Mark Hanna was not sanguine. His worst fears had been realized. "Now, look," he exclaimed, "that damned cowboy is President of the United States." Secretary of the Navy Long amended his diary entry of April 25, 1898, where he had excoriated Roosevelt for resigning his position as assistant secretary of the navy to rush off on a fool's venture. "P.S.," he wrote, "Roosevelt was right and we his friends were all wrong."

The Roosevelts moved into the White House bag and baggage. Edith Roosevelt found the hectic atmosphere of the presidential mansion uncongenial. It was, she declared, "like living over the store." The comment delighted Roosevelt. That, obviously, was just where he wanted to live.

45

Retrospections

This is probably as good a point as any to reiterate some of the basic assumptions underlying this work. First, there is the conviction that, as Carlyle said, "history is the essence of innumerable biographies." What ultimately enthralls us is what people *said*. What they did was influenced, in large measure, by the ways in which the ideas they had in their heads engaged the landscape, the physical, material world, the landscape of ideas reacting to the geographical landscape.

I have written about the relationship between events—what I have called *existential history*—and expository or *analytical history*; between, in the simplest terms, those events named by the participants and those more extensive and protracted unfoldings which the historians name in reflecting upon their meaning.

History is so vast, chaotic, and, in the final analysis, incomprehensible that the historian's almost irrepressible impulse is to "tidy it up." He commonly approaches the writing of it as though he understood it (or at least that segment which he has selected for specialized investigation or "research"). He has a businesslike, no-nonsense determination to kick or hammer it into some shape commonly called a thesis or a hypothesis. I have seen it as at least in part my function to "untidy" our past, to reveal it as the strange, crude, and often violent events or congeries of events it in fact was. I am at the same time well aware that I cannot myself avoid some ordering of that mysterious concatenation of facts. On the most rudimentary level history has to be crammed into things called chapters (John Bach McMaster refused, in large part, to do so and made his history thereby almost unreadable) and then stuffed into books, a completely arbitrary process. History obviously does not happen in chapters or even, unfortunately, in books or topics. Yet it is only so that we can begin to get a modest grasp of it.

The historian's most basic responsibility is, of course, as Leopold von Ranke said, "To tell what happened." Everything is subordinate to that; all theorizings and conjectures follow upon an effort to reconstruct faithfully and fairly *what happened*. That is by no means an easy task. Since the historian cannot, obviously, tell *everything* that happened, he is constrained to tell what seem to him the most important things. Some are obvious—the Civil War, for example—but beyond those inescapable and inevitable "great events," the historian finds himself at once in troubled waters. If, for example, he believes that economic factors are the real vectors of history, he must devote considerable time to unraveling the economic history, and he can never for a moment admit that religious perceptions or abstract ideas might, in fact, be more important in one era or another.

But the narrative historian, committed, above all, to viewing history through the eyes of the men and women who made it, will take comfort in Erich Auerbach's comment that the story of the past fully and fairly told must contain all possible theories as to its meaning (the past, after all, is our only source for theories about meaning). We may not make the meaning or meanings explicit or even be aware that there is/are a meaning/meanings, but they will be there for readers and critics to discern.

Certainly for me the most intoxicating aspect of history is listening to the marvelously resonant voices of our predecessors and entering into a kind of fellowship with the dead. I see my role rather as that of the doorman who announces to the guests, "Lord and Lady Salisbury; Mr. Alexander Berkman and Ms. Emma Goldman; Mr. William James and Ms. Jane Addams; Mr. William Haywood," or the cruise director who encourages the guests on the SS History to mix and get to know each other better. Or the stage manager of that inexhaustible and tragic drama we call history.

My intention is to stuff into this chapter themes and topics that

I have dealt with in earlier volumes but that, for the most part, have not found a convenient lodging place in this one, and also to add some reflections on the war between capital and labor.

For the basic American schizophrenia—slavery in the land of the free—the Civil War was an expensive therapy. The patient was slow to recover; indeed, the schizophrenia of slavery was replaced by the almost equally demoralizing war between capital and labor that divided the nation into two opposing factions. Yet the psychological stress was never as acute as it had been in the slavery issue. The connecting tissue was stronger and more resilient; the remedies were more apparent.

Earlier in this work I suggested two opposing "sets" of ideas—the Classical-Christian Consciousness and the Secular Democratic. The Classical-Christian Consciousness viewed history as a tragic drama in which all "progress" was painfully slow and, beyond that, "provisional" or reversible because of the human propensity to "self-aggrandizement," as William Manning, the Billerica farmer, put it, the tendency toward the satisfaction of selfish impulses at the expense of others. The Classical-Christians believed, moreover, in a transcendental dimension to life: the gods, or Fate, with the Greeks; the triune God, or Providence, with the Christians. The Secular Democratic Consciousness subscribed to the natural goodness of man/woman and the perfectibility of human beings and of society—what Carl Becker called the Heavenly City of the Eighteenth-Century Philosophers. In the period prior to the Civil War the Secular Democratic Consciousness established itself in the Jefferson-Jackson tradition as the dominant world view of the majority of Americans (most of whom remained, in their own minds at least, thoroughly orthodox Christians). After the Civil War, as we have seen, "Science" and Darwinism sealed the victory.

In the period covered by this volume many of the most influential reformers were exemplars of the Secular Democratic Consciousness, the most notable exception being the Populists and the Christian Socialists.

Henry Demarest Lloyd gave a classic summary of that consciousness in his diary. Under the heading "Summary of New Forces at Work to Produce the New Era," Lloyd listed:

> "The new woman. The new child.
> "The new man—the laborer.
> *"The new democracy—without politics*
> "The new industry—collective
> "The new religion—*man the redeemer* . . .

"The new Church—of the deed . . .
"The new education—of Fit Fabricando Faber—of doing while learning and learning by doing, of school and livelihood woven into one web."

"The consent of the governed is the political realization of this *divinity of democracy*," Lloyd added, "—*the creative will of the people* which is to be substituted for the old God."

Lester Ward was another prominent prophet of the new Secular Democratic religion, the religion of science, while his rival, William Graham Sumner, was a recapitulation of the Classical-Christian Consciousness, devoid of the millennial Christian element. John Jay Chapman, on the other hand, was a bearer of the Classical-Christian Consciousness put in the service of reform, as indeed was George Herron, the Christian Socialist evangelist.

It is evident that the Secular Democratic Consciousness, be it reformist or Marxist, derived its notion of a perfected social order from the millennial expectations of Christianity.

We spoke earlier of a "civil religion" in America which attributed to the United States the qualities of the Almighty—omniscience, omnipotence, justness, and eternalness. While such an image of America continued to be evoked, especially in official political oratory, the chaotic state of the economy and the desperate circumstances of farmers and laborers muted this familiar theme. When revolution threatened the status quo, it was hard to continue to project an image of America as the perfection of human wisdom and divine beneficence.

Perhaps the most compelling single development in our period was the emergence of the city as both the hope and the despair of the larger society. The nation's creative energies centered there, but the city was at the same time the most problematic area of American life. Poverty, crime, disease, the war between capital and labor, the threatening presence of immigrants, the demoralizing impact of the "new" all were dramatically apparent in the American cities. Yet the concentration of the nation's manifold problems in specific geographical locations encouraged the hope that they would prove susceptible to science. Careful investigations (and research), the close attention of experts, the intelligent activities of reformers must produce "solutions." When Abram Hewitt assumed the chairmanship of the Small Parks Association, he noted that all substantial reforms required at least ten years (short by geologic time); Jacob Riis observed that it took fourteen years plus Theodore Roosevelt to get rid of the flophouses run in conjunction with police stations.

Finally, the city created and marketed culture, its most conspicuous product. In Chicago the Art Institute was founded in 1879, the American Conservatory of Music four years later. Sullivan & Adler's Chicago Auditorium was opened in 1889, and the Chicago Symphony Orchestra was founded in 1891. The University of Chicago opened its doors in 1892, and the Field Museum the following year. In less than a decade cultural agencies requiring a combination of capital and culture of staggering magnitude made their appearance in a city that had been virtually destroyed in 1871.

The level of anxiety remained high. Indeed, there were those who believed it had been substantially elevated by the nature of American life in the decades following the Civil War. To the classic anxieties about sex and money, about "getting ahead" were added anxieties created by the virtual disappearance of traditional religious faith among upper- and middle-class intellectuals from the Adamses and the Jameses through the Ray Stannard Bakers, Twains, and Howes.

The influx of immigrants, especially the new strains from Eastern Europe; the rising crime rate associated with immigration and poverty; the growing signs of impending revolution as a consequence of the increasingly bitter warfare between capital and labor; the tension, or at least increased self-consciousness, in the relations between the sexes and in the concern about the deteriorating family; the deep divisions between North and South and East and West; the depression of 1873 and the Panic and severe depression of 1893—all contributed to a high anxiety level with a consequent dependence on such "tranquilizers" as alcohol and drugs and such psychological supports as the various New Thought and mind cure sects and the continued interest in spiritualism.

Another source of anxiety was the increasing disposition of Americans to introspection. Americans had, from the first, been disposed to the examination of their state of grace or lack of it. The ubiquitous diary keeping of which successive generations of Adamses had been exemplars had been a kind of running audit of spiritual profit and loss. But such internal audits had been, after all, directed at the soul's salvation.

Now began introspection of a different kind. Unquestionably derived from the Puritan soul audit, it asked the self questions to which there seemed no longer to be clear answers. Henry Adams considered introspection the great disease of the late nineteenth century. "Of all studies," he wrote, "the one he would rather have avoided was that of his own mind. He knew no tragedy so heartrending as introspection. . . . Ever since 1870 friends by the score had fallen victim to it." There was a whole new discipline—psychology—derived from it. There were hospitals, libraries, magazines devoted to it. Through the efforts primarily of William James "Harvard College was a focus of the study. . . . Nothing was easier than to take one's mind in one's hand, and ask one's psychological friends what they made of it. . . ." To all the truly important questions psychology seemed to have no answer. Were the soul and mind a unit? Were mind and body separate forms of a single human reality? Most unnerving of all, psychologists professed to have been able to distinguish "several personalities in the same mind, each conscious and constant, individual and exclusive." What did this discovery signify in terms of the instability of the "self" that was now the subject of such feverish examination? The world of dreams was understood as a symbol of that instability, capable of producing images that were not part of the conscious experience of the individual. "The new psychology," Adams wrote, "went further and seemed convinced that it had actually split personality not only into dualism, but also into complex groups, like telephonic centres and systems, that might be isolated and called up at will, and whose physical action might be occult in the sense of strangeness of any known form of force." The individual appeared to be "mechanically balancing himself by inhibiting all his inferior personalities, and sure to fall into sub-conscious chaos below, if one of his inferior personalities got on top. The only absolute truth was the sub-conscious chaos below, which everyone could feel when he sought it."

S. Weir Mitchell's book on neurasthenia entitled *Wear and Tear*, published in 1871, sold out in ten days and went through four subsequent editions in ten years. His *Fat and Blood* was equally successful. The search went on for antidotes. Mitchell had gotten mescaline from a tribe of Southwest Indians and sent some on to William James to try. Mitchell had been "in fairyland, lost among the most glorious visions of color—every object . . . appears in a jeweled splendor unknown to the natural world," but when James tried a bud, he was violently sick for twenty-four hours. No visions at all. Sidney George Fisher's doctor prescribed a drug to relieve the pain of his gout. The drug was "Indian hemp, or Hasheesh," which caused Fisher "an agreeable mental excitement . . ." he wrote his wife. It seemed a likely remedy for the nervous depressions that plagued him.

Many upper-class urban Americans suffered from what George Templeton Strong's doctor told him the French had identified as the "malady of forty years," which attacked "men who have led a dull, monotonous-lived routine. They suddenly or gradually lose vital force and get somehow all wrong. This disease is partly physical, partly moral," Strong wrote. "Its only remedy is total change of scene and atmosphere." In somewhat the same spirit Edward Bellamy described his fellow American males in *Looking Backward*: "For thirty years I had lived among them, and yet I seemed to have never noted before how drawn and anxious were their faces, of the rich as well as the poor, the refined, acute faces of the educated as well as the dull masks of the ignorant. And well it might be so, for I saw now, as never before I had seen so plainly, that each as he walked constantly turned to catch the whispers of a specter at his ear, the specter of Uncertainty."

George M. Beard was another "alienist" who undertook to treat American nervousness. His most influential books were: *A Practical Treatise on Nervous Exhaustion (Neurasthenia)*, published in 1880, and *American Nervousness*: *Its Causes and Consequences*, published the following year. Beard believed that nervousness was the consequence of the pace of American life, the rapid growth of the "periodical press," the telegraph, electricity, and railroad trains as well as the increased involvement of women in all aspects of American life. He recommended work as the best way of avoiding neurasthenia, whereas Mitchell insisted on complete rest as the cure.

Cocaine was the nerve cure of the 1890s. Doctors prescribed it; the surgeon general took it with wine at meals. It was in soda pop, medicine, and cigarettes, in ointments, and tablets. It was given, along with heroin, as a cure for alcoholism and morphine addiction. The per capita consumption rose from 12 grams in 1850 to 52 grams by the mid-1890s. It was widely prescribed as a remedy for hay fever (when sniffed, it shrank the nasal membranes and permitted the sinuses to drain). It was especially popular in dry states as a substitute for whiskey; in wet states it was often added to liquor.

Exercise, deep breathing, meditation, water cures (hot tubs), relaxation, and a hundred other panaceas were offered to moderate nervousness/anxiety. Each had its advocate. Some Americans followed the example of Catharine Beecher and tried them all in succession (or as many as time and money would permit).

We have taken frequent note of the widespread anxiety about the breakdown of the American family. Perhaps the only thing that Victoria Woodhull and Henry Adams agreed upon was the perilous state of that essential institution, though their diagnoses of the causes and their proposed remedies differed widely. It has been a major thesis of this work, however, that in the absence of a traditional aristocracy, families have transmitted values and provided the leadership cadres for the work of reforms—families as different as the Beechers and the Adamses. And of all the families the most potent have been the families born and bred in the abolitionist tradition. I have had occasion to note almost monotonously of the leading reformers and intellectuals of the last half of the century, "So-and-so was an abolitionist or the son (or daughter) of abolitionists."

While historians have recently given more weight to the role of individuals in the fight against slavery, they have paid far less attention to the effect of that agitation on the agitators. It now seems clear that the rigors of that struggle, the obloquy and public hostility that the abolitionists and their families endured, the verbal and physical violence constantly directed against them produced a quality of mind and character that proved singularly enduring and that distinguished the members of such families generation after generation by a reformist zeal and the will capable of sustaining it.

What this proposition does, of course, is to give increased importance to the issue of slavery (if that is possible). Not only has American history been formed to a disconcerting degree around the issue of slavery and its terrible quasi resolution in the Civil War, but it turns out that a very substantial portion of the more general passion for reform which distinguished the latter part of the nineteenth century and the early part of the twentieth and which, it is a thesis of this work, saved the nation from violent social upheaval was the direct result of a temper or a temper-ing produced in abolitionist families and sustained by them from generation to generation. There was, of course, more to it than that, but that lay at the very heart of the matter. To run against the current of public opinion, to espouse unpopular causes, to speak fearlessly for one's convictions are not common to mankind in general. Most of us are "natural" cowards. Social cowardice is instinctive; courage is learned behavior; it is best transmitted through and by families and communities. Tocqueville saw what I have called social cowardice, conformity, going along with the crowd, as the greatest danger to American democracy. The abolitionist movement trained tens of thousands of Americans to follow their own convictions regardless of the consequences. The abolitionists and their children, "forged in the fires of adversity," were the shock troops in the continuing fight for a just and equitable society long after slavery was only a memory. It cannot be too much emphasized that an essential ingredient in their capacity to sustain protest was the fact that they had triumphed; from being despised and rejected, they had come to be honored and admired. Many had even ascended from the lower middle class (in some instances the working class) to the highest rungs on the social ladder— Fanny Garrison Villard, for example. Indeed, under the banner of the Radical Republicans, they had run the country for a decade or more.

In the language of the social psychologist, we might say that their social behavior, their courage and tenacity in the face of public opprobrium, had received positive reinforcement by virtue of being successful. The abolitionist families had "learned," in the most dramatic fashion, that evil could be overcome, that justice could triumph, that the most basic institutions of a society could be transformed if the will to transform them was strong enough. The instinct of conformity was thereby counterbalanced or, more accurately, overbalanced by the conviction that positive social change was possible and that, moreover, it was the responsibility of enlightened Christian people to take up the long, grueling fight to bring it about. That, it would turn out, was the most important moral that the eradication of slavery made, and it was etched into the neural circuitry of the abolitionists and their offspring. It produced a character type and taught an invaluable lesson.

In most families one parent stood for discipline and self-denial while the other represented the loving, accepting, and nonjudgmental aspect of the parental relationship. In Oswald Garrison Villard's home, for instance, his father was the stern, demanding one; his mother, Fanny, daughter of William Lloyd Garrison, was the gentle and forgiving one, although the line was sometimes fine.

In a reformed family the rules for children were often as direct and simple as those that Frances Willard recalled from her childhood:

"Simple food, mostly of vegetables, fish and fowls.
"Plenty of sleep, with very early hours for retiring.
"Flannel clothing next the skin all year round; feet kept warm, head cool, and nothing worn tight.
"Just as much exercise as possible, only let fresh air and sunshine go together.

"No tea or coffee for the children, no alcoholic drink or tobacco for
    anybody.
"Tell the truth and mind your parents."

Not, on the whole, bad precepts.

In the training of children, great emphasis was placed on the
development of character. Character was composed primarily of self-
control in all matters having to do with physical and material desires
and of a rigorous abstinence, what we call today deferred gratification.
"As to some of the dangers of our times," Richard Henry Dana, Jr.,
wrote of his father, "he [Dana, Sr.] taught me to believe that science,
philosophy, art, literature and the brotherhood of man were the glory
of the human race; but luxury its debasement."

Parental letters poured out in an endless stream, most typically
from fathers to sons, advising, exhorting, admonishing. Dana cautioned his son: "In speaking, do not make gestures, unless you *feel that
you must.* . . ." Excessive gesturing was common and pretentious. "Correct yourself in little things," Dana wrote his son a year later, "and if
you have told any one what is not true, go to him and correct it. This
will mortify your pride and be a good discipline." As for academic
excellence, Dana felt that could be overdone. If young Richard was
graduated "with character, health, and knowledge," that was sufficient.

Control remained the major preoccupation of middle- and upper-
class families: first and foremost control of one's self and then control
of others—of wives, of children, of employees. One of the primary
functions of the family was to instill in children the psychological mechanisms of control. The age's ideal of self-control is perhaps best illustrated in John Forney's novel *The New Nobility.* Just as the hero, Henry
Harris, is on the point of "taking" his beloved, he realizes he is in
danger of losing control. "He had been trained as an engineer. When
driving his locomotive sixty miles an hour, his eye had learned to live,
as it were, along the rails in advance. As far as he could see, if a spike
had started, a rail had broken . . . he would have detected it. . . . His
hand would have been prompt . . . to open the valve which applied the
brake, to grasp the lever, and reverse the wheels. . . . This resulted
from a habit which went before everything else—the habit of self-
control, instant and in every emergency. So it was now. . . . Even in
that supreme moment, he grasped and held himself, saying to himself:
'Perhaps she has given her heart to Prince Kalitzoff. Even if she has

not, I can not commit myself even to her until I have consulted my mother!' "

The values of propriety, self-control, and conformity, inculcated by the family, were reinforced by the community. Frederic Howe recalled: "What the neighbors might think seriously conditioned our lives. Watchful eyes observed us in all we did. There was a sense of being clamped down, stiff in a mould made for one. . . . I rebelled against espionage, hated it, chafed under it. . . . Right living was living carefully, avoiding debts of any kind, and husbanding for some distant future when sickness and old age would overtake one. . . . To question Boss Quay, the protective tariff, or the prevailing system was to be outcast. . . . On Sunday the heads of . . . respectable families talked about religion; after six o'clock on Sunday, and from then on until Saturday night, they talked business and baseball."

The scholars and intellectuals of the era—men like William James, Charles Sanders Peirce, Josiah Royce, Richard Ely, John Fiske, Louis Agassiz and his son, Alexander, Nathaniel Shaler, the geologist, Clarence King, and Joseph Henry—identified themselves (as did the poets) with a large literate public. They wrote books and articles for them and lectured to them interminably at Chautauquas, at the Sunset Club in Chicago, at the People's Institute in New York, at Cooper Union, at Ethical Culture camps, and a thousand other spots and spas.

In doing so, they perpetuated what we might call the preacherly tradition of New England Puritanism. The minister of the Congregational Church was only the first among equals. He preached to a literate and theologically sophisticated flock. He had no priestly mysteries or secret formularies, no private rituals, no special language up his ecclesiastical sleeve. The preacherly teachers of the post-Puritan era—the poets, the moralists, the scholars, the lecturers—identified themselves with that Puritan tradition, Calvin's priesthood of all believers.

But by the end of the century the "expert" began to be defined as someone who commanded specialized, esoteric knowledge, commonly the result of research; knowledge inaccessible to the laity, to amateurs and nonprofessionals. The great divorce, the withdrawal of scholars and intellectuals into a private, hermetic world, was a development the consequences of which were almost beyond calculation.

Some reflections on the war between capital and labor are appropriate. It is important, first of all, to keep in mind the fact that

America had a long tradition of radical thinking and radical action as well. John Adams enjoyed the company of three radical friends in Worcester, Massachusetts, when he was teaching school there in the 1750s. "Equality and Deism" were their cardinal principles. The Antichrist was all forms of rank and distinction in society. "A perfect equality of suffrage was essential to liberty." When an indignant Adams raised the question "of women, of children, of idiots, of madmen, of criminals, of prisoners for debt or for crimes," his friends were unshaken. "An entire level of power, property, consideration were essential to Liberty and would be introduced and established in the millennium."

The radical credentials of the American Revolution are perhaps sufficiently well established not to require arguing here (although it must be said some historians have questioned how far the American Revolution might properly be called radical or even revolutionary). James Madison's tenth Federalist Paper is the classic statement of the proposition that those groups, classes, or economic interests that can, through the acquisition of power, exploit those without power or with less power will invariably do so. Thus, Madison argued, no system of government that did not take as its primary responsibility the protection of the legitimate rights of all classes and interests in the society, those of the poor (and weak) as well as those of the well-to-do (and powerful), could validate itself. It was to this problem that William Manning, the semiliterate farmer from Billerica, Massachusetts, addressed himself at the time of Jay's Treaty (1796). In his *Key to Libberty* Manning made a remarkably sophisticated analysis of the means by which the "few" maintained their power over the "many" and used that power for the purposes of economic exploitation. Manning's critique was, in a real sense, more sophisticated than Madison's since he went beyond political forms to describe the social and cultural arrangements which enabled the few to hold onto power and work their will on the far more numerous many.

The most radical proposals for maintaining a degree of economic equality in a society rapidly evolving toward sharper and more rigid class distinctions were those of Thomas Jefferson. He proposed that all laws and constitutions be rewritten every fifteen (or nineteen) years, observing that "a little rebellion now and then" was salutary and that the "tree of liberty" should be periodically "watered by the blood of patriots." In addition, he was attracted to the idea that private property should be appropriated by the state on the death of its owner and redistributed to the needy and deserving. If a farmer was displaced to make room for a factory, Jefferson declared, other work must be found for him.

Most important of all was what the English critic Wyndham Lewis has called the "radical universalism" of the American Revolution—the notion that the Revolution marked the beginning of the "emancipation" of the world. "All hail, coming revolutions," the Reverend Samuel Thacher exclaimed at a Fourth of July celebration in Concord, Massachusetts, in 1796. "Lawless power"—that is to say, power not derived directly and legitimately from the people—must crumple everywhere as the depressed and exploited peoples over the world toppled their masters and freed themselves from servitude, tyrannical kings, and oppressive aristocracies.

The revolutionary upheavals in Europe in 1848 and 1849 gave tremendous impetus to secular, "scientific" critiques of industrial capitalism. Heretofore the attacks on capitalism had been primarily on "moral" grounds. It was "wrong." Now the attacks took on a more complex character. Karl Marx had pointed out the relationship between the economic order and the whole array of ideas, precepts, "immutable truths," and simple prejudices that supported it. Socialism was no longer utopian, a dream or vision of a better and more harmonious life; it was coldly scientific, the result of a determined process or dialectic. It was 1872 before Marx's *Communist Manifesto* was published in the United States (in *Woodhull's and Claflin's Weekly* apparently); but Marx was, after all, only one exponent of socialism, and a wide variety of socialist ideas circulated in the United States well before its publication. When the women's rights movement split into two divisions after the Civil War, the more radical wing, with its base in New York, called its magazine *Revolution*. Lester Ward and his wife were subscribers, and when Ward and his friends formed the National Liberal Reform League in the fall of 1869, "for the dissemination of Liberal Ideas," the reader may recall that he appealed to "Liberals, Skeptics, Infidels, Secularists, Utilitarians, Socialists, Positivists, Spiritualists, Deists, Theists, Pantheists, Atheists, Freethinkers, all who desire the mental emancipation from the trammels of superstition and the domination of priestcraft. . . ."

Believing that all human institutions and constitutions to be legitimate must be consistent with divine ordinances, Wendell Phillips and Thaddeus Stevens had no qualms about stating that if, in fact, the Constitution should prove to be incompatible with the most basic doc-

trines of Christianity (in the case of Phillips) and/or of human brotherhood, it must be amended or discarded. But in the resurgence of
the states' rights dogma that followed the "arrangement" of 1876, the
debate was carried on as though the states' rights issue were to be
decided by reference to a sacred text, the Constitution. Undoubtedly
millions of Americans who wished to see justice done to freed blacks
and even to the exploited white victims of capitalism were distressed
to learn that the Constitution of the United States precluded Congress's
passing effective legislation (that at least was what the leaders of their
respective parties told them), leaving matters in the hands of the states,
where piecemeal social and economic reforms, won by heroic efforts,
were almost invariably evaded or ignored by the "interests" they were
designed to control.

Historians have generally been disposed to the view that the ruthlessly acquisitive behavior of the so-called robber barons and the attendant suffering that it caused were the price the United States had
to pay for a period of unparalleled growth and technological progress.
This was an idea that had substantial support among contemporary
critics of capitalism. "Misgovernment in the United States," John Jay
Chapman wrote, "is an incident in the history of commerce. It is part
of the triumph of industrial progress. . . . The growth and concentration of capital which the railroad and the telegraph made possible
is the salient fact in the history of the last quarter-century. That fact
is at the bottom of our political troubles. It was inevitable that the
enormous masses of wealth, springing out of new conditions and requiring new laws, should strive to control the legislation and the administration which touched them at every point. At the present time, we
cannot say just what changes were or were not required. . . . It is
enough to see that such changes as came were inevitable; and nothing
can blind us to the fact that the methods by which they were obtained
were subversive of free government." Indeed, whatever "form of government had been in force in America during this era would have run
the risk of being controlled by capital, of being bought and run for
revenue. It happened that the beginning of the period found the
machinery of our government in a particularly purchasable
state. . . . Party name and party symbols were of an almost religious
importance. . . . Political power had by the war been condensed and
packed for delivery. . . . The change of motive power behind the party
organizations—from principles, to money—was silently effected dur-

ing the thirty years which followed the war. Like all organic change, it was unconscious. It was understood by no one."

The "new American" was to Henry Adams "the child of incalculable coal-power, chemical power, electric power, and radiating energy, as well as of new forces yet undetermined. . . ." Henry's brother Brooks identified the railroads as the primary instrument of capitalist domination. They had established their control over the "public highways" and thus over the total life of the nation. Since "movement is life, and the stoppage of movement is death, and the movement of every people flows along its highways," the owners of the railroads were able to tax the American people far more ruthlessly and irresponsibly than any king or tyrant, who, after all, could be deposed by angry subjects. "Indeed," Adams wrote, "it grew to be considered a mark of efficient railroad management to extract the largest revenue possible from the people, along the lines of least resistance; that is by taxing most heavily those individuals and localities which could least resist." The same was true of the regulation of the currency, traditionally one of the most jealously guarded prerogatives of sovereignty, surrendered in the United States, "in moments of financial panic, [to] the handful of financiers who, directly or indirectly, govern the Clearing House." It was small wonder that the financiers had used every stratagem at their command to prevent the curtailment of their powers. The privilege "of subjecting the debtor class to such pressure as the creditor may think necessary, in order to force the debtor to surrender his property to the creditor at the creditor's price, is a wonder beside which Aladdin's lamp burns dim. . . . Nature," he added, "has cast the United States into the vortex of the fiercest struggle which the world has ever known. She has become the heart of the economic system of the age, and she must maintain her supremacy by wit and by force, or share the fate of the discarded."

When Brooks Adams wrote *The New Empire* in 1902, he argued that the "mass" in the form of corporations was the determinant "and the men who rise to the control of these corporations rise because they are the fittest. The process is natural selection. The life of the community lies in these masses. Derange them, and there would immediately follow an equivalent loss of energy. They are there because the conditions of our civilization are such as to make it cheaper that they should be there. . . ." If their presence comported ill with the country's political institutions, "the political institutions must be readjusted," or the whole fabric of society would become unraveled. "America," Adams wrote, "holds its tenure of prosperity only on condition that she can undersell her rivals, and she cannot do so if her administrative machinery generates friction unduly."

Had an alliance of farmers and workers and the forces of reform in general been able to impose substantial governmental constraints on exploitative entrepreneurial behavior, the economic and industrial development of the nation would have been seriously inhibited. Or so the argument ran. But the notion that decent wages, reasonable hours of work, and safe and sanitary working conditions would have put a crimp in industrial growth has been refuted by the fact that the proximate achievement of such conditions in the United States, immediately following World War II, was accompanied by a notable increase in the productivity of American workers. The fact that state intervention in the economy, even, indeed, highly authoritarian intervention, could be salutary was demonstrated first by Germany, where the state sponsored research related to industrial development with spectacular results, and more recently by Japan, where the government in an alliance with industry and within the framework of political democracy has created the most successful industrial nation in the world.

The fact is that there was abundant evidence to contradict the opponents of government intervention. The Department of Agriculture, as we have seen, helped materially to make American agriculture the most productive in the world. The Army Corps of Engineers, the Signal Corps, and the Smithsonian Institution under the leadership of Joseph Henry accomplished far more in the realm of the sciences, pure and applied, than all the private agencies in the country prior to the end of the nineteenth century.

Nor was the notion of a creative role for the Federal government a novel or un-American one. It was, in America at least, as old as the unabashed nationalism of the Founding Fathers or, more specifically, of those among them who took the lead in drafting the Federal Constitution. It was the political doctrine of Henry Clay, and its most brilliant spokesman was John Quincy Adams.

Adams had dreamed of the United States as a great nation using its vast resources for the good of all its citizens, for a system of "internal improvements" which would have "checkered over with railroads and canals" the whole Union, which would "have afforded high wages and constant employment to hundreds of thousands of laborers, and in which every dollar expended would have repaid itself fourfold in the enhanced value of public lands." But slavery—"the Sable Genius of the South"—brought about the downfall of Adams's dream. "The American Union, as a moral person in the family of nations," he wrote shortly before his death, "is to live from hand to mouth, and to cast away instead of using for the improvement of its own condition, the bounties of Providence." The curse of slavery was not limited to the slaves and the slaveholders or, indeed, to the South. It lay at the heart of the states' rights doctrine, which constantly impeded efforts to deal with national problems on a national level. The fact was that the only thing that hindered the effective use of the powers of the Federal government to ensure some modest degree of social justice was the mischievous doctrine of states' rights, which had shielded the institution of slavery from the earliest days of the Republic and, after the demise of slavery, was used to deny the former slaves their rights as citizens and to block all efforts to impose effective checks on rampant capitalism.

But this, of course, is only half the story. Political theory bows to political reality. There were a great many Americans of all classes and sections who understood perfectly well that states' rights was, in most instances, a code word for reactionary politics. Until the state and Federal courts were captured by the capitalists, staffed with corporation lawyers, and subverted to the end of protecting privilege, the courts gave short shrift to states' rights. So the problem was not simply that capitalism masqueraded as a tender regard for the rights of the states; it was that those of quite a different persuasion, primarily the embattled farmers and the workingmen and women of the nation, were unable to form an alliance that could take power and install a new ideology, one that would encourage the Federal government to intervene both to protect the rights of the residents of individual states and to pass Federal legislation to improve the lot of workers and farmers and, indeed, any group in the society that suffered from inequities that were a consequence of the social arrangements that were highly beneficial to others. In a single word—justice.

So the critical question is why that alliance, from which much good was expected and which for a brief and intoxicating moment in the years between 1892 and 1896 seemed indeed about to achieve power, failed?

In considering the reasons for the failure of the radical farmer and the dispossessed worker to form an alliance, we must start with their specific physical situation. The farmer existed on a particular piece of geography, as either owner or tenant. If he was a tenant, he aspired to be an owner. Therefore, he had a profound regard for property rights. He belonged, typically, to a church and a community. He owned his own tools and usually his own livestock and was, in that degree, a capitalist. He was usually literate, with at least a grammar school education. He had absorbed through his education, however rudimentary, at least a modicum of American history, especially the history of the American Revolution, and this had, in many instances, been reinforced by the teachings and precepts of his family and ex-emplified in many of the institutions of his community, such as Fourth of July celebrations and the observance of patriotic occasions and hol-idays. He had been schooled in politics, in party meetings and rural barbecues. At best he had a college education and a degree of learning comparable to that of the more politically sophisticated urban middle and upper class.

While it was true that he had some counterparts among labor leaders, in the rank and file of workingmen the case was very different. The industrial worker was almost invariably a renter, often in a crowded tenement, with little or no feeling for the land as "property." He was typically illiterate or semiliterate. Increasingly he was an immigrant, who, to his other handicaps and incapacities, added a language barrier. He knew and cared little about American history, although he un-doubtedly had a set of rather conventional images of America as a land of freedom and opportunity, images in disorienting conflict with the realities of American life. He was lacking in political experience, seldom voted, and was confused and demoralized by the machinery of party politics. His principal political schooling came from the ma-chine politicians of his ward, who provided him with small favors and herded him off to vote as instructed. The farmer's rage and hostility, frustration, and despair were tempered by a host of still workable symbols—the Declaration of Independence, the Founding Fathers, the ballot, the ideal of equality, and perhaps above all, the teachings of Scripture, which, if they contained the seeds of revolution, also en-joined patience, forbearance, and the love of one's enemies. For the industrial worker, on the other hand, the political process seemed unmanageable.

These disparities were reinforced by a basic hostility on the part of Protestant farmers toward immigrants in general and Catholic im-migrants in particular. In addition, the ranks of labor were deeply split on both ethnic and ideological grounds. Every successive wave of immigrants, especially those of a "new" nationality, were perceived as a threat to the livelihoods of those already here.

Another major impediment to a political solution to the inequities in American society was, as we have noted earlier, the legacy of the Civil War itself and the manner in which it set the Republican and Democratic parties in concrete. The Republican Party grew to maturity as, among other things, a kind of antiworkingman, anti-Western, anti-Southern party. Its only positive affirmations were for gold and high tariffs. Otherwise it was characterized mainly by its "againstism." It was against workingmen—labor—generally described as the "dangerous classes"; it was against the radicalism of the West; and of course, it was against the South and the Democratic Party in all its manifestations. The fact that it was all these things was not in itself remarkable and would not, under ordinary circumstances, have been nearly enough to assure it an almost uninterrupted hold on political power had it not been that it had inherited a constituency from the war that was unflinchingly loyal to the name Republican. With the Republican Party the pliant tool of capitalism and the Democratic Party beyond the pale, the forces of reform were demoralized and confused. Meanwhile, the People's Party had risen, astonishingly, as a revolt against both parties and then, with the appearance of the charismatic Bryan, been swallowed up or "fusioned" by the Democrats, infatuated and distracted by the silver issue. It is easy to underestimate the consequences of the fact that the two issues that most engaged partisan political passions in this period—gold versus silver and free trade versus protection—had little or nothing to do with the real problems faced by American society.

Finally, in the words of John Jay Chapman, "Political power had by the war been condensed and packed for delivery." Lincoln himself realized that fact and expressed alarm at its prospective consequences. The reassertion of states' rights dogma (it represented a kind of unholy realliance of Northern capitalists and Southerners who wished to be free to work out their own postwar alternative to slavery) and the abyss between Democrats and Republicans effectively stymied any use of the powers of government to discipline or modify the exploitative activities of individual capitalists or corporations.

In the rhetoric of the disaffected from the latter years of the eighties to the end of the century, the choice of "ballots or bullets" was constantly reiterated: substantive reform or social transformation through peaceful democratic means or, that failing, through revolutionary violence. Why, when the ballot failed in 1896 and more conclusively in 1900, were there not bullets? Certainly talk of revolution was everywhere in the air and not, of course, just in the United States— in Great Britain, France, Italy, even, most bizarrely, czarist Russia. But bullets did, after all, play a more important role than ballots; the bullets fired from the Iver Johnson revolver of Leon Czolgosz changed the political climate of the United States in a moment.

The "bottom line," as we say today, may well have been the fact that intense as the criticism of capitalism was, especially among intellectuals, Christian Socialists, radical working-class leaders, and farmers, there can be little doubt that the mass of middle-class Americans were decidedly "capitalistic" in their own aspirations. "Ask any man you meet," Moses Harman wrote in *Lucifer*, "whether he would like to stand in the shoes of Jay Gould, of Senator Stanford, or of Col. King. . . . Nine cases in ten he will eagerly answer, Yes! So then most poor men are simply underdeveloped stock gamblers, railroad kings, or land monopolists." To Frederic Howe, growing up in Meadville, Pennsylvania, "Life meant business, getting on in the world; the business one was in determined one's social position. My ambition," he wrote, "was to make money and enjoy the pleasures that possessors of wealth enjoyed. . . . My mind was empty of enthusiasm. I thought as those about me thought. My world was bounded by the block in which I lived, by my relatives, by the Methodist church. . . ." Howe escaped from that world, but it remained the world of a vast number of his compatriots. In the last analysis, radical reform of American capitalism would wait upon fundamental changes in the attitudes or "consciousness" of the inhabitants of innumerable Meadvilles scattered across the continent. But at least the process had begun.

In the midst of so much that was negative—the oppressive aspects of industrial capitalism, the continuing revelations of municipal corruption, the raging war between capital and labor, the increasing radicalization of desperate farmers of the South and Midwest, and the swelling tide of "dangerous" aliens—Americans clung stubbornly to their faith in the "greatness" of the United States, to the conviction that they were the Lord's Chosen People, the elect, whose mission it was to redeem the world. That mission seemed confirmed by the "wretched refuse of foreign shores," who, by coming year after year in enormous numbers, gave the most dramatic possible testimony to the power of that vision. Dismal as conditions were for the dwellers in big-city slums, for miners and factory workers and farmers, for Southern (and, to a somewhat lesser degree, Northern) blacks, there was always, like a tantalizing mirage on a distant horizon, the hope of something better. The government of the United States might be securely in the hands of the determined defenders of the status quo or the status quo ante, but it was abundantly evident that America was a different reality. "The United States"—if we take it to be, narrowly defined, the various structures of municipal, state, and Federal government, with their respective codes, constitutions, and laws—was, like most governments, generally obtuse and inept. "America" was far more basic and more elemental. It was a mind-boggling geography, a temper, an ethos, an ethic, a dream, and, above all, a *promise*. Mary Antin called her autobiography *The Promised Land*. Young Herbert Croly, the son of abolitionists David and Jane Cunningham Croly, would soon write a book called *The Promise of American Life*. It was the promise that was irresistible, that no reality, however grim, could tarnish or obscure. The fact was that America, with all its flaws and blemishes, was a larger, freer world. "Freedom" and "promise" were talismanic words, words that had the power to counterbalance, it might be argued—indeed, in time to overbalance—all the negative forces of late-nineteenth-century America. "The land of the free," "freedom-loving," "liberty-loving"— such phrases had a peculiar potency for Americans. In their preoccupation with the grosser inequities of American life, "freedom" seemed to many reformers tainted by the freedom of predatory capitalists to exploit their fellow citizens. The reformers were thus often less concerned with "freedom" than with "social justice." Yet "freedom"— freedom of speech, of writing, of assembly—was clearly an essential precondition for the long and arduous battle to achieve a more equitable society. Mary Antin's ecstasy at her ready admission to her Boston public school was as real a fact of American life as the big-city tenement, the Southern lynching, or the shooting of strikers by Pinkerton thugs, as real and, in the long run, far more *defining*. The institutional structures of the Old World were stifling, the accumulated social detritus of centuries of oppression. In America there was, after all, this powerful and perpetual referent to the Ur document of the nation, the rights and freedoms guaranteed to Americans by the Constitution. However ignored or abused, that document could, in the hands of the enlightened judge, demolish a tower of wrongs in an instant. "To breathe the air of a free people" may be a worn phrase, scoffed at by the cynical, but it describes an essential, a palpable reality. Generation after generation of newcomers to these shores drew such a breath, draw it still.

Were, we might ask, the majority of middle-class Americans "happy" in the waning decades of the century? The question is stubbornly resistant to an answer. The problem lies, in part, in defining happiness, in determining of what happiness consists and, beyond that, of deciding whether happiness is in itself a legitimate or even an obtainable goal. The Protestant Ethic, to which we attribute so much influence in shaping the American psyche, held that the purpose of life was to know and to do God's will—an extremely demanding exercise in itself. In this work we have inclined to the view that history is, above all, a tragic drama. If that is its most quintessential nature, then the issue of "happiness" appears irrelevant, if not frivolous, capable of being framed only by the Secular Democratic Consciousness. If a nineteenth-century equivalent of George Gallup had asked a substantial segment of middle-class small-town white Protestant Americans the question "Are you happy?" I suspect that the answer would have been overwhelmingly in the affirmative because even then Americans appear to have considered it very close to unpatriotic to confess to being less than euphoric at their good fortune in being citizens of the United States. Furthermore, as we have suggested, there was a very substantial body of evidence of the kind collected by Andrew Carnegie in *Triumphant Democracy* to support the superior advantages of such a status. But that, of course, begs the question of whether that status had, as an inevitable accompaniment, happiness. Proud to the point of perpetual boastfulness and clearly addicted to a constantly expanding range of creature comforts (the vaunted American standard of living), Americans, by every relatively objective criterion—their ancient and continuing dependence on alcohol and drugs, for example—appear to have been a restless, "nervous," "high anxiety" breed.

Perhaps we can get a better perspective on the question by addressing it to present-day America, which has, without question, attained a much higher level of material well-being and social justice. Again, we can be confident that most Americans wish to think of themselves as "happy"; they have, in fact, been polled more than once on that question, and the answer has always been affirmative by a great majority. On the other hand, there is a large body of data which suggest that the level of anxiety in the United States today may be as high as it was a century ago (or, conceivably, even higher).

But if we cannot answer the question of the American "happiness quotient" with any confidence, we can say that "America was promises." Promises bound the generations together despite the forces that worked strongly to pull them apart. The promise extended beyond the life of any single individual. It is true of America as of no other nation that we can understand it fully only in integuments of at least two generations because the promise was always that things would be better for the sons and daughters than for the fathers and mothers. The story of America is thus "generational"; it is only *between* the generations that we can begin to discern it. We have always lived more in the future than in the present. In the era covered by this volume it was as though the very harshness of the social and economic system had inspired the reformers to nobler visions of a new human order. In the struggle for justice of the oppressed and exploited and their advocates lay germinating the seeds of the future.

ACKNOWLEDGMENTS

I wish to express my gratitude to David Stanford for his role as my special adviser on American Indians. Though I fear I have not always pleased him in my interpretations, he has been unfailingly helpful and tolerant.

Sara Boutelle has passed along numerous useful items.

Frances Rydell gave the manuscript that loving attention which, as with earlier volumes, has done so much to make that phase of their preparation a pleasure.

I found Hal Sears's excellent study, *The Sex Radicals*, most helpful as was Jeanne Madeline Weimann's *The Fair Women* and Dolores Hayden's *Grand Domestic Revolution: A History of Feminist Designs for American Homes, Neighborhoods and Cities*.

The manuscript benefited greatly from the attentions of Benjamin Custer.

Index

Abbot, Alice Asbury, 498
Abbott, Lyman, 17–18, 483, 561, 605
Abbott, Mrs. Lyman, 399
Abolitionist movement, 93, 259, 283, 827
  capacity to sustain protest, 915
  effect on mind and character, 914–915
  Indian policy, 15–16
Academic freedom, 603–606
Academy of Political and Social Science, 151
Accidents and disasters, 191
Adams, Brooks, 123, 213, 296–297, 318, 486–487
  The Emancipation of Massachusetts, 327
  The Law of Civilization and Decay, 327–329, 553
  The New Empire, 921–922
Adams, Charles Francis, Sr., 296, 331
  Ambassador to Great Britain, ix, 296
Adams, Charles Francis, Jr., 59, 108–110, 295–297,
  305, 307, 318, 329–331, 458, 464
  Autobiography, 330–331
  on Harvard, 593–594
  on New England Sabbaths, 557
  ownership of Kansas stockyard, 801
  physical arduousness of war, 841–842
  railroads, 4, 108–110, 329–330
  writings, 330–331
Adams, Henry, 110–113, 296–297, 317–318
  on breakdown of American family, 914
  on Chicago's World's Fair, 503–504
  death of wife, 323–325
  on disappearance of religion, 556

The Education of Henry Adams, 318, 325
election of 1896, 552–553
election of President McKinley, 864–865
on "feminization" of American literature, 757
friendships, 319–331, 861
on future of country, 902
on Grant Administration, 454–455
John Hay and, 319–331
  Hay and Adams houses, 321–322, 324
on industrialism and capitalism, 534
on Jewish capitalists, 359
letter-writing, 319, 326
marriage to Marion Hooper ("Clover"), 320, 323,
  789
  Saint-Gaudens memorial to his wife, 789
on "new Americans," 921
Panic of 1893, 486–489, 491, 508–509
on politics, 454–455
professor of American history at Harvard, 320–
  321, 594
on railroads, 90
on relations with Great Britain, 889–890
Washington years, 321–322
on women, 690–691, 694–695
writings, 323–324
Adams, John, 142, 270, 296, 331
  radical friends, 918
Adams, John Quincy, 296–297, 331
  on Indian rights, 1
  on "internal improvements," 798–799, 922–923

Adams, Louisa Catherine, 296
Adams, Marion Hooper ("Clover"), 320, 323, 789
Adams, Samuel, 327
Adams family, 296, 317–331
  family life, 296–297
  Puritan heritage, 327, 330–331
Addams, Jane, 455, 483, 503, 681
  Democracy and Social Ethics, 412–416
  dream of universal fellowship, 407–408
  education, 404–407, 545
  Hull House, 404–421
  on Pullman strike, 525–526
  religion, 405–407
  "Why the Ward Boss Rules," 372–374
  on women's suffrage, 662
Addams, John H., 404–405
Adler, Dankmar, 792–793
Adler, Felix, 357
Adventist Church, 568
African emigration of blacks, 642–643
African Methodist Church, 633, 650, 752
Agassiz, Alexander, 917
Agassiz, Louis, 304, 592, 595, 670, 917
Agriculture, Department of, 423–424, 463, 922
Agricultural Wheel, 432–433
Aguinaldo, Emilio, 868, 873, 885
Albertson, Ralph, 565–566
Alcoholism, 665–666, 911, 913
Alcott, Bronson, 720, 763
Alcott, Louisa May, 720, 751, 763–764
Aldrich, Truman, 834–835
Allegheny College, 595–597
Alliance, farm-labor, 436–438, 446–448, 923–924
  (*See also* Farmer's Alliance)
Altgeld, John P., 416, 418, 484–495, 518, 520
American Association for the Advancement of Science, 592
American Association of Spiritualists, 263
American Federation of Labor (AF of L), 237, 255, 490
  craft unions, 237
  eight-hour day campaign, 237–238
  guiding principles, 526–527
  Pullman strike, 526
  socialist issue, 527–528
American Protective Association, 450, 533, 696
American Railway Union, 257, 517–535, 700, 706
American Revolution:
  economic equality, 918–919
  radical credentials of, 918–919
American Steel and Wire Company, 124
American Sugar Refining Company, 130
American Union, 113–114
Anarchism and anarchists, 186, 214, 245, 256, 258
  "American" or "individualist," 287
  attentât or political assassination, 472
  Alexander Berkman, 471–476
  Christian divisions, 284

communities, 291–294
  European, 287
  female, 288–290
  Samuel Fielden, 247
  free love movement and, 267
  free thought and, 285–294
  goals of, 287
  Haymarket Affair and, 246–247, 249–250
  importance of grass-roots anarchism, 293
  individualist, 164, 287, 294
  newspapers, 251
  number of anarchists, 290–291
  presidents assassinated by, 903–904
  August Spies, 238, 242–245, 247, 289
Andrews, Stephen Pearl, 258–259, 265–266, 271, 273, 276, 294, 298, 842
  free love movement, 259
Anglo-American Cattle Company, 804–805
Anglo-Saxon Americans, 540, 658–659
Anthony, Maj. Scott, 11–13
Anthony, Susan B., 264–265, 282, 493, 499
Anthropology, 43, 159, 601
Antin, Mary, 344–353, 927
  essay on George Washington, 352–353
  The Promised Land, 346–353
Antioch College, 679
Antitrust Act, 463–464
Anxiety and nervousness, 911–914, 928–929
  introspection and, 911–912
Apache Indians, 1–2, 34, 83
  raids by, 2, 38
Arapaho Indians:
  raids by, 10–11, 51–52
Arbeiter Zeitung, 243, 247, 251
Arbitration of labor disputes, 229, 460, 484, 707
Architects and architecture, 492–498, 789–796
  landscape architects, 779–780, 795–796
  New York City, 97
  skyscrapers, 792–793
  women, 794
Arizona Territory, 1, 34, 99
Armot, Pennsylvania:
  mining strikes, 480–481
Armour, Philip, 371, 647
Armstrong, Gen. Samuel, 621
Arthur, President Chester, 83, 94, 454–458
Arts and artists, 295, 492–498, 504, 772–797
  architects, 789–796
  collectors and collections, 773, 784
  cowboys and Indians, 780, 782–784
  Eastern art, 779, 784
  feminism and, 773
  "high society" painters, 784–786
  Impressionists, 775, 796
  landscapes and seascapes, 775, 779–780, 795–796
  museums and galleries, 495, 796–797
  photography, 777–779
  sculptors, 788–789

Arts and artists (*cont.*):
  "Western art," 779–782, 784
  women artists, 773, 787–788
Astor, Mrs. John Jacob, 84
Atchison, Topeka and Santa Fe, 97, 100, 112
Atlanta, Georgia, 835
Atlanta University, 634
Atlantic Monthly, 134, 251, 551, 692, 722, 725, 748
Attentât or political assassination, 472
Atwood, Charles B., 492
Austen, Kate, 288, 426
Austro-Hungarian Empire, 891
  emigration from, 332
Aveling, Eleanor Marx and husband, 198, 211–212, 214, 248, 436–437, 735

Bagby, George, 833
Bagehot, Walter, 598
Baker, Ray Stannard, 370, 377–378, 395, 400–401, 749
  on Coxey's march, 508–512
  on East-West differences, 821–822
  education, 596
  on Germany's industrial might, 891–892
  on irrigation, 816–817
  on Pullman strike, 520–521, 527
Bakunin, Mikhail, 166
Baltimore, electric street railroads, 119
Baltimore and Ohio railroad, 168–170, 191
Bancroft, George, 321–322
Banks, Nathaniel, 187
Baptists, 554, 580, 833
Barbed-wire fencing, 123–124
Bascom, Lt., 35, 40
Baseball, 845–846
Basketball, 850
Bear Republic, 467
Beard, George M., 913
Beaux, Cecilia, 496
Beaux-Arts, École des, Paris, 776, 789, 791, 794
Beecher, Catharine, 696, 914
  on health of women, 674–675
  reform of American home, 668–670
Beecher, Lt. Frederick Henry, 52
Beecher, Henry Ward, 16, 17, 161, 177–178, 238, 382, 398, 757–758
Beeson, John, 8, 31–32
Bell, Alexander Graham, 115
Bell Telephone Company, 115–116
Bellamy, Edward, 164, 483, 503, 556–557, 692, 698, 708–711
  Looking Backward, 292, 708–711, 738, 913
  national socialism, 164, 292, 483, 503, 698, 709–711, 724
  nationalist clubs, 483, 711
  new thought and, 692–695
Bemis, Edward W., 566, 603–605

Bennett, William, 494
Bent, Robert, 12–14
Benteen, Capt. Frederick, 69–72
Berea College in Kentucky, 634
Berkman, Alexander (anarchist), 471–476
  Frick shot by, 471–476
  Prison Memoirs of an Anarchist, 476
Bernard, Reuben, 35–36
Bethune, Robert, 794
Beveridge, Albert, 865–866
Bicycling, popularity of, 392–393, 844–845
Bierce, Ambrose, 754–755, 901
Bierstadt, Albert, 779–782
Bigelow, Poultney, 783
Bigelow, William Sturgis, 860
Billy the Kid, 810–811
Bingham, George Caleb (American painter), 774–776, 786
Birmingham, Alabama, iron and steel industry, 123
Birth control, 261, 273, 279, 693
Bishop, Isabella Lucy Bird, 818–819
Bismarck, Count Otto von, 891, 893
Black, William Perkins, 248–250, 254
Black Codes, 615
Black Hills expedition of 1874, 46
Black Hills Reservation, 61–73
  allotments of food, 65–66
  Cheyenne and Sioux on, 61–62
  Indians sent to Fort Laramie, 66
  military post established, 62
  peace conference, 73
  Sheridan's campaign against Indians, 66–73
  treaty meeting, 64–65
  White River parley, 64–66
Blackfoot Indians, 6
Blacks, 614–660
  advancement, 622
  African Emigrationists, 642–643
  American "prejudice," 878–879
  athletes, 846
  black regiments, 46, 52, 642
  civil rights, 658–659
  colleges for, 634
  consciousness for black people, 635–636
  cowboys, 647
  discrimination against, 621, 651
  disfranchisement of, 620–621, 650
  Dred Scott decision, 166
  education, 621
    industrial, 622–623
    missionary teachers, 633–634
  efforts to unionize, 645–646
  emancipation of slaves, 614–615
  emigration West and North, 637, 640–647
  employed on trains, 108
  erosion of rights and status, 614–615
  farmers' movement and, 446–448
  hopes for black equality, 614
  in Oklahoma Territory, 648–649

Blacks (cont.):
  intimidation of, 615–618
  "Jim Crow" laws, 625, 650
  leaders and spokesmen, 621–640
    W.E.B. Du Bois, 625–640
    Booker T. Washington, 621–640
  lynching mobs, 631–649, 651–653
  male suffrage, 662
  New Orleans race riots, 651–652
  on Indian Territory, 83
  Philippine occupation, 883–884
  police harassment of, 651
  political power destroyed, 619–621
  "poor whites" and, 632
  race relations, 624, 631, 650, 658–659
  radicalism of Northern blacks, 634
  rape charges, 650–651
  Reconstruction politics, 615–618, 642–643
  religion, 627, 632–633
  social segregation, 629–630
  Southern black Republicans, 619
  in Spanish-American War, 870–871, 874–879
  spirituals, 627
  treatment in post-Reconstruction period, 659–660
  white hostility, 638–639, 649, 657–658
  women, role of, 654–657
    black women's clubs, 655–656
    financial security, 654
    Southern white men and, 654
  World's Columbian Exposition, 501–502, 655–656
  writers, 737–738, 752
Blackwell, Antoinette Brown, 499–500
Blackwell, Dr. Elizabeth, 685–687
Blackwell, Henry, 662
Blaine, James G., 456, 458–459, 465
Blair, Lewis Harvie, 836–837
Blanc, Madame (French journalist), 668, 682
Bland, Richard Parks, 547
Blavatsky, Helena, 579, 698
Bliss, William Dwight Porter, 566
Blood, Col. James Harvey, 265
Bloomer, Amelia, 682
Bloomers, 689
Blythe, David Gilmour, 786
Body, interest in movement and postures, 776, 841
Boer War, 890
Bohemianism, 860
Bok, Edward, 397–399
Bonanza Kings (mining barons), 124–125
Bonfield, John, 241
Bonsal, Stephen, 877
Bonus incentive systems, 191
Bosses, political, 372–374
Boston, Mass., 826–827
  financial center, 827
  infatuation with British, 828
  Italian immigrants, 338–339
  literary scene, 721, 747, 753–754, 827
  slums, 419
  spiritual life, 826–827
  support for Indians, 58–60, 84
Boston Advertiser, 17
Boston Evening Transcript, 17, 378
Boston Public Library, 793
  murals painted by Sargent, 785–786
Boutelle, Charles A., 433
Boutwell, George, 866
Bowles, Samuel, 20, 733
Boxer Rebellion of 1900, 578, 895–896
Boyce, Neith, 354–355, 389
Bozeman Trail, 23–24, 29, 34
  abandonment of forts, 5, 60
Brady, Edgar, 394
Brandes, Georg, 361
Brent, John, 807–808
Bridger, Jim, 19, 24
Briggs, Charles, 568
Brisbane, Arthur, 402
Brook Farm, 165, 266
Brooks, Phillips, 789
Broos, William, 699
Brotherhood of Locomotive Engineers, 238
Brotherhood of Locomotive Firemen, 435
Brown, Alice, 764
Brown, John, 93
Brown, Leonard, 430
Brown, Preston, 883
Brown, Maj. William, 43
Brown University, 605
Browne, Carl, 509–510
Brownell, Capt. Cornelius, 883
Brush, Charles, 116–118
Bryan, William Jennings, 464–465, 487, 605, 719, 900
  Chautauqua lectures, 611
  "Cross of Gold" speech, 545, 548
  election of 1896, 544–553
  election of 1900, 897
  free silver issue, 465, 545, 548
Bryant, William Cullen, 717, 719
  The Library of World Poetry, 717
  Whitman and, 719
Bryce, James, 94, 873
Buchanan, President James, 8, 542
Buchanan, Jasper Johnson, 511
Buchanan, Joseph, 236, 255
Buchanan, Joseph Rodes, 341
Buffalo, New York, 179, 903–904
Buffalo Bill (Will Cody), 51, 73, 817
Buffalo hunting, 51, 102
  destroyed by railroads, 57–60
Buffalo soldiers, 46
Buntline, Ned, 817
Burchard, Rev. Samuel, 459
Burgess, John W., 658–659
Burnett, Dr. Mary Weeks, 665

Bushnell, Horace, 562–563
Bushnell, Kate, 687–688
Business interests:
  acts of tyranny and oppression, 179
  corrupt, 384
  effect on Haymarket Affair, 253–254
  influence on education, 601–606
  paramilitary organizations formed by, 236
  (See also Corporations)
Butler, Benjamin, 251, 458–459, 723
Butler, Nicholas Murray, 849
Butte, (Montana) copper mines, 479

Cable, George Washington, 749–750
  on integration of blacks and whites, 837
  Old Creole Days, 749–750
Cahan, Abraham, 354–355, 357, 389
Calhoun, James, 68
California:
  Chinese immigrants, 334–335
  gold rush, 467
Calvin, John, 556, 828, 917
Cambridge Cooperative Housekeeping Society,
  671–672, 738
Camp, Walter, 847–850
Camp Supply, Indian Territory, 45, 47
Canals, barge traffic, 112
Canby, Gen. E. R. S., 59–60
Cameron, Elizabeth Sherman, 325
Captain Jack, Modoc Indian chief, 59–60
Capitalism and capitalists, 144, 213
  attacks on, 111, 919
  Andrew Carnegie as exponent of, 134–139
  control over government, 920–921
  criticism of, 926
  Darwinism and, 140–163
  effect of Great Strikes, 185–186
  emphasis on profits, 131–133
  entrepreneurial daring, 131
  farmers versus, 430–431
  ideology of, 133–140
  inequities of, 701–703
  influence of bankers on corporations, 131–132
  opponents of, 213, 701–702
  political power and, 920–921
  "robber barons," xiii, 820
  Weaver's critique of, 443
  (See also War between capital and labor)
Capital punishment, 256
Carlisle, (Pennsylvania) school for Indians, 51
Carnegie, Andrew, 104, 120–123, 334, 384, 422–
  423, 466, 884, 900
  exponent of capitalism, 121, 134–138
  on growth of railroads, 98–99
  Homestead Strike, 122, 469
    (See also Homestead Strike)
  production genius, 122
  public indignation over Homestead Strike, 477–
    478

  public libraries given by, 478
  relations with workers, 121–122
  relief fund for Homestead workers, 478
  retirement in Scotland, 137, 469
  scabs and strikebreakers rejected by, 469
  servants, 855–856
  termed moral coward, 477–478
  Triumphant Democracy, 426, 469, 928
Carnegie Steel Company, 122
  Homestead Strike, 469–481
  immigrant labor, 224–225
  Edgar Thomson plant, 121–122, 470
Carpetmaking, 124
Carrington, Col. Henry, 24–26, 34
Carroll, Lewis, 751
Carson, Kit, 13–14
Case, Lyman, 266
Cassatt, Alexander, 495
Cassatt, Mary, 495
Catholic Church, 229, 580–586
  anti-Catholic hostility, 533, 580–586, 604
  ethnic groups, 580–581
  educational institutions, 363
  rights of labor, 581
  role of laity, 582–583
  women's suffrage, 662–663
Catholic Columbian Congress, 582
Catlin, George, 774
Cattle business, 97–98, 102–103, 804–805, 809
Centennial Exhibition in Philadelphia, 1
  telephone display, 115
Central America, 541
  revolutionary upheavals in, 894
Central Labor Union, 236, 242
Central Pacific, 90
Centralization of power, 130
Century magazine, 190, 390
  illustrations, 783
Chamberlain, Joseph, 889
Channing, Edward, 594–595
Chapman, Elizabeth Chanler, 419–420
Chapman, John Jay, 308, 313, 356, 365, 828–829
  on American literature, 764
  Classical-Christian Consciousness, 910
  on Cleveland, 459
  distinguished parentage, 711–712
  education of children, 419
  infatuation with British, 828–829
  William James and, 313, 601–602
  on Lowell, 721–722
  on New York City, 365
  poem on death of Bismarck, 893
  political activism and reform, 551, 711–714, 925
  Political Nursery, 388, 713, 887–888
  Practical Agitation, 713–714
  on preparatory schools, 589
  on Progress and Poverty, 209
  romantic reputation, 712
  scorn of convention, 860

Chapman, John Jay (*cont.*):
  settlement work, 419–420
  Roosevelt and, 388, 887–888
Chapman, Maria Weston, 711
Chapman, Minna Timmins, 711–712, 860
Charity, personal versus organized, 136, 165, 368,
  420–421
Charles, Robert, 651–652
Chautauqua movement, 608–611, 698, 917
Cherokee Indians, 85
Chesnut, Mary, 838
Chesnutt, Charles, 737–738, 752
Cheyenne Indians:
  raids and counterraids, 4–14, 51–52, 54–55
  reservation issue, 79–81
  surrender of, 83
Chicago, 369–372
  Jane Addams and Hull House, 404–421
  architecture, 790–793
  crime and criminals, 369–370
  cultural agencies, 911
  Great Fire, 369, 371
  Haymarket Affair, 241–257
  Italian immigrants, 336, 338
  labor radicalism, 236
  meat-packing business, 371
  meetings of labor groups, 242
  political bosses, 370–374
  radical organizations, 234, 247
  railroad center, 98
  railroad strikes, 180–183
    Halsted Street Viaduct, 181–182
  settlement houses, 404–421
  woman's club movement, 667–668
Chicago, Burlington and Quincy, 98
Chicago, Milwaukee and St. Paul, 98
Chicago, Rock Island and Pacific, 98
Chicago and North Western Railroad, 98, 464
Chicago Civil Federation, 503
Chicago Daily News, 177
Chicago Edison Company, 371
Chicago Mail, 242
Chicago Relief Aid Association, 503
Chicago Tribune, 522, 699
Chicago Union League, 134
Chicago's World's Columbian Exposition in 1893,
  326, 491–505
  American power and progress, 491–492
  architects and artists, 492–493, 794
  beneficial effects, 505
  black participation, 501–502, 655–656
  Cleveland's address, 496–497
  Ferris wheel, 504–505
  Midway, 505
  Parliament of Religions, 579
  role of women, 493–498, 655–656, 787–788,
  794
  Women's Building, 493–502

Child, Lydia Maria, 16, 28, 31–32, 55–56, 60
  An Appeal for the Indians, 31
Children and child care, 262
  child labor, 168, 217, 220–222, 417–418
  education, 419–420
  parental authority, 683–684
  rules for, 915–916
  working conditions, 217
China, 893–894
  Boxer Rebellion, 895–896
  Germany's ambitions in, 895
  missionary activity, 578–579
  Open Door policy, 896
Chinese immigrants, 87, 334–336
  cooks, 46
  worked on railroads, 91–92
Chinese Revolution, 576–577
Chivington, John, 9–14, 54
Chiricahua Apaches, 35–41
Chisholm Trail, 102–103
Choate, Joseph, 131, 895
Chopin, Kate O'Flaherty, 766–769, 851
  stories of feminine discontent, 769
Chopin, Oscar, 767
Christian radicalism, 431
Christian relief organizations, 165
Christian Science, 572–575
Christian Socialists, 102, 158, 164–165, 239, 439–
  440, 483, 909
  George Herron, 563–567
  journals, 566
  Pullman strike and, 523
Christianity, 554–586
  churches and sects, 554–555
  compatibility of evolution with, 160
  "fundamental," 586
  muscular Christianity, 842
  scientific principles, 202
  sin, 562–563
  (*See also* Religion)
Christmas, at Fort Lyon, 45
Church, Frederick, 781
Church of Christ, Scientists, 572–574
Church of the Latter-Day Saints, 813
Cigarmaking operations, 218
Cities, 364–375
  beautification of, 415
  creative energies, 910
  cultural agencies, 911
  emergence of, 910
  Far West, 813
  graft and corruption, 378, 400
  immigrants, 910
  municipal reform, 374–375, 385, 697
  New York City, 364–369
  political bosses, 372–374
  problems facing, 910–911
  wealth and poverty, 364

Civil Service reform, 460, 468
Civil War:
  consequences of, ix–xiii
  Indian participants, 8–9
Civilized Tribes, 83
Claflin, Roxy, 265
Claflin, Tennessee C., 166, 258–262, 267, 767
Clark, John Bates, 161
Clark, Dr. W. S., 576
Clark University at Worcester, 600
Class struggle, xi–xii
Classical-Christian Consciousness, 158, 714, 909–
  910
Clay, Henry, 922
Clayton-Bulwer Treaty of 1850, 894
Cleveland, President Grover, 83, 239, 454, 536–537
  Cuba's struggle for independence, 542–543
  disillusionment with, 530–531
  distribution of patronage, 460–461
  election of 1884, 458–463, 466–468
  election of 1892, 466–467, 482–488
  foreign affairs, 537–540
  inaugural address, 460
  Pullman strike, 518
  Republican charges against, 463
  tariff issue, 462
Clothes and clothing, 351–352, 689–690
  of Westerners, 799
  (See also Garment industry)
Club movement, 666–668
Coal mining:
  breaker boys, 222–223
  labor conditions, 214–215
  Spring Valley strike, 700
  (See also Mines and mining)
Cochise, Apache chief, 34–41
  refusal to go to Tularosa Reservation, 37–38, 40
Cody, Will (Buffalo Bill), 51, 73, 817
Coeur d'Alene, Idaho, mines, 479
Coffin, Charles, 117
Cole, Thomas, 786
Colgate, Samuel, 277
Colleges:
  for blacks, 634
  coeducational, 679–680, 682
  enrollments, 590–591
  private men's colleges, 679–680
  sport programs, 847–850
  women, 678–682
  (See also Institutions of higher learning)
Colorado:
  black homesteaders, 647
  women's vote, 532–533
Colorado Springs, 799, 818
Colorado Territory, 45
  Indian raids, 9–14
Colored Farmers' National Alliance and Coopera-
  tive Union, 433

Colored National Labor Union, 645–646
Colored Women's League, 501–502
Columbian World's Exposition (see Chicago World's
  Columbian Exposition)
Colyer, Vincent, 31, 37
Comanche Indians, 1–2
  raids and counterraids, 50–51
Comic supplements, newspapers, 402
Commercial Advertiser, 389
Common, John R., 606
Commonwealth Colony in Georgia, 706
Communism, 178, 180, 230, 256
  public attitudes toward, 242
Communities:
  communist, 165, 259
  free love, 266–267, 276
  immigrant, 339–340
  Jewish agricultural, 360–361
  model industrial towns, 191–192
  socialist-anarchist, 291–294
  utopian socialist, 165
Competition:
  attitudes toward, 113–114
  Carnegie on, 135
  free, 129
Comstock, Anthony, 270, 277–279, 285, 294
Comstock Act (1873), 277
Comstock lode, 127
Comte, Auguste, 307
Conditions of labor (see Labor conditions)
Conformity, 915, 917
Congregational Church, 917
Congregationalists, 284, 554
Congress:
  Indian affairs, 2, 15
  Sand Creek massacre investigation, 13–14
Conkling, Roscoe, 456
Connecticut Indian Association, 84
Connor, Gen. Patrick, 11
Consciousness movement:
  anxiety about the "dangerous classes," 514
  Classical-Christian, 158, 714, 909–910
  effect of exposé journalists and editors, 403
  effects of railroad strikes, 185
  forms of, 158
  grass-roots anarchism and, 293
  growth of new, xv
  public imagination or, 455
  Secular Democratic, 148, 158, 714, 909–910, 928
Conservatism, 483
Constitution, 376, 919–920, 922
  debates over articles, 376
Contraceptive information, 278–279
Control of one's self, 916–917
Converse, Rev. James, 566
Cooke, Jay, 108–109
Cooke, Gen. Philip St. George, 26
Cooke, Rollin Hillyer, 760

Cooke, Rose Terry, 760
Consumerism, 161
Cooper, Anna Julia, 501–502, 656–657, 685
Cooper, James Fenimore, 86, 314, 766
Cooper Union, NYC, 231–232, 237, 359, 625, 917
Cooperative movement, 228, 598
  enterprises, 121, 230–231
  living arrangements, 671–673
  Henry Demarest Lloyd and, 703–707
Cooperative Union of America, 432
Copperheads, 453, 459
Corcoran, William Wilson, 321
Corporations:
  corrupting influence of, 444–445
  growth of power, 444–445, 468
  influence of bankers and financiers, 131–132
  Panic of 1893, 485–486
  (See also Business interests)
Cotton mills, Southern, 835
Courts and justice, 923
Cowboys, 808–809
  black, 647
  union of rodeo performers, 808–809
  working conditions, 222
Cox, Kenyon, 788–789
Coxey, Jacob, 508–516
  "Address of Protest," 514–515
Coxey's Army, 508–516
  farmers and workingmen, 512–513
  supporters, 515
Craddock, Charles Egbert, 771
Cramer, Lt. Joseph, 12
Crane, Mary Helen, 747
Crane, Stephen, 395, 747–748, 875
  The Red Badge of Courage, 748
Crazy Horse, Oglala chieftain, 65, 68–71, 73, 77
  killing of, 73–74
Crédit Mobilier scandals, 90, 92
Creel, George, 402, 830
Crime and criminals, 911
  organized lawlessness, x
  train robberies, 105–107
Crocker, Charles, 91, 93, 97, 755
Crocker, William, 479, 495
Croker, Dick, 374–375, 386
Croly, David and Jane Cunningham, 266, 927
Croly, Herbert, 927
Crook, Gen. George, 38, 67–69, 73
  pacification of Indians, 42–44
  at Rosebud Creek, 68–69
  winter campaigning, 43
Crow Indians, 94–95
Cuba, 539–544, 873–879
  attack on Santiago, 875–876
  disease, 878, 880
  independence from Spain, 541–542
  invasion of, 873–879
  newspapers and, 880–881

San Juan Hill, 876–877
Spain and, 865
Spanish-American War, 873–881
struggle for independence, 541–543
Culture and customs, 492–493
  city agencies, 911
  democracy and, 492
  of immigrants, 339–340
  Indians, 20, 43, 84–86
  industrial, 89
Curie, Marie, 396
Curtis, Cyrus, 398
Curtis, George William, 458, 782, 849–850
Curtis, Gen. Martin, 12
Curtis, William Eleroy, 62–63
Curtis Publishing Company, 398
Custer, Elizabeth, 64
Custer, Gen. George, 1, 46, 52–55
  campaign against Indians, 62, 67–72
  defeat at Little Bighorn, 70–71
  worst military disaster, 71
"Custer's Last Stand," 72
Customers, treatment of, 115
Cutting, R. Fulton, 888
Czech immigrants, 332
  Great Plains states, 341–342
Czech-language newspapers, 342
Czolgosz, Leon, 903–904, 926

Dacus, J. A., on Great Strikes, 169–173, 178–186
Daft, Leo, 119
Dakota Territory, 62, 99
  Czech migration to, 341
  railroads, 100
Damrosch, Walter, 854
Dana, Charles, 176, 300, 381
Dana, Richard Henry, 330, 591–592, 722
  Two Years Before the Mast, 729
Dana, Richard Henry, Jr., 850, 916
Danish immigrants, 332
Darrow, Clarence, 288, 416, 485, 707
Darwin, Charles, 210–211
  Origin of Species, 211
  survival of fittest, 130, 201
Darwinism, xiii, 137, 139, 140–163, 273, 328, 559–560, 586, 601
  John Bates Clark, 161
  John Fiske, 158–160
  Charles Sander Peirce, 161–163
  Josiah Strong, 160–161
  William Graham Sumner, 140–147, 151, 157–158
  Lester Ward, 140–144, 147–158
Daudet, Alphonse, 396
Davidson, Thomas, 612
Davis, Andrew Jackson, 294
Davis, David, 444–445
Davis, James H., 451
Davis, Jefferson, 95, 182, 628, 831

Davis, L. Clarke, 769
Davis, Maria Louisa, 786
Davis, Rebecca Harding, 769–770, 875
Davis, Richard Harding, 875
Dawes, Sen. Henry, 239
Dawes Act in 1887, 84
Day, William Rufus, Secretary of State, 882, 889
De Bardeleben, Henry Fairchild, 835
Debating and literary societies, 258, 698
De Bow, L. D. B., 834
Debs, Eugene V., 257, 519–532, 897
    cooperative movement, 706
    Pullman strike, 517, 519–527
de Claire, Hector, 288
de Cleyre, Voltairine (anarchist), 288–290, 356,
    485, 904
De Lamar, Joseph, 125
De Leon, Daniel, 253
De Mille, Agnes, 195
Democracy, x–xi
Democratic Party, 453–468, 925
    conservative elements, 453
    divisions in, 503
    election of 1878, 456–457
    election of 1880, 456–457
    election of 1884, 458–463
    election of 1892, 465–466
    election of 1896, 544–553
    election of 1900, 900
    hard money versus free silver wing, 450
    Midwest, 467–468, 544
Denver, Colorado, 813
Depew, Chauncey, 372
Depression of 1873, 167
Depression of 1879, 213–214
Depression of 1892, 450
Depression of 1893, 131–132, 911
Depression of 1894, 529–530
Depressions, cause of, 199–200, 203
    failure of banks and financial houses, 464
Dewey, Capt. George, 868, 871–872
    popular hero, 879–880
    victor at Manila, 871–872
Dewey, John, 311, 589, 698
Diaries and letter-writing, 319, 326, 861–862,
    911
Dibble, Martha Cleveland, 501
Dickens, Charles, 403, 802–803
    Hard Times, 380
Dickinson, Anna, 449, 819
Dickinson, Emily, 723, 731–735
Dickinson, Dr. Frances, 493
Die Freiheit journal, 231, 251
Diggs, Annie, 285–286, 515
Dill, James B., 384
Dillon, Sidney, 92, 109
Disasters and accidents, 191
    natural, 428–429
    railroad, 103

Divorce, 259
    (See also Marriage and divorce)
Dodd, Anna Bowman, 739
Dodge, William, 29, 58–59
Dodge City, 97, 103
Doggett, Kate Newell, 557
Dole, Sanford, 878
Dolliver, J. P., 433
Doniphan, Col. Alexander, 3
Donnelly, Ignatius (Populist leader), 440–443, 450,
    460–461, 549–550, 897
    Caesar's Column (1891), 441
    The Golden Bottle, 442
Dooley, Mr., 371
Douglass, Frederick, 16, 56, 500, 502, 622, 640–
    641, 645, 656, 662
Dow, Neal, 457, 459
Drake, Elmina, 273–274
Dred Scott decision, 166
Drexel, Elizabeth, 857
Drug abuse, 911–913
    cocaine and heroin, 913
Du Bois, William Edward Burghardt, 313, 625–
    640
    academic career, 629–640
    attack on Booker T. Washington, 636–640
    early life, 626
    education, 626–629
    friend of William James, 627–628
    The Philadelphia Negro, 629–631
    The Souls of Black Folk, 627, 635–636, 840
Duck hunting, 843
Dull Knife, Cheyenne chief, 79–80
Dunbar, Paul Laurence, 502, 629, 753
Dunning, William, 658–659
Durant, Henry Fowle, 678–679
Dynamic Sociology (Ward), 150–157

Eakins, Thomas Cowperthwaite, 775–777
    paintings of sporting activities, 776–777
    portraits, 776
East and Easterners:
    East-West differences, 799–800, 820–821, 911
    "Eastern art," 779
    investors in West, 805–806
    role of women, 682
Easton Greys (Philadelphia), 175–176, 187
École des Beaux-Arts in Paris, 776, 789, 791, 794
Economics, 566, 922
    capital preceded and created labor, 202
    classical, 138–139
    Malthusian-Ricardian-Smithian, 200–203
    new and old, 598, 601
Eddy, Asa Gilbert, 574
Eddy, Mary Baker, 572–575
Edgar Thomson Steel Company, 121–122, 470
Edison, Thomas Alva, 117–118
    inventions, 117–118
Edmonds, Richard, 834

Education, 587–613
  academic freedom, 603–606
  adult education, 608, 611–612
  of blacks, 633–634
  Chautauqua movement, 608–611
  college preparatory schools, 588–589
  colleges, 589–590, 606
    curriculum, 601–605
    doctrine of objectivity, 606–607
  denominational colleges, 593, 607
  doctrine of objectivity, 606–607
  enrollments in public schools, 589–591
  Federal agencies and, 592
  forms of, 155–156
  free public, 165, 589–591, 612
  German scholarship and, 596–597
  graduate studies, 588, 612–613
  Harvard, 592–595
  influence of business interests, 601–606
  Institutions of Higher Learning (IHLs), 590,
    595–606
  instruction, 591
  medical schools, 593
  Midwest institutions, 593
  "new" versus "old," 587–588
  pedagogy, 589
  playgrounds, 591
  private versus public, 612
  redemptive power, 587
  scientific, 588
  scientists, 592–593
  state universities, 593, 612
  Sunday school education, 609
  teachers, 589–590
    women, 590
  teachers' colleges and normal schools, 591
  universal, 152
  wooing of capitalists, 601–602
Eight-hour-day issue, 133, 237–240
  instituted by Carnegie, 121, 123
  negative reaction to, 238–239
  pay issue, 238–239
1893 (dramatic year), 482–507
  Chicago World's Columbian Exposition, 491–505
  Panic of 1893, 482–491
  poor and poverty, 503
  railroad bankruptcies, 485
  repeal of Silver Purchase Act, 487–488
Elections, 454–468, 532–533
  1872, 59
  1878, 456
  1880, 456
  1884, 458
  1888, 462
  1890, 464–465
  1892, 450, 454, 456, 465–466, 482–484
  1894, 530, 532, 534–535, 544
  1896, 536–553, 864
  1897, 553

  1898, 869
  1900, 897, 901–904
Electric power companies, 117–120
Electric street railroads, 119
Electricity, 113, 116–118
  alternating current, 118–119
  development and growth, 116–118
  dynamos, 117–118
  generator problems, 116
  incandescent lamps, 118
Electromagnetism, 283
Elevators and skyscrapers, 792
Eliot, Charles William, 303, 594–595
  President of Harvard, 307–309, 601–602
Eliot, T. S., 730
Elites, 295–296
  Adams family, 296
  James family, 296
Ellinger, Moritz, 285
Elliot, Ethel Stewart, 857
Elliott, Joel, 54–55, 70
Ellis, Elizabeth Warder, 859
Ely, Richard, 419, 483, 503, 550, 598–599, 603, 917
Ely, Mayor Smith, 178
Emancipation Proclamation, 93
Emerson, Ralph Waldo, 112, 263, 297–298, 316,
    701, 716–718, 720–721, 822
  "The American Scholar," 210
Employee benefits programs, 191
Engel, George, 251, 254
Engels, Friedrich, 417
  The Condition of the Working Class in England, 215
Engineers and engineering, 791
England (see Great Britain)
Enlightenment philosophers, 152
  rationalism, 282
Entrepreneurs, xi
  exploitative behavior, 444–445
  origins of leading, 124
Episcopalians, 284, 554
Equal Rights Association, 32
Erie Canal, 296–297
Erie Railroad, 108–109
  scandal, 330
Estes Park, Colorado, 799, 818–819
Ethical Culture Society, 357, 407, 410
Eugenics, 260–261, 276, 341
Europe, revolutionary upheavals, 919
European travels, 857–859
Evans, Chris, 106–107
Evans, Gov. John, 11
Evarts, Secretary of State William, 95–96, 169
Evolution, xiii, 159
  compatibility with Christianity, 160
  process of natural selection, 142
  (See also Darwinism)
Ewert, Theodore, 63
Expansionists, 882–883
Experts, 910, 917

Fabian Socialists of Great Britain, 211, 286
Fairbank, John, 577
Fall River, Mass., 215–218
  housing conditions, 218
  labor conditions, 215, 217
Families and family life, 263
  breakdown of, 911, 914
  effect of abolition movement on, 914–915
  parental relationships, 915
  reformers, 684
  rules for children, 915–916
  values transmitted by, 296, 914, 917
Far West, xiii–xiv
  cities, 813
  education, 593
  journalists, 402
Farmers' Alliance, 286, 432, 453, 839
  Lecture Bureau, 449
  Ocala (Florida) Convention, 448
Farmers' movement, 420–451
  aims of, 432–433
  alliance between black and white farmers, 447–448
  alliance between workers and farmers, 436–438, 446–448
    failure of, 923–924
  associations, 429–432
  cooperative activities, 431
  Department of Agriculture and, 423–424
  drought and bust of 1887, 424–425, 437
  Granger movement, 429–432
  economic distress, 425, 437
  enterprise and ingenuity of farmers, 424
  farm machinery, 423
  grains and wheat, 422–423
  grievances, 432
  large-scale agriculture, 102, 111
  leaders:
    Ignatius Donnelly, 440–443, 450
    W. Scott Morgan, 433–434
    Thomas Nugent, 439–440
    John Swinton, 436
    Tom Watson, 436–439
    James B. Weaver, 443–445
  live stock, 422–423
  living conditions, 425–427
  natural disasters, 428–429
  organizers of, 437
  plight of farm wives, 426–427
  productivity, 422–423
  railroad versus, 430
  subtreasury plan, 433
Farmers' Mutual Benefit Association, 432
Farmers' Union, 432
Farnham, Eliza, 274
Farragut, Admiral David G., 789
Farrington brothers (train robbers), 105
Faulkner, William, 730
Federal Steel Company, 124

Federal troops, as strikebreakers, 170–172, 178, 187–188, 518–520, 528
Federalist Papers, 918
Federation of Organized Trades and Labor Unions, 237
Feminism, 286, 676–677
Ferrell, Frank J., 230
Ferris, George Washington Gale, 504
Ferris wheel, 504–505
Fetterman, Capt. James, 24–27, 56, 66
Field, Kate, 498
Field, Marshall, 253
Fielden, Sam, 245, 247, 254
Financial policies:
  free silver, 450, 466, 468, 547
  hard versus soft money, 450, 453–454
  monetary policy, 443
Finney, John, 419
Fischer, Adolph, 250, 251, 254
Fish, Hamilton, 875
Fisher, Sidney George, 133, 305, 588, 842, 912–913
Fisk, Clinton, 463
Fisk, Jim, 57, 101, 108, 857
Fisk University at Nashville, 126, 634
Fiske, John, 158–160, 558, 917
  The Idea of God as Affected by Modern Knowledge, 159
  Outlines of Cosmic Philosophy, 159
Fitzmaurice, John W., 223
Fitzpatrick, Thomas, 4–7, 19
Five of Hearts Club, 323
Flexner, Simon, 419
Flower, Benjamin Orange, 580
Football, 847–850
  college teams, 847–850
  reforms, 849–850
Foote, Dr. Edward Bliss, 278–279
Foote, Edward Bond, 278
Forbes-Robertson, Beatrice, 667
Ford, Bob, 106
Foreign policy, 889–905
  Cleveland era, 537–540
  (*See also* Spanish-American War)
Forney, John, 745
  The New Nobility, 745–746, 784, 916
Forster, Dora, 275–276
Forsyth, Maj. George, 52
Fort Atkinson, Indians at, 5
Fort Benton, 6
Fort Phil Kearny, 24, 63
Fort Laramie, 64, 66
  Indian council meeting, 4–5
  Indian raids, 7
  treaty with Sioux and Cheyenne (1868), 29
Fort Lincoln, 64, 68, 78
Fort Lyon, 11–13, 45–49
Fort Riley, 53
Fort Wayne, Indiana, railroad strikes, 179–180
Fort Wise, Indian treaty, 10

Forts:
    in Indian territory, 5
    life in frontier posts, 44–49
Fortune, T. Thomas, 628–630, 655
Foster, John Watson, 895
Founding Fathers, 922
Fourier, Charles, 266
Fox, Anna, 194–195
Fox, Sam, 120
France–U.S. relations, 896
Franklin Institute, 116
"Free alliance," 259
Free love movement, 258–283, 567
    advocates of, 268–269
    "Affinity," 260
    alliances, 266–269
    attacks on conventional marriages, 268–271
    children and child-rearing, 262
    Christian divisions, 284, 287
    communities, 266–267, 276
    contraceptives and birth control, 261
    contracts for housework, 275
    grass-roots strain, 267
    journals, 268–270
    in Midwest, 267
    potency of, 264–265
    reforms and reformers, 264–283
    revolution in domestic life, 261
    scientific principles in mate selection, 260–261,
        276, 341
    sex reforms, 270–273, 275, 282–283
    taboos on "sexual" words, 271
Free Religious Association, 285
Free (coinage of) silver, 450, 466, 468, 547
    Bryan and, 465
    greenback–free silver–gold controversy,
        453
Free Soil cause, 9
Free speech, 256, 268, 270
    opposition to Comstock, 278
Free thought and freethinkers, 149–150, 258, 268–
        269, 273, 556
    communities, 292–293
    Czech-language newspapers, 342
    journals, 284
    Midwest meetings, 284–287
    newspaper editors, 294
    publication of obscene words, 285
    spiritualism and, 283
Freedman's Bureau, 38
Freedom, magic word, 258–259
    and rights, 927
Freeman, Mary Wilkins, 761–763
    life in New England towns, 761–763
    A New England Nun, 762–763
Freemasons, 359
French, Daniel Chester, 492
French Revolution, 473
    Great Fear in France, 184–185

Frewen, Moreton, 805
Frick, Henry, 122–123, 339, 773
    manager of Carnegie Steel Company, 469–470
    public indignation at strikebreaking efforts, 477
    shot by Berkman, 471–476
Frick Coke Company, strike in 1887, 469–470
Friends and friendships, 861
Frontier settlers:
    Indian raids, 56
    life in frontier posts, 44–49
Fuller, Melville, 461

Gage, Lyman, 253–254, 503
Gall, leader of Hunkpapa Sioux, 66, 70–71, 73
Galloway, John, 883–884
Gardner, Asa, 553
Gardner, Elizabeth, 495
Gardner, Isabella, 495
Gardner, William Amory, 862–863
Garfield, President James A., 186–187, 208, 456–
        457
    assassination of, 454, 457
Garland, Hamlin, 746–747, 765
Garment industry, 351–352
Garrison, Frances, 93
Garrison, William Lloyd, 21, 83, 93
Gary, Joseph, 248, 253
Gas, demand for natural gas, 120
Gates, George A., 563, 821
Gates, John W. ("Bet-a-Million"), 123–124
Gatling guns, 876
General Managers' Association, 518
Genetic issues, 658
Geology, study of, 592
George, Henry, 158, 164, 483, 529, 797, 820
    early life, 193–194
    on financial insecurity, 204
    Haymarket Affair and, 252
    on individual life, 206–207
    interest in becoming college professor, 198–
        199
    The Irish Land Question, 208
    on land and rents, 197–198, 204–205
    marriage, 194–195
    nationalization of land, 211–212
    opposed to Chinese immigration, 334
    opposed to Malthusian-Ricardian-Smithian eco-
        nomics, 200–203
    Our Land and Land Policy, 197–198
    Progress and Poverty, 150–151, 192–212, 605
        influence of, 211–212
        success of, 208–209
    public speaking career, 198
    reflections on immortality, 207–208
    Single Tax Clubs, 698
    single tax theories, 204–205, 211
    social law and moral law, 201
    "The Study of Political Economy," 198–199
    style of writing, 209–210

George, Henry (*cont.*):
  theories, 199–212
  writings, 196–212
George, Henry, Jr., 208
Georgia Commonwealth, 565
"German Bureau," 467
German immigrants, 165, 332–333
  Black Sea Germans, 343
  hostility toward, 246
  "liberationists," 93
  political activity, 467
  radical segment, 333
  in Texas, 341
  Volga Germans, 342–343
Germany, 891–893, 922
  Ray Stannard Baker on, 891–892
  centralization of power, 893
  influence on American education, 596–597
  militant nationalism, 892
  scientific research, 891
  U.S. relations and, 890–891
Geronimo, 83
Ghost Dance uprising, 83, 823–825
Gibbon, Col. John, 67–69, 71
Gibbons, James Cardinal, 581–583
Gibson, Charles Dana, 875
Gildersleeve, Basil, 597
Gillette, King Camp, 291–292
Gillette's "safety" razor, 292
Gilman, Arthur, 679
Gilman, Caroline Howard, 670
Gilman, Charlotte Perkins, 275–276, 668, 672–673,
    694, 764–765
  on servant problems, 855–856
  "The Yellow Wall Paper," 765–767
Gilman, Daniel Coit, 592–593, 597–600, 750
Gilman, Samuel, 670
Gladden, Washington, 560–562, 585, 660, 885–886
Glidden, Joseph, 123–124
Goddard, Martha, 82
Goddard, Morrill, 402
Godkin, E. L., 79, 94, 228, 458, 538
  editor of *Nation*, 79, 97
  on Indian problem, 17, 79
  on Great Strikes, 188–189, 228
Gold Creek, 94–95
Gold rush of '49, 53, 103
Gold strike on Black Hills, 61
Goldbugs, 464, 466
Golf, 137
Goldman, Emma (anarchist), 288, 426, 458, 471–
    473, 476, 505–506, 683, 903–904
  attack on Johann Most, 476
  description of Debs, 521–522
  Mother Earth, 904
Gompers, Samuel, 237, 252–253, 255, 483, 490–
    491
  clemency appeal for Haymarket anarchists, 251–
    252

craft-union patterns, 257
  eight-hour day campaign, 237–238
  Haymarket Affair, 251–253
  Pullman strike, 526–532
  refusal to call general strike, 526–529
Goo-goos, 713
Good Government Clubs, 713
"Good Government" reforms, 374
Gordon, Samuel, 290
Gorman, Arthur Pue, 530
Gould, Jay, 90, 134, 229, 397–398, 602
Government, Federal, 922–923
  intervention, 922
  purposes of, 153
  troops used as strikebreakers, 170–172, 177–178,
    187–188, 479, 518–520, 528
Grady, Henry, 833, 835
Graft and corruption, municipal, 400–401
Grand Canyon, 799
Granger, Gen. Gordon, 37
Granger movement, 429–432
Grant, Frederick Dent, 63–64, 387
Grant, President Ulysses S., 18, 94–95
  Indian peace policy, 18–19, 31–33, 36–40, 50–
    60, 62, 78–79
  restores Custer's command, 67
Grant, Julia Dent, 493–494
Grasshopper plague, 428–429
Gray, Asa, 592
Gray, Elisha, 115
Great Britain:
  American relations, 537–539, 828, 889–890
  investors in Western lands, 804–805
  labor conditions, 214–215
  social life, 828–829
  Venezuela affair, 537–539
Great Desert West, 799, 814–816
Great Northern Railway, 98, 468
Great Plains West, 799, 805
  Czech farmers, 342
  immigrants, 333, 341–343
  Kansas, 801–802
  Volga Germans, 342–343
Great Rock Island Route, 101
Great Strikes (1877), 164–192, 228, 456
  concessions by railroad companies, 180–182
  congressional reaction, 186–187
  consequences of, 183, 191–192
  fear of revolution, 171
  Federal troops as strikebreakers, 170–172, 178,
    187–188
  grievances, 175, 178–179, 183
  public opinion favored, 176–178
  right to strike, 186–187
  riots and violence, 170–174, 178, 189–190
  significance of, 177, 184–185
  spontaneous outbreaks, 168, 184, 528
  women involved in, 171–172, 174, 182
Greek civilization, preoccupation with, 852

Greek immigrants, 332
Greeley, Horace, 59, 194
Green, Norvin, 113–114
Greenback-free silver-gold controversy, 453
Greenback-Labor Party, 456, 458–459, 616
Greenbackers, 432
Greener, Richard, 641, 646
Grinell, Julius, 253
Grisham, G. N., 625
Grover, A. J., 20
Guggenheim interests, 358, 805
Gunton, George, 605, 705
Gurney, Ephraim, 320

Haggin, James, 125
Hale, Beatrice Forbes-Robertson, 693–694
Hale, Edward Everett, 723
Hall, Abraham Oakey, 506
Hall, G. Stanley, 600
Hallowell, Sara, 495, 796
Halstead, Murat, 93
Hamilton, Agnes, 419
Hamilton, Alice, 418–419
Hamilton, Norah, 419
Hammond, John Hays, 479
Hampton, Wade, 615
Hampton Institute, Virginia, 51, 621
Hancock, Gen. Winfield Scott, 178, 456–457
Hanna, Marcus Alonzo, 864–865
  (See also Mark Hanna)
Hanna, Mark, 454, 522, 545–547, 864–866, 904–
    906
  appointed to Senate, 864–866
  McKinley and, 454, 546–547, 864–866, 905
  opposed TR, 898–899, 905–906
  presidential campaign of 1900, 897
Hapgood, Hutchins, 313, 354–355, 389, 404
Happiness, issue of, 928
  organization of, 154–155
Hard money versus soft money, 450, 453–454, 466
Hare, William, 62
Harlan, Justice John, 659
Harman, Lillian, 268, 270, 275, 281
Harman, Moses, 267–268, 279–280, 427, 926
  charged with obscenity, 280
  individualist anarchists, 287
  Lucifer, published by, 268–269, 279–281, 284–
    288
Harney, Col. William, 7, 28
Harper, William Rainey, 370, 600–605
Harper's Magazine, 723
Harper's Weekly, 17, 114, 246
  illustrations, 774, 781–782
Harriman, Borden, 691
Harriman, Florence, 666–667, 793, 854, 859
Harriman, Joe, 897
Harris, Joel Chandler, 631, 748–749, 822, 832
  Uncle Remus stories, 748
Harris, Thomas Lake, 293, 755

Harris, Townsend, 575–576
Harrison, President Benjamin, 454, 462–464, 479,
    516
Harrison, Carter, 234
Harrison, President William Henry, 462, 899
Hart, Albert Bushnell, 594–595
Harte, Bret, 727
Harvard College, 159, 553–595
  Charles Francis Adams, Jr., 593–594
  faculty, 592–595
  history department, 594–595
  William James appointed professor of philosophy,
    303, 307, 308
  Lawrence Scientific School, 303
  Medical School, 602
  philosophy department, 308–312
Harvey, William Hope, 536
Harvey restaurants and Harvey Girls, 98
Haskell, Burnette, 235–236, 292
Haskins, Charles Homer, 599
Havemeyer, H. O., 530–531
Hawaiian Islands:
  annexation of, 54, 873, 877–878
  missionaries, 877–878
Hawthorne, Nathaniel, 316, 731, 751
Hay, John, 189–190, 228, 402, 766
  and Henry Adams, 319–331, 789
    camping expedition to Yellowstone, 843–844
    houses, 321–322, 324
  ambassador to Great Britain, 865, 889
  appointed secretary of state, 889, 896–905
  biography of Lincoln, 320
  The Bread-Winners, 190, 745
  diplomatic triumphs, 889–905
  on McKinley-Bryan campaigns, 552
  relations with Congress, 894–895
  Roosevelt's Cabinet, 905
  on Spanish-American War, 881
Hay and Adams houses, 321–322, 324
Hayden, Sophia, 493–494, 794
Hayes, President Rutherford B., 79, 270, 321–322,
    454
  Great Strikes, 169–171
  use of Federal troops to suppress strikes, 177–
    178
Haymarket Affair (1886), 215, 241–257, 290
  anarchists, pardoned by Altgeld, 485
  bombing, 244–245
  campaign for clemency, 250–254
  effect on labor movement, 249
  guilty verdict, 249
  imprint on history, 255
  interest in England, 253–254
  martyrs, 255
  popular reaction, 245–247, 253–255
  riot and bloodshed, 244–248
  Spies's "call to arms," 243–244
  trials, 247–249
Haywood, William ("Big Bill"), 225, 479, 516

Hazen, Charles, 599
Health of Americans, 674–678, 841–842
Hearst, George, 125, 370
Hearst, Phoebe Apperson, 813
Hearst, William Randolph, 370, 402, 901
  Journal, 402, 867–868, 876–877
  rivalry between Pulitzer and, 402, 871–872
Hegermann-Lindencrone, Lillie Greenough, 806–808
Hemingway, Ernest, 730
Henderson, Sen. John B., 28
Henrotin, Ellen, 667
Henry, Joseph, 592, 917, 922
Herbert, Victor, 871, 879
Herron, George (Christian Socialist), 102, 483–484, 555, 601, 735–736
  Kingdom magazine, 564–565
Hewitt, Abram, 208, 820, 910
Heywood, Angela Tilton, 269–272, 694
Heywood, Ezra, 269–270, 279
  convicted of publishing obscene material, 279
  free love movement, 269
Hickok, Wild Bill, 817
Higginson, Thomas Wentworth, 402, 659, 848
  literary critic, 722–724, 734–735, 766
Hill, Sen. David Bennet, 488
Hill, James Jerome (railroad baron), 98, 461, 468, 485, 523
Hillis, Rev. Newell Dwight, 652
Hinduism, 579
Historians, 320–321, 324, 328
  basic responsibility, 907–908
  existential and analytical, 907–908
  narrative, 908
Hoar, Sen. George, 132, 894, 900
Hobart, Garret A., 550, 897
Holliday, Doc, 811
Holmes, Emma, 8–9
Holmes, John, 20–21
Holmes, Lizzie, 234
Holmes, Oliver Wendell, 724–725, 757–758
Holmes, William, 247, 256
Holt, Henry, 324, 398
Homer, Winslow, 774–776
Homestead (Pennsylvania) Strike, 122, 469–481
  Frick shot by Berkman, 471–476
  Frick's attempts to break union, 470–471
  Pinkerton agents, 471, 473–477
  public opinion in support of, 476–478
  state militia to restore order, 471, 474
  town founded by Carnegie, 469
Homestead Act, 99
Homesteading, 99–100
Hooker, Isabella Beecher, 674
Hooper, Marion, 320
  (*See also* Adams, Marion Hooper "Clover")
Hopkins, Johns (*see* Johns Hopkins University)
Hopkins, Mark, 91, 93, 97, 133
Horse racing, 846–847

Hose, Sam, 631, 649
Houdini, Harry, 505
Hours and wages, 216–217
  eight-hour-day campaign, 121, 122, 133, 237–240
Housing, New York City, 218
Houston, Edwin, 117
Howard, J. Imogen, 655–656
Howard, Milford, 435, 531–532
Howard, Gen. Oliver Otis, 38–40, 44, 75–77
Howard University, 38, 619
Howe, E. W., 786
Howe, Frederic, 133–134, 371–372, 385–386, 453, 691–692
  on education, 595–600
  on Mark Hanna, 545–547
  on Johns Hopkins, 597–600
  on religion, 557–558
  settlement house work, 420
Howe, Julia Ward, 16, 500, 662, 723
Howe, Lois, 493, 794
Howells, William Dean, 251, 297, 402, 483, 535, 671, 723–725, 827
  literary influence, 724–725
  The Rise of Silas Lapham, 741
  A Traveler from Altruria, 237–238
Howison, George Holmes, 310
Howland, Marie Stevens, 265–267
Hoxie, Vinnie Ream, 494–495
Hubbard, Elbert, 510
Hudson's Bay Company, 98
Hull, Moses, 268–269
Hull House settlement, Chicago, 404–421, 681
  assistance of scholars and professionals, 316
  center of radical reform, 416
  day nursery, 41
  educational courses, 411–412
  in immigrant neighborhood, 409
  Social and Economic Conference (1896), 715
  staffed by upper-class young women, 408–409
Hunt, Hannah, free love movement, 269
Hunt, Lillie (Populist), 269
Hunt, Richard Morris, 492, 504
Hunt, William, 303
Hunt, William Morris, 781
Huntington, Collis Potter, 90–93, 495, 622
Hurd, Harriet, 391–393
Hyde, James Hazen, 854

Idaho Territory, 38
IHLs (*see* Institutions of higher learning)
Illinois:
  child labor, 418
  railroad strikes, 179
Illinois State Register, 241–242
Immigration and immigrants, 332–343, 657–658
  assimilation of emigrant groups, 362–363
  British immigrants, 332–333
  causes of, 333
  coal mine workers, 224

Immigration and immigrants (*cont.*):
  Chinese immigrants, 334–336
  after Civil War, 165
  communities, 339–340
  customs and culture, 339–340
  early classes, 332–333
  freedom to eat, 276
  hostility toward, 924–925
  increased tide of, 332–333
  Jewish, 344–363
  in Middle West and Great Plains states, 341–342
  need for cheap labor, 332
  women, 683
  working conditions, 224–225
Imperialism, 864–886
  Christian, 540
  corporate, 540–541
Impressionists, 775, 796
Independent (journal), 161
India, missionary activity, 579
Indian Bureau, 8, 27, 80
Indian College at Carlisle, Pa., 842
"Indian Fighter," 46
Indian Rights Association, 84
Indian Ring (private traders), 44
Indian Territory, 6, 8–9
  Confederate and Union forays, 9
  life at frontier posts, 45–48
  number of Indians, 83
  rights of ex-slaves, 22
Indian wars:
  cost of, 74
  Battle of Wounded Knee, 825
  Bozeman Trail massacre, 24–27
  captive white women and children, 55
  casualties, 41
  death of Sitting Bull, 824–825
  end of, 61–88
  Fetterman's party, annihilation of, 24–27
  to force Indians to accept reservation life, 61
  life of U.S. soldiers, 44–49
  Sand Creek Massacre, 12–14
  scattered campaigns, 50–60
  in Southwest, 34–39, 50–52
  war tactics, 52
  warfare between tribes, 15, 73
Indians:
  abuse and exploitation, 2–14, 44, 50–60, 85
  American aborigines, 85–87
  assimilation policy, 17–18
  attitudes of whites, 4, 19–22, 28
  buffalo hunting, 51
  Christianization, 6, 16–17, 33
  Civil War participation, 8–9
  "civilizing" attempts, 58, 82
  culture, 20, 43, 84–86
  dancing and storytelling, 48
  dependency of whites, 65

diseases, 81
educational programs, 16–17, 84–85
  agricultural training, 16
ex-slaves, rights of, 22
extermination policy, 16, 19–21, 23, 42, 52–56
Fort Laramie gathering of tribes, 4
Ghost Dance religion, 83, 823–825
government policies (1865–1900), 15–33, 85
  civilization fund, 32
grievances presented in East, 58–59
heroes, 77
hostility of whites, 2–14
Indian agents, 33, 63
Indian Commission, 31–32
Indian lobby, 50
Indian Removal, 1, 7, 17
mutilation of bodies, 72
organizations supporting, 57, 83–84
peace policy, 15–16, 27–29
Plains tribes, 823–824
pro-Indian sentiment, 7–8
Quaker policy, 33, 59
racism, 87
raids and counterraids, 1–15, 20, 50–60
  (*See also* Indian wars)
railroads destroyed tribes, 53–56, 89
red-white clash, 85–86
reformers and friends, 17, 83–85
reservation issue, 2–4, 17–19, 33, 42, 83
  forced acceptance of, 61
  individual landholdings, 60
  "revolts" from reservations, 51–60
Sand Creek Massacre, 12–14
scalp locks, 47
state versus Federal rights, 1–2
subsidies and presents, 3, 6, 65
surveillance of whites, 63
treachery of white man, 40
treaties, 4–7, 10, 64
  breakdown in (1868–1869), 53
  treaty payments, 65–66
Westerners and, 19–20
white prejudices, 28
white treachery, 12–14
winter campaigning, 43, 53–54
women and children, 54, 77–78
Wovoka, Indian messiah, 823–825
Individualism, xiii, 17, 210, 598
  sovereignty of the individual, 294
Individualist anarchism, 164
Industrial Army, 516
Industrial Brotherhood, 227
Industrialism, 599
  capitalism, 534–535
  government and, 920–921
  railroads stimulus to growth, 102
Industrial Union, 433
Inequities in American society, 923–925
Information, dissemination of essential, 403

Information Bureau of the Socialist Federation of North America, 232–234
Ingersoll, Charles, 133
Ingersoll, Col. Robert, 556
Institutions of higher learning (IHLs), 590, 595–606
  curriculum, 591, 601
  enrollments, 590
  facilities, 591
  growth of, 590–593
  Harvard, 593–595
  sciences, 592
  (*See also* under name of institution)
Insull, Samuel, 371
Insurance, employee, 191
Intellectuals, 309, 558
  criticism of capitalism, 926
  disappearance of religious faith, 911
  James family, 295–316
  Jewish, 353–358
  scholars and, 917
International Congress of Women, 498–499
International Labor Congress, 493
International Woman's Council, 276–277
International Workers of the World, 255
International Working People's Association (IWPA), 233–238
  German membership, 234
  journals, 234–235
International Workingmen's Association, 166, 242, 267, 645
  Pacific Coast Division, 235–236
Internationalists, 180–181, 184–185
Interstate Commerce Act of 1887, 461–462
Introspection, 911–912
Inventors and investors, 113–117
Ireland, Archbishop John, of St. Paul, 582
Irish immigrants, 45, 87, 165, 189, 332–333, 359, 363
  saloons and saloonkeepers, 385–386
Irish Land Question, The (George), 208
Iron and steel industry, 123
  Bessemer process, 121
  Southern mills, 834–835
Iron Bull, Crow chief, 95–96
Iron-Moulders International Union, 167
Iron ore mines, 122–123
Irons, Martin, 229
Irrigation movement, 815–816
Irving, Washington, 315
Ise, John, 425, 428–429
Italian immigrants, 165, 332–333, 363
  in Boston, 338–339
  customs and culture, 339
  in New York City, 336–338
  strikebreakers, 224, 339
Ives, Halsey, 495
IWPA (*see* International Working People's Association)

Jackson, Andrew, 454–455
Jackson, Helen Hunt, 82, 732, 735, 766
  A Century of Dishonor, 82, 84
  Ramona, 766
James, Alice, 296, 301
James, Frank and Jesse, 105–106, 811
James, Garth Wilkinson, 296, 299–300, 863
James, Henry, Jr., 247, 296, 314–316, 725–727, 766
  on English country houses, 858
  "A Landscape Painter," 748
  novelist, 296–297
  The Portrait of a Lady, 726
  Roderick Hudson, 725–726
  The Turn of the Screw, 726
  writer as artist, 315
James, Henry, Sr., 296–301, 331
  religious writings, 301–303
James, Robertson, 296, 299–301, 314, 863
James, William (the "first"), 296–297
James, William (the "second"), 158, 247, 296–315, 317, 415, 917
James, William:
  artistic ability, 303
  John Jay Chapman and, 712–713
  edited Henry Sr.'s writings, 301–303
  education, 303–307
  Father of Pragmatism, 296
  friends and friendships, 308, 314
  generosity of spirit, 308
  on Harvard faculty, 307–308
  on Haymarket affair, 247
  on intellectual climate, 558
  letter-writing, 862
  mind cure movement, 571–572
  philosophical thinking, 309
  The Principles of Psychology, 308
  scientific spirit, 303
  study of psychology, 308, 912
  teaching and thinking, 312–313
  The Varieties of Religious Experience, 304–305, 313–314, 571
  war between science and religion, 307
  on war with Spain, 872, 884–885
  on West, 823
  Yoga discipline, 579–580
James family, 295–317
  family life, 297–299
Jameson, John Franklin, 599
Japan, 893–894, 922
  missionary activity, 575–576
Jay, John, 313, 711
Jay, William, 313, 711–712
Jehovah's Witnesses, 569
Jefferson, Thomas, 4, 142–143
  on "a little rebellion," 918–919
  vision of farmers, 425–426
Jeffersonian Republicans, xi
Jefford, Tom (Indian scout), 36, 38–41

Jenney, Marie, 691–692
Jerome, Clara, 805
Jerome, William Travers, 857
Jewett, Sarah Orne, 760–763
  The Country of the Pointed Firs, 761
Jewish immigrants, 344–363
  agricultural settlements, 360–361
  Mary Antin on, 344–353
  anti-Semitism, 358–359
  assimilation, 352–353, 362
  characteristic traits, 346
  clothing and customs, 347–348
  in clothing industry, 351–352
  Eastern European Jews, 344–345
  educational opportunities, 347, 352–353
  escape from Russia, 344–345
  farm colonies in New Jersey, 360–361
  financiers and bankers, 358–359
  in free thought groups, 285
  generational conflicts, 357–358
  intellectuals and journalists, 353–354
  New York City ghetto, 344, 349–355
  philanthropy, 356, 359
  from Poland and Russia, 332, 344–345
  preoccupation with money, 350–351
  promised land, 344–363
  religious problems, 345–346, 356–358
  socialism, 361
  upper-class Jews, 358–359
  women, 348–349
Johns Hopkins University, 597–600
  German scholarship methods, 597–598
  graduates, 599–600
  Frederick Howe on, 597–600
  Medical School, 419
John Swinton's Paper, 167, 178, 246, 485–486
Johnson, President Andrew, 615
Johnson, Eastman, 495, 781
Johnson, Rev. Herrick, 523
Johnson, James Weldon, 505, 636
Johnson County War, 809–810
Jones, Mary ("Mother"), 222, 241–242, 255
  organizer for the United Mine Workers, 480–481
Joplin, Scott, 505
Jordan, David Starr, 841
Joseph, Chief of Nez Percé, 74–78
Josephson, Matthew, 102
Journalism and journalists, 376–403
  advocates of reform, 378–379
  Ray Stannard Baker, 377–378, 400–401
  Edward Bok, 397–399
  exposé, 378, 389, 400–401
  "investigative reporting," 378
  Frederic Howe, 385–386
  Jewish, 353–354
  S. S. McClure, 389–401
  from Midwest or Far West, 402
  reform, 378–379
  Jacob Riis, 377–389

Lincoln Steffens, 378, 384–389, 399
  Frances Willard, 377
  yellow journalists, 402
  (*See also* under name of journalist)
Judah, Theodore Dehone, 91, 93, 97
Judaic Passion, 356
Junior League, 855

Kansas:
  character of, 801–802
  farm areas, 449, 801
  migration to, 341, 343
  free thought movement, 284–286
  reforms, 802
Kansas City Stock Yards Company, 109
Kansas Liberals, 267–268
Kansas Pacific Railroad, 23, 51, 93, 102
Kearns, Thomas, 125–126
Kearny, Gen. Stephen, 2–3
Kearny (Nebraska) Herald, 19
Keenan, George, 156
Kelley, Charles, 516
Kelley, Florence, 417–418
Kelley, Oliver Hudson, 429
Kelley, Sarah, 417
Kelley's Industrial Army, 516
Kelly, Patrick, 461
Kent, William, 369
Key, Ellen, 693, 751
Kindergartens, 664
King, Clarence, 322–323, 464, 489, 917
  Panic of 1890 and, 464–465
King, Edward, 743–744
King, Grace, 770–771
Kiowa Indians, 5–6, 50–51
Kipling, Rudyard, 395–396
Kirkland, Dr. Cyclone, 511
"Kitchen reformers," 673–674
Kittredge, George, 595
Klein, Isaac, 887
Kneeland, Abner, 284
Knight, Jesse, 125
Knights of Labor, 211, 216, 219, 222, 227–230, 236, 450
  declaration of principles, 227–228
  demise of, 255–256, 528
  membership, 229
  militant leaders, 229–230
  radical talk, 229–230
  reaction against Haymarket Affair, 246–257
  socialistic aims, 227–229
  strikes, 229–230
  talk of revolution, 229–231
  union-cum-temperance organization, 230
Knights of St. Crispin, 225
Knox College in Galesburg, Illinois, 390, 679
Kropotkin, Piotr, 287, 290
Kuhn, Loeb and Company, 358, 488

Labor conditions, 213–226
  arbitration of labor disputes, 229, 460, 484, 707
  Eleanor Aveling's survey of, 214–222
  blacklists and intimidation, 216
  British and American, compared, 214–216
  cowboys, 222
  employees replaced by machines, 217–218
  enemy of capital, 134
  exploitation of, 213–226
  farm-labor alliance, 436–438, 446–448, 923–924
  fire hazards, 221
  Great Strikes, 164–192
  in "hard times," 213–215
  health hazards, 218–220
  hours and wages, 216–217, 223
  housing conditions, 218
  militancy, 192
  New York clothing industry, 219
  strikes, 223
  sweatshops, 219
  unemployment, 217
  use of company script in lieu of money, 216–217
  war between capital and labor, 139
  women and children, 217
  working class, 134
  (See also Unions)
Labor consciousness, development of, 192
Labor movement, 214
  beginning of, 186
  effect of Haymarket Affair, 249, 252, 255–256
  growth of unions, 192
  newspapers and journals, 214
  radical political action, 214
Labor Party, 212
Labor-saving machinery, 217–218
Ladies' Home Journal, 398–399
La Farge, John, 322, 324, 786–787, 789, 793
  murals in Trinity Church, 789
La Farge, Mabel Hooper, 325
La Flesche, Susette, 81–82
Lamar, Lucius Quintus Cincinnatus, 461
Lamont, Thomas, 372
Land grants, 99
  homesteading, 99–100
Land Reform League of California, 198
Lane, Mary Bradley, 739
Langston, John Mercer, 621
Lapwai Reservation, 75
Lathrop, Julia, 416–417
Lawrence, William, 137–138
Lawsuits, 115
  mines and mine owners, 127
Leadville, Colorado, 126
Lease, Mary, 449–451
Lecture business, 449, 464
  (See also Chautauqua movement)
Lehr, Harry, 854, 857
Leigh, William, 784
Leisure time, 852

Leiter, Joseph, 371–373
Leiter, Levi, 468
Leo XIII, Pope, 581
Letter-writing, 319, 326, 861–862
Levering, Joshua, 550
Lewelling, Lorenzo Dow, 484, 489, 532
Lewis, Dr. Dio, 93, 663
Lewis, Wyndham, 919
Liberal, Missouri (free-thought community), 292
"Liberals," 258
Liberty, 142–143
  civil, 143
  under law, 143
Liberty (Benjamin Tucker's journal), 285, 287–288, 294
Life-styles:
  drugs and alcohol, 911–913
  nervousness/anxiety, 911–914, 928–929
  pace of American life, 913
Lincoln, President Abraham, 190, 250, 252, 404
  on Indian problem, 8–9
Lingg, Louis, 248, 251, 254, 289
Lippman, Walter, 313
Literature, 716–756
  black writers, 737–738, 752
  Boston literary scene, 721, 747, 753–754, 827
  children's literature, 751, 760–761
  Emily Dickinson, 731–735
  feminist social reform novels, 758–759
  "feminization" of American literature, 757
  immigrant novel, 743–744
  Henry James, 725–727
  literary criticism, 316
  marriage relationship, 767–769
  New England literary establishment, 724
    small-town short-story genre, 760–764
    women writers, 757–763
  novelist-journalists, 769–770
  novels of miscegenation, 737, 770
  poetry, 717, 719–720
  procapitalism school, 745–746
  psychological studies, 766–769
  on redemption, 209–210
  satiric novels, 739
  serials in magazines, 736
  short stories, 748, 757–758
  "social protest" novels and short stories, 735–756
  Southern writers, 766–769
  tearjerkers, 736–739
  travel sketches, 739–741
  Mark Twain, 727–731
  utopian novels, 738–739
  women writers, 757–771
  (See also under name of writer)
Little Bighorn, Battle of, 1, 69, 71–72
Little Landers movement, 816
Lloyd, Henry Demarest, 254, 416, 418, 482–485, 490, 503, 550, 565, 773
  cooperative methods, 703–707

Lloyd, Henry Demarest (*cont.*):
  denunciations of capitalism, 701–702, 705
  editor of *Chicago Tribune*, 699–700
  on occupation of Cuba, 867
  reform spirit, 698–708, 715
  Spring Valley strike, 700–701
  summary of Secular-Democratic Consciousness, 909–910
  wayside home, at Winnetka, 699–700
  Wealth Against Commonwealth, 602, 701–702, 705
Lloyd, Jessie Bross, 699
Locomotives, 104
Lodge, George ("Bay") Cabot, 860
Lodge, Sen. Henry Cabot, 320, 322, 540–541, 594
  Cuban question, 543
London, Jack, 395, 516
London Times, 208
Long, John (secretary of the navy), 871, 873–874, 906
Long, Stephen, 62
Long Island Railroad, 178
Longfellow, William Wadsworth, 718–719, 752
  The Song of Hiawatha, 752, 755
Looking Backward (Bellamy), 292, 708–711, 738, 913
Lopez, Narciso, 541–542
Lord, Judge Otis, 732
"Lost Cause" myth, 830–832
Louisiana Farmers' Union, 432
Louisiana People's Party, 447
Louisville and Nashville Railroad, 834–835
Love, Alfred, 32
Lovejoy, Arthur, 606
Low, Mayor Seth, 697
Lowell, James Russell, x, 108, 402, 721–725
Lowell, labor conditions, 218, 265–266
"Lowell girls," 265–266
Lucifer (Moses Harman's journal), 268–269, 279–281, 284–288
Ludlow, Fitzhugh, 781
Lum, Dyer Daniel, 289–290
Lumber camps, hazardous work, 223
Lynch, John Roy, 617–619
Lynching of blacks, 631–632, 642, 656

McAllister, Ward, 853–854
Machinery, labor-saving, 200–201
Machinists and Blacksmiths Union, 228
McClure, S. S., 389–401
  early life, 389–391
  syndicated articles for magazines, 393–394
  Wheelman edited by, 392–393
McClure's Magazine, 394–397
  exposure articles, 396–397
  staff, 395–400
McConnell, Samuel, 252
McCormick, Cyrus, 242, 479
McCormick Harvester Company, 242–243
McCosh, James, 133
McCoy, Joseph, 102, 801

McGlynn, Father Edward, 612
McGuffey *Readers*, 545, 591
McKim, Charles Follen, 793
McKim, Mead & White, 793–794
McKinley, President William, 454
  assassination of, 901, 903–904
  "campaign," 547, 552
  creation of Marcus Hanna, 864–865
  election of 1896, 546–547, 552–553, 864
  election of 1900, 897, 901–904
  funeral, 904
  message calling for war, 866, 869–870
  opposition to, 884–885
McLeod, Margaret Perle, 291
MacMonnies, Frederick, 492
MacMonnies, Mary Fairchild, 495–496, 857
Macrae, Rev. David, 88, 107–108
Madison, James, 918
Magazines and journals:
  effect of new printing technology, 797
  illustrations, 783, 797
  juvenile, 783
  syndicated articles, 393–394
  (*See also* under name of magazine)
Mahan, Alfred Thayer, naval policy, 541, 868, 877
Mahony, Frances, 794
Maloney, Joseph, 897
Maine (U.S. battleship), 866–869
  sinking of, 868–869
Males, 692
  characteristics and traits, 501
  clothing, 689
  differences between sexes, 682, 692
  father-daughter relationships, 404–405, 694
  "malady of forty years," 913
  marriage, 691
  masculine anxiety, 692
  mother-son relationship, 694–695
Malthus *Principles of Population*, 211
Malthusian-Darwinian system, 446
  Henry George and, 200–203
Mangas Coloradas ("Red Sleeves"), 36
Mann, Horace, 591
Manning, William, xii, 131, 152, 239, 909
  Key to Liberty, 431, 918
Mariposa, California, 812–813
Marketing methods, 128
Markham, Edwin, 293, 755–756
Marriage and divorce, 259–260, 857
  free love movement, 259–260
    attacks on conventional marriage, 268–271
  mate selection, 260–264
  sexual exploitation of women, 262
  in short stories and novels, 767–769
  upper classes, 857
  (*See also* Free love movement)
Marshall, Chief Justice John, 376
Martin, Edward, 429–430
Martinsburg (West Virginia) railroad strike, 169

Marx, Karl, 165, 214–215, 231, 417, 645
  Capital, 215
  Communist Manifesto, 919
  on *Progress and Poverty*, 212
Marxism, 164–166, 181, 184–185
Mass-production techniques, 103
Massachusetts:
  Board of Railroad Commissioners, 109, 330
  labor conditions, 215
  (*See also* Boston; New England)
Massillon, Ohio, Coxey's Army, 508, 511
Matchett, Charles H., 547, 552
Matthews, Prentiss, 615–617
Matthiessen, F. O., 297
Mazzini, Giuseppe, 406, 410
Meacham, Alfred B., 59–60, 84
Mead, George, 600
Mead, William Rutherford, 793
Medicine Lodge Creek, Kansas, 29–30
Medill, Joseph, 94, 463
Meditation and Mind Cure, 572
Meeker, Jim, 19
Melville, Herman, 316, 716–717, 724, 731
  "Billy Budd," 717
Memphis, boycott of streetcars, 644
Mencken, H. L., 730
Mendle, Gregor, 658
Meres, Merle (sculptor), 494
Meriwether, Elizabeth Avery, 674
Merrill, Isabel Trowbridge, 577–578
Merwin, Samuel, 742
Methodists, 284, 554, 580, 833
Meyers, Isaac, 645–646
Mexican War, 1, 34
  Apache raiding parties, 40–41
Michigan, child labor, 220
Middle-class Americans, 145
Middle West (Midwest), xiii
  educational institutions, 593, 596
    colleges, 607–608
  free love movement, 267–268
  freethinkers, 284–287
  immigrants, 333, 341–342
  journalists, 402
  patronage, distribution of, 460
  radical farmers, 450
  Republican Party, xiv
  social and political conditions, 801
Miles, Gen. Nelson A., 51, 73, 77–78, 94–95, 519–520, 877
Mill, John Stuart, 307, 417
Millennium, x, 567–569
Miller, Joaquin, 92, 765, 817
Miller, Lewis, 609
Miller, Thomas Ezekiel, 620–621
Millerites, 568
Mills, B. Fay, 483
Mind cure movement, 571–572
  Christian Science, 572–575

Mine Owners Protective Association, 479
Mineral resources, 120
Mines and mining:
  attempts to break unions, 533–534
  conditions of labor, 214
  disputed claims, 127
  grubstaking, 126
  Italian immigrants, 339
  mining barons or Bonanza Kings, 124–125
  mining developers, 125–126
  prospectors, 125
  silver mines, 125–126
  stock fluctuations, 125
  strikes, 479–481, 533–534
    use of Federal troops, 170–172, 177–178, 187–188, 479, 518–520, 528
Minnesota: population growth, 800
  Sioux uprising, 9
Miscegenation in novels and short stories, 737, 770
Missionary movement, 555, 575–579
  role of women, 579–580
Mississippi Valley West, 799
Missouri Pacific, strike in 1885, 229
Mitchell, David, 5
Mitchell, S. Weir, 764–765, 912–913
Modjeska, Helena, 292–293
Modoc War in California, 59–60
Molly Maguire episode, 175, 533
Monetary policies, 443
  clamor for cheap money, 203
  hard versus soft, 450, 453–454, 466
  Jewish preoccupation with, 350–351
  sex and, 275
Monopolies, 114, 129
  (*See also* Trusts and monopolies)
Monroe Doctrine, 537–539, 891
Monroe League, 196
Mont St. Michel, 326
Montana: Clark and Daly feud, 804
  copper mines, 804
  sheep raising, 804
Moody, Dwight, 569–570
Morgan, Clement, 628
Morgan, J. Pierpont, 124, 277, 384, 488, 659
  gifts to Harvard, 602
Morgan, Julia, 794
Morgan, Tom, 490–491, 527–528, 700
Morgan, W. Scott (Farmer-journalist), 433–434, 446
Mormons, xiv, 460, 813–814
  issue of polygamy, 813–814
Morris, Gouverneur, xi–xii
Morris, William (English reformer), 247, 253, 256
Morrison, Col. Pitcairn, 34
Morse, Jedidiah, 284, 359
Morse, Samuel F. B., 92, 115, 119, 592
Morton, J. Sterling, 460, 464–465, 503
Morton, Levi, 466
Mosby's Rangers, 877

Most, Johann (anarchist leader), 231–236, 251–252, 357, 471
  attack by Emma Goldman, 476
  German revolutionary, 231–232
  Revolutionary Catechism, 232
Mott, Lucretia, 16, 32, 83
  father-daughter relationship, 694
Mount Holyoke College, 678–679, 731
Muckraking, 385
Muggeridge, Edward James, 777–779
Mugwumps, 458–459
Muir, John, 822
Muirhead, James Fullerton, 757
Munsey, Frank, 751–752
Murfree, Mary Noailles, 771
Museums and galleries, 495, 796–797
Music and musicians, 505
Muybridge, Edward, 777–779
  photographs of horse in motion, 777

Naismith, James, 850
Nast, Thomas, 506, 775
Nation (periodical), 17, 79, 97, 188, 878
National Agricultural Wheel, 432–433
  aims of farmers' movement, 432–433
National Biscuit Company, 129
National Christian Citizenship League, 566
National Cordage Company, 485
National Defense Association, 270, 278–279
National Farmers' Alliance, 433
National Grange of the Patrons of Husbandry, 429–431
National Greenback-Labor Party, 458–459
National Labor Union, 227
  black unions, 645
National Liberal League, 140, 285
National Liberal Reform League, 288, 292, 556, 919
National parks, 795–796, 818
National Reform Association, 286
National Woman Suffrage Association, 258, 264
Nationalism (Bellamy's), 164, 292, 483, 503, 698, 709–711, 724
Natural selection versus scientific breeding, 260–261, 276, 341, 658
Navaho Indians, 3
Naval policy, Mahan's two-ocean navy, 541, 868
Nebraska: immigrants, 341, 343
  railroads, 100
Neebe, Oscar, 250
Nelson, Henry Loomis, 94
Nervousness/anxiety, 911–914, 928–929
Nesbit, Evelyn, 857
Neurasthenia, 912–913
New American Empire, 864–886
New England, 826–829
  Boston, 826–827
  (*See also* Boston)

  character, 827–828
  literary establishment, 402, 724
  mills, 827
  Puritan ethic, 826
  Puritanism, 917
New England Free Love League, 270
New England Labor Reform League, 270
New Jersey: labor conditions, 217, 219
  railroad strikes, 176
New Mexico, 1, 3, 99, 810
  Lincoln County Wars, 810
New Orleans: Creole life, 767–769
  race riots, 651
New products, 128
New Thought, 570–572
  sects, 572–575
New York Academy of Design, 780
New York City, 364–369
  adult education, 611–612
  Art Students League, 788
  Central Park, 795–796
  charitable organizations, 368
  child abuse, 367–368
  Children's Aid Society, 697
  Chinese immigrants, 335–336
  clothing industry, 219, 365
  Colony Club, 666–667
  Cooper Union, 231–232, 237, 359, 625, 917
  crime and criminals, 365–368
  exodus of Southern blacks to, 644
  Fifth Avenue, 793
  Foundling Hospital, 367–368
  free love movement, 266–267
  garment industry, 219, 365
  Good Government Club, 713
  housing, 381–382
  Indian chiefs visit to, 56–57
  infant death rate, 367–368
  Italian immigrants, 336–337
  Jewish immigrants, 344
    ghetto life, 344, 353–355
  Metropolitan Museum of Art, 796
  municipal reforms, 697
  New York Infirmary, 685
  police station lodgings, 381–383, 387
  population, 365
  railroad strike, 178
  reforms and reformers, 385–386, 697
  settlement houses, 419–420
  slums, 344, 353–355, 365
  Tammany Hall, 385, 456, 459
  tenement buildings, 366–367, 381–382
  Tweed ring, 374, 401, 506
New York Herald, 176, 238
New York *Journal*, 402, 876–877
  for war with Spain, 867–868
New York Press Association, 378
New York State: political bosses, 372

New York Times, The, 16, 17, 55, 96, 246, 523
  on railroad strikes, 176–177, 183
New York Tribune, 17, 64, 176, 319
  on Haymarket Affair, 245
New York World, 62, 402, 467, 524, 879
  rivalry between *Journal* and, 871–872
  sentiment for war with Spain, 867–868, 879–880
New Zealand, reforms, 707
Newell, Frederick Haynes, 816
Newspapers and journals:
  adaptation to democratic needs, 403
  comic supplements, 402
  Czech-language, 342
  freethinkers, 294
  independent press, 378–379
  journalists, 376–403
  labor movement and, 214
  liberal, 378
  role in Spanish-American War, 402, 867
  sensationalism, 880–881
  syndicating articles for, 393–394
  war between Hearst and Pulitzer, 402, 871–872
Nez Percé in Oregon, 8
  campaign against, 73–78
Nicaraguan Canal, plans to build, 878
Nichols, Thomas and Mary, 276
Nicolay, John G., 190, 319
Nock, Albert Jay, 208
Norris, Benjamin Franklin (Frank), 395
North:
  black migration to, 631–642, 839
  deep divisions between South and, 911
  reformers, 453
North American Review, 108, 134, 320
North Dakota, 94
Northern Pacific Railroad, 58, 94, 485
  bankruptcy, 96–97
  route of, 99
Northwest, 799
Norton, Charles Eliot, 108, 595, 722
Norwegian immigrants, 332
Noyes, John Humphrey, 165, 263, 671
Nugent, Jim (Mountain Jim), 818–819
Nugent, Thomas, 439–440
Nye, Bill (humorist), 521

Oakley, Annie ("Little Sure Shot"), 817–818
Oates, Joyce Carol, 296
Oberlin College, 679
Obscenity, campaign against, 277–279
Ocala Convention of Farmers' Alliance, 448
O'Donnell, Hugh, 473–474, 511
Oelrichs, Harry, 804–805
O'Flaherty, Kate, 766–769, 851
Oglesby, Gov. Richard James, 251–254
Ohio, railroad strikes, 179
Ohio & Mississippi Railroad, 105
Oil and gas industry, 120
  development of, 122

monopolistic conditions, 122–123
  trusts, 129–131
Oklahoma Territory, 99, 648–649
  black settlers, 648
  Czech migration to, 341
  opening of, 648–649
Olcott, Col. H. S., 579
Old-boy network, 402
Older, Fremont, 416
Olerich, Henry, 738–739
Olmsted, Frederick Law, 334, 491
  Central Park designed by, 795–796
  on social relations in Mariposa, 812–813
Olney, O., 286
Olney, Richard (attorney general), 518–520, 536–539
Olympic games, 852
Omaha Convention, Populist Party, 466–467
Omaha Indians, 48–49, 81
Oneida Community, 165
Open Door policy, 896
Ord, Gen. E. O. C., 61–62
Oregon and California Railroad, 93–94
Oregon and Transcontinental Company, 96–97
Oregon Railway and Navigation Company, 97
Oregon Steamship Company, 94
Oregon Trail, 5, 7, 23
Osler, William, 419
Ostend Manifesto, 537, 542
Owen, Albert Kimsey, 267
Owen, Robert Dale, 191

Pacific Railroad, 182
Pacific West, 821–822
Page, Thomas Nelson, 766
  "Lost Cause," myth, 830–832
  The Negro: The Southerner's Problem, 831
Page, Walter Hines, 551, 600, 622, 829, 873
Paine, Tom, 142–143, 150, 267
  Common Sense, 210
Palmer, Bertha, 493–498, 522, 855
Palmer, George Herbert, 308, 679
Palmer, Sen. J. M., 478–479, 550, 552
Panama Canal, 894–895
Panic and Depression of 1837, 165
Panic and Depression of 1873, 61
Panic of 1890, 464–465
Panic of 1893, 482–491
Pantarchy group, 259, 270
Papago Indians, 36
Paper money issue, 443
Park, Robert, 340–341
Park movement, 795–796, 818
Parker, Minerva, 794
Parkhurst, Dr. Charles, 382–386, 420
Parkhurst, Henry, 273
Parkman, Francis, 326
Parsons, Albert, 234–237, 242–248, 254, 289
  Haymarket Affair, 251

Parsons, Frank, 566
Patriotism, 145
Patronage, 460
Patrons of Husbandry, 431
Pawnee Indians, 3
Payne, David, 648
Payne, William Norton, 742–743
Peabody, Robert, 794
Peace Commission, 27–31
　treaty with Sioux and Cheyenne, 29–30
Peale, Rembrandt, 775
Peary, Admiral Robert, 396, 857
Peck, Bradford, 291
Peffer, Sen. William Alfred, 515
Peirce, Benjamin, 592
Peirce, Charles Sanders, 161–163, 309–310, 558–559, 670, 917
Peirce, Melusina "Zinna" Fay, 670–672, 738, 765
Pennsylvania:
　Molly Maguire episode, 175, 533
　oil fields, 120
　political bosses, 372
　railroad strikes, 171–175
Pennsylvania & Reading Railroad, 175
Pennsylvania coal mines:
　child labor, 220–221
　conditions of labor, 214
　immigrant workers, 224, 339
Pennsylvania Railroad, 104, 121
　railroad strike, 171–174
Pensions for veterans, 462–463
People's Party, 439, 443, 447–448, 453, 489, 497, 925
　formation of, 448–449
　Omaha Convention, 466–467
　platform, 466
Peperson, Richard, 125
Perkins, Frances, 383
Perkins, Frederic Beecher, 764
Perry, Bliss, 396
Perry, Matthew, 575
Philadelphia: anarchists, 290–291
　Centennial Exposition (1876), 1, 115
　exodus of blacks to, 644
Philadelphia & Reading Railroad, 485
Philanthropy, 165
　Carnegie on, 136
　Jewish, 356, 359
　(See also Charity)
Philippine Islands:
　American military action, 871
　black soldiers, 883
　criticism of American invasion, 884–886
　Dewey's victory at Manila, 871
　occupation of, 882–883
　"pacification" of, 880–881, 900
　revolt against Spanish rule, 868
　(See also Spanish-American War)
Phillips, John S., 394–396, 399

Phillips, Wendell, 16, 20, 55, 58–60, 87–88, 289, 334, 444, 919–920
　on labor unions, 225–226
　The Ponca Chiefs, 82
Phonograph, invention of, 117
Photographers and photography, 777–779
　horses in motion, 777–779
　nudes, 778–779
Pickering, Edward Charles, 595
Pickett, Virginia, 684
Piegan Massacre (1870), 55–56
Pierce, Franklin, 542
Pinchback, Pinckney Benton Stewart, 625
Pine Ridge Reservation, 80–81
Pinkerton detectives, 105–106, 127, 236, 242, 244, 518
　reaction against use of, 478–479
Pinkham, Lydia E., 571
Pinney, Lucien V., 270
Pitt River expedition, 38
Pittsburgh, Pa., 473
　railroad strike, 171–174, 178
Plain Home Talk (Foote), 278
Plains Indians, 4–7
　campaigns against, 54–60
Platt, Thomas (political boss), 372, 887–888, 898–899, 905
"Play instinct" in Americans, 415, 828–829, 852
Playgrounds, 591
Pluralism, 311
Plutocracy versus democracy, 144, 531, 551
Poe, Edgar Allan, 402
Poetry and poets, 719, 772–773
　William Cullen Bryant, 719
　Emily Dickinson, 723, 731–735
　James Russell Lowell, 721, 724–725
　Walt Whitman, 717–721, 723
　John Greenleaf Whittier, 717, 719, 723–725
Poland, persecution of Jews, 344–346
Polish immigrants, 332, 363
Political developments, 452–468
Political economy, study of, 198–199
Political radicalism, 258
Politics, 452–468
　capital versus labor, 452
　Cleveland re-election, 466–467
　distribution of patronage, 460
　election of 1894, 465–466
　hard money versus soft money, 453–454
　Panic of 1890, 464
　political bosses, 370–374, 455
　politicians, 295, 384
　　graft and corruption, 384
　presidential candidates, 454–455
　Sherman Antitrust Act, 463–464
　signs of revolt (1890), 465
　tariff question, 453–454
Polk, James, 541–542
Polk, Leonidas Lafayette, 448

Ponca Indians controversy, 81–82
Poor, working-class:
    attitude of Wasps, 413–414
    attitude toward life, 413–414
    fear of starvation and old age, 414–415
Pope, Col. Albert, 392–393
Pope Leo XIII, 581
Population growth, 141, 275, 279
Populist Party, 454, 838
Populists, 269, 279, 467, 503, 897, 909
    Convention in 1894, 533–534
    election of 1892, 484
    election of 1896, 549–550
    farmer's movement, 420–451
    leaders, 450–451
    political attacks on, 532–533
    Pullman strike supported by, 525–535
    writings of, 446
Pork-barrel appropriations, 462
"Positivists," 258
Potter, Henry Codman, 561, 628
Poverty, 156
    association with progress, 201
    (See also Poor, working-class)
Powder River, 67
Powderly, Terence, 227–231, 252, 255–256, 450, 487
    head of Knights of Labor, 227
Powell, Capt. James, 24
Powell, John Wesley, 150, 816
Power, Susan O., 676–677
Power, centralization of, 130
Pragmatism, 161–162, 310–312
Prairie Cattle Company, 805
Pratt, Bela Lyon, 788
Pratt, Daniel, 834–835
Pratt, Enoch, 136
Pratt, Richard Henry, 18, 51, 86, 842
Presbyterians, 554, 580
Presidential candidates, 454–455
Presser v. the State of Illinois, 236
Price-fixing agreements, 128, 131
Princeton University, 592
Printing, new technological developments, 797
Prioleau, George, 874, 876
Prison reforms, 697–698
Private preparatory schools, 842
Proctor, Sen. Redfield, 867–868
Progress, 141–142, 163
Progress and Poverty (George), 192, 193–212
Progressive Party, 385
Prohibition movement, 286, 802
    election of 1896, 550
Prohibition Party, 457, 459, 463, 467, 663
Promised land, 344–363
Promontory Point, Utah, 91
Property rights, 133, 139
Prostitution, 219, 685–689
Protestant ethic, 17, 928

Protestant Passion, 330, 356, 554–557, 575
Protestantism, 554–586
    Creation in the Book of Genesis, 586
    defections of liberal denominations, 284
    Fatherhood of God, 560
    liberal, 284, 579
Pryor, Robert, 251
Psychology, 600–601
    study of, 912–913
Public good, 135
    Carnegie's devotion to, 121
"Public improvements," 516
Public ownerships of natural resources, 603
Pueblo Indians, 3
Puerto Rico, 872, 877, 880
Pulitzer, Joseph, 94, 402
    New York World, 62, 402, 467, 524, 879
    rivalry between Hearst and, 402, 871–872
Pulitzer, Ralph, 853
Pullman, George, 104, 191, 522, 524
Pullman Palace Car Company, 191
Pullman strike, 517–532
    American Railway Union, 526–527
    arbitration proposed by union, 518
    Christian Socialists and, 523
    consequences of, 527–529
    economic causes, 529–530
    effect on families of strikers, 527–528
    General Managers' Association, 518, 526–527
    jurisdictional issue, 528
    newspapers hostile to union, 522–523
    Populist support of, 525
    rents on company-owned houses, 517
    riots and violence, 519–520
    strikebreaking, 603
        use of Federal troops, 518–520, 528–529
    sympathy for strikers, 522–524
Puritan ethic, 826
Puritanism, 145, 277, 327, 330, 355, 828, 917

Quakers, Indian policy, 33, 59
Quay, Matthew, 372
Quimby, Phineas, 573, 575
Quinn, James, 254

Race riots, 651–652
    New Orleans, 651–652
    Wilmington, North Carolina, 653
Racial prejudice, 87, 452, 657–658
Radcliffe College, 679
Radicalism, 164, 483, 918
    journals, 258
    political, 214, 258, 294
    radicals, 255–256
Railroads:
    accidents and disasters, 103–104
    Charles Francis Adams expert on, 328–330
    air brakes, 118–119
    bankruptcies, 100–102

Railroads (*cont.*):
  black redcaps, 108
  capitalist domination, 921
  cattle business, 97–98, 102–103
  Chinese labor, 91–92
  competition by, 101
  congressional legislation, 90
  Crédit Mobilier scandal, 90, 92
  destruction of Indian lands, 53–60, 89, 92
  dining cars, 104, 111
  electric street cars, 119
  failures in 1893, 485
  farmers versus, 430
  fraud and corruption, 90, 92–93, 177
  government ownership of, 110, 525
  Great Strikes (1877), 164–192
    (*See also* Great Strikes)
  growth of, 89–90
  importance of, 107–110
  industrial growth stimulated by, 102, 110
  Interstate Commerce Act of 1887, 461–
    462
  laborers and workmen, 91–92
  land grants, 99–100
    to populate Western states, 99
  locomotives, 104
  names of, 111–112
  nationalization issue, 110, 525
  network of, 100–101
  passenger cars, 104, 111–112
  Pullman sleepers, 104
  Pullman strike (*see* Pullman strike)
  railroad barons, 90–93, 97, 108–112
    private cars, 105–107
  rate wars, 101, 462
  restaurants, 98
  routes of western roads, 100–101
  social-economic effect, 107–108
  statehood and, 99
  symbol of American progress, 110–111
  telegraph offices, 113–116
  train robberies, 105–107
  train stations, 108
  transcontinental, 3–23, 90–103
    completion of, 92
    official spike driven at Gold Creek, 94–96
    second transcontinental, 94–96
  wages and working conditions, 165–166
  workers, 91–92, 103–104
Ralph, Julian, 811
Ranches and ranchers, 806–807
  cattle, 97–98, 102–103
Rand, Carrie, 567
Rand, Mrs. E. D., 563
Rand School, 567
Rape charges, 286, 650–651
Rauschenbusch, Walter, 563
Reading (Pennsylvania) railroad strike, 175
Reconstruction, x, 658–659

  politics, 615–618, 642–643
  racial prejudice, 658–659
Red Cloud, Chief of Sioux, 24–29, 32, 58, 63–66
  trip to Washington, 56–57
Red Dog, 57, 65
Red Internationals, 236
Red River War (1874–75), 61
Redemption movement, 318, 540, 584, 599,
    681
  literature of, 210
  search for redemption, 262
  social action, 356
  zeal for reforming, 827
Redfield, Dr. William, 592
Reed, Thomas, 866, 904
Reeder, Brig. Gen. Frank, 175
Reese, Cara, 500–501
Reform schools, 698
Reforms and reformers, 696–715
  abolitionists and, 914
  Edward Bellamy, 699, 708–711
  John Jay Chapman, 699, 711–714
  Christian Socialism, 483
  effect of TR's presidency, 904–905
  Frederic Howe, 385–386
  Henry Demarest Lloyd, 698–708, 715
  longevity of reformers, 281
  municipal reforms, 374–375, 385, 697
  organizations, 696–697, 715
  political, 697
  prison, 697–698
  Protestant Passion and, 555
  radical, 503
  Jacob Riis, 377–389
  role in Great Strikes, 188–189
  Secular Democratic Consciousness and, 909–910
  secular-minded, x
  social, 696
  Lincoln Steffens, 378, 384–389, 399
  upper-class reformers, 855
Reid, Whitelaw, 176, 238, 319–320, 466, 839–840,
    864, 884, 900
Relief agencies, 464
Religion, 159–160, 554–586
  "Biblical scholarship," 567–568
  bigotry, 469
  Catholic Church, 580–586
  Christian Science, 572–575
  churches and sects, 554–555
  "civil religion," 910
  Darwin and evolution, 559–560
  driving force of American history, 584
  economics and, 210
  freethinkers, 556
  income distribution, 561
  Jewish, 612
  loss of faith, 556–557, 586, 911
  mission movement, 555, 575–579
  morality and, 154, 557

Religion (*cont.*):
"New Thought" or "Science of the Mind," 559–560, 570–572
pragmatism and, 311–312
revivals and revivalism, 569–570
science versus, 144, 202, 307, 555–556, 910
sin, 562
Southerners, 833
war between capital and labor, 562
wealth and, 138–139
Remington, Frederic, 780, 782–784, 879
cowboy and Indian paintings, 782–784
Remsen, Ira, 597
Reno, Maj. Marcus, 69–71
Reno Gang (train robbers), 105
Replogles, Georgina and Henry, 292
Repressive instincts, 277–278
Republican Party, xi, xiv, 212, 452–468, 925
conservative elements, 453
election of 1878, 456
election of 1880, 456
election of 1884, 458–459
election of 1888, 462–463
election of 1892, 465–467
election of 1896, 547–553
election of 1900, 897–898
founding of, 450
Liberal Republicans, 59
Mugwumps, 458–459
Radical Republicans, 15, 27–28, 915
under domination of capitalists, 452–453
Research and development, 115
Retirement benefits for workers, 191
Retrospections, 907–929
farmer-worker alliance, 923–924
history and historians, 907–908
war between capital and labor, 909, 917–918
Revivals and revivalism, 569–570, 596, 803, 833
Revolution:
fear of, 513
middle- and upper-class revolutionaries, 473
talk of, 229–231, 450, 482, 544, 926
(*See also* American Revolution)
Revolution (journal), 258
Revolutionary idealism, 471
Revolutionary upheavals in Europe, 919
Rhodes, James Ford, 618–619, 658
Richard, Ellen Swallow, 673–674
Richardson, Henry Hobson, 324, 789–790
Richardson, Sid, 784
Richter, Eugene, 739
Rickett, Dr. M. O., 647
Rideout, Alice, 494
Riesman, David, 588
Riis, Jacob, 176, 335, 338, 363, 377–389, 420, 867, 910–911
on conditions in New York City, 366–369
documentaries, 383–384

education reform, 668
How the Other Half Lives, 350, 382–383
on Jewish immigrants, 349–350
playground movement, 591
reform journalist, 379
Roosevelt and, 381–383, 387, 389
Riley, James Whitcomb, 521, 753
Rimmer, William, 787
Ripley, George, 300
Rischin, Moses, 352
Road-building programs, 515–516
"Robber barons," xiii, 102, 920
Robins, Mrs. Raymond, 683
Rockefeller, John D., 122, 129–130, 137, 701, 705, 805
University of Chicago and, 603–605
Rockford (Illinois) Female Seminary, 417
Rocky Mountain West, xiii, 799, 805, 814
Roe, Lt. Faye, 45
Roe, Frances, 45–49
Roentgen, Wilhelm, 397
Rogers, Farman, 778
Rogue River expedition, 38
Roman Catholic Church (*see* Catholic Church)
Roosevelt, Alice, 322
Roosevelt, Edith, 906
Roosevelt, Theodore, 247, 320, 329, 538
assistant secretary of navy, 388, 553, 865
effect of war with Spain, 881
football reforms, 849
governor of New York, 887–889
on hostility of West for East, 822–823
infatuation with West, 779–780, 783, 819–820, 899–900
marriage to Edith Kermit Carow, 820
police commissioner, 387–388
presidency, 905–906
Riis and, 381–383, 387, 389
Rough Riders, 875–879
Spanish-American War, 865–882, 889
supported Philippine conquest, 889
vice-presidential candidate, 898–899
The Winning of the West, 820
Root, Elihu, 869
Rosewater, Edward, 342
Rosicky, Jan, 342
Ross, Edward Alsworth, 599, 606
Rough Riders, 875–879
Rousseau, Jean Jacques, 152, 473
Royce, Josiah, 308–310, 312, 558, 917
Rumanian immigrants, 346
Rush, Benjamin, 278, 587
Russell, Charles Edward, 456, 611, 784
Russell, Charles Taze, 569
Russell, Edward, 443
Russia, 893
Jewish emigration, 344–346
Russian immigrants, 332
Ryan, Father Abram, 831

Ryder, Albert Pinkham, 786–787
Ryerson, Martin, 793

Sackville-West, Lionel, 463
Sage Foundation, 224
Saint-Gaudens, Augustus, 322, 491–492, 781, 788–789, 793, 857
St. Louis: graft and corruption, 378, 400–401
    railroad strike, 182
St. Nicholas Magazine, 390
Saloons and saloonkeepers, 385–386
Salt, price-fixing agreements, 128–129
Salt Lake City, 813
Salt River Canyon, 43
San Francisco: earthquake, 823
    literary scene, 753–756
    railroad strikes, 182–183
San Francisco Times, 197
Sand Creek Massacre, 12–14
Sandwich Islands (see Hawaiian Islands)
Santa Fe Trail, 5, 23
Santayana, George, 312
Sargent, John Singer, 322, 495, 785–786, 788
Satanta (Kiowa chief), 50–51
Saturday Evening Post, 398
Savage, M. J., 516
Sawyer, Mattie, 268–269
Scandinavian immigrants, 332–333
Schiff, Jacob, 360, 488
Schizophrenia, American, 909
Schmitt, Max, 776
Scholars and intellectuals, 917
Schurz, Carl, 59, 79, 82, 93–94, 97, 109, 363, 458, 669, 866, 900–901
Schwab, Michael, 251, 254
Science and religion, 144, 202, 309–310, 910
    war between, 307, 555–556
    (See also Darwinism)
Scott, Thomas, 104, 176
Sculptors, 788–789
    women, 494
Sears, Sarah Choate, 787–788
Secular Democratic Consciousness, 158, 714, 909–910
    issue of "happiness," 928
Secular Democratic (Enlightenment) notion of man, 148
Self-control, ideal of, 916–917
Seligman, Edwin, 612
Semple, Etta, 285
Sentimentalism, 162
Servant problems, 855–856
Settlement house movement, 404–421
    attitude of WASPs, 413
    boards of trustees, 420–421
    forces behind, 410
    popularity of, 419
Sexual issues, 258–283
    attitudes toward, 267

free love, 258–283
eugenics, 276
reforms, 286
taboos on "sexual" words, 271
Shaler, Nathaniel, 595, 917
Shaw, Rev. Anna, 499
Shaw, George Bernard, 211, 253, 287–288
    Fabian Essays, 292
    on Moses Harman, 280–281
Shaw, Robert, 789
Shays's Rebellion, 431, 709
Sheedy, Dennis, 126
Sheldon, Charles M., 566
Sheridan, Gen. Philip, 50, 54–55, 62–72, 94
Sherman, Sen. John, 52, 325, 458, 463, 488, 889
    antitrust bill, 132, 463
    secretary of state, 864–865
Sherman, Gen. William Tecumseh, 22–29, 34, 38, 62
    Indian campaigns, 50–54
Sherman Antitrust Act, 132, 463
Sherman Silver Purchase Act, 463–464
    repeal of, 487–488
Shoe and boot industry, 124, 215
Shorthand, development of, 259
Shoshone Indians, 42
Silliman, Benjamin, 592
Silver issue, 544, 547–550, 906
    (See also Free silver)
Simpson, Jeremiah ("Jerry"), 437–438
Sinclair, Upton, 754
Sinclair, William, 452, 619–620, 649
Singleton, Benjamin, 647
Sioux Indians, 1, 7, 9, 73–74, 83
    death of Sitting Bull, 824–825
    peace conferences, 5, 16, 73–74
    raids and counterraids, 7, 24
Sitting Bull, 65, 68, 70, 73, 77, 94
    death of, 824–825
Skyscrapers, 792–793
Sladen, Capt. John, 38
Slenker, Elmina, 273–274, 279
Slenker, Isaac, 273–274
Slogans, "waving the bloody shirt," 459
Slough, Col. John, 10
Small, Albion, 604
Smith, Adam, 211
    Wealth of Nations, 139
Smith, Charles Sprague, 612
Smith, Gerrit, 32
Smith, Hannah Whitall, 665
Smith, J. Allen, 605–606
Smith, Jedediah, 4
Smith College, 678–679
Smithsonian Institution, 592, 922
Smoky Hill Trail, 23
Smyth, Newman, 560
Smythe, William E., 798, 802–803, 814–816, 820–821

Social behavior, 915
Social Crusade, 566–567
Social Gospel, 483, 560–562, 568
Social justice, 613
Social protests: anarchism and, 293
  novels and short stories, 733–756
Social reform, 185
  (*See also* Reform and reformers)
Social Reform Union, 566
Social Register, 854–855
Social science, 601
Social service, 409–410
Socialism, xiii, 164, 180, 184, 210, 214, 247, 256,
  258, 464, 919
  "American," 164
  Bellamy's "national" socialism, 164, 483, 503, 698,
    709–711
  Christian, 164–165, 239, 483
    (*See also* Christian Socialists)
  difference between anarchism and, 214–215
  doctrines of, 214–215
  growth of, 482
  William Holmes, 247
  Jewish, 361
  ignorance of American labor, 215
  influence of socialists, 232
  John Most and, 231–236
  Albert Payson, 247–248
  "single tax," 164
  union and, 215, 490–491
Socialist Federation of North America, 232–233
Socialist Labor Party, 232, 436, 467, 897
  election of 1896, 547
  growth of, 527–528
Sociologists, 142
Sociology, 140–158, 566, 599
  applied, 156, 158
Sontag, John, 106–107
South, 829–840
  blacks, 836–840
  businessmen, 833–834
  cotton mills, 835
  Democratic Party, 838
  economic progress, 835–836
  farmers' movement, 432, 838–839
  industrialization, 834
  iron and coal, 834–835
  investments, 834
  "Lost Cause" myth, 830–832
  New South, 835–840
  nostalgia syndrome, 829–830
  poor whites, 838
  postwar agrarian, 453
  racial attitudes, 836–840
  radical political ideas, 453
  religious life, 823
  Republican Party, 838
  segregated schools, 837
  Southern consciousness, 833

Southern literature, 832–833
  state of mind, 829
  states' rights issue, 839, 923
  struggle for survival, 839–840
  tobacco, 835
South America policy, 541
Southern Alliance, 433, 448–450
Southern Pacific, 806
Southwest, xiv, 799
  Indian wars, 34–39, 50–52, 83
Spain, Cuban policy, 866
Spanish-American War, 865–866
  attack on Santiago, 875–876
  black soldiers, 877–879, 883–884
  casualties, 880
  charges and countercharges, 880–881
  Dewey's victory at Manila, 871–872
  enlistments, 470–471
  invasion of Cuba, 873
  newspapers and, 867–868
    journalistic sensationalism, 871–872, 880–881
    rivalry between Hearst and Pulitzer, 871–872
    yellow journalism, 402, 871–872
  opposition to, 872–873
  Roosevelt's Rough Riders, 875–879
  San Juan Hill battle, 876–877
  territorial acquisition, 873
  sentiment for, 865–866
  treaty ending, 882
Spencer, Herbert, 136, 151, 159, 601
  First Principles and Social Statics, 211
Spengler, Oswald, 295
Spies, August, 238, 242–245, 247, 289
  Haymarket Affair, 242, 247
Spiritualism, 180, 259–260, 275, 570
  importance of, 282–283
  Victoria Woodhull and, 262–268
Spofford, Harriet, 393
Sports, 841–852
  baseball, 845–846
  basketball, 850
  bicycling, 844–845
  black athletes, 846
  boxing contests, 845
  Coaching Club, 843
  duck-hunting, 843
  Eakins's paintings, 775–777
  English influence on, 842–843
  football, 847–850
  golf, 843
  horse racing, 846–847
  "Olympic games," 852
  role in building character, 851
  roller skating, 845
  tennis, 843
Sprague, Frank Julian, 119
Sprague Electric Railway and Motor Company, 119
Spring-Rice, Cecil, 325
Spring Valley (Illinois) coal strike, 700–701

Springfield (Mass.) *Republican*, 20, 733
Stagecoaches, 95, 106
Standard of living, 928
Standard Oil Company, 11, 123, 701, 705
Standard Oil Company of Ohio, 129–131
 antitrust violations, 131
Standing Bear, Chief of Poncas, 81
Stanford, Jane Lathrop, 606
Stanford, Leland, 91–93, 97, 136–137, 777–778
 photographs of horse in motion, 777
Stanford University, 606, 796, 823
Stanton, Elizabeth, 264–265, 282, 499–500
Starr, Ellen Gates, 407, 416–417
State universities, 680
States' rights, xii–xiii, 452, 456, 461, 529, 615, 798,
  826, 920
 code word for reactionary politics, 923
 politics and, 452, 456, 923
 Supreme Court decisions, 642, 839
Stead, William, 370
Steel and iron workers, 121, 123, 834–835
 Homestead strike, 469–481
Steel barons, 102
Steffens, Lincoln, 353–358, 374–375, 378, 384–
  389, 399, 596
 Roosevelt and, 888, 904–906
 The Shame of the Cities, 400–401
Stephens, Alexander, 461
Stetson, Charles Walter, 764–765
Stetson, Charlotte, 764–765
Stevens, Alzina (Populist), 416
Stevens, Isaac, 6
Stevens, Marie, 265–267
Stevens, Thaddeus, 775, 919
Stevenson, Adlai E., 900
Stevenson, Robert Louis, 92
Stickney, Joseph Trumbull, 860
Stock markets, 902
 mining stock, 125
Stockham, Alice B., 272
Stone, Amasa, 189
Stone, Clara, 319–320
Stone, Lucy, 500, 562, 685
Storey, Moorfield, 882–883
Stowe, Harriet Beecher, 261–262, 412–413, 716,
  757–758, 760–761
 American Woman's Home . . . , 668–669
 birthday party in 1882, 757–758
 home reformers, 668–670
 on Indian policy, 16, 84
 Uncle Tom's Cabin, 210, 413, 636
Straight University at New Orleans, 634
Straus, Isador, 468
Strikes:
 Federal troops used as strikebreakers, 170–172,
  178, 187–188, 518–520, 528
 Homestead, Pennsylvania, 469–481
 increase in number of, 223
 lock-outs, 700
  in mining states, 479–481
 Pullman strike, 517–532
 right to strike, 186–187
 riots and, 136
 Spring Valley (Illinois) coal mines, 700–701
 strikebreakers, 122, 236, 469
 strike-leaders, 134
 telegraph operators, 114
 (*See also* Great Strikes)
Strong, George Templeton, 166, 305, 367, 591,
  772, 913
Strong, Josiah, 160–161, 382, 540, 658, 842
Strong, Temple, 772
Strong, William, 98, 386
Suffrage movement, 264–265
 black males, 662
 organizations, 663–666
 Seneca Falls Convention, 499
 women's movement and, 150, 231, 264–265,
  662–666, 682
Sugar trusts, 129–131, 530–531
Sullivan, Louis Henri (architect), 369, 492, 790–793
Sully, Thomas, 775
Sulzberger, Mayer, 360
Sumner, William Graham, 140–147, 151, 458, 538–
  539, 823
 Classical-Christian Consciousness, 910
 compared with Lester Ward, 157–158
 denounced Spanish-American War, 872
 "Sociology," essay, 143
 on wars and revolutions, 145–146
Sun Yat-sen, 576–577
 influence of Henry George, 211
Supreme Court decisions, 250, 376, 527
 doctrine of states' rights, 642, 839
 Dred Scott decision, 166
 Granger cases, 642
 Indian affairs, 1
 Slaughterhouse Cases, 642
 transformation of, 445
Sweatshops, 349, 352, 408, 418
 wages, 446
Swedenborgians, 297–298
Swedish immigrants, 332
Swett, Leonard, 250
Swinton, John, 167, 178–181, 189, 198, 378, 436
 John Swinton's Paper, 167, 178, 246, 485–486
Sylvis, William, 167
Syndicalism, 164
Syndicating articles, 393–394
Syracuse, railroad strikes, 179

Tabor, Horace, 126
Taft, Lorado, 492
Tammany Hall, 385, 456, 459
Tappan, Samuel, 28
Tarbell, Ida, 394–395, 399–400, 557, 610
Tariff issue, 453–458, 462–463, 530–531
 antiprotectionists, 458

Tariff issue (cont.):
  Cleveland and, 462
  congressional hearings, 457–458
  McKinley tariff, 465–467, 531
  reciprocity, 465
Tarkington, Booth, 395
Taussig, Frank, 595
Tawney, R. H., 586
Taxes and taxation, 136
  single tax theories of Henry George, 204–205, 211
Taylor, Bayard, 300
Taylor, Henry Osborn, 594
Taylor, Jim (cowboy), 647
Taylor, Myron, 372
Taylor, Susie King, 549–660
Taylor, Zachary, 899
Technological innovations, 202
  future shock and, xv
  growth of, 113–127
Tecumseh, Indian chief, 77
Telegraph, 113–116
  first message (1844), 92, 115, 119
  nationalization issue, 114
  strike of operators, 114
Telephone, 115
  "long distance" lines, 116
Teller, Sen. Henry Moore, 487
Temperance movement, 663–666
  Knights of Labor and, 230
Tennis, introduction of, 843
Terrorism, political, 471
Terry, Gen. Alfred H., 22, 28, 44, 62, 67, 72–73, 94
Teton Range, 799
Texas: annexation of, 1
  immigrant settlers, 341
  Indian raids, 2, 50–51
Texas Alliance, 432
Texas Emigration and Land Company, 2
Texas Rangers, 2
Textile industry, 124
  cotton mills, 835
Thacher, Rev. Samuel, 919
Thaw, Harry, 857
Thayer, Abbott Handerson, 778
Thayer, William Roscoe, 189–190, 547–549, 894, 896
Theosophical Society, 579
Theosophists, 579, 698
Thomson, Elihu, 117–119
Thomson-Houston Electric Company, 117–119
Thomson Steel Company, 121–122, 470
Thoreau, Henry David, 267, 316, 720, 764
Thorn, Frederick, 794
Tibbles, Thomas Henry, 48–49, 81–82
Ticknor, George, 590, 596
Tidewater Pipe Line Company, 130
Tilden, Samuel, 198, 454, 468
Tillman, Sen. Benjamin, 619–620

Tilton, Angela, 269–270
Tilton, Theodore, 251
Timmins, Minna (see Chapman, Minna Timmins)
Tinford, Jack, 475–476
Tobacco, 835
Tocqueville, Alexis de, xii, 282, 394, 716, 852
  on writers, 716
Todd, Mabel Loomis, 734–735
Tongue River Reservation, 73, 81
Tougaloo University in Mississippi, 634
Tourgée, Judge Albion, 646, 650, 736, 758, 832
Trade unions (see Unions)
Train, George Francis, 252, 285
Train robberies, 105–107
Trall, Dr. R. T., 674
Tramps and criminals, 508, 744–745
Transcendentalism, 151, 263, 579
  spiritualism and, 283
Treaty of Guadaloupe Hidalgo (1848), 1
Trine, R. W., 572
Trinity Church, Boston, 789
Trumbull, Lyman, 252, 533
Trumbull, Matthew, 289
Trusts and monopolies, 128–131, 507
  antitrust law violations, 130–131
  New York State, 130–131
  "pools," formation of, 128
  price-fixing agreements, 128
  rise of, 128–129
  sugar, 129
Tucker, Benjamin, 287
  Liberty, 285
Tucson, Arizona, 36
Tularosa Reservation, 37
Turner, Bishop Henry, 642–643, 651
Turner, Nat, 637
Tuskegee Normal and Industrial Institute, 521, 640
Twain, Mark, 20, 195, 335, 575, 723, 727–731, 739, 750, 833
  The Adventures of Huckleberry Finn, 729–731
  books and stories for children, 751
  The Innocents Abroad, 727–728, 740
  Roughing It, 728
Tweed, William Marcy (Boss Tweed), 374, 401, 506

Uncle Tom's Cabin (Stowe), 210, 413, 636
Unemployment, 217, 446, 464, 485–486, 508
  Coxey's march on Washington, 508–516
Union Labor Party, 437
Union League, 32
Union Pacific Railroad, 23, 29, 90–92, 94, 109, 485, 805–806
  failure of, 464
Unions, 214, 227–240
  American Railway Union, 257
  black, 108, 645
  campaign to break power of, 532–534
  craft-union pattern, 256–257
  doctrine of violence, 234

Unions (*cont.*):
  Federal power to suppress union activity, 170–
    172, 178, 187–188, 518–520, 528–529
  following Civil War, 166
  formation of, 214, 223–224
  importance of organization, 225–226
  International Workingmen's Association, 231–236
  Knights of Labor (*see* Knights of Labor)
  rise of, 165
  socialism issue, 490–491
  (*See also* Labor conditions; Strikes)
Unitarians, 284
United Mine Workers, 256, 480–481
United States:
  faith in "greatness" of, 926–927
  "freedom" and "promise," 927, 929
  Geological Survey, 323
  Indian Commission, 31–32, 56–57
  life of soldiers in Indian country, 44–49
  relations with Great Britain, 537–539
  Strike Commission, 257
United States Steel Corporation, 384
Universal Peace Union, 60
"Universal Science," 259
Universalism, philosophy of, 259
University of California, 592, 596–597
University of Chicago, 371
  Rockefeller influence, 600, 613
University of Michigan, 419
University of Wisconsin, 599, 603
Universology, doctrine of, 258
Upper classes, 853–863
  bohemianism, 860
  clothes and clothing, 860
  conspicuousness, 853–854
  European tours, 857–859
  friends and friendships, 861
  infatuation with British, 828–829
  Jewish immigrants, 358–359
  letter-writing, 861–862
  marriage and divorce, 857
  morals and behavior, 857, 860
  old rich versus new rich, 854–855
  reform activities, 419, 855
  revolutionaries, 473
  scandals, 854, 857
  servant problems, 855
  settlement house work, 408–409, 419
  social obligations, 408–409
  Social Register, 854–855
  Veblen on, 860–861
  yachts, 854
Utah, 99
  transcontinental railroad joined, 91, 94–96
Ute Indians, 45, 85
Utopian socialist communities, 165

Vail, Alfred, 115
Vail, Theodore Newton, 115–116

Van Depoele, Charles, 119
Van Dyke, John, 789
Van Rensselaer, Mariana Griswold, 790, 796
Vanderbilt, Consuelo, 854
Vanderbilt, Cornelius, 101
Vanderbilt, Mrs. William, 854
Vardaman, James, 621
Vassar College, 678
Vatican Council of 1870, 581–582
Veblen, Thorstein, 690, 795
  criticism of upper classes, 860–861
Vedder, Elihu, 786–787
Venezuela affair, 537–539
Vernon, Leroy, 584
Vesey, Denmark, 637
Veterans, pensions for, 463
Vice squads, 277–279
  Society for the Suppression of Vice, 277–278
Vilas, William Freeman, 460, 468, 487–488, 536
Villard, Frances Garrison, 93, 915
Villard, Henry, 93–97, 363, 450, 465
  German "liberationist," 93
  home on Madison Avenue, New York City, 793,
    853
  railroad tycoon, 97
  transcontinental railroad built by, 94–97
    collapse of financial empire, 96–97
Villard, Oswald Garrison, 93, 372, 557, 595, 773
  on John Jay Chapman, 714
  on Chicago's exposition, 505
  education, 588
  on New York City, 365
  on newspapers and Cuban invasion, 867, 869–
    870, 880
  parental relationships, 93, 915
  transcontinental railroad, 95
Vincent, John Heyl, 609
Virginia City, 23
Volga Germans, 342–343
Voltaire, 150
von Ranke Leopold, 908
Voorhees, Daniel, 54
Vought, Lizzie, 145–150
Vrooman, Walter and Harry, 436–437

Wabash, Indiana, first electric street lights,
    116
Wadsworth, Charles, 732
Wages and working conditions, 133, 136–137, 165,
    219
  (*See also* Eight-hour-day issue; Labor conditions;
    Unions)
Wagon trains, 4, 53
Waisbrooker, Lois, 274–276, 281
  writings, 274
Waite, Catherine Van Valkenburg, 493
Waite, Davis, 484, 488, 532
Wald, Lillian, 697
Walker, Edwin Cox, 268, 285, 427, 519

Wall, Edward C., 467
Wallace, Alfred Russel, 210, 810
Walser, G. H., 292
Walters, Alexander, 650
Wanamaker, John, 116
War between capital and labor, xiii, 139, 203–204,
    549, 555, 599, 926
    capital supported by Federal administration, 525,
        534
    cities and, 910–911
    education and, 599
    labor conditions, 213–226
    W. Scott Morgan on, 433–434
    political issue, 452, 454
    retrospections, 909, 917–918
    unions and, 228
War between science and religion, 144, 202, 307,
    555–556, 910
Ward, Artemus, 727
Ward, Elizabeth Stuart Phelps, 759–760
    The Silent Partner, 759–760
Ward, Lester, x, 110, 258, 288, 556, 589, 612
    compared with Sumner, 157–158
    dissemination of liberal ideas, 919
    Dynamic Sociology, 150–157
    Father of American sociology, 146
    government clerkship, 149
    National Liberal Reform League, 292, 919
    romance with Lizzie Vought, 145–150, 258
    Secular Democratic Consciousness and, 910
Ward, Thomas, 305–306
Warner, Charles Dudley, 728–729, 739
    The Gilded Age, 739–740
Warren, Josiah, 263, 294
Washington, Booker T., 621–640, 835
    attack by Du Bois, 636–640
    compact with white South, 636–638
    critics of, 639–640
    program of industrial education, 636–640
Washington, D.C.:
    Coxey's march on, 508–516
    defense against strikers, 171
    visit of Indian chiefs, 56–57
Washington Post, 522–523, 865
WASPs (White Anglo-Saxon Protestants), 658–659
    attitude toward working class, 413–414
Watson, David, 131
Watson, Tom, 111, 435–439, 550, 838–839
    alliance between white and black farmers, 447
    handbook written by, 438–439
    leader of farmers' movement in South, 435–439
Watterson, Henry, 467, 831, 833–834
"Waving the bloody shirt" slogan, 459
Wayland, J. A., 706
Wealth, 138
    concentrations of, 534
    distribution of, 161
    religion and, 138
    (See also Upper classes)

Weather forecasting, 592
Weaver, James B., 443–446, 461, 508
    candidate of Greenback-Labor Party, 456–457,
        459
    nominated by People's Party, 467
Webb, Sidney and Beatrice, 416, 503, 612
Webster, Henry Kitchell, 741–742, 949
    social protest writings, 741–742
Welch, William, 419
Welles, Gideon, 9
Wellesley College, 678–679
Wells, Ida, 502, 643–644, 654–656
Welsh, Herbert, 84
Wendell, Barrett, 595
West and Westerners, xiii
    art and artists, 779–784
    cattle and sheep, 804
    company towns, 813–814
    cowboys, 808–809
    East-West differences, 799–800, 820–823
    Eastern investments, 804–805
    English investors and settlers, 804–805
    Fantasy West, 817–818
    Great Desert West, 799, 814–816
    Great Plains West, 799
    hardships and violence, 811–812
    health and disease, 810–811
    hostility toward East, 822–823
    immigrant communities, 804
    Indians, 823–824
    investments in, 800–801, 804–805
    Johnson County War, 809–810
    Lincoln County Wars, 810
    migration West, 4, 34, 53, 74, 798–799
        of Southern blacks, 641–642, 646–647
    mines and mining, 806
        strikes, 479
    Mississippi Valley West, 799
    New England influences, 801
    Northwest, 799
    obsessed with East, xiv–xv, 822–823
    political and social conditions, 801–803, 811
    population growth, 800–801
    public lands, 799
    ranches and ranchers, 806–807
    Rocky Mountain West, 799, 814
    Roosevelt's infatuation with, 899–900
    social life, 802–803, 811
    Southwest, 799
    town life, 802–804
    "Western art," 779–784
    women, role of, 682
Western Federation of Miners, 479
Western Union Telegraph Company, 113–115, 397
    labor conditions, 216
Westinghouse, George, 118, 132
Westinghouse Air Brake Company, 118
Westinghouse Electric Company, 132
Weyler y Nicolau, Gen. Valeriano, 543–544

Wheeler, Benjamin Ide, 821
Wheeler, Gen. "Fighting Joe," 875
Whipple, Bishop Henry Benjamin, 8, 31, 78
Whistler, James Abbott McNeil, 495, 784–785
White, George, 619, 653–654
White, Henry, 898
White, Horace, 699
White, Stanford, 666, 793, 854, 857
White, Thomas Earle, 291
White, William Allen, 395, 437–438, 549, 551, 904–905
  on Mary Lease, 449
  on Jeremiah ("Jerry") Simpson, 437–438
  "What's the Matter with Kansas?" 549
Whites, Anglo-Saxon Protestant (WASPs), 658–659
  attitudes toward working class, 413–414
Whitman, Albery, 191, 752
Whitman, Sarah, 319
Whitman, Walt, 316, 378, 690–691, 717–723, 752
  DemocraticVistas, 718
  Emerson and, 719–721
  Leaves of Grass, 210, 279, 717, 721, 723
  "Song of Myself," 263
Whitney, Elihu, 118
Whittier, John Greenleaf, 260, 717, 719, 757–758
Wilberforce University in Ohio, 629
Wilbur, Sibyl, 574
Wilcox, Ella Wheeler, 398
Willard, Frances (journalist), 18, 377, 482–483, 699, 721
  rules for children, 915–916
  WCTU and, 482, 499, 663–665
Willard, Josiah Flynt, 744
Williams, Consul Oscar, 871, 873
Wilshire, Gaylord, 612
Wilson, Edmund, 714
Wilson, J. Stitt, 566
Wilson, Sen. William Lyne, 530–531
Wilson, Woodrow, xi, 137, 553, 597
Windom, William, 28
Wing, Simon, 467
Winslow, Forbes, 902
Winthrop, John, 355, 430
  "A Modell of Christian Charity," 209, 584
Wischnewetsky, Lazare, 417–418
Wisconsin, Democratic Party struggle, 467–468
Wise, Rabbi Isaac, 285, 360
Wise, J. B., 285
Woman's Christian Temperance Union (WCTU), 482–483, 663–666
  Frances Willard and, 482, 499, 663–664
Woman's Union Missionary Society of New York, 578
Woman's World magazine, 214
Women, 661–695
  architects, 794
  arts and artists, 495–496, 680, 773
  bicycling, 844–845
  black women, 654–657

career-oriented, 500, 670
Chicago World's Columbian Exposition and, 493–502, 787–788
child-care, 693–694
clothing, 689–690
club movement, 666–668
colleges, 678–682
  curriculum, 680–681
cooperative living arrangements, 671–673
culture, 680–681
emancipation of women, 692
family and home, 684–685
  reformers, 668–672
father-daughter relations, 404–405, 694
  female achievers with supportive fathers, 404–405
"feminine mystique," 676–677
grand tour taken by, 681
health of American women, 674–678
hours and wages, 219
immigrants, 683
International Congress of Women, 498–499
Jewish immigrants, 348–349
journalists, 377
"kitchen reformers," 673–674
legal rights of, 667, 842
marriage and divorce, 669–670, 684–685, 692
masculine attitude toward, 690
mother-daughter relationship, 694
motherhood, 687, 693–694
orators, 275
parental authority and, 683–684
physical exercise, 678
prostitution, 219, 685–688
role in American life, 661
role in Great Strikes, 171–172, 174, 480–481
role in missionary activities, 579–580
sculptors, 788–789
sexuality, 258, 262–263, 689–690, 692–693
social obligation of upper class, 408–409
social purity movement, 687–688
sports and, 851
suffrage movement, 150, 231, 258, 264, 662–666, 682
teachers, 590
temperance movements, 482–483, 663–666
unmarried women, 684–685
women's rights movement, 499–500, 661–662, 919
working conditions, 217–219, 694
writers and writings, 398–399, 757–771
Women in American Society (Woolson), 259
Women's National Indian Association, 84
Women's rights movement, 499–500, 661–662, 919
  Revolution magazine, 919
Wood, Henry, 572
Woodford, Gen. Stewart Lyndon, 866, 869–879
Woodhull, Canning, 265

Woodhull, Victoria, 166, 231, 270–271, 282, 842
  on breakdown of American family, 914
  espousal of free love, 260–265
  lecturer on spiritualism, 262–265
Woodhull and Claflin's Weekly, 258
Woodruff, T. T., 104
Woodward, C. Vann, 833
Woolley, John, 901
Woolson, Alba, 259, 426–427, 669–670
  on health of American women, 675–678
Woolson, Constance Fenimore, 725, 766
Woolson, Moses, 790, 792
Worcester, Mass., 471
  free love movement, 270
Workers and working class:
  attitudes toward, 231, 239
  barrier between WASPs and, 413–414
  failure to form alliance with radical farmers, 923–924
  Great Strikes (1877), 164–192
  immigrants, 133–134
  industrial, 133–134
  role in politics, 165
  revolution, 471
Working conditions, 165, 213–226
  (*See also* Labor conditions)
Working-Class Movement in America, The (Jones), 222

Workingmen's Party of New York, 178–181
Workingmen's Party of the United States, 167–168
World Labor Congress, 502–503
World's Columbian Exposition (*see* Chicago World's Columbian Exposition in 1893)
Wounded Knee, Battle of, 825
Wright, Elizur, 270
Wright, Frances, 165
Wright, Henry, 389
Wyman, Jeffries, 303
Wynkoop, Maj., 11–13
Wyoming: railroads, 99
  Stock Grower's Association, 809–810

Yale University, 592
Yandell, Enid, 493–494
Yellowstone Park, xiv, 23, 48, 66, 77, 799, 818
  camping expeditions, 843–844
Yerkes, Charles Tyson, 370–371
Yiddish theater, 349, 357
Yoga, 579–580
Yosemite, 799
  photographs of, 777
Young, Brigham, 813–814
Young Men's Christian Associations, 842
Younger brothers, 105–107

FOR THE BEST IN PAPERBACKS, LOOK FOR THE Ⓟ

In every corner of the world, on every subject under the sun, Penguin represents quality and variety—the very best in publishing today.

For complete information about books available from Penguin—including Pelicans, Puffins, Peregrines, and Penguin Classics—and how to order them, write to us at the appropriate address below. Please note that for copyright reasons the selection of books varies from country to country.

In the United Kingdom: For a complete list of books available from Penguin in the U.K., please write to *Dept E.P., Penguin Books Ltd, Harmondsworth, Middlesex, UB7 0DA.*

In the United States: For a complete list of books available from Penguin in the U.S., please write to *Dept BA, Penguin,* Box 120, Bergenfield, New Jersey 07621-0120.

In Canada: For a complete list of books available from Penguin in Canada, please write to *Penguin Books Ltd, 2801 John Street, Markham, Ontario L3R 1B4.*

In Australia: For a complete list of books available from Penguin in Australia, please write to the *Marketing Department, Penguin Books Ltd, P.O. Box 257, Ringwood, Victoria 3134.*

In New Zealand: For a complete list of books available from Penguin in New Zealand, please write to the *Marketing Department, Penguin Books (NZ) Ltd, Private Bag, Takapuna, Auckland 9.*

In India: For a complete list of books available from Penguin, please write to *Penguin Overseas Ltd, 706 Eros Apartments, 56 Nehru Place, New Delhi, 110019.*

In Holland: For a complete list of books available from Penguin in Holland, please write to *Penguin Books Nederland B.V., Postbus 195, NL-1380AD Weesp, Netherlands.*

In Germany: For a complete list of books available from Penguin, please write to *Penguin Books Ltd, Friedrichstrasse 10-12, D-6000 Frankfurt Main I, Federal Republic of Germany.*

In Spain: For a complete list of books available from Penguin in Spain, please write to *Longman, Penguin España, Calle San Nicolas 15, E-28013 Madrid, Spain.*

In Japan: For a complete list of books available from Penguin in Japan, please write to *Longman Penguin Japan Co Ltd, Yamaguchi Building, 2-12-9 Kanda Jimbocho, Chiyoda-Ku, Tokyo 101, Japan.*